133

170-171   168-169

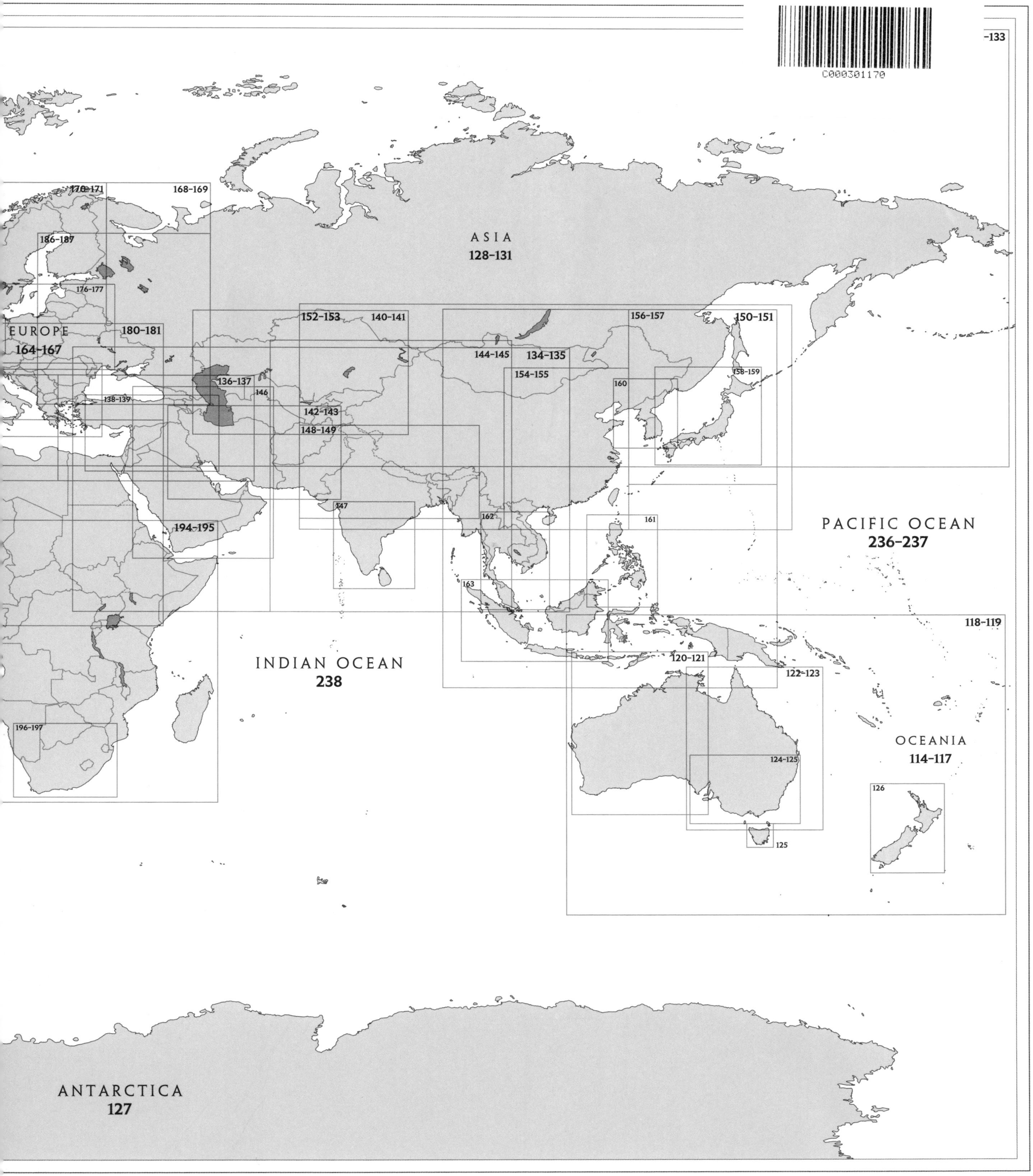

186-187

176-177

ASIA
128-131

152-153   140-141

156-157   150-151

EUROPE
164-167   180-181

144-145   134-135

158-159

136-137   154-155

138-139   146   160

142-143

148-149

147

194-195   162   161   PACIFIC OCEAN
236-237

163

118-119

INDIAN OCEAN
238   120-121   122-123

OCEANIA
114-117

124-125

196-197   126

125

ANTARCTICA
127

UNIVERSAL
ATLAS
OF THE WORLD

Published by Times Books
An imprint of HarperCollins Publishers
Westerhill Road, Bishopbriggs, Glasgow G64 2QT

First Published 2008
Second Edition 2012

Third edition 2015

Copyright © Times Books Group Ltd 2015

Maps © Collins Bartholomew Ltd 2015

The Times is a registered trademark of Times Newspapers Ltd

A catalogue record for this book is available from the British Library

ISBN 978-0-00-813884-4

10 9 8 7 6 5 4 3 2 1

Printed and bound in Hong Kong

All mapping in this atlas is generated from Collins Bartholomew digital databases.
Collins Bartholomew, the UK's leading independent geographical information supplier,
can provide a digital, custom, and premium mapping service to a variety of markets.
For further information:
Tel: +44 (0) 208 307 4515
e-mail: collinsbartholomew@harpercollins.co.uk
or visit our website at: www.collinsbartholomew.com

If you would like to comment on any aspect of this atlas,
please contact us at the above address or online.

www.timesatlas.com
e-mail: timesatlas@harpercollins.co.uk

🐦 @timesatlas
📘 Facebook.com/thetimesatlas

THE TIMES

UNIVERSAL
ATLAS
OF THE WORLD

TIMES BOOKS

LONDON

CONTENTS

ATLAS OF THE WORLD

Page	Title	Scale
154–155	**CHINA** Central and East	1:7 500 000
	Hong Kong	1:750 000
156–157	**JAPAN, NORTH KOREA AND SOUTH KOREA**	1:7 000 000
158–159	**JAPAN**	1:5 000 000
160	**CHINA** Northeast, **NORTH KOREA AND SOUTH KOREA**	1:5 000 000
161	**PHILIPPINES**	1:7 000 000
162	**THAILAND, CAMBODIA AND PENINSULAR MALAYSIA**	1:7 500 000
163	**INDONESIA** West	1:10 000 000

EUROPE

Page	Title	Scale
164–165	**EUROPE** Physical	1:17 500 000
166–167	**EUROPE** Political	1:17 500 000
168–169	**NORTHERN EUROPE**	1:10 000 000
170–171	**SCANDINAVIA AND THE BALTIC STATES**	1:5 000 000
	Iceland	1:5 000 000
	Faroe Islands	1:5 000 000
172–173	**ENGLAND AND WALES**	1:2 000 000
174	**SCOTLAND**	1:2 000 000
	Shetland Islands	1:2 000 000
175	**IRELAND**	1:2 000 000
176–177	**EUROPE** North Central	1:5 000 000

Page	Title	Scale
178–179	**BELGIUM, NETHERLANDS AND GERMANY** North	1:2 000 000
180–181	**SOUTHERN EUROPE AND THE MEDITERRANEAN**	1:10 000 000
182	**FRANCE**	1:5 000 000
183	**SPAIN AND PORTUGAL**	1:5 000 000
184–185	**ITALY AND THE BALKANS**	1:5 000 000
186–187	**RUSSIA** West	1:7 000 000

AFRICA

Page	Title	Scale
188–189	**AFRICA** Physical	1:28 000 000
190–191	**AFRICA** Political	1:28 000 000
192–193	**AFRICA** North	1:16 000 000
	Cape Verde	1:16 000 000
194–195	**AFRICA** Central and South	1:16 000 000
196–197	**SOUTH AFRICA**	1:5 000 000

NORTH AMERICA

Page	Title	Scale
198–199	**NORTH AMERICA** Physical	1:32 000 000
200–201	**NORTH AMERICA** Political	1:32 000 000
202–203	**CANADA**	1:17 000 000
204–205	**CANADA** West	1:7 000 000
206–207	**CANADA** East	1:7 000 000

VI

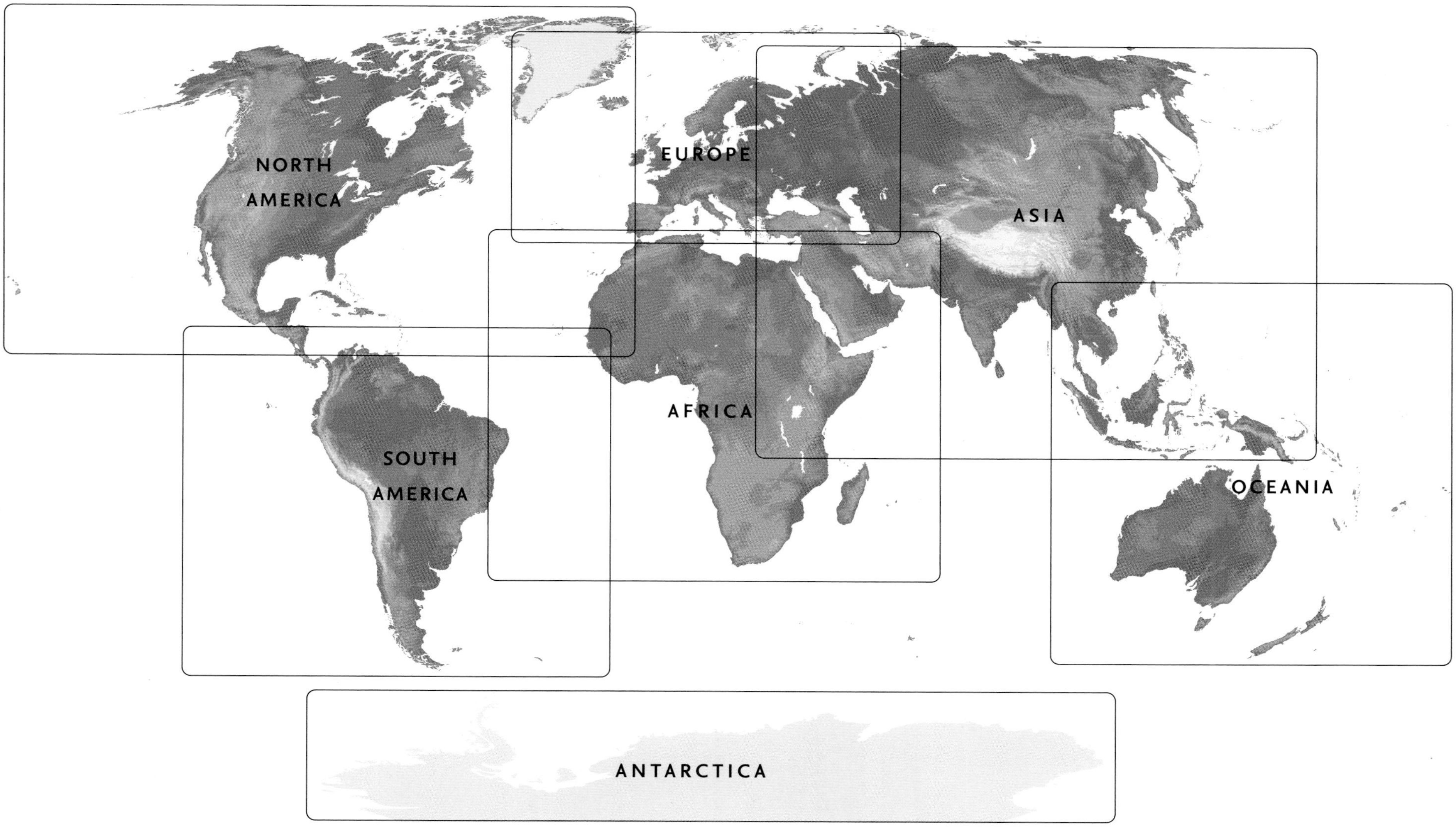

NORTH
AMERICA

EUROPE

ASIA

AFRICA

SOUTH
AMERICA

OCEANIA

ANTARCTICA

SATELLITE IMAGES

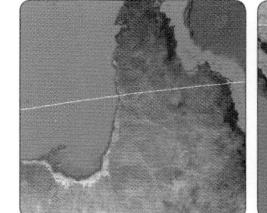
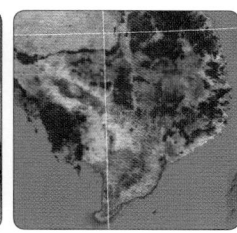

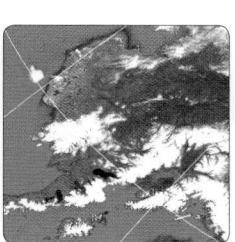

OCEANIA

The continent of Oceania comprises Australia, New Guinea, New Zealand and the islands of the Pacific Ocean. The main Pacific island groups of Melanesia, Micronesia and Polynesia sit among the complex of ridges and troughs which make up the Pacific sea floor. Notable among these, and visible extending northwards from New Zealand, are the Kermadec and Tonga trenches – the latter reaching a depth of 10 800 m at Horizon Deep. Australia itself appears largely dry and barren, its vast interior consisting of several deserts, with brighter salt lakes in the low artesian basin of the east central area. The east coast of Australia, separated from the interior by the Great Dividing Range – the source of the continent's longest rivers the Murray and the Darling – is more densely vegetated. New Guinea is covered by dense tropical forest, while New Zealand displays a great variety of land cover types, most prominent being the snow-capped Southern Alps on South Island.

RING OF FIRE

This image shows the western portion of the 'Ring of Fire' – the 35 000 km boundary between the Pacific oceanic crustal plate and its neighbouring continental plates which is characterized by the frequent occurrence of earthquakes and volcanoes. Approximately 70 per cent of historically recorded active volcanoes have occurred within this belt. The ocean floor topography reveals the plate boundaries running north from New Zealand, through the islands of the West Pacific, eastern Indonesia, the Philippines and Japan. In the far northeast of the image, the remarkable Hawaiian-Emperor chain of volcanic islands is visible. Over 5800 km long, this chain of islands has formed over the last 70 million years as the Pacific plate has moved across an area of high volcanic activity known as a hotspot. This has created a chain of volcanoes which get progressively younger and higher in elevation towards the southeast. The island of Hawaii is the most recent addition to the chain with active volcanoes Mauna Loa and Kilauea.

AUSTRALIAN DESERTS

Australia is the driest inhabited continent on earth, 70 per cent of it is arid or semi-arid. Deserts occupy 30 per cent of land, mainly on the western plateau and the interior lowlands. The orange area near the centre of the country is the Simpson Desert where the world's longest parallel sand dunes run for hundreds of kilometres. The light yellow area to the southeast of this is the inhospitable area of the Tirari, Strzelecki and Sturt Stony Deserts. Salt lakes occur in many lowland areas. The largest is Kati-Thanda-Lake Eyre, its dry lake bed appearing white on the image. Until recently, Kati Thanda-Lake Eyre was thought to be permanently dry. In the last forty years, however, it has been spectacularly filled several times, becoming, temporarily, Australia's largest lake.

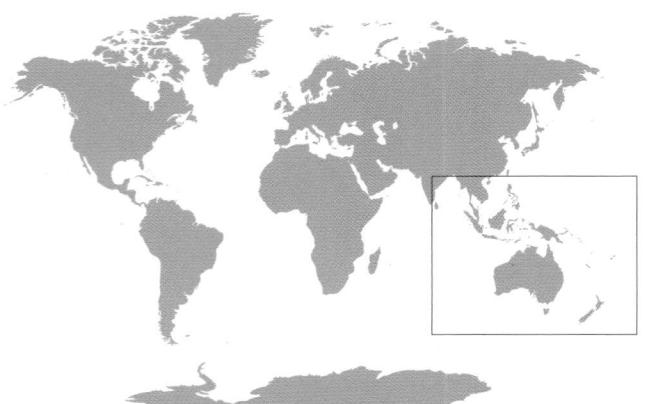

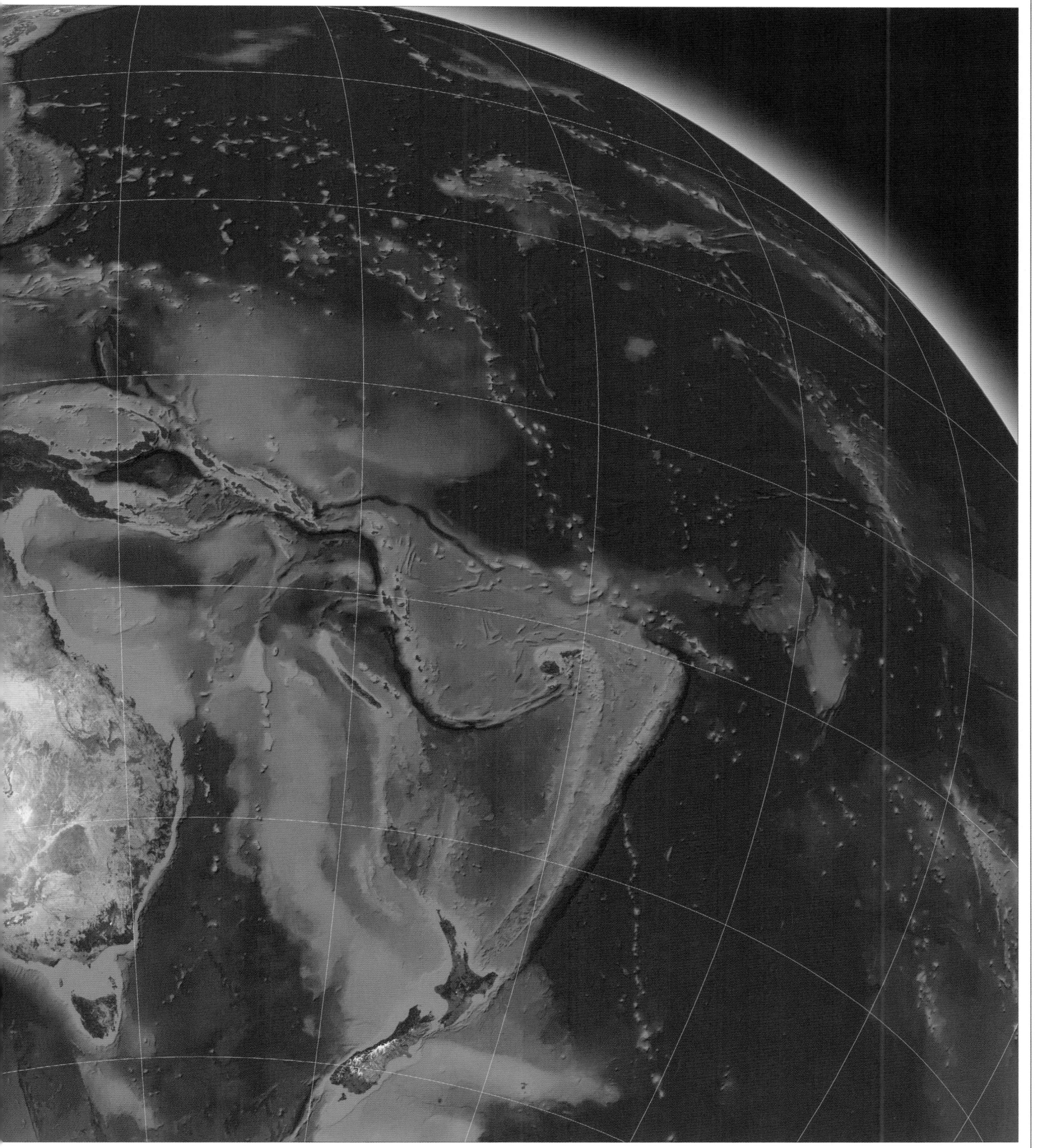

ASIA

This vast continent – the world's largest – covers an enormous area and contains a great variety of landscapes, evident on this image. It stretches from the Mediterranean Sea in the west to the far east of the Russia and Japan, and from arctic Siberia in the north to the tropical islands of Indonesia. The Caspian Sea – the world's largest lake – is prominent in the west. The snow-capped Caucasus mountains stretching from the Caspian Sea to the Black Sea clearly mark the divide between Asia and Europe. Just east of the Caspian Sea lies the complex shape of the Aral Sea. This was once the world's fourth largest lake, but is now drastically reduced in size because of climate change and the extraction of water for irrigation.

THE HIMALAYA

The great Asian mountain system of the Himalaya can be seen as a snow-covered arc on the image as it stretches for over 2000 km in a series of parallel ridges from the Ganges basin in the east to the Plateau of Tibet in the west. Formed 25–70 million years ago, as the earth's crust folded due to the northward push of the Indian subcontinent, the system is still growing and is subject to severe earthquakes. All fourteen of the world's peaks above 8000 m are found in the Himalaya and adjoining ranges. The main range, in which the highest peaks are found, is permanently snow-covered and there are extensive glaciers which give rise to the Indian subcontinent's major rivers. The image clearly shows the contrast between the aridity of the Plateau of Tibet and the Tarim Basin to the north, shown in yellow tones in this image, and the more vegetated land to the south, appearing green-brown. This is a result of the interception of the moisture-laden monsoon weather system by the south-facing slopes of the Himalaya.

RIVERS OF BANGLADESH

The courses and confluence of the Ganges and Brahmaputra Rivers can be seen in the centre of the image. Bangladesh, the country in which they meet, is dominated by rivers and, as most of the country lies less than 110 m above sea level, is prone to flooding. Many of India's largest cities lie in the valley of the Ganges where its flood plains support over 8 per cent of the world's population. The Ganges, considered sacred by Hindus, discharges into the Bay of Bengal, nearly 2500 km downstream from its source in the Gangotri Glacier in the Himalaya. It carries with it 2 billion tons of sediment every year which has led to the formation of the world's largest river delta. Dense wetland forests, known as the Sundarbans, grow along the coast and appear as a dark green strip on this image.

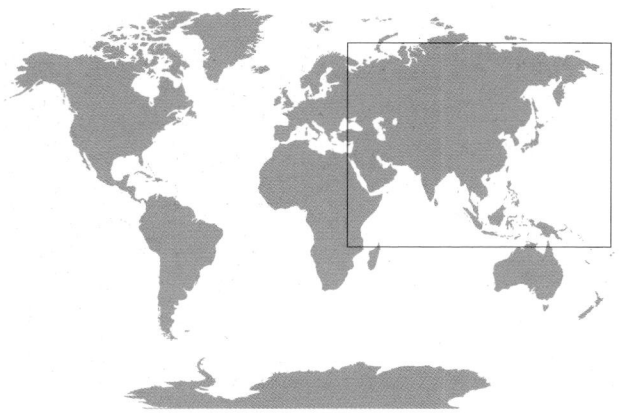

EUROPE

The generally densely vegetated continent of Europe contains some dramatic geographical features. The complex coastlines of Iceland, Scandinavia and northwestern Russia mark its northern and western limits, while the British Isles sit on the flat, wide continental shelf. Europe's mountain ranges divide the continent – in the southwest, the Pyrenees separate France from the drier Iberian Peninsula; the wide arc of the Alps separates Italy from the rest of western Europe; the Carpathian Mountains, appearing as a dark curve between the Alps and the Black Sea, mark the edge of the vast European plains; and the Caucasus, stretching between the Black Sea and the Caspian Sea, create a prominent barrier between Europe and Asia. Two of Europe's greatest rivers are also clearly visible on this image – the Volga, Europe's longest river, flowing south from the Ural Mountains into the Caspian Sea and the Dnieper flowing across the plains into the northern Black Sea.

THE ALPS

Highlighted by snow cover on this image, this 800 km long mountain system in south central Europe has been formed in the last 55 million years by the northward movement of the African landmass crumpling up the rocks of the Eurasian landmass. This squeezing action formed huge folds in the rock many kilometres in size. The folds would often break and slide over one another to form huge thrust faults as they pushed northwards. The resultant mountain range has Mont Blanc (4810 m) as its highest peak, and is the source of several of Europe's major rivers, including the Rhine, the Rhone and the Po. The highest peaks are permanently snow-capped and there are numerous glaciers. Glaciation was more extensive in the past and carved a unique Alpine mountain landscape characterized by U-shaped valleys and long, moraine-blocked lakes, several of which appear black on this image.

CASPIAN SEA

Seen near the eastern edge of this image is the Caspian Sea – the world's largest body of inland water. Like the much smaller Aral Sea, to its northeast, the Caspian Sea was once connected to the Mediterranean before falling sea levels during the ice age cut it off. The Volga river supplies over 75 per cent of its inflow. Water levels have fluctuated greatly as a result of dam construction and water extraction from the Volga. Rapid lowering of its level was seen between 1929 and 1978 but since then levels have risen by 2.5 m, pushing the Volga delta (the dark area on the northwest shore of the sea) 100 km inland. The Caspian Sea has no outflow and salinity levels vary across it. Highest levels of 20 per cent are found in the very shallow Garabogazköl Aýlagy – the prominent grey inlet on the eastern shoreline – which is exploited for salt.

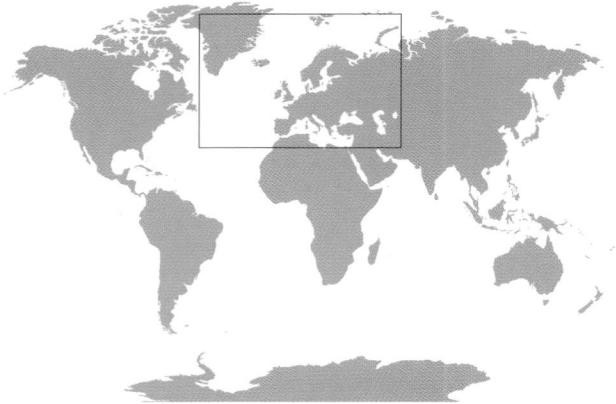

AFRICA

This image of Africa clearly shows the change in vegetation through the equatorial regions from the vast, dry Sahara desert covering much of the north of the continent, through the rich forests of the Congo basin – the second largest drainage basin in the world – to the high plateau of southern Africa. Lake Victoria dominates central east Africa and the Nile and its delta create a distinctive feature in the desert in the northeast. The path of the Great Rift Valley can be traced by the pattern of linear lakes in east Africa, to Ethiopia, and along the Red Sea. The small, dark fan-shaped feature in central southern Africa is the Okavango Delta in Botswana – one of the world's most ecologically sensitive areas. To the east of the continent lies Madagascar, and in the Indian Ocean northeast of this is the Mascarene Ridge sea feature stretching from the Seychelles in the north to Mauritius and Réunion in the south.

EAST AFRICA RIFT VALLEY

More than 6700 km long, the East African Rift was formed 30 million years ago when the African and Arabian continental plates separated. The two branches of the Rift, each of which is about 50 km wide, are visible on this image. The western branch is dominated by larger lakes, including Lake Albert in the north and Lake Tanganyika in the south, while the eastern branch is dotted with smaller lakes including Lake Natron. The land here is mostly 1000 m above sea level, and drier and less densely vegetated than west Africa. Lake Victoria, the third largest lake in the world, lies on the equatorial plain between the two branches of the Rift. One of the main headwater reservoirs of the River Nile, its lake basin is heavily populated and intensely cultivated. Mount Kilimanjaro and Mount Kenya – the two highest mountains in Africa – lie to the east of Lake Victoria.

SAHEL

The Sahel is a thin band of dry savanna grassland stretching 5000 km from Senegal and Mauritania in northwest Africa to the Red Sea coast of Sudan and Eritrea in the northeast. It appears on this image as a light green and tan strip running across the continent between the yellow desert sands of the Sahara, and the dark green densely vegetated area of equatorial Africa. The Sahel region is one of Africa's most productive crop areas but it has a history of famine due to highly erratic rainfall. A dry period from the early 1970s to the mid 1990s left many wondering if the Sahara was creeping south. Satellite images are being used to study the area over time and, although the area is not becoming a desert on a large scale, areas of land degradation are being identified.

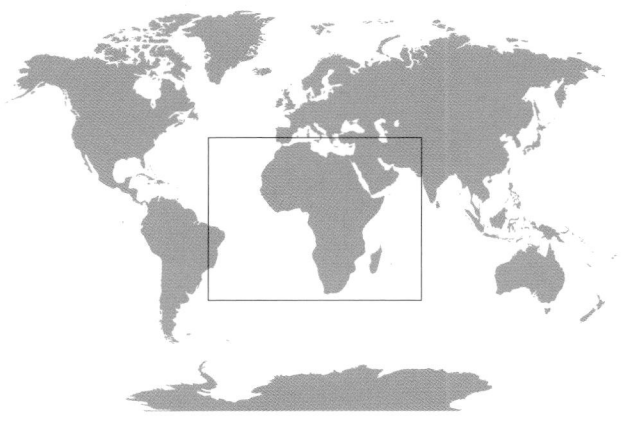

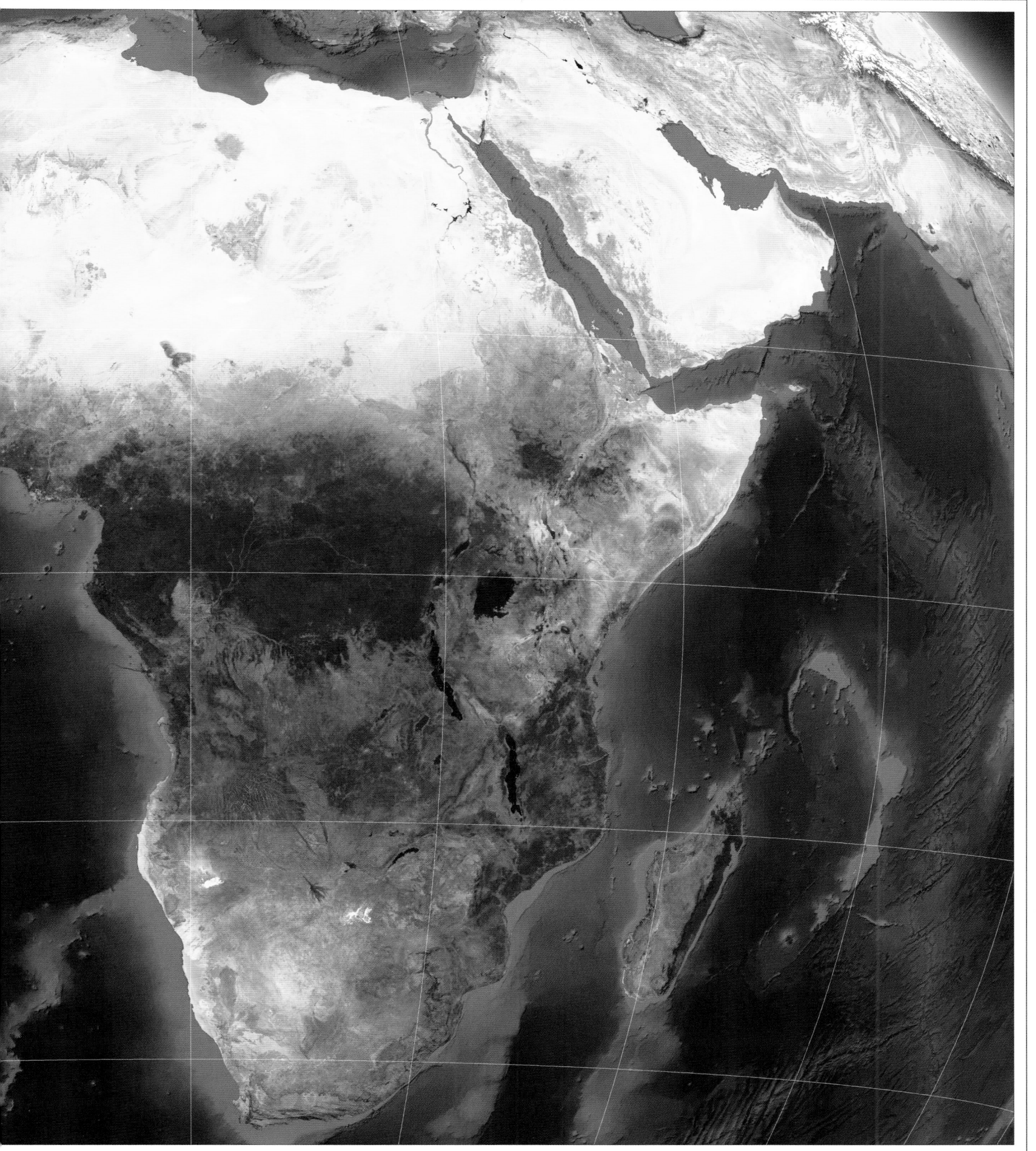

NORTH AMERICA

Many well-known geographical features are identifiable on this image of North America, which also illustrates the contrasts in landscapes across the continent. Greenland – the world's largest island – sits off the northeast coast while the dramatic chain of the Aleutian Islands in the northwest stretches from Alaska across the Bering Sea to the Kamchatka Peninsula in Russia. Further south in the Pacific Ocean, at the far left of the image, lie the Hawai'ian Islands and their very distinctive ocean ridge. There is a strong west-east contrast across the continent. The west is dominated by the Rocky Mountains which give way to the Great Plains. In the east, the Great Lakes, the largest of which, Lake Superior, is second in size only to the Caspian Sea in Asia, the valley of the Mississippi and the Coastal Plain are prominent. In the southeast the complex floor of the Caribbean Sea is visible, particularly the dramatic Cayman Trench, stretching from the Gulf of Honduras to southern Cuba.

GREAT LAKES

During a succession of ice ages in the last 2 million years, much of Canada was covered by a vast ice sheet. When it melted, a huge volume of water was released southwards and some of this remains trapped in the glacier-carved lake basins of the Great Lakes and numerous smaller lakes on the Canadian Shield – a plateau in eastern Canada and the northeast USA. Four of the five Great Lakes mark the boundary between the USA and Canada. The lakes are connected by canals and short rivers creating a 1867 km waterway from the western end of Lake Superior to the St Lawrence river outflow at the eastern end of Lake Ontario. The St Lawrence Seaway, opened in 1959, allowed deep draft shipping direct access to the lakes from the Atlantic Ocean. The height above sea level of the lake surfaces varies. The greatest height difference, of 51 m, occurs between Lakes Erie and Ontario at Niagara Falls.

GREENLAND ICE SHEET

The ice sheet which covers more than 80 per cent of Greenland is the northern hemisphere's largest remaining relic of the last ice age. The ice sheet has shrunk noticeably since 1978. Studies of satellite data reveal that it has lost 20 per cent more mass than it received in recent years due to melting and iceberg calving. There are fears that the rate of melting is increasing due to global warming, and that this could have serious implications for world sea levels, ocean currents and weather patterns. If the Greenland ice sheet were to melt completely, the sea level would rise by more than 7 m. In 2007, a new island Uunartoq Qeqertoq (Warming Island) was discovered. This was previously thought to be part of mainland Greenland, but as ice melted it was revealed as an island.

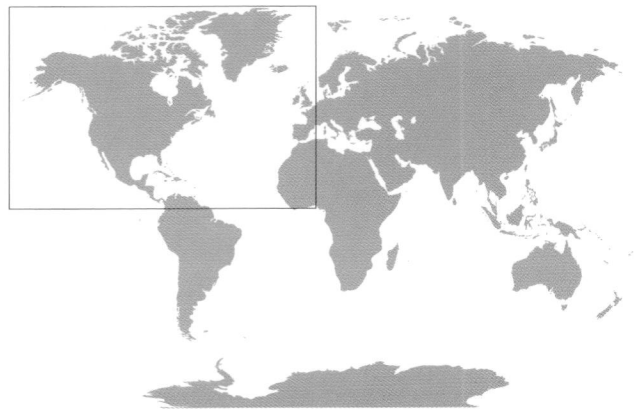

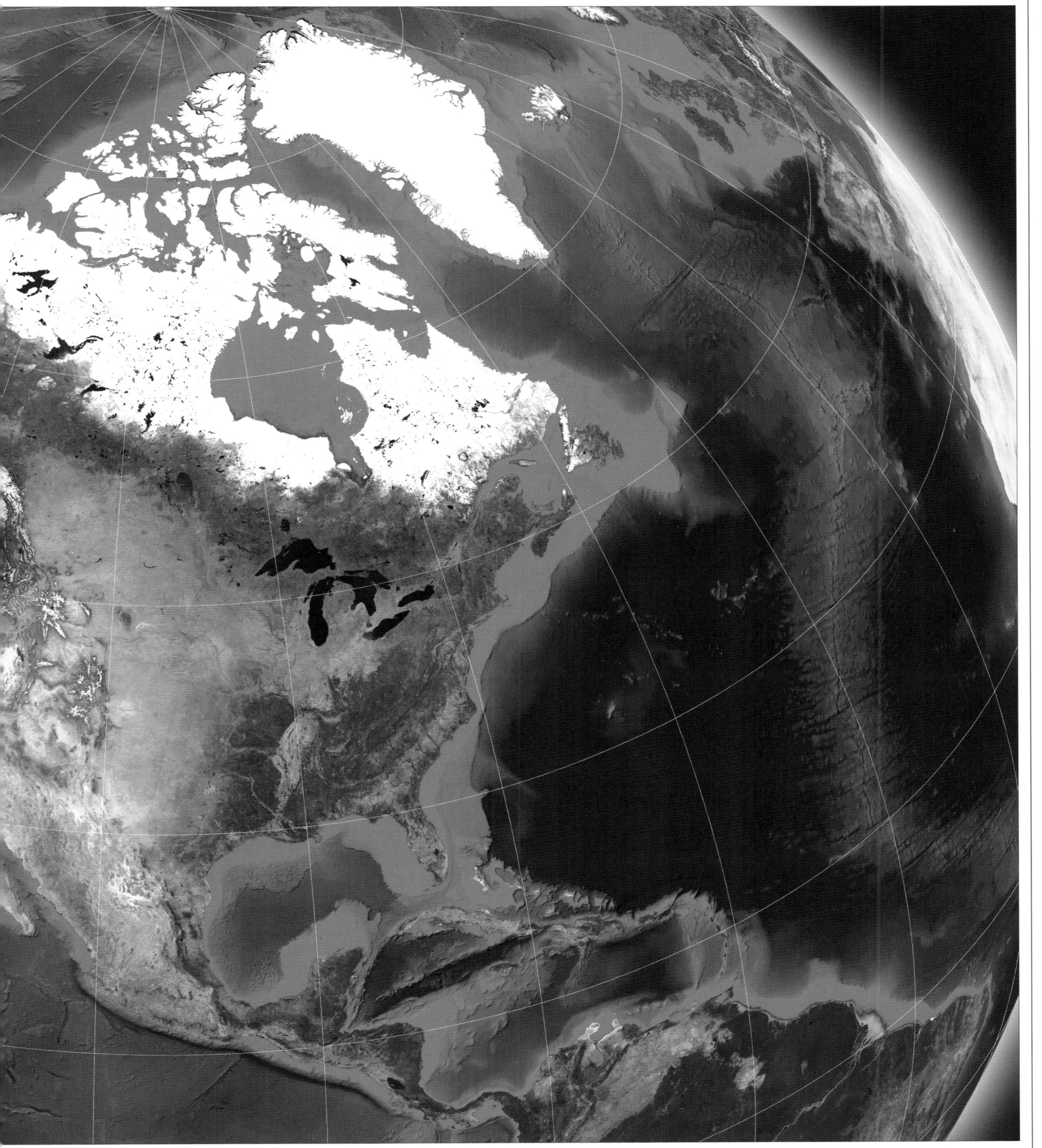

SOUTH AMERICA

The Andes mountains stretch along the whole length of the west coast of South America, widening into the high plains of the Altiplano in Bolivia and Peru in the centre of the continent. Lake Titicaca, the world's highest large navigable lake, lies on the Altiplano, straddling the Bolivia-Peru border. Running parallel to the Andes, just off the west coast, is the Peru-Chile Trench which marks the active boundary between the Nazca and South American tectonic plates. Movement between these plates gives rise to numerous volcanoes in the Andes. The Amazon river runs across almost the whole width of the continent in the north, meeting the Atlantic Ocean in its wide delta on the northeast coast. The vast Amazon basin is one of the most ecologically diverse areas of the Earth. In the south, the wide continental shelf stretches eastwards from the tip of the continent to the Falkland Islands and South Georgia on the bottom edge of the image.

AMAZON

The world's second longest river, the 6516 km long Amazon, discharges one-fifth of the total fresh water entering the world's oceans. The enormous Amazon Basin covers most of northern Brazil, as well as parts of five other South American countries and supports the world's largest rainforest, its rich plant life shown in dark green tones on this image. The Andes define the western rim of the Basin and supply the headwaters of many of the Amazon's 500 tributaries. The confluence of the Rio Negro (appearing black on the image) and the Amazon (appearing yellow) is visible near the centre of the Basin. The difference in appearance between the rivers is a result of the low sediment content of the Rio Negro. In contrast, the Amazon empties approximately 1.3 million tons of sediment into the Atlantic Ocean every day. The vast delta which has formed from this sediment is seen as a bright yellow area on the image.

ANDES

The world's longest mountain range, the Andes, stretches more than 8000 km from Venezuela to Chile. Higher than any other mountains, with the exception of the Himalaya, they are home to many areas of volcanic activity. Earthquakes, mudflows and landslides present additional hazards. The bright area in the centre of the image, near the west coast of the continent, is the driest place on earth – the Atacama Desert. This is a large area of saltpans and bare rock, some parts of which have not had rain for more than a century. Other, smaller salt flats are also visible as light areas. These are remnants of a vast inland sea which once covered the area. White areas on the southern part of the image are glaciers in the southern Andes.

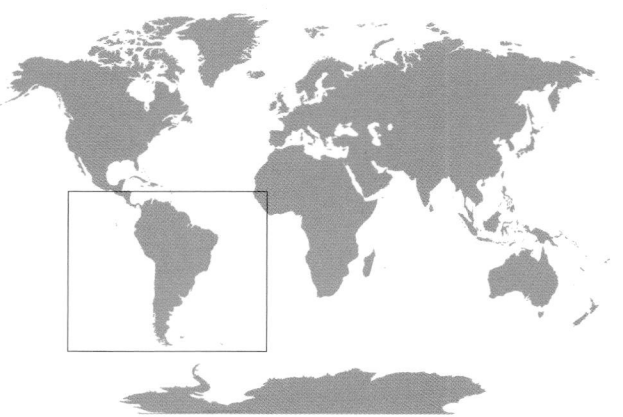

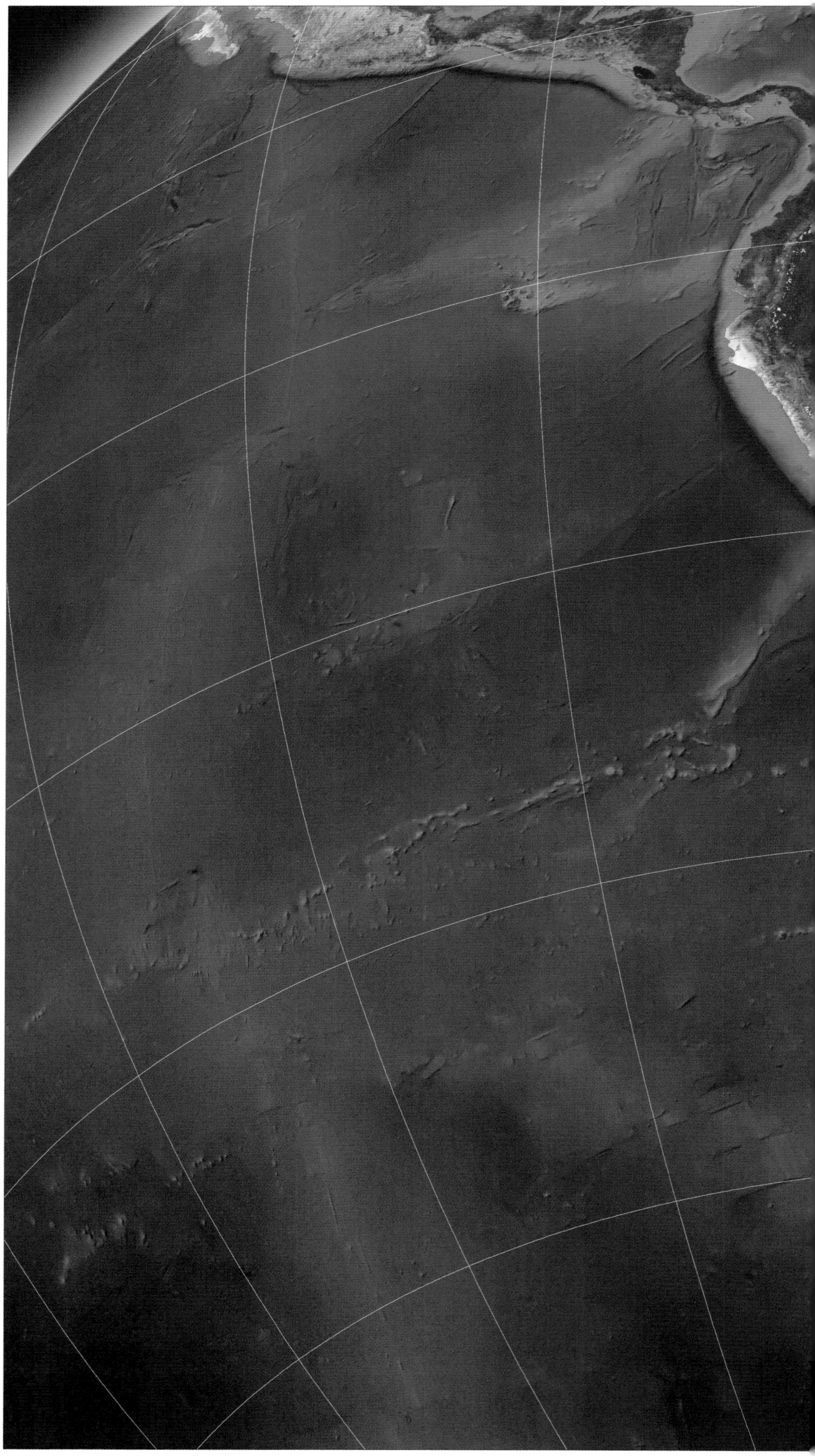

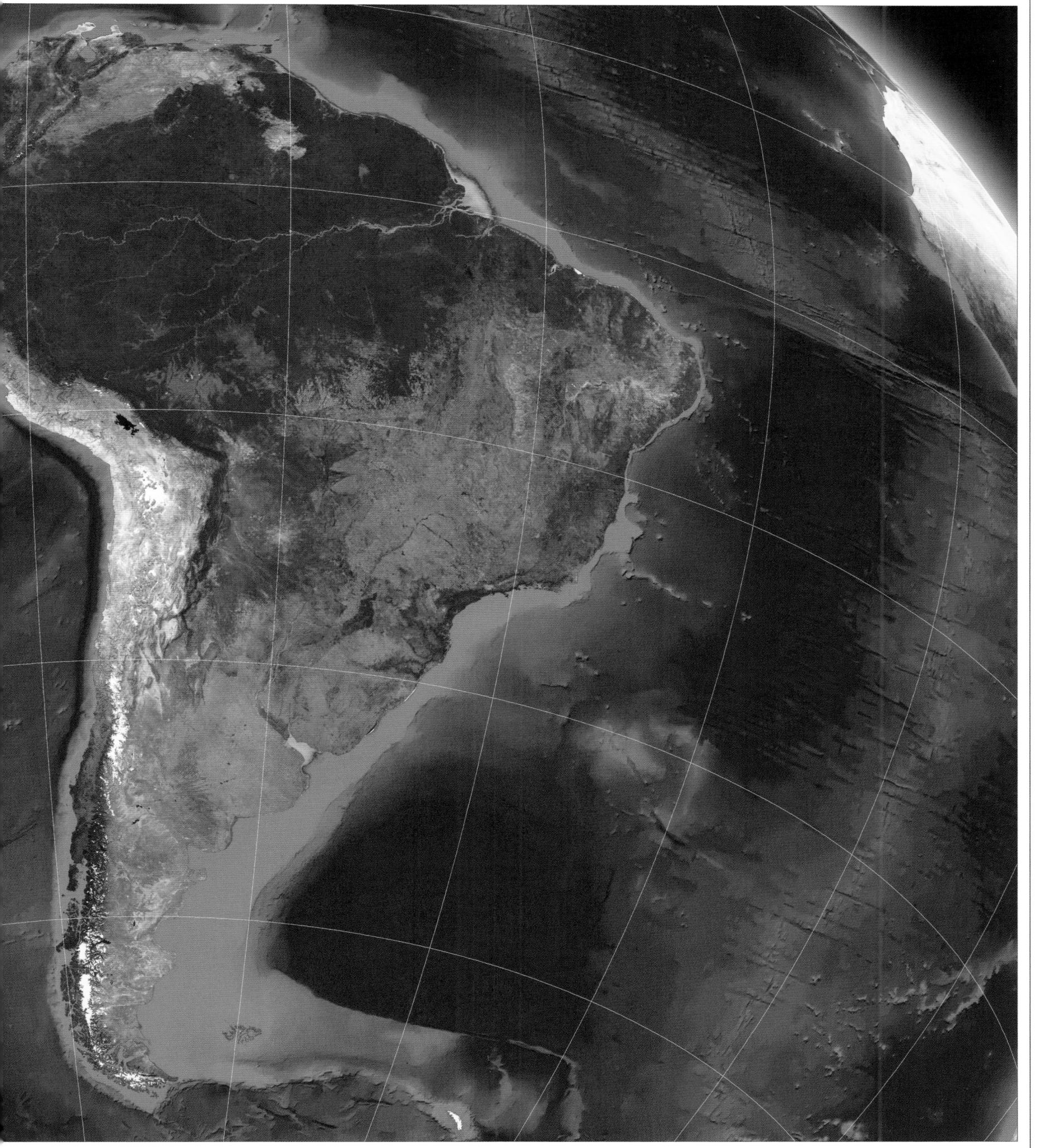

ANTARCTICA

Protected by the Antarctic Treaty, implemented in 1959, from commercial exploitation and from the realization of territorial claims, Antarctica is perhaps the world's greatest unspoilt, and relatively unexplored, wilderness. This image combines bathymetric data (incomplete in some black areas) with a mosaic of over a thousand Landsat ETM+ scenes to show the extent of the continental ice sheet in an austral summer. Floating sea ice is not shown. The Antarctic Peninsula – home to numerous scientific research stations – in the top left of the image reaching towards South America, the huge Ronne and Ross ice shelves, and the Transantarctic Mountains – dividing the continent into West and East Antarctica – are the dominant physical features.

ANTARCTICA ICE SHEET UNDER THREAT

The largest mass of ice on earth, the Antarctic ice sheet contains over 70 per cent of the earth's fresh water. On Antarctica's high inland plateau the ice sheet is up to 4.5 km thick and feeds massive ice shelves which float out onto the surrounding seas. This particular image does not show floating sea ice but the analysis of satellite images (commonly known as the science of remote sensing) provides valuable data for scientists studying the extent and characteristics of the ice. The stability of the ice sheet is being threatened by global warming and in the 1990s it was predicted that the ice shelves that surround Antarctica were in danger of becoming unstable.

Studies of the extent of seven ice shelves along the Antarctic Peninsula, in the top left of this image, reveal a decline of 13 500 sq km since 1974. In 1998, over only thirty-one days, the Larsen B ice shelf disintegrated into thousands of icebergs and it is now a mere 40 per cent of its previous extent. After analyzing twenty years of satellite data of the continent as a whole, scientists have concluded that persistent melting of the ice has been occurring further inland and at higher altitudes over the past two decades. These changes are attributed to a steady warming of the climate in the region. The rate of warming is approximately 0.5 Centigrade degrees (C°) per decade and the trend has been present since the late 1940s.

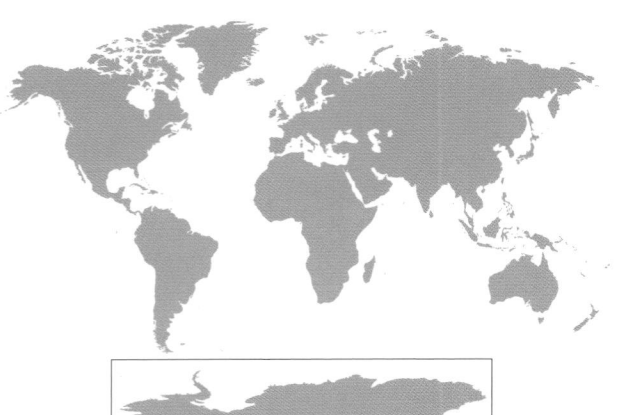

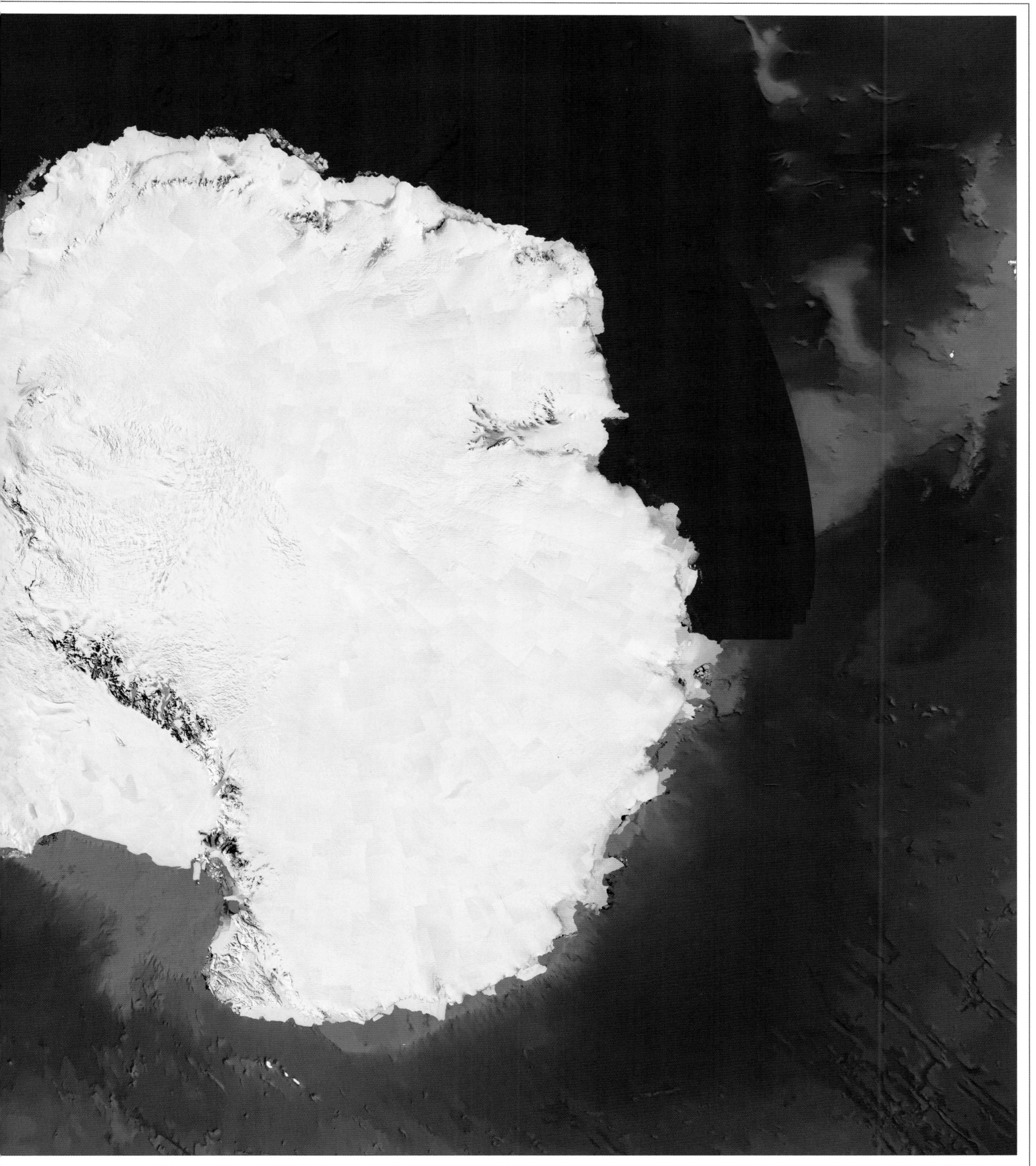

THE WORLD ON MERCATOR'S PROJECTION 1858

From the *Family Atlas of Physical, General and Classical Geography*.
Drawn and engraved by J. Bartholomew Jr F.R.G.S.

The nineteenth century was the Age of Empire, when all the major European powers harboured imperial ambitions and used their commercial and military might to extend their influence in known parts of the world and open up new regions.

In the first half of the century, the process had been gradual. Britain had emerged as the pre-eminent overseas power, extending the boundaries of her established colonial possessions in North America, India and Australia and acquiring new footholds in Singapore (1819), Hong Kong (1842), and Natal (1843). Meanwhile, imperial rivals were weakened in the post-Napoleonic period. France, Spain and the Netherlands had all ceded colonial territory to Britain while Spain and Portugal were weakened by the loss of their Latin American colonies: Brazil seceded peacefully from Portugal in 1822, while the former Spanish colonies of Paraguay, Argentina (La Plata as recorded on the map), Chile, Colombia (New Granada), Venezuela, Ecuador, Peru, and Bolivia had fought their way to independence between 1811 and 1825. Mexico had secured its freedom from Spain in 1821 and two years later, Central America had seceded from it to create a federal republic which then further divided in 1839 into the independent states of Costa Rica, El Salvador, Guatemala, Honduras and Nicaragua (although interestingly, the cartographers have not recorded this).

In the second half of the century, the pace of imperial expansion increased markedly. By 1858, it is clear that Europeans had made few inroads into Africa; fifty years later, however, the map would show a multicoloured mosaic of colonial territories belonging to Britain, France, Portugal, and the newly unified nations of Germany and Italy. Asia was also a focus for European expansion, chiefly by the French, who secured control of Indo-China (1884–93) and by the British, who gained significant portions of the East Indies (1875–95). India also remained a focus of British interest. However, imperialism was not a solely European trait: Japan would acquire Formosa from China in 1895 and forcibly annex Korea in 1910, while the USA would secure the Philippines from Spain in 1898.

Other changes to this map during the second half of the century include the borders of the once-mighty Turkish or Ottoman Empire receding from the Balkans, north Africa and parts of the Persian Gulf. In North America, Russia abandoned its sole American colony, Alaska, which it would sell to the US Government in 1867 for $7.2 million. Elsewhere on the continent, the British colonies of North America were granted legislative autonomy under the Crown as part of a process begun by the establishment of the federal Dominion of Canada in 1867, while Britain's Australian possessions were already largely self-governing.

EVENTS	
14 January	Felice Orsini and three accomplices fail to assassinate Napoleon III in Paris, France, but the bombs kill and injure bystanders
2 July	*The Great Stink*, the stench of untreated sewage in the Thames, affects the work of Parliament, in London (UK), leading eventually to proposals for a sewerage system for London
11 August	First ascent of the Eiger, Switzerland, by two Swiss guides and an Irishman, Charles Barrington

BIRTHS	
18 March	Rudolf Diesel, German inventor of the diesel engine (d. 1913)
27 October	Theodore Roosevelt, 26th President of United States (1901–1909), Nobel Peace Prize 1906 (d. 1919)

DEATHS	
16 June	John Snow, British physician, one of the fathers of epidemiology, famous for promoting anaesthesia and medical hygiene (b. 1813)
17 November	Robert Owen, Welsh-born social reformer and one of the founders of the cooperative movement (b. 1771)

THE WORLD ON MERCATOR'S PROJECTION.

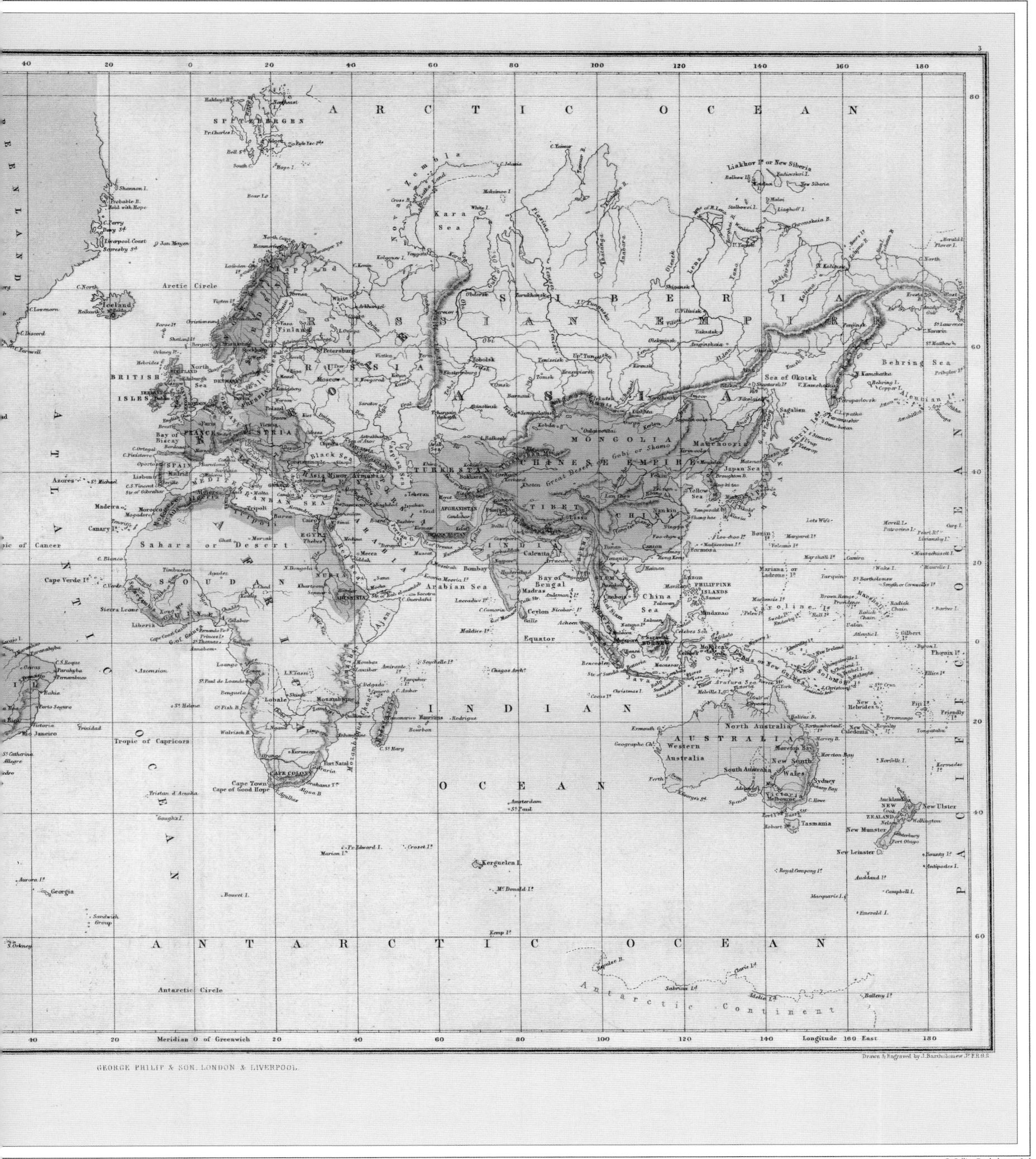

POLITICAL MAP OF THE WORLD 1914

From the *International Reference Atlas of the World*, cartography by
J. G. Bartholomew LL.D., F.R.G.S., Cartographer to the King.

This map shows the imperial divisions of the world at the onset of the
First World War in 1914. European colonial empires had grown rapidly
over the past century and by now the Great Powers of Europe had
engrossed nine-tenths of Africa and much of Asia.

Prior to 1914, Europe had been run on balance-of-power politics,
where a status quo was maintained between the major powers, often
with unofficial agreements and alliances. However, the power system
was changing and there was now less collaboration and more rivalry
because empire powers wanted to preserve imperialism and control
competitors (seen, for example, with the naval arms race between Britain
and Germany). Imperial ambitions, shifting powers and rising tensions
engulfed Europe.

The Balkans became a key area: this was the one region where the
Habsburg empire of Austria-Hungary had a chance of maintaining
its ascendancy. But, on 28 June 1914, the Archduke Franz Ferdinand,
heir to the Habsburg throne, was assassinated in Sarajevo by a Serb
nationalist, Gavrilo Princip. This incident threw Europe into turmoil.
Austria-Hungary sought revenge, and invaded Serbia. German support
for Austria and Russian support for Serbia gave way to a series of alliances
and declarations of war involving global powers, and beginning the First
World War.

Two major alliances emerged. The Allied (Entente) Powers consisted
primarily of France, Britain, Russia and their associated empires and
dependencies. They were later joined by, among others, Italy and, in 1917,
the United States (the force of which would ultimately tip the balance).
The Central Powers comprised Germany and Austria-Hungary and their
empires, later joined by the Ottoman Empire and Bulgaria.

The war was expected to be short-lived, but four years of particularly
bloody warfare later, millions of lives had been lost, both military and
civilian. An armistice on 11 November 1918 between the Allied Powers (the
victors) and Germany, and the Treaty of Versailles in 1919, finally brought
an end to the conflict.

Following the Great War, the map would change completely, with the
defeat of the German and Austro-Hungarian Empires and the collapse
of the Russian Empire following the communist revolution. Territories
in grey on this map belong to the German Empire, and would, five years
later, be reapportioned to the victors in the war by the Treaty of Versailles:
Tanganyika would go to Britain; Togoland and German Cameroon would
be shared between France and Britain; German South West Africa would
go to South Africa; the Pacific Islands to New Zealand; and New Guinea to
Australia.

EVENTS	
2 February	Charlie Chaplin's first film 'Making a Living' is released in USA
29 May	Ocean liner Empress of Ireland sinks in the Gulf of St Lawrence, Canada, causing the loss of 1012 lives
4 August	Germany invades neutral Belgium, Britain declares war on Germany, USA declares neutrality
15 August	Panama Canal, Central America, opens
28 August	In the Battle of Heligoland Bight, off the northwest coast of Germany, the first naval battle of World War I, the British under Admiral Beatty sink three German light cruisers
5–12 September	The First Battle of the Marne begins northeast of Paris, France. 500 000 are killed or injured in an Allied victory. The counterattack ends the German advance on Paris

BIRTHS	
2 April	Sir Alec Guinness, British actor (d. 2000)
15 June	Yuri Andropov, Russian politician, leader of Soviet Union Nov 1982-Feb 1984 (d. 1984)

DEATHS	
21 June	Bertha von Suttner, Austrian novelist and pacifist, first woman to win Nobel Peace Prize, 1905, (b. 1843)
28 June	Archduke Franz Ferdinand of Austria, with wife Sophie, assassinated (b. 1863)

POLITICAL
MAP OF THE WORLD
ON MERCATORS PROJECTION.
Steamship distances are given in Nautical Miles
Principal Railways shown thus

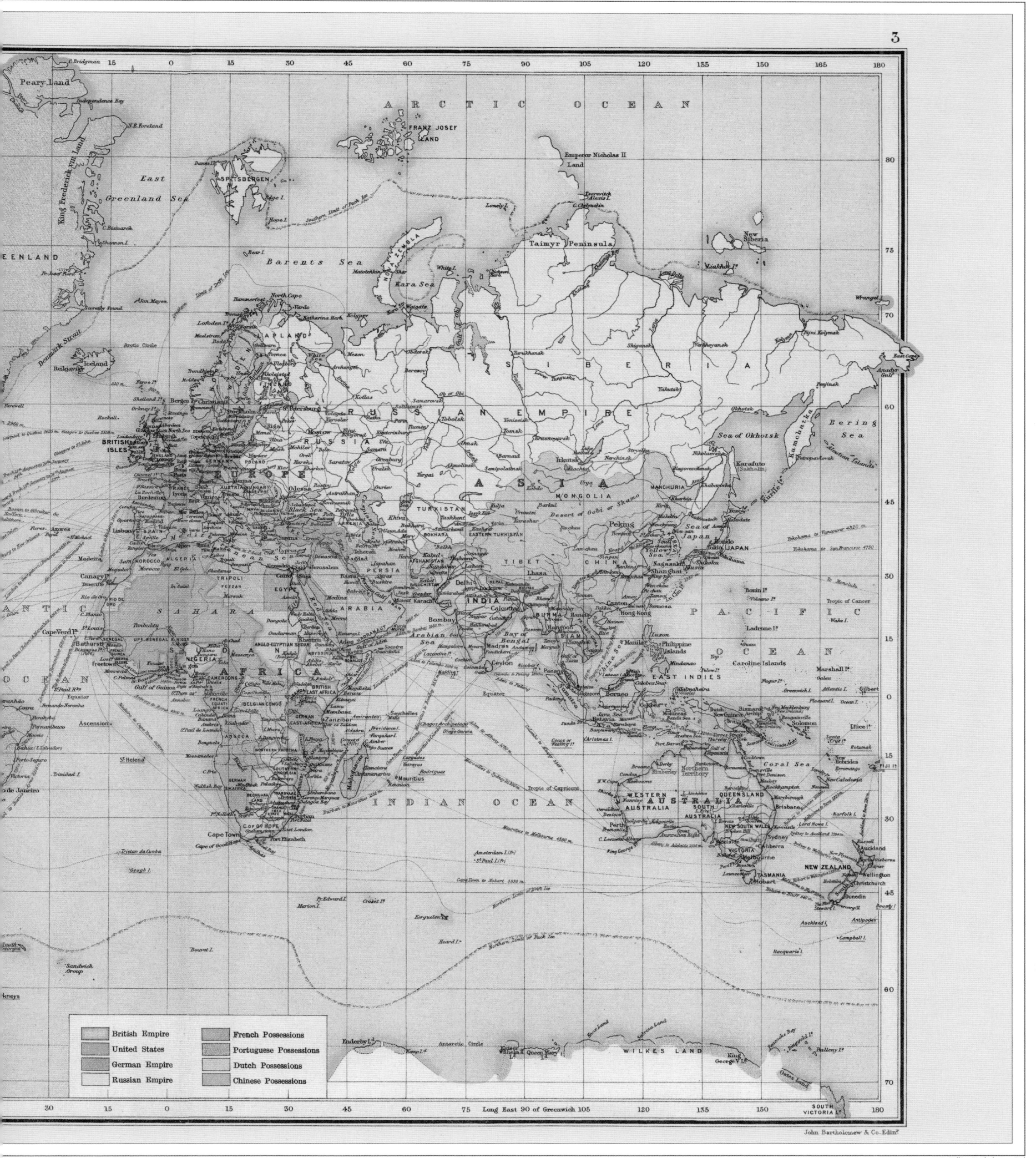

British Empire
United States
German Empire
Russian Empire

French Possessions
Portuguese Possessions
Dutch Possessions
Chinese Possessions

John Bartholomew & Co. Edinᵣ

WORLD POLITICAL DIVISIONS 1936

From the *Advanced Atlas, Fifth Edition*, cartography by
John Bartholomew M.C., M.A., F.R.S.E., F.R.G.S., Cartographer to the King.

The political situation of the world three years before the outbreak
of the Second World War can be seen from this map. The power
of empires had waned significantly after the First World War, and
a number of treaties and pacts were signed between countries to
safeguard against military attacks. Growing political and social conflict
was leading to nationalist uprisings, while both communism and
fascism were on the rise in Europe.

At the time this map was produced, General Franco and his nationalist
troops had rebelled against the Spanish Republic. The resulting Spanish
Civil War pitted Nationalists against Republicans. Republicans were
supported mainly by secular and urban power bases such as Catalonia
and the Basque Country, and also by peasants living in poverty under
aristocratic landowners. The Nationalists, on the other hand, drew
support mostly from the Catholic clergy and wealthier, conservative
landowners. Their anti-communist stance also attracted international
support from fascist Italy under Mussolini and Nazi Germany under
Hitler. The last of the Republican forces surrendered on 1 April 1939,
dissolving the Spanish Republic and leading to a dictatorship under
Franco which was to last for many years to come.

On 25 November 1936, a pact was signed between Nazi Germany and
the Empire of Japan, directed immediately against the Communist
International (Comintern) but more subtly against the Soviet Union.
The Anti-Comintern Pact would protect Germany and Japan's common
interests, safeguarding them against Soviet attacks. Meanwhile, the
Soviet Union was forging closer links with the countries of Western
Europe.

On the African continent, Egypt had been granted independence from
the British Empire in 1922, but fearing attack from Italy, Egypt signed
the Anglo-Egyptian Treaty with the UK in 1936, under which the UK
would have to supply and train Egypt's army and assist in its defence
should war occur.

As can be seen from the shipping routes marked in blue on the inset
map, it was impossible to transport goods between Europe and Asia
without circumnavigating Africa one way or the other. Running
between Port Said on the Mediterranean Sea and Suez on the Red Sea,
the Suez Canal, which had been completed in 1869, was pivotal as it
provided the shorter of the two routes. Military protection of this area
was therefore vital, and it was for this reason that, although the UK
withdrew its troops from the rest of Egypt as a result of the treaty, UK
garrisons remained on the Suez Canal.

Worldwide, the scene was being set for a major conflict, which erupted
in 1939 as the Second World War.

EVENTS	
1 March	Construction of the Hoover Dam, USA, is completed
7 March	Nazi Germany occupies the Rhineland, Germany, in violation of the Treaty of Versailles
30 June	Publication of 'Gone with the Wind' by Margaret Mitchell, in USA
1 July	Maiden voyage of the luxury liner Queen Mary across the Atlantic from Southampton, UK
1 August	Summer Olympics begin in Berlin, Germany
2 November	BBC starts world's first regular TV broadcasting, from Alexandra Palace, north London, UK
10–11 December	Edward VIII, king of Great Britain abdicates

BIRTHS	
1 August	Yves St Laurent, Algerian-born French fashion designer
5 October	Vaclav Havel, Czech writer and politician, first President of the Czech Republic 1993–2003

DEATHS	
20 January	King George V of Great Britain (b. 1865)
19 August	Federico García Lorca, Spanish writer, poet and dramatist (b. 1898)

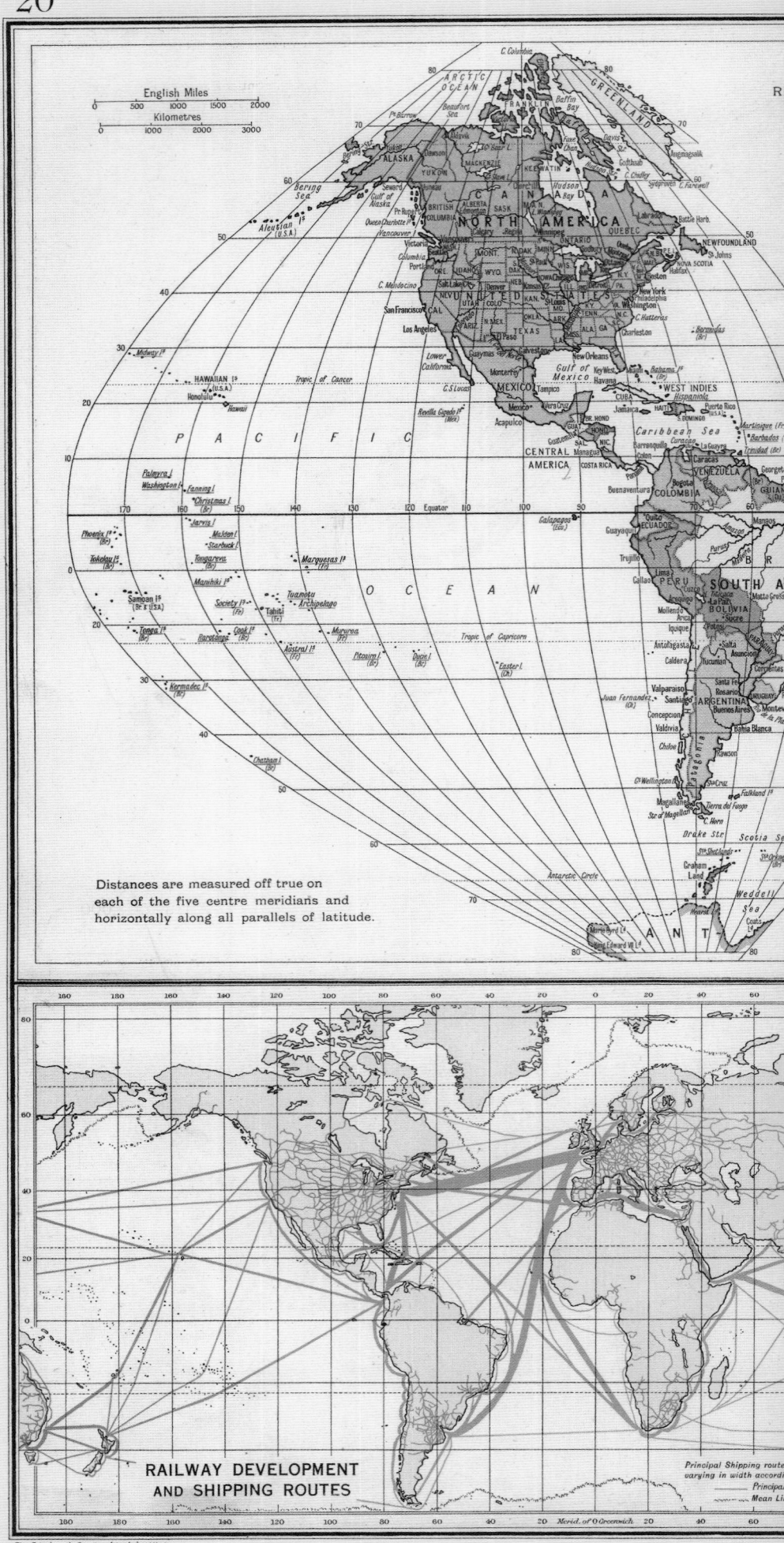

Distances are measured off true on
each of the five centre meridians and
horizontally along all parallels of latitude.

RAILWAY DEVELOPMENT
AND SHIPPING ROUTES

The Edinburgh Geographical Institute

WORLD POLITICAL DIVISIONS

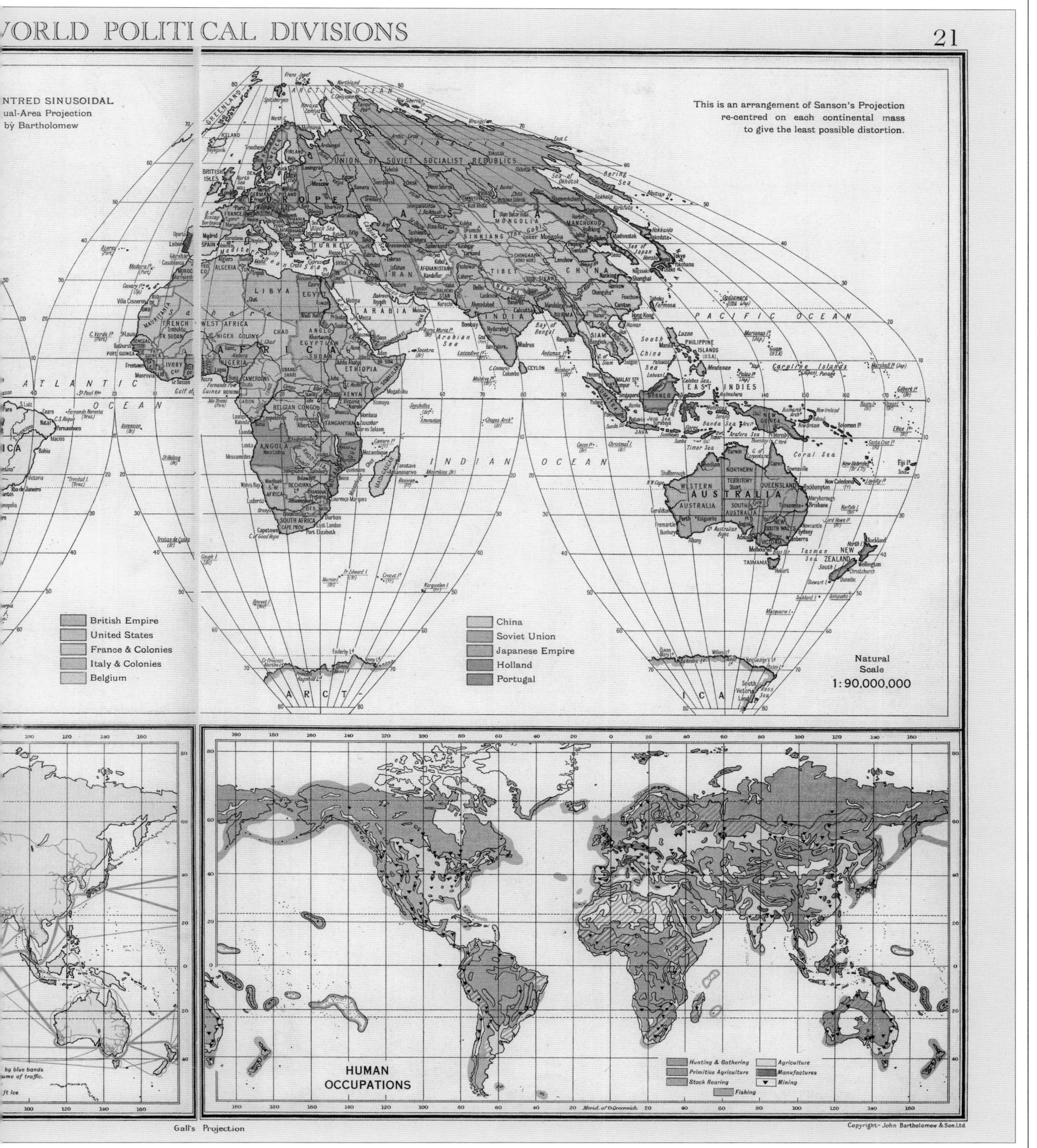

NTRED SINUSOIDAL
ual-Area Projection
by Bartholomew

This is an arrangement of Sanson's Projection
re-centred on each continental mass
to give the least possible distortion.

British Empire	China
United States	Soviet Union
France & Colonies	Japanese Empire
Italy & Colonies	Holland
Belgium	Portugal

Natural
Scale
1:90,000,000

HUMAN OCCUPATIONS

Hunting & Gathering	Agriculture
Primitive Agriculture	Manufactures
Stock Rearing	Mining
Fishing	

by blue bands
ume of traffic.

ft Ice

Gall's Projection

Copyright- John Bartholomew & Son.Ltd.

WORLD ROUTES OF COMMERCE
1950

From the *Advanced Atlas of Modern Geography*, cartography by
John Bartholomew, M.C., Director, the Geographical Institute, Edinburgh.

Just as the First World War had acted as a catalyst for massive change to
the existing world order, so too the fallout from the Second World War
brought significant political, territorial and economic upheaval across
the globe. The interplay of these elements accounted for much of the
tension in international relations for the remainder of the century. The
rate of geopolitical change in the years after 1945 was so rapid that this
map would soon be out-of-date.

The most significant development in world politics post-1945 was
the emergence of the USA and USSR as hostile superpowers, and the
ideological alignment of other nations with each respective camp. The
armed stand-off which emerged between the two power blocs became
known as the Cold War and lasted until the fall of Soviet communism
in the early 1990s. Inevitably, Europe was the principal contact point
between these conflicting ideologies.

For their part, the Soviets had extended their 1939 borders westwards
towards Poland, incorporating Finland and the Baltic states en route.
Moreover, they had created a buffer zone of satellite communist states
in Eastern Europe to protect the motherland from further invasions
from the west. From 1947, the USA sought to rebuild western Europe,
economically and militarily, as a bulwark against the further spread of
communism. Germany formed the boundary between these conflicting
power bases, and in 1949, after several years of mounting tension, the
country was formally partitioned between the occupying powers. The
Soviet sector became East Germany (the GDR) and the Allies' sectors
West Germany (the FDR). Interestingly, the map still records Germany as
a single entity.

Beyond Europe, there were other flashpoints. The communist People's
Republic of China had been established in 1949 after a lengthy civil war,
and the following year, China invaded Tibet, over which it had always
claimed authority – although this was and still is disputed. At about the
same time, in neighbouring Korea, the first armed conflict of the Cold
War began. Like the Great Powers of old, the superpowers intervened in
a civil war, backing the respective forces of the communist North and
the pro-western South, and creating a template for later conflict in
Indo-China that would continue for decades.

Yet if the new emerging power blocs were to be the main source of
future international tensions, issues from the past of the old imperial
powers were also still to surface. As the map shows, in 1950, France,
Britain, the Netherlands and Portugal still had a hold on their
nineteenth-century colonies, particularly in Africa. In the following
decade, each would gradually relinquish this control, peacefully in some
cases and after bloody revolution in others. Britain's successor to empire,
the Commonwealth of Nations, had dropped 'British' from its title in
1949 in acknowledgement of the shifting power balance in its relationship
with its former colonies – though the map's legend has yet to catch up
with this change.

EVENTS	
26 January	India becomes a republic, Rajendra Prasad is the first President
8 March	First Volkswagen Type 2 van (camper van) produced in Wolfsburg, Germany, the forerunner of modern passenger vans
13 May	First race in the inaugural season of the Formula One World Championship is held at Silverstone, England, and is won by Nino Farina
7 October	Beginning of the 1950–51 invasion of Tibet by China

BIRTHS	
18 July	Sir Richard Branson, British businessman, best known for his Virgin brand of companies

DEATHS	
21 January	Eric Blair, pen name George Orwell, English writer and journalist (1984, Animal Farm) (b. 1903)

ROUTES OF COMMERCE

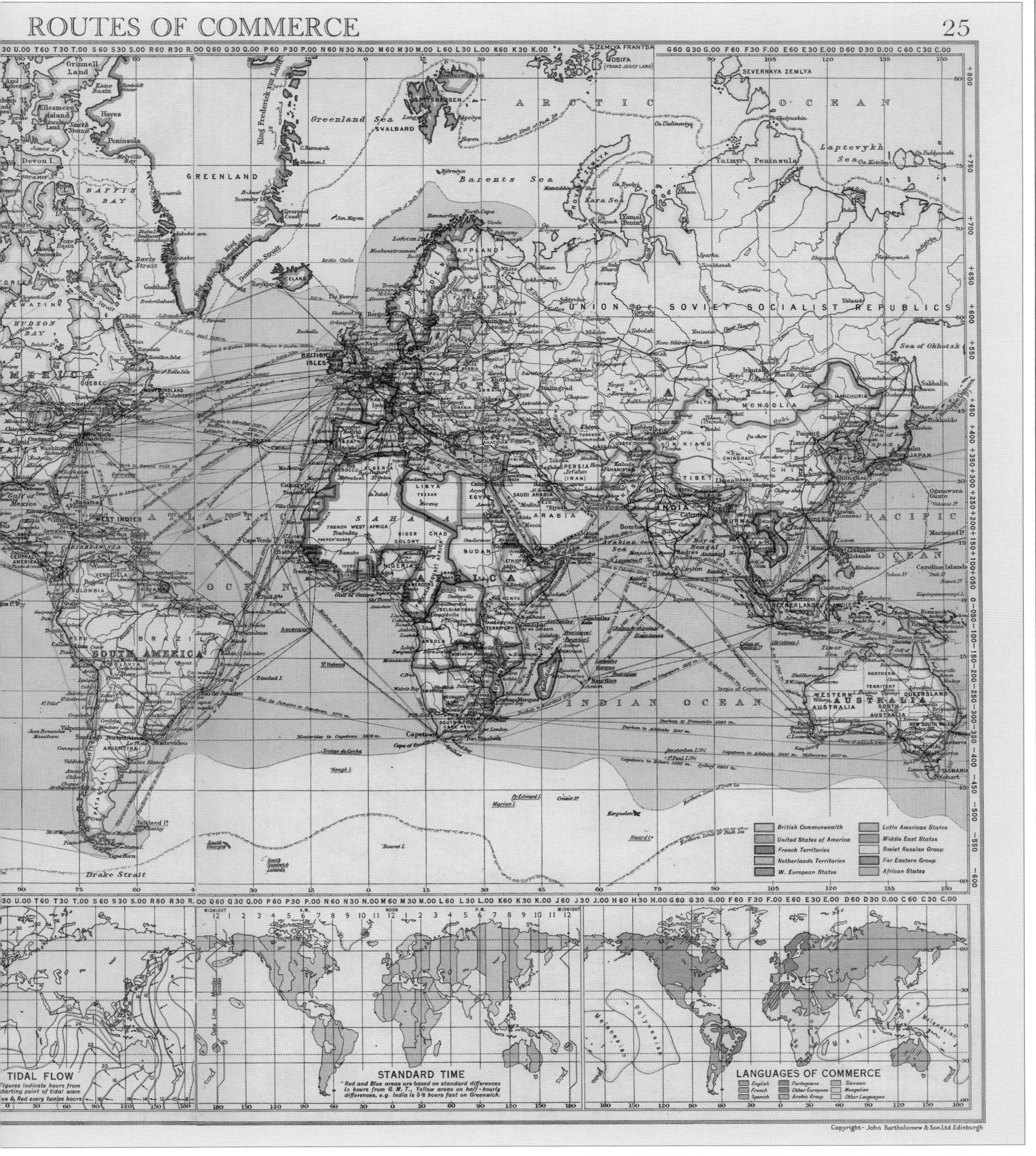

British Commonwealth
United States of America
French Territories
Netherlands Territories
W. European States
Latin American States
Middle East States
Soviet Russian Group
Far Eastern Group
African States

TIDAL FLOW

Figures indicate hours from starting point of tidal wave Blue & Red every twelve hours

STANDARD TIME

Red and Blue areas are based on standard differences in hours from G.M.T., Yellow areas on half-hourly differences, e.g. India is 5½ hours fast on Greenwich.

LANGUAGES OF COMMERCE

English
French
Spanish
Portuguese
Other-European
Arabic Group
Slavonic
Mongolian
Other Languages

THE WORLD POLITICAL CHART 1963

From the Edinburgh World Atlas, Fifth Edition, cartography by
John Bartholomew C.B.E., M.C., LL.D., F.R.S.E., F.R.G.S.

Almost twenty years on from the end of the Second World War, the 'age of empire' was close to its end. International politics had instead become dominated by two superpowers – the United States and the Union of Soviet Socialist Republics (USSR) – who were opposed to each other during the lengthy Cold War.

Significant changes affected French and British possessions worldwide at this time. After the devastation of the war, European powers no longer had the military strength to defend against nationalist movements, nor the economic strength to enforce their rule; in addition, there was a groundswell of public opinion against overseas colonisation. The size and power of the British Empire had been much reduced by the independence of India in 1947, and during the late 1950s and early 1960s the pace of decolonisation had increased considerably, especially in Africa.

Rapid political change in Africa and various other parts of the world often led to violent internal conflicts. Following the Mau Mau uprising, Kenya was granted independence in 1963, the year this map was published. Also in Kenya, ethnic Somalians unsuccessfully strived to join the Northern Frontier District with neighbouring Somalia. By contrast, a communist revolution in Zanzibar, almost immediately after independence from Britain had been granted (also in 1963), successfully overthrew the reigning monarch and established the Republic of Zanzibar and Pemba – which shortly afterwards united with Tanganyika to form Tanzania.

The visual representation of Africa at this time is markedly different from when it was dominated by empires in the nineteenth and early twentieth centuries, with many independent states freed from imperial rule. African allegiances would prove critical during this period as the superpowers sought their loyalty during the Cold War: the poorer African nations were able to play them against each other and use them to their economic advantage.

Further east, nationalists and communists were also the biggest threat to the imperial powers. In South-East Asia, Malaya fought a long struggle against communist insurgents, and became independent from Britain in 1957. The British felt that Singapore would not be large enough to be securely independent, so it was joined with Malaya, Sarawak and North Borneo (renamed Sabah) to form the Federation of Malaysia in 1963. However, Singapore left this union shortly afterwards, in 1965, as an independent nation.

EVENTS	
22 March	The Beatles release their first album, 'Please Please Me' in UK
25 May	The Organisation of African Unity is created in Addis Ababa, Ethiopia
16 June	Soviet cosmonaut, Valentina Tereshkova, is the first woman in space, in Vostok 6
5 August	USA, UK and Soviet Union sign a Partial Nuclear Test Ban Treaty
28 August	Martin Luther King delivers his 'I have a dream' speech from the steps of the Lincoln Memorial, Washington D.C., USA
14–15 November	A volcanic eruption under the sea near Iceland creates a new island, Surtsey
22 November	John F. Kennedy, President of USA, assassinated in Dallas, Texas, USA (b. 1917)
23 November	The first episode of 'Dr Who' is broadcast by BBC, in UK

BIRTHS	
22 February	Vijay Singh, Fijian golfer
27 March	Quentin Tarantino, American director, actor and producer

DEATHS	
30 January	Francis Poulenc, French composer (b. 1899)
3 June	Pope John XXIII 1958-63 (b. 1881)

COMPASS VARIATION
1950

Gall's Projection

POLITICAL CHART

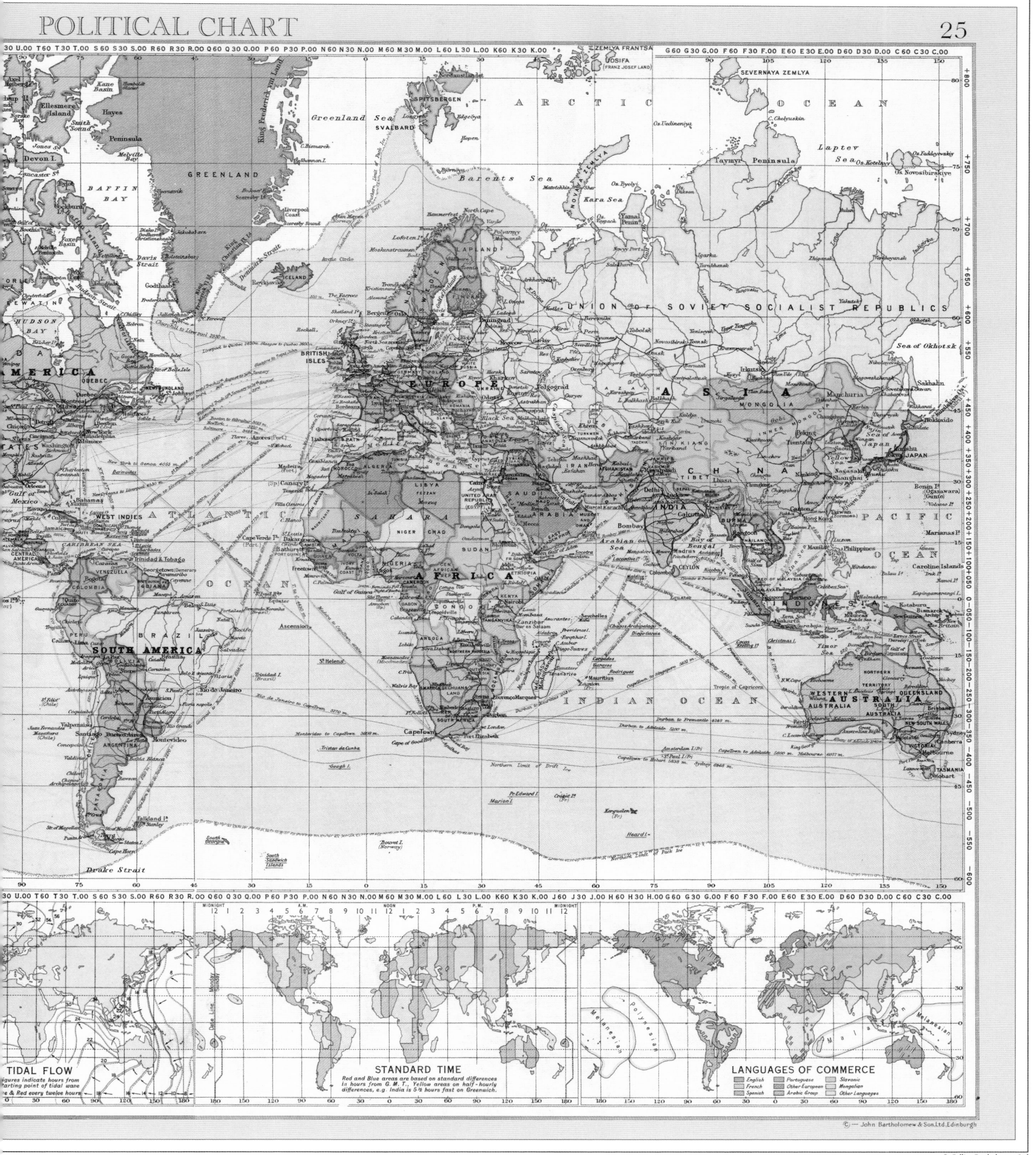

TIDAL FLOW

Figures indicate hours from starting point of tidal wave & Red every twelve hours.

STANDARD TIME

Red and Blue areas are based on standard differences in hours from G.M.T. Yellow areas are on half-hourly differences, e.g. India is 5½ hours fast on Greenwich.

LANGUAGES OF COMMERCE

English · Portuguese · Slavonic
French · Other European · Mongolian
Spanish · Arabic Group · Other Languages

STATES OF THE WORLD 1982

From the *Bartholomew World Atlas, Twelfth Edition*, cartography by
John Bartholomew, M.A. F.R.S.E., Director, the Geographical Institute, Edinburgh.

This map represents an intermediate stage between one extensive series of changes and another – beforehand, the decolonisation that had gone on in previous decades, especially in Africa; and afterwards, the collapse of communist regimes in the 1990s. Compared with earlier maps, the monolithic slabs of colour which represented a (usually European) country's overseas possessions are gone.

The inset map on the left plots the changes of sovereignty that had occurred since 1939. The aftermath of the First World War had started the retreat from empire by the European powers, and the Second World War accelerated the process. Britain sought to maintain association with its former colonies through the Commonwealth, albeit as an equal partner rather than as overlord.

The changes that came after this map was published mostly resulted from political changes in the Soviet Union and its Warsaw Pact allies in Eastern Europe between 1989 and 1991. These dramatic developments resulted in the reunification of Germany, the bloody break-up of Yugoslavia, the peaceful break-up of Czechoslovakia, and independence for all fifteen former Soviet republics, including the Ukraine, Armenia and the Baltic States, and several nations in central Asia – leaving the Russia as a separate country much reduced in size compared with the former USSR. In addition, the new nations of Eritrea and East Timor came into being.

Yet while the age of empire was over by 1982, a number of wars being fought across the globe had distinctly old-style colonial overtones. In Afghanistan, the mighty Soviet Red Army had been embroiled since 1978 in a bloody conflict with native resistance fighters, the mujahideen, to prop up an ailing puppet government in a struggle reminiscent of Russian and British machinations in the region during much of the nineteenth century. And in 1982, just as Israel completed its withdrawal from the Sinai Peninsula in accordance with the Egyptian-Israeli peace treaty of 1979, it became an active participant in the Lebanese Civil War, invading southern Lebanon to oust the Palestinian Liberation Organization from the region.

Also that year, the UK fought its last 'colonial' war, in the South Atlantic. Argentina had long harboured claims to the Falkland Islands off its eastern coast, which Britain had exercised jurisdiction over since at least 1833. Partly as a distraction from serious economic hardships at home, Argentina's ruling military junta invaded first South Georgia and then the Falkland Islands themselves. To the junta's surprise, Britain responded by launching a massive military task force to retake this tiny possession some 8000 miles distant. After a number of brief but bloody air, sea and land battles, the British triumphed, but the issue of sovereignty continues to be a matter of dispute.

While Britain was fighting to regain lost possessions at one end of the globe, at the other it was drawing a final line under its political involvement with another former colony. In 1982, the remaining vestiges of Canada's legislative dependence on the UK ended and the country secured complete constitutional sovereignty for the first time in its history.

EVENTS	
14 June	Falklands War between UK and Argentina ends with formal surrender by Argentina
17 April	Canada changes its constitution, establishing full political independence from Great Britain

BIRTHS	
22 April	Kaká, Brazilian footballer, FIFA World Player of the Year 2007

DEATHS	
14 September	Grace Kelly, American actress, Princess of Monaco (b. 1929)

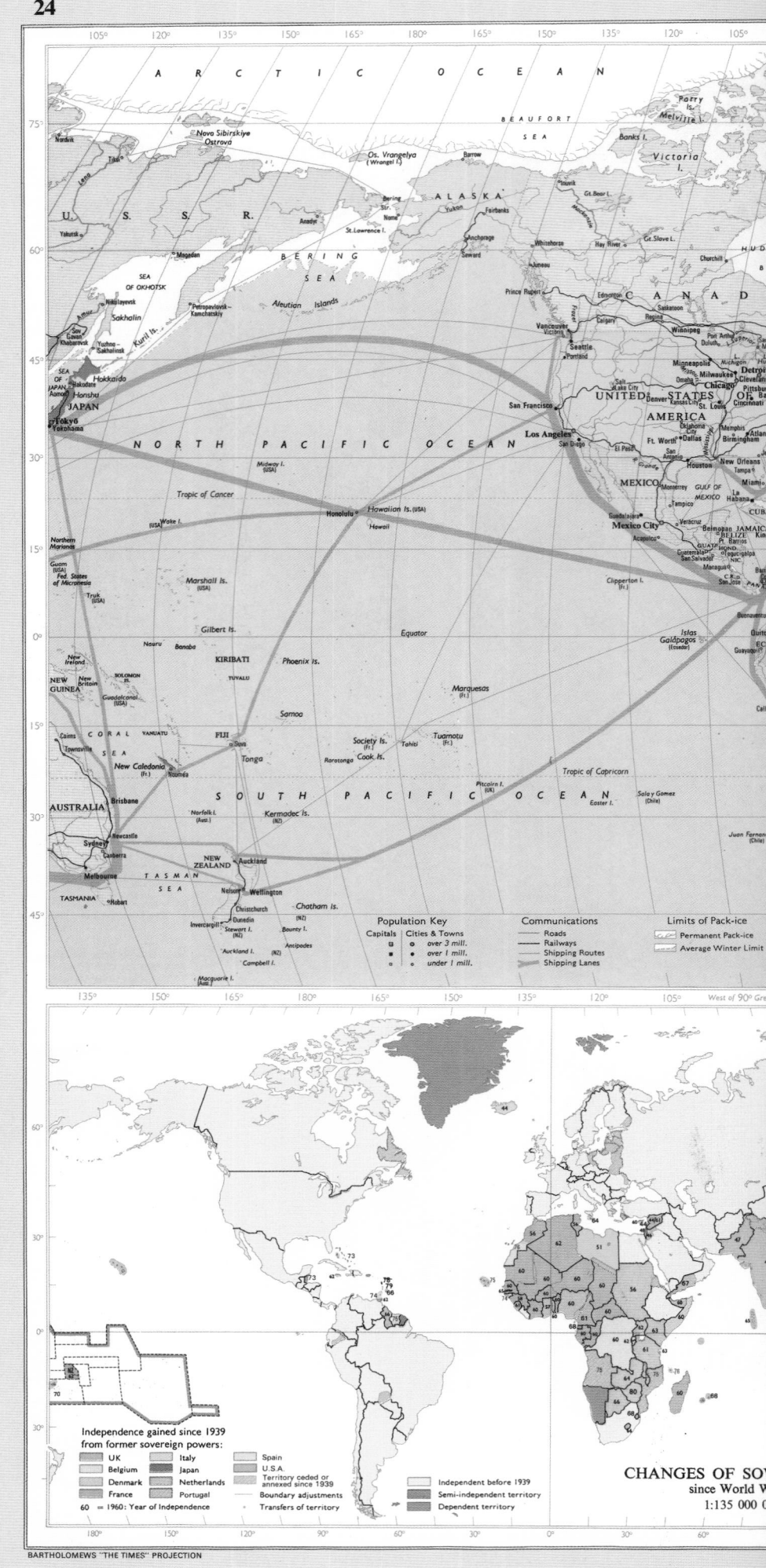

24

Population Key
Capitals | Cities & Towns
over 3 mill.
over 1 mill.
under 1 mill.

Communications
Roads
Railways
Shipping Routes
Shipping Lanes

Limits of Pack-ice
Permanent Pack-ice
Average Winter Limit

Independence gained since 1939
from former sovereign powers:
UK
Belgium
Denmark
France
Italy
Japan
Netherlands
Portugal
Spain
U.S.A.
Territory ceded or annexed since 1939
60 = 1960: Year of Independence
Boundary adjustments
Transfers of territory
Independent before 1939
Semi-independent territory
Dependent territory

CHANGES OF SOV
since World W
1:135 000 0

BARTHOLOMEWS "THE TIMES" PROJECTION

STATES OF THE WORLD

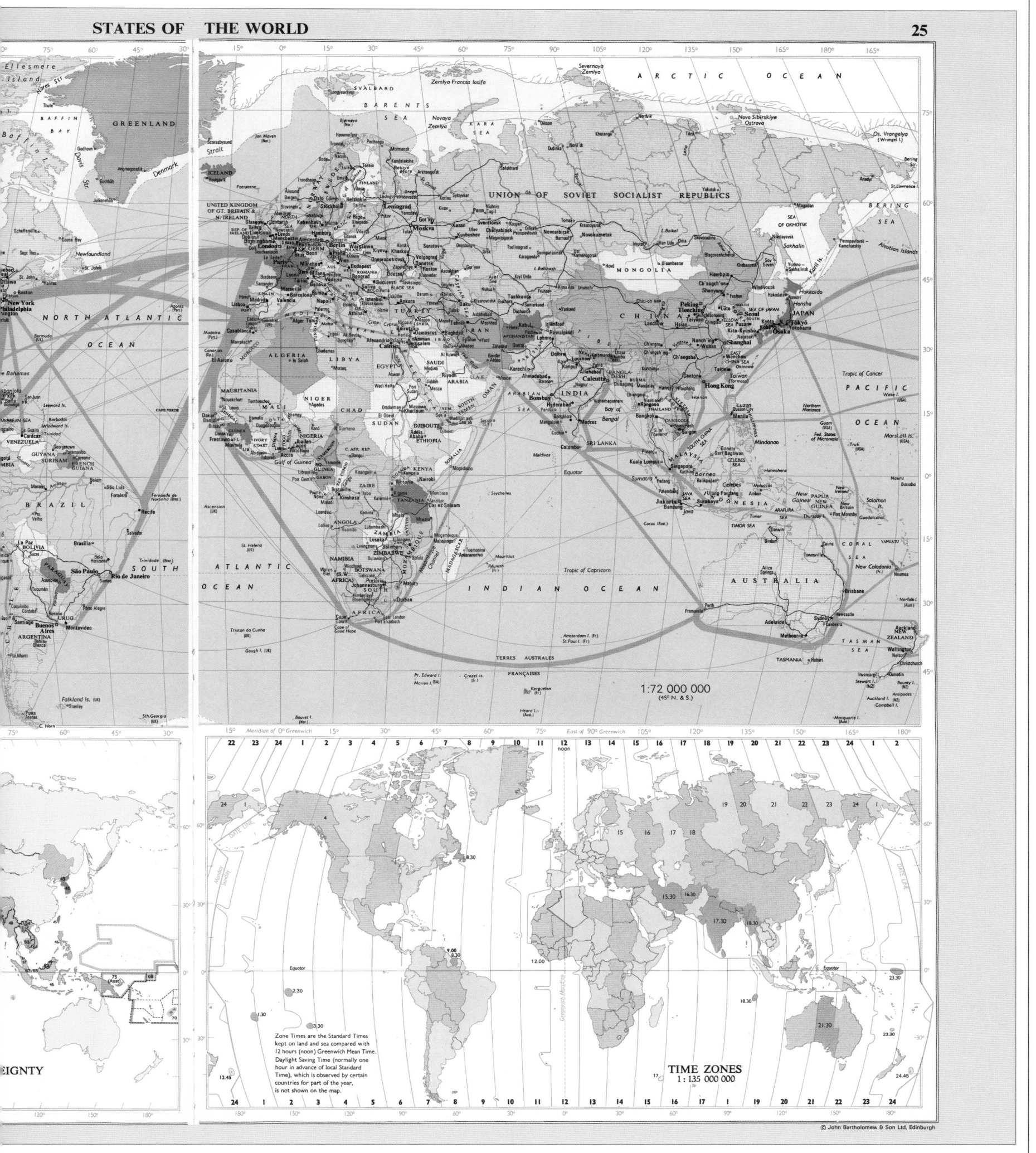

1:72 000 000
(45° N. & S.)

Zone Times are the Standard Times
kept on land and sea compared with
12 hours (noon) Greenwich Mean Time.
Daylight Saving Time (normally one
hour in advance of local Standard
Time), which is observed by certain
countries for part of the year,
is not shown on the map.

TIME ZONES
1 : 135 000 000

EIGNTY

© John Bartholomew & Son Ltd, Edinburgh

AFRICA 1852

From *The College Atlas for Schools and Families.*

Although European occupation of the African continent would not begin in earnest until the later nineteenth century, this was the period during which the basic groundwork was laid. Colour-coding around the coastline indicates areas of influence divided up between Britain, France, Portugal and Spain, but there was virtually no ingress into the interior. Recorded European exploration had begun with the Greeks and Romans. The Greek cartographer Ptolemy was the first known to recognise a large landmass in Africa but it was not until medieval times that systematic exploration of the coast began.

Ultimately, European mapping of Africa took place over four centuries. Portuguese explorers sailed around the coasts of Senegal and Guinea in the 1440s but it would be the dying years of the century before Vasco da Gama finally found the route around Africa, reaching Mozambique and ultimately India in the face of fierce opposition from Arab slave traders, in 1498.

As well as the lure of the unknown, explorers were spurred on by mythology that had grown up around Africa, from the Christian kingdom of Prester John to the search for the fabled Mountains of the Moon, presumed source of the Nile. These are marked on the map north of the Equator. The interior remained unexplored for over 300 years, until adventurous individuals took it upon themselves to explore the continent's unknown elements. David Livingstone crossed the Kalahari Desert and at the time the map was made, was crossing the Zambezi river region.

In 1852 the map was marked with best-guesswork, such as the 'supposed source of the river Zaire' and 'Ptolemy's source of the Nile'. In the later 1850s and 1860s, Richard Burton, John Speke and James Grant would find Lake Tanganyika and Lake Victoria and the source of the Nile; and in 1877, Henry Morton Stanley would follow the Congo to its mouth at the Atlantic.

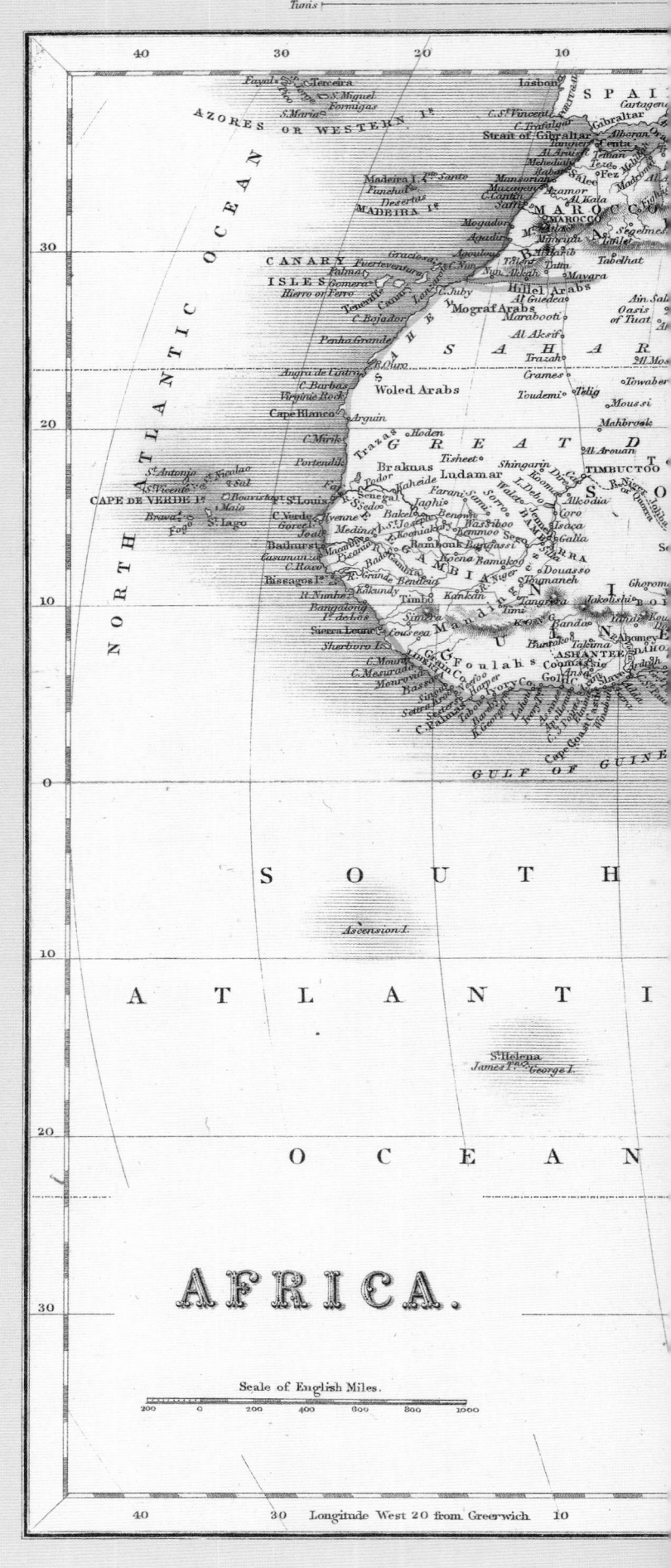

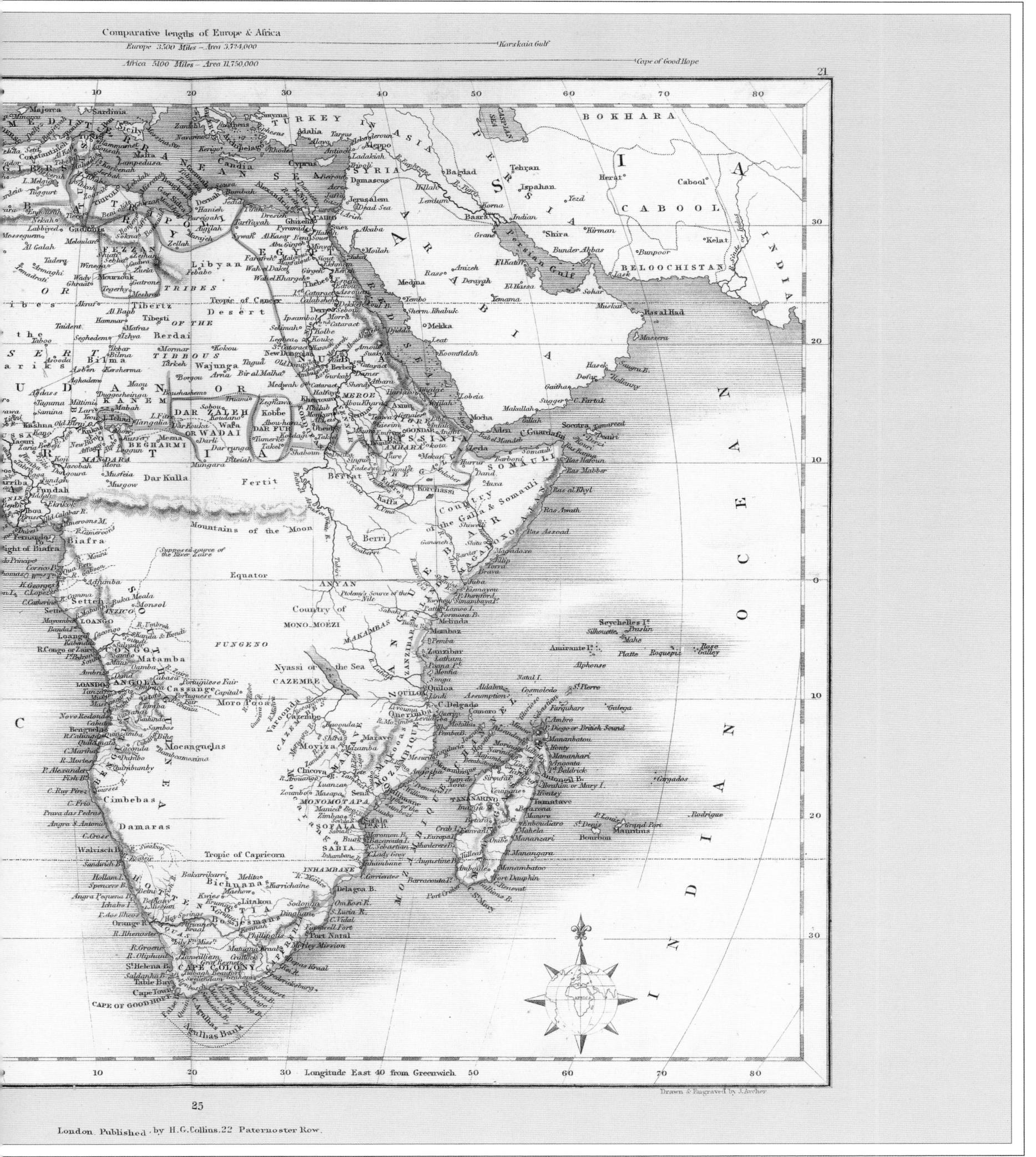

Comparative lengths of Europe & Africa

Europe 3500 Miles — Area 3,724,000

Africa 5100 Miles — Area 11,750,000

Karskaia Gulf

Cape of Good Hope

21

London. Published by H.G.Collins, 22 Paternoster Row.

25

Drawn & Engraved by J. Archer

Longitude East 40 from Greenwich

PRUSSIA 1852

From *The College Atlas for Schools and Families.*

This map dates from 1852 and shows the borders of Prussia, the state that was arguably the most dynamic in post-Napoleonic Europe. By the twentieth century, Prussia would be considered so dangerous that it would be officially broken up by the victorious Allies after the Second World War on the grounds of being 'a bearer of militarism and reaction in Germany'.

In 1852, Germany as a nation did not officially exist. There were thirty-eight German states, a collection of regions with a common linguistic, cultural and legal heritage, cemented by a shared history – the remnants of the Holy Roman Empire of the German Nation, an institution that had existed in various and evolving forms since the era of Charlemagne in the ninth century and which had ended in 1806 as a result of the stresses of the Napoleonic Wars.

By the time the map was drawn up, Prussia was the dominant state of the German nations, eclipsing the status claimed at the start of the century by the kingdom of Austria. Prussia's lands stretched from the border with the Netherlands in the west to Russia in the east, comprising the vast part of northern Germany and more than half the area of Germany north of Austria. As the map shows, it was not a contiguous territory but all the prosperous northern German cities, including Berlin, lay within its borders, as did the industrial powerhouse of the Ruhr.

The catalyst of growing Prussian domination would prove decisive. In 1862, Prince Wilhelm I would appoint as premier Otto von Bismarck, a political and strategic genius. Under his Machiavellian policy of Realpolitik, Prussia fought a series of carefully planned wars culminating in the Franco-Prussian War of 1870–71 after which the Unification of Germany, the Kaiserreich, was proclaimed. Austria was excluded, leaving Prussia the dominant power in a greater Germany for seventy-five years.

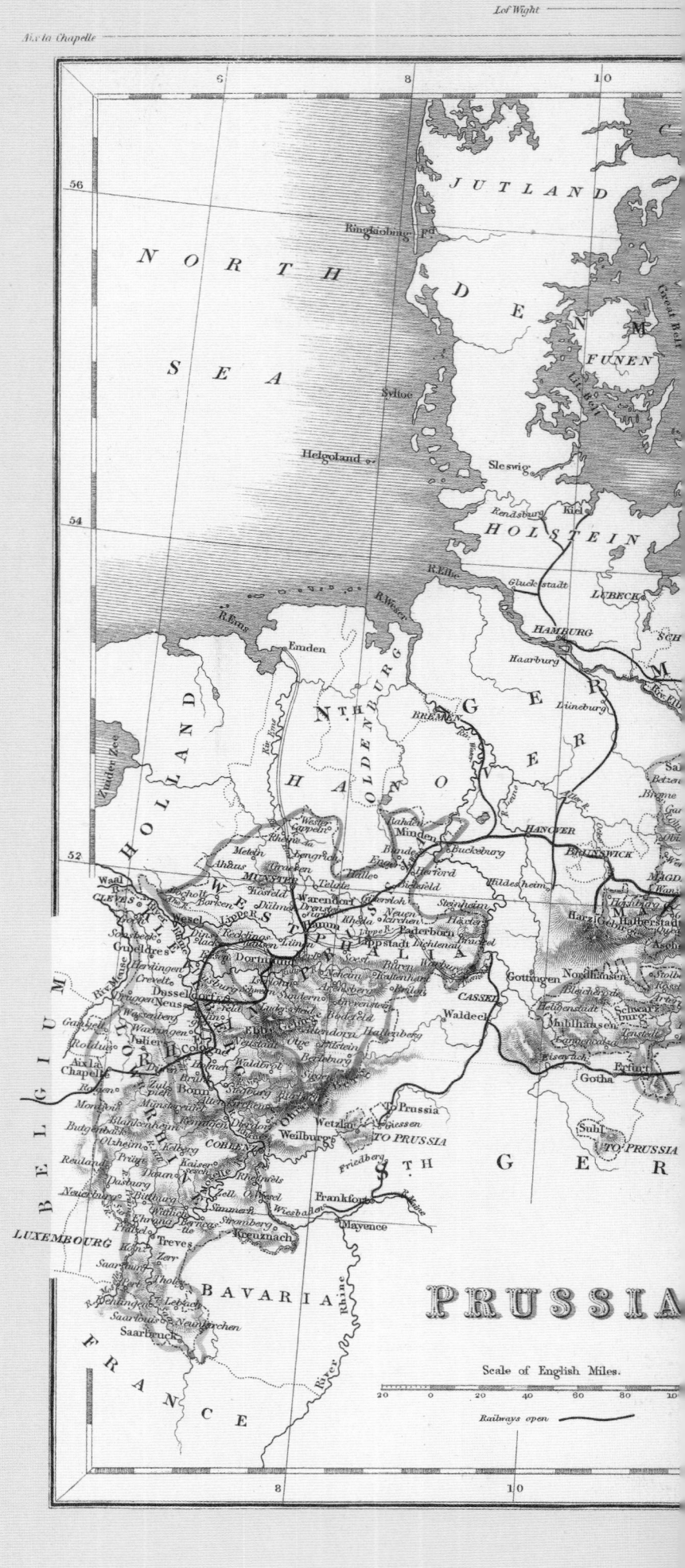

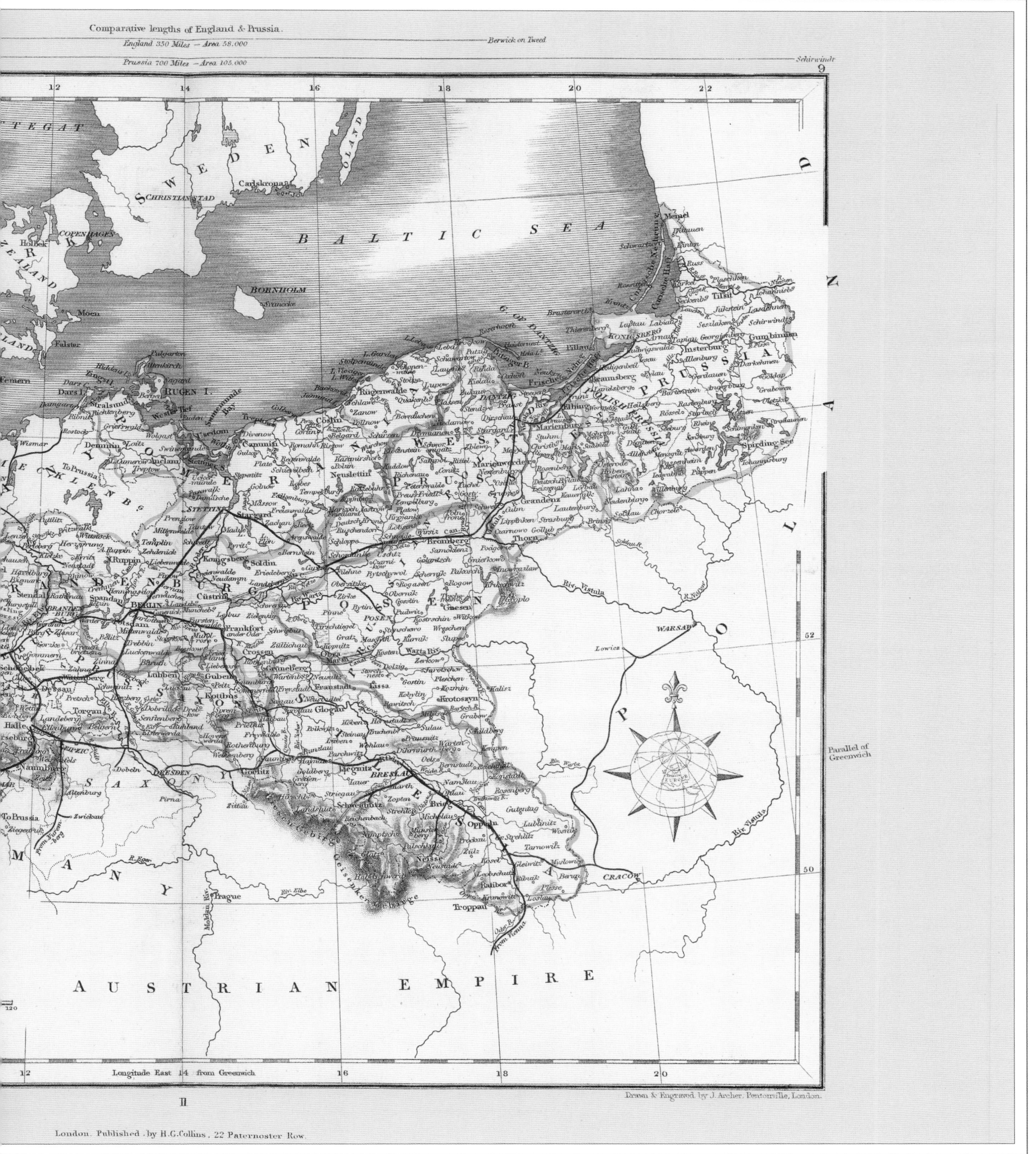

Comparative lengths of England & Prussia.

England 350 Miles — Area 58,000

Prussia 700 Miles — Area 105,000

Berwick on Tweed

Schirwindt

Drawn & Engraved by J. Archer, Pentonville, London.

II

London. Published by H.G.Collins, 22 Paternoster Row.

UNITED STATES OF AMERICA 1879

From the *Handy General Atlas of America, Philip's.* Cartography by
J. G. Bartholomew, F.R.G.S.

This 1879 map of the United States of America depicts the country
at a particularly interesting time in its history. Following the
Union victory in the civil war in 1865 the southern states were very
slow to re-build. The northern states by comparison, driven by an
unprecedented influx of immigrants from Europe, forged ahead with
rapid urbanization, infrastructure development and economic growth.

One of the main barriers to westward expansion into California
was the Sierra Nevada mountain range. Emigrants attempting to
cross the range by wagon faced a long and dangerous journey that
many did not survive. In 1844 a party travelling westward into the
mountains followed the Truckee River. This led them to what is
now called the Donner Pass 2 160 m (7 085 ft). This low narrow pass
became the gateway west into California for thousands of emigrants.
A direct rail connection came in 1869 with the completion of the First
Transcontinental Railroad through the Donner Pass. While the pass is
not named on the map, the railroad can be seen crossing the Nevada/
California state boundary and then the Sierra Nevada mountains to
the northwest of Carson City.

The map is also interesting as it pre-dates the formation of some
of the states. North and South Dakota are shown as Huron Dakota.
During the 1870s attempts were made to bring the Dakota Territory
into the Union, both as a single state and as two states, but it was
not until 1889 that both North and South Dakota were admitted.
The other state not named on the map is Oklahoma. The map
shows this as Indian Territory. During much of the nineteenth
century, thousands of Native American Indians were forced from
their ancestral homelands from across North America, and by the
1890s more than thirty Native American nations and tribes had
been concentrated within the area occupied by present day
Oklahoma. Cattle ranchers and other white settlers increasingly
pushed further into the area, as did the railroad companies, and by
1890 the Native Americans had lost more than half their territory. It
was not until 1907 that Oklahoma was established as the forty-sixth
state of the Union.

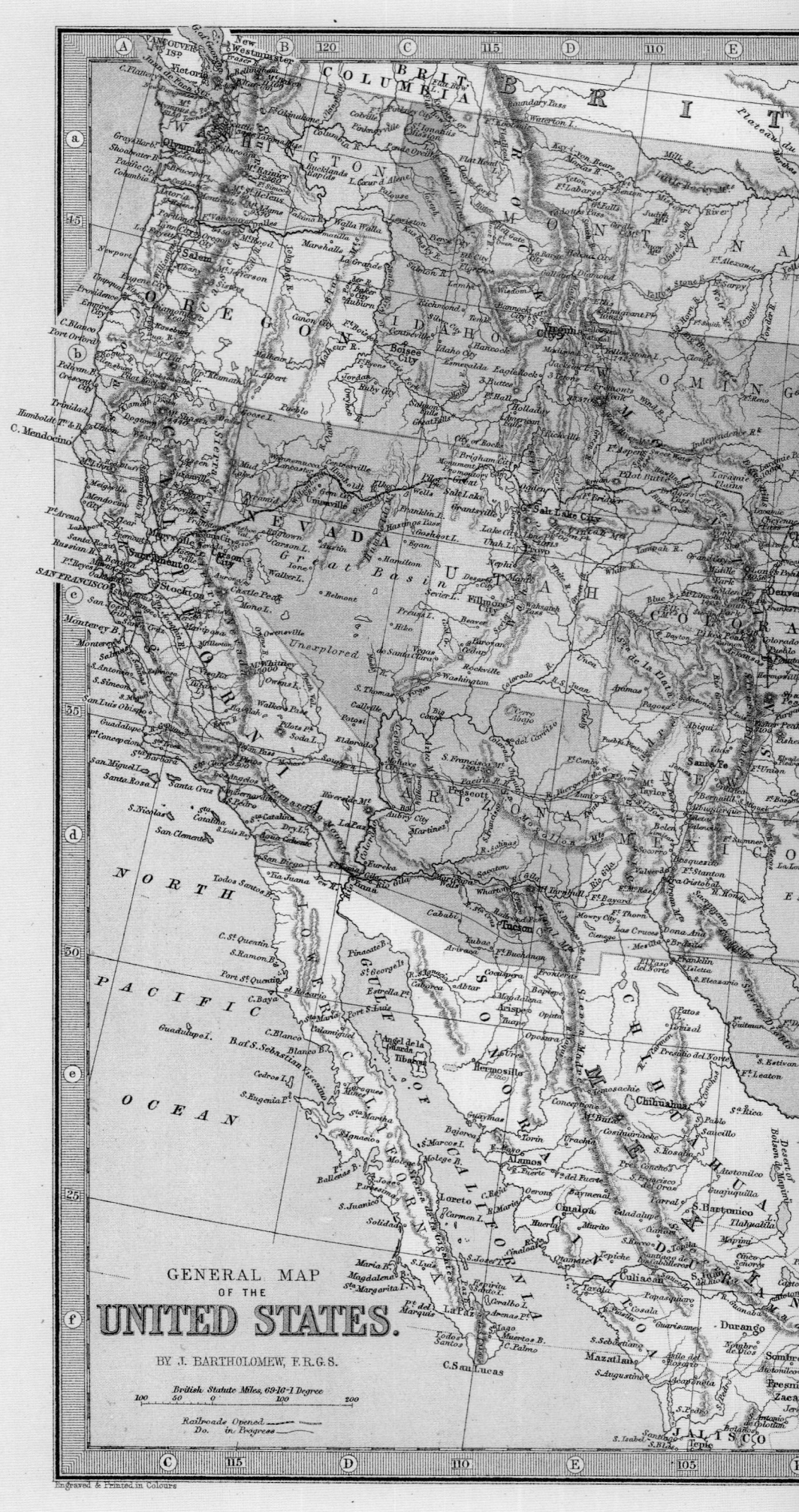

NEW ZEALAND 1879

From the Collins New Complete Atlas.

To forestall growing French interest in the islands and control the increasingly lawless trading settlements there, the British Government had signed the Treaty of Waitangi with the indigenous Maori chieftains in 1840, as a first step to claiming full sovereignty over New Zealand. The following year, it became a colony in its own right, having previously been administered as part of the Australian colony of New South Wales.

European colonisation then began in earnest, with most immigrants opting to settle on South Island. However, on North Island, where the Maoris were greatest in number, a steady influx of settlers led to intense competition for land with the indigenous tribes. Disputes over territory were exacerbated by disagreements over the precise terms of the Waitangi treaty and these boiled over into outright war in the mid-1840s and throughout much of the 1860s. Following the latter of these Land Wars, large tracts of land were confiscated from the local Maori by the government, a source of resentment that continues to the present day.

The map also shows in insets each of New Zealand's four main population centres which had grown up in the preceding forty years: Wellington had been established in the first flush of European settlement in 1840 and became the national capital in 1865. Auckland was the port where most European settlers arrived to spread their influence across North Island. Christchurch, New Zealand's first city, was named after the eponymous Oxford college and was first settled in the late 1840s. Dunedin's Scottish origins are revealed in its name which derives from the Gaelic for Edinburgh.

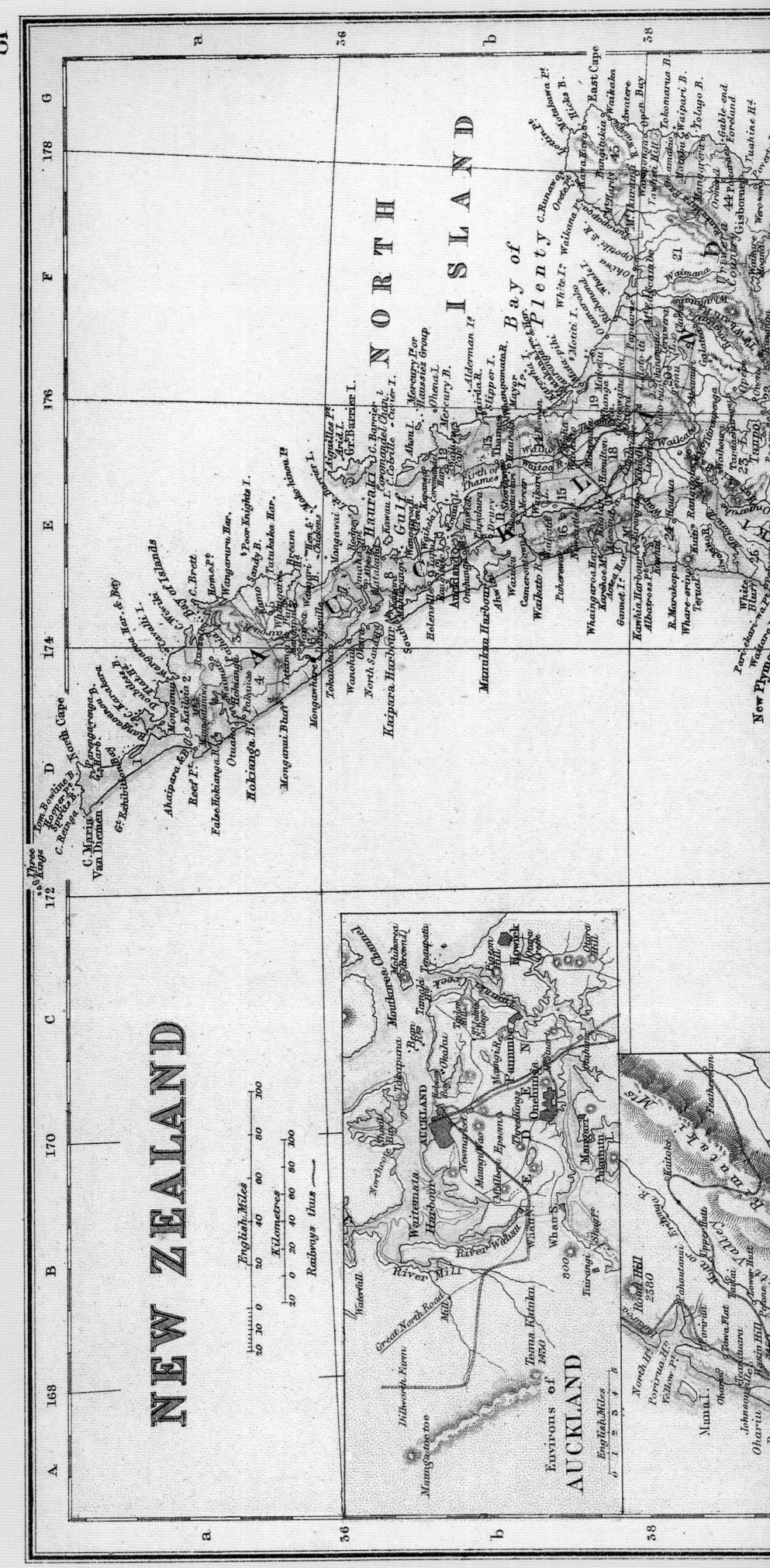

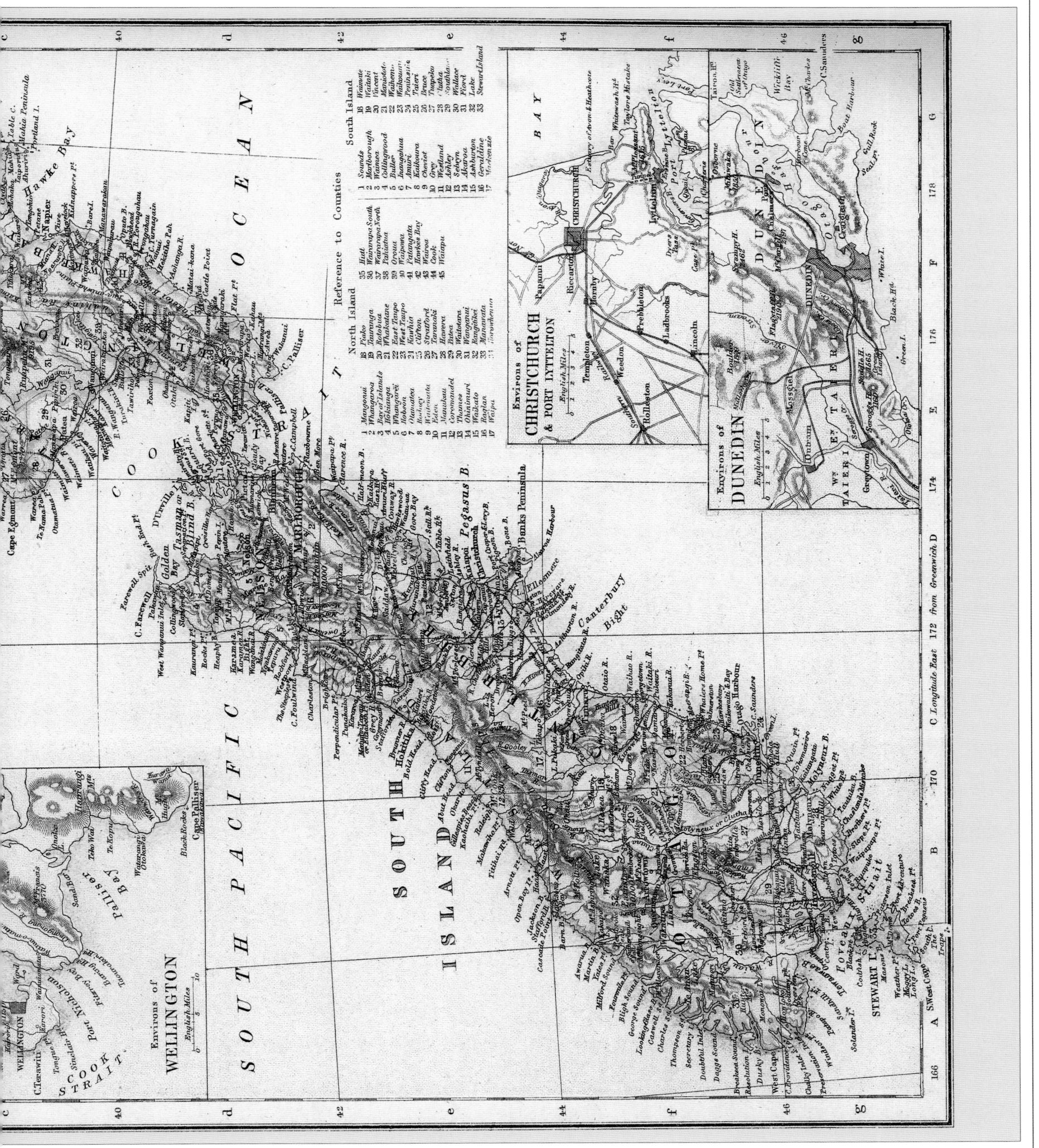

Reference to Counties

North Island
1 Mongonui
2 Whangaroa
3 Bay of Islands
4 Hokianga
5 Whangarei
6 Hobson
7 Otamatea
8 Rodney
9 Waitemata
10 Eden
11 Manukau
12 Coromandel
13 Thames
14 Ohinemuri
15 Waikato
16 Raglan
17 Waipa

18 Piako
19 Tauranga
20 Rotorua
21 Whakatane
22 East Taupo
23 West Taupo
24 Kawhia
25 Clifton
26 Stratford
27 Taranaki
28 Hawera
29 Patea
30 Waitotara
31 Wanganui
32 Rangitikei
33 Manawatu
34 Horowhenua

35 Hutt
36 Wairarapa South
37 Wairarapa North
38 Pahiatua
39 Orua
40 Waipawa
41 Patangata
42 Hawkes Bay
43 Wairoa
44 Cook
45 Waiapu

South Island
18 Waimate
19 Waitaki
20 Vincent
21 Maniototo
22 Waihemo
23 Waikouaiti
24 Peninsula
25 Taieri
26 Bruce
27 Clutha
28 Tuapeka
29 Southland
30 Wallace
31 Fiord
32 Lake
33 Stewart Island

1 Sounds
2 Marlborough
3 Waimea
4 Collingwood
5 Buller
6 Inangahua
7 Amuri
8 Kaikoura
9 Cheviot
10 Grey
11 Westland
12 Ashley
13 Selwyn
14 Akaroa
15 Ashburton
16 Geraldine
17 Waimate

Environs of
CHRISTCHURCH
& PORT LYTTELTON

English Miles

Environs of
DUNEDIN

English Miles

Environs of
WELLINGTON

English Miles

CANADIAN CITIES 1891

From *The English Imperial Atlas of the World*, cartography by
J. G. Bartholomew, F.R.G.S.

This plate shows a series of six of Canada's major urban areas at
the end of the nineteenth century. Vancouver is notable by its
absence (as indeed are any other cities from the west of the continent).
At this time the vast majority of Canadians were located to the east.
In 1891 when the plans were drawn Vancouver's population was only
around 8 000.

One of the more interesting inclusions is the plan of Halifax. It shows
Halifax Peninsula, the site on which the town was originally founded,
and the downtown district. The peninsula is joined to the western
shore, jutting out towards the eastern shore and forming one of the
world's largest natural harbours.

The plan shows a heavily fortified city, with forts at the Citadel
(Fort George) and Fort Needham, barracks, Admiralty House and a
naval dockyard. The park overlooking the North-West Arm was also
a military reserve. These represent the core of a series of fortifications
that have surrounded Halifax through its history, providing defence
against the French and then Americans and overseeing the North
Atlantic shipping routes. The city had been founded by the British
in 1749 in response to a continuing French presence in Cape Breton
and was a base for the British army and navy until 1906, when control
passed to Canada; it remains of primary importance to the Canadian
navy and army today.

The fringe of wharves lining the harbourside illustrate Halifax's
important commercial status. The dockside Intercolonial Railway,
which opened in 1872, provided Halifax's ice-free harbour with
access to the Canadian interior, processing the movement of goods,
people and military into and out of the country. In 1917 the city was
devastated when a loaded munitions ship exploded in the harbour.
Over 2 000 people died and 9 000 (an estimated 20 per cent of
Halifax's population) were maimed or injured. In particular, the
areas of Richmond and Dartmouth (across the harbour) were utterly
destroyed by the force of the blast, by a tsunami that rose up from
the harbour and by fires that broke out. It remains the world's largest
accidental explosion and a memorial today stands in Fort Needham
Memorial Park.

The 1891 map of Toronto shows a city centre laid out in a grid pattern
that was common to both North American cities and British colonial
cities of the time. Known as York from the time of its founding by
the British in 1793, the town had from 1796 been the capital of Upper
Canada, the British colony that covered most of present-day southern
Ontario. The original Fort York was destroyed in the British-American
War of 1812; both it and its replacement are marked on the waterfront.
However, land reclamation has left the site several hundred metres
inland today. Partly to avoid confusion with other Yorks in North
America, in 1834 the town was renamed Toronto, originally a name
given to the area by the indigenous Mohawk people. The grid layout
of Toronto's streets emerged as blocks of the land were carved out
from the natural forest west of the River Don.

In 1867 Ottawa became the capital of the united Dominion of Canada
and Toronto the capital of the new province of Ontario with its
legislature in the New Parliament Buildings in Queen's Park, at the
head of College Street (now University Avenue). A previous incarnation
of the Parliament Buildings can be seen on Wellington Street, on
the Ottawa plan. University College in Queen's Park was founded in
1827 as King's College and is now part of the University of Toronto.
Other colleges that would become part of the university, such as Knox
College and Trinity College, are also mapped. Other municipal and
urban structures are also shown. Wharves line the waterfront with the
railway and Union Station behind. The station and twenty acres of the
area around would later be destroyed in the Great Fire of Toronto in
1904, the largest known fire in the city to
that date.

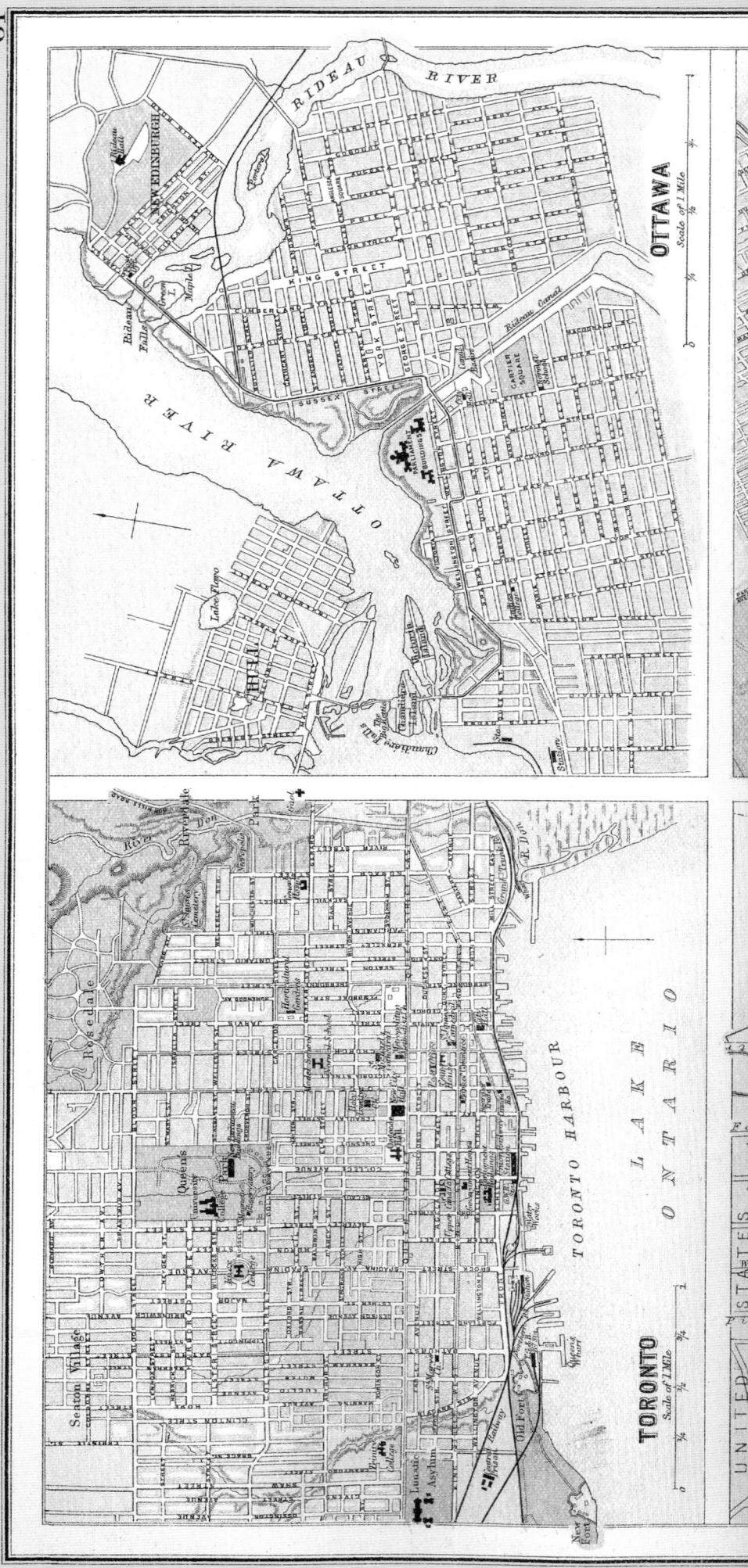

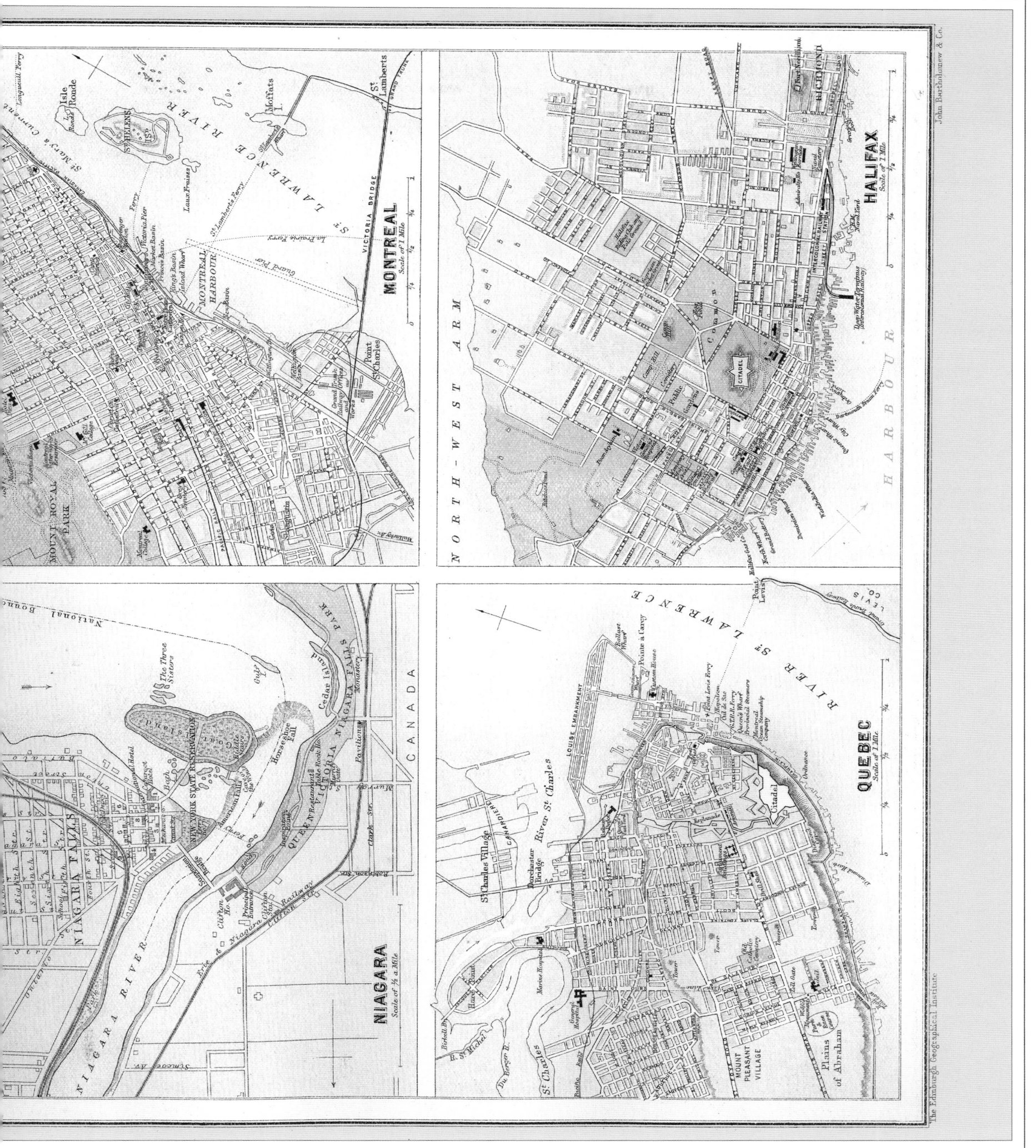

MONTREAL
Scale of 1 Mile

HALIFAX
Scale of 1 Mile

NIAGARA
Scale of ⅔ a Mile

QUEBEC
Scale of 1 Mile

John Bartholomew & Co.

The Edinburgh Geographical Institute

SOUTH AMERICA 1895

From *The Times Atlas of the World*. First Edition.

The South America map of 1895 depicts a continent whose borders are mostly recognisable today. The political forces that shaped national boundaries throughout the nineteenth century were virtually spent. The Spanish and Portuguese empires had been driven off the continental mainland and in their former colonies local establishment alliances ran the new republics. Greater political stability allowed increased economic development and South America became a major exporter of minerals and commodities including beef, coffee, wheat, rubber and sugar to the industrialised world.

Border changes after 1895 were largely contained to disputed territories between neighbours. The exception was Panama, which appears on the 1895 map as a region of Colombia. Panama declared independence in 1903 with the backing of the USA; in return, the USA agreed to build and maintain a canal within a predesignated zone across the isthmus. The Panama Canal was completed in 1914.

The colony of British Honduras, bordering the Caribbean on the west of the isthmus, would gain independence as Belize in 1981. It was the last British colony on the American continent, although like France and the Netherlands, Britain retained island possessions, from the Falkland Islands in the South Atlantic, to the islands of the Lesser Antilles and Jamaica in the Caribbean.

Only in the extremities of South America were territorial and colonial skirmishes still playing out in 1895 yet these were of symbolic significance. The first was in Spain's remaining American territorial possessions, Cuba and Puerto Rico, shown in the map in the Greater Antilles. Spanish inability to contain nationalist unrest, and US concern over its economic interests on the islands, would lead in 1898 to the Spanish-American War. The conflict was over within weeks. The settlement, in the Treaty of Paris in the same year, recognised Cuban independence, while Puerto Rico became an American protectorate. The Spanish empire, a major power on the American continent for four centuries, was at an end.

The second was on the northeast mainland, where the border between Venezuela and British Guiana was the subject of a seemingly minor, longrunning dispute. The confrontation took a different turn in 1895 with the direct intervention of the USA, which forced Britain into the independent arbitration the country had hitherto refused.

American interest was justified in terms of the Monroe Doctrine of 1823 which sought to end to European interference in the Americas. Drawn up at a time when the South American empires were breaking up, the Doctrine was intended to prevent any further European land grabs on the American continent. The 1895 Venezuela Boundary Dispute was one of the first instances of the United States' asserting its hegemony over the entire American hemisphere and the Doctrine would become a cornerstone of American foreign policy throughout the twentieth century.

SOUTH AMERICA

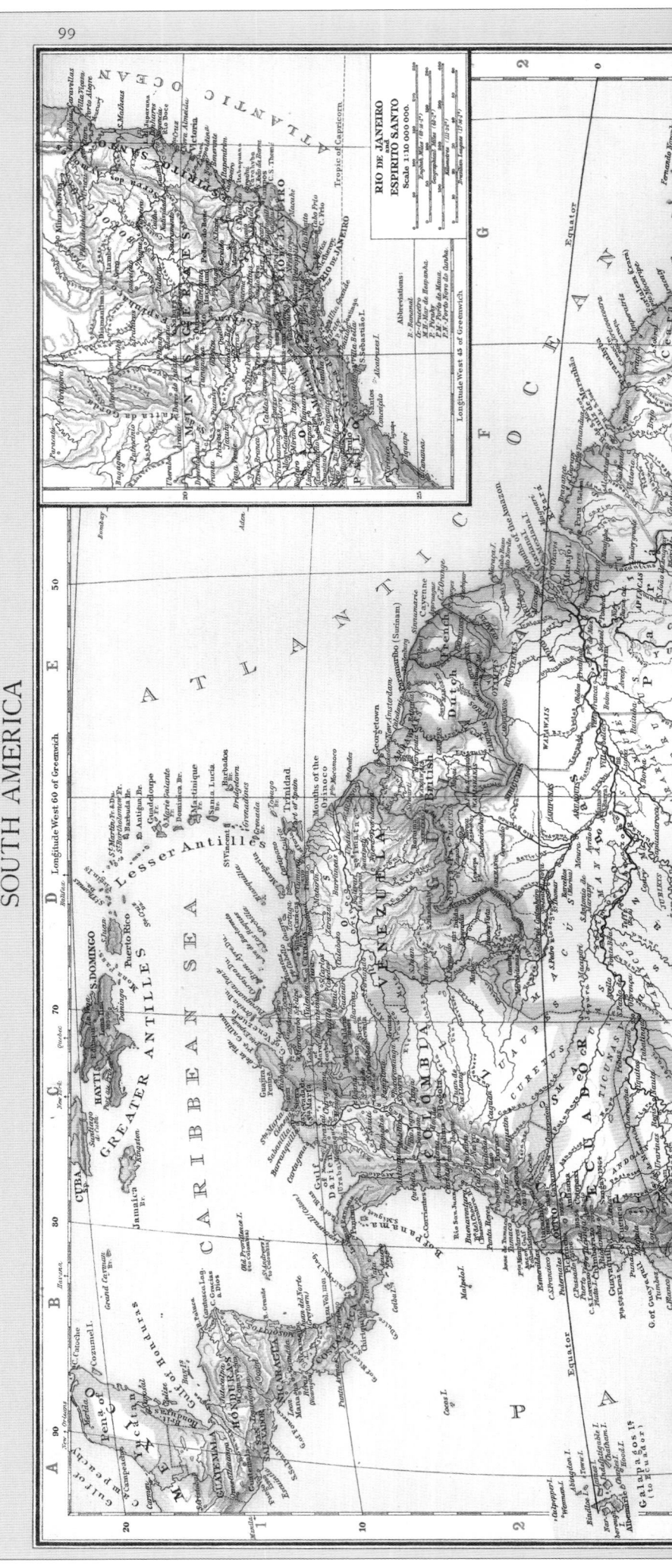

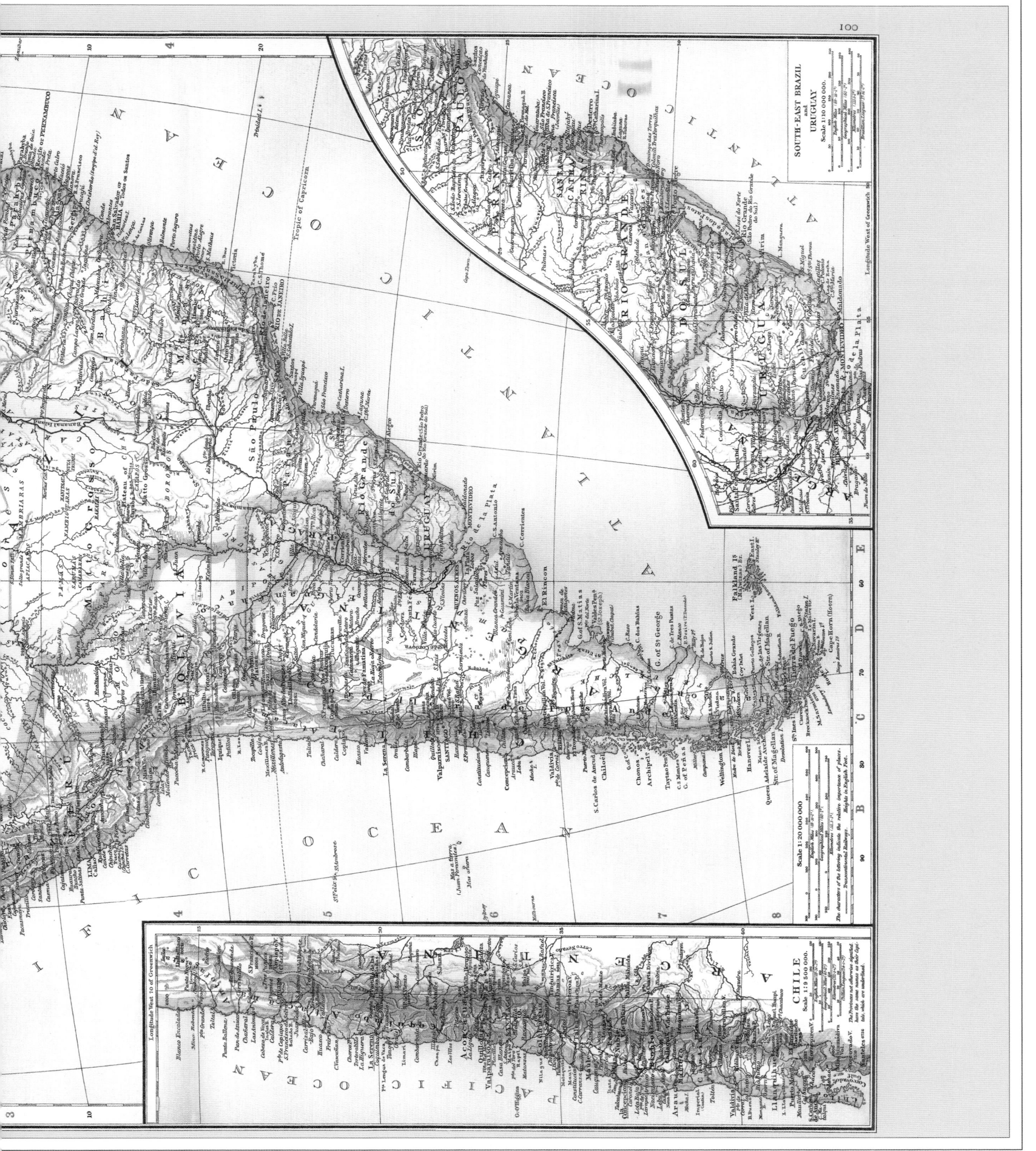

SOUTH-EAST BRAZIL
and
URUGUAY
Scale 1:10 000 000.

CHILE
Scale 1:9 500 000.

SOUTHERN AFRICA 1895

From *The Times Atlas of the World*. First Edition.

This map of Southern Africa was published between the two Boer wars. The first Boer War, also known as the Transvaal War, was a brief conflict against the British spanning 1880–1881 in which the Boers fought to re-establish their independence which they had originally lost in 1877 as a consequence of accepting British help against the Zulus. The second Boer War was a much more lengthy and brutal conflict spanning 1899–1902. With British victory over the Transvaal and Orange Free State the Boer republics became British colonies which later became the Union of South Africa. During the conflict military and civilian casualties were high.

France was also very active in Africa and the Indian Ocean at this time. It invaded the island nation of Madagascar in 1883. The result of the conflict was that Madagascar ceded the Antsiranana Bay and surrounding land to France. In 1895 French forces again landed on the island, this time marching on the capital, Antananarivo. They encountered little resistance and the city's defenders quickly surrendered. France annexed Madagascar in 1896 and the royal family was sent into exile in Algeria.

The map also reveals that many other European powers had significant possessions in this part of Africa. German possessions included the area of present day Namibia. It also conquered the regions that are now Rwanda, Burundi and Tanzania, and incorporated them into German East Africa. Portugal similarly had significant possessions in Angola and Mozambique.

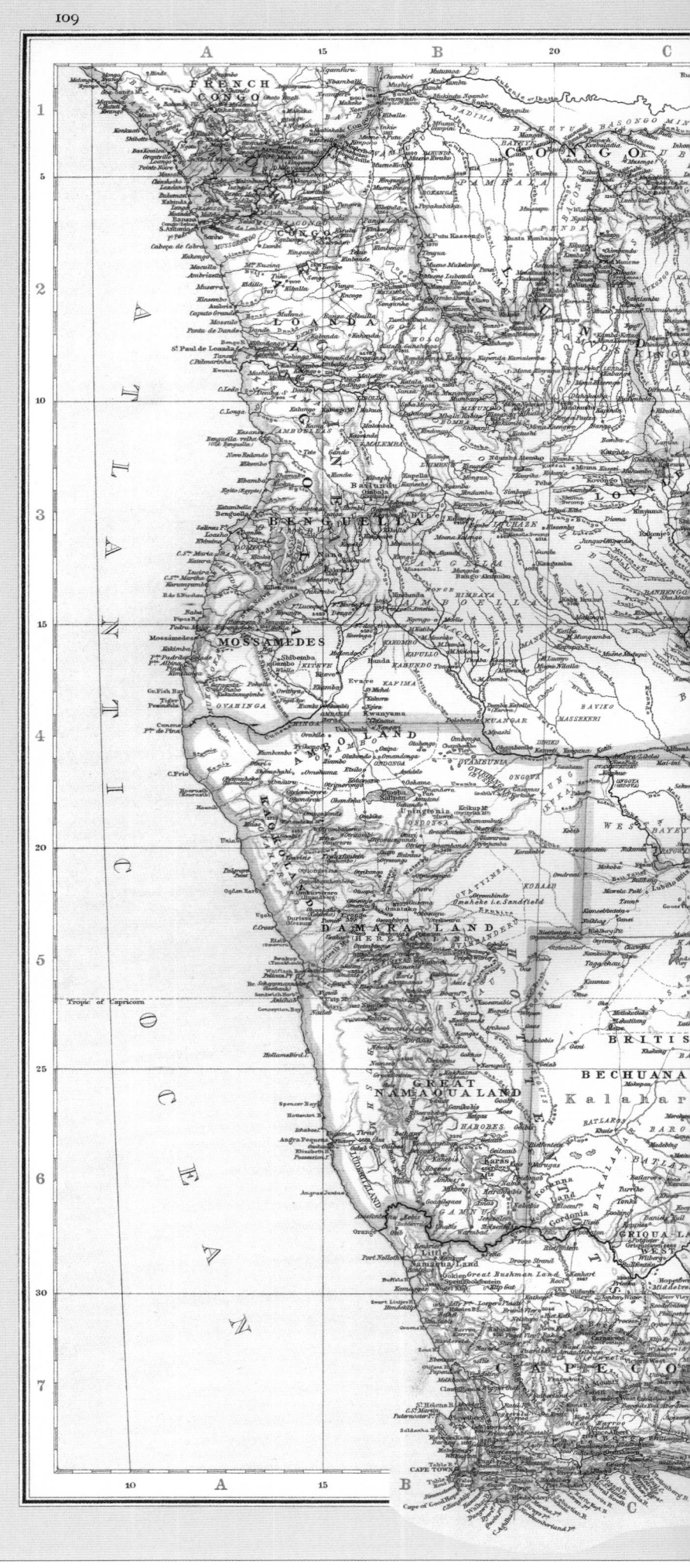

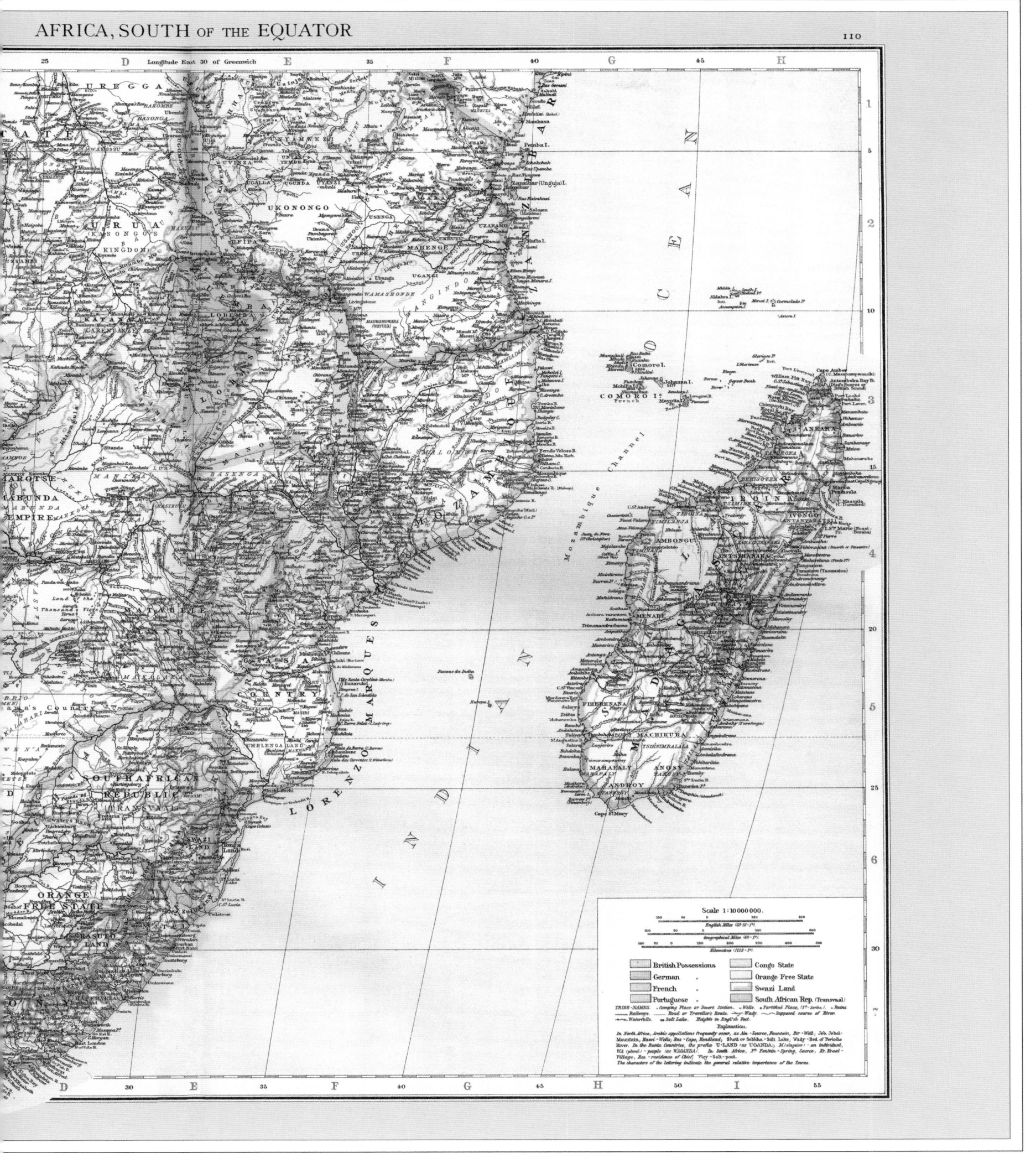

AFRICA, SOUTH OF THE EQUATOR

110

AFGHANISTAN 1896

From *The Times Atlas of the World*. First Edition.

The most striking feature of this topographical map is the great 800-km-(500-mile-)long stretch of the Hindu Kush mountain system, whose central ridge extends from the northwest of the modern-day Pakistan down into central and eastern Afghanistan.

The immense detail of settlements and physical features included on the map does not make it easy to read but close inspection of the central Afghan region reveals many place names familiar from the daily news reports of the current conflict there.

In fact, Afghanistan has been a battleground for European nations for long periods of its recent history, particularly during the nineteenth century from when this map dates (1896). The coloured borders on the map graphically illustrate Afghanistan's strategic position as buffer zone between British India in the southeast and Tsarist Russia in the north and west. For much of the century, Russia and Britain attempted to out-manoeuvre each other politically, diplomatically and militarily to secure control of this territory and so thwart each other's imperial ambitions. 'The Great Game' as this was known, drew each power increasingly into conflict in the region and destabilized it as a succession of puppet regimes exploited tensions among generations of ambitious local rulers.

An attempt was made in 1893 to establish a boundary line that would place physical limits on the spheres of influence of British India and local Afghan rulers. The Durand Line as it was called does not feature on the map, as the demarcation survey that plotted its 500-km-(800-mile-)long course from Chitral to Baluchistan only reported in the same year the map was published. However, far from defusing tensions in the region as it was intended to do, it actually triggered a long-running and often bloody dispute between the governments of Afghanistan and British India and would subsequently threaten Afghan–Pakistani relations.

AFGHANISTAN AND BALUCHISTAN

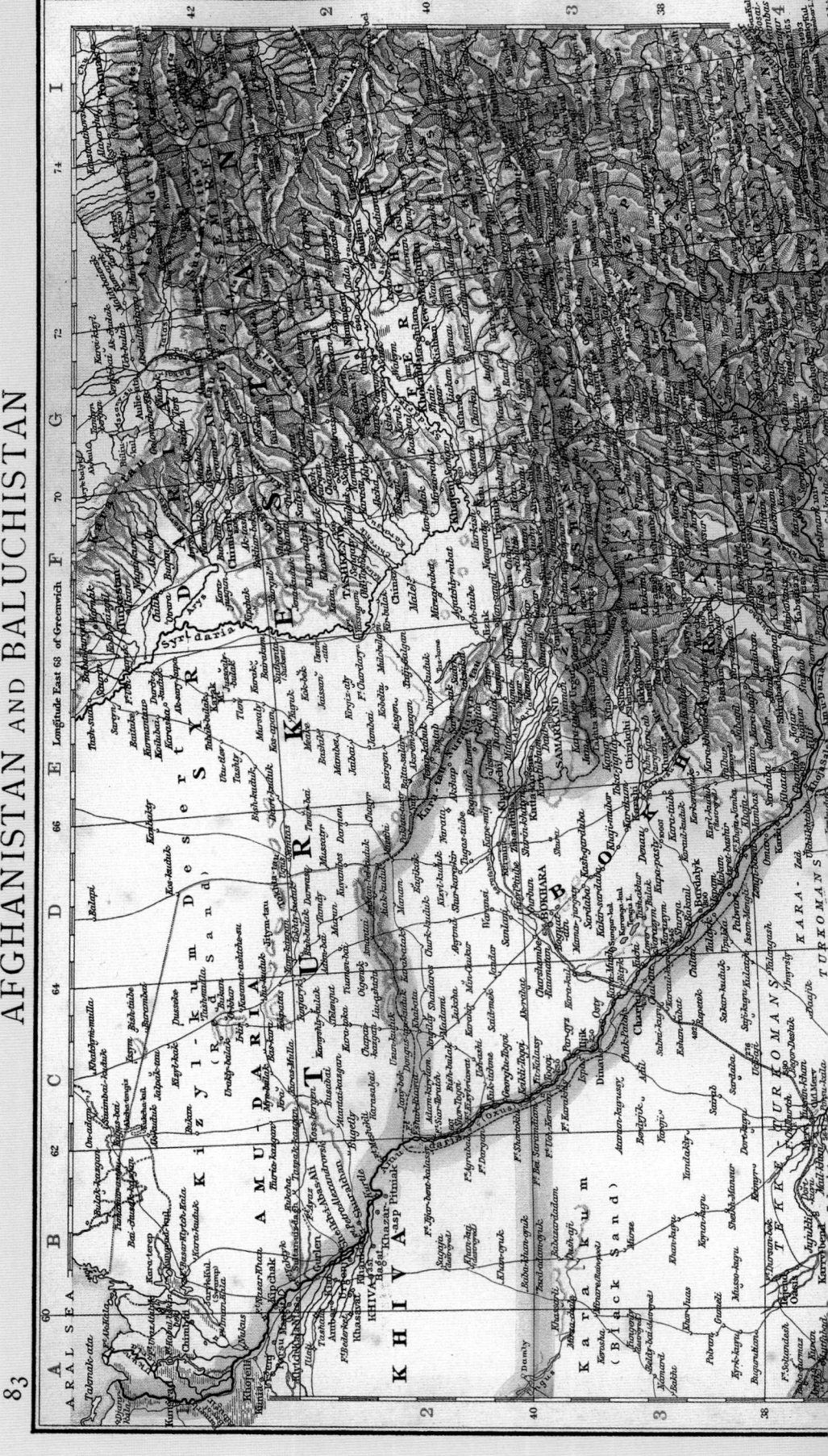

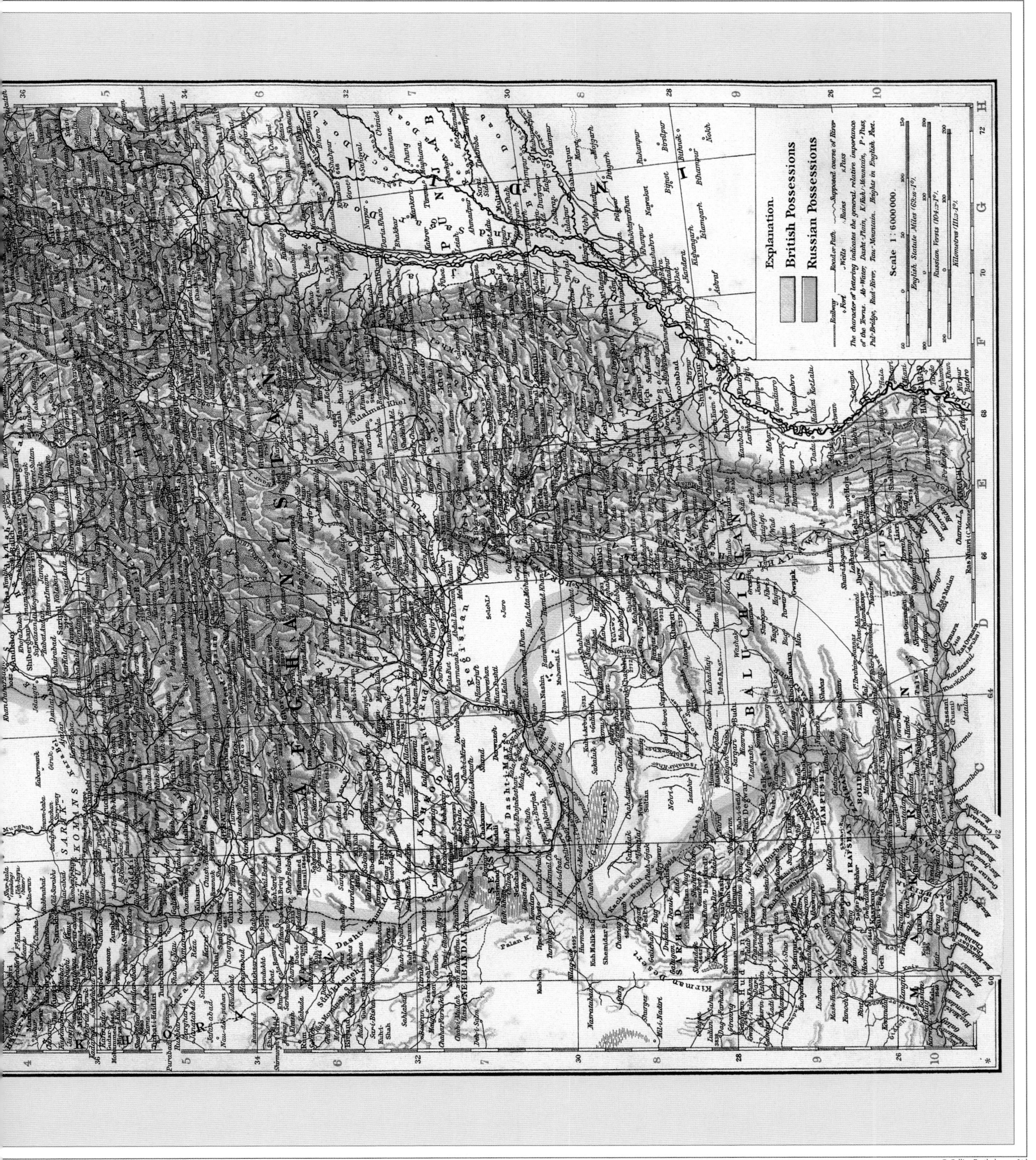

Explanation.

British Possessions
Russian Possessions

Scale 1 : 6000000.

NORTH POLAR REGIONS AND SOUTH POLAR REGIONS 1898

From the *Citizen's Atlas*, cartography by J. G. Bartholomew, F.R.G.S.

These maps of the polar regions allow a variety of interesting comparisons to be drawn about these extremes of the Earth and how they were being explored.

Far from being homogeneous ice masses, the northern and southern polar regions are physically very different. The North Pole is at the centre of the Arctic Ocean and is an almost landlocked body of water largely composed of drifting pack ice; the South Pole, by contrast, lies on a continental land mass. Reflecting this, the motivations of those who ventured into these unexplored regions were also different.

For many northern polar explorers, the intention was to find a navigable passage through the ice to open up a trade route to link the Atlantic and Pacific Oceans – the so-called Northwest Passage. During the nineteenth century several expeditions had ventured into the area and in 1851, British naval captain Sir Robert McClure was credited with the discovery of the Passage route, although it was not actually navigable by sea alone. Separate unsuccessful expeditions were also mounted during this period with the express purpose of reaching the North Pole itself. One of the most prominent of these is recorded on the map, that of the Norwegian Fridtjof Nansen. The closest point to the Pole that Nansen reached – 86°14' N, in April 1895 – was then the highest recorded latitude ever reached. The North Magnetic Pole had been first identified in 1831 by James Clark Ross on the Boothia Peninsula in the far north of Canada, and it can just be seen on the map at approximately 70°N 94°W.

Unlike the northern polar region, whose boundaries – Greenland and the North American and Eurasian continental masses – were mostly well mapped, the physical boundaries of the southern polar region were very poorly understood, as is evident from the map. The existence of Terra Australis Incognita – the unknown southern lands – had been assumed for centuries, but it was not until Cook's voyages in the 1770s that exploration of the region began in earnest. Sealers and whalers followed in his wake, but it was not until the 1820s that Antarctica was first actually sighted, probably by the Russian explorer, Bellingshausen. From the 1830s a series of national expeditions embarked for Antarctica: the French expedition of 1837–40 under Jules Dumont D'Urville; the United States Exploring Expedition of 1838–42 commanded by Charles Wilkes; and the British expedition of 1839–43 under James Clark Ross. The progress of these and other earlier explorations is plotted on the map, as are the varying attempts to find the South Magnetic Pole near Victoria Land. In spite of these efforts, it is obvious that the southern lands were still a largely unknown quantity when Scott, Shackleton, Amundsen and others began their drives to the Pole in the first decade of the new century.

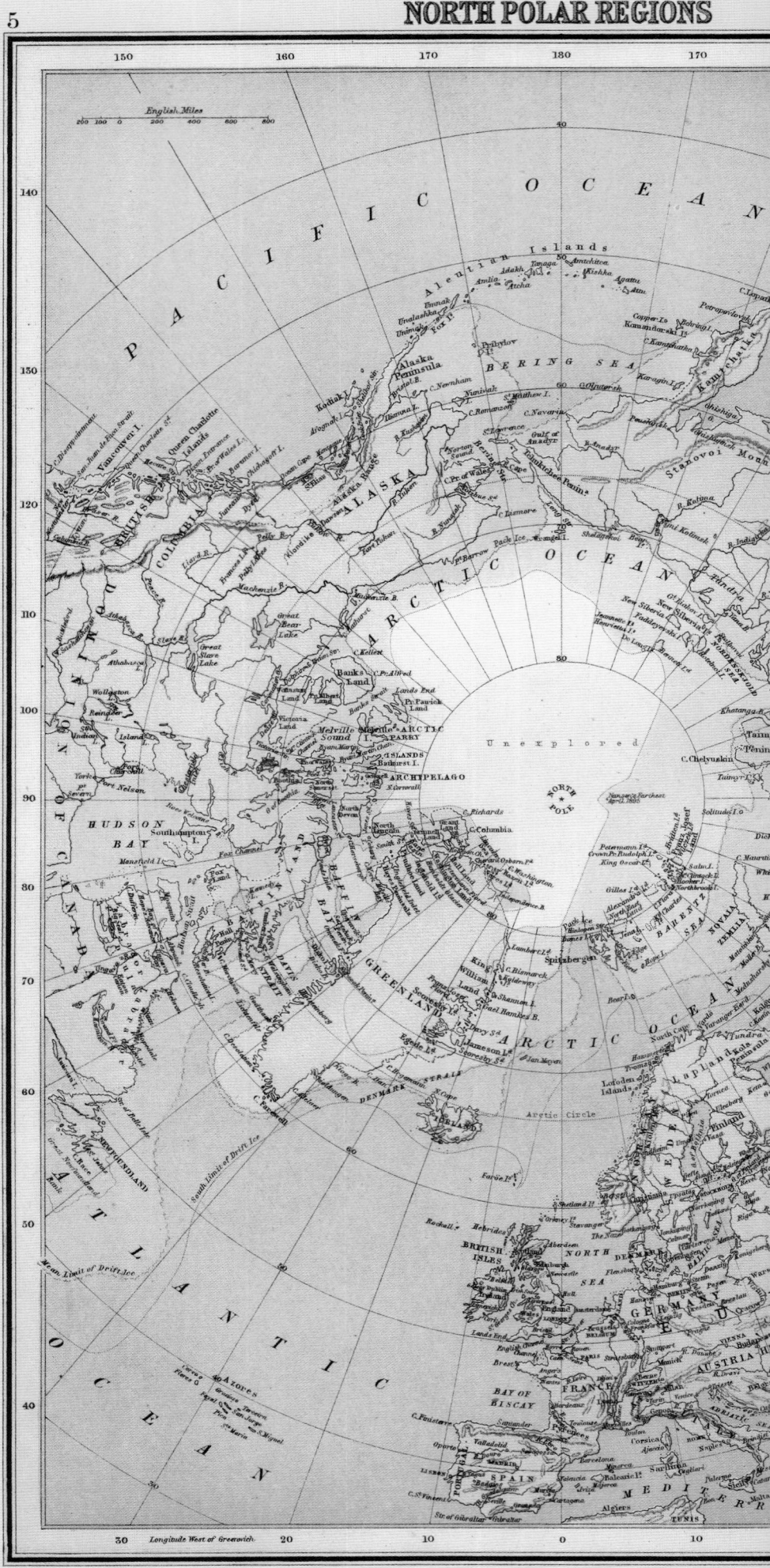

SOUTH POLAR REGIONS

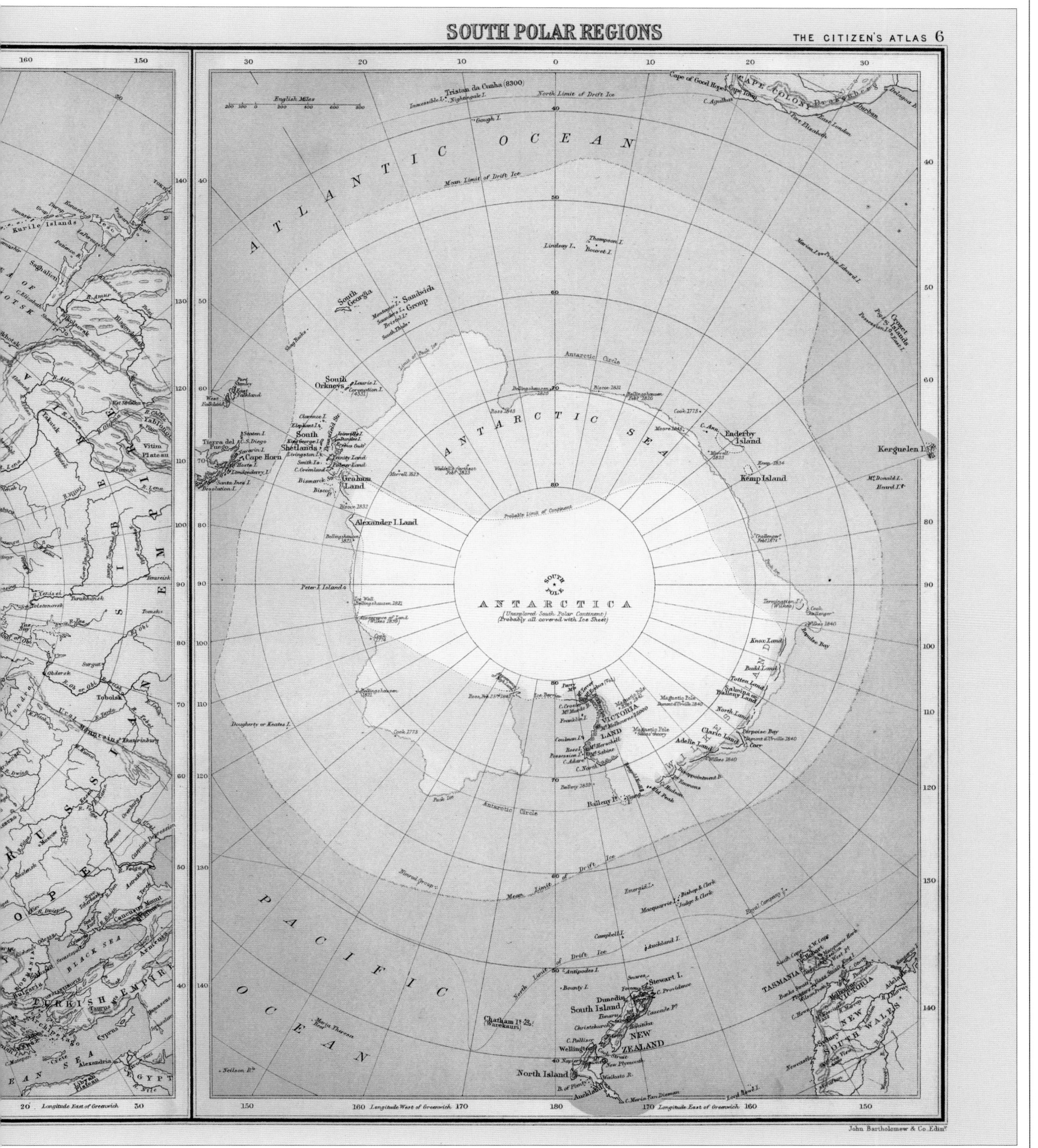

AUSTRALIA 1898

From the *Citizen's Atlas*, cartography by J. G. Bartholomew, F.R.G.S.

This map records the geopolitical make-up of Australia immediately prior to the ending of British colonial rule. Three years after it was drawn, the federal Commonwealth of Australia came into being, holding Dominion status under the British Crown.

The political boundaries depicted here had been established during the course of the nineteenth century, and with minor exceptions have remained unchanged to the present day.

Captain James Cook first recorded what he called New South Wales (NSW) in 1770 and the first settlement of the Crown Colony began eight years later, primarily as a penal colony for convicts transported from Britain and Ireland. The infamous Botany Bay, whose name became synonymous with the deprivations and hardship of penal servitude here, can be seen immediately to the south of Sydney (151°E 34°S). The original NSW was a vast tract, covering more than half the continent, and between 1803 and 1851 four largely self-governing colonies were carved from it: South Australia, Victoria, Queensland, and Tasmania.

South Australia came into being in 1834 and was unique amongst the colonies in being the only one to be settled entirely by free immigrants, rather than convicts. Victoria and Queensland, both named in honour of the reigning monarch, were granted full colonial status in 1851 and 1859 respectively. Curiously, the first of the new colonies to be separated from NSW (in 1825), the island of Tasmania off the southeast coast, is not featured here. Western Australia, the only colony not part of the original NSW lands, was established in 1826 as counter to possible French expansion in the region.

The only subsequent territorial developments to change the map of modern Australia from that depicted here occurred in 1911: the Northern Territory was formally separated from South Australia, and the Australian Capital Territory was created as a politically neutral area to host the soon-to-be-constructed new capital, Canberra. While Canberra was in development, Melbourne served as the temporary seat of government.

A particularly striking feature of the map is the pattern of settlement. The temperate and subtropical climates of the southwestern and eastern coastal areas attracted the original European settlers and 60 per cent of the Australian population still lives there. The drive inland was accelerated by a series of goldrushes beginning in the 1850s, and supported by the development of the first railways and telegraphs, although much of the central desert and grasslands remained uninhabited and unexplored (as the map indicates).

The exception to this pattern is the swath of habitations running almost continuously through the centre of the country from Darwin in the far north to Adelaide on the south coast. These had grown up bordering the main communication route opened up in the 1860s which was later to become one of the major highways. This passes through Alice Springs (or as it was called then Stuart), while relatively nearby (131°E 26°S) is the world-famous Ayers Rock (now known by its Aboriginal name, Uluru).

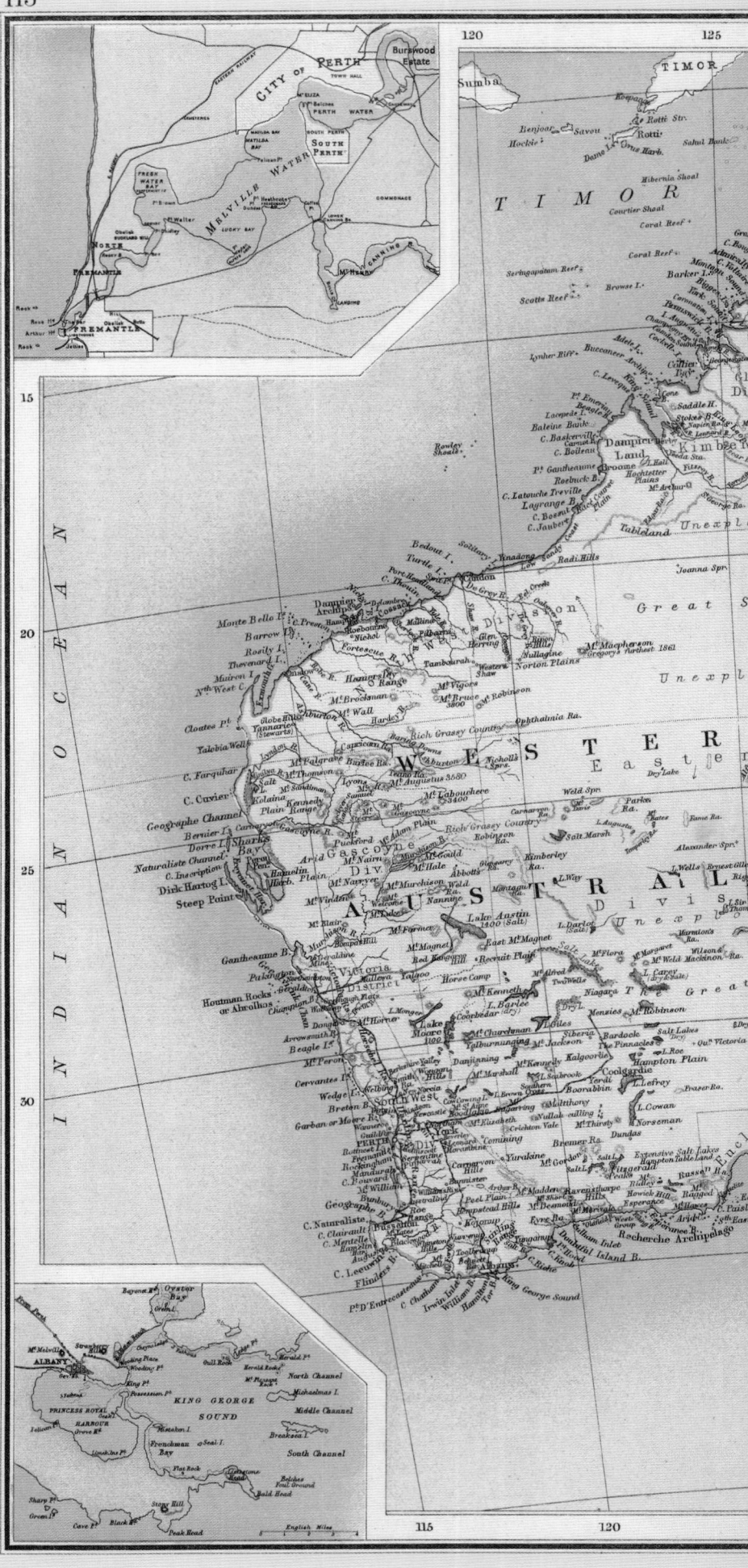

AUSTRALIA

TURKEY IN EUROPE, GREECE &c.
1898

From the *Citizen's Atlas*, cartography by J. G. Bartholomew, F.R.G.S.

By the end of the nineteenth century, the Ottoman or Turkish Empire had existed for 600 years. It was an Islamic successor to both the Roman and Holy Roman Empires, and at the peak of its powers in the seventeenth century had stretched from Gibraltar to the Caspian Sea, and from Vienna to the mouth of the Persian Gulf. Its strategic bridging of Europe and Asia Minor had given Turkey a pivotal role in virtually every aspect of East-West relations throughout its existence.

By 1898, however, the 'Sick Man of Europe' (as Tsar Nicholas I had called it) was in terminal decline, financially bankrupt and losing territory to foreign incursions and nationalist unrest in its fringe provinces. The Great Powers – Britain, France, Germany, Austria-Hungary and Russia – were keen to exploit Ottoman difficulties, intervening regularly in the complex political and military disputes in the region to further their respective, and often conflicting, interests.

In Europe, Greece was the first to secure its independence – in 1829, after a bloody revolution whose success was in no small part due to the interventions of Britain, France and Russia. The success of the Greeks acted as a catalyst for other nationalist movements in the region and neither internal reform nor brutal repression could prevent the progressive slackening of the Empire's hold on its European provinces.

However, it took the international settlements following the Russo-Turkish War of 1877–78 for the independence of many of Turkey's Balkan states to be internationally recognised. Under the Treaty of Berlin of 1878, the Great Powers and the Ottomans agreed to the complete independence of Romania (created in 1862 by the union of the semi-autonomous principalities of Moldavia and Wallachia) and of Serbia and Montenegro, which had enjoyed de facto independence since 1858 and 1867 respectively. The treaty also established the autonomous principalities of Bulgaria and Eastern Roumelia under nominal Ottoman suzerainty but with local leadership approved by the Powers; the two states were subsequently united in 1885 following a Bulgarian coup. The Ottomans were also forced to cede Bosnia and Herzegovina to Austria-Hungary but retained Macedonia. The treaty thereby set the seal on the disintegration of the Ottoman Empire in Europe, so that by 1898 its territory had been reduced to a section of the southern Balkans. In the following decade, this would be eroded even further as Greece, Bulgaria, Serbia and Albania fought one another and the Turks to expand their borders.

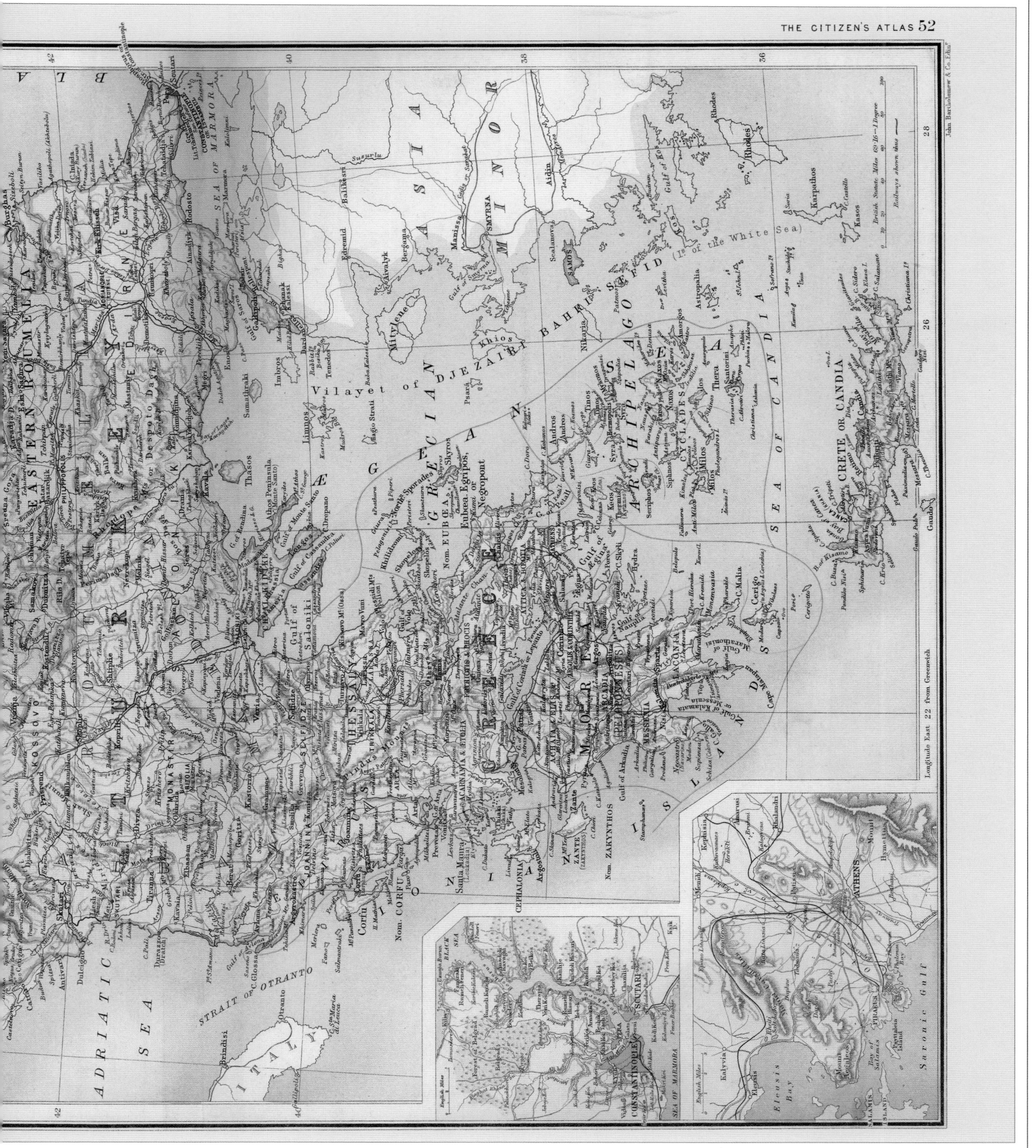

AFRICA 1898

From the *Citizen's Atlas*, cartography by J. G. Bartholomew, F.R.G.S.

A comparison between the maps of Africa in 1852 on pages 28–29, and that here dramatically illustrates the speed with which the continent was parcelled up between the competing European powers in the latter half of the nineteenth century.

For the first three-quarters of the century, little of Africa was ruled directly by Europeans, the major exceptions being French Algeria and the British Cape Colony. The British, French and Portuguese all possessed smaller footholds in western and southern parts of the continent but these were restricted to coastal territories with little penetration inland. Yet the interior had been explored and mapped for more than a century by the likes of Mungo Park, David Livingstone, H.M. Stanley, Serpa Pinto, Richard Burton, John Speke and James Grant, and it was as a result of their expeditions that Europeans came to realise the vast resources waiting to be seized.

In 1880, the 'Scramble for Africa' began in earnest. Fuelled by strategic rivalries, national ambitions and a commercial imperative to source new markets and raw materials, the major European powers set about a speedy partitioning of the continent.

Britain was in many ways the chief beneficiary of the partitioning of Africa. A primary motivation was to secure communication channels with India, the keystone of her empire. It was for this reason that Egypt was effectively annexed in 1882 to protect the strategically vital Suez Canal, and neighbouring Sudan was similarly annexed in 1898. Further advancements around the horn of Africa and northwards from the Cape Colony would continue to reinforce the vital trade routes to the East.

The French, still smarting from their defeat by Germany in the Franco-Prussian War of 1870, sought to re-establish national pride with overseas conquests. They advanced inland from Senegal, their coastal foothold in west Africa, and by 1898 controlled large swaths of land in north and west Africa, parts of the Congo in central Africa and the island of Madagascar in the Indian Ocean. Newly unified, Germany had begun its world expansion under Bismarck in the 1880s, and within a decade had established itself as the third-largest colonial power in Africa with the acquisition of South West Africa, Togoland, Cameroon and East Africa.

Italy, Portugal, Spain and Belgium also carved out parcels of territory for themselves until finally only Abyssinia (now Ethiopia) remained in the hands of indigenous rulers, while Liberia was already established as an independent republic (in 1847) to resettle former slaves from North America.

Throughout the colonisation process, the Europeans had encountered localised and piecemeal opposition but a policy of divide-and-conquer married to technological superiority generally saw them prevail. Ironically, Britain would shortly face its sternest military test in Africa, not from local tribes but from the Dutch Boers, who from 1899 to 1902 would fight to re-establish the autonomy of their republics in southern Africa.

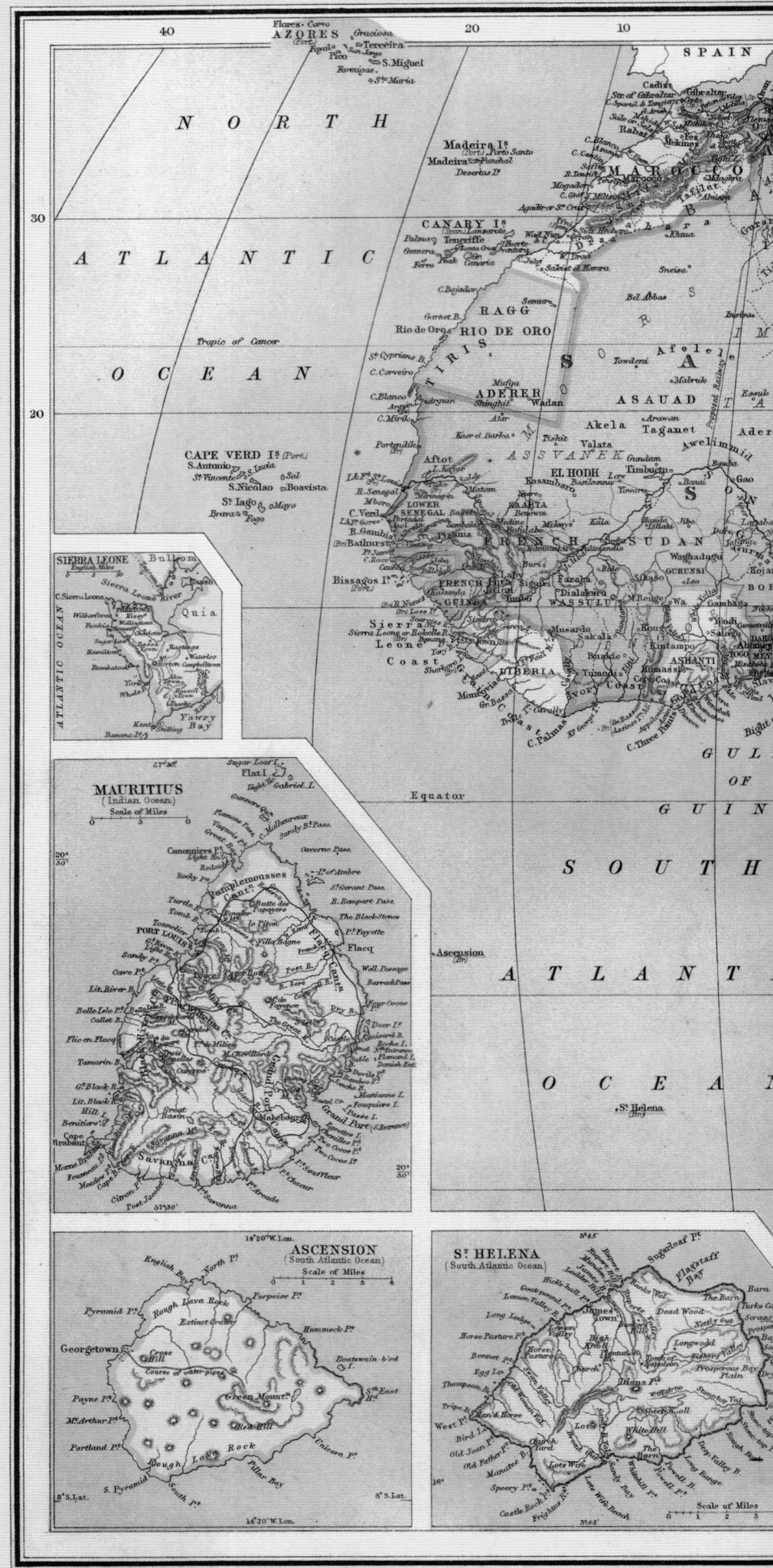

AFRICA

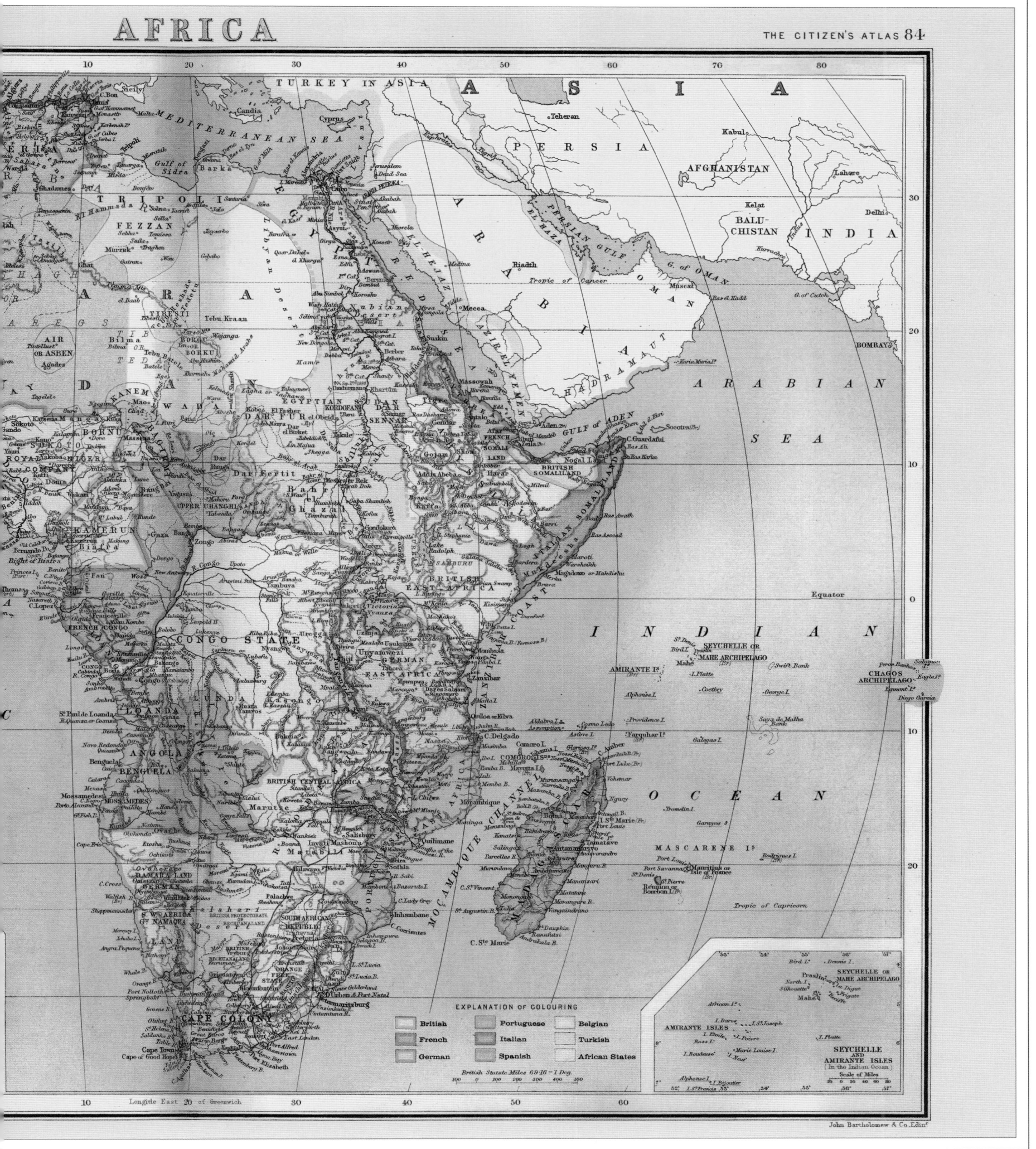

EXPLANATION OF COLOURING

British	Portuguese	Belgian
French	Italian	Turkish
German	Spanish	African States

British Statute Miles 69·16 = 1 Deg.

Longitude East 20 of Greenwich

SEYCHELLE OR MAIRE ARCHIPELAGO

AMIRANTE ISLES

SEYCHELLE AND AMIRANTE ISLES
(In the Indian Ocean)
Scale of Miles

John Bartholomew & Co. Edin.

DOMINION OF CANADA 1898

From the *Citizen's Atlas*, cartography by J. G. Bartholomew, F.R.G.S.

This map provides a fascinating snapshot of the development of modern Canada barely thirty years after the British colonies of North America were united and granted legislative autonomy under the Crown. This confederation was the first stage in the development of the independent nation.

At first glance, many of the territorial names on the map such as Quebec, Ontario, Nova Scotia, and Manitoba echo those of the country's modern provinces. Others – Assiniboia, Athabasca and Keewatin amongst them – are much less familiar.

Following the British North America Act of 1867, the Canadian Confederation initially comprised only the four eastern provinces of Ontario, Quebec, New Brunswick and Nova Scotia. The remainder of this vast land remained under direct British control: on the east coast Newfoundland and Labrador, and Prince Edward Island were held as colonies, as was British Columbia in the west – while the territory in between was owned by the powerful commercial agency, the Hudson's Bay Company, and was divided into Rupert's Land and the North-Western Territory.

By 1873, British Columbia and Prince Edward Island had both entered the Confederation. In 1870, after the British Government had ended its trading monopoly, the Hudson's Bay Company transferred all its land holdings to the Dominion, and out of these emerged the North-West Territories and the new province of Manitoba.

The scale of the new North-West Territories was immense. At its greatest extent, it stretched from the Alaskan border in the west to the maritime lands of Labrador in the east and from above the Arctic Circle to the United States border. In size, it was close to that of Western Europe. Instead of depicting this vast territory as a single entity, the map shows the various districts into which it was then divided to ease its administration.

Between 1876 and 1895, the North-West Territories were progressively subdivided until there were a total of nine districts, and it was from these that much of the rest of Canada's current political geography emerged in the early years of the twentieth century. In 1898, following the celebrated gold rush in the Klondyke near the Alaskan border, the district of Yukon was elevated to its current Territorial status. In 1905, the provinces of Alberta and Saskatchewan were created from Alberta, Assiniboia, Athabasca, and Saskatchewan districts. By 1912, Quebec had assumed its current boundaries following its acquisition of the district of Ungava. The remaining pieces of Canada's geopolitical landscape fell into place in 1949 when Newfoundland and Labrador became its tenth province, and in 1999, with a final subdivision of the Northwest Territories to create Nunavut, a new territory composed of parts of Franklin, Mackenzie and Keewatin districts.

Although the cultural influence of France remains strong in its former colony of Quebec, the tiny archipelago of Saint Pierre and Miquelon off Newfoundland's southern coast is the only part of what was once known as New France still under French control.

93

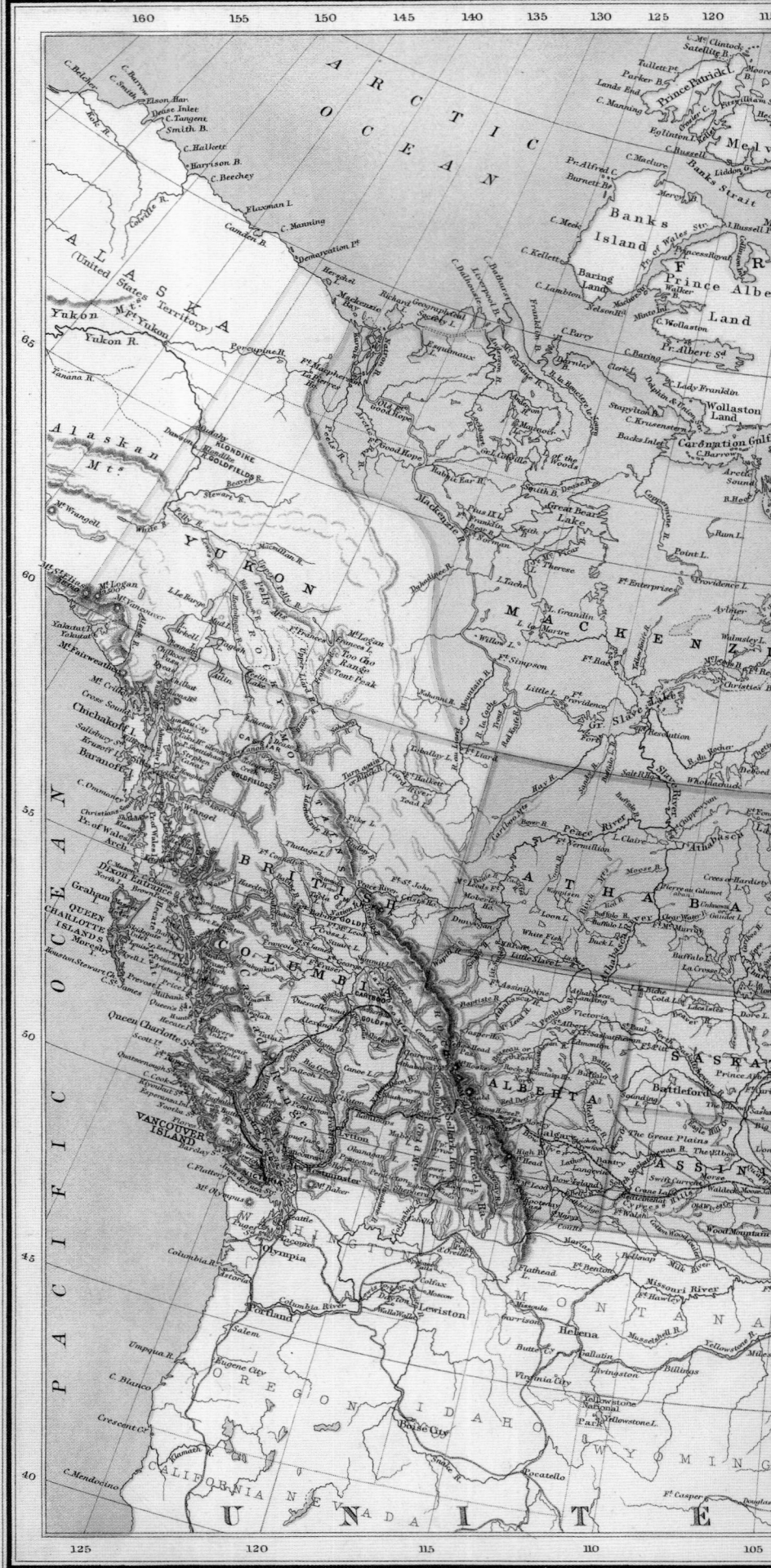

DOMINION OF CANADA

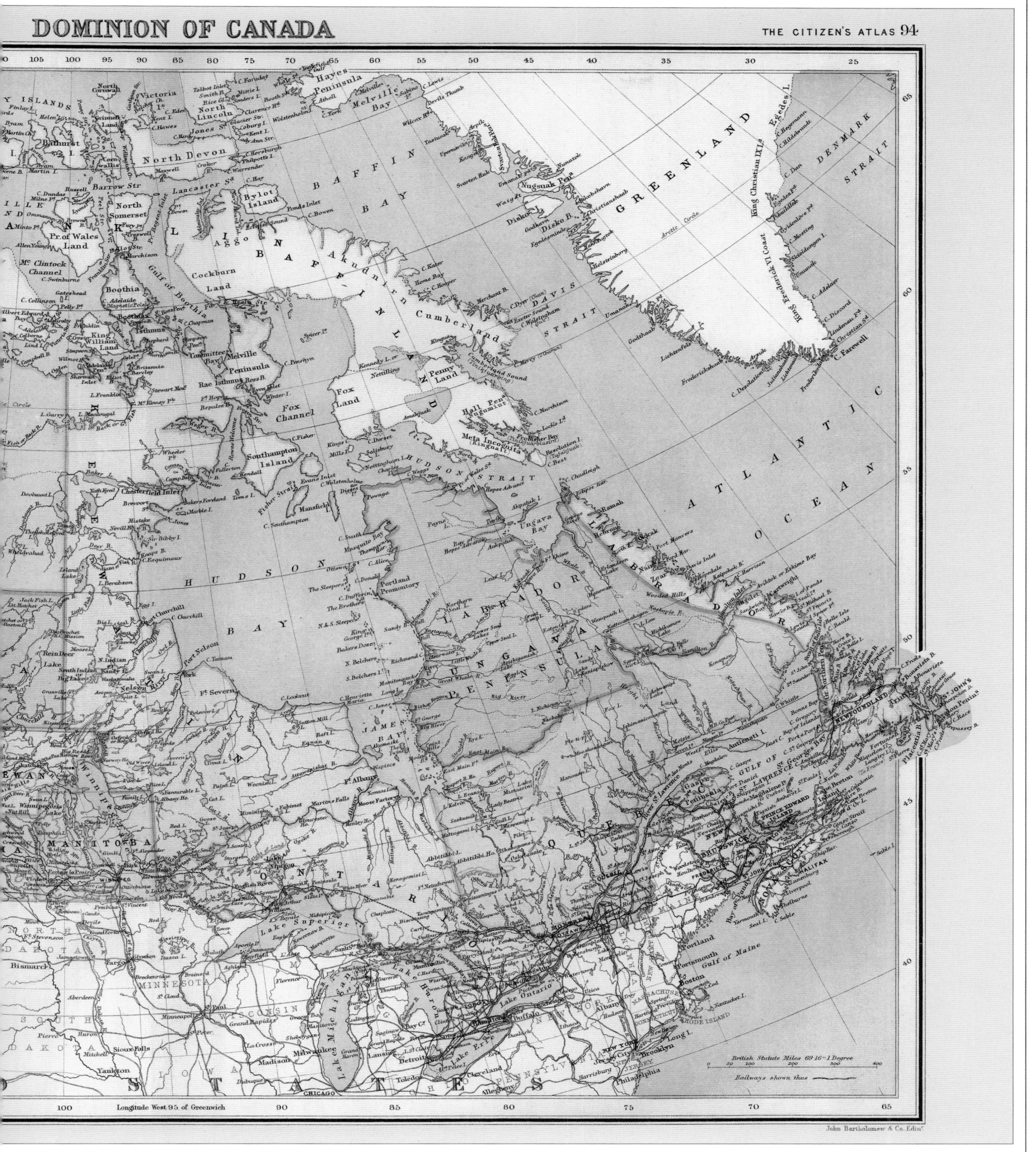

British Statute Miles 69·16=1 Degree

Railways shown thus

Longitude West 95 of Greenwich

John Bartholomew & Co. Edin.

TURKEY IN ASIA, PERSIA, ARABIA, &c. 1914

From the *International Reference Atlas of the World*, cartography by J. G. Bartholomew LL.D., F.R.G.S., Cartographer to the King.

The late nineteenth and early twentieth centuries had seen a dramatic contraction of the Ottoman Empire, particularly in the Balkans but also in North Africa, where Algeria and Tunisia had been ceded to France, and Libya to Italy.

Nevertheless, the Empire's possessions in Asia and the Middle East remained considerable. In addition to its Anatolian homeland stretching between the Black Sea and the Mediterranean, Constantinople's rule extended to Palestine, Syria, Iraq and the western coastal edge of the Arabian Peninsula, although with varying degrees of authority. For example, although nominally under Ottoman control, Egypt had in fact been self-governing for most of the nineteenth century and had even annexed its neighbouring Ottoman province of the Sudan from 1820 to 1885.

During the nineteenth century, the Great Powers – Britain, France, Germany, Austria-Hungary and Russia – had been happy to exploit local tensions and nationalist uprisings in the Balkans to destabilise the Ottoman Empire. In the Middle Eastern theatre, however, France, Italy and particularly Britain were all prepared to intervene more directly to advance their strategic interests.

Egypt has been styled on this map as an unaligned state, neither Turkish nor British, although in practice the British had been de facto rulers since 1882, following their seizure of power to protect their strategic and financial interests in the Suez Canal. Similar motives had led them to establish nominal joint control over Sudan with Egypt in 1899, although again the country was effectively administered as a Crown colony. Britain had also established footholds at various locations on the Arabian Peninsula: in Aden at the critical juncture of the Red and Arabian Seas; in neighbouring Oman; and in Kuwait ('El Kuweit') at the head of the Persian Gulf. Both Aden and Kuwait had been made protectorates, in 1886 and 1899 respectively, although only the former is recorded as such on the map.

Italy and France had also sought a presence in the region, establishing colonies in Eritrea (in 1890) and in French Somaliland (1896). France also developed considerable influence in Syria and Lebanon. Throughout this period, the bulk of the Arabian Peninsula was controlled by the Saud dynasty and was not politically aligned with any of the Great Powers. Although never formally invaded, Persia was economically dependent on Europe, and as a result, Britain and Russia effectively divided the country between them from 1907 into two spheres of economic interest in which each power could exert its influence.

As this map was being published, the world plunged into the horrors of the First World War. In Turkey, a modernist liberal government had been ousted by a military coup the previous year and had been replaced by a hardline nationalist and Islamist regime. In October 1914, Turkey entered the war on Germany's side, setting in motion the train of events that would bring about the final dissolution of the Ottoman Empire and the ultimate creation of the modern Turkish republic.

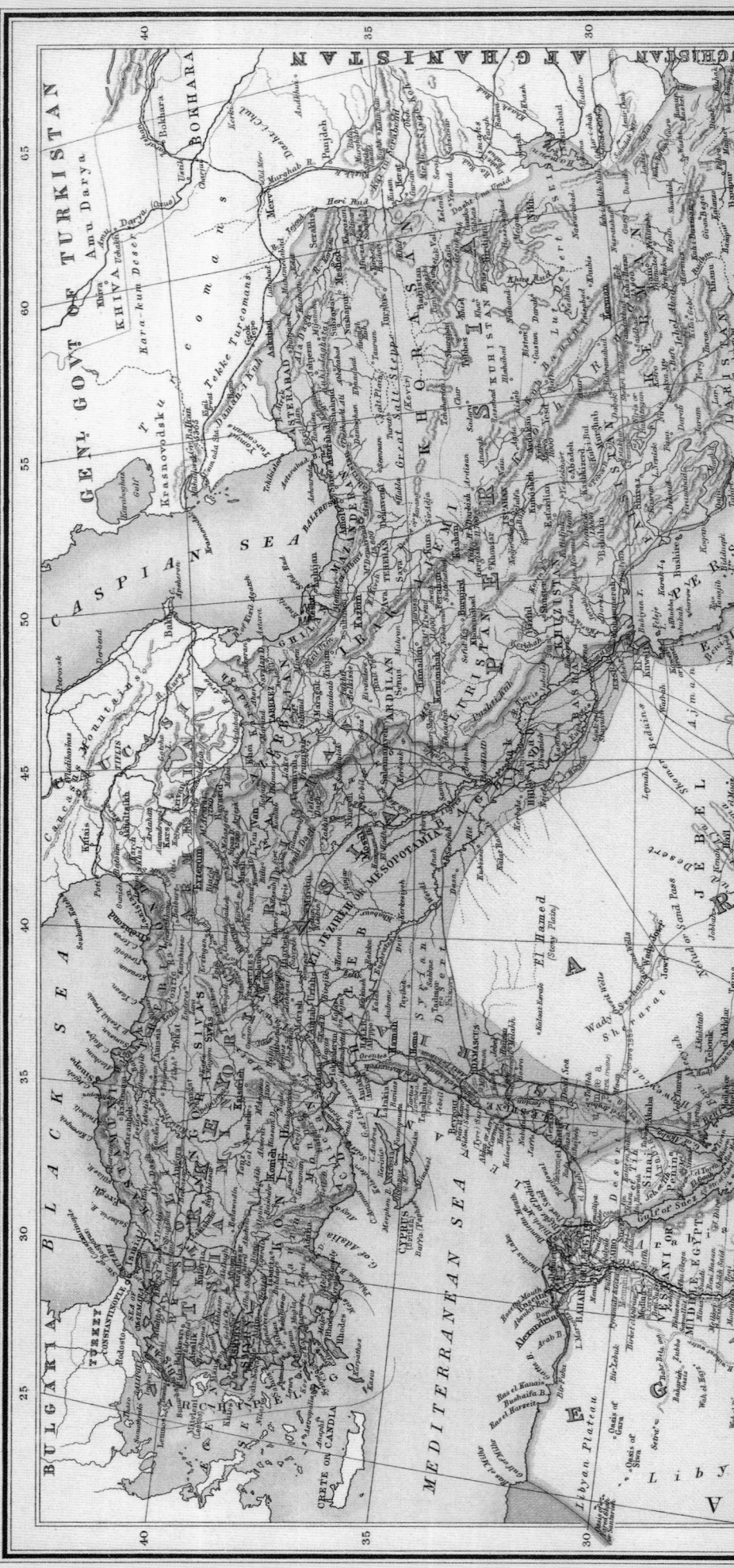

62

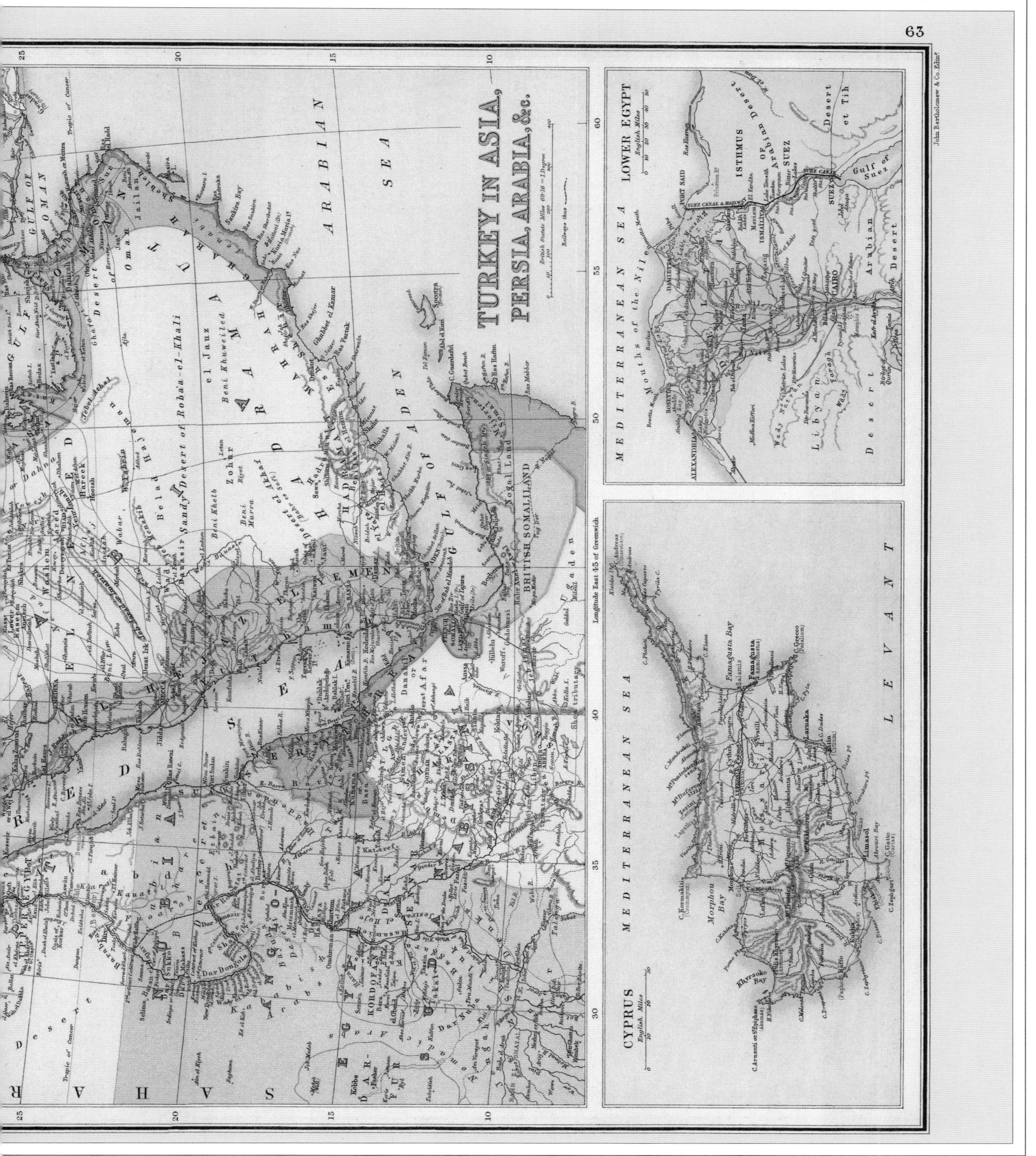

TURKEY IN ASIA, PERSIA, ARABIA, &c.

LOWER EGYPT

CYPRUS

John Bartholomew & Co. Edin.

INDIAN EMPIRE 1914

From the *International Reference Atlas of the World*, cartography by
J. G. Bartholomew LL.D., F.R.G.S., Cartographer to the King.

Dating from immediately before the outbreak of the First World War, this map graphically illustrates the reach of British imperial power on the Indian subcontinent.

Extending far beyond the political borders of modern India, the writ of the King Emperor George V ran across a territory that also encompassed the present-day states of Pakistan, Bangladesh and Myanmar (Burma). Although not officially recognised as part of British India, the strategically vital Crown colony of Ceylon (now Sri Lanka) and the northern kingdoms of Nepal and Bhutan also fell under its influence.

The map also demonstrates the complex interplay of direct rule and local autonomy that was essential to the smooth administration of such a vast and diverse territory. Britain's occupation of and rule in India had begun early in the seventeenth century through the activities of the commercial trading company, the Honourable East India Company. Having monopolised trade with the East Indies, the Company subsequently acquired military and administrative responsibilities in the region until it had become the de facto ruler. By means of diplomacy and military activity, it brought many of the hundreds of independent native states into the British sphere of colonial influence.

Areas marked in pink represent those administered directly by London through its principal representative, the Governor-General, the head of the British Administration in India, based in Calcutta. Known collectively as the British Provinces of India, these areas included the United Provinces in the north, the Central Provinces, Madras in the south, Bombay in the west and Bengal in the east.

By contrast, those areas in yellow mark out the clusters of Princely States, those nominally sovereign territories outside the direct control of the British Government who had entered into personal treaties with the Crown. These treaties allowed each state a degree of local autonomy and freedom to issue its own laws and set its own government. However, each was essentially a vassal state under British protection. As the monarch's personal representative to these Princely States, the Governor-General was also known as the Viceroy.

Also evident from the map is the extent of India's rail network. It was begun in 1853 under private enterprise, and by 1907, when all rail companies were brought under government control, the network extended over 9000 miles, mostly spreading inland from the major ports and termini of Calcutta, Bombay and Madras.

The historical snapshot presented here represents the high-water mark of Britain's imperial control in the region. As with many other states, the political, cultural and social consequences of the First World War in India would lead to greater calls for self-government and begin the process that would eventually lead to independence.

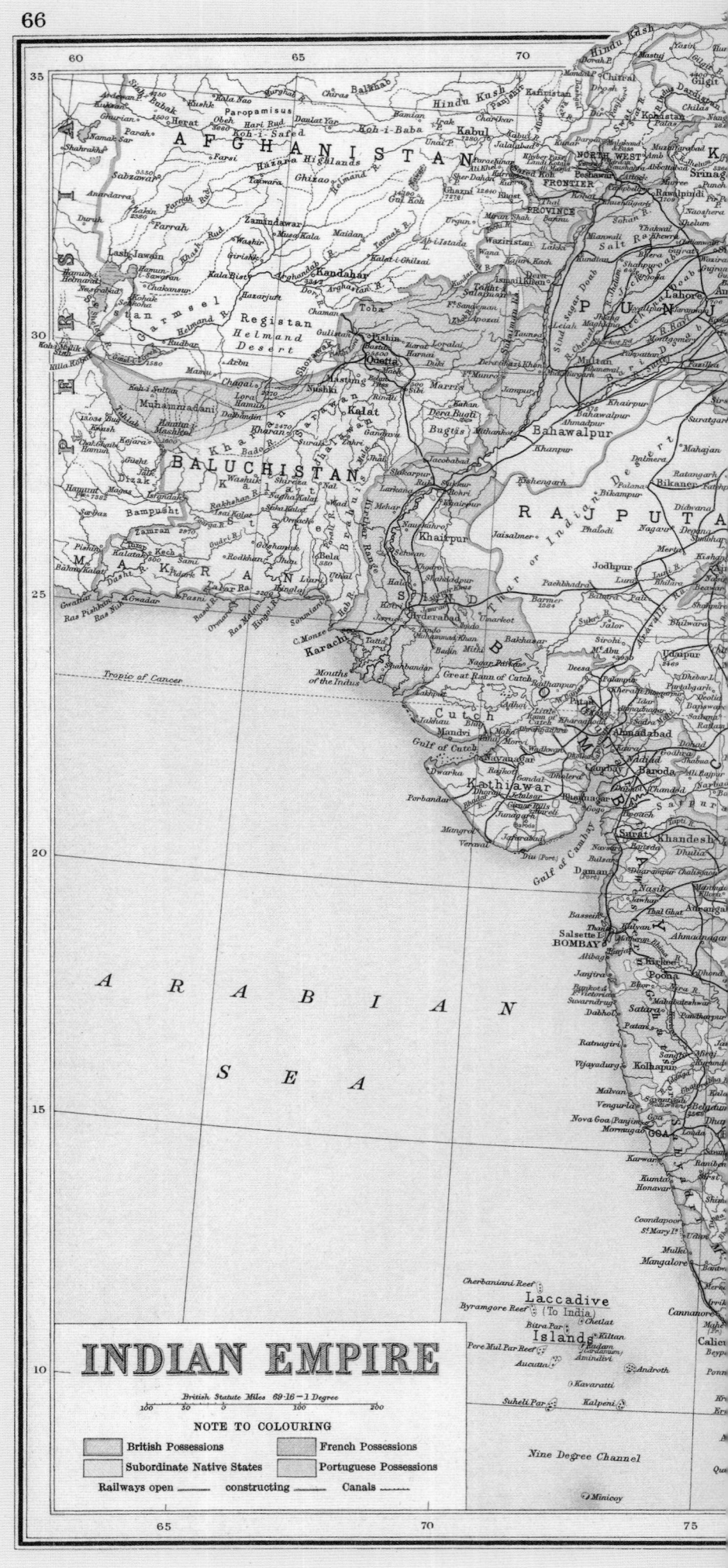

EUROPE POLITICAL 1922

From *The Times Survey Atlas of the World*, prepared at
"The Edinburgh Geographical Institute" under the direction of
J.G. Bartholomew, LL.D. F.R.S.E., F.R.G.S., Cartographer to the King.

The aftermath of the First World War and the Treaty of Versailles
in 1919 forged a new world order, completely redrawing the world
map and bringing an end to centuries of dynastic power that had
previously dominated central and eastern Europe. At the same time,
a rise in ethnic nationalism was threatening European colonial
empires. People were becoming more drawn towards democracy and
against aristocracies and military elites, who shunned social reform.

Geographically, Austria-Hungary had been the second largest country
in Europe (after the Russian Empire). Defeated in the war, however,
Austria-Hungary and its Habsburg dynasty lost its territory, and
was replaced by new successor states. Czechoslovakia, for example,
declared independence from the Austro-Hungarian Empire in 1918.
The new separate states of Austria, Hungary, Czechoslovakia and
Yugoslavia can all be seen on this map, which dates from 1922.

Following the Russian Revolution in 1917, another great empire,
the largest in Europe, collapsed. The Russian Empire lost much of
its western frontier – the new Baltic states of Estonia, Latvia and
Lithuania successfully fought independence wars against Bolshevist
Russia and German right-wing Freikorps, and were recognised as
independent countries in 1920.

The map, however, shows these states during only a brief spell of
independence. The communist Union of Soviet Socialist Republics
(USSR) was established in the same year this map was produced, and
with Stalin as leader from 1923, it would become one of the great world
superpowers. Following rigged elections and occupation by the Soviet
Army, the three independent Baltic states were swallowed up by the
USSR in 1940.

Further west, the British Empire lost most of one of its territories
through nationalism. In 1921, following the Irish War of
Independence, twenty-six of Ireland's thirty-two counties became
the self-governing Irish Free State. This was not a completely
independent republic, however; instead, it was granted Dominion
status within the British Empire, under the Anglo-Irish Treaty,
retaining the British monarch as head of state but having its own
army and police. The six counties in the north-east immediately opted
out of this agreement and remained part of the UK, as
Northern Ireland.

The treaty, however, led to internecine strife. It split the nationalist
Irish Republican Army (IRA) and its political branch, Sinn Féin, into
pro- and anti-treaty factions. This situation evolved into the Irish
Civil War, fought between June 1922 and May 1923. It was a vicious and
bitter war, marked by executions and a battle in Dublin, and ended in
defeat for the anti-treaty IRA forces and confirmation of the existence
of the Irish Free State.

"The Times" ATLAS

THE EDINBURGH GEOGRAPHICAL INSTITUTE

EUROPE - POLITICAL

PLATE 10

JOHN BARTHOLOMEW & SON, LTD.

CHINA 1922

From *The Times Survey Atlas of the World*, prepared at
"The Edinburgh Geographical Institute" under the direction of
J.G. Bartholomew, LL.D. F.R.S.E., F.R.G.S., Cartographer to the King.

The map shows how English-speakers were used to seeing Chinese place names long before modern 'Pinyin' spellings, which are characterised by frequent occurrences of q, x, y and z. Most obviously, some main names are in English – eg Inner Mongolia, Eastern Gobi – and some are partly English, eg Gulf of Liao-tung. Peking is used for what is now Beijing.

Hyphens (Shan-tung, Shan-hsi, Tsing-tao, Miao-tao) are used in the old Wade-Giles spelling system to show sounds that come from separate characters. Usually, the more well-known a place or a feature is to the Western reader, the more likely it is to be a single word, eg Tientsin, Dairen, Chinwangtao – but plenty of smaller names are also one word, perhaps because native sources following Post Office spellings were not fully standardised. If there were any mistakes by the cartographer, it would have been difficult to change them: everything was engraved by hand, on metal plates, in mirror writing. Some names are simple to engrave, eg Shan-tung, but others quite complex, eg the bay on the south side of the Shan-tung peninsula, given here as Ting-tsze-tswi-kou. To ease the task somewhat, these maps both omit the apostrophes with which Wade-Giles distinguishes the different sorts of 'T' and 'Ch'.

The inset map from 1958 shows how the cartographer's view of Chinese names had evolved in the meantime: the names look somewhat more familiar to the modern eye, the hyphens have mostly gone, and some spellings are simpler. The coastal feature previously given as Ting-tsze-tswi-kou has become Tingtze Wan (evidently now regarded as a bay rather than a river mouth). But the most striking difference between the two maps is that the important places are in much bigger type, aiding clarity and legibility. On the 1922 map Tientsin is almost indistinguishable from a village, though nowadays it has ten million people. Tientsin and Peking are still the only name shown for those cities, but in other cases a policy is emerging to give more than one version of a name. Another trend is to name features more in the local language – so for instance Liaotung Wan replaces Gulf of Liao-tung.

The next quantum leap would, of course, be the adoption of Pinyin by the Chinese themselves – producing names in a style which is now more familiar to the Western reader, such as Beijing, Tianjin, Dalian, and Liaodong Wan. The small bay on what is now the Shandong peninsula has become Dingzi Gang (*see* 153 F2) – a very different name from Ting-tsze-tswi-kou on the map of 1922.

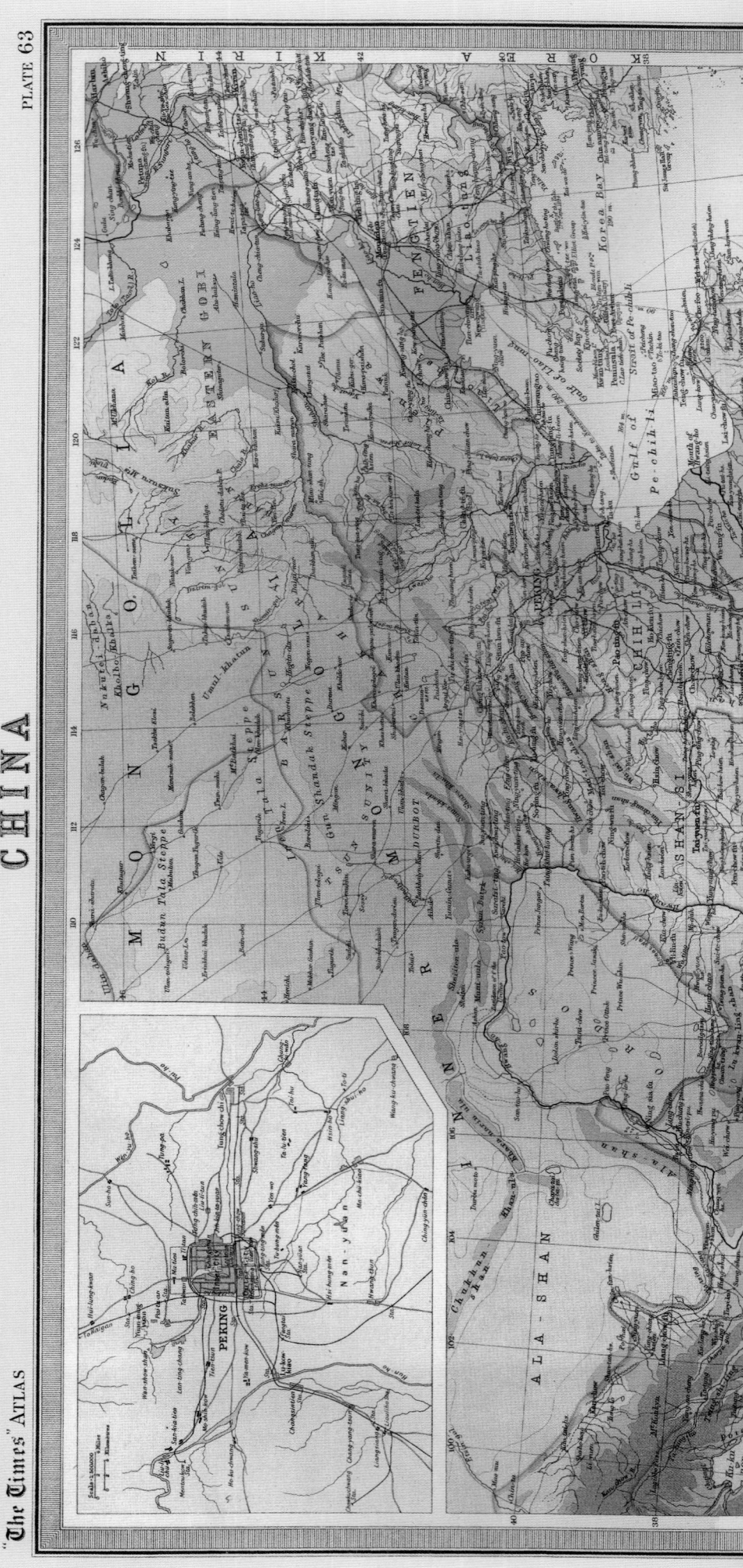

PLATE 63

CHINA

"The Times" ATLAS

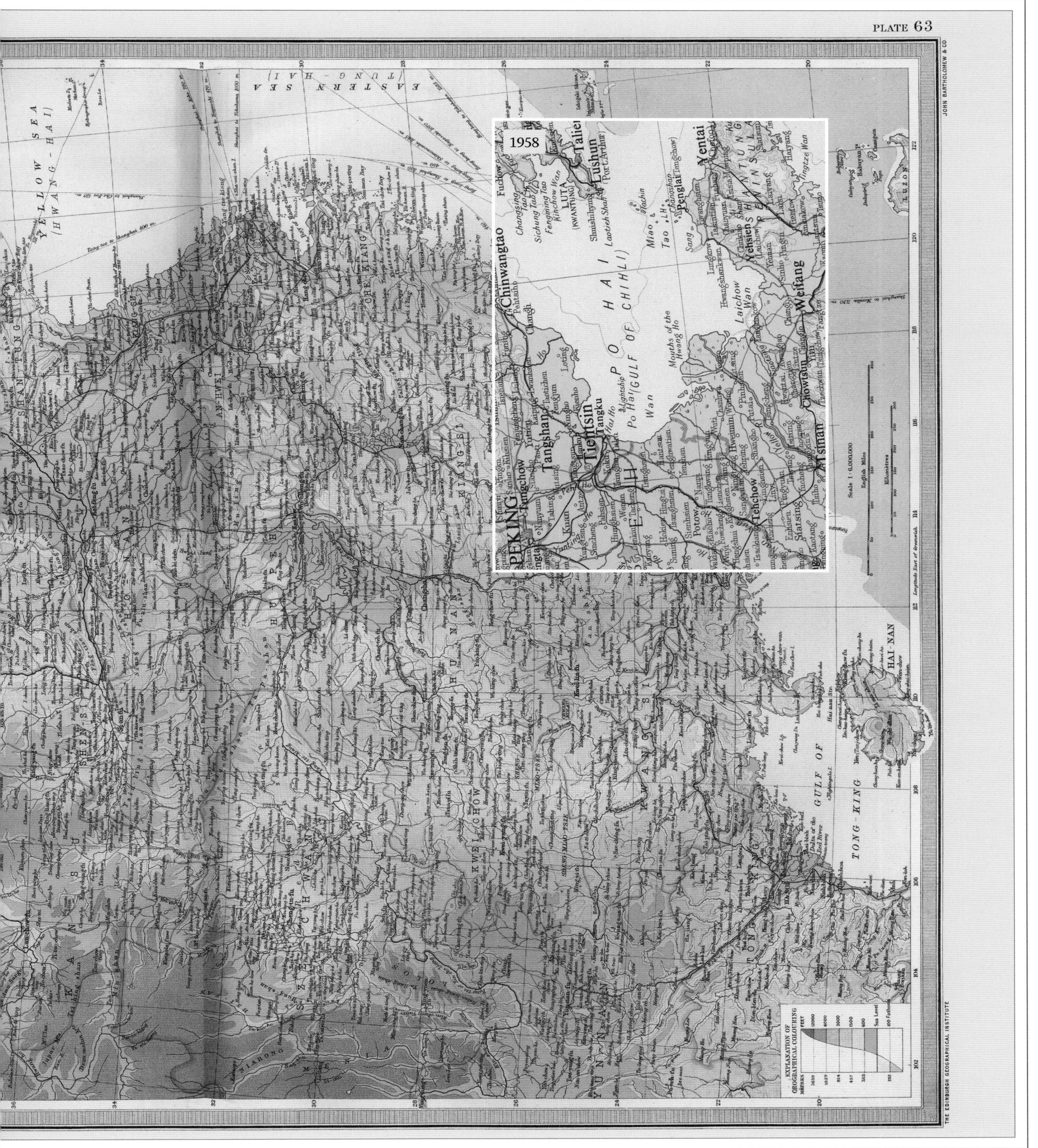

WORLD POWERS 1957

From *The Times Atlas of the World, Mid-Century Edition 1958*, cartography by
John Bartholomew, M.C., LL.D.

The most striking feature of this map is its unusual viewpoint
(or projection). Devised in 1948 by John Bartholomew of the famous
cartographic dynasty, the Atlantis Projection abandons the common
atlas convention of depicting maps that show the Arctic at the top
and the Antarctic at the bottom, with the Atlantic in between. Here the
projection is tilted and centred at 30°W 45°N to allow a focus on the
world's oceans, in particular the Atlantic.

The use of the Atlantis Projection in this instance is particularly
effective in conveying the combative nature of relations between
the United States and the Soviet Union, the two superpowers which
emerged to dominate the new world order following the Second
World War. Like giant beasts poised to grapple, the major landmasses
of the capitalist West and the communist East face each other across
the Arctic and North Atlantic Oceans: this was an accurate reflection
of the state of international politics at this time.

With the defeat of Fascism in 1945, any sense of unity and common
purpose between the Soviet Union and the other Allied powers swiftly
evaporated. This was soon replaced by a growing mutual distrust
and outright hostility that was underpinned by the polarising effects
of their respective political ideologies. Both power blocs possessed
nuclear arsenals but were reluctant to confront each other in either
nuclear or conventional warfare. The uneasy armed truce that
emerged became known as the Cold War.

In spite of these geopolitical tensions, the United Nations
Organization had been founded in 1947 as a vehicle for maintaining
international peace and security and developing international
economic and social cooperation. Ten years later, the UN had over
eighty member nations, although their division into hostile armed
camps did little to further the aims of the organization.

Both the USA and the Soviets sought to build economic, military
and diplomatic alliances to support their particular strategic
ambitions. In 1949, the USA established the North Atlantic Treaty
Organization (NATO), formally allying itself to Western Europe in
order to contain the spread of Communism there. Elsewhere in
the world, in 1954–55, two similar alliances were formed to counter
communist expansion – the South East Asian Treaty Organization
(SEATO) in the Philippines and Indo-China, and the Baghdad Pact
in the Middle East. The USSR and Communist China retaliated
by providing military and economic support to anti-colonial or
nationalist struggles in Africa, Asia and Latin America, while in 1955,
the Soviets established the Warsaw Pact, their own military alliance
among the communist countries of Eastern Europe.

Within a few short years of this particular map being drawn,
significant colour changes would be required for a number of
countries: Alaska would become a full member state of the USA (1959);
Fidel Castro would establish a Marxist government on America's
doorstep in Cuba (1959), and the process by which many African
nations would shake off the last remnants of European colonialism
would begin in earnest.

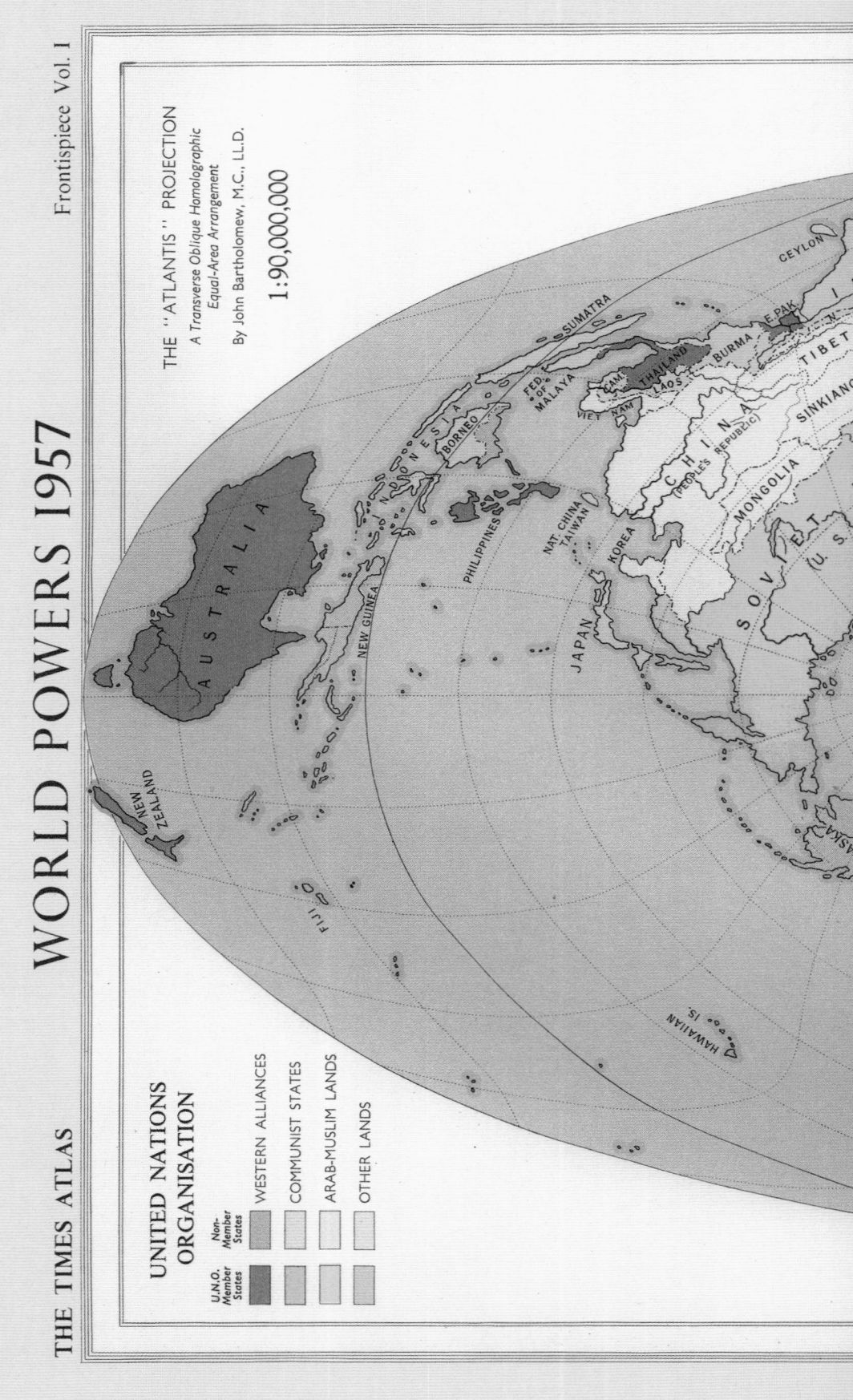

Frontispiece Vol. I

WORLD POWERS 1957

THE TIMES ATLAS

THE "ATLANTIS" PROJECTION
*A Transverse Oblique Homolographic
Equal-Area Arrangement*
By John Bartholomew, M.C., LL.D.

1:90,000,000

UNITED NATIONS
ORGANISATION

U.N.O.
Member
States

Non-
Member
States

WESTERN ALLIANCES

COMMUNIST STATES

ARAB-MUSLIM LANDS

OTHER LANDS

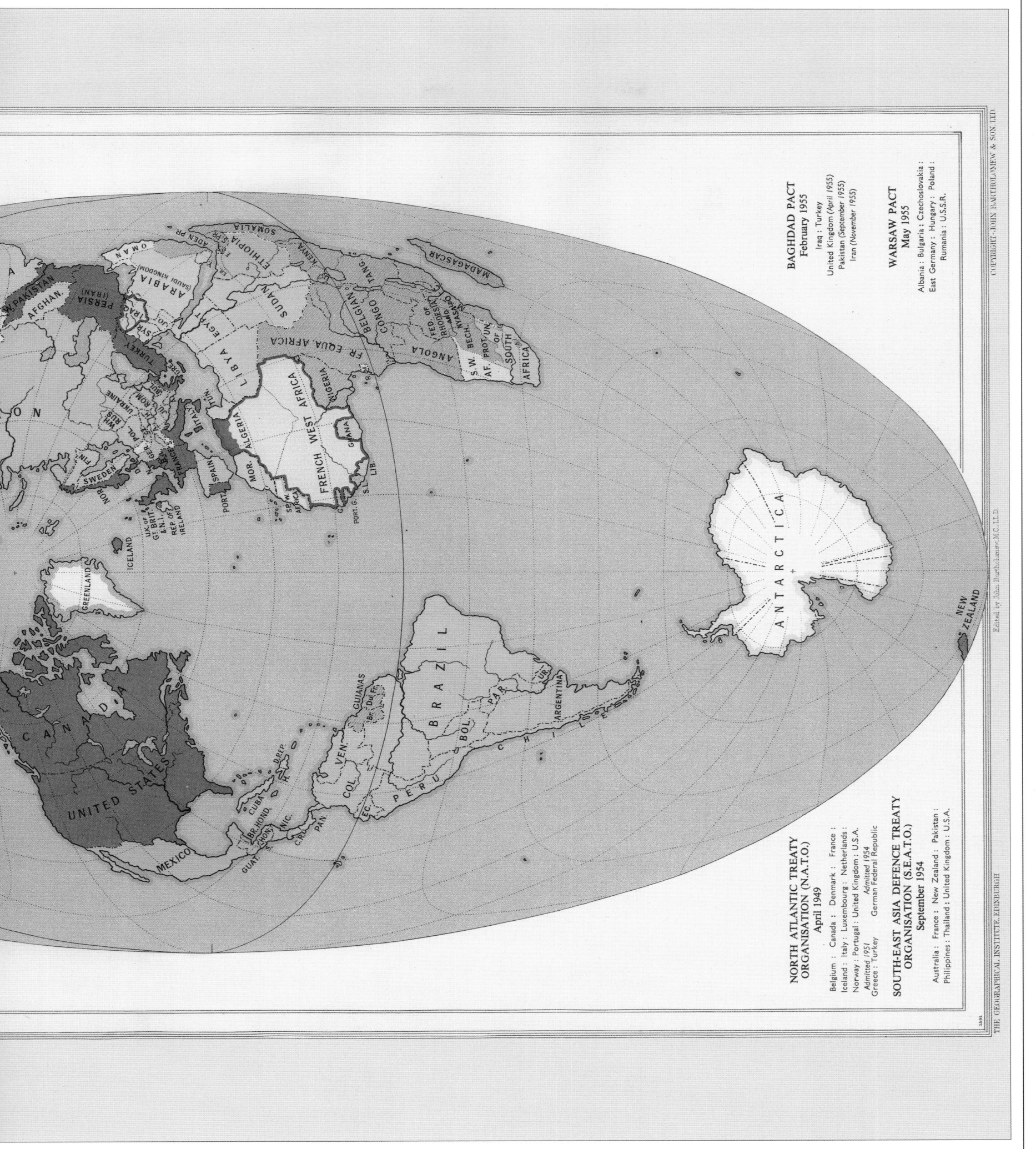

BAGHDAD PACT
February 1955

Iraq : Turkey :
United Kingdom (April 1955) :
Pakistan (September 1955) :
Iran (November 1955)

WARSAW PACT
May 1955

Albania : Bulgaria : Czechoslovakia :
East Germany : Hungary : Poland :
Rumania : U.S.S.R.

NORTH ATLANTIC TREATY
ORGANISATION (N.A.T.O.)
April 1949

Belgium : Canada : Denmark : France :
Iceland : Italy : Luxembourg : Netherlands :
Norway : Portugal : United Kingdom : U.S.A.

Admitted 1951   Admitted 1954
Greece : Turkey   German Federal Republic

SOUTH-EAST ASIA DEFENCE TREATY
ORGANISATION (S.E.A.T.O.)
September 1954

Australia : France : New Zealand : Pakistan :
Philippines : Thailand : United Kingdom : U.S.A.

THE GEOGRAPHICAL INSTITUTE, EDINBURGH

Edited by John Bartholomew, M.C., LL.D.

COPYRIGHT : JOHN BARTHOLOMEW & SON LTD.

MAPPING SCIENCE

For millennia, maps have been important for reflecting people's ideas and knowledge of their world, their social and cultural environments, and the growing complexity of the spatial challenges they faced, especially during recent centuries. Rather than evolving, maps appeared in various forms, in different parts of the world at different times and to meet different needs. Technical improvements also came in stages, often in response to contemporary advances in science and technology.

The fact that most geospatial and map information is now stored digitally has not changed the fundamental uses of cartography, it just means that spatial data handling is now carried out more effectively. Maps have long been recognized as primarily communicative devices, but they have had equally significant roles in support of spatial data exploration and analysis. It is the latter two which have gained importance recently as technologies have allowed new ways of 'visualizing' the world.

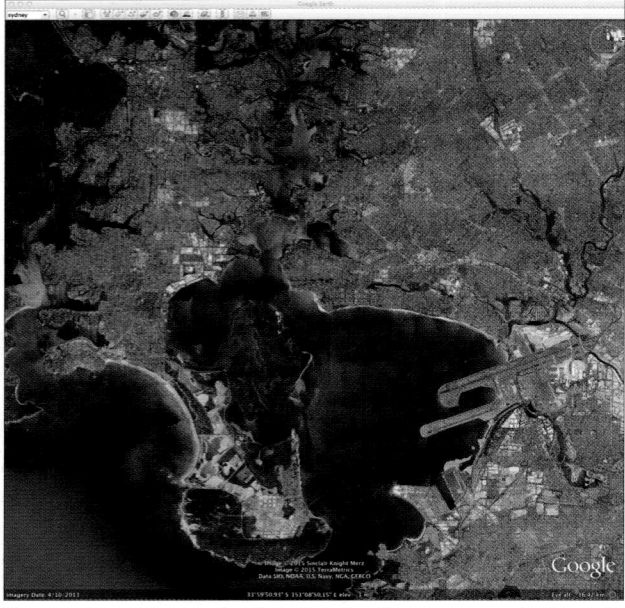

The powerful and dramatic Google Earth application brings easy navigation and visualization of the globe through progressively higher resolution satellite images, aerial photographs and mapping to any web user. Interactivity includes the ability for users to add their own data as overlays to the Google Earth images.

The last four centuries of the second millennium AD saw a massive increase in world population, urbanization, and industrialization. They have also been characterized by an increasing recognition of the importance of mapping, and by developing technologies in the fields of surveying, navigation, printing, communications, and computers.

The development of aviation and then satellite remote sensing, from the early 1970s, offered new forms of imagery and measurement techniques, which have been particularly significant in recent cartographic developments. They allowed a new view of the Earth and spawned a new age in mapping. The introduction of the computer led to the production of digital maps and the rapid recoding of spatial data from paper to digital databases. This, in turn, supported the development of Geographical Information Systems (GIS), which allow users to select their own spatially referenced data and carry out exploratory and analytical manipulations to degrees of speed and complexity previously unimagined. The digital era has also changed the ways in which new spatially-related data are acquired. Global Positioning System (GPS) technology now provides much greater potential for the rapid and precise measurement of position. Most recently, the growth of the Internet and World-wide Web, and GPS-enabled mobile technologies, have created opportunities for high-speed access to any data from anywhere at any time.

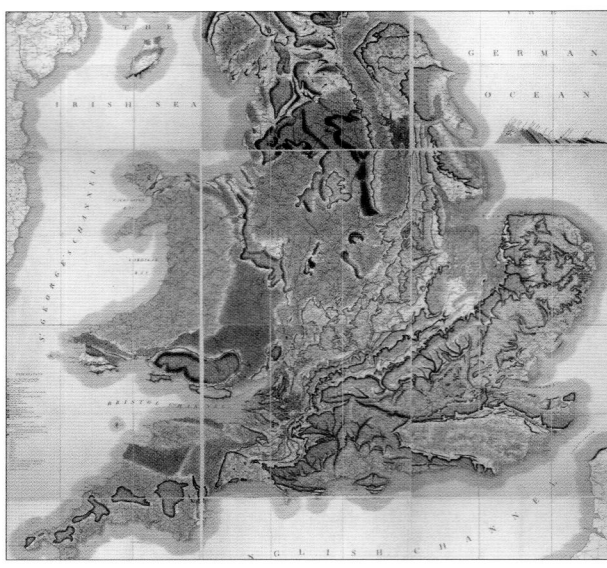

This early world map is carved on a Babylonian clay tablet, c. 600 BC. Babylon is shown as a rectangle intersected by vertical lines representing the Euphrates river. Small circles show other cities and countries, and the world is encircled by an ocean – the 'Bitter River'. British Museum, Department of Western Asiatic Antiquities, London, UK.

Called *A Delineation of Strata of England and Wales, with part of Scotland*, produced by William Smith and published in 1815, this was the first geological map of Britain. Natural History Museum, London, UK.

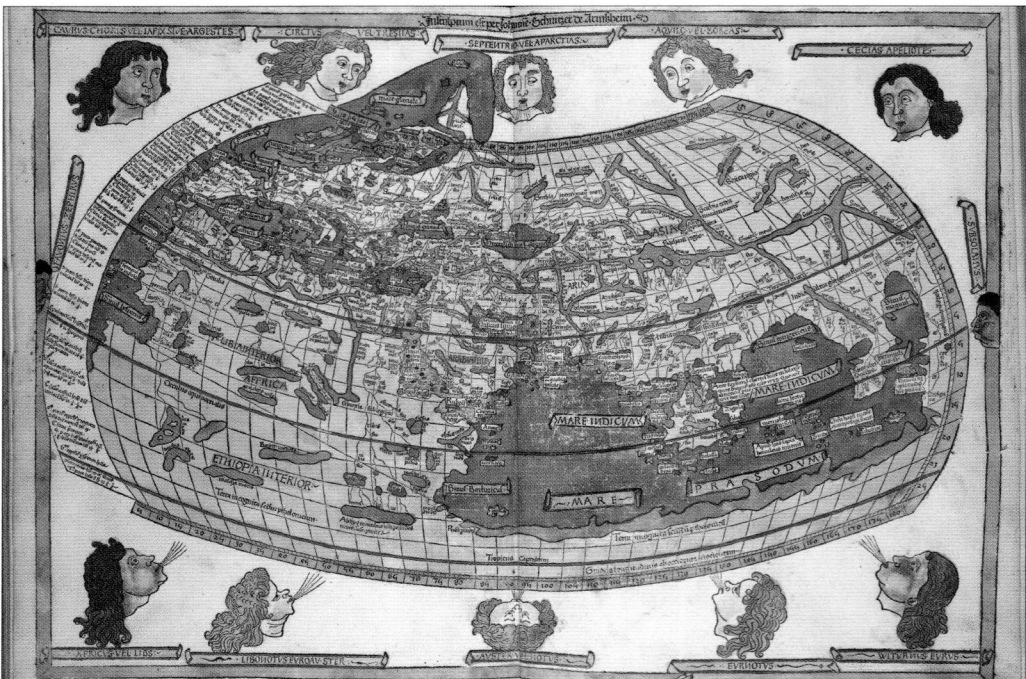

This world map is based on the work of Claudius Ptolemy, produced by Donis Nicolaus in Ulm, Germany, 1630. The map includes lines of latitude and longitude which give a sense of accuracy. The figures represent different wind directions. British Library, London, UK.

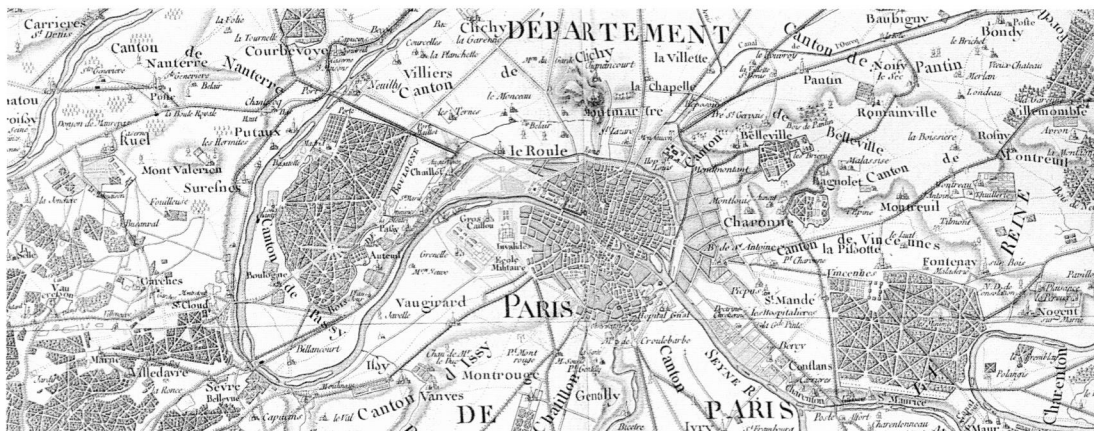

This is a detail from the first sheet – Sheet No. 1 Paris – of a map of France by Cassini de Thury, 1736. Original scale 1:86 400. National Library of Scotland, Edinburgh, UK.

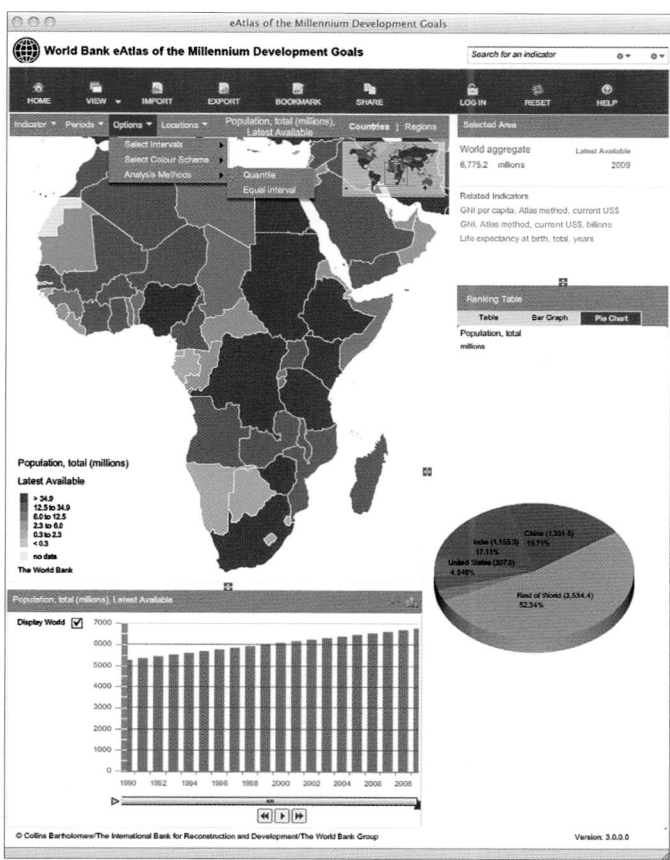

The quality of satellite images has greatly improved over time. Landsat images go back to 1972 and are now an unmatched historical archive held by the United States Geological Survey (USGS). The image above is of Venice taken in June 2000 by the Enhanced Thematic Mapper+ on Landsat 7 at 60 m resolution. It was launched in 1999.

By the time Landsat 8 was launched in 2013 with improved sensors and technology, the resolution possible had greatly improved as a much crisper image is captured. The image above from September 2013 was taken from the Operational Land Imager on Landsat 8 with a 30 m resolution. Some satellites can now capture very high resolution images at better than 0.5 m.

Some mapping applications allow high levels of user interactivity – allowing selection of the specific data to be mapped, how these data should be classified and depicted, what background map detail should be included, etc. The World Bank e-Atlas of Global Development also incorporates tables and graphs generated from the same data.

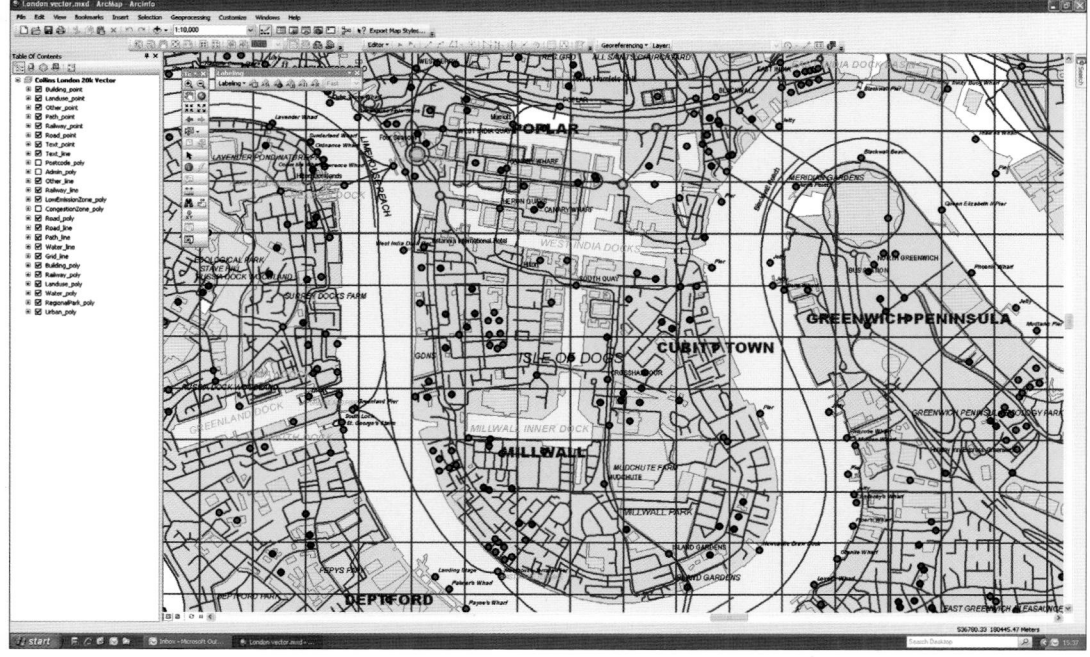

Geographic Information Systems (GIS) analyse data spatially and allow comparisons of numerous, complex datasets for the purposes of analysis, planning and mapping. An increasing amount of data is now 'geo-referenced', and can be used in this way – in fact almost all data could be described as geographical, referring to events or phenomena which occur somewhere in the world.

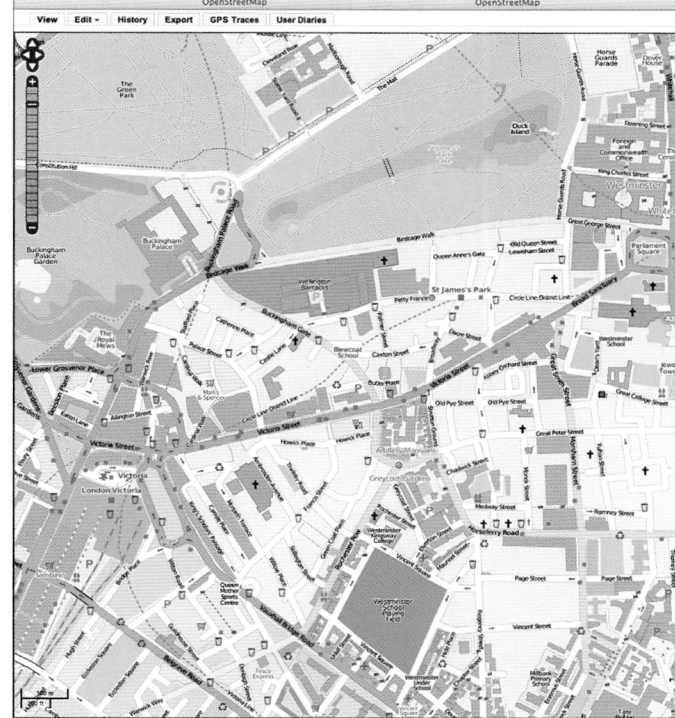

Maps free from normal copyright restrictions are created through the OpenStreetMap project. In what is a collaborative effort, participants gather geographic data in the field and create 'tracklogs' from Global Positioning System (GPS) receivers. Cartographic techniques are then applied to convert these into meaningful maps for free use. Such mapping is now forming the basis for web-based and mobile mapping applications.

THE EARTH

Before the end of the 19th century, earth scientists had no way of discovering the composition of the interior of the Earth. Ideas about the internal structure were therefore based almost entirely on speculation. The only evidence related to phenomena apparent at the Earth's surface, but which seemed to arise from within. These consisted of earthquakes, volcanoes, and geysers. To early thinkers, earthquakes indicated that the Earth could not be made entirely of solid rock, but might contain underground caverns full of air. Geysers and springs also suggested that the interior of the Earth was partly, or largely, made up of water. On the other hand, volcanic eruptions seemed to indicate that fire existed underground. For a long time, debate continued between the neptunists who favoured a watery interior and the volcanists favouring a fiery one. With the development of instrumental seismology and worldwide seismic monitoring, starting around 1900, a more soundly based answer began to appear. Careful study of the time differences of different earthquake waves showed that features of the Earth's structure could be deduced by analysing the way in which waves travel through it. Boundaries between different layers within the Earth were identified by the way waves were reflected or refracted by them. It was also possible to tell which parts of the Earth's interior must be liquid, since some types of wave can only travel through solid regions. As a result, the basic internal structure of the Earth became known.

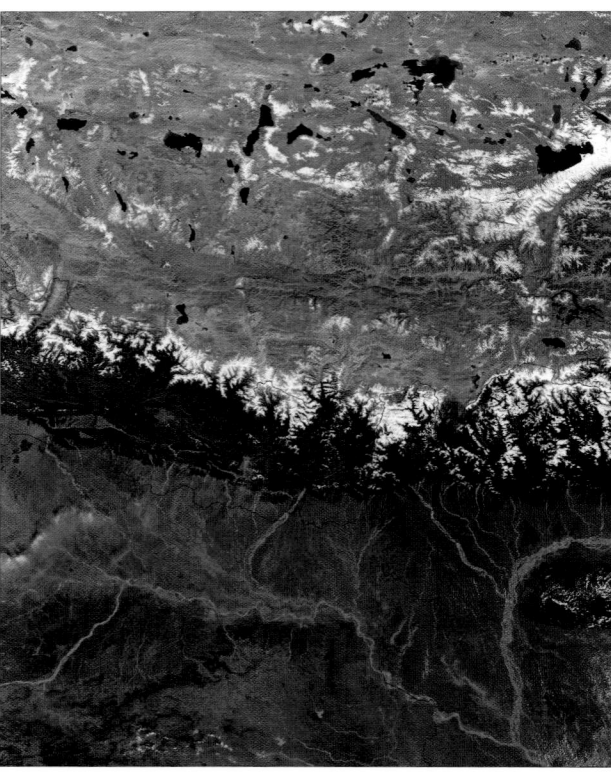

The Himalaya can be clearly seen in this image. They are being formed as the Indian continental plate to the south collides with the Asian plate to the north. This is an example of a continental destructive plate boundary.

PLATE TECTONICS

Over the course of geological time the Earth's crust has broken up into large fragments, which are known as lithospheric or tectonic plates. These plates are slowly moving relative to one another at rates of a few centimetres per year. This process – originally described as continental drift, a term coined by the meteorologist Alfred Wegener who first proposed the idea in the 1920s – is known as plate tectonics. The interaction of plates along their boundaries causes volcanic and seismic activity. The fact that the shapes of South America and Africa dovetail neatly into one another was noticed as early as the 17th century, and this has proved to be no coincidence.

THE EARTH'S INTERNAL STRUCTURE

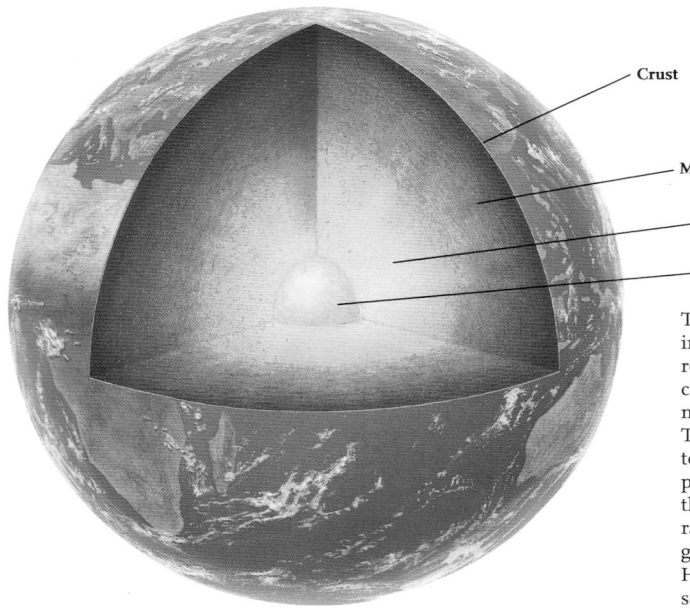

Crust

Mantle

Outer Core

Inner Core

The interior of the Earth can be divided into three principal regions. The outermost region is the crust which is extremely thin compared to the Earth as a whole. The next layer down is known as the mantle. This is about 2850 km thick and is believed to consist mostly of the minerals olivine, pyroxene and garnet. Below the mantle is the Earth's core, which is about 3470 km in radius, and is mainly made up of iron. The greater part of the core is completely liquid. However, there is an inner core which is solid, and about 1220 km in radius.

Mass	5.974 x 10²¹ tonnes
Total area	509 450 000 sq km / 196 698 645 sq miles
Land area	149 450 000 sq km / 57 702 645 sq miles
Water area	360 000 000 sq km / 138 996 000 sq miles
Volume	1 083 207 x 10⁶ cubic km / 259 911 x 10⁶ cubic miles
Equatorial diameter	12 756 km / 7 927 miles
Polar diameter	12 714 km / 7 900 miles
Equatorial circumference	40 075 km / 24 903 miles
Meridional circumference	40 008 km / 24 861 miles

PLATE TECTONICS

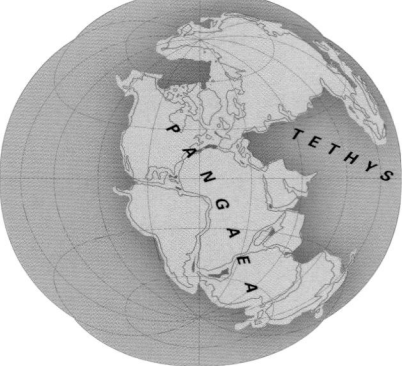

The Earth looked very different 200 million years ago. All the continents were at one time joined together in a great landmass called Pangaea.

By 100 million years ago Africa had split away from the Americas. Antarctica and Australia then broke away from Africa and subsequently from each other.

About 165 million years ago this super-continent began to break up.

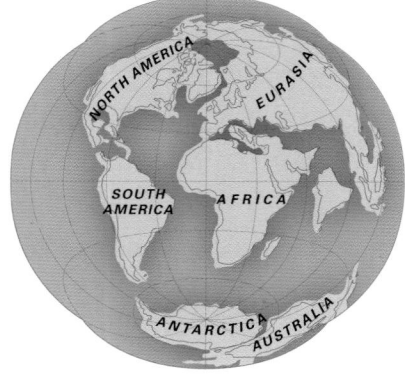

Around 50 million years ago, North America and Europe separated, and India, which was formerly attached to Antarctica, moved northwards to collide with Asia.

TYPES OF PLATE BOUNDARY

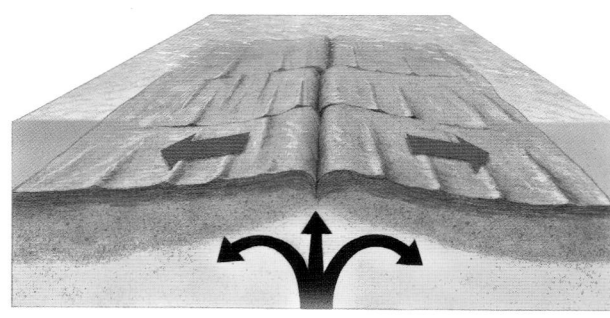

A constructive (or divergent) plate boundary occurs where two plates are moving away from each other, with new crust being formed along the ridge between them. One place where such a boundary occurs on land is in Iceland. Here the mid-Atlantic ridge creates a dramatic rift in the landscape at Thingvellir, the site of the old Icelandic parliament.

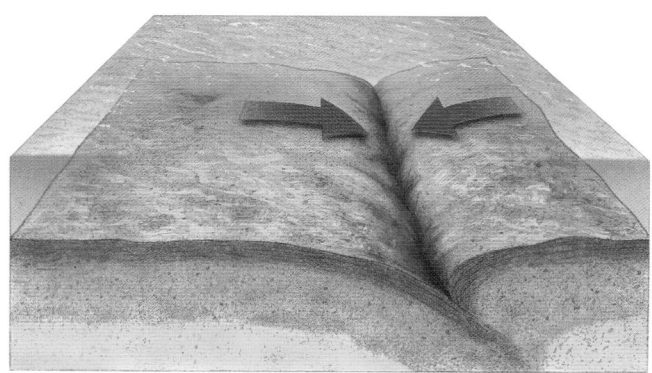

With a destructive (or convergent) boundary, two plates are colliding. When an oceanic crust meets another piece of oceanic crust it sinks under it, creating a subduction zone (usually accompanied by a deep ocean trench) as it does so.

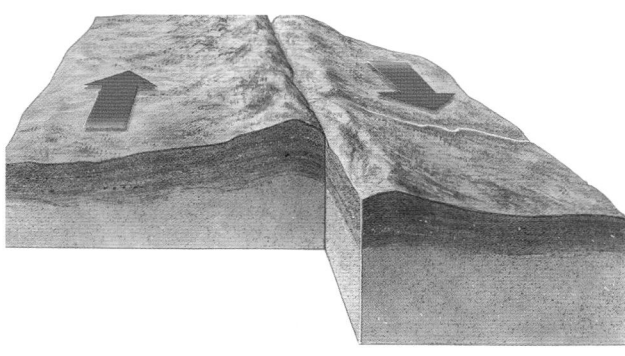

In some places, two plates slide past one another, with neither being destroyed. This is known as a conservative (or transform) boundary. The classic example is in California, where the Pacific Plate is sliding northwest relative to the North American Plate, along the line of the San Andreas Fault.

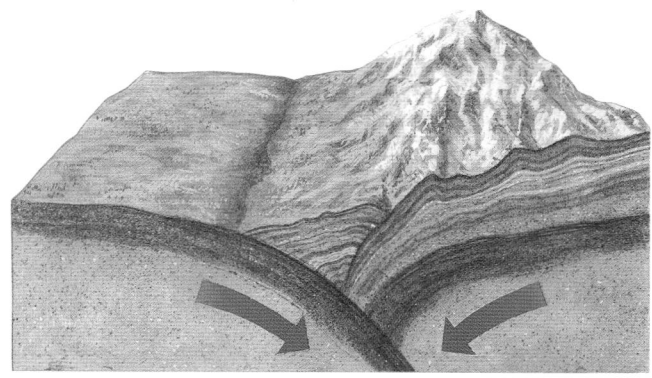

Occasionally, with a destructive (or convergent) boundary a continental crust meets another continental crust, and the two crumple up, one eventually being forced under the other. This is what is happening between India and Asia, with the Himalaya being formed as a result.

TECTONIC PLATE BOUNDARIES

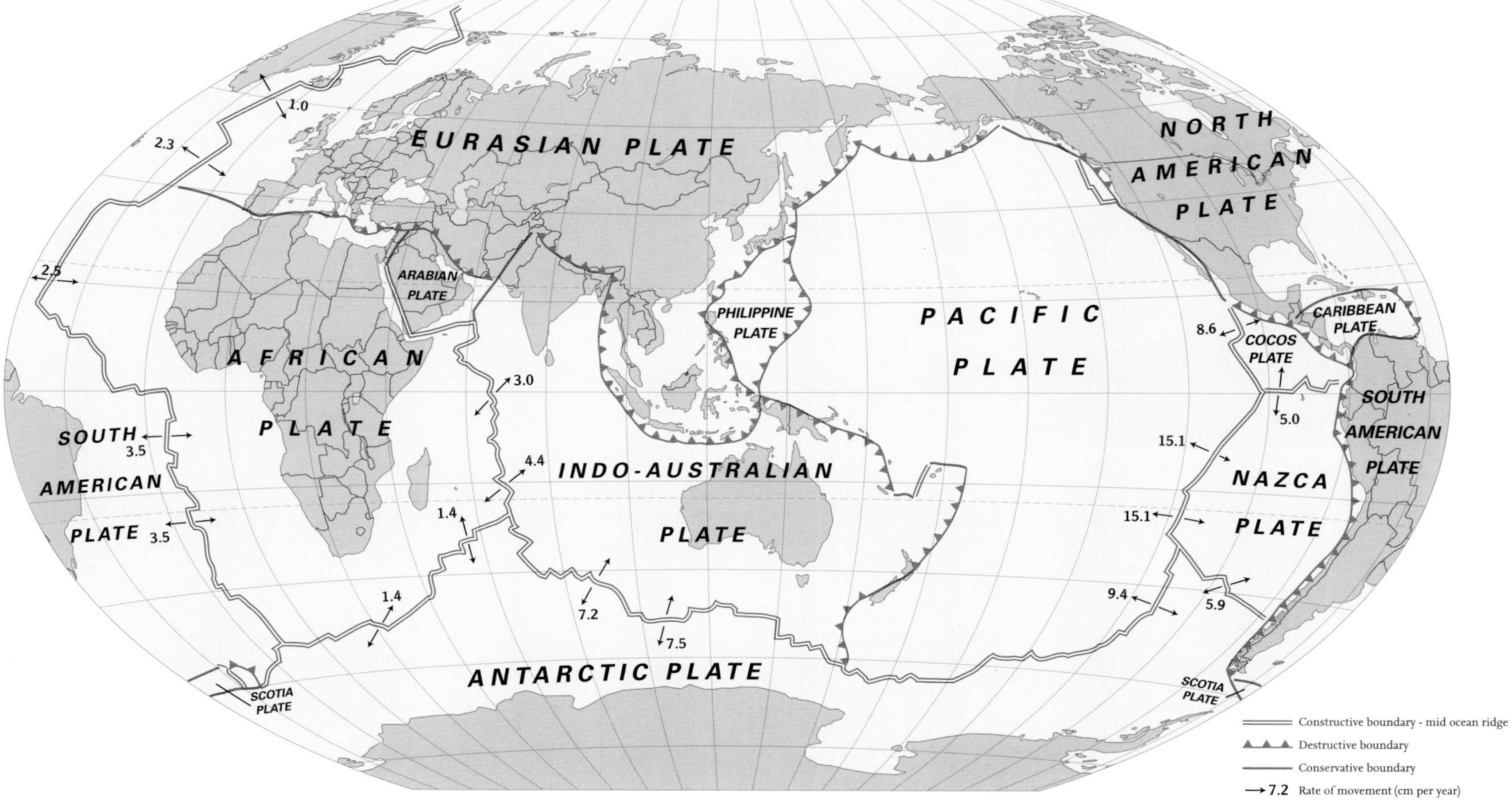

EURASIAN PLATE

NORTH AMERICAN PLATE

ARABIAN PLATE

AFRICAN PLATE

PHILIPPINE PLATE

PACIFIC PLATE

CARIBBEAN PLATE

COCOS PLATE

SOUTH AMERICAN PLATE

SOUTH AMERICAN PLATE

INDO-AUSTRALIAN PLATE

NAZCA PLATE

ANTARCTIC PLATE

SCOTIA PLATE

SCOTIA PLATE

1.0
2.3
2.5
3.0
3.5
3.5
1.4
4.4
1.4
7.2
7.5
8.6
5.0
15.1
15.1
9.4
5.9

Constructive boundary - mid ocean ridge
Destructive boundary
Conservative boundary
→ 7.2 Rate of movement (cm per year)

© Collins Bartholomew Ltd

EARTHQUAKES AND VOLCANOES

Any map showing the distribution of earthquakes and volcanoes will inevitably look very similar to a map showing the boundaries of the tectonic plates. This is because both phenomena are largely controlled by the processes of plate tectonics. The vast majority of the world's earthquakes occur at plate boundaries as a result of one plate pushing past, or under, another. Even those earthquakes which occur away from plate margins are still mostly due to stresses in the rocks which result indirectly from plate movements.

TSUNAMIS

Earthquakes can sometimes give rise to another phenomenon which can cause even more destruction and loss of life – the tsunami. Tsunami is a Japanese word, meaning 'harbour wave', and is used today in preference to the expression 'tidal wave' (tides are not involved). When an earthquake occurs offshore, it may cause a sudden change in the shape of the ocean floor, as a result of submarine landslides or vertical fault movement. This causes a massive displacement of water, which in turn produces a powerful wave or series of waves, able to travel over huge distances.

On 11 March 2011, an earthquake of 9.0 magnitude took place around 70 km (43 miles) off the east coast of Japan. This triggered a tsunami wave that reached up to 40 m (133 feet) in height and travelled up to 10 km (6 miles) inland. The upper image, taken in August 2008, is of Ishinomaki, a city with around 147 000 inhabitants. In this area the tsunami was about 10 m (over 30 feet) in height and reached about 5 km (3.1 miles) inland. In the lower image taken three days after the tsunami struck the lower lying land is still flooded and many buildings have been swept away. The earthquake affected the land lowering the height by around 1.2 metres (nearly 4 feet) in some areas, where it now floods twice each day at high tide.

DISTRIBUTION OF EARTHQUAKES AND VOLCANOES

- ● Deadliest earthquake
- ● Earthquake of magnitude >=7.5
- ○ Earthquake of magnitude 5.5 – 7.5
- ▲ Major volcano
- ▲ Other volcano

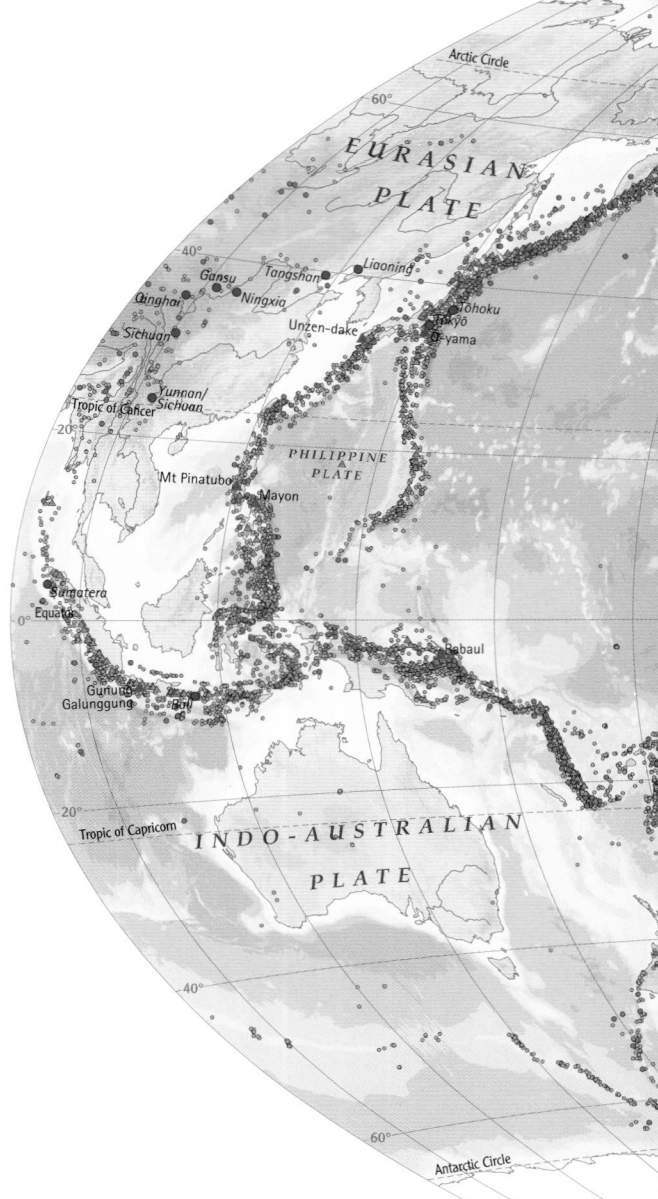

DEADLIEST EARTHQUAKES 1900–2015

Year	Location	Deaths
1905	**Kangra**, India	19 000
1907	west of **Dushanbe**, Tajikistan	12 000
1908	**Messina**, Italy	110 000
1915	**Abruzzo**, Italy	35 000
1917	**Bali**, Indonesia	15 000
1920	**Ningxia Province**, China	200 000
1923	**Tōkyō**, Japan	142 807
1927	**Qinghai Province**, China	200 000
1932	**Gansu Province**, China	70 000
1933	**Sichuan Province**, China	10 000
1934	**Nepal/India**	10 700
1935	**Quetta**, Pakistan	30 000
1939	**Chillán**, Chile	28 000
1939	**Erzincan**, Turkey	32 700
1948	**Aşgabat**, Turkmenistan	19 800
1962	northwest **Iran**	12 225
1970	**Huánuco Province**, Peru	66 794
1974	**Yunnan** and **Sichuan Provinces**, China	20 000
1976	central **Guatemala**	22 778
1976	**Tangshan**, Hebei Province, China	255 000
1978	**Khorāsān Province**, Iran	20 000
1980	**Ech Chélif**, Algeria	11 000
1988	**Spitak**, Armenia	25 000
1990	**Manjil**, Iran	50 000
1999	**İzmit (Kocaeli)**, Turkey	17 000
2001	**Gujarat**, India	20 000
2003	**Bam**, Iran	26 271
2004	**Sumatra**, Indonesia/Indian Ocean	>225 000
2005	northwest **Pakistan**	74 648
2008	**Sichuan Province**, China	>60 000
2010	**Léogâne**, Haiti	222 570
2011	**Tōhoku**, Japan	14 500
2015	**Gorkha**, Nepal	>8 000

RICHTER SCALE

The scale measures the energy released by an earthquake. The scale is logarithmic – a quake measuring 4 is 30 times more powerful than one measuring 3, and a quake measuring 6 is 27 000 times more powerful than one measuring 3.

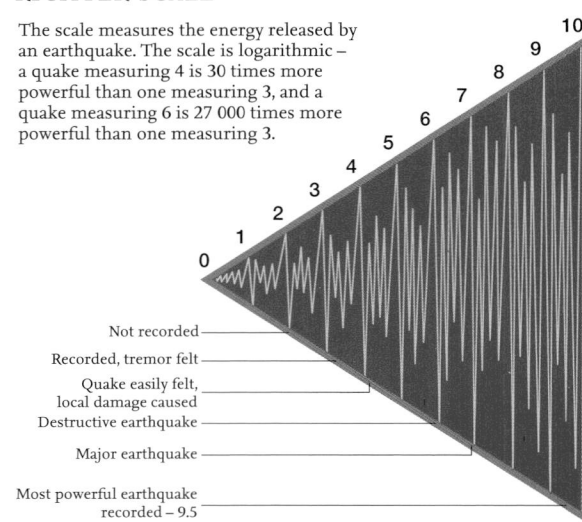

Not recorded

Recorded, tremor felt

Quake easily felt, local damage caused

Destructive earthquake

Major earthquake

Most powerful earthquake recorded – 9.5

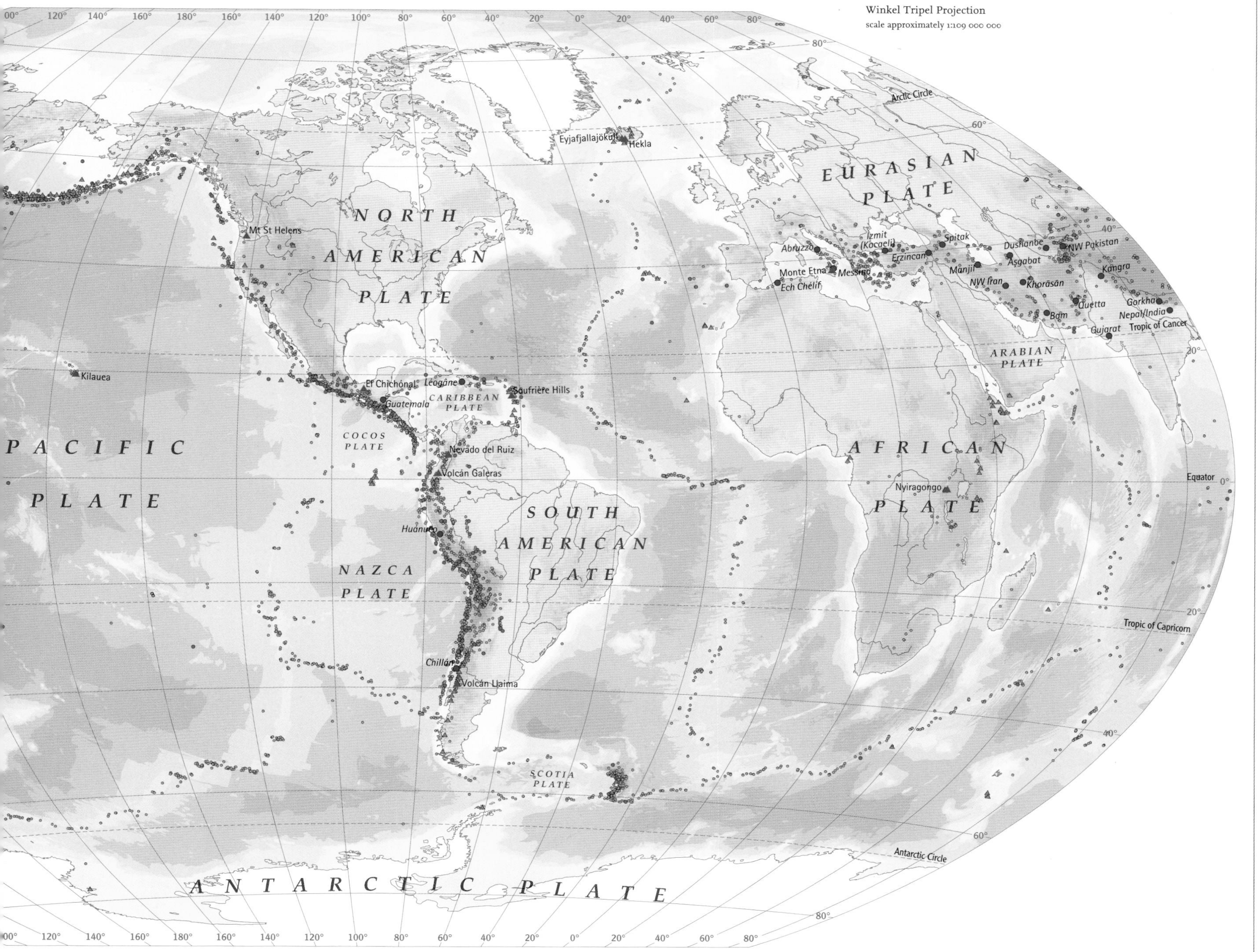

Winkel Tripel Projection
scale approximately 1:109 000 000

EURASIAN PLATE

NORTH AMERICAN PLATE

Eyjafjallajökull · Hekla

Arctic Circle

Mt St Helens

Izmit (Kocaeli) Spitak Dushanbe
Abruzzo Erzincan Manjil NW Pakistan
Monte Etna Messina NW Iran Khorāsān Kangra
Ech Chélif Bam Quetta Gorkha
Gujarat Nepal/India
Tropic of Cancer

ARABIAN PLATE

Kilauea

PACIFIC PLATE

El Chichónal · Leogáne Soufrière Hills
Guatemala CARIBBEAN PLATE

COCOS PLATE

Nevado del Ruiz

Volcán Galeras

AFRICAN PLATE

Nyiragongo

Equator

Huánuco

SOUTH AMERICAN PLATE

NAZCA PLATE

Tropic of Capricorn

Chillán

Volcán Llaima

SCOTIA PLATE

Antarctic Circle

ANTARCTIC PLATE

MAJOR VOLCANIC ERUPTIONS 1980–2014

Year	Volcano	Country
1980	Mt St Helens	USA
1982	El Chichónal	Mexico
1982	Gunung Galunggung	Indonesia
1983	Kilauea	Hawai'i, USA
1983	Ō-yama	Japan
1985	Nevado del Ruiz	Colombia
1991	Mt Pinatubo	Philippines
1991	Unzen-dake	Japan
1993	Mayon	Philippines
1993	Volcán Galeras	Colombia
1994	Volcán Llaima	Chile
1994	Rabaul	Papua New Guinea
1997	Soufrière Hills	Montserrat
2000	Hekla	Iceland
2001	Monte Etna	Italy
2002	Nyiragongo	Democratic Republic of the Congo
2010	Eyjafjallajökull	Iceland

Bárðarbunga is a subglacial stratovolcano under the Vatnajökull Glacier on Iceland. Local seismic activity had been gradually increasing from 2007, and this fissure opened in the Holuhraun lava field north east of the caldera in 2014.

CLIMATE

The climate classification shown on the main map is a simplified version of the system developed by W. Köppen. It is based on the relationship between temperature and precipitation data, and on vegetation characteristics. Extremes of climate, particularly tropical storms and tornadoes, are significant because of their destructive power. Increasing knowledge of these phenomena – particularly through the use of satellite imagery – will help in their prediction and will allow action to minimize their destructive effects.

TORNADOES

A tornado is a violent rotating column of air extending from a thunderstorm to the ground. The most violent tornadoes can cause massive destruction with wind speeds of 400 km per hr (249 miles per hr) or more. Although tornadoes occur in many parts of the world, they are found most frequently in the USA east of the Rocky Mountains and west of the Appalachian Mountains. They occur during the spring and summer months. In the USA in an average year 800 tornadoes are reported.

On 27 April 2014, thunderstorms created a powerful tornado that touched down in Arkansas destroying parts of the towns of Mayflower and Vilonia, including here near Lake Conway.

TROPICAL STORMS

Tropical storms have different names in different parts of the world: hurricanes in the north Atlantic and east Pacific; typhoons in the northwest Pacific; and cyclones in the Indian Ocean region. There are also many other local names for these often catastrophic events. Tropical storms are among the most powerful and destructive weather systems on Earth. Of the eighty to one hundred which develop annually over the tropical oceans, many make landfall and cause considerable damage to property and loss of life as a result of high winds and heavy rain.

MAJOR CLIMATIC REGIONS 2006 AND OCEAN SURFACE CURRENTS

Polar
- Ice cap
- Tundra

Cooler humid
- Subarctic
- Continental cool summer
- Continental warm summer

Warmer humid
- Temperate
- Humid subtropical
- Mediterranean

Dry
- Steppe
- Desert

Tropical humid
- Savanna
- Rain forest

- • Weather extreme location
- → Warm current
- → Cold current
- → Seasonal drift during northern winter

Arctic Circle

Mount Rainier

California

Oklahoma City

Yuma

Tropic of Cancer

• Mount Waialeale

North Equatorial

Equator

South Equatorial

Peru

Tropic of Capricorn

Antarctic Circumpolar

Antarctic Circle

TRACKS OF TROPICAL STORMS

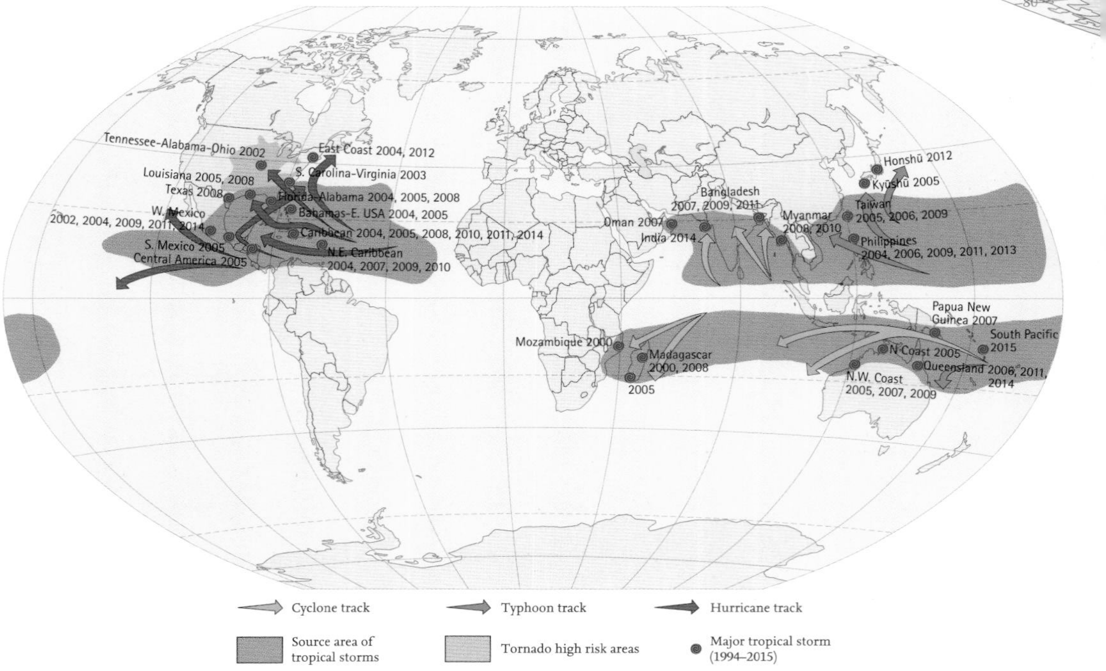

Tennessee-Alabama-Ohio 2002
East Coast 2004, 2012
Louisiana 2005, 2008
S. Carolina-Virginia 2003
Texas 2008
Honshū 2012
W. Mexico 2002, 2004, 2009, 2011, 2014
Florida-Alabama 2004, 2005, 2008
Kyūshū 2005
Bangladesh 2007, 2009, 2011
Taiwan 2005, 2006, 2009
S. Mexico 2005
Caribbean 2004, 2005, 2008, 2010, 2011, 2014
Oman 2007
Myanmar 2008, 2010
Central America 2005
N.E. Caribbean 2004, 2007, 2009, 2010
India 2014
Philippines 2004, 2006, 2009, 2011, 2013
Papua New Guinea 2007
Mozambique 2000
Madagascar 2000, 2008
South Pacific 2015
N Coast 2006
N.W. Coast 2005, 2007, 2009
Queensland 2008, 2011, 2014
2005

- ⇒ Cyclone track
- ⇒ Typhoon track
- ⇒ Hurricane track
- Source area of tropical storms
- Tornado high risk areas
- • Major tropical storm (1994–2015)

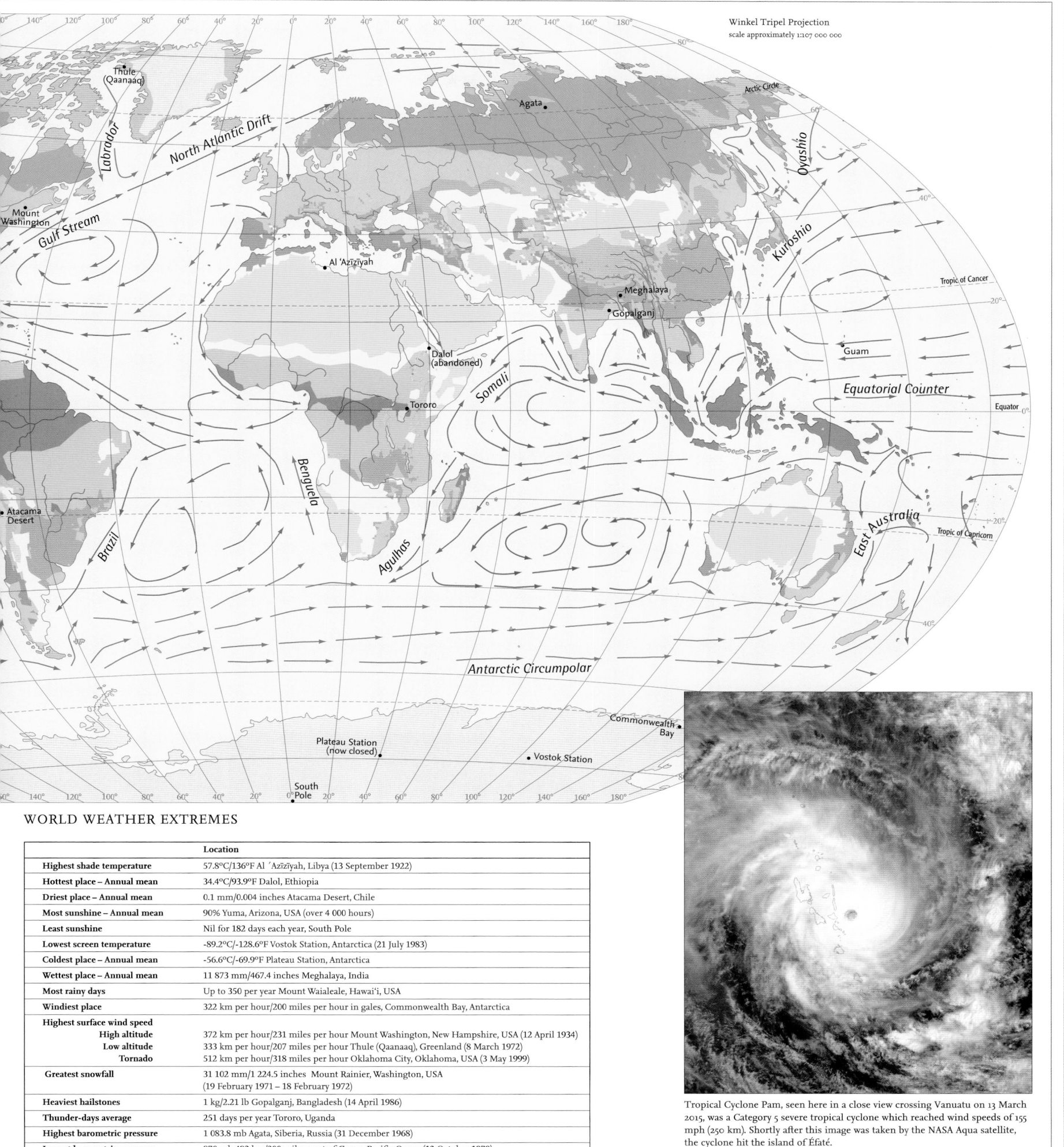

Winkel Tripel Projection
scale approximately 1:107 000 000

WORLD WEATHER EXTREMES

	Location
Highest shade temperature	57.8ºC/136ºF Al ʿAzīzīyah, Libya (13 September 1922)
Hottest place – Annual mean	34.4ºC/93.9ºF Dalol, Ethiopia
Driest place – Annual mean	0.1 mm/0.004 inches Atacama Desert, Chile
Most sunshine – Annual mean	90% Yuma, Arizona, USA (over 4 000 hours)
Least sunshine	Nil for 182 days each year, South Pole
Lowest screen temperature	-89.2ºC/-128.6ºF Vostok Station, Antarctica (21 July 1983)
Coldest place – Annual mean	-56.6ºC/-69.9ºF Plateau Station, Antarctica
Wettest place – Annual mean	11 873 mm/467.4 inches Meghalaya, India
Most rainy days	Up to 350 per year Mount Waialeale, Hawaiʻi, USA
Windiest place	322 km per hour/200 miles per hour in gales, Commonwealth Bay, Antarctica
Highest surface wind speed	
High altitude	372 km per hour/231 miles per hour Mount Washington, New Hampshire, USA (12 April 1934)
Low altitude	333 km per hour/207 miles per hour Thule (Qaanaaq), Greenland (8 March 1972)
Tornado	512 km per hour/318 miles per hour Oklahoma City, Oklahoma, USA (3 May 1999)
Greatest snowfall	31 102 mm/1 224.5 inches Mount Rainier, Washington, USA (19 February 1971 – 18 February 1972)
Heaviest hailstones	1 kg/2.21 lb Gopalganj, Bangladesh (14 April 1986)
Thunder-days average	251 days per year Tororo, Uganda
Highest barometric pressure	1 083.8 mb Agata, Siberia, Russia (31 December 1968)
Lowest barometric pressure	870 mb 483 km/300 miles west of Guam, Pacific Ocean (12 October 1979)

Tropical Cyclone Pam, seen here in a close view crossing Vanuatu on 13 March 2015, was a Category 5 severe tropical cyclone which reached wind speeds of 155 mph (250 km). Shortly after this image was taken by the NASA Aqua satellite, the cyclone hit the island of Éfaté.

CLIMATE CHANGE

The global average temperature can be established for approximately the last 150 years from the worldwide network of weather stations on land and observations made on board ships. The period 2000-2009 was the warmest decade since measurements began. This warming is observed over the oceans as well as over land, suggesting that it is a truly global phenomenon and not a conglomeration of 'local' increases in temperature caused by some small-scale process such as the urban heat island effect.

OBSERVING CLIMATE CHANGE

Changes have also been seen in various areas of the climate system. Snow cover and mountain glaciers have shrunk, and some melting of the Greenland and Antarctic ice sheets has been measured. Global average sea level rose by approximately 17 cm through the 20th century, partly because of the additional water in the ocean basins resulting from the melting of ice on land, and partly because water expands when it heats up. Patterns of precipitation (rainfall and snowfall) have also changed, with parts of North and South America, Europe and northern and central Asia becoming wetter while the Sahel region of central Africa, southern Africa, the Mediterranean and southern Asia have become drier. Intense rainfall events have become more frequent. In Europe, Asia and North America, growing seasons have extended, with flowers emerging and trees coming into leaf several days earlier in the year than in the mid-twentieth century.

Male, the capital of the Maldives, is approximately 2 m above the sea, but its reclaimed land is lower leaving it very vulnerable to a sustained rise in sea level.

THE CAUSES OF CLIMATE CHANGE

Climate can change naturally, but over the last century the industrial and agricultural activities of humans have become additional causes of climate change. Climate change can also result from changes in the concentration of 'greenhouse gases' which absorb and re-emit some of the heat radiation given off by the Earth's surface and hence warm the lower atmosphere. The most important greenhouse gas is water vapour, followed by carbon dioxide. While many of these gases occur naturally in the atmosphere, humans are responsible for increasing the concentration of many of them through the burning of fossil fuels, deforestation and other industrial and agricultural processes. We have also introduced new greenhouse gases, the 'halocarbons' such as chlorofluorocarbons (CFCs) which have damaged the ozone layer in the stratosphere.

The Pedersen Glacier in the Kenai Mountains, Alaska. The terminus has retreated by more than 2 km between 1917 (top) and 2005 (bottom).

PROJECTION OF GLOBAL TEMPERATURE CHANGE 2081–2100

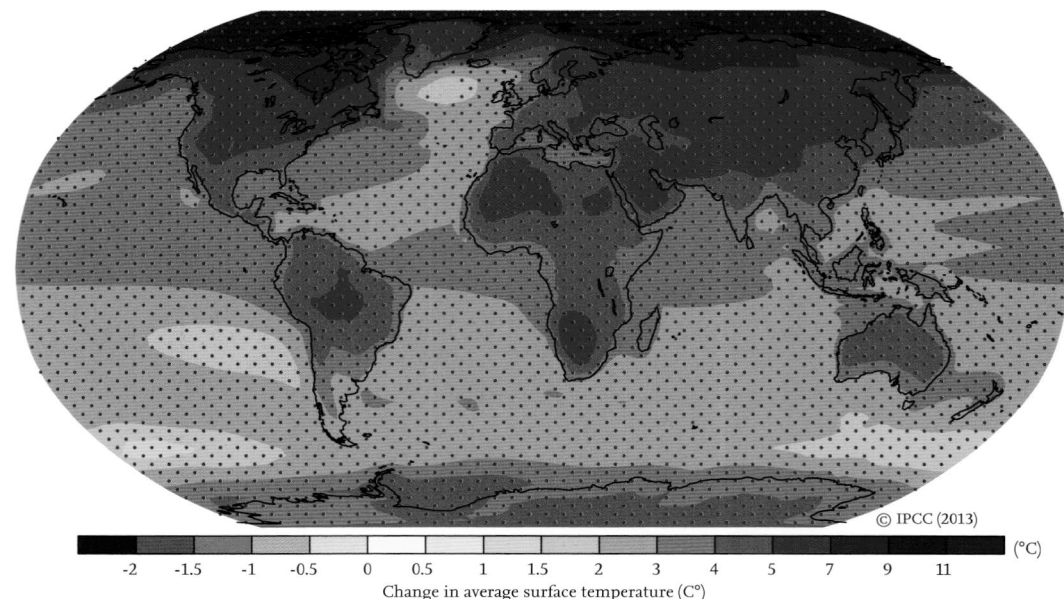

© IPCC (2013)

Faster warming is expected near the poles, as the melting snow and sea ice exposes the darker underlying land and ocean surfaces which then absorb more of the sun's radiation instead of reflecting it back to space in the way that brighter ice and snow do.

THREAT OF RISING SEA LEVEL

It has been suggested that further global warming of between
1.0 and 6.4 C° may occur by the end of the 21st century. Sea level
is projected to rise by between 28 cm and 58 cm, threatening
a number of coastal cities, low-lying deltas and small islands.
Larger rises are predicted in some locations than others.

AREAS AT RISK OF SUBMERSION

○ Major cities

  Coastal areas at greatest risk

  Islands and archipelagos

  Areas of low-lying islands

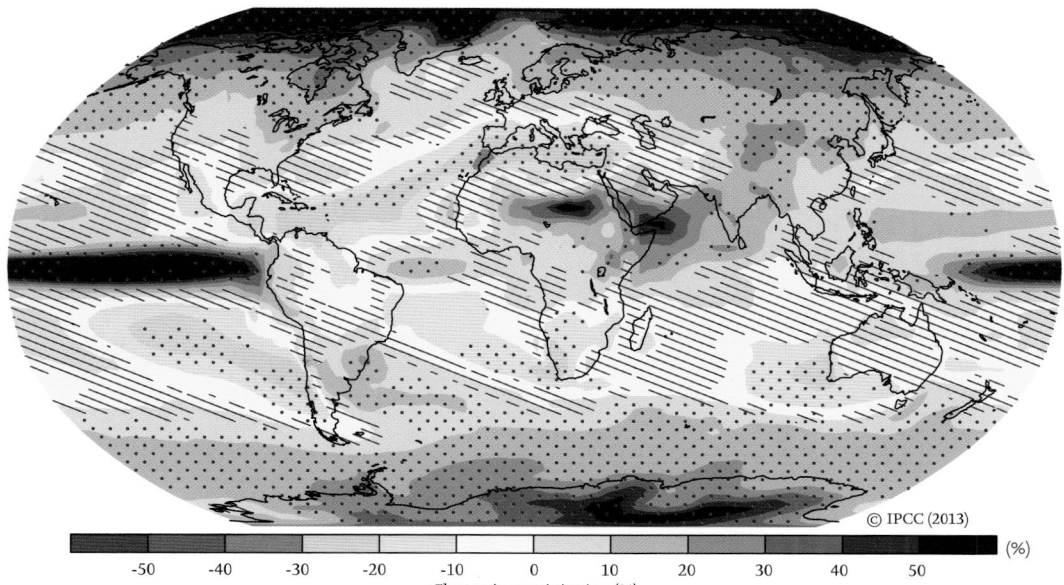

LOWEST PACIFIC ISLANDS

Location	Maximum height above sea level	Land area sq km	sq miles	Population
Kingman Reef	1 m (3 ft)	1	0.4	0
Palmyra Atoll	2 m (7 ft)	12	5	0
Ashmore and Cartier Islands	3 m (10 ft)	5	2	0
Howland Island	3 m (10 ft)	2	1	0
Johnston Atoll	5 m (16 ft)	3	1	0
Tokelau	5 m (16 ft)	10	4	1 466
Tuvalu	5 m (16 ft)	25	10	10 000
Coral Sea Islands Territory	6 m (20 ft)	22	8	0
Wake Island	6 m (20 ft)	7	3	0
Jarvis Island	7 m (23 ft)	5	2	0

HISTORICAL CLIMATE RECORDS

Observed change in surface temperature 1901–2012

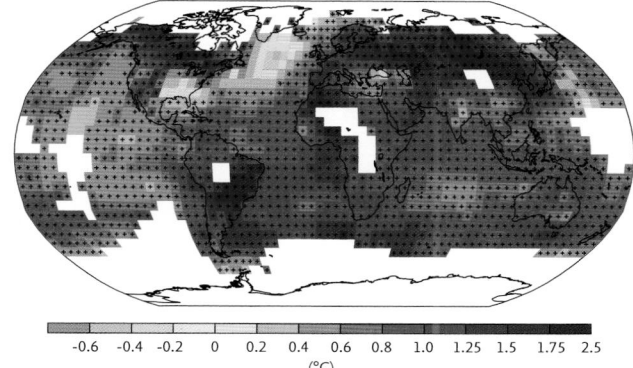

-0.6 -0.4 -0.2 0 0.2 0.4 0.6 0.8 1.0 1.25 1.5 1.75 2.5
(°C)

PROJECTION OF CHANGE IN AVERAGE PRECIPITATION 2081–2100

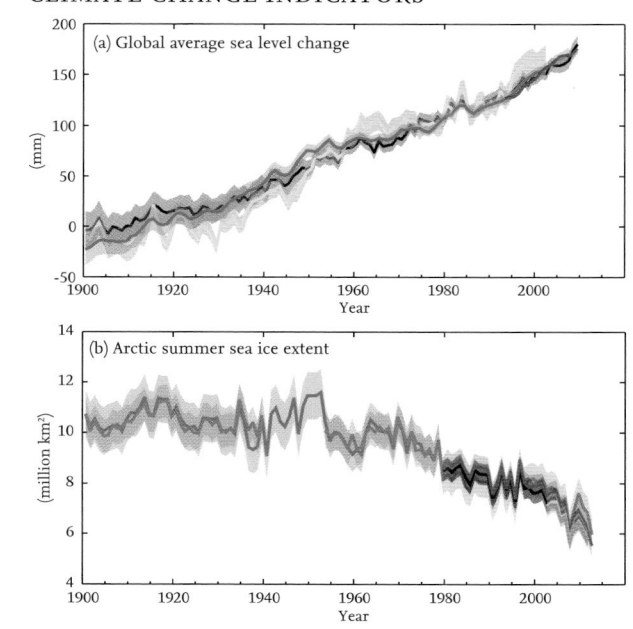

© IPCC (2013)

-50 -40 -30 -20 -10 0 10 20 30 40 50 (%)
Change in precipitation (%)

In the high-latitude regions (central and northern Europe, Asia and North America) the year-round average precipitation
is projected to increase, while in most sub-tropical land regions it is projected to decrease by as much as 20 per cent. This
would increase the risk of drought and, in combination with higher temperatures, threaten agricultural productivity.

CLIMATE CHANGE INDICATORS

(a) Global average sea level change

(b) Arctic summer sea ice extent

ENVIRONMENT AND BIODIVERSITY

Throughout history people have altered the natural environment, influencing landscapes, land cover, biodiversity, and the chemical composition of air, land, and water. The rate of change has accelerated dramatically since the industrial revolution, as a result of advances in technology, changing lifestyles and associated patterns of production and consumption, and the rapidly growing global population. As the human population has increased, so too has demand for the Earth's natural resources, leading in many areas to environmental degradation which has had significant impacts on people's lives in many parts of the world.

 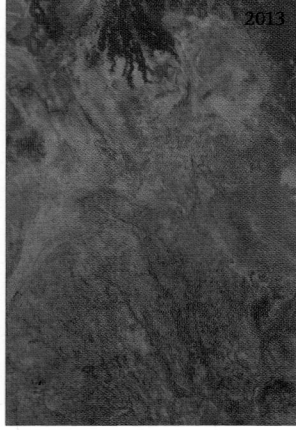

For many thousands of years the Hamoun wetlands have been a major source of food and shelter in the middle of vast arid plains in central Asia. From the mid 1990s however, the Helmand river was increasingly used for irrigation and diverted into dams leaving the area vulnerable to a prolonged drought. These images of the northern area in 1998 and 2013 show the extent of the devastation.

ENVIRONMENTAL CHANGE

Land cover has changed more over the past fifty years than at any time in human history. Much of this change has been due to the conversion of natural ecosystems to agricultural land to help meet demand for food production, particularly in developing regions. Wetlands and other freshwater environments have also been dramatically affected by changes in land cover and use. It is speculated that approximately one-third of all mangroves and half of all inland wetlands were converted during the 20th century. Fragmentation and the modification of river flow have resulted from the construction of dams and other structures along rivers, affecting almost 60 per cent of the large river systems in the world.

BIODIVERSITY

Biodiversity, derived from the term 'biological diversity', is the name given to the variety and processes of all life on Earth, including individual living organisms, their genes, and the habitats or ecosystems of which they are part, whether terrestrial, freshwater or marine. The diversity of life is not evenly distributed around the world, and based on the number of species in a location, or 'species richness', a general pattern emerges of considerably more biodiversity in the tropics than at higher latitudes. To date approximately two million species have been identified and described.

ECOLOGICAL FOOTPRINT
Humanity's ecological footprint by component 1961–2009.

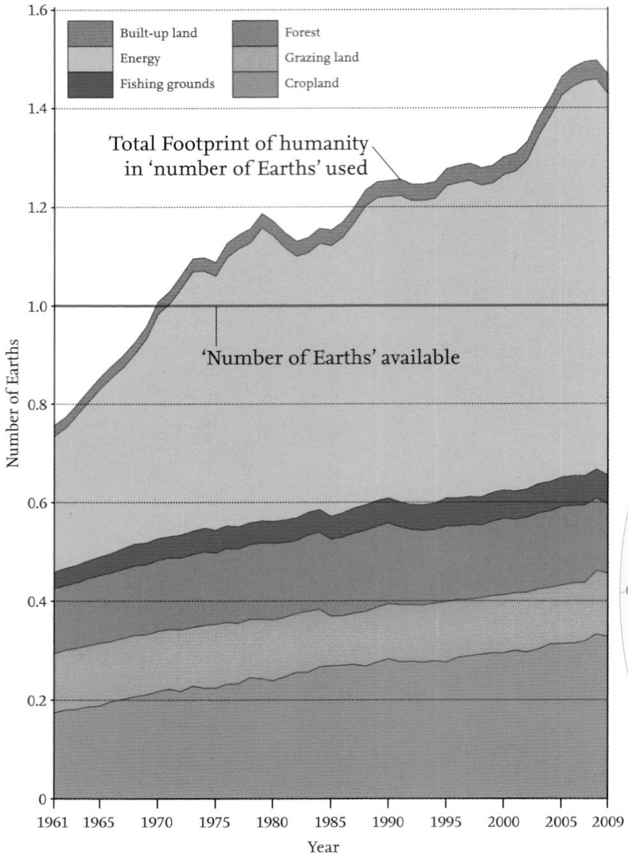

Built-up land
Energy
Fishing grounds
Forest
Grazing land
Cropland

Total Footprint of humanity in 'number of Earths' used

'Number of Earths' available

Number of Earths

1961 1965 1970 1975 1980 1985 1990 1995 2000 2005 2009
Year

WORLD LAND COVER
© ESA 2010 and UCLouvain

Winkel Tripel Projection
scale approximately 1:112 000 000

Arctic Circle
60°
40°
Tropic of Cancer
20°
0° Equator
20°
Tropic of Capricorn
40°
60°
Antarctic Circle

GLOBAL FRESH WATER AVAILABILITY
Cubic metres per person per year.

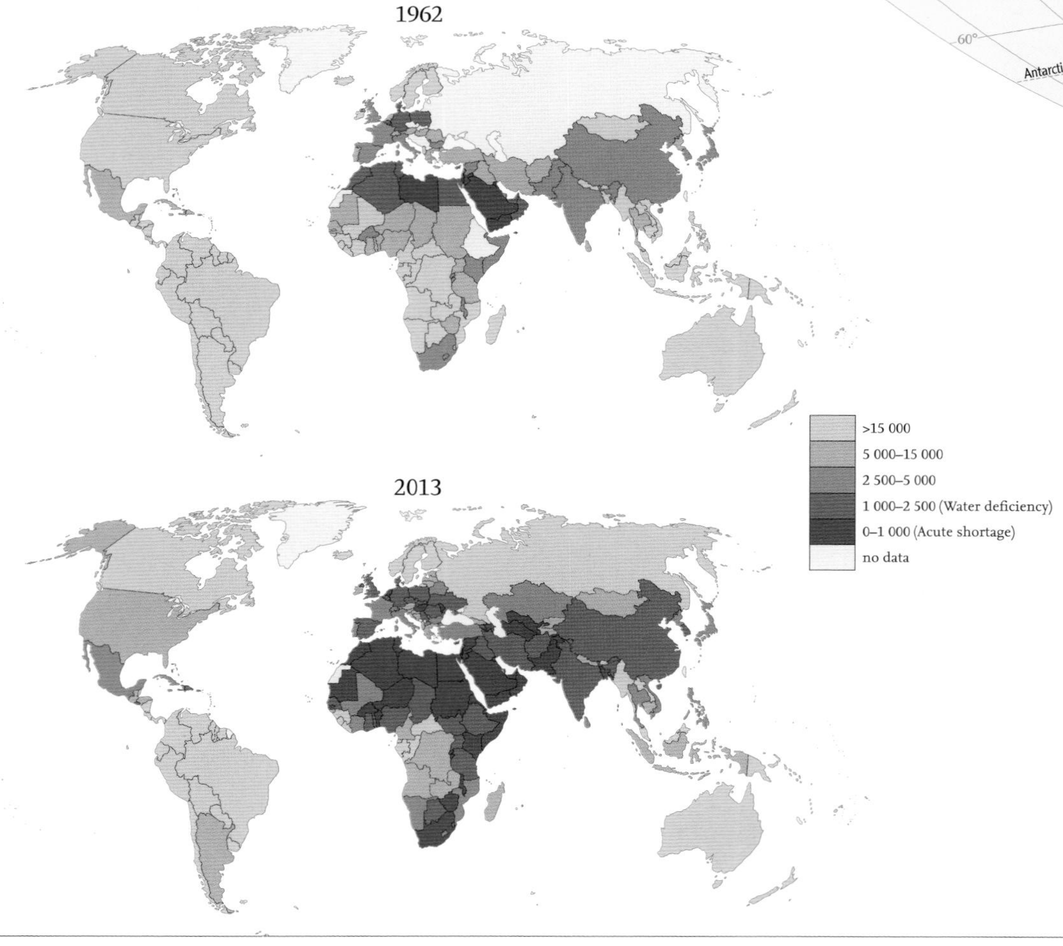

1962

2013

>15 000
5 000–15 000
2 500–5 000
1 000–2 500 (Water deficiency)
0–1 000 (Acute shortage)
no data

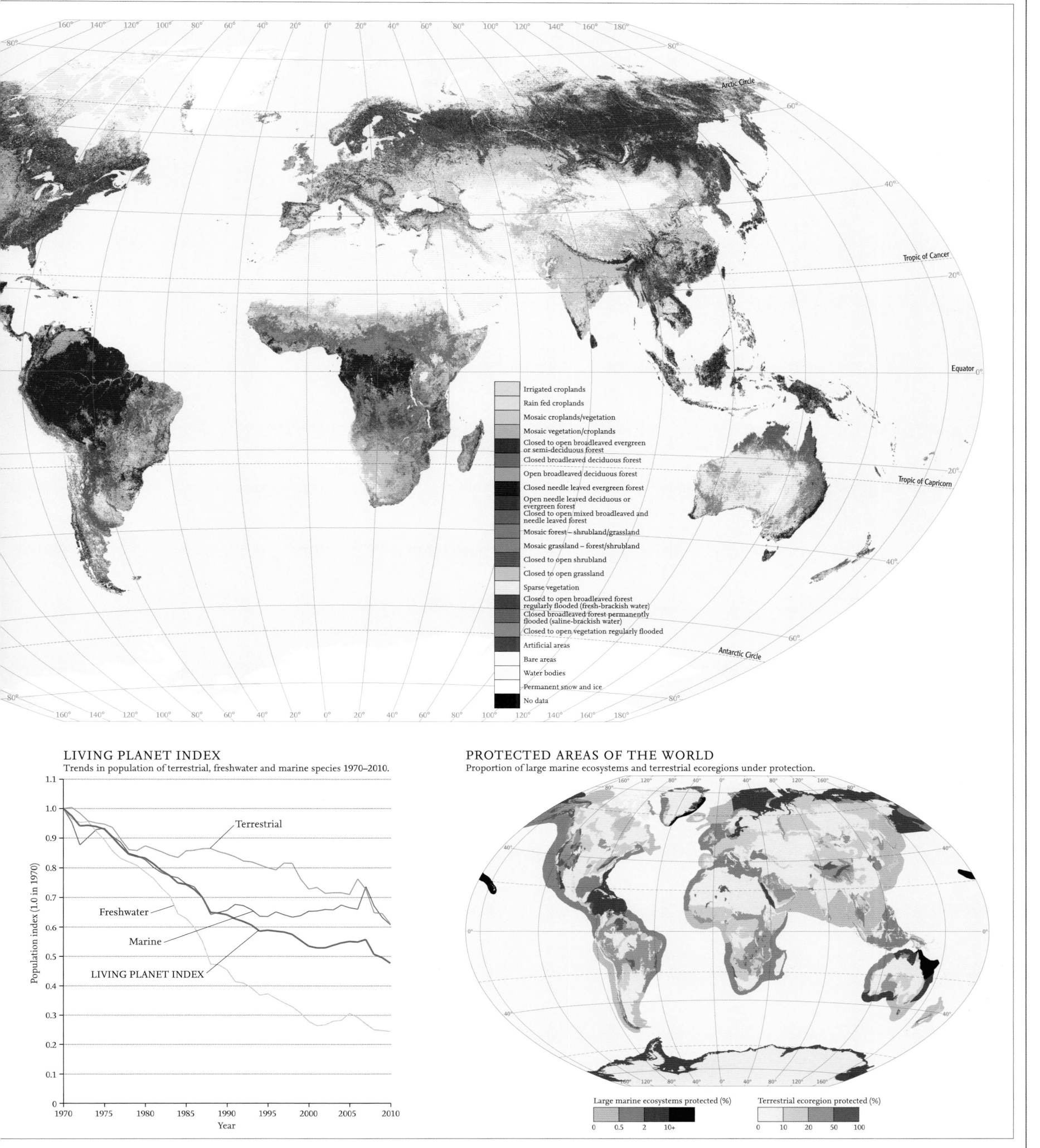

Irrigated croplands
Rain fed croplands
Mosaic croplands/vegetation
Mosaic vegetation/croplands
Closed to open broadleaved evergreen or semi-deciduous forest
Closed broadleaved deciduous forest
Open broadleaved deciduous forest
Closed needle leaved evergreen forest
Open needle leaved deciduous or evergreen forest
Closed to open mixed broadleaved and needle leaved forest
Mosaic forest – shrubland/grassland
Mosaic grassland – forest/shrubland
Closed to open shrubland
Closed to open grassland
Sparse vegetation
Closed to open broadleaved forest regularly flooded (fresh-brackish water)
Closed broadleaved forest permanently flooded (saline-brackish water)
Closed to open vegetation regularly flooded
Artificial areas
Bare areas
Water bodies
Permanent snow and ice
No data

LIVING PLANET INDEX
Trends in population of terrestrial, freshwater and marine species 1970–2010.

Terrestrial
Freshwater
Marine
LIVING PLANET INDEX

Population index (1.0 in 1970)

Year

PROTECTED AREAS OF THE WORLD
Proportion of large marine ecosystems and terrestrial ecoregions under protection.

Large marine ecosystems protected (%)
0   0.5   2   10+

Terrestrial ecoregion protected (%)
0   10   20   50   100

© Collins Bartholomew Ltd

75

POPULATION

World population is currently undergoing the biggest transformation that it has ever seen, but this process is impacting very unevenly. While overall numbers have been growing extremely rapidly since 1950, almost nine-tenths of the increase has taken place in the less developed regions, especially southern and eastern Asia, while Europe's population is now estimated to be in overall decline and ageing rapidly. India and China alone are responsible for over one-third of current growth, but most of the highest percentage rates of growth are to be found in Sub-Saharan Africa, where the demographic transition process is still at a relatively early stage.

Population growth in the 20th century was rapid and continued growth has carried the world's population past seven billion in 2011.

POPULATION DISTRIBUTION

People are distributed very unevenly over the face of the planet, even after allowing for the two-thirds that is covered by water. As shown on the main map, over a quarter of the land area is uninhabited or has extremely low population density, notably the polar regions, the Amazon basin and the dry deserts of Saharan Africa, southwest and central Asia, and Australia.

POPULATION GROWTH

Over the past half century world population has been growing faster than it has ever done before. While world population did not pass the one billion mark until 1804 and took another 123 years to reach two billion, it then added the third billion in 33 years, the fourth in 14 years and the fifth in 13 years, the sixth in 12 years with the 7 billionth person added in October 2011. The latest trends in population growth at country level emphasize the continuing contrast between the more and less developed regions. Annual growth rates of 1.3 per cent or more remain common in Latin America, Africa and southern Asia. A number of countries have rates in excess of 3.0 per cent, which if continued would lead to the doubling of population in 23 years or less. Ten countries account for 60 per cent of the world's current population growth, with India and China responsible for over half.

WORLD POPULATION DISTRIBUTION
Winkel Tripel Projection
scale approximately 1:109 000 000

TOP TWENTY COUNTRIES BY POPULATION AND POPULATION DENSITY 2013

Total population	Country	Rank	Country*	Inhabitants per sq mile	Inhabitants per sq km
1 369 993 000	China	1	Bangladesh	2 817	1 087
1 252 140 000	India	2	Taiwan	1 671	645
320 051 000	United States of America	3	South Korea	1 285	496
249 866 000	Indonesia	4	Rwanda	1 158	447
200 362 000	Brazil	5	Netherlands	1 045	404
182 143 000	Pakistan	6	India	1 024	395
173 615 000	Nigeria	7	Haiti	963	372
156 595 000	Bangladesh	8	Burundi	946	365
142 834 000	Russia	9	Belgium	942	364
127 144 000	Japan	10	Japan	872	337
122 332 000	Mexico	11	Philippines	849	328
98 394 000	Philippines	12	Sri Lanka	840	324
94 101 000	Ethiopia	13	Vietnam	720	278
91 680 000	Vietnam	14	United Kingdom	671	259
82 727 000	Germany	15	Germany	600	232
82 056 000	Egypt	16	Dominican Republic	556	215
77 447 000	Iran	17	Pakistan	535	207
74 933 000	Turkey	18	North Korea	535	207
67 514 000	Democratic Republic of the Congo	19	Italy	524	202
67 011 000	Thailand	20	Nepal	489	189

*Only countries with a population of over 10 million are considered.

AGE PYRAMIDS
World population by five-year age group and sex.

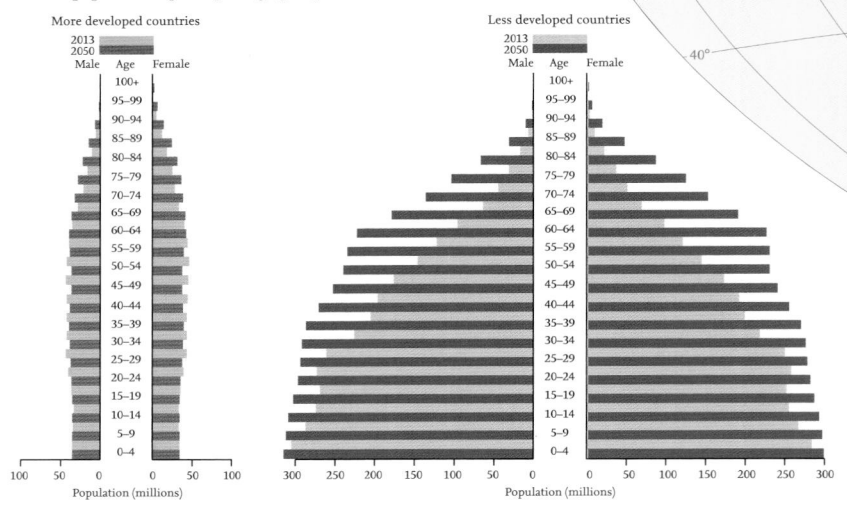

KEY POPULATION STATISTICS FOR MAJOR REGIONS

	Population 2013 (millions)	Growth (per cent)	Infant mortality rate	Total fertility rate	Life expectancy (years)	% aged 60 and over 2010	% aged 60 and over 2050
World	7 162	1.1	37	2.5	70	11	22
More developed regions[1]	1 253	0.3	6	1.7	78	22	32
Less developed regions[2]	5 909	1.3	40	2.6	67	9	19
Africa	1 111	2.5	64	4.7	58	5	9
Asia	4 299	1.0	31	2.2	71	10	24
Europe[3]	742	0.1	6	1.6	76	22	34
Latin America and the Caribbean[4]	617	1.1	18	2.2	75	10	25
North America	355	0.9	6	1.9	79	19	27
Oceania	38	1.4	20	2.4	78	15	23

Except for population and % aged 60 and over figures, the data are annual averages projected for the period 2010–2015.

1. Europe, North America, Australia, New Zealand and Japan.
2. Africa, Asia (excluding Japan), Latin America and the Caribbean, and Oceania (excluding Australia and New Zealand).
3. Includes Russia.
4. South America, Central America (including Mexico) and all Caribbean Islands.

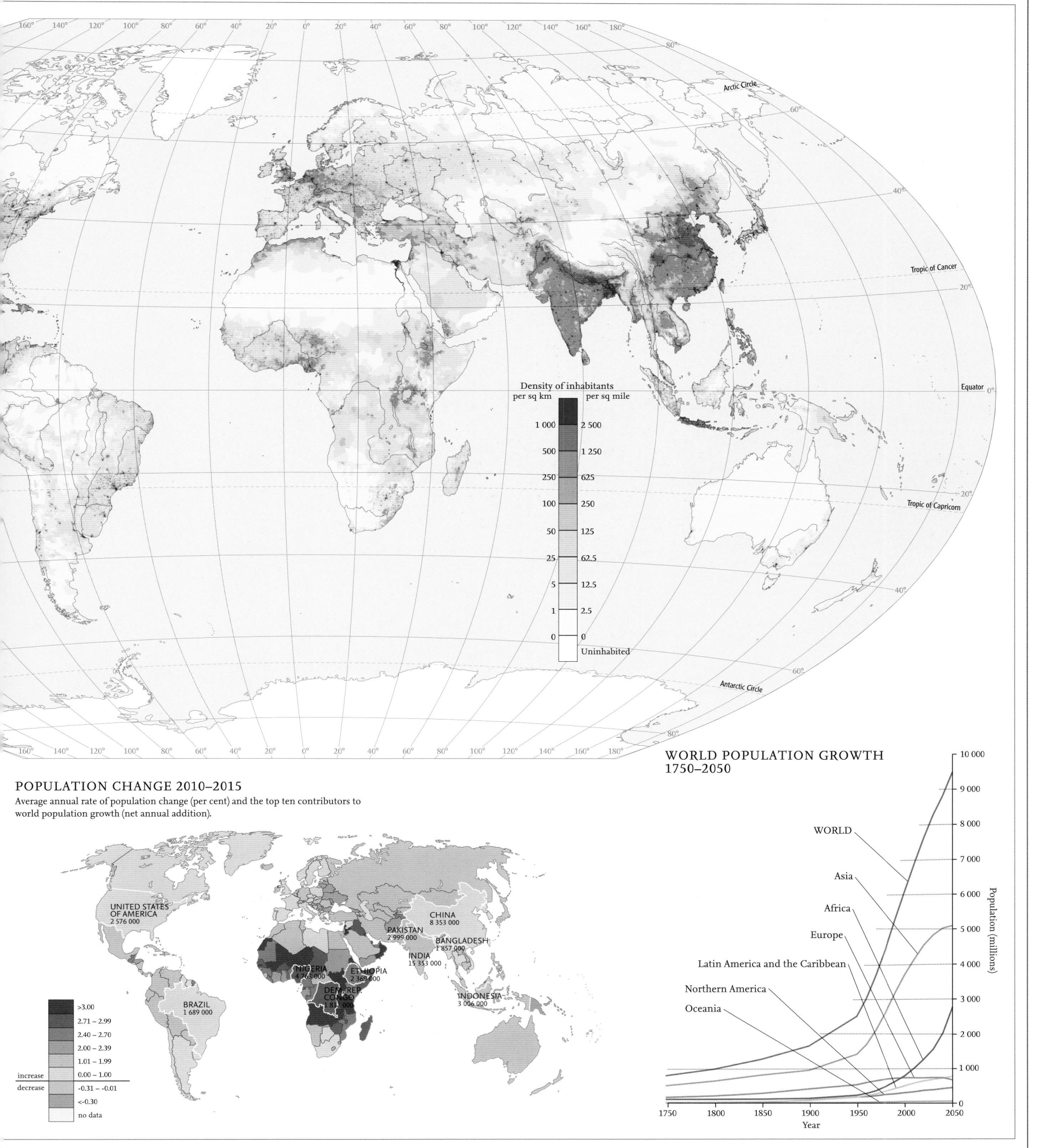

Density of inhabitants

per sq km	per sq mile
1 000	2 500
500	1 250
250	625
100	250
50	125
25	62.5
5	12.5
1	2.5
0	0

Uninhabited

POPULATION CHANGE 2010–2015

Average annual rate of population change (per cent) and the top ten contributors to world population growth (net annual addition).

UNITED STATES OF AMERICA 2 576 000
CHINA 8 353 000
PAKISTAN 2 999 000
BANGLADESH 1 857 000
INDIA 15 353 000
NIGERIA 4 363 000
ETHIOPIA 2 369 000
DEM. REP. CONGO 2 611 000
INDONESIA 3 006 000
BRAZIL 1 689 000

>3.00
2.71 – 2.99
2.40 – 2.70
2.00 – 2.39
1.01 – 1.99
0.00 – 1.00
increase
decrease
-0.31 – -0.01
<-0.30
no data

WORLD POPULATION GROWTH 1750–2050

WORLD
Asia
Africa
Europe
Latin America and the Caribbean
Northern America
Oceania

Population (millions)

Year

© Collins Bartholomew Ltd

77

URBANIZATION

World population is urbanizing rapidly and, in this respect, 2009 was a momentous point in world history. According to UN data, in mid 2009, for the first time urban dwellers outnumbered those living in traditionally rural areas. But the current level of urbanization varies greatly across the world, as too does its rate of increase. In the hundred years up to 1950 the greatest changes took place in Europe and North America. Relatively few large cities developed elsewhere and most of these were in coastal locations with good trading connections with the imperial and industrial nations. The main feature of the past half century has been the massive growth in the numbers of urban dwellers in the less developed regions.

Tōkyō is the largest city in the world and more than a quarter of the population of Japan live here. The city was established in 1603 and has been growing steadily ever since then.

TOWARDS AN URBANIZED WORLD

The annual rise in the percentage of the world's population living in cities has been accelerating steadily since the 1970s and it will be running at unprecedentedly high levels until at least 2030. As a result, by then, 3 in 5 people (59.9 per cent) will be urbanites compared to 36.6 per cent in 1970 and 51.6 per cent in 2010. In absolute terms, the global urban population almost trebled between 1970 and 2010, adding 2.16 billion to its 1970 total of 1.33 billion, and it is expected to grow by a further 1.4 billion by 2030. There is a broad contrast in the level of urbanization between the more and less developed regions, but also a great deal of variation within them. In the more developed regions as a whole, three-quarters of the population now live in urban areas.

THE GROWTH OF LARGE CITIES

Alongside the rise in the world's urban population has occurred a massive increase in the number and size of cities, especially of the very large cities or 'megacities'. In 1950, New York was the only agglomeration with over 10 million inhabitants, and there were still only three cities of this size by 1975 – New York, Tōkyō and Mexico City. By 2000, there were eighteen and there are expected to be thirty-seven by 2025. Urban areas are also becoming more diffuse and polycentric, making the task of defining separate cities on the ground even more difficult.

WORLD'S LARGEST CITIES 2015

Figures are for the urban agglomeration, defined as the population contained within the contours of a contiguous territory inhabited at urban levels without regard to administrative boundaries. They incorporate the population within a city plus the suburban fringe lying outside of, but adjacent to, the city boundaries.

City	Country	Population
Tōkyō	Japan	38 197 000
Delhi	India	25 629 000
Shanghai	China	22 963 000
Mexico City	Mexico	21 706 000
New York	USA	21 326 000
Mumbai	India	21 214 000
São Paulo	Brazil	21 028 000
Beijing	China	18 079 000
Dhaka	Bangladesh	17 382 000
Karachi	Pakistan	15 500 000
Kolkata	India	15 076 000
Buenos Aires	Argentina	14 151 000
Los Angeles	USA	14 081 000
Lagos	Nigeria	13 121 000
Manila	Philippines	12 856 000
İstanbul	Turkey	12 459 000
Guangzhou	China	12 385 000
Rio de Janeiro	Brazil	12 380 000
Shenzhen	China	12 337 000
Moscow	Russia	12 144 000
Cairo	Egypt	11 944 000
Ōsaka	Japan	11 783 000
Paris	France	11 097 000
Chongqing	China	11 054 000
Jakarta	Indonesia	10 470 000
Kinshasa	Dem. Rep. Congo	10 312 000
Wuhan	China	10 256 000
Chicago	USA	10 199 000
Bengaluru	India	10 016 000
Chennai	India	9 887 000
Lima	Peru	9 843 000
Seoul	South Korea	9 740 000
Tianjin	China	9 670 000
Bogotá	Colombia	9 650 000
London	United Kingdom	9 348 000
Bangkok	Thailand	9 281 000
Hyderabad	India	8 921 000
Lahore	Pakistan	8 491 000
Dongguan	China	7 859 000
Chengdu	China	7 815 000
Foshan	China	7 650 000

WORLD'S MAJOR CITIES

Urban agglomerations with over 2.5 million inhabitants.

2.5 million - 5 million

5 million - 10 million

10 million - 20 million

over 20 million

LEVEL OF URBANIZATION

Percentage of total population living in urban areas 2015. The world's urban population exceeded 50 per cent of the total population during 2009.

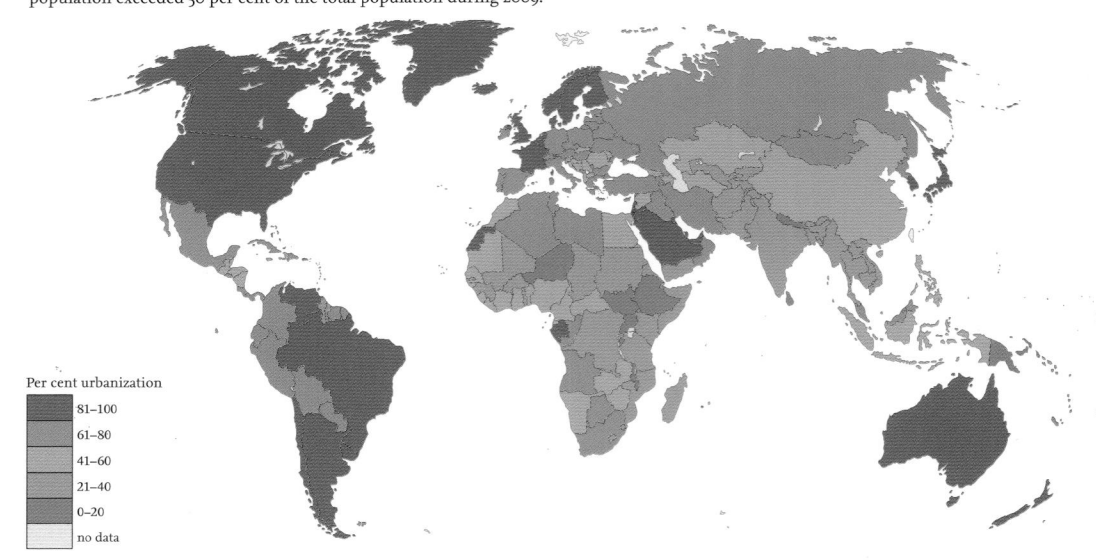

Per cent urbanization

- 81–100
- 61–80
- 41–60
- 21–40
- 0–20
- no data

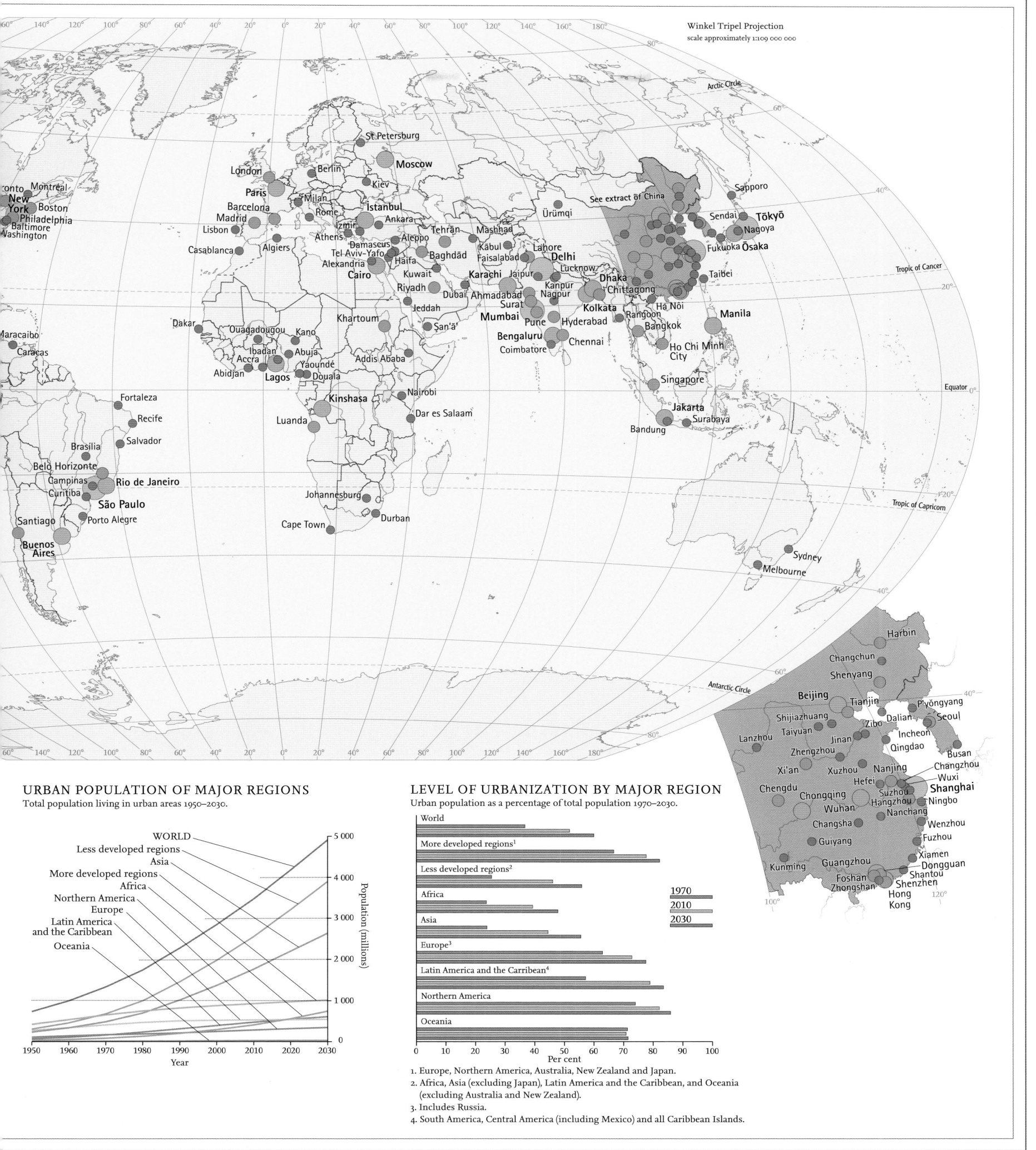

Winkel Tripel Projection
scale approximately 1:109 000 000

See extract of China

URBAN POPULATION OF MAJOR REGIONS
Total population living in urban areas 1950–2030.

WORLD
Less developed regions
Asia
More developed regions
Africa
Northern America
Europe
Latin America and the Caribbean
Oceania

Population (millions)

Year

LEVEL OF URBANIZATION BY MAJOR REGION
Urban population as a percentage of total population 1970–2030.

World
More developed regions[1]
Less developed regions[2]
Africa
Asia
Europe[3]
Latin America and the Carribean[4]
Northern America
Oceania

1970
2010
2030

Per cent

1. Europe, Northern America, Australia, New Zealand and Japan.
2. Africa, Asia (excluding Japan), Latin America and the Caribbean, and Oceania (excluding Australia and New Zealand).
3. Includes Russia.
4. South America, Central America (including Mexico) and all Caribbean Islands.

© Collins Bartholomew Ltd

79

WEALTH, POVERTY AND TRADE

In 2012 the world economy produced $97 trillion in goods and services. Since 2000, global output has increased by 2.7 per cent a year with the fastest growth occurring in the developing countries of Asia. But growth has been uneven. While China's average output per person grew by 10 per cent and India's grew by 6.2 per cent, many fragile and conflict-affected countries saw average incomes decrease. Large inequalities in income exist within countries as well, and these are often closely associated with inequalities in education and health outcomes. The great challenge for economic development is to sustain high rates of growth over long periods, with the benefits of growth broadly shared, including through the creation of new and sustainable jobs in emerging sectors, thus reducing poverty and making permanent improvements in human welfare.

Poverty, hunger, and environmental degradation are problems experienced in areas such as this in Freetown, capital of Sierra Leone, one of the world's poorest countries.

POVERTY AND INEQUALITY

In 2005, 25 per cent of the population of low- and middle-income economies, still lived in extreme poverty. With continued growth of average incomes, that number was expected to fall to less than 900 million by 2015. Even then there will be more than 2 billion people living on less than $2.00 a day or $730 a year. The greatest number of the extreme poor live in the large, lower-middle income economies of Asia – India and China – which together account for almost half of the people living in extreme poverty. But these are fast growing economies, where poverty rates have been falling rapidly. The highest rates of poverty are found in Sub-Saharan Africa, where economic growth was slowest in the 1990s and the regional poverty rate has only recently fallen below 50 per cent. Since the mid-1990s, income inequality, as measured by the Gini index, has increased in slightly more than half of developing countries with available data.

FOREIGN AID

For the poorest countries to fund their development, aid provided by richer countries and organizations such as the World Bank, IMF and the UN helps to fill the gap. Since 2000, net ODA flows have increased in real terms from $81.9 billion to $134.5 billion in 2013. To meet pledges made for 2010, the assistance provided by DAC donors would have had to rise to 0.35 per cent of GNI but has instead fallen short to 0.30 per cent in 2013, as domestic fiscal constraints are putting significant pressure on donors to reduce their aid budgets. In 2013 only five countries provided more than 0.7 per cent of their GNI as aid.

AVERAGE INCOME
Gross National Income (GNI) per capita 2013

Winkel Tripel Projection
scale 1 : 107 000 000

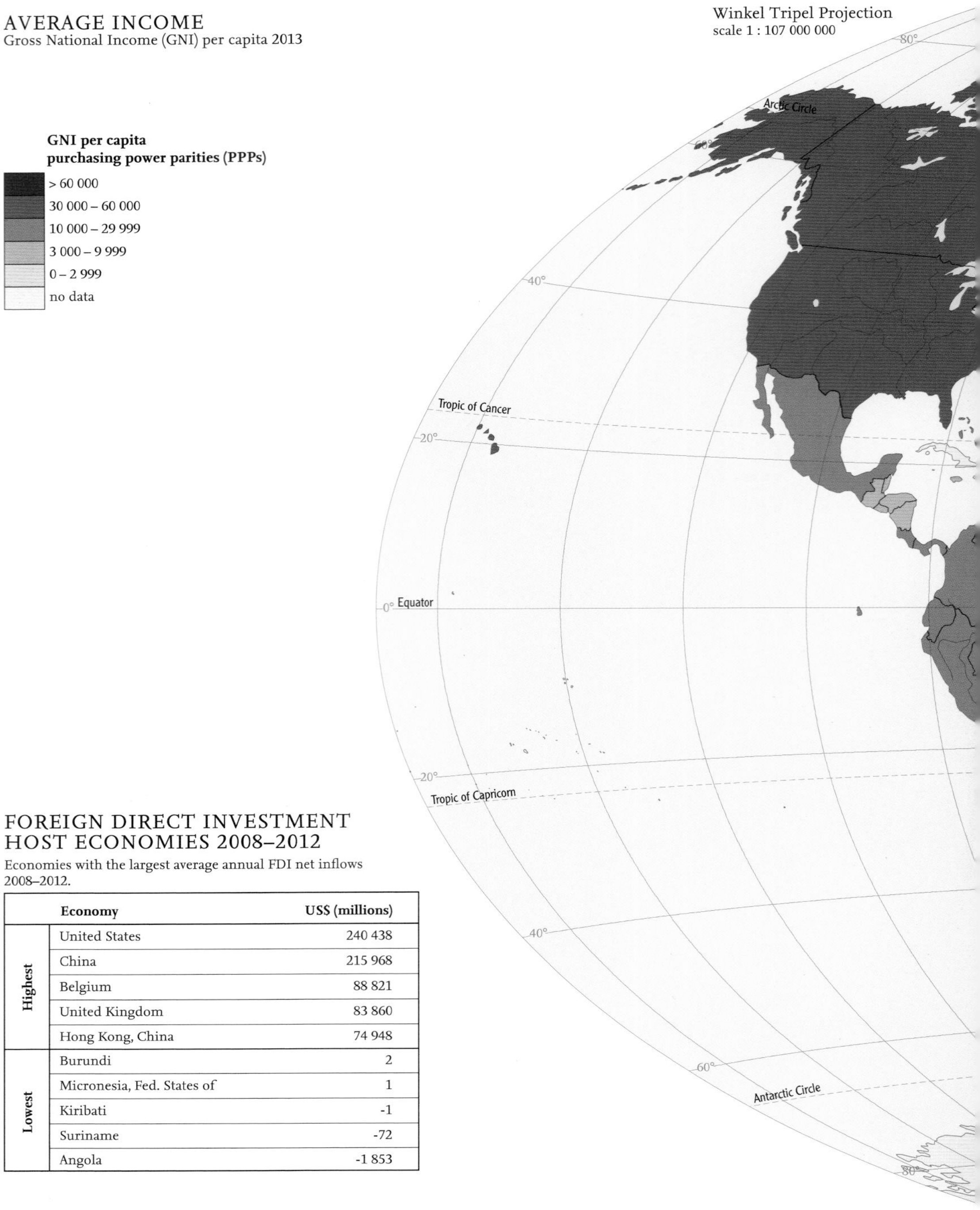

**GNI per capita
purchasing power parities (PPPs)**

- > 60 000
- 30 000 – 60 000
- 10 000 – 29 999
- 3 000 – 9 999
- 0 – 2 999
- no data

FOREIGN DIRECT INVESTMENT HOST ECONOMIES 2008–2012
Economies with the largest average annual FDI net inflows 2008–2012.

	Economy	US$ (millions)
Highest	United States	240 438
	China	215 968
	Belgium	88 821
	United Kingdom	83 860
	Hong Kong, China	74 948
Lowest	Burundi	2
	Micronesia, Fed. States of	1
	Kiribati	-1
	Suriname	-72
	Angola	-1 853

INCOME INEQUALITY
Most recent value 2000–2012

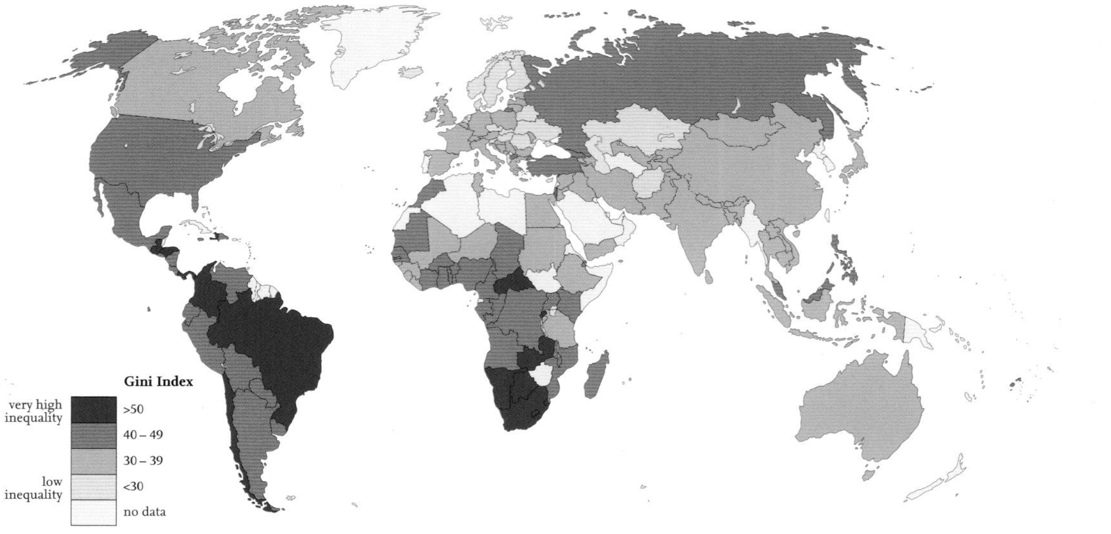

Gini Index

very high inequality
- >50
- 40 – 49
- 30 – 39
- <30
low inequality
- no data

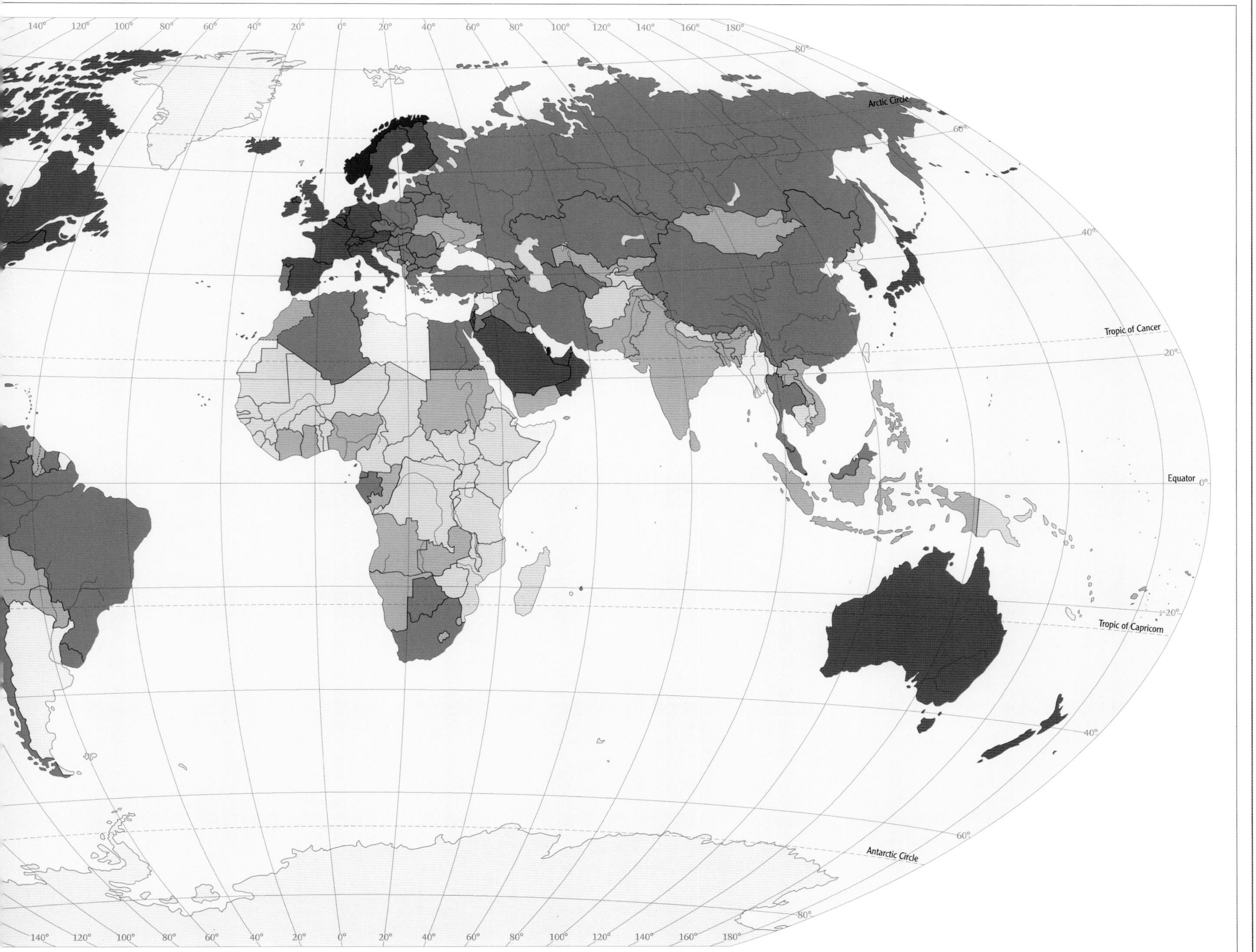

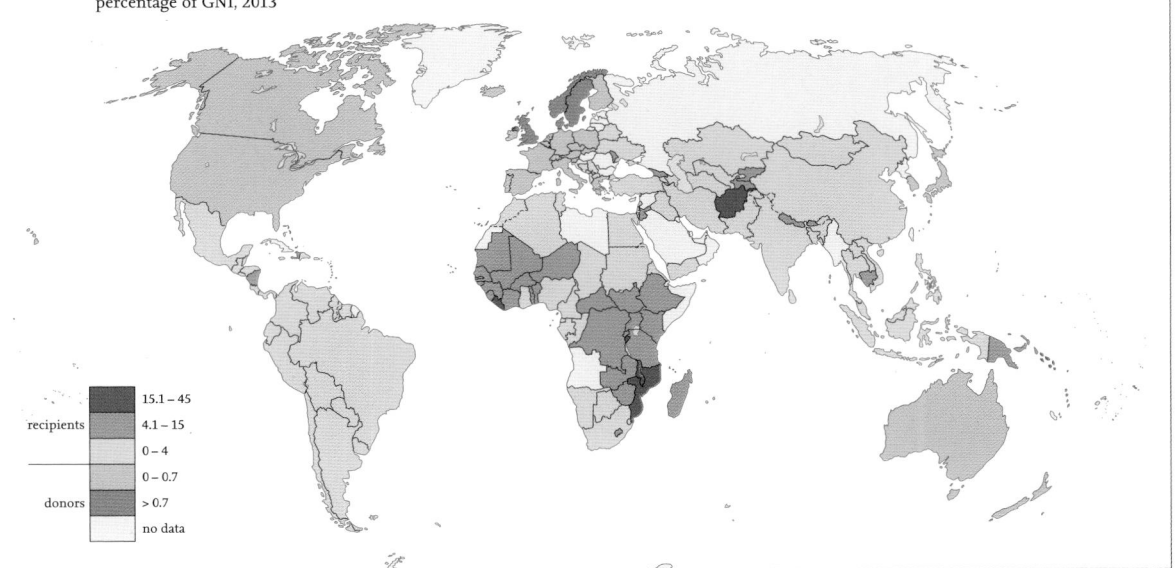

TRADE OPENNESS 2013

Trade as a percentage share of GDP, 2013
Countries with a population of over 2 million

Rank	Country	Trade as a share of GDP (%)
1	Hong Kong, China	458
2	Singapore	358
3	Ireland	190
4	Slovakia	181
5	United Arab Emirates	176
6	Hungary	170
7	Belgium	164
8	Vietnam	164
9	Netherlands	156
10	Malaysia	154
11	Czech Republic	149
12	Thailand	144
13	Slovenia	143
14	Kyrgyzstan	143
15	Congo	143
16	Cambodia	140

AID FOR DEVELOPMENT

Net Official Development Assistance (ODA) as a
percentage of GNI, 2013

recipients
15.1 – 45
4.1 – 15
0 – 4
0 – 0.7
donors
> 0.7
no data

COMMUNICATIONS

The rapid growth of the telecommunications industry over the last two decades, has contributed to the 'death of distance' by linking different parts of the world ever more cheaply and reliably due to improvements in technology. This process has meant that millions of virtual places, identified by telephone numbers, e-mail addresses, and World Wide Web sites, have become an essential part of the world's social and economic landscape. The huge demand for mobile and satellite telephones has contributed to satellite demand and to the building of ground stations. The parallel demand for electronic addresses has also triggered a construction boom for international submarine cables as well as adding to the demand for satellites. Initially, most of these networks served an information belt running from western Europe across North America to eastern Asia, but now the rest of the world is becoming much more connected.

INTERNET COMMUNICATIONS

Internet users have been increasing rapidly since 1991. However, access levels vary, with twenty-two countries and territories reporting less than 5 per cent internet penetration. Around 45 per cent of the world's internet users are from the Asia-Pacific region, making it the largest internet market. In contrast, almost 20 per cent of Africans are online (up from 10 per cent in 2010), while the developing country average is 32 per cent. Constraints include the high costs of international bandwidth to developing countries if they have to pay for a link to a hub in a developed country. International bandwidth is a critical part of the infrastructure as it is the most important factor in the speed of access to websites in other countries.

BROADBAND COMMUNICATIONS

Broadband connections for access to the internet are relatively recent, but in that short time huge developments have been made in the technology and access speeds have shown a steady rise which is still continuing. Broadband access has had an impact on the delivery of electronic services in many areas such as health, education and finance through the use of Information and Communication Technologies (ICTs). It has also been recognized that broadband and ICTs have an important role in the realization of the Millennium Development Goals (MDGs). As a result these technologies are receiving a high level of attention from policy makers at national and international levels. Mobile broadband (or mobile internet) is wireless high-speed internet access available through a portable modem device on a laptop computer and increasingly widely on mobile cellular telephones.

THE RISE OF 4G

Source: GMSA Intelligence

Some countries started to offer fourth generation (4G) mobile telecommunications services in 2010. Now, 4G covers the majority of countries with an estimated 35 per cent of the world's population covered in early 2015. 4G services offer much faster connection speeds than 3G along with high quality service and security levels. 3G reached over 70 per cent of the world's population in late 2014.

WORLD COMMUNICATION EQUIPMENT 1996–2014

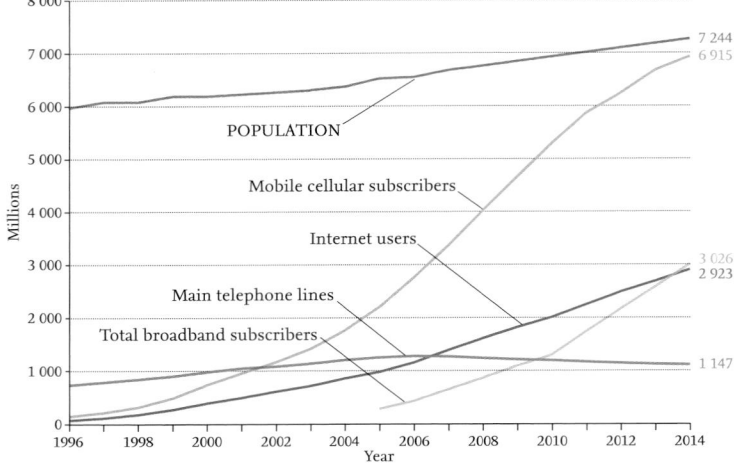

INTERNATIONAL TELECOMMUNICATIONS INDICATORS BY REGION 2014

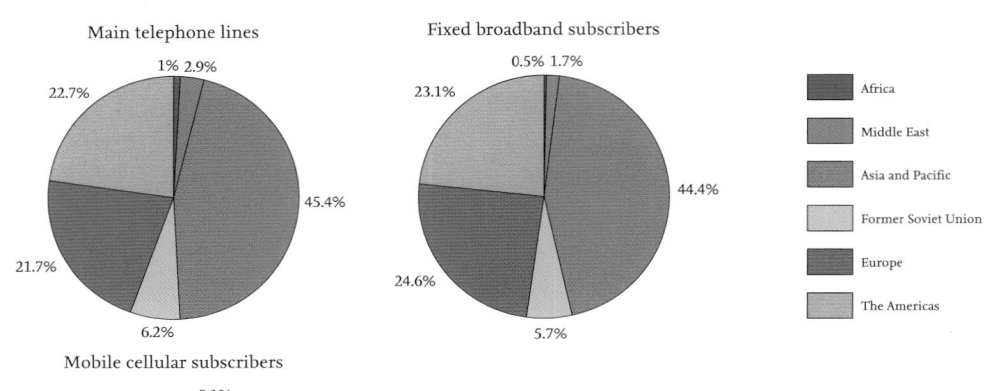

Main telephone lines — Fixed broadband subscribers

Africa · Middle East · Asia and Pacific · Former Soviet Union · Europe · The Americas

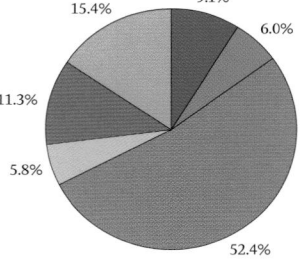

Mobile cellular subscribers

FIXED BROADBAND SUBSCRIBERS 2013

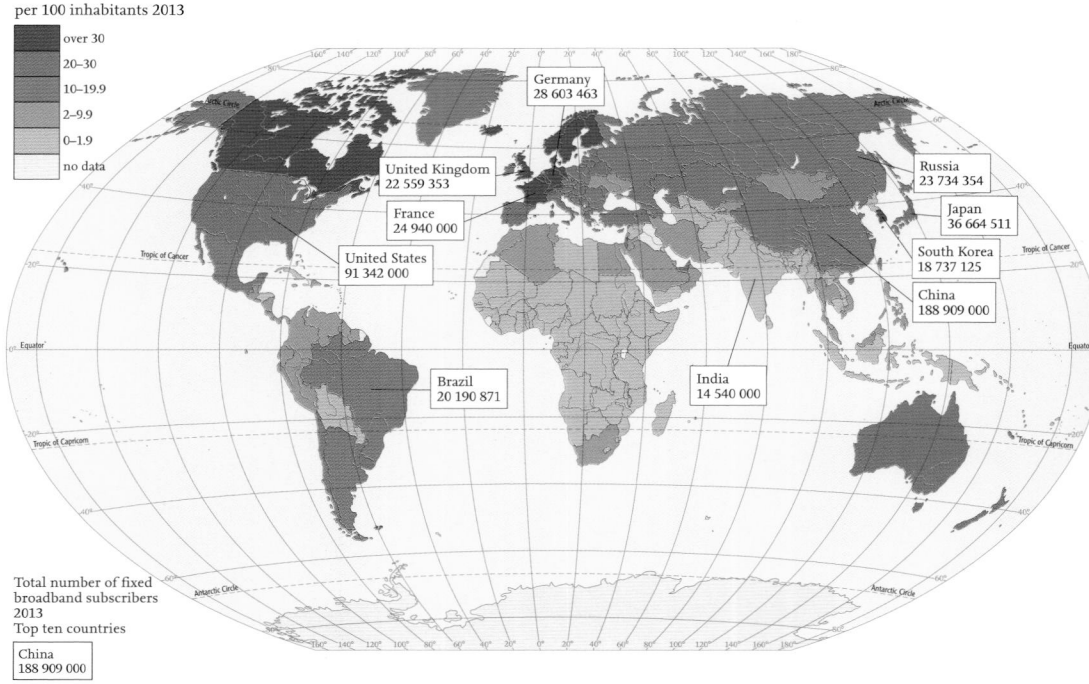

Fixed broadband subscribers per 100 inhabitants 2013
- over 30
- 20–30
- 10–19.9
- 2–9.9
- 0–1.9
- no data

Germany 28 603 463
United Kingdom 22 559 353
France 24 940 000
United States 91 342 000
Russia 23 734 354
Japan 36 664 511
South Korea 18 737 125
China 188 909 000
Brazil 20 190 871
India 14 540 000

Total number of fixed broadband subscribers 2013
Top ten countries
China 188 909 000

FIXED TELEPHONE SUBSCRIBERS 2013

Fixed telephone subscriptions per 100 inhabitants 2013

- over 50
- 35 – 50
- 20 – 34.9
- 10 – 19.9
- 5 – 9.9
- 1 – 4.9
- 0 – 0.9
- no data

Total telephone lines 2013
Top ten countries

China
266 985 000

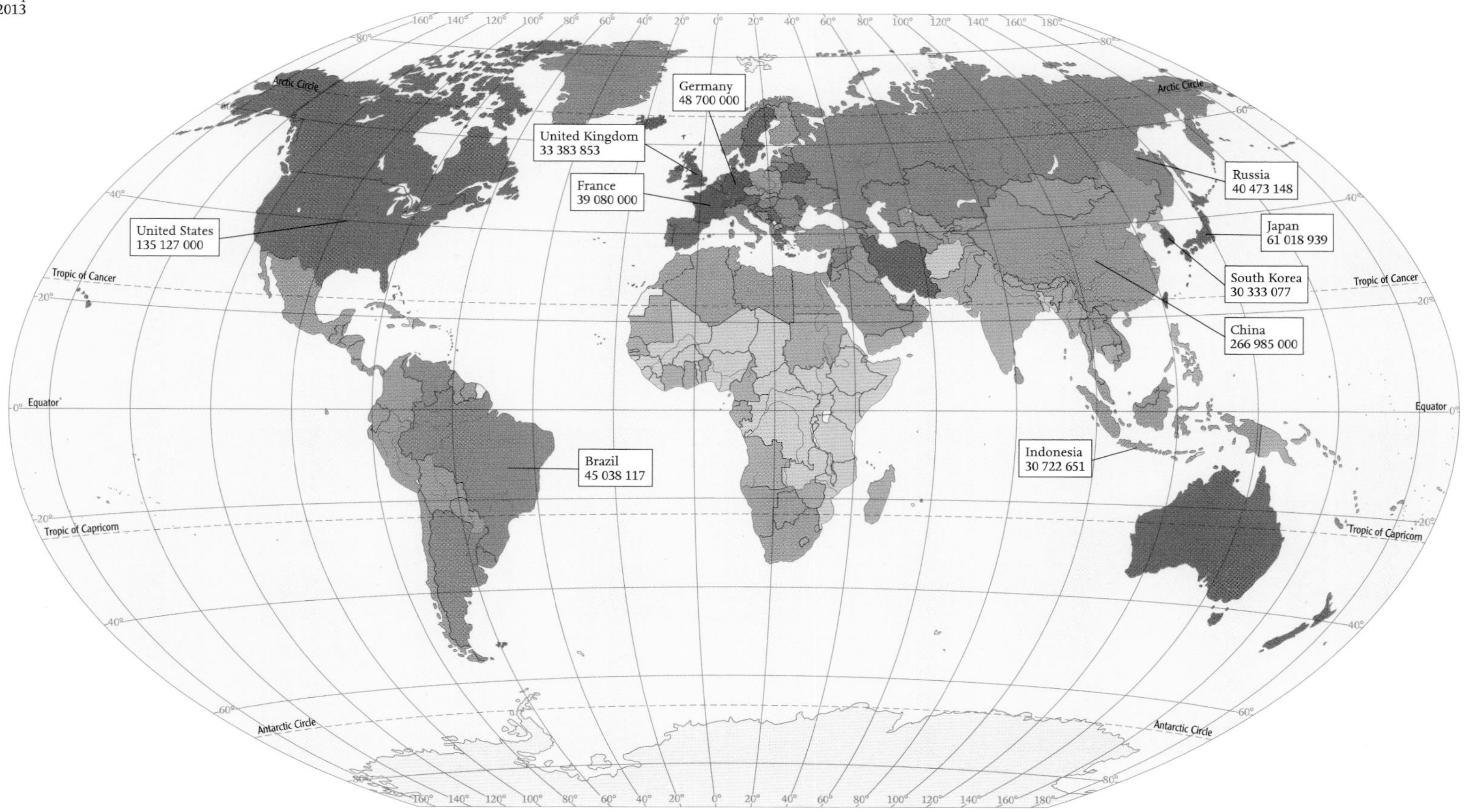
Germany
48 700 000
United Kingdom
33 383 853
France
39 080 000
United States
135 127 000
Russia
40 473 148
Japan
61 018 939
South Korea
30 333 077
China
266 985 000
Brazil
45 038 117
Indonesia
30 722 651
Arctic Circle
Tropic of Cancer
Equator
Tropic of Capricorn
Antarctic Circle

MOBILE CELLULAR SUBSCRIBERS 2013

Mobile cellular subscribers per 100 inhabitants 2013

- over 150
- 120–150
- 90–119.9
- 60–89.9
- 30–59.9
- 0–29.9
- no data

Total mobile cellular subscribers 2013
Top ten countries

China
1 229 113 000

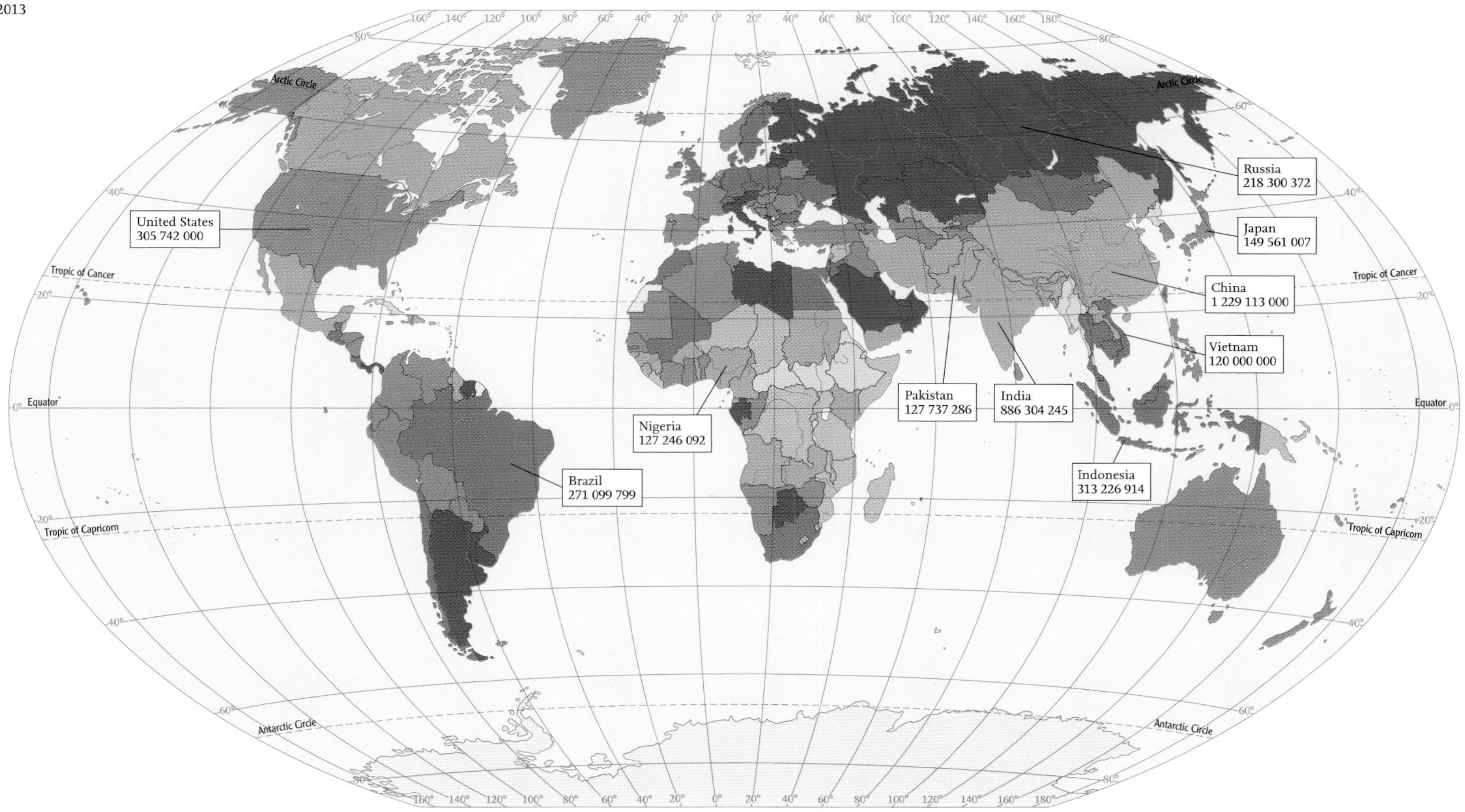
United States
305 742 000
Russia
218 300 372
Japan
149 561 007
China
1 229 113 000
Vietnam
120 000 000
Pakistan
127 737 286
India
886 304 245
Nigeria
127 246 092
Brazil
271 099 799
Indonesia
313 226 914
Arctic Circle
Tropic of Cancer
Equator
Tropic of Capricorn
Antarctic Circle

PHYSICAL FEATURES

The images below illustrate some of the major physical features of Oceania, Asia, Europe and Africa.

AUSTRALASIA

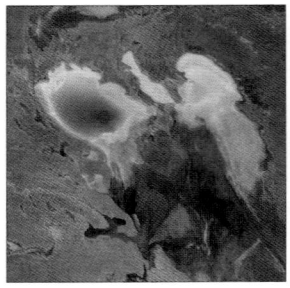

Kati Thanda-Lake Eyre,
South Australia

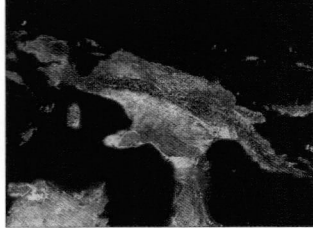

The island of New Guinea

ASIA

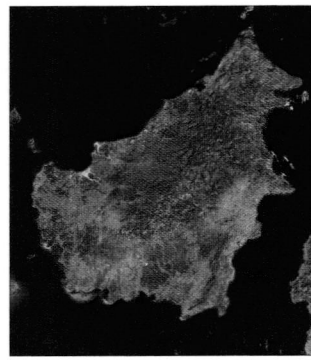

The island of Borneo

Mt Everest, China/Nepal

EUROPE

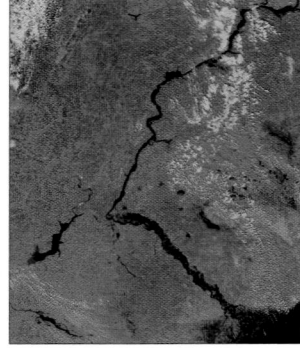

The river Volga, Russia

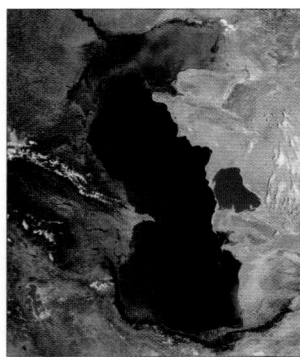

The Caspian Sea

AFRICA

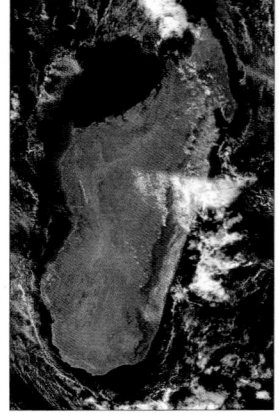

The island of Madagascar

Kilimanjaro, Tanzania

OCEANIA
Total Land Area
8 844 516 sq km / 3 414 868 sq miles (includes New Guinea and Pacific Island nations)

HIGHEST MOUNTAINS	metres	feet
Puncak Jaya, Indonesia	4 884	16 023
Puncak Trikora, Indonesia	4 730	15 518
Puncak Mandala, Indonesia	4 700	15 420
Puncak Yamin, Indonesia	4 595	15 075
Mt Wilhelm, Papua New Guinea	4 509	14 793
Mt Kubor, Papua New Guinea	4 359	14 301

LARGEST ISLANDS	sq km	sq miles
New Guinea	808 510	312 166
South Island (Te Waipounamu), New Zealand	151 215	58 384
North Island (Te Ika-a-Māui), New Zealand	115 777	44 701
Tasmania	67 800	26 178

HIGHEST MOUNTAIN
Puncak Jaya

LARGEST ISLAND
New Guinea

LARGEST LAKE AND
LOWEST POINT
Kati Thanda-Lake Eyre

ASIA
Total Land Area
45 036 492 sq km / 17 388 590 sq miles

HIGHEST MOUNTAINS	metres	feet
Mt Everest (Sagarmatha/ Qomolangma Feng), China/Nepal	8 848	29 028
K2 (Chogori Feng), China/Pakistan	8 611	28 251
Kangchenjunga, India/Nepal	8 586	28 169
Lhotse, China/Nepal	8 516	27 939
Makalu, China/Nepal	8 463	27 765
Cho Oyu, China/Nepal	8 201	26 906

LARGEST ISLANDS	sq km	sq miles
Borneo	745 561	287 861
Sumatra (Sumatera)	473 606	182 859
Honshū	227 414	87 805
Celebes (Sulawesi)	189 216	73 056
Java (Jawa)	132 188	51 038
Luzon	104 690	40 421

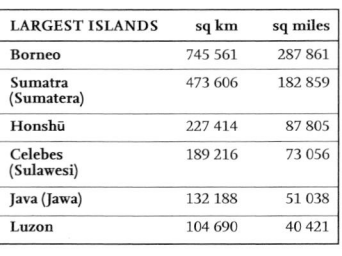

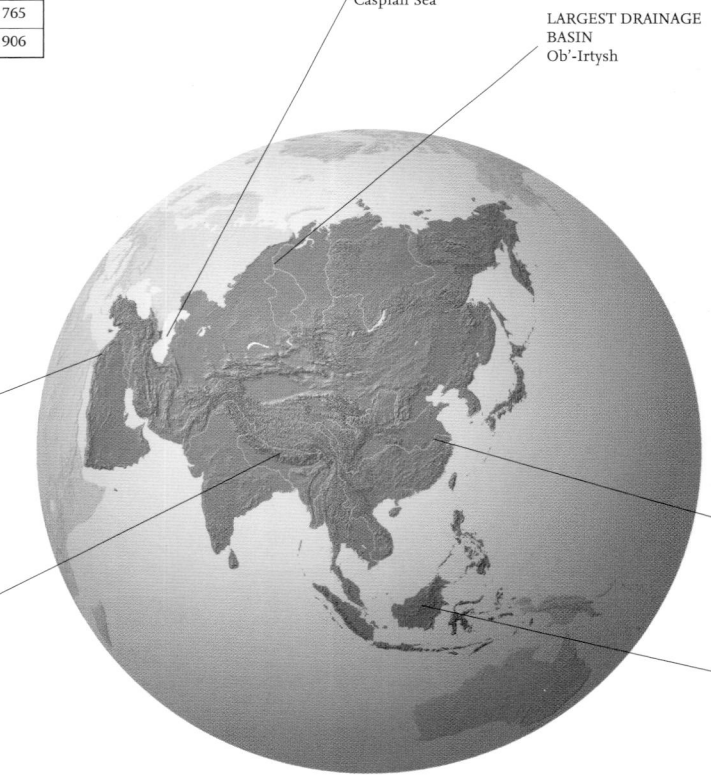

LARGEST LAKE
Caspian Sea

LARGEST DRAINAGE
BASIN
Ob'-Irtysh

LOWEST POINT
Dead Sea

HIGHEST MOUNTAIN
Mt Everest

EUROPE

Total Land Area
9 908 599 sq km / 3 825 710 sq miles

LONGEST RIVERS	km	miles
Murray-Darling	3 672	2 282
Darling	2 844	1 767
Murray	2 375	1 476
Murrumbidgee	1 485	923
Lachlan	1 339	832
Cooper Creek	1 113	692

LARGEST LAKES	sq km	sq miles
Kati Thanda-Lake Eyre	0–8 900	0–3 436
Lake Torrens	0–5 780	0–2 232

HIGHEST MOUNTAINS	metres	feet
El'brus, Russia	5 642	18 510
Gora Dykh-Tau, Russia	5 204	17 073
Shkhara, Georgia/Russia	5 201	17 063
Kazbek, Georgia/Russia	5 047	16 558
Mont Blanc, France/Italy	4 810	15 781
Dufourspitze, Italy/Switzerland	4 634	15 203

LARGEST ISLANDS	sq km	sq miles
Great Britain	218 476	84 354
Iceland	102 820	39 699
Ireland	83 045	32 064
Ostrov Severnyy	47 079	18 177
Spitsbergen	37 814	14 600
Ostrov Yuzhnyy	33 246	12 836
Sicily (Sicilia)	25 426	9 817

LONGEST RIVERS	km	miles
Volga	3 688	2 292
Danube	2 850	1 771
Dnieper	2 285	1 420
Kama	2 028	1 260
Don	1 931	1 200
Pechora	1 802	1 120

LARGEST LAKES	sq km	sq miles
Caspian Sea	371 000	143 243
Lake Ladoga (Ladozhskoye Ozero)	18 390	7 100
Lake Onega (Onezhskoye Ozero)	9 600	3 707
Vänern	5 585	2 156
Rybinskoye Vodokhranilishche	5 180	2 000

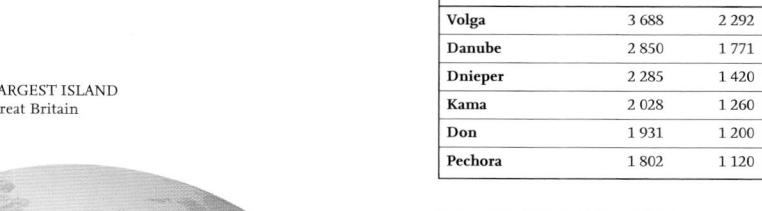

LARGEST ISLAND
Great Britain

LONGEST RIVER AND
LARGEST DRAINAGE BASIN
Volga

LONGEST RIVER AND
LARGEST DRAINAGE BASIN
Murray-Darling

HIGHEST MOUNTAIN
El'brus

LARGEST LAKE AND
LOWEST POINT
Caspian Sea

AFRICA

Total Land Area
30 343 578 sq km / 11 715 655 sq miles

LONGEST RIVERS	km	miles
Yangtze (Chang Jiang)	6 380	3 965
Ob'-Irtysh	5 568	3 460
Yenisey-Angara-Selenga	5 550	3 449
Yellow (Huang He)	5 464	3 395
Irtysh (Yertis)	4 440	2 759
Mekong	4 425	2 750

LARGEST LAKES	sq km	sq miles
Caspian Sea	371 000	143 243
Lake Baikal (Ozero Baykal)	30 500	11 776
Lake Balkhash (Ozero Balkash)	17 400	6 718
Aral Sea (Aral'skoye More)	17 158	6 625
Ysyk-Köl	6 200	2 394

HIGHEST MOUNTAINS	metres	feet
Kilimanjaro, Tanzania	5 892	19 330
Mt Kenya (Kirinyaga), Kenya	5 199	17 057
Margherita Peak, Democratic Republic of the Congo/Uganda	5 110	16 765
Meru, Tanzania	4 565	14 977
Ras Dejen, Ethiopia	4 533	14 872
Mt Karisimbi, Rwanda	4 510	14 796

LARGEST LAKES	sq km	sq miles
Lake Victoria	68 870	26 591
Lake Tanganyika	32 600	12 587
Lake Nyasa (Lake Malawi)	29 500	11 390
Lake Volta	8 482	3 275
Lake Turkana	6 500	2 510
Lake Albert	5 600	2 162

LONGEST RIVERS	km	miles
Nile	6 695	4 160
Congo	4 667	2 900
Niger	4 184	2 600
Zambezi	2 736	1 700
Wabē Shebelē Wenz	2 490	1 547
Ubangi	2 250	1 398

LARGEST ISLANDS	sq km	sq miles
Madagascar	587 040	226 656

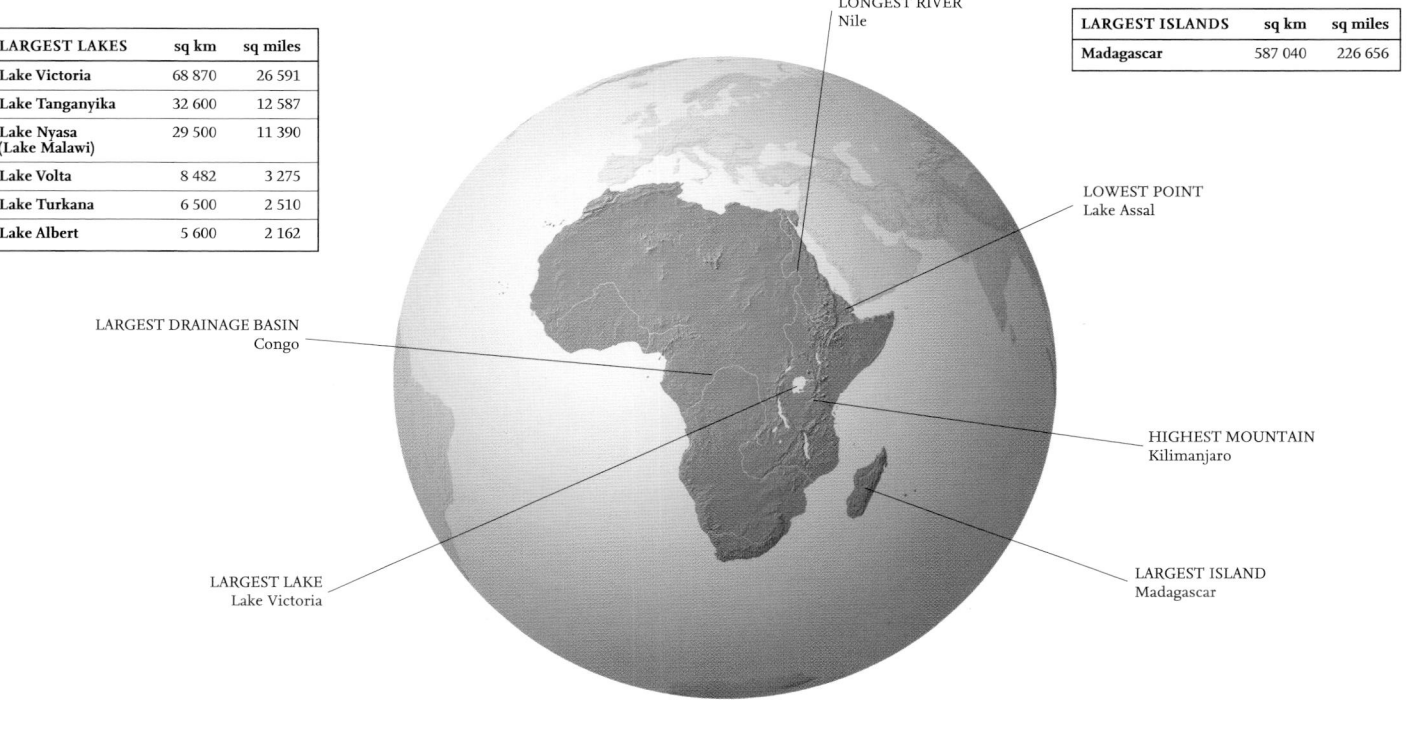

LONGEST RIVER
Nile

LONGEST RIVER
Yangtze
(Chang Jiang)

LARGEST ISLAND
Borneo

LOWEST POINT
Lake Assal

LARGEST DRAINAGE BASIN
Congo

HIGHEST MOUNTAIN
Kilimanjaro

LARGEST LAKE
Lake Victoria

LARGEST ISLAND
Madagascar

PHYSICAL FEATURES

The images below illustrate some of the major physical
features of North America, South America, and Antarctica.

NORTH AMERICA

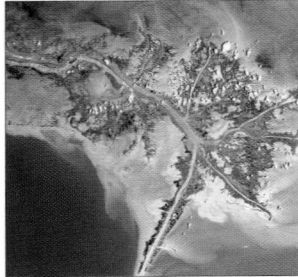

Mississippi-Missouri,
United States of America

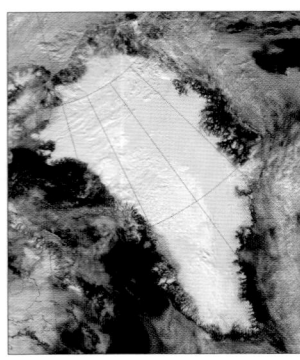

The island of Greenland

Mt McKinley, United States of America

SOUTH AMERICA

Lake Titicaca, Bolivia/Peru

Cerro Aconcagua,
Argentina

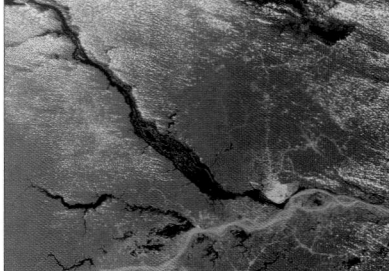

The river Amazon

ANTARCTICA

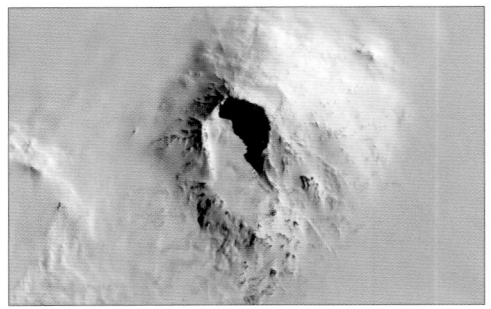

Mt Sidley, West Antarctica

NORTH AMERICA
Total Land Area
24 680 331 sq km / 9 529 076 sq miles (including Hawaiian Islands)

HIGHEST MOUNTAINS	metres	feet
Mt McKinley, USA	6 194	20 321
Mt Logan, Canada	5 959	19 550
Pico de Orizaba, Mexico	5 610	18 405
Mt St Elias, USA	5 489	18 008
Volcán Popocatépetl, Mexico	5 452	17 887
Mt Foraker, USA	5 303	17 398

LARGEST ISLANDS	sq km	sq miles
Greenland	2 175 600	839 999
Baffin Island	507 451	195 927
Victoria Island	217 291	83 896
Ellesmere Island	196 236	75 767
Cuba	110 860	42 803
Newfoundland	108 860	42 031
Hispaniola	76 192	29 418

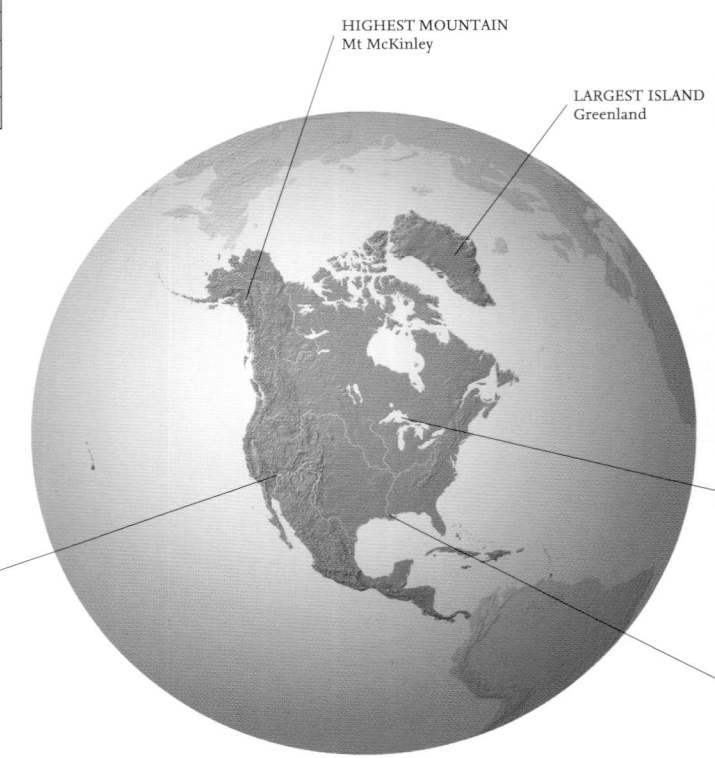

HIGHEST MOUNTAIN
Mt McKinley

LARGEST ISLAND
Greenland

LOWEST POINT
Death Valley

SOUTH AMERICA
Total Land Area
17 815 420 sq km / 6 878 534 sq miles

HIGHEST MOUNTAINS	metres	feet
Cerro Aconcagua, Argentina	6 959	22 831
Nevado Ojos del Salado, Argentina/Chile	6 908	22 664
Cerro Bonete, Argentina	6 872	22 546
Cerro Pissis, Argentina	6 858	22 500
Cerro Tupungato, Argentina/Chile	6 800	22 309
Cerro Mercedario, Argentina	6 770	22 211

LARGEST ISLANDS	sq km	sq miles
Isla Grande de Tierra del Fuego	47 000	18 147
Isla de Chiloé	8 394	3 241
East Falkland	6 760	2 610
West Falkland	5 413	2 090

LONGEST RIVER AND
LARGEST DRAINAGE BASIN
Amazon (Amazonas)

LARGEST LAKE
Lake Titicaca

HIGHEST MOUNTAIN
Cerro Aconcagua

LONGEST RIVERS	km	miles
Mississippi-Missouri	5 969	3 709
Mackenzie-Peace-Finlay	4 241	2 635
Missouri	4 086	2 539
Mississippi	3 765	2 340
Yukon	3 185	1 979
St Lawrence	3 058	1 900

LARGEST LAKES	sq km	sq miles
Lake Superior	82 100	31 699
Lake Huron	59 600	23 012
Lake Michigan	57 800	22 317
Great Bear Lake	31 328	12 096
Great Slave Lake	28 568	11 030
Lake Erie	25 700	9 923
Lake Winnipeg	24 387	9 416
Lake Ontario	18 960	7 320

LARGEST LAKE
Lake Superior

LONGEST RIVER AND
LARGEST DRAINAGE BASIN
Mississippi-Missouri

LONGEST RIVERS	km	miles
Amazon (Amazonas)	6 516	4 049
Río de la Plata-Paraná	4 500	2 796
Purus	3 218	2 000
Madeira	3 200	1 988
São Francisco	2 900	1 802
Tocantins	2 750	1 709

LARGEST LAKES	sq km	sq miles
Lake Titicaca	8 340	3 220

LOWEST POINT
Laguna del Carbón

LARGEST ISLAND
Isla Grande de Tierra del Fuego

ANTARCTICA
Total Land Area
12 093 000 sq km / 4 669 107 sq miles (excluding ice shelves)

HIGHEST MOUNTAIN
Mt Vinson

HIGHEST MOUNTAINS	metres	feet
Mt Vinson	4 897	16 066
Mt Tyree	4 852	15 918
Mt Kirkpatrick	4 528	14 855
Mt Markham	4 351	14 275
Mt Sidley	4 285	14 058
Mt Minto	4 165	13 665

ATLANTIC OCEAN
Total Area
86 557 000 sq km / 33 420 000 sq miles

ATLANTIC OCEAN	Area square km	square miles	Deepest Point metres	feet
Extent	86 557 000	33 420 000	8 605	28 231
Arctic Ocean	9 485 000	3 662 000	5 450	17 880
Caribbean Sea	2 512 000	970 000	7 680	25 197
Mediterranean Sea	2 510 000	969 000	5 121	16 801
Gulf of Mexico	1 544 000	596 000	3 504	11 496
Hudson Bay	1 233 000	476 000	259	850
North Sea	575 000	222 000	661	2 169
Black Sea	508 000	196 000	2 245	7 365
Baltic Sea	382 000	147 000	460	1 509

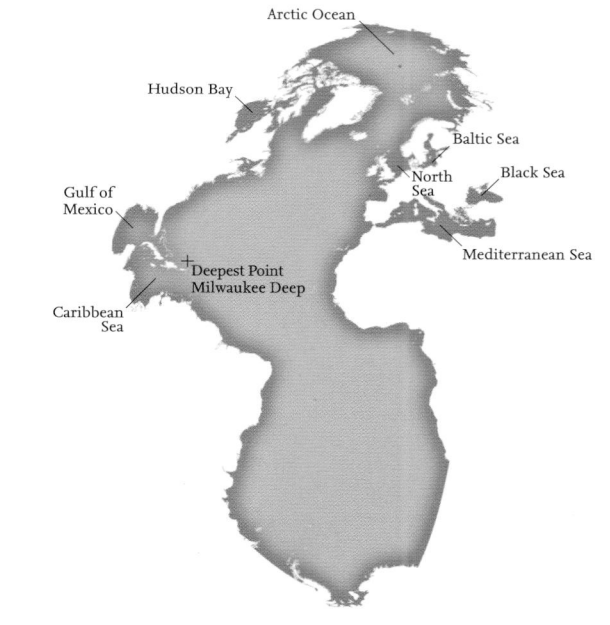

Arctic Ocean

Hudson Bay

Baltic Sea

Gulf of
Mexico

North
Sea

Black Sea

Deepest Point
Milwaukee Deep

Mediterranean Sea

Caribbean
Sea

INDIAN OCEAN
Total Area
73 427 000 sq km / 28 350 000 sq miles

Red
Sea

The Gulf

Bay of Bengal

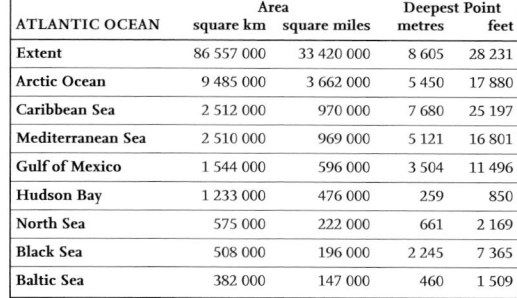

Deepest Point
Java Trench

INDIAN OCEAN	Area square km	square miles	Deepest Point metres	feet
Extent	73 427 000	28 350 000	7 125	23 376
Bay of Bengal	2 172 000	839 000	4 500	14 764
Red Sea	453 000	175 000	3 040	9 974
The Gulf	238 000	92 000	73	239

PACIFIC OCEAN
Total Area
166 241 000 sq km / 64 186 000 sq miles

PACIFIC OCEAN	Area square km	square miles	Deepest Point metres	feet
Extent	166 241 000	64 186 000	10 920	35 826
South China Sea	2 590 000	1 000 000	5 514	18 090
Bering Sea	2 261 000	873 000	4 150	13 615
Sea of Okhotsk	1 392 000	537 000	3 363	11 033
East China Sea and Yellow Sea	1 202 000	464 000	2 717	8 914
Sea of Japan (East Sea)	1 013 000	391 000	3 743	12 280

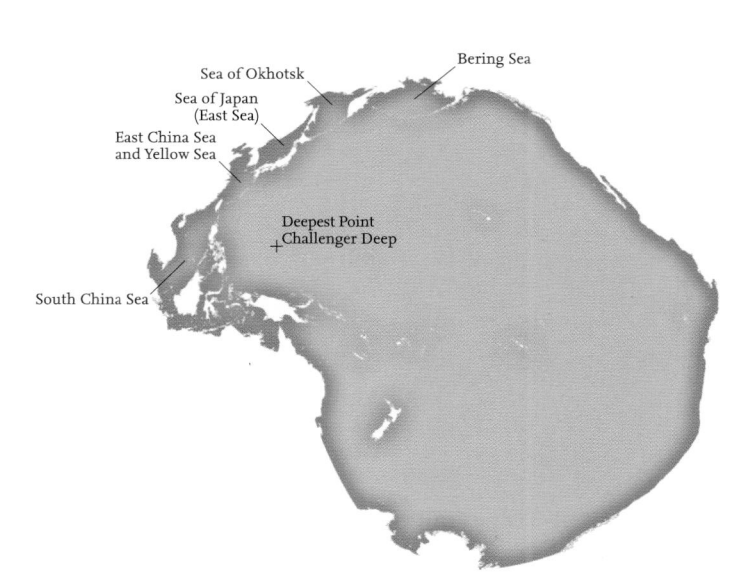

Sea of Okhotsk

Bering Sea

Sea of Japan
(East Sea)

East China Sea
and Yellow Sea

Deepest Point
Challenger Deep

South China Sea

STATES AND TERRITORIES

All 196 independent countries and all populated dependent and disputed territories are included in this list of the states and territories of the world; the list is arranged in alphabetical order by the conventional name form. For independent states, the full name is given below the conventional name, if this is different; for territories, the status is given. The capital city name is given in conventional English form with selected alternative, usually local, form in brackets.

Area and population statistics are the latest available and include estimates. The information on languages and religions is based on the latest information on 'de facto' speakers of the language or 'de facto' adherents of the religion. This varies greatly from country to country because some countries include questions in censuses while others do not, in which case best estimates are used. The order of the languages and religions reflects their relative importance within the country; generally, languages or religions are included when more than one per cent of the population are estimated to be speakers or adherents.

ABBREVIATIONS

CURRENCIES

CFA	Communauté Financière Africaine
CFP	Comptoirs Français du Pacifique

Membership of selected international organizations is shown by the abbreviations below; dependent territories do not normally have separate memberships of these organizations.

ORGANIZATIONS

APEC	Asia-Pacific Economic Cooperation
ASEAN	Association of Southeast Asian Nations
CARICOM	Caribbean Community
CIS	Commonwealth of Independent States
Comm.	The Commonwealth
EU	European Union
NATO	North Atlantic Treaty Organization
OECD	Organisation for Economic Co-operation and Development
OPEC	Organization of the Petroleum Exporting Countries
SADC	Southern African Development Community
UN	United Nations

Abkhazia
Disputed territory

Area Sq Km	8 700	**Languages**	Abkhaz, Russian, Georgian
Area Sq Miles	3 359	**Religions**	Abkhaz Orthodox Christianity, Sunni Muslim
Population	180 000		
Capital	Sokhumi (Aq"a)	**Currency**	Russian rouble, Abkhaz apsar

Map page 187 An autonomous republic within Georgia, Abkhazia has an active separatist movement seeking independence from Georgia. Although it is de jure part of Georgia, it effectively currently functions as an independent state with backing from Russia. This dispute has led to intermittent, but serious, armed conflict over the last twenty years. Abkhazia voted to separate from Georgia in 1992, a move rejected by Georgia and prompting a Georgian invasion. Abkhazian and Russian forces ousted Georgia and a cease-fire was established in 1994.

AFGHANISTAN
Islamic Republic of Afghanistan

Area Sq Km	652 225	**Languages**	Dari, Pashtu (Pushtu), Uzbek, Turkmen
Area Sq Miles	251 825	**Religions**	Sunni Muslim, Shi'a Muslim
Population	30 552 000	**Currency**	Afghani
Capital	Kābul	**Organizations**	UN

Map page 143

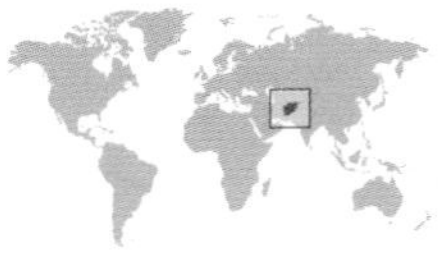

A landlocked country in central Asia with central highlands bordered by plains in the north and southwest, and by the Hindu Kush mountains in the northeast. The climate is dry continental. Over the last twenty-five years war has disrupted the economy, which is highly dependent on farming and livestock rearing. Most trade is with the former USSR, Pakistan and Iran.

ALBANIA
Republic of Albania

Area Sq Km	28 748	**Languages**	Albanian, Greek
Area Sq Miles	11 100	**Religions**	Sunni Muslim, Albanian Orthodox, Roman Catholic
Population	3 173 000	**Currency**	Lek
Capital	Tirana (Tiranë)	**Organizations**	NATO, UN

Map page 185

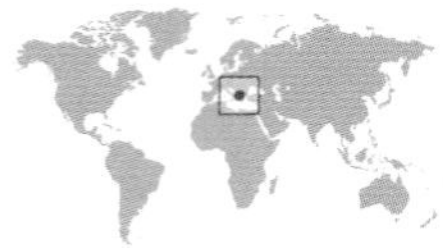

Albania lies in the western Balkan Mountains in southeastern Europe, bordering the Adriatic Sea. It is mountainous, with coastal plains where half the population lives. The economy is based on agriculture and mining. Albania is one of the poorest countries in Europe and relies heavily on foreign aid.

ALGERIA
People's Democratic Republic of Algeria

Area Sq Km	2 381 741	**Languages**	Arabic, French, Berber
Area Sq Miles	919 595	**Religions**	Sunni Muslim
Population	39 208 000	**Currency**	Algerian dinar
Capital	Algiers (Alger)	**Organizations**	OPEC, UN

Map page 192

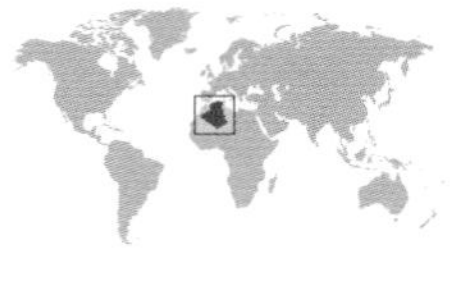

Algeria, the largest country in Africa, lies on the Mediterranean coast of northwest Africa and extends southwards to the Atlas Mountains and the dry sandstone plateau and desert of the Sahara. The climate ranges from Mediterranean on the coast to semi-arid and arid inland. The most populated areas are the coastal plains and the fertile northern slopes of the Atlas Mountains. Oil, natural gas and related products account for over ninety-five per cent of export earnings. Agriculture employs about a fifth of the workforce, producing mainly food crops. Algeria's main trading partners are Italy, France and the USA.

American Samoa
United States Unincorporated Territory

Area Sq Km	197	**Languages**	Samoan, English
Area Sq Miles	76	**Religions**	Protestant, Roman Catholic
Population	55 000	**Currency**	United States dollar
Capital	Fagatogo		

Map page 117

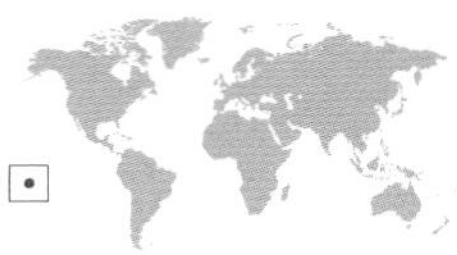

Lying in the south Pacific Ocean, American Samoa consists of five main islands and two coral atolls. The largest island is Tutuila. Tuna and tuna products are the main exports, and the main trading partner is the USA.

ANDORRA
Principality of Andorra

Area Sq Km	465	**Languages**	Catalan, Spanish, French
Area Sq Miles	180	**Religions**	Roman Catholic
Population	79 000	**Currency**	Euro
Capital	Andorra la Vella	**Organizations**	UN

Map page 183

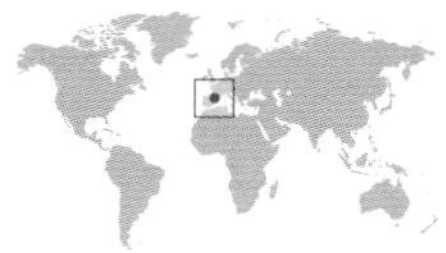

A landlocked state in southwest Europe, Andorra lies in the Pyrenees mountain range between France and Spain. It consists of deep valleys and gorges, surrounded by mountains. Tourism, encouraged by the development of ski resorts, is the mainstay of the economy. Banking is also an important economic activity.

ANGOLA
Republic of Angola

Area Sq Km	1 246 700	**Languages**	Portuguese, Bantu, other local languages
Area Sq Miles	481 354	**Religions**	Roman Catholic, Protestant, traditional beliefs
Population	21 472 000	**Currency**	Kwanza
Capital	Luanda	**Organizations**	OPEC, SADC, UN

Map page 195

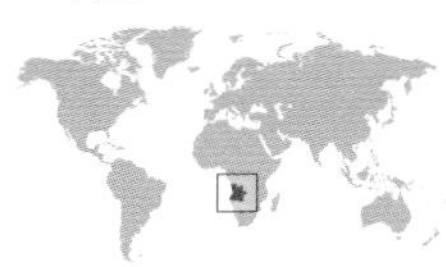

Angola lies on the Atlantic coast of south central Africa. Its small northern province, Cabinda, is separated from the rest of the country by part of the Democratic Republic of the Congo. Much of Angola is high plateau. In the west is a narrow coastal plain and in the southwest is desert. The climate is equatorial in the north but desert in the south. Around seventy per cent of the population relies on subsistence agriculture. Angola is rich in minerals (particularly diamonds), and oil accounts for approximately ninety per cent of export earnings. The USA, South Korea and Portugal are its main trading partners.

Anguilla
United Kingdom Overseas Territory

Area Sq Km	155	**Languages**	English
Area Sq Miles	60	**Religions**	Protestant, Roman Catholic
Population	14 000	**Currency**	East Caribbean dollar
Capital	The Valley		

Map page 223 Anguilla lies at the northern end of the Leeward Islands in the eastern Caribbean. Tourism and fishing form the basis of the economy.

ANTIGUA AND BARBUDA

Area Sq Km	442	**Languages**	English, Creole
Area Sq Miles	171	**Religions**	Protestant, Roman Catholic
Population	90 000	**Currency**	East Caribbean dollar
Capital	St John's	**Organizations**	CARICOM, Comm., UN

Map page 223

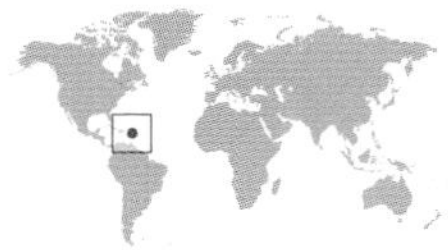

The state comprises the islands of Antigua, Barbuda and the tiny rocky outcrop of Redonda, in the Leeward Islands in the eastern Caribbean. Antigua, the largest and most populous island, is mainly hilly scrubland, with many beaches. The climate is tropical, and the economy relies heavily on tourism. Most trade is with other eastern Caribbean states and the USA.

ARGENTINA
Argentine Republic

Area Sq Km	2 766 889	**Languages**	Spanish, Italian, Amerindian languages
Area Sq Miles	1 068 302	**Religions**	Roman Catholic, Protestant
Population	41 446 000	**Currency**	Argentinian peso
Capital	Buenos Aires	**Organizations**	UN

Map page 232

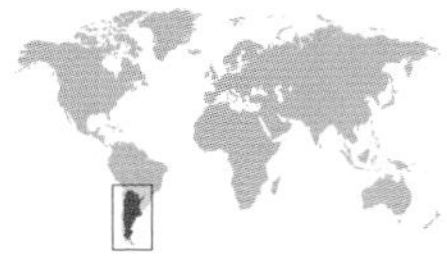

Argentina, the second largest state in South America, extends from Bolivia to Cape Horn and from the Andes mountains to the Atlantic Ocean. It has four geographical regions: subtropical forests and swampland in the northeast; temperate fertile plains or Pampas in the centre; the wooded foothills and valleys of the Andes in the west; and the cold, semi-arid plateaus of Patagonia in the south. The highest mountain in South America, Cerro Aconcagua, is in Argentina. Over ninety per cent of the population lives in towns and cities. The country is rich in natural resources including petroleum, natural gas, ores and precious metals. Agricultural products dominate exports, which also include motor vehicles and crude oil. Most trade is with Brazil and the USA.

ARMENIA
Republic of Armenia

Area Sq Km	29 800	**Languages**	Armenian, Kurdish
Area Sq Miles	11 506	**Religions**	Armenian Orthodox
Population	2 977 000	**Currency**	Dram
Capital	Yerevan (Erevan)	**Organizations**	CIS, UN

Map page 139

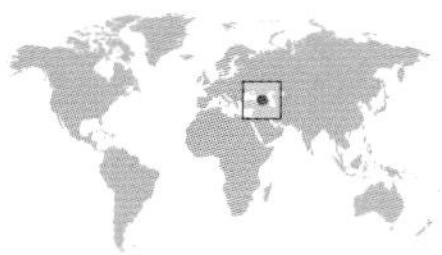

A landlocked state in southwest Asia, Armenia lies in the south of the Lesser Caucasus mountains. It is a mountainous country with a continental climate. One-third of the population lives in the capital, Yerevan. Exports include diamonds, scrap metal and machinery. Many Armenians depend on remittances from abroad.

Aruba
Self-governing Netherlands Territory

Area Sq Km	193	**Languages**	Papiamento, Dutch, English
Area Sq Miles	75	**Religions**	Roman Catholic, Protestant
Population	103 000	**Currency**	Aruban florin
Capital	Oranjestad		

Map page 233 The most southwesterly of the islands in the Lesser Antilles in the Caribbean, Aruba lies just off the coast of Venezuela. Tourism, offshore finance and oil refining are the most important sectors of the economy. The USA is the main trading partner.

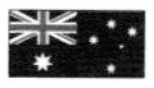

AUSTRALIA
Commonwealth of Australia

Area Sq Km	7 692 024	**Languages**	English, Italian, Greek
Area Sq Miles	2 969 907	**Religions**	Protestant, Roman Catholic, Orthodox
Population	23 343 000	**Currency**	Australian dollar
Capital	Canberra	**Organizations**	APEC, Comm., OECD, UN

Map page 118

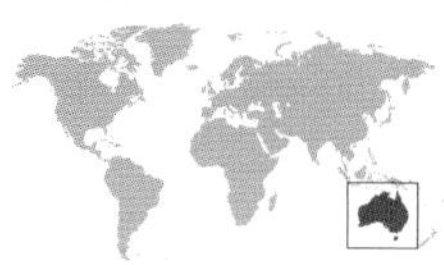

Australia, the world's sixth largest country, occupies the smallest, flattest and driest continent. The western half of the continent is mostly arid plateaus, ridges and vast deserts. The central eastern area comprises the lowlands of river systems draining into Lake Eyre, while to the east is the Great Dividing Range, a belt of ridges and plateaus running from Queensland to Tasmania. Climatically, more than two-thirds of the country is arid or semi-arid. The north is tropical monsoon, the east subtropical, and the southwest and southeast temperate. The majority of Australia's highly urbanized population lives along the east, southeast and southwest coasts. Australia has vast mineral deposits and various sources of energy. It is among the world's leading producers of iron ore, bauxite, nickel, copper and uranium. It is a major producer of coal, and oil and natural gas are also being exploited. Although accounting for under four per cent of the workforce, agriculture continues to be an important sector of the economy, with food and agricultural raw materials making up most of Australia's export earnings. Fuel, ores and metals, and manufactured goods, account for the remainder of exports. Japan and the USA are Australia's main trading partners.

Australian Capital Territory (Federal Territory)
Area Sq Km (Sq Miles) 2 358 (910) | Population 379 600 | Capital Canberra

Jervis Bay Territory (Territory)
Area Sq Km (Sq Miles) 73 (28) | Population 378

New South Wales (State)
Area Sq Km (Sq Miles) 800 642 (309 130) | Population 7 348 900 | Capital Sydney

Northern Territory (Territory)
Area Sq Km (Sq Miles) 1 349 129 (520 902) | Population 236 900 | Capital Darwin

Queensland (State)
Area Sq Km (Sq Miles) 1 730 648 (668 207) | Population 4 610 900 | Capital Brisbane

South Australia (State)
Area Sq Km (Sq Miles) 983 482 (379 725) | Population 1 662 200 | Capital Adelaide

Tasmania (State)
Area Sq Km (Sq Miles) 68 401 (26 410) | Population 512 400 | Capital Hobart

Victoria (State)
Area Sq Km (Sq Miles) 227 416 (87 806) | Population 5 679 600 | Capital Melbourne

Western Australia (State)
Area Sq Km (Sq Miles) 2 529 875 (976 790) | Population 2 472 700 | Capital Perth

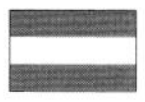

AUSTRIA
Republic of Austria

Area Sq Km	83 855	**Languages**	German, Croatian, Turkish
Area Sq Miles	32 377	**Religions**	Roman Catholic, Protestant
Population	8 495 000	**Currency**	Euro
Capital	Vienna (Wien)	**Organizations**	EU, OECD, UN

Map page 176

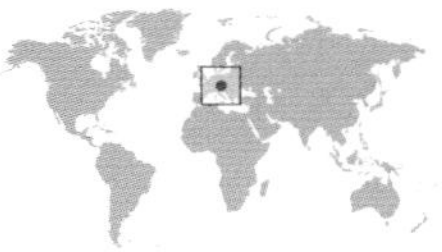

Two-thirds of Austria, a landlocked state in central Europe, lies within the Alps, with lower mountains to the north. The only lowlands are in the east. The Danube river valley in the northeast contains almost all the agricultural land and most of the population. Although the climate varies with altitude, in general summers are warm and winters cold with heavy snowfalls. Manufacturing industry and tourism are the most important sectors of the economy. Exports are dominated by manufactured goods. Germany is Austria's main trading partner.

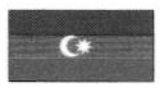

AZERBAIJAN
Republic of Azerbaijan

Area Sq Km	86 600	**Languages**	Azeri, Armenian, Russian, Lezgian
Area Sq Miles	33 436	**Religions**	Shi'a Muslim, Sunni Muslim, Russian and Armenian Orthodox
Population	9 413 000	**Currency**	Azerbaijani manat
Capital	Baku	**Organizations**	CIS, UN

Map page 139

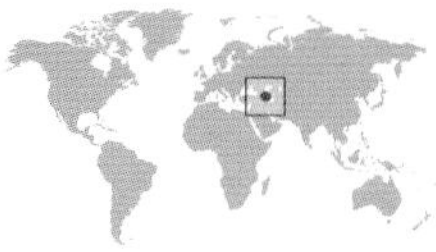

Azerbaijan lies to the southeast of the Caucasus mountains, on the Caspian Sea. Its region of Naxçıvan is separated from the rest of the country by part of Armenia. It has mountains in the northeast and west, valleys in the centre, and a low coastal plain. The climate is continental. It is rich in energy and mineral resources. Oil production, onshore and offshore, is the main industry and the basis of heavy industries. Agriculture is important, with cotton and tobacco the main cash crops.

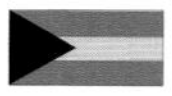

THE BAHAMAS
Commonwealth of The Bahamas

Area Sq Km	13 939	**Languages**	English, Creole
Area Sq Miles	5 382	**Religions**	Protestant, Roman Catholic
Population	377 000	**Currency**	Bahamian dollar
Capital	Nassau	**Organizations**	CARICOM, Comm., UN

Map page 223

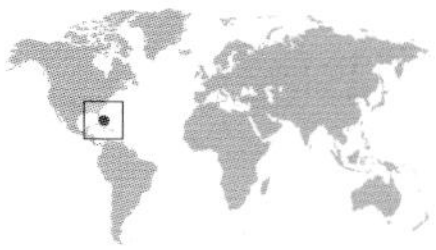

The Bahamas, an archipelago made up of approximately seven hundred islands and over two thousand cays, lies to the northeast of Cuba and east of the Florida coast of the USA. Twenty-two islands are inhabited, and seventy per cent of the population lives on the main island of New Providence. The climate is warm for much of the year, with heavy rainfall in the summer. Tourism is the islands' main industry. Offshore banking, insurance and ship registration are also major foreign exchange earners.

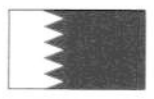

BAHRAIN
Kingdom of Bahrain

Area Sq Km	691	**Languages**	Arabic, English
Area Sq Miles	267	**Religions**	Shi'a Muslim, Sunni Muslim, Christian
Population	1 332 000	**Currency**	Bahraini dinar
Capital	Manama (Al Manāmah)	**Organizations**	UN

Map page 142

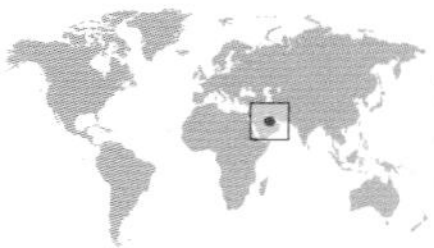

Bahrain consists of more than thirty islands lying in a bay in The Gulf, off the coasts of Saudi Arabia and Qatar. Bahrain Island, the largest island, is connected to other islands and to the mainland of Arabia by causeways. Oil production and processing are the main sectors of the economy.

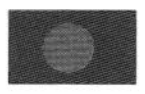

BANGLADESH
People's Republic of Bangladesh

Area Sq Km	143 998	**Languages**	Bengali, English
Area Sq Miles	55 598	**Religions**	Sunni Muslim, Hindu
Population	156 595 000	**Currency**	Taka
Capital	Dhaka (Dacca)	**Organizations**	Comm., UN

Map page 149

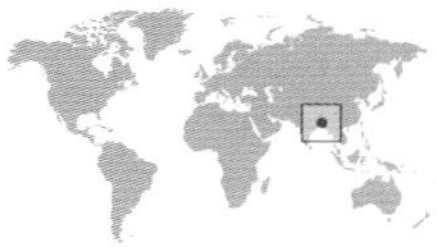

The south Asian state of Bangladesh is in the northeast of the Indian subcontinent, on the Bay of Bengal. It consists almost entirely of the low-lying alluvial plains and deltas of the Ganges and Brahmaputra rivers. The southwest is swampy, with mangrove forests in the delta area. The north, northeast and southeast have low forested hills. Bangladesh is one of the world's most densely populated and least developed countries. The economy is based on agriculture, though the garment industry is the main export sector. Storms during the summer monsoon season often cause devastating flooding and crop destruction. The country relies on large-scale foreign aid and remittances from workers abroad.

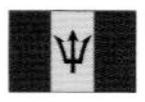

BARBADOS

Area Sq Km	430	**Languages**	English, Creole
Area Sq Miles	166	**Religions**	Protestant, Roman Catholic
Population	285 000	**Currency**	Barbadian dollar
Capital	Bridgetown	**Organizations**	CARICOM, Comm., UN

Map page 223

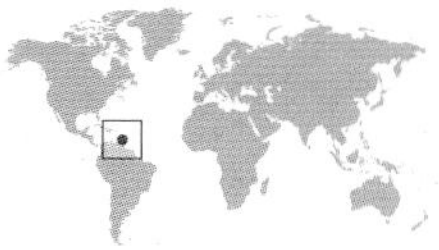

The most easterly of the Caribbean islands, Barbados is small and densely populated. It has a tropical climate and is subject to hurricanes. The economy is based on tourism, financial services, light industries and sugar production.

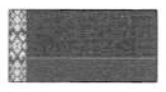

BELARUS
Republic of Belarus

Area Sq Km	207 600	**Languages**	Belarusian, Russian
Area Sq Miles	80 155	**Religions**	Belarusian Orthodox, Roman Catholic
Population	9 357 000	**Currency**	Belarusian rouble
Capital	Minsk	**Organizations**	CIS, UN

Map page 177

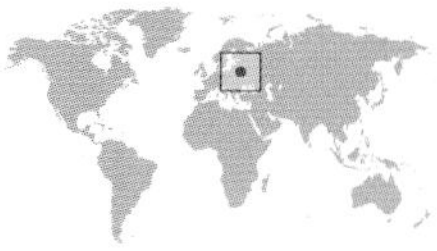

Belarus, a landlocked state in eastern Europe, consists of low hills and plains, with many lakes, rivers and, in the south, extensive marshes. Forests cover approximately one-third of the country. It has a continental climate. Agriculture contributes one-third of national income, with beef cattle and grains as the major products. Manufacturing industries produce a range of items, from construction equipment to textiles. Russia and Ukraine are the main trading partners.

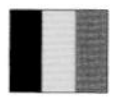

BELGIUM
Kingdom of Belgium

Area Sq Km	30 520	**Languages**	Dutch (Flemish), French (Walloon), German
Area Sq Miles	11 784	**Religions**	Roman Catholic, Protestant
Population	11 104 000	**Currency**	Euro
Capital	Brussels (Brussel/Bruxelles)	**Organizations**	EU, NATO, OECD, UN

Map page 178

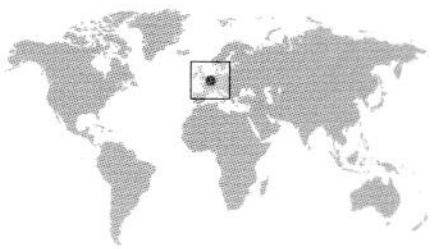

Belgium lies on the North Sea coast of western Europe. Beyond low sand dunes and a narrow belt of reclaimed land, fertile plains extend to the Sambre-Meuse river valley. The land rises to the forested Ardennes plateau in the southeast. Belgium has mild winters and cool summers. It is densely populated and has a highly urbanized population. With few mineral resources, Belgium imports raw materials for processing and manufacture. The agricultural sector is small, but provides for most food needs. A large services sector reflects Belgium's position as the home base for over eight hundred international institutions. The headquarters of the European Union are in the capital, Brussels.

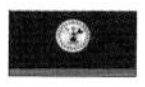

BELIZE

Area Sq Km	22 965	**Languages**	English, Spanish, Mayan, Creole
Area Sq Miles	8 867	**Religions**	Roman Catholic, Protestant
Population	332 000	**Currency**	Belizean dollar
Capital	Belmopan	**Organizations**	CARICOM, Comm., UN

Map page 225

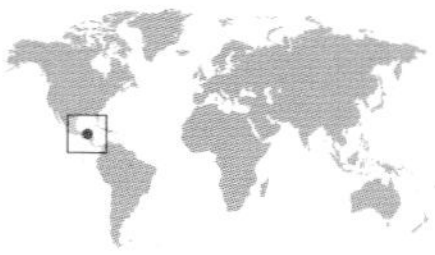

Belize lies on the Caribbean coast of central America and includes numerous cays and a large barrier reef offshore. The coastal areas are flat and swampy. To the southwest are the Maya Mountains. Tropical jungle covers much of the country and the climate is humid tropical, but tempered by sea breezes. A fifth of the population lives in the former capital Belize City. The economy is based primarily on agriculture, forestry and fishing, and exports include raw sugar, orange concentrate and bananas.

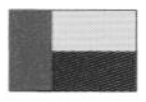

BENIN
Republic of Benin

Area Sq Km	112 620	**Languages**	French, Fon, Yoruba, Adja, other local languages
Area Sq Miles	43 483	**Religions**	Traditional beliefs, Roman Catholic, Sunni Muslim
Population	10 323 000	**Currency**	CFA franc
Capital	Porto-Novo	**Organizations**	UN

Map page 192

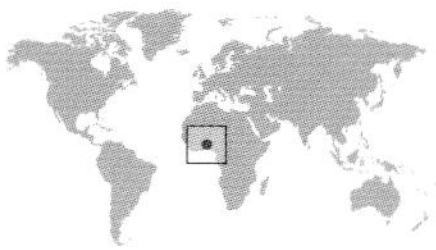

Benin is in west Africa, on the Gulf of Guinea. The climate is tropical in the north, equatorial in the south. The economy is based mainly on agriculture and transit trade. Agricultural products account for two-thirds of export earnings. Oil, produced offshore, is also a major export.

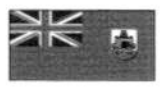

Bermuda
United Kingdom Overseas Territory

Area Sq Km	54	**Languages**	English
Area Sq Miles	21	**Religions**	Protestant, Roman Catholic
Population	65 000	**Currency**	Bermuda dollar
Capital	Hamilton		

Map page 223 In the Atlantic Ocean to the east of the USA, Bermuda comprises a group of small islands with a warm and humid climate. The economy is based on international business and tourism.

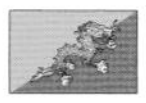

BHUTAN
Kingdom of Bhutan

Area Sq Km	46 620	**Languages**	Dzongkha, Nepali, Assamese
Area Sq Miles	18 000	**Religions**	Buddhist, Hindu
Population	754 000	**Currency**	Ngultrum, Indian rupee
Capital	Thimphu	**Organizations**	UN

Map page 149

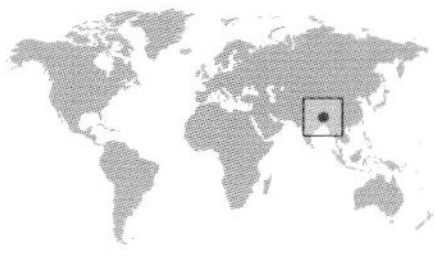

Bhutan lies in the eastern Himalaya mountains, between China and India. It is mountainous in the north, with fertile valleys. The climate ranges between permanently cold in the far north and subtropical in the south. Most of the population is involved in livestock rearing and subsistence farming. Bhutan is a producer of cardamom. Tourism is an increasingly important foreign currency earner, and hydroelectric power is also sold to India from the Tala site in the south-west.

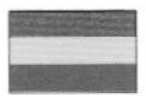

BOLIVIA
Plurinational State of Bolivia

Area Sq Km	1 098 581	**Languages**	Spanish, Quechua, Aymara
Area Sq Miles	424 164	**Religions**	Roman Catholic, Protestant, Baha'i
Population	10 671 000	**Currency**	Boliviano
Capital	La Paz/Sucre	**Organizations**	UN

Map page 230

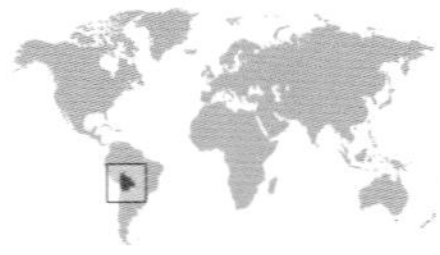

Bolivia is a landlocked state in central South America. Most Bolivians live on the high plateau within the Andes mountains. The lowlands range between dense rainforest in the northeast and semi-arid grasslands in the southeast. Bolivia is rich in minerals (zinc, tin and gold), and sales generate approximately half of export income. Natural gas, timber and soya beans are also exported. The USA is the main trading partner.

BOSNIA AND HERZEGOVINA

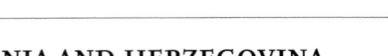

Area Sq Km	51 130	**Languages**	Bosnian, Serbian, Croatian
Area Sq Miles	19 741	**Religions**	Sunni Muslim, Serbian Orthodox, Roman Catholic, Protestant
Population	3 829 000	**Currency**	Convertible mark
Capital	Sarajevo	**Organizations**	UN

Map page 185

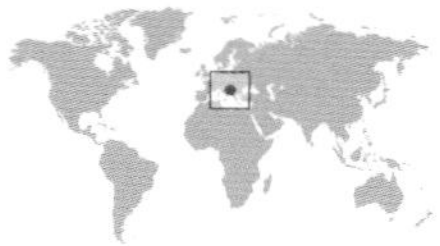

Bosnia and Herzegovina lies in the western Balkan Mountains of southern Europe, on the Adriatic Sea. It is mountainous, with ridges running northwest-southeast. The main lowlands are around the Sava valley in the north. Summers are warm, but winters can be very cold. The economy relies heavily on overseas aid.

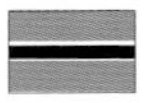

BOTSWANA
Republic of Botswana

Area Sq Km	581 370	**Languages**	English, Setswana, Shona, other local languages
Area Sq Miles	224 468	**Religions**	Traditional beliefs, Protestant, Roman Catholic
Population	2 021 000	**Currency**	Pula
Capital	Gaborone	**Organizations**	Comm., SADC, UN

Map page 195

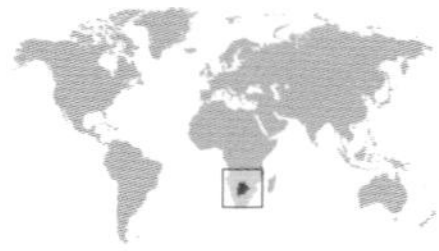

Botswana is a landlocked state in southern Africa. Over half of the country lies within the Kalahari Desert, with swamps to the north and salt-pans to the northeast. Most of the population lives near the eastern border. The climate is subtropical, but drought-prone. The economy was founded on cattle rearing, and although beef remains an important export, the economy is now based on mining. Diamonds account for seventy per cent of export earnings. Copper-nickel matte is also exported. The main trading partners are the UK and South Africa.

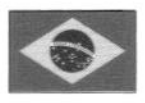

BRAZIL
Federative Republic of Brazil

Area Sq Km	8 514 879	**Languages**	Portuguese
Area Sq Miles	3 287 613	**Religions**	Roman Catholic, Protestant
Population	200 362 000	**Currency**	Real
Capital	Brasília	**Organizations**	UN

Map page 230–231

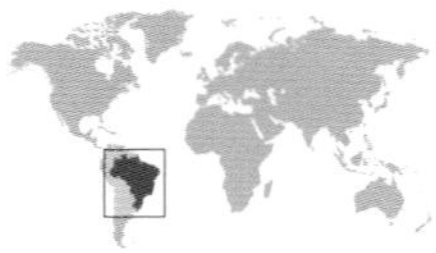

Brazil, in eastern South America, covers almost half of the continent, and is the world's fifth largest country. The northwest contains the vast basin of the Amazon, while the centre-west is largely a vast plateau of savanna and rock escarpments. The northeast is mostly semi-arid plateaus, while to the east and south are rugged mountains, fertile valleys and narrow, fertile coastal plains. The Amazon basin is hot, humid and wet; the rest of the country is cooler and drier, with seasonal variations. The northeast is drought-prone. Most Brazilians live in urban areas along the coast and on the central plateau. Brazil has well-developed agricultural, mining and service sectors, and the economy is larger than that of all other South American countries combined. Brazil is the world's biggest producer of coffee, and other agricultural crops include grains and sugar cane. Mineral production includes iron, aluminium and gold. Manufactured goods include food products, transport equipment, machinery and industrial chemicals. The main trading partners are the USA and Argentina. Economic reforms in Brazil have turned it into one of the fastest growing economies.

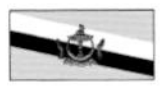

BRUNEI
Brunei Darussalam

Area Sq Km	5 765	**Languages**	Malay, English, Chinese
Area Sq Miles	2 226	**Religions**	Sunni Muslim, Buddhist, Christian
Population	418 000	**Currency**	Bruneian dollar
Capital	Bandar Seri Begawan	**Organizations**	APEC, ASEAN, Comm., UN

Map page 163

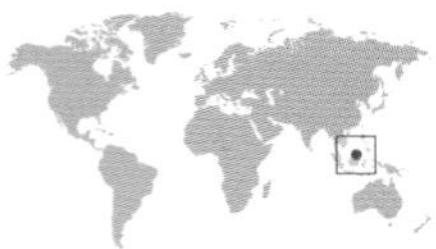

The southeast Asian oil-rich state of Brunei lies on the northwest coast of the island of Borneo, on the South China Sea. Its two enclaves are surrounded by the Malaysian state of Sarawak. Tropical rainforest covers over two-thirds of the country. The economy is dominated by the oil and gas industries.

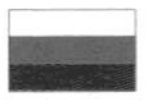

BULGARIA
Republic of Bulgaria

Area Sq Km	110 994	**Languages**	Bulgarian, Turkish, Romany, Macedonian
Area Sq Miles	42 855	**Religions**	Bulgarian Orthodox, Sunni Muslim
Population	7 223 000	**Currency**	Lev
Capital	Sofia	**Organizations**	EU, NATO, UN

Map page 185

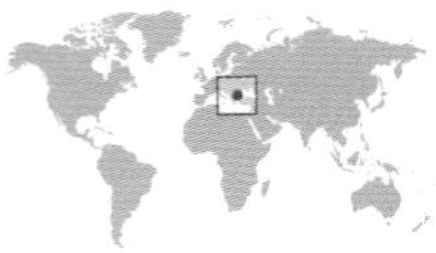

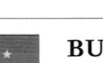

Bulgaria, in southern Europe, borders the western shore of the Black Sea. The Balkan Mountains separate the Danube plains in the north from the Rhodope Mountains and the lowlands in the south. The economy has a strong agricultural base. Manufacturing industries include machinery, consumer goods, chemicals and metals. Most trade is with Russia, Italy and Germany.

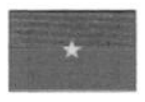

BURKINA FASO

Area Sq Km	274 200	**Languages**	French, Moore (Mossi), Fulani, other local languages
Area Sq Miles	105 869	**Religions**	Sunni Muslim, traditional beliefs, Roman Catholic
Population	16 935 000	**Currency**	CFA franc
Capital	Ouagadougou	**Organizations**	UN

Map page 192

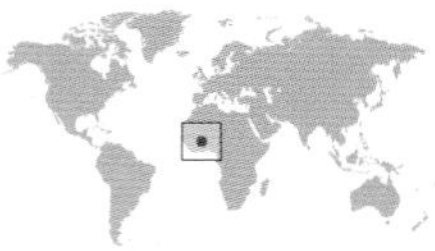

Burkina Faso, a landlocked country in west Africa, lies within the Sahara desert to the north and semi-arid savanna to the south. Rainfall is erratic, and droughts are common. Livestock rearing and farming are the main activities, and cotton, livestock, groundnuts and some minerals are exported. Burkina Faso relies heavily on foreign aid, and is one of the poorest and least developed countries in the world.

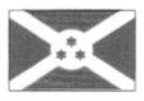

BURUNDI
Republic of Burundi

Area Sq Km	27 835	**Languages**	Kirundi (Hutu, Tutsi), French
Area Sq Miles	10 747	**Religions**	Roman Catholic, traditional beliefs, Protestant
Population	10 163 000	**Currency**	Burundian franc
Capital	Bujumbura	**Organizations**	UN

Map page 194

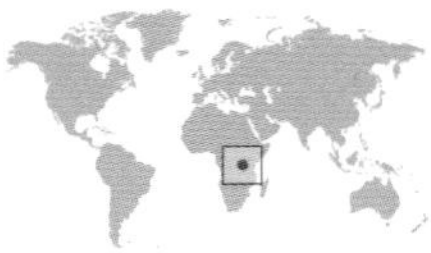

The densely populated east African state of Burundi consists of high plateaus rising from the shores of Lake Tanganyika in the southwest. It has a tropical climate and depends on subsistence farming. Coffee is its main export, and its main trading partners are Germany and Belgium. The country has been badly affected by internal conflict since the early 1990s.

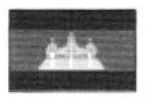

CAMBODIA
Kingdom of Cambodia

Area Sq Km	181 000	**Languages**	Khmer
Area Sq Miles	69 884	**Religions**	Buddhist, Roman Catholic, Sunni Muslim
Population	15 135 000	**Currency**	Riel
Capital	Phnom Penh	**Organizations**	ASEAN, UN

Map page 162

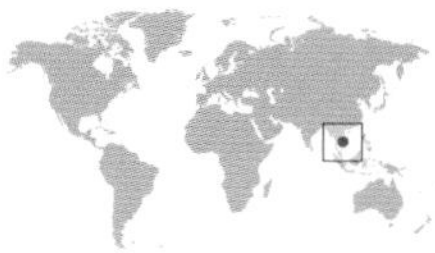

Cambodia lies in southeast Asia on the Gulf of Thailand, and occupies the Mekong river basin, with the Tônlé Sap (Great Lake) at its centre. The climate is tropical monsoon. Forests cover half the country. Most of the population lives on the plains and is engaged in farming (chiefly rice growing), fishing and forestry. The economy is recovering following the devastation of civil war in the 1970s, with rapid progress since 2000. Mineral resources are starting to be identified for development.

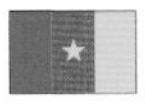

CAMEROON
Republic of Cameroon

Area Sq Km	475 442	**Languages**	French, English, Fang, Bamileke, other local languages
Area Sq Miles	183 569	**Religions**	Roman Catholic, traditional beliefs, Sunni Muslim, Protestant
Population	22 254 000	**Currency**	CFA franc
Capital	Yaoundé	**Organizations**	Comm., UN

Map page 193

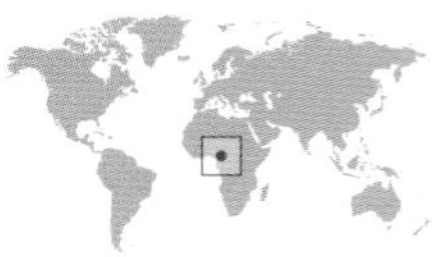

Cameroon is in west Africa, on the Gulf of Guinea. The coastal plains and southern and central plateaus are covered with tropical forest. Despite oil resources and favourable agricultural conditions Cameroon still faces problems of underdevelopment. Oil, timber and cocoa are the main exports. France is the main trading partner.

CANADA

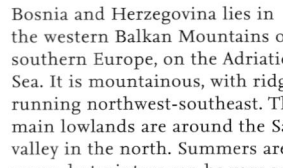

Area Sq Km	9 984 670	**Languages**	English, French
Area Sq Miles	3 855 103	**Religions**	Roman Catholic, Protestant, Eastern Orthodox, Jewish
Population	35 182 000	**Currency**	Canadian dollar
Capital	Ottawa	**Organizations**	APEC, Comm., NATO, OECD, UN

Map page 202–203

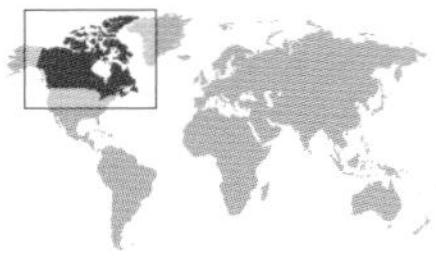

The world's second largest country, Canada covers the northern two-fifths of North America and has coastlines on the Atlantic, Arctic and Pacific Oceans. In the west are the Coast Mountains, the Rocky Mountains and interior plateaus. In the centre lie the fertile Prairies. Further east, covering about half the total land area, is the Canadian Shield, a relatively flat area of infertile lowlands around Hudson Bay, extending to Labrador on the east coast. The Shield is bordered to the south by the fertile Great Lakes-St Lawrence lowlands. In the far north climatic conditions are polar, while the rest has a continental climate. Most Canadians live in the urban areas of the Great Lakes-St Lawrence basin. Canada is rich in mineral and energy resources. Only five per cent of land is arable. Canada is among the world's leading producers of wheat, of wood from its vast coniferous forests, and of fish and seafood from its Atlantic and Pacific fishing grounds. It is a major producer of nickel, uranium, copper, iron ore, zinc and other minerals, as well as oil and natural gas. Its abundant raw materials are the basis for many manufacturing industries. Main exports are machinery, motor vehicles, oil, timber, newsprint and paper, wood pulp and wheat. Since the 1989 free trade agreement with the USA and the 1994 North America Free Trade Agreement, trade with the USA has grown and now accounts for around fifty per cent of imports and around seventy-five per cent of exports.

Alberta (Province)
Area Sq Km (Sq Miles) 661 848 (255 541) **Population** 3 965 339 **Capital** Edmonton

British Columbia (Province)
Area Sq Km (Sq Miles) 944 735 (364 764) **Population** 4 650 004 **Capital** Victoria

Manitoba (Province)
Area Sq Km (Sq Miles) 647 797 (250 116) **Population** 1 277 339 **Capital** Winnipeg

New Brunswick (Province)
Area Sq Km (Sq Miles) 72 908 (28 150) **Population** 754 039 **Capital** Fredericton

Newfoundland and Labrador (Province)
Area Sq Km (Sq Miles) 405 212 (156 453) **Population** 513 568 **Capital** St John's

Northwest Territories (Territory)
Area Sq Km (Sq Miles) 1 346 106 (519 734) **Population** 43 349 **Capital** Yellowknife

Nova Scotia (Province)
Area Sq Km (Sq Miles) 55 284 (21 345) **Population** 945 015 **Capital** Halifax

Nunavut (Territory)
Area Sq Km (Sq Miles) 2 093 190 (808 185) **Population** 34 023 **Capital** Iqaluit

Ontario (Province)
Area Sq Km (Sq Miles) 1 076 395 (415 598) **Population** 13 583 710 **Capital** Toronto

Prince Edward Island (Province)
Area Sq Km (Sq Miles) 5 660 (2 185) **Population** 145 763 **Capital** Charlottetown

Québec (Province)
Area Sq Km (Sq Miles) 1 542 056 (595 391) **Population** 8 099 095 **Capital** Québec

Saskatchewan (Province)
Area Sq Km (Sq Miles) 651 036 (251 366) **Population** 1 093 880 **Capital** Regina

Yukon (Territory)
Area Sq Km (Sq Miles) 482 443 (186 272) **Population** 36 418 **Capital** Whitehorse

CAPE VERDE (Cabo Verde)
Republic of Cabo Verde

Area Sq Km	4 033	**Languages**	Portuguese, Creole
Area Sq Miles	1 557	**Religions**	Roman Catholic, Protestant
Population	499 000	**Currency**	Cape Verdean escudo
Capital	Praia	**Organizations**	UN

Map page 192

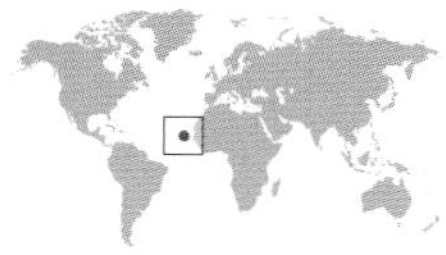

Cape Verde is a group of semi-arid volcanic islands lying off the coast of west Africa. The economy is based on fishing, subsistence farming and service industries. Windfarms on four islands supply around a quarter of all electricity.

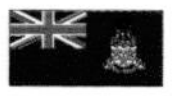

Cayman Islands
United Kingdom Overseas Territory

Area Sq Km	259	**Languages**	English
Area Sq Miles	100	**Religions**	Protestant, Roman Catholic
Population	58 000	**Currency**	Cayman Islands dollar
Capital	George Town		

Map page 223 A group of islands in the Caribbean, northwest of Jamaica. There are three main islands: Grand Cayman, Little Cayman and Cayman Brac. The Cayman Islands are one of the world's major offshore financial centres. Tourism is also important to the economy.

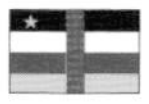

CENTRAL AFRICAN REPUBLIC

Area Sq Km	622 436	**Languages**	French, Sango, Banda, Baya, other local languages
Area Sq Miles	240 324	**Religions**	Protestant, Roman Catholic, traditional beliefs, Sunni Muslim
Population	4 616 000	**Currency**	CFA franc
Capital	Bangui	**Organizations**	UN

Map page 193

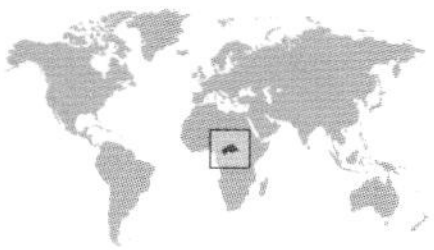

A landlocked country in central Africa, the Central African Republic is mainly savanna plateau, drained by the Ubangi and Chari river systems, with mountains to the east and west. The climate is tropical, with high rainfall. Most of the population lives in the south and west, and a majority of the workforce is involved in subsistence farming. Some cotton, coffee, tobacco and timber are exported, but diamonds account for around half of export earnings.

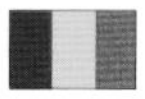

CHAD
Republic of Chad

Area Sq Km	1 284 000	**Languages**	Arabic, French, Sara, other local languages
Area Sq Miles	495 755	**Religions**	Sunni Muslim, Roman Catholic, Protestant, traditional beliefs
Population	12 825 000	**Currency**	CFA franc
Capital	Ndjamena	**Organizations**	UN

Map page 193

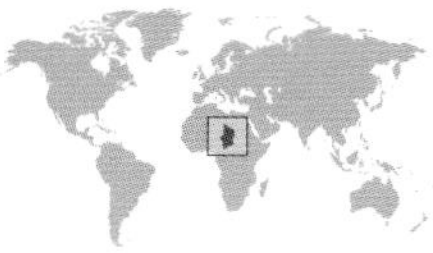

Chad is a landlocked state of north-central Africa. It consists of plateaus, the Tibesti mountains in the north and the Lake Chad basin in the west. Climatic conditions range between desert in the north and tropical forest in the southwest. With few natural resources, Chad relies on subsistence farming, exports of raw cotton, and foreign aid. The main trading partners are France, Portugal and Cameroon.

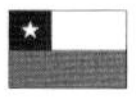

CHILE
Republic of Chile

Area Sq Km	756 945	**Languages**	Spanish, Amerindian languages
Area Sq Miles	292 258	**Religions**	Roman Catholic, Protestant
Population	17 620 000	**Currency**	Chilean peso
Capital	Santiago	**Organizations**	APEC, OECD, UN

Map page 232

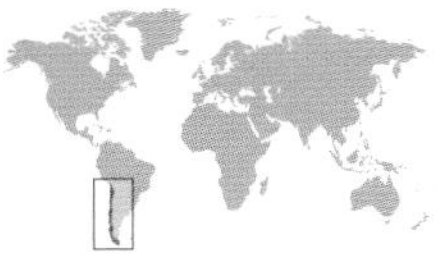

Chile lies along the Pacific coast of the southern half of South America. Between the Andes in the east and the lower coastal ranges is a central valley, with a mild climate, where most Chileans live. To the north is the arid Atacama Desert and to the south is cold, wet forested grassland. Chile has considerable mineral resources and is the world's leading exporter of copper. Nitrates, molybdenum, gold and iron ore are also mined. Agriculture (particularly viticulture), forestry and fishing are also important to the economy.

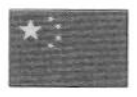

CHINA
People's Republic of China

Area Sq Km	9 606 802	**Languages**	Mandarin (Putonghua), Wu, Cantonese, Hsiang, regional languages
Area Sq Miles	3 709 186	**Religions**	Confucian, Taoist, Buddhist, Christian, Sunni Muslim
Population	1 369 993 000	**Currency**	Yuan, Hong Kong dollar, Macao pataca
Capital	Beijing (Peking)	**Organizations**	APEC, UN

Map page 150

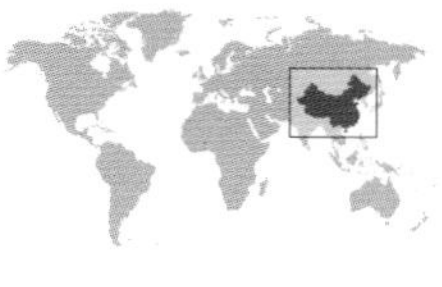

China, the world's most populous and fourth largest country, occupies a large part of east Asia, borders fourteen states and has coastlines on the Yellow, East China and South China Seas. It has a huge variety of landscapes. The southwest contains the high Plateau of Tibet, flanked by the Himalaya and Kunlun Shan mountains. The north is mountainous with arid basins and extends from the Tien Shan and Altai Mountains and the vast Taklimakan Desert in the west to the plateau and Gobi Desert in the centre-east. Eastern China is predominantly lowland and is divided broadly into the basins of the Yellow River (Huang He) in the north, the Yangtze (Chang Jiang) in the centre and the Pearl River (Xi Jiang) in the southeast. Climatic conditions and vegetation are as diverse as the topography: much of the country experiences temperate conditions, while the southwest has an extreme mountain climate and the southeast enjoys a moist, warm subtropical climate. Just under fifty per cent of China's huge population lives in rural areas, and agriculture employs around thirty-five per cent of the working population. The main crops are rice, wheat, soya beans, peanuts, cotton, tobacco and hemp. China is rich in coal, oil and natural gas and has the world's largest potential in hydroelectric power. It is a major world producer of iron ore, molybdenum, copper, asbestos and gold. Economic reforms from the early 1980's led to an explosion in manufacturing development concentrated on the 'coastal economic open region'. The main exports are machinery, textiles, footwear, toys and sports goods. Japan and the USA are China's main trading partners.

Anhui (Province)
Area Sq Km (Sq Miles) 139 000 (53 900) **Population** 59 680 000 **Capital** Hefei

Beijing (Municipality)
Area Sq Km (Sq Miles) 16 411 (6 336) **Population** 20 186 000 **Capital** Beijing (Peking)

Chongqing (Municipality)
Area Sq Km (Sq Miles) 82 400 (31 815) **Population** 29 190 000 **Capital** Chongqing

Fujian (Province)
Area Sq Km (Sq Miles) 124 000 (47 876) **Population** 37 200 000 **Capital** Fuzhou

Gansu (Province)
Area Sq Km (Sq Miles) 425 800 (164 401) **Population** 25 642 000 **Capital** Lanzhou

Guangdong (Province)
Area Sq Km (Sq Miles) 179 800 (69 421) **Population** 105 048 000 **Capital** Guangzhou (Canton)

Guangxi Zhuangzu Zizhiqu (Autonomous Region)
Area Sq Km (Sq Miles) 237 600 (91 737) **Population** 46 450 000 **Capital** Nanning

Guizhou (Province)
Area Sq Km (Sq Miles) 176 000 (67 954) **Population** 34 687 000 **Capital** Guiyang

Hainan (Province)
Area Sq Km (Sq Miles) 35 000 (13 514) **Population** 8 773 000 **Capital** Haikou

Hebei (Province)
Area Sq Km (Sq Miles) 188 000 (72 587) **Population** 72 405 000 **Capital** Shijiazhuang

Heilongjiang (Province)
Area Sq Km (Sq Miles) 473 000 (182 625) **Population** 38 340 000 **Capital** Harbin

Henan (Province)
Area Sq Km (Sq Miles) 167 000 (64 479) **Population** 93 880 000 **Capital** Zhengzhou

Hong Kong (Xianggang) (Special Administrative Region)
Area Sq Km (Sq Miles) 1 104 (426) **Population** 7 112 000 **Capital** Hong Kong (Xianggang)

Hubei (Province)
Area Sq Km (Sq Miles) 185 900 (71 776) **Population** 57 575 000 **Capital** Wuhan

Hunan (Province)
Area Sq Km (Sq Miles) 211 800 (81 776) **Population** 65 956 000 **Capital** Changsha

Jiangsu (Province)
Area Sq Km (Sq Miles) 102 600 (39 614) **Population** 78 988 000 **Capital** Nanjing

Jiangxi (Province)
Area Sq Km (Sq Miles) 166 900 (64 440) **Population** 44 884 000 **Capital** Nanchang

Jilin (Province)
Area Sq Km (Sq Miles) 187 400 (72 355) **Population** 27 494 000 **Capital** Changchun

Liaoning (Province)
Area Sq Km (Sq Miles) 148 000 (57 143) **Population** 43 830 000 **Capital** Shenyang

Macao (Special Administrative Region)
Area Sq Km (Sq Miles) 30 (12) **Population** 557 000 **Capital** Macao

Nei Mongol Zizhiqu Inner Mongolia **(Autonomous Region)**
Area Sq Km (Sq Miles) 1 183 000 (456 756) **Population** 24 817 000 **Capital** Hohhot

Ningxia Huizu Zizhiqu (Autonomous Region)
Area Sq Km (Sq Miles) 66 400 (25 637) **Population** 6 395 000 **Capital** Yinchuan

Qinghai (Province)
Area Sq Km (Sq Miles) 722 300 (278 880) **Population** 5 682 000 **Capital** Xining

Shaanxi (Province)
Area Sq Km (Sq Miles) 205 800 (79 459) **Population** 37 426 000 **Capital** Xi'an

Shandong (Province)
Area Sq Km (Sq Miles) 157 100 (60 656) **Population** 96 370 000 **Capital** Jinan

Shanghai (Municipality)
Area Sq Km (Sq Miles) 6 340 (2 448) **Population** 23 475 000 **Capital** Shanghai

Shanxi (Province)
Area Sq Km (Sq Miles) 156 700 (60 502) **Population** 35 930 000 **Capital** Taiyuan

Sichuan (Province)
Area Sq Km (Sq Miles) 486 000 (187 645) **Population** 80 500 000 **Capital** Chengdu

Tianjin (Municipality)
Area Sq Km (Sq Miles) 11 917 (4 601) **Population** 13 550 000 **Capital** Tianjin

Xinjiang Uygur Zizhiqu Sinkiang **(Autonomous Region)**
Area Sq Km (Sq Miles) 1 664 900 (642 818) **Population** 22 087 000 **Capital** Ürümqi

Xizang Zizhiqu Tibet **(Autonomous Region)**
Area Sq Km (Sq Miles) 1 202 200 (464 169) **Population** 3 033 000 **Capital** Lhasa

Yunnan (Province)
Area Sq Km (Sq Miles) 394 000 (152 123) **Population** 46 308 000 **Capital** Kunming

Zhejiang (Province)
Area Sq Km (Sq Miles) 101 800 (39 305) **Population** 54 630 000 **Capital** Hangzhou

Taiwan: The People's Republic of China claims Taiwan as its 23rd Province

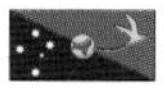

Christmas Island
Australian External Territory

Area Sq Km	135	**Languages**	English
Area Sq Miles	52	**Religions**	Buddhist, Sunni Muslim, Protestant, Roman Catholic
Population	2 072	**Currency**	Australian dollar
Capital	The Settlement (Flying Fish Cove)		

Map page 151 The island is situated in the east of the Indian Ocean, to the south of Indonesia. The economy was formerly based on phosphate extraction, although the mine is now closed. Tourism is developing and is a major employer.

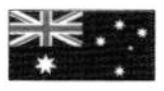

Cocos (Keeling) Islands
Australian External Territory

Area Sq Km	14	**Languages**	English
Area Sq Miles	5	**Religions**	Sunni Muslim, Christian
Population	550	**Currency**	Australian dollar
Capital	West Island		

Map page 151 The Cocos Islands consist of numerous islands on two coral atolls in the eastern Indian Ocean between Sri Lanka and Australia. Most of the population lives on West Island or Home Island. Coconuts are the only cash crop, and the main export.

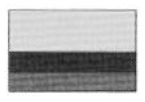

COLOMBIA
Republic of Colombia

Area Sq Km	1 141 748	**Languages**	Spanish, Amerindian languages
Area Sq Miles	440 831	**Religions**	Roman Catholic, Protestant
Population	48 321 000	**Currency**	Colombian peso
Capital	Bogotá	**Organizations**	UN

Map page 233

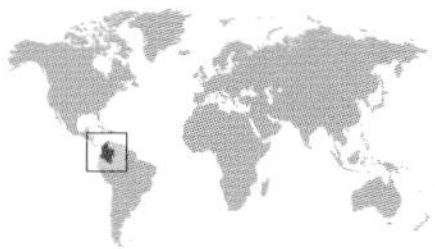

Colombia, in northwest South America, has coastlines on the Pacific and the Caribbean. Most Colombians live in high valleys and plateaus within the Andes. To the southeast are grasslands and the forests of the Amazon. The climate is tropical, varying with altitude. Only five per cent of land is cultivable. Colombia is the world's second largest producer of coffee and the largest producer of emeralds. Also important are sugar, bananas, cotton and flowers for export; and coal, nickel, gold, silver and platinum. Oil and its products are the main export. The main trade partner is the USA. Internal violence - both politically motivated and drugs-related - continues to hinder development.

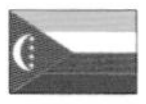

COMOROS
Union of the Comoros

Area Sq Km	1 862	**Languages**	Shikomor (Comorian), French, Arabic
Area Sq Miles	719	**Religions**	Sunni Muslim, Roman Catholic
Population	735 000	**Currency**	Comorian franc
Capital	Moroni	**Organizations**	UN

Map page 195

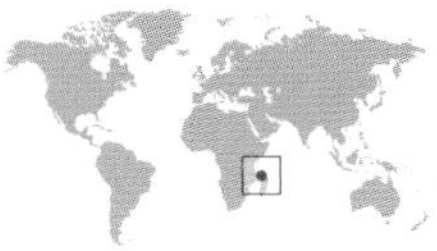

This state, in the Indian Ocean off the east African coast, comprises three volcanic islands of Ngazidja (Grande Comore), Nzwani (Anjouan) and Mwali (Mohéli), and some coral atolls. These tropical islands are mountainous, with poor soil and few natural resources. Subsistence farming predominates. Vanilla, cloves and ylang-ylang (an essential oil) are exported, and the economy relies heavily on workers' remittances from abroad.

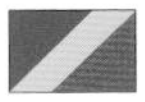

CONGO
Republic of the Congo

Area Sq Km	342 000	**Languages**	French, Kongo, Monokutuba, other local languages
Area Sq Miles	132 047	**Religions**	Roman Catholic, Protestant, traditional beliefs, Sunni Muslim
Population	4 448 000	**Currency**	CFA franc
Capital	Brazzaville	**Organizations**	UN

Map page 194–195

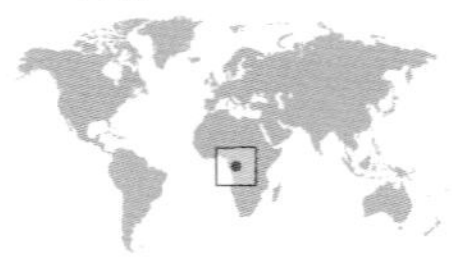

Congo, in central Africa, is mostly a forest or savanna-covered plateau drained by the Ubangi-Congo river systems. Sand dunes and lagoons line the short Atlantic coast. The climate is hot and tropical. Most Congolese live in the southern third of the country. Half of the workforce are farmers, growing food and cash crops including sugar, coffee, cocoa and oil palms. Oil and timber are the mainstays of the economy, and oil generates over fifty per cent of the country's export revenues.

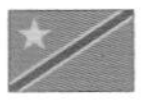

CONGO, DEMOCRATIC REPUBLIC OF THE

Area Sq Km	2 345 410	**Languages**	French, Lingala, Swahili, Kongo, other local languages
Area Sq Miles	905 568	**Religions**	Christian, Sunni Muslim
Population	67 514 000	**Currency**	Congolese franc
Capital	Kinshasa	**Organizations**	SADC, UN

Map page 194–195

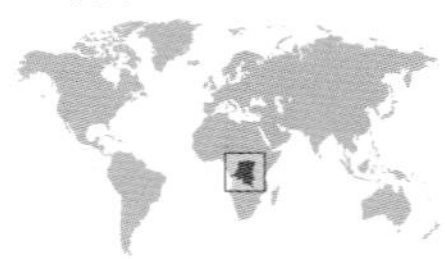

This central African state, formerly Zaire, consists of the basin of the Congo river flanked by plateaus, with high mountain ranges to the east and a short Atlantic coastline to the west. The climate is tropical, with rainforest close to the Equator and savanna to the north and south. Fertile land allows a range of food and cash crops to be grown, chiefly coffee. The country has vast mineral resources, with copper, cobalt and diamonds being the most important.

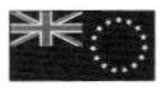

Cook Islands
Self-governing New Zealand Overseas Territory

Area Sq Km	293	**Languages**	English, Maori
Area Sq Miles	113	**Religions**	Protestant, Roman Catholic
Population	21 000	**Currency**	New Zealand dollar
Capital	Avarua		

Map page 117 These consist of groups of coral atolls and volcanic islands in the southwest Pacific Ocean. The main island is Rarotonga. Distance from foreign markets and restricted natural resources hinder development.

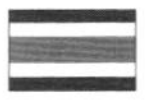

COSTA RICA
Republic of Costa Rica

Area Sq Km	51 100	**Languages**	Spanish
Area Sq Miles	19 730	**Religions**	Roman Catholic, Protestant
Population	4 872 000	**Currency**	Costa Rican colón
Capital	San José	**Organizations**	UN

Map page 224

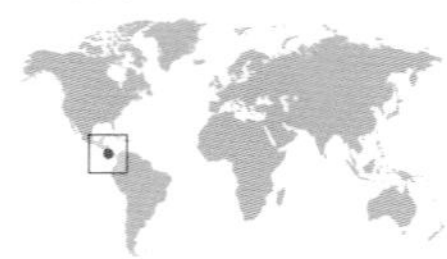

Costa Rica, in central America, has coastlines on the Caribbean Sea and Pacific Ocean. From tropical coastal plains, the land rises to mountains and a temperate central plateau, where most of the population lives. The economy depends on agriculture and tourism, with ecotourism becoming increasingly important. Main exports are textiles, coffee and bananas, and the USA is the main trading partner..

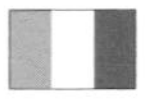

CÔTE D'IVOIRE (Ivory Coast)
Republic of Côte d'Ivoire

Area Sq Km	322 463	**Languages**	French, Creole, Akan, other local languages
Area Sq Miles	124 504	**Religions**	Sunni Muslim, Roman Catholic, traditional beliefs, Protestant
Population	20 316 000	**Currency**	CFA franc
Capital	Yamoussoukro	**Organizations**	UN

Map page 192

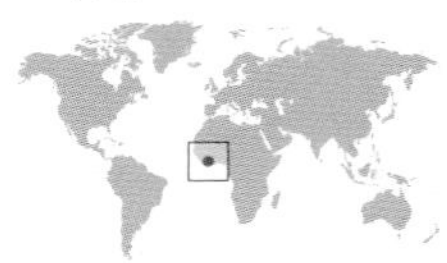

Côte d'Ivoire (Ivory Coast) is in west Africa, on the Gulf of Guinea. In the north are plateaus and savanna; in the south are low undulating plains and rainforest, with sand-bars and lagoons on the coast. Temperatures are warm, and rainfall is heavier in the south. Most of the workforce is engaged in farming. Côte d'Ivoire is a major producer of cocoa and coffee, and agricultural products (also including cotton and timber) are the main exports. Oil and gas have begun to be exploited.

Crimea
Disputed territory

Area Sq Km	27 000	**Languages**	Ukrainian, Russian
Area Sq Miles	10 400	**Religions**	Russian Orthodox, Sunni Muslim
Population	2 348 600	**Currency**	Russian Rouble
Capital	Simferopol'		

Map page 187 Following internal unrest in Ukraine in 2014, Russian-supported separatists in Crimea in southern Ukraine seized power in that region and a quickly arranged referendum resulted in the two administrative divisions in Crimea – the Autonomous Republic of Crimea (Respublika Krym) and the municipality of Sevastopol' – declaring independence from Ukraine as the Republic of Crimea. The referendum and its outcome were not recognized by the majority of the international community. Russia then passed a law in March 2014 annexing the Republic of Crimea, declaring it to be part of Russia – a move similarly not recognized, and strongly condemned by the majority of the international community. Ukrainian forces withdrew from Crimea soon after this annexation.

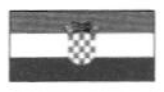

CROATIA
Republic of Croatia

Area Sq Km	56 538	**Languages**	Croatian, Serbian
Area Sq Miles	21 829	**Religions**	Roman Catholic, Serbian Orthodox, Sunni Muslim
Population	4 290 000	**Currency**	Kuna
Capital	Zagreb	**Organizations**	EU, NATO, UN

Map page 184

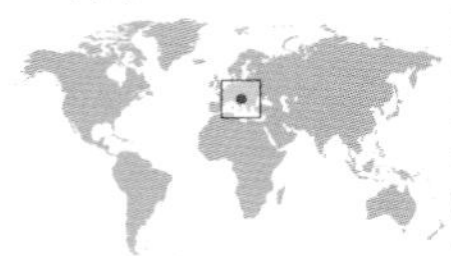

The southern European state of Croatia has a long coastline on the Adriatic Sea, with many offshore islands. Coastal areas have a Mediterranean climate; inland is cooler and wetter. Croatia was once strong agriculturally and industrially, but conflict in the early 1990s, and associated loss of markets and a fall in tourist revenue, caused economic difficulties from which recovery has been slow.

CUBA
Republic of Cuba

Area Sq Km	110 860	**Languages**	Spanish
Area Sq Miles	42 803	**Religions**	Roman Catholic, Protestant
Population	11 266 000	**Currency**	Cuban peso
Capital	Havana (La Habana)	**Organizations**	UN

Map page 223

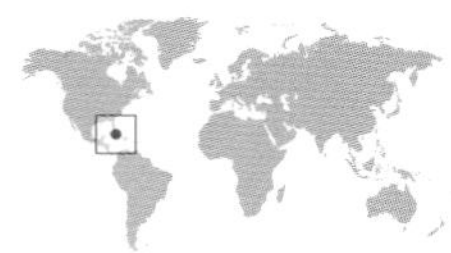

The country comprises the island of Cuba (the largest island in the Caribbean), and many islets and cays. A fifth of Cubans live in and around Havana. Cuba is slowly recovering from the withdrawal of aid and subsidies from the former USSR. Sugar remains the basis of the economy, although tourism is developing and is, together with remittances from workers abroad, an important source of revenue.

Curaçao
Self-governing Netherlands territory

Area Sq Km	444	**Languages**	Dutch, Papiamento
Area Sq Miles	171	**Religions**	Roman Catholic, Protestant
Population	159 000	**Currency**	Caribbean guilder
Capital	Willemstad		

Map page 233 Situated in the Caribbean Sea off the north coast of Venezuela, Curaçao was previously part of the Netherlands Antilles until they were dissolved in October 2010. It consists of the main island and the smaller uninhabited Kelin Curaçao and is the largest and most populous of the Lesser Antilles. Oil refining and tourism form the basis of the economy.

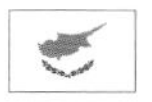

CYPRUS
Republic of Cyprus

Area Sq Km	9 251	**Languages**	Greek, Turkish, English
Area Sq Miles	3 572	**Religions**	Greek Orthodox, Sunni Muslim
Population	1 141 000	**Currency**	Euro
Capital	Nicosia (Lefkosia)	**Organizations**	Comm., EU, UN

Map page 138

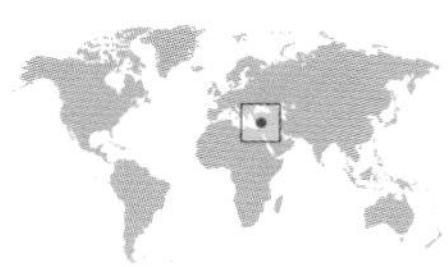

The eastern Mediterranean island of Cyprus has effectively been divided into two since 1974. The economy of the Greek-speaking south is based mainly on specialist agriculture and tourism, with shipping and offshore banking. The ethnically Turkish north depends on agriculture, tourism and aid from Turkey. The island has hot dry summers and mild winters. Cyprus joined the European Union in May 2004.

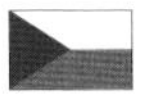

CZECH REPUBLIC

Area Sq Km	78 864	**Languages**	Czech, Moravian, Slovakian
Area Sq Miles	30 450	**Religions**	Roman Catholic, Protestant
Population	10 702 000	**Currency**	Koruna
Capital	Prague (Praha)	**Organizations**	EU, NATO, OECD, UN

Map page 176

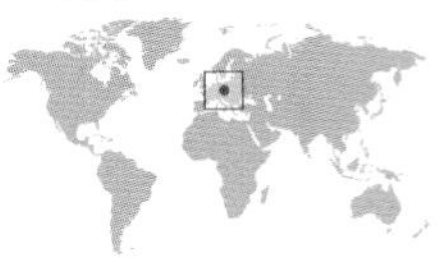

The landlocked Czech Republic in central Europe consists of rolling countryside, wooded hills and fertile valleys. The climate is continental. The country has substantial reserves of coal and lignite, timber and some minerals, chiefly iron ore. It is highly industrialized, and major manufactured goods include industrial machinery, consumer goods, cars, iron and steel, chemicals and glass. Germany is the main trading partner. The Czech Republic joined the European Union in May 2004.

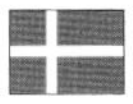

DENMARK
Kingdom of Denmark

Area Sq Km	43 075	**Languages**	Danish
Area Sq Miles	16 631	**Religions**	Protestant
Population	5 619 000	**Currency**	Danish krone
Capital	Copenhagen (København)	**Organizations**	EU, NATO, OECD, UN

Map page 171

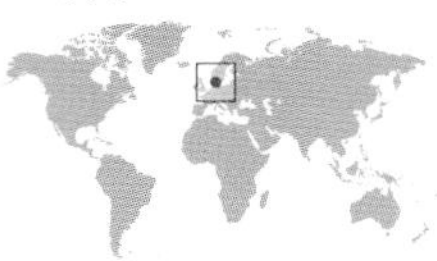

Denmark occupies the Jutland peninsula (Jylland) and nearly five hundred islands between the North and Baltic Seas in northern Europe. The country is low-lying. The climate is cool and temperate. A fifth of the population lives in and around the capital, Copenhagen (København), on the island of Zealand (Sjælland). Two-thirds of the area is fertile farmland, though agriculture only employs around six per cent of the workforce. Denmark is self-sufficient in oil and natural gas from the North Sea. Manufacturing, largely based on imported materials, accounts for over half of all exports, which include machinery, food, furniture, and pharmaceuticals. The main trading partners are Germany and Sweden.

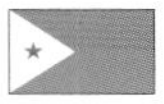

DJIBOUTI
Republic of Djibouti

Area Sq Km	23 200	**Languages**	Somali, Afar, French, Arabic
Area Sq Miles	8 958	**Religions**	Sunni Muslim, Christian
Population	873 000	**Currency**	Djiboutian franc
Capital	Djibouti	**Organizations**	UN

Map page 194

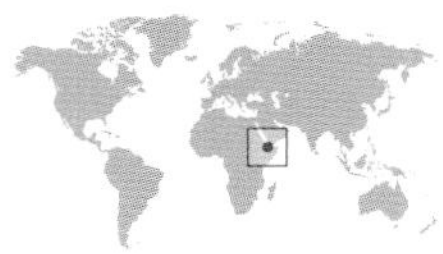

Djibouti lies in northeast Africa, on the Gulf of Aden at the entrance to the Red Sea. Most of the country is semi-arid desert with high temperatures and low rainfall. More than two-thirds of the population live in the capital. There is some camel, sheep and goat herding, but with few natural resources the economy is based on services and trade. Djibouti serves as a free trade zone for northern Africa, and the capital's port is a major transhipment and refuelling destination. It is linked by rail to Addis Ababa in Ethiopia.

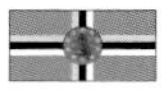

DOMINICA
Commonwealth of Dominica

Area Sq Km	750	**Languages**	English, Creole
Area Sq Miles	290	**Religions**	Roman Catholic, Protestant
Population	72 000	**Currency**	East Caribbean dollar
Capital	Roseau	**Organizations**	CARICOM, Comm., UN

Map page 223

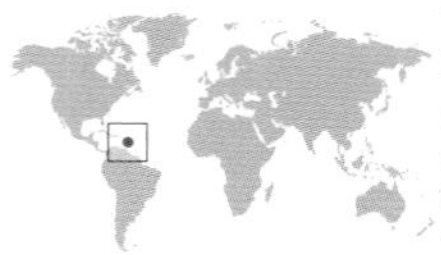

Dominica is the most northerly of the Windward Islands, in the eastern Caribbean. It is very mountainous and forested, with a coastline of steep cliffs. The climate is tropical and rainfall is abundant. Approximately a quarter of Dominicans live in the capital. The economy is based on agriculture, with bananas (the major export), coconuts and citrus fruits the most important crops. Tourism is a developing industry.

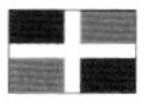

DOMINICAN REPUBLIC

Area Sq Km	48 442	**Languages**	Spanish, Creole
Area Sq Miles	18 704	**Religions**	Roman Catholic, Protestant
Population	10 404 000	**Currency**	Dominican peso
Capital	Santo Domingo	**Organizations**	UN

Map page 223

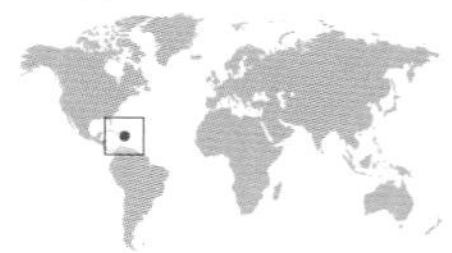

The state occupies the eastern two-thirds of the Caribbean island of Hispaniola (the western third is Haiti). It has a series of mountain ranges, fertile valleys and a large coastal plain in the east. The climate is hot tropical, with heavy rainfall. Sugar, coffee and cocoa are the

main cash crops. Nickel (the main export), and gold are mined, and there is some light industry. The USA is the main trading partner. Tourism is the main foreign exchange earner.

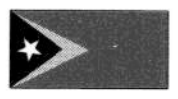

EAST TIMOR (Timor-Leste)

Democratic Republic of Timor-Leste

Area Sq Km	14 874	**Languages**	Portuguese, Tetun, English
Area Sq Miles	5 743	**Religions**	Roman Catholic
Population	1 133 000	**Currency**	United States dollar
Capital	Dili	**Organizations**	UN

Map page 151

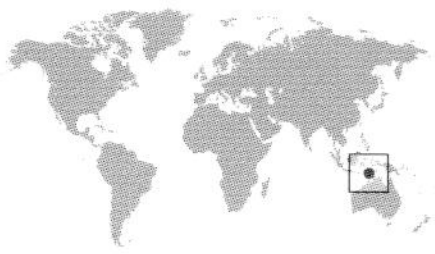

The island of Timor is part of the Indonesian archipelago, to the north of western Australia. East Timor occupies the eastern section of the island, and a small coastal enclave (Ocussi) to the west. A referendum in 1999 ended Indonesia's occupation, after which the country was under UN transitional administration until full independence was achieved in 2002. The economy is in a poor state and East Timor is heavily dependent on foreign aid.

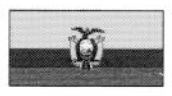

ECUADOR

Republic of Ecuador

Area Sq Km	272 045	**Languages**	Spanish, Quechua, and other Amerindian languages
Area Sq Miles	105 037	**Religions**	Roman Catholic
Population	15 738 000	**Currency**	United States dollar
Capital	Quito	**Organizations**	OPEC, UN

Map page 230

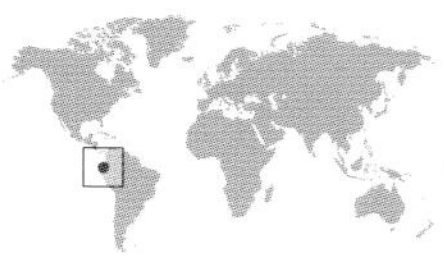

Ecuador is in northwest South America, on the Pacific coast. It consists of a broad coastal plain, high mountain ranges in the Andes, and part of the forested upper Amazon basin to the east. The climate is tropical, moderated by altitude. Most people live on the coast or in the mountain valleys. Ecuador is one of South America's main oil producers, and mineral reserves include gold. Most of the workforce depends on agriculture. Petroleum, bananas, shrimps, coffee and cocoa are exported. The USA is the main trading partner.

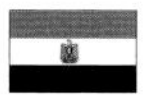

EGYPT

Arab Republic of Egypt

Area Sq Km	1 101 450	**Languages**	Arabic
Area Sq Miles	386 660	**Religions**	Sunni Muslim, Coptic Christian
Population	82 056 000	**Currency**	Egyptian pound
Capital	Cairo (Al Qāhirah)	**Organizations**	UN

Map page 193

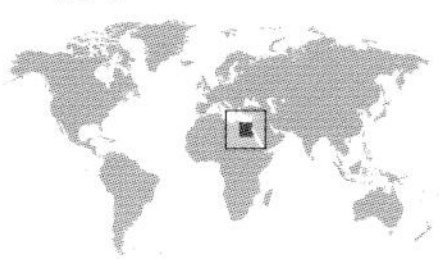

Egypt, on the eastern Mediterranean coast of north Africa, is low-lying, with areas below sea level in the Qattara depression. It is a land of desert and semi-desert except for the Nile valley, where ninety-nine per cent of Egyptians live. The Sinai peninsula in the northeast forms a land bridge between Africa and Asia. The summers are hot, the winters mild and rainfall is negligible. Less than four per cent of the land (chiefly around the Nile) is cultivated. Farming employs about one-third of the workforce; cotton is the main cash crop. Hydroelectric power is important. Main exports are oil and oil products, cotton, textiles and clothing..

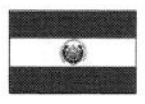

EL SALVADOR

Republic of El Salvador

Area Sq Km	21 041	**Languages**	Spanish
Area Sq Miles	8 124	**Religions**	Roman Catholic, Protestant
Population	6 340 000	**Currency**	United States dollar
Capital	San Salvador	**Organizations**	UN

Map page 225

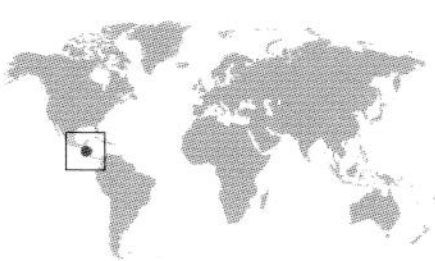

Located on the Pacific coast of central America, El Salvador consists of a coastal plain and volcanic mountain ranges which enclose a densely populated plateau area. The coast is hot, with heavy summer rainfall; the highlands are cooler. Coffee (the chief export), sugar and cotton are the main cash crops. The main trading partners are the USA and Guatemala.

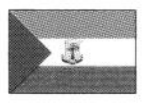

EQUATORIAL GUINEA

Republic of Equatorial Guinea

Area Sq Km	28 051	**Languages**	Spanish, French, Fang
Area Sq Miles	10 831	**Religions**	Roman Catholic, traditional beliefs
Population	757 000	**Currency**	CFA franc
Capital	Malabo	**Organizations**	UN

Map page 193

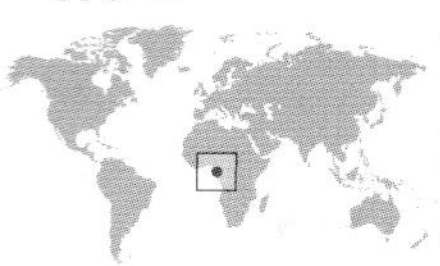

The state consists of Rio Muni, an enclave on the Atlantic coast of central Africa, and the islands of Bioco, Annobón and the Corisco group. Most of the population lives on the coastal plain and upland plateau of Rio Muni. The capital city, Malabo, is on the fertile volcanic island of Bioco. The climate is hot, humid and wet. Oil production started in 1992, and oil is now the main export, along with timber. The economy depends heavily on foreign aid.

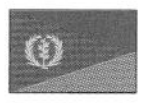

ERITREA

State of Eritrea

Area Sq Km	117 400	**Languages**	Tigrinya, Tigre
Area Sq Miles	45 328	**Religions**	Sunni Muslim, Coptic Christian
Population	6 333 000	**Currency**	Nakfa
Capital	Asmara	**Organizations**	UN

Map page 194

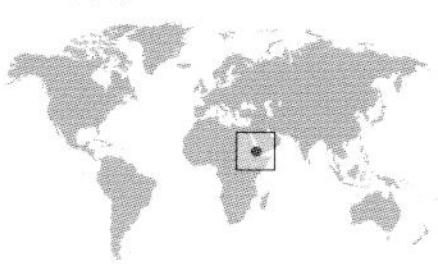

Eritrea, on the Red Sea coast of northeast Africa, consists of a high plateau in the north with a coastal plain which widens to the south. The coast is hot; inland is cooler. Rainfall is unreliable. The agriculture-based economy has suffered from over thirty years of war and occasional poor rains. Eritrea is one of the least developed countries in the world.

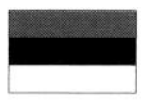

ESTONIA

Republic of Estonia

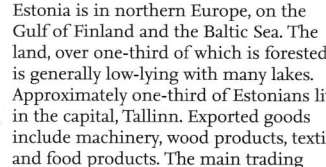

Area Sq Km	45 200	**Languages**	Estonian, Russian
Area Sq Miles	17 452	**Religions**	Protestant, Estonian and Russian Orthodox
Population	1 287 000	**Currency**	Euro
Capital	Tallinn	**Organizations**	EU, NATO, OECD, UN

Map page 171

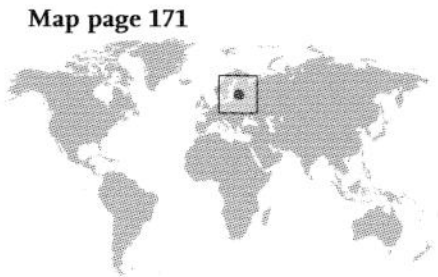

Estonia is in northern Europe, on the Gulf of Finland and the Baltic Sea. The land, over one-third of which is forested, is generally low-lying with many lakes. Approximately one-third of Estonians live in the capital, Tallinn. Exported goods include machinery, wood products, textiles and food products. The main trading partners are Russia, Finland and Sweden. Estonia joined the European Union in May 2004.

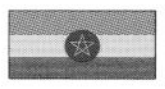

ETHIOPIA

Federal Democratic Republic of Ethiopia

Area Sq Km	1 133 880	**Languages**	Oromo, Amharic, Tigrinya, other local languages
Area Sq Miles	437 794	**Religions**	Ethiopian Orthodox, Sunni Muslim, traditional beliefs
Population	94 101 000	**Currency**	Birr
Capital	Addis Ababa (Ādīs Ābeba)	**Organizations**	UN

Map page 194

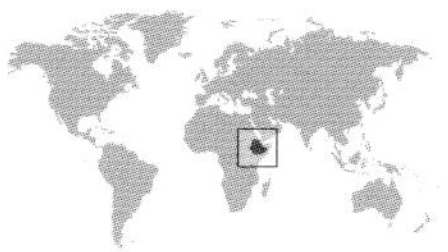

A landlocked country in northeast Africa, Ethiopia comprises a mountainous region in the west which is traversed by the Great Rift Valley. The east is mostly arid plateau land. The highlands are warm with summer rainfall. Most people live in the central–northern area. In recent years civil war, conflict with Eritrea and poor infrastructure have hampered economic development. Subsistence farming is the main activity, although droughts have led to frequent famines. Coffee is the main export and there is some light industry. Ethiopia is one of the least developed countries in the world.

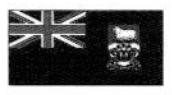

Falkland Islands (Islas Malvinas)

United Kingdom Overseas Territory

Area Sq Km	12 170	**Languages**	English
Area Sq Miles	4 699	**Religions**	Protestant, Roman Catholic
Population	2 931	**Currency**	Falkland Islands pound
Capital	Stanley		

Map page 232 Lying in the southwest Atlantic Ocean, northeast of Cape Horn, two main islands, West Falkland and East Falkland and many smaller islands, form the territory of the Falkland Islands. The economy is based on sheep farming and the sale of fishing licences.

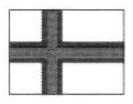

Faroe Islands

Self-governing Danish Territory

Area Sq Km	1 399	**Languages**	Faroese, Danish
Area Sq Miles	540	**Religions**	Protestant
Population	49 000	**Currency**	Danish krone
Capital	Thorshavn (Tórshavn)		

Map page 170 A self-governing territory, the Faroe Islands lie in the north Atlantic Ocean between the UK and Iceland. The islands benefit from the North Atlantic Drift ocean current, which has a moderating effect on the climate. The economy is based on deep-sea fishing.

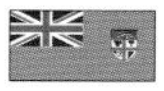

FIJI

Republic of Fiji

Area Sq Km	18 330	**Languages**	English, Fijian, Hindi
Area Sq Miles	7 077	**Religions**	Christian, Hindu, Sunni Muslim
Population	881 000	**Currency**	Fijian dollar
Capital	Suva	**Organizations**	Comm., UN

Map page 119

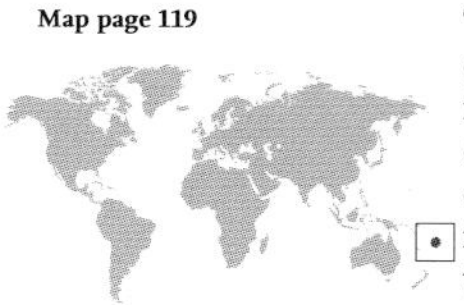

The southwest Pacific republic of Fiji comprises two mountainous and volcanic islands, Vanua Levu and Viti Levu, and over three hundred smaller islands. The climate is tropical and the economy is based on agriculture (chiefly sugar, the main export), fishing, forestry, gold mining and tourism.

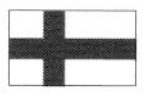

FINLAND

Republic of Finland

Area Sq Km	338 145	**Languages**	Finnish, Swedish, Sami languages
Area Sq Miles	130 559	**Religions**	Protestant, Greek Orthodox
Population	5 426 000	**Currency**	Euro
Capital	Helsinki (Helsingfors)	**Organizations**	EU, OECD, UN

Map page 170–171

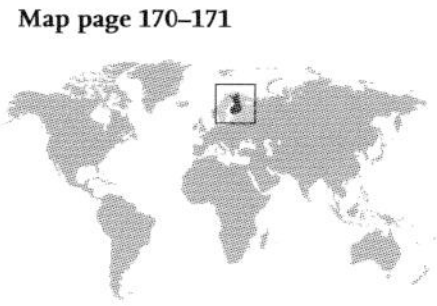

Finland is in northern Europe, and nearly one-third of the country lies north of the Arctic Circle. Forests cover over seventy per cent of the land area, and ten per cent is covered by lakes. Summers are short and warm, and winters are long and severe, particularly in the north. Most of the population lives in the southern third of the country, along the coast or near the lakes. Timber is a major resource and there are important minerals, chiefly chromium. Main industries include metal working, electronics, paper and paper products, and chemicals. The main trading partners are Germany, Sweden and the UK..

FRANCE

French Republic

Area Sq Km	543 965	**Languages**	French, German dialects, Italian, Arabic, Breton
Area Sq Miles	210 026	**Religions**	Roman Catholic, Protestant, Sunni Muslim
Population	64 291 000	**Currency**	Euro
Capital	Paris	**Organizations**	EU, NATO, OECD, UN

Map page 182

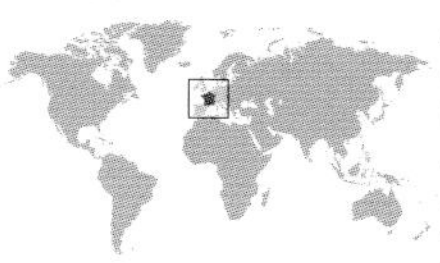

France lies in western Europe, on the Atlantic and the Mediterranean. There are mountain ranges in the southwest (the Pyrenees) and the east (the Alps, Jura and Vosges), and the Massif Central is an extensive hill region. The climate is temperate, the Mediterranean coast having hotter summers and milder winters. Over seventy per cent of the population lives in towns. There are coal reserves, and some oil and gas, but nuclear and hydroelectric power and imported fuels are vital. Industries include food processing, iron, steel and aluminium, chemicals, cars, electronics, oil refining, and tourism. Transport equipment, plastics and chemicals are exported. Trade is mainly with other EU countries.

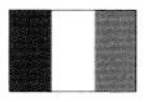

French Guiana

French Overseas Department

Area Sq Km	90 000	**Languages**	French, Creole
Area Sq Miles	34 749	**Religions**	Roman Catholic
Population	249 000	**Currency**	Euro
Capital	Cayenne		

Map page 231 French Guiana, on the north coast of South America, is densely forested. The climate is tropical, with high rainfall. Most people live in the coastal strip, and agriculture is mostly subsistence farming. Forestry and fishing are important, but mineral resources are largely unexploited and industry is limited. French Guiana depends on French aid. The main trading partners are France and the USA.

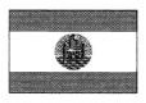

French Polynesia

French Overseas Collectivity

Area Sq Km	3 265	**Languages**	French, Tahitian, other Polynesian languages
Area Sq Miles	1 261	**Religions**	Protestant, Roman Catholic
Population	277 000	**Currency**	CFP franc
Capital	Papeete		

Map page 117 Extending over a vast area of the southeast Pacific Ocean, French Polynesia comprises more than one hundred and thirty islands and coral atolls. The main island groups are the Marquesas Islands, the Tuamotu Archipelago and the Society Islands. The capital, Papeete, is on Tahiti in the Society Islands. The climate is subtropical, and the economy is based on tourism. The main export is cultured pearls.

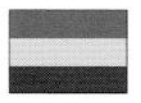

GABON

Gabonese Republic

Area Sq Km	267 667	**Languages**	French, Fang, other local languages
Area Sq Miles	103 347	**Religions**	Roman Catholic, Protestant, traditional beliefs
Population	1 672 000	**Currency**	CFA franc
Capital	Libreville	**Organizations**	UN

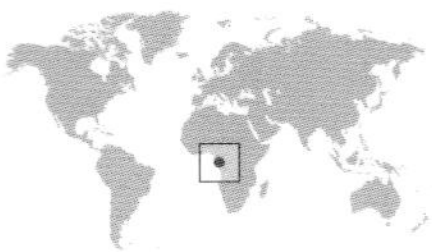

Map page 194 Gabon, on the Atlantic coast of central Africa, consists of low plateaus and a coastal plain lined by lagoons and mangrove swamps. The climate is tropical and rainforests cover over three-quarters of the land area. Nearly ninety per cent of the population lives in towns. The economy is heavily dependent on oil, which accounts for around seventy-five per cent of exports; manganese, uranium and timber are the other main exports. Agriculture is mainly at subsistence level.

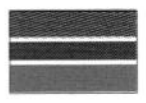

THE GAMBIA
Republic of The Gambia

Area Sq Km	11 295	**Languages**	English, Malinke, Fulani, Wolof
Area Sq Miles	4 361	**Religions**	Sunni Muslim, Protestant
Population	1 849 000	**Currency**	Dalasi
Capital	Banjul	**Organizations**	UN

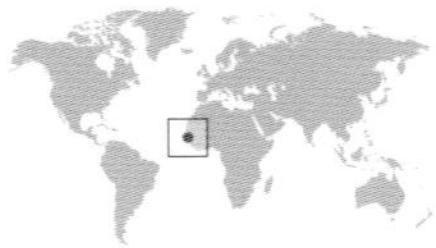

Map page 192 The Gambia, on the coast of west Africa, occupies a strip of land along the lower Gambia river. Sandy beaches are backed by mangrove swamps, beyond which is savanna. The climate is tropical, with most rainfall in the summer. Over seventy per cent of Gambians are farmers, growing chiefly groundnuts (the main export), cotton, oil palms and food crops. Livestock rearing and fishing are important, while manufacturing is limited. Re-exports, mainly from Senegal, and tourism are major sources of income.

Gaza
Disputed territory

Area Sq Km	363	**Languages**	Arabic
Area Sq Miles	140	**Religions**	Sunni Muslim, Shi'a Muslim
Population	1 701 437	**Currency**	Israeli shekel
Capital	Gaza		

Map page 138 Gaza is a narrow strip of land on the southeast corner of the Mediterranean Sea, between Egypt and Israel. This Palestinian territory has limited autonomy from Israel, but hostilities between Israel and the indigenous Arab population continue to restrict its economic development.

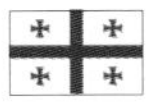

GEORGIA

Area Sq Km	69 700	**Languages**	Georgian, Russian, Armenian, Azeri, Ossetian, Abkhaz
Area Sq Miles	26 911	**Religions**	Georgian Orthodox, Russian Orthodox, Sunni Muslim
Population	4 341 000	**Currency**	Lari
Capital	Tbilisi	**Organizations**	UN

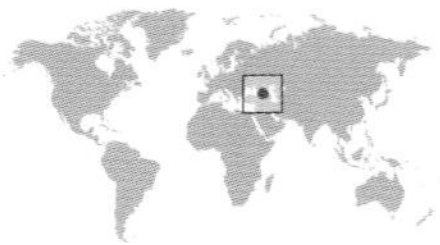

Map page 187 Georgia is in the northwest Caucasus area of southwest Asia, on the eastern coast of the Black Sea. Mountain ranges in the north and south flank the Kura and Rioni valleys. The climate is generally mild, and along the coast it is subtropical. Agriculture is important, with tea, grapes, and citrus fruits the main crops. Mineral resources include manganese ore and oil, and the main industries are steel, oil refining and machine building. The main trading partners are and Turkey, Ukraine and Azerbaijan.

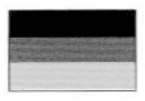

GERMANY
Federal Republic of Germany

Area Sq Km	357 022	**Languages**	German, Turkish
Area Sq Miles	137 847	**Religions**	Protestant, Roman Catholic
Population	82 727 000	**Currency**	Euro
Capital	Berlin	**Organizations**	EU, NATO, OECD, UN

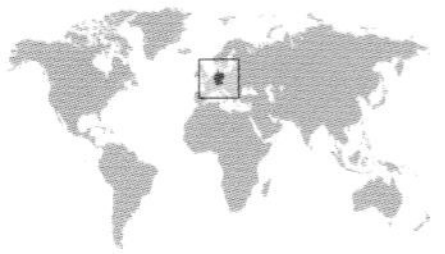

Map page 176 The central European state of Germany borders nine countries and has coastlines on the North and Baltic Seas. Behind the indented coastline, and covering about one-third of the country, is the north German plain, a region of fertile farmland and sandy heaths drained by the country's major rivers. The central highlands are a belt of forested hills and plateaus which stretch from the Eifel region in the west to the Erzgebirge mountains along the border with the Czech Republic. Farther south the land rises to the Swabian Alps (Schwäbische Alb), with the high rugged and forested Black Forest (Schwarzwald) in the southwest. In the far south the Bavarian Alps form the border with Austria. The climate is temperate, with continental conditions in eastern areas. The population is highly urbanized, with over seventy-five per cent living in cities and towns. With the exception of coal, lignite, potash and baryte, Germany lacks minerals and other industrial raw materials. It has a small agricultural base, although a few products (chiefly wines and beers) enjoy an international reputation. Germany is the world's fourth ranking economy after the USA, China and Japan. Its industries are amongst the world's most technologically advanced. Exports include machinery, vehicles and chemicals. The majority of trade is with other countries in the European Union, the USA and Japan.

State	Area Sq Km (Sq Miles)	Population	Capital
Baden-Württemberg (State)	35 752 (13 804)	10 842 000	Stuttgart
Bayern (State)	70 550 (27 240)	12 670 000	Munich (München)
Berlin (State)	892 (344)	3 544 000	Berlin
Brandenburg (State)	29 476 (11 381)	2 492 000	Potsdam
Bremen	404 (156)	663 000	Bremen
Hamburg (State)	755 (292)	1 814 000	Hamburg
Hessen (State)	21 114 (8 152)	6 116 000	Wiesbaden
Mecklenburg-Vorpommern (State)	23 173 (8 947)	1 629 000	Schwerin
Niedersachsen (State)	47 616 (18 385)	7 919 000	Hannover
Nordrhein-Westfalen (State)	34 082 (13 159)	17 853 000	Düsseldorf
Rheinland-Pfalz (State)	19 847 (7 663)	4 000 000	Mainz
Saarland (State)	2 568 (992)	1 010 000	Saarbrücken
Sachsen (State)	18 413 (7 109)	4 134 000	Dresden
Sachsen-Anhalt (State)	20 447 (7 895)	2 297 000	Magdeburg
Schleswig-Holstein (State)	15 761 (6 085)	2 842 000	Kiel
Thüringen (State)	16 172 (6 244)	2 211 000	Erfurt

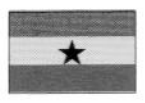

GHANA
Republic of Ghana

Area Sq Km	238 537	**Languages**	English, Hausa, Akan, other local languages
Area Sq Miles	92 100	**Religions**	Christian, Sunni Muslim, traditional beliefs
Population	25 905 000	**Currency**	Cedi
Capital	Accra	**Organizations**	Comm., UN

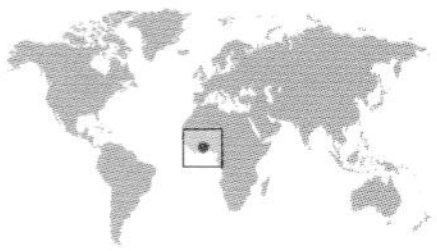

Map page 192 A west African state on the Gulf of Guinea, Ghana is a land of plains and low plateaus covered with savanna and rainforest. In the east is the Volta basin and Lake Volta. The climate is tropical, with the highest rainfall in the south, where most of the population lives. Agriculture employs over fifty per cent of the workforce. Main exports are gold, timber, cocoa, bauxite and manganese ore.

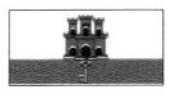

Gibraltar
United Kingdom Overseas Territory

Area Sq Km	7	**Languages**	English, Spanish
Area Sq Miles	3	**Religions**	Roman Catholic, Protestant, Sunni Muslim
Population	29 000		
Capital	Gibraltar	**Currency**	Gibraltar pound

Map page 183 Gibraltar lies on the south coast of Spain at the western entrance to the Mediterranean Sea. The economy depends on tourism, offshore banking and shipping services.

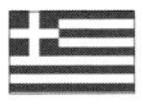

GREECE
Hellenic Republic

Area Sq Km	131 957	**Languages**	Greek
Area Sq Miles	50 949	**Religions**	Greek Orthodox, Sunni Muslim
Population	11 128 000	**Currency**	Euro
Capital	Athens (Athina)	**Organizations**	EU, NATO, OECD, UN

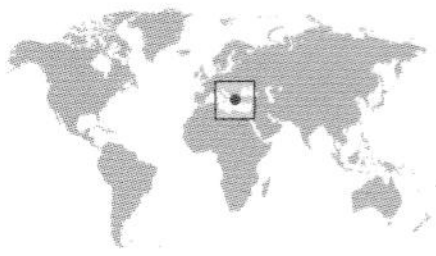

Map page 185 Greece comprises a mountainous peninsula in the Balkan region of southeastern Europe and many islands in the Ionian, Aegean and Mediterranean Seas. The islands make up over one-fifth of its area. Mountains and hills cover much of the country. The main lowland areas are the plains of Thessaly in the centre and around Thessaloniki in the northeast. Summers are hot and dry while winters are mild and wet, but colder in the north with heavy snowfalls in the mountains. One-third of Greeks live in the Athens area. Employment in agriculture accounts for approximately twenty per cent of the workforce, and exports include citrus fruits, raisins, wine, olives and olive oil. Aluminium and nickel are mined and a wide range of manufactures are produced, including food products and tobacco, textiles, clothing, and chemicals. Tourism is an important industry and there is a large services sector. Most trade is with other European Union countries.

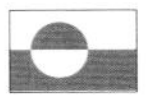

Greenland
Self-governing Danish Territory

Area Sq Km	2 175 600	**Languages**	Greenlandic, Danish
Area Sq Miles	840 004	**Religions**	Protestant
Population	57 000	**Currency**	Danish krone
Capital	Nuuk (Godthåb)		

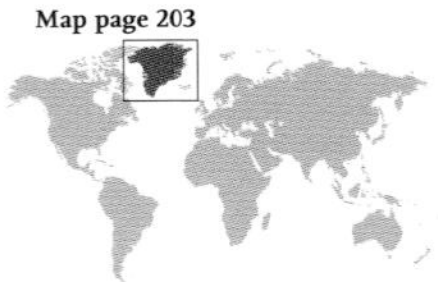

Map page 203 Situated to the northeast of North America between the Atlantic and Arctic Oceans, Greenland is the largest island in the world. It has a polar climate and over eighty per cent of the land area is covered by permanent ice cap. The economy is based on fishing and fish processing.

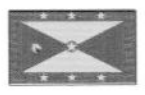

GRENADA

Area Sq Km	378	**Languages**	English, Creole
Area Sq Miles	146	**Religions**	Roman Catholic, Protestant
Population	106 000	**Currency**	East Caribbean dollar
Capital	St George's	**Organizations**	CARICOM, Comm., UN

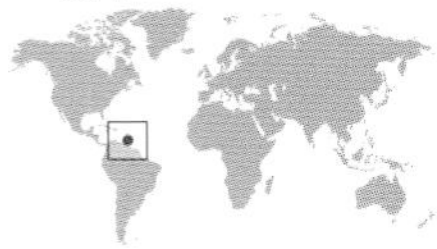

Map page 233 The Caribbean state comprises Grenada, the most southerly of the Windward Islands, and the southern islands of the Grenadines. Grenada has wooded hills, with beaches in the southwest. The climate is warm and wet. Agriculture is the main activity, with bananas, nutmeg and cocoa the main exports. Tourism is the main foreign exchange earner.

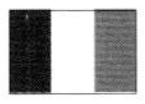

Guadeloupe
French Overseas Department

Area Sq Km	1 780	**Languages**	French, Creole
Area Sq Miles	687	**Religions**	Roman Catholic
Population	466 000	**Currency**	Euro
Capital	Basse-Terre		

Map page 223 Guadeloupe, in the Leeward Islands in the Caribbean, consists of two main islands (Basse-Terre and Grande-Terre, connected by a bridge), Marie-Galante, and a few outer islands. The climate is tropical, but moderated by trade winds. Bananas, sugar and rum are the main exports and tourism is a major source of income.

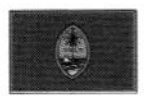

Guam
United States Unincorporated Territory

Area Sq Km	541	**Languages**	Chamorro, English, Tagalog
Area Sq Miles	209	**Religions**	Roman Catholic
Population	165 000	**Currency**	United States dollar
Capital	Hagåtña		

Map page 151 Lying at the south end of the Northern Mariana Islands in the western Pacific Ocean, Guam has a humid tropical climate. The island has a large US military base and the economy relies on that and on tourism.

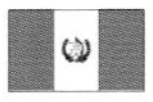

GUATEMALA
Republic of Guatemala

Area Sq Km	108 890	**Languages**	Spanish, Mayan languages
Area Sq Miles	42 043	**Religions**	Roman Catholic, Protestant
Population	15 468 000	**Currency**	Quetzal
Capital	Guatemala City	**Organizations**	UN

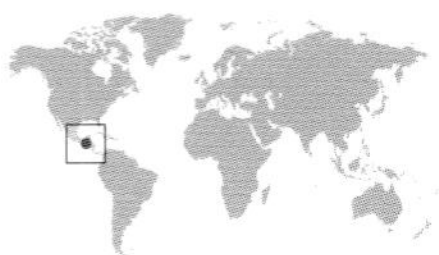

Map page 225 The most populous country in Central America after Mexico, Guatemala has long Pacific and short Caribbean coasts separated by a mountain chain which includes several active volcanoes. The climate is hot tropical in the lowlands and cooler in the highlands, where most of the population lives. Farming is the main activity and coffee, sugar and bananas are the main exports. There is some manufacturing of clothing and textiles. The main trading partner is the USA.

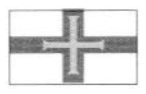

Guernsey
United Kingdom Crown Dependency

Area Sq Km	78	**Languages**	English, French
Area Sq Miles	30	**Religions**	Protestant, Roman Catholic
Population	65 578	**Currency**	Pound sterling
Capital	St Peter Port		

Map page 182 Guernsey is one of the Channel Islands, lying off northern France. The dependency also includes the nearby islands of Alderney, Sark and Herm. Financial services are an important part of the island's economy.

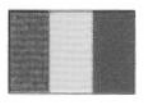

GUINEA
Republic of Guinea

Area Sq Km	245 857	**Languages**	French, Fulani, Malinke, other local languages
Area Sq Miles	94 926	**Religions**	Sunni Muslim, traditional beliefs, Christian
Population	11 745 000	**Currency**	Guinean franc
Capital	Conakry	**Organizations**	UN

Map page 192

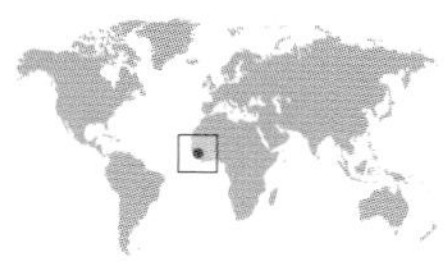

Guinea is in west Africa, on the Atlantic Ocean. There are mangrove swamps along the coast, while inland are lowlands and the Fouta Djallon mountains and plateaus. To the east are savanna plains drained by the upper Niger river system. The southeast is hilly. The climate is tropical, with high coastal rainfall. Agriculture is the main activity, employing nearly eighty per cent of the workforce, with coffee, bananas and pineapples the chief cash crops. There are huge reserves of bauxite, which accounts for more than seventy per cent of exports. Other exports include aluminium oxide, gold, coffee and diamonds.

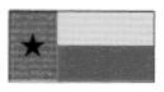

GUINEA-BISSAU
Republic of Guinea-Bissau

Area Sq Km	36 125	**Languages**	Portuguese, Crioulo, other local languages
Area Sq Miles	13 948	**Religions**	Traditional beliefs, Sunni Muslim, Christian
Population	1 704 000	**Currency**	CFA franc
Capital	Bissau	**Organizations**	UN

Map page 192

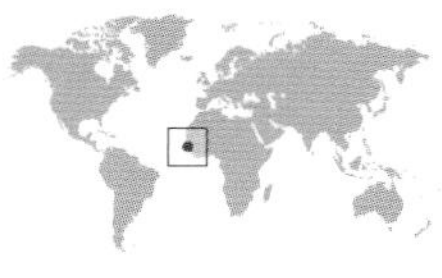

Guinea-Bissau is on the Atlantic coast of west Africa. The mainland coast is swampy and contains many estuaries. Inland are forested plains, and to the east are savanna plateaus. The climate is tropical. The economy is based mainly on subsistence farming. There is little industry, and timber and mineral resources are largely unexploited. Cashews account for seventy per cent of exports. Guinea-Bissau is one of the least developed countries in the world.

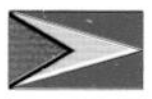

GUYANA
Co-operative Republic of Guyana

Area Sq Km	214 969	**Languages**	English, Creole, Amerindian languages
Area Sq Miles	83 000	**Religions**	Protestant, Hindu, Roman Catholic, Sunni Muslim
Population	800 000	**Currency**	Guyanese dollar
Capital	Georgetown	**Organizations**	CARICOM, Comm., UN

Map page 230–231

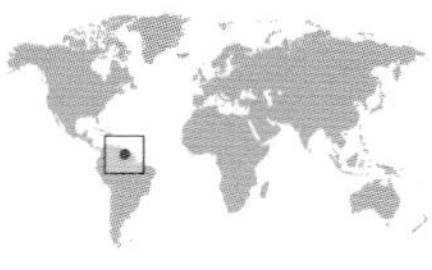

Guyana, on the northeast coast of South America, consists of highlands in the west and savanna uplands in the southwest. Most of the country is densely forested. A lowland coastal belt supports crops and most of the population. The generally hot, humid and wet conditions are modified along the coast by sea breezes. The economy is based on agriculture, bauxite, and forestry. Sugar, bauxite, gold, rice and timber are the main exports.

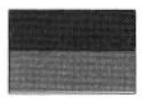

HAITI
Republic of Haiti

Area Sq Km	27 750	**Languages**	French, Creole
Area Sq Miles	10 714	**Religions**	Roman Catholic, Protestant, Voodoo
Population	10 317 000	**Currency**	Gourde
Capital	Port-au-Prince	**Organizations**	CARICOM, UN

Map page 223

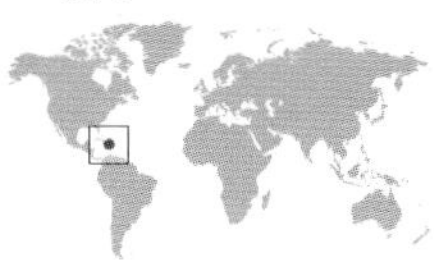

Haiti, occupying the western third of the Caribbean island of Hispaniola, is a mountainous state with small coastal plains and a central valley. The Dominican Republic occupies the rest of the island. The climate is tropical, and is hottest in coastal areas. Haiti has few natural resources, is densely populated and relies on exports of local crafts and coffee, and remittances from workers abroad. The country has not yet recovered from the 2010 earthquake.

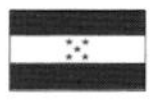

HONDURAS
Republic of Honduras

Area Sq Km	112 088	**Languages**	Spanish, Amerindian languages
Area Sq Miles	43 277	**Religions**	Roman Catholic, Protestant
Population	8 098 000	**Currency**	Lempira
Capital	Tegucigalpa	**Organizations**	UN

Map page 224

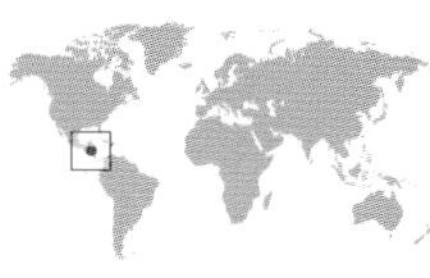

Honduras, in central America, is a mountainous and forested country with lowland areas along its long Caribbean and short Pacific coasts. Coastal areas are hot and humid with heavy summer rainfall; inland is cooler and drier. Most of the population lives in the central valleys. Coffee and bananas are the main exports, along with shellfish and zinc. Industry involves mainly agricultural processing.

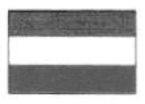

HUNGARY

Area Sq Km	93 030	**Languages**	Hungarian
Area Sq Miles	35 919	**Religions**	Roman Catholic, Protestant
Population	9 955 000	**Currency**	Forint
Capital	Budapest	**Organizations**	EU, NATO, OECD, UN

Map page 177

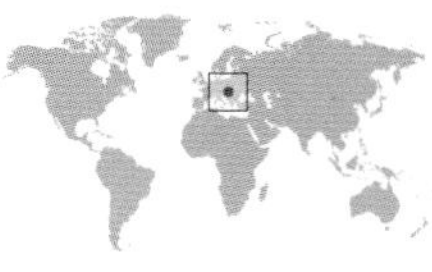

The Danube river flows north-south through central Hungary, a landlocked country in eastern Europe. In the east lies a great plain, flanked by highlands in the north. In the west low mountains and Lake Balaton separate a smaller plain and southern uplands. The climate is continental. Seventy per cent of the population lives in urban areas, and one-sixth lives in the capital, Budapest. Some minerals and energy resources are exploited, chiefly bauxite, coal and natural gas. Hungary has an industrial economy based on metals, machinery, transport equipment, chemicals and food products. The main trading partners are Germany and Austria. Hungary joined the European Union in May 2004.

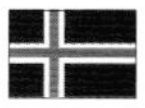

ICELAND
Republic of Iceland

Area Sq Km	102 820	**Languages**	Icelandic
Area Sq Miles	39 699	**Religions**	Protestant
Population	330 000	**Currency**	Icelandic króna
Capital	Reykjavík	**Organizations**	NATO, OECD, UN

Map page 170

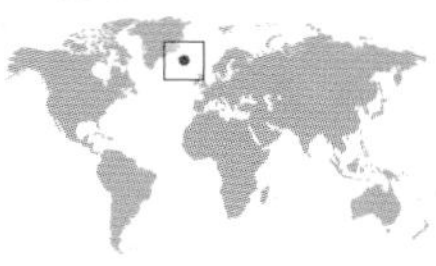

Iceland lies in the north Atlantic Ocean near the Arctic Circle, to the northwest of Scandinavia. The landscape is volcanic, with numerous hot springs, geysers, and approximately two hundred volcanoes. One-tenth of the country is covered by ice caps. Only coastal lowlands are cultivated and settled, and over half the population lives in the Reykjavik area. The climate is mild, moderated by the North Atlantic Drift ocean current and by southwesterly winds. The mainstays of the economy are fishing and fish processing, which account for seventy per cent of exports. Agriculture involves mainly sheep and dairy farming. Hydroelectric and geothermal energy resources are considerable. The main industries produce aluminium, ferro-silicon and fertilizers. Tourism, including ecotourism, is growing in importance.

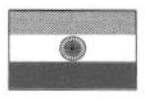

INDIA
Republic of India

Area Sq Km	3 166 620	**Languages**	Hindi, English, many regional languages
Area Sq Miles	1 222 632	**Religions**	Hindu, Sunni Muslim, Shi'a Muslim, Sikh, Christian
Population	1 252 140 000	**Currency**	Indian rupee
Capital	New Delhi	**Organizations**	Comm., UN

Map page 135

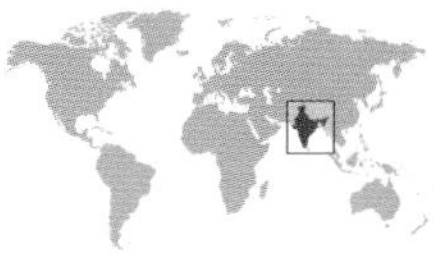

The south Asian country of India occupies a peninsula that juts out into the Indian Ocean between the Arabian Sea and Bay of Bengal. The heart of the peninsula is the Deccan plateau, bordered on either side by ranges of hills, the western Ghats and the lower eastern Ghats, which fall away to narrow coastal plains. To the north is a broad plain, drained by the Indus, Ganges and Brahmaputra rivers and their tributaries. The plain is intensively farmed and is the most populous region. In the west is the Thar Desert. The mountains of the Himalaya form India's northern border, together with parts of the Karakoram and Hindu Kush ranges in the northwest. The climate shows marked seasonal variation: a hot season from March to June; a monsoon season from June to October; and a cold season from November to February. Rainfall ranges between very high in the northeast Assam region to negligible in the Thar Desert. Temperatures range from very cold in the Himalaya to tropical heat over much of the south. Over sixty-seven per cent of the huge population – the second largest in the world – is rural, although Delhi, Mumbai (Bombay) and Kolkata (Calcutta) all rank among the ten largest cities in the world. Agriculture, forestry and fishing account for a quarter of national output and two-thirds of employment. Much of the farming is on a subsistence basis and involves mainly rice and wheat. India is a major world producer of tea, sugar, jute, cotton and tobacco. Livestock is reared mainly for dairy products and hides. There are major reserves of coal, reserves of oil and natural gas, and many minerals, including iron, manganese, bauxite, diamonds and gold. The manufacturing sector is large and diverse – mainly chemicals and chemical products, textiles, iron and steel, food products, electrical goods and transport equipment; software and pharmaceuticals are also important. All the main manufactured products are exported, together with diamonds and jewellery. The USA, Germany, Japan and the UK are the main trading partners.

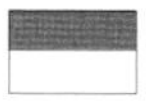

INDONESIA
Republic of Indonesia

Area Sq Km	1 919 445	**Languages**	Indonesian, other local languages
Area Sq Miles	741 102	**Religions**	Sunni Muslim, Protestant, Roman Catholic, Hindu, Buddhist
Population	249 866 000	**Currency**	Rupiah
Capital	Jakarta	**Organizations**	APEC, ASEAN, OPEC, UN

Map page 151

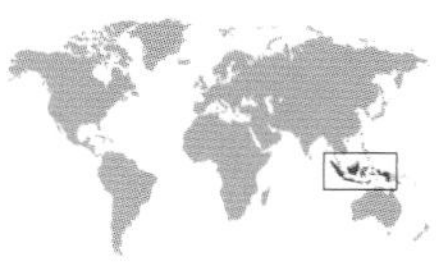

Indonesia consists of over thirteen thousand islands in Southeast Asia, between the Pacific and Indian Oceans. Sumatra, Java, Sulawesi (Celebes), Kalimantan (two-thirds of Borneo) and Papua (formerly Irian Jaya, western New Guinea) make up ninety per cent of the area. Most of Indonesia is covered with rainforest or mangrove swamps, and there are over three hundred volcanoes. Two-thirds of the population lives in the lowland areas of Java and Madura. The climate is tropical monsoon. Chief products are rice, palm oil, tea, coffee, rubber, tobacco, textiles, clothing, cement, tin, fertilizers and vehicles. Oil, gas, timber products and clothing are exported. Main trading partners are Japan, the USA and Singapore..

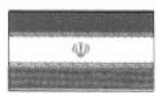

IRAN
Islamic Republic of Iran

Area Sq Km	1 648 000	**Languages**	Farsi, Azeri, Kurdish, regional languages
Area Sq Miles	636 296	**Religions**	Shi'a Muslim, Sunni Muslim
Population	77 447 000	**Currency**	Iranian rial
Capital	Tehrān	**Organizations**	OPEC, UN

Map page 142–143

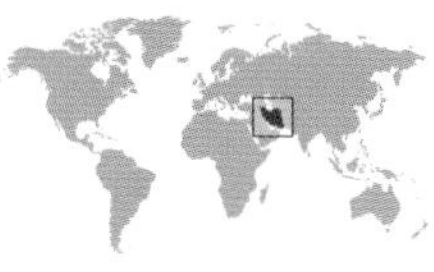

Iran is in southwest Asia, and has coasts on The Gulf, the Caspian Sea and the Gulf of Oman. In the east is a high plateau, with large salt pans and a vast sand desert. In the west the Zagros Mountains form a series of ridges, and to the north lie the Elburz Mountains. Most farming and settlement is on the narrow plain along the Caspian Sea and in the foothills of the north and west. The climate is one of extremes, with hot summers and very cold winters. Most of the light rainfall is in the winter months. Agriculture involves approximately one-fifth of the workforce. Wheat is the main crop, but fruit (especially dates) and pistachio nuts are grown for export. Petroleum (the main export) and natural gas are Iran's leading natural resources. Manufactured goods include carpets, clothing, food products and construction materials.

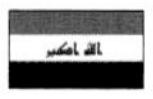

IRAQ
Republic of Iraq

Area Sq Km	438 317	**Languages**	Arabic, Kurdish, Turkmen
Area Sq Miles	169 235	**Religions**	Shi'a Muslim, Sunni Muslim, Christian
Population	33 765 000	**Currency**	Iraqi dinar
Capital	Baghdād	**Organizations**	OPEC, UN

Map page 139

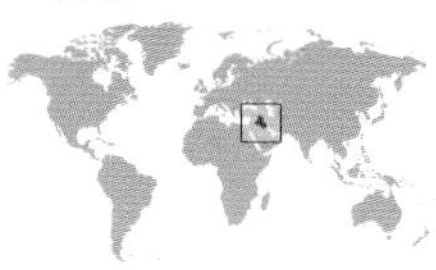

Iraq, in southwest Asia, has at its heart the lowland valley of the Tigris and Euphrates rivers. In the southeast, where the two rivers join, are the Mesopotamian marshes and the Shaṭṭ al 'Arab waterway leading to The Gulf. The north is hilly, while the west is mostly desert. Summers are hot and dry, and winters are mild with light, unreliable rainfall. The Tigris-Euphrates valley contains most of the country's arable land. One in five of the population lives in the capital, Baghdad. The economy has suffered following the 1991 Gulf War and the invasion of US-led coalition forces in 2005. The latter resulted in the overthrow of the dictator Saddam Hussein, but there is continuing internal instability. Oil is normally the main export.

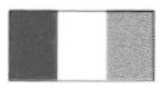

IRELAND

Area Sq Km	70 282	**Languages**	English, Irish
Area Sq Miles	27 136	**Religions**	Roman Catholic, Protestant
Population	4 627 000	**Currency**	Euro
Capital	Dublin (Baile Átha Cliath)	**Organizations**	EU, OECD, UN

Map page 175

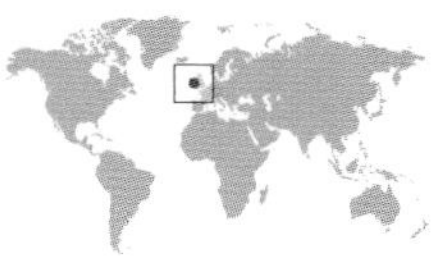

The Irish Republic occupies eighty per cent of the island of Ireland, in northwest Europe. It is a lowland country of wide valleys, lakes and peat bogs, with isolated mountain ranges around the coast. The climate is mild, modified by the North Atlantic Drift ocean current, and rainfall is plentiful, although highest in the west. Over sixty per cent of the population lives in urban areas. Resources include natural gas, peat, lead and zinc. Agriculture now employs less than six per cent of the workforce. The main industries are electronics, pharmaceuticals, engineering, food processing, brewing and textiles. Service industries and tourism are also important. The UK is the main trading partner.

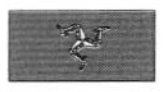

Isle of Man
United Kingdom Crown Dependency

Area Sq Km	572	**Languages**	English
Area Sq Miles	221	**Religions**	Protestant, Roman Catholic
Population	86 000	**Currency**	Pound sterling
Capital	Douglas		

Map page 172

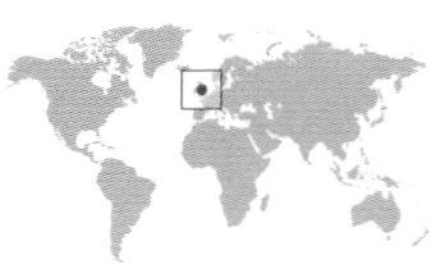

The Isle of Man lies in the Irish Sea between England and Northern Ireland. The island is self-governing, although the UK is responsible for its defence and foreign affairs. It is not part of the European Union, but has a special relationship with the EU which allows for free trade. Eighty per cent of the economy is based on the service sector, particularly financial services.

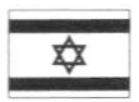

ISRAEL
State of Israel

Area Sq Km	22 072	**Languages**	Hebrew, Arabic
Area Sq Miles	8 522	**Religions**	Jewish, Sunni Muslim, Christian, Druze
Population	7 733 000	**Currency**	Shekel
Capital	Jerusalem (Yerushalayim) (El Quds) De facto capital. Disputed.	**Organizations**	OECD, UN

Map page 138

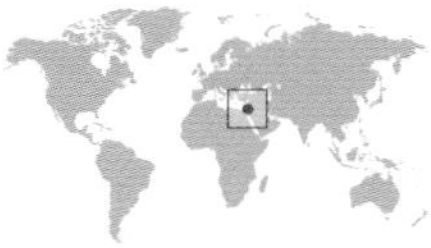

Israel lies on the Mediterranean coast of southwest Asia. Beyond the coastal Plain of Sharon are the hills and valleys of Samaria, with the Galilee highlands to the north. In the east is a rift valley, which extends from Lake Tiberias (Sea of Galilee) to the Gulf of Aqaba and contains the Jordan river and the Dead Sea. In the south is the Negev, a triangular semi-desert plateau. Most of the population lives on the coastal plain or in northern and central areas. Much of Israel has warm summers and mild, wet winters. The south is hot and dry. Agricultural production was boosted by the occupation of the West Bank in 1967. Manufacturing makes the largest contribution to the economy, and tourism is also important. Israel's main exports are machinery and transport equipment, software, diamonds, clothing, fruit and vegetables. The country relies heavily on foreign aid. Security issues relating to territorial disputes over the West Bank and Gaza have still to be resolved.

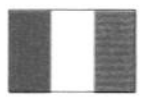

ITALY
Italian Republic

Area Sq Km	301 245	**Languages**	Italian
Area Sq Miles	116 311	**Religions**	Roman Catholic
Population	60 990 000	**Currency**	Euro
Capital	Rome (Roma)	**Organizations**	EU, NATO, OECD, UN

Map page 184–185

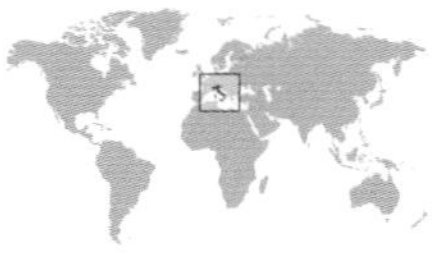

Italy occupies a peninsula in southern Europe jutting out into the Mediterranean. It includes Sicily and Sardinia and many smaller islands. The Alps are in the north, and the Apennines run along the peninsula. Population, agriculture and industry are concentrated in the northern lowlands. The climate is Mediterranean, but with colder, wetter winters in the north. Only one-fifth of the land is cultivated. Some oil, gas and coal are produced. Cereals, vines, fruit and vegetables are grown: Italy is the world's largest wine producer. Manufactures include industrial and domestic equipment, cars, textiles, chemicals and metal products. Tourism, finance and service industries are important. Most trade is with other EU countries.

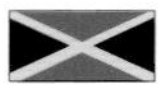

JAMAICA

Area Sq Km	10 991	**Languages**	English, Creole
Area Sq Miles	4 244	**Religions**	Protestant, Roman Catholic
Population	2 784 000	**Currency**	Jamaican dollar
Capital	Kingston	**Organizations**	CARICOM, Comm., UN

Map page 223

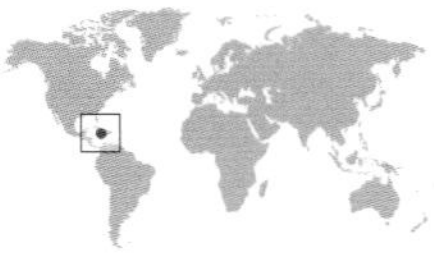

Jamaica, the third largest Caribbean island, has beaches and densely populated coastal plains traversed by hills and plateaus rising to the forested Blue Mountains in the east. The climate is tropical, but cooler and wetter on high ground. The economy is based on tourism, agriculture, mining and light manufacturing. Bauxite, aluminium oxide, sugar and bananas are the main exports. The USA is the main trading partner. Foreign aid is also significant.

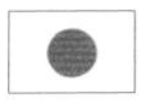

JAPAN

Area Sq Km	377 727	**Languages**	Japanese
Area Sq Miles	145 841	**Religions**	Shintoist, Buddhist, Christian
Population	127 144 000	**Currency**	Yen
Capital	Tōkyō	**Organizations**	APEC, OECD, UN

Map page 158–159

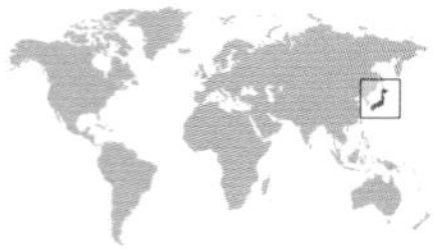

Japan lies in the Pacific Ocean off the coast of eastern Asia and consists of four main islands – Hokkaidō, Honshū, Shikoku and Kyūshū – and more than three thousand smaller islands in the surrounding Sea of Japan, East China Sea and Pacific Ocean. The central island of Honshū accounts for sixty per cent of the total land area and contains eighty per cent of the population. Behind the long and deeply indented coastline, nearly three-quarters of the country is mountainous and heavily forested. Japan has over sixty active volcanoes, and is subject to frequent earthquakes and typhoons. The climate is generally temperate maritime, with warm summers and mild winters, except in western Hokkaidō and northwest Honshū, where the winters are very cold with heavy snow. Only fourteen per cent of the land area is suitable for cultivation, and its few raw materials (coal, oil, natural gas, lead, zinc and copper) are insufficient for its industry. Most materials must be imported, including about ninety per cent of energy requirements. Yet Japan has the world's third largest industrial economy, with a range of modern heavy and light industries centred mainly around the major ports of Yokohama, Ōsaka and Tōkyō. It is the world's largest manufacturer of cars, motorcycles and merchant ships, and a major producer of steel, textiles, chemicals and cement. It is also a leading producer of many consumer durables, such as washing machines, and electronic equipment, chiefly office equipment and computers. Japan has a strong service sector, banking and finance being particularly important, and Tōkyō has one of the world's major stock exchanges. Owing to intensive agricultural production, Japan is seventy per cent self-sufficient in food. The main food crops are rice, barley, fruit, wheat and soya beans. Livestock rearing (chiefly cattle, pigs and chickens) and fishing are also important, and Japan has one of the largest fishing fleets in the world. A major trading nation, Japan has trade links with many countries in southeast Asia and in Europe, although its main trading partner is the USA.

Jersey
United Kingdom Crown Dependency

Area Sq Km	116	**Languages**	English, French
Area Sq Miles	45	**Religions**	Protestant, Roman Catholic
Population	99 000	**Currency**	Pound sterling
Capital	St Helier		

Map page 182

One of the Channel Islands lying off the west coast of the Cherbourg peninsula in northern France. Financial services are the most important part of the economy.

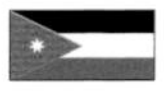

JORDAN
Hashemite Kingdom of Jordan

Area Sq Km	89 206	**Languages**	Arabic
Area Sq Miles	34 443	**Religions**	Sunni Muslim, Christian
Population	7 274 000	**Currency**	Jordanian dinar
Capital	'Ammān	**Organizations**	UN

Map page 138–139

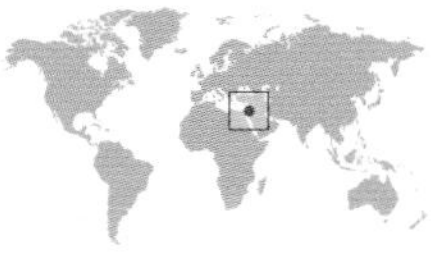

Jordan, in southwest Asia, is landlocked apart from a short coastline on the Gulf of Aqaba. Much of the country is rocky desert plateau. To the west of the mountains, the land falls below sea level to the Dead Sea and the Jordan river. The climate is hot and dry. Most people live in the northwest. Phosphates, potash, pharmaceuticals, fruit and vegetables are the main exports. The tourist industry is important, and the economy relies on workers' remittances from abroad and foreign aid.

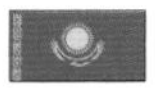

KAZAKHSTAN
Republic of Kazakhstan

Area Sq Km	2 717 300	**Languages**	Kazakh, Russian, Ukrainian, German, Uzbek, Tatar
Area Sq Miles	1 049 155	**Religions**	Sunni Muslim, Russian Orthodox, Protestant
Population	16 441 000	**Currency**	Tenge
Capital	Astana (Akmola)	**Organizations**	CIS, UN

Map page 140–141

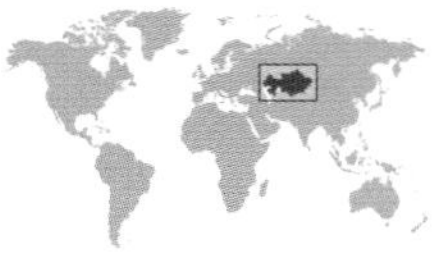

Stretching across central Asia, Kazakhstan covers a vast area of steppe land and semi-desert. The land is flat in the west, with large lowlands around the Caspian Sea, rising to mountains in the southeast. The climate is continental. Agriculture and livestock rearing are important, and cotton and tobacco are the main cash crops. Kazakhstan is very rich in minerals, including coal, chromium, gold, molybdenum, lead and zinc, and has substantial reserves of oil and gas. Mining, metallurgy, machine building and food processing are major industries. Oil, gas and minerals are the main exports, and Russia is the dominant trading partner.

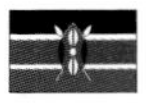

KENYA
Republic of Kenya

Area Sq Km	582 646	**Languages**	Swahili, English, other local languages
Area Sq Miles	224 961	**Religions**	Christian, traditional beliefs
Population	44 354 000	**Currency**	Kenyan shilling
Capital	Nairobi	**Organizations**	Comm., UN

Map page 194

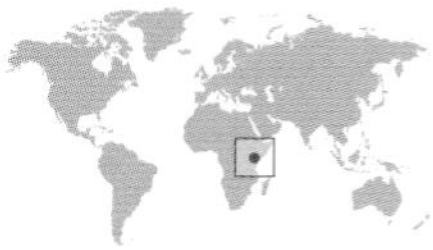

Kenya is in east Africa, on the Indian Ocean. Inland beyond the coastal plains the land rises to plateaus interrupted by volcanic mountains. The Great Rift Valley runs north-south to the west of the capital, Nairobi. Most of the population lives in the central area. Conditions are tropical on the coast, semi-desert in the north and savanna in the south. Hydroelectric power from the Upper Tana river provides most of the country's electricity. Agricultural products, mainly tea, coffee, fruit and vegetables, are the main exports. Light industry is important, and tourism, oil refining and re-exports for landlocked neighbours are major foreign exchange earners.

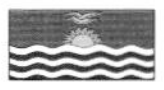

KIRIBATI
Republic of Kiribati

Area Sq Km	717	**Languages**	Gilbertese, English
Area Sq Miles	277	**Religions**	Roman Catholic, Protestant
Population	102 000	**Currency**	Australian dollar
Capital	Bairiki	**Organizations**	Comm., UN

Map page 117

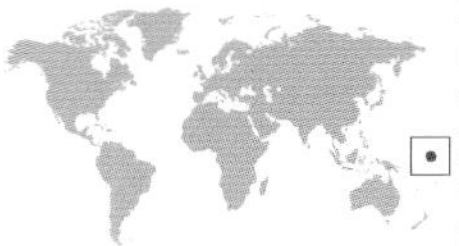

Kiribati, in the Pacific Ocean, straddles the Equator and comprises coral islands in the Gilbert, Phoenix and Line Island groups and the volcanic island of Banaba. Most people live on the Gilbert Islands, and the capital, Bairiki, is on Tarawa island in this group. The climate is hot, and wetter in the north. Copra and fish are exported. Kiribati relies on remittances from workers abroad and foreign aid.

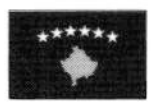

KOSOVO
Republic of Kosovo

Area Sq Km	10 908	**Languages**	Albanian, Serbian
Area Sq Miles	4 212	**Religions**	Sunni Muslim, Serbian Orthodox
Population	1 815 606	**Currency**	Euro
Capital	Prishtinë (Priština)		

Map page 185

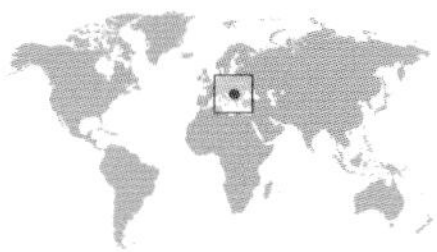

Kosovo, traditionally an autonomous southern province of Serbia, was the focus of ethnic conflict between Serbs and the majority ethnic Albanians in the 1990s until international intervention in 1999, after which it was administered by the UN. Kosovo declared its independence from Serbia in February 2008. The landscape is largely hilly or mountainous, especially along the southern and western borders.

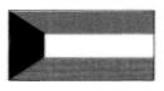

KUWAIT
State of Kuwait

Area Sq Km	17 818	**Languages**	Arabic
Area Sq Miles	6 880	**Religions**	Sunni Muslim, Shi'a Muslim, Christian, Hindu
Population	3 369 000	**Currency**	Kuwaiti dinar
Capital	Kuwait (Al Kuwayt)	**Organizations**	OPEC, UN

Map page 139

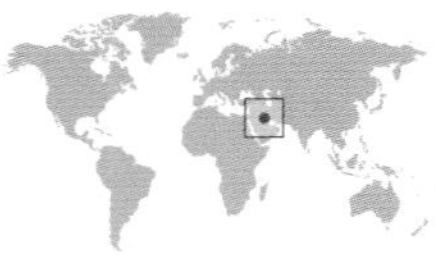

Kuwait lies on the northwest shores of The Gulf in southwest Asia. It is mainly low-lying desert, with irrigated areas along the bay, Kuwait Jun, where most people live. Summers are hot and dry, and winters are cool with some rainfall. The oil industry, which accounts for over ninety per cent of exports, has recovered from the damage caused by the Gulf War in 1991. Income is also derived from extensive overseas investments. Japan and the USA are the main trading partners.

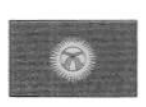

KYRGYZSTAN
Kyrgyz Republic

Area Sq Km	198 500	**Languages**	Kyrgyz, Russian, Uzbek
Area Sq Miles	76 641	**Religions**	Sunni Muslim, Russian Orthodox
Population	5 548 000	**Currency**	Kyrgyz som
Capital	Bishkek (Frunze)	**Organizations**	CIS, UN

Map page 141

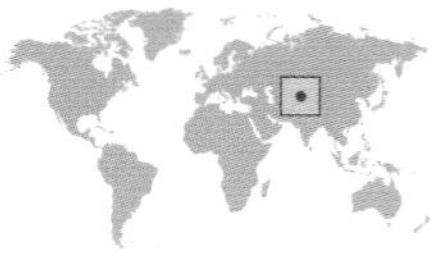

A landlocked central Asian state, Kyrgyzstan is rugged and mountainous, lying to the west of the Tien Shan mountain range. Most of the population lives in the valleys of the north and west. Summers are hot and winters cold. Agriculture (chiefly livestock farming) is the main activity. Some oil and gas, coal, gold, antimony and mercury are produced. Manufactured goods include machinery, metals and metal products, which are the main exports. Most trade is with Germany, Russia, Kazakhstan and Uzbekistan.

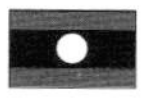

LAOS
Lao People's Democratic Republic

Area Sq Km	236 800	**Languages**	Lao, other local languages
Area Sq Miles	91 429	**Religions**	Buddhist, traditional beliefs
Population	6 770 000	**Currency**	Kip
Capital	Vientiane (Viangchan)	**Organizations**	ASEAN, UN

Map page 151

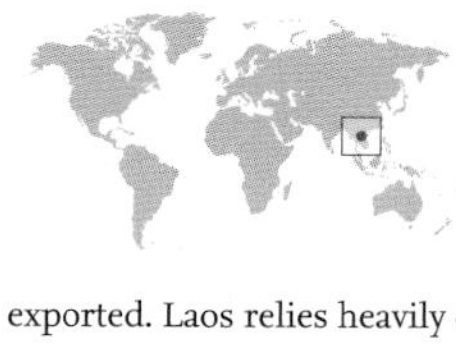

A landlocked country in southeast Asia, Laos is a land of mostly forested mountains and plateaus. The climate is tropical monsoon. Most of the population lives in the Mekong valley and the low plateau in the south, where food crops, chiefly rice, are grown. Hydroelectricity from a plant on the Mekong river, timber, coffee and tin are exported. Laos relies heavily on foreign aid.

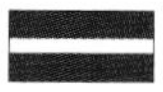

LATVIA
Republic of Latvia

Area Sq Km	64 589	**Languages**	Latvian, Russian
Area Sq Miles	24 938	**Religions**	Protestant, Roman Catholic, Russian Orthodox
Population	2 050 000	**Currency**	Euro
Capital	Rīga	**Organizations**	EU, NATO, UN

Map page 171

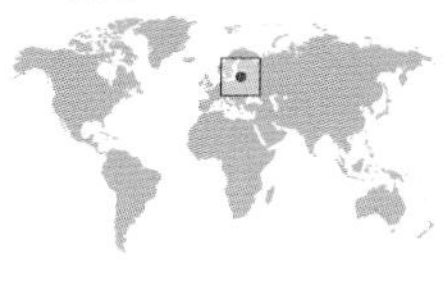

Latvia is in northern Europe, on the Baltic Sea and the Gulf of Riga. The land is flat near the coast but hilly with woods and lakes inland. The country has a modified continental climate. Over a quarter of the people live in the capital, Rīga. Crop and livestock farming are important. There are few natural resources. Industries and main exports include food products, transport equipment, wood and wood products and textiles. The main trading partners are Russia and Germany. Latvia joined the European Union in May 2004.

LEBANON
Lebanese Republic

Area Sq Km	10 452	**Languages**	Arabic, Armenian, French
Area Sq Miles	4 036	**Religions**	Shi'a Muslim, Sunni Muslim, Christian
Population	4 822 000	**Currency**	Lebanese pound
Capital	Beirut (Beyrouth)	**Organizations**	UN

Map page 138

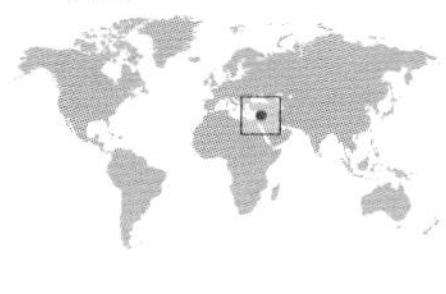

Lebanon lies on the Mediterranean coast of southwest Asia. Beyond the coastal strip, where most of the population lives, are two parallel mountain ranges, separated by the Bekaa Valley (El Beq'a). The economy and infrastructure have been recovering since the 1975–1991 civil war crippled the traditional sectors of financial services and tourism. Switzerland, the USA, France and the UAE are the main trading partners.

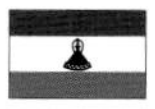

LESOTHO
Kingdom of Lesotho

Area Sq Km	30 355	**Languages**	Sesotho, English, Zulu
Area Sq Miles	11 720	**Religions**	Christian, traditional beliefs
Population	2 074 000	**Currency**	Loti, South African rand
Capital	Maseru	**Organizations**	Comm., SADC, UN

Map page 197

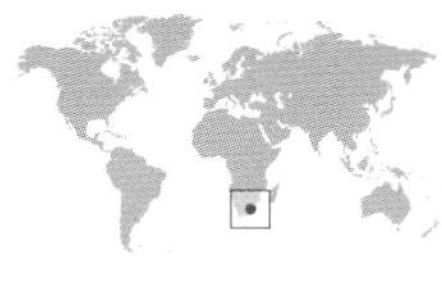

Lesotho is a landlocked state surrounded by South Africa. It is a mountainous country lying within the Drakensberg mountain range. Farming and herding are the main activities. The economy depends heavily on South Africa for transport links and employment. A major hydroelectric plant completed in 1998 allows the sale of water to South Africa. Exports include manufactured goods (mainly clothing and road vehicles), food, live animals, wool and mohair.

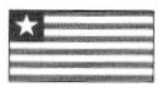

LIBERIA
Republic of Liberia

Area Sq Km	111 369	**Languages**	English, Creole, other local languages
Area Sq Miles	43 000	**Religions**	Traditional beliefs, Christian, Sunni Muslim
Population	4 294 000	**Currency**	Liberian dollar
Capital	Monrovia	**Organizations**	UN

Map page 192

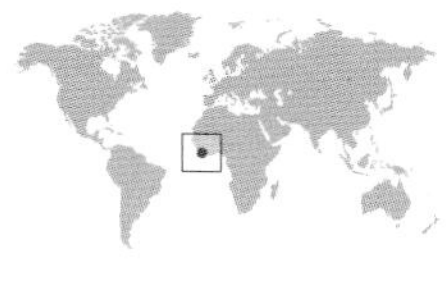

Liberia is on the Atlantic coast of west Africa. Beyond the coastal belt of sandy beaches and mangrove swamps the land rises to a forested plateau and highlands along the Guinea border. A quarter of the population lives along the coast. The climate is hot with heavy rainfall. Liberia is rich in mineral resources and forests. The economy is based on the production and export of basic products. Exports include diamonds, iron ore, rubber and timber. Liberia has a huge international debt and relies heavily on foreign aid.

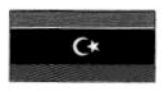

LIBYA
State of Libya

Area Sq Km	1 759 540	**Languages**	Arabic, Berber
Area Sq Miles	679 362	**Religions**	Sunni Muslim
Population	6 202 000	**Currency**	Libyan dinar
Capital	Tripoli (Ṭarābulus)	**Organizations**	OPEC, UN

Map page 193

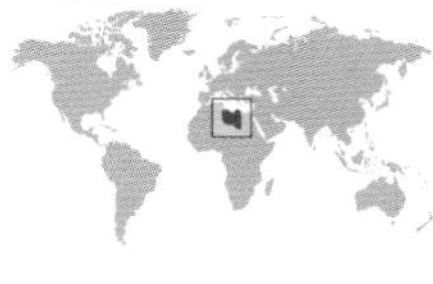

Libya lies on the Mediterranean coast of north Africa. The desert plains and hills of the Sahara dominate the landscape and the climate is hot and dry. Most of the population lives in cities near the coast, where the climate is cooler with moderate rainfall. Farming and herding, chiefly in the northwest, are important but the main industry is oil. Libya is a major producer, and oil accounts for virtually all of its export earnings. Italy and Germany are the main trading partners. As a result of the civil war in 2011 oil exports were disrupted and there was severe damage to the infrastructure of the country.

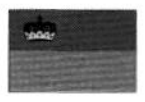

LIECHTENSTEIN
Principality of Liechtenstein

Area Sq Km	160	**Languages**	German
Area Sq Miles	62	**Religions**	Roman Catholic, Protestant
Population	37 000	**Currency**	Swiss franc
Capital	Vaduz	**Organizations**	UN

Map page 182

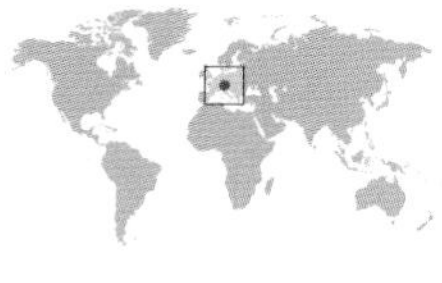

A landlocked state between Switzerland and Austria, Liechtenstein has an industrialized, free-enterprise economy. Low business taxes have attracted companies to establish offices which provide approximately one-third of state revenues. Banking is also important. Major products include precision instruments, ceramics and textiles.

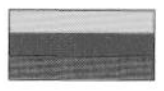

LITHUANIA
Republic of Lithuania

Area Sq Km	65 200	**Languages**	Lithuanian, Russian, Polish
Area Sq Miles	25 174	**Religions**	Roman Catholic, Protestant, Russian Orthodox
Population	3 017 000	**Currency**	Euro
Capital	Vilnius	**Organizations**	EU, NATO, UN

Map page 171

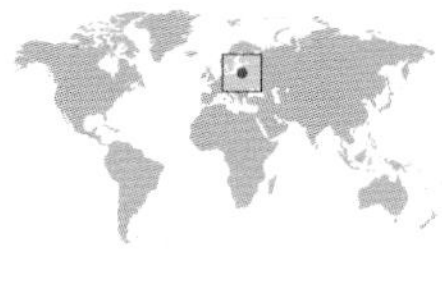

Lithuania is in northern Europe on the eastern shores of the Baltic Sea. It is mainly lowland with many lakes, rivers and marshes. Agriculture, fishing and forestry are important, but manufacturing dominates the economy. The main exports are machinery, mineral products and chemicals. Russia and Germany are the main trading partners. Lithuania joined the European Union in May 2004.

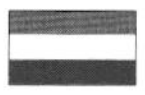

LUXEMBOURG
Grand Duchy of Luxembourg

Area Sq Km	2 586	**Languages**	Letzeburgish, German, French
Area Sq Miles	998	**Religions**	Roman Catholic
Population	530 000	**Currency**	Euro
Capital	Luxembourg	**Organizations**	EU, NATO, OECD, UN

Map page 178

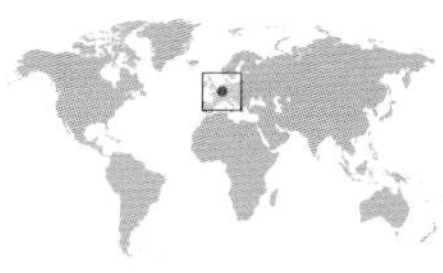

Luxembourg, a small landlocked country in western Europe, borders Belgium, France and Germany. The hills and forests of the Ardennes dominate the north, with rolling pasture to the south, where the main towns, farms and industries are found. The iron and steel industry is still important, but light industries (including textiles, chemicals and food products) are growing. Luxembourg is a major banking centre. Main trading partners are Belgium, Germany and France.

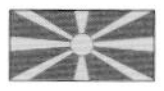

MACEDONIA (F.Y.R.O.M.)
Republic of Macedonia

Area Sq Km	25 713	**Languages**	Macedonian, Albanian, Turkish
Area Sq Miles	9 928	**Religions**	Macedonian Orthodox, Sunni Muslim
Population	2 107 000	**Currency**	Macedonian denar
Capital	Skopje	**Organizations**	NATO, UN

Map page 185

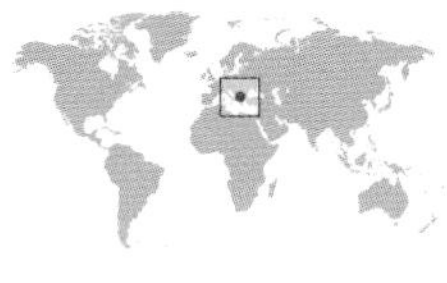

The Former Yugoslav Republic of Macedonia is a landlocked state in southern Europe. Lying within the southern Balkan Mountains, it is traversed northwest-southeast by the Vardar valley. The climate is continental. The economy is based on industry, mining and agriculture, but conflicts in the region have reduced trade and caused economic difficulties. Foreign aid and loans are now assisting in modernization and development of the country.

MADAGASCAR
Republic of Madagascar

Area Sq Km	587 041	**Languages**	Malagasy, French
Area Sq Miles	226 658	**Religions**	Traditional beliefs, Christian, Sunni Muslim
Population	22 925 000	**Currency**	Ariary
Capital	Antananarivo	**Organizations**	SADC, UN

Map page 195

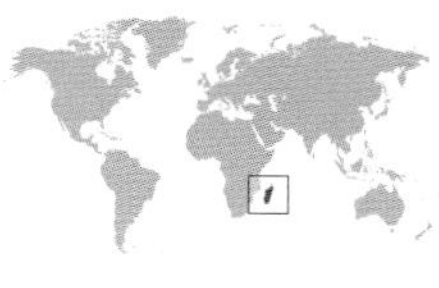

Madagascar lies off the east coast of southern Africa. The world's fourth largest island, it is mainly a high plateau, with a coastal strip to the east and scrubby plain to the west. The climate is tropical, with heavy rainfall in the north and east. Most of the population lives on the plateau. Although the amount of arable land is limited, the economy is based on agriculture. The main industries are agricultural processing, textile manufacturing and oil refining. Foreign aid is important. Exports include coffee, vanilla, cotton cloth, sugar and shrimps. France is the main trading partner.

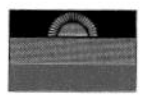

MALAWI
Republic of Malawi

Area Sq Km	118 484	**Languages**	Chichewa, English, other local languages
Area Sq Miles	45 747	**Religions**	Christian, traditional beliefs, Sunni Muslim
Population	16 363 000	**Currency**	Malawian kwacha
Capital	Lilongwe	**Organizations**	Comm., SADC, UN

Map page 195

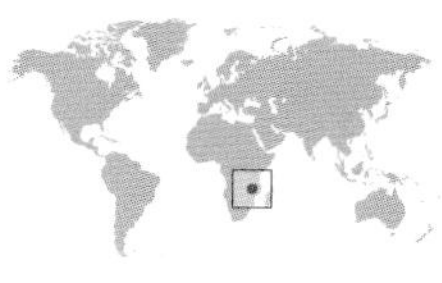

Landlocked Malawi in central Africa is a narrow hilly country at the southern end of the Great Rift Valley. One-fifth is covered by Lake Nyasa. Most of the population lives in rural areas in the southern regions. The climate is mainly subtropical, with varying rainfall. The economy is predominantly agricultural, with tobacco, tea and sugar the main exports. Malawi is one of the world's least developed countries and relies heavily on foreign aid. South Africa is the main trading partner.

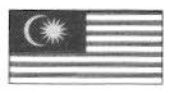

MALAYSIA

Area Sq Km	332 965	**Languages**	Malay, English, Chinese, Tamil, other local languages
Area Sq Miles	128 559	**Religions**	Sunni Muslim, Buddhist, Hindu, Christian, traditional beliefs
Population	29 717 000	**Currency**	Ringgit
Capital	Kuala Lumpur/ Putrajaya	**Organizations**	APEC, ASEAN, Comm., UN

Map page 163

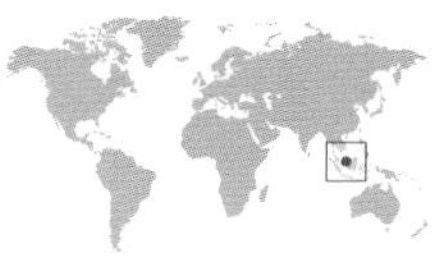

Malaysia, in southeast Asia, comprises two regions, separated by the South China Sea. The western region occupies the southern Malay Peninsula, which has a chain of mountains dividing the eastern coastal strip from wider plains to the west. East Malaysia, consisting of the states of Sabah and Sarawak in the north of the island of Borneo, is mainly rainforest-covered hills and mountains with mangrove swamps along the coast. Both regions have a tropical climate with heavy rainfall. About eighty per cent of the population lives in Peninsular Malaysia. The country is rich in natural resources and has reserves of minerals and fuels. It is an important producer of tin, oil, natural gas and tropical hardwoods. Agriculture remains a substantial part of the economy, but industry is the most important sector. The main exports are transport and electronic equipment, oil, chemicals, palm oil, wood and rubber. The main trading partners are Japan, the USA and Singapore.

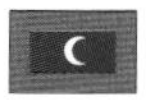

MALDIVES
Republic of the Maldives

Area Sq Km	298	**Languages**	Divehi (Maldivian)
Area Sq Miles	115	**Religions**	Sunni Muslim
Population	345 000	**Currency**	Rufiyaa
Capital	Male	**Organizations**	Comm., UN

Map page 130

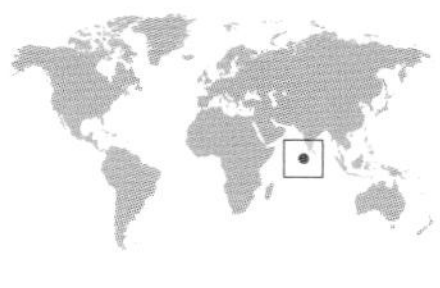

The Maldive archipelago comprises over a thousand coral atolls (around two hundred of which are inhabited), in the Indian Ocean, southwest of India. Over eighty per cent of the land area is less than one metre above sea level. The main atolls are North and South Male and Addu. The climate is hot, humid and monsoonal. There is little cultivation and almost all food is imported. Tourism has expanded rapidly and is the most important sector of the economy.

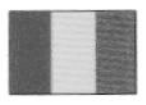

MALI
Republic of Mali

Area Sq Km	1 240 140	**Languages**	French, Bambara, other local languages
Area Sq Miles	478 821	**Religions**	Sunni Muslim, traditional beliefs, Christian
Population	15 302 000	**Currency**	CFA franc
Capital	Bamako	**Organizations**	UN

Map page 192

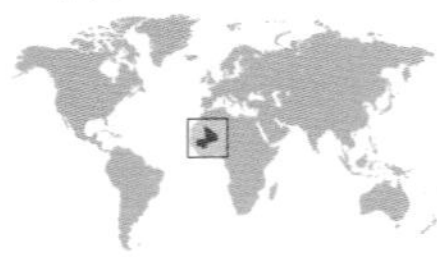

A landlocked state in west Africa, Mali is low-lying, with a few rugged hills in the northeast. Northern regions lie within the Sahara desert. To the south, around the Niger river, are marshes and savanna grassland. Rainfall is unreliable. Most of the population lives along the Niger and Falémé rivers. Exports include cotton, livestock and gold. Mali is one of the least developed countries in the world and relies heavily on foreign aid.

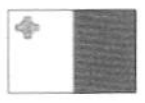

MALTA
Republic of Malta

Area Sq Km	316	**Languages**	Maltese, English
Area Sq Miles	122	**Religions**	Roman Catholic
Population	429 000	**Currency**	Euro
Capital	Valletta	**Organizations**	Comm., EU, UN

Map page 184

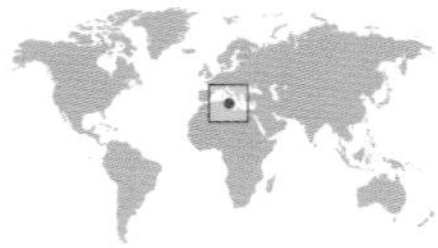

The islands of Malta and Gozo lie in the Mediterranean Sea, off the coast of southern Italy. The islands have hot, dry summers and mild winters. The economy depends on foreign trade, tourism and the manufacture of electronics and textiles. Main trading partners are the USA, France and Italy. Malta joined the European Union in May 2004.

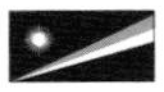

MARSHALL ISLANDS
Republic of the Marshall Islands

Area Sq Km	181	**Languages**	English, Marshallese
Area Sq Miles	70	**Religions**	Protestant, Roman Catholic
Population	53 000	**Currency**	United States dollar
Capital	Delap-Uliga-Djarrit	**Organizations**	UN

Map page 117

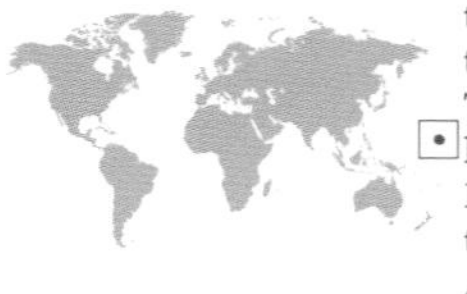

The Marshall Islands consist of over a thousand atolls, islands and islets, within two chains in the north Pacific Ocean. The main atolls are Majuro (home to half the population), Kwajalein, Jaluit, Enewetak and Bikini. The climate is tropical, with heavy autumn rainfall. About half the workforce is employed in farming or fishing. Tourism is a small source of foreign exchange and the islands depend heavily on aid from the USA.

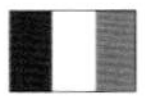

Martinique
French Overseas Department

Area Sq Km	1 079	**Languages**	French, Creole
Area Sq Miles	417	**Religions**	Roman Catholic, traditional beliefs
Population	404 000	**Currency**	Euro
Capital	Fort-de-France		

Map page 223 Martinique, one of the Caribbean Windward Islands, has volcanic peaks in the north, a populous central plain, and hills and beaches in the south. Tourism is a major source of foreign exchange, and substantial aid is received from France. The main trading partners are France and Guadeloupe.

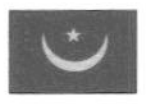

MAURITANIA
Islamic Republic of Mauritania

Area Sq Km	1 030 700	**Languages**	Arabic, French, other local languages
Area Sq Miles	397 955	**Religions**	Sunni Muslim
Population	3 890 000	**Currency**	Ouguiya
Capital	Nouakchott	**Organizations**	UN

Map page 192

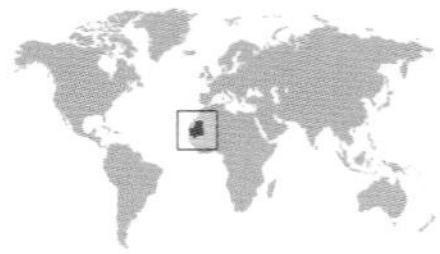

Mauritania is on the Atlantic coast of northwest Africa and lies almost entirely within the Sahara desert. Oases and a fertile strip along the Senegal river to the south are the only areas suitable for cultivation. The climate is generally hot and dry. About a quarter of Mauritanians live in the capital, Nouakchott. Most of the workforce depends on livestock rearing and subsistence farming. There are large deposits of iron ore which account for more than half of total exports. Mauritania's coastal waters are among the richest fishing grounds in the world. The main trading partners are France, Japan, China and Italy.

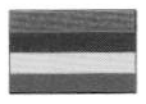

MAURITIUS
Republic of Mauritius

Area Sq Km	2 040	**Languages**	English, Creole, Hindi, Bhojpurī, French
Area Sq Miles	788	**Religions**	Hindu, Roman Catholic, Sunni Muslim
Population	1 244 000	**Currency**	Mauritian rupee
Capital	Port Louis	**Organizations**	Comm., SADC, UN

Map page 191

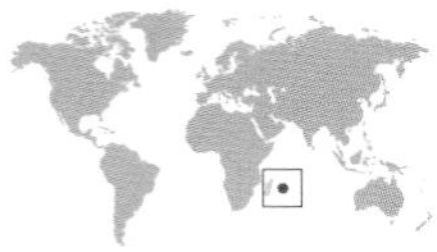

The state comprises Mauritius, Rodrigues and some twenty small islands in the Indian Ocean, east of Madagascar. The main island of Mauritius is volcanic in origin and has a coral coast, rising to a central plateau. Most of the population lives on the north and west sides of the island. The climate is warm and humid. The economy is based on sugar production, light manufacturing (chiefly clothing) and tourism.

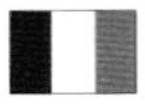

Mayotte
French Overseas Department

Area Sq Km	373	**Languages**	French, Mahorian (Shimaore), Kibushi
Area Sq Miles	144	**Religions**	Sunni Muslim, Christian
Population	222 000	**Currency**	Euro
Capital	Dzaoudzi		

Map page 195

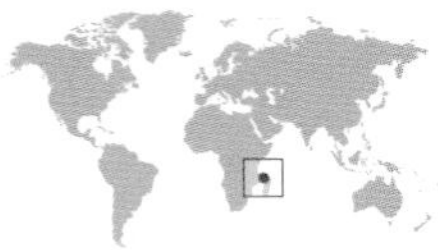

Lying in the Indian Ocean off the east coast of central Africa, Mayotte is geographically part of the Comoro archipelago. The economy is based on agriculture, but Mayotte depends heavily on aid from France.

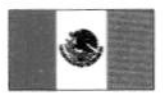

MEXICO
United Mexican States

Area Sq Km	1 972 545	**Languages**	Spanish, Amerindian languages
Area Sq Miles	761 604	**Religions**	Roman Catholic, Protestant
Population	122 332 000	**Currency**	Mexican peso
Capital	Mexico City	**Organizations**	APEC, OECD, UN

Map page 224–225

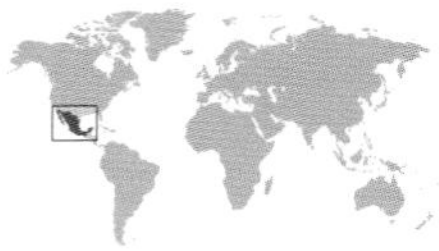

The largest country in Central America, Mexico extends south from the USA to Guatemala and Belize, and from the Pacific Ocean to the Gulf of Mexico. The greater part of the country is high plateau flanked by the western and eastern ranges of the Sierra Madre mountains. The principal lowland is the Yucatán peninsula in the southeast. The climate varies with latitude and altitude: hot and humid in the lowlands, warm on the plateau and cool with cold winters in the mountains. The north is arid, while the far south has heavy rainfall. Mexico City is the fourth largest conurbation in the world and the country's centre of trade and industry. Agriculture involves a sixth of the workforce; crops include grains, coffee, cotton and vegetables. Mexico is rich in minerals, including copper, zinc, lead, tin, sulphur, and silver. It is one of the world's largest producers of oil, from vast reserves in the Gulf of Mexico. The oil and petrochemical industries still dominate the economy, but a variety of manufactured goods are produced, including iron and steel, motor vehicles, textiles, chemicals and food and tobacco products. Tourism is growing in importance. Over three-quarters of all trade is with the USA.

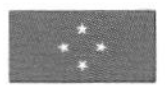

MICRONESIA, FEDERATED STATES OF

Area Sq Km	701	**Languages**	English, Chuukese, Pohnpeian, other local languages
Area Sq Miles	271	**Religions**	Roman Catholic, Protestant
Population	104 000	**Currency**	United States dollar
Capital	Palikir	**Organizations**	UN

Map page 116–117

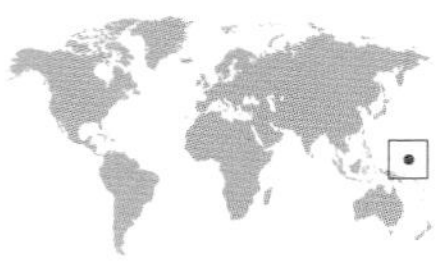

Micronesia comprises over six hundred atolls and islands of the Caroline Islands in the north Pacific Ocean. A third of the population lives on Pohnpei. The climate is tropical, with heavy rainfall. Fishing and subsistence farming are the main activities. Fish, garments and bananas are the main exports. Income is also derived from tourism and the licensing of foreign fishing fleets. The islands depend heavily on aid from the USA.

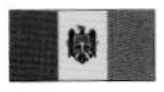

MOLDOVA
Republic of Moldova

Area Sq Km	33 700	**Languages**	Romanian, Ukrainian, Gagauz, Russian
Area Sq Miles	13 012	**Religions**	Romanian Orthodox, Russian Orthodox
Population	3 487 000	**Currency**	Moldovan leu
Capital	Chișinău (Kishinev)	**Organizations**	CIS, UN

Map page 187

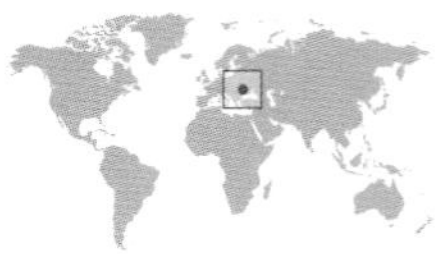

Moldova lies between Romania and Ukraine in eastern Europe. It consists of hilly steppe land, drained by the Prut and Dniester rivers. Moldova has no mineral resources, and the economy is mainly agricultural, with sugar beet, tobacco, wine and fruit the chief products. Food processing, machinery and textiles are the main industries. Russia is the main trading partner.

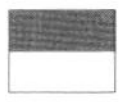

MONACO
Principality of Monaco

Area Sq Km	2	**Languages**	French, Monégasque, Italian
Area Sq Miles	1	**Religions**	Roman Catholic
Population	38 000	**Currency**	Euro
Capital	Monaco-Ville	**Organizations**	UN

Map page 182

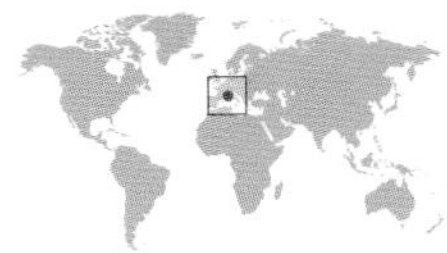

The principality occupies a rocky peninsula and a strip of land on France's Mediterranean coast. Monaco's economy depends on service industries (chiefly tourism, banking and finance) and light industry.

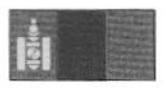

MONGOLIA

Area Sq Km	1 565 000	**Languages**	Khalka (Mongolian), Kazakh, other local languages
Area Sq Miles	604 250	**Religions**	Buddhist, Sunni Muslim
Population	2 839 000	**Currency**	Tugrik (tögrög)
Capital	Ulan Bator (Ulaanbaatar)	**Organizations**	UN

Map page 152–153

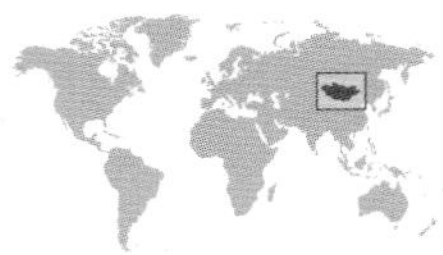

Mongolia is a landlocked country in eastern Asia between Russia and China. Much of it is high steppe land, with mountains and lakes in the west and north. In the south is the Gobi desert. Mongolia has long, cold winters and short, mild summers. A quarter of the population lives in the capital, Ulaanbaatar. Livestock breeding and agricultural processing are important. There are substantial mineral resources. Copper and textiles are the main exports. China and Russia are the main trading partners.

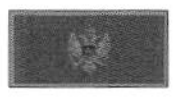

MONTENEGRO

Area Sq Km	13 812	**Languages**	Serbian (Montenegrin), Albanian
Area Sq Miles	5 333	**Religions**	Montenegrin Orthodox, Sunni Muslim
Population	621 000	**Currency**	Euro
Capital	Podgorica	**Organizations**	UN

Map page 185

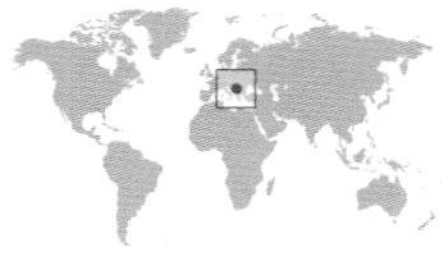

Montenegro, previously a constituent republic of the former Yugoslavia, became an independent nation in June 2006 when it opted to split from the state union of Serbia and Montenegro. Montenegro separates the much larger Serbia from the Adriatic coast. The landscape is rugged and mountainous, and the climate Mediterranean.

Montserrat
United Kingdom Overseas Territory

Area Sq Km	100	**Languages**	English
Area Sq Miles	39	**Religions**	Protestant, Roman Catholic
Population	4 922	**Currency**	East Caribbean dollar
Capital	Brades	**Organizations**	CARICOM

Map page 223

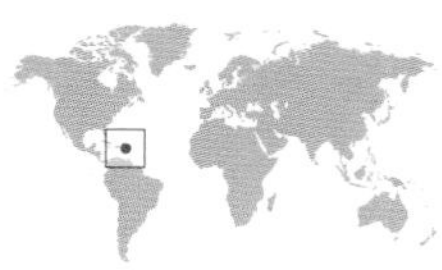

An island in the Leeward Islands group in the Lesser Antilles, in the Caribbean. From 1995 to 1997 the volcanoes in the Soufrière Hills erupted for the first time since 1630. Over sixty per cent of the island was covered in volcanic ash and Plymouth, the capital was, virtually destroyed. Many people emigrated, and the remaining population moved to the north of the island. Brades has replaced Plymouth as the temporary capital. Reconstruction is being funded by aid from the UK.

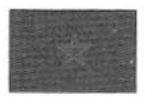

MOROCCO
Kingdom of Morocco

Area Sq Km	446 550	**Languages**	Arabic, Berber, French
Area Sq Miles	172 414	**Religions**	Sunni Muslim
Population	33 008 000	**Currency**	Moroccan dirham
Capital	Rabat	**Organizations**	UN

Map page 192

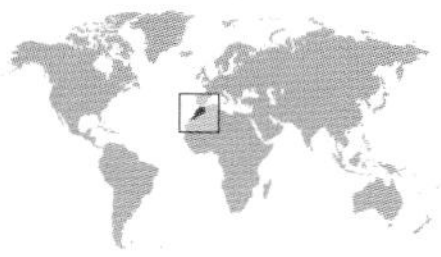

Lying in the northwest of Africa, Morocco has both Atlantic and Mediterranean coasts. The Atlas Mountains separate the arid south and disputed region of western Sahara from the fertile west and north, which have a milder climate. Most Moroccans live on the Atlantic coastal plain. The economy is based on agriculture, phosphate mining and tourism; the most important industries are food processing, textiles and chemicals.

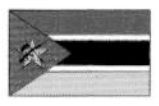

MOZAMBIQUE
Republic of Mozambique

Area Sq Km	799 380	**Languages**	Portuguese, Makua, Tsonga, other local languages
Area Sq Miles	308 642	**Religions**	Traditional beliefs, Roman Catholic, Sunni Muslim
Population	25 834 000	**Currency**	Metical
Capital	Maputo	**Organizations**	Comm., SADC, UN

Map page 195

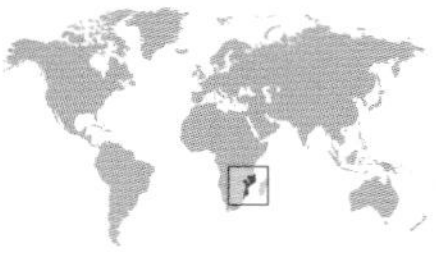

Mozambique lies on the east coast of southern Africa. The land is mainly a savanna plateau drained by the Zambezi and Limpopo rivers, with highlands to the north. Most of the population lives on the coast or in the river valleys. In general the climate is tropical with winter rainfall, but droughts occur. The economy is based on subsistence agriculture. Exports include shrimps, cashews, cotton and sugar, but Mozambique relies heavily on aid, and remains one of the least developed countries in the world.

MYANMAR (Burma)
Republic of the Union of Myanmar

Area Sq Km	676 577	**Languages**	Burmese, Shan, Karen, other local languages
Area Sq Miles	261 228	**Religions**	Buddhist, Christian, Sunni Muslim
Population	53 259 000	**Currency**	Kyat
Capital	Nay Pyi Taw	**Organizations**	ASEAN, UN

Map page 151

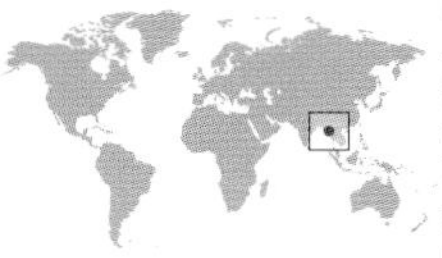

Myanmar (Burma) is in southeast Asia, bordering the Bay of Bengal and the Andaman Sea. Most of the population lives in the valley and delta of the Irrawaddy river, which is flanked by mountains and high plateaus. The climate is hot and monsoonal, and rainforest covers much of the land. Most of the workforce is employed in agriculture. Myanmar is rich in minerals, including zinc, lead, copper and silver. Political and social unrest and lack of foreign investment have affected economic development.

Nagorno-Karabakh
Disputed territory

Area Sq Km	6 000	**Languages**	Armenian
Area Sq Miles	2 317	**Religions**	Armenian Orthodox
Population	146 600	**Currency**	Armenian dram
Capital	Xankändi (Stepanakert)		

Map page 139 Established as an Autonomous Region within Azerbaijan in 1923, Nagorno-Karabakh is a disputed enclave of Azerbaijan. It is legally part of Azerbaijan, but is populated largely by ethnic Armenians who have established what amounts to a separatist de facto republic operating with support from Armenia. In 1991, the local Armenian population declared independence and Azerbaijan abolished the area's autonomous status. As a result of conflict, Nagorno-Karabakh/Armenia occupies approximately twenty per cent of Azerbaijan. A Russian-brokered cease-fire has been in place since 1994, with the cease-fire line enclosing the territory of Nagorno-Karabakh and the additional parts of Azerbaijan, up to the Armenian border, seized by Karabakh Armenians during the fighting. The area between the cease-fire line and the boundary of Nagorno-Karabakh is effectively a 'no-go' area.

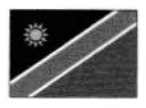

NAMIBIA
Republic of Namibia

Area Sq Km	824 292	**Languages**	English, Afrikaans, German, Ovambo, other local languages
Area Sq Miles	318 261	**Religions**	Protestant, Roman Catholic
Population	2 303 000	**Currency**	Namibian dollar
Capital	Windhoek	**Organizations**	Comm., SADC, UN

Map page 195

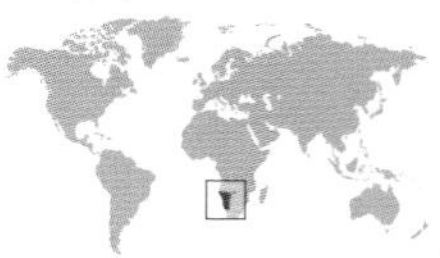

Namibia lies on the southern Atlantic coast of Africa. Mountain ranges separate the coastal Namib Desert from the interior plateau, bordered to the south and east by the Kalahari Desert. The country is hot and dry, but some summer rain in the north supports crops and livestock. Employment is in agriculture and fishing, although the economy is based on mineral extraction – diamonds, uranium, lead, zinc and silver. The economy is closely linked to South Africa.

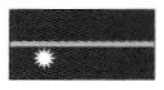

NAURU
Republic of Nauru

Area Sq Km	21	**Languages**	Nauruan, English
Area Sq Miles	8	**Religions**	Protestant, Roman Catholic
Population	10 000	**Currency**	Australian dollar
Capital	Yaren	**Organizations**	Comm., UN

Map page 119

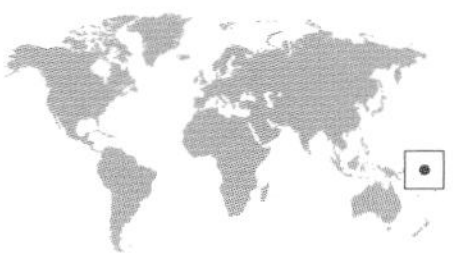

Nauru is a coral island near the Equator in the Pacific Ocean. It has a fertile coastal strip and a barren central plateau. The climate is tropical. The economy is based on phosphate mining, but reserves are exhausted and replacement of this income is a serious long-term problem.

NEPAL
Federal Democratic Republic of Nepal

Area Sq Km	147 181	**Languages**	Nepali, Maithili, Bhojpuri, English, other local languages
Area Sq Miles	56 827	**Religions**	Hindu, Buddhist, Sunni Muslim
Population	27 797 000	**Currency**	Nepalese rupee
Capital	Kathmandu	**Organizations**	UN

Map page 149

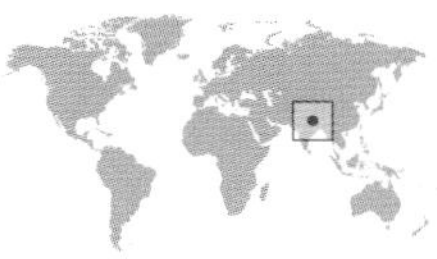

Nepal lies in the eastern Himalaya mountains between India and China. High mountains (including Everest) dominate the north. Most people live in the temperate central valleys and subtropical southern plains. The economy is based largely on agriculture and forestry. There is some manufacturing, chiefly of textiles and carpets, and tourism is important. Nepal relies heavily on foreign aid.

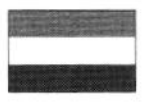

NETHERLANDS
Kingdom of the Netherlands

Area Sq Km	41 526	**Languages**	Dutch, Frisian
Area Sq Miles	16 033	**Religions**	Roman Catholic, Protestant, Sunni Muslim
Population	16 759 000	**Currency**	Euro
Capital	Amsterdam/ The Hague	**Organizations**	EU, NATO, OECD, UN

Map page 178

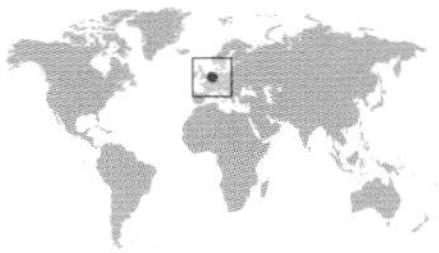

The Netherlands lies on the North Sea coast of western Europe. Apart from low hills in the far southeast, the land is flat and low-lying, much of it below sea level. The coastal region includes the delta of five rivers and polders (reclaimed land), protected by sand dunes, dykes and canals. The climate is temperate, with cool summers and mild winters. Rainfall is spread evenly throughout the year. The Netherlands is a populated and highly urbanized country, with the majority of the population living in the cities of Amsterdam, Rotterdam and The Hague. Horticulture and dairy farming are important activities, although they employ less than three per cent of the workforce. The Netherlands is an important agricultural exporter, and is a leading producer and exporter of natural gas from reserves in the North Sea. The economy is based mainly on international trade and manufacturing industry. The main industries produce food products, chemicals, machinery, electrical and electronic goods and transport equipment. Germany is the main trading partner, followed by other European Union countries.

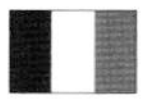

New Caledonia
French Overseas Country

Area Sq Km	19 058	**Languages**	French, other local languages
Area Sq Miles	7 358	**Religions**	Roman Catholic, Protestant, Sunni Muslim
Population	256 000		
Capital	Nouméa	**Currency**	CFP franc

Map page 119

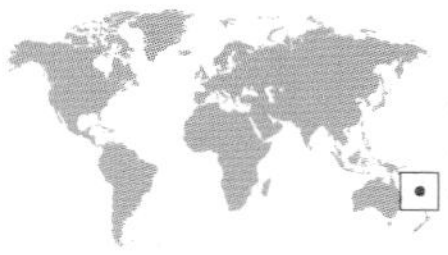

An island group lying in the southwest Pacific, with a sub-tropical climate. New Caledonia has over one-fifth of the world's nickel reserves, and the main economic activity is metal mining. Tourism is also important. New Caledonia relies on aid from France.

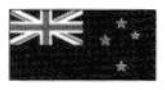

NEW ZEALAND

Area Sq Km	270 534	**Languages**	English, Maori
Area Sq Miles	104 454	**Religions**	Protestant, Roman Catholic
Population	4 506 000	**Currency**	New Zealand dollar
Capital	Wellington	**Organizations**	APEC, Comm., OECD, UN

Map page 126

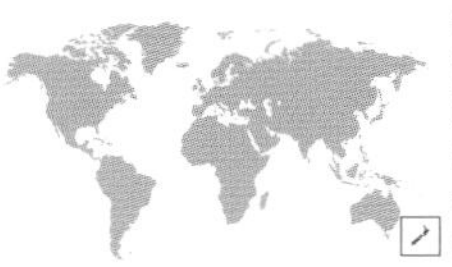

New Zealand comprises two main islands separated by the narrow Cook Strait, and a number of smaller islands. North Island, where three-quarters of the population lives, has mountain ranges, broad fertile valleys and a central plateau with hot springs and active volcanoes. South Island is also mountainous, with the Southern Alps running its entire length. The only major lowland area is the Canterbury Plains in the centre-east. The climate is generally temperate, although South Island has colder winters. Farming is the mainstay of the economy. New Zealand is one of the world's leading producers of meat (beef, lamb and mutton), wool and dairy products; fruit and fish are also important. Hydroelectric and geothermal power provide much of the country's energy needs. Other industries produce timber, wood pulp, iron, aluminium, machinery and chemicals. Tourism is the fastest growing sector of the economy. The main trading partners are Australia, the USA, China, the UK and Japan.

NICARAGUA
Republic of Nicaragua

Area Sq Km	130 000	**Languages**	Spanish, Amerindian languages
Area Sq Miles	50 193	**Religions**	Roman Catholic, Protestant
Population	6 080 000	**Currency**	Córdoba
Capital	Managua	**Organizations**	UN

Map page 224

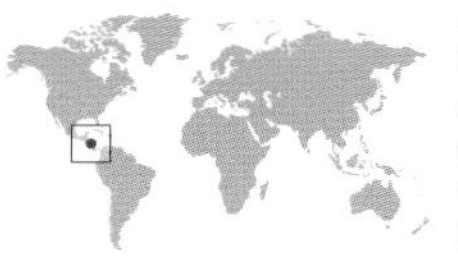

Nicaragua lies at the heart of Central America, with both Pacific and Caribbean coasts. Mountain ranges separate the east, which is largely rainforest, from the more developed western regions, which include Lake Nicaragua and some active volcanoes. The highest land is in the north. The climate is tropical. Nicaragua is one of the western hemisphere's poorest countries, and the economy is largely agricultural, but growth in tourism is having a positive effect in other areas. Exports include coffee, seafood, cotton and bananas. The USA is the main trading partner. Nicaragua has a huge national debt, and relies heavily on foreign aid.

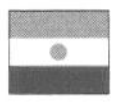

NIGER
Republic of Niger

Area Sq Km	1 267 000	**Languages**	French, Hausa, Fulani, other local languages
Area Sq Miles	489 191	**Religions**	Sunni Muslim, traditional beliefs
Population	17 831 000	**Currency**	CFA franc
Capital	Niamey	**Organizations**	UN

Map page 192–193

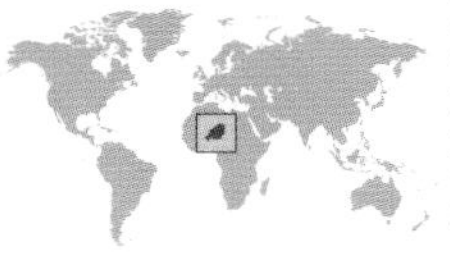

A landlocked state of west Africa, Niger lies mostly within the Sahara desert, but with savanna in the south and in the Niger valley area. The mountains of the Massif de l'Aïr dominate central regions. Much of the country is hot and dry. The south has some summer rainfall, although droughts occur. The economy depends on subsistence farming and herding, and uranium exports, but Niger is one of the world's least developed countries and relies heavily on foreign aid. France is the main trading partner.

NIGERIA
Federal Republic of Nigeria

Area Sq Km	923 768	**Languages**	English, Hausa, Yoruba, Ibo, Fulani, other local languages
Area Sq Miles	356 669	**Religions**	Sunni Muslim, Christian, traditional beliefs
Population	173 615 000	**Currency**	Naira
Capital	Abuja	**Organizations**	Comm., OPEC, UN

Map page 192–193

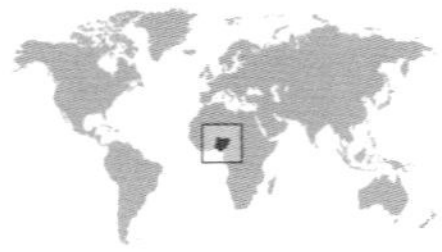

Nigeria is the most populous country in Africa. It includes the Niger delta on the Gulf of Guinea, a rainforest belt, wooded savanna plateaus inland, and semi-desert on the edge of the Sahara. The climate is tropical. Most people live on the coast or in the west. Agriculture is on a subsistence basis, but Nigeria is a net importer of food. Cocoa and rubber are exported. Oil is extremely important to the economy, while gas reserves and minerals are largely undeveloped. Industry involves oil refining, fertilizers, agricultural processing, textiles, vehicle assembly and steel. Political instability in the past has left Nigeria with heavy debts, poverty and unemployment but it is now the largest economy in Africa.

Niue
Self-governing New Zealand Overseas Territory

Area Sq Km	258	**Languages**	English, Nivean
Area Sq Miles	100	**Religions**	Christian
Population	1 460	**Currency**	New Zealand dollar
Capital	Alofi		

Map page 119

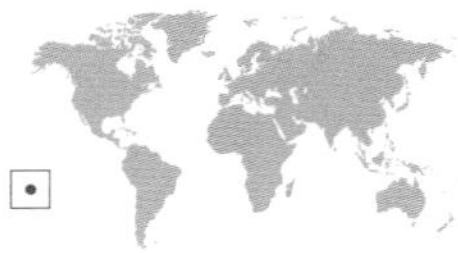

Niue, one of the largest coral islands in the world, lies in the south Pacific Ocean about 500 kilometres (300 miles) east of Tonga. The economy depends on aid and remittances from New Zealand. The population is declining because of migration to New Zealand.

Norfolk Island
Australian External Territory

Area Sq Km	35	**Languages**	English
Area Sq Miles	14	**Religions**	Protestant, Roman Catholic
Population	2 302	**Currency**	Australian dollar
Capital	Kingston		

Map page 119

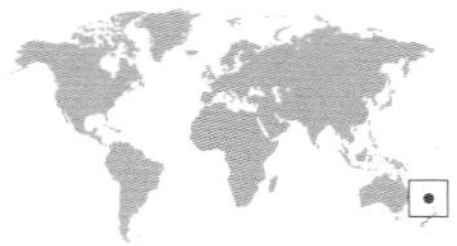

In the south Pacific Ocean, Norfolk Island lies between Vanuatu and New Zealand. Tourism has increased steadily and is the mainstay of the economy and provides revenues for agricultural development.

Northern Mariana Islands
United States Commonwealth

Area Sq Km	477	**Languages**	English, Chamorro, other local languages
Area Sq Miles	184	**Religions**	Roman Catholic
Population	54 000	**Currency**	United States dollar
Capital	Capitol Hill		

Map page 151

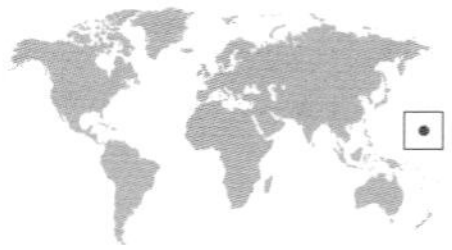

A chain of islands in the northwest Pacific Ocean, extending over 550 kilometres (350 miles) north to south. The main island is Saipan. Tourism is a major industry, employing approximately half the workforce.

NORTH KOREA
Democratic People's Republic of Korea

Area Sq Km	120 538	**Languages**	Korean
Area Sq Miles	46 540	**Religions**	Traditional beliefs, Chondoist, Buddhist
Population	24 895 000	**Currency**	North Korean won
Capital	P'yŏngyang	**Organizations**	UN

Map page 160

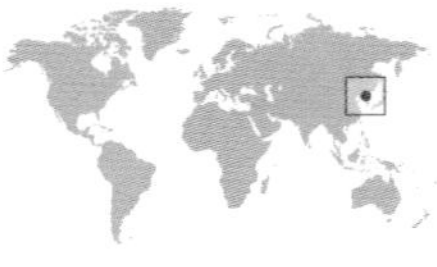

Occupying the northern half of the Korean peninsula in eastern Asia, North Korea is a rugged and mountainous country. The principal lowlands and the main agricultural areas are the plains in the southwest. Sixty per cent of the population lives in urban areas, mainly on the coastal plains. North Korea has a continental climate, with cold, dry winters and hot, wet summers. Approximately one-third of the workforce is involved in agriculture, mainly growing food crops on cooperative farms. Various minerals, notably iron ore, are mined and are the basis of the country's heavy industries. Exports include minerals (lead, magnesite and zinc) and metal products (chiefly iron and steel). The economy declined after 1991, when ties to the former USSR and eastern bloc collapsed, and there have been serious food shortages.

NORWAY
Kingdom of Norway

Area Sq Km	323 878	**Languages**	Norwegian, Sami languages
Area Sq Miles	125 050	**Religions**	Protestant, Roman Catholic
Population	5 043 000	**Currency**	Norwegian krone
Capital	Oslo	**Organizations**	NATO, OECD, UN

Map page 170–171

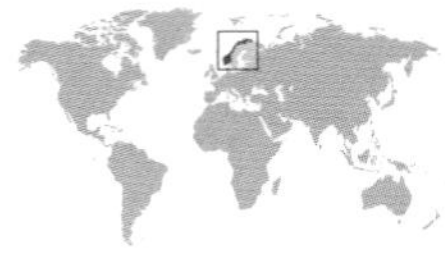

Norway stretches along the west coast of Scandinavia. Its extensive coastline is indented with fjords and fringed with islands. Inland, the terrain is mountainous, with forests and lakes in the south. The only major lowlands are in the south, where most of the population lives. The climate is modified by the North Atlantic Drift. Norway is one of western Europe's leading producers of oil and gas, from its North Sea fields, and oil contributes half of all export earnings. Industries include oil and gas platforms and petrochemicals, and the processing of fish, timber and minerals. Agriculture is limited. Fishing and fish farming, merchant shipping and tourism are also important.

OMAN
Sultanate of Oman

Area Sq Km	309 500	**Languages**	Arabic, Baluchi, Indian languages
Area Sq Miles	119 499	**Religions**	Ibadhi Muslim, Sunni Muslim
Population	3 632 000	**Currency**	Omani rial
Capital	Muscat (Masqaṭ)	**Organizations**	UN

Map page 146

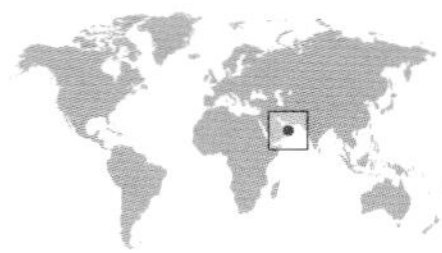

In southwest Asia, Oman occupies the east and southeast coasts of the Arabian Peninsula and an enclave north of the United Arab Emirates. Most of the land is desert, with mountains in the north and south. The climate is hot and mainly dry. Most of the population lives on the coastal strip on the Gulf of Oman. The majority depend on farming and fishing, but the oil and gas industries dominate the economy with around eighty per cent of export revenues coming from oil.

PAKISTAN
Islamic Republic of Pakistan

Area Sq Km	881 888	**Languages**	Urdu, Punjabi, Sindhi, Pashtu (Pushtu), English, Balochi
Area Sq Miles	340 497	**Religions**	Sunni Muslim, Shi'a Muslim, Christian, Hindu
Population	182 143 000	**Currency**	Pakistani rupee
Capital	Islamabad	**Organizations**	Comm., UN

Map page 144–145

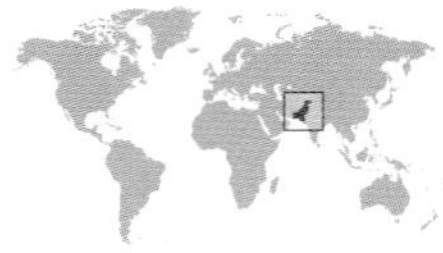

Pakistan is in the northwest part of the Indian subcontinent in south Asia, on the Arabian Sea. The east and south are dominated by the great basin of the Indus river system. This is the main agricultural area and contains most of the predominantly rural population. To the north the land rises to the mountains of the Karakoram, Hindu Kush and Himalaya mountains. The west is semi-desert plateaus and mountain ranges. The climate ranges between dry desert, and arctic tundra on the mountain tops. Temperatures are generally warm and rainfall is monsoonal. Agriculture is the main sector of the economy, employing over a third of the workforce, and is based on extensive irrigation schemes. Pakistan is one of the world's leading producers of cotton and a major exporter of rice. Pakistan produces natural gas and has a variety of mineral deposits including coal and gold, but they are little developed. The main industries are textiles and clothing manufacture and food processing, with fabrics and ready-made clothing the leading exports. Pakistan also produces leather goods, fertilizers, chemicals, paper and precision instruments. The country depends heavily on foreign aid and remittances from workers abroad.

PALAU
Republic of Palau

Area Sq Km	497	**Languages**	Palauan, English
Area Sq Miles	192	**Religions**	Roman Catholic, Protestant, traditional beliefs
Population	21 000	**Currency**	United States dollar
Capital	Melekeok (Ngerulmud)	**Organizations**	UN

Map page 151

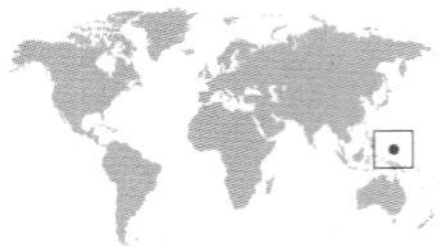

Palau comprises over three hundred islands in the western Caroline Islands, in the west Pacific Ocean. The climate is tropical. The economy is based on farming, fishing and tourism, but Palau is heavily dependent on aid from the USA.

PANAMA
Republic of Panama

Area Sq Km	77 082	**Languages**	Spanish, English, Amerindian languages
Area Sq Miles	29 762	**Religions**	Roman Catholic, Protestant, Sunni Muslim
Population	3 864 000	**Currency**	Balboa
Capital	Panama City	**Organizations**	UN

Map page 224

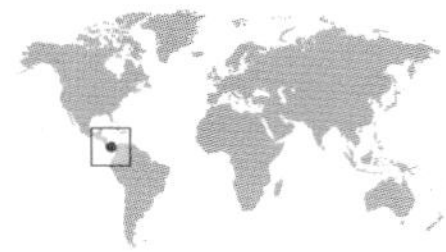

Panama is the most southerly state in central America and has Pacific and Caribbean coasts. It is hilly, with mountains in the west and jungle near the Colombian border. The climate is tropical. Most of the population lives on the drier Pacific side. The economy is based mainly on services related to the Panama Canal: shipping, banking and tourism. Exports include bananas, shrimps, coffee, clothing and fish products. The USA is the main trading partner.

PAPUA NEW GUINEA
Independent State of Papua New Guinea

Area Sq Km	462 840	**Languages**	English, Tok Pisin (Creole), other local languages
Area Sq Miles	178 704	**Religions**	Protestant, Roman Catholic, traditional beliefs
Population	7 321 000	**Currency**	Kina
Capital	Port Moresby	**Organizations**	APEC, Comm., UN

Map page 118–119

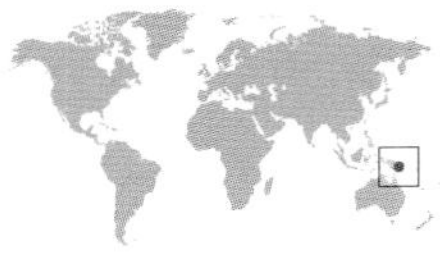

Papua New Guinea occupies the eastern half of the island of New Guinea and includes many island groups. It has a forested and mountainous interior, bordered by swampy plains, and a tropical monsoon climate. Most of the workforce are farmers. Timber, copra, coffee and cocoa are important, but exports are dominated by minerals, chiefly gold and copper. The country depends on foreign aid. Australia, Japan and Singapore are the main trading partners.

PARAGUAY
Republic of Paraguay

Area Sq Km	406 752	**Languages**	Spanish, Guaraní
Area Sq Miles	157 048	**Religions**	Roman Catholic, Protestant
Population	6 802 000	**Currency**	Guaraní
Capital	Asunción	**Organizations**	UN

Map page 232

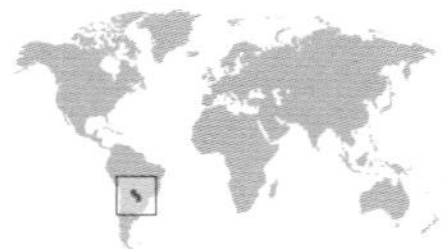

Paraguay is a landlocked country in central South America, bordering Bolivia, Brazil and Argentina. The Paraguay river separates a sparsely populated western zone of marsh and flat alluvial plains from a more developed, hilly and forested region to the east and south. The climate is subtropical. Virtually all electricity is produced by hydroelectric plants, and surplus power is exported to Brazil and Argentina. The hydroelectric dam at Itaipú is one of the largest in the world. The mainstay of the economy is agriculture and related industries. Exports include cotton, soya bean and edible oil products, timber and meat. Brazil and Argentina are the main trading partners.

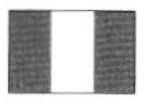

PERU
Republic of Peru

Area Sq Km	1 285 216	**Languages**	Spanish, Quechua, Aymara
Area Sq Miles	496 225	**Religions**	Roman Catholic, Protestant
Population	30 376 000	**Currency**	Nuevo sol
Capital	Lima	**Organizations**	APEC, UN

Map page 230

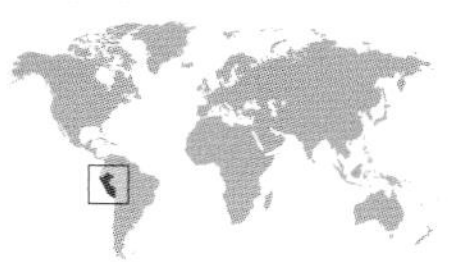

Peru lies on the Pacific coast of South America. Most Peruvians live on the coastal strip and on the plateaus of the high Andes mountains. East of the Andes is the Amazon rainforest. The coast is temperate with low rainfall while the east is hot, humid and wet. Agriculture involves one-third of the workforce and fishing is also important. Agriculture and fishing have both been disrupted by the El Niño climatic effect in recent years. Sugar, cotton, coffee and, illegally, coca are the main cash crops. Copper and copper products, fishmeal, zinc products, coffee, petroleum and its products, and textiles are the main exports. The USA and the European Union are the main trading partners.

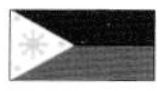

PHILIPPINES
Republic of the Philippines

Area Sq Km	300 000	**Languages**	English, Filipino, Tagalog, Cebuano, other local languages
Area Sq Miles	115 831	**Religions**	Roman Catholic, Protestant, Sunni Muslim, Aglipayan
Population	98 394 000	**Currency**	Philippine peso
Capital	Manila	**Organizations**	APEC, ASEAN, UN

Map page 161

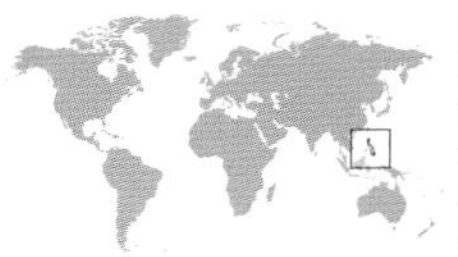

The Philippines, in southeast Asia, consists of over seven thousand islands lying between the South China Sea and the Pacific Ocean. The main islands are mountainous and forested. Volcanoes are active, and earthquakes and tropical storms are common. Most of the population lives on the plains or the coastal strips. The climate is hot and humid with monsoonal rainfall. Rice, coconuts, sugar cane, pineapples and bananas are the main crops, and fishing is important. Exports include electronic and transport equipment and machinery, clothing, and coconuts. Foreign aid and remittances from workers abroad are important to the economy. The USA and Japan are the main trading partners.

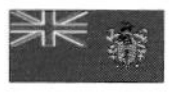

Pitcairn Islands
United Kingdom Overseas Territory

Area Sq Km	45	**Languages**	English
Area Sq Miles	17	**Religions**	Protestant
Population	50	**Currency**	New Zealand dollar
Capital	Adamstown		

Map page 117

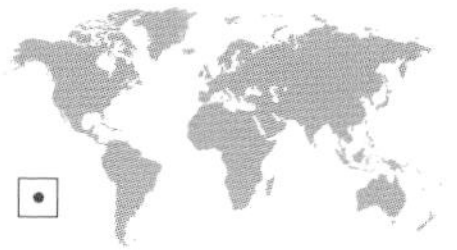

An island group in the southeast Pacific Ocean consisting of Pitcairn Island and three uninhabited islands, Henderson, Ducie and Oeno Islands. It was originally settled by mutineers from HMS *Bounty* in 1790.

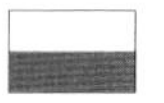

POLAND
Republic of Poland

Area Sq Km	312 683	**Languages**	Polish, German
Area Sq Miles	120 728	**Religions**	Roman Catholic, Polish Orthodox
Population	38 217 000	**Currency**	Złoty
Capital	Warsaw (Warszawa)	**Organizations**	EU, NATO, OECD, UN

Map page 176–177

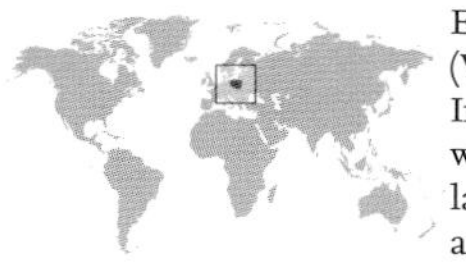

Poland lies on the Baltic coast of eastern Europe. The Oder (Odra) and Vistula (Wisła) river deltas dominate the coast. Inland, much of the country is low-lying, with woods and lakes. In the south the land rises to the Sudeten Mountains and the western part of the Carpathian Mountains, which form the borders with the Czech Republic and Slovakia respectively. The climate is continental. Around a sixth of the workforce is involved in agriculture, and exports include livestock products and sugar. The economy is heavily industrialized, with mining and manufacturing accounting for forty per cent of national income. Poland is one of the world's major producers of coal, and also produces copper, zinc, lead, sulphur and natural gas. The main industries are machinery and transport equipment, shipbuilding, and metal and chemical production. Exports include machinery and transport equipment, manufactured goods, food and live animals. Germany is the main trading partner. Poland joined the European Union in May 2004.

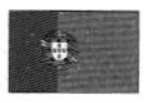

PORTUGAL
Portuguese Republic

Area Sq Km	88 940	**Languages**	Portuguese
Area Sq Miles	34 340	**Religions**	Roman Catholic, Protestant
Population	10 608 000	**Currency**	Euro
Capital	Lisbon (Lisboa)	**Organizations**	EU, NATO, OECD, UN

Map page 183

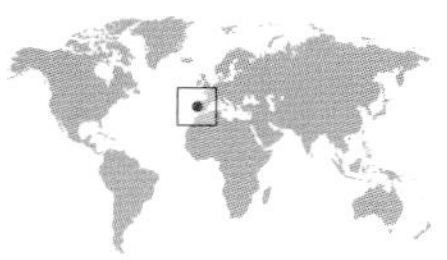

Portugal lies in the western part of the Iberian peninsula in southwest Europe, has an Atlantic coastline and is bordered by Spain to the north and east. The island groups of the Azores and Madeira are parts of Portugal. On the mainland, the land north of the river Tagus (Tejo) is mostly highland, with extensive forests of pine and cork. South of the river is undulating lowland. The climate in the north is cool and moist; the south is warmer, with dry, mild winters. Most Portuguese live near the coast, and more than one-third of the total population lives around the capital, Lisbon (Lisboa). Agriculture, fishing and forestry involve approximately ten per cent of the workforce. Mining and manufacturing are the main sectors of the economy. Portugal produces kaolin, copper, tin, zinc, tungsten and salt. Exports include textiles, clothing and footwear, electrical machinery and transport equipment, cork and wood products, and chemicals. Service industries, chiefly tourism and banking, are important to the economy, as are remittances from workers abroad. Most trade is with other European Union countries.

Puerto Rico
United States Commonwealth

Area Sq Km	9 104	**Languages**	Spanish, English
Area Sq Miles	3 515	**Religions**	Roman Catholic, Protestant
Population	3 688 000	**Currency**	United States dollar
Capital	San Juan		

Map page 223

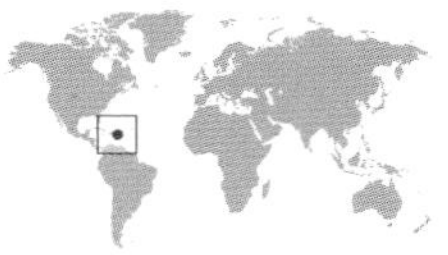

The Caribbean island of Puerto Rico has a forested, hilly interior, coastal plains and a tropical climate. Half of the population lives in the San Juan area. The economy is based on manufacturing (chiefly chemicals, electronics and food), tourism and agriculture. The USA is the main trading partner.

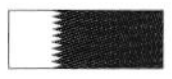

QATAR
State of Qatar

Area Sq Km	11 437	**Languages**	Arabic
Area Sq Miles	4 416	**Religions**	Sunni Muslim
Population	2 169 000	**Currency**	Qatari riyal
Capital	Doha (Ad Dawḩah)	**Organizations**	OPEC, UN

Map page 142

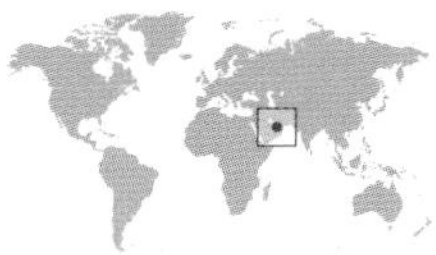

Qatar occupies a peninsula in southwest Asia that extends northwards from east-central Saudi Arabia into The Gulf. The land is flat and barren with sand dunes and salt pans. The climate is hot and mainly dry. Most people live in the area of the capital, Doha. The economy is heavily dependent on oil and natural gas production and the oil-refining industry. Income also comes from overseas investment. Japan is the largest trading partner.

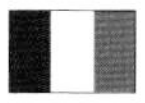

Réunion
French Overseas Department

Area Sq Km	2 551	**Languages**	French, Creole
Area Sq Miles	985	**Religions**	Roman Catholic
Population	875 000	**Currency**	Euro
Capital	St-Denis		

Map page 191

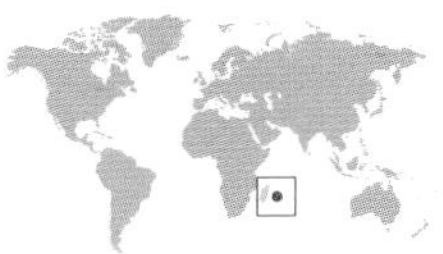

The Indian Ocean island of Réunion is mountainous, with coastal lowlands and a warm climate. The economy depends on tourism, French aid, and exports of sugar. In 2005 France transferred the administration of various small uninhabited islands in the seas around Madagascar from Réunion to the French Southern and Antarctic Lands.

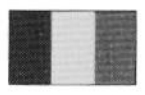

ROMANIA

Area Sq Km	237 500	**Languages**	Romanian, Hungarian
Area Sq Miles	91 699	**Religions**	Romanian Orthodox, Protestant, Roman Catholic
Population	21 699 000	**Currency**	Romanian leu
Capital	Bucharest (București)	**Organizations**	EU, NATO, UN

Map page 185

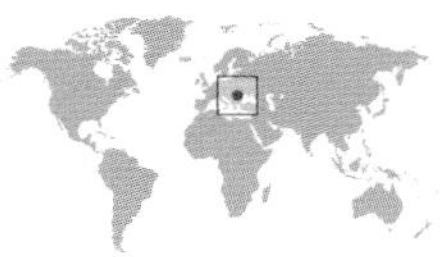

Romania lies in eastern Europe, on the northwest coast of the Black Sea. Mountains separate the Transylvanian Basin in the centre of the country from the populous plains of the east and south and from the Danube delta. The climate is continental. Romania has mineral resources (zinc, lead, silver and gold) and oil and natural gas reserves. Economic development has been slow and sporadic, but measures to accelerate change were introduced in 1999. Agricultural employment has since declined. The main exports are textiles, mineral products, chemicals, machinery and footwear. The main trading partners are Germany and Italy.

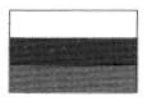

RUSSIA

Area Sq Km	17 075 400	**Languages**	Russian, Tatar, Ukrainian, other local languages
Area Sq Miles	6 592 849	**Religions**	Russian Orthodox, Sunni Muslim, Protestant
Population	142 834 000	**Currency**	Russian rouble
Capital	Moscow (Moskva)	**Organizations**	APEC, CIS, UN

Map page 132–133

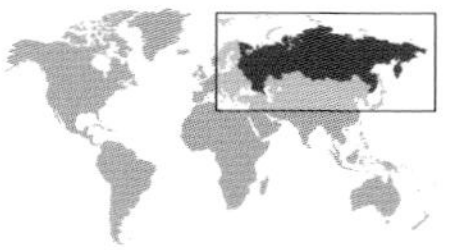

Russia occupies much of eastern Europe and all of northern Asia, and is the world's largest country. It borders fourteen countries to the west and south and has long coastlines on the Arctic and Pacific Oceans to the north and east. European Russia lies west of the Ural Mountains. To the south the land rises to uplands and the Caucasus mountains on the border with Georgia and Azerbaijan. East of the Urals lies the flat West Siberian Plain and the Central Siberian Plateau. In the south-east is Lake Baikal, the world's deepest lake, and the Sayan ranges on the border with Kazakhstan and Mongolia. Eastern Siberia is rugged and mountainous, with many active volcanoes in the Kamchatka Peninsula. The country's major rivers are the Volga in the west and the Ob', Irtysh, Yenisey, Lena and Amur in Siberia. The climate and vegetation range between arctic tundra in the north and semi-arid steppe towards the Black and Caspian Sea coasts in the south. In general, the climate is continental with extreme temperatures. The majority of the population (the tenth largest in the world), and industry and agriculture are concentrated in European Russia. The economy is dependent on exploitation of raw materials and on heavy industry. Russia has a wealth of mineral resources, although they are often difficult to exploit because of climate and remote locations. It is one of the world's leading producers of petroleum, natural gas and coal as well as iron ore, nickel, copper, bauxite, and many precious and rare metals. Forests cover over forty per cent of the land area and supply an important timber, paper and pulp industry. Approximately eight per cent of the land is suitable for cultivation. Agriculture has shown steady growth since 1999, with grain now exported. Fishing is important and Russia has a large fleet operating around the world. The transition to a market economy has been slow and difficult, with considerable underemployment. As well as mining and extractive industries there is a wide range of manufacturing industry, from steel mills to aircraft and space vehicles, shipbuilding, synthetic fabrics, plastics, cotton fabrics, consumer durables, chemicals and fertilizers. Exports include fuels, metals, machinery, chemicals and forest products. The most important trading partners include Germany, the USA and Belarus.

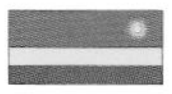

RWANDA
Republic of Rwanda

Area Sq Km	26 338	**Languages**	Kinyarwanda, French, English
Area Sq Miles	10 169	**Religions**	Roman Catholic, traditional beliefs, Protestant
Population	11 777 000	**Currency**	Rwandan franc
Capital	Kigali	**Organizations**	Comm., UN

Map page 195

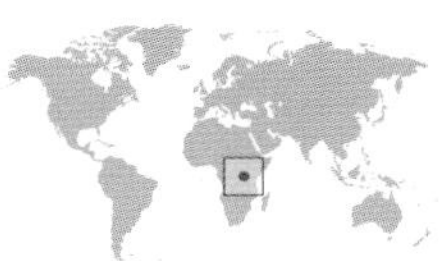

Rwanda, the most densely populated country in continental Africa, is situated in the mountains and plateaus to the east of the western branch of the Great Rift Valley in east Africa. The climate is warm with a summer dry season. Rwanda depends on subsistence farming, coffee and tea exports, light industry and foreign aid. The country is slowly recovering from serious internal conflict which caused devastation in the early 1990s.

St-Barthélemy
French Overseas Collectivity

Area Sq Km	21	**Languages**	French
Area Sq Miles	8	**Religions**	Roman Catholic
Population	9 072	**Currency**	Euro
Capital	Gustavia		

Map page 223

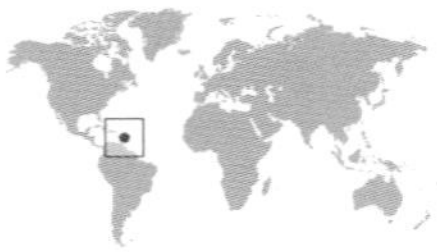

An island in the Leeward Islands in the Lesser Antilles, in the Caribbean south of St-Martin. It was separated from Guadeloupe politically in 2007. Tourism is the main economic activity.

St Helena, Ascension and Tristan da Cunha
United Kingdom Overseas Territory

Area Sq Km	410	**Languages**	English
Area Sq Miles	158	**Religions**	Protestant, Roman Catholic
Population	5 366	**Currency**	St Helena pound, Pound sterling
Capital	Jamestown		

Map page 190 Known until 2009 as St Helena and Dependencies, this UK territory lies in the south Atlantic Ocean. The islands, all of volcanic origin, are very remote from each other and from Africa and South America. The economy varies from island to island, but depends also on UK aid. Main trading partners are the UK and South Africa.

ST KITTS AND NEVIS
Federation of Saint Kitts and Nevis

Area Sq Km	261	**Languages**	English, Creole
Area Sq Miles	101	**Religions**	Protestant, Roman Catholic
Population	54 000	**Currency**	East Caribbean dollar
Capital	Basseterre	**Organizations**	CARICOM, Comm., UN

Map page 223

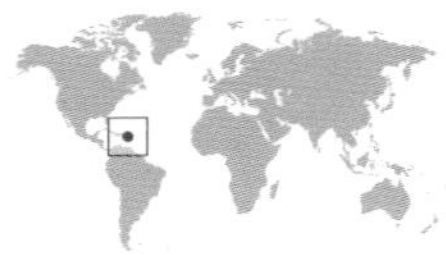

St Kitts and Nevis are in the Leeward Islands, in the Caribbean. Both volcanic islands are mountainous and forested, with sandy beaches and a warm, wet climate. About three-quarters of the population lives on St Kitts. Agriculture is the main activity, with sugar the main product. Tourism and manufacturing (chiefly garments and electronic components) and offshore banking are important activities.

ST LUCIA

Area Sq Km	616	**Languages**	English, Creole
Area Sq Miles	238	**Religions**	Roman Catholic, Protestant
Population	182 000	**Currency**	East Caribbean dollar
Capital	Castries	**Organizations**	CARICOM, Comm., UN

Map page 223

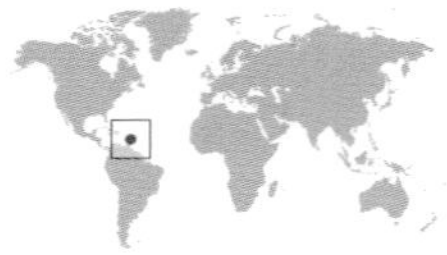

St Lucia, one of the Windward Islands in the Caribbean Sea, is a volcanic island with forested mountains, hot springs, sandy beaches and a wet tropical climate. Agriculture is the main activity, with bananas accounting for approximately forty per cent of export earnings. Tourism, agricultural processing and light manufacturing are increasingly important.

St-Martin
French Overseas Collectivity

Area Sq Km	54	**Languages**	French
Area Sq Miles	21	**Religions**	Roman Catholic
Population	37 630	**Currency**	Euro
Capital	Marigot		

Map page 223

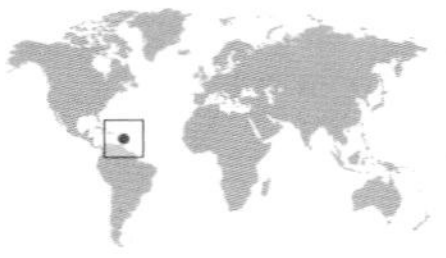

The northern part of St-Martin, one of the Leeward Islands, in the Caribbean. The other part of the island is a self-governing Netherlands territory (Sint Maarten). It was separated from Guadeloupe politically in 2007. Tourism is the main source of income.

St Pierre and Miquelon
French Territorial Collectivity

Area Sq Km	242	**Languages**	French
Area Sq Miles	93	**Religions**	Roman Catholic
Population	6 312	**Currency**	Euro
Capital	St-Pierre		

Map page 207

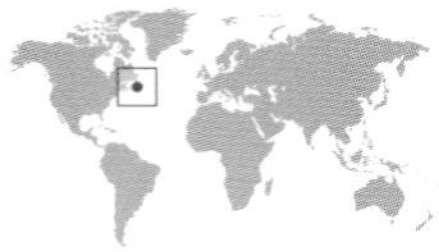

A group of islands off the south coast of Newfoundland in eastern Canada. The islands are largely unsuitable for agriculture, and fishing and fish processing are the most important activities. The islands rely heavily on financial assistance from France.

ST VINCENT AND THE GRENADINES

Area Sq Km	389	**Languages**	English, Creole
Area Sq Miles	150	**Religions**	Protestant, Roman Catholic
Population	109 000	**Currency**	East Caribbean dollar
Capital	Kingstown	**Organizations**	CARICOM, Comm., UN

Map page 223

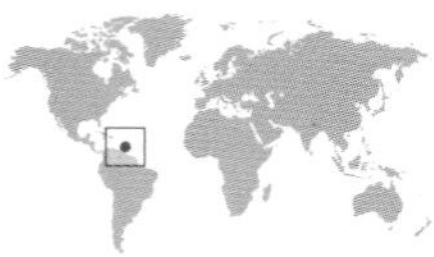

St Vincent, whose territory includes islets and cays in the Grenadines, is in the Windward Islands, in the Caribbean. St Vincent itself is forested and mountainous, with an active volcano, Soufrière. The climate is tropical and wet. The economy is based mainly on agriculture and tourism. Bananas account for approximately one-third of export earnings and arrowroot is also important. Most trade is with the USA and other CARICOM countries.

SAMOA
Independent State of Samoa

Area Sq Km	2 831	**Languages**	Samoan, English
Area Sq Miles	1 093	**Religions**	Protestant, Roman Catholic
Population	190 000	**Currency**	Tala
Capital	Apia	**Organizations**	Comm., UN

Map page 119

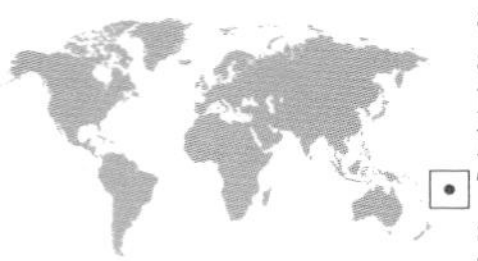

Samoa consists of two larger mountainous and forested islands, Savai'i and Upolu, and seven smaller islands, in the south Pacific Ocean. Over half the population lives on Upolu. The climate is tropical. The economy is based on agriculture, with some fishing and light manufacturing. Traditional exports are coconut products, fish and beer. Tourism is increasing, but the islands depend on workers' remittances and foreign aid.

SAN MARINO
Republic of San Marino

Area Sq Km	61	**Languages**	Italian
Area Sq Miles	24	**Religions**	Roman Catholic
Population	31 000	**Currency**	Euro
Capital	San Marino	**Organizations**	UN

Map page 184

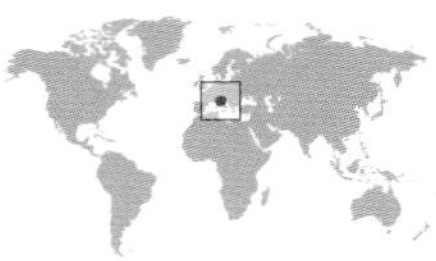

Landlocked San Marino lies in northeast Italy. A third of the people live in the capital. There is some agriculture and light industry, but most income comes from tourism. Italy is the main trading partner.

SÃO TOMÉ AND PRÍNCIPE
Democratic Republic of São Tomé and Príncipe

Area Sq Km	964	**Languages**	Portuguese, Creole
Area Sq Miles	372	**Religions**	Roman Catholic, Protestant
Population	193 000	**Currency**	Dobra
Capital	São Tomé	**Organizations**	UN

Map page 193

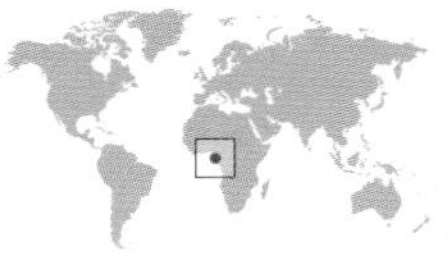

The two main islands and adjacent islets lie off the coast of west Africa in the Gulf of Guinea. São Tomé is the larger island, with over ninety per cent of the population. Both São Tomé and Príncipe are mountainous and tree-covered, and have a hot and humid climate. The economy is heavily dependent on cocoa, which accounts for around ninety per cent of export earnings.

SAUDI ARABIA
Kingdom of Saudi Arabia

Area Sq Km	2 200 000	**Languages**	Arabic
Area Sq Miles	849 425	**Religions**	Sunni Muslim, Shi'a Muslim
Population	28 829 000	**Currency**	Saudi Arabian riyal
Capital	Riyadh (Ar Riyāḍ)	**Organizations**	OPEC, UN

Map page 146

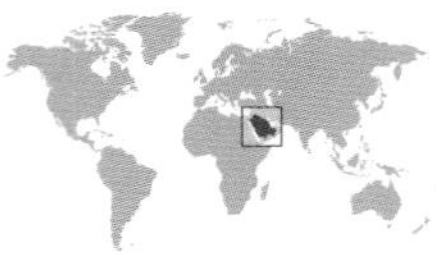

Saudi Arabia occupies most of the Arabian Peninsula in southwest Asia. The terrain is desert or semi-desert plateaus, which rise to mountains running parallel to the Red Sea in the west and slope down to plains in the southeast and along The Gulf in the east. Over eighty per cent of the population lives in urban areas. There are around four million foreign workers in Saudi Arabia, employed mainly in the oil and service industries. Summers are hot, winters are warm and rainfall is low. Saudi Arabia has the world's largest reserves of oil and significant natural gas reserves, both onshore and in The Gulf. Crude oil and refined products account for over ninety per cent of export earnings. Other industries and irrigated agriculture are being encouraged, but most food and raw materials are imported. Saudi Arabia has important banking and commercial interests. Japan and the USA are the main trading partners.

SENEGAL
Republic of Senegal

Area Sq Km	196 720	**Languages**	French, Wolof, Fulani, other local languages
Area Sq Miles	75 954	**Religions**	Sunni Muslim, Roman Catholic, traditional beliefs
Population	14 133 000	**Currency**	CFA franc
Capital	Dakar	**Organizations**	UN

Map page 192

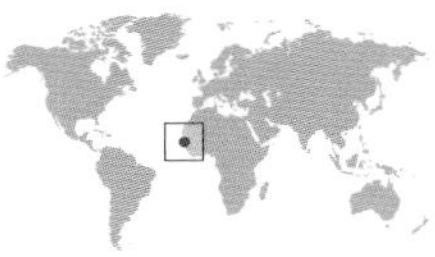

Senegal lies on the Atlantic coast of west Africa. The north is arid semi-desert, while the south is mainly fertile savanna bushland. The climate is tropical with summer rains, although droughts occur. One-fifth of the population lives in and around Dakar, the capital and main port. Fish, groundnuts and phosphates are the main exports. France is the main trading partner.

SERBIA
Republic of Serbia

Area Sq Km	77 453	**Languages**	Serbian, Hungarian
Area Sq Miles	29 904	**Religions**	Serbian Orthodox, Roman Catholic, Sunni Muslim
Population	7 181 505	**Currency**	Serbian dinar
Capital	Belgrade (Beograd)	**Organizations**	UN

Map page 185

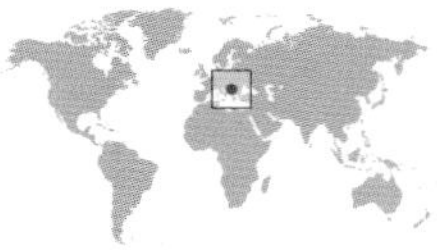

Following ethnic conflict and the break-up of Yugoslavia through the 1990s, the state union of Serbia and Montenegro retained the name Yugoslavia until 2003. The two then became separate independent countries in 2006. The southern Serbian province of Kosovo declared its independence from Serbia in February 2008. The landscape is rugged, mountainous and forested in the south, while the north is low-lying and drained by the Danube river system.

SEYCHELLES
Republic of Seychelles

Area Sq Km	455	**Languages**	English, French, Creole
Area Sq Miles	176	**Religions**	Roman Catholic, Protestant
Population	93 000	**Currency**	Seychelles rupee
Capital	Victoria	**Organizations**	Comm., SADC, UN

Map page 191

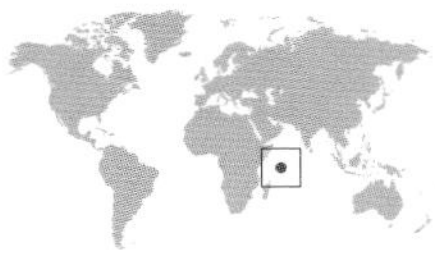

The Seychelles comprises an archipelago of over one hundred granitic and coral islands in the western Indian Ocean. Over ninety per cent of the population lives on the main island, Mahé. The climate is hot and humid with heavy rainfall. The economy is based mainly on tourism, fishing and light manufacturing.

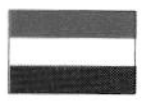

SIERRA LEONE
Republic of Sierra Leone

Area Sq Km	71 740	**Languages**	English, Creole, Mende, Temne, other local languages
Area Sq Miles	27 699	**Religions**	Sunni Muslim, traditional beliefs
Population	6 092 000	**Currency**	Leone
Capital	Freetown	**Organizations**	Comm., UN

Map page 192

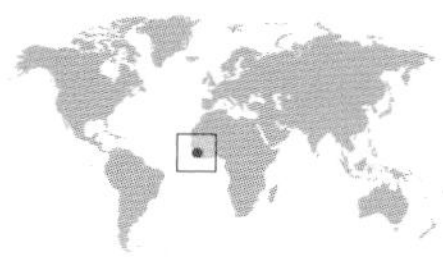

Sierra Leone lies on the Atlantic coast of west Africa. Its coastline is heavily indented and is lined with mangrove swamps. Inland is a forested area rising to savanna plateaus, with mountains to the northeast. The climate is tropical and rainfall is heavy. Most of the workforce is involved in subsistence farming. Cocoa and coffee are the main cash crops. Diamonds and rutile (titanium ore) are the main exports. Sierra Leone is one of the world's poorest countries, and the economy relies on substantial foreign aid.

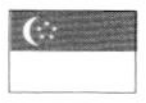

SINGAPORE
Republic of Singapore

Area Sq Km	639	**Languages**	Chinese, English, Malay, Tamil
Area Sq Mile	247	**Religions**	Buddhist, Taoist, Sunni Muslim, Christian, Hindu
Population	5 412 000	**Currency**	Singapore dollar
Capital	Singapore	**Organizations**	APEC, ASEAN, Comm., UN

Map page 162

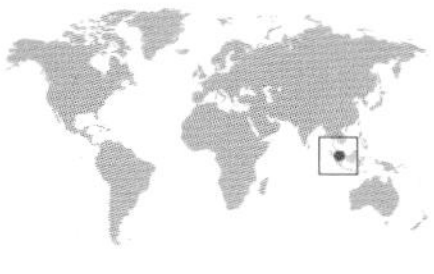

The state comprises the island of Singapore and over fifty others, at the tip of the Malay Peninsula in southeast Asia. Singapore is generally low-lying and includes areas of reclaimed land. The climate is hot and humid, with heavy rainfall all year. Most food has to be imported. Singapore lacks natural resources; industries and services have fuelled the nation's economic growth during recent decades. Main industries include electronics, oil refining, chemicals, pharmaceuticals, ship repair, food processing and textiles. Singapore is also a major financial centre. Its port is one of the world's largest and busiest. Tourism is also important. Japan, the USA and Malaysia are the main trading partners.

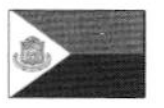

Sint Maarten
Self-governing Netherlands territory

Area Sq Km	34	**Languages**	Dutch, English
Area Sq Miles	13	**Religions**	Roman Catholic, Protestant
Population	45 000	**Currency**	Caribbean guilder
Capital	Philipsburg		

Map page 223 The southern part of one of the Leeward Islands, in the Caribbean; the other part of the island is a dependency of France. Sint Maarten was previously part of the Netherlands Antilles until they were dissolved in October 2010. Tourism and fishing are the most important industries.

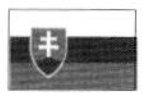

SLOVAKIA
Slovak Republic

Area Sq Km	49 035	**Languages**	Slovakian, Hungarian, Czech
Area Sq Miles	18 933	**Religions**	Roman Catholic, Protestant, Orthodox
Population	5 450 000	**Currency**	Euro
Capital	Bratislava	**Organizations**	EU, NATO, OECD, UN

Map page 177

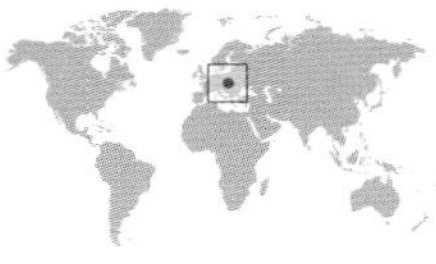

A landlocked country in central Europe, Slovakia is mountainous in the north, but low-lying in the southwest. The climate is continental. There is a range of manufacturing industries, and the main exports are machinery and transport equipment, but in recent years there have been economic difficulties and growth has been slow. Slovakia joined the European Union in May 2004. Most trade is with other EU countries, especially the Czech Republic and Germany.

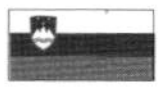

SLOVENIA
Republic of Slovenia

Area Sq Km	20 251	**Languages**	Slovenian, Croatian, Serbian
Area Sq Miles	7 819	**Religions**	Roman Catholic, Protestant
Population	2 072 000	**Currency**	Euro
Capital	Ljubljana	**Organizations**	EU, NATO, OECD, UN

Map page 184–185

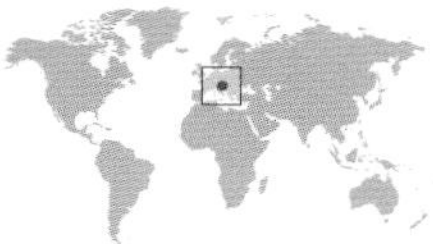

Slovenia lies in the northwest Balkan Mountains of southern Europe and has a short coastline on the Adriatic Sea. It is mountainous and hilly, with lowlands on the coast and in the Sava and Drava river valleys. The climate is generally continental inland and Mediterranean nearer the coast. The main agricultural products are potatoes, grain and sugar beet; the main industries include metal processing, electronics and consumer goods. Trade has been re-orientated towards western markets and the main trading partners are Germany and Italy. Slovenia joined the European Union in May 2004.

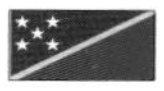

SOLOMON ISLANDS

Area Sq Km	28 370	**Languages**	English, Creole, other local languages
Area Sq Miles	10 954	**Religions**	Protestant, Roman Catholic
Population	561 000	**Currency**	Solomon Islands dollar
Capital	Honiara	**Organizations**	Comm., UN

Map page 119

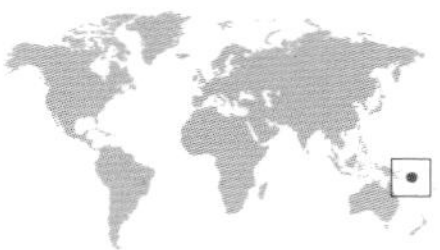

The state consists of the Solomon, Santa Cruz and Shortland Islands in the southwest Pacific Ocean. The six main islands are volcanic, mountainous and forested, although Guadalcanal, the most populous, has a large lowland area. The climate is generally hot and humid. Subsistence farming, forestry and fishing predominate. Exports include timber products, fish, copra and palm oil. The islands depend on foreign aid.

SOMALIA
Federal Republic of Somalia

Area Sq Km	637 657	**Languages**	Somali, Arabic
Area Sq Miles	246 201	**Religions**	Sunni Muslim
Population	10 496 000	**Currency**	Somali shilling
Capital	Mogadishu (Muqdisho)	**Organizations**	UN

Map page 194

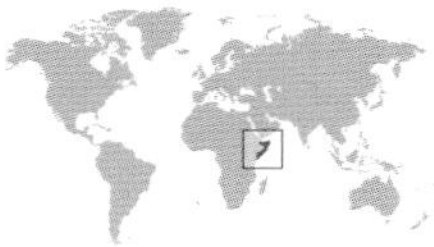

Somalia is in northeast Africa, on the Gulf of Aden and Indian Ocean. It consists of a dry scrubby plateau, rising to highlands in the north. The climate is hot and dry, but coastal areas and the Jubba and Wabē Shebelē Wenz river valleys support crops and most of the population. Subsistence farming and livestock rearing are the main activities. Exports include livestock and bananas. Frequent drought and civil war have prevented economic development. Somalia is one of the poorest, most unstable and least developed countries in the world.

Somaliland
Disputed territory

Area Sq Km	140 000	**Languages**	Somali, Arabic, English
Area Sq Miles	54 054	**Religions**	Sunni Muslim
Population	3 500 000	**Currency**	Somaliland shilling
Capital	Hargeysa		

Map page 194 After the collapse of the central Somali government in 1991 and at the start of the civil war, Somaliland, in the northwest of the country, covering the area of the former British Protectorate of Somaliland, declared its independence from Somalia as the Republic of Somaliland. A referendum in 2001 saw a majority vote for secession, and Somaliland currently operates as a de facto independent country, with fairly close relations with Ethiopia. The Transitional Federal Government of Somalia does not recognize its independence and conflicts still arise between Somaliland and the neighbouring region of Puntland over ownership of the administrative regions of Sanaag and Sool.

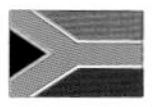

SOUTH AFRICA

Area Sq Km	1 219 090	**Languages**	Afrikaans, English, nine other official languages
Area Sq Miles	470 693	**Religions**	Protestant, Roman Catholic, Sunni Muslim, Hindu
Population	52 776 000	**Currency**	Rand
Capital	Bloemfontein/ Cape Town/ Pretoria (Tshwane)	**Organizations**	Comm., SADC, UN

Map page 196–197

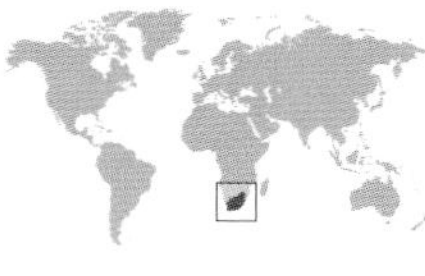

South Africa occupies most of the southern part of Africa. It surrounds Lesotho and has a long coastline on the Atlantic and Indian Oceans. Much of the land is a vast plateau, covered with grassland or bush and drained by the Orange and Limpopo river systems. A fertile coastal plain rises to mountain ridges in the south and east, including Table Mountain near Cape Town and the Drakensberg range in the east. Gauteng is the most populous province, with Johannesburg and Pretoria its main cities. South Africa has warm summers and mild winters. Most of the country has the majority of its rainfall in summer, but the coast around Cape Town has winter rains. South Africa has the largest economy in Africa, although wealth is unevenly distributed and unemployment is very high. Agriculture employs about six per cent of the workforce, and produce includes fruit, wine, wool and maize. The country is the world's leading producer of gold and chromium and an important producer of diamonds. Many other minerals are also mined. The main industries are mineral and food processing, chemicals, electrical equipment, textiles and motor vehicles. Financial services are also important.

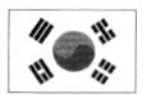

SOUTH KOREA
Republic of Korea

Area Sq Km	99 274	**Languages**	Korean
Area Sq Miles	38 330	**Religions**	Buddhist, Protestant, Roman Catholic
Population	49 263 000	**Currency**	South Korean won
Capital	Seoul (Sŏul)	**Organizations**	APEC, OECD, UN

Map page 160

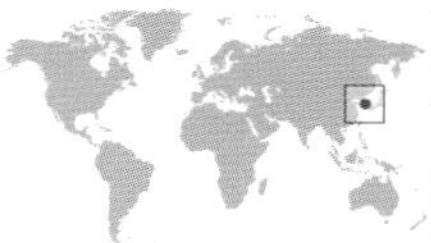

The state consists of the southern half of the Korean Peninsula in eastern Asia and many islands lying off the western and southern coasts in the Yellow Sea. The terrain is mountainous, although less rugged than that of North Korea. Population density is high and the country is highly urbanized; most of the population lives on the western coastal plains and in the river basins of the Han-gang in the northwest and the Naktong-gang in the southeast. The climate is continental, with hot, wet summers and dry, cold winters. Arable land is limited by the mountainous terrain, but because of intensive farming South Korea is nearly self-sufficient in food. Sericulture (silk) is important, as is fishing, which contributes to exports. South Korea has few mineral resources, except for coal and tungsten. It has achieved high economic growth based mainly on export manufacturing. The main manufactured goods are cars, electronic and electrical goods, ships, steel, chemicals and toys, as well as textiles, clothing, footwear and food products. The USA and Japan are the main trading partners.

South Ossetia
Disputed territory

Area Sq Km	4 000	**Languages**	Ossetian, Russian, Georgian
Area Sq Miles	1 544	**Religions**	Eastern Orthodox
Population	70 000	**Currency**	Russian rouble
Capital	Tskhinvali		

Map page 187 The formerly autonomous region of South Ossetia seeks independence from Georgia and looks to Russia, which recognizes its independence, as its principal ally. South Ossetia's autonomous status was removed in 1990. Violent conflicts followed between Georgia and the separatists, supported by Russia, who wished to unite with Russian North Ossetia. A cease-fire was agreed in 1992. Elections in 1996 were not recognized by Georgia, nor were elections and an independence referendum, voting in favour of independence, in 2006. Russian interference and interest in the area has continued to cause tensions with the Georgian government, the most recent conflict was in 2008 when Georgian troops attacked separatists. Russia responded and a week of fighting was ended by a cease-fire and resulted in Russia recognising South Ossetia's independence.

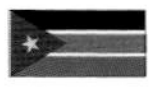

SOUTH SUDAN
Republic of South Sudan

Area Sq Km	644 329	**Languages**	English, Arabic, Dinka, Nuer, other local languages
Area Sq Miles	248 775	**Religions**	Traditional beliefs, Christian
Population	11 296 000	**Currency**	South Sudanese pound
Capital	Juba	**Organizations**	UN

Map page 193

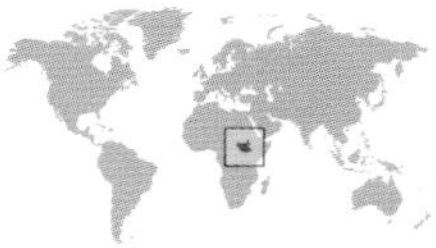

South Sudan in northeast Africa has grasslands, tropical forests and swamps in the north with higher lands in the south. The equatorial climate has moderate temperatures, high humidity and heavy rainfall. Independence from Sudan was gained in July 2011 as a result of a referendum held as part of the agreement which ended decades of civil war between north and south. The government plan to move the capital from Juba to Ramciel in the centre of the country. The economy is mostly agricultural, but the vast natural resources, including huge oil-reserves, are now being increasingly exploited. South Sudan is one of the world's least developed countries.

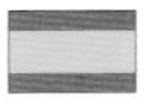

SPAIN
Kingdom of Spain

Area Sq Km	504 782	**Languages**	Spanish (Castilian), Catalan, Galician, Basque
Area Sq Miles	194 897	**Religions**	Roman Catholic
Population	46 927 000	**Currency**	Euro
Capital	Madrid	**Organizations**	EU, NATO, OECD, UN

Map page 183

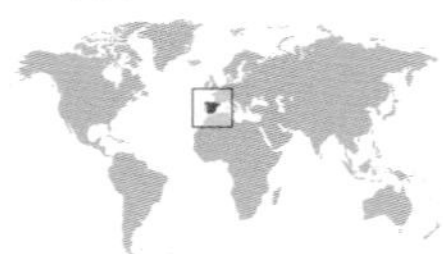

Spain occupies most of the Iberian peninsula in southwest Europe. It includes the Canary Islands, and two enclaves in north Africa. Much of the mainland is a high plateau, and the Pyrenees form the border with France. Summers are hot and winters cool, especially in the north. Most of the population is urban, and agriculture involves only a tenth of the workforce. Fruit, vegetables and wine are exported. Mineral resources include lead, copper, mercury and fluorspar. Some oil is produced, but Spain has to import energy. Manufacturing industries include machinery, transport equipment, vehicles and food products. Fishing, tourism and financial services are also important. Most trade is with other EU countries.

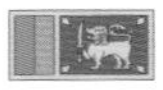

SRI LANKA
Democratic Socialist Republic of Sri Lanka

Area Sq Km	65 610	**Languages**	Sinhalese, Tamil, English
Area Sq Miles	25 332	**Religions**	Buddhist, Hindu, Sunni Muslim, Roman Catholic
Population	21 273 000	**Currency**	Sri Lankan rupee
Capital	Sri Jayewardenepura Kotte	**Organizations**	Comm., UN

Map page 147

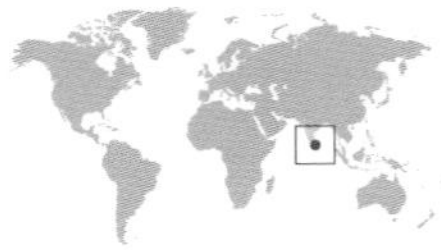

Sri Lanka lies in the Indian Ocean off the southeast coast of India in south Asia. It has rolling coastal plains, with mountains in the centre-south. The climate is hot and monsoonal. Most people live on the west coast. Manufactures (chiefly textiles and clothing), tea, rubber, copra and gems are exported. The economy relies on foreign aid and workers' remittances. The USA and the UK are the main trading partners.

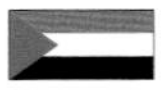

SUDAN
Republic of the Sudan

Area Sq Km	1 861 484	**Languages**	Arabic, English, Nubian, Beja, Fur, other local languages
Area Sq Miles	718 725	**Religions**	Sunni Muslim, traditional beliefs, Christian
Population	37 964 000	**Currency**	Sudanese pound (Sudani)
Capital	Khartoum	**Organizations**	UN

Map page 193

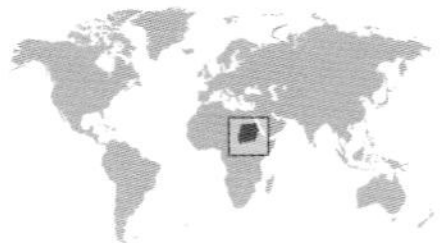

The Sudan is in the northeast of the continent of Africa, on the Red Sea. It lies within the upper Nile basin, much of which is arid plain but with swamps to the south. Mountains lie to the northeast, west and south. The climate is hot and arid with light summer rainfall, and droughts occur. Most people live along the Nile and are farmers and herders. Cotton, gum arabic, livestock and other agricultural products are exported. The government is working with foreign investors to develop oil resources, but the independence of South Sudan in July 2011 after civil war, and ethnic cleansing in Darfur continue to restrict the economy. Main trading partners are Saudi Arabia, China and UAE.

SURINAME
Republic of Suriname

Area Sq Km	163 820	**Languages**	Dutch, Surinamese, English, Hindi
Area Sq Miles	63 251	**Religions**	Hindu, Roman Catholic, Protestant, Sunni Muslim
Population	539 000	**Currency**	Surinamese dollar
Capital	Paramaribo	**Organizations**	CARICOM, UN

Map page 231

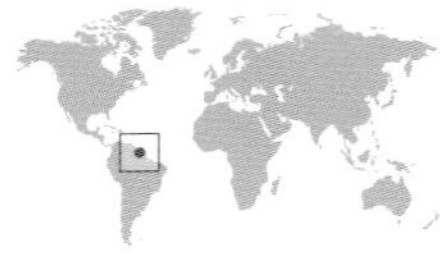

Suriname, on the Atlantic coast of northern South America, consists of a swampy coastal plain (where most of the population lives), central plateaus, and highlands in the south. The climate is tropical, and rainforest covers much of the land. Bauxite mining is the main industry, and alumina and aluminium are the chief exports, with shrimps, rice, bananas and timber also exported. The main trading partners are the Netherlands, Norway and the USA.

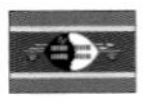

SWAZILAND
Kingdom of Swaziland

Area Sq Km	17 364	**Languages**	Swazi, English
Area Sq Miles	6 704	**Religions**	Christian, traditional beliefs
Population	1 250 000	**Currency**	Lilangeni, South African rand
Capital	Mbabane	**Organizations**	Comm., SADC, UN

Map page 197

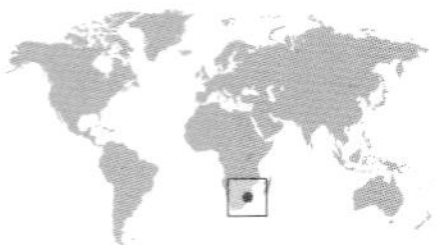

Landlocked Swaziland in southern Africa lies between Mozambique and South Africa. Savanna plateaus descend from mountains in the west towards hill country in the east. The climate is subtropical, but temperate in the mountains. Subsistence farming predominates. Asbestos and diamonds are mined. Exports include sugar, fruit and wood pulp. Tourism and workers' remittances are important to the economy. Most trade is with South Africa.

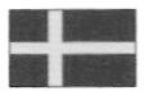

SWEDEN
Kingdom of Sweden

Area Sq Km	449 964	**Languages**	Swedish, Sami languages
Area Sq Miles	173 732	**Religions**	Protestant, Roman Catholic
Population	9 571 000	**Currency**	Swedish krona
Capital	Stockholm	**Organizations**	EU, OECD, UN

Map page 170–171

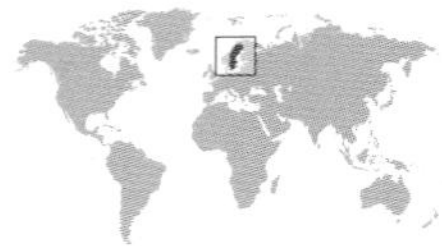

Sweden occupies the eastern part of the Scandinavian peninsula in northern Europe and borders the Baltic Sea, the Gulf of Bothnia, and the Kattegat and Skagerrak. Forested uplands cover the northern half, which extends beyond the Arctic Circle. The south is a lowland lake region where most of the population lives. Sweden has warm summers and cold winters, severe in the north. Natural resources include forests, minerals and water. Dairy products, meat, cereals and vegetables are produced. Iron and copper are mined, and also zinc, lead, silver and gold. Exports include machinery and transport equipment, chemicals, forest products, furniture and telecommunications equipment. Most trade is with other EU countries.

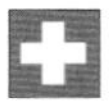

SWITZERLAND
Swiss Confederation

Area Sq Km	41 293	**Languages**	German, French, Italian, Romansch
Area Sq Miles	15 943	**Religions**	Roman Catholic, Protestant
Population	8 078 000	**Currency**	Swiss franc
Capital	Bern	**Organizations**	OECD, UN

Map page 182

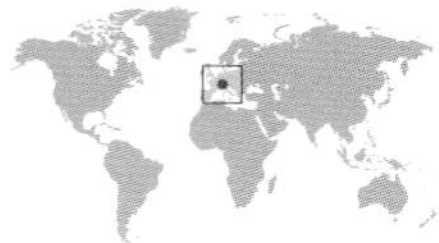

Switzerland is a mountainous, landlocked country in west-central Europe. The southern half lies within the Alps, and the Jura mountains are in the northwest. The rest is a high plateau, where most of the population lives. Climate varies depending on altitude, but in general summers are mild and winters are cold. Switzerland has a very high living standard, yet it has few mineral resources, and most food and raw materials are imported. Manufacturing (especially precision instruments and heavy machinery, chemicals and pharmaceuticals) and financial services are the mainstay of the economy. Tourism, and international organizations based in Switzerland, are also major foreign currency earners. Germany is the main trading partner.

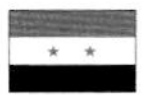

SYRIA
Syrian Arab Republic

Area Sq Km	184 026	**Languages**	Arabic, Kurdish, Armenian
Area Sq Miles	71 052	**Religions**	Sunni Muslim, Shi'a Muslim, Christian
Population	21 898 000	**Currency**	Syrian pound
Capital	Damascus (Dimashq)	**Organizations**	UN

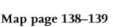

Map page 138–139

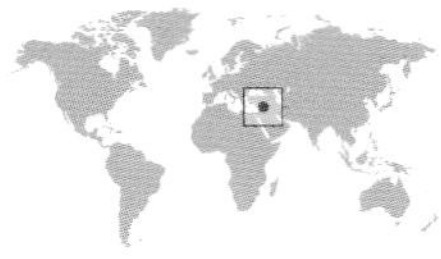

Syria is in southwest Asia, has a short coastline on the Mediterranean Sea, and stretches inland to a plateau traversed northwest-southeast by the Euphrates river. Mountains flank the southwest borders with Lebanon and Israel. The climate is Mediterranean in coastal regions, hotter and drier inland. Most Syrians live on the coast or in the river valleys. Syria's economy has been struggling since the start of the civil unrest in 2011 and the oil and gas industry has collapsed.

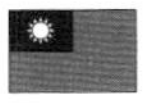

TAIWAN
Republic of China

Area Sq Km	36 179	**Languages**	Mandarin (Putonghua), Min, Hakka, other local languages
Area Sq Miles	13 969	**Religions**	Buddhist, Taoist, Confucian, Christian
Population	23 344 000	**Currency**	New Taiwan dollar
Capital	Taibei (T'aipei)	**Organizations**	APEC

Map page 155

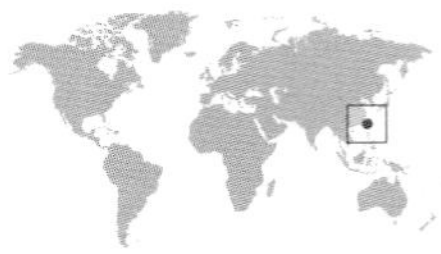

The east Asian state consists of the island of Taiwan, separated from mainland China by the Taiwan Strait, and several much smaller islands. Much of Taiwan is mountainous and forested. Densely populated coastal plains in the west contain most of the population and economic activity. The climate is tropical and monsoonal. The country is virtually self-sufficient in food, and exports some products. Coal, oil and gas are produced and a few minerals are mined. Taiwan depends heavily on imported raw materials. The main manufactures and exports are electrical goods (including televisions, computers and calculators), textiles, fertilizers, clothing, footwear and toys. The main trading partners are the USA, Japan and Germany. The People's Republic of China claims Taiwan as its 23rd Province.

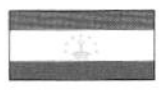

TAJIKISTAN
Republic of Tajikistan

Area Sq Km	143 100	**Languages**	Tajik, Uzbek, Russian
Area Sq Miles	55 251	**Religions**	Sunni Muslim
Population	8 208 000	**Currency**	Somoni
Capital	Dushanbe	**Organizations**	CIS, UN

Map page 141

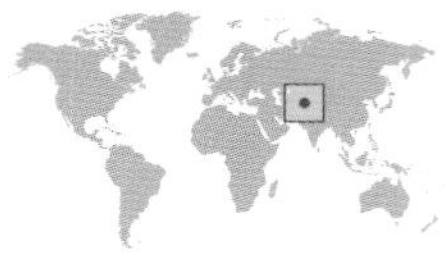

Landlocked Tajikistan in central Asia is a mountainous country, dominated by the mountains of the Alai Range and the Pamir. In the less mountainous western areas summers are warm, although winters are cold. Agriculture is the main sector of the economy, chiefly cotton growing and cattle breeding. Mineral deposits include lead, zinc, and uranium. Metal processing, textiles and clothing are the main manufactured goods; the main exports are aluminium and cotton. Uzbekistan, Kazakhstan and Russia are the main trading partners.

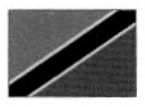

TANZANIA
United Republic of Tanzania

Area Sq Km	945 087	**Languages**	Swahili, English, Nyamwezi, other local languages
Area Sq Miles	364 900	**Religions**	Shi'a Muslim, Sunni Muslim, traditional beliefs, Christian
Population	49 253 000	**Currency**	Tanzanian shilling
Capital	Dodoma	**Organizations**	Comm., SADC, UN

Map page 195

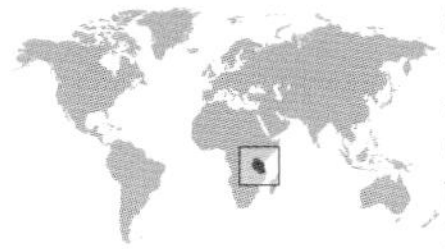

Tanzania lies on the coast of east Africa and includes the island of Zanzibar in the Indian Ocean. Most of the mainland is a savanna plateau lying east of the Great Rift Valley. In the north, near the border with Kenya, is Kilimanjaro, the highest mountain in Africa. The climate is tropical. The economy is based on agriculture, which employs about ninety per cent of the workforce. Agricultural processing and gold and diamond mining are the main industries, although tourism is growing. Coffee, cotton, cashew nuts and tobacco are the main exports, with cloves from Zanzibar. Most export trade is with India, China and Switzerland. Tanzania depends heavily on foreign aid.

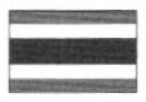

THAILAND
Kingdom of Thailand

Area Sq Km	513 115	**Languages**	Thai, Lao, Chinese, Malay, Mon-Khmer languages
Area Sq Miles	198 115	**Religions**	Buddhist, Sunni Muslim
Population	67 011 000	**Currency**	Baht
Capital	Bangkok (Krung Thep)	**Organizations**	APEC, ASEAN, UN

Map page 162

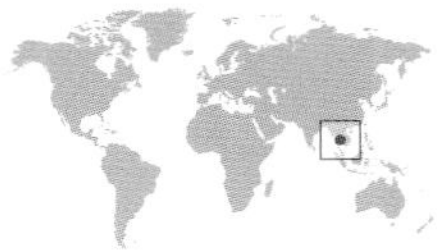

Thailand lies between the Gulf of Thailand and the Andaman Sea and includes the northern Malay Peninsula and many islands lining the coast. To the east of the extensive Chao Phraya basin is a plateau drained by the Mekong, while much of the rest is forested upland. The climate is hot, humid and monsoonal. Half the workforce is involved in agriculture, and fishing is also important, but tourism is the major earner. Minerals include gas, oil, lignite, tin, tungsten and baryte, and gemstones, and manufacturing includes electronics, clothing and food processing. Thailand is a leading exporter of rice, rubber, palm oil and cassava. Japan, China and the USA are the main trading partners.

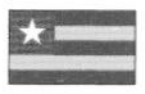

TOGO
Togolese Republic

Area Sq Km	56 785	**Languages**	French, Ewe, Kabre, other local languages
Area Sq Miles	21 925	**Religions**	Traditional beliefs, Christian, Sunni Muslim
Population	6 817 000	**Currency**	CFA franc
Capital	Lomé	**Organizations**	UN

Map page 192

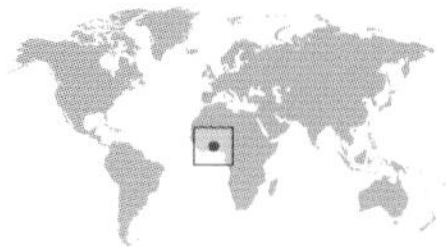

Togo is a long narrow country in west Africa with a short coastline on the Gulf of Guinea. The interior consists of plateaus rising to mountainous areas. The climate is tropical, and is drier inland. Agriculture is the mainstay of the economy. Phosphate mining and food processing are the main industries. Cotton, phosphates, coffee and cocoa are the main exports. Lomé, the capital, is an entrepôt trade centre.

Tokelau
New Zealand Overseas Territory

Area Sq Km	10	**Languages**	English, Tokelauan
Area Sq Miles	4	**Religions**	Christian
Population	1 411	**Currency**	New Zealand dollar

Map page 119 Tokelau consists of three atolls, Atafu, Nukunonu and Fakaofa, lying in the Pacific Ocean north of Samoa. Subsistence agriculture is the main activity, and the islands rely on aid from New Zealand and remittances from workers overseas.

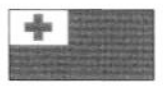

TONGA
Kingdom of Tonga

Area Sq Km	748	**Languages**	Tongan, English
Area Sq Miles	289	**Religions**	Protestant, Roman Catholic
Population	105 000	**Currency**	Pa'anga
Capital	Nuku'alofa	**Organizations**	Comm., UN

Map page 119

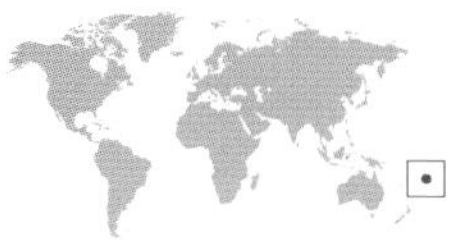

Tonga comprises some one hundred and seventy islands in the south Pacific Ocean, northeast of New Zealand. The three main groups are Tongatapu (where sixty per cent of Tongans live), Ha'apai and Vava'u. The climate is warm and wet, and the economy relies heavily on agriculture. Tourism and light industry are also important to the economy. Exports include squash, fish, vanilla beans and root crops. Most trade is with New Zealand, Japan and Australia.

Transnistria
Disputed territory

Area Sq Km	4 200	**Languages**	Russian, Ukrainian, Moldovan
Area Sq Miles	1 622	**Religions**	Eastern Orthodox, Roman Catholic
Population	520 000	**Currency**	Transnistrian rouble, Moldovan leu
Capital	Tiraspol		

Map page 187 Transnistria, the area of Moldova mainly between the Dniester river and the Ukrainian border, is a predominantly ethnic Russian, and Russian-speaking region. Campaigns for Transnistrian autonomy and independence led to civil war between Moldovan forces and separatists who had proclaimed the self-styled 'Dniester Republic', aligned to Russia, in 1990. A peace agreement with Russia in 1992 ended this war, granted Transnistria special status and established a security zone along its border with Moldova, controlled by Russian, Moldovan and Transnistrian troops. An agreement between Moldova and Transnistria in 1996 stated that Transnistria would remain a part of Moldova, but the campaign for independence continues and the status of the region remains to be resolved. It currently functions as a (predominantly Russian) de facto autonomous republic, separate from Moldova – the Pridnestrovian Moldavian Republic.

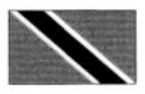

TRINIDAD AND TOBAGO
Republic of Trinidad and Tobago

Area Sq Km	5 130	**Languages**	English, Creole, Hindi
Area Sq Miles	1 981	**Religions**	Roman Catholic, Hindu, Protestant, Sunni Muslim
Population	1 341 000	**Currency**	Trinidad and Tobago dollar
Capital	Port of Spain	**Organizations**	CARICOM, Comm., UN

Map page 233

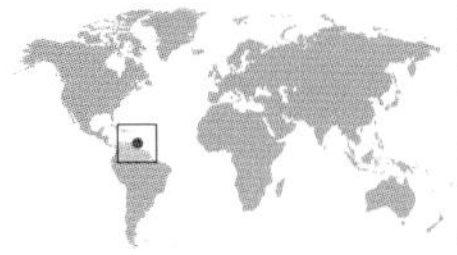

Trinidad, the most southerly Caribbean island, lies off the Venezuelan coast. It is hilly in the north, with a central plain. Tobago, to the northeast, is smaller, more mountainous and less developed. The climate is tropical. The main crops are cocoa, sugar cane, coffee, fruit and vegetables. Oil and petrochemical industries dominate the economy. Tourism is also important. The USA is the main trading partner.

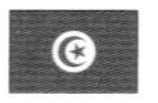

TUNISIA
Republic of Tunisia

Area Sq Km	164 150	**Languages**	Arabic, French
Area Sq Miles	63 379	**Religions**	Sunni Muslim
Population	10 997 000	**Currency**	Tunisian dinar
Capital	Tunis	**Organizations**	UN

Map page 193

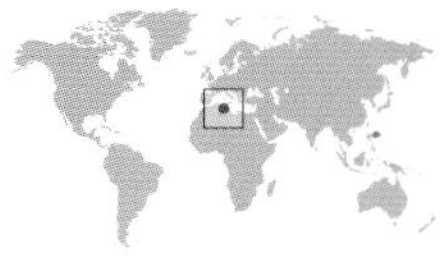

Tunisia is on the Mediterranean coast of north Africa. The north is mountainous with valleys and coastal plains, has a Mediterranean climate and is the most populous area. The south is hot and arid. Oil and phosphates are the main resources, and the main crops are olives and citrus fruit. Tourism is an important industry. Exports include petroleum products, textiles, fruit and phosphorus. Most trade is with European Union countries.

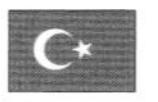

TURKEY
Republic of Turkey

Area Sq Km	779 452	**Languages**	Turkish, Kurdish
Area Sq Miles	300 948	**Religions**	Sunni Muslim, Shi'a Muslim
Population	74 933 000	**Currency**	Lira
Capital	Ankara	**Organizations**	NATO, OECD, UN

Map page 138–139

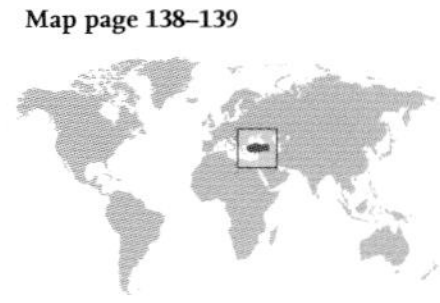

Turkey occupies a large peninsula in southwest Asia. It includes eastern Thrace, in southeastern Europe. The Asian mainland consists of the semi-arid Anatolian plateau, flanked to the north, south and east by mountains. The coast has a Mediterranean climate, but inland conditions are more extreme, with hot, dry summers and cold, snowy winters. Cotton, grains, tobacco, fruit, nuts and livestock are produced, and minerals include chromium, iron ore, lead, tin, borate, baryte, and some coal. Manufacturing includes clothing, textiles, food products, steel and vehicles. Tourism is a major industry, around forty milion visitors a year. Germany and the USA are the main trading partners. Remittances from workers abroad are important to the economy.

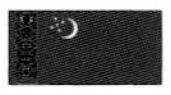

TURKMENISTAN

Area Sq Km	488 100	**Languages**	Turkmen, Uzbek, Russian
Area Sq Miles	188 456	**Religions**	Sunni Muslim, Russian Orthodox
Population	5 240 000	**Currency**	Turkmen manat
Capital	Aşgabat (Ashkhabad)	**Organizations**	UN

Map page 140

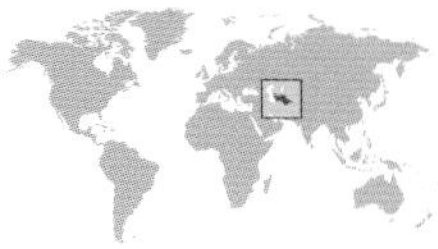

Turkmenistan, in central Asia, comprises the plains of the Karakum Desert, the foothills of the Kopet Dag mountains in the south, the Amudar'ya valley in the north and the Caspian Sea plains in the west. The climate is dry, with extreme temperatures. The economy is based mainly on irrigated agriculture (chiefly cotton growing), and natural gas and oil. Main exports are natural gas, oil and cotton fibre. Ukraine, Iran, Turkey and Russia are the main trading partners.

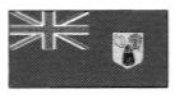

Turks and Caicos Islands
United Kingdom Overseas Territory

Area Sq Km	430	**Languages**	English
Area Sq Miles	166	**Religions**	Protestant
Population	33 000	**Currency**	United States dollar
Capital	Grand Turk (Cockburn Town)		

Map page 223 The state consists of over forty low-lying islands and cays in the northern Caribbean. Only eight islands are inhabited, and two-fifths of the people live on Grand Turk and Salt Cay. The climate is tropical, and the economy is based on tourism, fishing and offshore banking.

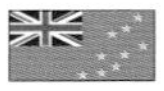

TUVALU

Area Sq Km	25	**Languages**	Tuvaluan, English
Area Sq Miles	10	**Religions**	Protestant
Population	10 000	**Currency**	Australian dollar
Capital	Vaiaku	**Organizations**	Comm., UN

Map page 119

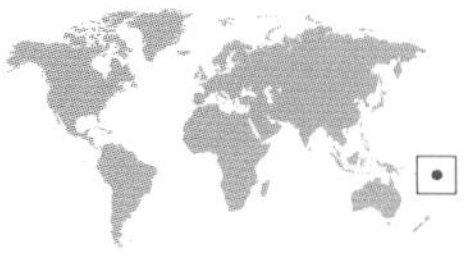

Tuvalu comprises nine low-lying coral atolls in the south Pacific Ocean. One-third of the population lives on Funafuti, and most people depend on subsistence farming and fishing. The islands export copra, stamps and clothing, but rely heavily on foreign aid. Most trade is with Fiji, Australia and New Zealand.

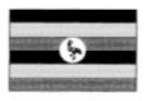

UGANDA
Republic of Uganda

Area Sq Km	241 038	**Languages**	English, Swahili, Luganda, other local languages
Area Sq Miles	93 065	**Religions**	Roman Catholic, Protestant, Sunni Muslim, traditional beliefs
Population	37 579 000	**Currency**	Ugandan shilling
Capital	Kampala	**Organizations**	Comm., UN

Map page 194

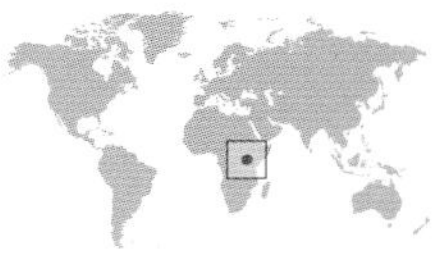

A landlocked country in east Africa, Uganda consists of a savanna plateau with mountains and lakes. The climate is warm and wet. Most people live in the southern half of the country. Agriculture employs around eighty per cent of the workforce and dominates the economy. Coffee, tea, fish and fish products are the main exports. Uganda relies heavily on aid.

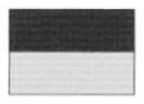

UKRAINE

Area Sq Km	603 700	**Languages**	Ukrainian, Russian
Area Sq Miles	233 090	**Religions**	Ukrainian Orthodox, Ukrainian Catholic, Roman Catholic
Population	45 239 000	**Currency**	Hryvnia
Capital	Kiev (Kyiv)	**Organizations**	UN

Map page 187

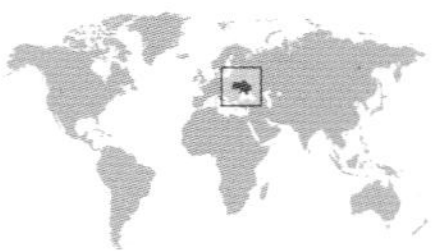

The country lies on the Black Sea coast of eastern Europe. Much of the land is steppe, generally flat and treeless, but with rich black soil, and it is drained by the river Dnieper. Along the border with Belarus are forested, marshy plains. The only uplands are the Carpathian Mountains in the west and smaller ranges on the Crimean peninsula. Summers are warm and winters are cold, with milder conditions in the Crimea. About a quarter of the population lives in the mainly industrial areas around Donets'k, Kiev and Dnipropetrovs'k. The Ukraine is rich in natural resources: fertile soil, substantial mineral and natural gas deposits, and forests. Agriculture and livestock rearing are important, but mining and manufacturing are the dominant sectors of the economy. Coal, iron and manganese mining, steel and metal production, machinery, chemicals and food processing are the main industries. The EU and Russia are the main trading partners but the economy is struggling.

UNITED ARAB EMIRATES
Federation of Emirates

Area Sq Km	77 700	**Languages**	Arabic, English
Area Sq Miles	30 000	**Religions**	Sunni Muslim, Shi'a Muslim
Population	9 346 000	**Currency**	United Arab Emirates dirham
Capital	Abu Dhabi (Abū Ẓaby)	**Organizations**	OPEC, UN

Map page 142–143

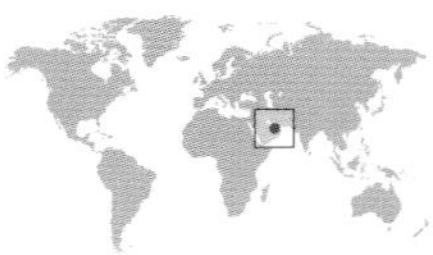

The UAE lies on the Gulf coast of the Arabian Peninsula. Six emirates are on The Gulf, while the seventh, Fujairah, is on the Gulf of Oman. Most of the land is flat desert with sand dunes and salt pans. The only hilly area is in the northeast. Over eighty per cent of the population lives in three of the emirates - Abu Dhabi, Dubai and Sharjah. Summers are hot and winters are mild, with occasional rainfall in coastal areas. Fruit and vegetables are grown in oases and irrigated areas, but the Emirates' wealth is based on hydrocarbons found in Abu Dhabi, Dubai, Sharjah and Ras al Khaimah. The UAE is one of the major oil producers in the Middle East. Dubai is an important entrepôt trade centre. The main trading partners are India, Iran, Iraq and China.

Abu Dhabi (Abū Ẓaby) (Emirate)
Area Sq Km (Sq Miles) 67 340 (26 000) **Population** 1 628 000 **Capital** Abu Dhabi (Abū Ẓaby)

Ajman (Emirate)
Area Sq Km (Sq Miles) 259 (100) **Population** 250 000 **Capital** Ajman

Dubai (Emirate)
Area Sq Km (Sq Miles) 3 885 (1 500) **Population** 1 722 000 **Capital** Dubai

Fujairah (Emirate)
Area Sq Km (Sq Miles) 1 165 (450) **Population** 152 000 **Capital** Fujairah

Ra's al Khaymah (Emirate)
Area Sq Km (Sq Miles) 1 684 (650) **Population** 241 000 **Capital** Ra's al Khaymah

Sharjah (Emirate)
Area Sq Km (Sq Miles) 2 590 (1 000) **Population** 1 017 000 **Capital** Sharjah

Umm al Qaywayn (Emirate)
Area Sq Km (Sq Miles) 777 (300) **Population** 56 000 **Capital** Umm al Qaywayn

UNITED KINGDOM
United Kingdom of Great Britain and Northern Ireland

Area Sq Km	243 609	**Languages**	English, Welsh, Gaelic
Area Sq Miles	94 058	**Religions**	Protestant, Roman Catholic, Muslim
Population	63 136 000	**Currency**	Pound sterling
Capital	London	**Organizations**	Comm., EU, NATO, OECD, UN

Map page 172–175

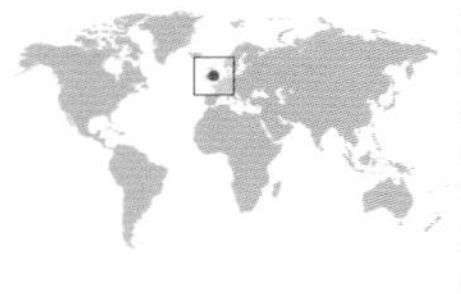

The United Kingdom, in northwest Europe, occupies the island of Great Britain, part of Ireland, and many small adjacent islands. Great Britain comprises England, Scotland and Wales. England covers over half the land area and supports over four-fifths of the population, at its densest in the southeast. The English landscape is flat or rolling with some uplands, notably the Cheviot Hills on the Scottish border, the Pennines in the centre-north, and the hills of the Lake District in the northwest. Scotland consists of southern uplands, central lowlands, the Highlands (which include the UK's highest peak) and many islands. Wales is a land of hills, mountains and river valleys. Northern Ireland contains uplands, plains and the UK's largest lake, Lough Neagh. The climate of the UK is mild, wet and variable. There are few mineral deposits, but important energy resources. Agricultural activities involve sheep and cattle rearing, dairy farming, and crop and fruit growing in the east and southeast. Productivity is high, but approximately one-third of food is imported. The UK produces petroleum and natural gas from reserves in the North Sea and is self-sufficient in energy in net terms. Major manufactures are food and drinks, motor vehicles and parts, aerospace equipment, machinery, electronic and electrical equipment, and chemicals and chemical products. However, the economy is dominated by service industries, including banking, insurance, finance and business services. London, the capital, is one of the world's major financial centres. Tourism is also a major industry, with approximately thirty-two million visitors a year. International trade is also important, equivalent to around forty per cent of national income. Main trading partners and the USA and other European Union countries.

England (Constituent country)
Area Sq Km (Sq Miles) 130 433 (50 360) **Population** 53 493 700 **Capital** London

Northern Ireland (Province)
Area Sq Km (Sq Miles) 13 576 (5 242) **Population** 1 823 600 **Capital** Belfast

Scotland (Constituent country)
Area Sq Km (Sq Miles) 78 822 (30 433) **Population** 5 313 600 **Capital** Edinburgh

Wales (Principality)
Area Sq Km (Sq Miles) 20 778 (8 022) **Population** 3 074 100 **Capital** Cardiff

UNITED STATES OF AMERICA

Area Sq Km	9 826 635	**Languages**	English, Spanish
Area Sq Miles	3 794 085	**Religions**	Protestant, Roman Catholic, Sunni Muslim, Jewish
Population	320 051 000	**Currency**	United States dollar
Capital	Washington D.C.	**Organizations**	APEC, NATO, OECD, UN

Map page 210–211

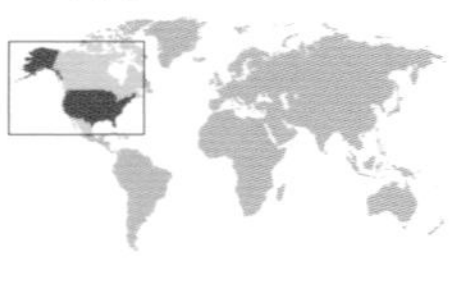

The USA comprises forty-eight contiguous states in North America, bounded by Canada and Mexico, plus the states of Alaska, to the northwest of Canada, and Hawaii, in the north Pacific Ocean. The populous eastern states cover the Atlantic coastal plain (which includes the Florida peninsula and the Gulf of Mexico coast) and the Appalachian Mountains. The central states occupy a vast interior plain drained by the Mississippi-Missouri river system. To the west lie the Rocky Mountains, separated from the Pacific coastal ranges by intermontane plateaus. The Pacific coastal zone is also mountainous, and prone to earthquakes. Hawaii is a group of some twenty volcanic islands. Climatic conditions range between arctic in Alaska to desert in the intermontane plateaus. Most of the USA has a temperate climate, although the interior has continental conditions. There are abundant natural resources, including major reserves of minerals and energy resources. The USA has the largest and most technologically advanced economy in the world, based on manufacturing and services. Although agriculture accounts for approximately two per cent of national income, productivity is high and the USA is a net exporter of food, chiefly grains and fruit. Cotton is the major industrial crop. The USA produces iron ore, copper, lead, zinc, and many other minerals. It is a major producer of coal, petroleum and natural gas, although being the world's biggest energy user it imports significant quantities of petroleum and its products. Manufacturing is diverse. The main industries are petroleum, steel, motor vehicles, aerospace, telecommunications, electronics, food processing, chemicals and consumer goods. Tourism is a major foreign currency earner, with approximately seventy-four million visitors a year. Other important service industries are banking and finance, Wall Street in New York being one of the world's major stock exchanges. Canada and Mexico are the main trading partners.

Alabama (State)
Area Sq Km (Sq Miles) 135 765 (52 419) **Population** 4 822 023 **Capital** Montgomery

Alaska (State)
Area Sq Km (Sq Miles) 1 717 854 (663 267) **Population** 731 449 **Capital** Juneau

Arizona (State)
Area Sq Km (Sq Miles) 295 253 (113 998) **Population** 6 553 255 **Capital** Phoenix

Arkansas (State)
Area Sq Km (Sq Miles) 137 733 (53 179) **Population** 2 949 131 **Capital** Little Rock

California (State)
Area Sq Km (Sq Miles) 423 971 (163 696) **Population** 38 041 430 **Capital** Sacramento

Colorado (State)
Area Sq Km (Sq Miles) 269 602 (104 094) **Population** 5 187 582 **Capital** Denver

Connecticut (State)
Area Sq Km (Sq Miles) 14 356 (5 543) **Population** 3 590 347 **Capital** Hartford

Delaware (State)
Area Sq Km (Sq Miles) 6 446 (2 489) **Population** 917 092 **Capital** Dover

District of Columbia (District)
Area Sq Km (Sq Miles) 176 (68) **Population** 632 323 **Capital** Washington

Florida (State)
Area Sq Km (Sq Miles) 170 305 (65 755) **Population** 19 317 568 **Capital** Tallahassee

Georgia (State)
Area Sq Km (Sq Miles) 153 910 (59 425) **Population** 9 919 945 **Capital** Atlanta

Hawaii (State)
Area Sq Km (Sq Miles) 28 311 (10 931) **Population** 1 392 313 **Capital** Honolulu

Idaho (State)
Area Sq Km (Sq Miles) 216 445 (83 570) **Population** 1 595 728 **Capital** Boise

Illinois (State)
Area Sq Km (Sq Miles) 149 997 (57 914) **Population** 12 875 255 **Capital** Springfield

Indiana (State)
Area Sq Km (Sq Miles) 94 322 (36 418) **Population** 6 537 334 **Capital** Indianapolis

Iowa (State)
Area Sq Km (Sq Miles) 145 744 (56 272) **Population** 3 074 186 **Capital** Des Moines

Kansas (State)
Area Sq Km (Sq Miles) 213 096 (82 277) **Population** 2 885 905 **Capital** Topeka

Kentucky (State)
Area Sq Km (Sq Miles) 104 659 (40 409) **Population** 4 380 415 **Capital** Frankfort

Louisiana (State)
Area Sq Km (Sq Miles) 134 265 (51 840) **Population** 4 601 893 **Capital** Baton Rouge

Maine (State)
Area Sq Km (Sq Miles) 91 647 (35 385) **Population** 1 329 192 **Capital** Augusta

Maryland (State)
Area Sq Km (Sq Miles) 32 134 (12 407) **Population** 5 884 563 **Capital** Annapolis

Massachusetts (State)
Area Sq Km (Sq Miles) 27 337 (10 555) **Population** 6 646 144 **Capital** Boston

Michigan (State)
Area Sq Km (Sq Miles) 250 493 (96 716) **Population** 9 883 360 **Capital** Lansing

Minnesota (State)
Area Sq Km (Sq Miles) 225 171 (86 939) **Population** 5 379 139 **Capital** St Paul

Mississippi (State)
Area Sq Km (Sq Miles) 125 433 (48 430) **Population** 2 984 926 **Capital** Jackson

Missouri (State)
Area Sq Km (Sq Miles) 180 533 (69 704) **Population** 6 021 988 **Capital** Jefferson City

Montana (State)
Area Sq Km (Sq Miles) 380 837 (147 042) **Population** 1 005 141 **Capital** Helena

Nebraska (State)
Area Sq Km (Sq Miles) 200 346 (77 354) **Population** 1 855 525 **Capital** Lincoln

Nevada (State)
Area Sq Km (Sq Miles) 286 352 (110 561) **Population** 2 758 931 **Capital** Carson City

New Hampshire (State)
Area Sq Km (Sq Miles) 24 216 (9 350) **Population** 1 320 718 **Capital** Concord

New Jersey (State)
Area Sq Km (Sq Miles) 22 587 (8 721) **Population** 8 864 590 **Capital** Trenton

New Mexico (State)
Area Sq Km (Sq Miles) 314 914 (121 589) **Population** 2 085 538 **Capital** Santa Fe

New York (State)
Area Sq Km (Sq Miles) 141 299 (54 556) **Population** 19 570 261 **Capital** Albany

North Carolina (State)
Area Sq Km (Sq Miles) 139 391 (53 819) **Population** 9 752 073 **Capital** Raleigh

North Dakota (State)
Area Sq Km (Sq Miles) 183 112 (70 700) **Population** 699 628 **Capital** Bismarck

Ohio (State)
Area Sq Km (Sq Miles) 116 096 (44 825) **Population** 11 544 225 **Capital** Columbus

Oklahoma (State)
Area Sq Km (Sq Miles) 181 035 (69 898) **Population** 3 814 820 **Capital** Oklahoma City

Oregon (State)
Area Sq Km (Sq Miles) 254 806 (98 381) **Population** 3 899 353 **Capital** Salem

Pennsylvania (State)
Area Sq Km (Sq Miles) 119 282 (46 055) **Population** 12 763 536 **Capital** Harrisburg

Rhode Island (State)
Area Sq Km (Sq Miles) 4 002 (1 545) **Population** 1 050 292 **Capital** Providence

South Carolina (State)
Area Sq Km (Sq Miles) 82 931 (32 020) **Population** 4 723 723 **Capital** Columbia

South Dakota (State)
Area Sq Km (Sq Miles) 199 730 (77 116) **Population** 833 354 **Capital** Pierre

Tennessee (State)
Area Sq Km (Sq Miles) 109 150 (42 143) **Population** 6 456 243 **Capital** Nashville

Texas (State)
Area Sq Km (Sq Miles) 695 622 (268 581) **Population** 26 059 203 **Capital** Austin

Utah (State)
Area Sq Km (Sq Miles) 219 887 (84 899) **Population** 2 855 287 **Capital** Salt Lake City

Vermont (State)
Area Sq Km (Sq Miles) 24 900 (9 614) **Population** 626 011 **Capital** Montpelier

Virginia (State)
Area Sq Km (Sq Miles) 110 784 (42 774) **Population** 8 185 867 **Capital** Richmond

Washington (State)
Area Sq Km (Sq Miles) 184 666 (71 300) **Population** 6 897 012 **Capital** Olympia

West Virginia (State)
Area Sq Km (Sq Miles) 62 755 (24 230) **Population** 1 855 413 **Capital** Charleston

Wisconsin (State)
Area Sq Km (Sq Miles) 169 639 (65 498) **Population** 5 726 398 **Capital** Madison

Wyoming (State)
Area Sq Km (Sq Miles) 253 337 (97 814) **Population** 576 412 **Capital** Cheyenne

URUGUAY
Oriental Republic of Uruguay

Area Sq Km	176 215	**Languages**	Spanish
Area Sq Miles	68 037	**Religions**	Roman Catholic, Protestant, Jewish
Population	3 407 000	**Currency**	Uruguayan peso
Capital	Montevideo	**Organizations**	UN

Map page 235

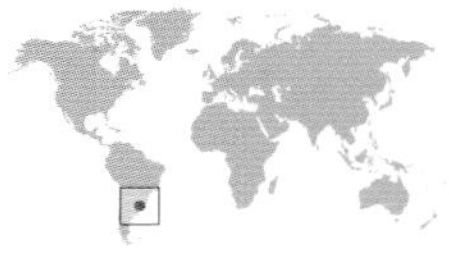

Uruguay, on the Atlantic coast of central South America, is a low-lying land of prairies. The coast and the River Plate estuary in the south are fringed with lagoons and sand dunes. Almost half the population lives in the capital, Montevideo. Uruguay has warm summers and mild winters. The economy is based on cattle and sheep ranching, and the main industries produce food products, textiles, and petroleum products. Meat, wool, hides, textiles and agricultural products are the main exports. Brazil and Argentina are the main trading partners.

UZBEKISTAN
Republic of Uzbekistan

Area Sq Km	447 400	**Languages**	Uzbek, Russian, Tajik, Kazakh
Area Sq Miles	172 742	**Religions**	Sunni Muslim, Russian Orthodox
Population	28 934 000	**Currency**	Uzbek som
Capital	Toshkent (Tashkent)	**Organizations**	CIS, UN

Map page 140–141

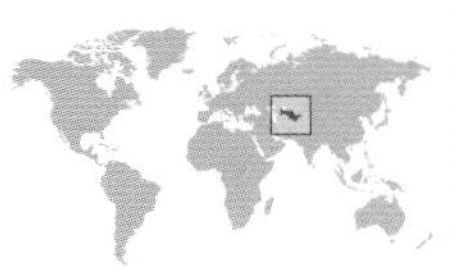

A landlocked country of central Asia, Uzbekistan consists mainly of the flat Kyzylkum Desert. High mountains and valleys are found towards the southeast borders with Kyrgyzstan and Tajikistan. Most settlement is in the Fergana basin. The climate is hot and dry. The economy is based mainly on irrigated agriculture, chiefly cotton production. Uzbekistan is rich in minerals, including gold, copper, lead, zinc and uranium, and it has one of the largest gold mines in the world. Industry specializes in fertilizers and machinery for cotton harvesting and textile manufacture. Russia is the main trading partner.

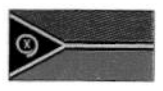

VANUATU
Republic of Vanuatu

Area Sq Km	12 190	**Languages**	English, Bislama (Creole), French
Area Sq Miles	4 707	**Religions**	Protestant, Roman Catholic, traditional beliefs
Population	253 000	**Currency**	Vatu
Capital	Port Vila	**Organizations**	Comm., UN

Map page 119

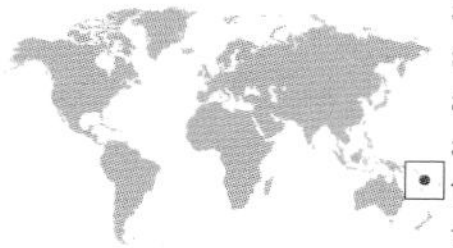

Vanuatu occupies an archipelago of approximately eighty islands in the southwest Pacific. Many of the islands are mountainous, of volcanic origin and densely forested. The climate is tropical, with heavy rainfall. Half of the population lives on the main islands of Éfaté and Espíritu Santo, and the majority of people are employed in agriculture. Copra, beef, timber, vegetables, and cocoa are the main exports. In March 2015 Cyclone Pam caused catastrophic damage to the islands.

VATICAN CITY
Vatican City State or Holy See

Area Sq Km	0.5	**Languages**	Italian
Area Sq Miles	0.2	**Religions**	Roman Catholic
Population	800	**Currency**	Euro
Capital	Vatican City		

Map page 184

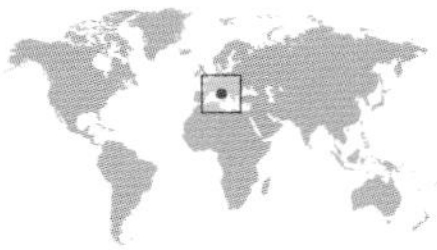

The world's smallest sovereign state, the Vatican City occupies a hill to the west of the river Tiber within the Italian capital, Rome. It is the headquarters of the Roman Catholic church, and income comes from investments, voluntary contributions and tourism.

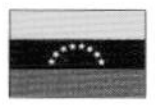

VENEZUELA
Bolivarian Republic of Venezuela

Area Sq Km	912 050	**Languages**	Spanish, Amerindian languages
Area Sq Miles	352 144	**Religions**	Roman Catholic, Protestant
Population	30 405 000	**Currency**	Bolívar
Capital	Caracas	**Organizations**	OPEC, UN

Map page 233

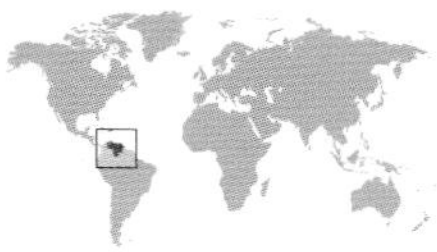

Venezuela is in northern South America, on the Caribbean. Its coast is much indented, with the oil-rich area of Lake Maracaibo at the western end, and the swampy Orinoco Delta to the east. Mountain ranges run parallel to the coast, and turn southwestwards to form a northern extension of the Andes. Central Venezuela is an area of lowland grasslands drained by the Orinoco river system. To the south are the Guiana Highlands, which contain the Angel Falls, the world's highest waterfall. Almost ninety per cent of the population lives in towns, mostly in the coastal mountain areas. The climate is tropical, with most rainfall in summer. Farming is important, particularly cattle ranching and dairy farming; coffee, maize, rice and sugar cane are the main crops. Venezuela is a major oil producer, and oil accounts for about seventy-five per cent of export earnings. Aluminium, iron ore, copper and gold are also mined, and manufactures include petrochemicals, aluminium, steel, textiles and food products. The USA, China and Brazil are the main trading partners.

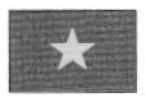

VIETNAM
Socialist Republic of Việtnam

Area Sq Km	329 565	**Languages**	Vietnamese, Thai, Khmer, Chinese, other local languages
Area Sq Miles	127 246	**Religions**	Buddhist, Taoist, Roman Catholic, Cao Dai, Hoa Hao
Population	91 680 000	**Currency**	Dong
Capital	Ha Nôi	**Organizations**	APEC, ASEAN, UN

Map page 151

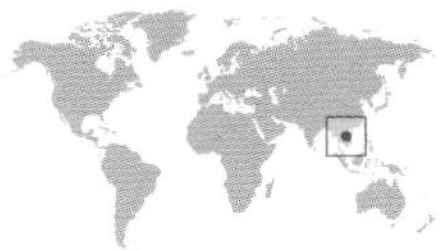

Vietnam lies in southeast Asia, on the South China Sea. The Red River lowlands in the north and the Mekong delta in the south are separated by narrow coastal plains backed by the Annam Highlands. Most people live in the river deltas. The climate is tropical. Over three-quarters of the workforce is involved in agriculture, forestry or fishing. Coffee, tea and rubber are important, but Vietnam is the world's second largest rice exporter. Oil, coal and copper are produced, and other main industries are food processing, clothing and footwear, cement and fertilizers. Exports include oil, coffee, rice, clothing and fish. Japan and Singapore are the main trading partners.

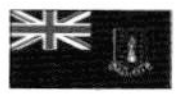

Virgin Islands (U.K.)
United Kingdom Overseas Territory

Area Sq Km	153	**Languages**	English
Area Sq Miles	59	**Religions**	Protestant, Roman Catholic
Population	28 000	**Currency**	United States dollar
Capital	Road Town		

Map page 223

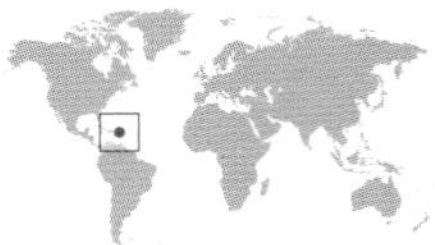

The Caribbean territory comprises four main islands and over thirty islets at the eastern end of the Virgin Islands group. Apart from the flat coral atoll of Anegada, the islands are volcanic in origin and hilly. The climate is subtropical, and tourism is the main industry.

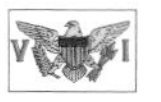

Virgin Islands (U.S.A.)
United States Unincorporated Territory

Area Sq Km	352	**Languages**	English, Spanish
Area Sq Miles	136	**Religions**	Protestant, Roman Catholic
Population	107 000	**Currency**	United States dollar
Capital	Charlotte Amalie		

Map page 223

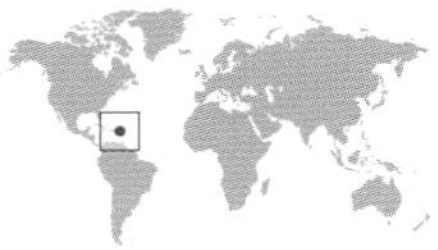

The territory consists of three main islands and over fifty islets in the Caribbean's western Virgin Islands. The islands are hilly, of volcanic origin, and the climate is subtropical. The economy is based on tourism, with some manufacturing, including a major oil refinery on St Croix.

Wallis and Futuna Islands
French Overseas Territory

Area Sq Km	274	**Languages**	French, Wallisian, Futunian
Area Sq Miles	106	**Religions**	Roman Catholic
Population	13 000	**Currency**	CFP franc
Capital	Matā'utu		

Map page 119

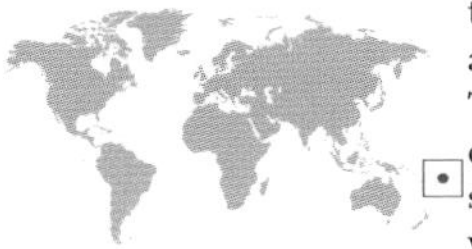

The south Pacific territory comprises the volcanic islands of the Wallis archipelago and the Hoorn Islands. The climate is tropical. The islands depend on subsistence farming, the sale of licences to foreign fishing fleets, workers' remittances from abroad and French aid.

West Bank
Disputed territory

Area Sq Km	5 860	**Languages**	Arabic, Hebrew
Area Sq Miles	2 263	**Religions**	Sunni Muslim, Jewish, Shi'a Muslim, Christian
Population	2 719 112	**Currency**	Jordanian dinar, Israeli shekel

Map page 138

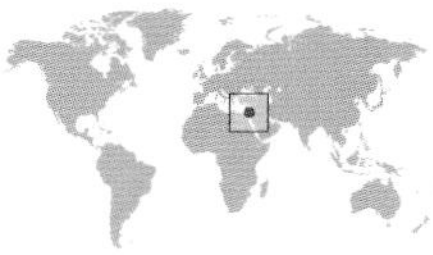

The territory consists of the west bank of the river Jordan and parts of Judea and Samaria. The land was annexed by Israel in 1967, but some areas have been granted autonomy under agreements between Israel and the Palestinian Authority. Conflict between the Israelis and the Palestinians continues to restrict economic development.

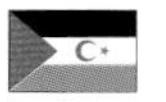

Western Sahara
Disputed territory

Area Sq Km	266 000	**Languages**	Arabic
Area Sq Miles	102 703	**Religions**	Sunni Muslim
Population	567 000	**Currency**	Moroccan dirham
Capital	Laâyoune		

Map page 192

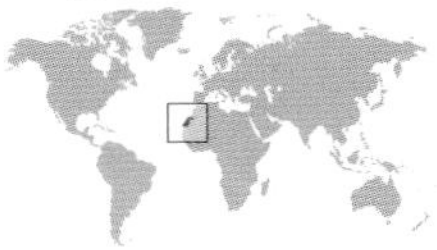

Situated on the northwest coast of Africa, the territory of the Western Sahara is now effectively controlled by Morocco. The land is low, flat desert with higher land in the northeast. There is little cultivation and only about twenty per cent of the land is pasture. Livestock herding, fishing and phosphate mining are the main activities. All trade is controlled by Morocco.

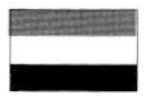

YEMEN
Republic of Yemen

Area Sq Km	527 968	**Languages**	Arabic
Area Sq Miles	203 850	**Religions**	Sunni Muslim, Shi'a Muslim
Population	24 407 000	**Currency**	Yemeni riyal
Capital	Şan'ā'	**Organizations**	UN

Map page 146

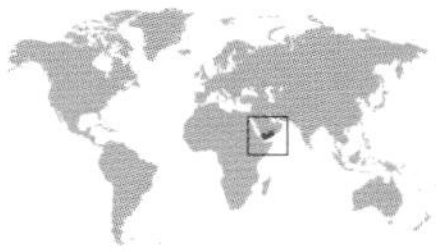

Yemen occupies the southwestern part of the Arabian Peninsula, on the Red Sea and the Gulf of Aden. Beyond the Red Sea coastal plain the land rises to a mountain range and then descends to desert plateaus. Much of the country is hot and arid, but there is more rainfall in the west, where most of the population lives. Farming and fishing are the main activities, with cotton the main cash crop. The main exports are crude oil, fish, coffee and dried fruit. Despite some oil resources Yemen is one of the poorest countries in the Arab world. Main trading partners are Thailand, China, South Korea and Saudi Arabia.

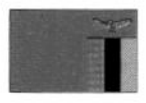

ZAMBIA
Republic of Zambia

Area Sq Km	752 614	**Languages**	English, Bemba, Nyanja, Tonga, other local languages
Area Sq Miles	290 586	**Religions**	Christian, traditional beliefs
Population	14 539 000	**Currency**	Zambian kwacha
Capital	Lusaka	**Organizations**	Comm., SADC, UN

Map page 195

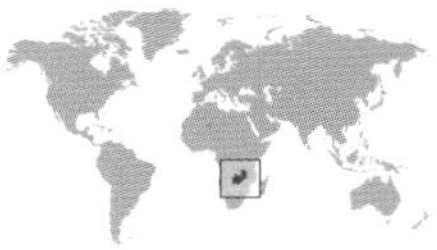

A landlocked state in south central Africa, Zambia consists principally of high savanna plateaus and is bordered by the Zambezi river in the south. Most people live in the Copperbelt area in the centre-north. The climate is tropical, with a rainy season from November to May. Agriculture employs over sixty per cent of the workforce, but is mainly at subsistence level. Copper mining is the mainstay of the economy, although reserves are declining. Copper and cobalt are the main exports. Most trade is with South Africa.

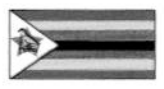

ZIMBABWE
Republic of Zimbabwe

Area Sq Km	390 759	**Languages**	English, Shona, Ndebele
Area Sq Miles	150 873	**Religions**	Christian, traditional beliefs
Population	14 150 000	**Currency**	US dollar and other currencies
Capital	Harare	**Organizations**	SADC, UN

Map page 195

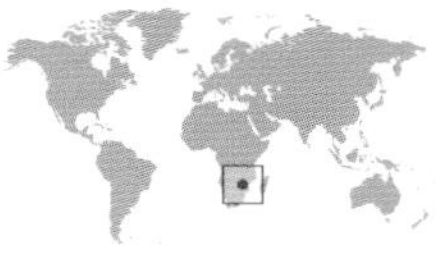

Zimbabwe, a landlocked state in south-central Africa, consists of high plateaus flanked by the Zambezi river valley and Lake Kariba in the north and the Limpopo river in the south. Most of the population lives in the centre of the country. There are significant mineral resources, including gold, nickel, copper, asbestos, platinum and chromium. Agriculture is a major sector of the economy, with crops including tobacco, maize, sugar cane and cotton. Beef cattle are also important. Exports include tobacco, gold, ferroalloys, nickel and cotton. South Africa is the main trading partner. The economy has suffered recently through significant political unrest and instability.

INTRODUCTION TO THE ATLAS AND MAP SYMBOLS

These pages explain the editorial policies followed for map pages 110 to 240 and the map symbols used on the maps are also explained here. In the tradition of The Times Atlas of the World, the map sequence starts at the International Date Line in the Pacific Ocean and broadly works westwards, moving from Oceania through Asia, Europe, Africa, North America and finally to South America. The alphanumeric reference system used in the index is based on latitude and longitude, and the number and letter for each graticule square are shown within each map frame. The numbers of adjoining or overlapping plates are shown by arrows in the frame and accompanying numbers in the margin.

BOUNDARIES

The status of nations, their names and their boundaries, are shown in this atlas as they are at the time of going to press, as far as can be ascertained. The atlas includes any recent changes of status of nations and their boundaries. Where an international boundary symbol appears in the sea or ocean it does not necessarily infer a legal maritime boundary, but shows which islands belong to which country.

Where international boundaries are the subject of dispute it may be that no portrayal of them will meet with the approval of any of the countries involved. It is not seen as the function of this atlas to try to adjudicate between the rights and wrongs of political issues, and reference mapping at atlas scales is not the ideal medium for indicating the claims of many separatist and irredentist movements. However, every reasonable attempt is made to show where an active territorial dispute exists, and where there is an important difference between 'de facto' (existing in fact, on the ground) and 'de jure' (according to law) boundaries. This is done by the use of a different symbol where international boundaries are disputed, or where the alignment is unconfirmed, to that used for settled international boundaries. Ceasefire lines are also shown by a separate symbol. For clarity, disputed boundaries and areas are annotated where this is considered necessary. The atlas aims to take a strictly neutral viewpoint of all such cases, based on advice from expert consultants.

SCALE

In order to directly compare areas throughout the world it would be necessary to maintain a single map scale throughout the atlas. However, the desirability of mapping more densely populated and more significant areas of the world at larger, and therefore more detailed, scales means that a range of scales have been used. Scales for continental maps range from 1:17 500 000 to 1:32 000 000, depending on the size of the continental land mass being covered. Scales for regional maps are typically in the range 1:12 000 000 to 1:20 000 000, although smaller scales are used for a few remoter areas such as northern Asia. Mapping for most countries is at scales between 1:5 000 000 and 1:7 000 000, although for the most densely populated areas of Europe the scale increases to 1:2 000 000.

MAP PROJECTIONS

The representation or 'projection' of the Earth into only two dimensions is a perennial problem for the cartographer. Distortions are inevitable and all map projections are compromises. Some projections seek to maintain correct area relationships (equal area projections), true distances and bearings from a point (equidistant projections) or correct angles and shapes (conformal projections). Others attempt to achieve a balance between these properties. The choice of projections used in this atlas has been made on an individual continental and regional basis. Projections used, and their individual parameters, have been defined to provide the best representation of the area mapped, to minimize distortion and to reduce scale errors as much as possible. The projection used is indicated at the bottom left of each map plate.

PLACE NAMES

The spelling of place names on maps has always been a matter of great complexity, because of the variety of the world's languages and the systems used to write them down. There is no standard way of spelling names or of converting them from one alphabet, or symbol set, to another. Instead, conventional ways of spelling have evolved in each of the world's major languages, and the results often differ significantly from the name as it is

spelled in the original language. Familiar examples of English conventional names include Munich (München), Florence (Firenze) and Moscow (from the transliterated form, Moskva).

In this atlas, local name forms are used where these are in the Roman alphabet, though for major cities and main physical features, conventional English names are given first. The local forms are those which are officially recognized by the government of the country concerned, usually as represented by its official mapping agency. This is a basic principle laid down by the United Kingdom government's Permanent Committee on Geographical Names (PCGN) and the equivalent United States Board on Geographic Names (BGN). Prominent English-language and historic names are not neglected, however. These, and significant superseded names and alternate spellings, are included in brackets on the maps where space permits, and are cross-referenced in the index.

Country names are shown in conventional English form and include any recent changes promulgated by national governments and adopted by the United Nations. The names of continents, oceans, seas and under-water features in international waters also appear in English throughout the atlas, as do those of other international features where such an English form exists and is in common use. International features are defined as features crossing one or more international boundary.

For languages in non-Roman alphabets or symbol sets, names need to be 'Romanized' through a process of transliteration (the conversion of characters or symbols from one alphabet into another) or transcription (conversion of names based on pronunciation). Different systems often exist for this process, but PCGN and its United States counterpart, the Board on Geographic Names (BGN), usually follow the same Romanization principles, and the general policy for this atlas is to follow their lead.

ABBREVIATIONS

Arch.	Archipelago			L.	Lake			Ra.	Range		mountain range
B.	Bay				Loch	(Scotland)	lake	S.	South, Southern		
	Bahia, Baía	Portuguese	bay		Lough	(Ireland)	lake		Salar, Salina,		
	Bahía	Spanish	bay		Lac	French	lake		Salinas	Spanish	salt pan, salt pans
	Baie	French	bay		Lago	Portuguese, Spanish	lake	Sa	Serra	Portuguese,	mountain range
C.	Cape			M.	Mys	Russian	cape, point		Sierra	Spanish	mountain range
	Cabo	Portuguese,		Mt	Mount			Sd	Sound		
		Spanish	cape, headland		Mont	French	hill, mountain	S.E.	Southeast,		
	Cap	French	cape, headland	Mt.	Mountain				Southeastern		
Co	Cerro	Spanish	hill, peak, summit	Mte	Monte	Portuguese, Spanish	hill, mountain	St	Saint		
E.	East, Eastern			Mts	Mountains				Sankt	German	Saint
Est.	Estrecho	Spanish	strait		Monts	French	hills, mountains		Sint	Dutch	Saint
G.	Gebel	Arabic	hill, mountain	N.	North, Northern			Sta	Santa	Italian, Portuguese,	
Gt	Great			O.	Ostrov	Russian	island			Spanish	Saint
I.	Island, Isle			Pk	Puncak	Indonesian, Malay	hill, mountain	Ste	Sainte	French	Saint
	Ilha	Portuguese	island	Pt	Point			Str.	Strait		
	Islas	Spanish	island	Pta	Punta	Italian, Spanish	cape, point	Tk	Teluk	Indonesian, Malay	bay, gulf
Is	Islands, Isles			R.	River			Tg	Tanjong, Tanjung	Indonesian, Malay	cape, point
	Islas	Spanish	islands		Rio	Portuguese	river	Vdkhr.	Vodokhranilishche	Russian	reservoir
Kep.	Kepulauan	Indonesian	islands		Río	Spanish	river	W.	West, Western		strait
Khr.	Khrebet	Russian	mountain range		Rivière	French	river		Wadi, Wâdi, Wādī	Arabic	watercourse

RELIEF

Contour intervals used in layer-colouring for
land height and sea depth

Ocean maps   Reference maps

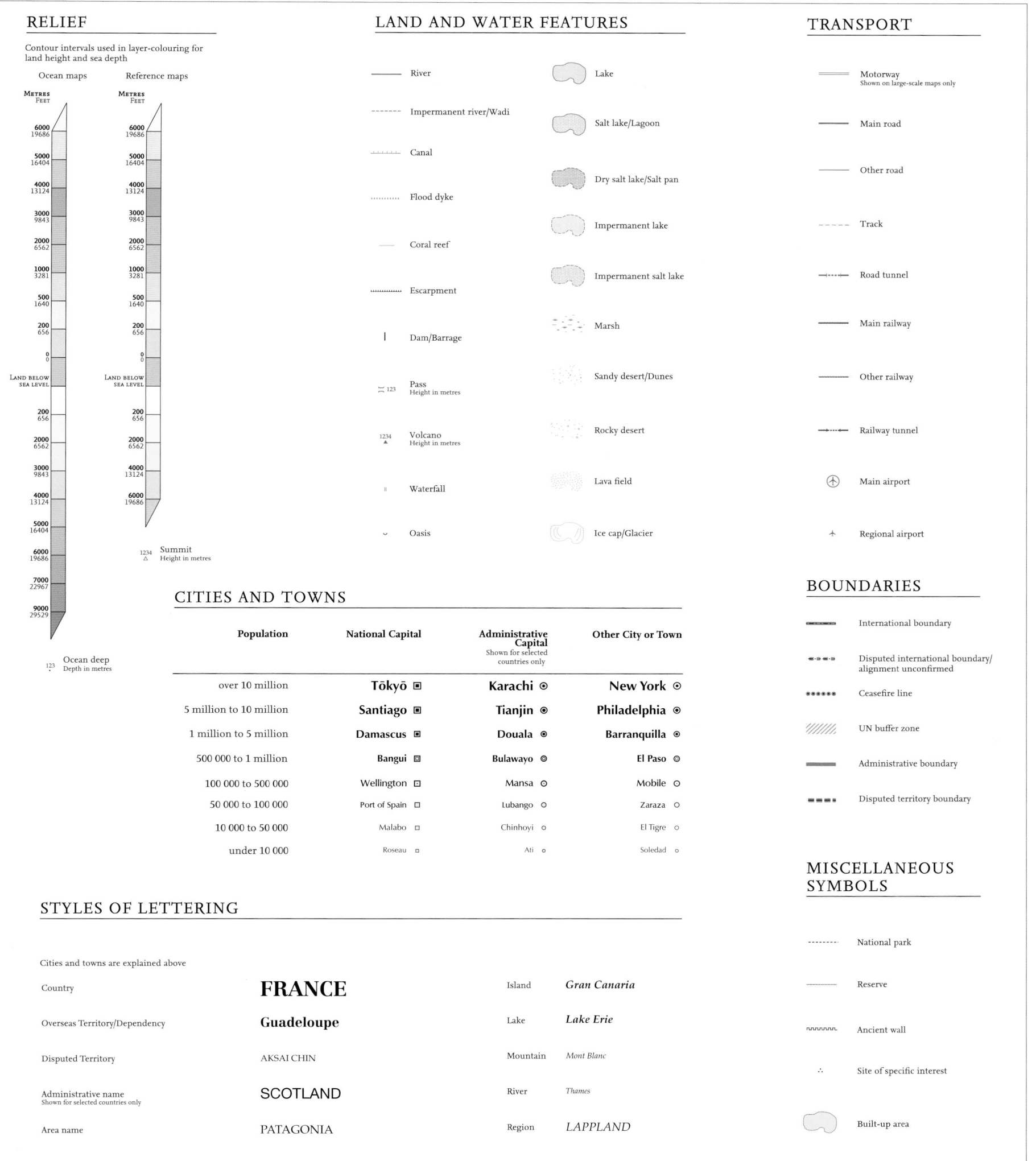

Metres Feet	
6000 / 19686	
5000 / 16404	
4000 / 13124	
3000 / 9843	
2000 / 6562	
1000 / 3281	
500 / 1640	
200 / 656	
0 / 0	

Land below sea level

123   Ocean deep
    Depth in metres

LAND AND WATER FEATURES

—— River

------- Impermanent river/Wadi

········· Canal

·········· Flood dyke

—— Coral reef

············· Escarpment

| Dam/Barrage

≍ 123   Pass
     Height in metres

1234 ▲   Volcano
     Height in metres

Waterfall

˘   Oasis

Lake

Salt lake/Lagoon

Dry salt lake/Salt pan

Impermanent lake

Impermanent salt lake

Marsh

Sandy desert/Dunes

Rocky desert

Lava field

Ice cap/Glacier

1234 △   Summit
     Height in metres

CITIES AND TOWNS

Population	National Capital	Administrative Capital *Shown for selected countries only*	Other City or Town
over 10 million	**Tōkyō** ▣	**Karachi** ◉	**New York** ◉
5 million to 10 million	**Santiago** ▣	**Tianjin** ◉	**Philadelphia** ◉
1 million to 5 million	**Damascus** ▣	**Douala** ◉	**Barranquilla** ◉
500 000 to 1 million	**Bangui** ▣	**Bulawayo** ◎	**El Paso** ◎
100 000 to 500 000	Wellington ▢	Mansa ○	Mobile ○
50 000 to 100 000	Port of Spain ▢	Lubango ○	Zaraza ○
10 000 to 50 000	Malabo ▫	Chinhoyi ○	El Tigre ○
under 10 000	Roseau ▫	Ati ○	Soledad ○

STYLES OF LETTERING

Cities and towns are explained above

Country	**FRANCE**	Island	*Gran Canaria*
Overseas Territory/Dependency	**Guadeloupe**	Lake	*Lake Erie*
Disputed Territory	AKSAI CHIN	Mountain	*Mont Blanc*
Administrative name *Shown for selected countries only*	SCOTLAND	River	*Thames*
Area name	PATAGONIA	Region	*LAPPLAND*

TRANSPORT

═══ Motorway
     Shown on large-scale maps only

—— Main road

—— Other road

----- Track

—•—•— Road tunnel

—— Main railway

—— Other railway

—•—•— Railway tunnel

⊕   Main airport

✦   Regional airport

BOUNDARIES

━━━ International boundary

◄-■-►-► Disputed international boundary/ alignment unconfirmed

✴✴✴✴✴✴ Ceasefire line

//////// UN buffer zone

━━━━ Administrative boundary

▬ ▬ ▬ ▬ Disputed territory boundary

MISCELLANEOUS SYMBOLS

-------- National park

·············· Reserve

∿∿∿∿∿ Ancient wall

∴   Site of specific interest

Built-up area

WORLD PHYSICAL

The shapes of the continents and oceans have evolved over millions of years. Movement of the tectonic plates which make up the Earth's crust has created some of the best known land features. From the highest point of Mount Everest to the deepest in the Mariana Trench is a height of almost 20 000 m /over 65 000 ft. Earthquakes, volcanoes, erosion, climatic variations and man's intervention all continue to affect the Earth's landscapes. Different landscapes reflect great variations in climate from deserts such as the Sahara, to the frozen ice cap of Antarctica.

FACTS

• The Pacific Ocean is larger than the continents' land areas combined.

• The average height of the Earth's land surface is 840 m (2755 ft) above sea level and 52 per cent of the land is below 500 m (1640 ft). Approximately 10 per cent of the surface is permanently covered by ice.

• The Ural Mountains define part of the boundary between Europe and Asia.

• The collision of two tectonic plates – the Indo-Australia and the Eurasian Plates – formed the Himalaya mountains. The mountains are still rising at a rate of approximately 5 mm (0.2 inch) a year.

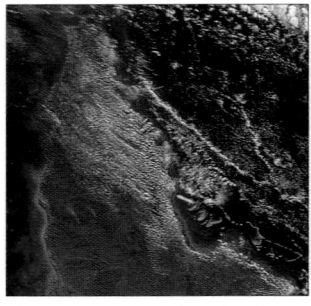
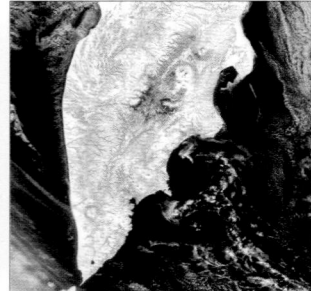

The Great Barrier Reef stretches for over 2000 km (1249 miles) over an area of approximately 344 400 sq km (132 974 sq miles). The reef is located off the eastern coast of Queensland, Australia and can be seen from space.

The Kamchatka Peninsula in northeastern Asia is a mountainous landscape with numerous active volcanoes.

High sand dunes, sculpted by the wind, dwarf houses at the edge of the Sahara.

The lowland Pampas grasslands of South America stretch across central Argentina and most of Uruguay.

1 : 90 000 000

PHYSICAL EXTREMES

EARTH'S DIMENSIONS		HIGHEST MOUNTAINS	metres	feet	location
Mass	5.974 x 10²¹ tonnes	Mt Everest	8 848	29 028	China/Nepa
Volume	1 083 207 x 10⁶ cu km / 259 911 x 10⁶ cu miles	K2	8 611	28 251	China/Pakistan
Total area	509 450 000 sq km / 196 699 000 sq miles	Kangchenjunga	8 586	28 169	India/Nepa
Land area	149 450 000 sq km / 57 703 000 sq miles	Lhotse	8 516	27 939	China/Nepa
Water area	360 000 000 sq km / 138 996 000 sq miles	Makalu	8 463	27 765	China/Nepa
Water volume	1 389 500 x 10³ cu km / 333 405 x 10³ cu miles	Cho Oyu	8 201	26 906	China/Nepa
Equatorial diameter	12 756 km / 7 927 miles	Dhaulagiri I	8 167	26 794	Nepa
Polar diameter	12 714 km / 7 900 miles	Manaslu	8 163	26 781	Nepa
Equatorial circumference	40 075 km / 24 903 miles	Nanga Parbat	8 126	26 660	Pakistan
Meridional circumference	40 008 km / 24 861 miles	Annapurna I	8 091	26 545	Nepa

Winkel Tripel Projection

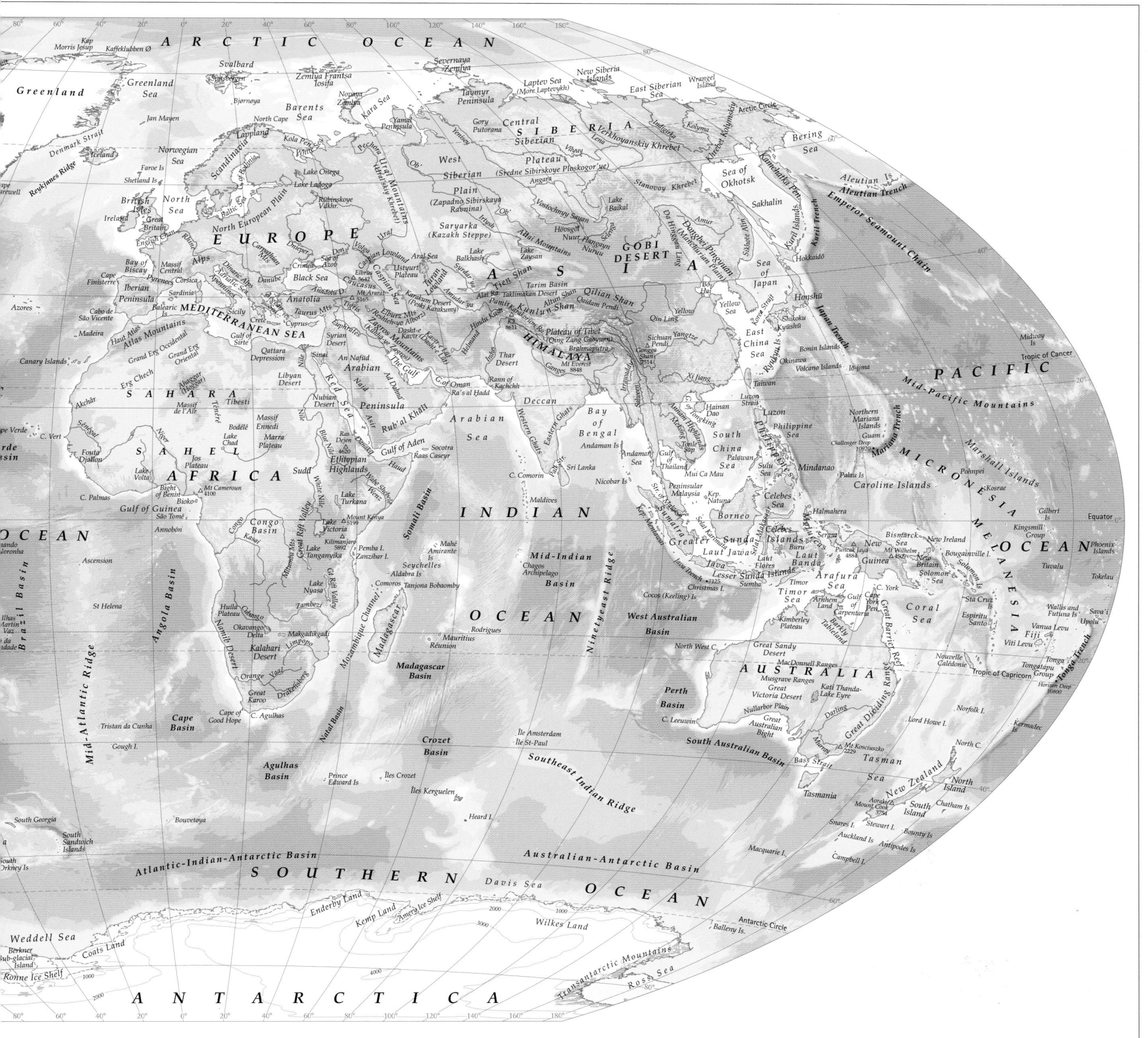

LONGEST RIVERS	km	miles	location	LARGEST ISLANDS	sq km	sq miles	location	LARGEST LAKES	sq km	sq miles	location	OCEANS AND SEAS	Area sq km	sq miles	Deepest point metres	feet
Nile	6 695	4 160	Africa	Greenland	2 175 600	839 999	North America	Caspian Sea	371 000	143 243	Asia/Europe	Pacific Ocean	166 241 000	64 186 000	10 920	35 826
Amazon	6 516	4 049	South America	New Guinea	808 510	312 166	Oceania	Lake Superior	82 100	31 699	North America	Atlantic Ocean	86 557 000	33 420 000	8 605	28 231
Yangtze	6 380	3 965	Asia	Borneo	745 561	287 861	Asia	Lake Victoria	68 870	26 591	Africa	Indian Ocean	73 427 000	28 350 000	7 125	23 376
Mississippi-Missouri	5 969	3 709	North America	Madagascar	587 040	226 656	Africa	Lake Huron	59 600	23 012	North America	Arctic Ocean	9 485 000	3 662 000	5 450	17 880
Ob'-Irtysh	5 568	3 460	Asia	Baffin Island	507 451	195 927	North America	Lake Michigan	57 800	22 317	North America	South China Sea	2 590 000	1 000 000	5 514	18 090
Yenisey-Angara-Selenga	5 550	3 449	Asia	Sumatra	473 606	182 859	Asia	Lake Tanganyika	32 600	12 587	Africa	Caribbean Sea	2 512 000	970 000	7 680	25 197
Yellow	5 464	3 395	Asia	Honshū	227 414	87 805	Asia	Great Bear Lake	31 328	12 096	North America	Mediterranean Sea	2 510 000	969 000	5 121	16 801
Congo	4 667	2 900	Africa	Great Britain	218 476	84 354	Europe	Lake Baikal	30 500	11 776	Asia	Bering Sea	2 261 000	873 000	4 150	13 615
Río de la Plata-Paraná	4 500	2 796	South America	Victoria Island	217 291	83 896	North America	Lake Nyasa	29 500	11 390	Africa	Bay of Bengal	2 172 000	839 000	4 500	14 764
Irtysh	4 440	2 759	Asia	Ellesmere Island	196 236	75 767	North America	Great Slave Lake	28 568	11 030	North America	Gulf of Mexico	1 544 000	596 000	3 504	11 496

WORLD POLITICAL

The present picture of the political world is the result of a long history of exploration, colonialism, conflict and negotiation. In 1950 there were eighty-two independent countries. Since then there has been a significant trend away from colonial influences and, although many dependent territories still exist, there are now 196 independent countries. The newest country is South Sudan which gained independence from Sudan in July 2011. The shapes of countries reflect a combination of natural features, such as mountain ranges, and political agreements. There are still areas of the world where boundaries are disputed or only temporarily settled as ceasefire lines.

FACTS

• Since 1990 thirty-four new countries have been created. The break up of the Soviet Union (or the U.S.S.R. – Union of Soviet Socialist Republics) in 1991 created fifteen of these countries including Russia.

• The Maldives in the Indian Ocean consist of approximately 1200 low-lying islands, all under 2 m (6.5 ft) in elevation.

• The Commonwealth, first defined in 1926, has evolved from communities within the British Empire, to a free association of fifty-three member countries.

• Both China and Russia have borders with fourteen different countries.

THE UNITED NATIONS

The name "United Nations" was coined by United States President Franklin D. Roosevelt, and was first used in the "Declaration by United Nations" of 1 January 1942. The United Nations (UN) officially came into existence on 24 October 1945, when the United Nations Charter was ratified by China, France, the Soviet Union, the United Kingdom, the United States and a majority of other signatories. It was a successor to the League of Nations which had been unsuccessful in preventing the Second World War.

All *de facto* independent countries of the world, except Taiwan and Vatican City, are members – 193 in total. Kosovo is also not a member. The principal headquarters of the UN are in New York but other major agencies of the Organization are found in Geneva, The Hague, Vienna and other locations.

The United Nations building, New York, USA.

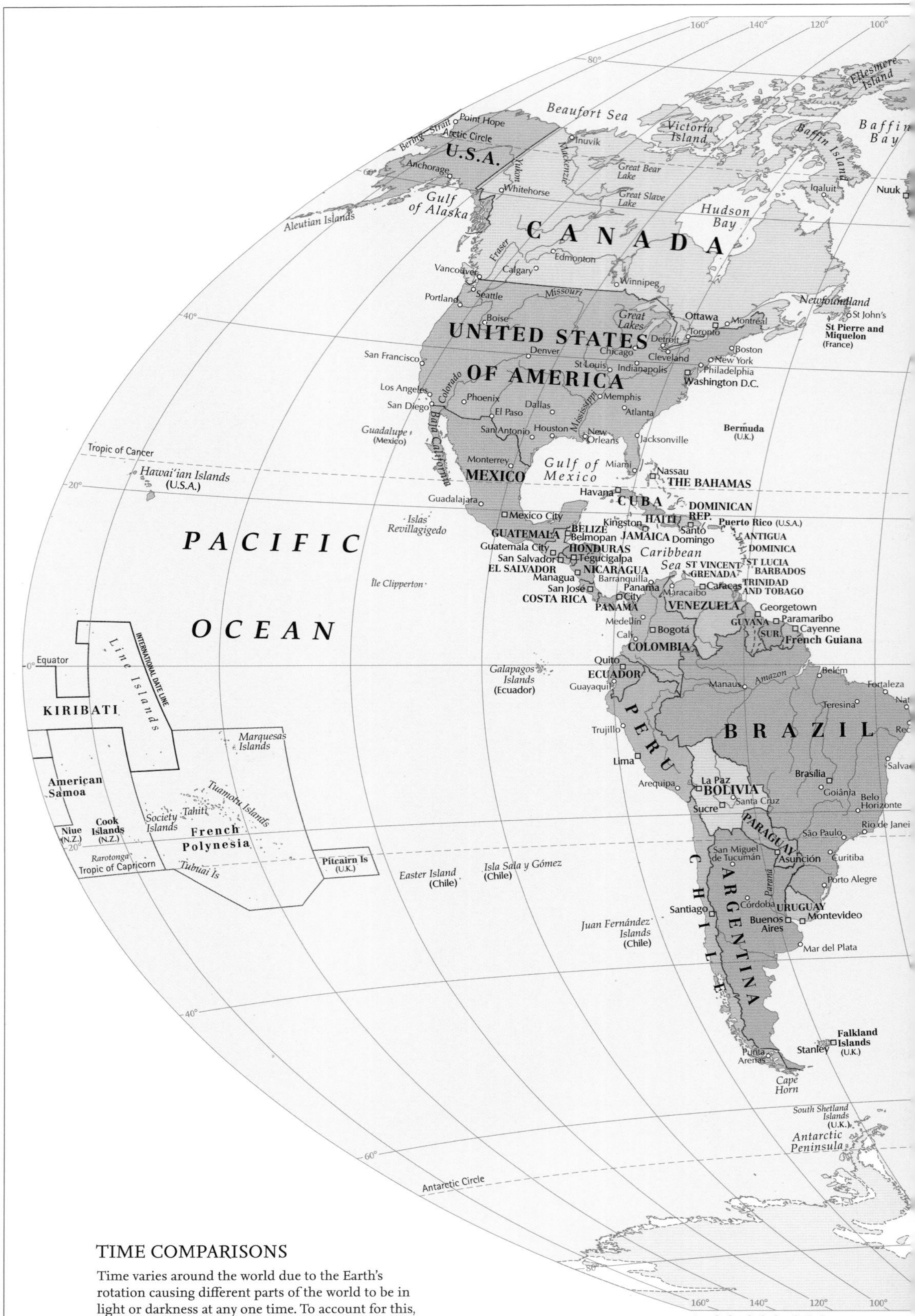

1 : 90 000 000

TIME COMPARISONS

Time varies around the world due to the Earth's rotation causing different parts of the world to be in light or darkness at any one time. To account for this, the world is divided into twenty-four Standard Time Zones based on 15° intervals of longitude.
The table below gives examples of times observed at different parts of the world when it is 12 noon in the zone at the Greenwich Meridian (0° longitude).
Daylight Saving Time, normally one hour ahead of local Standard Time, observed by certain countries for parts of the year, is not considered.

01:00	02:00	03:00	04:00	05:00	06:00	07:00	08:00	09:00
American Samoa	Cook Islands	Anchorage	Vancouver	Edmonton	Winnipeg	Ottawa	Puerto Rico	Nuuk
	Hawai'ian Islands		Seattle	Denver	Chicago	Toronto	Manaus	Recife
	Society Islands		San Francisco		Dallas	New York	La Paz	Brasília
	Tahiti		Los Angeles		Houston	Philadelphia	Sucre	Rio de Janeiro
			Pitcairn Islands		Monterrey	Washington D.C.	Asunción	São Paulo
					Mexico City	Havana		Montevideo
					San Salvador	Bogotá		Buenos Aires
					San José	Quito		
					Easter Island	Lima		

Winkel Tripel Projection

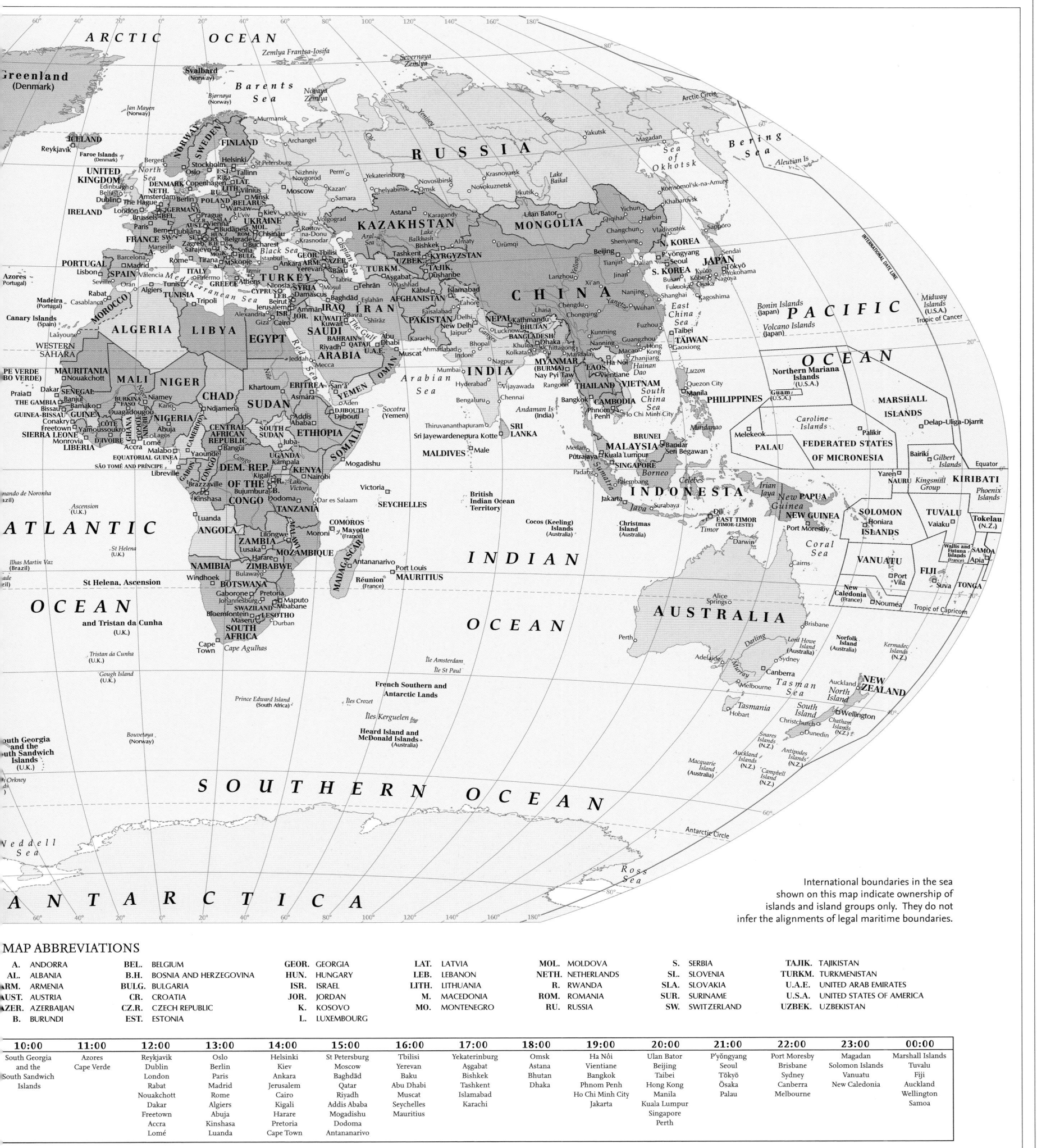

International boundaries in the sea shown on this map indicate ownership of islands and island groups only. They do not infer the alignments of legal maritime boundaries.

MAP ABBREVIATIONS

A.	ANDORRA	BEL.	BELGIUM	GEOR.	GEORGIA	LAT.	LATVIA	MOL.	MOLDOVA
AL.	ALBANIA	B.H.	BOSNIA AND HERZEGOVINA	HUN.	HUNGARY	LEB.	LEBANON	NETH.	NETHERLANDS
ARM.	ARMENIA	BULG.	BULGARIA	ISR.	ISRAEL	LITH.	LITHUANIA	R.	RWANDA
AUST.	AUSTRIA	CR.	CROATIA	JOR.	JORDAN	M.	MACEDONIA	ROM.	ROMANIA
AZER.	AZERBAIJAN	CZ.R.	CZECH REPUBLIC	K.	KOSOVO	MO.	MONTENEGRO	RU.	RUSSIA
B.	BURUNDI	EST.	ESTONIA	L.	LUXEMBOURG				

S.	SERBIA	TAJIK.	TAJIKISTAN	
SL.	SLOVENIA	TURKM.	TURKMENISTAN	
SLA.	SLOVAKIA	U.A.E.	UNITED ARAB EMIRATES	
SUR.	SURINAME	U.S.A.	UNITED STATES OF AMERICA	
SW.	SWITZERLAND	UZBEK.	UZBEKISTAN	

10:00	11:00	12:00	13:00	14:00	15:00	16:00	17:00	18:00	19:00	20:00	21:00	22:00	23:00	00:00
South Georgia and the South Sandwich Islands	Azores Cape Verde	Reykjavik Dublin London Nouakchott Dakar Freetown Accra Lomé	Oslo Berlin Paris Madrid Rome Algiers Abuja Kinshasa Luanda	Helsinki Kiev Ankara Jerusalem Cairo Kigali Harare Pretoria Cape Town	St Petersburg Moscow Baghdad Qatar Riyadh Addis Ababa Mogadishu Dodoma Antananarivo	Tbilisi Yerevan Baku Abu Dhabi Muscat Seychelles Mauritius	Yekaterinburg Aşgabat Bishkek Tashkent Islamabad Karachi	Omsk Astana Bhutan Dhaka	Ha Nôi Vientiane Bangkok Phnom Penh Ho Chi Minh City Jakarta	Ulan Bator Beijing Taibei Hong Kong Manila Kuala Lumpur Singapore Perth	P'yŏngyang Seoul Tōkyō Ōsaka Palau	Port Moresby Brisbane Sydney Canberra Melbourne	Magadan Solomon Islands Vanuatu New Caledonia	Marshall Islands Tuvalu Fiji Auckland Wellington Samoa

OCEANIA PHYSICAL

The map highlights the three major island groupings traditionally used to categorise the enormously extensive Pacific island chains and their people: Micronesia ('small islands'), in the northwest, covering chiefly the North Mariana, Marshall and Caroline Islands; Melanesia ('black islands'), in the middle, mainly consisting of the Solomon Islands and Papua New Guinea; and Polynesia ('many islands'), encompassing all the rest across much of the Pacific. The Great Dividing Range, running down the eastern side of Australia, is prominent, as is the mountainous ridge forming the backbone of New Guinea. New Guinea in our definition is shared between Oceania and Asia.

FACTS

• Tasmania, and the Tasman Sea to the east of it, are named after Abel Tasman, a 17th century Dutch explorer. Tasmania was originally named Van Diemen's Land (by Tasman himself). The Cook Islands, in the middle of Polynesia, are named after the 18th century British sea captain, James Cook.

• It has been proved by genetic research that the Pacific islands were originally populated over hundreds of years by adventurous seafarers from the Asian side, although the Norwegian Thor Heyerdahl's 'Kon-Tiki' expedition of the 1950s had strongly suggested that the people came from the Americas.

• Pitcairn Island, in the far east of Polynesia, was uninhabited until it was occupied by mutineers from the 18th century British ship 'Bounty'. The present-day inhabitants are descended from them.

HIGHEST MOUNTAINS	m	ft
Puncak Jaya, Indonesia	4 884	16 023
Puncak Trikora, Indonesia	4 730	15 518
Puncak Mandala, Indonesia	4 700	15 420
Puncak Yamin, Indonesia	4 595	15 075
Mt Wilhelm, Papua New Guinea	4 509	14 793
Mt Kubor, Papua New Guinea	4 359	14 301

LARGEST ISLANDS	sq km	sq miles
New Guinea	808 510	312 167
South Island, New Zealand	151 215	58 384
North Island, New Zealand	115 777	44 701
Tasmania	67 800	26 178

LONGEST RIVERS	km	miles
Murray-Darling	3 672	2 282
Darling	2 844	1 767
Murray	2 375	1 476
Murrumbidgee	1 485	923
Lachlan	1 339	832
Cooper Creek	1 113	692

LARGEST LAKES	sq km	sq miles
Kati Thanda-Lake Eyre	0–8 900	0–3 436
Lake Torrens	0–5 780	0–2 232

Orthographic Projection

1 : 32 000 000

MILES 0   400   800   1200

E   F   G   H   I   J

Hokkaidō   Kuril Islands

Bonin Islands

Volcano Islands

North
Mariana
Islands   Pagan

Tinian   Saipan
Rota
Guam

M i c r o n e s i a

Farauleb   Pikelot
Hall Is
Chuuk
ne Islands

Eauripik

Mortlock
Islands   Pohnpei

Kosrae

Bikini

Ralik Chain
Ratak Chain

Kwajalein

Maloelap

Mili

Marshall
Islands

Gilbert
Islands   Tarawa

M e l a n e s i a

Nauru   Banaba

Aranuka
Nonouti
Tabiteuea   Beru Nikunau
Onotoa   Kingsmill Group
Tamana
Arorae

Nanumea
Nanumanga   Niutao
Nui Vaitupu

Nukufetau   Funafuti

Nukulaelae

Niulakita

PACIFIC

OCEAN

Wake Island

Kure
Atoll

Midway
Islands   Pearl and Hermes
Atoll
Lisianski   Laysan
Island   Island

Gardner
Pinnacles
Necker Island

H a w a i i a n   I s l a n d s

Kaua'i
O'ahu Maui

Hawai'i

Tropic of Cancer

Johnston Atoll

Kingman Reef

Palmyra Atoll

Teraina

Tabuaeran

L i n e   I s l a n d s

Kiritimati

1

2

3

Admiralty
Islands   New Hanover
New
Ireland

B i s m a r c k
S e a

Sepik

Mt Wilhelm
4509   New Britain

ea

Gulf
of Papua   Owen Stanley Range

Cape York   D'Entrecasteaux
Islands   Louisiade
Archipelago

Cape
York
Peninsula

Bougainville
Island

Choiseul
New Georgia
New Georgia
Islands   Santa Isabel

Solomon Islands

Guadalcanal

Makira
(San Cristobal)

Rennell

Nukumanu Islands

Ontong Java Atoll

S o l o m o n   S e a

Malaita

Duff Islands

Santa Cruz
Islands

Banks
Islands

Howland Island

Baker Island

Phoenix Islands
McKean
Nikumaroro   Kanton

Orona   Rawaki
Manra

Nukunono
Atafu
Fakaofo

Swains Island

Îles Wallis   Savai'i   Upolu
Niuafo'ou   Samoa
Tafahi

Jarvis Island

Malden Island
Starbuck Island

Vostok Island

Flint Island

Rakahanga
Pukapuka   Manihiki
Nassau

Caroline Island
(Millennium Island)

4

Coral
Sea

Gregory Range

Great Dividing Range

Great Barrier Reef

Espiritu Santo   Maéwo

Malakula   Ambrym
Epi
Erromango   Éfaté
Tanna

Anatom

Îles Chesterfield

Cato Island
and Bank

Nouvelle-
Calédonie

Îles Loyauté

Rotuma

Yasawa
Group   Vanua Levu
Viti Levu   Koro
Fiji
Kadavu   Totoya
Ono-i-Lau
Hunter I.   Ceva-i-Ra

Îles de Hoorn

Niuafo'ou
Niuatoputapu   Tutuila Manu'a Is

Vava'u
Group

Tofua

Tongatapu

Penrhyn

Suvarrow

Manihiki
Mauke

Society Islands
Tahiti

5

Darling
Downs

Grey Range   Barrier Range

Sturt Stony Desert

Darling

Lachlan

Murray

Mt Kosciuszko
2229

Botany
Bay

Cape Howe

Sandy Cape

Île des Pins

Norfolk
Island

Lord Howe
Island

Ata
Group

Niue

Raoul Island

Kermadec Islands

Palmerston
Aitutaki   Cook
Islands
Rarotonga   Mangaia   Mauke
Maria

Îles du Duc de Gloucester

Hereheretue

Rurutu   Anaa

Mangareva   Makatea

T u b u a i   I s l a n d s   Tubuai

Marquesas Islands
Nuku Hiva   Hiva Oa

Îles du
Roi-Georges
Rangiroa   Ra'iatea
Fakarava   Rangiroa
Rarotonga   Puka Puka

T u a m o t u   I s l a n d s

Hao

Îles
Gambier

Rapa   Marotiri

Acteon

6

Cape Otway   Bass Strait
King Island

Tasmania

South East
Cape

Flinders Island

T A S M A N

S E A

Cape Maria   North
van Diemen   Cape

North Island
(Te Ika-a-Māui)

Great Barrier
Island

East Cape

Cook Strait

Aoraki/
Mount Cook   Southern Alps
3724

South Island
(Te Waipounamu)   Cape
Providence

Stewart Island

Snares Islands

Chatham Islands

Pitt Island

Bounty Islands

Antipodes Islands

Auckland Islands

Campbell Island

Macquarie Island

Henderson I.
Ducie I.

Pitcairn Island

Tropic of Capricorn

7

E   F   G   H   I   J

© Collins Bartholomew Ltd

0   400   800   1200   1600   2000 KILOMETRES

OCEANIA POLITICAL

Oceania is defined here as covering Australia, New Zealand and all the independent nations of the Pacific Ocean, along with various islands in the southwestern Pacific which remain as dependent territories. We also count the whole of Papua New Guinea as being within Oceania, following a common convention – although this does result in dividing the large island of New Guinea arbitrarily into two along the political boundary. Such definitions are not regarded by geographers as hard and fast, however. The political boundaries shown on this map are intended to clarify the physical coverage of island countries and dependencies rather than actually defining strict territorial limits, which are very much more complex and sometimes as yet unsettled.

FACTS

- The former UN Trust Territory of the Pacific Islands, administered by the USA, was divided during the 1980s to form the independent nations of Micronesia, the Marshall Islands, and Palau (see p.131) – plus Guam and the Northern Mariana Islands, which remain as US dependencies.

- Several small uninhabited islands and atolls scattered across the Pacific are also under US control: those shown on this map are Wake, Howland, Baker, Jarvis and Palmyra. Hawaii has been a state of the USA since the late 1950s.

- Kiribati (pronounced 'Kiribass') was formerly known as the Gilbert Islands. (The name Kiribati is a local phonetic variation on 'Gilbert'). Tuvalu used to be a UK dependency known as the Ellice Islands. Vanuatu was once a UK/French territory, the New Hebrides.

LARGEST COUNTRIES	Area sq km	sq miles
Australia	7 692 024	2 969 907
Papua New Guinea	462 840	178 704
New Zealand	270 534	104 454
Solomon Islands	28 370	10 954
Fiji	18 330	7 077
Vanuatu	12 190	4 707
Samoa	2 831	1 093
Tonga	748	289
Kiribati	717	277
Federated States of Micronesia	701	271

MOST POPULATED COUNTRIES	Population
Australia	23 343 000
Papua New Guinea	7 321 000
New Zealand	4 506 000
Fiji	881 000
Solomon Islands	561 000
Vanuatu	253 000
Samoa	190 000
Tonga	105 000
Federated States of Micronesia	104 000
Kiribati	102 000

CAPITALS		
Largest population	**Canberra**, Australia	358 000
Smallest population	**Vaiaku**, Tuvalu	516
Most northerly	**Delap-Uliga-Djarrit**, Marshall Islands	7° 07' N
Most southerly	**Wellington**, New Zealand	41° 18' S
Highest	**Canberra**, Australia	581 m/1906 ft

Orthographic Projection

1 : 32 000 000

MILES 0   400   800   1200

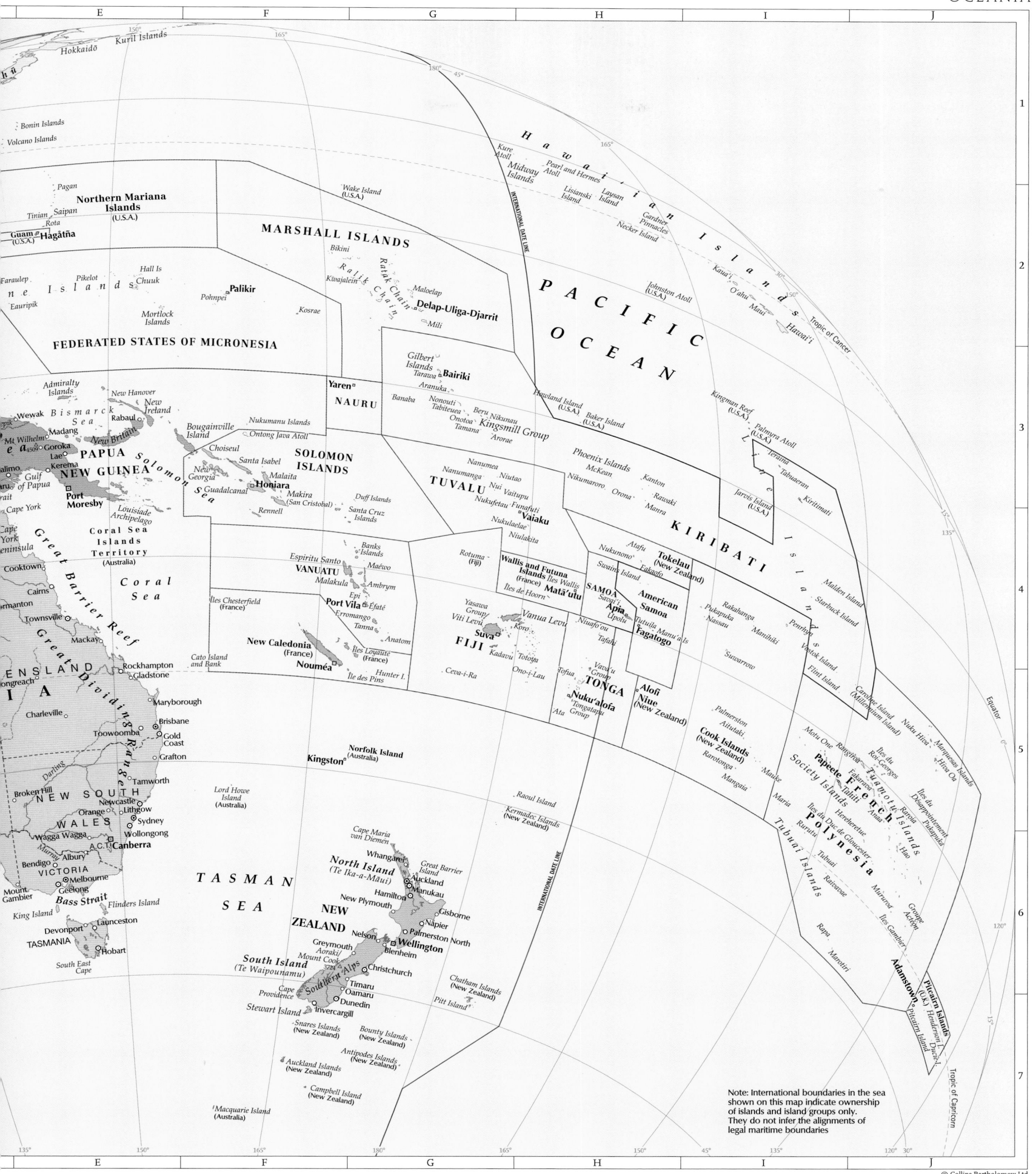

Note: International boundaries in the sea
shown on this map indicate ownership
of islands and island groups only.
They do not infer the alignments of
legal maritime boundaries

0   400   800   1200   1600   2000 KILOMETRES

© Collins Bartholomew Ltd

AUSTRALASIA AND SOUTHWEST PACIFIC

The western half of the map is dominated by the huge landmass of Australia, often regarded as a continent in its own right. To the north is part of Indonesia and the large island of New Guinea, divided politically between Indonesia and Papua New Guinea. The eastern half of the map, by contrast, is largely oceanic and covers the islands of Melanesia (which includes the Solomon Islands), much of Polynesia, and New Zealand in the south. Political boundaries shown in the Pacific are indicative of land ownership rather than being legal territorial limits.

FACTS

• Canberra became Australia's capital as a compromise, after a long dispute between Sydney and Melbourne.

• The 1420 km long, Alice Springs to Darwin railway line, opened in January 2004 creating a 3000 km line from Adelaide in the south to Darwin on the north coast (a two day journey).

• Auckland, New Zealand, has the largest Polynesian population of any city in Oceania.

• Polynesia means many islands, and there are over 1000, which are mostly low lying reefs and atolls.

GLOSSARY

FRENCH

Île; Îles	island; islands
Récif, Récifs	reef, reefs

INDONESIAN

Kepulauan	islands
Laut	sea
Puncak	hill, mountain, summit
Selat	strait
Teluk	gulf, bay

Most early European voyages of discovery in the Pacific were searches for a habitable southern continent or for a useable northern strait between the Pacific and Atlantic oceans. Both proved imaginary. The expeditions instead confirmed the immensity of the Pacific and revealed the islands of New Zealand, a habitable eastern Australia, numerous island groups and a valuable whale fishery.

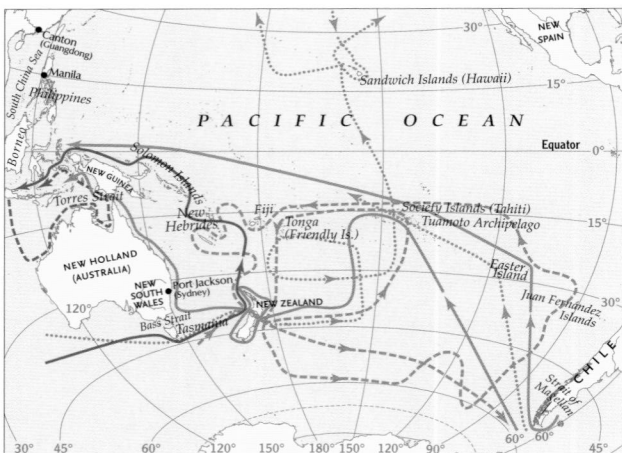

→ **Tasman** 1642–3 the first European expedition to reach Van Diemen's Land (now Tasmania), New Zealand and to see the islands of Fiji.

-→ **Tasman** 1644 Mapped a significant portion of the west of Australia

→ **Roggeveen** 1722 discovered Easter Island and some of the Samoan group; circumnavigated globe.

····· **Wallis** 1766–8 discovered Society Islands (Tahiti), encouraged hope of habitable southern continent; circumnavigated globe.

→ **Cook** 1768–71 charted coasts of New Zealand, explored east coast of Australia, confirmed existence of Torres Strait; circumnavigated globe.

-→ **Cook** 1772–5 made circuit of southern oceans in high latitude, charted New Hebrides, discovered many islands, ended hope of habitable southern continent; circumnavigated globe.

····· **Cook and Clerke** 1776–80 extensive exploration of the Pacific Ocean.

Lambert Azimuthal Equal Area Projection

1 : 20 000 000

MILES 0   200   400   600

© Collins Bartholomew Ltd

AUSTRALIA WEST

Western Australia is characterized by huge desert areas. The interior is sparsely populated – over 90 per cent of Australia's population lives in its coastal cities. Western Australia only contains around 10 per cent of the population of Australia. In the Northern Territory is Uluru (Ayers Rock), one of Australia's most recognisable icons and a UNESCO World Heritage site. The name Uluru comes from the local Pitjantjatjara people.

FACTS

- Western Australia is Australia's largest state in area, covering the western third of the mainland. It is, after the Sakha Republic in Russia, the second largest sub-national entity in the world.

- Large areas of the interior (or 'outback') are desert. Most of Australia's lakes are impermanent and salty, and their size and outline – or even their existence – may change from year to year owing to the varying aridity of the climate.

- The longest straight railway line in the world crosses the Nullarbor Plain (meaning 'treeless'), between South Australia and Western Australia.

GLOSSARY

INDONESIAN			
Gunung	mountain	**Selat**	strait
Kepulauan	islands	**Tanjung**	cape, point
Laut	sea		

The mineral industry in Western Australia exploits over fifty different minerals – more than any other State or Territory in Australia. There are over a thousand mines including those producing alumina, diamonds, iron ore and mineral sands. This area also produces around 70 per cent of Australia's gold and significant amounts of salt, nickel, tantalum and numerous other metals. Iron ore, petroleum and gold are the most important commodities by value. New projects include the Gorgon development off the northwest coast of Western Australia – Australia's largest minerals project and one of the world's largest natural gas projects. Centred on the development of several large gas fields off Barrow Island it incorporates subsea pipelines, gas treatment plants and shipping facilities.

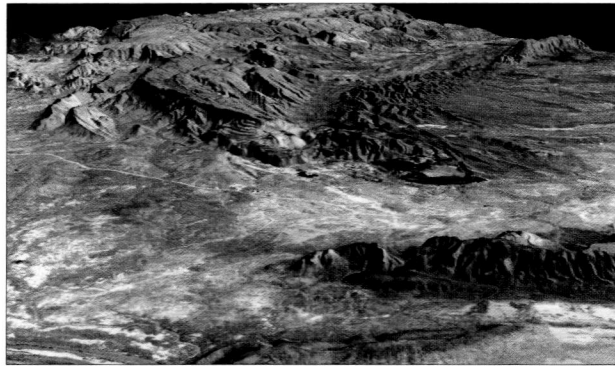

This satellite image is a 3-D perspective view of the Argyle opencast diamond mine in the Kimberley area of Western Australia. The mine is the largest diamond producer in the world by volume although it does not produce a large proportion of high quality stones. However it does produce over 90 per cent of the world's supply of rare pink diamonds.

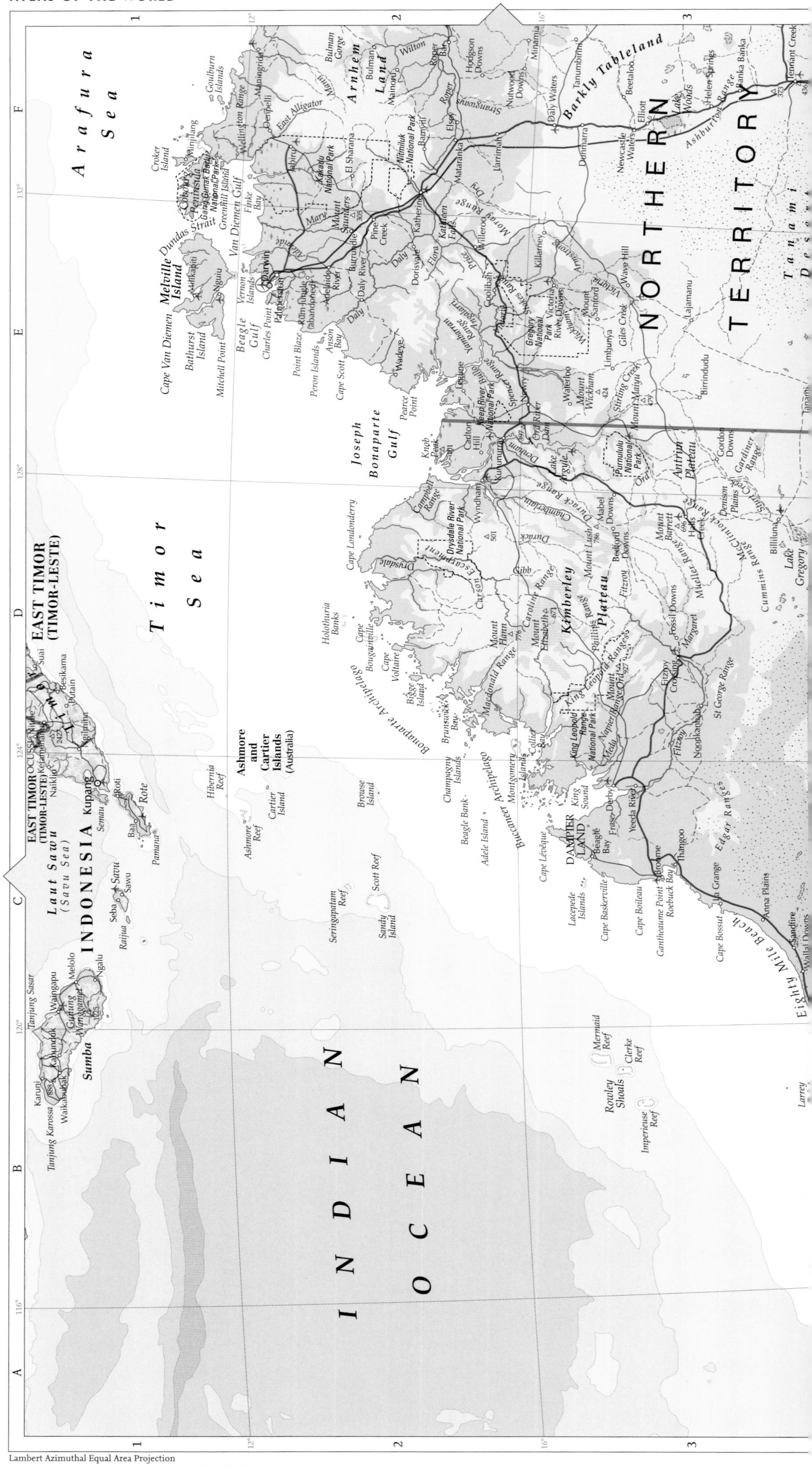

Lambert Azimuthal Equal Area Projection

1 : 8 000 000

MILES 0   100   200   300

123

© Collins Bartholomew Ltd

0   100   200   300   400   500 KILOMETRES

AUSTRALIA EAST

The eastern coast of Australia is the most populated part of the country. This coast is dominated by the Great Barrier Reef, which is the largest coral reef in the world, stretching for over 2000 km (1249 miles). The other major physical feature of this part of Australia is the Great Dividing Range which continues for more than 3500 km (2175 miles) from the northeastern tip of Queensland, down the length of the eastern coastline where it turns west, before finally fading in western Victoria. It consists of an area of mountain ranges, plateaus, upland areas and escarpments with a complex geological history.

FACTS

- Australia is divided administratively into various large States or Territories. Western Australia is the largest, with Queensland second, while the island of Tasmania ranks as a state in its own right. The Northern Territory (not a state) occupies most of the north-central area of the country. The small area round Canberra is designated as the Australian Capital Territory (A.C.T. on the map).

- Kati Thanda-Lake Eyre is the largest salt lake in Australia. Salt has been washed into the lake from underlying marine sediments, and in its usual dry state, the lake bed is a glistening sheet of white salt. Flooding of Kati Thanda-Lake Eyre is sporadic with a complete fill occurring only about every fifty years.

- Brisbane, the capital of Queensland, lies on the coast almost at the southern boundary of the state. A distance of well over 2000 km (1249 miles) separates it from Cape York, the northernmost point of the state and of Australia.

- The distribution of cane toads in Australia is expanding. In parts of Northern Territory this invasive species is spreading west at a rate of up to 50 km (30 miles) a year.

Much of Australia typically receives low rainfall leaving it open to regular periods of drought where water use is restricted. This has led to water and feed shortages for animals, dust storms and a huge reduction in some areas of agricultural production, such as cotton, which require a lot of water.

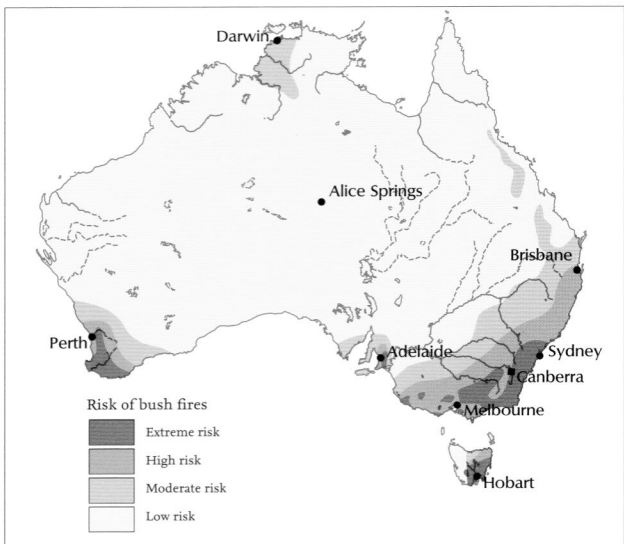

Risk of bush fires

- Extreme risk
- High risk
- Moderate risk
- Low risk

Southeast Australia is one of the most fire prone areas in the world. Bush fires are common and can be severe. About a quarter of bush fires are naturally occurring, usually started by lightning. Unfortunately the remaining three-quarters are the result of human activity. Until 2009 the worst bush fires in Australia were the Ash Wednesday fires of February 1983 when widespread drought, strong winds and low humidity triggered a series of fires across Victoria and southeast South Australia, many started by arsonists. In early 2009 intense heat wave conditions again followed weeks of drought and combined with high winds to create even more extreme bush fire conditions. On 7 February, known as Black Saturday, as many as 400 individual fires were recorded. Ignition has been attributed to a variety of causes including faulty power lines and other human activity. Entire towns were destroyed and altogether there were 173 fatalities in Victoria, the highest loss of life ever recorded from bush fires.

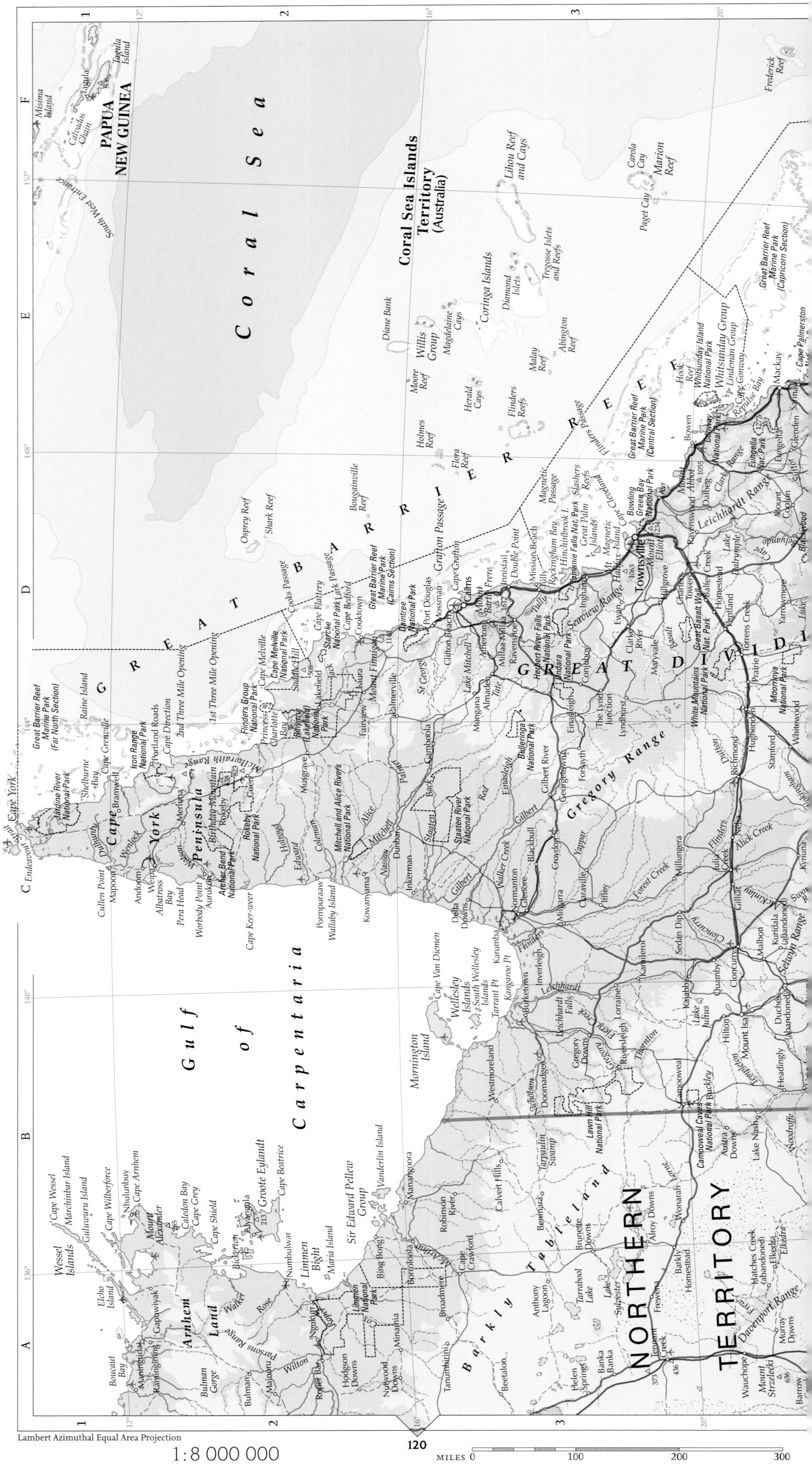

Lambert Azimuthal Equal Area Projection

1 : 8 000 000

MILES 0   100   200   300

© Collins Bartholomew Ltd

0   100   200   300   400   500 KILOMETRES

AUSTRALIA SOUTHEAST

This map homes in on the country's most densely populated states, on the south-eastern mainland – New South Wales (capital Sydney, the largest city in Australia and in Oceania in general), and the smaller Victoria (capital Melbourne). All along the eastern coast lies the Great Dividing Range, the highest and most extensive mountain range in Australia: the highest point is Mount Kosciuszko. In the northwest the most prominent map features are several major salt lakes, of which one is Kati Thanda-Lake Eyre, divided into two parts whose sizes vary throughout the year and according to rainfall.

FACTS

• The Australian Capital Territory, round Canberra, has an offshoot in the Jervis Bay Territory on the coast, although for some purposes Jervis Bay counts as a separate administrative Territory in its own right.

• Administrative boundaries on this map and on the map of Australia in general indicate the relative emptiness of the interior in human terms, with very few settlements, usually widely spaced. Where boundaries are more sinuous they are often following rivers, of which the Murray (with its tributary the Darling) is the most important in the country.

• In 1859, twenty-four rabbits were released for hunting near Geelong. Now an estimated 200–300 million plague Australia.

• In Tasmania around 45 per cent of all native forests are protected in World Heritage areas, National Parks and other reserves. Tasmania also has one of the world's oldest living organisms, a stand of Tasmanian Huon Pines, which appear to have been reproducing vegetatively for over 10 500 years.

Sydney is the largest city in Australia, and the state capital of New South Wales. It is the site of the first European colony in Australia, established in 1788 at Sydney Cove. The city is built around Port Jackson, which includes Sydney Harbour and it is well known because of the Sydney Opera House and the Sydney Harbour Bridge both of which can be seen here. Sydney is one of the most multicultural cities in the world as it is a major destination for immigration in Australia. It has also hosted several international sporting events, including the 1938 British Empire Games, the 2000 Summer Olympics and the 2003 Rugby World Cup.

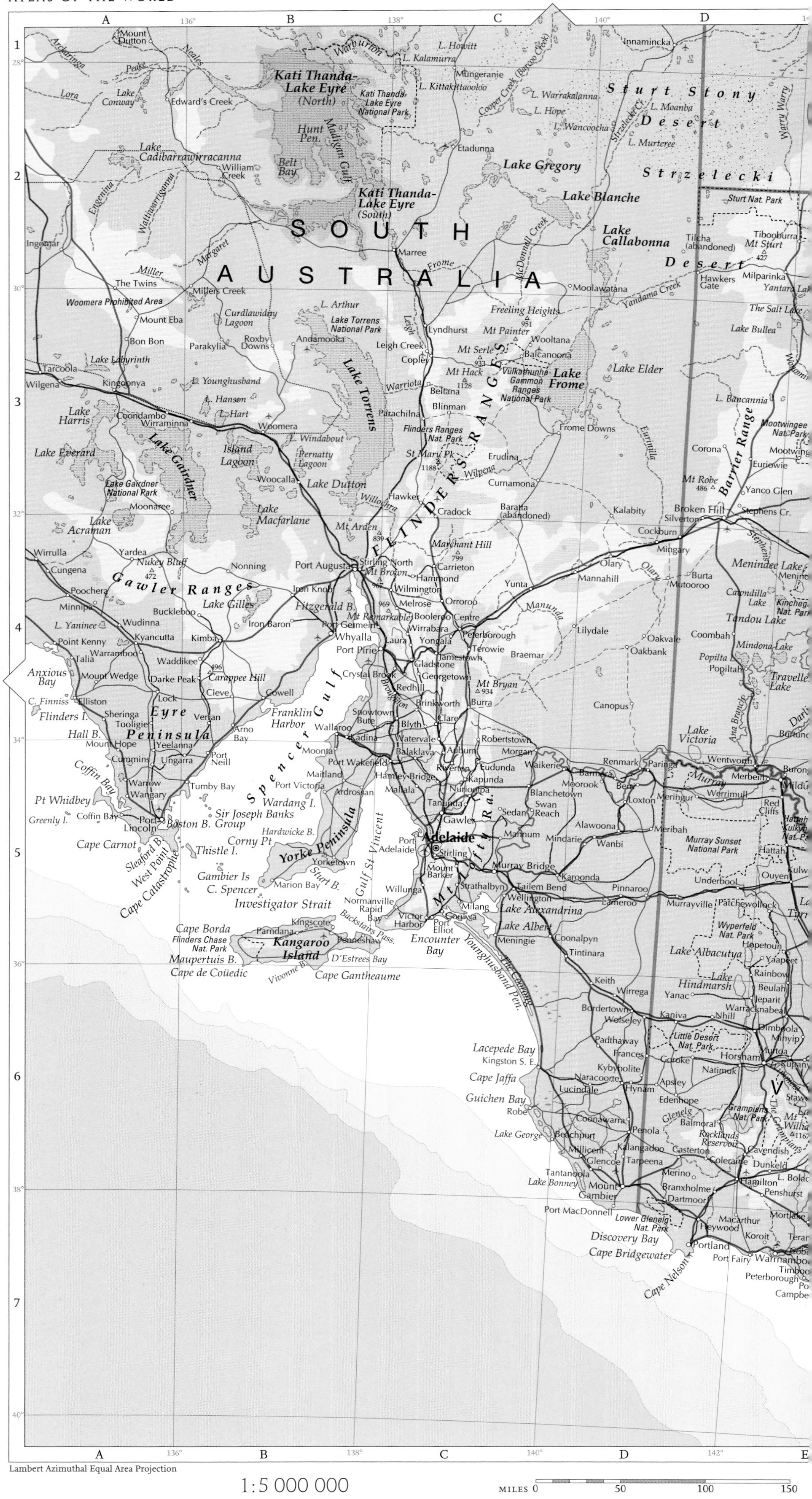

123

121

Lambert Azimuthal Equal Area Projection

1:5 000 000

MILES 0   50   100   150

NEW ZEALAND
ANTARCTICA

New Zealand is divided into two main islands, known simply as North Island and South Island. The capital, Wellington, is situated on the North Island facing the Cook Strait, which divides it from the South Island. Dominating the South Island are the Southern Alps, famous for its scenery including glaciers and some notable mountain peaks. There are volcanoes in the north. Antarctica is a continent occupying the area round the South Pole. It has always been uninhabited apart from temporary research station staff. The permanent Antarctic ice cap is over 4 km (2.5 miles) thick at its maximum.

ANTARCTICA

The Antarctic is a continental land mass covered in ice. Much of it is insulated from wider global changes by the circumpolar winds and ocean currents. However the Antarctic Peninsula is more exposed and its climate records for the past fifty years show a worrying 3C° (5.4F°) rise in average temperatures.

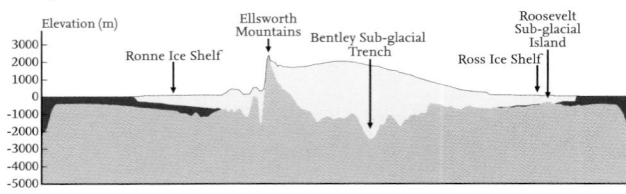

Cross-section of West Antarctica from the Ronne Ice Shelf to the Ross Ice Shelf. This profile is quite different to the Arctic Ocean (*see* p.240).

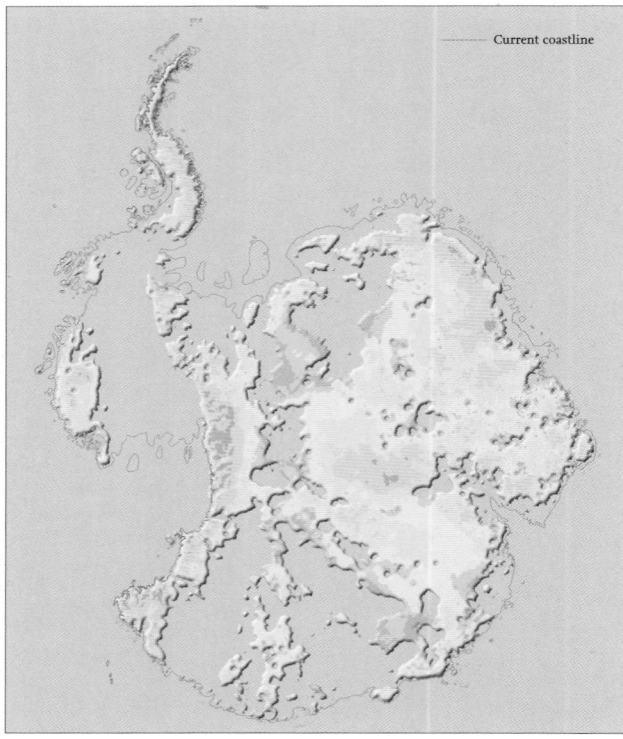

If Antarctica's ice were to melt completely, the shape of the continent would change dramatically, with its new coastline being defined by its bedrock. In reality, the land mass would rise as a result of being relieved of the weight of its ice, the effects of which are very difficult to predict.

FACTS

• Before its discovery by Europeans, New Zealand had long been populated by Maoris, of Polynesian origin. Aoraki ("cloud-piercer") is the Maori name for Mount Cook, the country's highest mountain.

• New Zealand's North Island is world-famous for its geysers and hot springs – most notably at Rotorua.

• New Zealand has benefited from a tourist boom resulting from J.R.R. Tolkien's 'Lord of the Rings' having been largely filmed there.

• All territorial claims to parts of Antarctica are suspended, under the Antarctic Treaty of 1959.

• Some areas of Antarctica are never snow-covered and consist of bare rock, (The 'Dry Valleys').

• In 2012 a borehole reached the surface of Lake Vostok, one of over 140 freshwater lakes that had been sealed under Antarctic ice for over fifteen million years.

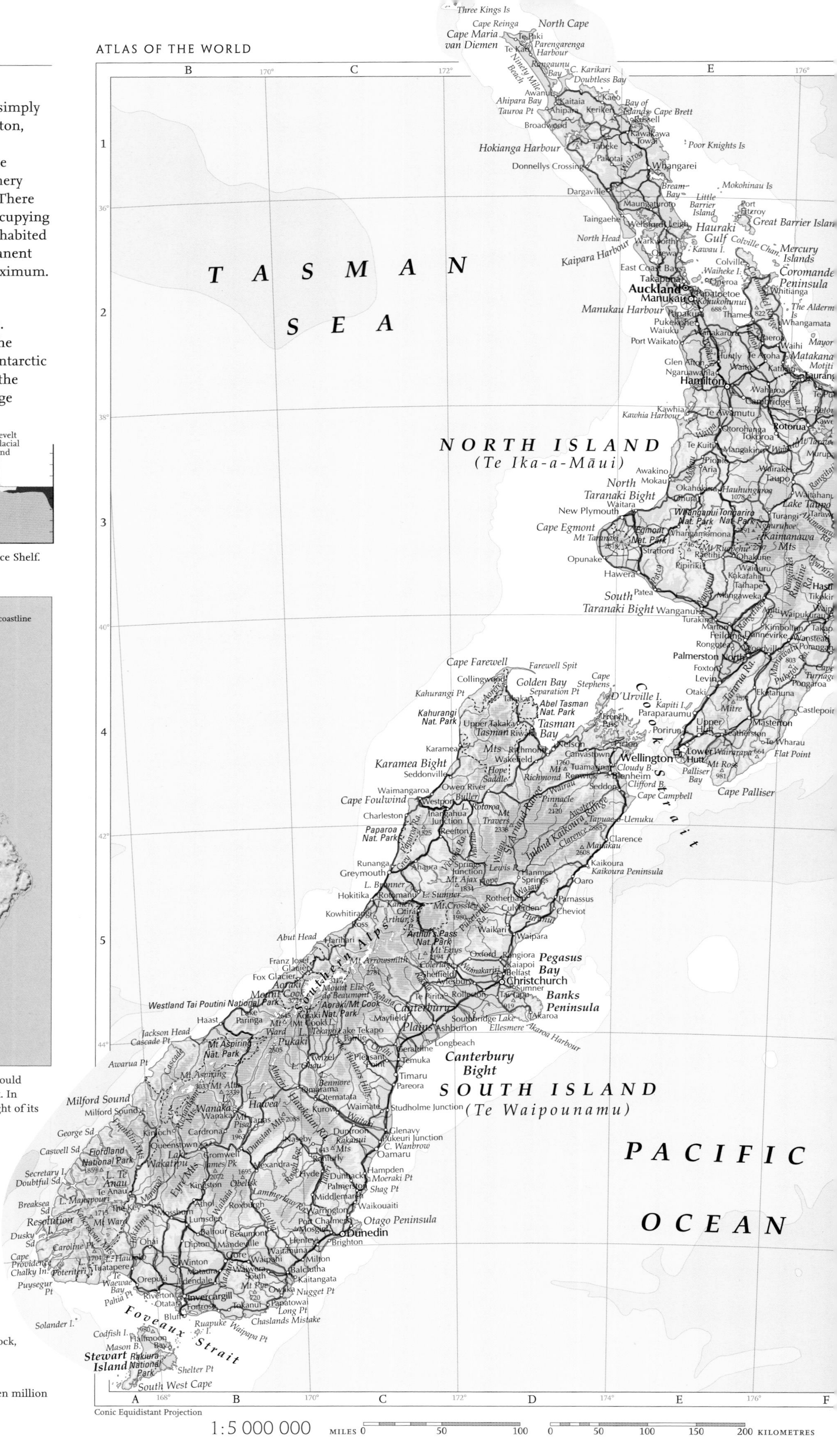

TASMAN SEA

NORTH ISLAND
(Te Ika-a-Māui)

SOUTH ISLAND
(Te Waipounamu)

PACIFIC OCEAN

Foveaux Strait

Conic Equidistant Projection

1 : 5 000 000

MILES 0   50   100   0   50   100   150   200 KILOMETRES

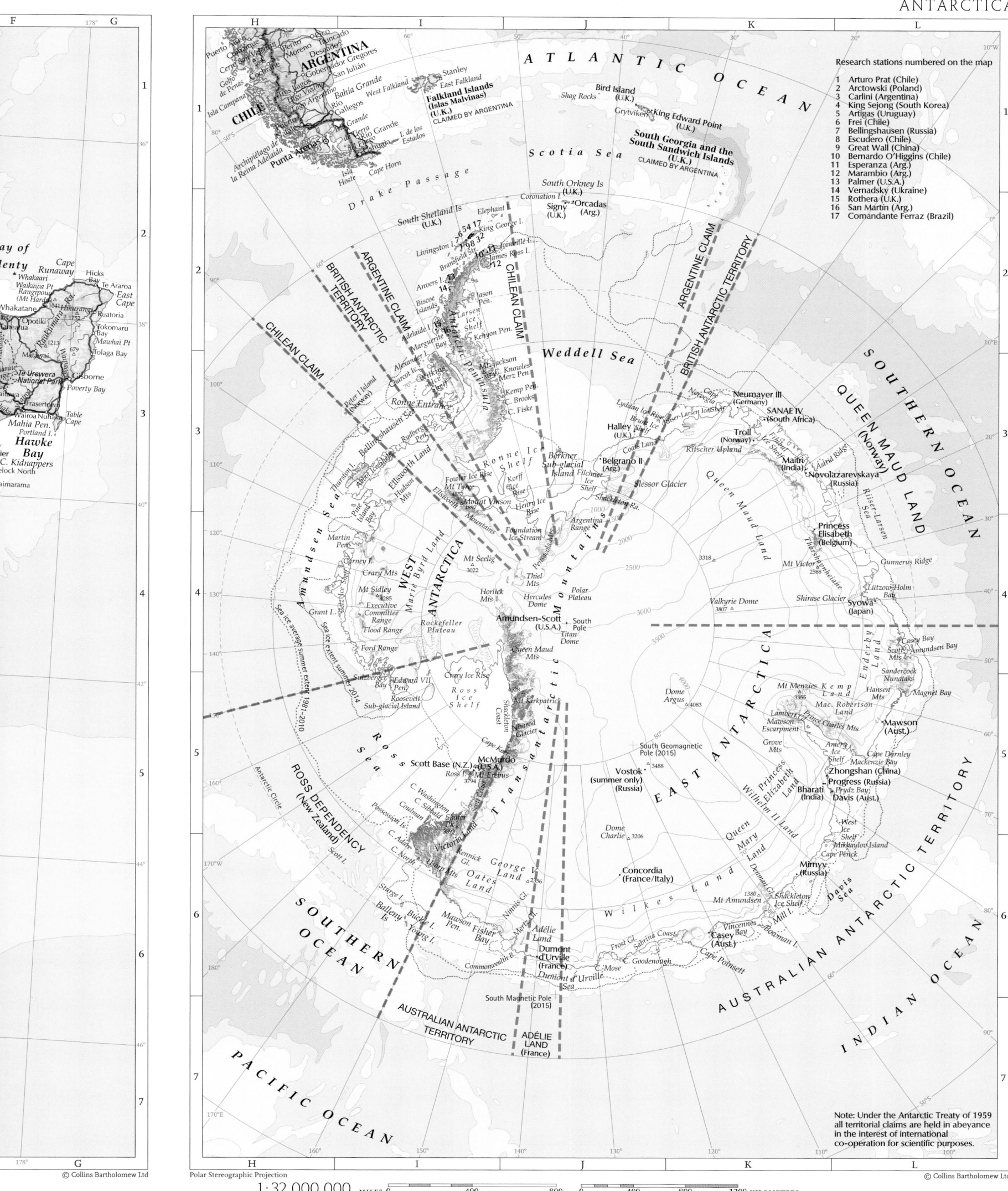

ATLANTIC OCEAN

Research stations numbered on the map

1 Arturo Prat (Chile)
2 Arctowski (Poland)
3 Carlini (Argentina)
4 King Sejong (South Korea)
5 Artigas (Uruguay)
6 Frei (Chile)
7 Bellingshausen (Russia)
8 Escudero (Chile)
9 Great Wall (China)
10 Bernardo O'Higgins (Chile)
11 Esperanza (Arg.)
12 Marambio (Arg.)
13 Palmer (U.S.A.)
14 Vernadsky (Ukraine)
15 Rothera (U.K.)
16 San Martin (Arg.)
17 Comandante Ferraz (Brazil)

Bay of Plenty

CHILE
ARGENTINA

Falkland Islands
(Islas Malvinas)
(U.K.)
CLAIMED BY ARGENTINA

South Georgia and the
South Sandwich Islands
(U.K.)
CLAIMED BY ARGENTINA

Scotia Sea

Drake Passage

Hawke Bay

Weddell Sea

SOUTHERN OCEAN
QUEEN MAUD LAND
(Norway)

BRITISH ANTARCTIC TERRITORY

ARGENTINE CLAIM

CHILEAN CLAIM

Antarctic Peninsula

Ronne Ice Shelf

Filchner Ice Shelf

WEST ANTARCTICA
Marie Byrd Land
Ellsworth Land

EAST ANTARCTICA

Amundsen-Scott (U.S.A.)
South Pole

Ross Ice Shelf

Transantarctic Mountains

ROSS DEPENDENCY
(New Zealand)

McMurdo (U.S.A.)
Scott Base (N.Z.)

Vostok (summer only) (Russia)

Concordia (France/Italy)

AUSTRALIAN ANTARCTIC TERRITORY

SOUTHERN OCEAN

PACIFIC OCEAN

INDIAN OCEAN

ADÉLIE LAND (France)
Dumont d'Urville (France)

AUSTRALIAN ANTARCTIC TERRITORY

Note: Under the Antarctic Treaty of 1959
all territorial claims are held in abeyance
in the interest of international
co-operation for scientific purposes.

© Collins Bartholomew Ltd

Polar Stereographic Projection

© Collins Bartholomew Ltd

1 : 32 000 000   MILES 0   400   800   0   400   800   1200 KILOMETRES

127

ASIA PHYSICAL

The map highlights the many major mountain ranges – in particular the Himalaya – and plateaus which make up much of Asia. These contrast with enormous low-lying plains, especially in the far north (Siberia) and on the Yellow Sea coast of China. The Ganges and Indus rivers on the Indian subcontinent also occupy extensive lowlands. Indonesia represents by far the most complex archipelago, although there are also many other large and important islands, most notably, Sri Lanka (formerly Ceylon), the Philippines, Taiwan, Japan, and the various island groups in the Arctic Ocean.

FACTS

- The outline of Asia is characterised by a number of major peninsulas, including Arabia, the Indian subcontinent, Indo-China and its offshoot the Malay Peninsula, Korea, and the highly volcanic Kamchatka Peninsula.

- Ninety of the world's 100 highest mountains are in Asia. Many lie in the Himalayan kingdom of Nepal where the height of the land ranges from 60 m to 8848 m (200 ft to 29 028 ft).

- The Indonesian archipelago is made up of over 13 000 islands.

- The deepest lake in the world is Lake Baikal in Russia which is over 1600 m (5250 ft) deep.

- The Gobi Desert, one of the world's biggest areas of desert and semi-desert, occupies a large zone of northern China and Mongolia.

HIGHEST MOUNTAINS	m	ft
Mt Everest (Sagarmatha/Qomolangma Feng), China/Nepal	8 848	29 028
K2 (Chogori Feng), China/Pakistan	8 611	28 251
Kangchenjunga, India/Nepal	8 586	28 169
Lhotse, China/Nepal	8 516	27 939
Makalu, China/Nepal	8 463	27 765
Cho Oyu, China/Nepal	8 201	26 906

LARGEST ISLANDS	sq km	sq miles
Borneo	745 561	287 861
Sumatra (Sumatera)	473 606	182 859
Honshū	227 414	87 805
Celebes (Sulawesi)	189 216	73 056
Java (Jawa)	132 188	51 038
Luzon	104 690	40 421

LONGEST RIVERS	km	miles
Yangtze (Chang Jiang)	6 380	3 965
Ob'-Irtysh	5 568	3 460
Yenisey-Angara-Selenga	5 550	3 449
Yellow (Huang He)	5 464	3 395
Irtysh	4 440	2 759
Mekong	4 425	2 750

LARGEST LAKES	sq km	sq miles
Caspian Sea	371 000	143 243
Lake Baikal (Ozero Baykal)	30 500	11 776
Lake Balkhash (Ozero Balkash)	17 400	6 718
Aral Sea (Aral'skoye More)	17 158	6 625
Ysyk-Köl	6 200	2 394

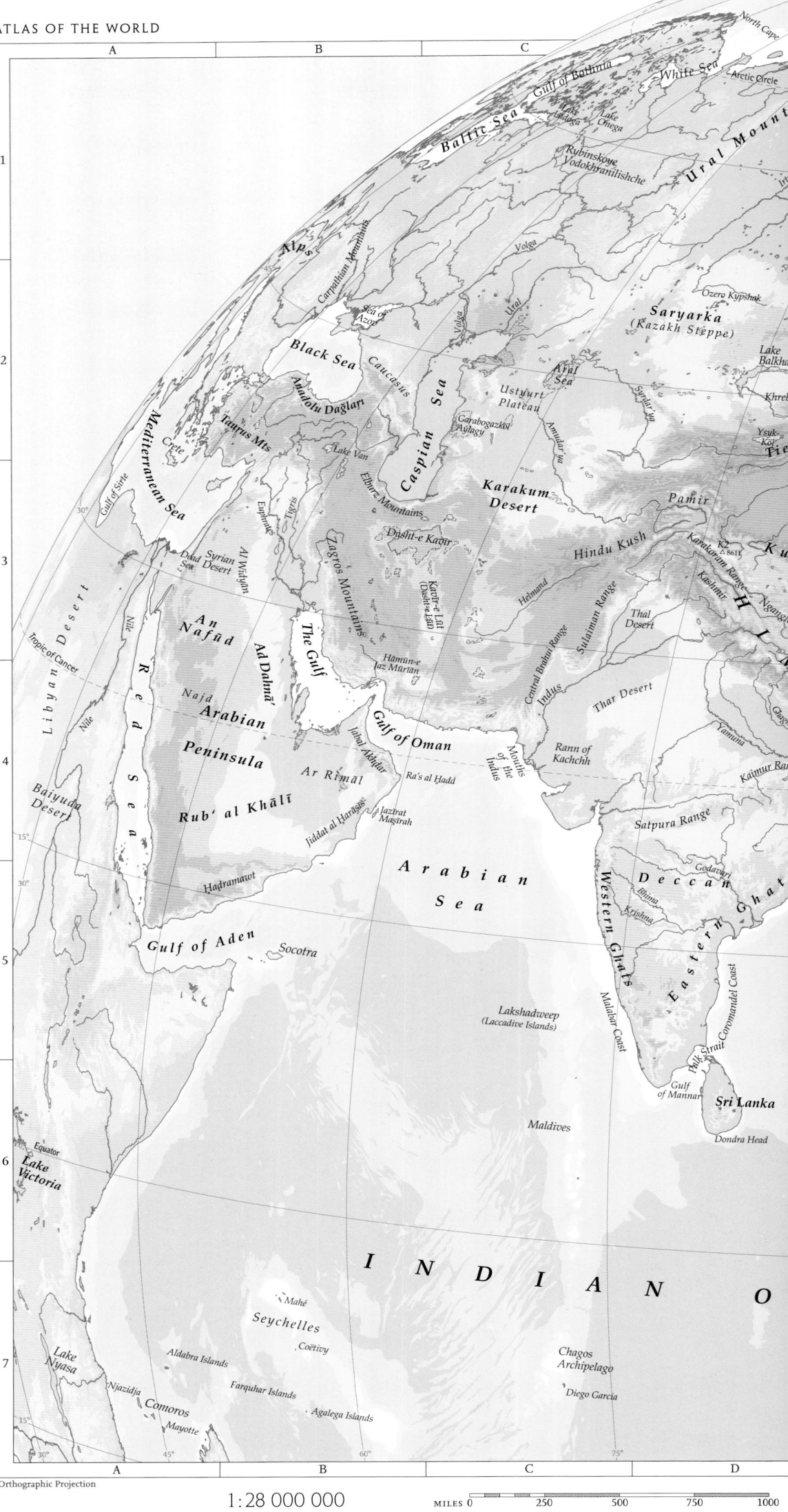

Orthographic Projection

1 : 28 000 000

MILES 0   250   500   750   1000

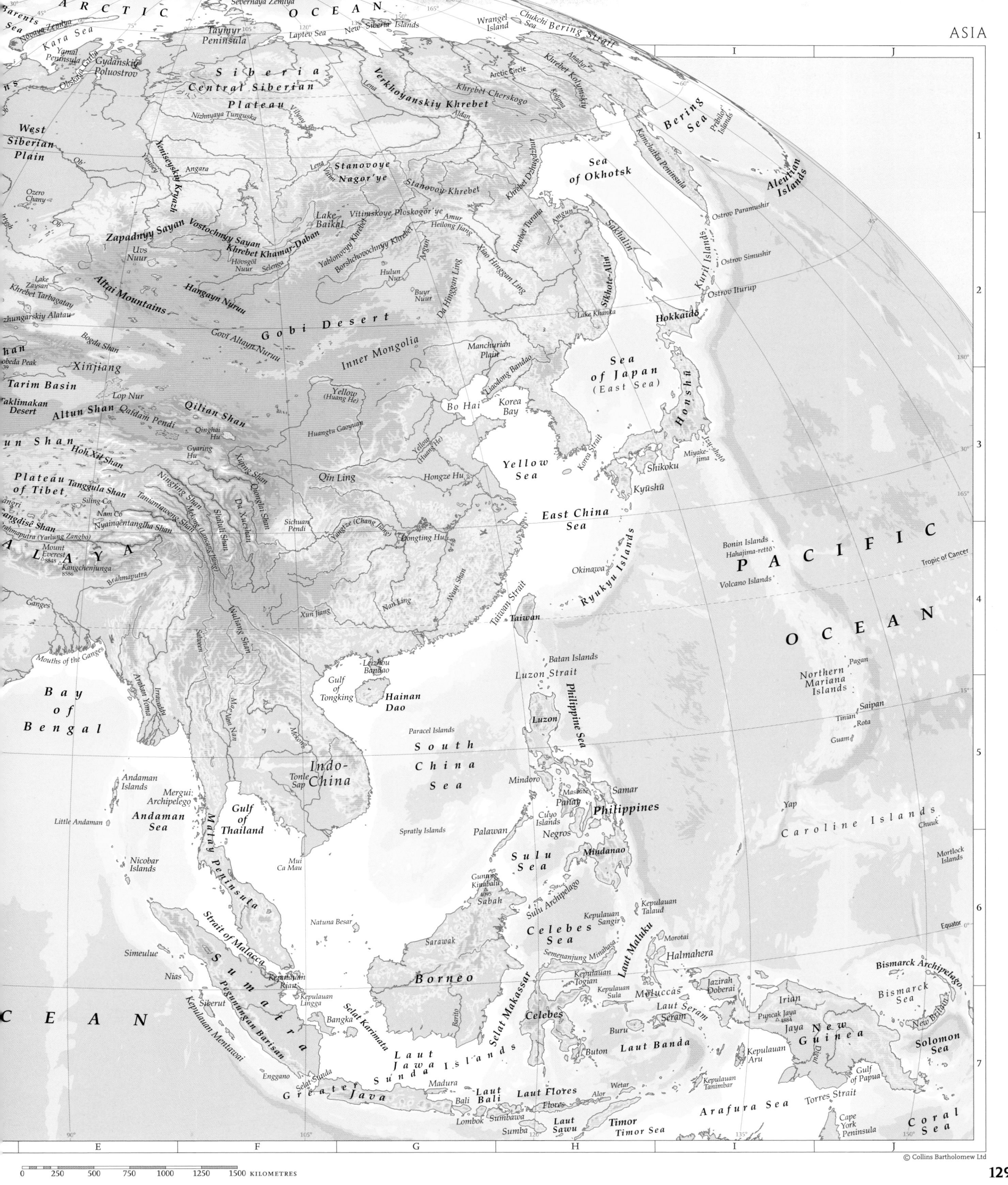

ARCTIC OCEAN

Barents Sea
Novaya Zemlya
Kara Sea
Yamal Peninsula
Gydanskiy Poluostrov
Obskaya Guba
Severnaya Zemlya
Taymyr Peninsula
Laptev Sea
New Siberian Islands
Wrangel Island
Chukchi Sea
Bering Strait
Anadyr'

West Siberian Plain

Siberia
Central Siberian Plateau
Nizhnyaya Tunguska
Lena
Vilyuy
Verkhoyanskiy Khrebet
Aldan
Khrebet Cherskogo
Kolyma
Khrebet Kolymskiy

Arctic Circle

Bering Sea
Kamchatka Peninsula
Pribilof Islands
Aleutian Islands

Ozero Chany
Ob'
Yeniseyskiy Kryazh
Angara
Yenisey

Stanovoye Nagor'ye
Lake Baikal
Vitimskoye Ploskogor'ye
Stanovoy Khrebet
Amur
Heilong Jiang
Khrebet Dzhugdzhur
Amgun'
Sea of Okhotsk

Ostrov Paramushir
Ostrov Simushir
Ostrov Iturup
Kuril Islands
Sakhalin

Zapadnyy Sayan
Vostochnyy Sayan
Khrebet Khamar-Daban
Hövsgöl Nuur
Selenga
Yablonovyy Khrebet
Borshchovochnyy Khrebet
Argun'
Da Hinggan Ling
Hulun Nur

Altai Mountains
Uvs Nuur
Hangayn Nuruu
Buyr Nuur
Xiao Hinggan Ling

Sikhote-Alin'
Hokkaidō

Lake Zaysan
Khrebet Tarbagatay
zhungarskiy Alatau
Bogda Shan
Govĭ Altayn Nuruu
Gobi Desert
Inner Mongolia
Manchurian Plain
Lake Khanka
Sea of Japan (East Sea)
Honshū

han
obeda Peak
Xinjiang
Yellow (Huang He)
Huangtu Gaoyuan
Liaodong Bandao
Bo Hai
Korea Bay

Tarim Basin
Taklimakan Desert
Lop Nur
Qilian Shan
Qinghai Hu
Yellow (Huang He)
Hongze Hu
Korea Strait
Shikoku

Altun Shan
Qaidam Pendi
Xining Shan

un Shan
Hoh Xil Shan
Tanggula Shan
Ningjing Shan
Da Xueshan
Sichuan Pendi
Dongting Hu
Yangtze (Chang Jiang)
Qin Ling
Hongze Hu
Yellow Sea
Okinawa
Kyūshū
Iwo-shima
Miyake-jima

Plateau of Tibet
Siling Co
Tongtian Heng
Nam Co
Nyainqêntanglha Shan
Tanlantaweng Shan
Shaluli Shan

ANALAYA
Mount Everest 8848
Kangchenjunga 8586
Brahmaputra (Yarlung Zangbo)

East China Sea

PACIFIC
Bonin Islands
Hahajima-rettō
Tropic of Cancer

Ganges
Brahmaputra
Wuliang Shan
Xun Jiang
Nan Ling
Wugi Shan
Taiwan Strait

Volcano Islands
Ryukyu Islands

Mouths of the Ganges
Arakan Yoma
Irrawaddy
Salween
Mekong
Mae Nam Nan
Taiwan

OCEAN

Bay of Bengal

Andaman Islands
Little Andaman
Mergui Archipelego

Tonle Sap
Indo-China

Leizhou Bandao
Gulf of Tongking
Hainan Dao

Paracel Islands

Batan Islands
Luzon Strait

Northern Mariana Islands
Pagan
Saipan
Tinian
Rota
Guam

South China Sea

Philippine Sea

Luzon

Andaman Sea
Nicobar Islands
Malay Peninsula
Gulf of Thailand
Mui Ca Mau
Mekong

Mindoro
Masbate
Samar
Panay
Cuyo Islands
Negros
Philippines

Yap

Caroline Islands
Chuuk

Mortlock Islands

Spratly Islands
Palawan

Sulu Sea
Mindanao

Simeulue
Nias
Strait of Malacca

Gunung Kinabalu 4095
Sabah
Sulu Archipelago
Kepulauan Talaud
Kepulauan Sangir

Natuna Besar

Kepulauan Riau
Sumatra
Pegunungan Barisan
Kepulauan Mentawai
Siberut
Kepulauan Lingga
Bangka
Selat Karimata
Sarawak
Borneo
Celebes Sea
Kepulauan Togian
Semenanjung Minahasa
Kepulauan Sula
Morotai
Halmahera
Jazirah Doberai
Irian
New Guinea

Bismarck Archipelago
Bismarck Sea
New Britain

Equator

OCEAN

Enggano
Greater
Java
Madura
Selat Sunda
Sunda Islands
Lesser Sunda Islands
Laut Jawa
Bali
Lombok
Sumbawa
Baritō
Selat Makassar
Celebes
Buru
Moluccas
Laut Seram
Seram
Laut Banda
Buton
Kepulauan Togian
Puncak Jaya 4884
Jaya
Kepulauan Aru
Gulf of Papua

Solomon Sea

Laut Bali
Laut Flores
Sumba
Wetar
Alor
Flores
Laut Sawu
Timor
Timor Sea

Arafura Sea
Torres Strait
Cape York Peninsula

Coral Sea

© Collins Bartholomew Ltd

0 250 500 750 1000 1250 1500 KILOMETRES

ASIA POLITICAL

With approximately sixty per cent of the world's population, Asia is home to numerous cultures, people groups and lifestyles. It also has a great variety of physical regions which can be defined by the cultural, economic and political systems they support. The major regions are: the arid, oil-rich, mainly Islamic southwest; southern Asia, isolated from the rest of Asia by major mountain ranges; the Indian- and Chinese-influenced monsoon region of southeast Asia; the mainly Chinese-influenced industrialized areas of eastern Asia; and Soviet Asia, made up of most of the former Soviet Union.

FACTS

- The line dividing Asia from Oceania is taken as the political boundary between Indonesia and Papua New Guinea. This results in the island of New Guinea being divided between the two continents.

- The break-up of the former Soviet Union in 1991 created two groups of countries in Asia: Kazakhstan, Uzbekistan, Turkmenistan, Tajikistan and Kyrgyzstan on the one hand and Georgia, Armenia and Azerbaijan on the other. This still left Russia as by far the largest country in the world.

- Cyprus, although part of the European Union and having long-standing cultural links with Europe, is classed as being within Asia.

- Both China and Russia have borders with fourteen different countries.

LARGEST COUNTRIES	Area sq km	sq miles
Russia	17 075 400	6 592 849
China	9 606 802	3 709 186
India	3 166 620	1 222 632
Kazakhstan	2 717 300	1 049 155
Saudi Arabia	2 200 000	849 425
Indonesia	1 919 445	741 102
Iran	1 648 000	636 296
Mongolia	1 565 000	604 250
Pakistan	881 888	340 497
Turkey	779 452	300 948

MOST POPULATED COUNTRIES	Population
China	1 369 993 000
India	1 252 140 000
Indonesia	249 866 000
Pakistan	182 143 000
Bangladesh	156 595 000
Russia	142 834 000
Japan	127 144 000
Philippines	98 394 000
Vietnam	91 680 000
Iran	77 447 000

CAPITALS		
Largest population	**Tōkyō,** Japan	37 049 000
Smallest population	**Melekeok,** Palau	391
Most northerly	**Astana,** Kazakhstan	51° 10' N
Most southerly	**Dili,** East Timor	8° 35' S
Highest	**Thimphu,** Bhutan	2 423 m/ 7 949 ft

Orthographic Projection

1 : 28 000 000

MILES 0   250   500   750   1000

ARCTIC OCEAN

Kara Sea

CENTRAL SIBERIAN PLATEAU

Verkhoyanskiy Khrebet

Bering Strait

Bering Sea

R U S S I A

Sea of Okhotsk

Kamchatka Peninsula

Aleutian Islands

MONGOLIA

GOBI DESERT

INNER MONGOLIA

Ulan Bator

NORTH KOREA

P'yŏngyang

Sea of Japan (East Sea)

Hokkaidō

Sapporo

XINJIANG

Tarim Basin

Qilian Shan

Qaidam Pendi

TIBET

C H I N A

Beijing

Seoul

SOUTH KOREA

Yellow Sea

Tōkyō

J A P A N

Honshū

Shikoku

Kyūshū

East China Sea

HIMALAYA

Mount Everest

Kathmandu

Thimphu

BHUTAN

BANGLADESH

Dhaka

MYANMAR (BURMA)

Nay Pyi Taw

Bay of Bengal

THAILAND

Bangkok

LAOS

Vientiane

VIETNAM

Ha Nôi

Hainan Dao

Taibei

TAIWAN

Ryukyu Islands

PACIFIC OCEAN

Tropic of Cancer

Bonin Islands (Japan)

Volcano Islands (Japan)

Northern Mariana Islands

Luzon

PHILIPPINES

Manila

Saipan

Guam

CAMBODIA

Phnom Penh

Ho Chi Minh City

SOUTH CHINA SEA

Andaman Sea

Andaman Islands (India)

Nicobar Islands (India)

Gulf of Thailand

Malay Peninsula

Mindoro

Palawan

Samar

Negros

Mindanao

PALAU

Melekeok

Caroline Islands

Yap

Mortlock Islands

Kuala Lumpur

Singapore

MALAYSIA

BRUNEI

Bandar Seri Begawan

SABAH

SARAWAK

Celebes Sea

Sulu Sea

Sulu Archipelago

Sumatra

Borneo

KALIMANTAN

Celebes

I N D O N E S I A

Moluccas

Halmahera

New Guinea

Bismarck Archipelago

Bismarck Sea

Jayapura

Jakarta

Java

Laut Jawa

Laut Flores

Laut Banda

East Timor (Timor-Leste)

Dili

Timor

Arafura Sea

Torres Strait

Cape York Peninsula

Coral Sea

Gulf of Papua

Equator

OCEAN

0   250   500   750   1000   1250   1500 KILOMETRES

© Collins Bartholomew Ltd

131

RUSSIA

Russia is split between Asia and Europe primarily along the
Ural Mountains. It is easily the largest country in the world –
almost twice the size of Canada, the second largest. It stretches
almost half way around the globe and has borders with
fourteen different countries – a record shared with China.
There is a marked contrast in the spread of the population
of Russia between the densely populated west and the more
sparsely populated north and east.

FACTS

- Some of Russia's Arctic islands are named after famous people including Zemlya
  Frantsa-Iosifa (after the emperor Franz Josef), Ostrov Greem-Bell (Graham Bell)
  and Ostrova De-Longa (de Long, a Frenchman).

- The emptiness of huge areas of Siberia is emphasised here by the lack of
  settlements, roads and railways. Two important rail routes join east with west:
  the Trans-Siberian and Baikal-Amur Railways.

- Svalbard, a Norwegian territory in the Arctic Ocean whose main island is
  Spitsbergen, has a high proportion of young and temporary residents, many of
  them employed in mining and tourism.

GLOSSARY

RUSSIAN			
Guba	bay, gulf	**Ozero**	lake
Khrebet	mountain range	**Ploskogor'ye**	plateau
Mys	cape, point	**Zaliv**	gulf, bay
Ostrov	island	**Zemlya**	land
Ostrova	islands		

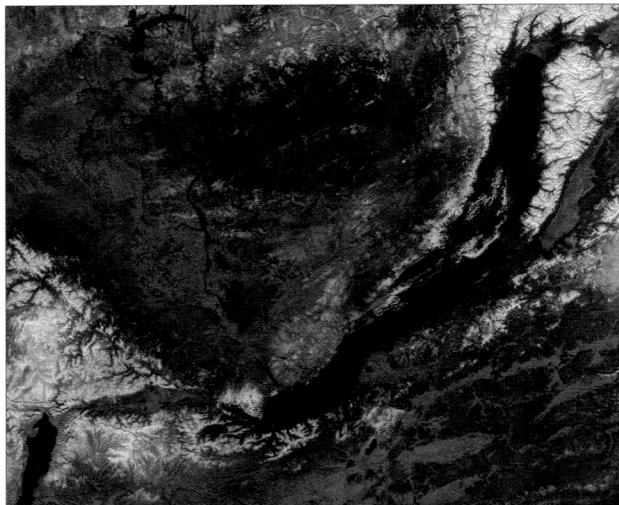

Lake Baikal, Asia's second largest lake after the Caspian Sea, is renowned as the
world's oldest and deepest freshwater lake. It reaches a depth of over 1.6 km
(1 mile). It is also the world's largest lake by volume, holding over 23 000 cu km
(5518 cu miles) of water – over 20 per cent of the world's unfrozen freshwater
reserves. Lake Baikal is designated as a UNESCO world heritage site because of
its rich wildlife, which includes the nerpa – the world's only freshwater seal.
The lake is under threat from pollution from the cities and factories within its
catchment area.

169

Conic Equidistant Projection

134

1 : 21 000 000

MILES 0   200   400   600   800

ARCTIC OCEAN

Ostrov Rudol'fa
Zemlya H. Vil'cheka
Ostrov Green-Bell
O. Schmidta
O. Komsomolets
O. Ushakova
Severnaya
O. Pioner
Zemlya
Ostrov Vize
O. Oktyabr'skoy Revolyutsii
O. Bol'shevik

Zemlya Frantsa-Iosifa

Kara Sea (Karskoye More)

Mys Zhelaniya

Belyy

Gydanskiy Poluostrov
Yamal Peninsula
Seyakha
Tazovskiy

New Siberia Islands (Novosibirskiye Ostrova)
Ostrov De-Longa
O. Bennetta
O. Zhokhova
O. Mal. Lyakhovskiy
Ostrov Kotel'nyy

East Siberian Sea (Vostochno-Sibirskoye More)

Wrangel I. (Ostrov Vrangelya)

Chukchi Sea

Bering Strait

U.S.A.

Prolio Longa

BERING SEA

Taymyr Peninsula
Gory Byrranga
Ozero Taymyr

Laptev Sea (More Laptevykh)

Khrebet Cherskogo

Koryakskoye Nagor'ye

Karaginskiy
Zaliv

Noril'sk
Plato Putorana

Kamchatka Peninsula

Sredinnyy Khrebet

Petropavlovsk-Kamchatskiy

R U S S I A

Central Siberian Plateau (Sredne-Sibirskoye Ploskogor'ye)

Yakutsk

Sea of Okhotsk (Okhotskoye More)

Sakhalin

West Siberian Plain (Zapadno-Sibirskaya Ravnina)

S I B E R I A (S I B I R ')

Stanovoy Khrebet

Kuril Islands (Kuril'skiye Ostrova)

ADMINISTERED BY RUSSIA, CLAIMED BY JAPAN

Tomsk
Krasnoyarsk
Kemerovo
Novosibirsk
Novokuznetsk
Barnaul

Lake Baikal

Hokkaidō
Sapporo

Irkutsk
Ulan-Ude

Khabarovsk
Komsomol'sk-na-Amure

Yuzhno-Sakhalinsk

Ürümqi

MONGOLIA
Ulan Bator (Ulaanbaatar)

GOBI DESERT

Vladivostok

Sea of Japan (East Sea)

JAPAN
Tōkyō
Yokohama
Nagoya
Ōsaka
Kyōto
Kōbe

Harbin
Changchun

NORTH KOREA
P'yŏngyang

SOUTH KOREA
Seoul (Sŏul)
Busan

Shenyang

INNER MONGOLIA

Hohhot
Beijing (Peking)
Baotou
Datong
Tianjin

C H I N A

Yellow Sea (Huang Hai)

Qingdao (Tsingtao)

Taiyuan

ASIA CENTRAL AND SOUTH

The map covers a vast zone from the edges of Europe and Africa to the Pacific Ocean. It includes the whole of the Middle East, with Iran and Afghanistan; the Indian subcontinent; all of mainland Southeast Asia; Mongolia and most of China; plus Kazakhstan and its central Asian neighbours. The physical colouring draws attention to the huge tract of mountainous territory which stretches from Turkey and the Caucasus to the Himalaya and western China. Major deserts occupy large parts of the Arabian Peninsula, Kazakhstan, western China and Mongolia.

FACTS

• Toxic waste still contaminates the site of the world's worst chemical factory accident at Bhopal near the centre of India. Thousands of people died and over half a million have suffered related health disorders after a leak of toxic gas from the Union Carbide plant in 1984.

• India is the world's second most populous country after China, although its population is growing at a faster rate than China's – it grows by over 16 million people each year.

• Mecca was the birthplace of the prophet Mohammed and is the holiest city of Islam. Over one million pilgrims visit the Great Mosque each year – a journey known as the Hajj.

Asia is a focus for the increasingly sensitive, and potentially explosive, issue of decreasing water resources. Countries in central and southern Asia have some of the lowest rates in the world for available freshwater per capita. The region also has some of the highest rates in the world for irrigated land as a percentage of agricultural land. As demand for water steadily increases, the potential for international disputes over its use also rises. Irrigation and the extraction of water for industry put great strain on an already limited resource.

AGRICULTURAL IRRIGATED LAND (% OF TOTAL AGRICULTURAL LAND) latest figures 2009-2012					
1	Pakistan	70.2	9	United Arab Emirates	19.1
2	India	35.2	10	Albania	17.0
3	Japan	34.7	11	Greece	16.9
4	Malta	34.0	12	Italy	16.9
5	Israel	31.8	13	Tajikistan	14.8
6	Azerbaijan	29.5	14	Turkey	13.6
7	Cyprus	21.9	15	St. Kitts & Nevis	13.3
8	Mauritius	21.8	16	Portugal	12.7

The Tigris and Euphrates rivers have been dammed in many places, affecting the volume and flow of water in several countries. Attempts have been made to formulate treaties between the countries affected, but the issue remains a source of tension.

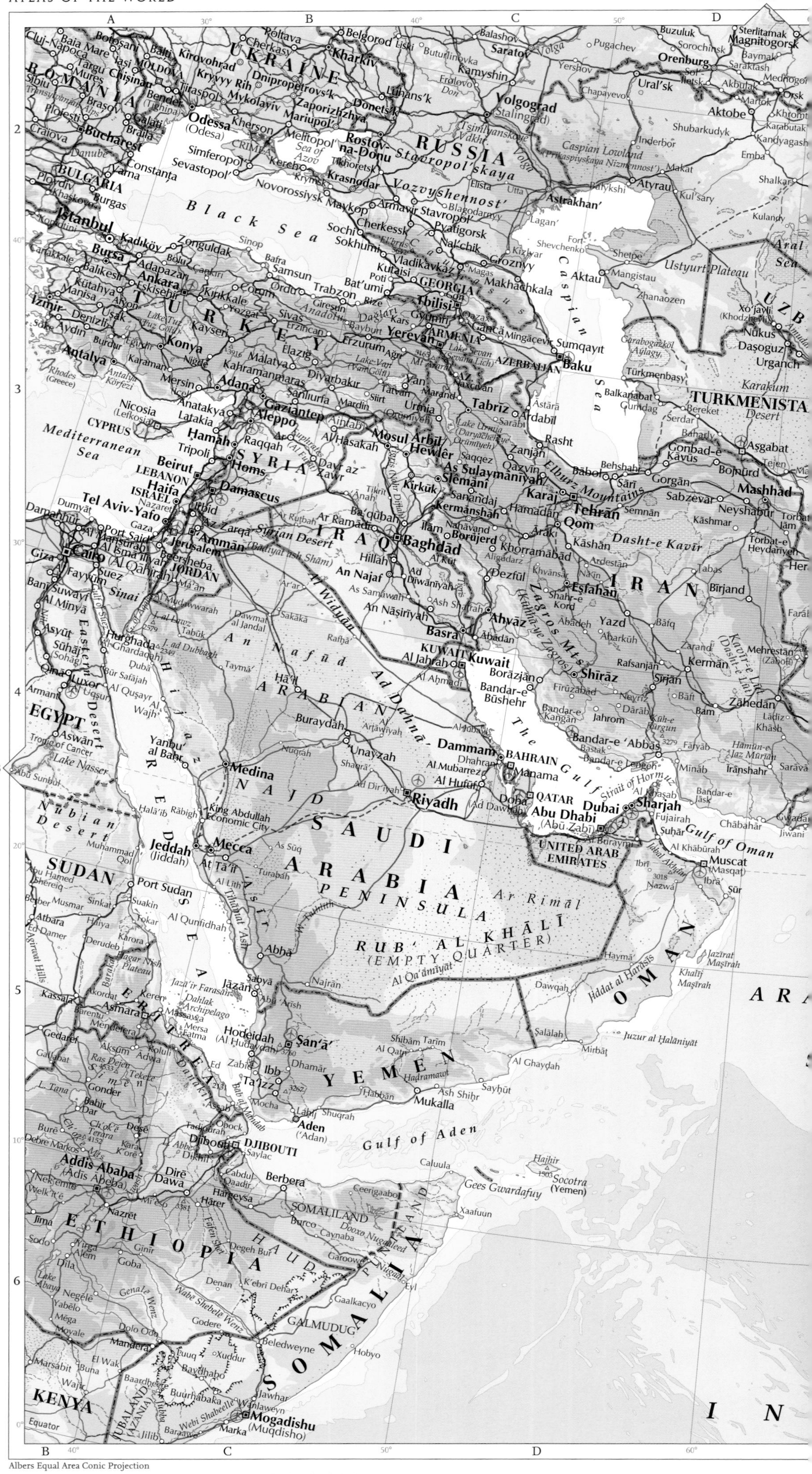

Tigris-Euphrates catchment area
Ataturk ▲ Dam
1 Barrage

Albers Equal Area Conic Projection

1 : 20 000 000   MILES 0   200   400   600   800

EASTERN MEDITERRANEAN, THE CAUCASUS AND IRAQ

The map includes the area of the eastern shore of the Mediterranean Sea traditionally known as the Levant. This area contains the West Bank (between Israel and Jordan) and Gaza (between Israel and Egypt), the two zones which are the scene of the long-running conflict between Israel and the Palestinians. The map covers several other geopolitical 'hot spots' including the Caucasus region between the Black and Caspian Seas (which contains the Russian republic of Chechnia), Iraq and Cyprus.

FACTS

- The level of the Caspian Sea can fluctuate by several metres. As a result, the large Kara Bogaz Gol inlet can be left almost dry.

- The Israeli government has encouraged immigration of Jews to Israel, and the building of new Jewish settlements in the occupied territories.

- The level of the Dead Sea, between Israel, the West Bank and Jordan, has dropped by over 16 m in the last thirty years through extraction of water for agriculture and industry.

GLOSSARY

ARABIC	
Buḥayrat	lake
Hawr	lake

FARSI (Iran)	
Daryācheh	lake
Dasht	desert

TURKISH	
Dağ; Dağı	mountain
Dağları	mountain range
Körfezi	gulf, bay

The continents of Asia and Europe are physically separated by the narrow strait of water known as the Bosporus. The strait also divides Turkey, and its largest city and former capital of Istanbul, between the two continents. The strait itself is less than 1 km (0.6 miles) wide, is 31 km (19 miles) long and connects the Sea of Marmara in the south to the Black Sea in the north. It has long been a crucial route for commercial transport between Asia and Europe. A second narrow strait – the Dardanelles – lies to the west, linking the Sea of Marmara to the Mediterranean Sea.

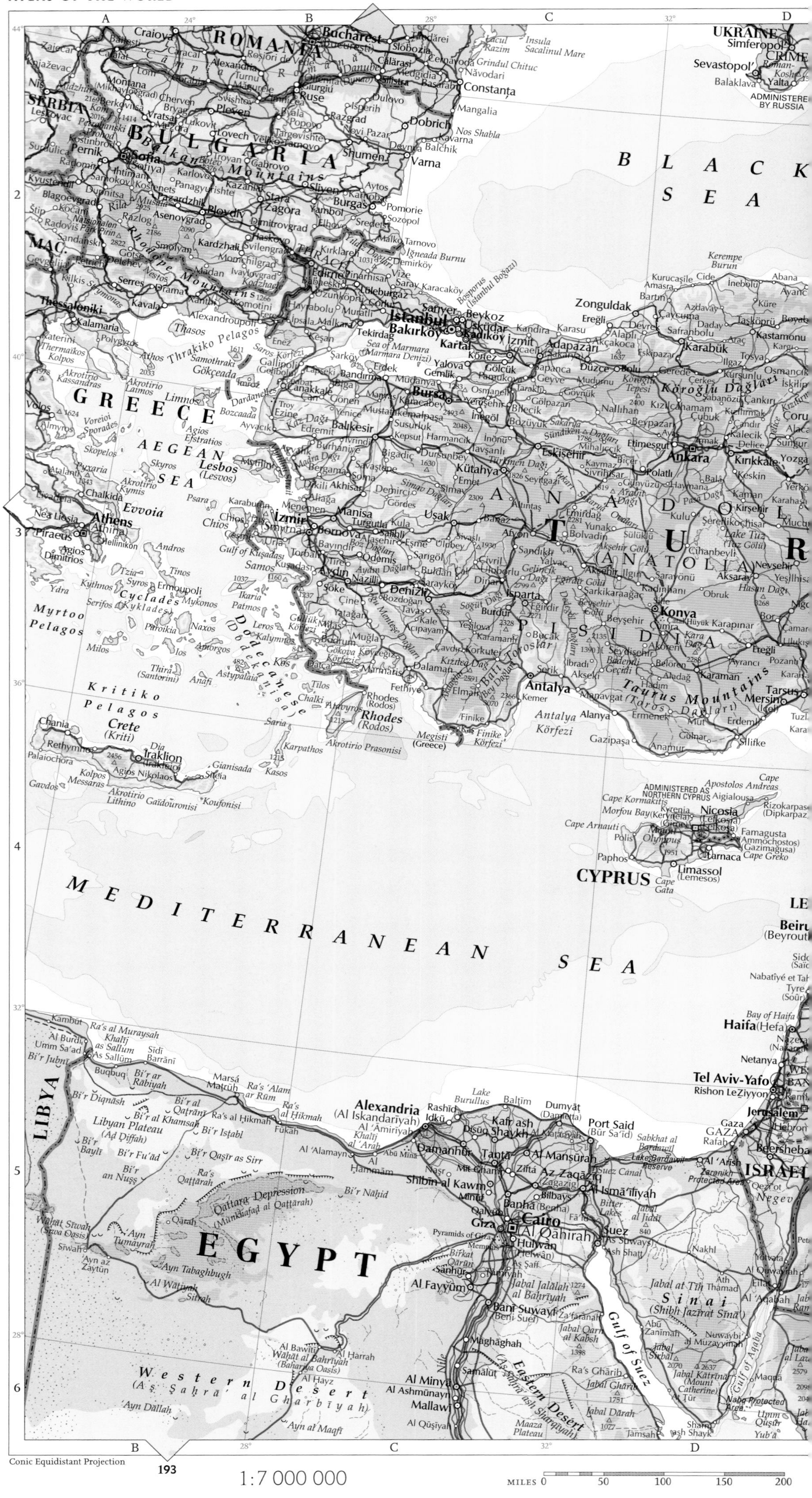

Conic Equidistant Projection

1 : 7 000 000

MILES 0   50   100   150   200

visions of Russia numbered on the map
RESPUBLIKA KALMYKIYA-KHALM'G-TANGCH (G1)
RESPUBLIKA DAGESTAN (G2)
CHECHENSKAYA RESPUBLIKA (G2)
RESPUBLIKA INGUSHETIYA (G2)
RESPUBLIKA SEVERNAYA OSETIYA-ALANIYA (G2)
KABARDINO-BALKARSKAYA RESPUBLIKA (F2)
KARACHAYEVO-CHERKESSKAYA RESPUBLIKA (F2)
RESPUBLIKA ADYGEYA (F1)

RUSSIA

KAZAKHSTAN

STAVROPOL'SKIY KRAY

KRASNODARSKIY

MANGYSTAUSKAYA
OBLAST'

GEORGIA

ARMENIA

AZERBAIJAN

NAGORNO-
KARABAKH

AZER.

C A S P I A N   S E A

TURKMENISTAN

TURKEY

SYRIA

IRAQ

IRAN

JORDAN

SAUDI ARABIA

KUWAIT

Syrian Desert

MESOPOTAMIA

An Nafūd

Elburz Mountains

ZAGROS

T H E   G U L F

Tbilisi
Yerevan
Baku
Tehrān
Baghdad
Damascus
Amman
Kuwait
Aleppo
Mosul
Basra
Esfahān
Shiraz
Ahvāz

0 50 100 150 200 250 300 350 KILOMETRES

© Collins Bartholomew Ltd

THE MIDDLE EAST

The map homes in on the core of the Middle East, an area of southwest Asia which can be defined in various ways. Almost all of Turkey is shown, all of Iraq and Kuwait, and Armenia and Azerbaijan in the northeast, among other countries. The scale emphasizes the relatively small size of Israel, Lebanon and the West Bank, contrasting sharply with their high political profile in modern times. Cyprus, now in the European Union and often culturally associated with Europe, belongs in a physical sense to Asia.

FACTS

- The name 'West Bank' refers the territory's location on the west bank of the river Jordan. It was part of the Kingdom of Jordan until it relinquished its claim to the area in 1988.

- The whole of Jerusalem is treated by Israel as its national capital but this is not recognized by the international community. The native Palestinians share a direct interest in the city and claim it as theirs.

- Kuwait, one of several oil-rich countries in the Gulf area, was invaded by Iraq in 1990, following which the country was liberated by a US-led international force in Operation Desert Storm.

GLOSSARY

ARABIC	
Buḩayrat	lake
Hawr	lake
Jabal, Jebel	mountain

FARSI (Iran)	
Dāgh (D.)	hill(s), mountain(s)
Daryācheh	lake

TURKISH	
Dağ; Dağı	mountain
Dağları	mountain range
Körfezi	gulf, bay

After the First World War, Palestine was under British control and in 1947 the United Nations proposed the creation of separate Jewish and Arab states. This plan was rejected by the Palestinians and Arab nations, and in 1948, after Britain had withdrawn, Israel declared its independence. Most of the territory gained during the ensuing war, and also during the Six Day War in 1967, remains occupied by Israel. The barrier being built around the West Bank is seen by Israel as essential to maintaining its security, but it has had a devastating effect on the lives of Palestinians, and its legality is still contested.

Conic Equidistant Projection

1 : 5 000 000

MILES 0   50   100   150   200

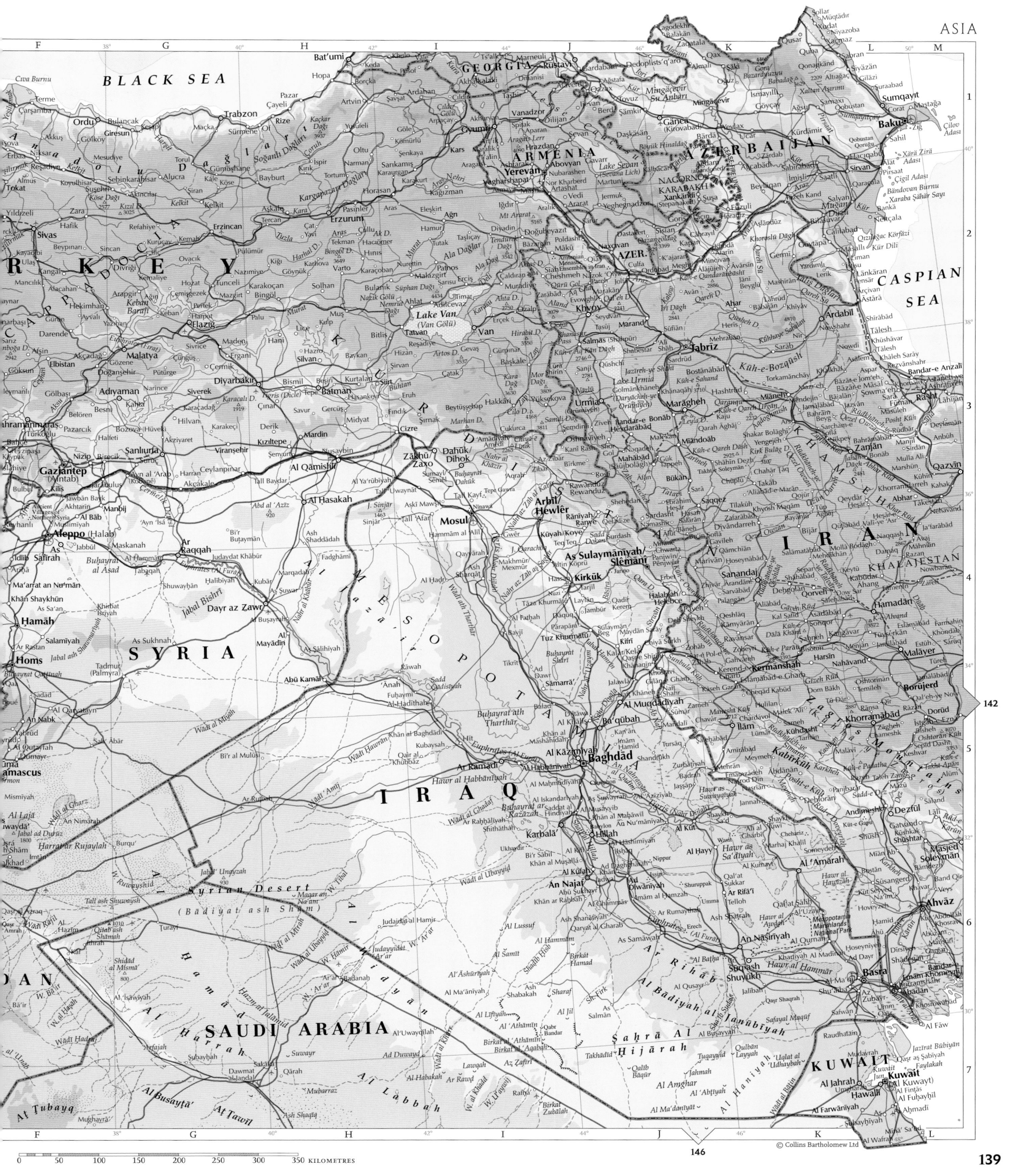

BLACK SEA

GEORGIA

ARMENIA

AZERBAIJAN

CASPIAN SEA

T U R K E Y

AZER.

I R A N

S Y R I A

I R A Q

A l   J a z ī r a h

M E S O P O T A M I A

KHALAJESTAN

SAUDI ARABIA

KUWAIT

Kuwait
(Al Kuwayt)

Baghdad

Basra

Tabrīz

Aleppo (Halab)

Gaziantep (Antab)

Mosul

Damascus

Ḥamāh

Homs

Syrian Desert
(Bādiyat ash Shām)

Sivas

Erzurum

Erzincan

Diyarbakır

Malatya

Van

Lake Van
(Van Gölü)

Yerevan

Baku

Sumqayıt

Karbalā'

An Najaf

Al Kūt

Al 'Amārah

An Nāṣirīyah

Ahvāz

Kirkūk

As Sulaymānīyah/Slēmānī

Arbīl/Hewlēr

Dahūk/Dihok

Al Qāmishlī

Al Ḥasakah

Ar Raqqah

Dayr az Zawr

Hamadān

Kermānshāh

Khorramābād

Sanandaj

Zanjān

Qazvīn

Rasht

Bandar-e Anzalī

Ardabīl

Marāgheh

Urmia

Lake Urmia
(Orūmīyeh)

ASIA CENTRAL

The centre of attention on this map is the extensive region between China and the Caspian Sea which used to be known as Soviet Central Asia, in the days before the Soviet Union (the USSR) was dissolved in 1991. The five now-independent republics of Kazakhstan, Uzbekistan, Turkmenistan, Tajikistan and Kyrgyzstan were formerly under direct Soviet control. On the border of Kazakhstan and Uzbekistan is the Aral Sea, in its own drainage basin. Much of the region is either semi-arid or mountainous.

FACTS

• The Aral Sea has shrunk by almost 40 000 sq km as a result of climate change and water extraction for agriculture. This has led to various ecological, economic and health problems.

• The Kazakh, Uzbek, Turkmen and Kyrgyz (Kirghiz) languages are all closely linked to Turkish, while Tajik is a relative of Farsi (or Persian), the language of Iran.

• Kazakhstan moved its capital in 1997 from the traditional Alma-Ata in the southeast (now spelt Almaty) to Astana in the north. Astana itself has been renamed several times over the years, most recently being changed from Akmola.

GLOSSARY

KAZAKH, KYRGYZ	
Köl	lake

TAJIK	
Küli	lake
Qullai	mountain

UZBEK	
Tog'lari	hills, mountains

RUSSIAN	
Gory	mountains
Khrebet	mountain range
Ozero	lake
Peski	desert
Zaliv	gulf, bay

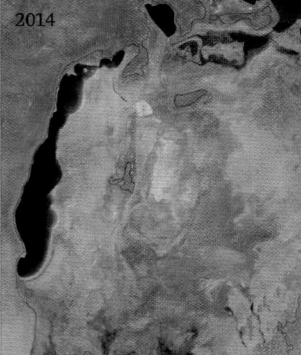

1973   2014

The Aral Sea was once the world's fourth largest lake. It is now reduced to a narrow area at the far west of the former sea, having shrunk as a result of the diversion of water for ill-fated agricultural schemes, and climate change. The local fishing industry has been devastated and the change has had a serious effect on the health of the local population, due to the exposure of chemicals on the dry sea bed. A dam has been constructed to help preserve the northern part of the lake, but the once larger southern part continues to shrink. Water resources are a growing issue throughout Asia, and a similar fate is threatening Lake Balkhash.

MAPPING CHANGE

The Aral Sea shoreline from 1958 is shown on the map. It is similar to the image above from 1973.

Conic Equidistant Projection

1:7 000 000

MILES 0   50   100   150   200

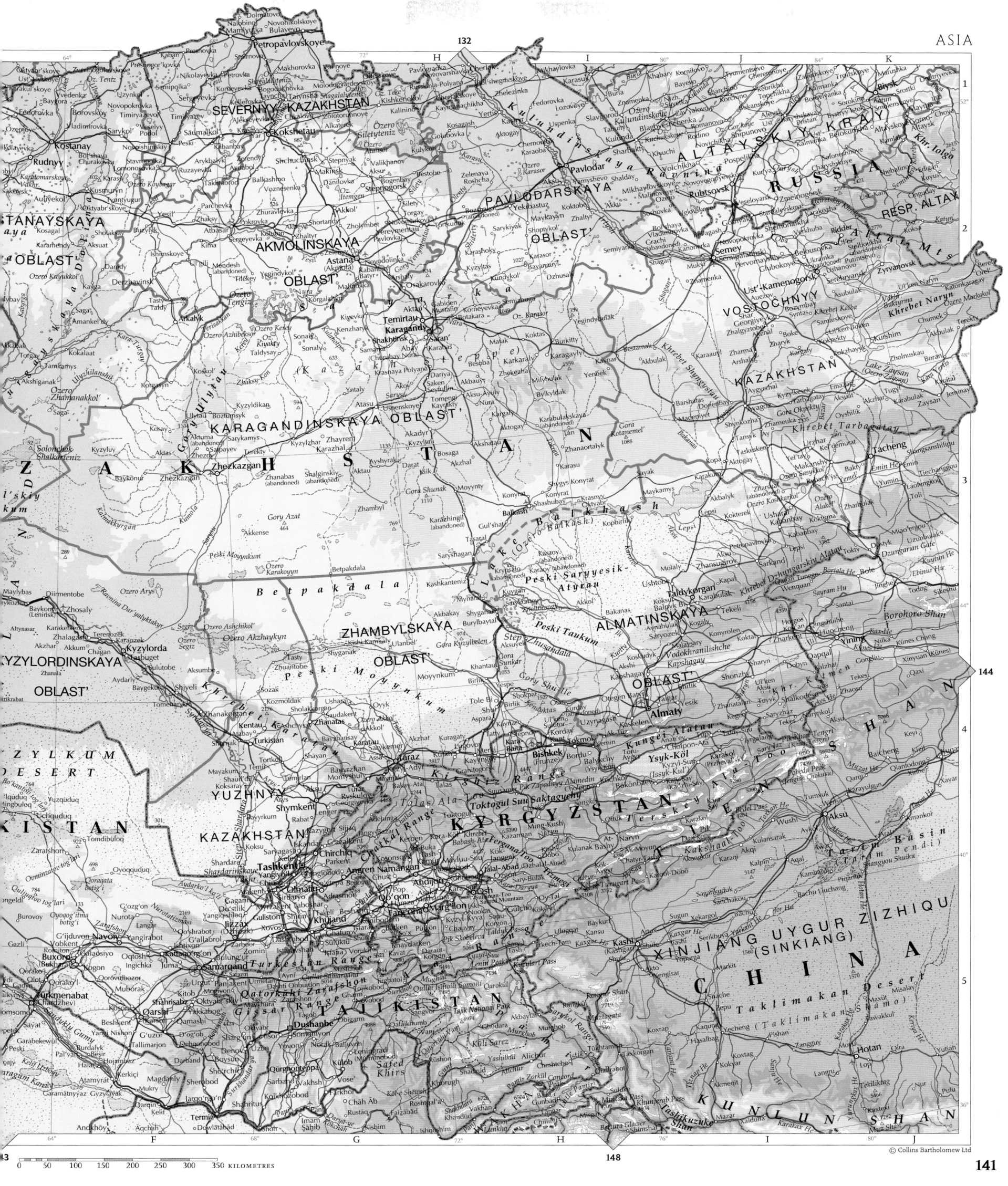

THE GULF, IRAN AND AFGHANISTAN

Covering Iran and Afghanistan, and stretching from the Caspian Sea in the north to The Gulf in the south, the map emphasizes the high plateau and mountainous nature of much of the landscape of this region. In contrast to these areas, it also shows the flat lowlands in the Tigris and Euphrates basins of Iraq, the Caspian Sea basin (lying partly below sea level) and the deserts of Turkmenistan, the Gulf coast, and the lower Indus valley in Pakistan.

FACTS

- Oil is the chief source of revenue in Iran, its major oilfields lying in the western foothills of the Zagros Mountains.

- The mountains of the Hindu Kush dominate more than three quarters of Afghanistan, with peaks rising to over 6400 m.

- The alluvial plains of the ancient region of Mesopotamia, lying between the Tigris and Euphrates Rivers in modern-day Iraq, were the site of the ancient Babylonian and Assyrian civilizations.

GLOSSARY

FARSI (Iran), DARI (Afghanistan)		TAJIK	
Daryācheh	lake	**Qatorkuhi**	mountain, mountain range
Dasht	desert	**Qullai**	mountain
Kūh; Kūhha	mountain, mountains		
Rūd, Rūdkhāneh	river		

This striking image of the Kavir Desert in Iran shows the geological structure clearly because of the lack of soil or vegetation. Gentle folding of many thin layers of rock was followed by the erosion of the top layers exposing the light and dark folds of the layers beneath. The lake in the centre, shown by the dark S-shape, lies to the right of a sandy area where the sand is thin enough to allow the darker rock to be seen below.

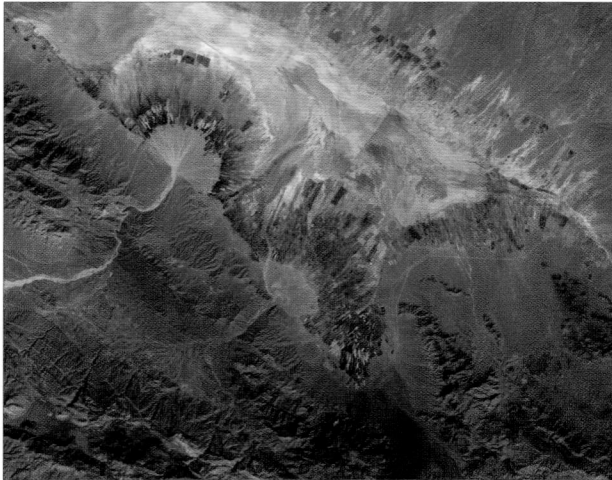

The valleys of the Zagros Mountains in southern Iran are abundant with dry salt lakes and ephemeral and subterranean streams. Water is a valuable commodity for agriculture – where these subterranean streams surface, the water table is higher and water more accessible through wells. This image shows a dry river fanning out as it reaches the flat valley, where it would have slowed and deposited sediments, creating a swathe of fertile land that has been exploited for agriculture.

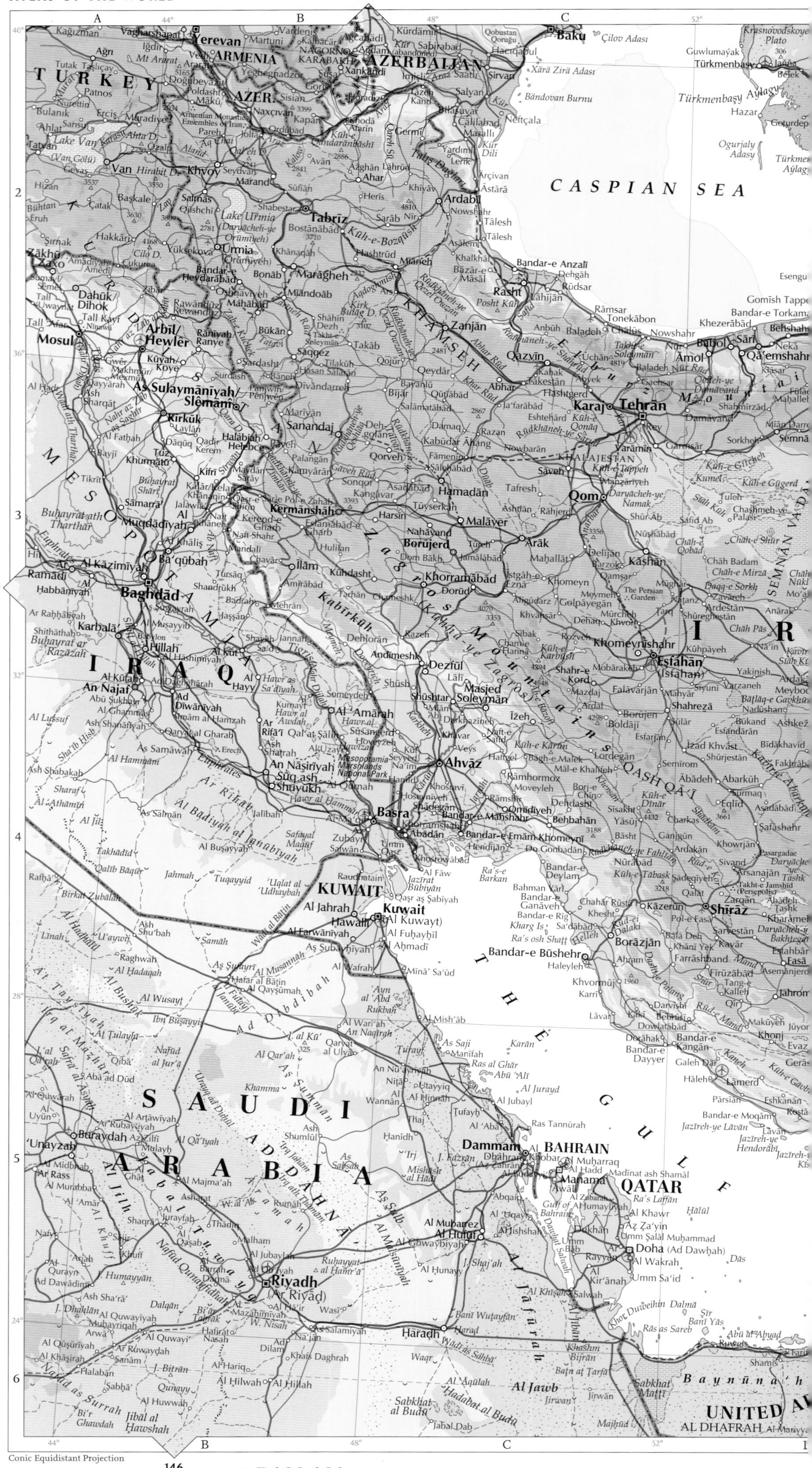

Conic Equidistant Projection

1:7 000 000

MILES 0   50   100   150   200

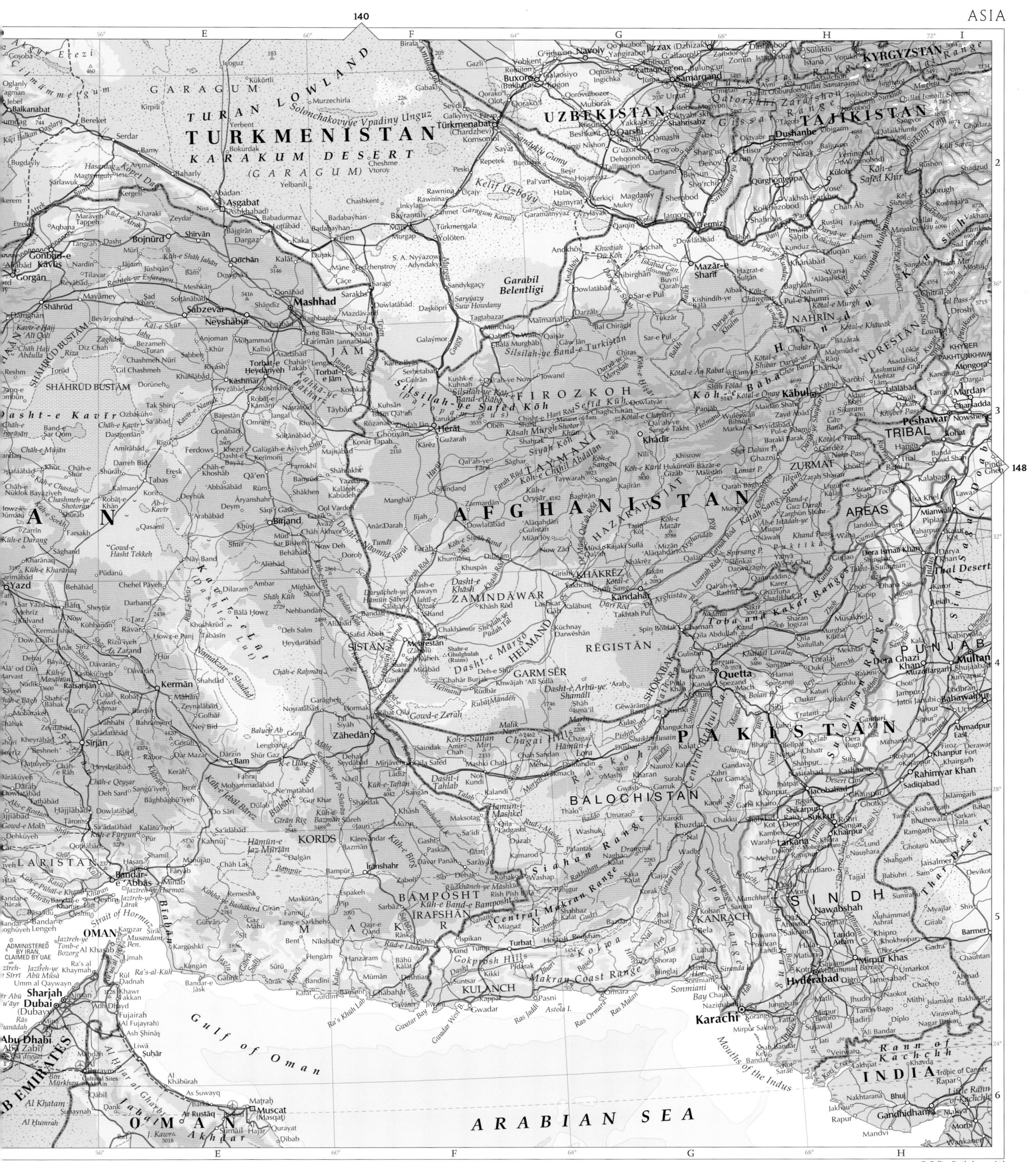

© Collins Bartholomew Ltd

0 50 100 150 200 250 300 350 KILOMETRES

SOUTHERN ASIA

The focus of the map is the Indian subcontinent. India is the largest and most populous country in the subcontinent and the second most populous in the world behind China. The map also shows sparsely populated western China, including the vast Himalaya and the Plateau of Tibet. Pakistan is shown in its entirety. Sri Lanka occupies the teardrop-shaped island off the southern coast of India. The complex patterns of international boundaries in this region hint at mountainous terrain, a turbulent past and on-going territorial disputes.

FACTS

- Approximately two thirds of Bangladesh is fertile arable land served by the Ganges and Brahmaputra Rivers. During the monsoon these rivers can seriously flood the area.

- Mount Everest, the highest mountain in the world, was first climbed in 1953 and lies in the great Himalaya mountain range on the border between China and Nepal.

- The height of the land in Nepal ranges from 60 m to 8848 m.

GLOSSARY

CHINESE	
He	river
Hu	lake
Jiang	river
Shan	mountain(s)

DARI (Afghanistan)	
Dasht	desert
Kūh	mountain, mountains

RUSSIAN	
Khrebet	mountain range
Ozero	lake

TIBETAN	
Co	lake
Kangri	mountain, peak

Myanmar's national capital of Nay Pyi Taw is a planned city. Rangoon (Yangôn) had been the country's capital since 1885 until, in late 2005, the military government announced that a new capital was to be built in the jungle to the north. The reasons for the move were not clear although there were suggestions that it was on the advice of astrologers, and that it was to reduce the likelihood of attack from other countries. Hundreds of workers were 'recruited' for the major construction project. It was one of the host cities of the 2013 Southeast Asian Games. Uppatasanti Pagoda – the 'Peace Pagoda' – is a prominent landmark standing 99 m (325 ft) high. Its precinct includes gardens, hostels, a museum and statues and also a Buddha tooth relic from China.

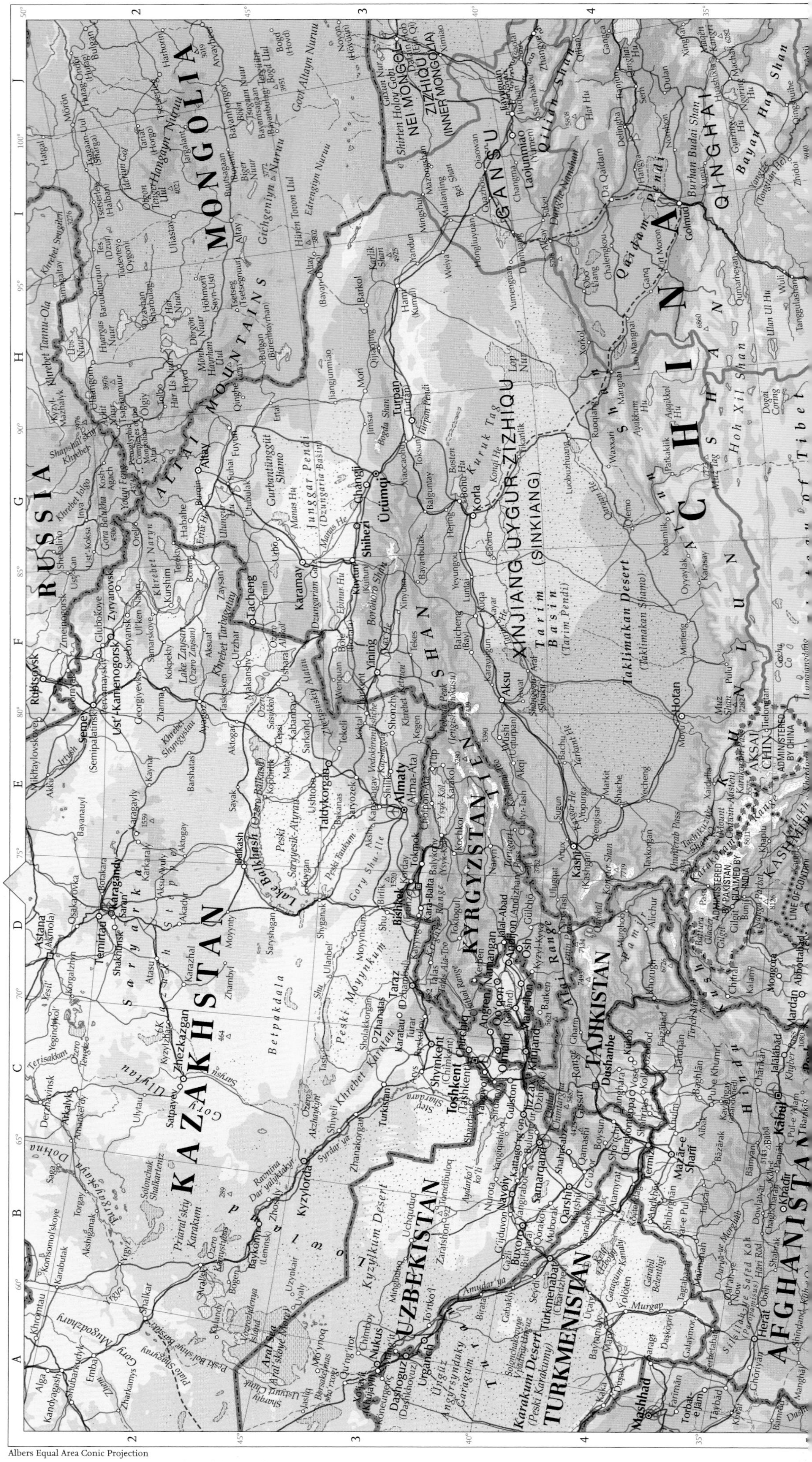

132

Albers Equal Area Conic Projection

1:13 000 000

MILES 0   100   200   300   400   500

0 100 200 300 400 500 600 700 800 KILOMETRES

ARABIAN PENINSULA
INDIA SOUTH AND SRI LANKA

The Arabian Peninsula is a largely desert area of southwest Asia, framed by the Red Sea, the Arabian Sea (part of the Indian Ocean), and The Gulf (also often referred to as the Persian Gulf). The southernmost point of the peninsula, in Yemen, is only narrowly separated from Africa. The focus of the right-hand map is southern India and the island nation of Sri Lanka, formerly known as Ceylon. Part of the Maldives, consisting of numerous low-lying islands, is also shown.

FACTS
- The name Saudi Arabia is derived from the name of the ruling royal family, Saud.
- Bahrain, an independent island kingdom in The Gulf, is connected by a causeway to the Saudi Arabian mainland.
- The country name Sri Lanka is phonetically related to the country's earlier name, Ceylon. Ceylon is still sometimes used to refer to the island itself. Sri Lanka has designated a new national capital adjacent to Colombo: Sri Jayewardenepura Kotte.

GLOSSARY

ARABIC

Bāb	strait	**Ra's**	cape, point
Jabal	mountain(s)	**Wādī**	watercourse
Jazā'ir, Juzur	islands		

1930

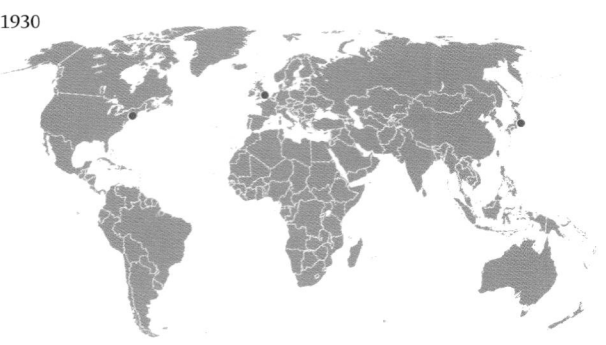

1975

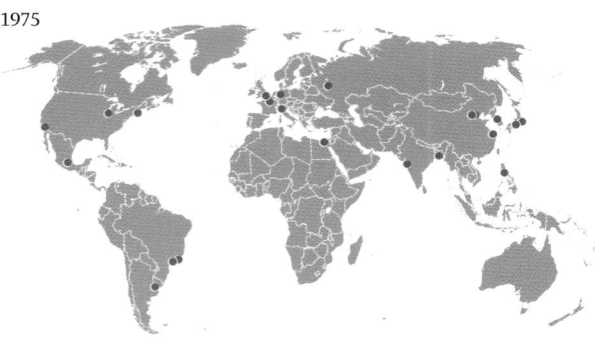

2015

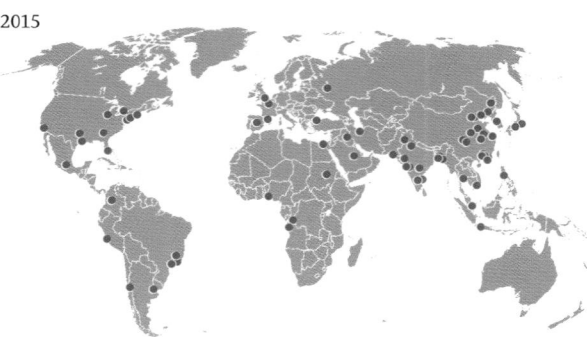

In 2010, for the first time in history, it was estimated that more people lived in cities than in rural areas. This growth in the urban population has largely been an Asian phenomenon, in which India and China have been key players. In 1975, throughout Asia, there were only nine cities with populations over 5 million. By 2015 this figure was forty out of a world total of sixty-nine. India itself has seen massive urban growth, with steady rural-urban migration. By 2015 India had nine cities of over 5 million inhabitants, with four of these – Delhi, Mumbai, Kolkata and Bengaluru – having over 10 million inhabitants.

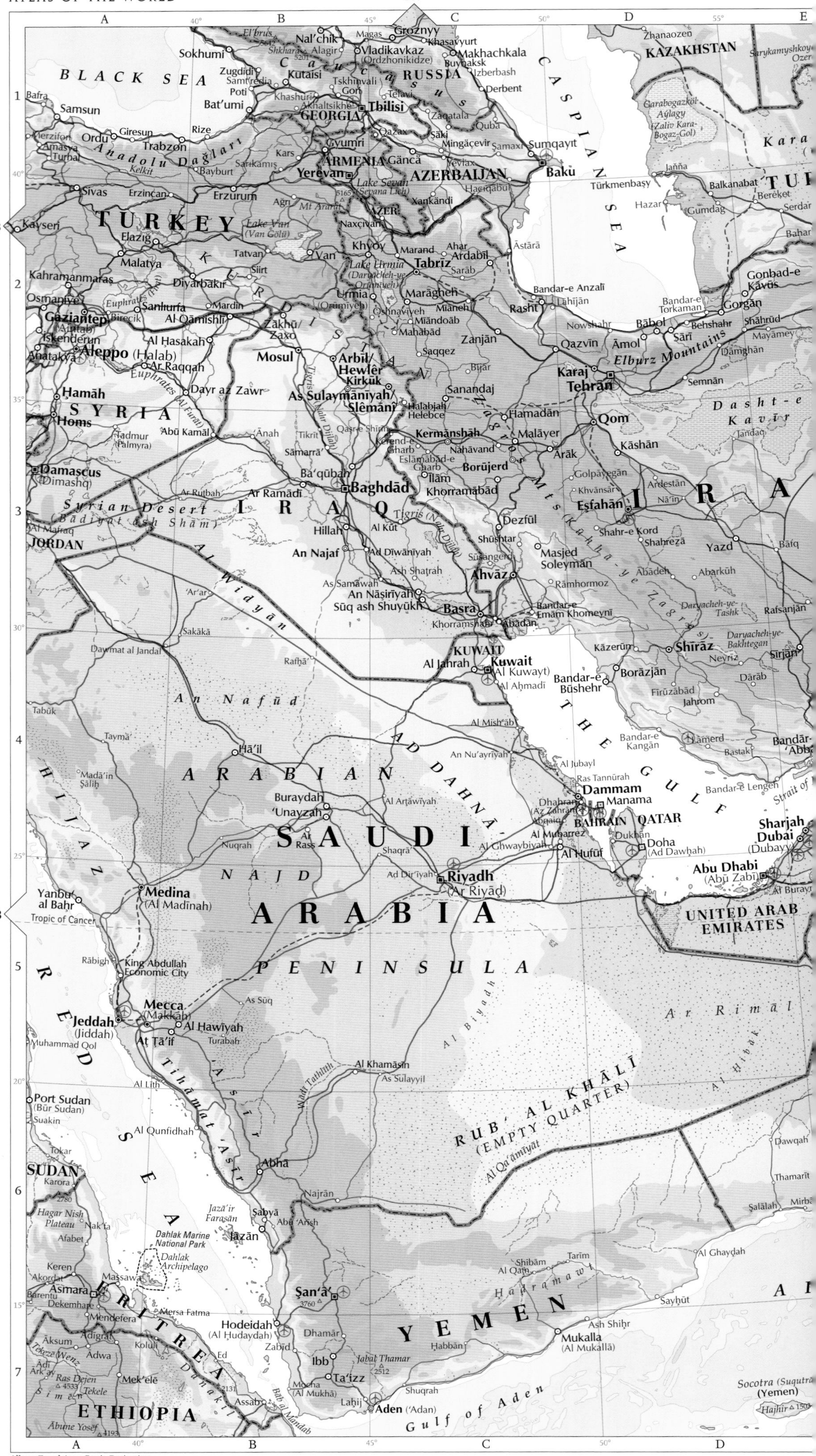

Albers Equal Area Conic Projection

1:12 500 000   MILES 0   100   200   300   0   100   200   300   400 KILOMETRES

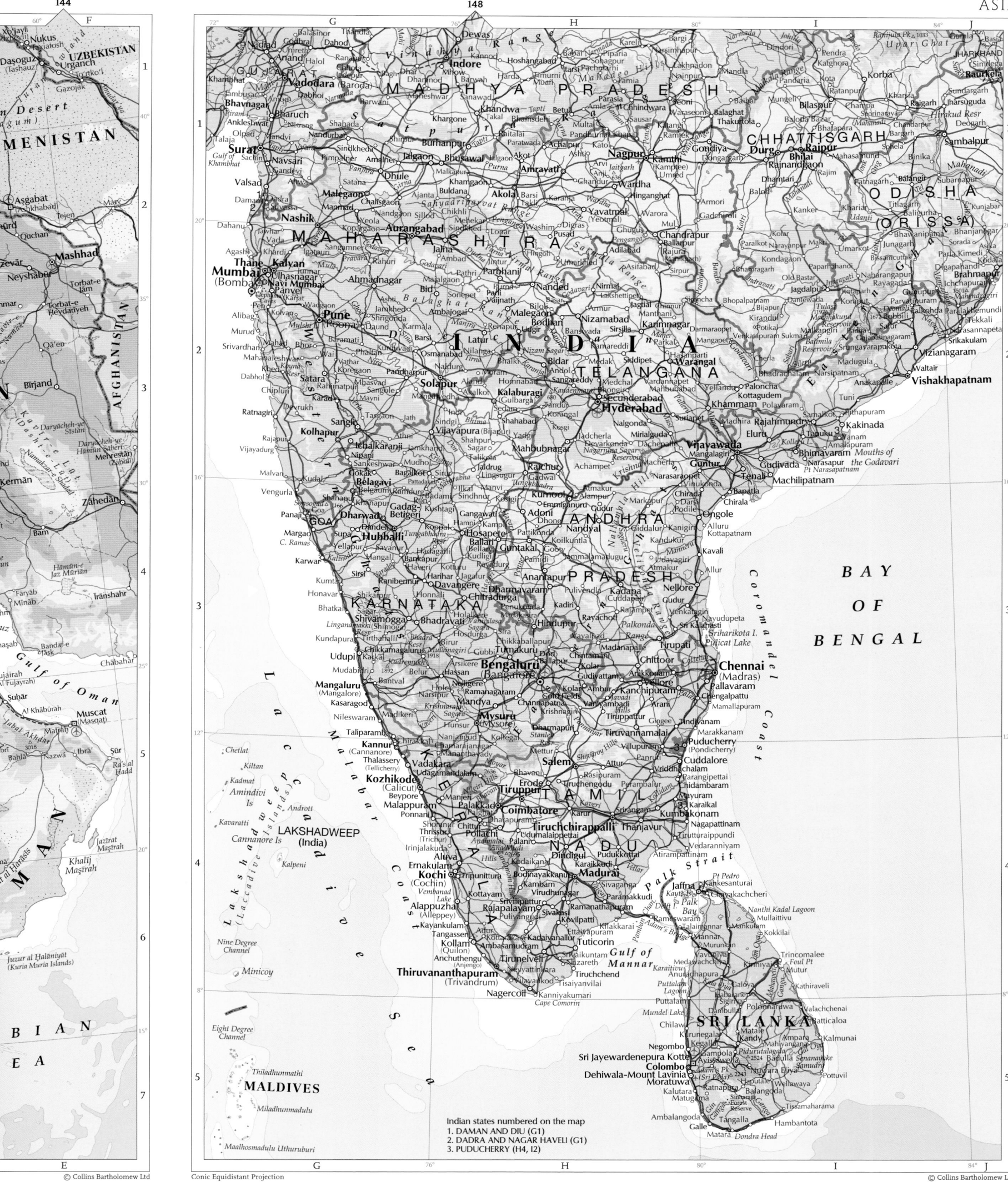

144

148

F

1

40°

35°

m Desert
agum)

TURKMENISTAN

AFGHANISTAN

Mashhad

Neyshābūr

Birjand

Kermān

Zāhedan

Gulf of Oman

Muscat
(Masqat)

OMAN

ARABIAN
SEA

UZBEKISTAN

Nukus
Urganch

Daşoguz
(Tashauz)

G

76°

GUJARAT

Vadodara (Baroda)

Indore

MADHYA   PRADESH

Surat

Bhavnagar

Nashik

MAHARASHTRA

Mumbai
(Bombay)

Navi Mumbai

Pune

Nagpur

Amravati

Akola

Solapur

Kalaburagi
(Gulbarga)

Kolhapur

Vijayapura (Bijapur)

Hyderabad
Secunderabad

TELANGANA

Warangal

INDIA

CHHATTISGARH

Durg   Raipur
Bhilai

ODISHA
(ORISSA)

Brahmapur

Vishakhapatnam

Vijayawada

Guntur

Machilipatnam

Kurnool

ANDHRA

PRADESH

Nellore

H

80°

Raurkela

JHARKHAND

Sambalpur

Rajahmundry

Kakinada

Mouths of
the Godavari

BAY

OF

BENGAL

I

J

84°

2

16°

Belagavi

Hubballi

Dharwad

GOA

Panaji

KARNATAKA

Shivamogga

Bhadravati

Mangaluru
(Mangalore)

Udupi

Bengaluru
(Bangalore)

Mysuru
(Mysore)

Chitradurga

Hosapete

Ballari

Guntakal

Anantapur

Hindupur

Tirupati

Chennai
(Madras)

Kanchipuram

KERALA

Kozhikode
(Calicut)

Kannur
(Cannanore)

Coimbatore

Tiruppur

TAMIL

NADU

Salem

Puducherry
(Pondicherry)

Cuddalore

Coromandel Coast

3

12°

Kochi
(Cochin)

Madurai

Tiruchchirappalli

Thanjavur

Palk Strait

Jaffna

Palk
Bay

4

Thiruvananthapuram
(Trivandrum)

Kollam
(Quilon)

Tuticorin

Tirunelveli

Cape Comorin

Gulf of
Mannar

Trincomalee

SRI LANKA

Kandy

Colombo
Sri Jayewardenepura Kotte
Dehiwala-Mount Lavinia
Moratuwa

Galle

Dondra Head

8°

LAKSHADWEEP
(India)

Lakshadweep (Laccadive Islands)

Laccadive Coast

Minicoy

Eight Degree
Channel

MALDIVES

Nine Degree
Channel

5

7

Indian states numbered on the map
1. DAMAN AND DIU (G1)
2. DADRA AND NAGAR HAVELI (G1)
3. PUDUCHERRY (H4, I2)

G

H

I

J

© Collins Bartholomew Ltd

Conic Equidistant Projection

© Collins Bartholomew Ltd

1:7 000 000

MILES 0   50   100   150

0   50   100   150   200   250   300 KILOMETRES

147

INDIA NORTH AND BANGLADESH

The map shows in detail the densely-populated areas of northern India, along with the whole of Pakistan, Nepal and Bhutan, and virtually all of Afghanistan and Bangladesh. This is a volatile region. Jammu and Kashmir, in the north, has long been the basis of a major territorial dispute between India and Pakistan, and the Line of Control named on the map represents the present de facto boundary between the countries. The nearby zone called the Aksai Chin is disputed between China and India.

FACTS

- India's capital can be regarded as Delhi or New Delhi. The latter is an area within Delhi itself, containing most of the government buildings.

- The area between Nepal and Bhutan, known as Sikkim (capital Gangtok shown on the map) was independent until it became an Indian state in 1975.

- Darjiling, in the far northeast of India, is famous as a tea-growing area whose traditional spelling of Darjeeling is more familiar.

GLOSSARY

CHINESE	
He	river
Hu	lake
Jiang	river
Shan	mountain(s)

TIBETAN	
Co	lake
Kangri	mountain, peak
Qu	river
Tso	lake

DARI (Afghanistan)	
Darreh	valley
Küh	mountain, mountains

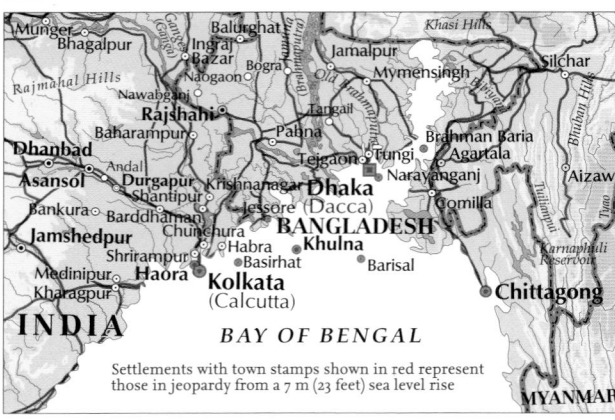

Settlements with town stamps shown in red represent those in jeopardy from a 7 m (23 feet) sea level rise

Bangladesh, with its population of over 150 million people, is a very low-lying country and frequently suffers from major flooding in the monsoon season. Together with neighbouring parts of India, it is also at great risk from rising sea level due to climate change. Many major cities, including Kolkata and Dhaka, both of which have more than 10 million inhabitants, lie in the vulnerable coastal region. The effects of a sea level rise of 7 m (23 feet) would be devastating for this region.

Indian states numbered on the map
1. DAMAN AND DIU (B5, C5)
2. DADRA AND NAGAR HAVELI (C5)
Pakistani administrative divisions numbered on map
3. AZAD KASHMIR (C2)

Conic Equidistant Projection

1 : 7 000 000

MILES 0   50   100   150   200

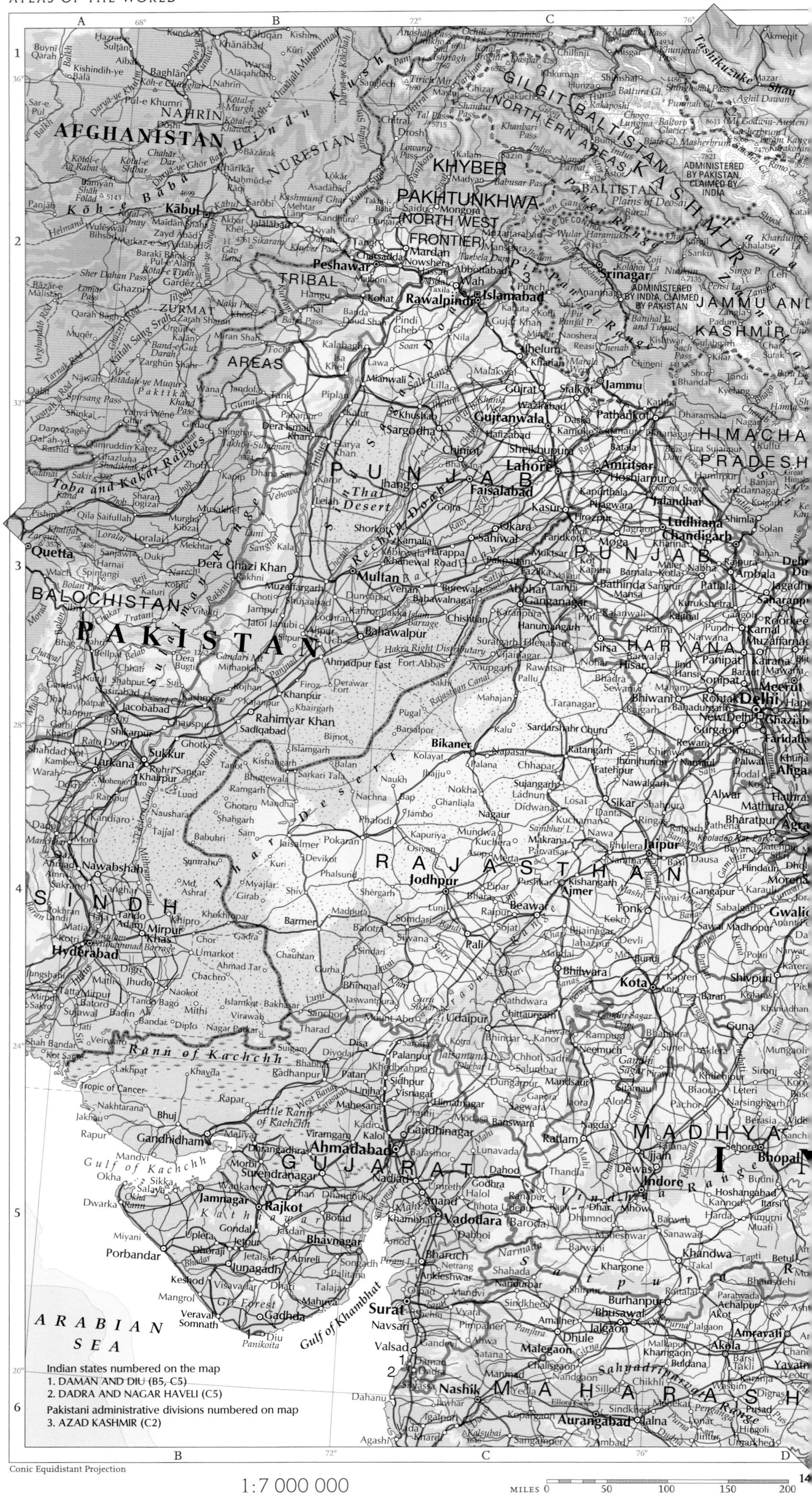

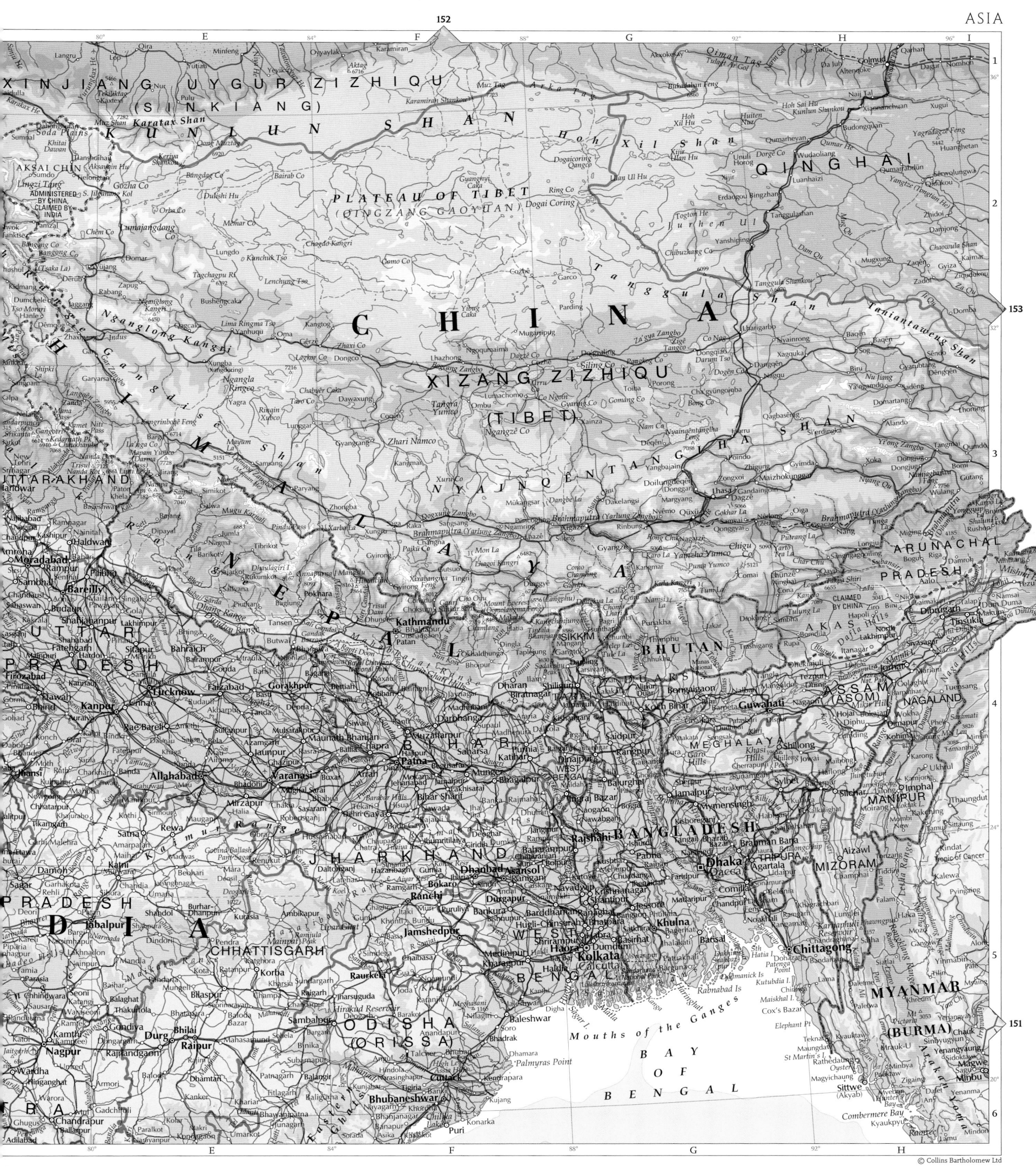

© Collins Bartholomew Ltd

0 50 100 150 200 250 300 350 KILOMETRES

ASIA EAST AND SOUTHEAST

Southeast Asia is physically divided into two parts. The mainland section consists largely of two very prominent peninsulas: Indo-China, covering Vietnam, Laos and Cambodia; and the Malay Peninsula, occupied by Malaysia and by the southerly extensions of Thailand and Myanmar (Burma). Almost all of the rest of the region consists of large groups of islands: chiefly Indonesia, stretching from east to west across the map for almost 3000 miles, and the Philippines to the north.

FACTS

- The Indonesian archipelago is made up of over 13 000 islands, approximately 6000 of which are inhabited.

- East Timor, part of the island of Timor in the southeast of the map, was a Portuguese possession (Portuguese Timor), but was absorbed by Indonesia in the 1970s. It gained its independence as a new member of the United Nations in 2002, using its Portuguese-based name Timor-Leste.

- Indonesia has the fourth biggest population of any country – only exceeded by China, India and the United States. Java is one of the most densely populated parts of the globe.

GLOSSARY

INDONESIAN

Kepulauan	islands	Selat	strait
Laut	sea	Tanjung	cape, point
Pegunungan	mountain range	Teluk	bay, gulf

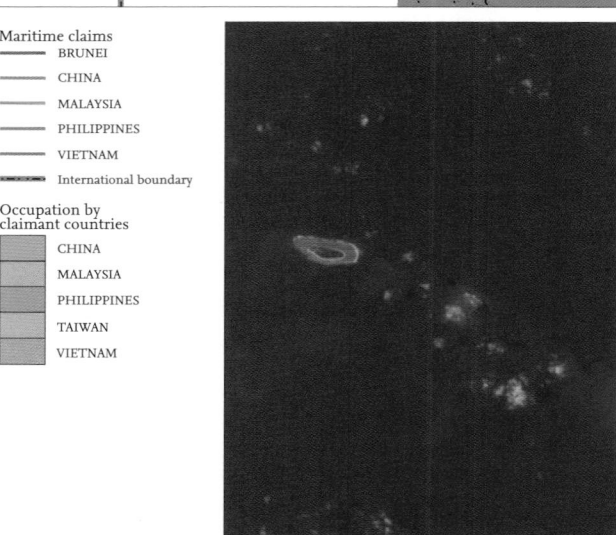

Maritime claims
- ———— BRUNEI
- ———— CHINA
- ———— MALAYSIA
- ———— PHILIPPINES
- ———— VIETNAM
- ━━━━ International boundary

Occupation by claimant countries
- CHINA
- MALAYSIA
- PHILIPPINES
- TAIWAN
- VIETNAM

The seemingly insignificant reefs of the Spratly Islands in the South China Sea are the scene of a territorial dispute between six countries. Although tiny – the largest is less than half a square kilometre in size – they are seen as strategically and economically important by each of the claimants. About forty-five of the tiny islands are occupied, in order to endorse the various claims. Ownership would mean access to the vast fishing grounds and oil-rich seafloor of the area. Despite some encouraging cooperation between the countries involved, a long-term, permanent agreement on the sovereignty of the islands still appears some way off.

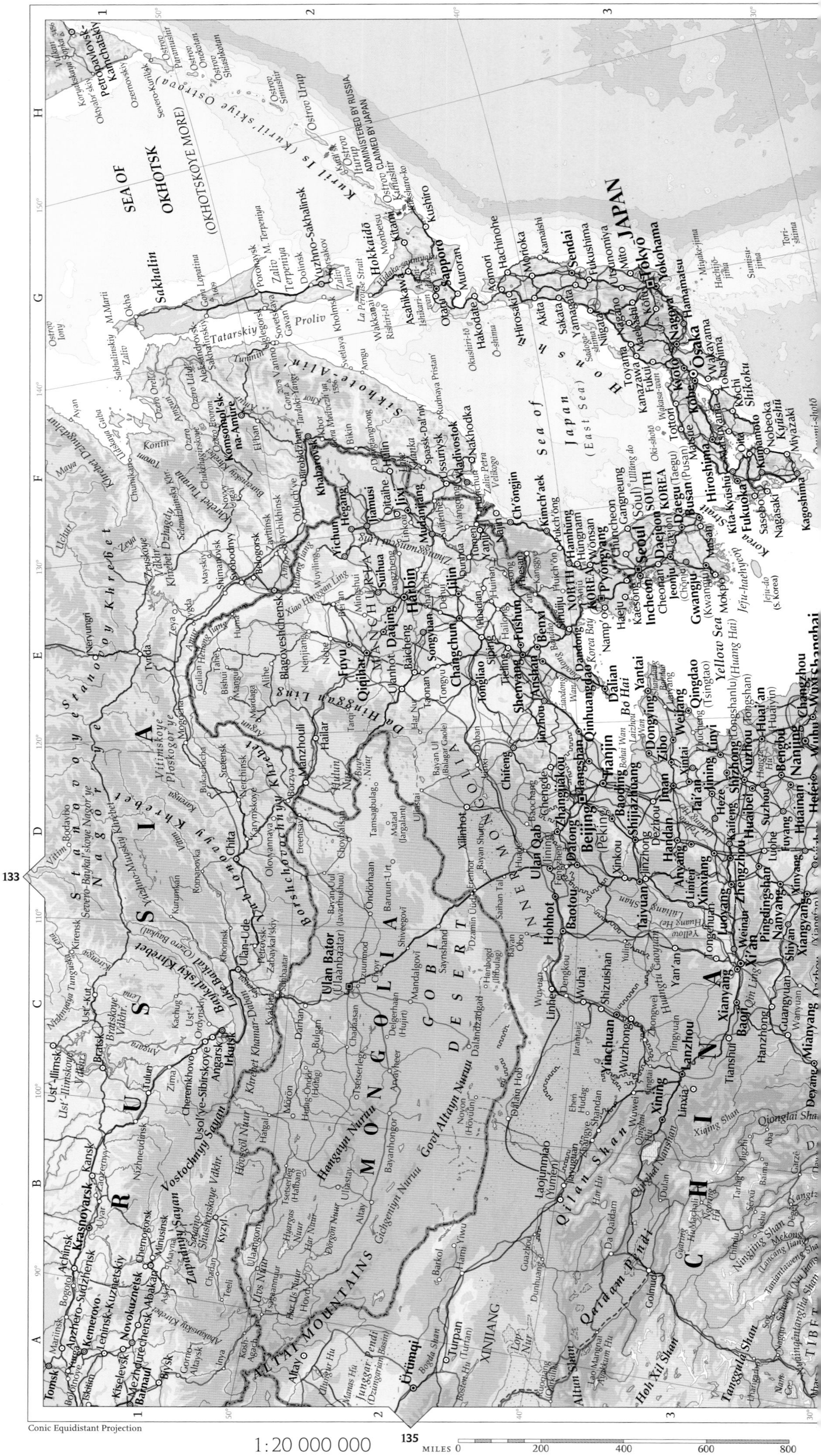

150

Conic Equidistant Projection

1 : 20 000 000

MILES 0   200   400   600   800

133

135

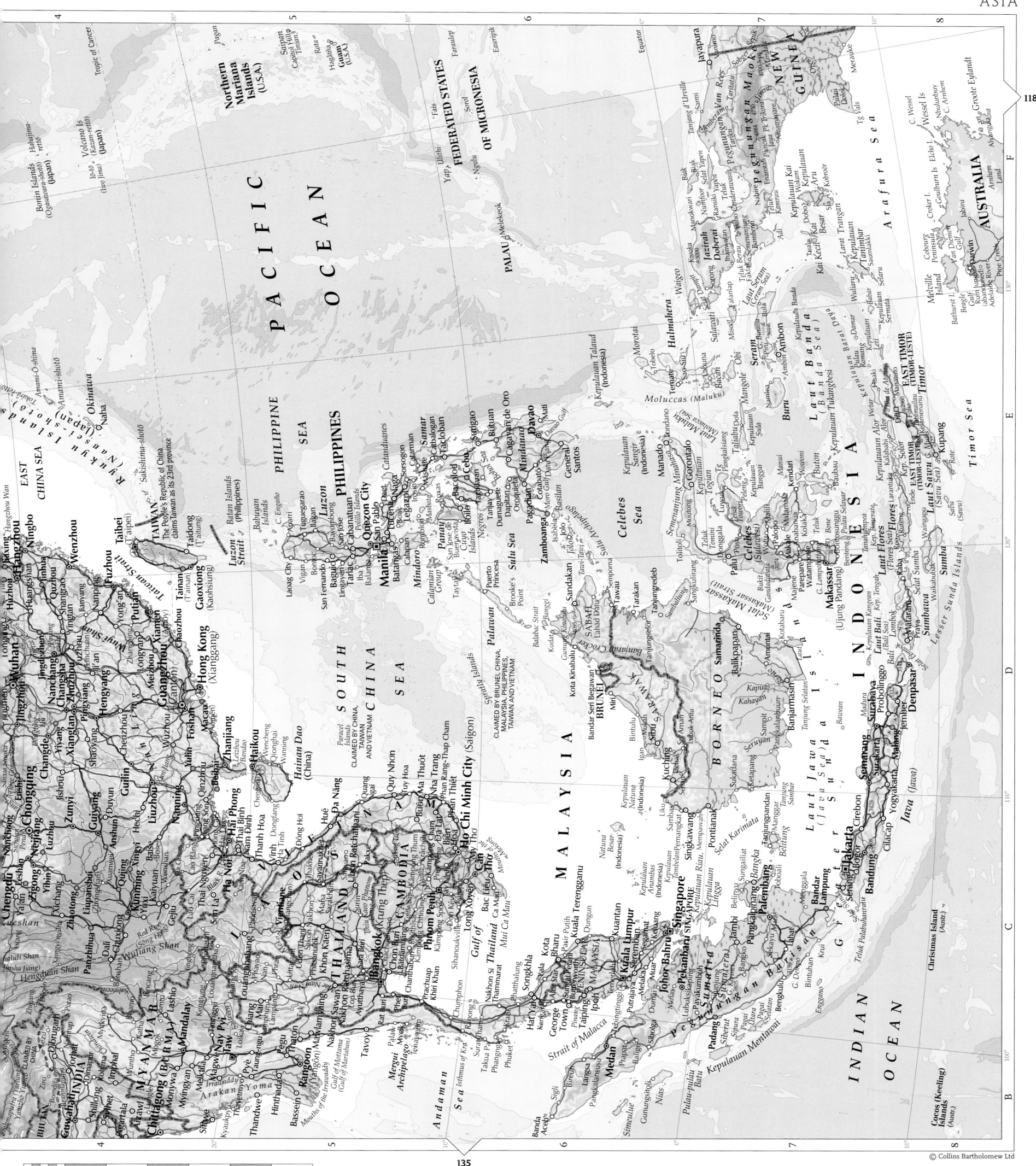

PACIFIC

OCEAN

PHILIPPINE

SEA

FEDERATED STATES

OF MICRONESIA

NEW

GUINEA

AUSTRALIA

Arafura

Sea

Timor Sea

EAST TIMOR
(TIMOR-LESTE)

I N D O N E S I A

Celebes

Sea

Sulu

Sea

PHILIPPINES

Banda Sea

Laut Banda
(Banda Sea)

Laut Maluku
(Molucca Sea)

Moluccas (Maluku)

Halmahera

TAIWAN
The People's Republic of China
claims Taiwan as its 23rd province

EAST

CHINA SEA

Ryukyu Islands

Hong Kong
(Xianggang)

Macao

Hainan Dao
(China)

S O U T H

C H I N A

S E A

Spratly Islands

Paracel
Islands
CLAIMED BY CHINA,
VIETNAM

CLAIMED BY BRUNEI, CHINA,
MALAYSIA, PHILIPPINES,
TAIWAN AND VIETNAM

BRUNEI

B O R N E O

SARAWAK

SABAH

Palawan

M A L A Y S I A

Ho Chi Minh City (Saigon)

V I E T N A M

CAMBODIA

Phnom Penh

THAILAND

Bangkok

Gulf of
Thailand

MYANMAR
(BURMA)

Mandalay

Rangoon

LAOS

Vientiane

Hà Nôi

Hai Phong

Andaman

Sea

Bay
of
Bengal

INDIA

BHUTAN

Chongqing

Chengdu

Kunming

Guangzhou
(Canton)

Nanchang

Wuhan

Changsha

Fuzhou

Taibei
(Taipei)

Gaoxiong
(Kaohsiung)

Tainan
(Tainan)

Luzon

Manila

Quezon City

Mindanao

Davao

Celebes
(Sulawesi)

Makassar

Borneo

Kalimantan
(Indonesia)

Balikpapan

Banjarmasin

Kuching

Pontianak

Singapore

Kuala Lumpur

MALAYSIA

Medan

Sumatra

Palembang

Bandar
Lampung

Jakarta

Bandung

Semarang

Surabaya

Java (Jawa)

Laut Jawa
(Java Sea)

Denpasar

Mataram

Sumbawa

Sumba

Flores

Timor

Kupang

Strait of Malacca

Pegunungan Barisan

Greater

Sunda

Islands

Lesser Sunda Islands

Darwin

INDIAN

OCEAN

Christmas Island
(Aust.)

Cocos (Keeling)
Islands
(Aust.)

© Collins Bartholomew Ltd

0   200   400   600   800   1000   1200   1400 KILOMETRES

EASTERN ASIA

This map centres on China – the world's most populous country – and the wider region known as the Far East. The density of settlements in the eastern half of China contrasts sharply with the relatively sparsely inhabited western areas of Tibet and Xinjiang, and the north of the country adjacent to Mongolia. There are great physical contrasts within this region, from the Himalaya, the highest mountains in the world, and the vast, high Plateau of Tibet, to the Gobi and the deserts of western China.

FACTS

- Mongolia was traditionally referred to as Outer Mongolia while a large zone of northern China is still known as Inner Mongolia. China actually extends further north than any part of Mongolia.

- Tibet, formerly an independent nation, was taken over by China in the 1950s, and its spiritual ruler, the Dalai Lama, has lived abroad since then.

- The system now used for converting Chinese characters into our alphabet, called Pinyin, involves frequent use of the letters q, x and z, which gives some spellings still relatively unfamiliar in the West (e.g. Xinjiang, Guangzhou). Other Pinyin spellings, such as Beijing, are more well known. For more details see page 60.

GLOSSARY

CHINESE	
Hai	sea
He	river
Hu	lake
Shan	mountain(s)

MONGOLIAN	
Nuruu	mountain range
Nuur	lake

China's economy has been growing faster than that of any other major nation for over a quarter of a century to become the world's second largest economy after the USA and the largest exporter of goods in the world. Per capita income has grown at an average annual rate of more than 10 per cent over the last three decades. The rapid development does have its problems however. Estimates indicate that there are over 100 million people living below the poverty line in China, with great inequalities between the more highly developed coastal provinces and the poorer inland regions. Development also raises environmental concerns with China as the world's greatest emitter of carbon dioxide, largely through its industrial growth.

CHINA'S ECONOMY	2000	2013
Gross National Income (GNI) (International $)	2.9 trillion	16.0 trillion
GNI per capita (International $)	2 340	11 850
Annual GDP growth (per cent)	8.4	7.7
Exports of goods and services (per cent of GDP)	23.3	26.4

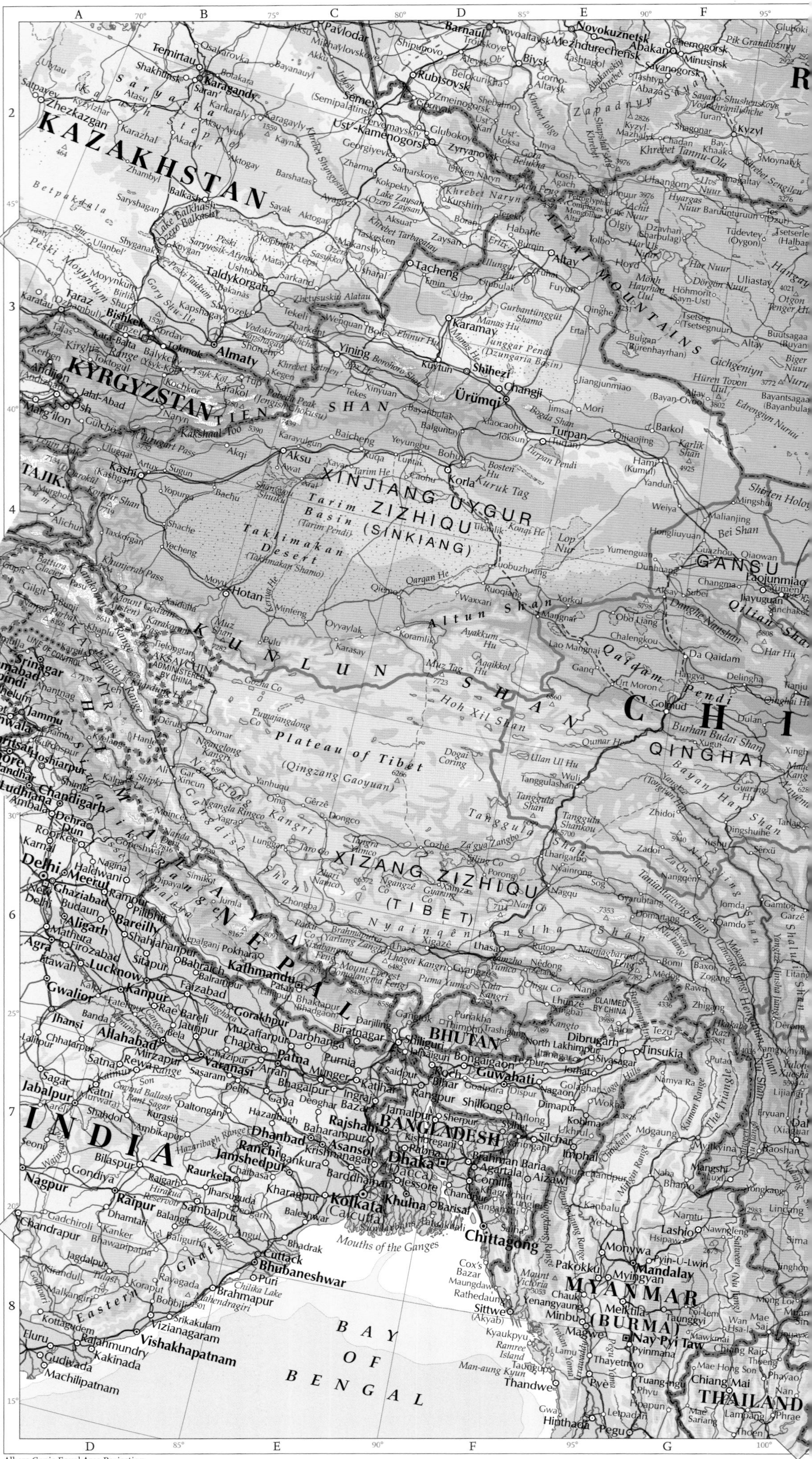

Albers Conic Equal Area Projection

1:15 000 000

MILES 0   200   400

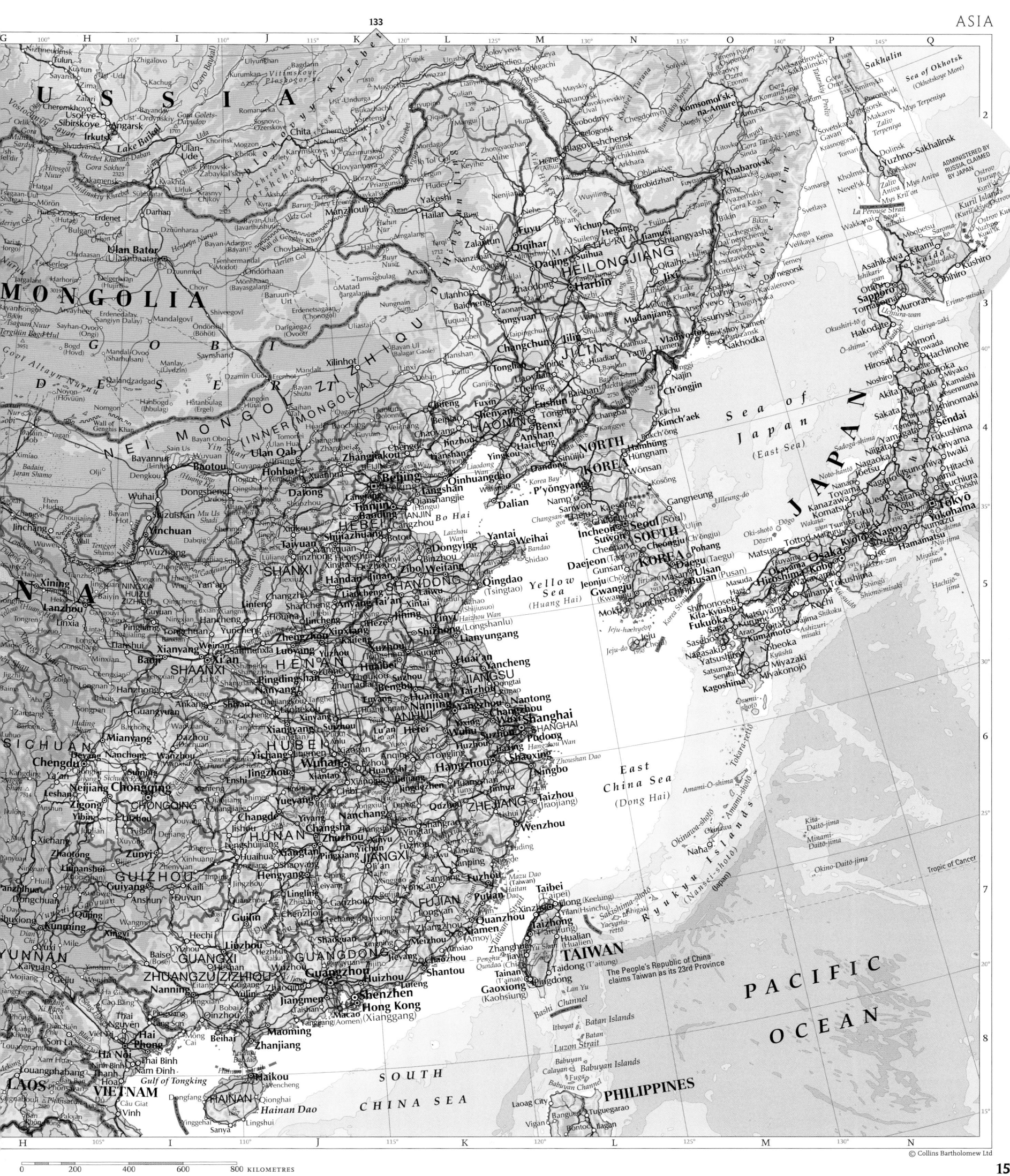

133

G 100° H 105° I 110° J 115° K 120° L 125° M 130° N 135° O 140° P 145° Q

U S S I A

MONGOLIA

G O B I   D E S E R T

Ulan Bator
(Ulaanbaatar)

NEI MONGOL

INNER MONGOLIA

MANCHURIA

HEILONGJIANG

Harbin

JILIN

Changchun

Vladivostok

NORTH KOREA

P'yŏngyang

Sea of
Japan
(East Sea)

J A P A N

Tōkyō
Yokohama

Sapporo

LIAONING

Shenyang

SOUTH KOREA

Seoul (Sŏul)

Baotou

Hohhot

Datong

Beijing
(Peking)

Tianjin

TIANJIN

HEBEI

Tangshan

Dalian

Incheon

Daejeon (Taejŏn)

Busan (Pusan)

Hiroshima

Ōsaka

Kyōto
Nagoya

Yinchuan

Taiyuan

SHANXI

Shijiazhuang

Jinan

SHANDONG

Qingdao
(Tsingtao)

Yellow
Sea
(Huang Hai)

Fukuoka

Kita-Kyūshū

Lanzhou

Xining

NINGXIA HUIZU ZIZHIQU

Xi'an

SHAANXI

Luoyang

Zhengzhou

HENAN

Nanjing

JIANGSU

Lianyungang

Kagoshima

SICHUAN

Chengdu

Chongqing

CHONGQING

HUBEI

Wuhan

ANHUI

Hefei

Shanghai

SHANGHAI

Hangzhou

Suzhou

East
China Sea
(Dong Hai)

Ningbo

ZHEJIANG

GUIZHOU

Guiyang

HUNAN

Changsha

JIANGXI

Nanchang

Wenzhou

Kunming

YUNNAN

GUANGXI

ZHUANGZU ZIZHIQU

Nanning

GUANGDONG

Guangzhou

FUJIAN

Fuzhou

Quanzhou

Xiamen
(Amoy)

Taibei
(Taipei)

TAIWAN

The People's Republic of China
claims Taiwan as its 23rd Province

Gaoxiong
(Kaohsiung)

Tropic of Cancer

Shenzhen

Hong Kong

Macao
(Xianggang)
(Aomen)

Maoming

Zhanjiang

LAOS

VIETNAM

Ha Noi

Hai Phong

Beihai

Haikou

HAINAN

Hainan Dao

Gulf of Tongking

P A C I F I C

O C E A N

S O U T H

C H I N A   S E A

PHILIPPINES

0   200   400   600   800 KILOMETRES

© Collins Bartholomew Ltd

CHINA CENTRAL AND EAST

This is the most heavily populated part of China, as shown by the numerous cities and the dense network of roads and railways. The relative sparseness of population in the north (Inner Mongolia) stands out. The island of Hainan, in the south, is a province of China in its own right. The other large island shown, Taiwan, functions as an independent nation. Two of China's great rivers are in this region: the Yangtze (or Chang Jiang) and the Yellow River (Huang He).

FACTS

• Taiwan (Republic of China) has been claimed by China since the People's Republic was established in 1949. It is not a member of the United Nations – now the only *de facto* independent country in the world not to be so, other than the Vatican City.

• Hong Kong, formerly a UK possession, was returned to China in 1997 as a Special Administrative Region. Macau (formerly Portuguese) was similarly returned in 1999.

• The Three Gorges Dam project on the Yangtze river is the largest of its kind. Millions of people were relocated and over 100 towns and villages were destroyed during its construction.

GLOSSARY

CHINESE			
Bandao	peninsula	**Jiang**	river
Dao	island	**Ling**	mountain range
He	river	**Shan**	mountain(s)
Hu	lake	**Wan**	bay

1993

2013

The Three Gorges Dam Project on the Yangtze river in central China is the largest hydro-electric scheme in the world in terms of installed generating capacity. Construction of the huge dam created a reservoir 660 km (410 miles) long at its maximum fill, which it reached for the first time in 2010. The project provides large amounts of electricity for a huge area but as with many large dam-building schemes, it has not been without controversy. During its construction over a million people were displaced, the disturbed flow of the Yangtze has affected communities downstream and the full environmental effects of the changes, including silting and landslides, are yet to be seen.

UPON COMPLETION OF THE THREE GORGES DAM PROJECT	
Population resettled	1.2 million
Area inundated	1084 sq km (418 sq miles)
Number of historic sites inundated	1200
Generating capacity	22 500 MW
Money invested	180 billion yuan (22.5 billion $US)

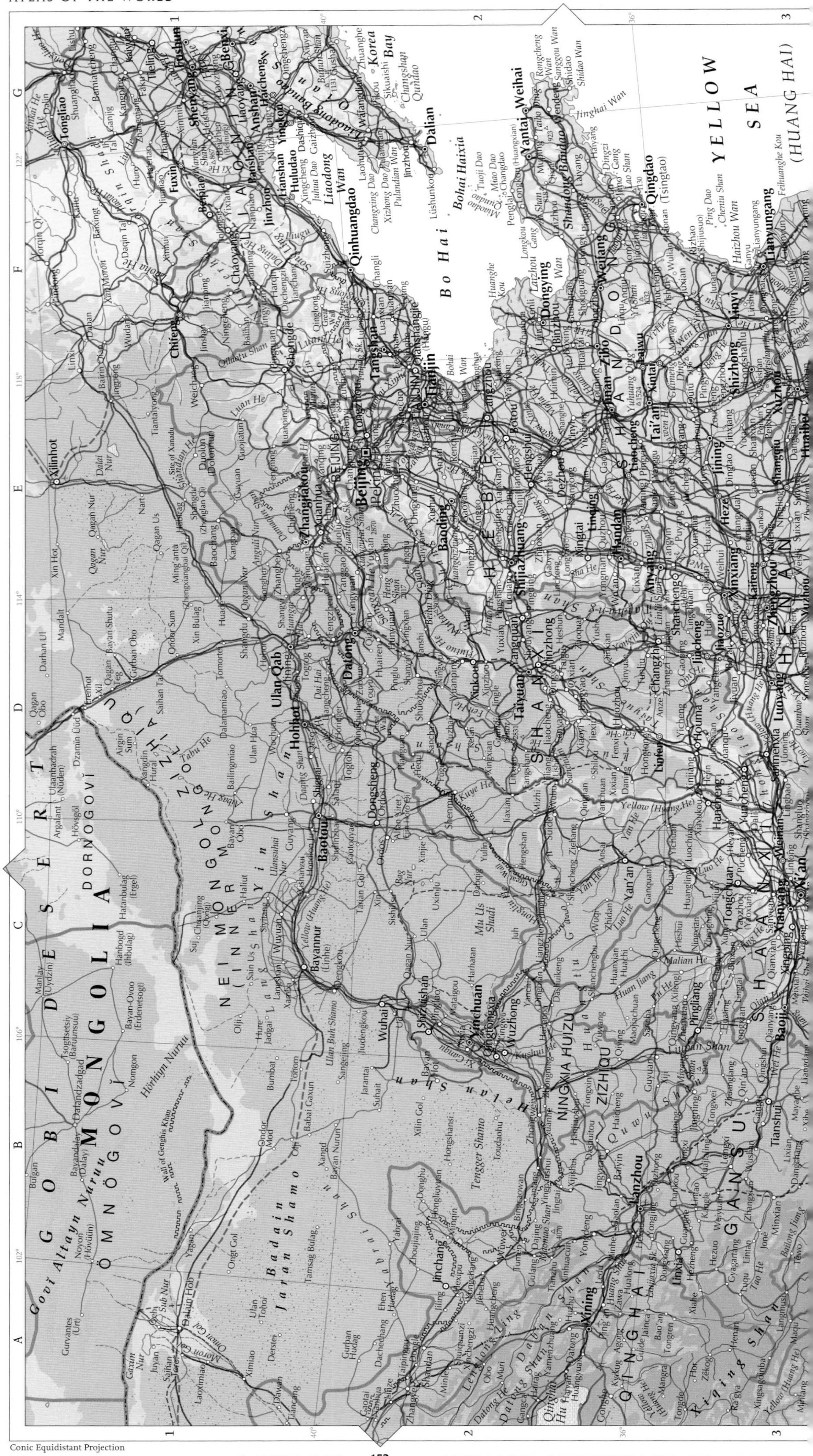

Conic Equidistant Projection

1 : 7 500 000

MILES 0   100   200   300

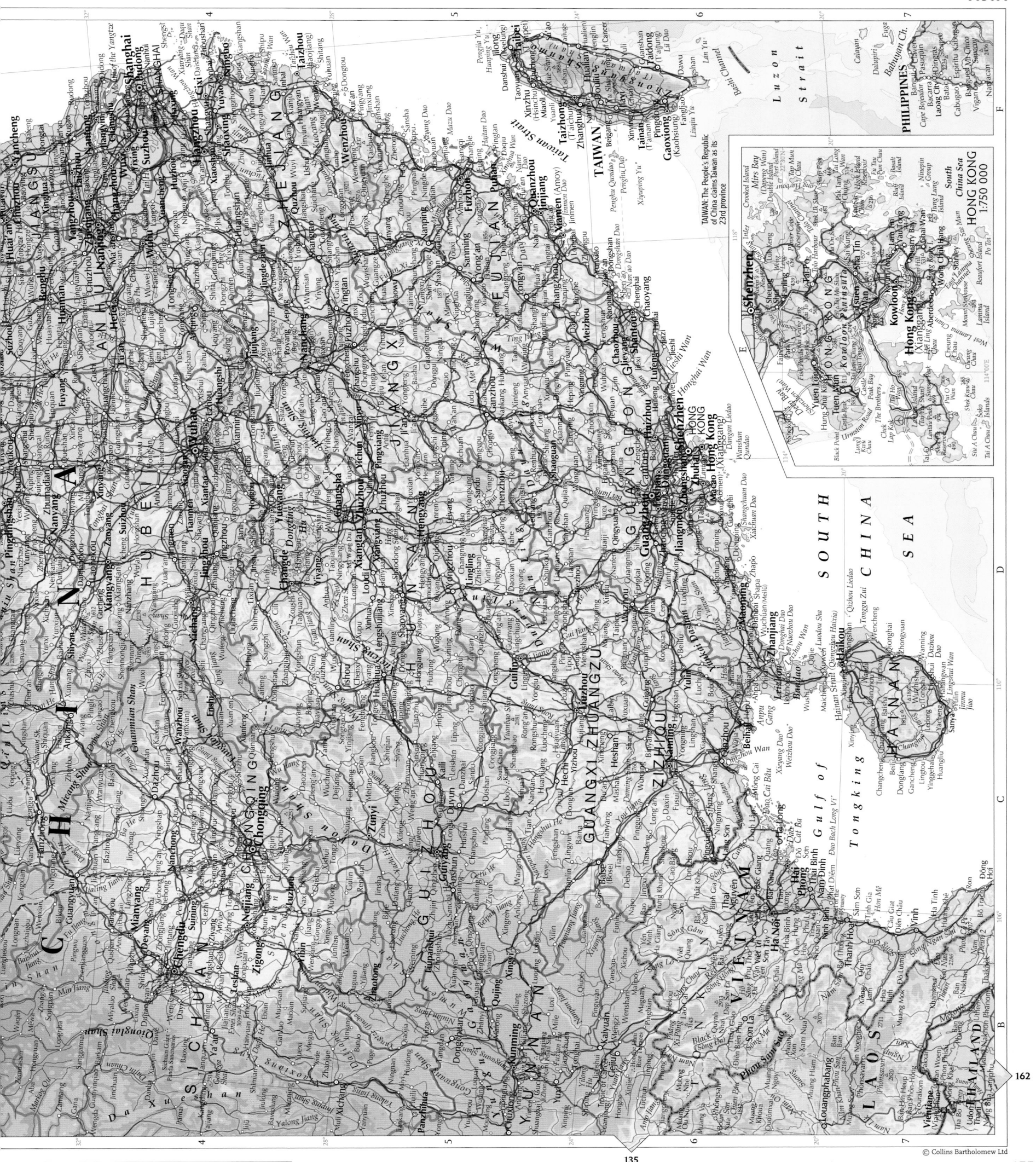

0   100   200   300   400   500 KILOMETRES

JAPAN, NORTH KOREA AND SOUTH KOREA

The map shows Japan, North and South Korea, and neighbouring parts of China and Russia. The area has seen some significant territorial disputes over the years, most notably that between the two Koreas which led to the Korean War in the 1950s, the ownership of the small islets known as Liancourt Rocks (Dok-do to the Koreans and Take-shima to the Japanese)' and the status of the southern Kuril Islands – under Russian control but claimed by Japan. There is also an ongoing disagreement over the naming of the Sea of Japan (known to the Koreans as the East Sea).

FACTS

• In 1964 Japan introduced the world's first high speed train service, called the Shinkansen (bullet train) with a purpose-built line from Tōkyō to Ōsaka. The network has since been expanded and trains can reach 300 km/hr.

• The Korean language is spoken throughout the peninsula and is written with its own set of characters, distinct from either Chinese or Japanese.

• Vladivostock, near the Russo-Chinese border, is Russia's largest port city on the Pacific Ocean and the home port of the Russian Pacific Fleet.

GLOSSARY

CHINESE	
He	river
Ling	mountain range
Shan	mountain(s)

JAPANESE	
-jima	island
-misaki	cape, point
-san	mountain
-shima	island

KOREAN	
-do	island
-kundo	islands
-man	bay
-san	mountain

RUSSIAN	
Khrebet	mountain range
Mys	cape, point
Ostrov	island
Vodokhranilishche	reservoir

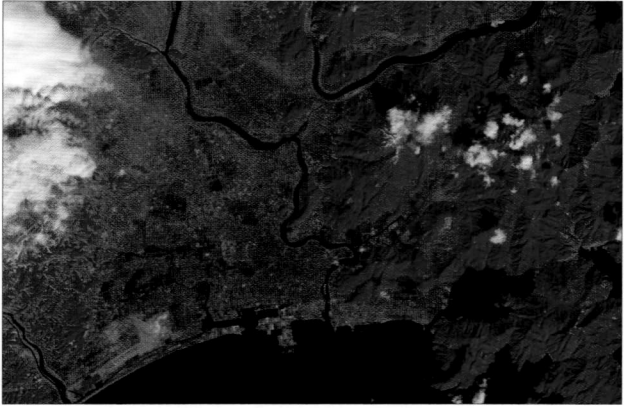

Japan lies directly on the boundary between the Eurasian, Philippine and Pacific tectonic plates. This boundary forms part of the 'Ring of Fire' – the zone around the edge of the Pacific Ocean marked by plate boundaries and therefore highly susceptible to earthquakes and volcanoes. Japan experiences approximately 1500 earthquakes each year but the 9.0 magnitude Tōhoku earthquake that struck on 11th March 2011 was the largest to hit Japan in recorded history. These false-colour images of the city of Ishinomaki show water as blue and vegetation as red. They show the city immediately after the earthquake and subsequent tsunami, and the same area 11 months later. This area is low-lying and well-populated and was one of the areas most affected by the tsunami. The floodwater around the airfield on the coast to the west and also along the rivers can be clearly seen. The later image shows this flooding to have retreated.

Conic Equidistant Projection

1:7 000 000

MILES 0   50   100   150   200

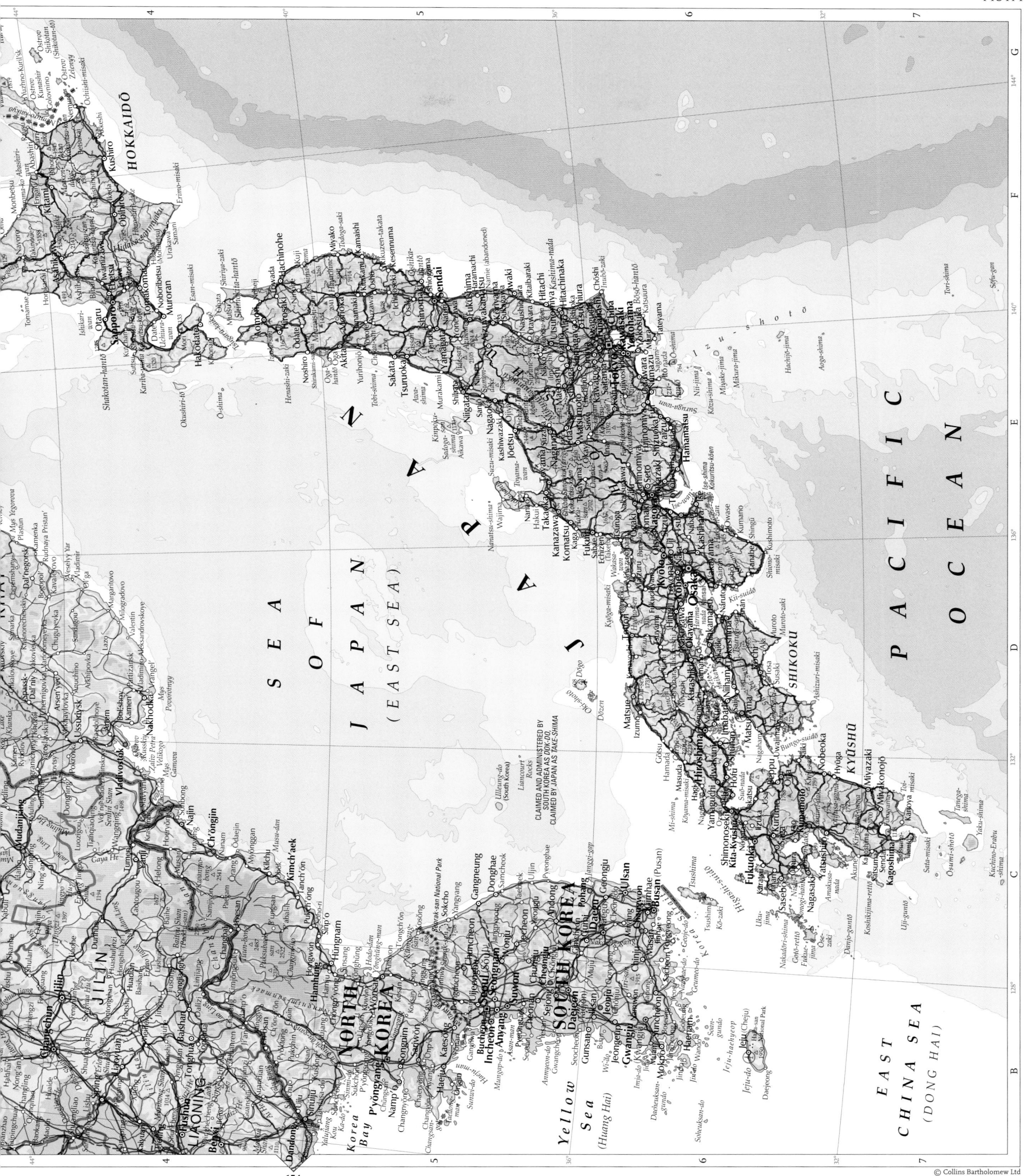

PACIFIC OCEAN

SEA OF JAPAN (EAST SEA)

Yellow Sea (Huang Hai)

EAST CHINA SEA (DONG HAI)

HOKKAIDŌ

JILIN

LIAONING

NORTH KOREA

SOUTH KOREA

SHIKOKU

KYŪSHŪ

CLAIMED AND ADMINISTERED BY
SOUTH KOREA AS DOK-DO,
CLAIMED BY JAPAN AS TAKE-SHIMA

JAPAN

The main islands of Japan form a large, curving archipelago lying off the east coast of Asia. Very much the biggest island is Honshū; to the south are Kyūshū and Shikoku (separated from Honshū by the now-bridged Inland Sea). To the north is Hokkaidō, connected by a long rail tunnel. The islands are volcanic and the region is prone to earthquakes. Japan also controls a far-flung spread of much smaller islands across a large area of the northwest Pacific Ocean.

FACTS

- The Japanese name for Japan, which can be spelt either Nippon or Nihon, means 'Land of the Rising Sun'. The national flag symbolises this, with a red disc on a white background.

- Japan has a long-standing territorial dispute with Russia since the former Soviet Union occupied several previously Japanese-controlled islands at the end of the Kuril island chain, including Kunashir, shown on the far northeast margin of this map.

- The Japanese language is written using three different sets of characters, one of which is derived from Chinese.

- Japanese food, in all its exciting forms, is an increasingly popular cultural export of Japan.

GLOSSARY

JAPANESE			
-dake	mountain	-sanmyaku	mountain range
-jima	island	-shima	island
-misaki	cape, point	-shotō	islands
-san	mountain		

Tōkyō, the capital city of Japan, has been the largest city in the world since 1970. United Nations projections predict that in 2015 it will remain the world's largest city with a metropolitan area population of over 38 million. The image here shows only a small part of the vast conurbation. The pressure on the land has led to major land reclamation projects in Tōkyō Bay – obvious from the angular shape of the coastline. Tōkyō International (Haneda) airport is built entirely on reclaimed land. Vegetation shows as red in this 'false colour' image, making the grounds of the Imperial Palace prominent in the top left.

Conic Equidistant Projection

1:5 000 000

MILES 0   50   100   150   200

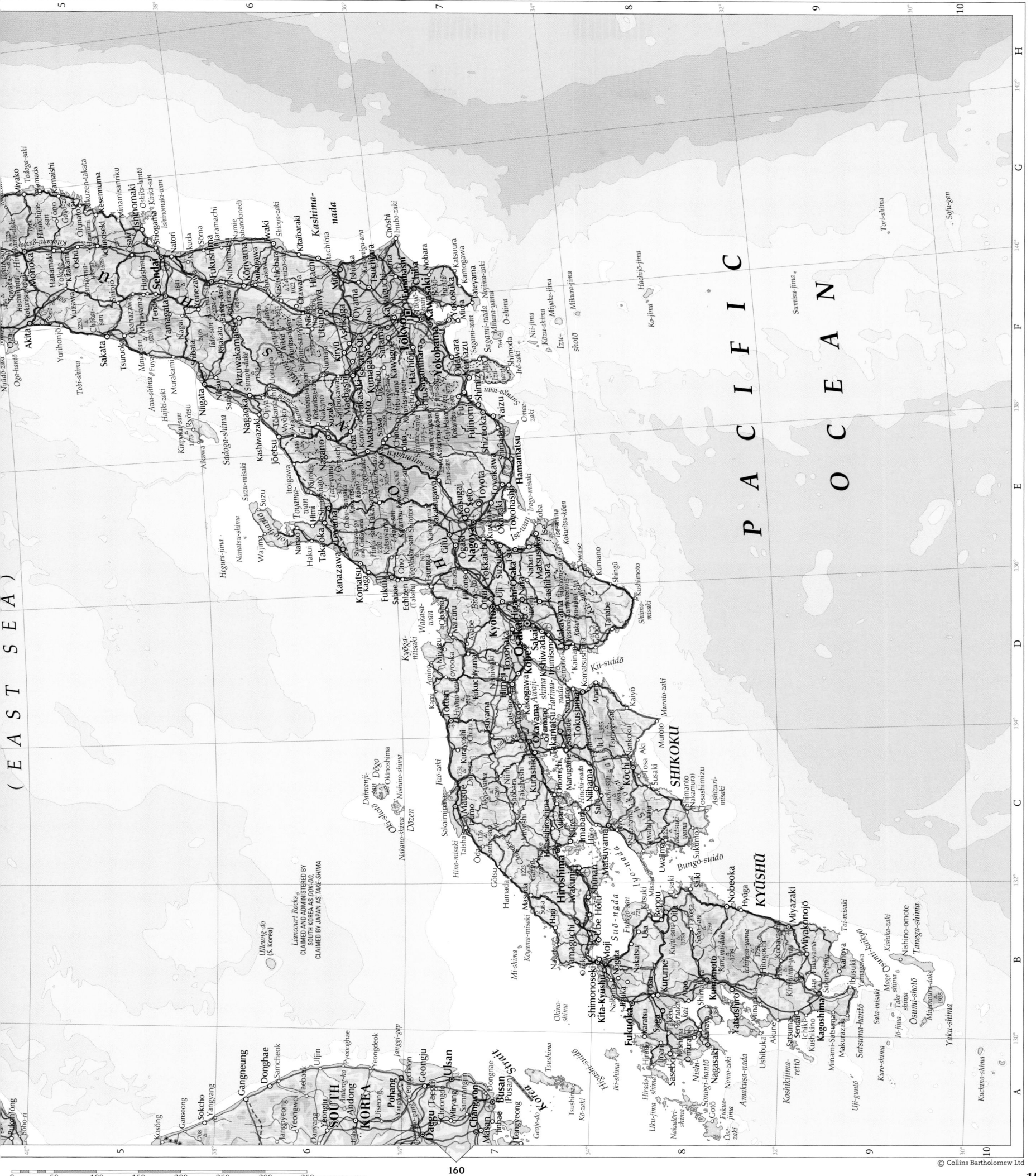

PACIFIC OCEAN

(EAST SEA)

KYŪSHŪ

SHIKOKU

SOUTH KOREA

Korea Strait

© Collins Bartholomew Ltd

0 50 100 150 200 250 300 350 KILOMETRES

160

CHINA NORTHEAST, NORTH KOREA AND SOUTH KOREA PHILIPPINES

The map of Korea shows how the two separate countries of North and South Korea occupy a large peninsula between China and Japan, separating the Yellow Sea from the Sea of Japan (known to the Koreans as the East Sea). The Philippines is a single country consisting of a large group of islands which separates the South China Sea from the Pacific Ocean and which lies between Taiwan and East Malaysia. The two island arcs almost connect with the Malaysian part of Borneo.

FACTS

- The Korean peninsula was divided into North Korea and South Korea in 1948, approximately along the thirty-eighth parallel.

- North Korea retains one of the world's few remaining communist governments. Kim Jong-il, the son of the original president, was known officially as the 'Dear Leader' until his death and succession by his son, Kim Jong-un, in 2011.

- The Philippines is largely English-speaking, but also has an official language known as Filipino (or Pilipino), derived from the native Tagalog language.

- Mount Pinatubo on the island of Luzon erupted violently in 1991, the second largest volcanic eruption of the twentieth century. The resulting cloud of volcanic ash was hundreds of miles wide.

GLOSSARY

INDONESIAN	
Kepulauan	islands

MALAY	
Bukit	hill, mountain
Gunung	mountain
Tanjong	cape, point
Teluk	bay, gulf

KOREAN	
-bong	mountain
-do	island
-gang	river
-haehyŏp	strait
-ho	lake
-man	bay
-san	mountain
-sanmaek	mountain range

The world's largest land reclamation project is the Saemankeum project in southwestern South Korea, just southwest of Kunsan. The 33 km (20.5 miles) sea wall was completed in 2010 as the longest man-made sea barrier in the world. It was built to reclaim land in the estuaries of two rivers, the Mankyung and Tongjin. Once filled, the area will be transformed into new farmland and a large freshwater reservoir. The area affected however, is a sensitive and significant area of tidal marshland. It is an important habitat for hundreds of thousands of migratory birds, and for fish and shellfish – a habitat which will be lost by the creation of 400 sq km (154 sq miles) of new land.

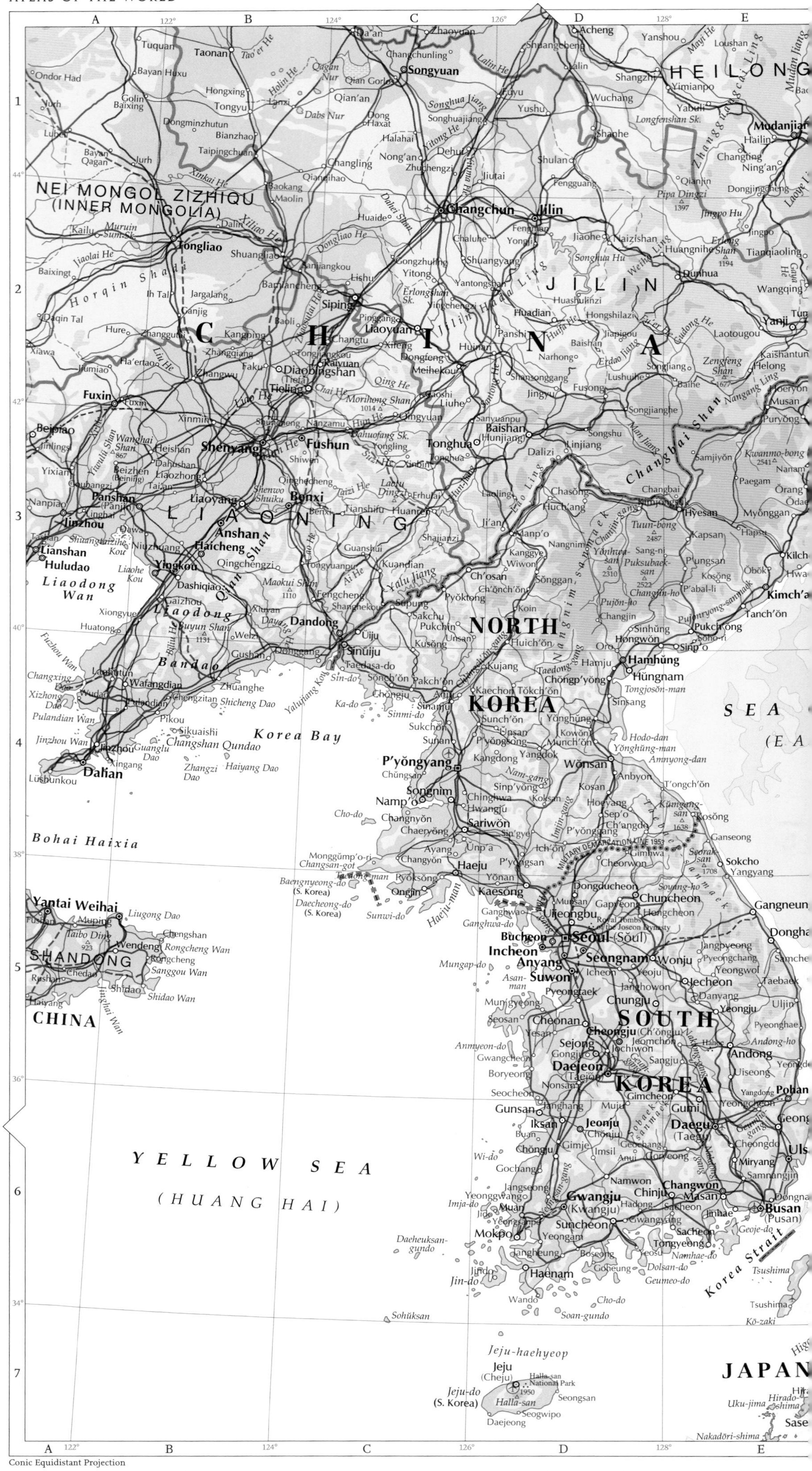

Conic Equidistant Projection

1:5 000 000   MILES 0   50   100   150   0   50   100   150 KILOMETRE

PHILIPPINES

South China Sea / Luzon

LUZON STRAIT
Balintang Channel
Babuyan Channel
PHILIPPINE SEA

North I.
Mabudis
Itbayat
Batan Islands
Basco Batan
Ibuhos Sabtang

Calayan
Dalupiri Babuyan Islands Didicas
Fuga Camiguin
Babuyan
Cape Bojeador
Pasuquin
Bacarra Bangui Claveria
Laoag City Cape Engaño
Batac Escarpada Point
Espiritu Sicapoo San Vicente
Bangued Abulug Aparri Palaui
Cabugao Buguey
Vigan Tuguegarao Cape San Ildefonso
Narvacan Mt Chico Enrile
Santa Cruz Bontoc Ilagan
Candon Roxas Divilican Bay
Bangar Echague San Ildefonso Peninsula
Luna Santiago Palanan Point
San Fernando Trinidad Bayombong Palanan
Bolinao Baguio Bambang Casiguran
Lingayen Bani Fabian Cape Encanto
Gulf Dagupan Baler Bay
Alaminos Rosario San Jose Baler
Lingayen San Carlos Laur Cape Encanto
Caiman Point Camiling Cuyapo Palayan
Santa Cruz Tarlac Cabanatuan LUZON
Masinloc Palauig Capas Gapan
Iba Angeles Mabalacat Polillo
Mt Pinatubo San Fernando Angat Polillo Islands
1660 Mexico Valenzuela
San Antonio Orani Quezon City Patnanongan
Olongapo Balanga Manila Jomalig
Sampaloc Point Cavite Pasig Pacete Calagua Islands
Taytay Santa Cruz Paracale Pandan
Maragondon Tagaytay City San Cruz Alabat Panay Catanduanes
Nasugbu Lipa Lucena Calauag San Andres Virac
Lubang Islands Batangas San Pablo Libmanan Nagumbuaya Point
Lubang Rosario Tayabas Bay Lucban Naga Lagonoy
Golo Verde I. Pass Mulanay Pili Buhi Gulf
Lubang Paluan Boac Pasacao Iriga Tabaco
Cape Calavite Calapan Bondoc Pen. Ligao Mayon Rapurapu
Mamburao Naujan Pola Simara Daraga Legazpi
Mindoro Mt Halcon Marinduque Banton Donsol Sorsogon
2585 Pinamalayan Burias Magallanes Bulusan
Sablayan San Teresa Romblon Bulan Irosin
San Jose Bongabong Roxas Tablas Masbate Batag
Calauit New Buenavista Sibuyan Ticao Laoang
Busuanga Busuanga Looc Cajidiocan Sea San Palapag
Calamian Coron Bulalacao Tablas Cataingan Lapinig
Group Culion Semirara Masbate Placer Catarman
Culion Culion Islands Borocay Esperanza Calbayog Oras
Linapacan Strait Sibay Nabas Catbalogan SAMAR
Linapacan El Nido Iloc Pandan Panay Naval Borongan
Taytay Pandan B. San Isidro Calbiga
Tuluran Cuyo Agutaya Dit Kalibo Biliran Catarman General MacArthur
Imuruan Bay Islands Cuyo Sigma Ormoc Calicoan
Roxas Cuyo Roxas Barbaza Roxas Baybay Guiuan
Green Island San Jose de VISAYAN Madridejos Handig Point
Cleopatra Buenavista PANAY Passi Cadiz Leyte Gulf
Needle Peaked Point Dumaran Tobias Fornier Ajuy Silay Cebu Abuyog Desolation Point
Babuyan Honda Bay Dalangaman Islands Pototan Bacolod San Carlos Silago
Apurahuan Dumaran Bayo Point Iloilo Bago Tanjay Lapu-Lapu Sogod
Puerto Princesa Panay Gulf Guihulngan Cebu Mansin Joroto
Panagtaran Point Calusa Cagayan Aguisan Talisay Camotes Sea Dinagat
Aborlan Cavili Cagayan Islands Sipalay Cadiz Cargar Bohol Str. Siargao
Malabang Arena NEGROS Bais Carmen General Luna
Quezon The Teeth Cantilan Pahaon Bucas Grande
Dumaran Hinoba-an Pamplona Tagbilaran Guindulman Dapa Siargao
Tubbataha Reefs Basay Bohol Surigao Placer
North Islet Siaton Dumaguete Panglao Bohol Sea Mambajao General Luna
Mantalingajan South Islet Siquijor Tanjay Lake Mainit Madrid
Brooke's Point Talisayan Diuata Pt Cauit Pt
Rio Tuba Tagolo Pt Cantilan
Bancalan Sulu Sea Dipolog Lianga
Bonobono Manukan El Salvador Oroquieta Cagayan Bay Bislig
Balabac Presidente Manuel A Roxas Iligan de Oro Prosperidad Hinatuan
Balabac Sindangan Ozamiz MINDANAO Malaybalay Lingig
C. Melville Liloy Aurora Pagadian Marawi Mt Ragang Cateel Bay
Bancoran Siocon Tubod Lala Lake 2954 Bangai Bay
Balambangan Banggi Aliacu Malabang Kibawe Panabo Caraga
San Miguel Is Sibuco Tungawan Iligan Bay Baguio Compostela
Keenapusan Zamboanga Peninsula Bongo Cotabato Kapuntakan Tagum Pantukan
Cagayan de Zamboanga Olutanga Bay Kidapawan Babak
Tawi-Tawi Sangboy Islands Moro Gulf Pikit Davao Manay
Zamboanga Basilan Strait Gulf Talayan Diolog Samal Mayo Bay
Malawali Isabela Matanal Pt Upi Buluan Lapon Mount Hamiguitan
Pangutaran Pilas Lebak Norala Palatia Range Wildlife Sanctuary
Kudat Kulassein Basilan Banga Davao Governor Generoso
Tandek Pangutaran Group Bubuan Bolod Is Tapiantana Palimbang Kalaong Surup Cape San Agustin
Teluk Paitan Tongquil Kiamba General Santos
Gunung Langkon Laparan Cap Parang Glan Jose Abad
Tambuyukon Doc Can Jolo Samales Group Santos
Jambongan Dammai Lugus Jolo Tapul Group Kalibo Sarangani
Teluk Labuk Siasi Tandubas Sarangani
Beluran Tanjong Sugut Lapac Miangas (Indonesia)
Lingkabau Parang Siasi Sarangani Kepulauan
Sandakan Balimbing Tapul Group Balut Islands Nanusa
Labuk Panglima Sugala Tapul Islands Karatung Marampit
Tambisan Sugala Manuk Manka
SABAH Gunung Bagahak Tawi-Tawi Sulu Archipelago Kepulauan
MALAYSIA Magdalena Sibutu Passage Essang Mangupung Kepulauan
Melau Bukit Panglima Simunul Karkaralong Gemeh Talaud
Kinabatangan Lokan Ubian Sumber Sonsorol Pulutan Niampak
Lanas Kuamut Balung Bum-Bum Salibabu Lirung
Bunyu Tawau Semporna Celebes Karakelong Mangarang
Tenom Kalabakan Sebatik Sea Sangir Kaburuang
INDONESIA Sembakung Mandul Awu Bukide Tahuna
Tarakan Tapahmerah Damar
Tarakan Sangir Galipaeng Kaloma

INDONESIA

Scale

Mercator Projection
1:7 000 000
© Collins Bartholomew Ltd

MILES 0   50   100   150
0   50   100   150   200   250   300 KILOMETRES

161

THAILAND, CAMBODIA AND PENINSULAR MALAYSIA
INDONESIA WEST

The left-hand map shows Indo-China, Thailand, southern Myanmar (or Burma) and Malaysia. The city state of Singapore is also featured. Indo-China – whose name relates to former influences from India and China – consists of Laos, Vietnam and Cambodia. Malaysia is divided into Peninsular Malaysia on the Asian mainland, and East Malaysia (shown on the right-hand map), which consists of Sabah and Sarawak, on the mainly Indonesian island of Borneo, and Labuan, just off the coast of Sabah. The very wealthy, independent sultanate of Brunei lies on the north coast of Borneo.

FACTS

- Country names change: Cambodia used to be Kampuchea; Myanmar was officially adopted in the 1980s and is now used in place of Burma; Thailand used to be called Siam.

- Cambodia suffered huge problems, including widespread massacres, under the Khmer Rouge régime in the late 1970s. It now once again attracts many visitors to its notable historic sites such as Angkor.

- The small island of Krakatau (more well known as Krakatoa), between Java and Sumatra, exploded in a devastating volcanic eruption in 1883. The resultant tsunami claimed around 33 000 lives; 90 per cent of the total death toll.

GLOSSARY

BURMESE	
Kyun	island

INDONESIAN	
Gunung	mountain
Kepulauan	islands
Tanjong, Tanjung (Tg)	cape, point
Teluk (Tk)	gulf, bay

MALAY	
Gunung	mountain
Kuala	river mouth

THAI	
Ko	island

VIETNAMESE	
Dao	island
Mui	cape, point
Sông	river

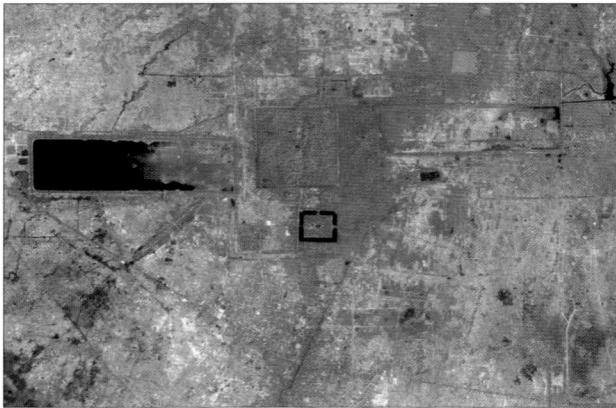

The ruins of Angkor, in western Cambodia, are an UNESCO world heritage site and are among the most important archaeological sites in Asia. The site was originally founded in the first century and consists of the ruins of successive Khmer capitals. The ruins remained buried in the jungle until they were rediscovered and brought to the world's attention by a French missionary in the mid-nineteenth century. The town of Angkor Thom, and the huge temple of Angkor Wat, were highly elaborate and spectacular constructions which even as ruins draw around a million visitors each year – a situation which brings major challenges to the conservation of this important site.

1 : 7 500 000

Mercator Projection

MILES 0   100   150

0   100   200 KILOMETRE

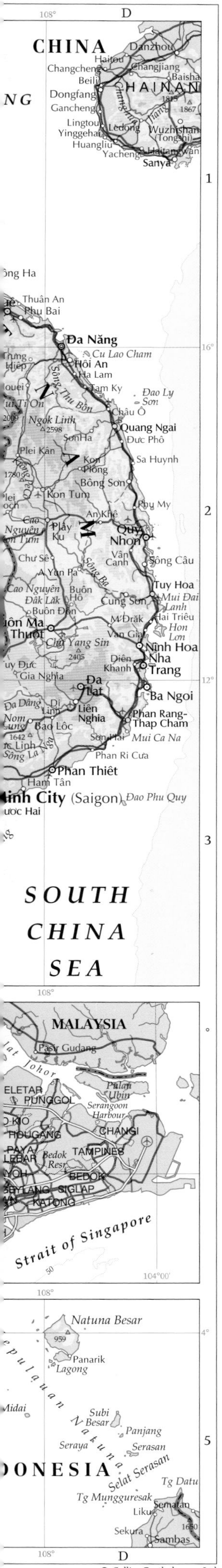

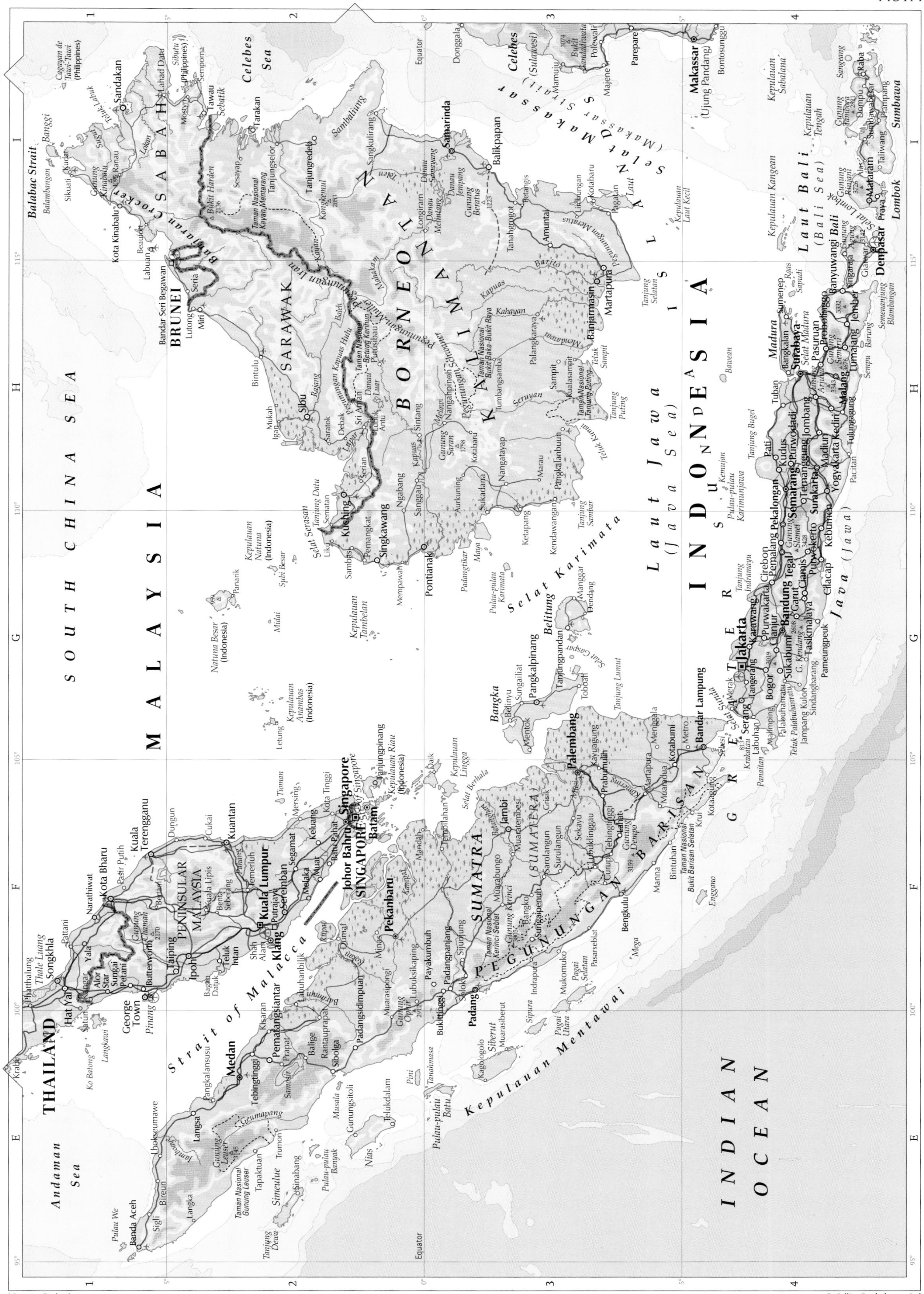

CHINA

HAINAN

SOUTH CHINA SEA

SOUTH CHINA SEA

Balabac Strait

Cagayan de Tawi-Tawi (Philippines)

Celebes Sea

SABAH

Kota Kinabalu
Sandakan
Lahad Datu
Tawau
Tarakan

Banjur Crocker

BRUNEI
Bandar Seri Begawan
Miri
Seria
Lutong

SARAWAK

Bintulu
Sibu
Mukah

KALIMANTAN

BORNEO

Samarinda
Balikpapan
Banjarmasin
Martapura

Celebes (Sulawesi)

Makassar (Ujung Pandang)

Laut Bali (Bali Sea)

Denpasar
Mataram
Lombok
Sumbawa

Madura
Surabaya
Malang
Kediri
Yogyakarta
Surakarta
Semarang

INDONESIA

Pontianak
Kuching
Singkawang
Sambas

Laut Jawa (Java Sea)

Kepulauan Natuna (Indonesia)

Natuna Besar (Indonesia)

Kepulauan Anambas (Indonesia)

MALAYSIA

Bangka
Pangkalpinang

Belitung

Selat Karimata

Jakarta
Bandung
Bogor
Serang
Bandar Lampung

Palembang

Jambi

SUMATERA (SUMATRA)

PEGUNUNGAN BARISAN

Java (Jawa)

THAILAND

Narathiwat
Pattani
Yala
Songkhla
Hat Yai
Alor Star
Kota Bharu
Kuala Terengganu
George Town
Pinang
Ipoh
Taiping
Butterworth
Kuantan

PENINSULAR MALAYSIA

Kuala Lumpur
Klang
Seremban
Melaka
Muar
Johor Bahru

SINGAPORE
Singapore
Batam

Pekanbaru

Strait of Malacca

Medan
Pematangsiantar
Sibolga
Padang
Bukittinggi

Andaman Sea

Banda Aceh
Sigli
Langsa
Lhokseumawe

Pulau We

Nias

Kepulauan Mentawai

INDIAN OCEAN

MALAYSIA

Strait of Singapore

CHANGI

Natuna Besar
Panarik

INDONESIA

Selat Serasan

Mercator Projection

1:10 000 000   MILES 0   100   200

0   100   200   300   400 KILOMETRES

© Collins Bartholomew Ltd

163

EUROPE PHYSICAL

The continent consists of a complex, irregular arrangement of extensive plains, plateaus, and mountain ranges. There are several significant island groups – notably the British Isles and Iceland in the Atlantic, and in the Mediterranean the Balearic Islands, Corsica and Sardinia, Sicily, and Crete. The general outline of the continent is complicated further by a number of prominent peninsulas, among which are the Balkan Peninsula (principally occupied by Greece), Italy, the Iberian Peninsula (Spain and Portugal), Denmark, and Scandinavia consisting of Norway and Sweden.

FACTS

• The Danube flows through seven countries and has six different local names – Donau (Austria and Germany), Dunaj (Slovakia), Duna (Hungary), Dunav (Serbia), Dunarea (Romania) and Dunay (Ukraine). 'Danube' is the conventional English name.

• All the seas on this map (except the Caspian) are in effect branches of the Atlantic Ocean.

• Europe's four highest mountains – El'brus, Gora Dykh-Tau, Shkhara and Kazbek – are in the Caucasus. Mont Blanc, the highest mountain in the Alps, is fifth.

• By stretching north–south over more than 45 degrees of latitude, Europe has a greatly varied climate, from the hot Mediterranean to the frozen Arctic.

HIGHEST MOUNTAINS	m	ft
El'brus, Russia	5 642	18 510
Gora Dykh-Tau, Russia	5 204	17 073
Shkhara, Georgia/Russia	5 201	17 063
Kazbek, Georgia/Russia	5 047	16 558
Mont Blanc, France/Italy	4 810	15 781
Dufourspitze, Italy/Switzerland	4 634	15 203

LARGEST ISLANDS	sq km	sq miles
Great Britain	218 476	84 354
Iceland	102 820	39 699
Ireland	83 045	32 064
Ostrov Severnyy (Novaya Zemlya North Island)	47 079	18 177
Spitsbergen	37 814	14 600
Ostrov Yuzhnyy (Novaya Zemlya South Island)	33 246	12 836
Sicily (Sicilia)	25 426	9 817

LONGEST RIVERS	km	miles
Volga	3 688	2 292
Danube	2 850	1 771
Dnieper	2 285	1 420
Kama	2 028	1 260
Don	1 931	1 200
Pechora	1 802	1 120

LARGEST LAKES	sq km	sq miles
Caspian Sea	371 000	143 243
Lake Ladoga (Ladozhskoye Ozero)	18 390	7 100
Lake Onega (Onezhskoye Ozero)	9 600	3 707
Vänern	5 585	2 156
Rybinskoye Vodokhranilishche	5 180	2 000

Orthographic Projection

1:17 500 000   MILES 0   200   400   600   800

Bjørnøya

Barents Sea

North Cape
Varangerhalvøya
Poluostrov
Rybachiy

Zemlya
Frantsa-Iosifa

Ostrov
Severnyy

Novaya Zemlya

*Kara
Sea*

Ostrov
Yuzhnyy

Ostrov
Kolguyev

Cheshskaya Guba

Pechora

Yenisey

Arctic Circle

75°

75°

90°

105°

Inarijärvi

Lapland

Ozero
Ekostrovskaya
Imandra

**Kola
Peninsula**

White Sea

Mezen

Severnaya Dvina

Vychegda

Ob'

Irtysh

Vesterålen
Lofoten
Vestfjorden

Scandinavia

Oulujärvi

Lule
Ume
Inalls

Pielinen

Lake
Onega

Kamskoye
Vodokhranilishche

Kuybyshevskoye
Vodokhranilishche

Ural Mountains

Altai Mountains

Gulf of Bothnia

Saimaa

Lake
Ladoga

Rybinskoye
Vodokhranilishche

Volga

Lake Balkhash

Tien Shan

Åland

Gulf of Finland

Ozero
Il'men'

Lake
Peipus

Kama

Vänern

Hiiumaa

Saaremaa

Gulf
of Riga

Central Russian Upland

Volga

Aral Sea

Ysyk-Köl

90°

Vättern

Gotland

Baltic Sea

Öland

Bornholm

Gulf of
Gdansk

Dnieper

Kuybyshevskoye
Vodoskhovyshche

Don

*North
Sea*

Jutland
Zealand
Fyn
Lolland

Kattegat

Skagerrak

North European Plain

Vistula

Bug

Warta

Odra

Elbe

*Pripet
Marshes*

Kremenchuts'ke
Vodoskhovyshche

Tsimlyanskoye
Vodokhranilishche

Volga

*Caspian
Sea*

Hindu Kush

Frisian Islands

IJsselmeer

Weser

Erzgebirge

Sudety

Vistula

Tisa

Kakhovs'ke
Vodoskhovyshche

Gulf of
Kohtla

Stavropol'skaya
Vozvyshennost'

Garabogazköl
Aylagy

Plateau
de l'Ardenne

Rhine

Moselle
Saône

Böhmer Wald

Tatra Mts

Carpathian Mountains

Dnister

Dnieper

Sea
of Azov

Karkinits'ka
Zatoka

Crimea

Caucasus

Elbrus
5642
Gora Dykh-Tau
5204

Massif
Central

Vosges

Danube

Danube

Lake
Constance

Balaton

Sava

Transylvanian Alps

Morava

Danube

Black Sea

The Gulf

Lake
Geneva

A L P S

Mont Blanc
4810

Dolomites

Lago di
Garda

Po

*Dinaric
Alps*

Balkan Mountains

Zagros Mountains

ees

Golfe
du Lion

Ligurian
Sea

Apennines

Adriatic Sea

Rhône

Costa Brava

Corsica

Rhodope Mountains

Sea of
Marmara

Tigris

60°

30°

45°

Balearic Islands

Sardinia

**Tyrrhenian
Sea**

Capo Carbonara

Isole
Lipari

Strait of
Otranto

Thasos

Pindus Mts

**Aegean
Sea**

Limnos

Chios

Euphrates

Minorca

Majorca

Corfu

Evvoia

Andros

Ionian Islands

Ibiza

Formentera

Sicilian Channel

Sicily

*Ionian
Sea*

Peloponnisos

Cyclades

Dodecanese

Rhodes

Karpathos

Cyprus

M E D I T E R R A N E A N   S E A

Malta

Kythira

Kritiko Pelagos

Crete

15°

30°

30°

45°

0   200   400   600   800   1000   1200 KILOMETRES

EUROPE POLITICAL

Europe's dense jigsaw of countries reflects the complex history of its many national groupings. The political map was redrawn significantly after the First and Second World Wars, and changes have continued since – Germany reunified in 1990, Yugoslavia and the former Soviet Union broke up in 1991, and Czechoslovakia was divided into two in 1993. Many European countries are small by world standards – some are among the world's smallest – but European Russia is part of the largest country in the world.

FACTS

• The European Union increased its membership from fifteen to twenty-eight members in 2013, with several other countries keen to join. It now includes Bulgaria, Romania and Croatia, and several eastern European countries, but not Norway, Switzerland or Iceland.

• Iceland and the Faroe Islands belong culturally and linguistically to Scandinavia.

• Europe has the two smallest independent countries in the world – Vatican City and Monaco.

• Since the Yugoslav civil war of 1991–1995 the country has been broken up. The most recent area to declare independence from Serbia is Kosovo, in February 2008.

LARGEST COUNTRIES	Area	
	sq km	sq miles
Russia	17 075 400	6 592 849
Ukraine	603 700	233 090
France	543 965	210 026
Spain	504 782	194 897
Sweden	449 964	173 732
Germany	357 022	137 849
Finland	338 145	130 559
Norway	323 878	125 050
Poland	312 683	120 728
Italy	301 245	116 311

MOST POPULATED COUNTRIES	Population
Russia	142 834 000
Germany	82 727 000
France	64 291 000
United Kingdom	63 136 000
Italy	60 990 000
Spain	46 927 000
Ukraine	45 239 000
Poland	38 217 000
Romania	21 699 000
Netherlands	16 759 000

CAPITALS		
Largest population	**Moscow,** Russia	12 144 000
Smallest population	**Vatican City**	800
Most northerly	**Reykjavík,** Iceland	64° 39' N
Most southerly	**Valletta,** Malta	35° 54' N
Highest	**Andorra la Vella,** Andorra	1 029 m/ 3 376 ft

NORTH AMERICA

Baffin Bay

Greenland

Spitsbergen

Longyearbyen

Greenland Sea

Arctic Circle

Jan Mayen (Norway)

Denmark Strait

ICELAND

Reykjavík

NORWAY SI

Faroe Islands (Denmark)
Tórshavn

Shetland Islands

Orkney Islands

Rockall

Outer Hebrides

SCOTLAND

Glasgow   Edinburgh

NORTHERN IRELAND
Belfast

UNITED KINGDOM

Dublin   Manchester   Leeds
Liverpool
IRELAND

WALES   Birmingham
ENGLAND
Cardiff

London

English Channel

Channel Islands

Brest   Rennes

Nantes

F

ATLANTIC

OCEAN

Bay of Biscay

Bordeaux

A Coruña   Bilbao
P
Zaragoza

Flores

Azores (Portugal)

São Jorge   Terceira

Ponta do Pico   Ponta Delgada
São Miguel

Oporto   Salamanca
Madrid

PORTUGAL   SPAIN
Tagus
Valenci

Arquipélago dos Açores

Santa Maria

Lisbon

Córdoba
Seville   Cartage

Cádiz   Málaga
Gibraltar (U.K.)
Ceuta (Spain)
Melilla (Spain)

Madeira (Portugal)   Ilha de Porto Santo
Funchal

Orthographic Projection

1 : 17 500 000   MILES 0   200   400   600   800

0   200   400   600   800   1000   1200 KILOMETRES

NORTHERN EUROPE

The map emphasizes the sheer size of European Russia (ending at the Ural Mountains in the east) relative to the rest of northern Europe. Also apparent are the extensive plains of Eastern Europe and the mountain ranges of Scandinavia, the Alps and the Carpathian Mountains. To the south and east of the Scandinavian peninsula is an intricate network of seas and straits centred on the Baltic Sea. Also prominent are Iceland, far to the north-west, the British Isles – separated from the continental mainland by only about 34 kilometres (21 miles) across the Strait of Dover – and the Danish-controlled Faroe Islands.

FACTS

- The Baltic Sea is truly international – the islands of Öland and Gotland belong to Sweden, Bornholm to Denmark, the Åland Islands to Finland, and Hiiumaa and Saaremaa to Estonia.

- Much of this area consists of the North European Plain. As a result, many of the major roads and railways run straight for great distances, and the map shows how Moscow in particular is a focus for these routes.

- The Russian city of St Petersburg, founded by the Tsar Peter the Great, was first renamed Petrograd in 1914, then Leningrad, after the communist leader, in 1924. It reverted to its original name in 1991.

GLOSSARY

FAROESE	
-oy	island

ICELANDIC	
-jökull	glacier, ice cap

RUSSIAN	
Guba	gulf, bay
Mys	cape, point
Ozero	lake
Poluostrov	peninsula
Vodokhranilishche	reservoir
Zaliv	gulf, bay

	EU member
	EU applicant
	Non EU member

The European Union (EU) was originally created as the European Economic Community (EEC) in 1957 by the Treaty of Rome. The six founder members were Belgium, France, West Germany, Italy, Luxembourg, and the Netherlands. Since 1957 the EU has grown and now has twenty-eight member states. The original EEC members cooperated over trade and the economy but the EU today is a political union dealing with many subjects of importance in everyday life, including regional development, security and justice and environmental protection. Nineteen of the current members also share a single currency, the Euro.

European Union (EU) Headquarters in Brussels.

Conic Equidistant Projection

1:10 000 000

MILES 0   100   150   200   250   300

169

SCANDINAVIA AND THE BALTIC STATES

Two groups of countries appear on this map: Scandinavia, and the Baltic states of Estonia, Latvia, and Lithuania. The latter three were parts of the former Soviet Union. Norway, Sweden and Denmark speak languages that are very closely related to each other, while Finland speaks a quite different language whose only close relative in the region is Estonian. Sami (Lappish) is spoken in parts of the north, an area known as Lappland. Faroese is the closest relative to the Icelandic language. A small enclave of Russia, centred on the city of Kaliningrad, is sandwiched between Lithuania and Poland.

FACTS

- Denmark and Sweden have been linked since 2000 by a major bridge over the Öresund strait. Denmark has also built long bridges between its main islands, notably over the Great Belt sea channel.

- The Åland Islands, although part of Finland, are Swedish-speaking and enjoy a considerable degree of autonomy. Swedish is also spoken widely in the southwestern coastal areas of Finland.

- Iceland is physically isolated in the North Atlantic, and is far closer to Greenland than to mainland Europe. Its capital, Reykjavík, is the world's northernmost national capital.

- Lakes cover almost 10 per cent of the total land area of Finland.

GLOSSARY

FINNISH	
-järvi	lake
kansallispuisto	national park

ICELANDIC	
-flói	gulf, bay
-jökull	glacier, ice cap

NORWEGIAN	
-dal	valley
-halvøya	peninsula

SWEDISH	
älven	river
-bukten	gulf, bay

Iceland's location on the Mid-Atlantic Ridge makes it a hotspot for active volcanoes. The boundary between the American and Eurasian plates crosses the 'land of ice and fire' from north to south and the country's largest volcanoes – Katla, Grimsvotn and Hekla – all lie along this boundary. Also on the boundary is Eyjafjallajökull. Although not a major volcanic event compared to many others, the eruption of Eyjafjallajökull in 2010 was notable because of the subsequent ash cloud that disrupted air travel across western and northern Europe. There were fears of similar disruption when Bárðarbunga, Iceland's second highest mountain, erupted in late 2014 (see image). However, even though air quality was affected, there was no disruption to flights. The eruption ended at the end of February 2015.

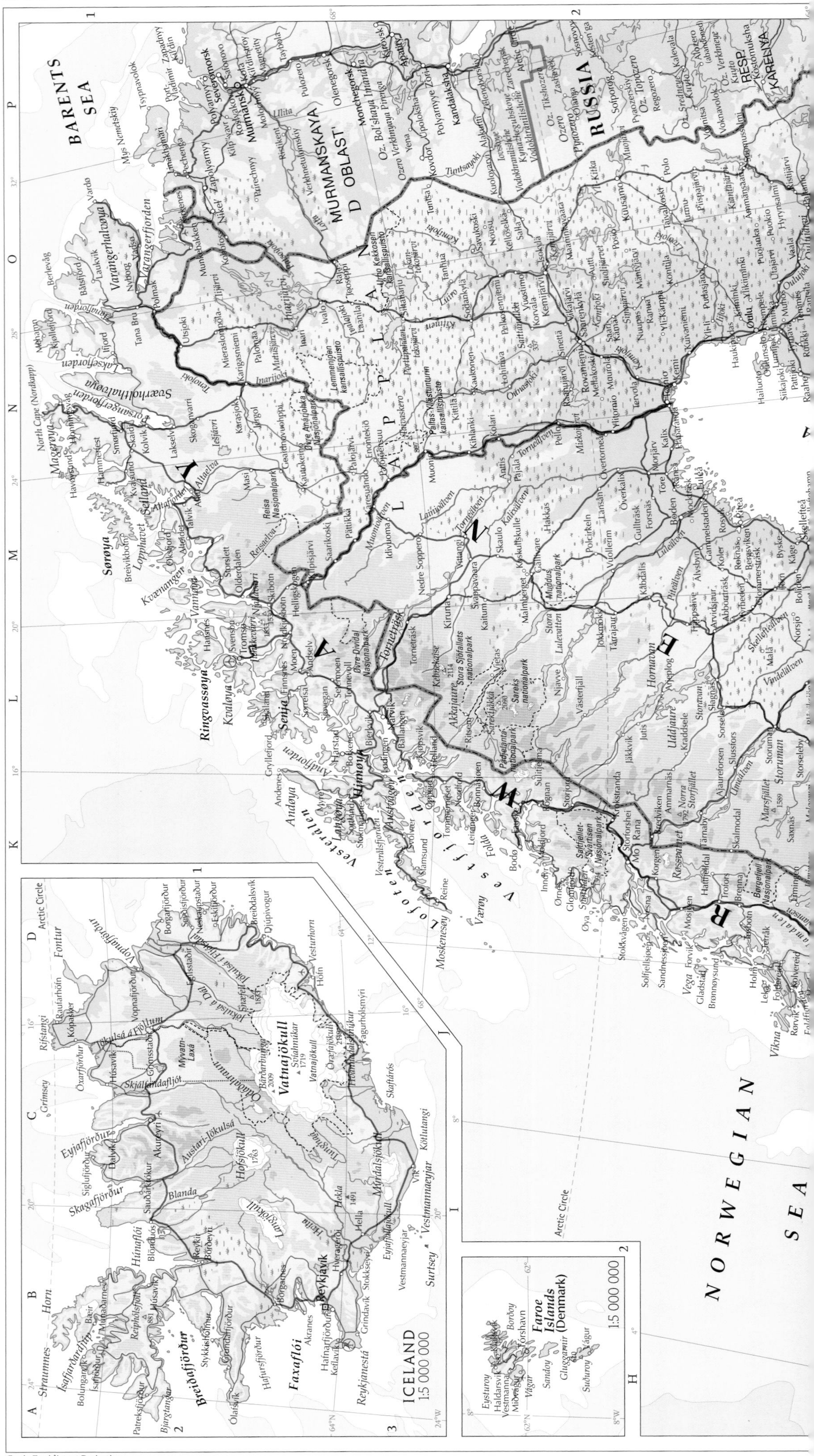

Conic Equidistant Projection

1 : 5 000 000

MILES 0   50   100   150   200

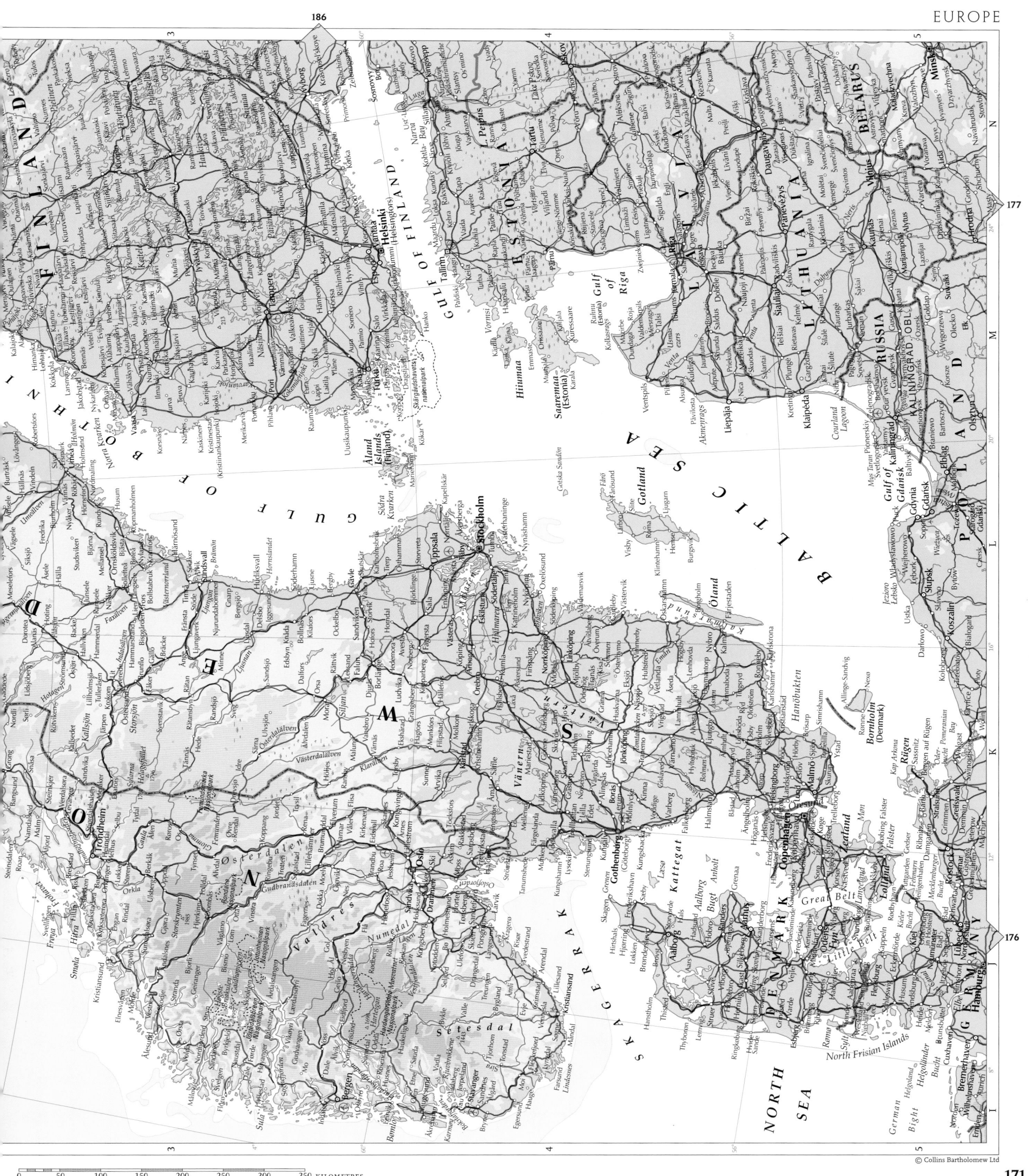

0   50   100   150   200   250   300   350 KILOMETRES

ENGLAND AND WALES

England and Wales together form the southern part of Great Britain – the largest island of the British Isles and the largest in Europe. England is separated from the rest of mainland Europe by the English Channel and the North Sea, and from Ireland by the Irish Sea. The backbone of Wales is the broad range of the Cambrian Mountains, while northern England has the Pennines as its main chain of hills, with a rugged, mountainous offshoot in the Lake District of Cumbria.

FACTS

- The term 'British Isles' signifies the group of islands of which Great Britain is the major component. The term 'Britain' refers only to the main island, although the terms 'Britain' and 'British' are commonly used when referring to the UK as a whole.

- The Isle of Man is a separate entity from the United Kingdom, and has a parliament (the Tynwald) which is much older than that of the UK – over 1000 years old.

- The English Channel is known in French as 'La Manche', meaning 'the sleeve'.

- The Channel Tunnel, which provides a rail link between England and France, was opened in 1994 – almost 200 years after the idea was first proposed in 1806.

GLOSSARY

GAELIC	
Ben	mountain
Creag	mountain
Loch	lake

WELSH	
Moel	hill
Mynydd	mountain

The Strait of Dover forms the narrowest part of the English Channel, where Great Britain is separated from the rest of Europe by only 34 km (21 miles). Linking the North Sea with the Atlantic Ocean, the strait is one of the busiest waterways in the world with approximately 400 commercial vessels passing through it every day. The short, white streaks in the water on this image are ships' wakes. The white lines along both the English and French coastlines are white chalk cliffs, including, on the British side, the famous White Cliffs of Dover.

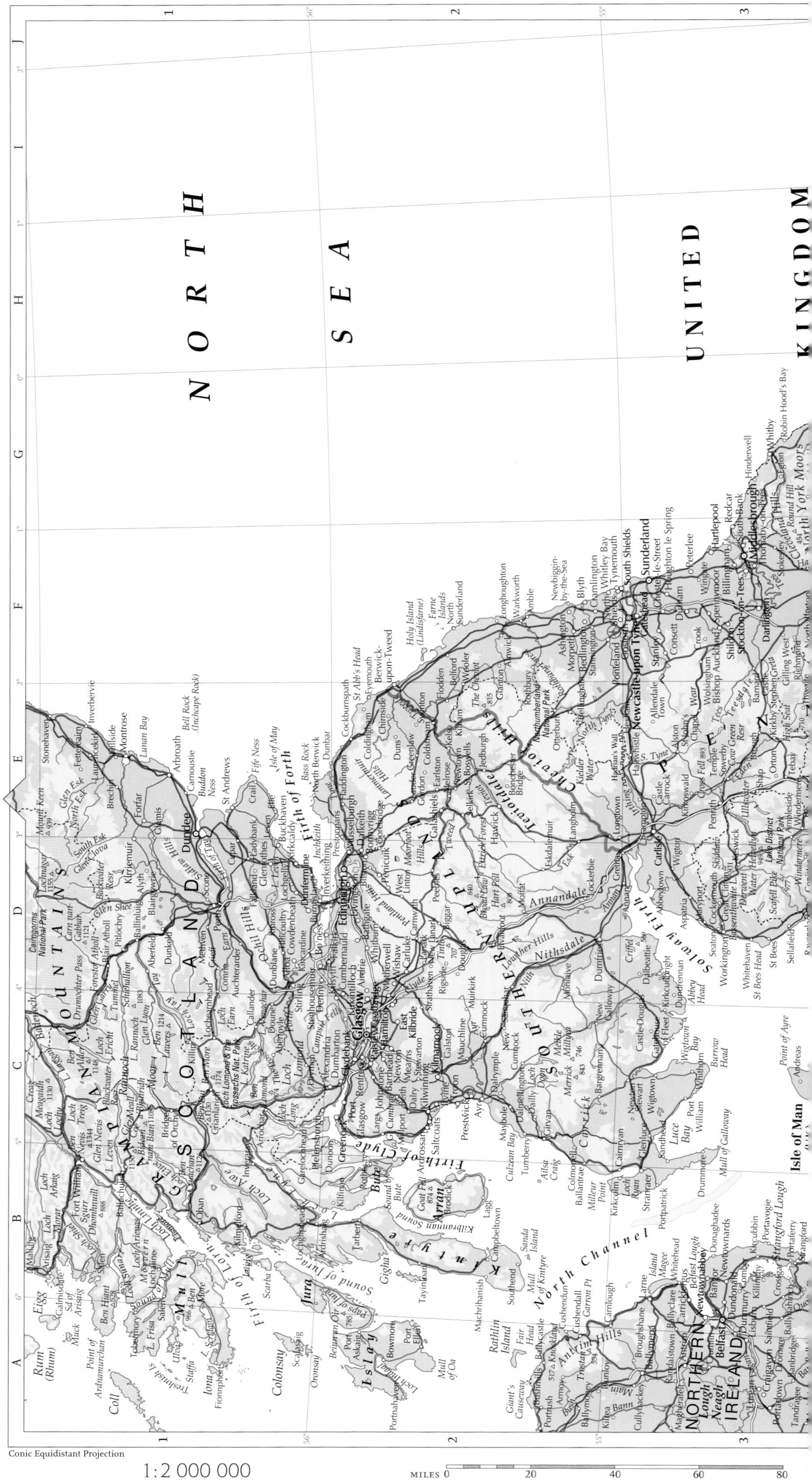

Conic Equidistant Projection

1 : 2 000 000

MILES 0   20   40   60   80

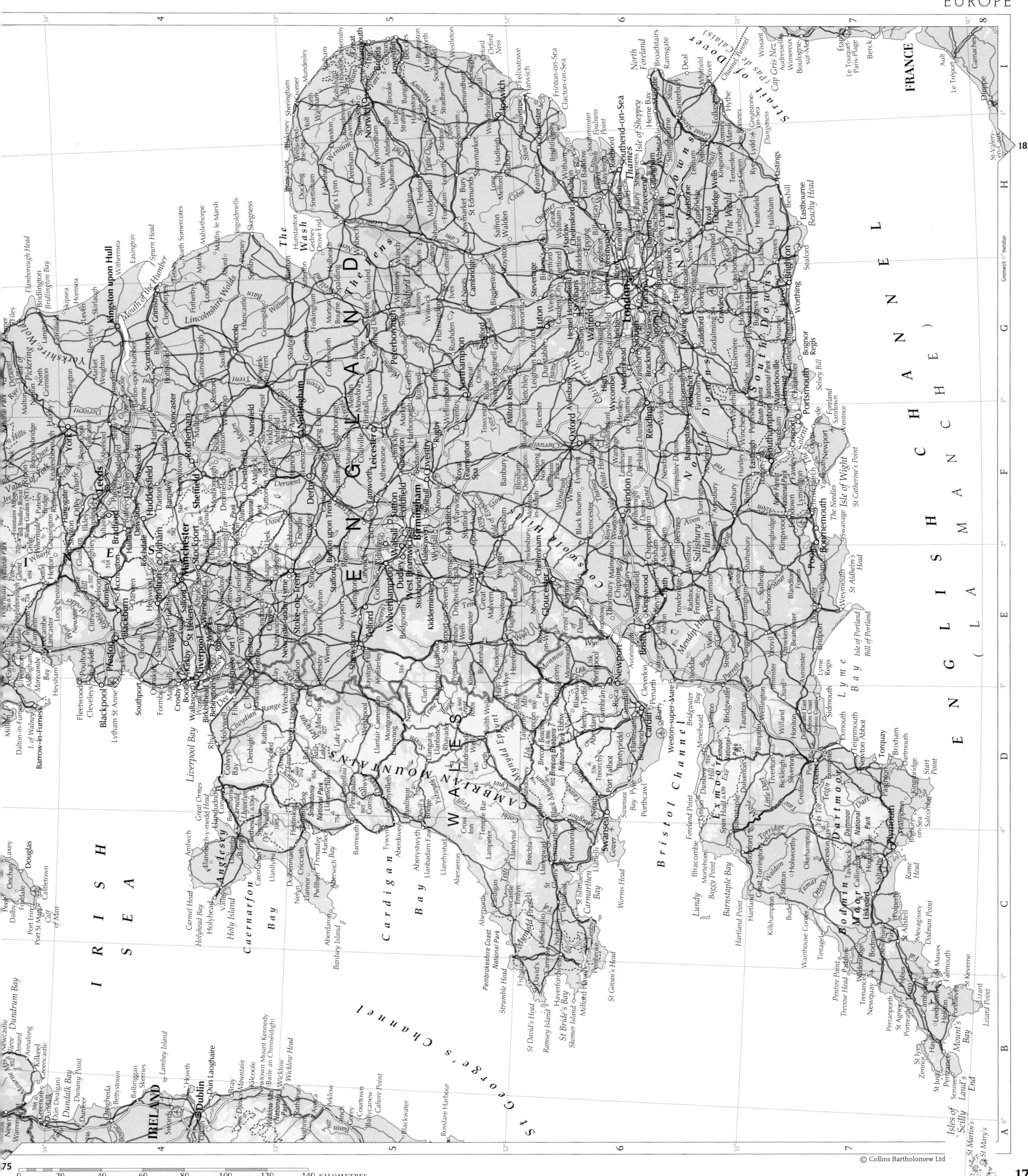

FRANCE

ENGLAND

WALES

IRELAND

I R I S H   S E A

Liverpool Bay

Cardigan   Bay

Caernarfon   Bay

S t   G e o r g e ' s   C h a n n e l

Bristol   Channel

E N G L I S H   C H A N N E L

(L A   M A N C H E)

Strait of Dover (Pas de Calais)

The Wash

CAMBRIAN MOUNTAINS

© Collins Bartholomew Ltd

0   20   40   60   80   100   120   140 KILOMETRES

SCOTLAND

IRELAND

Scotland forms the northernmost part of the United Kingdom. It includes many islands, among which are the Inner and Outer Hebrides to the west, and the Shetland Islands, located well to the north of the Orkney Islands. Ireland, which is the second largest island in the British Isles after Great Britain, is politically divided into two parts: the Republic of Ireland occupies most of the south and the northwest, while Northern Ireland in the northeast is part of the United Kingdom.

FACTS

- Scotland represents about 34 per cent of the land area of Great Britain, but has less than 9 per cent of the UK's population.

- Scotland established its own parliament in 1999, for the first time since 1707. A referendum on Scottish independence took place in 2014 which resulted in Scotland remaining part of the United Kingdom.

- Ireland is separated from the closest point in Great Britain (the Mull of Kintyre) by only 20 km (12 miles).

- Different forms of Gaelic, a Celtic language related to Welsh and Breton, are spoken, and actively encouraged, in parts of both Scotland and Ireland.

GLOSSARY

GAELIC	
Ben	mountain
Creag	mountain
Loch	lake

IRISH	
Inish	island
Lough	lake
Slieve	hill, mountain

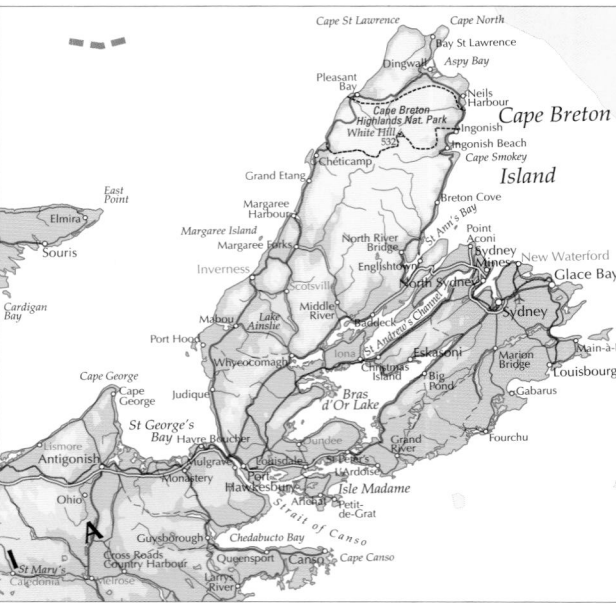

The historical and geographical extents of the Scottish and Irish diasporas can often be traced through the occurrence of 'local' place names around the world. The 18th century in particular was marked by extensive migrations from the Scottish Highlands due to the Highland Clearances. Many emigrants settled in the New World and named their new villages and towns in memory of places back home. Examples can be found throughout North America, with Nova Scotia (whose name itself means 'New Scotland') being typical, as indicated by the highlighted names on this map extract from the *Times Comprehensive Atlas of the World*. Similarly, Irish emigrants followed the same practice – the example here of New Waterford having been named by settlers from Waterford.

174

Conic Equidistant Projection

1 : 2 000 000

MILES 0   20   40   0   20   40   60   80 KILOMETRES

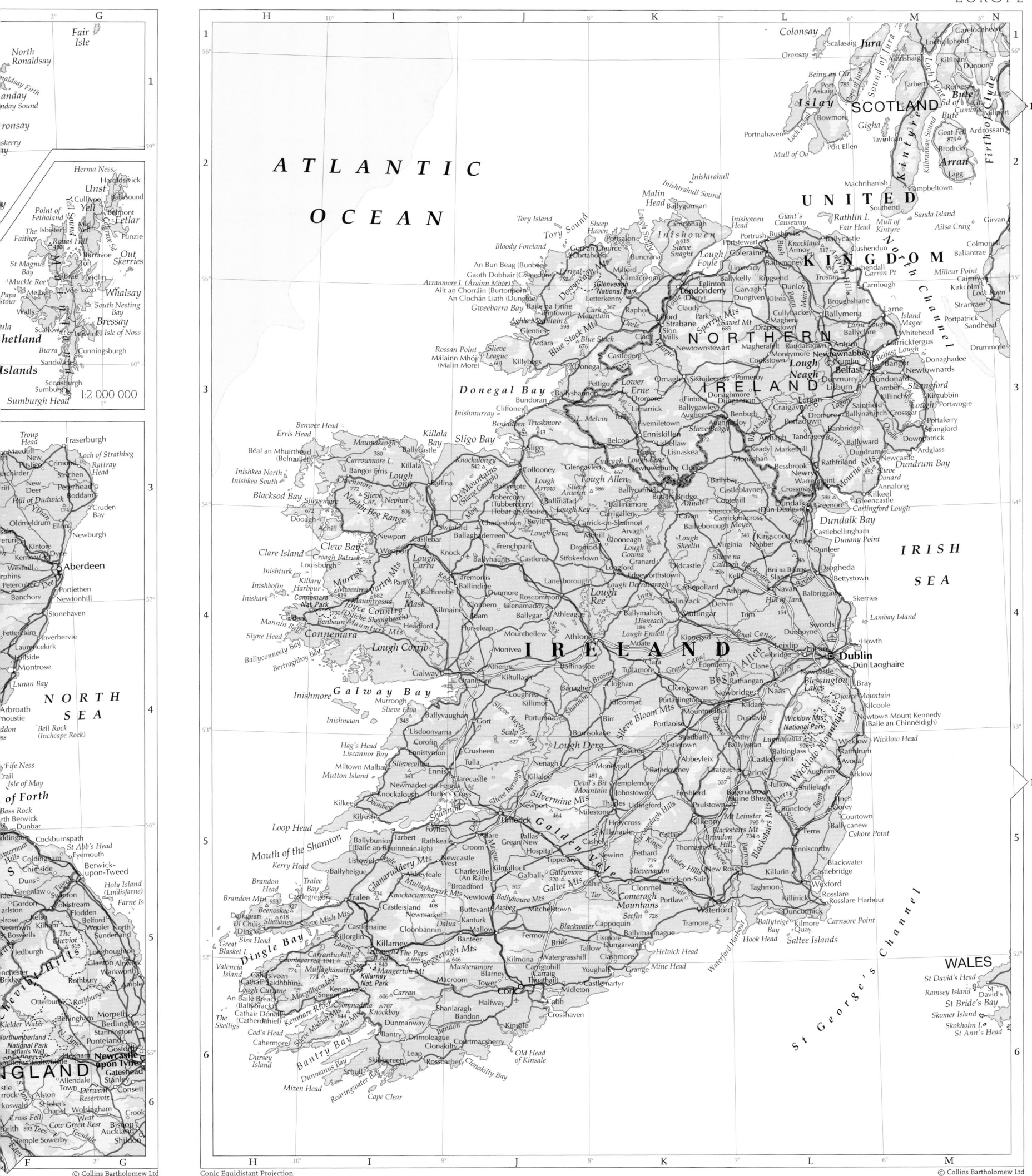

ATLANTIC OCEAN

SCOTLAND

UNITED KINGDOM

NORTHERN IRELAND

IRELAND

IRISH SEA

NORTH SEA

WALES

ENGLAND

St George's Channel

© Collins Bartholomew Ltd

Conic Equidistant Projection

1:2 000 000   MILES 0   20   40   0   20   40   60   80 KILOMETRES

© Collins Bartholomew Ltd

EUROPE NORTH CENTRAL

Central Europe consists of an extensive plain bordered in the south by the Alps (principally in Switzerland and Austria); in the east by the Carpathian and Tatra Mountains; in the west by the Low Countries (Belgium and the Netherlands); and in the north by the North and Baltic Seas. Germany and Austria are at the core of Central Europe, together with some of the countries traditionally identified as being in Eastern Europe, such as Poland, Hungary, Slovakia, and the Czech Republic.

FACTS

• The Rhine and Danube rivers both have a wide variety of local names, including Rhin and Rhein (the Rhine in France and Germany), and Duna and Dunaj (the Danube in Hungary and Slovakia).

• Following the reunification of East and West Germany in 1990, Berlin was designated again as the capital of Germany, a title it relinquished at the end of the Second World War.

• The map shows the Slavic-speaking countries of Poland, the Czech Republic, Slovakia, Slovenia, the Ukraine, Belarus, and Lithuania. Romanian is a Latin-based language related to French and Italian, while Hungarian is unique and largely unrelated to any of its neighbours.

GLOSSARY

GERMAN	
Alb	mountain region
Bucht	gulf, bay
-gebirge	mountains
Wald	forest
-wald	forest

POLISH	
Jezioro	lake

SLOVAK	
Malé	small

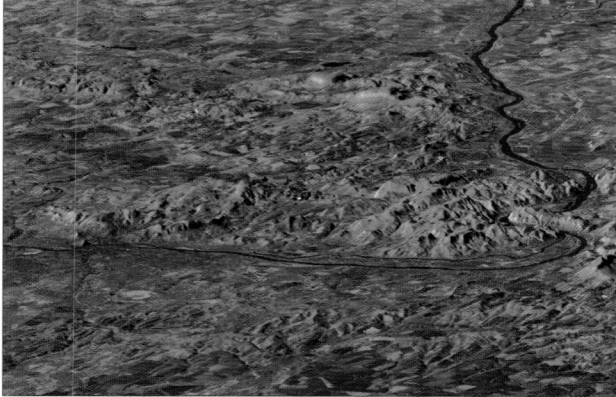

The Danube is Europe's second longest river, and the only major river on the continent to flow from west to east. It rises in the Black Forest of southwest Germany and flows generally southeastwards for 2857 km (1775 miles), passing through, or along the boundaries of, ten countries, before forming a large delta on the Black Sea coast. This west-facing perspective view shows the Danube near Budapest – one of four European capitals along its course. The river enters the image in the top right where it forms the border between Slovakia and Hungary. It then leaves the border, transecting the Transdanubian Mountains before turning southward past Budapest (the purple-blue area in the bottom left of the image).

Conic Equidistant Projection

1:5 000 000

MILES 0   50   100   150   200

BALTIC SEA

ESTONIA

LATVIA

LITHUANIA

RUSSIA

KALININGRAD OBL.

POLAND

BELARUS

RUSSIA

NOVGOROD. OBL.

PSKOV. OBL.

TVERSKAYA OBL.

SMOLENSK. OBL.

BRYANSK. OBL.

UKRAINE

SLOVAKIA

HUNGARY

ROMANIA

MOLDOVA

TRANSNISTRIA

Black Sea

Gotland

Öland

Gulf of Riga

Saaremaa (Estonia)

Gulf of Gdańsk

Warsaw (Warszawa)

Vienna (Wien)

Budapest

Minsk

Kiev

Odessa

171

185

186

187

© Collins Bartholomew Ltd

177

0 50 100 150 200 250 300 350 KILOMETRES

BELGIUM, NETHERLANDS AND GERMANY NORTH

Almost all of the eastern half of the map covers Germany, the largest country in western and central Europe. The western part of the map covers the three Benelux countries, Belgium, the Netherlands and Luxembourg, which are also commonly known as the Low Countries. In the Netherlands, a prominent feature is the artificially-dammed IJsselmeer, which was formerly an inlet of the North Sea called the Zuider Zee.

FACTS

- Along the North Sea coast is the long chain of the Frisian Islands, which are divided between the Netherlands, Germany and Denmark to the north.

- Significant parts of the Netherlands were reclaimed from the sea over several centuries. The largest of the resultant polders are to the east of Amsterdam, where the new town of Lelystad is shown on the map.

- Luxembourg was one of the original six members of the European Economic Community, now the European Union. It is predominantly French-speaking, but Luxembourg's own language (Letzeburgish), and German, are also in use.

GLOSSARY

CZECH	
hory	hills, mountains

DUTCH	
-meer	lake
-zee	sea

GERMAN	
-berg	hill, mountain
Heide	heath, moor
-wald	forest

A quarter of the Netherlands land area is below sea level, mostly made up of 3000 reclaimed 'polders'. The largest of these are within the IJsselmeer (top), a large lake created in the 1930s by barricading off the Zuider Zee from the North Sea. The satellite image (bottom) shows Flevoland, the world's largest man-made island, in 2005, the reclamation complete and the polder under cultivation with towns and infrastructure well-developed. The green area of water is Markermeer, an undrained polder which serves as a freshwater reservoir and flood control.

Conic Equidistant Projection

1:2 000 000

MILES 0   20   40   60   80

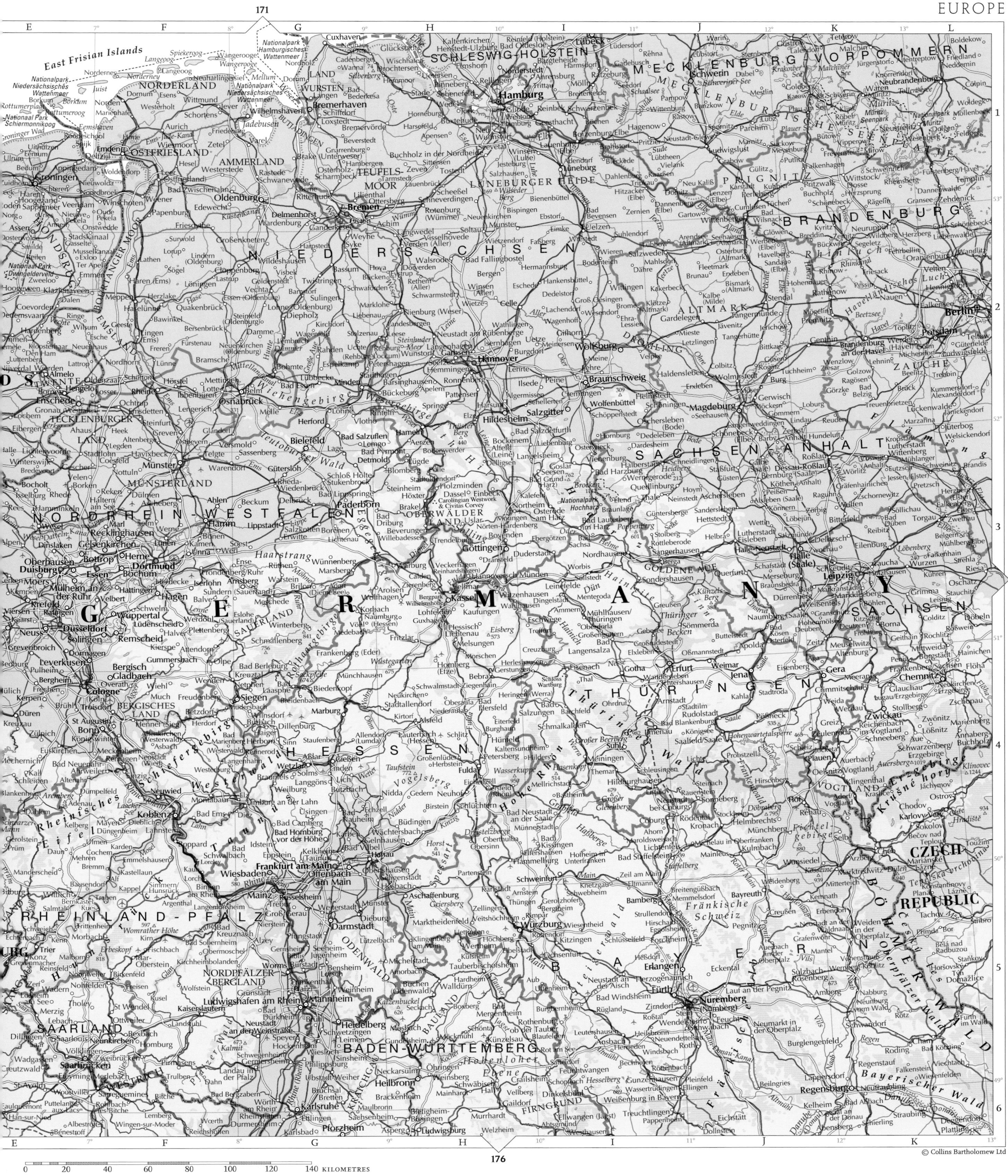

G E R M A N Y

SCHLESWIG-HOLSTEIN

MECKLENBURG-VORPOMMERN

NIEDERSACHSEN

BRANDENBURG

SACHSEN-ANHALT

NORDRHEIN-WESTFALEN

HESSEN

THÜRINGEN

SACHSEN

RHEINLAND-PFALZ

SAARLAND

BADEN-WÜRTTEMBERG

BAYERN

CZECH REPUBLIC

OSTFRIESLAND · NORDERLAND · AMMERLAND · MÜNSTERLAND · BERGISCHES LAND · SAUERLAND · VOGELSBERG · ODENWALD · VOGTLAND

East Frisian Islands

Hamburg · Bremen · Hannover · Braunschweig · Magdeburg · Berlin · Potsdam · Leipzig · Halle (Saale) · Chemnitz · Nuremberg · Würzburg · Frankfurt am Main · Wiesbaden · Mainz · Mannheim · Karlsruhe · Cologne · Düsseldorf · Essen · Dortmund · Duisburg · Erfurt · Jena · Gera · Zwickau

0 20 40 60 80 100 120 140 KILOMETRES

© Collins Bartholomew Ltd

SOUTHERN EUROPE AND THE MEDITERRANEAN

The map shows much of Europe, putting the continent in context with the Mediterranean Sea – Europe's natural southern limit. The proximity of North Africa, Turkey, and the Middle Eastern countries of Syria, Lebanon, Jordan and Israel is clear. Large islands characterize the Mediterranean Sea, the Aegean particularly being peppered with small islands and archipelagos. The mountainous regions of the Alps, the Carpathian Mountains, and the Balkan Mountains are prominent, and the map also shows the upland plateau nature of Spain and Turkey.

FACTS

• The Channel Islands consist of two separate dependencies of the UK – the Bailiwicks of Jersey and Guernsey. UK ownership of the islands is the last remnant of England's historical connections with France.

• The spectacular mountain range of the Alps is the source for several of Europe's major rivers including the Rhine, the Rhône, and the Po.

• Gibraltar has been a possession of the UK since the early 18th century, although ownership is disputed by Spain.

• San Marino, a tiny independent nation within the borders of northeast Italy, is unique in having survived the unification of Italy as a single country in the 19th century.

GLOSSARY

ARABIC	
Jabal; Jebel	mountain(s)
Ra's	cape, point
Wādī	watercourse

ITALIAN	
Golfo	gulf, bay
Isola; Isole	island; islands

SPANISH	
Cabo	cape, point
Cordillera	mountain range

TURKISH	
Dağ; Dağı	mountain
Gölü	lake
Körfezi	gulf, bay

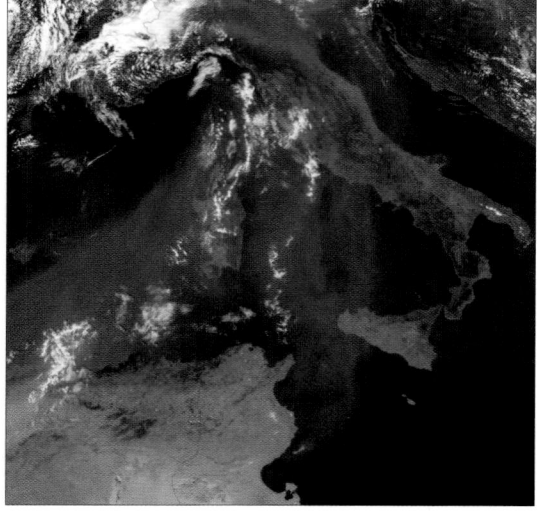

Southern Europe is affected by dust storms like the one shown in this image sweeping northward and eastward from Morocco, Algeria, and Tunisia across the Mediterranean Sea towards Italy.

To the south, Africa's Sahara desert stretches across 4800 km (2983 miles). A quarter of the desert is covered by sand seas which provide ample material for such storms. A severe storm can advance as a swirling wall of dust which reduces visibility to almost zero. Southern Europe is also prone to storms caused by the Sirocco, a hot, usually dry and dust-laden wind which comes from the Sahara and which can reach hurricane force.

Conic Equidistant Projection

1:10 000 000

MILES 0   100   150   200   250   300

169

193

136

0   100   200   300   400   500 KILOMETRES

FRANCE
SPAIN AND PORTUGAL

Mountain ranges are prominent in the map of France, with the Alps dividing France from Italy in the southeast and the Pyrenees separating it from Spain. The small nation of Andorra is located high in the Pyrenees between France and Spain. Spain and Portugal cover the Iberian Peninsula to the southwest of France. Gibraltar, a tiny enclave in the far south, remains a UK Overseas Territory, and just across the Strait of Gibraltar, on the Moroccan coast, lies the small Spanish exclave of Ceuta.

FACTS

- Corsica, the large island shown in the Mediterranean to the southeast of the French mainland, is an integral part of France, with its own distinct culture and dialect.

- Monaco is set on the Mediterranean coast close to the Italian border. It is the second smallest country in the world. Its chief town, Monte-Carlo, is renowned for its casinos.

- Andorra's government is subject to a special arrangement between France and Spain. Since 1278, the two joint rulers are the President of France and the Bishop of La Seu d'Urgell in Spain.

- The narrowness of the Strait of Gibraltar is mainly responsible for the low tidal range found throughout the Mediterranean.

GLOSSARY

CATALAN	
Golf	gulf, bay

FRENCH	
Baie	bay
Golfe	gulf, bay
Île; Îles	island; islands
Massif	mountains, upland
Pointe (Pte)	cape, point

PORTUGUESE	
Baía	bay
Serra	mountain range

SPANISH	
Cordillera	mountain range
Embalse	reservoir
Mar	sea
Sierra	mountain range

World's top 10 tourist destinations (arrivals), 2013

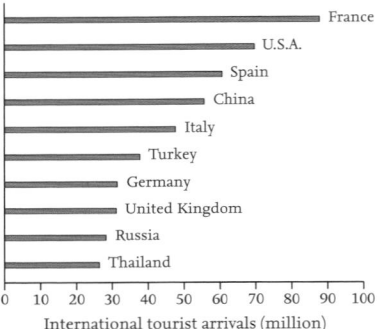

International tourist arrivals (million)

World's top 10 tourist destinations (tourism receipts), 2013

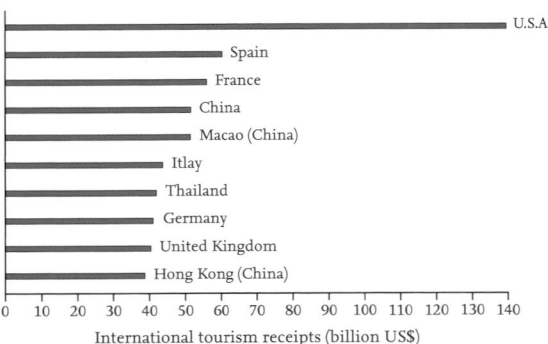

International tourism receipts (billion US$)

Although the pace of growth is slowing Europe remains a major tourist destination, receiving over 563 million visitors in 2013. This continuing popularity is driven by several factors, including the appeal of traditional sun and sea holidays, the prominence of low-cost airlines, the diversity of destinations, and the high number of major cultural and sporting events which commonly happen throughout Europe. The Mediterranean region remains particularly popular, with France ranked as the world's top tourist destination for international visitors and with several destinations emerging in the Balkans and southern Caucasus.

Conic Equidistant Projection

1:5 000 000

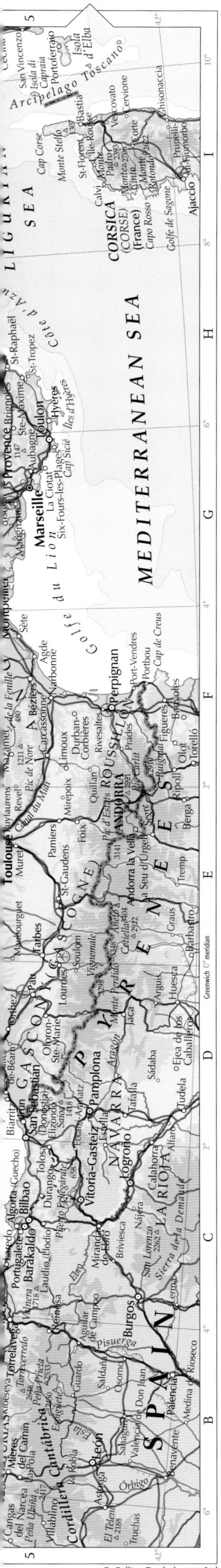

MEDITERRANEAN SEA

LIGURIAN SEA

CORSICA (CORSE) (France)

FRANCE

SPAIN

PORTUGAL

ANDORRA

PYRENEES

GALICIA

ASTURIAS

CANTABRIA

NAVARRA

LA RIOJA

ARAGON

CATALUNA

CASTILLA Y LEON

CASTILLA-LA MANCHA

EXTREMADURA

ANDALUCIA

MURCIA

SIERRA MORENA

GASCOGNE

GASCONY

ROUSSILLON

Bay of Biscay

Mar Cantábrico

ATLANTIC OCEAN

Balearic Islands (Islas Baleares)

Mallorca (Majorca)

Ibiza (Eivissa)

Formentera

Costa Brava

Costa Blanca

Costa del Sol

Costa de la Luz

Golfo de Valencia

Golfo de Cádiz

Alborán Sea

Strait of Gibraltar

ALGERIA

MOROCCO

Algiers (Alger)

Oran

Madrid

Barcelona

Valencia

Sevilla

Zaragoza

Málaga

Bilbao

Oporto (Porto)

Lisbon (Lisboa)

Gibraltar (U.K.)

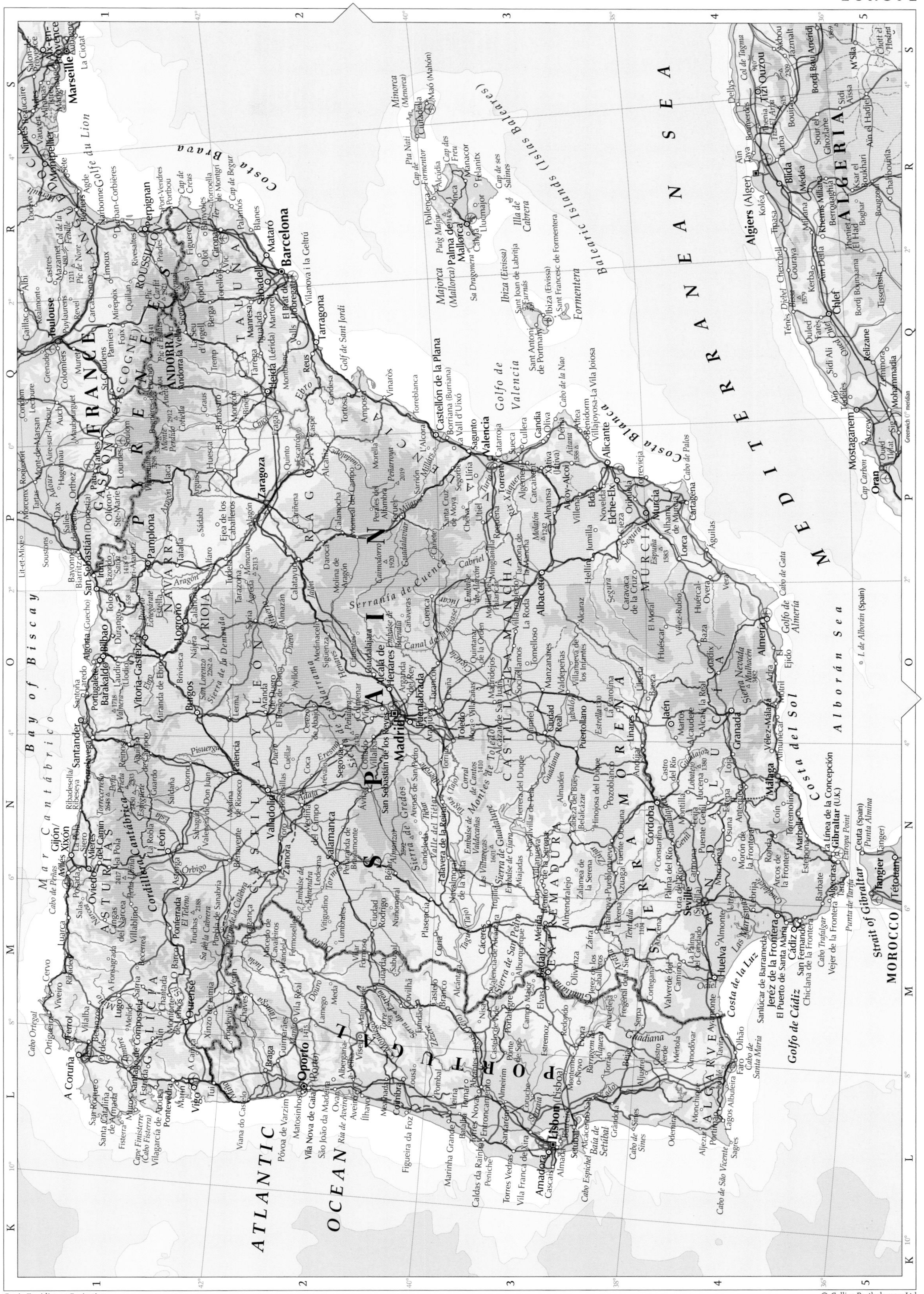

Ceuta (Spain)

Marseille

Toulouse

Perpignan

Pamplona

Santander

Gijón

A Coruña

Granada

Córdoba

Murcia

Alicante

Tarragona

León

Valladolid

Salamanca

Badajoz

Cádiz

Huelva

Jaén

Albacete

Vitoria-Gasteiz

Logroño

San Sebastián (Donostia)

Castellón de la Plana

1 : 5 000 000

MILES 0   50   100

0   50   100   150   200 KILOMETRES

184   184   180

ITALY and THE BALKANS

The western half of this map shows the familiar peninsula of Italy, culminating in a 'boot' pointing to a 'football' in the shape of Sicily, which along with the other large island of Sardinia is an integral part of the Italian Republic. Corsica, to the north of Sardinia, is an administrative region of France. In the east, the patchwork of countries on the modern map has been made more complex in recent years by the dissolution of the former Yugoslavia into seven separate countries – the most recent change being Kosovo's independence from Serbia.

FACTS

• The Balkans are usually regarded as consisting of mainland Greece, Albania, Bulgaria, the countries of the former Yugoslavia, and southern Romania.

• The Vatican City is the world's smallest independent nation. It was formed by agreement with the Italian government in the 1920s from part of central Rome.

• The Sea of Marmara links the Mediterranean with the Black Sea via the Bosporus, on which stands Istanbul, and the Dardanelles, adjacent to Gallipoli, scene of fierce fighting during the First World War.

GLOSSARY

BULGARIAN	
Nos	cape, point
Planina	hills, mountains

GREEK	
Kolpos	gulf, bay
Pelagos	sea

ROMANIAN	
Lacul (L.)	lake
Vârful	mountain

ITALIAN	
Arcipelago	archipelago
Capo	cape, point
Golfo	gulf, bay
Isola; Isole	island; islands
Monte	mountain
Monti	mountains

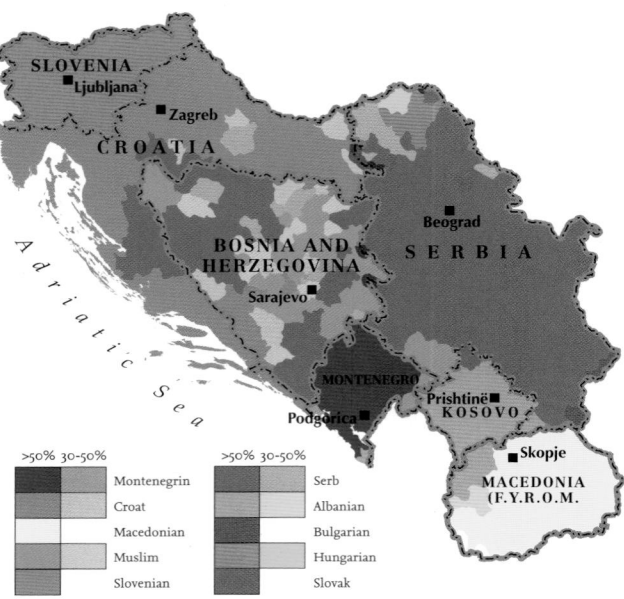

The Balkan region has a long history of instability and ethnic conflict as a result of the underlying complexity of the ethnic composition of what was once Yugoslavia. The early 1990s saw civil war in the region and four Yugoslav republics – Croatia, Slovenia, Bosnia and Herzegovina and Macedonia – each declared their independence. The war continued until the Dayton Peace Accord was established in 1995. Conflict continued in Kosovo, however, where the ruling (but minority) Serbs carried out ethnic cleansing of the native Albanian population until NATO intervention in 1999. The break-up of Yugoslavia is now complete, with Montenegro (May 2006), and Kosovo (February 2008) both having declared their independence from Serbia.

Conic Equidistant Projection

1:5 000 000

MILES 0   50   100   150   200

187

138

© Collins Bartholomew Ltd

0   50   100   150   200   250   300   350 KILOMETRES

RUSSIA WEST

European Russia is conventionally defined as ending at the
Ural Mountains, just off the northeast corner of the map, the
Caspian Sea and the Caucasus mountains, shown in the far
southeast of the map. Many countries shown were republics
within the former Soviet Union until its demise in 1991. The
coastline of the Black Sea includes the Crimea peninsula –
scene of the Crimean War in the 1850s – and the delta of the
river Danube, which up to this point has flowed through,
or along the borders of ten countries from its source in
southwest Germany.

FACTS

- Although the majority of the population of Russia are ethnic Russians it
  encompasses many other ethnic groups including Tatars, Ukrainians, and
  Chechens.

- Moldova and the Ukraine both opted to give their own languages precedence in
  the early 1990s, before which Russian had been dominant. Ukrainian is closely
  related to Russian, written in the Cyrillic alphabet. Moldova and Romania both
  mainly speak Romanian, which is written in the Roman alphabet.

- In the north of the Ukraine lies the town of Chornobyl', notorious for a
  disastrous explosion at its nuclear power station in 1986.

GLOSSARY

RUSSIAN	
Bol'shoy	big
Guba	gulf, bay
Nizmennost'	lowland
Ozero	lake
Vodokhranilishche, Vdkhr.	reservoir
Vozvyshennost'	upland

UKRAINIAN	
Vodoskhovyshche, Vdskh.	reservoir
Zatoka	gulf, bay

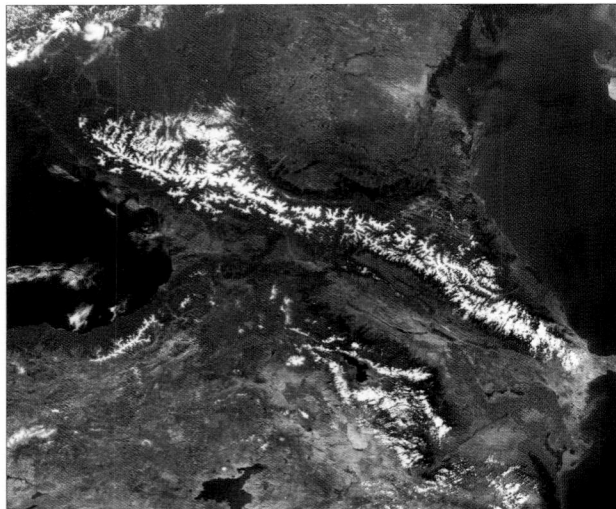

The snow-capped Caucasus mountains, between the Black Sea in the west and
the Caspian Sea in the east, mark the southwestern boundary of Russia. The
ethnically mixed North Caucasus is a region used to violence. Chechnia has seen
on-and-off conflict since the early 1990s in its efforts to secede from Russia. Tens
of thousands have been killed and hundreds of thousands displaced. The violence
has spilled over into neighbouring republics (Ingushetia, Dagestan and North
Ossetia in Russia, South Ossetia in Georgia). Dagestan has seen terrorist attacks
and kidnappings while North Ossetia was the scene of the siege of the school at
Beslan in 2004 which left 344 civilians dead.

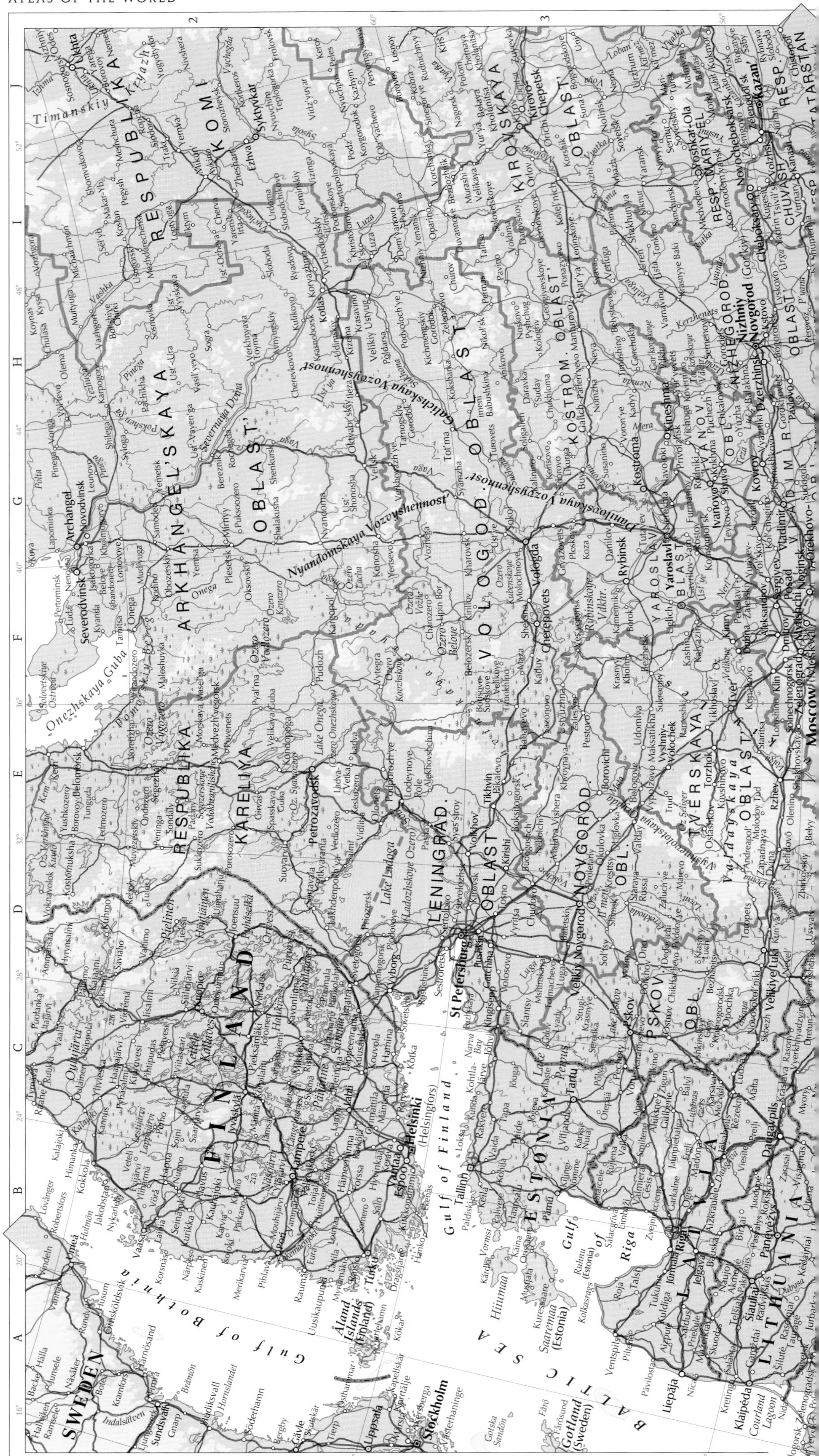

170

Conic Equidistant Projection

1:7 000 000

MILES 0   50   100   150   200

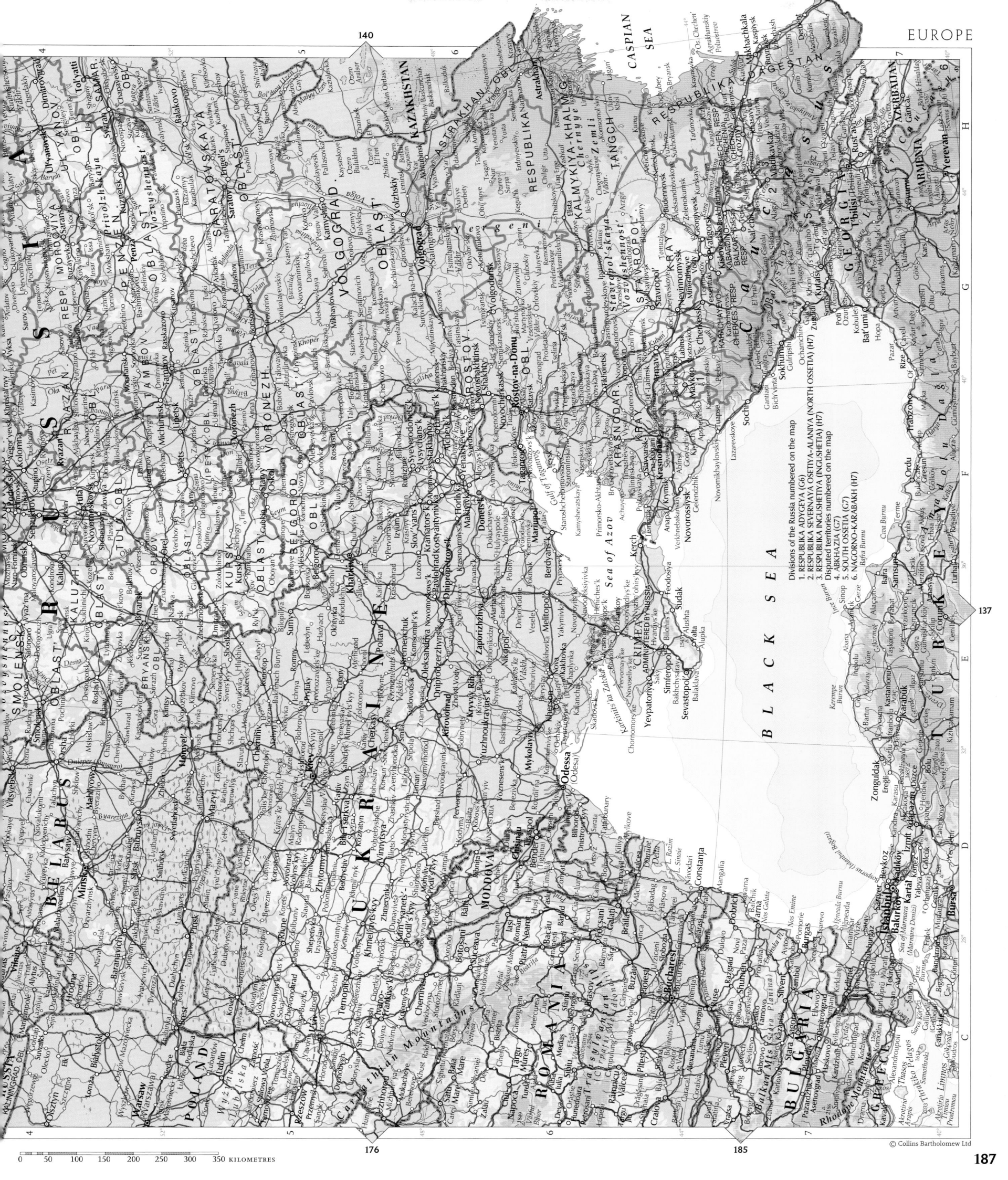

Divisions of the Russia numbered on the map
1. RESPUBLIKA ADYGEYA (G6)
2. RESPUBLIKA SEVERNAYA OSETIYA-ALANIYA (NORTH OSSETIA) (H7)
3. RESPUBLIKA INGUSHETIYA (INGUSHETIA) (H7)
Disputed territories numbered on the map
4. ABKHAZIA (G7)
5. SOUTH OSSETIA (G7)
6. NAGORNO-KARABAKH (H7)

ADMINISTERED BY RUSSIA

0   50 100 150 200 250 300   350 KILOMETRES

© Collins Bartholomew Ltd

AFRICA PHYSICAL

Africa is connected to Asia at the narrow Sinai peninsula. It is also separated narrowly from Europe at the Strait of Gibraltar. It contains some of the world's greatest physical features. The north is dominated by the Sahara desert and the semi-arid Sahel region, while the mountainous zone of the Great Rift Valley runs down much of the east. The chief feature of central Africa is the vast Congo Basin, while the Kalahari and Namib deserts occupy large parts of the southwest.

FACTS

- The Suez Canal, a crucial shipping route between the Atlantic and Indian Oceans, links the Mediterranean Sea to the Red Sea. It opened in 1869 and is 163 km (101 miles) long.

- The Sahara desert covers 9 million sq km (3.5 million sq miles), approximately 30 per cent of Africa's total land area.

- The floor of the Great Rift Valley varies from nearly 400 m (1300 ft) below sea level to over 1800 m (5900 ft) above sea level.

HIGHEST MOUNTAINS	m	ft
Kilimanjaro, Tanzania	5 892	19 330
Mt Kenya (Kirinyaga), Kenya	5 199	17 057
Margherita Peak, Dem. Rep. of the Congo/Uganda	5 110	16 765
Meru, Tanzania	4 565	14 977
Ras Dejen, Ethiopia	4 533	14 872
Mt Karisimbi, Rwanda	4 510	14 796

LARGEST ISLANDS	sq km	sq miles
Madagascar	587 040	226 656

LONGEST RIVERS	km	miles
Nile	6 695	4 160
Congo	4 667	2 900
Niger	4 184	2 600
Zambezi	2 736	1 700
Wabē Shebelē Wenz	2 490	1 547
Ubangi	2 250	1 398

LARGEST LAKES	sq km	sq miles
Lake Victoria	68 870	26 591
Lake Tanganyika	32 600	12 587
Lake Nyasa (Lake Malawi)	29 500	11 390
Lake Volta	8 482	3 275
Lake Turkana	6 500	2 510
Lake Albert	5 600	2 162

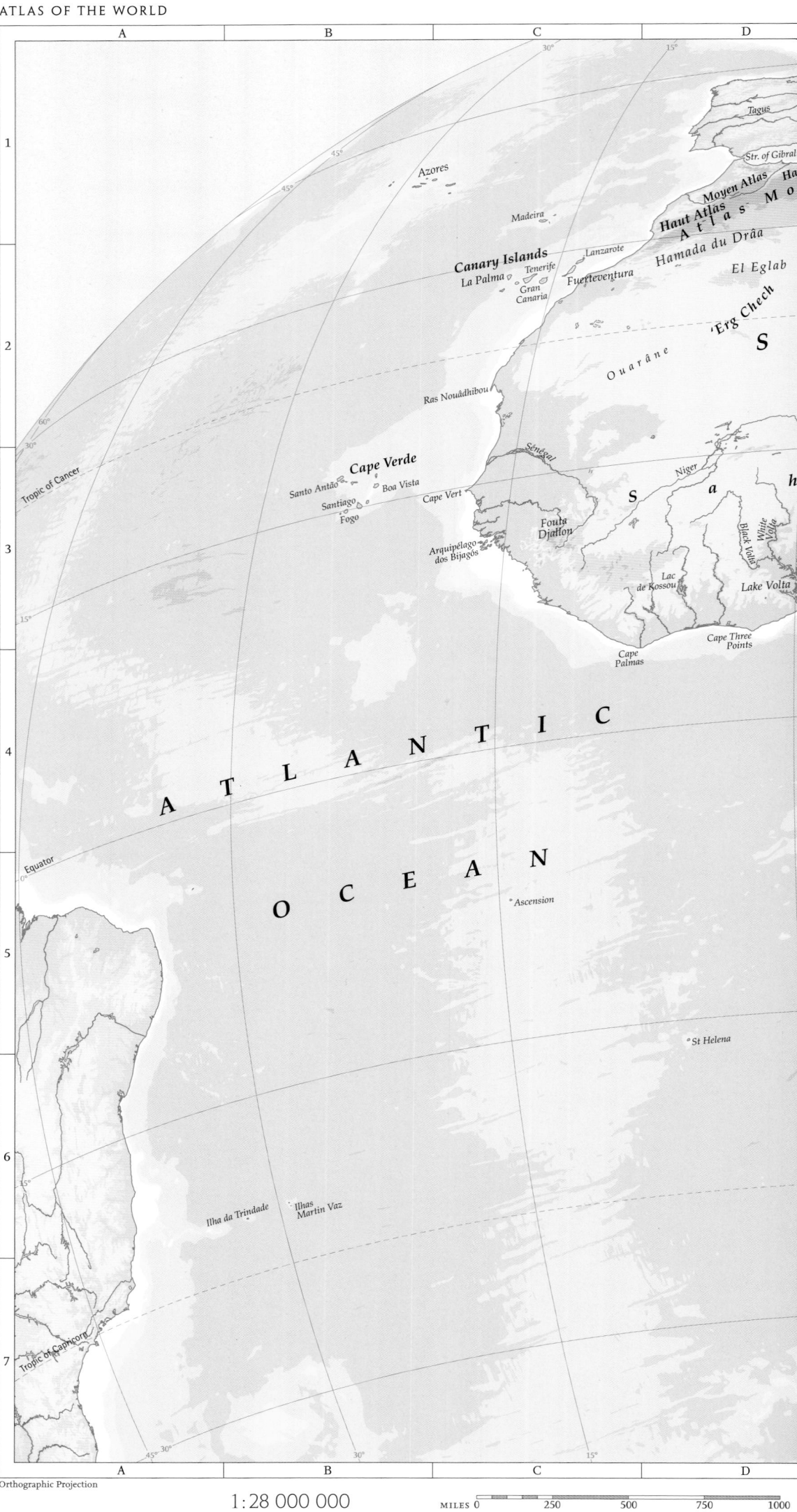

Orthographic Projection

1 : 28 000 000

MILES 0   250   500   750   1000

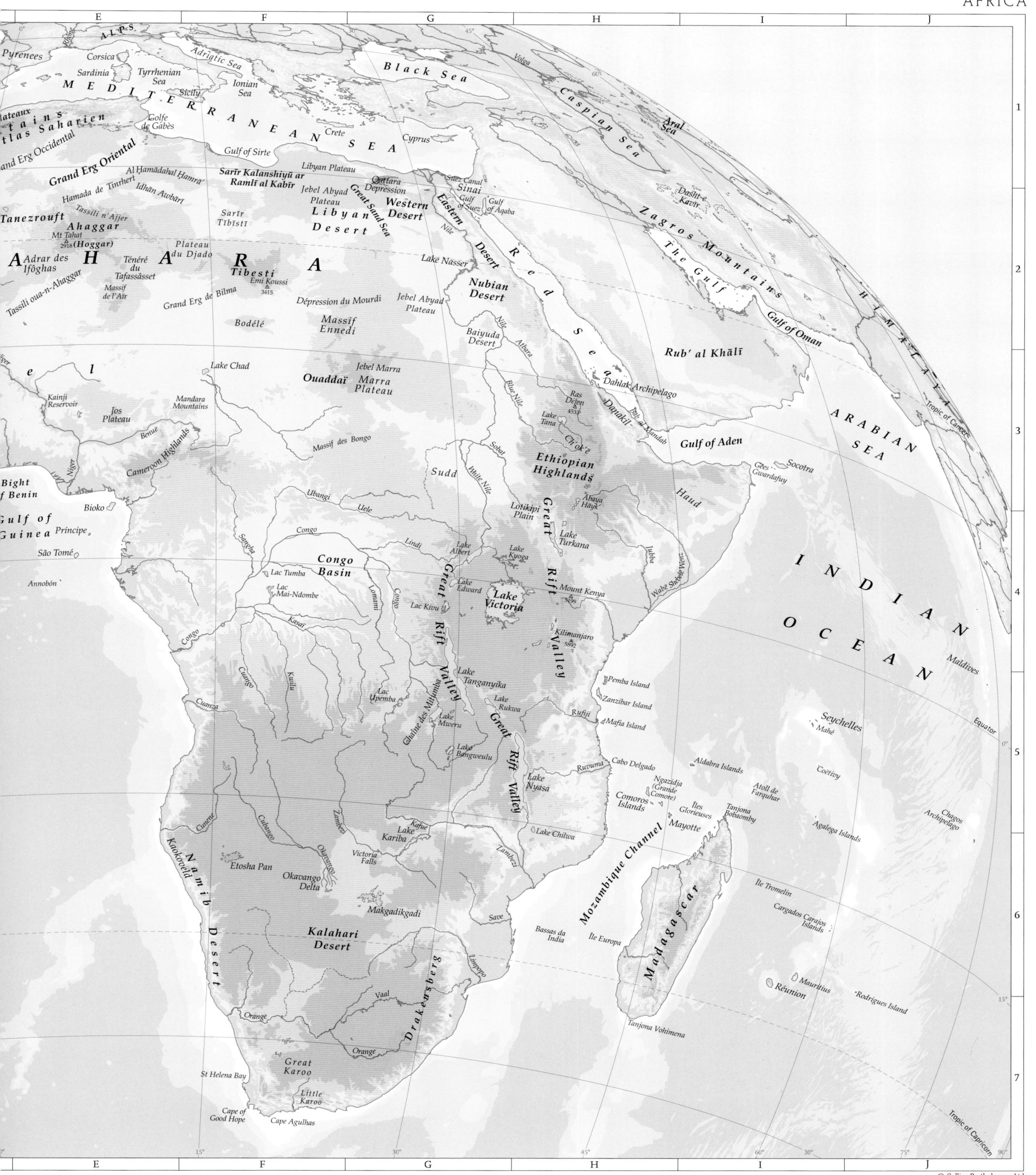

Pyrenees
Corsica
Sardinia
Tyrrhenian
Sea
Adriatic Sea
Ionian
Sea
Black Sea
Volga
Caspian Sea
Aral Sea
ALPS
Plateaus
tains
tlas Sahariern
M E D I T E R R A N E A N   S E A
Sicily
Crete
Cyprus
Golfe
de Gâbes
Gulf of Sirte
Libyan Plateau
Qattara
Depression
Suez Canal
Sinai
Gulf
of Suez
Gulf of Aqaba
Z a g r o s   M o u n t a i n s
The Gulf
Dasht-e
Kavir
Grand Erg Oriental
Al Ḥamādah al Ḥamrā'
Sarīr Kalanshiyū ar
Ramlī al Kabīr
Jebel Abyad
Plateau
Great Sand Sea
Western
Desert
Eastern
Nile
Grand Erg Occidental
Hamada de Tinrhert
Idhān Awbārī
Sarīr
Tībīstī
Western
Desert
Gulf of Oman
Tanezrouft
Ahaggar
Tassili n'Ajjer
L i b y a n
D e s e r t
A R A B I A N
S E A
Mt Tahat
2918 (Hoggar)
Plateau
du Djado
Lake Nasser
Nubian
Desert
R e d   S e a
Rub' al Khālī
Tropic of Cancer
A
Adrar des
Ifôghas
H
Ténéré
du
Tafassâsset
A
Tibesti
Emi Koussi
3415
R
Jebel Abyad
Plateau
A
Baiyuda
Desert
Dahlak Archipelago
HIMALAYA
Tassili oua-n-Ahaggar
Massif
de l'Aïr
Dépression du Mourdi
Nile
Atbara
Bāb al Mandab
Grand Erg de Bilma
Bodélé
Massif
Ennedi
Blue Nile
Ras
Dejen
4533
Danakil
Gulf of Aden
Socotra
River
e
l
Lake Chad
Jebel Marra
Ouaddaï   Marra
Plateau
Lake
Tana
Ch'ok'e
Ethiopian
Highlands
Raas
Gwardafuy
Kainji
Reservoir
Jos
Plateau
Mandara
Mountains
Massif des Bongo
Sobat
White Nile
Abaya
Hayk'
Haud
Bight
of Benin
Niger
Benue
Cameroon Highlands
Sudd
Ubangi
Uele
Lotikipi
Plain
Great Rift Valley
Wabē Shebelē Wenz
Jubba
Gulf of
Guinea
Bioko
Príncipe
Sangha
Congo
Lindi
Lake
Albert
Lake
Kyoga
Mount Kenya
5199
São Tomé
Lac Tumba
Congo
Basin
Lac
Mai-Ndombe
Lomami
Congo
Kasai
Lac Kivu
Lake
Edward
Lake
Victoria
Kilimanjaro
5892
Annobón
Great Rift Valley
Great Rift Valley
Lake
Turkana
INDIAN
Cuango
Kwilu
Chaîne des Mitumba
Lac
Upemba
Lake
Tanganyika
Maldives
OCEAN
Cuanza
Kasai
Lake
Mweru
Lake
Rukwa
Pemba Island
Zanzibar Island
Rufiji
Mafia Island
Equator
Lake
Bangweulu
Great Rift Valley
Lake
Nyasa
Ruvuma
Cabo Delgado
Aldabra Islands
Seychelles
Mahé
Coëtivy
Cunene
Cubango
Zambezi
Kafue
Lake
Kariba
Lake Chilwa
Ngazidja
(Grande
Comore)
Comoros
Islands
Îles
Glorieuses
Mayotte
Tanjona
Bobaomby
Atoll de
Farquhar
Agalega Islands
Chagos
Archipelago
Kaokoveld
Okavango
Etosha Pan
Okavango
Delta
Victoria
Falls
Zambezi
Save
Mozambique Channel
Île Tromelin
Cargados Carajos
Islands
Namib
Desert
Makgadikgadi
Bassas da
India
Île Europa
Madagascar
Mauritius
Réunion
Rodrigues Island
Kalahari
Desert
Drakensberg
Limpopo
Tanjona Vohimena
Tropic of Capricorn
Vaal
Orange
St Helena Bay
Great
Karoo
Orange
Cape of
Good Hope
Little
Karoo
Cape Agulhas

AFRICA POLITICAL

The political patchwork of Africa is a result of a complex history and of boundaries formed largely during the colonial era, which saw European control of the majority of the continent from the 15th century until widespread moves to independence began in the 1950s. The colonial era effectively came to an end in the 1970s. The status of Western Sahara, formerly Spanish but now effectively under Moroccan control, remains to be agreed internationally. Today there are once again two countries called Congo, since Zaire reverted to the name Democratic Republic of the Congo in 1997.

FACTS

- Many languages are spoken in different parts of Africa, although Arabic is the main native language all across the north. In most other areas, the languages of European powers (mainly English, French, Portuguese and Spanish, along with Afrikaans) remain in common use.

- Only Liberia and Ethiopia have remained free from colonial rule throughout their history.

- Less than half the population of Africa has access to safe drinking water.

- Of the ten countries in the world with children under-five mortality rates of more than 200 per 1000 live births, nine are in Africa.

LARGEST COUNTRIES	Area	
	sq km	sq miles
Algeria	2 381 741	919 595
Democratic Republic of the Congo	2 345 410	905 568
Sudan	1 861 484	718 725
Libya	1 759 540	679 362
Chad	1 284 000	495 755
Niger	1 267 000	489 191
Angola	1 246 700	481 354
Mali	1 240 140	478 821
South Africa	1 219 090	470 693
Ethiopia	1 133 880	437 794

MOST POPULATED COUNTRIES	Population
Nigeria	173 615 000
Ethiopia	94 101 000
Egypt	82 056 000
Democratic Republic of the Congo	67 514 000
South Africa	52 776 000
Tanzania	49 253 000
Kenya	44 354 000
Algeria	39 208 000
Sudan	37 964 000
Uganda	37 579 000

CAPITALS		
Largest population	**Cairo**, Egypt	11 944 000
Smallest population	**Victoria**, Seychelles	26 000
Most northerly	**Tunis**, Tunisia	36° 46′ N
Most southerly	**Cape Town**, South Africa	33° 57′ S
Highest	**Addis Ababa**, Ethiopia	2 408 m/ 7 900 ft

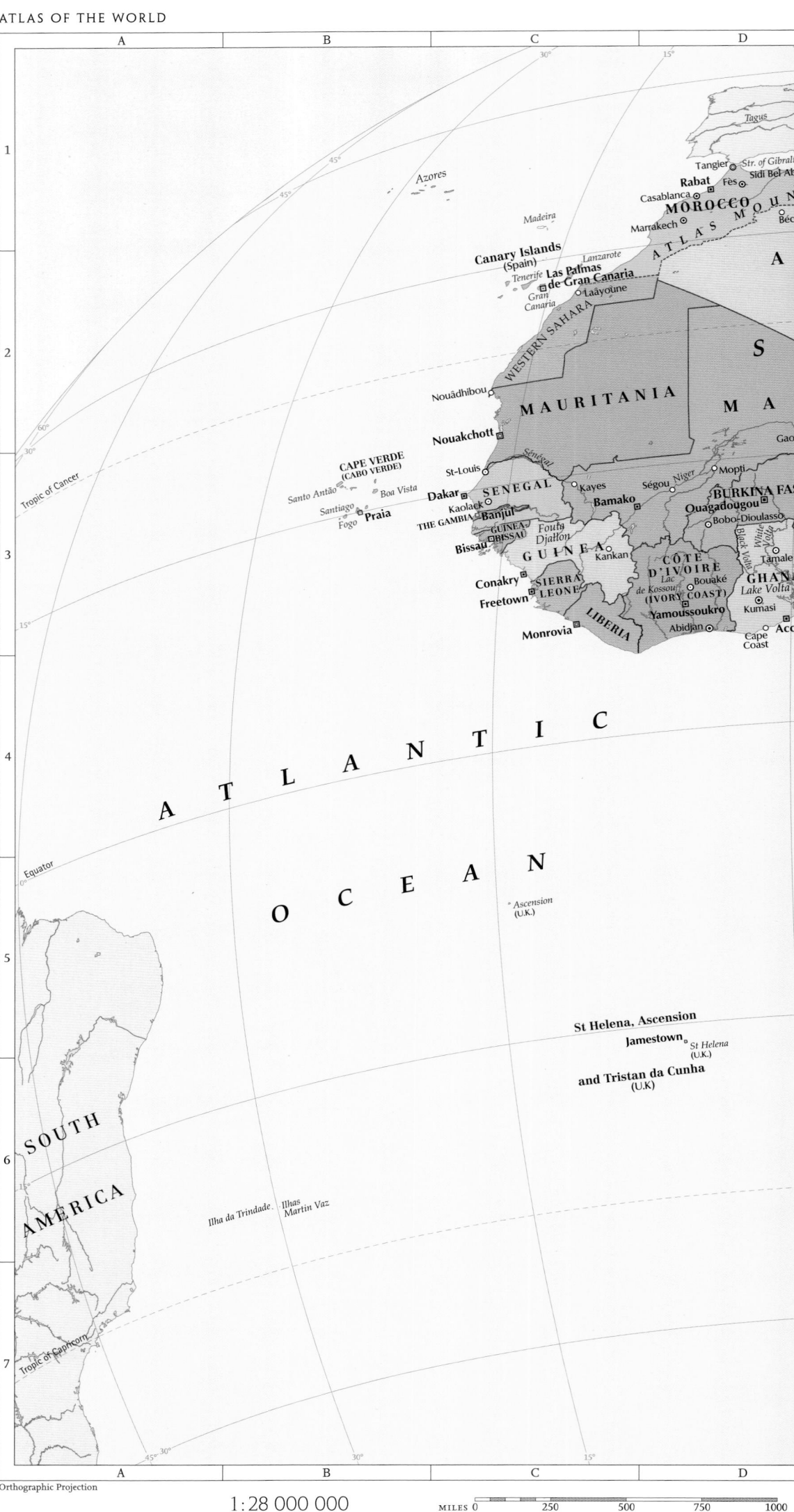

Orthographic Projection

1 : 28 000 000

MILES 0   250   500   750   1000

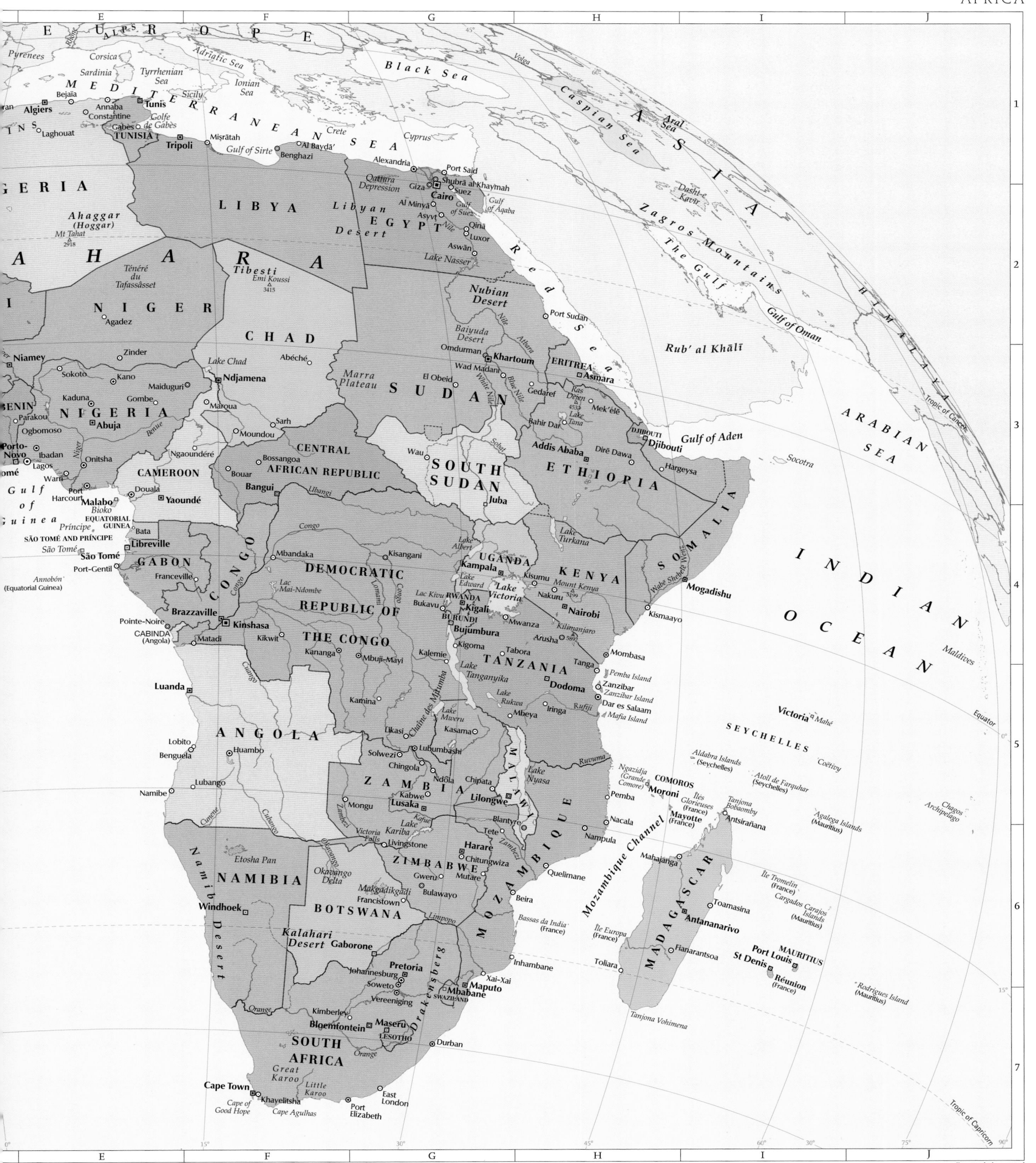

© Collins Bartholomew Ltd

0   250   500   750   1000   1250   1500 KILOMETRES

AFRICA NORTH

The Sahara desert and the huge countries covering it occupy the north of this map. Ahaggar and Tibesti are major rocky uplands within the desert. The countries along the southern coast of West Africa are more densely populated and significantly smaller. In the north, the Atlas Mountains – geologically a continuation of the Alps – are the chief physical feature. The Spanish-owned Canary Islands and the Portuguese island of Madeira lie off the northwest coast. Lake Chad is now a relatively insignificant feature, having shrunk dramatically as a result of a drying climate and the extraction of water for irrigation.

FACTS

- Names of parts of the West African coast relate to former trading connections dating from the colonial era. For example, the Gold Coast (also the former name of Ghana), Ivory Coast (which gave its name to the country now known as Côte d'Ivoire) and the Slave Coast.

- Long, straight boundaries are usually an indication that the territory involved is largely flat, empty desert.

- Ethnic conflict has dogged the modern history of Sudan. Black-African tribal groups in the south sought autonomy from the largely Arab north until independence was finally achieved by South Sudan in July 2011. Despite the peaceful process of separation several issues between the two countries remain unresolved, including disputes in the oil-rich border areas.

- More than 90 per cent of the 82 million inhabitants of Egypt live around the River Nile.

GLOSSARY

AMHARIC (Ethiopia)	
Wenz	river

BERBER (Algeria, Morocco)	
Adrar	hills, mountains

FRENCH	
Monts	mountains

ARABIC	
Bahr	river
Erg	sand dunes
Jabal; Jebel	mountain(s)
Wadi	watercourse
Wāḥāt	oasis

MAPPING CHANGE

Lake Chad (see D3) was previously much larger than it is today. The lake extent in 1922 is marked on the map to show how much it has shrunk.

THE NILE

Since the Stone Age the Nile has been the lifeblood for Egyptian civilization. The fertile silt deposited by the river as it flooded every summer led to the development of settlements along its banks and today the great majority of Egypt's population is still supported by it. The fertile area can be clearly seen in the image below as a ribbon of green cutting through the desert. Constructed to regulate the flow of the river, the Aswan High Dam was opened in 1971, and behind it Lake Nasser formed. The dam also provided hydroelectricity and improved navigation on the river which was previously hindered by a series of cataracts between northern Sudan and southern Egypt.

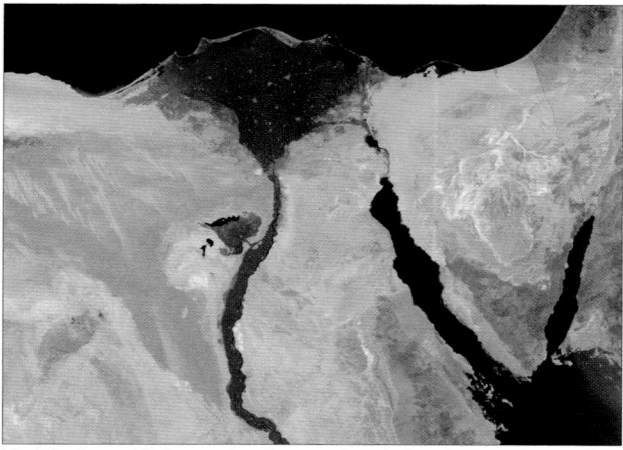

The Nile, the world's longest river, flows northwards from its source in central Africa to reach the Mediterranean Sea through its delta north of Cairo. Its major tributaries, the White Nile and Blue Nile join near to the Sudanese capital Khartoum and further north the river is joined by its other major tributary the Atbara. From there the river flows through a desert landscape until it splits into its two distributaries, the Rashid (Rosetta) and Dumyat (Damietta) branches at Cairo.

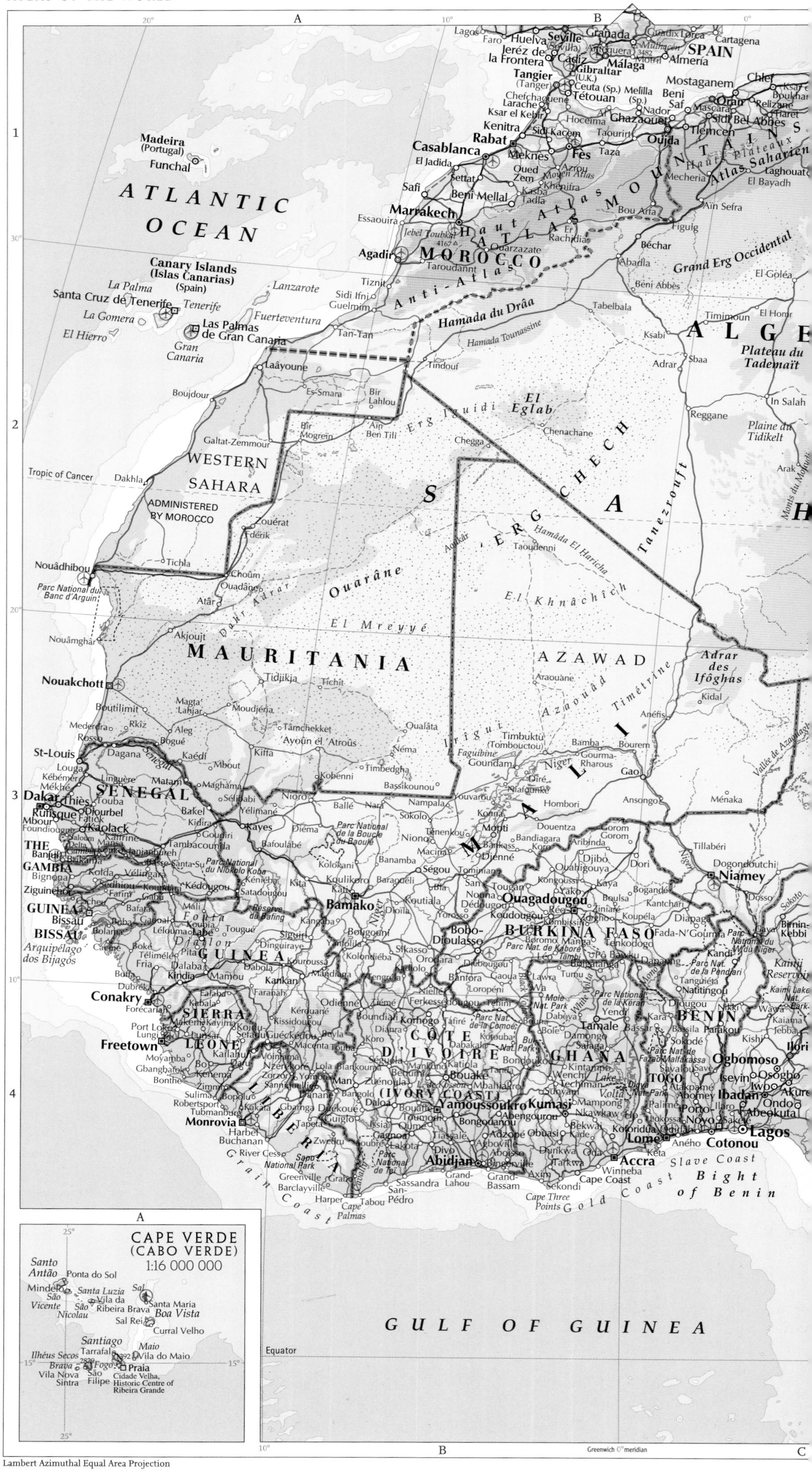

CAPE VERDE
(CABO VERDE)
1:16 000 000

Lambert Azimuthal Equal Area Projection

1 : 16 000 000

MILES 0   200   400   600

181

MEDITERRANEAN SEA

ITALY — Palermo, Trapani, Messina, Reggio di Calabria, Catania, Syracuse, Ragusa, Sicily, Gela, Agrigento, Mt Etna

Ionian Sea

MALTA — Valletta

GREECE — Athens (Athina), Patras, Corinth, Piraeus, Sparti, Milos, Crete (Kriti), Iraklion, Karpathos, Rhodes (Rodos)

TURKEY — Antalya, Denizli, Konya, Adana, Gaziantep, Şanlıurfa, Mersin, Tarsus, Iskenderun, Antakya, Mosul, Kirkük, Arbil/Hewlêr

CYPRUS (Lefkosia) — Nicosia, Limassol (Lemesos), Larnaka, Famagusta

SYRIA — Aleppo, Hamāh, Homs, Damascus, Dayr az Zawr, Tadmur, Latakia

LEBANON — Beirut, Tripoli, Sidon, Tyre

IRAQ — Ar Ramādī, Samarra, Tikrit

ISRAEL — Tel Aviv-Yafo, Haifa, Nazareth, Jerusalem (Al Quds / Yerushalayim), Beersheba

JORDAN — Amman, Irbid, Az Zarqā', Ma'an, Al Karak, As Salt, Sakākā

EGYPT — Alexandria (Al Iskandarīyah), Cairo (Al Qāhirah), Port Said, Suez, Giza, Tanta, Damanhūr, Al Mansūrah, Ismâilîya, Az Zaqāzīq, Al Fayyūm, Banī Suwayf, Al Minyā, Asyūt, Sūhaj, Qina, Luxor, Aswān, Hurghada, Marsā al 'Alam, Al Quşayr, Al Khārijah, Marsā Matrūh, Sinai

Western Desert (As Sahrā' al Gharbīyah), Eastern Desert, Wāhāt al Bahrīyah (Bahariya Oasis), Wāhāt al Farāfirah (Farafra Oasis), Wāhāt ad Dākhilah (Dakhla Oasis), Wāhāt al Khārijah (The Great Oasis)

Qattara Depression, Libyan Plateau, Great Sand Sea, Gulf of Suez, Gulf of Aqaba

SAUDI ARABIA — HIJAZ, Medina (Al Madīnah), Mecca (Makkah), Jeddah (Jiddah), Ta'if, Yanbu' al Bahr, Hā'il, Taymā', Tabūk, Dūba, Al Wajh, An Nafūd, King Abdullah Economic City

LIBYA — Tripoli (Tarābulus), Benghazi, Mişrātah, Al Khums, Tarhūnah, Sabhā, Murzuq, Al Jawf, Al Kufrah, Waddān, Ghadāmis, Ghāt, TRIPOLITANIA, FEZZAN, Tāzirbū, Sirte (Surt), Ajdābiyā, Al Marj, Darnah, Tubruq

Gulf of Sirte (Khalīj Surt), As Sarīr, Sarīr Tibesti, Rebiana Sand Sea (Ramlat Rabyānah), Idhān Murzuq, Idhān Awbārī, Hadabat al Jilf al Kabīr

ALGERIA — Algiers (Alger), Constantine, Annaba, Skikda, Bejaïa, Biskra, Touggourt, El Oued, Ouargla, Ghardaïa, Hassi Messaoud, In Aménas, In Amguid, Tamanrasset, Djanet, HOGGAR, Grand Erg Oriental, Hamada de Tinrhert, Tassili n'Ajjer, Plateau du Tademaït, Adrar, Mt Tahat 2918

TUNISIA — Tunis, Sfax, Sousse, Gabès, Kairouan, Bizerte, Gafsa, Medenine, Zarzis, Nabeul, Golfe de Gabès, Golfe de Hammamet

NIGER — Agadez, Zinder, Maradi, Tahoua, Arlit, Bilma, Fachi, Nguigmi, Diffa, Tessaoua, Goudoumaria, Réserve Naturelle Nationale de l'Aïr et du Ténéré, Massif de l'Aïr (Azbine), Erg du Ténéré, Grand Erg de Bilma, Ténéré du Tafassâsset, Plateau de Manguéni, Plateau du Djado, Termit and Tin Toumma National Nature and Cultural Reserve

CHAD — Ndjamena, Abéché, Faya, Moussoro, Ati, Biltine, Zouar, Bardaï, Oum-Hadjer, Mao, Bokoro, Massakory, Bol, Lake Chad, Bodélé, Tibesti, Emi Koussi 3415, Erdi, Massif Ennedi, Erg du Djourab, Dépression du Mourdi, Ounianga Kébir, Lakes of Ounianga, Koro Toro, Am-Djarass, Ouaddaï, Bahr el Ghazal, Extent of Lake Chad shoreline in 1922

NIGERIA — Abuja, Kano, Kaduna, Maiduguri, Zaria, Katsina, Jos, Maradi, Lafia, Makurdi, Lokoja, Enugu, Onitsha, Abakaliki, Yola, Bauchi, Gombe, Damaturu, Gashua, Nguru, Potiskum, Dutse, Wukari, Takum, Gusau, Funtua, Calabar, Uyo, Aba, Owerri, Umuahia, Port Harcourt, Warri, Benin City, Bioko, Mouths of the Niger, Yankari National Park

CAMEROON — Yaoundé, Douala, Maroua, Garoua, Ngaoundéré, Bamenda, Bafoussam, Bertoua, Edéa, Kribi, Ebolowa, Nkongsamba, Kumba, Mbouda, Foumban, Batouri, Mt Cameroun 4100, Cameroon Highlands, Parc National de la Bénoué, Parc National de Waza, Parc National de Bouba Ndjida, Parc National de Kalamaloué

CENTRAL AFRICAN REPUBLIC — Bangui, Bossangoa, Bouar, Bambari, Berbérati, Carnot, Bozoum, Kaga Bandoro, Sibut, Bria, Bouca, Ndélé, Obo, Bangassou, Zémio, Rafaï, Mobaye, Nola, Bimbo, Batangafo, Paoua, Parc National du Manovo-Gounda Saint Floris, Parc National de Bamingui-Bangoran, Parc National André Félix, Massif des Bongo

SUDAN — Khartoum, Omdurman, Port Sudan (Bür Sūdān), Kassala, El Obeid, Nyala, El Fasher, Wad Madani, Kosti, Sennar, Ed Dueim, Atbara, Berber, Dongola, Shendi, Ed Damer, El Geneina, Zalingei, Kadugli, Talodi, El Muglad, Ed Da'ein, Abu Zabad, En Nahud, Sinkat, Tokar, Suakin, Kerma, Merowe, Kareima, Merowe Dam, Shereiq, Kassala, Gedaref, Al Qadārif, Singa, Ad Damazin, Roseires Reservoir, Jebel Marra 3070, DARFUR, KORDOFAN, Nubian Desert, Bayuda Desert, Nuba Mountains, Wadi Howar National Park, Merga Oasis, Jebel Abyad Plateau, Bir en Natrûn, Selima Oasis, Wadi Halfa, Lake Nasser, Abu Hamed, Muhammad Qol, 'Uwaynāt (J. Uweinat 1893)

SOUTH SUDAN — Juba, Wau, Malakal, Bentiu, Aweil, Rumbek, Yei, Bor, Kuajok, Torit, Yambio, Renk, Nasir, Kodok, Pibor Post, Raga, Tambura, Nimule, White Nile, Sudd, Jonglei Canal, Boma National Park, Southern National Park, Bandingilo National Park, Lantoto National Park, Radom National Park, ADMINISTERED BY SUDAN, CLAIMED BY SOUTH SUDAN, Abyei

ERITREA — Asmara, Keren, Mersa Fatma, Assab, Barentu, Teseney, Dahlak Archipelago, Dahlak Marine National Park

ETHIOPIA — Addis Ababa (Ādīs Ābeba), Mek'ele, Gonder, Bahir Dar, Desē, Nazrēt, Jima, Gambēla, Debre Birhan, Dembī Dolo, Gimbi, Nek'emtē, Hosa'ina, Dilla, Negēlē, Goba, Āwash, Lake Tana, Chok'ē Mts, Simēn Mountains, Ras Dashen 4533, Great Rift Valley, Abaya Hāyk', Blue Nile (Ābay Wenz)

DEMOCRATIC REPUBLIC OF THE CONGO — Kisangani, Mbandaka, Bumba, Buta, Isiro, Bunia, Gemena, Lisala, Aketi, Basankusu, Businga, Bondo, Watsa, Faradje, Dungu, Boende, Ikela, Basoko, Banalia, Parc National de la Garamba, Parc National de la Maiko, Parc National de l'Okapi, Parc National des Virunga, Parc National de la Salonga Nord, Congo, Parc National de la Lomami

CONGO — Brazzaville, Ouésso, Impfondo, Dongou, Liranga, Epéna, Parc National de Nouabalé-Ndoki, Parc National d'Odzala, Parc National de la Léfini

GABON — Libreville, Port-Gentil, Parc National de la Lopé, Parc National de Minkébé, Parc National de Moukalaba-Doudou

EQUATORIAL GUINEA — Bata, Mongomo, Ebebiyin, Mbini

SÃO TOMÉ AND PRÍNCIPE — São Tomé, Príncipe

UGANDA — Kampala, Lake Albert, Lake Edward, Murchison Falls National Park, Queen Elizabeth National Park, Lake Kyoga, Gulu, Soroti, Mbale, Tororo, Lake Victoria

KENYA — Nairobi, Kisumu, Nakuru, Eldoret, Garissa, Kitale, Lodwar, Marsabit, Wajir, Mt Kenya (Kirinyaga), Lake Turkana, Mount Elgon National Park, Central Island National Park, South Island National Park, Sibiloi National Park, Tsavo East National Park, Machakos, Thika

TANZANIA — Serengeti National Park, Musoma, Lake Victoria

RWANDA — Kigali

UNDER EGYPTIAN ADMIN. / Halā'ib

UNDER KENYAN ADMIN. / Lokichokio, Ilemi Triangle

SCALE 0 200 400 600 800 KILOMETRES

137
1
144
2
194
3
194
4
5

194

AFRICA CENTRAL AND SOUTH

The map covers central and southern Africa, centring on the Democratic Republic of the Congo, formerly known as Zaïre and Belgian Congo. The African Great Lakes, and the Great Rift Valley in which they sit, feature prominently, in particular Lake Victoria, the world's third largest lake and the largest in Africa. Important features of southern Africa include the Makgadikgadi salt flats and the Okavango Delta, both in Botswana. Madagascar, in the Indian Ocean, is the fourth largest island in the world and is renowned for its unique flora and fauna.

FACTS

• The capital cities of the two Congos – Kinshasa and Brazzaville – face each other across the river Congo. The river was also known as the Zaïre when the dictator President Mobutu was in power in Zaïre between 1965 and 1997.

• Zanzibar was one of the main ports of Tanzania involved in the slave trade. It is estimated that about 600 000 slaves were sold through the Zanzibar market between 1830 and 1873.

• The term Great Rift Valley refers to a dramatic and extensive zone of geological faulting, mountain-building and volcanic activity stretching much of the way up eastern Africa and into the Red Sea and beyond.

GLOSSARY

AFRIKAANS		FRENCH	
-berg	mountain(s)	Chaîne	mountain range

ARABIC		MALAGASY (Madagascar)	
Bahr	river	Nosy	island
Jebel	mountain(s)	Tanjona	cape, point

Population living with HIV/AIDS, 2013

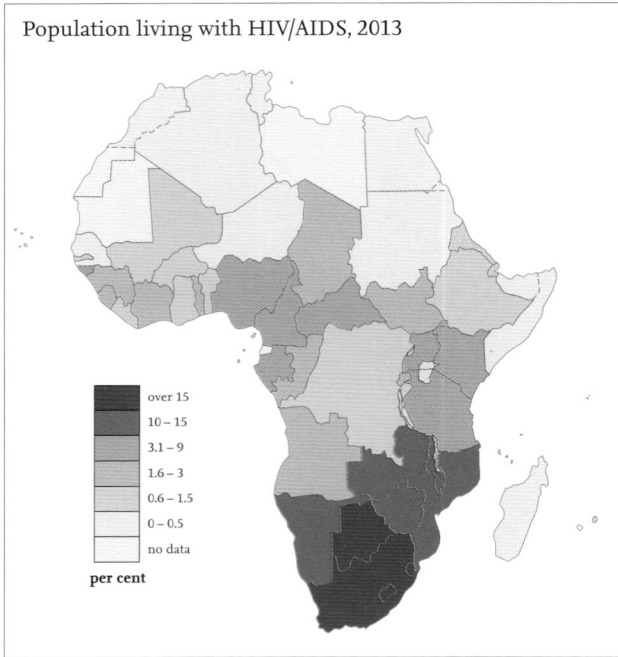

over 15
10 – 15
3.1 – 9
1.6 – 3
0.6 – 1.5
0 – 0.5
no data

per cent

With over 35 million people living with HIV/AIDS (Human Immunodeficiency Virus/Acquired Immune Deficiency Syndrome) worldwide and more than 29 million deaths from the disease, the AIDS epidemic poses one of the biggest threats to public health. The UNAIDS project estimated that 2.3 million people were newly infected in 2012 and that 1.6 million AIDS sufferers died. This is 28 per cent fewer new infections than the peak of 3.2 million in 1997. As well as the death count itself, in 2012 there were almost 15 million living African children, under the age of 18, that had been orphaned as a result of the disease. Treatment to prevent HIV transmission to children has resulted in a 52 per cent drop in infections worldwide between 2001 and 2012.

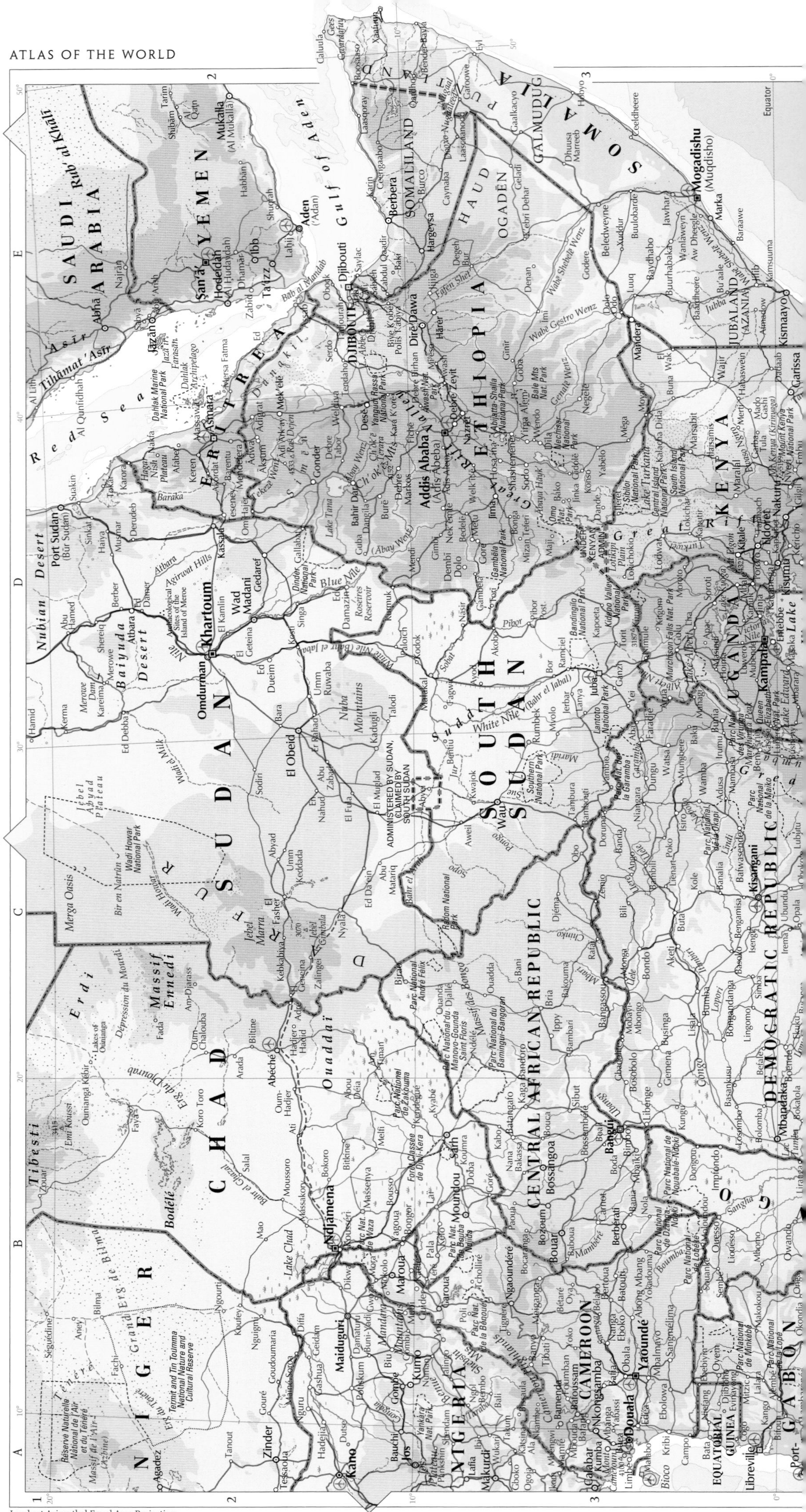

Lambert Azimuthal Equal Area Projection

1 : 16 000 000

MILES 0   200   400   600

© Collins Bartholomew Ltd

0   200   400   600   800 KILOMETRES

SOUTH AFRICA

The map focuses on South Africa – an important country in the politics and economy of the African continent. The country consists of nine provinces, which replaced the long-established four provinces in 1994. The independent kingdom of Lesotho is entirely enclosed within South Africa, while another kingdom, Swaziland, is almost so, located against the border with Mozambique. Dense urban areas, especially around Johannesburg, contrast with the sparsely-populated areas in the northwest towards the Kalahari and Namib deserts.

FACTS

- South Africa's former political system based on apartheid (separation of the races) was brought to an end at the election of 1994. The controversial system of semi-independent black homelands was abandoned at the same time.

- South Africa's overall administrative capital is Pretoria, but Cape Town (legislative capital) and Bloemfontein (judicial capital) share some of the functions of the national capital.

- South Africa's rich mineral resources make it the world's leading producer of gold and chromium, and a leading source of diamonds.

GLOSSARY

AFRIKAANS	
-berg; -berge	mountain(s)
-fontein	spring, well
Groot	big
-punt	cape, point
-veld	field

PORTUGUESE	
Cabo	cape, point
Ilhas	islands
Praia	beach, shore

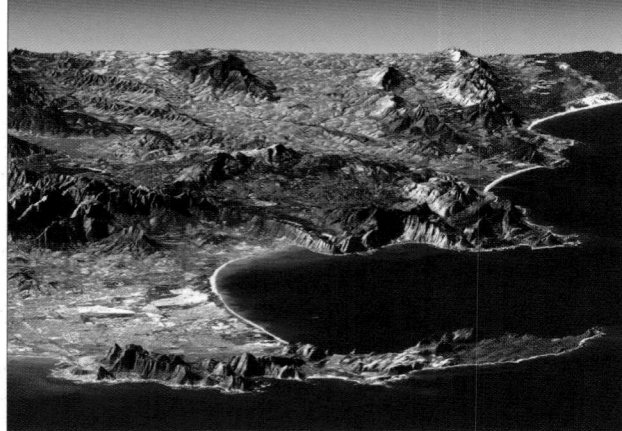

South Africa's legislative capital of Cape Town, seen in the bottom left of this 3-D perspective view, was originally founded in 1652 as a watering and supply station for the Dutch East India Company to serve its ships travelling between Europe and India. This route involves sailing around the Cape of Good Hope, renowned for wild weather and high seas.

The Cape of Good Hope is often mistaken as the southernmost tip of Africa (Cape Agulhas has this honour, as seen in this satellite image showing both capes). The cape was first rounded by the Portuguese navigator Bartolomeu Dias in 1488. He originally named it the 'Cape of Storms' but his king renamed it to reflect the hope of discovering India.

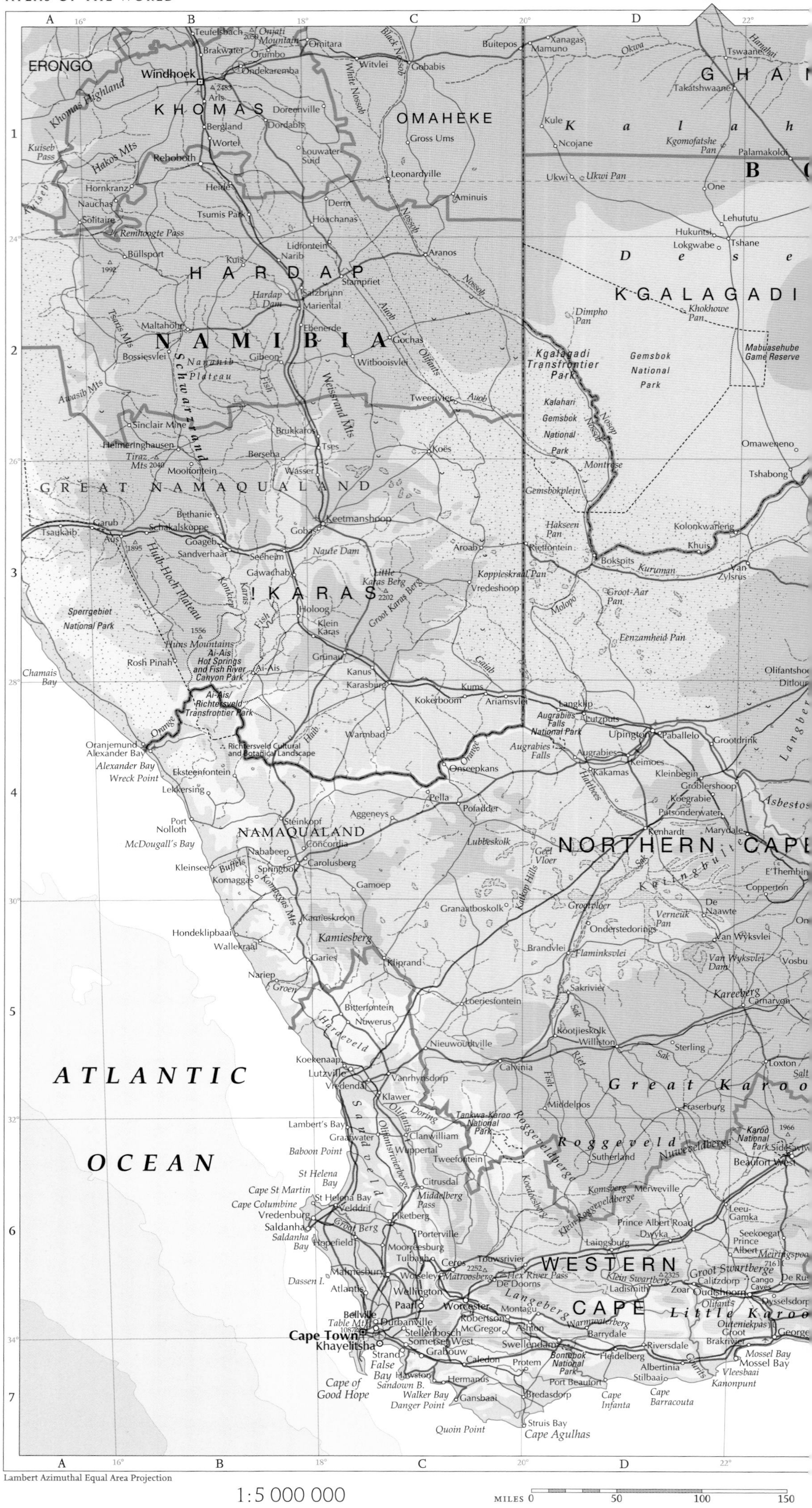

Lambert Azimuthal Equal Area Projection

1 : 5 000 000

MILES 0   50   100   150

195

© Collins Bartholomew Ltd

0   50   100   150   200   250 KILOMETRES

NORTH AMERICA PHYSICAL

The continent of North America is taken to include Mexico, Central America and the Caribbean. Mexico is physically part of the continent, but since it is Spanish-speaking its cultural and linguistic links connect it closely with South and Central America. The mostly ice-covered island of Greenland – a dependency of Denmark – lies to the northeast. The continent contains a wide range of landscapes, from the Arctic north to sub-tropical Central America, and from the high mountains of the west, to the central Great Plains.

FACTS

- The term Rocky Mountains is often applied to the whole mountain zone in the west. This area does, however, include many other significant mountain ranges and extensive plateaus.

- The Aleutian Islands, stretching in an arc across the northern Pacific, are part of Alaska.

- Lake Superior is the world's largest freshwater lake.

- Over 320 000 sq km (124 000 sq miles) of the USA is protected for conservation purposes.

- The inlet of the Pacific Ocean known as the Gulf of California is entirely within Mexico. The peninsula which defines it is known as Baja California, meaning Lower California.

HIGHEST MOUNTAINS	m	ft
Mt McKinley, USA	6 194	20 321
Mt Logan, Canada	5 959	19 550
Pico de Orizaba, Mexico	5 610	18 405
Mt St Elias, USA	5 489	18 008
Volcán Popocatépetl, Mexico	5 452	17 887
Mt Foraker, USA	5 303	17 398

LARGEST ISLANDS	sq km	sq miles
Greenland	2 175 600	839 999
Baffin Island	507 451	195 927
Victoria Island	217 291	83 896
Ellesmere Island	196 236	75 767
Cuba	110 860	42 803
Newfoundland	108 860	42 031
Hispaniola	76 192	29 418

LONGEST RIVERS	km	miles
Mississippi-Missouri	5 969	3 709
Mackenzie-Peace-Finlay	4 241	2 635
Missouri	4 086	2 539
Mississippi	3 765	2 340
Yukon	3 185	1 979
St Lawrence	3 058	1 900

LARGEST LAKES	sq km	sq miles
Lake Superior	82 100	31 699
Lake Huron	59 600	23 012
Lake Michigan	57 800	22 317
Great Bear Lake	31 328	12 096
Great Slave Lake	28 568	11 030
Lake Erie	25 700	9 923
Lake Winnipeg	24 387	9 416
Lake Ontario	18 960	7 320

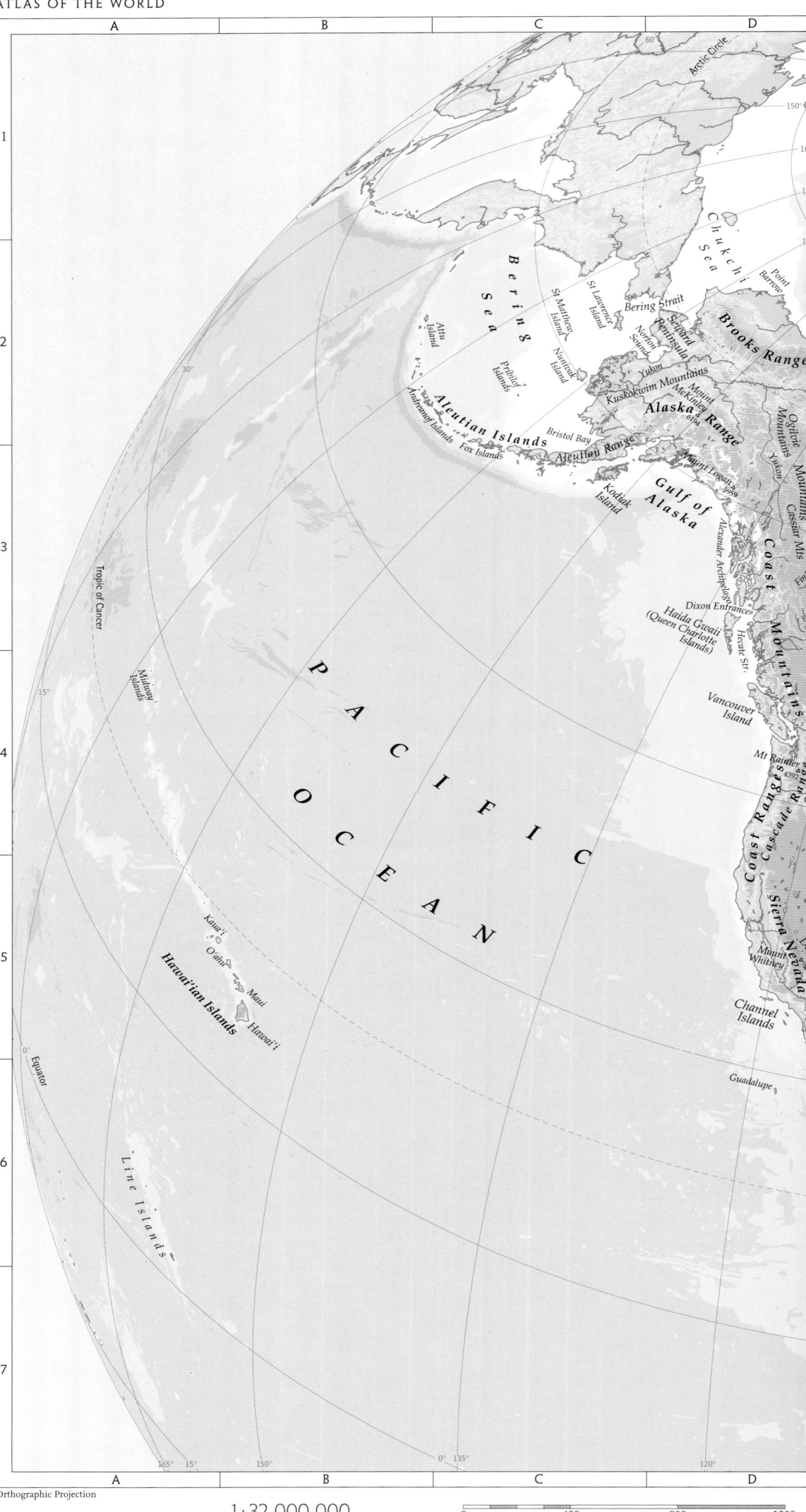

Orthographic Projection

1:32 000 000

MILES 0   400   800

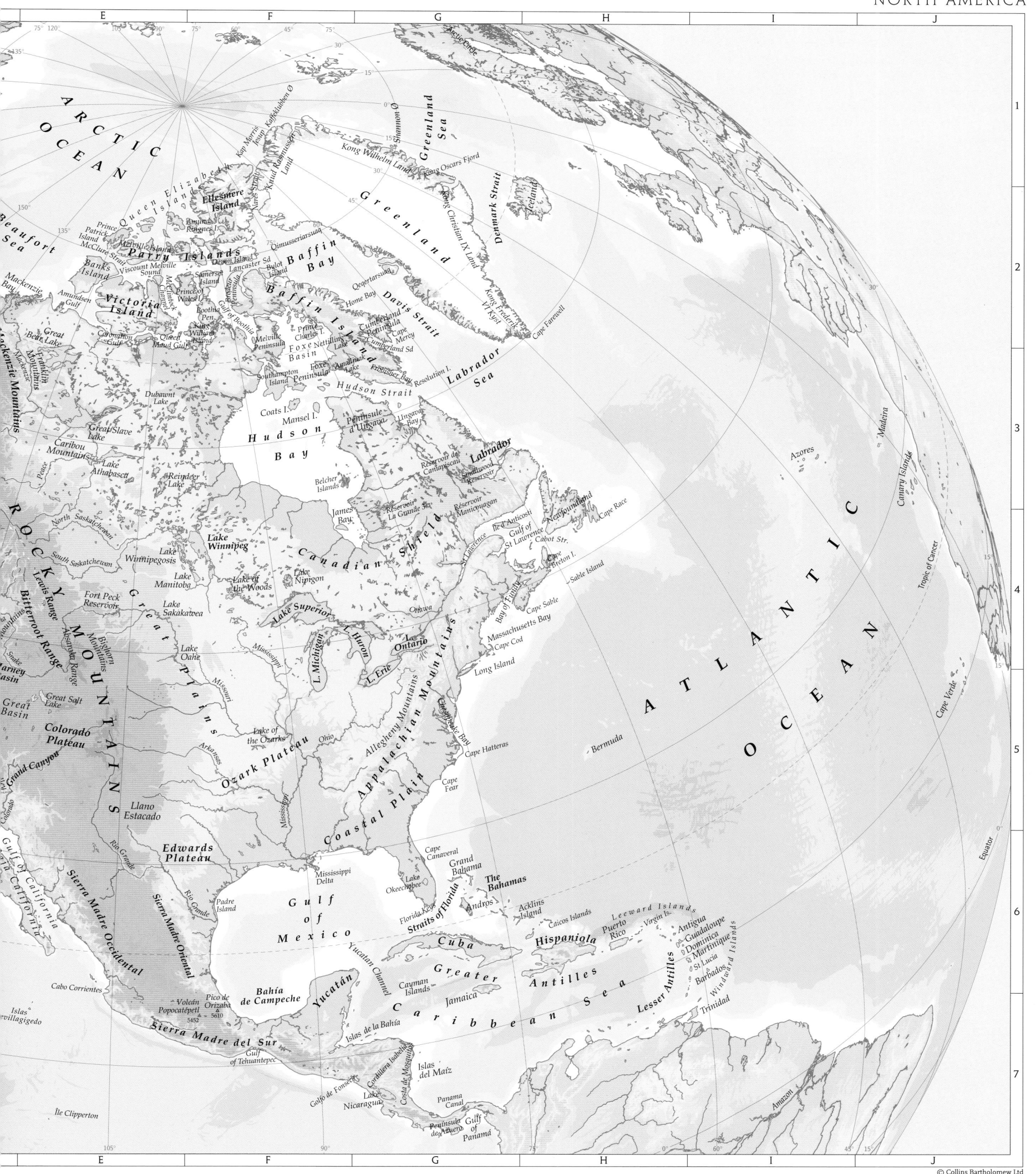

ARCTIC OCEAN

Beaufort Sea

Greenland Sea

Arctic Circle

Queen Elizabeth Islands

Ellesmere Island

Greenland

Kong Wilhelm Land

Kong Oscars Fjord

Kong Christian IX Land

Denmark Strait

Iceland

Prince Patrick Island

Melville Island

Banks Island

McClure Strait

Viscount Melville Sound

Parry Islands

Devon Island

Lancaster Sd

Baffin Bay

Qimusseriarsuaq

Home Bay

Davis Strait

Cape Farewell

Victoria Island

Great Bear Lake

Coronation Gulf

Amundsen Gulf

Franklin Mountains

Boothia Pen.

Gulf of Boothia

King William Island

Queen Maud Gulf

Somerset Island

Prince of Wales Island

Baffin Island

Melville Peninsula

Prince Charles I.

Foxe Basin

Foxe Channel

Cumberland Peninsula

Cumberland Sd

Cape Mercy

Frobisher Bay

Resolution I.

Labrador Sea

Mackenzie Mountains

Mackenzie Bay

Mackenzie

Dubawnt Lake

Southampton Island

Foxe Peninsula

Hudson Strait

Caribou Mountains

Great Slave Lake

Peace

Lake Athabasca

Reindeer Lake

Coats I.

Mansel I.

Peninsule d'Ungava

Ungava Bay

Hudson Bay

Labrador

ROCKY MOUNTAINS

North Saskatchewan

South Saskatchewan

Lake Winnipegosis

Lake Manitoba

Lake Winnipeg

Belcher Islands

James Bay

Réservoir La Grande

Canadian Shield

Réservoir de Caniapiscau

Smallwood Reservoir

Réservoir Manicouagan

Azores

Canary Islands

Madeira

Fort Peck Reservoir

Lewis Range

Bitterroot Range

Bighorn Mountains

Absaroka Range

Great Plains

Lake of the Woods

Lake Nipigon

Lake Superior

L. Michigan

L. Huron

Ottawa

Île d'Anticosti

Gulf of St Lawrence

Cabot Str.

Newfoundland

Cape Race

St Lawrence

C. Breton I.

Lake Sakakawea

Lake Oahe

Mississippi

Missouri

Lake Erie

Lake Ontario

Bay of Fundy

Cape Sable

Sable Island

Snake

Harney Basin

Great Salt Lake

Great Basin

Colorado Plateau

Grand Canyon

Colorado

Ohio

Arkansas

Lake of the Ozarks

Ozark Plateau

Appalachian Mountains

Allegheny Mountains

Massachusetts Bay

Cape Cod

Long Island

Chesapeake Bay

Cape Hatteras

ATLANTIC OCEAN

Bermuda

Cape Verde

Tropic of Cancer

Llano Estacado

Mississippi

Coastal Plain

Cape Fear

Edwards Plateau

Rio Grande

Padre Island

Cape Canaveral

Lake Okeechobee

Grand Bahama

The Bahamas

Gulf of California

Sierra Madre Occidental

Sierra Madre Oriental

Gulf of Mexico

Mississippi Delta

Florida Keys

Straits of Florida

Andros

Acklins Island

Caicos Islands

Puerto Rico

Virgin Is.

Leeward Islands

Antigua

Guadaloupe

Dominica

Martinique

St Lucia

Barbados

Cabo Corrientes

Bahía de Campeche

Yucatán

Yucatán Channel

Cuba

Cayman Islands

Jamaica

Greater Antilles

Hispaniola

Caribbean Sea

Lesser Antilles

Windward Islands

Trinidad

Islas Revillagigedo

Volcán Popocatépetl 5452

Pico de Orizaba 5610

Islas de la Bahía

Sierra Madre del Sur

Gulf of Tehuantepec

Golfo de Fonseca

Cordillera Isabelia

Islas del Maíz

Lago Nicaragua

Costa de Mosquitos

Panama Canal

Île Clipperton

Península de Azuero

Gulf of Panama

Amazon

Equator

0 400 800 1200 1600 2000 KILOMETRES

NORTH AMERICA POLITICAL

The United States of America consists of the states south of the '49th Parallel', plus Hawaii, far out in the Pacific Ocean, and Alaska, the large peninsula in the northwest of the continent. Alaska lies partly within the Arctic Circle, and faces Russia across the narrow Bering Strait. Canada, formerly a dominion of the UK, occupies the north of the Continent. The region includes numerous overseas territories, from enormous Greenland to tiny islands in the Caribbean Sea.

FACTS

- St Pierre and Miquelon is a small French dependent territory off the coast of Newfoundland and Labrador.

- The Caribbean Sea is defined as the area between the mainland of South America and the two major island arcs of the Greater Antilles (Cuba, Jamaica, Hispaniola, Puerto Rico) and the Lesser Antilles, which between them form the West Indies.

- Some islands of the West Indies remain as overseas dependencies of France, the Netherlands, the UK, and the USA.

- The world's longest single continuous land border stretches for 6416 km (3987 miles) between Canada and the USA.

LARGEST COUNTRIES	Area sq km	sq miles
Canada	9 984 670	3 855 103
United States of America	9 826 635	3 794 085
Mexico	1 972 545	761 604
Nicaragua	130 000	50 193
Honduras	112 088	43 277
Cuba	110 860	42 803
Guatemala	108 890	42 043
Panama	77 082	29 762
Costa Rica	51 100	19 730
Dominican Republic	48 442	18 704

MOST POPULATED COUNTRIES	Population
United States of America	320 051 000
Mexico	122 332 000
Canada	35 182 000
Guatemala	15 468 000
Cuba	11 266 000
Dominican Republic	10 404 000
Haiti	10 317 000
Honduras	8 098 000
El Salvador	6 340 000
Nicaragua	6 080 000

CAPITALS		
Largest population	**Mexico City,** Mexico	21 706 000
Smallest population	**Brades,** Montserrat	13 600
Most northerly	**Nuuk,** Greenland	64° 11' N
Most southerly	**Panama City,** Panama	8° 56' N
Highest	**Mexico City,** Mexico	2 300 m/ 7 546 ft

Administrative divisions abbreviated on the map:

U.S.A.		CANADA	
CONN.	CONNECTICUT	P.E.I.	PRINCE EDWARD ISLAND
DEL.	DELAWARE		
MD	MARYLAND		
MASS.	MASSACHUSETTS		
N.H.	NEW HAMPSHIRE		
N.J.	NEW JERSEY		
R.I.	RHODE ISLAND		
VER.	VERMONT		

Orthographic Projection

1 : 32 000 000

MILES 0   400   800   1200

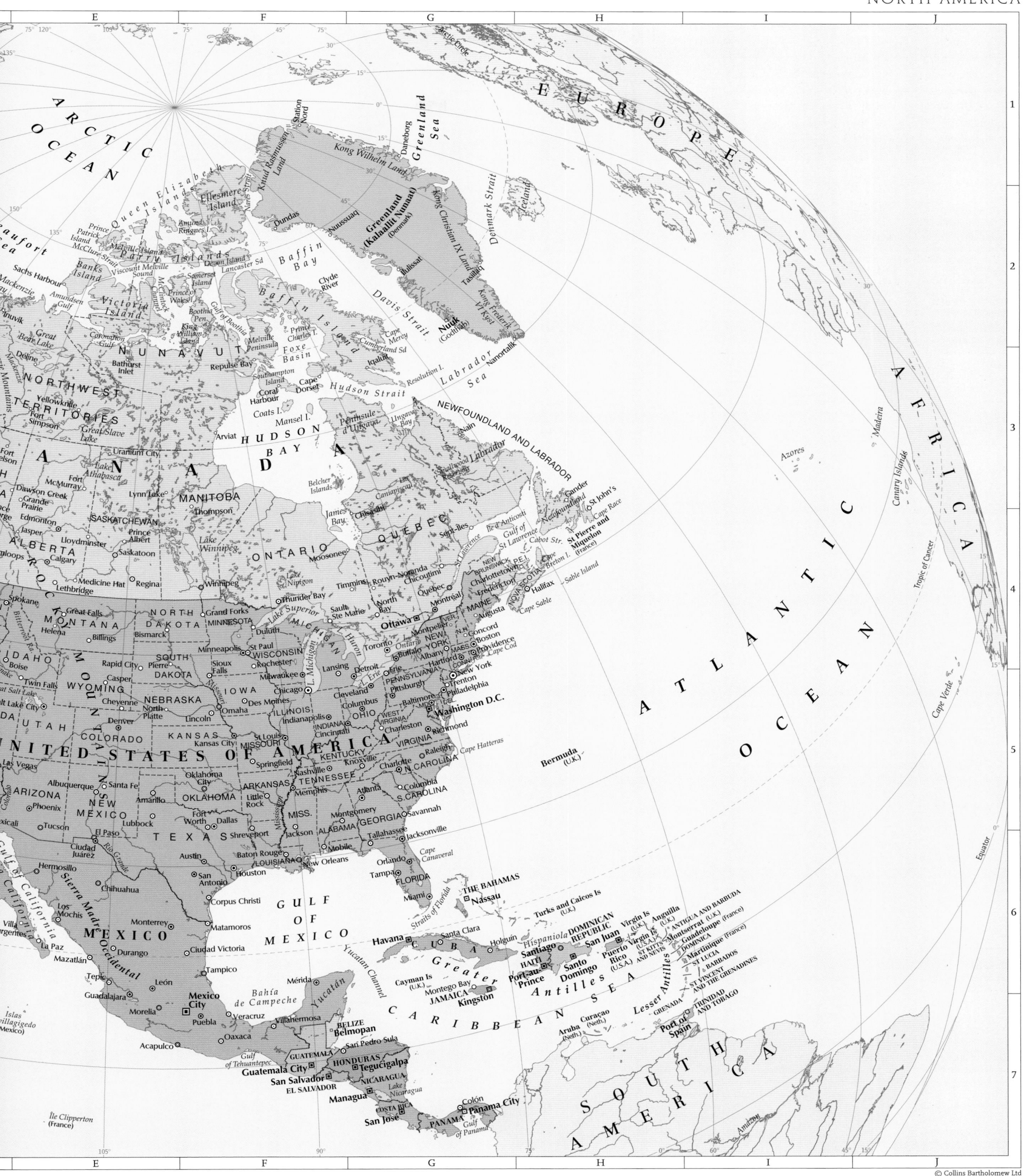

© Collins Bartholomew Ltd

0   400   800   1200   1600   2000 KILOMETRES

CANADA

Canada and Alaska occupy the northern half of North America. The Arctic north consists of a vast group of islands, the largest of which is Baffin Island. Hudson Bay forms a huge inlet in the east, while the west is dominated by major mountain ranges, particularly the Rocky Mountains. Much of the rest is lowland or plateau, dotted by thousands of lakes. Part of the boundary with the USA passes through the Great Lakes, west of which it runs along the 49th parallel.

FACTS

- Canada has the longest coastline of any country in the world.

- The territory of Nunavut is Canada's newest administrative division, created in 1999 from the eastern part of the Northwest Territories.

- The term Inuit is now used to refer to the Arctic people formerly called Eskimos. An individual is called an Inuk, and the language of the Inuit, with its own special alphabet, is Inuktitut.

- The Canadian province of Québec is largely French-speaking, a legacy of its French ownership in the 18th century.

- The state of Alaska was bought by the USA from Russia in 1867.

GLOSSARY

DANISH	
Kyst	coastal area

FRENCH	
Île; Îles	island; islands
Péninsule	peninsula

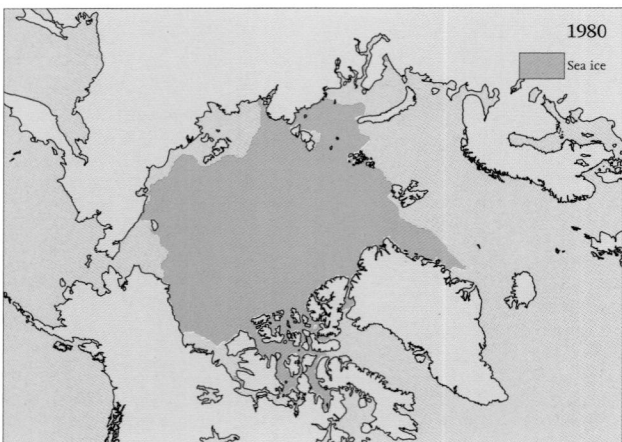

1980 — Sea ice

The Northwest Passage has been sought out by explorers for many centuries as a possible trade route through the Arctic Ocean and between the many islands of northern Canada. On the map from 1980, we can see that on any given year there was no guaranteed route through. This did not stop colonial powers in Europe and Asia trying to find a commercial sea route from as early as the 15th century. By the 19th century various expeditions had explored parts of the route but the final section was not located until 1854. However, it still took until 1906 for the Norwegian explorer Roald Amundsen to conquer the route by sea, but some parts of it were so shallow they could not be used for commercial traffic.

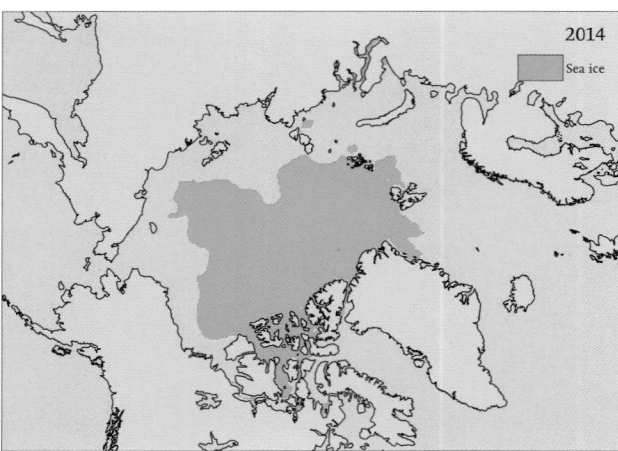

2014 — Sea ice

In this map from 2014 we can see the effect of climate change on the Arctic sea ice, which is now much reduced. It is thought that this change may keep the passage open for significant amounts of time, but the investment in escort ships and staging posts may mean it is 10 or 20 years before the route could be a viable alternative to the Panama Canal.

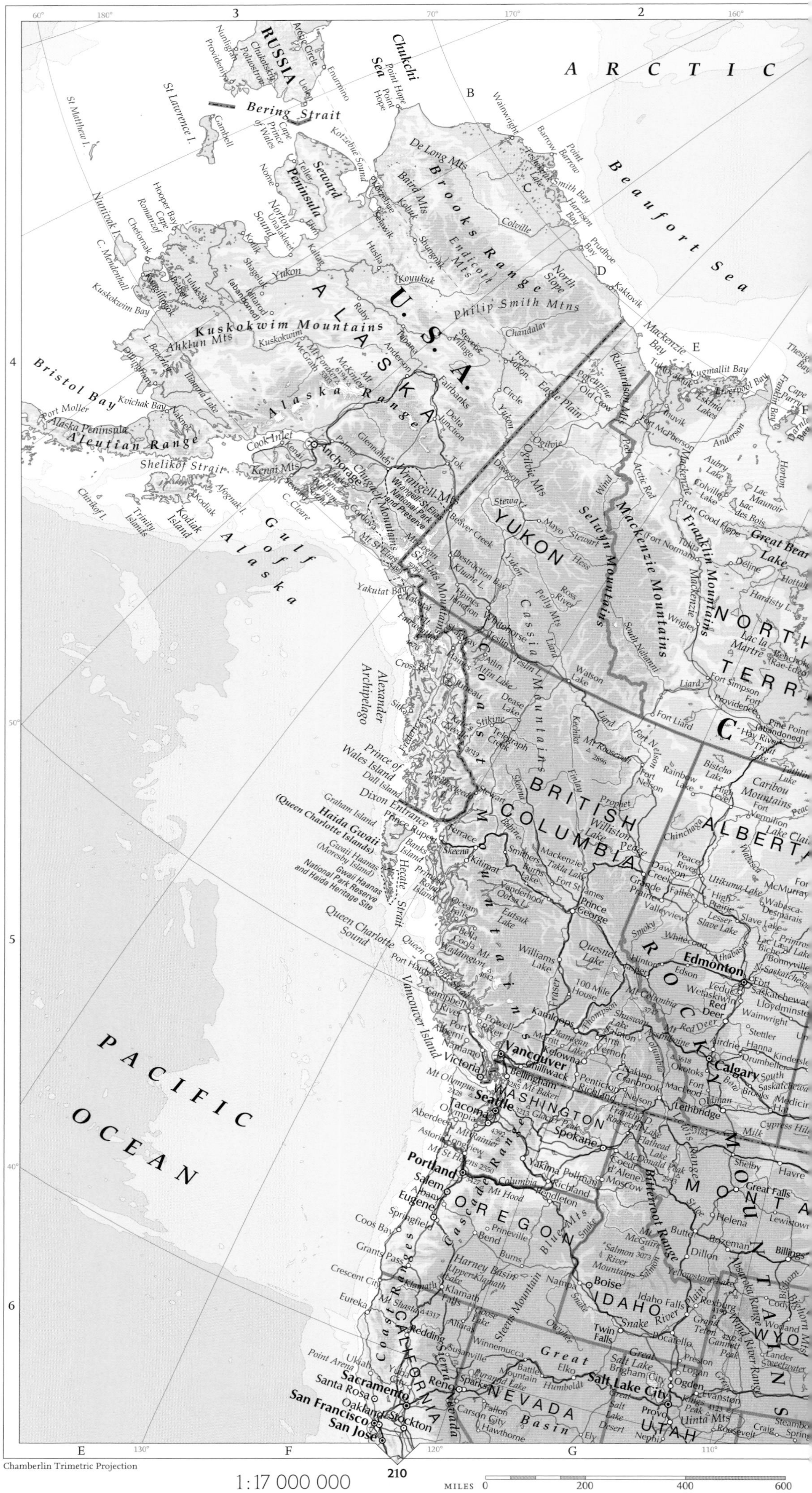

Chamberlin Trimetric Projection

1 : 17 000 000

MILES 0   200   400   600

© Collins Bartholomew Ltd

0 200 400 600 800 1000 KILOMETRES

CANADA WEST

This map shows the western half of Canada (with the exception of the extreme north), concentrating on the large provinces of British Columbia, Alberta, Saskatchewan, and Manitoba. British Columbia includes Vancouver Island and the Queen Charlotte Islands. Manitoba contains numerous lakes, notably lakes Winnipeg and Winnipegosis, while in the Northwest Territories are the Great Slave Lake and Great Bear Lake. The broad chain of the Rocky Mountains dominates the west. In contrast Manitoba, Saskatchewan, and eastern Alberta cover the extensive, flat plains known as the Prairies.

FACTS

- The Prairies of Canada and the USA are among the world's most productive agricultural lands, famous for wheat production.

- While Vancouver is the largest city in British Columbia it is not the capital. This is Victoria, which is on Vancouver Island.

- Straight-line boundaries often indicate vast stretches of plain or very sparsely populated territory. The boundaries of Saskatchewan are entirely straight which follow lines of latitude and longitude.

- The map highlights the great profusion of lakes in central and western Canada. In the three Prairie provinces alone there are well over 5000.

- Calgary in Alberta, hosted the 1988 Winter Olympics and Vancouver hosted them in 2010.

- Lake Winnipeg in Manitoba is the fifth-largest freshwater lake in Canada and although it has a relatively shallow average depth at 12 m (39ft) it was an important transport link before the railway arrived.

The international boundary between Canada and the USA is shown here in a forested area between Montana in the USA and British Columbia in Canada. In common with most forested areas the boundary is maintained as a cleared section of forest stretching into the distance in both directions with occasional white markers at regular intervals. The line extends across North America as a peaceful marker, which while undefended is well maintained.

BOUNDARY FACTS

- The boundary is maintained by the International Boundary Commission which was set up under the Treaty of 1908 to re-establish and map the boundary from coast to coast. The Treaty of 1925 established the commission as the permanent caretaker of the boundary and its markers.

- In forested areas the boundary is kept clear for 6 m (20 ft). It must be kept free of any obstruction and clearly marked so that laws can be properly enforced.

- The forested boundary is 2172 km (1350 miles) in length. The early clearing operation used manual tools such as saws and axes.

- The land boundary has a total length of 5061 km (3145 miles) with 5528 monuments and 5700 triangulation stations. The shortest distance between boundary monuments is 46 cm (18 inches).

- The Commission regulates any building work within 3 m (10 ft) of the boundary and defines the boundary in any legal situation involving the border.

Conic Equidistant Projection

1:7 000 000

MILES 0   50   100   150   200

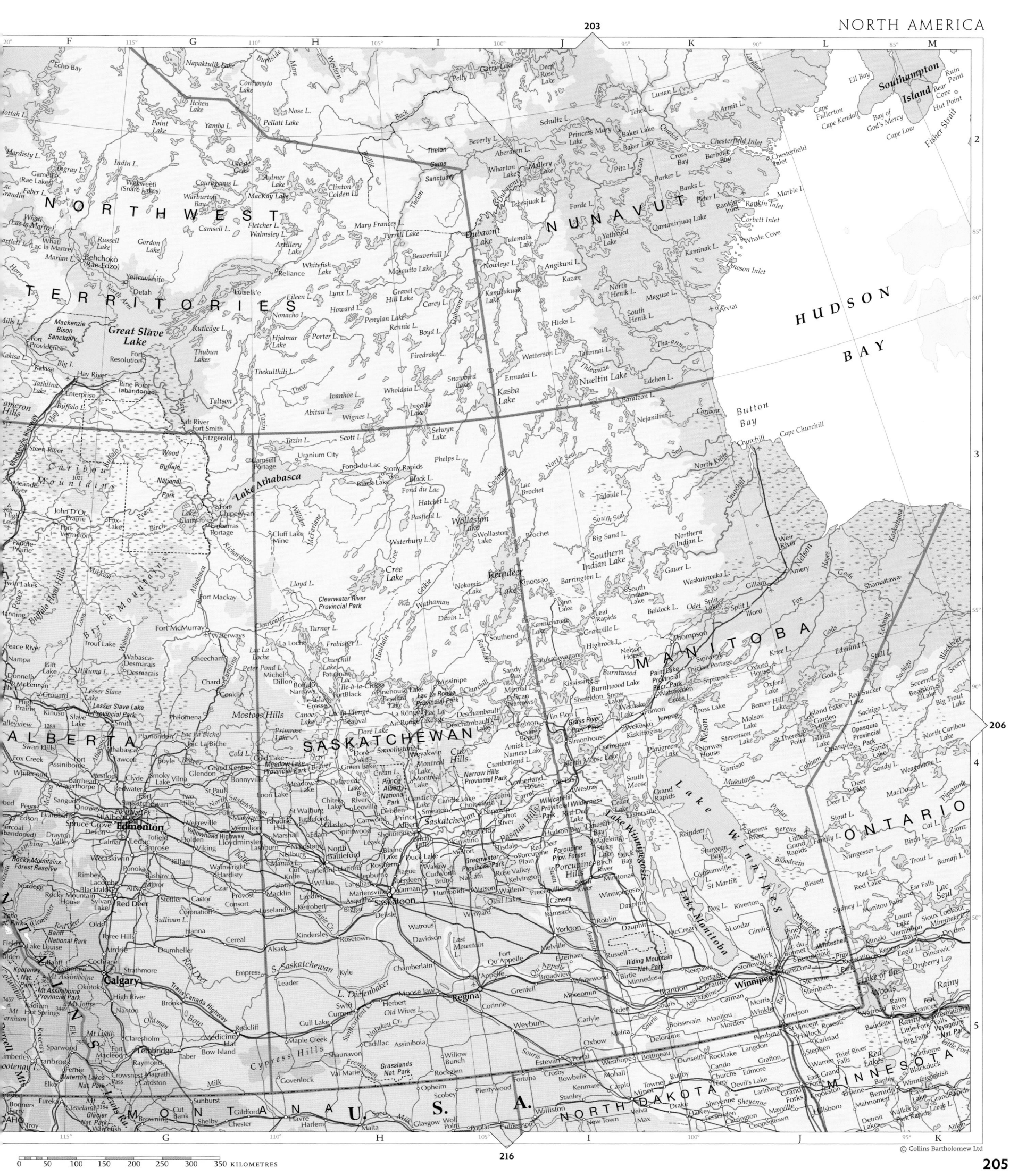

CANADA EAST

The large eastern provinces of Ontario and Québec are the chief focus of this map. Also shown are Newfoundland and Labrador, and the much smaller Nova Scotia, New Brunswick, and Prince Edward Island – Canada's Maritime Provinces. Ontario borders the USA along the Great Lakes which form the dominant physical feature of this map and are one of the most prominent features of the whole North American continent. Canada's national capital, Ottawa, is located within Ontario but is on the border with Québec.

FACTS

• French spellings are used throughout Québec. Indian languages and Inuktitut (formerly Eskimo) are also spoken here, particularly in the north.

• The province of Newfoundland and Labrador was officially renamed (from just Newfoundland) in 2001. It has always, however, included the large mainland region of Labrador, adjoining Québec.

• All the islands in Hudson Bay, even those very close against the Québec shore, belong to the northern province of Nunavut (see page 203).

• Nova Scotia means 'New Scotland' in Latin. Scots Gaelic language and culture are still prevalent in some areas of the province.

GLOSSARY

FRENCH			
Île; Îles	island; islands	Mont	mountain
Lac	lake	Rivière	river

The Bay of Fundy is a famous location to view the dramatic difference between high and low tides (see map G5). This bay and Ungava Bay (see map G2) have the largest tides on Earth. The high tide water level can be 17 m (56 feet) higher than low tide and can be more if there is a storm surge.

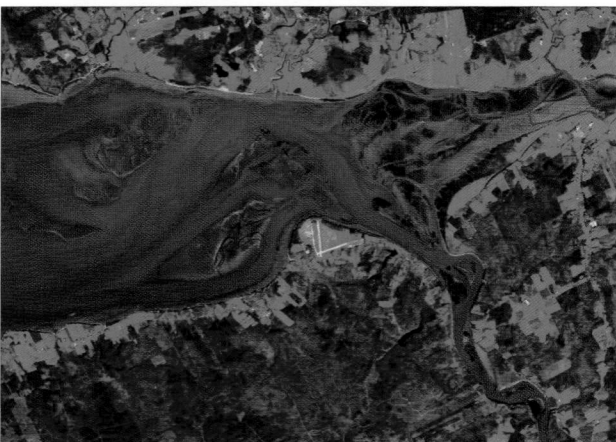

The pair of images shown here cover the area of the Minas Basin, (see map H4) which is the southern arm of the Bay of Fundy. Here during low tide, much of Cobequid Bay becomes exposed and the landscape looks more like a series of braided rivers in a wide channel.

The large tides are a result of tidal resonance. This occurs when the time between the high and low tides is the same, or almost the same as the time it takes a large wave to travel from the mouth of the bay all the way to the far shore and back. This allows the water moving around the bay to become synchronized with the lunar tides and so the tidal effect is amplified.

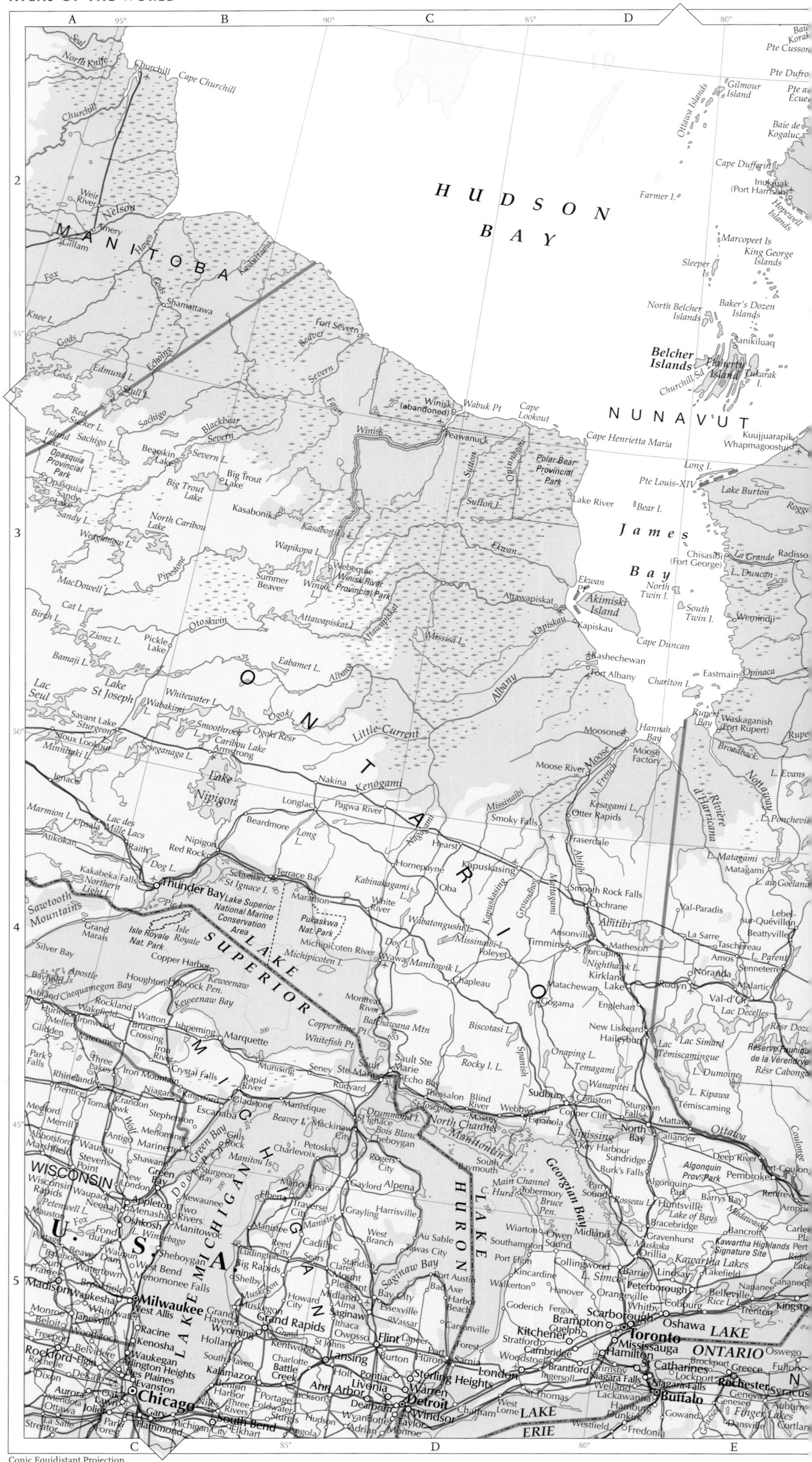

Conic Equidistant Projection

1:7 000 000

MILES 0   50   100   150   200

© Collins Bartholomew Ltd

THE GREAT LAKES

The map shows at large scale the interconnected Great Lakes of North America. Four of the lakes are shared between the USA and Canada, the fifth (Lake Michigan) lies entirely within the USA. The lakes have played a significant role in the economic development of North America and the region hosts some of the continent's largest cities and industrial centres. Niagara Falls are between Lake Erie and Lake Ontario, while numerous small lakes dot the landscape of the Canadian Shield in the top right of the map.

FACTS

• The Great Lakes contain one-fifth of the world's fresh water, only the Polar ice caps and Lake Baikal in Siberia contain more.

• The coastline of the lakes is 17 549 km (10 905 miles) and the area covered is 244 000 sq km (94 200 sq miles).

• Lake Superior is the largest lake by volume and also the deepest and coldest.

• The Great Lakes Legacy Act of 2002 provides money to clean up contaminated sediments from the lakes and to educate people about the issue.

Snow is important in many areas as a fresh water resource. Satellite images of snow extent can help to estimate the amount of water the snow contains, which helps to manage reservoirs and assists with flood prediction. The Great Lakes are a huge area of water and as such they have an effect on snowfall known as lake-effect snow. As a winter storm passes there is usually a strong cold air-flow behind the cold front and in areas south of the Great Lakes there will be heavy squalls, blowing snow and reduced visibility. The cold air picks up moisture as it passes over the lakes and the resulting snow can be heavier than the storm that preceded it.

In the satellite images above we can see how the snow cover moves south as winter passes. At the top we are in early December 2002 , while at the bottom we are in February 2014. These show well how the lake-effect snowfall has a major effect on the eastern and southern shores of the Great Lakes and how the effect is visible even although snow cover varies from year to year.

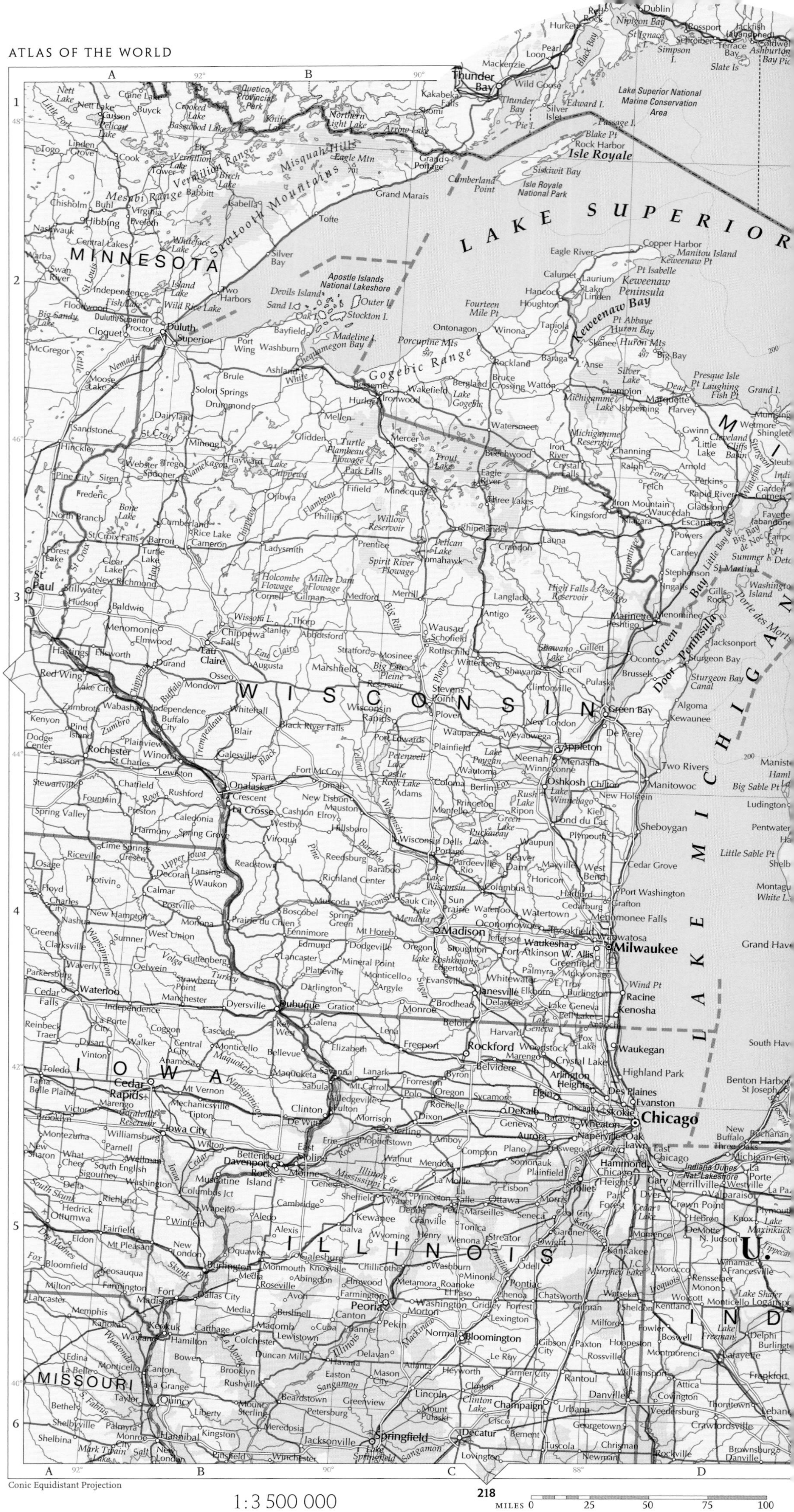

216

218

Conic Equidistant Projection

1 : 3 500 000

MILES 0   25   50   75   100

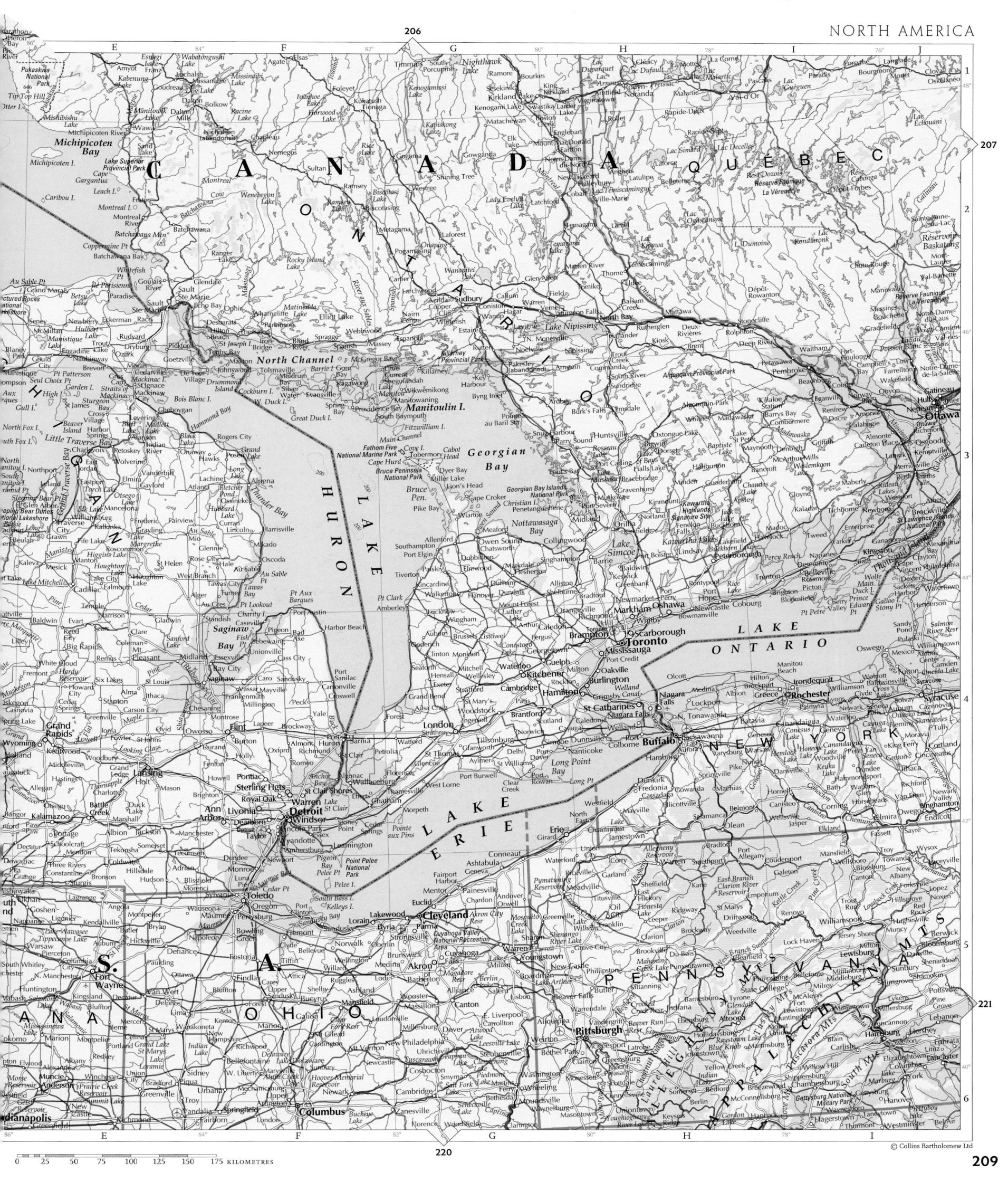

207

C A N A D A

Q U É B E C

O N T A R I O

Michipicoten Bay

Lake Superior Provincial Park

North Channel

Manitoulin I.

Fathom Five National Marine Park
Bruce Peninsula National Park

Bruce Pen.

L A K E H U R O N

Georgian Bay

Georgian Bay Islands National Park

Saginaw Bay

Nottawasaga Bay

Lake Simcoe

Toronto

Mississauga
Brampton
Markham
Scarborough
Oshawa

L A K E O N T A R I O

Burlington
Hamilton
Kitchener
Cambridge

St Catharines
Niagara Falls
Welland

Buffalo

N E W Y O R K

Rochester

Syracuse

Niagara Falls

Grand Rapids

Lansing

Flint

Detroit
Windsor
Dearborn
Ann Arbor
Livonia
Warren
Sterling Hgts

L A K E E R I E

Erie

Cleveland
Lakewood
Parma
Euclid

Lorain
Elyria

Akron

Toledo

U. S. A.

O H I O

Fort Wayne

Columbus

Pittsburgh

P E N N S Y L V A N I A

A L L E G H E N Y   M T S

A P P A L A C H I A N   M T S

Indianapolis

221

220

© Collins Bartholomew Ltd

0 25 50 75 100 125 150 175 KILOMETRES

209

UNITED STATES OF AMERICA

This map shows the forty-eight 'contiguous states' of the USA (including District of Columbia). The remaining states are Alaska (see page 202) and Hawaii (see page 214). Squeezing the USA onto a single map like this gives a 'snapshot' of the country and the locations of the individual states. It also shows the extents within the country of some of the world's most notable physical features, from the Rocky Mountains to the Mississippi-Missouri river – together the fourth longest in the world.

FACTS

- The Great Lakes, all shared with Canada apart from Lake Michigan, include the three biggest lakes in North America. Lake Superior is also the second biggest lake in the world, Lake Huron fourth, and Lake Michigan fifth.

- All the administrative divisions of the USA are designated as States except the area immediately surrounding the national capital, Washington, which is known as the District of Columbia – hence the expression 'Washington, D.C.'.

- Washington is not only the name of the capital, but also of one of the states – on the opposite side of the country, in the far northwest.

GLOSSARY

SPANISH			
Bahía	bay	**Punta**	cape, point
Isla	island	**San; Santa**	saint
Presa	reservoir	**Sierra**	mountain range

PRIMARY ENERGY CONSUMPTION

In 2008-9 energy markets became relatively volatile as a result of global economic and geopolitical instability. The increase in energy consumption slowed dramatically or even decreased in the developed parts of the world. The geography of energy production and consumption is highly uneven and a small number of countries dominate energy production and consumption. China is now the largest primary energy consumer having overtaken the USA in 2009. It consumes almost a fifth of the global primary energy. Although even in China this rate of growth is slowing. While the consumption of energy in Europe and North America has remained fairly constant between 2003 and 2013, there has been a huge increase in consumption of energy in the developing regions.

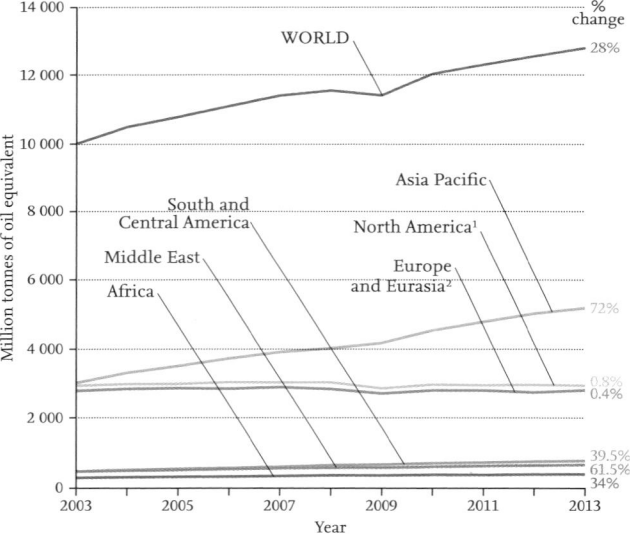

1. Canada, USA and Mexico.
2. Comprises: Russia, Estonia, Latvia, Lithuania, Belarus, Ukraine, Moldova, Georgia, Armenia, Azerbaijan, Kazakhstan, Uzbekistan, Turkmenistan, Tajikistan and Kyrgyzstan.

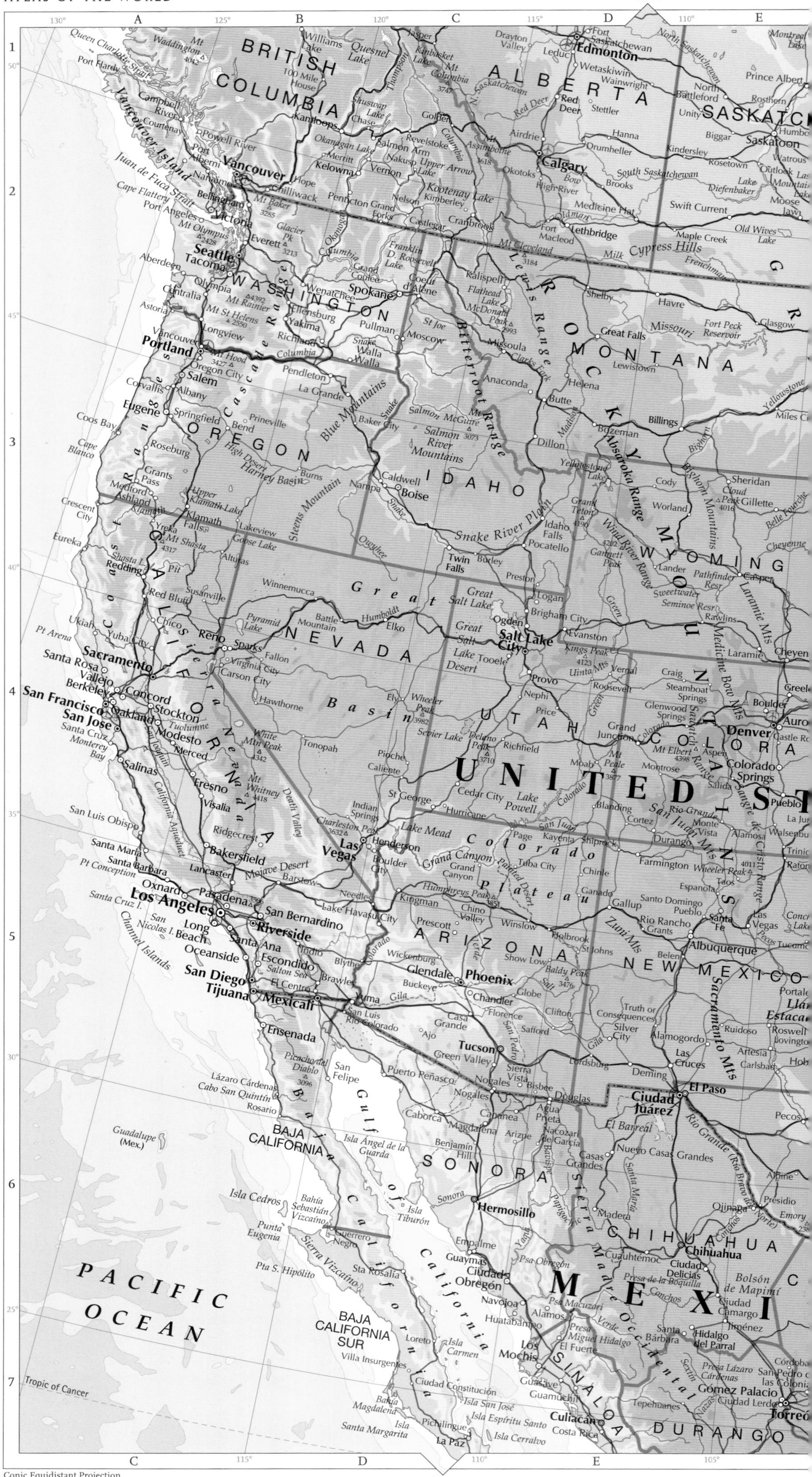

Conic Equidistant Projection

1 : 12 000 000

MILES 0   100   200   300   400

USA WEST

The area of the country covered here is the zone west of the Rocky Mountains, consisting of various mountain ranges separated by extensive plains and plateaus. The most important mountains apart from the Rockies themselves are the Sierra Nevada and the Coast Ranges. One large basin is occupied by the Great Salt Lake, next to which is Salt Lake City. The world famous Grand Canyon lies in the south of the map. Death Valley, notorious for its harsh climate lies to its west.

FACTS

- California is the most populous state of the USA with a population of over 38 million in 2014. Next in rank is Texas, with over 27 million and New York is third with more than 19 million.

- Spanish place names (such as Los Angeles and San Francisco) derive from early colonial times when Spain controlled large parts of what is now the western USA. The Spanish language is still widely spoken today.

- The huge western extension of the Great Salt Lake is an area of desert which is allowed to flood when the main lake becomes particularly full. It is known as the Newfoundland Evaporation Basin.

GLOSSARY

SPANISH			
Bahía	bay	**Punta**	cape, point
Desierto	desert	**San; Santa**	saint
Isla	island	**Sierra**	mountain range
Presa	reservoir		

The USA now has fifty-seven areas fully designated as a National Park with two more in it's dependent territories. In the USA a National Park is generally a large natural area with many different attributes, some of which may be historically significant. Hunting, mining, and some other destructive activities are not authorized. There are many other protected area designations within the USA, including national forests at federal level and a system of parks managed at state level.

Yellowstone National Park, the very first American National Park, was established in 1872. This image shows the lower Yellowstone Falls which are part of the Yellowstone Grand Canyon area. Other notable park features are the popular geyser known as "Old Faithful", the hot springs, and the varied wildlife.

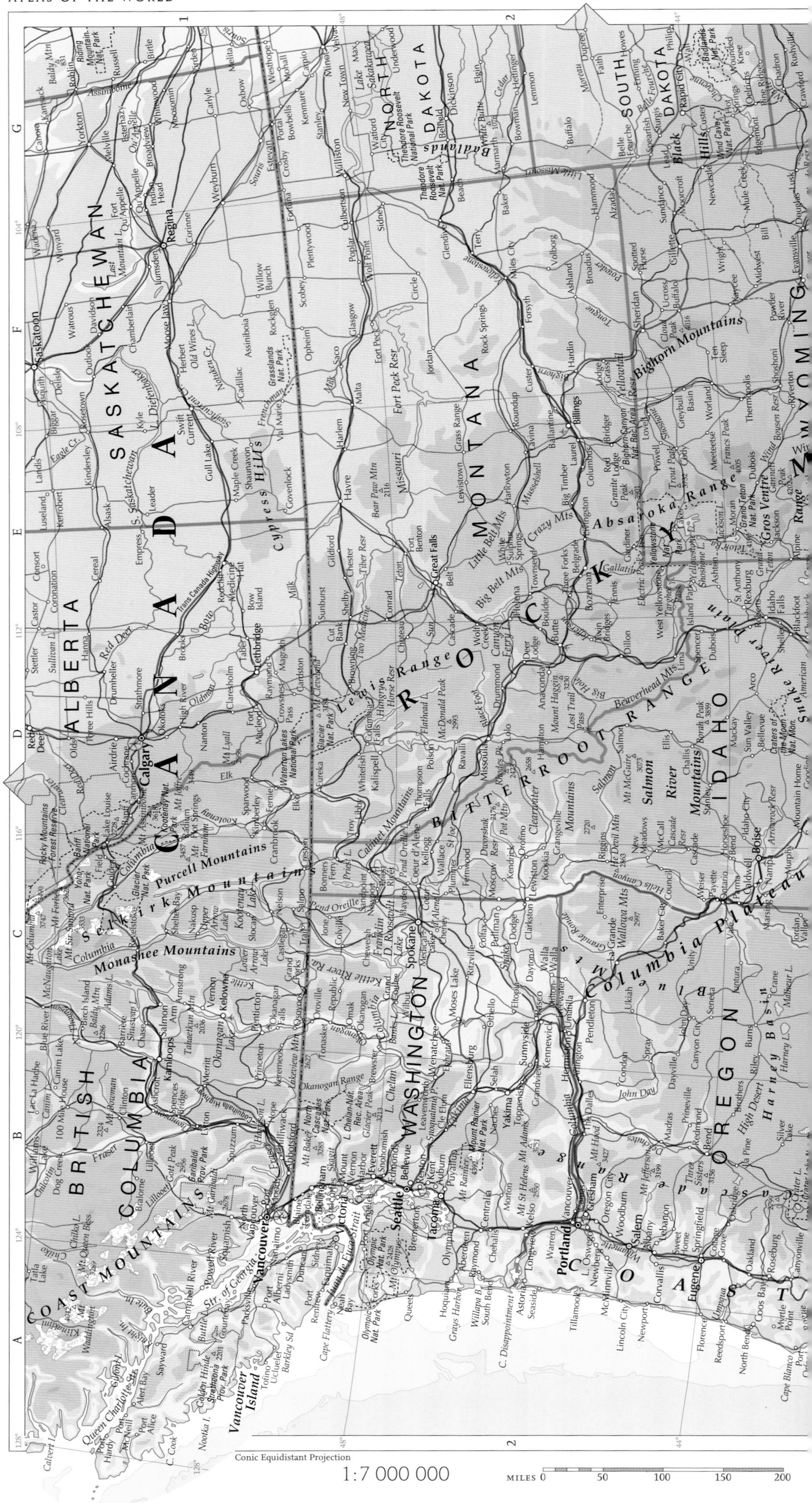

Conic Equidistant Projection

1:7 000 000

MILES 0   50   100   150   200

217

224

© Collins Bartholomew Ltd

0   50   100   150   200   250   300   350   KILOMETRES

USA SOUTHWEST

This large-scale map of the southwestern United States contrasts the high plateaus and deserts of Nevada, Arizona, and Utah with the broad lowland of California's central valley and the mountains of the Sierra Nevada. The Grand Canyon is shown in the east-centre, with lengthy reservoirs at each end. Death Valley, west of the centre of the map, lies below sea level and is the lowest point in North America. The many national park names describe other internationally famous landscapes. The inset highlights the chain of volcanic islands forming the state of Hawaii in the Pacific Ocean.

FACTS

• Mt Whitney (*see* map C3) is the highest point in the contiguous states at 4418 m (14 495 ft) and was named after Josiah Whitney, the State Geologist of California.

• The lowest point in North America is found in Death Valley (*see* map D3) where the land is -86 m (282 ft) below sea level.

• Death Valley is the hottest and driest place in the USA, where temperatures can reach more than 46 °C (115 °F) in the summer.

• The Grand Canyon (*see* map F3) was cut over many millennia by the Colorado river. The canyon is 446 km (277 miles) long, has a width from 6.4–29 km (4–18 miles) wide and reaches a depth of over 1.6 km (1 mile) in some places.

• San Francisco Bay (*see* map A3) is considered to be the largest landlocked harbour in the world.

• The state of Hawaii is an archipelago made up of over 130 points of land from Kure Atoll (*see* page 115) in the north to the main island of Hawai'i in the south. The state was the fiftieth to be admitted to the union on 20th August 1959.

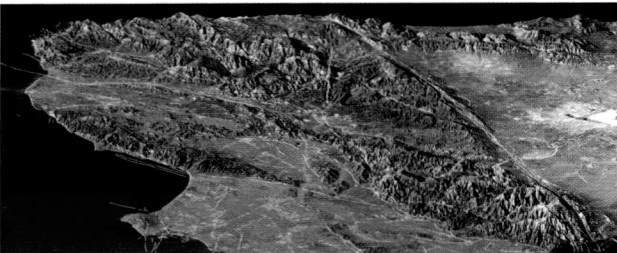

This is a satellite image of Los Angeles, where topographic shading has been added. It shows the southern end of the San Andreas fault which extends from northern California southward to Cajon Pass near San Bernardino (*see* map D4). Over much of its length, a linear trough reveals the presence of the fault from the air. Inside the trough there are distinctive lakes, bays, and valleys. On the ground, the fault is less obvious but can be recognized by interpreting the signs in the landscape. The fault zone has some distinctive landforms that include long straight escarpments, narrow ridges, and small ponds.

This is Wallace Creek, in San Luis Obisbo County. It is an excellent example of a stream channel making a dramatic right turn where it crosses the San Andreas fault. It is possible to use the offset of the stream from its original position to measure the movement of the fault over time.

PACIFIC OCEAN

O'AHU (Hawaii)
1:1 500 000

HAWAI'IAN ISLANDS (U.S.A.)
1:6 000 000

Lambert Conformal Conic Projection

1:3 500 000

MILES 0   25   50   75   200

D | E | F | G | H

UTAH

NEVADA

ARIZONA

COLORADO

NEW MEXICO

MEXICO

SONORA

BAJA CALIFORNIA

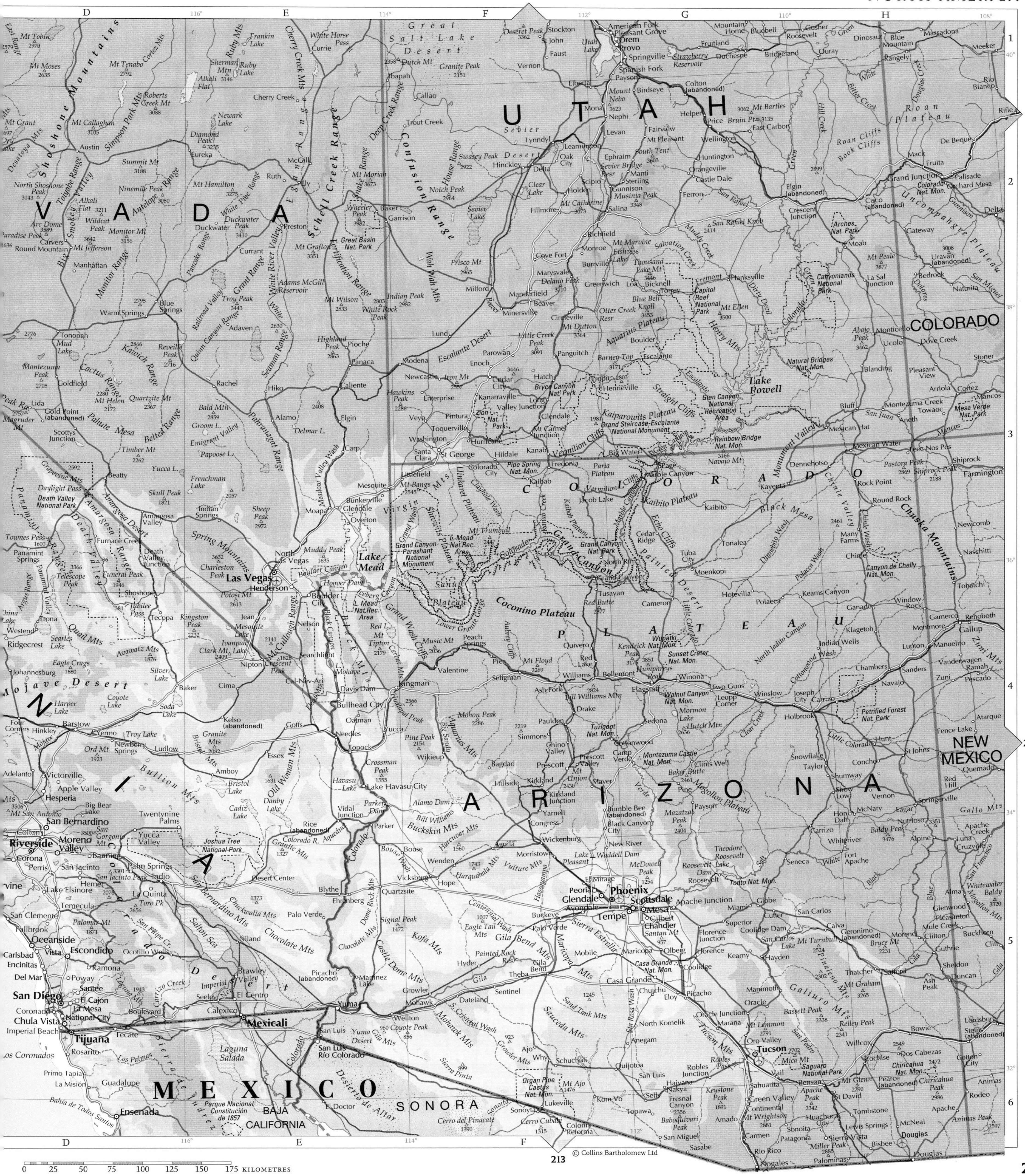

CALIFORNIA

Great Salt Lake Desert

Shoshone Mountains

Death Valley National Park

Mojave Desert

Lake Mead

Lake Powell

Grand Canyon

Coconino Plateau

Painted Desert

Las Vegas
North Las Vegas
Henderson
Boulder City
Hoover Dam

Phoenix
Glendale
Peoria
Scottsdale
Mesa
Tempe
Chandler
Gilbert
Avondale

Tucson

San Diego
Chula Vista
Tijuana
Mexicali
Yuma
Calexico

San Bernardino
Riverside
Moreno Valley
Oceanside
Escondido
Carlsbad
Palm Springs

Flagstaff
Prescott
Kingman
Bullhead City
Lake Havasu City

Gallup

St George
Cedar City

Tonopah
Goldfield
Beatty

Provo
Orem

Grand Canyon National Park

Petrified Forest Nat. Park

Joshua Tree National Park

Salton Sea

Colorado River

Gila River

Organ Pipe Cactus Nat. Mon.

© Collins Bartholomew Ltd

0 25 50 75 100 125 150 175 KILOMETRES

USA CENTRAL

The map focuses on the Great Plains – the extensive grassland zone in the centre of the USA. The plains rise gently from the valleys of the Mississippi and Missouri rivers to the Rocky Mountains, the southern end of which can be seen in Colorado and New Mexico. The Mississippi and Missouri together make up the longest river system in North America. The map shows about half of the border area between Mexico and the USA. The boundary here is defined by the course of the Rio Grande river.

FACTS

- The Mississippi-Missouri is the longest river in North America – at nearly 6000 km (around 3700 miles) – and the fourth longest in the world. (This includes lengthy headstreams which have other names).

- Kansas City is divided by the Missouri river between the states of Kansas and Missouri. By far the larger of the two cities is in Missouri.

- The eastern half of this map and the western part of the following map, cover what is known as the American 'Midwest'.

- As in California, there is considerable Spanish influence in this part of the USA resulting from its proximity to Mexico. The cross-border relationship has given rise to a culture and cuisine commonly referred to as Tex-Mex.

GLOSSARY

SPANISH			
Desierto	desert	**San; Santa**	saint
Llano	plain, prairie	**Serranía**	mountain range
Presa	reservoir	**Sierra (Sa)**	mountain range

The Mississippi river loses energy as it enters the Gulf of Mexico (*see* map F6) and this has accumulated over time to form the classic bird's-foot delta we have today – *see* image page 86. The delta changes shape over time and as it is very unstable there is little human settlement. However further inland cities such as New Orleans were built by the river and as a result the meanders of the river have been managed by a series of dams, locks, and canals.

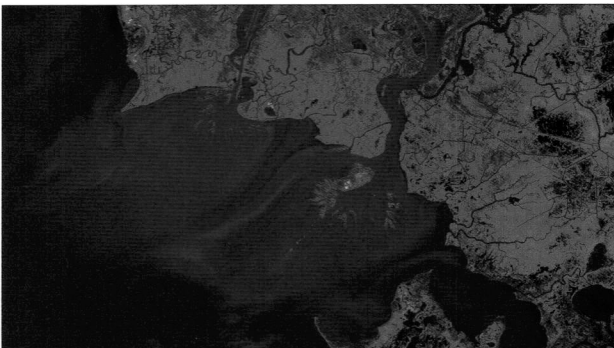

In these images dating from 1984 (top) and 2014 (bottom), the 2014 image shows how two new river deltas have developed at the mouths of the Atchafalaya River (right) and the Wax Lake Outlet (left). The slow-moving waters allow sediment to settle near the shore rather than being carried out into the Gulf of Mexico. During the floods of 2012, water was diverted from the Mississippi into the Atchafalaya, resulting in an increase in the sediment being carried by the river. This process raises the hope that land and water management could help to reclaim other areas of the Mississippi Delta.

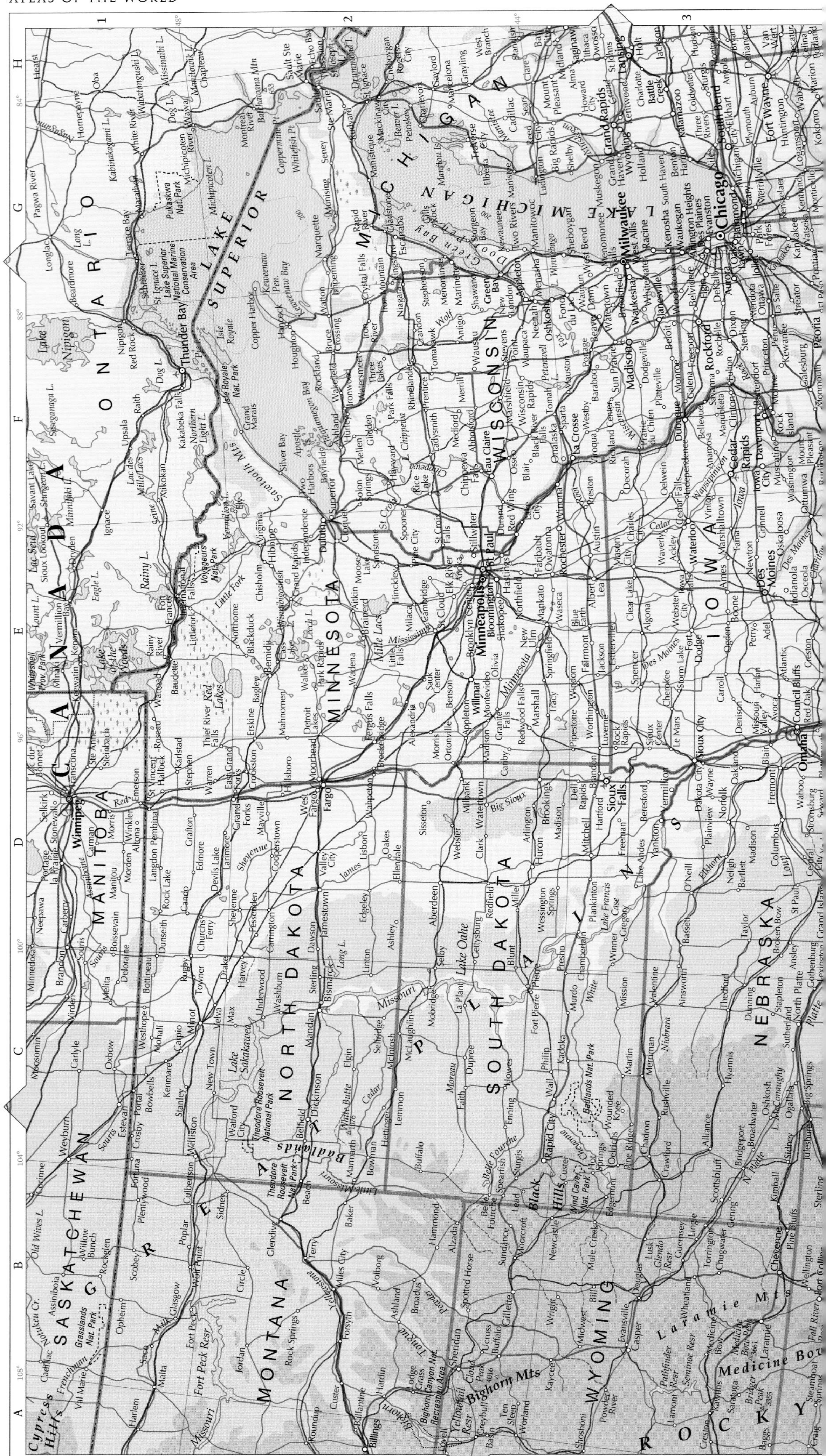

Lambert Conformal Conic Projection

1 : 7 000 000

MILES 0   50   100   150   200

© Collins Bartholomew Ltd

USA EAST

The map is dominated in the north by the Great Lakes and in the south by the peninsula of Florida, which defines the eastern side of the Gulf of Mexico. Not far offshore from Florida, the Bahamas form an independent country which used to be a possession of the United Kingdom. The Appalachian Mountains are the main feature inland, while on the coast Cape Hatteras shows prominently. The eastern seaboard has many barrier islands which protect the main coast, but which are themselves constantly changing in size and position due to wind and sea forces.

FACTS

- Florida is one of the world's major holiday destinations, most notably the cities of Orlando (of Disney World fame), Miami and West Palm Beach, and the wildlife-rich wetlands known as the Everglades.

- Western Florida is nicknamed the Panhandle because of its shape.

- Giovanni da Verrazano, an Italian explorer, is renowned as the first European to explore the Atlantic coast of North America between South Carolina and Newfoundland in 1524. In New York Harbour the Verrazano-Narrows Bridge is named in his honour.

- The coasts of Florida and North Carolina have long chains of narrow reefs or islands, often referred to as keys or cays.

There are hurricanes every year in the Caribbean and the Gulf of Mexico. The worst in terms of death toll was the Great Hurricane which swept over the Lesser Antilles in 1780, killing over 25 000 people. This map shows the tracks of more recent major hurricanes, including the second most deadly, Hurricane Mitch, which left a death toll of over 19 000 in 1998.

1980–2014 HURRICANE TRACKS

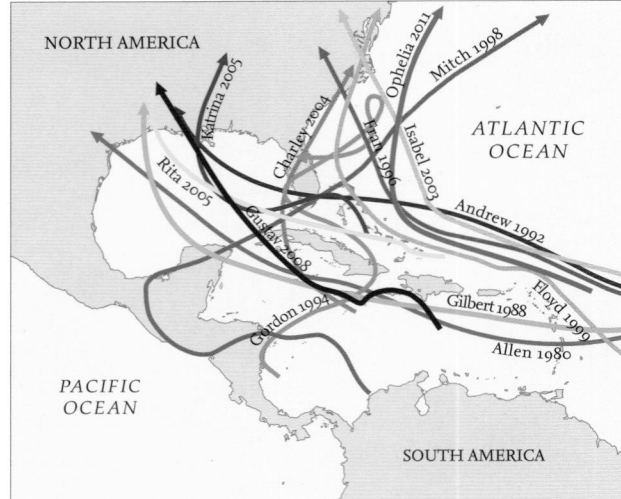

For the USA the most devastating hurricane in recent years was Katrina in 2005 which swept across Florida then crossed the Gulf of Mexico, intensifying as it did so. It made landfall in Louisiana, then again near the Louisiana-Mississippi border before breaching the levees that protect New Orleans. Hurricanes generate ferocious winds, but it is water, not wind, which causes the greatest damage and loss of life. As well as the heavy rain, the low pressure at the core of the storm allows the sea to bulge upward and the winds drive huge waves toward the shore. Together these produce a storm surge which can cause coastal flooding. Katrina produced a 9 m (30 feet) storm surge. About 80 per cent of New Orleans was flooded and there has been a long-lasting impact on the economy of the region.

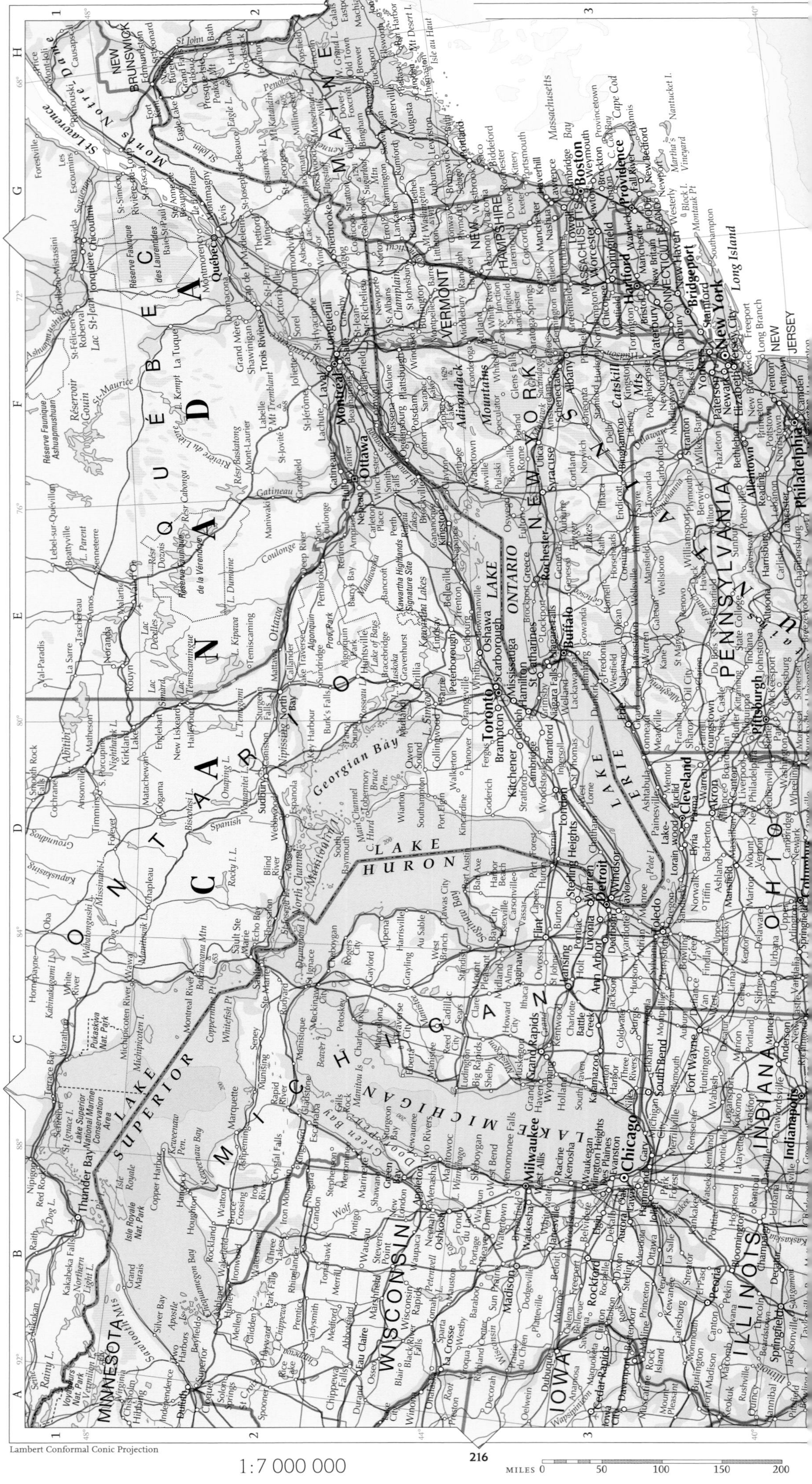

Lambert Conformal Conic Projection

1:7 000 000

MILES 0   50   100   150   200

© Collins Bartholomew Ltd

USA NORTHEAST

This map brings the densely-populated northeastern USA into focus. The great cities of the northeast are covered here, from Detroit (between Lakes Huron and Lake Erie) to Boston, New York, Philadelphia, Baltimore, and the capital, Washington D.C., ranged in a line down the east coast. The northeastern part of the map is New England, a region consisting of the states of Connecticut, Rhode Island, Massachusetts, Vermont, New Hampshire, and Maine.

FACTS

- New York, although the biggest city in the USA, is not the capital of New York state – this is the more central town of Albany.

- The USA's smallest state, Rhode Island, is not an island. The name is a shortening of a historic title which includes the small offshore island of that name.

- Niagara Falls (see map D3), on the USA/Canadian border, is commonly regarded as the second biggest waterfall in the world, by volume of water, after Khone falls on the Mekong river in Asia.

'MEGALOPOLIS'

Derived from Greek and meaning 'very large city', Megalopolis was first applied by the French geographer Jean Gottman in 1961 to the region of northeast USA extending from Boston in the north to Washington D.C. in the south. It is also often referred to as 'BosWash'. It has formed through the growth of individual large cities such as Boston, New York, Philadelphia, and Washington D.C. and their merging into one another to form an almost contiguous built-up area.

This 'map of paved surfaces' in the Washington-Baltimore area has been produced from satellite imagery and by means of the application of 'false colour' shows the areas of impervious surfaces – buildings and roads. The extent of the built-up area can be easily seen by the red and purple colours.

The region has a population in excess of 52 million – about 16 per cent of the total of the USA in an area of less than 2 per cent of the country's land area. It is the commercial centre of the country and home to many major domestic and international companies.

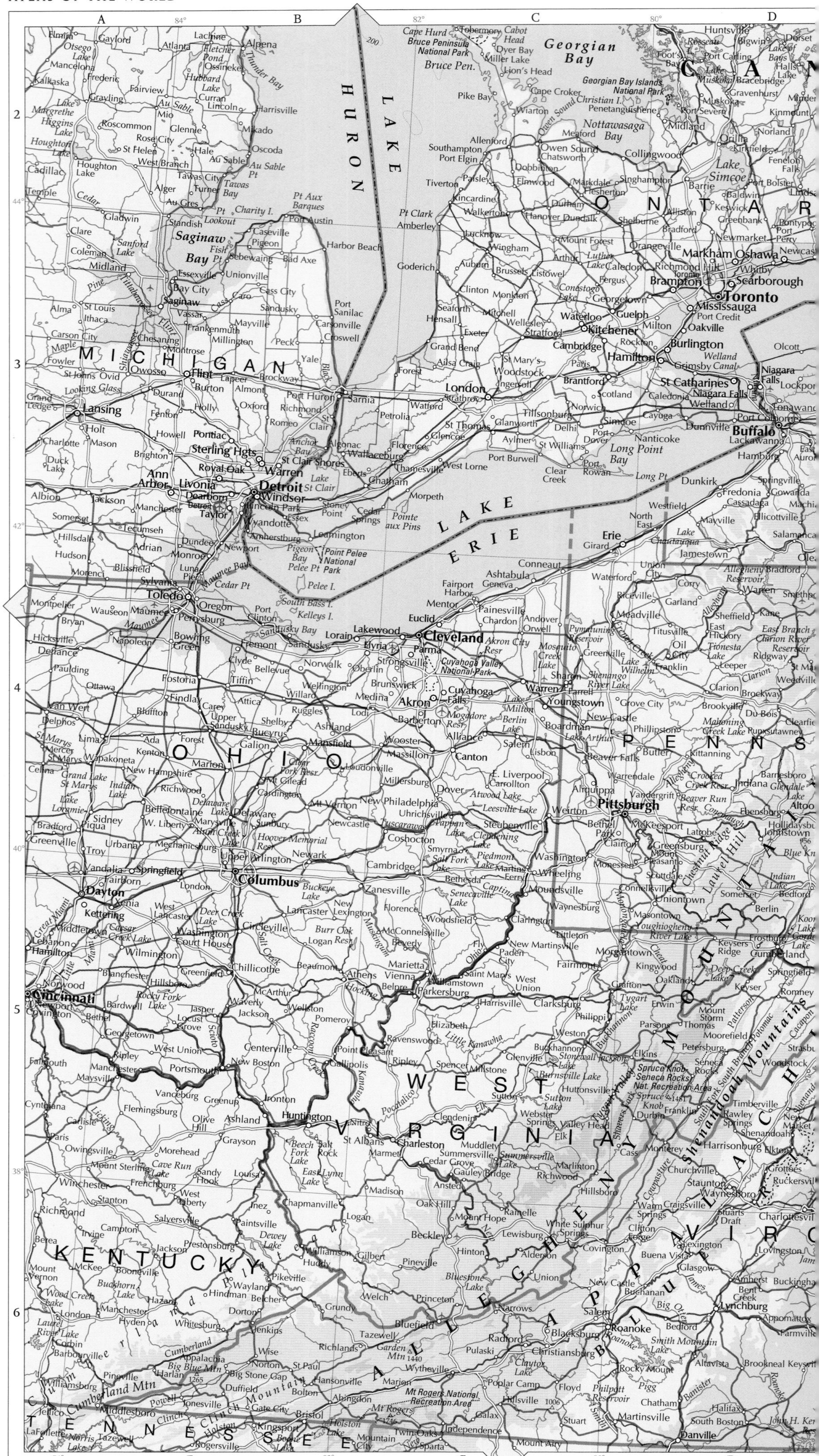

Lambert Conformal Conic Projection

1:3 500 000

MILES 0   25   50   75   100

CENTRAL AMERICA AND THE CARIBBEAN

The map shows the whole chain of islands constituting the West Indies, including all the islands of the Greater and Lesser Antilles, and the countries of mainland Central America. With the southern coast of the USA and the northern coast of South America, these encircle the Caribbean Sea and the Gulf of Mexico – both branches of the Atlantic Ocean. Central America's countries take up the narrow neck of land linking North and South America.

FACTS

- Cuba is the largest island in the region. For several decades, it was seen as a security threat to the USA, owing to its extreme proximity and its close alliance with the former Soviet Union.

- The USA maintains a military base on the coast of Cuba, at Guantánamo Bay – well-known in recent years as a detention camp for suspected terrorists.

- Guadeloupe and Martinique are governed as integral parts of France, rather than as dependent overseas territories in the usual sense.

- The narrowness of Panama has been taken advantage of by the Panama Canal – a vital shipping route opened in 1914.

GLOSSARY

SPANISH			
Bahía	bay	**Isla**	island
Cabo	cape	**Islas**	islands
Cayos	islands	**Punta**	cape, point
Costa	coastal area	**San; Santa**	saint
Golfo	gulf, bay		

This satellite image combines visible and near-infrared wavelengths and clearly shows changes in land use across the United States/Mexico border. Areas of vegetation are displayed in red. The grid pattern of the lush agricultural fields of southern California is in stark contrast to the more barren area of northwest Mexico on the lower half of the image. The street pattern of the border town of Mexicali is also clearly seen. The border is patrolled by United States border guards as there is a major problem with illegal entry and smuggling into the United States. The border patrol only intercepts around sixty per cent of illegal immigrants. However, the total number of illegal border crossings has fallen in recent years. A security fence has been built along much of the border and this has been a contributory factor in this reduction in numbers.

Lambert Azimuthal Equal Area Projection

1 : 14 000 000

MILES 0   200   400

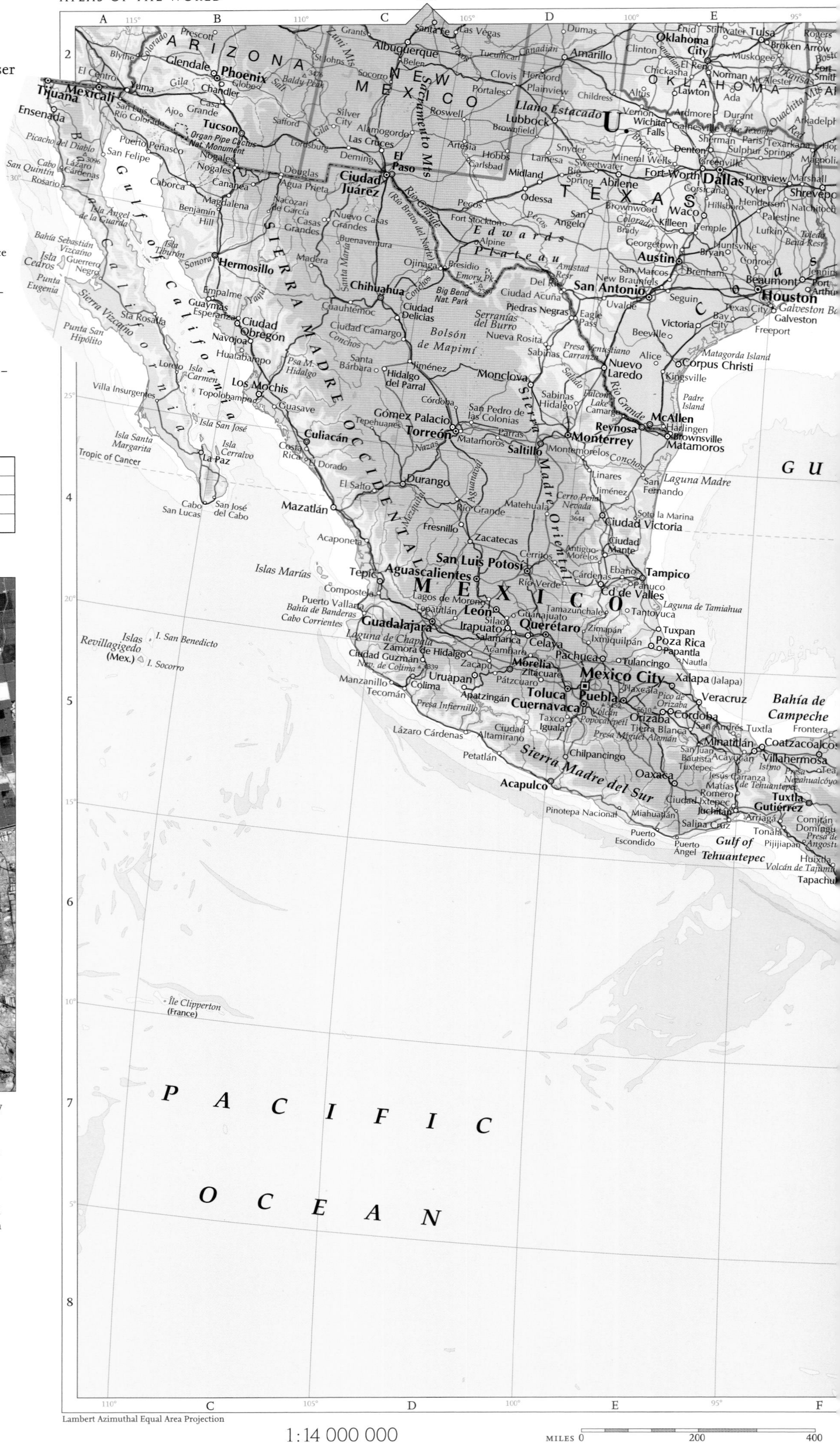

211

ATLANTIC OCEAN

GULF OF MEXICO

THE BAHAMAS

CARIBBEAN SEA

Tropic of Cancer

Bermuda (U.K.) Hamilton

TENNESSEE
Nashville
Memphis
Chattanooga
Knoxville
Asheville
ALABAMA
Birmingham
Atlanta
GEORGIA
Columbus
Montgomery
Mobile
New Orleans
MISSISSIPPI
Jackson
LOUISIANA
Baton Rouge
Little Rock
KANSAS

NORTH CAROLINA
Charlotte
Raleigh
Durham
Greensboro
Winston-Salem
SOUTH CAROLINA
Columbia
Charleston
Savannah
Jacksonville
Tallahassee
Panama City
Pensacola
Cape Hatteras
Cape Fear
Cape Lookout
Wilmington
Myrtle Beach
Hilton Head Island

Orlando
Tampa
St Petersburg
Clearwater
Sarasota
Fort Myers
West Palm Beach
Fort Lauderdale
Hollywood
Miami
Miami Beach
Key West
Daytona Beach
Melbourne
Cape Canaveral
Lake Okeechobee
Everglades Nat. Park
Big Cypress Nat. Reserve
Cape Sable
Gainesville
Ocala

Grand Bahama
Freeport
Little Abaco
Great Abaco
Eleuthera
Nassau
Andros
Cat Island
San Salvador
Rum Cay
Long Island
Crooked Island
Acklins Island
Mayaguana
Great Inagua
Turks and Caicos Islands (U.K.)
Grand Turk (Cockburn Town)
Turks Is

Havana (La Habana)
Matanzas
Pinar del Río
Santa Clara
Cienfuegos
Trinidad
CUBA
Camagüey
Ciego de Ávila
Holguín
Bayamo
Santiago de Cuba
Guantánamo
Las Tunas
Isla de la Juventud
Yucatan Channel

Mérida
Cancún
Cozumel
YUCATÁN
Chetumal
BELIZE
Belmopan
GUATEMALA
Guatemala City
HONDURAS
Tegucigalpa
San Pedro Sula
La Ceiba
EL SALVADOR
San Salvador
San Miguel
NICARAGUA
Managua
León
COSTA RICA
San José
Puerto Limón

HISPANIOLA
HAITI
Port-au-Prince
Cap-Haïtien
Gonaïves
Jacmel
DOMINICAN REPUBLIC
Santo Domingo
Santiago
Puerto Plata
La Romana
San Francisco de Macorís
JAMAICA
Kingston
Montego Bay
Spanish Town
Cayman Islands (U.K.)
George Town
Grand Cayman
Little Cayman
Cayman Brac

Pico Duarte
Puerto Rico (U.S.A.)
San Juan
Ponce
Mayagüez
Mona Passage
Virgin Is (U.K.)
Virgin Is (U.S.A.)
Charlotte Amalie
St Croix
Anguilla (U.K.)
St-Martin (Fr.)
St Maarten (Neth.)
St-Barthélemy (Fr.)
ANTIGUA AND BARBUDA
St John's
ST KITTS AND NEVIS
Basseterre
Montserrat (U.K.)
GUADELOUPE (Fr.)
Basse-Terre
Marie-Galante
DOMINICA
Roseau
MARTINIQUE (Fr.)
Fort-de-France
ST LUCIA
Castries
ST VINCENT & THE GRENADINES
Kingstown
BARBADOS
Bridgetown
GRENADA
St George's
TRINIDAD AND TOBAGO
Port of Spain
Scarborough
LEEWARD ISLANDS
LESSER ANTILLES
WINDWARD ISLANDS
GREATER ANTILLES

Aruba (Neth.)
Oranjestad
Curaçao (Neth.)
Willemstad
Bonaire (Neth.)
Islas Los Roques (Ven.)
I. de Margarita (Ven.)
I. La Tortuga (Ven.)
I. Blanquilla (Ven.)

PANAMA
Panama City
Colón
David
Golfo de Panamá

COLOMBIA
Barranquilla
Cartagena
Medellín
Bogotá
Cali
Cúcuta
Bucaramanga
Manizales
Pereira
Armenia
Ibagué
Santa Marta
Valledupar
Sincelejo
Montería
Quibdó
Buenaventura
Popayán
Neiva
Villavicencio
Tunja

VENEZUELA
Caracas
Maracaibo
Valencia
Barquisimeto
Maracay
Barcelona
Cumaná
Maturín
Ciudad Guayana
Ciudad Bolívar
Barinas
San Cristóbal
Mérida
Puerto Cabello
Los Teques
El Tigre
La Gran Sabana
Orinoco

BRAZIL
Pakaraima Mts

© Collins Bartholomew Ltd

0 200 400 600 KILOMETRES

230

231

223

MEXICO AND CENTRAL AMERICA

This map covers the Mexico and Central America. It stretches from Chihuahua in the north, along the Rio Grande and the border with the USA, to the Gulf of Mexico, and southeastwards through the Central American states to the narrow Istmo de Panamá (Isthmus of Panama), the link to the South American continent. The Yucatán is the large peninsula which extends northwards into the Gulf of Mexico, forming the large bay Bahía de Campeche. The Pacific Ocean lies to the west and southwest.

FACTS

• Mexico was colonized by the Spanish in the 16th century, and gained independence in 1821.

• Mexico City, located in the south-centre of the country, is the largest city in North America, with a population of over 21 million.

• Several historic native cultures in Mexico are represented by important archaeological remains, some involving pyramids and evidence of bloodthirsty religious practices, including Chichén Itzá, near Pisté, a major Maya site in the Yucatán peninsula (see map G3).

• Mexico City was founded on the site of the Aztec city of Tenochtitlán. It is amongst many major world tourist destinations throughout the country.

• Work has started on a new $50 billion inter-ocean canal in Nicaragua, which is planned to go through Lake Nicaragua the largest lake in Central America.

GLOSSARY

SPANISH			
Bahía	bay	**Presa**	reservoir
Cerro	mountain	**Sierra**	mountain range
Isla; Islas	island; islands	**Volcán**	volcano
Laguna	lagoon		

It took 34 years, from 1880 to 1914, and cost over 30 000 lives to construct the Panama Canal which links the Atlantic Ocean to the Pacific Ocean. The 82 km (51 mile) sea way saves a 12 500 km (7800 mile) sea journey around South America. The images above show the Galliard (Culebra) Cut under construction in 1911 and the first lock of the canal, popular with cruise ships, nearly a century later. Current capacity of canal traffic far exceeds the expectations of a hundred years ago and construction is underway to double capacity by widening and deepening channels and by building two new lock complexes.

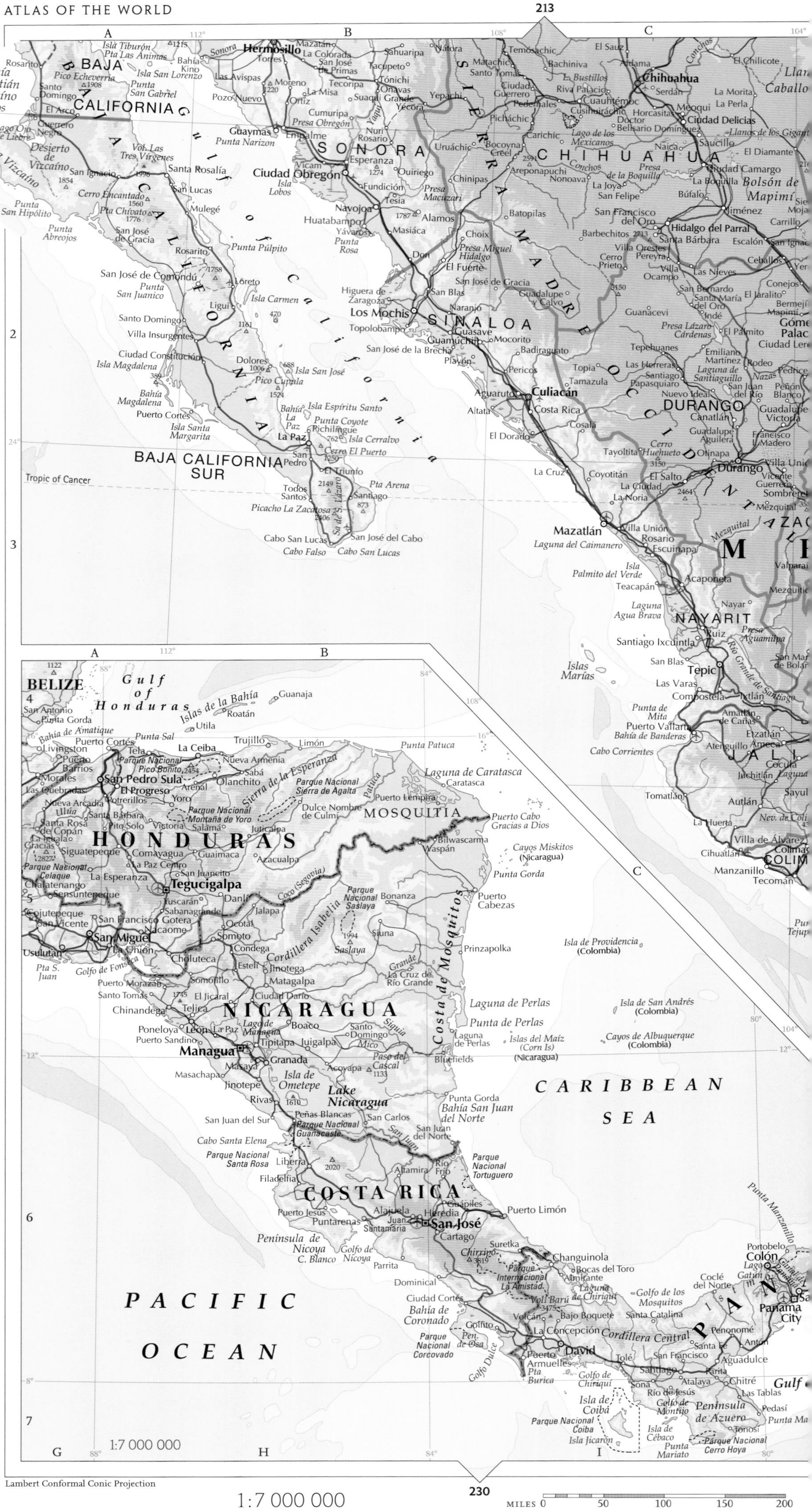

1:7 000 000

Lambert Conformal Conic Projection

1:7 000 000

MILES 0   50   100   150   200

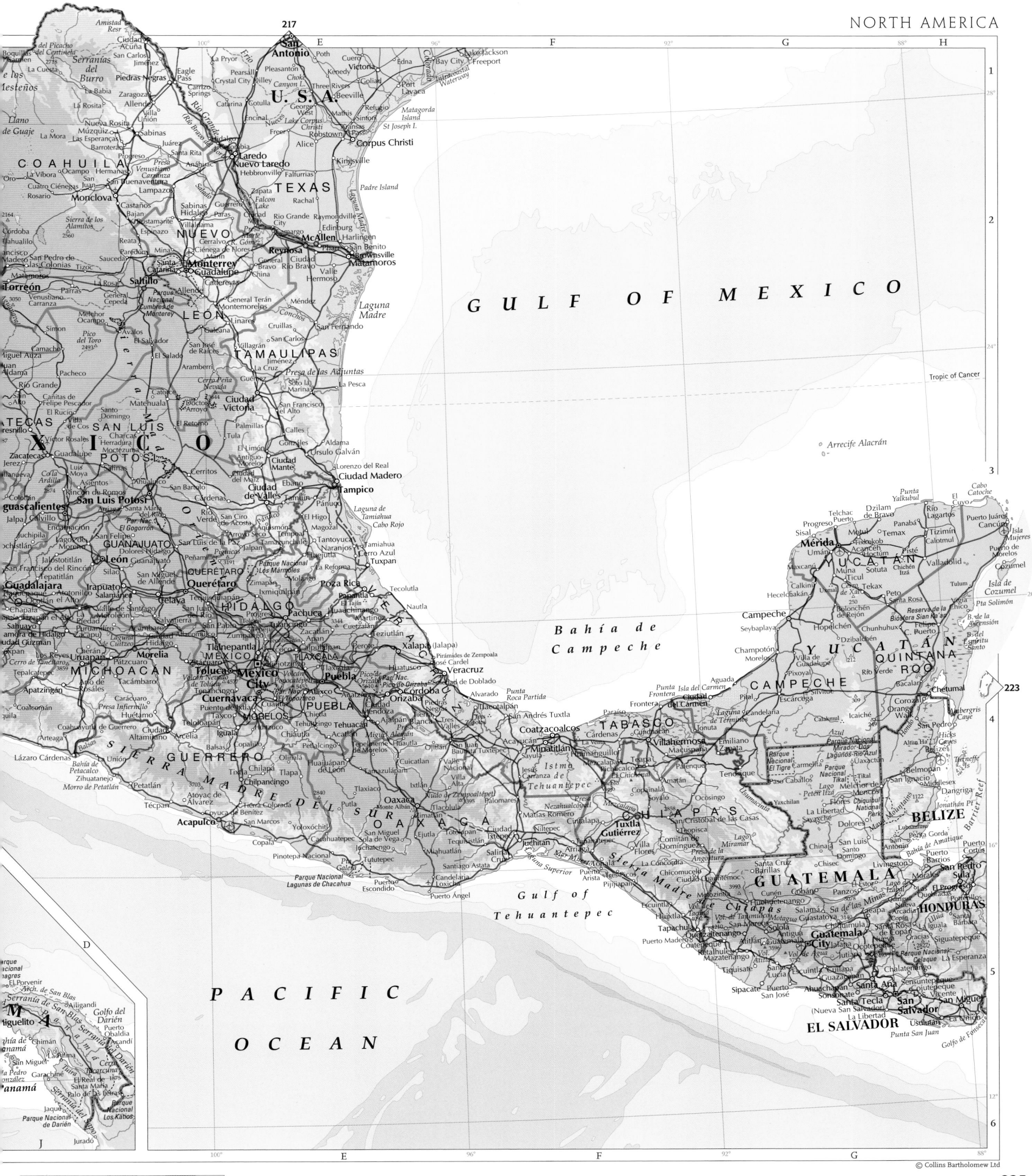

217

223

GULF OF MEXICO

Tropic of Cancer

Bahía de Campeche

Gulf of Tehuantepec

PACIFIC OCEAN

U.S.A.

TEXAS

COAHUILA

NUEVO LEÓN

TAMAULIPAS

MEXICO

ZACATECAS

SAN LUIS POTOSÍ

GUANAJUATO

QUERÉTARO

HIDALGO

MICHOACÁN

MEXICO CITY

TLAXCALA

PUEBLA

MORELOS

GUERRERO

OAXACA

VERACRUZ

TABASCO

CHIAPAS

CAMPECHE

YUCATÁN

QUINTANA ROO

BELIZE

GUATEMALA

HONDURAS

EL SALVADOR

SIERRA MADRE DEL SUR

SIERRA MADRE

Monterrey

Saltillo

Torreón

Guadalajara

Morelia

Toluca

Cuernavaca

Puebla

Acapulco

Oaxaca

Veracruz

Villahermosa

Mérida

Campeche

Chetumal

Belmopan

Guatemala City

San Salvador

Tegucigalpa

Corpus Christi

Matamoros

Reynosa

Nuevo Laredo

Laredo

San Antonio

Tampico

Ciudad Madero

Tuxtla Gutiérrez

Coatzacoalcos

Chihuahua

Durango

San Luis Potosí

Aguascalientes

León

Guanajuato

Querétaro

Pachuca

Irapuato

Celaya

Arrecife Alacrán

© Collins Bartholomew Ltd

0 50 100 150 200 250 300 350 KILOMETRES

PANAMÁ

225

SOUTH AMERICA PHYSICAL

South America stretches from north of the Equator to a point
less than 1000 km (621 miles) away from Antarctica at Cape
Horn. The most dominant physical features are the Andes,
stretching down the western side, and the enormous Amazon
Basin. Vast plains occupy much of the south and southeast
– in the Pampas grasslands and the region of Patagonia
in southern Argentina. Much of the rest of the continent
consists of dissected plateaus, undulating lowlands, and lesser
mountain ranges.

FACTS

- The Galapagos Islands, made famous by the research of Charles Darwin and
renowned for its wildlife and biodiversity, are a far-flung part of Ecuador,
situated about 750 km (466 miles) out in the Pacific Ocean.

- Cerro Aconcagua, at 6959 m (22 831 ft), is the highest point in the
western hemisphere.

- South Georgia and the South Sandwich Islands, lying between South America
and Antarctica, are collectively a UK dependency, with no permanent
population.

- The world's driest desert is the Atacama, where only 1 mm of rain may
fall as infrequently as once every five to twenty years.

HIGHEST MOUNTAINS	m	ft
Cerro Aconcagua, Argentina	6 959	22 831
Nevado Ojos del Salado, Argentina/Chile	6 908	22 664
Cerro Bonete, Argentina	6 872	22 546
Cerro Pissis, Argentina	6 858	22 500
Cerro Tupungato, Argentina/Chile	6 800	22 309
Cerro Mercedario, Argentina	6 770	22 211

LARGEST ISLANDS	sq km	sq miles
Isla Grande de Tierra del Fuego	47 000	18 147
Isla de Chiloé	8 394	3 241
East Falkland	6 760	2 610
West Falkland	5 413	2 090

LONGEST RIVERS	km	miles
Amazon (Amazonas)	6 516	4 049
Río de la Plata-Paraná	4 500	2 796
Purus	3 218	2 000
Madeira	3 200	1 988
São Francisco	2 900	1 802
Tocantins	2 750	1 709

LARGEST LAKES	sq km	sq miles
Lake Titicaca	8 340	3 220

Orthographic Projection

1:32 000 000

MILES 0   400   800   1200

Cuba
Greater
Jamaica
Antilles
Caribbean Sea
Hispaniola
Puerto Rico
Anguilla
Antigua
Dominica
Guadeloupe
Martinique
St Lucia
Barbados
St Vincent
and the Grenadines
Tobago
Trinidad
Lesser Antilles
Grenada
Isla de Margarita
Punta
Gallinas
Golfo de
Venezuela
Aruba
Sa de Perijá
Lake
Maracaibo
Golfo del
Darién
Gulf of Panama
Isla de Malpelo
Cordillera Occidental
Cordillera Central
Cordillera Oriental
Llanos
Orinoco
Guaviare
Orinoco
Delta del
Orinoco
Guiana Highlands
La Gran
Sabana
Pakaraima Mountains
Negro
Branco
Serra
Tumucumaque
Gulf of Guayaquil
Putumayo
Japurá
Amazon
Marañón
Purus
Napo
Ucayali
Juruá
Amazon
Basin
Amazon
Mouths of
the Amazon
Ilha de Marajó
Represa
de Balbina
Punta
Negra
Cordillera Central
Cordillera Oriental
Cordillera Occidental
A
Selvas
Madeira
Tapajós
Represa de
Tucuruí
Serra do Cachimbo
Serra dos Parecis
Beni
Guaporé
Xingu
Serra dos Caiabis
Serra do Roncador
Araguaia
Tocantins
Serra Geral de Goiás
Parnaíba
Barragem de
Sobradinho
Cabo de
São Roque
Fernando
de Noronha
N
Lake Titicaca
Cordillera Oriental
Altiplano
Lago de
Poopó
Salar de Uyuni
Bañados
del Izozog
Pantanal
Serra da Mesa
Serra do Caiapó
Represa
Chapada
Diamantina
São Francisco
Serra do Espinhaço
Cabo Santo
Antonio
D
Atacama Desert
Paraguay
Serra de Maracaju
Paraná
Represa Porto
Primavera
Brazilian
Highlands
Serra da Mantiqueira
Ponta de Baleia
6908
Nevado
Ojos del Salado
6872
Cerro
Bonete
Gran Chaco
Teuco
Serra da Mantiqueira
Cabo de São Tomé
Ilha da Trindade
Islas
de los Desventurados
Isla San
Félix
Isla San
Ambrosio
Salinas Grandes
Sierras de Córdoba
Laguna Mar
Chiquita
Paraná
Uruguay
Lagoa
dos Patos
Illas
Martin Vaz
E
Juan Fernández
Islands
Cerro Aconcagua
6959
Pampas
Salado
Lagoa
Mirim
Río de la Plata
Embalse Ezequiel
Ramos Mexía
Negro
Bahía Blanca
Punta Rasa
Golfo San Matías
Isla de Chiloé
Chubut
Península
Valdés
Archipiélago
de los Chonos
Lago Buenos
Aires
Golfo de
San Jorge
Cabo Tres
Puntas
Golfo de Penas
Patagonia
ANDES
Archipiélago de la
Reina Adelaida
Bahía
Grande
Strait of Magellan
Isla Grande
de Tierra del Fuego
Isla de los Estados
Cape Horn
West
Falkland
Falkland
Islands
East Falkland
Shag
Rocks
South Georgia
Drake Passage
Scotia Sea
South Shetland
Islands
South Orkney
Islands
Antarctic Peninsula
South
Sandwich
Islands
Traversay Islands
Candlemas Island
Saunders Island
Montagu Island
Southern Thule
Bristol Island

ATLANTIC
OCEAN

Madeira
Canary
Islands
Gran
Canaria
Tropic of Cancer
Cape Verde
Santo Antão
Boa Vista
São Tiago
Senegal
Niger
Gulf of Guinea
Equator
Ascension
St Helena
Tristan
da Cunha
Cape of Good Hope
Orange
Tropic of Capricorn

0   400   800   1200   1600   2000 KILOMETRES

© Collins Bartholomew Ltd

227

SOUTH AMERICA POLITICAL

Brazil fills most of the north of the continent, while Argentina is the largest country in the narrower south. Chile consists of a long, narrow strip along the Pacific coast. French Guiana is the only remaining territory under overseas control, on a continent which has a long colonial history. Spanish is the language of the majority of the continent, although Brazil is largely Portuguese-speaking. There has been a steady process of urbanization and the majority of South America's population live in the major cities and close to the coast.

FACTS

- South America is often referred to as Latin America, reflecting the historic influences of Spain and Portugal.

- Bolivia and Paraguay are the only landlocked countries on the continent.

- The Falkland Islands were first settled by the British, although Argentina retains a claim over them and calls them the Malvinas Islands (Islas Malvinas in Spanish). This claim resulted in a war in 1982 between Argentina and the UK.

- The Juan Fernández Islands (Archipiélago Juan Fernández), a group of Chilean islands in the Pacific, are known for having been the location of the famous 'castaway' novel, Robinson Crusoe.

LARGEST COUNTRIES	Area	
	sq km	sq miles
Brazil	8 514 879	3 287 613
Argentina	2 766 889	1 068 302
Peru	1 285 216	496 225
Colombia	1 141 748	440 831
Bolivia	1 098 581	424 164
Venezuela	912 050	352 144
Chile	756 945	292 258
Paraguay	406 752	157 048
Ecuador	272 045	105 037
Guyana	214 969	83 000

MOST POPULATED COUNTRIES	Population
Brazil	200 362 000
Colombia	48 321 000
Argentina	41 446 000
Venezuela	30 405 000
Peru	30 376 000
Chile	17 620 000
Ecuador	15 738 000
Bolivia	10 671 000
Paraguay	6 802 000
Uruguay	3 407 000

CAPITALS		
Largest population	**Buenos Aires,** Argentina	13 401 000
Smallest population	**Sucre,** Bolivia	358 000
Most northerly	**Caracas,** Venezuela	10° 28' N
Most southerly	**Stanley,** Falkland Islands	51° 43' S
Highest	**La Paz,** Bolivia	3 630 m/ 11 909 ft

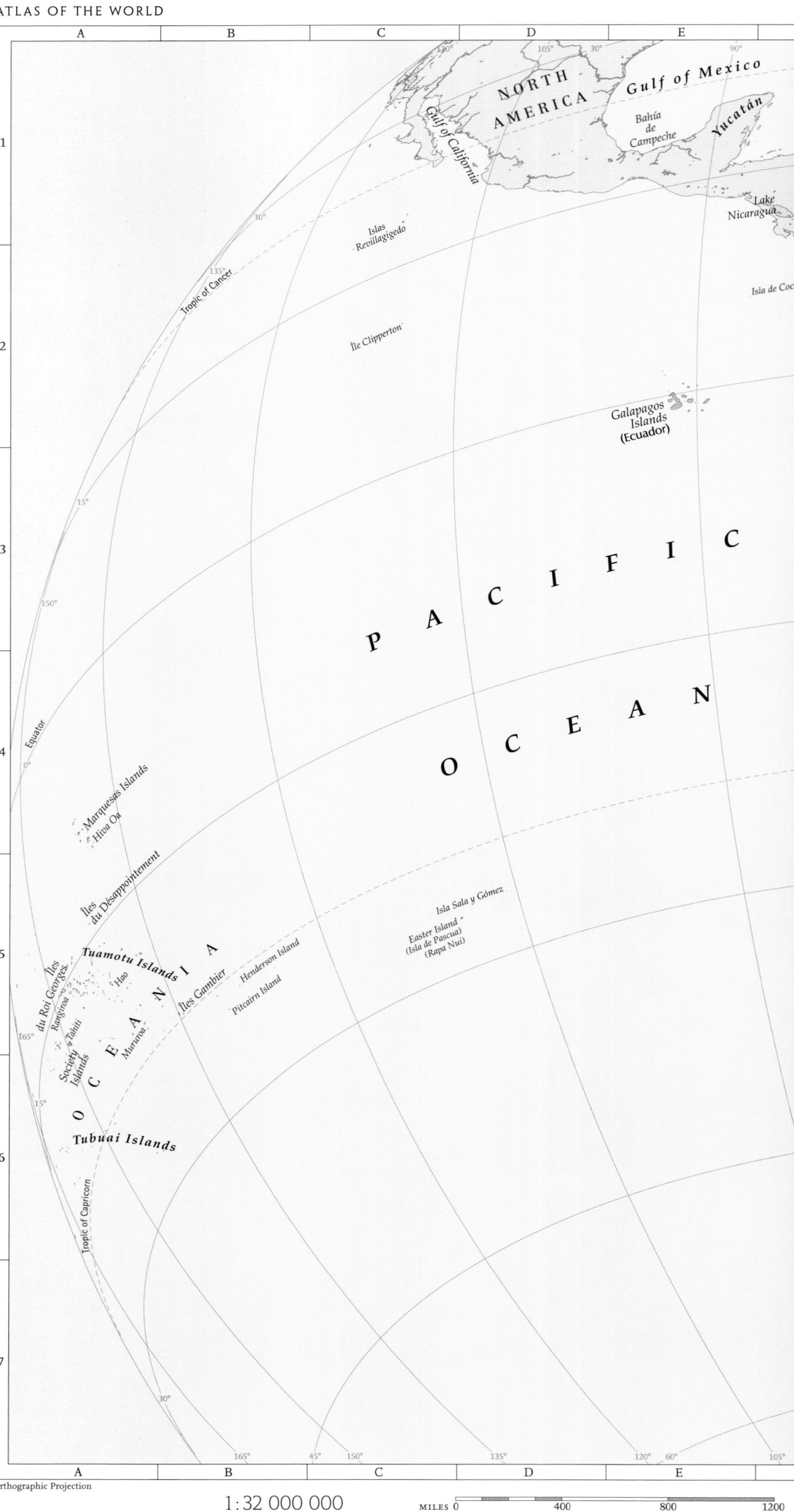

Orthographic Projection

1 : 32 000 000

MILES 0   400   800   1200

0   400   800   1200   1600   2000 KILOMETRES

SOUTH AMERICA NORTH

This wide, northern section of the continent is dominated by Brazil, the greater part of which consists of the tropical rain forest zone of the Amazon river basin. Ecuador is named after its position straddling the equator. The northern part of Bolivia also comes into the map area, with Lake Titicaca – the largest in South America – featuring prominently on the border with Peru. The sprawling delta of the Amazon, along with the mouth of the nearby river Tocantins, is a notable feature of the northeast coast.

FACTS

- The mountains collectively known as the Andes, contain a number of major active volcanoes, including Cotopaxi and Chimborazo in Ecuador.
- Machu Picchu, located near Cusco in Peru, is one of the world's most famous archaeological sites. It is a former capital of the Inca empire.
- Colombia is a major producer of illegal drugs and the world's largest producer of cocaine.
- Bolivia is named after an anti-colonial fighter of the 19th century, Simón Bolívar.
- Water flow along the Amazon is over 1500 times that of the River Thames.

GLOSSARY

PORTUGUESE	
Baía	bay
Cabo	cape, point
Chapada	hills, uplands
Represa	reservoir
São; Santa; Santo	saint
Serra	mountain range

SPANISH	
Bahía	bay
Cordillera	mountain range
Embalse	reservoir
Isla	island

In the Amazon rainforest deforestation has occurred every year since the 1960s. One per cent of the tropical rainforest is lost every year in South America. The countries affected are Bolivia, Brazil, Colombia, Ecuador, French Guiana, Guyana, Peru, Suriname, Venezuela. Lawlessness is a major problem in the large remote forest. The rights of indigenous communities to manage the forest are often abused and conservation laws widely flouted. In recent years, the Brazilian government has said that due to law enforcement and strict environmental controls, the rate of destruction of the rainforest has slowed. However, environmentalists are still concerned at the rate of tree felling.

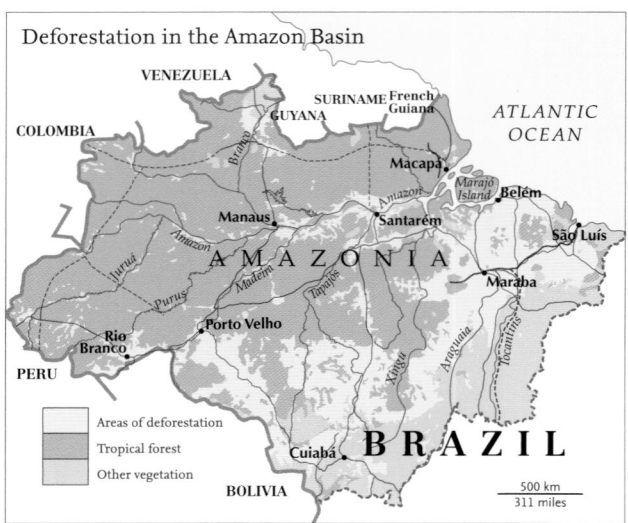

Deforestation in the Amazon Basin

Landowners are clearing forests to make way for cattle ranching, soya bean production, mineral exploration and logging. For poor farmers the 'slash-and-burn' agricultural system is a short-term solution as the soil becomes infertile after about three years and a new area has to be cleared. Commercial agricultural methods work on a larger scale and have a greater effect. Where land is abandoned it takes fifty years or more for the forest to grow again.

223

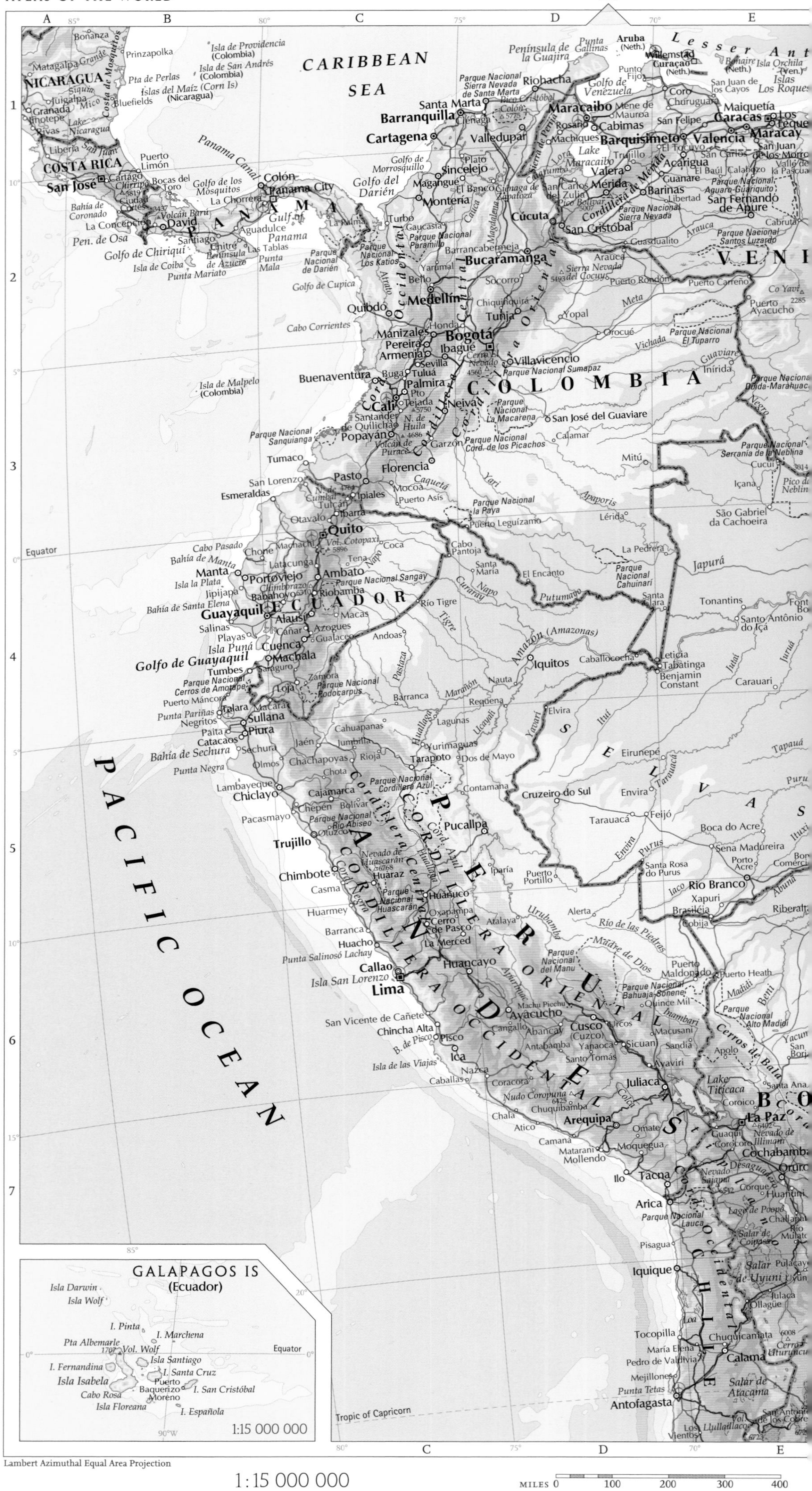

Lambert Azimuthal Equal Area Projection

1:15 000 000

MILES 0 100 200 300 400

ATLANTIC

OCEAN

GRENADA
Isla Blanquilla
(Ven.)
Isla de
Margarita
(Ven.)
St George's
Los Testigos
(Ven.)
Tobago
Scarborough
La Asunción
Porlamar
Port of Spain
Trinidad
TRINIDAD
AND TOBAGO
Carúpano
Güiria
Gulf of
Paria
San Fernando
Cumaná
Pampatar
Barcelona
Maturin
Zaraza
El Tigre
Tucupita
Delta del
Orinoco
Ciudad Guayana
Barrancas
Mabaruma
Ciudad Bolívar
Upata
Mapire
El Callao
La Paragua
Port Kaituma
Matthews Ridge
Anna Regina
Tumereng
Bartica
New Amsterdam
Georgetown
ZUELA
Pakaraima Mountains
La Gran
Sabana
Mt Roraima
2810
Linden
Paramaribo
Nieuw Amsterdam
Nieuw Nickerie
Apoera
Albina
St Laurent
Sinnamary
Kourou
Cayenne
Parque Nacional
Canaima
SURINAME
Professor van
Blommestein Meer
Juliana Top
1230
French
Guiana
Boa Vista
Lethem
CLAIMED BY
VENEZUELA
GUYANA
CLAIMED BY
SURINAME
Serra Tumucumaque
Pointe Béhague
Cabo Orange
Oiapoque
Diapoque
Parque Nacional
de Cabo Orange
Calçoene
Ilha de Maracá
Amapá
Parque Nacional
Montanhas do
Tumucumaque
Serra do Navio
Santana
Macapá
Morro Grande
Paru
Arere
Afuá
Ilha
Queimada
Boca do Jari
Chaves
Cabo
Maguarinho
Baía de
Maracã
Salinópolis
Curuçá
Capanema
Bragança
Mouths
of the
Amazon
Parque Nacional
dos Lençóis Maranhenses
Mazagão
Almeirim
Breves
Castanhal
Viseu
Parque Nacional
Jaú-Sarisariñama
Obidos
Santa
Maria
Faro
Alenquer
Monte
Alegre
Santarém
Amazon (Amazonas)
Xingu
Portel
Abaetetuba
Belém
Acará
Irituia
Cametá
Cândido Mendes
Pinheiro
São Luís
Barreirinhas
Parnaíba
Camocim
Itapipoca
Caucaia
Fortaleza
Aracati
Macau
Ponta do Calcanhar
Touros
Cabo de São Roque
Natal

BRAZIL

© Collins Bartholomew Ltd

0   200   400   600   800 KILOMETRES

SOUTH AMERICA SOUTH

VENEZUELA AND COLOMBIA

This southern section of South America tapers down through Argentina and Chile to its curving 'tail' at Cape Horn. Paraguay is sandwiched between Brazil and Argentina on the great plain known as the Gran Chaco. Northwestern South America (right-hand map) contains extensive lowlands around the Orinoco river and its delta, and part of the huge Amazon Basin. Southern parts of the West Indies lie off the coast in the Caribbean Sea, while the Isthmus of Panama connects the region to Central and North America.

FACTS

- Bolivia shares the functions of its national capital between two cities – La Paz and Sucre.

- Cape Horn (Cabo de Hornos in Spanish) was notorious for centuries as a particularly dangerous passage for ocean-going vessels. There is no other land between here and Antarctica.

- Patagonia, the southern part of Argentina, has a long history of Welsh settlement.

- The Pantanal, in western Brazil, is the largest area of wetland in the world.

GLOSSARY

PORTUGUESE	
Lagoa	lagoon
Represa	reservoir
Rio	river
Serra	mountain range

SPANISH	
Cabo	cape, point
Embalse	reservoir
Estrecho	strait
Laguna	lagoon
Nevado	snow-covered mountain
Salar	salt pan
Volcán	volcano

The Iguaçu Falls are the most famous feature of the Iguaçu Falls National Park and they divide the river into the upper and lower Iguazu. The waterfall system is along 2.7 km (1.67 miles) of the river and consists of 275 falls. Some of the falls are up to 82 m (269 ft) in height, best of which is Devil's Throat.

Spanish Conquistador Álvar Núñez Cabeza de Vaca was the the first European to find the falls in 1541, one of which on the Argentine side is named after him. In the late nineteenth century they were rediscovered by Boselli, and he also has one of the falls on the Argentina side named after him.

The Iguaçu Falls lie on the Iguaçu River which forms the border between Brazil and Argentina. The falls are about three times as wide as Niagara Falls – this prompted the former president's wife, Eleanor Roosevelt to utter 'poor Niagara' on first sight of the falls. The Iguaçu National Park is a UNESCO World Heritage Site, shared between Argentina and Brazil and is a popular tourist destination. It is one of South America's largest forest preservation areas.

Lambert Azimuthal Equal Area Projection

1:15 000 000   MILES 0   100   200   300   0   200   400   600 KILOMETRES

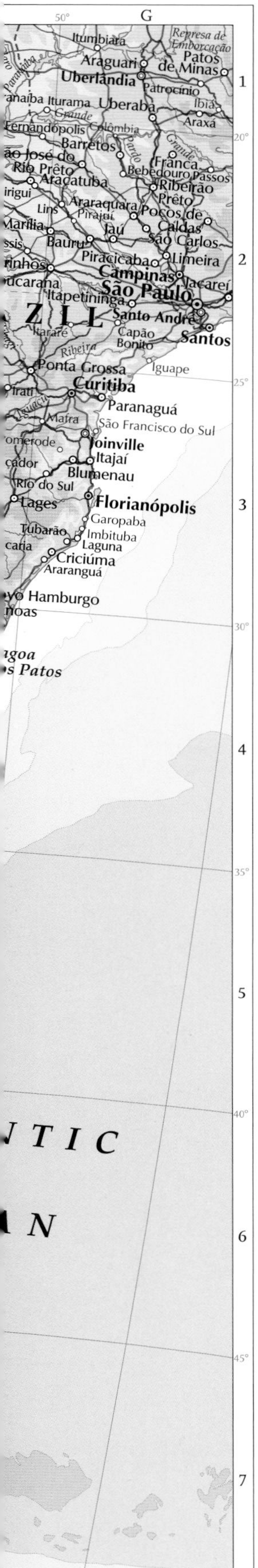

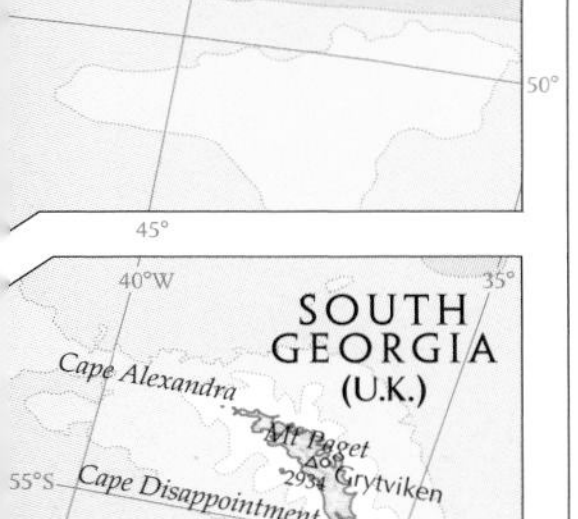

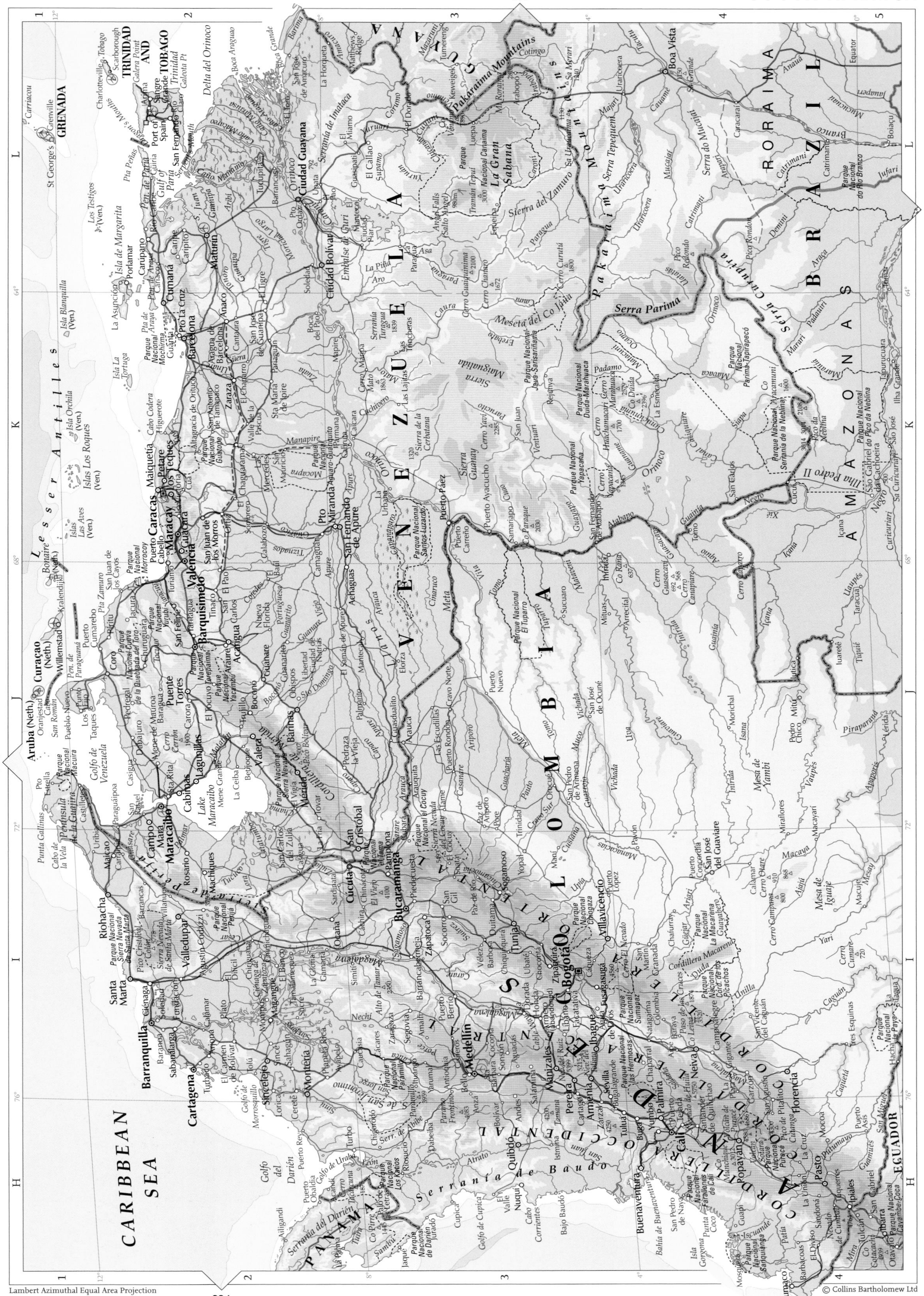

231

CARIBBEAN SEA

VENEZUELA

COLOMBIA

BRAZIL

GUYANA

TRINIDAD AND TOBAGO

GRENADA

ECUADOR

PANAMA

Lesser Antilles

Caracas
Maracaibo
Valencia
Barquisimeto
Ciudad Bolívar
Ciudad Guayana
Cumaná
Barcelona
Maturín
Puerto Cabello

Bogotá
Medellín
Cali
Cartagena
Barranquilla
Santa Marta
Bucaramanga
Cúcuta
Pereira
Manizales
Armenia
Ibagué
Popayán
Pasto
Valledupar
Riohacha
Sincelejo
Montería
Tunja
Villavicencio

Aruba (Neth.)
Curaçao (Neth.)
Willemstad
Oranjestad

Serra Parima
Pakáraima Mountains
La Gran Sabana
Lake Maracaibo
Golfo de Venezuela
Delta del Orinoco

RORAIMA
AMAZONAS

CORDILLERA OCCIDENTAL
CORDILLERA ORIENTAL
CORDILLERA CENTRAL

São Paulo
Santos
Curitiba
Florianópolis
Uberlândia

Lambert Azimuthal Equal Area Projection

1:7 500 000

MILES 0   50   100   150
KILOMETRES 0 50 100 150 200 250 300

223
224
231

© Collins Bartholomew Ltd

BRAZIL SOUTHEAST

CHILE CENTRAL, ARGENTINA CENTRAL AND URUGUAY

These two maps concentrate on the densely populated parts of Brazil, Chile, Argentina and Uruguay. Southeastern Brazil consists of approximately 11 per cent of the country's area but contains over 40 per cent of its population. The interior of the region is characterized by an array of enormous reservoirs, most notably on the Paraná river. Santiago (right-hand map) is set in the high mountains of the Andes, while Buenos Aires and Montevideo are on either side of the inlet of the river Plate (Río de la Plata). Great bays and lagoons indent the eastern coastline, while inland lie the extensive grassland plains of the Pampas.

FACTS

- São Paulo has a population of over twenty-one million. It was the first city in South America to exceed the ten million mark. Rio de Janeiro, the former national capital (before Brasília), has over twelve million inhabitants.

- Numerous large dams lie along the course of the Paraná river. They generate huge amounts of hydro-electricity for the cities of the region.

- Rio de Janeiro is one of the world's most attractive cities, with dramatic hills and bays. Corcovado peak is topped by the famous statue of Christ, *Cristo Redentor*, which overlooks the wide inlet of Guanabara Bay.

GLOSSARY

PORTUGUESE	
Baía	bay
Cabo	cape, point
Lago	lake
Lagoa	lagoon
Ponta	cape, point
Represa	reservoir
Serra	mountain range

SPANISH	
Cerro (Co)	mountain
Cordillera (Cord.)	mountain range
Embalse	reservoir
Nevado (Nev.)	snow-covered mountain
Punta	cape, point
Salina	salt pan
Sierra (Sa)	mountain range
Volcán (Vol.)	volcano

The first two capital cities of Brazil were Salvador and Rio de Janeiro. As far back as the eighteenth century there was the suggestion of moving the capital inland. Construction of Brasília as the administrative and political centre of Brazil began in 1956 and in 1960 it became the capital city. The architect was Oscar Niemeyer and Lúcio Costa was the urban planner. It is located on the Paraná, a headstream of the Tocantins river. Lake Paranoá, an artificial lake has been created on the east side of the city.

Though Brasília was primarily built for government authorities, there were many migrants from other parts of Brazil who came and settled in the new city, as they wanted a better quality of life. It is the fifth largest city in Brazil with a population in 2015 of 4 249 000

With many innovative buildings, Brasília is listed as a World Heritage Site, the only city built in the twentieth century to hold that status. This image shows the twin administrative towers and the bowl and dome shaped buildings of the National Congress in the Square of Three Powers at the heart of the city.

Lambert Azimuthal Equal Area Projection

1 : 7 500 000   **232**

MILES 0   50   100   150   0   50   100   150   200   250   300 KILOMETRES

231

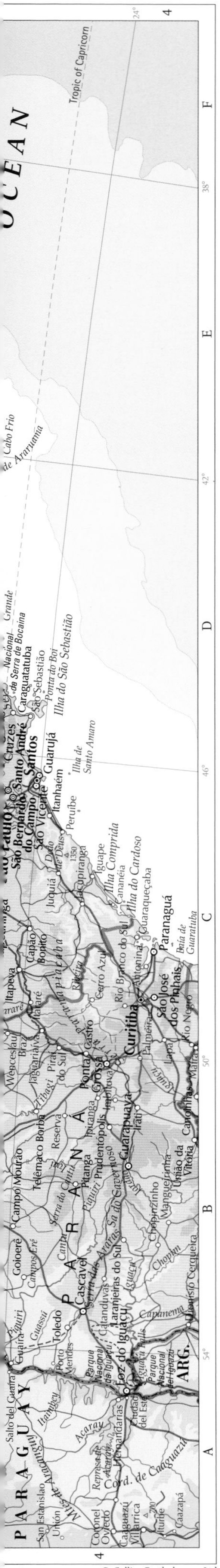
OCEAN
PARAGUAY
PARANÁ
ARG.
Curitiba
Paranaguá
Santos
Foz do Iguaçu
Tropic of Capricorn

© Collins Bartholomew Ltd

232

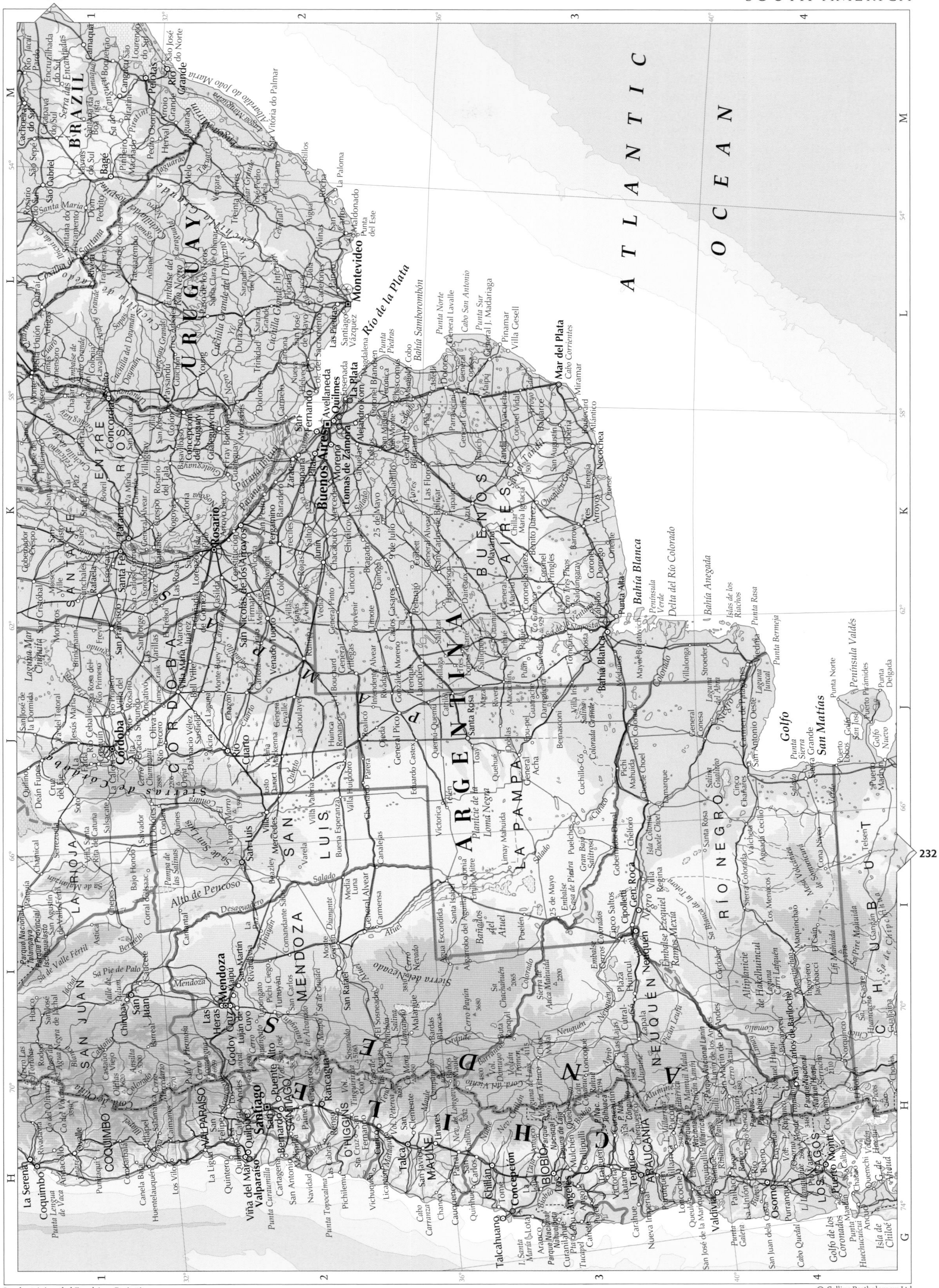
ATLANTIC
OCEAN
BRAZIL
URUGUAY
ARGENTINA
CHILE
BUENOS AIRES
SANTA FE
ENTRE RÍOS
CÓRDOBA
SAN LUIS
MENDOZA
SAN JUAN
LA RIOJA
LA PAMPA
NEUQUÉN
RÍO NEGRO
CHUBUT
Buenos Aires
Montevideo
Río de la Plata
Rosario
Córdoba
Mendoza
Santiago
Valparaíso
Concepción
Mar del Plata
Bahía Blanca
La Plata
Santa Fe
Paraná
San Luis
San Juan
Neuquén
Temuco
Valdivia
Osorno
Puerto Montt
Pelotas
Rio Grande
Golfo San Matías
Península Valdés
232

© Collins Bartholomew Ltd

Lambert Azimuthal Equal Area Projection

1:7 500 000

MILES 0 50 100 150

0 50 100 150 200 250 300 KILOMETRES

PACIFIC OCEAN

Stretching half way around the globe, the Pacific is the world's largest ocean and contains 45 per cent of the earth's water area. It is larger than all of the continents combined and contains the earth's deepest point – Challenger Deep in the Mariana Trench 10 920 m (35 826 ft) deep. It includes hundreds of islands, including the main Pacific island groups of Polynesia (meaning many islands), Micronesia (small islands) and Melanesia (black islands). The ocean has an enormous effect on the world's climate, as a breeding ground for tropical storms and the source of the climatic phenomenon El Niño.

FACTS

- The Pacific was named by the 16th-century explorer Ferdinand Magellan after the calm waters he experienced there.

- The Panama Canal, 65 km (40 miles) long, is part of an 82 km (51 miles) long seaway that opened in 1914 and carries over 14 000 ships each year between the Pacific and Atlantic Oceans. It saves a journey of over 12 000 km (7457 miles) around the hazardous Cape Horn.

- The Pacific is estimated to contain over 315 million cu km (76 million cubic miles) of water and has an average depth of over 4000 m (13 123 ft).

- The countries adjoining the Pacific are often collectively referred to as the Pacific Rim.

TIME ZONES

The system of timekeeping throughout the world is based on twenty-four time zones, each stretching over fifteen degrees of longitude – the distance equivalent to a time difference of one hour. The prime, or Greenwich Meridian (zero degrees longitude), is the basis for Greenwich Mean Time (GMT), also known as Universal Coordinated Time (UTC), by which other time zones are measured.

This universal reference point was agreed by delegates from twenty-six countries at the International Meridian Conference in Washington D.C., in 1884. Prior to this, many separate central meridians were in use, for navigational and reference purposes, including London, Paris, Cadiz and Stockholm. Time zone boundaries can be altered to suit international or internal boundaries.

THE INTERNATIONAL DATE LINE

The International Date Line is an imaginary line passing down the Pacific Ocean at approximately 180 degrees west (or east) of Greenwich, across which the date changes by one day. To the left (west) of the line the date is always one day ahead of the right (east). If travelling eastwards across the line, travellers must move their calendars back one day.

The position and status of the line was agreed at the same conference at which Greenwich was adopted as the prime meridian. The line has no international legal status and countries near to it can choose which date they will observe. It was amended most recently in 2011 when Samoa and Tokelau both shifted from east to west of the dateline, omitting the day 30 December 2011 entirely. The changes were made to align dates with their main trading partners, New Zealand and Australia.

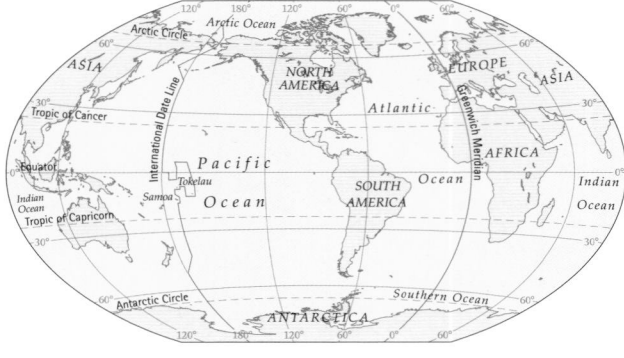

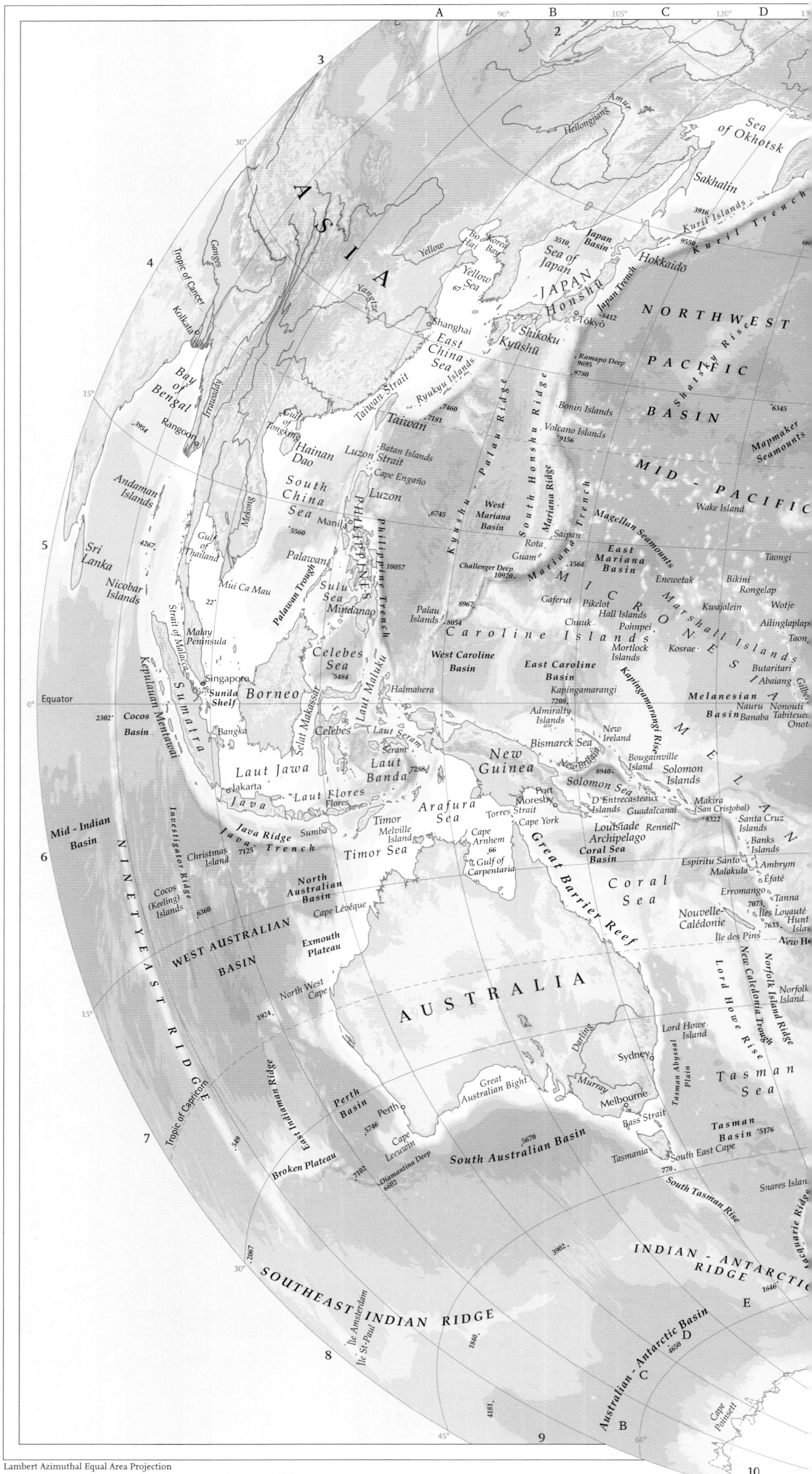

Lambert Azimuthal Equal Area Projection

1:58 000 000   MILES 0   500   1000   1500   2000

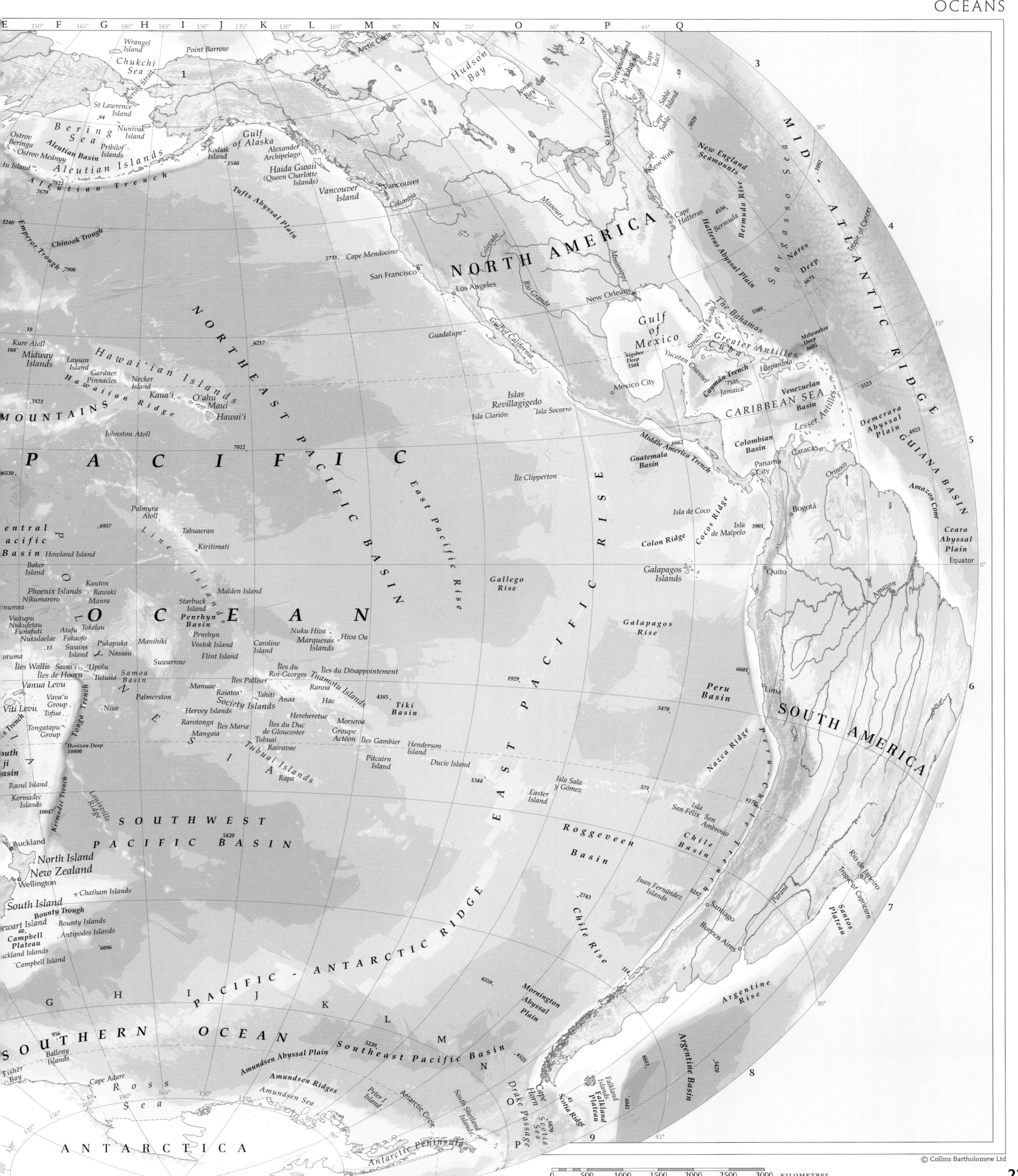

Wrangel Island
Chukchi Sea
Point Barrow
Arctic Circle
Hudson Bay
Newfoundland
St John's
Cape Race
.69
1

MID

St Lawrence
.84
Bering Strait
Nunivak Island
Mackenzie
James Bay
Sable Island
St Lawrence
New England Seamounts
.5023
ATLANTIC
.1002
3

Ostrov Beringa
Ostrov Medny
Bering Sea
Pribilof Islands
Gulf of Alaska
Kodiak Island
Alexander Archipelago
.1546
Vancouver Island
Vancouver
Columbia
Missouri
New York
Cape Hatteras
Bermuda Rise
Bermuda
.4556
Nares Deep
.6671
Tropic of Cancer
30°
4

Aleutian Basin
Aleutian Islands
.7822
.7679
Aleutian Trench
Haida Gwaii (Queen Charlotte Islands)
Tufts Abyssal Plain
Hatteras Abyssal Plain

tu Island
.1240
Emperor Trough
Chinook Trough
.7900
.2733
Cape Mendocino
San Francisco
Los Angeles
Rio Grande
New Orleans
Gulf of Mexico
Sigsbee Deep 3504
The Bahamas
.5508
Straits of Florida
Cuba
Greater Antilles
Milwaukee Deep 8605
RIDGE
15°
5

.18
Kure Atoll
.104
Midway Islands
Laysan Island
Hawai'ian Islands
.6217
Guadalupe
Gulf of California
Mexico City
Yucatan Channel
Hispaniola
.5523
Venezuelan Basin
CARIBBEAN SEA
Demerara Abyssal Plain
GUIANA BASIN

MOUNTAINS
Gardner Pinnacles
Necker Island
Kaua'i
O'ahu
Maui
Hawai'i
Islas Revillagigedo
Isla Clarión
Isla Socorro
Middle America Trench
.6661
Guatemala Basin
Colombian Basin
Panama City
Caracas
Lesser Antilles
.4923

.1823
Hawai'ian Ridge
Johnston Atoll
.7022
Île Clipperton
Isla de Coco
Cocos Ridge
Colon Ridge
Isla de Malpelo
Bogotá
Amazon Cone
Ceara Abyssal Plain

.6530
PACIFIC
East Pacific Rise
Gallego Rise
Galapagos Islands
.3901
Isla
Quito
Equator
0°

Central Pacific Basin
Palmyra Atoll
.6957
Tabuaeran
Kiritimati
Galapagos Rise
.6601

Baker Island
Howland Island
OCEAN
Kanton Rawaki
Manra
Malden Island
Starbuck Island
Penrhyn Basin
Penrhyn
Vostok Island
Flint Island
Peru Basin
Lima
6

Phoenix Islands
Nikumaroro
numea
Vaitupu
Nukufetau
Funafuti
Nukulaelae
.13
Atafu
Fakaofo
Tokelau
Swains Island
Pukapuka
Nassau
Manihiki
Suwarrow
Nuku Hiva
Marquesas Islands
Hiva Oa
.1929
SOUTH AMERICA

otuma
Îles Wallis
Îles de Hoorn
Sava'i
Upolu
Tutuila
Samoa Basin
Îles du Roi-Georges
Îles du Désappointement
Tuamotu Islands
.4385
Tiki Basin
EAST
Nazca Ridge

Vanua Levu
Vava'u Group
Tofua
Niue
Palmerston
Manuae
Îles Palliser
Raroia
Hao
.5470
PACIFIC
15°

Viti Levu
s Trench
Tongatapu Group
Tonga Trench
Rarotonga
Hervey Islands
Îles Maria
Mangaia
Raiatea
Tahiti
Society Islands
Anaa
Hereheretue
Îles du Duc de Gloucester
Tubuai
Raivavae
Moruroa
Groupe Actéon
Îles Gambier
Easter Island
Isla Sala y Gómez
.571
RISE
Isla San Félix
San Ambrosio
Chile Basin
.8170

South Fiji Basin
Horizon Deep 10800
Tubuai Islands
Rapa
Pitcairn Island
Ducie Island
Henderson Island
.1344
Roggeveen Basin
.114
7

Raoul Island
Kermadec Islands
Louisville Ridge
Kermadec Trench
.10047
Chile Rise
.2743
Juan Fernández Islands
.5259
Santiago
Buenos Aires
Santos Plateau
Tropic of Capricorn

Auckland
SOUTHWEST
.5420
PACIFIC BASIN
Mornington Abyssal Plain
Argentine Rise

North Island
New Zealand
Wellington
Chatham Islands
.4359
.4225
8

South Island
Bounty Trough
Bounty Islands
.6096
Argentine Basin
.6041

ewart Island
Campbell Plateau
Antipodes Islands
PACIFIC - ANTARCTIC RIDGE
.5230
Southeast Pacific Basin
30°

ckland Islands
Campbell Island
.956
Balleny Islands
SOUTHERN OCEAN
Amundsen Abyssal Plain
Falkland Islands
Falkland Plateau
.5420

Fisher Bay
Cape Adare
Ross Sea
Amundsen Ridges
Amundsen Sea
Peter I Island
Antarctic Circle
South Shetland Islands
Cape Horn
Scotia Plateau
.5570
Scotia Ridge
.45
9

ANTARCTICA
Antarctic Peninsula
Drake Passage
45°

0   500   1000 1500 2000 2500 3000 KILOMETRES

INDIAN OCEAN
ATLANTIC OCEAN

The Indian Ocean, which contains the Arabian Sea, the Bay of Bengal, the Red Sea and The Gulf, south of Cape Agulhas, the southernmost tip of Africa and also through the Suez Canal between the Mediterranean Sea and the Red Sea, joins the Atlantic Ocean. The Atlantic Ocean is the warmest and saltiest of the world's oceans. The Mediterranean Sea, the Gulf of Mexico, the Caribbean Sea and the Arctic Ocean are generally described as parts of the Atlantic. When combined together, these two oceans are still smaller than the Pacific.

FACTS

- The Mid-Atlantic ridge runs down the centre of the Atlantic. It marks the boundary between two of the Earth's tectonic plates and is an active volcanic zone which is pulling Europe and America apart at a rate of over 2 cm (almost one inch) per year.

- The major tsunami of December 2004 originated just off the coast of Sumatra and travelled the whole width of the Indian Ocean, hitting north Africa over six hours later.

- The North Atlantic Drift is an ocean current originating in the Gulf of Mexico. It carries warm water towards the Arctic Ocean and modifies the climate of northwest Europe.

OCEAN CONVEYOR BELT

All five of the world's oceans, Arctic, Atlantic, Indian, Pacific, and Southern are interlinked. Water is able to move freely creating one global ocean which covers more than 70 per cent of the earth's surface.

While surface winds drive ocean currents in the upper part of the ocean, the global Ocean Conveyor Belt, also know as the Thermohaline Circulation, moves water slowly thousands of metres below the surface.

As warm water moves north towards the Arctic it gradually cools. As sea ice forms, the remaining water becomes saltier and sinks. This initiates the circulation of the conveyor belt. However, this ocean circulation pattern could potentially be disrupted in the future. If increasing amounts of freshwater from melting glaciers and sea ice enter the ocean altering ocean salinity, this could have an impact on global climate.

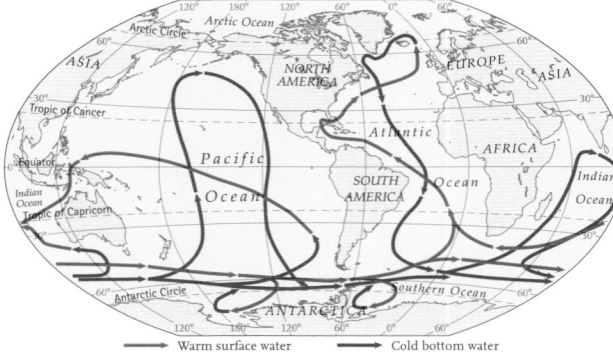

Ocean Conveyor Belt circulation

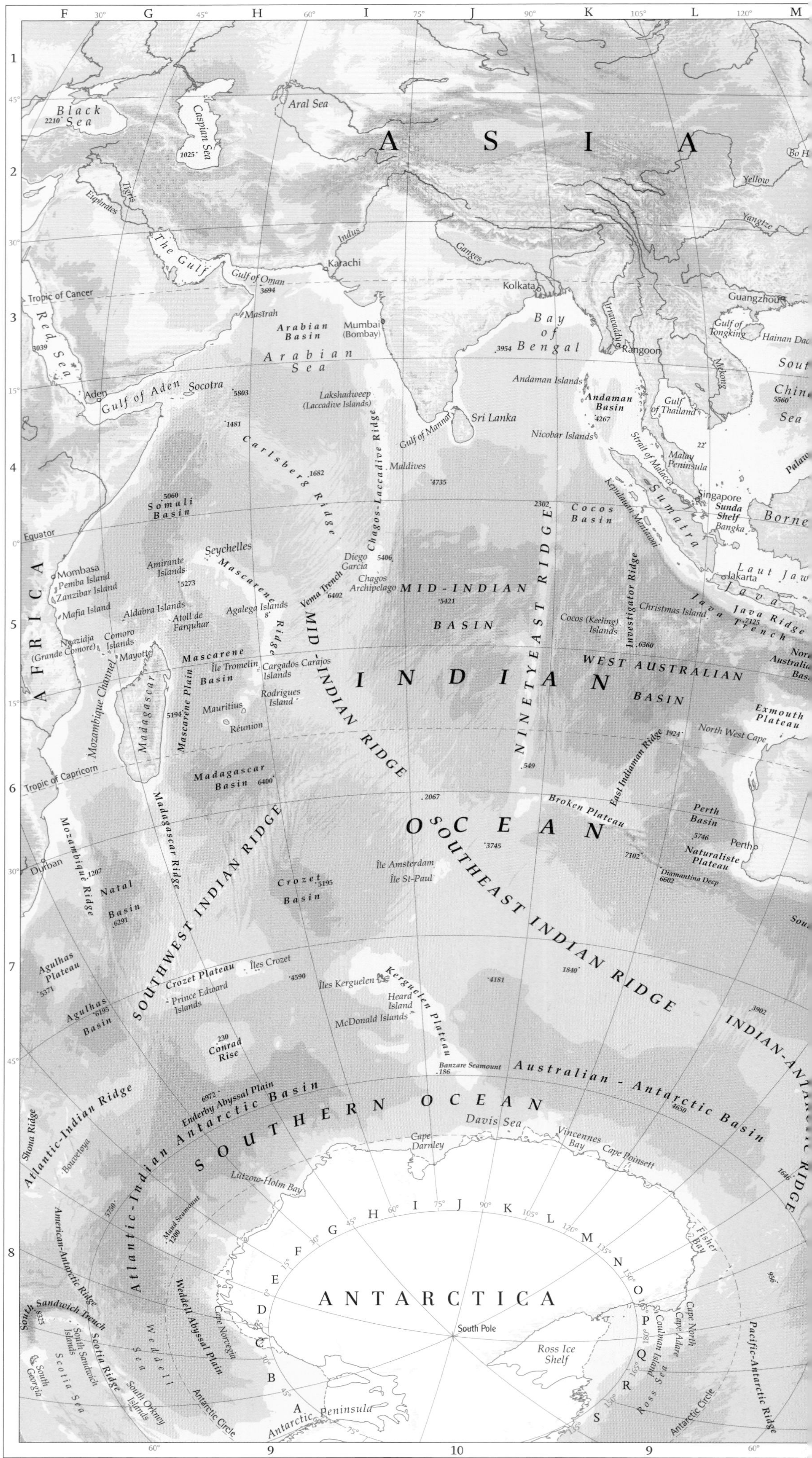

— Warm surface water   — Cold bottom water

Lambert Azimuthal Equal Area Projection

1 : 58 000 000   MILES 0   500   1000   1500   0   500   1000   1500   2000   2500   KILOMETRES

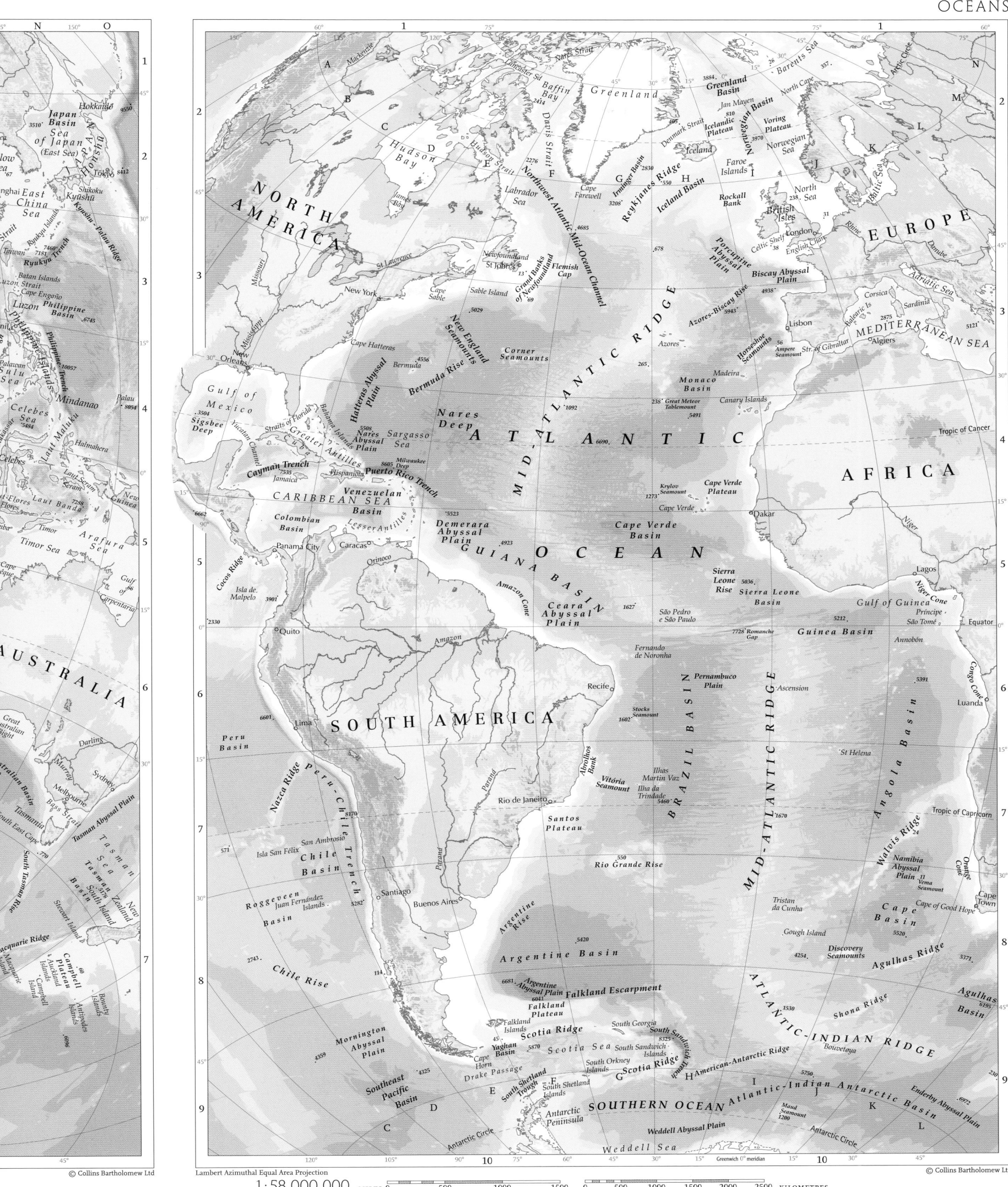

ARCTIC OCEAN

Lying entirely within the Arctic Circle, a large proportion of the Arctic Ocean is permanently covered in sea ice, which in some places reaches a thickness of over 4 m (13 ft). It generates up to 50 000 icebergs per year. The ocean is almost landlocked, and is connected to the Pacific Ocean only by the narrow Bering Strait – an important shipping route for Russian merchant ships. Its main connection with the Atlantic Ocean is the Greenland Sea. It is the smallest and shallowest of the oceans, and is often considered to be an extension of the Atlantic Ocean.

FACTS

- Sea ice extent varies seasonally. For monitoring of sea ice go to www.nsidc.org

- Many features in the Arctic are named after early explorers, including the Englishman John Davis, the Dutchman Willem Barents, Vitus Bering from Denmark and the Norwegian Fridtjof Nansen.

- The North Pole is believed to have been first visited by the American Robert Peary in 1909. The Magnetic Pole – north on a compass – lies approximately 900 km (560 miles) to the south, towards Canada.

- Due to the number of major rivers flowing into it and its low evaporation rate, the Arctic is the least salty of all the oceans. For details on polar research visit www.spri.cam.ac.uk

Aerial view of melting sea ice floes in the Arctic Ocean.

The Arctic regions of Alaska, northern Canada, Greenland, northern Scandinavia and Russia contain the homelands of a diverse range of indigenous peoples. They are heavily dependent on the natural resources in the region. Recently conflicts have arisen with governments eager to exploit these rich resources. Some countries bordering the Arctic Ocean have also initiated claims to the sea floor below the Arctic Ocean, and Canada and the USA are in dispute over the seasonal waterway known as the Northwest Passage (see page 202).

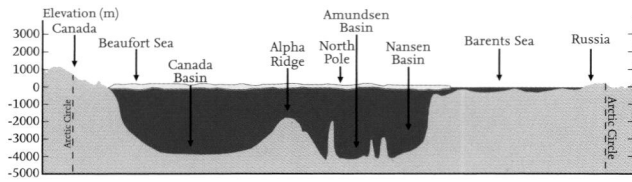

Cross-section of the Arctic Ocean from northwest Canada to northwest Russia.

Polar Stereographic Projection

1:38 500 000

MILES 0   200   400   600   800   0   400   800   1200   1600   KILOMETRES

© Collins Bartholomew Ltd

NORTH
AMERICA

EUROPE

ASIA

AFRICA

SOUTH
AMERICA

OCEANIA

ANTARCTICA

Pribilof Islands

Colorado River

Bermuda

Hawai'i

Warsaw

Hanhowuz Reservoir

Lake Dundas

New Zealand

SATELLITE IMAGES

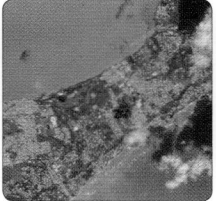

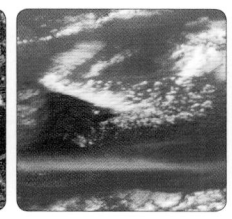
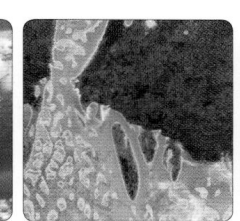
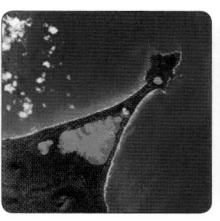
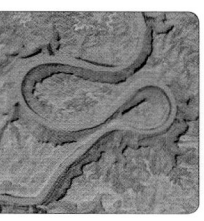

NEW ZEALAND IN SUNGLINT

This image, taken with a digital camera from the International Space Station (ISS), looks west over New Zealand. The sunglint centres on Wellington, the capital of New Zealand, at the southern end of North Island. Across Cook Strait down the length of South Island, the promontory of Banks Peninsula near Christchurch is easy to pick out. Unusually 'the land of the long white cloud' – the translation of Aotearoa, the Maori name for New Zealand – appears almost cloudless.

Sunglint is an effect created when the sun reflects off the surface of a body of water at the same angle as the satellite viewing it. It creates a mirror-like impression of calm waters, whereas rougher waters appear dark.

The ISS orbits the earth over fifteen times a day but the isolated position of New Zealand means that the astronauts are often resting when over this area of the planet.

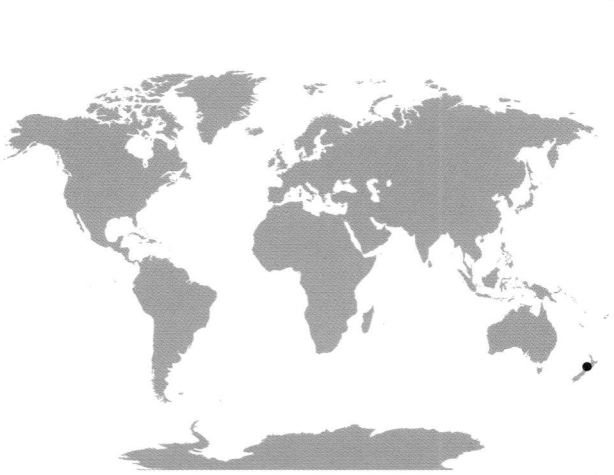

BERMUDA ATLANTIC OCEAN

Bermuda, a British Overseas Territory, is made up of approximately 180 islands formed from the rim of a caldera of a submarine volcano. It sits in the Atlantic Ocean on the western edge of the Sargasso Sea, 1030 km (640 miles) east of the U.S.A. On 17 October 2014 the eye of Hurricane Gonzalo passed over the islands causing power outages and $200–400 million of damage.

What can be seen clearly in this image is the sediment stirred up and transported up to 30 km (18 miles) away from the coast. The sediment is probably a mixture of beach sand and carbonate sediments lifted from the lagoons and reefs.

The movement of these sediments is important to the carbon cycle of the ocean. Calcium carbonate ($CaCO_3$) is a key component for marine animals that make shells. It is converted from the carbon in their diets. Over time shells of dead organisms collect and form reefs and islands of limestone. Once the limestone is exposed and weathered, carbon is released back into the atmosphere. Storm waters can move large quantities of sediment which are deposited on the deep ocean floor where it will mainly dissolve and help the neutralisation of excess amounts of carbon dioxide.

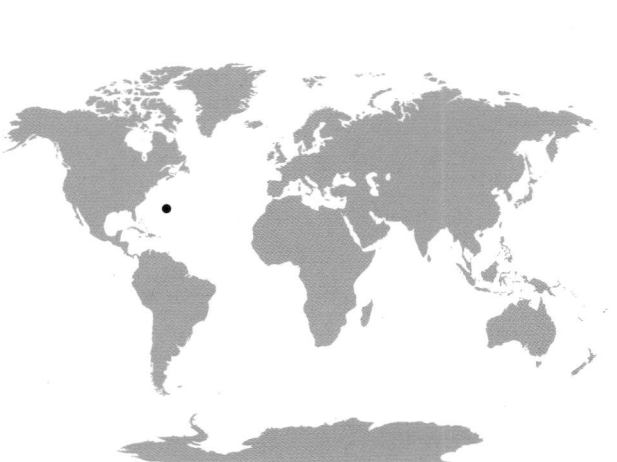

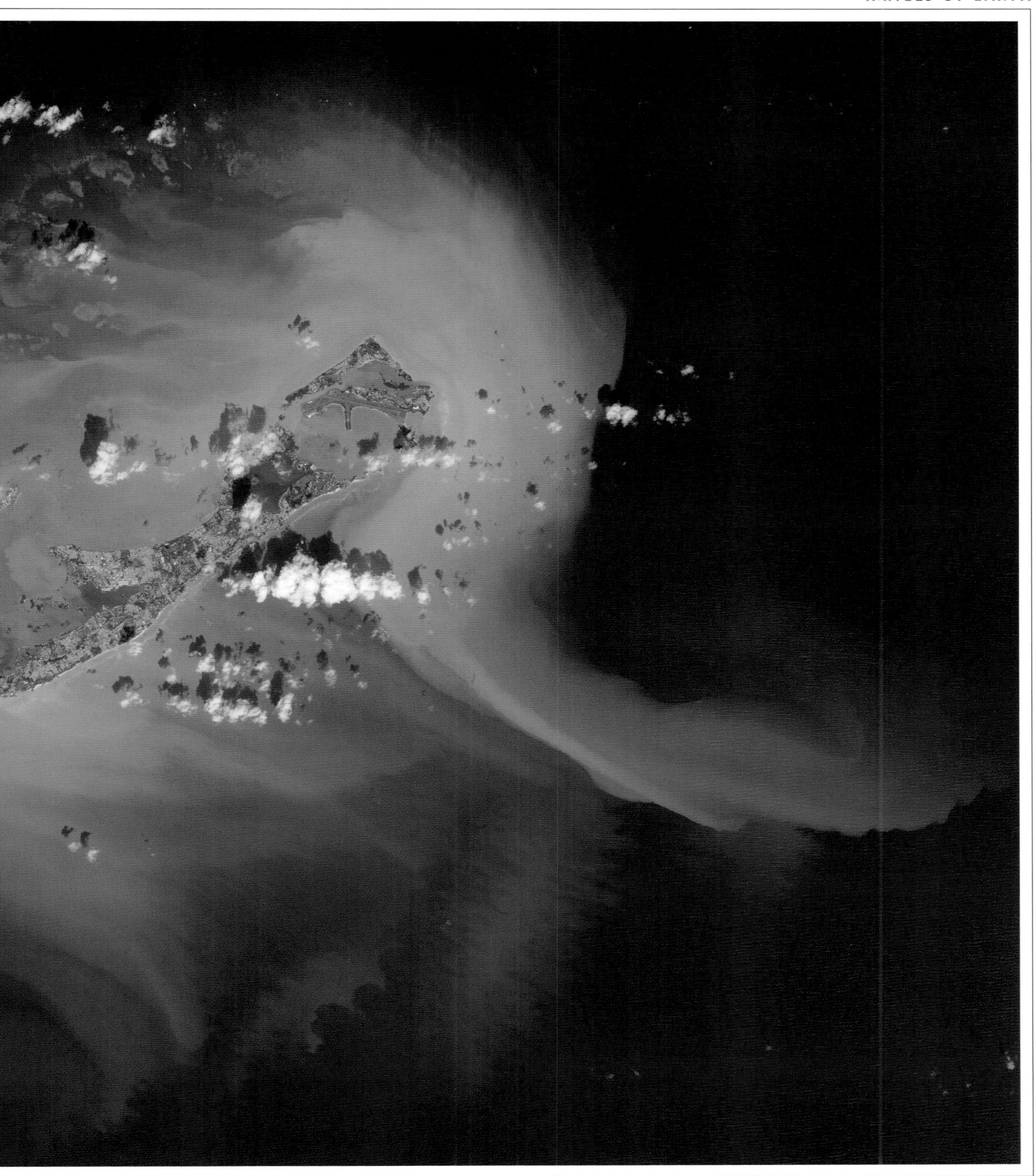

WARSAW POLAND

Warsaw, the capital of Poland, sits on the Vistula River. It is Poland's longest river and flows from the Czech Republic/Slovakia border to the Baltic Sea. The main city centre is on the higher west bank while the lower east bank has a sandy shore with woodlands. The surrounding countryside is a mixture of agriculture and woodland.

Warsaw suffered greatly in the Second World War; initially with the deportation of its Jewish population which in 1939 was nearly 30 per cent of the city. The Ghetto uprising in 1943 followed by the Warsaw uprising in the autumn of 1944 resulted in thousands of deaths and the city was razed to the ground with 85 per cent of its buildings destroyed. When the war finished the priority was to put up housing for returning citizens but also the decision was made to rebuild the Old Town – Stare Miasto – as closely to the original as possible. It is now a UNESCO World Heritage Site.

Śródmieście is the new centre. It is to the south and features the skyscrapers and high-rise buildings of a very modern city. The 'Royal Route', home to the Presidential Palace, joins the new and old towns. On the east bank, close to the river, the white dot is the Stadion Narodwy (National Stadium). It has a retractable roof and was used for football matches in the UEFA Euro 2012 tournament.

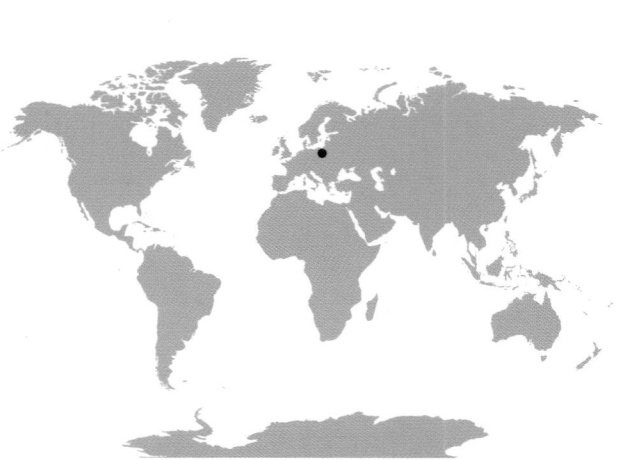

HAWAI'I PACIFIC OCEAN

The view of the islands of Hawai'i faces west with the largest island, Hawai'i, nearest the camera. It is made up of five shield-type volcanoes which have created the island from the sea floor over thousands of years. The most active volcano is Kilauea in the south. Its last major eruption was in 1983 but has been active on-and-off since then.

Apart from the clouds, what can be identified drifting west from the island is what is well-known to islanders as 'vog'. This haze is made up of fog, smog and volcanic gas. Sulphur dioxide and other gases chemically interact with the sunlight, atmospheric oxygen, moisture and dust to produce this haze which can be transported hundreds of kilometres when conditions allow. When there is high atmospheric pressure and slow wind speeds, alternating vortices start to appear, as seen here as the 'vog' moves past the next island of Maui. This pattern is called von Kármán vortices.

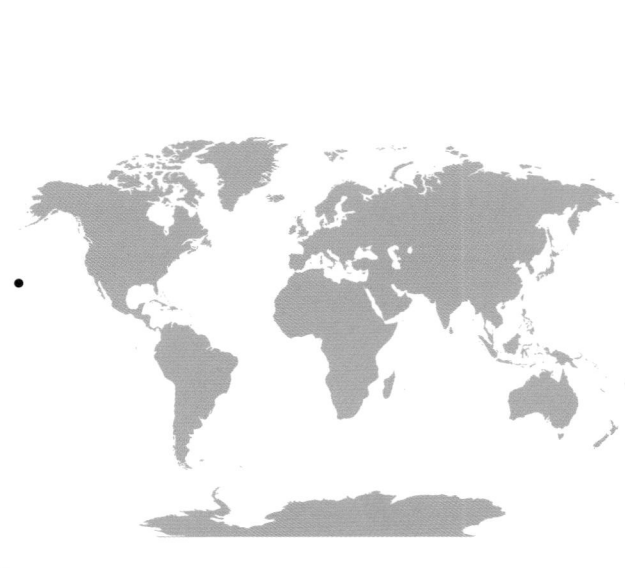

LAKE DUNDAS AUSTRALIA

This view looks west over Lake Dundas, one of the largest salt lakes in Western Australia. When it is full it covers 26 000 hectares. This area is notable for long hours of sunshine, high temperatures and low rainfall of about 250 mm (10 inches) a year. There are no rivers in the area and any agriculture, as depicted by the straight lined shapes at the top left of the image, requires high levels of fertilisers to improve the salty soil. It is calculated that one square mile of land is needed to sustain one sheep.

The main economy of the area centres on gold mining and processing, as well as nickel and platinum mining. Studies of the geology of the area suggest that in the Jurassic period Lake Dundas was one of a series of large drainage channels which connected to a string of salt lakes stretching north for about 170 km (105 miles).

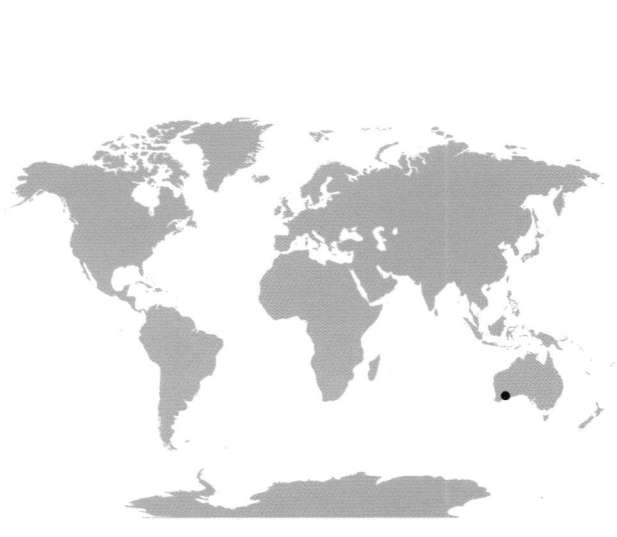

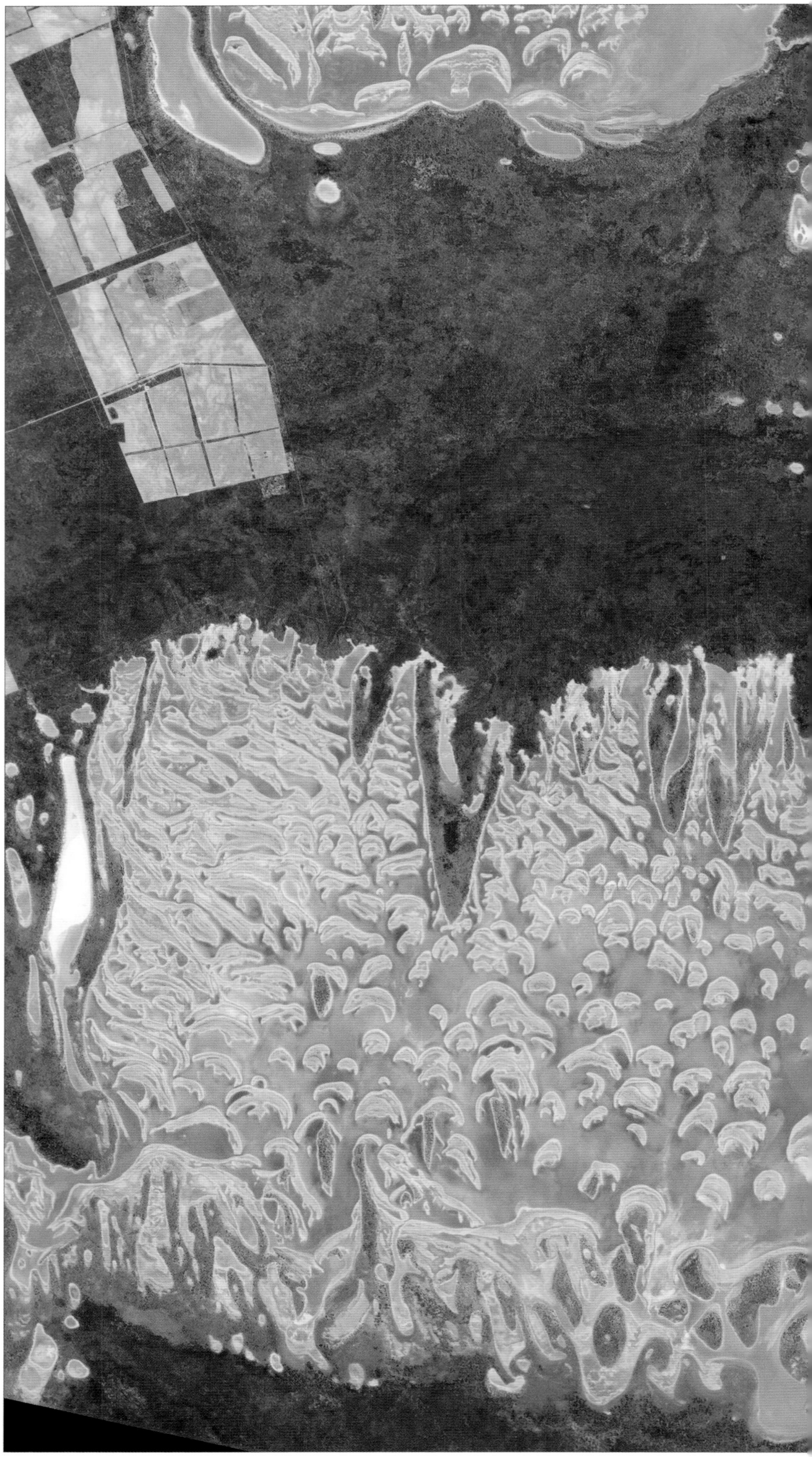

PRIBILOF ISLANDS USA

St Paul, to the right, and St George, to the left, are two of four islands which make up the Pribilof Islands. Formerly called the Fur Seal Islands, they lie in the Bering Sea, 500 km (300 miles) west of Alaska's mainland and 400 km (240 km) north of the Aleutian Islands archipelago.

The milky green and blue colour in the sea shows the extent of the microscopic phytoplankton bloom due to the nutrient rich waters. This bloom is the basis of a healthy habitat for fish and birds. In spring, when the Arctic winter ice melts, nutrients are released and the ocean water is freshened. This triggers the start of the phytoplankton blooms.

In summer the phytoplankton become food sources for zooplankton, fish and other marine life and as the waters warm up the nutrients in the sea diminish. In the autumn, storms can stir up the ocean bringing nutrients back up to the cooler surface and improving the conditions for a late increase in blooms. Recent research suggests a disturbance to the natural balance between phytoplankton and their predators can trigger the process of a bloom developing.

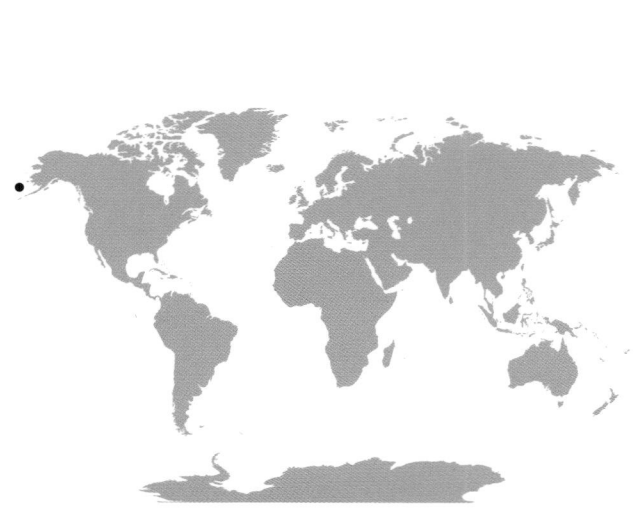

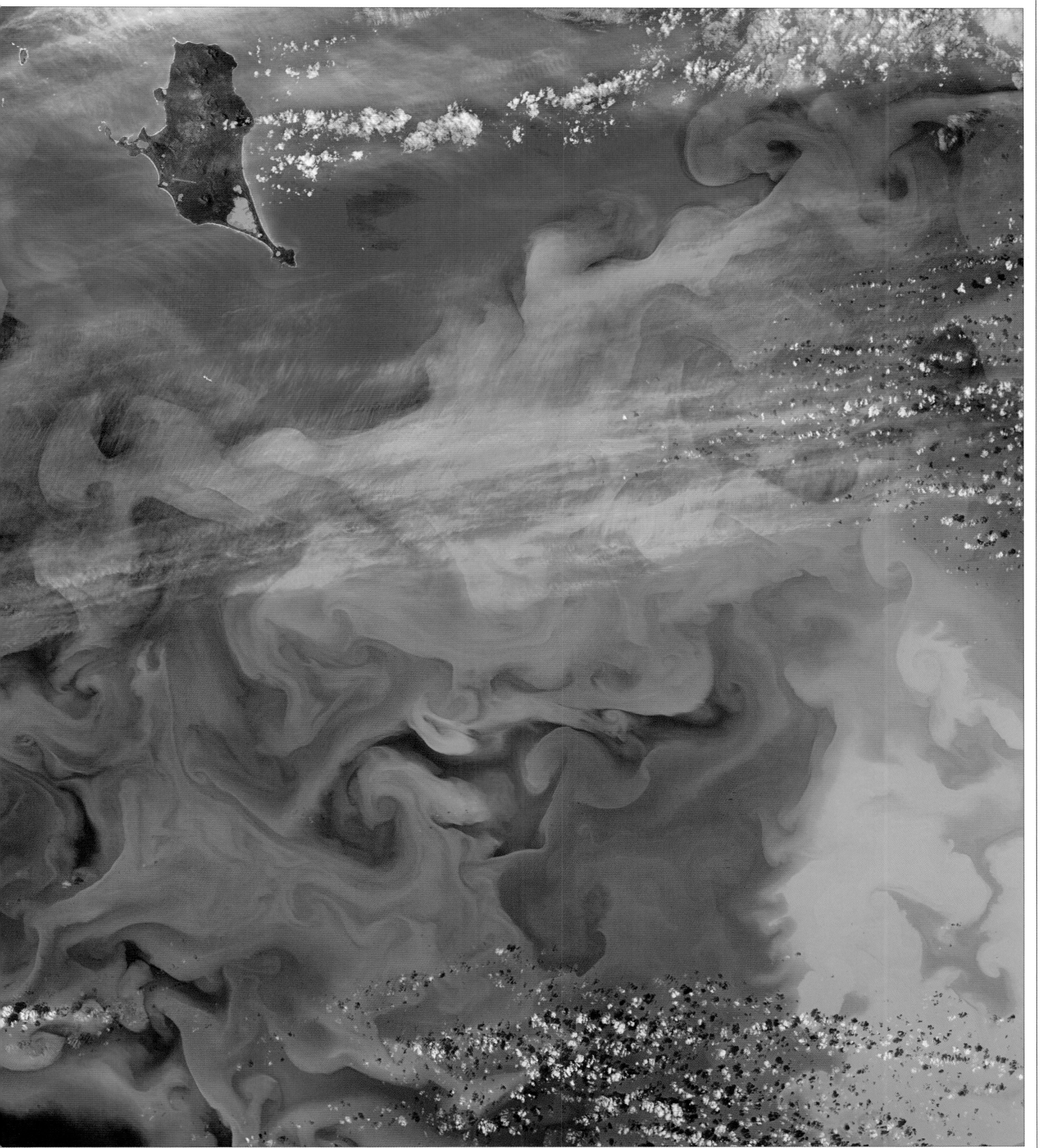

COLORADO RIVER USA

Utah is home to some of the most rugged terrain in the U.S.A. and here at the confluence of the Green River (on the left) and the Colorado River (on the right), the remote nature of the land is evident. The area includes the Canyonlands National Park, which despite its remoteness, attracts over 440 000 visitors a year who enjoy the scenery and tranquillity as well as white-water rafting and trekking.

Geologists have long been fascinated by the meandering nature of the rivers in this area. Such behaviour is usually associated with rivers such as the Mississippi where it crosses broad floodplains, cutting through soft alluvial soils. The Colorado River is best known for flowing through the Grand Canyon with sheer rock faces up to 1800 m (6000 ft) deep. Here canyons are about 150 m (500 ft) deep and reveal over 100 million years of geological history.

On the right-hand page there can be seen a double oxbow, known as The Loop. Geologists would call this an 'entrenched meander'. At its narrowest point there is only 150 m (500 ft) of land separating the two river channels. The action of the river and the wind continue to erode and reshape this landscape. At some point in the future the neck piece of land will collapse, redirecting the river and creating an oxbow lake.

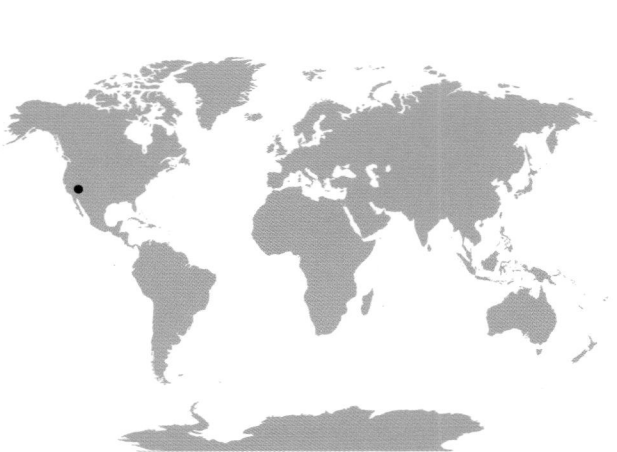

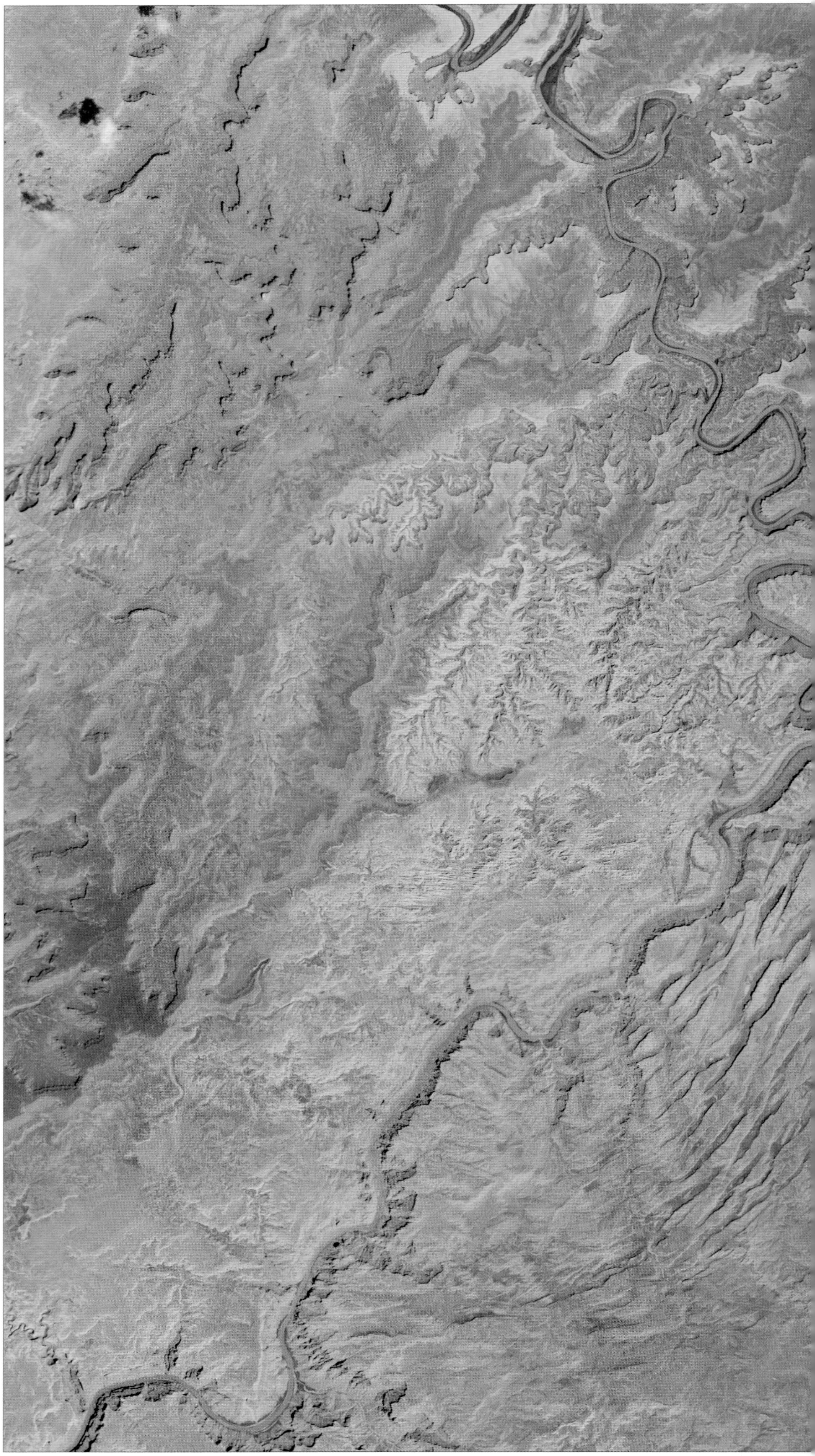

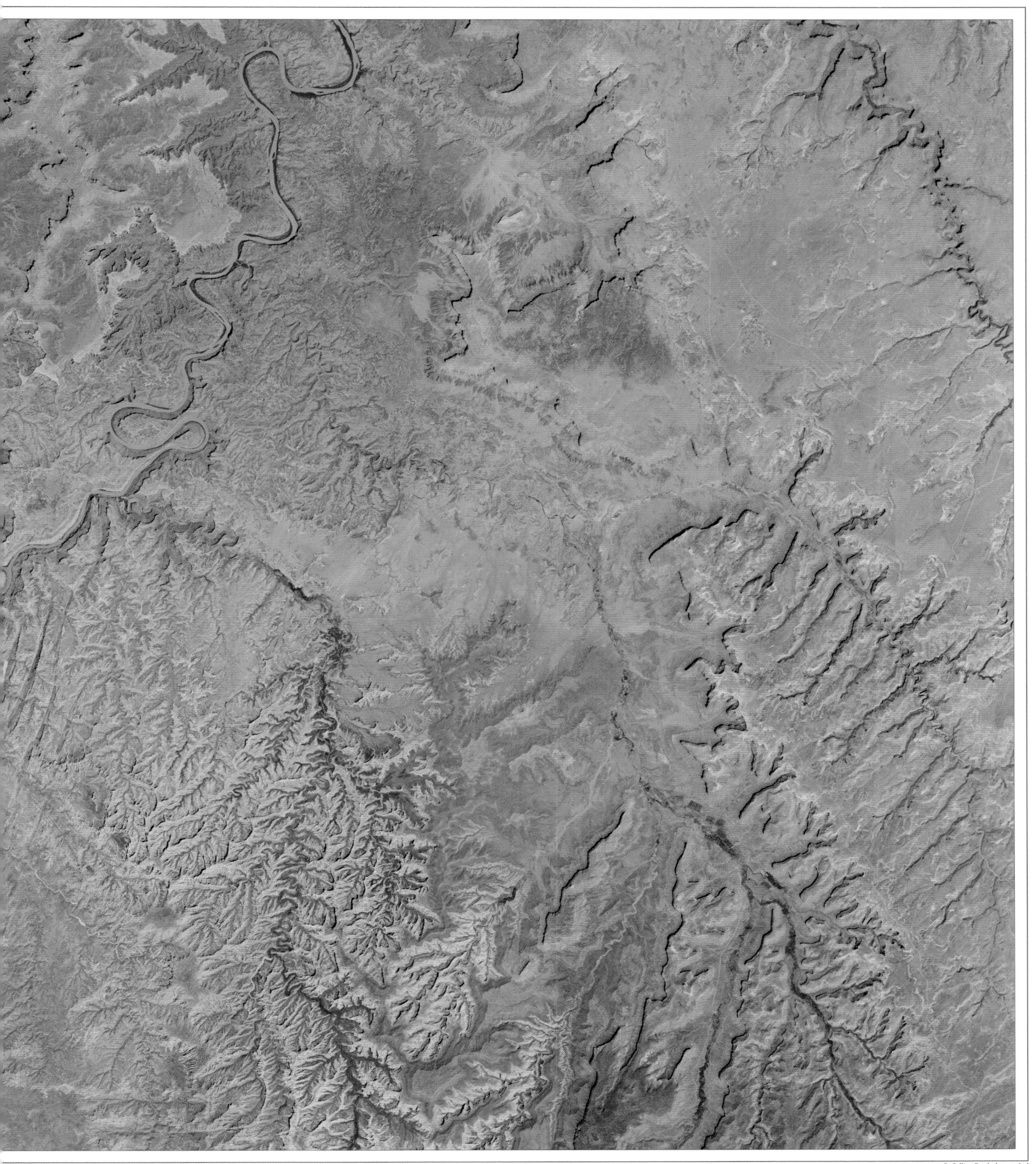

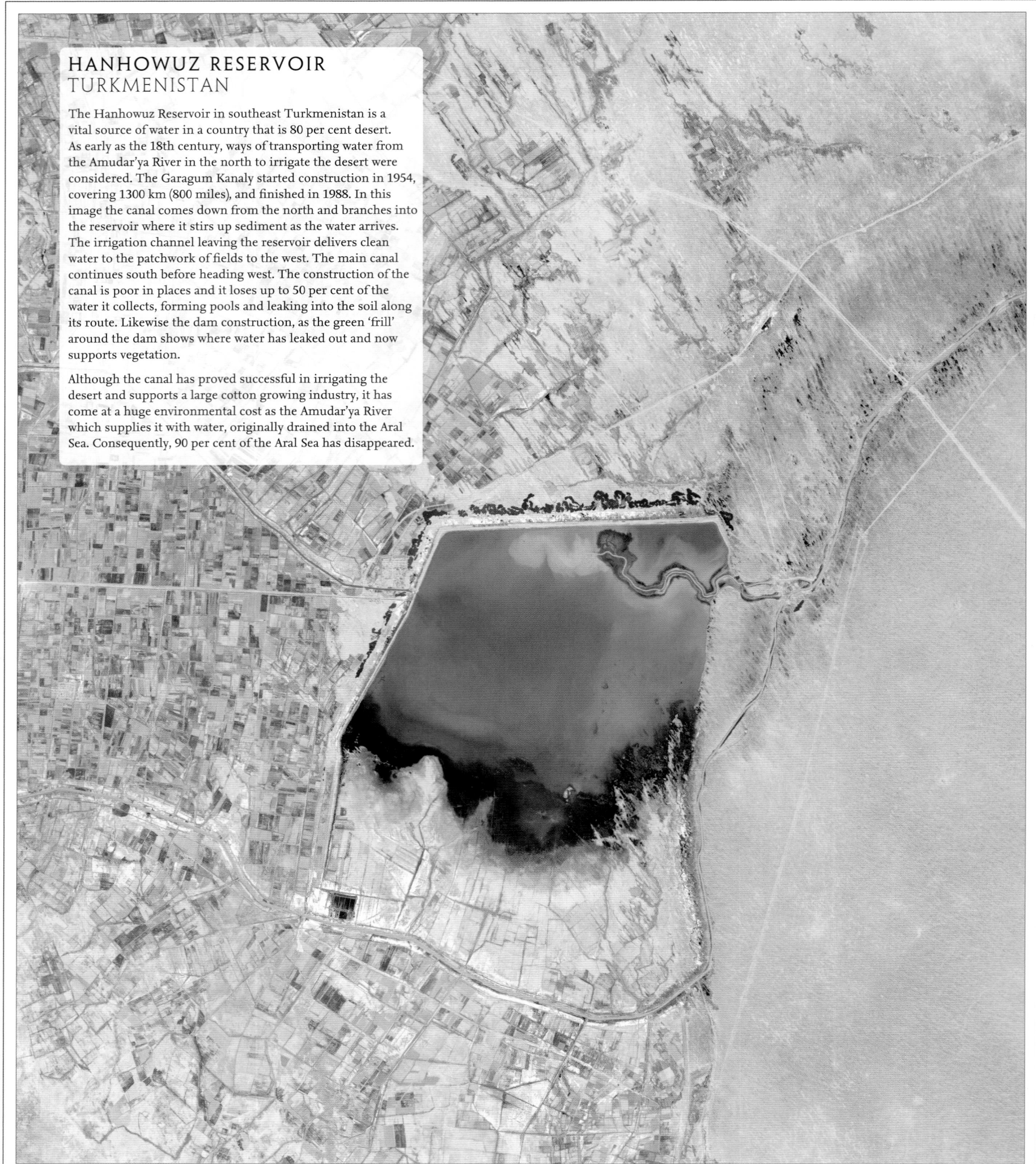

HANHOWUZ RESERVOIR
TURKMENISTAN

The Hanhowuz Reservoir in southeast Turkmenistan is a
vital source of water in a country that is 80 per cent desert.
As early as the 18th century, ways of transporting water from
the Amudar'ya River in the north to irrigate the desert were
considered. The Garagum Kanaly started construction in 1954,
covering 1300 km (800 miles), and finished in 1988. In this
image the canal comes down from the north and branches into
the reservoir where it stirs up sediment as the water arrives.
The irrigation channel leaving the reservoir delivers clean
water to the patchwork of fields to the west. The main canal
continues south before heading west. The construction of the
canal is poor in places and it loses up to 50 per cent of the
water it collects, forming pools and leaking into the soil along
its route. Likewise the dam construction, as the green 'frill'
around the dam shows where water has leaked out and now
supports vegetation.

Although the canal has proved successful in irrigating the
desert and supports a large cotton growing industry, it has
come at a huge environmental cost as the Amudar'ya River
which supplies it with water, originally drained into the Aral
Sea. Consequently, 90 per cent of the Aral Sea has disappeared.

INTRODUCTION TO THE INDEX

The index includes all names shown on the reference maps in the atlas. Each entry includes the country or geographical area in which the feature is located, a page number and an alphanumeric reference. Additional entry details and aspects of the index are explained below.

REFERENCING

Names are referenced by page number and by grid reference. The grid reference relates to the alphanumeric values which appear in the margin of each map. These reflect the graticule on the map – the letter relates to longitude divisions, the number to latitude divisions.

Names are generally referenced to the largest scale map page on which they appear. For large geographical features, including countries, the reference is to the largest scale map on which the feature appears in its entirety, or on which the majority of it appears.

Rivers are referenced to their lowest downstream point – either their mouth or their confluence with another river. The river name will generally be positioned as close to this point as possible.

Entries relating to names appearing on insets are indicated by a small box symbol: □ followed by a grid reference if the inset has its own alphanumeric values.

ALTERNATIVE NAMES

Alternative names appear as cross-references and refer the user to the index entry for the form of the name used on the map.

For rivers with multiple names – for example those which flow through several countries – all alternative name forms are included within the main index entries, with details of the countries in which each form applies.

ADMINISTRATIVE QUALIFIERS

Administrative divisions are included in an entry to differentiate duplicate names – entries of exactly the same name and feature type within the one country – where these division names are shown on the maps. In such cases, duplicate names are alphabetized in the order of the administrative division names. Additional qualifiers are included for names within selected geographical areas, to indicate more clearly their location.

DESCRIPTORS

Entries, other than those for towns and cities, include a descriptor indicating the type of geographical feature. Descriptors are not included where the type of feature is implicit in the name itself, unless there is a town or city of exactly the same name.

NAME FORMS AND ALPHABETICAL ORDER

Name forms are as they appear on the maps, with additional alternative forms included as cross-references. Names appear in full in the index, although they may appear in abbreviated form on the maps.

The German character ß is alphabetized as 'ss'. Names beginning with Mac or Mc are alphabetized exactly as they appear. The terms Saint, Sainte, etc, are abbreviated to St, Ste, etc, but alphabetized as if in the full form.

NUMERICAL ENTRIES

Entries beginning with numerals appear at the beginning of the index, in numerical order. Elsewhere, numerals are alphabetized before 'a'.

PERMUTED TERMS

Names beginning with generic, geographical terms are permuted – the descriptive term is placed after, and the index alphabetized by, the main part of the name. For example, Lake Superior is indexed as Superior, Lake; Mount Everest as Everest, Mount. This policy is applied to all languages. Permuting has not been applied to names of towns, cities or administrative divisions beginning with such geographical terms. These remain in their full form, for example, Lake Isabella, USA.

INDEX ABBREVIATIONS

admin. dist.	administrative district	IN	Indiana	Phil.	Philippines
admin. div.	administrative division	Indon.	Indonesia	plat.	plateau
admin. reg.	administrative region	is	islands	P.N.G.	Papua New Guinea
Afgh.	Afghanistan	isth.	isthmus	Port.	Portugal
AK	Alaska	Kazakh.	Kazakhstan	prov.	province
AL	Alabama	KS	Kansas	pt	point
Alg.	Algeria	KY	Kentucky	Qld	Queensland
Alta	Alberta	Kyrg.	Kyrgyzstan	Que.	Québec
AR	Arkansas	l.	lake	r.	river
Arg.	Argentina	LA	Louisiana	reg.	region
aut. comm.	autonomous community	lag.	lagoon	res.	reserve
aut. reg.	autonomous region	Lith.	Lithuania	resr	reservoir
aut. rep.	autonomous republic	Lux.	Luxembourg	RI	Rhode Island
AZ	Arizona	MA	Massachusetts	r. mouth	river mouth
Azer.	Azerbaijan	Madag.	Madagascar	S.	South
b.	bay	Man.	Manitoba	S.A.	South Australia
Bangl.	Bangladesh	MD	Maryland	salt l.	salt lake
B.C.	British Columbia	ME	Maine	Sask.	Saskatchewan
Bol.	Bolivia	Mex.	Mexico	SC	South Carolina
Bos. & Herz.	Bosnia and Herzegovina	MI	Michigan	SD	South Dakota
Bulg.	Bulgaria	MN	Minnesota	sea chan.	sea channel
c.	cape	MO	Missouri	Sing.	Singapore
CA	California	Moz.	Mozambique	Stn	station
C.A.R.	Central African Republic	MS	Mississippi	Str.	strait
CO	Colorado	MT	Montana	Switz.	Switzerland
Col.	Colombia	mt.	mountain	Tajik.	Tajikistan
CT	Connecticut	mts	mountains	Tanz.	Tanzania
Czech Rep.	Czech Republic	mun.	municipality	Tas.	Tasmania
DC	District of Columbia	N.	North, Northern	terr.	territory
DE	Delaware	nat. park	national park	Thai.	Thailand
Dem. Rep. Congo	Democratic Republic of the Congo	N.B.	New Brunswick	TN	Tennessee
depr.	depression	NC	North Carolina	Trin. and Tob.	Trinidad and Tobago
des.	desert	ND	North Dakota	Turkm.	Turkmenistan
disp. terr.	disputed territory	NE	Nebraska	TX	Texas
Dom. Rep.	Dominican Republic	Neth.	Netherlands	U.A.E.	United Arab Emirates
Equat. Guinea	Equatorial Guinea	Nfld. and Lab.	Newfoundland and Labrador	U.K.	United Kingdom
esc.	escarpment	NH	New Hampshire	Ukr.	Ukraine
est.	estuary	NJ	New Jersey	U.S.A.	United States of America
Eth.	Ethiopia	NM	New Mexico	UT	Utah
Fin.	Finland	N.S.	Nova Scotia	Uzbek.	Uzbekistan
FL	Florida	N.T.	Northern Territories	VA	Virginia
for.	forest	N.S.W.	New South Wales	Val.	Valley
Fr. Guiana	French Guiana	N.W.T.	Northwest Territories	Venez.	Venezuela
Fr. Polynesia	French Polynesia	N.Z.	New Zealand	Vic.	Victoria
g.	gulf	NV	Nevada	vol.	volcano
GA	Georgia	NY	New York	vol. crater	volcanic crater
Guat.	Guatemala	OH	Ohio	VT	Vermont
h.	hill	OK	Oklahoma	W.	West, Western
hd	headland	Ont.	Ontario	WA	Washington
HI	Hawaii	OR	Oregon	W.A.	Western Australia
Hond.	Honduras	PA	Pennsylvania	WI	Wisconsin
i.	island	Pak.	Pakistan	WV	West Virginia
IA	Iowa	Para.	Paraguay	WY	Wyoming
ID	Idaho	P.E.I.	Prince Edward Island	Y.T.	Yukon
IL	Illinois	pen.	peninsula		

1st Three Mile Opening

1

122 D2 1st Three Mile Opening *sea chan.* Australia
122 C2 2nd Three Mile Opening *sea chan.* Australia
235 K2 9 de Julio Arg.
235 K2 25 de Mayo *Buenos Aires* Arg.
235 I3 25 de Mayo *La Pampa* Arg.
204 E4 100 Mile House Canada

A

171 J5 Aabenraa Denmark
179 E4 Aachen Germany
171 J4 Aalborg Denmark
171 J4 Aalborg Bugt *b.* Denmark
176 E6 Aalen Germany
149 H3 Aalo India
178 C4 Aalst Belgium
171 J4 Aarhus Denmark
171 J4 Aars Denmark
178 C4 Aarschot Belgium
154 A3 Aba China
194 D3 Aba Dem. Rep. Congo
192 C4 Aba Nigeria
142 B5 Abā ad Dūd Saudi Arabia
142 C4 Ābādān Iran
140 D5 Abadan Turkm.
142 D4 Ābādeh Iran
142 D4 Ābādeh Ţashk Iran
192 B1 Abadla Alg.
234 D2 Abaeté *r.* Brazil
231 I4 Abaetetuba Brazil
236 G6 Abaiang *atoll* Kiribati
213 E4 Abajo Peak U.S.A.
192 C4 Abakaliki Nigeria
150 B1 Abakan Russia
150 A1 Abakanskiy Khrebet *mts* Russia
187 E7 Abana Turkey
230 D6 Abancay Peru
142 D4 Abarkūh Iran
142 D4 Abarkūh, Kavīr-e *des.* Iran
158 I2 Abashiri Japan
158 I2 Abashiri-wan *b.* Japan
119 E3 Abau P.N.G.
141 H2 Abay Kazakh.
Abaya, Lake Eth. *see* Ābaya Hāyk'
194 D3 Ābaya Hāyk' *l.* Eth.
193 F3 Ābay Wenz *r.* Eth. *alt.* Azraq, Bahr el (Sudan), *conv.* Blue Nile
133 K4 Abaza Russia
143 E3 'Abbāsābād Iran
184 C4 Abbasanta *Sardinia* Italy
208 C2 Abbaye, Point U.S.A.
194 E2 Abbe, Lake Eth.
182 E1 Abbeville France
217 E6 Abbeville *LA* U.S.A.
219 D5 Abbeville *SC* U.S.A.
175 I5 Abbeyfeale Ireland
174 E6 Abbey Head U.K.
175 K5 Abbeyleix Ireland
172 D3 Abbeytown U.K.
170 L2 Abborrträsk Sweden
123 D4 Abbot, Mount Australia
127 I3 Abbot Ice Shelf Antarctica
204 E5 Abbotsford Canada
208 B3 Abbotsford U.S.A.
213 F4 Abbott U.S.A.
148 C2 Abbottabad Pak.
139 H3 'Abd al 'Azīz *h.* Syria
139 K5 Ābdānān Iran
137 I4 'Abdollāhābād Iran
140 C1 Abdulino Russia
193 E3 Abéché Chad
126 D4 Abel Tasman National Park N.Z.
192 B4 Abengourou Côte d'Ivoire
Åbenrå Denmark *see* Aabenraa
179 J6 Abensberg Germany
192 C4 Abeokuta Nigeria
173 C5 Aberaeron U.K.
175 F3 Aberchirder U.K.
125 H5 Abercrombie *r.* Australia
173 D6 Aberdare U.K.
173 C5 Aberdaron U.K.
125 I4 Aberdeen Australia
205 H4 Aberdeen Canada
155 □ Aberdeen *Hong Kong* China
197 F6 Aberdeen S. Africa
175 F3 Aberdeen U.K.
221 E5 Aberdeen *MD* U.S.A.
217 F5 Aberdeen *MS* U.S.A.
216 D2 Aberdeen *SD* U.S.A.
212 B2 Aberdeen *WA* U.S.A.
205 I2 Aberdeen Lake Canada
173 C5 Aberdovey U.K.
Aberdyfi U.K. *see* Aberdovey
174 E4 Aberfeldy U.K.
173 F4 Aberford U.K.
174 D4 Aberfoyle U.K.
173 D6 Abergavenny U.K.
217 C5 Abernathy U.S.A.
173 C5 Aberporth U.K.
173 C5 Abersoch U.K.
173 C5 Aberystwyth U.K.
169 S2 Abez' Russia
146 B6 Abhā Saudi Arabia
142 C2 Abhar Iran
142 C2 Abhar Rūd *r.* Iran
233 H2 Abibe, Serranía de *mts* Col.
192 B4 Abidjan Côte d'Ivoire
194 D3 Abijatta-Shalla National Park Eth.
143 E3 Ab-i-Kavīr *salt flat* Iran
217 D4 Abilene *KS* U.S.A.
217 D5 Abilene *TX* U.S.A.
173 F6 Abingdon U.K.
208 B5 Abingdon *IL* U.S.A.
220 C6 Abingdon *VA* U.S.A.
122 E3 Abington Reef Australia
187 F6 Abinsk Russia
205 H2 Abitau Lake Canada
206 D4 Abitibi *r.* Canada
206 E4 Abitibi, Lake Canada
137 F2 Abkhazia *disp. terr* Georgia
121 F5 Abminga Australia
148 C3 Abohar India
192 B4 Aboisso Côte d'Ivoire
192 C4 Abomey Benin
193 D4 Abong Mbang Cameroon
161 H4 Aborlan Phil.
193 D3 Abou Déia Chad
139 J1 Abovyan Armenia
175 F3 Aboyne U.K.
146 C4 Abqaiq Saudi Arabia
235 J4 Abra, Laguna del *l.* Arg.
183 L3 Abrantes Port.
232 C2 Abra Pampa Arg.
224 A2 Abreojos, Punta *pt* Mex.
234 E2 Abrolhos, Arquipélago dos *is* Brazil
239 G7 Abrolhos Bank *sea feature* S. Atlantic Ocean
212 E2 Absaroka Range *mts* U.S.A.
179 H6 Abtsgmünd Germany
142 D5 Abū al Abyaḍ *i.* U.A.E.
142 C5 Abū 'Alī *i.* Saudi Arabia
Abū al Jirāb *i.* U.A.E. *see* Abū al Abyaḍ
146 B6 Abū 'Arīsh Saudi Arabia
146 D5 Abu Dhabi U.A.E.
Abu Haggag Egypt *see* Ra's al Ḩikmah
193 F3 Abu Hamed Sudan
192 C4 Abuja Nigeria
139 H4 Abū Kamāl Syria
193 E3 Abu Matariq Sudan
138 B6 Abū Mīnā *tourist site* Egypt
142 D5 Abū Mūsá, Jazīreh-ye *i.* U.A.E.
230 E6 Abunã *r.* Bol.
230 E5 Abunã Brazil
146 A7 Ābune Yosēf *mt.* Eth.
181 G5 Abū Nujaym Libya
138 C6 Abū Qīr, Khalīj *b.* Egypt
135 F4 Abu Road India
Abu Simbel Egypt *see* Abū Sunbul
139 J6 Abū Şukhayr Iraq
193 F2 Abū Sunbul Egypt
126 C5 Abut Head N.Z.
161 J4 Abuyog Phil.
193 E3 Abu Zabad Sudan
Abū Ẓabī U.A.E. *see* Abu Dhabi
139 L6 Abūzam Iran
136 D5 Abū Zanīmah Egypt
Abu Zenîma Egypt *see* Abū Zanīmah
193 E3 Abyad Sudan
121 B4 Abydos Australia
193 E4 Abyei Sudan
142 C2 Ābyek Iran
140 D1 Abzakovo Russia
140 D2 Abzanovo Russia
Academy Bay Russia *see* Akademii, Zaliv
221 I2 Acadia National Park U.S.A.
225 D3 Acambaro Mex.
225 G3 Acancéh Mex.
233 H2 Acandí Col.
183 L1 A Cañiza Spain
224 C3 Acaponeta Mex.
225 E4 Acapulco Mex.
231 I4 Acará Brazil
231 J4 Acaraú *r.* Brazil
235 A4 Acaray *r.* Para.
232 E3 Acaray, Represa de *resr* Para.
233 J2 Acarigua Venez.
225 E4 Acatlán Mex.
225 E4 Acatzingo Mex.
225 F4 Acayucán Mex.
192 B4 Accra Ghana
173 E4 Accrington U.K.
233 J3 Achaguas Venez.
148 D5 Achalpur India
147 H2 Achampet India
Achan Russia *see* Bolon'
133 S3 Achayvayam Russia
160 D1 Acheng China
178 A4 Achicourt France
175 I4 Achill Ireland
175 H4 Achill Island Ireland
174 C2 Achiltibuie U.K.
179 H1 Achim Germany
150 B1 Achinsk Russia
144 H2 Achit Nuur *l.* Mongolia
137 G2 Achkhoy-Martan Russia
174 C3 Achnasheen U.K.
174 C3 A'Chralaig *mt.* U.K.
187 F6 Achuyevo Russia
138 B3 Acıgöl *l.* Turkey
138 B3 Acıpayam Turkey
184 F6 Acireale *Sicily* Italy
216 E3 Ackley U.S.A.
223 J4 Acklins Island Bahamas
173 I5 Acle U.K.
235 H2 Aconcagua *r.* Chile
235 H2 Aconcagua, Cerro *mt.* Arg.
231 K5 Acopiara Brazil
166 A6 Açores, Arquipélago dos *is* N. Atlantic Ocean
183 L1 A Coruña Spain
224 H6 Acoyapa Nicaragua
184 G4 Acquaviva delle Fonti Italy
184 C2 Acqui Terme Italy
124 A4 Acraman, Lake *salt flat* Australia
Acre Israel *see* 'Akko
185 G5 Acri Italy
177 I7 Ács Hungary
117 J6 Actéon, Groupe *is* Fr. Polynesia
220 B4 Ada *OH* U.S.A.
217 D5 Ada *OK* U.S.A.
183 N2 Adaja *r.* Spain
232 E8 Adam, Mount *h.* Falkland Is
187 F6 Adamovka Russia
221 G3 Adams *MA* U.S.A.
208 C4 Adams *WI* U.S.A.
212 B2 Adams, Mount U.S.A.
147 H4 Adam's Bridge *sea feature* India/Sri Lanka
204 F4 Adams Lake Canada
215 E2 Adams McGill Reservoir U.S.A.
204 C3 Adams Mountain U.S.A.
214 B2 Adams Peak U.S.A.
147 I5 Adam's Pk Sri Lanka
117 J7 Adamstown Pitcairn Is
'Adan Yemen *see* Aden
138 E3 Adana Turkey
138 C1 Adapazarı Turkey
175 J5 Adare Ireland
127 I6 Adare, Cape Antarctica
123 D5 Adavale Australia
215 E2 Adaven U.S.A.
139 J5 Ad Daghghārah Iraq
146 C5 Ad Dahnā' *des.* Saudi Arabia
Ad Dammām Saudi Arabia *see* Dammam
142 B5 Ad Dawādimī Saudi Arabia
Ad Dawḩah Qatar *see* Doha
139 I4 Ad Dawr Iraq
139 K6 Ad Dayr Iraq
142 B5 Ad Dibdibah *plain* Saudi Arabia
142 B6 Ad Dilam Saudi Arabia
146 C5 Ad Dir'īyah Saudi Arabia
194 D3 Addis Ababa Eth.
221 J2 Addison U.S.A.
139 J6 Ad Dīwānīyah Iraq
173 G6 Addlestone U.K.
197 F6 Addo Elephant National Park S. Africa
139 I6 Ad Duwayd *well* Saudi Arabia
219 D6 Adel *GA* U.S.A.
216 E3 Adel *IA* U.S.A.
124 C5 Adelaide Australia
120 E2 Adelaide *r.* Australia
219 E7 Adelaide Bahamas
197 G6 Adelaide S. Africa
127 I2 Adelaide Island Antarctica
118 D3 Adelaide River Australia
215 D4 Adelanto U.S.A.
120 C2 Adele Island Australia
127 J6 Adélie Land *reg.* Antarctica
125 H5 Adelong Australia
141 G4 Adelunga Uzbek.
146 C7 Aden Yemen
146 C7 Aden, Gulf of Somalia/Yemen
179 E4 Adenau Germany
179 I1 Adendorf Germany
142 D5 Adh Dhayd U.A.E.
137 F5 'Adhfā' *well* Saudi Arabia
151 F7 Adi *i.* Indon.
194 D2 Ādī Ārk'ay Eth.
194 D2 Ādīgrat Eth.
148 D6 Adilabad India
139 I2 Adilcevaz Turkey
213 B3 Adin U.S.A.
193 D2 Adīrī Libya
221 F2 Adirondack Mountains U.S.A.
Ādīs Ābeba Eth. *see* Addis Ababa
194 D3 Ādīs Alem Eth.
139 G3 Adıyaman Turkey
177 M7 Adjud Romania
225 E3 Adjuntas, Presa de las *resr* Mex.
207 I3 Adlavik Islands Canada
118 C3 Admiralty Gulf Australia
203 J2 Admiralty Inlet Canada
204 C3 Admiralty Island U.S.A.
204 C3 Admiralty Island National Monument-Kootznoowoo Wilderness *nat. park* U.S.A.
119 E2 Admiralty Islands P.N.G.
147 H3 Adoni India
179 G3 Adorf (Diemelsee) Germany
179 K4 Adorf/Vogtland Germany
156 F2 Ado-Tymovo Russia
182 D5 Adour *r.* France
183 O4 Adra Spain
184 F6 Adrano *Sicily* Italy
192 B2 Adrar Alg.
192 A2 Adrar *mts* Alg.
192 A2 Adrar, Ḍahr *hills* Mauritania
141 G4 Adrasmon Tajik.
193 E3 Adré Chad
209 E5 Adrian *MI* U.S.A.
217 C5 Adrian *TX* U.S.A.
184 E2 Adriatic Sea Europe
147 H4 Adur India
194 C3 Adusa Dem. Rep. Congo
121 C4 Adverse Well Australia
194 D2 Ādwa Eth.
133 O3 Adycha *r.* Russia
187 F6 Adygeya, Respublika *aut. rep.* Russia
187 F6 Adygeysk Russia
187 H6 Adyk Russia
192 B4 Adzopé Côte d'Ivoire
185 K5 Aegean Sea Greece/Turkey
Aenus Turkey *see* Enez
179 H2 Aerzen Germany
183 L1 A Estrada Spain
194 D2 Afabet Eritrea
139 J3 Āfān Iran
169 Q4 Afanas'yevo Russia
143 F3 Afghanistan *country* Asia
171 J3 Åfjord Norway
180 D5 Aflou Alg.
194 E3 Afmadow Somalia
202 C4 Afognak Island U.S.A.
183 M1 A Fonsagrada Spain
190 Africa
139 F3 'Afrīn, Nahr *r.* Syria/Turkey
139 F2 Afşin Turkey
178 D2 Afsluitdijk *barrage* Neth.
213 E3 Afton U.S.A.
231 H4 Afuá Brazil
138 E5 'Afula Israel
138 C2 Afyon Turkey
179 K4 Aga Germany
192 C3 Agadez Niger
192 B1 Agadir Morocco
191 I5 Agalega Islands Mauritius
140 D1 Agapovka Russia
137 F2 Agara Georgia
149 G5 Agartala India
148 C6 Agashi India
209 F2 Agate Canada
185 L6 Agathonisi *i.* Greece
145 D9 Agatti *i.* India
192 B4 Agboville Côte d'Ivoire
139 K1 Ağcabädi Azer.
139 K2 Ağdam (abandoned) Azer.
137 G2 Ağdaş Azer.
Agdash Azer. *see* Ağdaş
183 F5 Agde France
182 E4 Agen France
196 C4 Aggeneys S. Africa
179 F4 Agger *r.* Germany
148 D1 Aghil Dawan China
175 J3 Aghla Mountain *h.* Ireland
185 K7 Agia Varvara Greece
139 G2 Ağın Turkey
185 J6 Agios Dimitrios Greece
185 K5 Agios Efstratios *i.* Greece
185 L5 Agios Fokas, Akrotirio *pt* Greece
185 J5 Agios Konstantinos Greece
185 K7 Agios Nikolaos Greece
185 J4 Agiou Orous, Kolpos *b.* Greece
193 F3 Agirwat Hills Sudan
197 F3 Agisanang S. Africa
121 E5 Agnes, Mount *h.* Australia
121 C5 Agnew Australia
192 B4 Agnibilékrou Côte d'Ivoire
185 K2 Agnita Romania
156 E2 Agniye-Afanas'yevsk Russia
154 A2 Agong China
148 D4 Agra India
187 H7 Agrakhanskiy Poluostrov *pen.* Russia
183 P2 Ágreda Spain
139 I2 Ağrı Turkey
185 J7 Agria Gramvousa *i.* Greece
184 E6 Agrigento *Sicily* Italy
185 I5 Agrinio Greece
235 H3 Agrio *r.* Arg.
184 F4 Agropoli Italy
139 J1 Ağstafa Azer.
139 L1 Ağsu Azer.
225 G5 Agua, Volcán de *vol.* Guat.
224 C3 Agua Brava, Laguna *lag.* Mex.
225 G4 Aguada Mex.
235 J4 Aguada Cecilio Arg.
233 I3 Aguadas Col.
233 I3 Agua de Dios Col.
223 K5 Aguadilla Puerto Rico
224 I6 Aguadulce Panama
235 I3 Agua Escondida Arg.
224 C3 Aguamilpa, Presa *l.* Mex.
222 D4 Aguanaval *r.* Mex.
235 I1 Agua Negra, Paso del *pass* Arg./Chile
234 B3 Aguapeí *r.* Brazil
222 C2 Agua Prieta Mex.
234 A3 Aguaray Guazú *r.* Para.
233 K2 Aguaro-Guariquito, Parque Nacional *nat. park* Venez.
224 C2 Aguaruto Mex.
225 D3 Aguascalientes Mex.
225 D3 Aguascalientes *state* Mex.
234 E2 Águas Formosas Brazil
234 C1 Águas Lindas de Goiás Brazil
234 C3 Agudos Brazil
215 F5 Aguila U.S.A.
183 N1 Aguilar de Campoo Spain
183 P4 Águilas Spain
161 I4 Aguisan Phil.
196 D7 Agulhas, Cape S. Africa
239 K9 Agulhas Basin *sea feature* Southern Ocean
234 D3 Agulhas Negras *mt.* Brazil
238 F7 Agulhas Plateau *sea feature* Southern Ocean
239 J8 Agulhas Ridge *sea feature* S. Atlantic Ocean
163 I4 Agung, Gunung *vol.* Indon.
161 J4 Agusan *r.* Phil.
233 I2 Agustín Codazzi Col.
161 I4 Agutaya Phil.
137 G2 Agvali Russia
192 C2 Ahaggar *plat.* Alg.
192 C2 Ahaggar, Tassili oua-n- *plat.* Alg.
142 B2 Ahar Iran
126 C5 Ahaura N.Z.
179 F2 Ahaus Germany
126 F3 Ahimanawa Range *mts* N.Z.
126 D1 Ahipara N.Z.
126 D1 Ahipara Bay N.Z.
202 B4 Ahklun Mountains U.S.A.
139 I2 Ahlat Turkey
179 F3 Ahlen Germany
148 C5 Ahmadabad India
147 G2 Ahmadnagar India
148 B3 Ahmadpur East Pak.
148 B4 Ahmad Tar Pak.
179 I4 Ahorn Germany
142 C4 Ahram Iran
179 I1 Ahrensburg Germany
139 I2 Ahta Dağı *mt.* Turkey
171 N3 Ähtäri Fin.
171 N4 Ahtme Estonia
139 L6 Āhū Iran
225 G5 Ahuachapán El Salvador
225 D3 Ahualulco Mex.
182 F3 Ahun France
126 B6 Ahuriri *r.* N.Z.
142 C4 Ahvāz Iran
148 C5 Ahwa India
196 B3 Ai-Ais Namibia
196 B3 Ai-Ais Hot Springs and Fish River Canyon Park Namibia
196 B4 Ai-Ais/Richtersveld Transfrontier Park Namibia/S. Africa
154 D1 Aibag He *r.* China
143 H2 Aībak Afgh.
Aidin Turkm. *see* Aýdyň
214 □1 'Aiea U.S.A.
138 E4 Aigialousa Cyprus
185 J6 Aigina *i.* Greece
185 J5 Aigio Greece
182 H4 Aigle de Chambeyron *mt.* France
235 L2 Aiguá Uruguay
160 C3 Ai He *r.* China
Aihui China *see* Heihe
159 F5 Aikawa Japan
219 D5 Aiken U.S.A.
121 F4 Aileron Australia
224 J6 Ailigandi Panama
236 G6 Ailinglaplap *atoll* Marshall Is
178 A5 Ailly-sur-Noye France
209 G4 Ailsa Craig Canada
174 C5 Ailsa Craig *i.* U.K.
175 J3 Ailt an Chorráin Ireland
234 E2 Aimorés, Serra dos *hills* Brazil
214 □1 'Āina Haina U.S.A.
192 C1 Aïn Beïda Alg.
192 B2 'Aïn Ben Tili Mauritania
'Ain Dâlla *spring* Egypt *see* 'Ayn Dāllah
183 R4 Aïn Defla Alg.
180 D5 Aïn Deheb Alg.
183 R5 Aïn el Hadjel Alg.
'Ain el Maqfi *spring* Egypt *see* 'Ayn al Maqfi
180 E4 Aïn-M'Lila Alg.
192 B1 Aïn Sefra Alg.
207 H4 Ainslie, Lake Canada
216 D3 Ainsworth U.S.A.
Aintab Turkey *see* Gaziantep
183 R4 Aïn Taya Alg.
183 Q5 Aïn Tédélès Alg.
'Ain Tibaghbagh *spring* Egypt *see* 'Ayn Tabaghbugh
'Ain Timeira *spring* Egypt *see* 'Ayn Tumayrah
'Ain Zeitûn Egypt *see* 'Ayn az Zaytūn
233 I4 Aipe Col.
162 C5 Air *i.* Indon.
192 C3 Aïr, Massif de l' *mts* Niger
205 G4 Airdrie Canada
174 E5 Airdrie U.K.
178 D6 Aire *r.* France
183 O5 Aire-sur-l'Adour France
192 C3 Aïr et du Ténéré, Réserve Naturelle Nationale de l' *nature res.* Niger
203 K3 Air Force Island Canada
154 D1 Airgin Sum China
205 H3 Air Ronge Canada
154 F2 Ai Shan *h.* China
204 B2 Aishihik Canada
204 B2 Aishihik Lake Canada
182 G2 Aisne *r.* France
180 C5 Aïssa, Djebel *mt.* Alg.
183 P3 Aitana *mt.* Spain
119 E2 Aitape P.N.G.
216 E2 Aitkin U.S.A.
140 C1 Aitovo Russia
117 I5 Aitutaki *i.* Pacific Ocean
177 K7 Aiud Romania
183 G5 Aix-en-Provence France
182 G4 Aix-les-Bains France
149 F5 Aiyar Reservoir India
149 H5 Aizawl India
171 N4 Aizkraukle Latvia
171 M4 Aizpute Latvia
159 F6 Aizuwakamatsu Japan
184 C4 Ajaccio *Corsica* France
233 I4 Ajajú *r.* Col.
225 E4 Ajalpán Mex.
147 G1 Ajanta India
170 K2 Ajaureforsen Sweden
126 D5 Ajax, Mount N.Z.
193 E1 Ajdābiyā Libya
158 G4 Ajigasawa Japan
192 C2 Ajjer, Tassili n' *plat.* Alg.
138 E5 'Ajlūn Jordan
142 D5 'Ajmān U.A.E.
148 C4 Ajmer India
215 F5 Ajo U.S.A.

'Alīābād

215 F5 Ajo, Mount U.S.A.
161 I4 Ajuy Phil.
158 H3 Akabira Japan
156 E1 Akademii, Zaliv b. Russia
141 H2 Akadyr Kazakh.
147 H2 Akalkot India
158 I3 Akan Kokuritsu-kōen nat. park Japan
138 D4 Akanthou Cyprus
126 D5 Akaroa N.Z.
126 D5 Akaroa Harbour N.Z.
149 H4 Akas reg. India
137 E4 Akāshat Iraq
141 H3 Akbakay Kazakh.
141 I3 Akbalyk Kazakh.
143 H3 Akbar Khēl Afgh.
149 E4 Akbarpur India
140 E3 Akbasty Kazakh.
141 H2 Akbaur Kazakh.
141 H5 Akbaytal Tajik.
141 G2 Akbeyit Kazakh.
183 S4 Akbou Alg.
141 I2 Akbulak Vostochnyy Kazakhstan Kazakh.
141 K2 Akbulak Vostochnyy Kazakhstan Kazakh.
140 B2 Akbulak Zapadnyy Kazakhstan Kazakh.
140 C2 Akbulak Russia
139 F2 Akçadağ Turkey
139 G3 Akçakale Turkey
138 C1 Akçakoca Turkey
138 D3 Akçali Dağ mt. Turkey
138 C3 Akdağ mt. Turkey
138 C3 Ak Dağı mt. Turkey
139 H2 Ak Dağı mts Turkey
136 C3 Akdağlar mts Turkey
138 E2 Akdağmadeni Turkey
140 D4 Akdepe Turkm.
171 L4 Åkersberga Sweden
178 C2 Akersloot Neth.
140 E3 Akespe Kazakh.
194 C3 Aketi Dem. Rep. Congo
140 C4 Akgyr Erezi hills Turkm.
Akhali-Afoni Georgia see Akhali Atoni
137 F2 Akhali Atoni Georgia
139 I1 Akhalkalaki Georgia
187 G7 Akhaltsikhe Georgia
149 G5 Akhaura Bangl.
193 E1 Akhḍar, Al Jabal al mts Libya
147 E5 Akhḍar, Jabal mts Oman
138 A2 Akhisar Turkey
139 F3 Akhtarīn Syria
187 H5 Akhtubinsk Russia
137 G2 Akhty Russia
140 D1 Akhunovo Russia
139 I1 Akhuryan Armenia
159 C8 Aki Japan
206 D3 Akimiski Island Canada
138 E3 Akıncı Burun pt Turkey
139 G3 Akıncılar Turkey
156 D1 Akishma r. Russia
159 G5 Akita Japan
192 A3 Akjoujt Mauritania
140 E2 Akkabak Kazakh.
170 L2 Akkajaure l. Sweden
Akkala Uzbek. see Oqqal'a
140 E2 Akkarga Kazakh.
141 G3 Akkense Kazakh.
140 D2 Akkermanovka Russia
158 I3 Akkeshi Japan
140 B3 Akkistau Kazakh.
138 E5 'Akko Israel
141 G2 Akkol' Akmolinskaya Oblast' Kazakh.
141 H3 Akkol' Almatinskaya Oblast' Kazakh.
140 B3 Akkol' Atyrauskaya Oblast' Kazakh.
141 G4 Akkol' Zhambylskaya Oblast' Kazakh.
141 G4 Akkol', Ozero salt l. Kazakh.
141 I2 Akku Kazakh.
141 F3 Akkum Kazakh.
139 F1 Akkuş Turkey
Akkyr, Gory hills Turkm. see Akgyr Erezi
148 D4 Aklera India
171 M4 Akmeņrags pt Latvia
148 D1 Akmeqit China
Akmola Kazakh. see Astana
141 G2 Akmolinskaya Oblast' admin. div. Kazakh.
141 I4 Ak-Moyun Kyrg.
159 D7 Akō Japan
193 F4 Akobo South Sudan
148 D5 Akola India
141 I4 Akongkür China
194 D2 Akordat Eritrea
138 D3 Akören Turkey
148 D5 Akot India
141 H2 Akoy Kazakh.
207 G1 Akpatok Island Canada
141 I4 Akqi China
170 B2 Akranes Iceland
171 I4 Åkrehamn Norway
213 G3 Akron CO U.S.A.
220 C4 Akron OH U.S.A.
220 C4 Akron City Reservoir U.S.A.
148 D2 Aksai Chin terr. Asia
138 E2 Aksaray Turkey
144 H4 Aksay China
141 H4 Ak-Say r. Kyrg.
187 F6 Aksay Russia
148 D2 Aksayqin Hu l. China
138 D3 Akşehir Turkey
138 C2 Akşehir Gölü l. Turkey
138 C3 Akseki Turkey
140 C1 Aksenovo Russia
142 D4 Aks-e Rostam r. Iran
153 J1 Aksha Russia
140 C2 Akshatau Aktyubinskaya Oblast' Kazakh.
141 H3 Akshatau Karagandinskaya Oblast' Kazakh.
141 I4 Akshi Kazakh.
140 E2 Akshiganak Kazakh.
140 B4 Akshukyr Kazakh.
140 C3 Akshymyrau Kazakh.
141 J4 Aksu Xinjiang Uygur Zizhiqu China
141 J4 Aksu Xinjiang Uygur Zizhiqu China
141 G1 Aksu Akmolinskaya Oblast' Kazakh.
141 I3 Aksu Almatinskaya Oblast' Kazakh.
141 I1 Aksu Pavlodarskaya Oblast' Kazakh.
141 G4 Aksu Yuzhnyy Kazakhstan Kazakh.
140 C2 Aksu Zapadnyy Kazakhstan Kazakh.
141 I3 Aksu r. Kazakh.
138 C3 Aksu r. Turkey
141 F2 Aksuat Kostanayskaya Oblast' Kazakh.
141 J3 Aksuat Vostochnyy Kazakhstan Kazakh.
141 H2 Aksu-Ayuly Kazakh.
141 J4 Aksu He r. China
194 D2 Āksum Eth.
141 F3 Aksumbe Kazakh.
141 H3 Aksuyek Kazakh.
149 F1 Aktag mt. China
141 F2 Aktas Kazakh.
139 J2 Aktas Dağı mt. Turkey
139 I1 Aktaş Gölü l. Georgia
Aktash Uzbek. see Oqtosh
141 G3 Aktau Karagandinskaya Oblast' Kazakh.
141 H2 Aktau Karagandinskaya Oblast' Kazakh.
140 B4 Aktau Mangystauskaya Oblast' Kazakh.
141 I5 Akto China
140 D2 Aktobe Kazakh.
141 H2 Aktogay Karagandinskaya Oblast' Kazakh.
141 H1 Aktogay Pavlodarskaya Oblast' Kazakh.
141 I3 Aktogay Vostochnyy Kazakhstan Kazakh.
177 N4 Aktsyabrski Belarus
141 F2 Aktuma (abandoned) Kazakh.
140 D3 Aktumsyk Kazakh.
140 D3 Aktumsyk, Mys pt Uzbek.
141 H4 Ak-Tüz Kyrg.
140 D2 Aktyubinskaya Oblast' admin. div. Kazakh.
159 B8 Akune Japan
192 C4 Akure Nigeria
170 C2 Akureyri Iceland
149 G1 Akxokesay China
Akyab Myanmar see Sittwe
141 H3 Akzhal Karagandinskaya Oblast' Kazakh.
141 J2 Akzhal Vostochnyy Kazakhstan Kazakh.
140 D2 Akzhar Aktyubinskaya Oblast' Kazakh.
141 F3 Akzhar Kyzylordinskaya Oblast' Kazakh.
141 J3 Akzhar Vostochnyy Kazakhstan Kazakh.
141 G4 Akzhar Zhambylskaya Oblast' Kazakh.
141 F3 Akzhaykyn, Ozero salt l. Kazakh.
139 G3 Akziyaret Turkey
171 J3 Ål Norway
142 C5 Al 'Abā Saudi Arabia
219 C6 Alabama r. U.S.A.
219 C5 Alabama state U.S.A.
219 C5 Alabaster U.S.A.
161 I3 Alabat i. Phil.
139 J7 Al 'Abṭīyah well Iraq
141 G4 Ala-Buka Kyrg.
192 E1 Al Abyār Libya
138 E1 Alaca Turkey
139 F2 Alacahan Turkey
138 E1 Alaçam Turkey
138 B2 Alaçam Dağları mts Turkey
225 G3 Alacrán, Arrecife reef Mex.
136 D3 Aladağ Turkey
139 I2 Ala Dag mt. Turkey
139 I2 Ala Dağlar mts Turkey
138 E3 Ala Dağları mts Turkey
187 H7 Alagir Russia
231 K6 Alagoinhas Brazil
183 P2 Alagón Spain
161 J5 Alah r. Phil.
171 M3 Alahärmä Fin.
139 K7 Al Aḥmadī Kuwait
141 G5 Alai Range mts Asia
171 M3 Alajärvi Fin.
224 H6 Alajuela Costa Rica
139 K2 Ālājūjeh Iran
137 E5 Al Akhḍar Saudi Arabia
148 D3 Alaknanda r. India
141 J3 Alakol', Ozero salt l. Kazakh.
170 O2 Alakurtti Russia
138 B6 Al 'Alamayn Egypt
231 F4 Alalaú r. Brazil
142 B5 Al 'Amār Saudi Arabia
139 K6 Al 'Amārah Iraq
136 B5 'Alam ar Rūm, Ra's pt Egypt
Alamdo China see Alando
'Alam el Rûm, Râs pt Egypt see 'Alam ar Rūm, Ra's
139 J7 Al Amghar waterhole Iraq
161 H2 Alaminos Phil.
138 B6 Al 'Āmirīyah Egypt
225 D2 Alamítos, Sierra de los mt. Mex.
215 E3 Alamo U.S.A.
215 F4 Alamo Dam U.S.A.
213 F5 Alamogordo U.S.A.
217 D6 Alamo Heights U.S.A.
213 E6 Alamos Sonora Mex.
224 B2 Alamos Sonora Mex.
213 F4 Alamosa U.S.A.
147 H3 Alampur India
170 K2 Alanäs Sweden
Åland is Fin. see Åland Islands
179 J1 Aland r. Germany
147 H2 Aland India
142 B2 Aland r. Iran
171 L3 Åland Islands Fin.
149 H3 Alando China
162 B5 Alang Besar i. Indon.
Alaniya aut. rep. Russia see Severnaya Osetiya-Alaniya, Respublika
209 E3 Alanson U.S.A.
138 D3 Alanya Turkey
142 D4 'Alā' od Dīn Iran
138 C1 Alaplı Turkey
147 H4 Alappuzha India
138 E7 Al 'Aqabah Jordan
143 F3 'Alāqahdārī Gulistān Afgh.
142 C6 Al 'Āqūlah well Saudi Arabia
183 O3 Alarcón, Embalse de resr Spain
138 D6 Al 'Arīsh Egypt
146 C4 Al Arṭāwīyah Saudi Arabia
163 I4 Alas Indon.
138 B2 Alaşehir Turkey
136 C6 Al Ashmūnayn Egypt
139 I6 Al 'Āshūrīyah well Iraq
202 D3 Alaska state U.S.A.
202 D4 Alaska, Gulf of U.S.A.
204 E3 Alaska Highway Canada/U.S.A.
202 B4 Alaska Peninsula U.S.A.
202 D3 Alaska Range mts U.S.A.
139 L2 Älät Azer.
Alat Uzbek. see Olot
139 I6 Al 'Athāmīn hills Iraq
137 F5 Al Atwā' well Saudi Arabia
187 H4 Alatyr' Russia
187 H4 Alatyr' r. Russia
230 C4 Alausí Ecuador
139 J1 Alaverdi Armenia
170 N2 Alavieska Fin.
171 M3 Alavus Fin.
124 D5 Alawoona Australia
139 K1 Alazani r. Azer./Georgia
139 J5 Al 'Azīzīyah Iraq
193 D1 Al 'Azīzīyah Libya
137 E5 Al Azraq al Janūbī Jordan
184 C2 Alba Italy
139 F3 Al Bāb Syria
183 P3 Albacete Spain
124 D5 Albacutya, Lake dry lake Australia
139 J6 Al Bādiyah al Janūbīyah des. Iraq
185 J1 Alba Iulia Romania
207 F3 Albanel, Lac Canada
185 I4 Albania country Europe
118 B5 Albany Australia
206 C3 Albany r. Canada
219 C6 Albany GA U.S.A.
209 E5 Albany IN U.S.A.
219 C4 Albany KY U.S.A.
221 G3 Albany NY U.S.A.
212 B2 Albany OR U.S.A.
125 H1 Albany Downs Australia
142 B5 Al Barrah Saudi Arabia
Al Başrah Iraq see Basra
139 J6 Al Baṭḥa' marsh Iraq
119 E3 Albatross Bay Australia
125 F8 Albatross Island Australia
193 E2 Al Bawīṭī Egypt
193 E1 Al Bayḍā' Libya
230 □ Albemarle, Punta pt Galapagos Is Ecuador
219 E5 Albemarle Sound sea chan. U.S.A.
184 C2 Albenga Italy
183 N3 Alberche r. Spain
123 A5 Alberga Australia
118 D4 Alberga watercourse Australia
183 L2 Albergaria-a-Velha Port.
125 G4 Albert Australia
182 F2 Albert France
124 C5 Albert, Lake Australia
194 D3 Albert, Lake Dem. Rep. Congo/Uganda
204 F4 Alberta prov. Canada
221 E6 Alberta U.S.A.
204 F4 Alberta, Mount Canada
196 D7 Albertinia S. Africa
178 D4 Albert Kanaal canal Belgium
216 E3 Albert Lea U.S.A.
194 D3 Albert Nile r. Africa
232 B8 Alberto de Agostini, Parque Nacional nat. park Chile
197 H3 Alberton S. Africa
182 H4 Albertville France
179 E6 Albestroff France
183 F5 Albi France
231 H2 Albina Suriname
214 A2 Albion CA U.S.A.
221 I2 Albion ME U.S.A.
209 E4 Albion MI U.S.A.
220 D3 Albion NY U.S.A.
137 E5 Al Bi'r Saudi Arabia
183 O5 Alborán, Isla de i. Spain
183 O4 Alboran Sea Europe
Ålborg Denmark see Aalborg
Ålborg Bugt b. Denmark see Aalborg Bugt
Alborz, Reshteh-ye mts Iran see Elburz Mountains
204 F4 Albreda Canada
123 D4 Albro Australia
142 C5 Al Budayyi' Bahrain
183 L4 Albufeira Port.
213 F5 Albuquerque U.S.A.
224 I5 Albuquerque, Cayos de is Col.
147 E5 Al Buraymī Oman
136 B5 Al Burdī Libya
183 M3 Alburquerque Spain
125 G6 Albury Australia
139 H4 Al Buşayrah Syria
139 G7 Al Busayṭā' plain Saudi Arabia
139 K6 Al Buşayyah Iraq
142 B4 Al Bushūk well Saudi Arabia
183 L3 Alcácer do Sal Port.
183 O2 Alcalá de Henares Spain
183 O4 Alcalá la Real Spain
184 E6 Alcamo Sicily Italy
183 P2 Alcañiz Spain
183 M3 Alcántara Spain
183 O3 Alcaraz Spain
183 N4 Alcaudete Spain
183 O3 Alcázar de San Juan Spain
187 F5 Alchevs'k Ukr.
235 J2 Alcira Arg.
234 E2 Alcobaça Brazil
121 F4 Alcoota Australia
235 K2 Alcorta Arg.
Alcoy Spain see Alcoy-Alcoi
183 P3 Alcoy-Alcoi Spain
183 R3 Alcúdia Spain
195 E4 Aldabra Islands Seychelles
224 C1 Aldama Chihuahua Mex.
225 E3 Aldama Tamaulipas Mex.
133 N4 Aldan Russia
133 O3 Aldan r. Russia
178 D1 Aldeboarn Neth.
173 I5 Aldeburgh U.K.
182 D2 Alderney i. U.K.
214 B4 Alder Peak U.S.A.
173 G6 Aldershot U.K.
220 C6 Alderson U.S.A.
142 D6 Al Dhafrah reg. U.A.E.
172 D3 Aldingham U.K.
173 F5 Aldridge U.K.
208 B5 Aledo U.S.A.
192 A3 Aleg Mauritania
234 E3 Alegre Brazil
232 E3 Alegrete Brazil
235 K2 Alejandro Korn Arg.
232 □ Alejandro Selkirk, Isla i. Atlantic Ocean
186 E2 Alekhovshchina Russia
156 E1 Aleksandra, Mys hd Russia
140 B4 Aleksandra Bekovicha-Cherkasskogo, Zaliv b. Kazakh.
186 F3 Aleksandrov Russia
187 I5 Aleksandrov Gay Russia
140 C1 Aleksandrovka Orenburgskaya Oblast' Russia
140 D1 Aleksandrovka Respublika Bashkortostan Russia
137 F1 Aleksandrovskoye Stavropol'skiy Kray Russia
187 H6 Aleksandrovskoye Stavropol'skiy Kray Russia
133 P4 Aleksandrovsk-Sakhalinskiy Russia
132 F1 Aleksandry, Zemlya i. Russia
141 G1 Alekseyevka Kazakh.
156 B1 Alekseyevka Amurskaya Oblast' Russia
187 F5 Alekseyevka Belgorodskaya Oblast' Russia
187 G5 Alekseyevskaya Russia
187 F4 Aleksin Russia
185 I3 Aleksinac Serbia
195 B4 Alèmbé Gabon
138 E1 Alembeyli Turkey
234 D3 Além Paraíba Brazil
171 J3 Ålen Norway
182 E2 Alençon France
231 H4 Alenquer Brazil
214 □[2] 'Alenuihāhā Channel U.S.A.
139 F3 Aleppo Syria
203 M1 Alert Canada
230 D6 Alerta Peru
204 D3 Alert Bay Canada
182 G4 Alès France
177 K7 Aleşd Romania
184 C2 Alessandria Italy
171 I3 Ålesund Norway
236 G2 Aleutian Basin sea feature Bering Sea
200 C2 Aleutian Islands U.S.A.
202 C4 Aleutian Range mts U.S.A.
237 H2 Aleutian Trench sea feature N. Pacific Ocean
133 Q4 Alevina, Mys c. Russia
221 J2 Alexander U.S.A.
122 B2 Alexander, Mount h. Australia
204 B3 Alexander Archipelago is U.S.A.
196 B4 Alexander Bay b. Namibia/S. Africa
196 B4 Alexander Bay S. Africa
219 C5 Alexander City U.S.A.
127 I3 Alexander Island Antarctica
125 F6 Alexandra Australia
126 B6 Alexandra N.Z.
232 □ Alexandra, Cape Atlantic Ocean
185 J4 Alexandreia Greece
221 F2 Alexandria Canada
193 E1 Alexandria Egypt
185 K3 Alexandria Romania
197 G6 Alexandria S. Africa
174 D5 Alexandria U.K.
209 E5 Alexandria IN U.S.A.
217 E6 Alexandria LA U.S.A.
216 E2 Alexandria MN U.S.A.
221 E5 Alexandria VA U.S.A.
221 F2 Alexandria Bay U.S.A.
124 C5 Alexandrina, Lake Australia
185 K4 Alexandroupoli Greece
207 I3 Alexis r. Canada
208 B5 Alexis U.S.A.
204 E4 Alexis Creek Canada
141 J1 Aley r. Russia
141 J1 Aleysk Russia
179 F4 Alf Germany
183 P1 Alfaro Spain
139 K7 Al Farwānīyah Kuwait
139 I4 Al Fatḥah Iraq
139 L7 Al Fāw Iraq
193 F2 Al Fayyūm Egypt
179 H3 Alfeld (Leine) Germany
234 D3 Alfenas Brazil
139 L7 Al Fintās Kuwait
177 J7 Alföld plain Hungary
173 H4 Alford U.K.
221 F2 Alfred Canada
221 H3 Alfred U.S.A.
121 D5 Alfred and Marie Range hills Australia
139 L7 Al Fuḥayḥīl Kuwait
Al Fujayrah U.A.E. see Fujairah
139 J6 Al Furāt r. Iraq/Syria alt. Fırat (Turkey), conv. Euphrates
140 D2 Alga Kazakh.
140 C2 Algabas Kazakh.
171 I4 Ålgård Norway
235 I3 Algarrobo del Aguilla Arg.
183 L4 Algarve reg. Port.
187 G4 Algasovo Russia
183 N4 Algeciras Spain
183 P3 Algemesí Spain
Alger Alg. see Algiers
209 E3 Alger U.S.A.
192 B2 Algeria country Africa
179 H2 Algermissen Germany
139 J6 Al Ghammās Iraq
Al Ghardaqah Egypt see Hurghada
142 B5 Al Ghāṭ Saudi Arabia
146 D6 Al Ghayḍah Yemen
184 C4 Alghero Sardinia Italy
146 C4 Al Ghwaybiyah Saudi Arabia
192 C1 Algiers Alg.
197 F6 Algoa Bay S. Africa
208 D3 Algoma U.S.A.
216 E3 Algona U.S.A.
209 F4 Algonac U.S.A.
209 H3 Algonquin Park Canada
209 H3 Algonquin Provincial Park Canada
183 O1 Algorta Spain
139 I7 Al Habakah well Saudi Arabia
139 I5 Al Ḥabbānīyah Iraq
142 B4 Al Ḥadaqah well Saudi Arabia
142 C5 Al Ḥadd Bahrain
142 A4 Al Hadhālīl plat. Saudi Arabia
139 I4 Al Ḥadīthah Iraq
Al Ḥaḍr Iraq see Hatra
137 F5 Al Ḥafār well Saudi Arabia
139 F4 Al Ḥaffah Syria
142 B5 Al Ḥā'ir Saudi Arabia
143 E6 Al Hajar Oman
143 E5 Al Ḥajar al Gharbī mts Oman
139 G6 Al Ḥamād plain Jordan/Saudi Arabia
183 P4 Alhama de Murcia Spain
138 B6 Al Ḥammām Egypt
139 I6 Al Ḥammām well Iraq
139 G4 Al Ḥammām Syria
139 J7 Al Haniyah esc. Iraq
142 B6 Al Hariq Saudi Arabia
136 C5 Al Ḥarrah Egypt
139 G6 Al Ḥarrah reg. Saudi Arabia
139 H3 Al Ḥasakah Syria
139 J5 Al Hāshimīyah Iraq
146 B5 Al Ḥawīyah Saudi Arabia
137 E5 Al Ḥawjā' Saudi Arabia
139 K5 Al Ḥayy Iraq
136 C5 Al Ḥayz Egypt
139 F6 Al Hazīm Jordan
137 E5 Al Ḥazm Saudi Arabia
142 B6 Al Ḥillah Saudi Arabia
142 B6 Al Ḥilwah Saudi Arabia
142 C5 Al Ḥinnāh Saudi Arabia
136 D5 Al Ḥismā plain Saudi Arabia
192 B1 Al Hoceima Morocco
Al Ḥudaydah Yemen see Hodeidah
137 E5 Al Ḥufrah reg. Saudi Arabia
146 C4 Al Hufūf Saudi Arabia
137 E5 Al Hūj hills Saudi Arabia
142 D6 Al Ḥumrah reg. U.A.E.
142 C5 Al Ḥunayy Saudi Arabia
142 B6 Al Huwwah Saudi Arabia
152 C5 Ali China
142 D2 'Alīābād Golestān Iran
143 E3 'Alīābād Khorāsān-e Jonūbī Iran
143 F4 'Alīābād Khorāsān-e Jonūbī Iran
139 K4 'Alīābād Kordestān Iran

'Alīābād, Kūh-e

137 H4 'Alīābād, Kūh-e *mt.* Iran
139 K3 'Alīābād-e Marān Iran
185 L5 Aliağa Turkey
185 J4 Aliakmonas *r.* Greece
139 K5 'Alī al Gharbī Iraq
147 G2 Alibag India
148 B4 Ali Bandar Pak.
183 P3 Alicante Spain
122 C2 Alice *r.* Australia
123 D5 Alice *watercourse* Australia
197 G6 Alice S. Africa
217 D7 Alice U.S.A.
204 D3 Alice Arm (abandoned) Canada
118 D4 Alice Springs Australia
219 E7 Alice Town Bahamas
141 H5 Alichur Tajik.
141 H5 Alichur *r.* Tajik.
161 I5 Alicia Phil.
123 C4 Alick Creek *r.* Australia
148 D4 Aligarh India
142 C3 Alīgūdarz Iran
150 E1 Alihe China
195 B4 Alima *r.* Congo
171 K4 Alingsås Sweden
138 B2 Aliova *r.* Turkey
148 B3 Alipur Pak.
149 G4 Alipur Duar India
220 C4 Aliquippa U.S.A.
194 E2 Ali Sabieh Djibouti
139 F6 Al 'Īsāwīyah Saudi Arabia
139 J2 'Alī Shāh Iran
Al Iskandarīyah Egypt *see* Alexandria
139 J5 Al Iskandarīyah Iraq
193 F1 Al Ismā'īlīyah Egypt
185 K5 Aliveri Greece
197 G5 Aliwal North S. Africa
205 G4 Alix Canada
139 F6 Al Jafr Jordan
142 C5 Al Jāfūrah *des.* Saudi Arabia
193 E2 Al Jaghbūb Libya
139 K7 Al Jahrah Kuwait
142 C6 Al Jawb *reg.* Saudi Arabia
192 E2 Al Jawf Libya
193 D1 Al Jawsh Libya
139 G3 Al Jazā'ir *reg.* Iraq/Syria
183 L4 Aljezur Port.
142 C5 Al Jībān *reg.* Saudi Arabia
139 I6 Al Jil *well* Iraq
142 B5 Al Jilh *esc.* Saudi Arabia
142 C5 Al Jishshah Saudi Arabia
Al Jīzah Egypt *see* Giza
138 E6 Al Jīzah Jordan
146 C4 Al Jubayl Saudi Arabia
142 B5 Al Jubaylah Saudi Arabia
142 C5 Al Jumaylīyah Qatar
142 C5 Al Jurayd *i.* Saudi Arabia
142 B5 Al Jurayfah Saudi Arabia
183 L4 Aljustrel Port.
138 E6 Al Karak Jordan
141 G1 Alkaterek Kazakh.
139 J5 Al Kāẓimīyah Iraq
147 E5 Al Khābūrah Oman
139 J5 Al Khāliş Iraq
146 B5 Al Khamāsīn Saudi Arabia
193 F2 Al Khārijah Egypt
147 E4 Al Khaşab Oman
142 A6 Al Khāşirah Saudi Arabia
142 D6 Al Khatam *reg.* U.A.E.
142 C5 Al Khawr Qatar
142 C5 Al Khīşah *well* Saudi Arabia
142 C5 Al Khobar Saudi Arabia
142 B5 Al Khuff *reg.* Saudi Arabia
193 D1 Al Khums Libya
137 E5 Al Khunfah *sand area* Saudi Arabia
139 J5 Al Kifl Iraq
142 C5 Al Kir'ānah Qatar
178 C2 Alkmaar Neth.
139 J5 Al Kūfah Iraq
193 E2 Al Kufrah Libya
139 K5 Al Kumayt Iraq
139 J5 Al Kūt Iraq
Al Kuwayt Kuwait *see* Kuwait
139 H7 Al Labbah *plain* Saudi Arabia
Al Lādhiqīyah Syria *see* Latakia
221 I1 Allagash U.S.A.
221 I1 Allagash *r.* U.S.A.
221 I1 Allagash Lake U.S.A.
149 E4 Allahabad India
139 F5 Al Lajā *lava field* Syria
133 O3 Allakh-Yun' Russia
197 G3 Allanridge S. Africa
197 H1 Alldays S. Africa
209 E4 Allegan U.S.A.
220 D4 Allegheny *r.* U.S.A.
220 C6 Allegheny Mountains U.S.A.
220 D4 Allegheny Reservoir U.S.A.
175 J3 Allen, Lough *l.* Ireland
219 D5 Allendale U.S.A.
172 E3 Allendale Town U.K.
225 D1 Allende *Coahuila* Mex.
225 D2 Allende *Nuevo León* Mex.
179 G4 Allendorf (Lumda) Germany
209 G3 Allenford Canada
221 F4 Allentown U.S.A.
Alleppey India *see* Alappuzha
179 I2 Aller *r.* Germany
216 C3 Alliance *NE* U.S.A.
220 C4 Alliance *OH* U.S.A.
139 I6 Al Līfīyah *well* Iraq
171 K5 Allinge-Sandvig Denmark
137 G6 Al Lişāfah *well* Saudi Arabia
209 H3 Alliston Canada
146 B5 Al Līth Saudi Arabia
174 E4 Alloa U.K.
125 J2 Allora Australia
147 I3 Allur India
147 I3 Alluru Kottapatnam India
139 I6 Al Lussuf *well* Iraq
207 F4 Alma Canada
209 E4 Alma *MI* U.S.A.
216 D3 Alma *NE* U.S.A.
215 H5 Alma *NM* U.S.A.
139 I6 Al Ma'ānīyah Iraq
Alma-Ata Kazakh. *see* Almaty
183 L3 Almada Port.
137 E5 Al Madāfi' *plat.* Saudi Arabia
139 J7 Al Ma'danīyāt *well* Iraq
122 D3 Almaden Australia
183 N3 Almadén Spain
139 K6 Al Madīnah Iraq
Al Madīnah Saudi Arabia *see* Medina
139 F5 Al Mafraq Jordan
139 J5 Al Maḥmūdīyah Iraq
142 B5 Al Majma'ah Saudi Arabia
139 K1 Almalı Azer.
142 C5 Al Malsūnīyah *reg.* Saudi Arabia
Almalyk Uzbek. *see* Olmaliq
Al Manāmah Bahrain *see* Manama
214 B1 Almanor, Lake U.S.A.
183 P3 Almansa Spain
193 F1 Al Manşūrah Egypt
183 N2 Almanzor *mt.* Spain
139 K6 Al Ma'qil Iraq
142 D6 Al Mariyyah U.A.E.
193 E1 Al Marj Libya
234 C1 Almas, Rio das *r.* Brazil
136 D5 Al Maţarīyah Egypt
141 H3 Almatinskaya Oblast' *admin. div.* Kazakh.
141 I4 Almaty Kazakh.
Al Mawşil Iraq *see* Mosul
139 H4 Al Mayādīn Syria
142 B5 Al Mazāḥimīyah Saudi Arabia
183 O2 Almazán Spain
133 M3 Almaznyy Russia
231 H4 Almeirim Brazil
183 L3 Almeirim Port.
179 E2 Almelo Neth.
234 E2 Almenara Brazil
183 M2 Almendra, Embalse de *resr* Spain
183 M3 Almendralejo Spain
178 D2 Almere Neth.
183 O4 Almería Spain
183 O4 Almería, Golfo de *b.* Spain
132 G4 Al'met'yevsk Russia
171 K4 Älmhult Sweden
142 B5 Al Midhnab Saudi Arabia
183 N5 Almina, Punta *pt* Morocco
193 F2 Al Minyā Egypt
224 I6 Almirante Panama
Almirós Greece *see* Almyros
146 C4 Al Mish'āb Saudi Arabia
139 F5 Al Mismīyah Syria
183 L4 Almodôvar Port.
209 F4 Almont U.S.A.
209 I3 Almonte Canada
183 M4 Almonte Spain
146 C4 Al Mubarrez Saudi Arabia
138 E7 Al Mudawwarah Jordan
142 C5 Al Muḥarraq Bahrain
Al Mukallā Yemen *see* Mukalla
Al Mukhā Yemen *see* Mocha
181 H5 Al Mukhaylī Libya
183 O4 Almuñécar Spain
139 J5 Al Muqdādīyah Iraq
142 B5 Al Murabba Saudi Arabia
137 E5 Al Murūt *well* Saudi Arabia
139 F1 Almus Turkey
142 B4 Al Musannāh *ridge* Saudi Arabia
139 J5 Al Musayyib Iraq
136 A3 Almyros Greece
185 K7 Almyrou, Ormos *b.* Greece
172 F2 Alnwick U.K.
119 J3 Alofi Niue
149 H5 Alon Myanmar
156 A2 Alongshan China
185 J5 Alonnisos *i.* Greece
151 E7 Alor *i.* Indon.
151 E7 Alor, Kepulauan *is* Indon.
163 B1 Alor Star Malaysia
Alost Belgium *see* Aalst
148 C5 Alot India
121 E5 Aloysius, Mount Australia
170 O2 Alozero (abandoned) Russia
214 C4 Alpaugh U.S.A.
179 E3 Alpen Germany
209 F3 Alpena U.S.A.
123 D4 Alpha Australia
240 P1 Alpha Ridge *sea feature* Arctic Ocean
215 H5 Alpine *AZ* U.S.A.
217 C6 Alpine *TX* U.S.A.
213 E3 Alpine *WY* U.S.A.
190 F4 Alpine National Park Australia
184 C1 Alps *mts* Europe
146 C6 Al Qa'āmīyāt *reg.* Saudi Arabia
193 D1 Al Qaddāḥīyah Libya
139 F4 Al Qadmūs Syria
Al Qāhirah Egypt *see* Cairo
142 B5 Al Qā'īyah *well* Saudi Arabia
137 E5 Al Qalībah Saudi Arabia
139 H3 Al Qāmishlī Syria
138 D6 Al Qanţarah Egypt
142 B5 Al Qar'ah *well* Saudi Arabia
139 F4 Al Qaryatayn Syria
142 B5 Al Qaşab Saudi Arabia
146 C6 Al Qaţn Yemen
139 F6 Al Qaţrānah Jordan
193 D2 Al Qaţrūn Libya
142 B4 Al Qayşūmah Saudi Arabia
137 F5 Al Qāyşūmah *well* Saudi Arabia
192 E1 Al Qubbah Libya
183 M3 Alqueva, Barragem de *resr* Port.
138 E5 Al Qunayţirah (abandoned) Syria
146 B6 Al Qunfidhah Saudi Arabia
142 A5 Al Qurayn Saudi Arabia
139 K6 Al Qurnah Iraq
193 F2 Al Quşayr Egypt
139 J6 Al Qusayr Iraq
136 C6 Al Qūşīyah Egypt
142 B6 Al Qūşūrīyah Saudi Arabia
139 F5 Al Quţayfah Syria
142 A5 Al Quwārah Saudi Arabia
142 B6 Al Quwayi' Saudi Arabia
142 B5 Al Quwayīyah Saudi Arabia
138 E7 Al Quwayrah Jordan
122 B3 Alroy Downs Australia
182 H2 Alsace *reg.* France
173 E4 Alsager U.K.
139 I6 Al Samīt *well* Iraq
205 H4 Alsask Canada
179 H4 Alsfeld Germany
179 J3 Alsleben (Saale) Germany
172 E3 Alston U.K.
125 J2 Alstonville Australia
171 M4 Alsunga Latvia
170 M1 Alta Norway
126 B6 Alta, Mount N.Z.
170 M1 Altaelva *r.* Norway
170 M1 Altafjorden *sea chan.* Norway
235 J1 Alta Gracia Arg.
233 K2 Altagracia de Orituco Venez.
135 G2 Altai Mountains China/Mongolia
219 D6 Altamaha *r.* U.S.A.
231 H4 Altamira Brazil
224 H6 Altamira Costa Rica
185 G4 Altamura Italy
154 C2 Altan Xiret China
224 C2 Altata Mex.
220 D6 Altavista U.S.A.
135 G2 Altay China
144 H3 Altay *Govĭ-Altay* Mongolia
150 B2 Altay *Govĭ-Altay* Mongolia
141 K2 Altay, Respublika *aut. rep.* Russia
141 J1 Altayskiy Kray *admin. div.* Russia
141 K2 Altayskoye Russia
183 P3 Altea Spain
170 M1 Alteidet Norway
179 E4 Altenahr Germany
179 F2 Altenberge Germany
179 K4 Altenburg Germany
179 F4 Altenkirchen (Westerwald) Germany
149 H1 Altenqoke China
179 L1 Altentreptow Germany
139 L1 Altıağaç Azer.
139 J4 Altin Köprü Iraq
185 L5 Altınoluk Turkey
138 C2 Altıntaş Turkey
230 E7 Altiplano *plain* Bol.
179 J2 Altmark *reg.* Germany
179 I5 Altmühl *r.* Germany
234 B2 Alto Araguaia Brazil
234 B2 Alto Garças Brazil
230 E6 Alto Madidi, Parque Nacional *nat. park* Bol.
195 D5 Alto Molócuè Moz.
219 B4 Alton *IL* U.S.A.
217 F4 Alton *MO* U.S.A.
221 H3 Alton *NH* U.S.A.
216 D1 Altona Canada
220 D4 Altoona U.S.A.
234 C1 Alto Paraíso de Goiás Brazil
234 B2 Alto Sucuriú Brazil
234 B2 Alto Taquari Brazil
176 F6 Altötting Germany
173 E4 Altrincham U.K.
179 K1 Alt Schwerin Germany
225 G4 Altun Ha *tourist site* Belize
150 A3 Altun Shan *mts* China
213 B3 Alturas U.S.A.
217 D5 Altus U.S.A.
140 E3 Altynasar *tourist site* Kazakh.
139 G1 Alucra Turkey
171 N4 Alūksne Latvia
139 L5 Alūm Iran
220 B4 Alum Creek Lake U.S.A.
235 H3 Aluminé *r.* Arg.
235 H3 Aluminé, Lago *l.* Arg.
187 E6 Alupka Crimea
193 D1 Al 'Uqaylah Libya
142 C5 Al 'Uqayr Saudi Arabia
Al Uqsur Egypt *see* Luxor
137 E5 Al 'Urayq *des.* Saudi Arabia
187 E6 Alushta Crimea
139 J4 Ālūt Iran
147 H4 Aluva India
193 E2 Al 'Uwaynāt Libya
139 I6 Al 'Uwayqīlah Saudi Arabia
142 A5 Al 'Uyūn Saudi Arabia
139 K6 Al 'Uzayr Iraq
217 D4 Alva U.S.A.
139 L4 Alvand, Kūh-e *mt.* Iran
225 F4 Alvarado Mex.
235 I2 Alvarado, Paso de *pass* Chile
231 F4 Alvarães Brazil
171 J3 Alvdal Norway
171 K3 Älvdalen Sweden
171 K4 Alvesta Sweden
171 I3 Ålvik Norway
171 L3 Alvik Sweden
217 E6 Alvin U.S.A.
170 M2 Älvsbyn Sweden
139 K7 Al Wafrah Kuwait
134 B4 Al Wajh Saudi Arabia
142 C5 Al Wakrah Qatar
142 C5 Al Wannān Saudi Arabia
137 G5 Al Waqbá *well* Saudi Arabia
148 D4 Alwar India
142 B5 Al Wari'ah Saudi Arabia
136 B5 Al Wāţiyah *well* Egypt
139 H5 Al Widyān *plat.* Iraq/Saudi Arabia
142 B4 Al Wusayţ *well* Saudi Arabia
118 D3 Alyangula Australia
139 I3 Al Ya'rūbīyah Syria
174 E4 Alyth U.K.
171 N5 Alytus Lith.
212 F2 Alzada U.S.A.
179 E5 Alzette *r.* Lux.
179 G5 Alzey Germany
142 C5 Al Zubarah *tourist site* Qatar
233 L3 Amacuro *r.* Guyana/Venez.
118 D4 Amadeus, Lake *salt flat* Australia
139 I3 'Amādīyah/Amêdî Iraq
203 K3 Amadjuak Lake Canada
215 G6 Amado U.S.A.
183 L3 Amadora Port.
159 A8 Amakusa-nada *b.* Japan
171 K4 Åmål Sweden
147 I2 Amalapuram India
150 D1 Amalat *r.* Russia
233 I3 Amalfi Col.
197 F3 Amalia S. Africa
185 I6 Amaliada Greece
148 C5 Amalner India
151 F7 Amamapare Indon.
234 A3 Amambaí Brazil
234 A3 Amambaí *r.* Brazil
234 A3 Amambaí, Serra de *hills* Brazil/Para.
151 E4 Amami-Ō-shima *i.* Japan
151 E4 Amami-shotō *is* Japan
140 D2 Amangel'dy Kazakh.
141 F2 Amankel'dy Kazakh.
141 J4 Amankol China
140 E3 Amanotkel' Kazakh.
185 G5 Amantea Italy
231 H3 Amapá Brazil
183 M3 Amareleja Port.
215 D3 Amargosa Desert U.S.A.
215 D3 Amargosa Range *mts* U.S.A.
215 D3 Amargosa Valley U.S.A.
217 C5 Amarillo U.S.A.
184 F3 Amaro, Monte *mt.* Italy
149 E4 Amarpatan India
136 D2 Amasra Turkey
138 E1 Amasya Turkey
121 E5 Amata Australia
225 F4 Amatán Mex.
224 G5 Amatique, Bahía de *b.* Guat.
224 C3 Amatlán de Cañas Mex.
178 D4 Amay Belgium
153 L1 Amazar Russia
156 A1 Amazar *r.* Russia
231 H4 Amazon *r.* S. America *alt.* Amazonas
231 I3 Amazon, Mouths of the Brazil
233 K4 Amazonas *state* Brazil
231 H4 Amazonas *r.* S. America *conv.* Amazon
239 F5 Amazon Cone *sea feature* S. Atlantic Ocean
231 G4 Amazònia, Parque Nacional *nat. park* Brazil
148 C6 Ambad India
147 H2 Ambajogai India
148 D3 Ambala India
147 I5 Ambalangoda Sri Lanka
195 E6 Ambalavao Madag.
195 E5 Ambanja Madag.
143 E4 Ambar Iran
147 H4 Ambasamudram India
123 D5 Ambathala Australia
230 C4 Ambato Ecuador
195 E5 Ambato Boeny Madag.
195 E6 Ambato Finandrahana Madag.
195 E5 Ambatolampy Madag.
195 E5 Ambatomainty Madag.
195 E5 Ambatondrazaka Madag.
179 J5 Amberg Germany
225 H4 Ambergris Caye *i.* Belize
182 G4 Ambérieu-en-Bugey France
209 G3 Amberley Canada
149 E5 Ambikapur India
195 E5 Ambilobe Madag.
204 C3 Ambition, Mount Canada
172 F2 Amble U.K.
172 E3 Ambleside U.K.
178 D4 Amblève *r.* Belgium
195 E6 Amboasary Madag.
195 E5 Ambohidratrimo Madag.
195 E6 Ambohimahasoa Madag.
151 E7 Ambon Indon.
151 E7 Ambon *i.* Indon.
195 E6 Ambositra Madag.
195 E6 Ambovombe Madag.
215 E4 Amboy *CA* U.S.A.
208 C5 Amboy *IL* U.S.A.
221 F3 Amboy Center U.S.A.
195 B4 Ambriz Angola
119 G3 Ambrym *i.* Vanuatu
147 H3 Ambur India
193 E3 Am-Djarass Chad
Amdo China *see* Lharigarbo
224 C3 Ameca Mex.
178 D1 Ameland *i.* Neth.
221 E6 Amelia Court House U.S.A.
221 G4 Amenia U.S.A.
214 B2 American, North Fork *r.* U.S.A.
239 H9 American-Antarctic Ridge *sea feature* S. Atlantic Ocean
213 D3 American Falls U.S.A.
213 D3 American Falls Reservoir U.S.A.
215 G1 American Fork U.S.A.
117 H4 American Samoa Pacific Ocean
219 C5 Americus U.S.A.
178 D2 Amersfoort Neth.
197 H3 Amersfoort S. Africa
173 G6 Amersham U.K.
205 K3 Amery Canada
127 K5 Amery Ice Shelf Antarctica
216 E3 Ames U.S.A.
173 F6 Amesbury U.K.
221 H3 Amesbury U.S.A.
149 E4 Amethi India
185 J5 Amfissa Greece
133 O3 Amga Russia
153 K2 Amgalang China
150 F2 Amgu Russia
192 C2 Amguid Alg.
150 F1 Amgun' *r.* Russia
207 H4 Amherst Canada
221 G3 Amherst *MA* U.S.A.
221 I2 Amherst *ME* U.S.A.
220 D6 Amherst *VA* U.S.A.
209 F4 Amherstburg Canada
184 D3 Amiata, Monte *mt.* Italy
182 F2 Amiens France
139 H5 'Amīj, Wādī *watercourse* Iraq
147 G4 Amindivi Islands India
159 D7 Amino Japan
196 C1 Aminuis Namibia
142 B3 Amīrābād *Īlām* Iran
143 E3 Amīrābād *Yazd* Iran
239 M6 Amirante Islands Seychelles
238 H5 Amirante Trench *sea feature* Indian Ocean
143 F4 Amir Chah Pak.
205 I4 Amisk Lake Canada
217 C6 Amistad Reservoir Mex./U.S.A.
125 J1 Amity Point Australia
148 D5 Amla India
171 J4 Åmli Norway
173 C4 Amlwch U.K.
138 E6 'Ammān Jordan
173 D6 Ammanford U.K.
170 O2 Ämmänsaari Fin.
170 L2 Ammarnäs Sweden
123 A4 Ammaroo Australia
179 F1 Ammerland *reg.* Germany
179 I3 Ammern Germany
176 E7 Ammersee *l.* Germany
Ammochostos Cyprus *see* Famagusta
162 C2 Amnat Charoen Thai.
160 D4 Amnyong-dan *hd* N. Korea
148 C5 Amod India
155 B6 Amo Jiang *r.* China
142 D2 Āmol Iran
179 H5 Amorbach Germany
185 K6 Amorgos *i.* Greece
206 E4 Amos Canada
Amoy China *see* Xiamen
147 I5 Ampara India
234 C3 Amparo Brazil
176 E6 Amper *r.* Germany
239 I3 Ampere Seamount *sea feature* N. Atlantic Ocean
183 Q2 Amposta Spain
139 F6 'Amrah, Qaşr *tourist site* Jordan
148 D5 Amravati India
148 B5 Amreli India
148 B4 Amri Pak.
138 E4 'Amrīt Syria
148 C3 Amritsar India
148 D3 Amroha India
170 L2 Åmsele Sweden
178 C2 Amstelveen Neth.
178 C2 Amsterdam Neth.
197 I3 Amsterdam S. Africa
221 F3 Amsterdam U.S.A.
238 J7 Amsterdam, Île *i.* Indian Ocean
176 G6 Amstetten Austria
193 E3 Am Timan Chad
140 D3 Amudar'ya *r.* Turkm./Uzbek.
203 I2 Amund Ringnes Island Canada
127 K6 Amundsen, Mount Antarctica
237 K10 Amundsen Abyssal Plain *sea feature* Southern Ocean
240 B1 Amundsen Basin *sea feature* Arctic Ocean
127 L4 Amundsen Bay Antarctica
202 F2 Amundsen Gulf Canada
237 K10 Amundsen Ridges *sea feature* Southern Ocean
127 J4 Amundsen-Scott *research stn* Antarctica
237 L10 Amundsen Sea Antarctica
163 I3 Amuntai Indon.
150 E2 Amur *r.* China/Russia *alt.* Heilong Jiang
156 B1 Amuro-Baltiysk Russia
Amur Oblast *admin. div.* Russia *see* Amurskaya Oblast'
133 O4 Amursk Russia
156 C1 Amurskaya Oblast' *admin. div.* Russia
156 F1 Amurskiy Liman *str.* Russia
156 C3 Amurzet Russia
187 F6 Amvrosiyivka Ukr.
209 E1 Amyot Canada

Aravalli Range

149 H6 An Myanmar
117 I5 Anaa atoll Fr. Polynesia
151 E7 Anabanua Indon.
133 M2 Anabar r. Russia
133 M2 Anabarskiy Zaliv b. Russia
124 D4 Ana Branch r. Australia
214 C4 Anacapa Island U.S.A.
233 K2 Anaco Venez.
215 D2 Anaconda U.S.A.
212 B1 Anacortes U.S.A.
217 D5 Anadarko U.S.A.
138 D2 Anadolu reg. Turkey
139 F1 Anadolu Dağları mts Turkey
133 S3 Anadyr' Russia
133 S3 Anadyr' r. Russia
133 T3 Anadyrskiy Zaliv b. Russia
185 K6 Anafi i. Greece
234 E1 Anagé Brazil
139 H4 'Ānah Iraq
215 D5 Anaheim U.S.A.
204 D4 Anahim Lake Canada
225 D2 Anáhuac Mex.
147 H4 Anaimalai Hills India
147 I2 Anakapalle India
123 D4 Anakie Australia
195 E5 Analalava Madag.
231 F4 Anamã Brazil
163 G2 Anambas, Kepulauan is Indon.
208 B4 Anamosa U.S.A.
147 H4 Ana Mudi India
138 D3 Anamur Turkey
138 D3 Anamur Burnu pt Turkey
159 D8 Anan Japan
148 C5 Anand India
149 F5 Anandapur India
149 F5 Anandpur r. India
141 I4 Anan'ev Kyrg.
147 H3 Anantapur India
148 C2 Anantnag India
148 D4 Anant Peth India
187 D6 Anan'yiv Ukr.
187 F6 Anapa Russia
234 C2 Anápolis Brazil
142 D4 Anār Iran
142 D3 Anārak Iran
142 C3 Anarbar r. Iran
143 F3 Anār Darah Afgh.
Anatolia reg. Turkey see Anadolu
119 G4 Anatom i. Vanuatu
232 D3 Añatuya Arg.
233 L4 Anauá r. Brazil
175 H6 An Baile Breac Ireland
142 C2 Anbūh Iran
175 J2 An Bun Beag Ireland
160 D4 Anbyon N. Korea
182 D3 Ancenis France
202 D3 Anchorage U.S.A.
209 F4 Anchor Bay U.S.A.
147 H4 Anchuthengu India
Anci China see Langfang
139 F3 Ancient Villages of Northern Syria tourist site Syria
175 J3 An Clochán Liath Ireland
An Cóbh Ireland see Cobh
184 E3 Ancona Italy
232 B6 Ancud Chile
235 H4 Ancud, Golfo de g. Chile
156 B3 Anda China
235 H1 Andacollo Chile
123 A5 Andado Australia
149 F5 Andal India
171 I3 Åndalsnes Norway
183 N4 Andalucía aut. comm. Spain
217 G6 Andalusia U.S.A.
135 H6 Andaman and Nicobar Islands union terr. India
238 K4 Andaman Basin sea feature Indian Ocean
135 H5 Andaman Islands India
135 H5 Andaman Sea Asia
124 B3 Andamooka Australia
195 E5 Andapa Madag.
234 E1 Andaraí Brazil
170 L1 Andenes Norway
178 D4 Andenne Belgium
178 C4 Anderlecht Belgium
182 D4 Andernos-les-Bains France
202 F3 Anderson r. Canada
202 D3 Anderson AK U.S.A.
209 E5 Anderson IN U.S.A.
217 E4 Anderson MO U.S.A.
219 D5 Anderson SC U.S.A.
125 G5 Anderson Bay Australia
230 C5 Andes mts S. America
170 L1 Andfjorden sea chan. Norway
147 H2 Andhra Pradesh state India
141 H4 Andijon Uzbek.
195 E5 Andilamena Madag.
195 E5 Andilanatoby Madag.
142 C3 Andīmeshk Iran
139 F3 Andırın Turkey
187 H7 Andiyskoye Koysu r. Russia
Andizhan Uzbek. see Andijon
143 G2 Andkhōy Afgh.
143 G2 Andkhōy r. Afgh.
195 E5 Andoany Madag.
230 C4 Andoas Peru
147 H2 Andol India
160 E5 Andong S. Korea
160 E5 Andong-ho l. S. Korea
122 C2 Andoom Australia
183 Q1 Andorra country Europe
183 Q1 Andorra la Vella Andorra
173 F6 Andover U.K.
221 H2 Andover ME U.S.A.
220 C4 Andover OH U.S.A.
170 K1 Andøya i. Norway
234 B3 Andradina Brazil
237 H2 Andreanof Islands U.S.A.
186 E3 Andreapol' Russia
172 C3 Andreas U.K.
194 C3 André Félix, Parc National nat. park C.A.R.
234 D3 Andrelândia Brazil
217 C5 Andrews U.S.A.
140 B1 Andreyevka Russia
185 G4 Andria Italy
195 E6 Androka Madag.
219 E7 Andros i. Bahamas
185 K6 Andros i. Greece
221 H2 Androscoggin r. U.S.A.
219 E7 Andros Town Bahamas
147 G4 Andrott i. India
187 D5 Andrushivka Ukr.
170 L1 Andselv Norway
183 N3 Andújar Spain
195 B5 Andulo Angola
121 E4 Anec, Lake salt flat Australia
192 C3 Anéfis Mali
223 L5 Anegada i. Virgin Is (U.K.)
235 J4 Anegada, Bahía b. Arg.
215 F5 Anegam U.S.A.
192 C4 Aného Togo
215 H3 Aneth U.S.A.
183 Q1 Aneto mt. Spain
193 D3 Aney Niger
155 E5 Anfu China
195 E5 Angadoka, Lohatanjona hd Madag.
120 E2 Angalarri r. Australia
156 A3 Ang'angxi China
150 B1 Angara r. Russia
150 C1 Angarsk Russia
121 F5 Angas Downs Australia
161 I3 Angat Phil.
171 K3 Ange Sweden
Angel, Salto waterfall Venez. see Angel Falls
222 B3 Ángel de la Guarda, Isla i. Mex.
161 I3 Angeles Phil.
233 L3 Angel Falls Venez.
171 K4 Ängelholm Sweden
123 D5 Angellala Creek r. Australia
214 B2 Angels Camp U.S.A.
171 L3 Ångermanälven r. Sweden
182 D3 Angers France
205 J2 Angikuni Lake Canada
162 B2 Angkor tourist site Cambodia
125 G2 Angledool Australia
173 C4 Anglesey i. U.K.
217 E6 Angleton U.S.A.
209 H2 Angliers Canada
162 □ Ang Mo Kio Sing.
194 C3 Ango Dem. Rep. Congo
195 D5 Angoche Moz.
235 H3 Angol Chile
195 B5 Angola country Africa
209 E5 Angola U.S.A.
239 I7 Angola Basin sea feature S. Atlantic Ocean
182 E4 Angoulême France
141 G4 Angren Uzbek.
162 B2 Ang Thong Thai.
156 A3 Anguang China
223 L5 Anguilla terr. Caribbean Sea
147 J1 Angul India
154 E1 Anguli Nur l. China
154 E2 Anguo China
234 A3 Anhanduí r. Brazil
171 J4 Anholt i. Denmark
155 D4 Anhua China
154 E3 Anhui prov. China
234 A2 Anhumas Brazil
234 C2 Anicuns Brazil
140 E2 Anikhovka Russia
186 G3 Anikovo Russia
215 H6 Animas U.S.A.
215 H6 Animas Peak U.S.A.
162 A2 Anin Myanmar
158 H1 Aniva Russia
158 H1 Aniva, Mys c. Russia
150 G2 Aniva, Zaliv b. Russia
119 G3 Aniwa i. Vanuatu
178 B5 Anizy-le-Château France
Anjengo India see Anchuthengu
155 F4 Anji China
148 D5 Anji India
155 D5 Anjiang China
143 E3 Anjoman Iran
182 D3 Anjou reg. France
Anjouan i. Comoros see Ndzuani
195 E5 Anjozorobe Madag.
160 C4 Anjŭ N. Korea
195 E6 Ankaboa, Tanjona pt Madag.
154 C3 Ankang China
138 D2 Ankara Turkey
195 E6 Ankazoabo Madag.
195 E5 Ankazobe Madag.
163 D2 An Khê Vietnam
148 C5 Ankleshwar India
162 C3 An Lôc Vietnam
155 B5 Anlong China
162 C2 Ânlóng Vêng Cambodia
155 D4 Anlu China
160 D5 Anmyeon-do i. S. Korea
221 H3 Ann, Cape U.S.A.
187 G5 Anna Russia
221 E5 Anna, Lake U.S.A.
192 C1 Annaba Alg.
179 L4 Annaberg-Buchholz Germany
139 F4 An Nabk Syria
146 B4 An Nafūd des. Saudi Arabia
139 J5 An Nahrawān al Qadīm canal Iraq
139 J6 An Najaf Iraq
175 K3 Annalee r. Ireland
175 M3 Annalong U.K.
111 Annam Highlands mts China
174 E6 Annan U.K.
174 E6 Annan r. U.K.
174 E5 Annandale val. U.K.
120 C3 Anna Plains Australia
221 E5 Annapolis U.S.A.
207 G5 Annapolis Royal Canada
149 E3 Annapurna I mt. Nepal
142 C5 An Naqīrah well Saudi Arabia
209 F4 Ann Arbor U.S.A.
231 G2 Anna Regina Guyana
139 K6 An Nāṣirīyah Iraq
121 B5 Annean, Lake salt flat Australia
182 H4 Annecy France
182 H3 Annemasse France
179 E1 Annen Neth.
204 C4 Annette Island U.S.A.
139 F5 An Nimārah Syria
155 B5 Anning China
219 C5 Anniston U.S.A.
191 E4 Annobón i. Equat. Guinea
182 G4 Annonay France
146 C4 An Nu'ayrīyah Saudi Arabia
139 J5 An Nu'mānīyah Iraq
216 E2 Anoka U.S.A.
195 E5 Anorontany, Tanjona hd Madag.
148 C1 Ānoshāh Pass Afgh.
155 D6 Anpu China
155 C6 Anpu Gang b. China
155 E4 Anqing China
154 F2 Anqiu China
An Ráth Ireland see Charleville
155 D5 Anren China
178 D4 Ans Belgium
154 C2 Ansai China
179 I5 Ansbach Germany
125 G7 Anser Group is Australia
160 B3 Anshan China
155 B5 Anshun Guizhou China
153 H6 Anshun Sichuan China
235 I1 Ansilta mt. Arg.
235 L1 Ansina Uruguay
216 D3 Ansley U.S.A.
217 D5 Anson U.S.A.
120 E2 Anson Bay Australia
192 C3 Ansongo Mali
206 D4 Ansonville Canada
220 C5 Ansted U.S.A.
148 D4 Anta India
230 D6 Antabamba Peru
139 F3 Antakya Turkey
195 F5 Antalaha Madag.
138 C3 Antalya Turkey
138 C3 Antalya Körfezi g. Turkey
195 E5 Antananarivo Madag.
127 Antarctica
127 I2 Antarctic Peninsula Antarctica
174 C3 An Teallach mt. U.K.
215 D2 Antelope Range mts U.S.A.
183 N4 Antequera Spain
213 F5 Anthony U.S.A.
122 A3 Anthony Lagoon Australia
192 B2 Anti-Atlas mts Morocco
183 H5 Antibes France
207 H4 Anticosti, Île d' i. Canada
208 C3 Antigo U.S.A.
207 H4 Antigonish Canada
223 L5 Antigua i. Antigua and Barbuda
Antigua Guat. see Antigua Guatemala
223 L5 Antigua and Barbuda country Caribbean Sea
225 G5 Antigua Guatemala Guat.
225 E3 Antiguo-Morelos Mex.
185 J7 Antikythira i. Greece
185 J7 Antikythiro, Steno sea chan. Greece
214 B3 Antioch CA U.S.A.
208 C3 Antioch IL U.S.A.
233 I3 Antioquia Col.
117 G7 Antipodes Islands N.Z.
185 K5 Antipsara i. Greece
217 E5 Antlers U.S.A.
232 B2 Antofagasta Chile
232 C3 Antofalla, Volcán vol. Arg.
178 B4 Antoing Belgium
224 I6 Antón Panama
235 C4 Antonina Brazil
234 E1 Antônio r. Brazil
213 F4 Antonito U.S.A.
175 L3 Antrim U.K.
175 L2 Antrim Hills U.K.
120 E3 Antrim Plateau Australia
195 E5 Antsalova Madag.
195 E5 Antsirabe Madag.
195 E5 Antsirañana Madag.
195 E5 Antsohihy Madag.
170 M2 Anttis Sweden
171 N3 Anttola Fin.
235 H3 Antuco Chile
235 H3 Antuco, Volcán vol. Chile
178 C3 Antwerp Belgium
221 F2 Antwerp U.S.A.
206 E3 Anuc, Lac l. Canada
158 C3 Anuchino Russia
160 D6 Anui S. Korea
148 C3 Anupgarh India
147 I4 Anuradhapura Sri Lanka
142 D5 Anveh Iran
127 I2 Anvers Island Antarctica
155 F5 Anxi China
155 B3 Anxian China
155 D4 Anxiang China
154 E2 Anxin China
124 A4 Anxious Bay Australia
154 E2 Anyang China
160 D5 Anyang S. Korea
185 K6 Anydros i. Greece
150 B3 A'nyêmaqên Shan mts China
155 E4 Anyi China
155 E5 Anyuan China
155 B4 Anyue China
156 E2 Anyuy r. Russia
133 R3 Anyuysk Russia
233 I3 Anzá Col.
154 D2 Anze China
150 A1 Anzhero-Sudzhensk Russia
195 C4 Anzi Dem. Rep. Congo
184 E4 Anzio Italy
119 G3 Aoba i. Vanuatu
157 E6 Aoga-shima i. Japan
162 A3 Ao Kham, Laem pt Thai.
Aomen China see Macao
158 G4 Aomori Japan
148 D3 Aonla India
126 C5 Aoraki N.Z.
126 C5 Aoraki/Mount Cook mt. N.Z.
126 C5 Aoraki/Mount Cook National Park N.Z.
162 C2 Aôral, Phnum mt. Cambodia
126 D4 Aorere r. N.Z.
184 B2 Aosta Italy
192 B2 Aoukâr reg. Mali/Mauritania
231 G8 Apa r. Brazil
194 D3 Apac Uganda
215 H6 Apache U.S.A.
215 H5 Apache Creek U.S.A.
215 G5 Apache Junction U.S.A.
215 G6 Apache Peak U.S.A.
219 C6 Apalachee Bay U.S.A.
219 C6 Apalachicola U.S.A.
225 E4 Apan Mex.
233 J4 Apaporis r. Col.
139 J1 Aparan Armenia
234 B3 Aparecida do Tabuado Brazil
161 I2 Aparri Phil.
170 P2 Apatity Russia
225 D4 Apatzingán Mex.
171 N4 Ape Latvia
178 D2 Apeldoorn Neth.
179 H2 Apelern Germany
180 E3 Apennines mts Italy
179 H1 Apensen Germany
149 E3 Api mt. Nepal
119 I3 Apia Samoa
126 E3 Apiti N.Z.
161 J5 Apo, Mount vol. Phil.
231 G2 Apoera Suriname
179 J3 Apolda Germany
125 E7 Apollo Bay Australia
230 E6 Apolo Bol.
219 D6 Apopka, Lake U.S.A.
234 B2 Aporé Brazil
234 B2 Aporé r. Brazil
218 B2 Apostle Islands U.S.A.
208 B2 Apostle Islands National Lakeshore nature res. U.S.A.
138 E4 Apostolos Andreas, Cape Cyprus
220 B6 Appalachia U.S.A.
220 C6 Appalachian Mountains U.S.A.
Appennino mts Italy see Apennines
184 E3 Appennino Abruzzese mts Italy
184 D2 Appennino Tosco-Emiliano mts Italy
184 E3 Appennino Umbro-Marchigiano mts Italy
125 I5 Appin Australia
179 E1 Appingedam Neth.
174 C3 Applecross U.K.
216 D2 Appleton MN U.S.A.
208 C3 Appleton WI U.S.A.
215 D4 Apple Valley U.S.A.
220 D6 Appomattox U.S.A.
184 E4 Aprilia Italy
187 F6 Apsheronsk Russia
124 D6 Apsley Australia
209 H3 Apsley Canada
183 G5 Apt France
234 B3 Apucarana Brazil
161 H4 Apurahuan Phil.
233 K3 Apure r. Venez.
230 D6 Apurímac r. Peru
193 F2 Aqaba, Gulf of Asia
139 I6 'Aqabah, Birkat al well Iraq
141 I4 Aqal China
142 D2 Aqbana Iran
143 G2 Āqchah Afgh.
142 B2 Aq Chai r. Iran
142 B2 Aqdoghmish r. Iran
139 J3 Āq Kān Dāgh, Kūh-e mt. Iran
140 C5 Āq Qalā Iran
152 E4 Aqqikkol Hu salt l. China
143 G3 Āq Rabat, Kōtal-e Afgh.
139 I3 'Aqrah Iraq
215 F4 Aquarius Mountains U.S.A.
215 G3 Aquarius Plateau U.S.A.
234 A3 Aquidauana Brazil
234 A2 Aquidauana r. Brazil
225 D4 Aquila Mex.
233 K4 Aquio r. Col.
225 E3 Aquismón Mex.
182 D4 Aquitaine reg. France
143 G4 'Arab Afgh.
219 C5 Arab U.S.A.
193 E3 Arab, Bahr el watercourse Sudan
138 B6 'Arab, Khalīj al b. Egypt
143 E3 'Arabābād Iran
238 I4 Arabian Basin sea feature Indian Ocean
Arabian Gulf Asia see The Gulf
146 B4 Arabian Peninsula Saudi Arabia
135 E5 Arabian Sea Indian Ocean
233 L3 Arabopó Venez.
233 L3 Arabopó r. Venez.
138 D1 Araç Turkey
233 L4 Araça r. Brazil
231 K6 Aracaju Brazil
233 K4 Aracamuni, Cerro h. Venez.
235 A4 Aracanguy, Montes de hills Para.
231 K4 Aracati Brazil
234 E1 Aracatu Brazil
234 B3 Araçatuba Brazil
183 M4 Aracena Spain
234 E2 Aracruz Brazil
234 D2 Araçuaí Brazil
234 D2 Araçuaí r. Brazil
185 I1 Arad Romania
193 E3 Arada Chad
118 D2 Arafura Sea Australia/Indon.
236 D6 Arafura Shelf sea feature Australia/Indon.
234 B1 Aragarças Brazil
139 I1 Aragats Armenia
139 J1 Aragats Lerr mt. Armenia
183 P2 Aragón aut. comm. Spain
183 P1 Aragón r. Spain
231 I5 Araguacema Brazil
233 K2 Aragua de Barcelona Venez.
231 I5 Araguaia r. Brazil
231 H6 Araguaia, Parque Nacional do nat. park Brazil
231 I5 Araguaína Brazil
233 L2 Araguao, Boca r. mouth Venez.
233 L2 Araguao, Caño r. Venez.
234 C2 Araguari Brazil
234 C2 Araguari r. Brazil
231 I5 Araguatins Brazil
187 H7 Aragvi r. Georgia
Arai Japan see Myōkō
Árainn Mhór Ireland see Arranmore Island
231 J4 Araioses Brazil
192 C2 Arak Alg.
142 C3 Arāk Iran
137 E4 Arak Syria
149 H5 Arakan Yoma mts Myanmar
147 H3 Arakkonam India
141 J4 Aral China
139 J2 Aralık Turkey
140 D3 Aral Sea salt l. Kazakh./Uzbek.
140 E3 Aral'sk Kazakh.
Aral'skoye More salt l. Kazakh./Uzbek. see Aral Sea
140 B2 Aralsor, Ozero l. Kazakh.
140 C2 Aralsor, Ozero salt l. Kazakh.
123 D4 Aramac Australia
123 D4 Aramac Creek watercourse Australia
142 B5 Aramah plat. Saudi Arabia
225 E2 Aramberri Mex.
148 D6 Aran r. India
183 O2 Aranda de Duero Spain
139 K4 Arandān Iran
185 I2 Aranđelovac Serbia
147 H3 Arani India
175 I4 Aran Islands Ireland
183 O2 Aranjuez Spain
195 B6 Aranos Namibia
217 D7 Aransas Pass U.S.A.
234 B2 Arantes r. Brazil
119 H1 Aranuka atoll Kiribati
162 B2 Aranyaprathet Thai.
159 B8 Arao Japan
192 B3 Araouane Mali
216 D3 Arapahoe U.S.A.
233 L4 Arapari r. Brazil
235 L1 Arapey Grande r. Uruguay
139 G2 Arapgir Turkey
231 K5 Arapiraca Brazil
185 K4 Arapis, Akrotirio pt Greece
234 B3 Arapongas Brazil
149 F4 A Rapti Doon r. Nepal
146 B3 'Ar'ar Saudi Arabia
139 I6 'Ar'ar, Wādī watercourse Iraq/Saudi Arabia
233 G3 Araranguá Brazil
234 C3 Araraquara Brazil
231 H5 Araras Brazil
235 B4 Araras, Serra das mts Brazil
139 J2 Ararat Armenia
125 E6 Ararat Australia
139 J2 Ararat, Mount Turkey
149 F4 Araria India
234 D3 Araruama, Lago de lag. Brazil
139 I2 Aras Turkey
139 I1 Aras Nehri r. Turkey alt. Araks (Armenia/Turkey), alt. Araz (Azerbaijan/Iran)
234 E1 Arataca Brazil
233 J3 Arauca Col.
233 J3 Arauca r. Venez.
235 H3 Araucanía admin. reg. Chile
235 H3 Arauco Chile
233 J3 Arauquita Col.
233 J2 Araure Venez.
148 C4 Aravalli Range mts India

Aravete

171 N4 Aravete Estonia
119 F2 Arawa P.N.G.
234 C2 Araxá Brazil
233 K2 Araya, Península de pen. Venez.
233 K2 Araya, Punta de pt Venez.
138 C2 Arayıt Dağı mt. Turkey
139 L2 Araz r. Azer./Iran alt. Araks (Armenia/Turkey), alt. Aras Nehri (Turkey)
186 I3 Arbazh Russia
139 J3 Arbīl/Hewlêr Iraq
171 K4 Arboga Sweden
205 I4 Arborfield Canada
175 F4 Arbroath U.K.
214 A2 Arbuckle U.S.A.
143 F4 Arbū-ye Shamālī, Dasht-e des. Afgh.
182 D4 Arcachon France
219 D7 Arcadia U.S.A.
213 A3 Arcata U.S.A.
215 D2 Arc Dome mt. U.S.A.
225 D4 Arcelia Mex.
193 F3 Archaeological Sites of the Island of Meroe tourist site Sudan
186 G1 Archangel Russia
119 E3 Archer r. Australia
122 C2 Archer Bend National Park Australia
215 H2 Arches National Park U.S.A.
Archman Turkm. see Arçman
139 L2 Ärçivan Azer.
124 A2 Arckaringa watercourse Australia
140 D5 Arçman Turkm.
213 D3 Arco U.S.A.
183 N4 Arcos de la Frontera Spain
203 J2 Arctic Bay Canada
240 B1 Arctic Mid-Ocean Ridge sea feature Arctic Ocean
240 Arctic Ocean
202 E3 Arctic Red r. Canada
127 L2 Arctowski research stn Antarctica
142 C2 Ardabīl Iran
139 I1 Ardahan Turkey
142 C4 Ardakān Fārs Iran
142 D3 Ardakān Yazd Iran
142 C4 Ardal Iran
171 I3 Årdalstangen Norway
175 J3 Ardara Ireland
185 K4 Ardas r. Bulg.
187 G4 Ardatov Nizhegorodskaya Oblast' Russia
187 H4 Ardatov Respublika Mordoviya Russia
209 G3 Ardbeg Canada
175 L4 Ardee Ireland
124 B4 Arden, Mount h. Australia
178 D5 Ardennes plat. Belgium
178 C5 Ardennes, Canal des France
142 D3 Ardestān Iran
175 M3 Ardglass U.K.
183 M3 Ardila r. Port.
125 G5 Ardlethan Australia
217 D5 Ardmore U.S.A.
174 B4 Ardnamurchan, Point of U.K.
137 G2 Ardon Russia
174 C4 Ardrishaig U.K.
124 B5 Ardrossan Australia
174 D5 Ardrossan U.K.
174 C3 Ardvasar U.K.
235 K2 Areco r. Arg.
232 E3 Areguá Para.
231 K4 Areia Branca Brazil
179 E4 Aremberg h. Germany
161 I4 Arena reef Phil.
214 A2 Arena, Point U.S.A.
224 B3 Arena, Punta pt Mex.
224 H5 Arenal Hond.
183 N2 Arenas de San Pedro Spain
171 J4 Arendal Norway
179 J2 Arendsee (Altmark) Germany
173 D5 Arenig Fawr h. U.K.
185 J6 Areopoli Greece
224 C2 Areponapuchi Mex.
230 D7 Arequipa Peru
231 H4 Arere Brazil
183 N2 Arévalo Spain
184 D3 Arezzo Italy
139 G6 'Arfajah well Saudi Arabia
123 B4 Argadargada Australia
154 D1 Argalant Mongolia
183 O2 Arganda del Rey Spain
161 I4 Argao Phil.
184 D2 Argenta Italy
182 D2 Argentan France
184 D3 Argentario, Monte h. Italy
184 B2 Argentera, Cima dell' mt. Italy
179 F5 Argenthal Germany
232 C5 Argentina country S. America
127 J4 Argentina Range mts Antarctica
239 F9 Argentine Abyssal Plain sea feature S. Atlantic Ocean
239 G8 Argentine Basin sea feature S. Atlantic Ocean
239 F8 Argentine Rise sea feature S. Atlantic Ocean
232 B8 Argentino, Lago l. Arg.
185 K2 Argeş r. Romania
143 G4 Arghandāb Rōd r. Afgh.
156 C1 Argi r. Russia
138 C2 Argıthanı Turkey
185 J6 Argolikos Kolpos b. Greece
185 J6 Argos Greece
185 I5 Argostoli Greece
183 P1 Arguis Spain
150 E1 Argun' r. China/Russia
187 H7 Argun Russia
127 K5 Argus, Dome ice feature Antarctica
215 D4 Argus Range mts U.S.A.
208 C4 Argyle U.S.A.
118 C3 Argyle, Lake Australia
174 C4 Argyll reg. U.K.
Ar Horqin Qi China see Tianshan
126 E3 Aria N.Z.
125 G5 Ariah Park Australia
159 B8 Ariake-kai b. Japan
195 B6 Ariamsvlei Namibia
184 F4 Ariano Irpino Italy
233 I4 Ariari r. Col.
235 J2 Arias Arg.
135 F6 Ari Atholhu Maldives
233 L2 Aribí r. Venez.
192 B3 Aribinda Burkina Faso
232 B1 Arica Chile
121 C7 Arid, Cape Australia
174 C4 Arienas, Loch l. U.K.
139 F4 Arīḥā Syria
213 G4 Arikaree r. U.S.A.
233 L2 Arima Trin. and Tob.
234 C1 Arinos Brazil
231 G6 Arinos r. Brazil
225 D4 Ario de Rosáles Mex.
233 J3 Ariporo r. Col.
231 F5 Aripuanã Brazil
231 F5 Aripuanã r. Brazil
231 F5 Ariquemes Brazil
234 B2 Ariranhá r. Brazil
196 B1 Aris Namibia
174 C4 Arisaig U.K.
174 C4 Arisaig, Sound of sea chan. U.K.
204 D4 Aristazabal Island Canada
232 C2 Arizaro, Salar de salt flat Arg.
215 G4 Arizona state U.S.A.
210 D5 Arizpe Mex.
142 B5 'Arjah Saudi Arabia
170 L2 Arjeplog Sweden
233 I2 Arjona Col.
163 H4 Arjuna, Gunung vol. Indon.
187 G5 Arkadak Russia
217 E5 Arkadelphia U.S.A.
174 C4 Arkaig, Loch l. U.K.
141 F2 Arkalyk Kazakh.
217 F5 Arkansas r. U.S.A.
217 E5 Arkansas state U.S.A.
217 D4 Arkansas City U.S.A.
149 G1 Arka Tag mts China
186 G2 Arkhangel'skaya Oblast' admin. div. Russia
187 F4 Arkhangel'skoye Russia
142 C2 Arkhara Russia
156 C3 Arkhipovka Russia
175 L5 Arklow Ireland
185 L6 Arkoi i. Greece
176 F3 Arkona, Kap c. Germany
133 J2 Arkticheskogo Instituta, Ostrova is Russia
221 F3 Arkville U.S.A.
183 G5 Arles France
197 G4 Arlington S. Africa
212 B2 Arlington OR U.S.A.
216 D2 Arlington SD U.S.A.
221 E5 Arlington VA U.S.A.
208 D4 Arlington Heights U.S.A.
192 C3 Arlit Niger
178 D5 Arlon Belgium
121 A7 Armadale Australia
161 J5 Armadores i. Indon.
175 L3 Armagh U.K.
193 F2 Armant Egypt
139 J1 Armavir Armenia
187 G6 Armavir Russia
139 J1 Armenia country Asia
233 I3 Armenia Col.
139 J2 Armenian Monastic Ensembles of Iran tourist site Iran
233 I3 Armero (abandoned) Col.
125 I3 Armidale Australia
205 K2 Armit Lake Canada
149 E5 Armori India
175 L2 Armoy U.K.
120 E3 Armstrong r. Australia
204 F4 Armstrong B.C. Canada
206 C3 Armstrong Ont. Canada
158 E1 Armu r. Russia
147 H2 Armur India
187 E6 Armyans'k Crimea
Arnaoutis, Cape Cyprus see Arnauti, Cape
207 F1 Arnaud r. Canada
138 D4 Arnauti, Cape Cyprus
171 J3 Årnes Norway
217 D4 Arnett U.S.A.
178 D3 Arnhem Neth.
118 D3 Arnhem, Cape Australia
118 D3 Arnhem Bay Australia
118 D3 Arnhem Land reg. Australia
184 D3 Arno r. Italy
124 B4 Arno Bay Australia
173 F4 Arnold U.K.
208 D2 Arnold U.S.A.
209 H1 Arnoux, Lac l. Canada
209 I3 Arnprior Canada
179 G3 Arnsberg Germany
179 I4 Arnstadt Germany
209 H3 Arnstein Canada
179 H5 Arnstein Germany
209 H1 Arntfield Canada
233 L3 Aro r. Venez.
195 B6 Aroab Namibia
179 H3 Arolsen Germany
184 C2 Arona Italy
221 J1 Aroostook Canada
221 I1 Aroostook r. U.S.A.
119 H2 Arorae i. Kiribati
161 I3 Aroroy Phil.
187 G7 Arpa r. Armenia/Turkey
139 I1 Arpaçay Turkey
143 G5 Arra r. Pak.
123 C5 Arrabury Australia
149 F4 Arrah India
139 I5 Ar Raḥḥālīyah Iraq
139 I5 Ar Ramādī Iraq
138 E7 Ar Ramlah Jordan
174 C5 Arran i. U.K.
175 J3 Arranmore Island Ireland
139 G4 Ar Raqqah Syria
182 F1 Arras France
142 A5 Ar Rass Saudi Arabia
139 F4 Ar Rastan Syria
139 I7 Ar Rawḍ well Saudi Arabia
142 C5 Ar Rayyān Qatar
233 J4 Arrecifal Col.
235 K2 Arrecifes Arg.
225 F4 Arriagá Mex.
225 D3 Arriaga Mex.
235 K2 Arribeños Arg.
139 K6 Ar Rifā'ī Iraq
139 J6 Ar Riḥāb salt flat Iraq
146 D5 Ar Rimāl reg. Saudi Arabia
215 H3 Arriola U.S.A.
Ar Riyāḍ Saudi Arabia see Riyadh
174 D4 Arrochar U.K.
235 M2 Arroio Grande Brazil
234 D1 Arrojado r. Brazil
175 J3 Arrow, Lough l. Ireland
208 B1 Arrow Lake Canada
213 D3 Arrowrock Reservoir U.S.A.
126 C5 Arrowsmith, Mount N.Z.
214 B4 Arroyo Grande U.S.A.
235 K2 Arroyo Seco Arg.
225 E3 Arroyo Seco Mex.
142 B5 Ar Rubay'iyah Saudi Arabia
234 A1 Arruda Brazil
139 J6 Ar Rumaythah Iraq
137 G5 Ar Ruq'ī well Saudi Arabia
143 E6 Ar Rustāq Oman
139 H5 Ar Ruṭbah Iraq
142 B6 Ar Ruwayḍah Saudi Arabia
Års Denmark see Aars
142 B2 Ars Iran
142 D4 Arsanajān Iran
158 C2 Arsen'yev Russia
141 H2 Arshaly Akmolinskaya Oblast' Kazakh.
141 J2 Arshaly Vostochnyy Kazakhstan Kazakh.
147 H3 Arsikere India
186 I3 Arsk Russia
138 E3 Arslanköy Turkey
194 E2 Arta Djibouti
185 I5 Arta Greece
139 J2 Artashat Armenia
225 D4 Arteaga Mex.
158 C3 Artem Russia
187 F5 Artemivs'k Ukr.
158 C3 Artemovskiy Russia
182 E2 Artenay France
213 F5 Artesia U.S.A.
209 G4 Arthur Canada
124 B3 Arthur, Lake salt flat Australia
220 C4 Arthur, Lake U.S.A.
125 G8 Arthur Lake Australia
119 F4 Arthur Point Australia
126 C5 Arthur's Pass N.Z.
126 C5 Arthur's Pass National Park N.Z.
219 F7 Arthur's Town Bahamas
127 L2 Artigas research stn Antarctica
235 L1 Artigas Uruguay
139 I1 Art'ik Armenia
205 H2 Artillery Lake Canada
197 G2 Artisia Botswana
182 F1 Artois reg. France
178 A4 Artois, Collines d' hills France
139 I2 Artos Dağı mt. Turkey
139 F1 Artova Turkey
187 D6 Artsyz Ukr.
127 I2 Arturo Prat research stn Antarctica
141 I5 Artux China
139 H1 Artvin Turkey
151 F7 Aru, Kepulauan is Indon.
194 D3 Arua Uganda
234 B1 Aruanã Brazil
233 J1 Aruba terr. Caribbean Sea
231 F4 Arumã Brazil
149 F4 Arun r. Nepal
149 H3 Arunachal Pradesh state India
173 G7 Arundel U.K.
Arun Gol r. China see Arun He
156 B3 Arun He r. China
195 D4 Arusha Tanz.
217 B4 Arvada U.S.A.
175 K4 Arvagh Ireland
150 C2 Arvayheer Mongolia
148 D5 Arvi India
205 K2 Arviat Canada
207 F4 Arvida Canada
170 L2 Arvidsjaur Sweden
171 K4 Arvika Sweden
214 C4 Arvin U.S.A.
142 B6 Arwā' Saudi Arabia
153 K2 Arxan China
143 E3 Āryanshahr Iran
141 G1 Arykbalyk Kazakh.
141 G4 Arys Kazakh.
141 G4 Arys' r. Kazakh.
141 F3 Arys, Ozero salt l. Kazakh.
187 G4 Arzamas Russia
179 K4 Arzberg Germany
183 P5 Arzew Alg.
187 H6 Arzgir Russia
179 K4 Aš Czech Rep.
233 L3 Asa r. Venez.
192 C4 Asaba Nigeria
139 G3 Asad, Buḥayrat al resr Syria
143 H3 Asadābād Afgh.
142 C3 Asadābād Hamadān Iran
143 E3 Asadābād Khorāsān-e Razavī Iran
142 D4 Asadābād Yazd Iran
162 A5 Asahan r. Indon.
158 H3 Asahi-dake vol. Japan
159 C7 Asahi-gawa r. Japan
158 H3 Asahikawa Japan
141 H4 Asaka Uzbek.
142 C2 Asālem Iran
160 D5 Asan-man b. S. Korea
149 F5 Asansol India
179 F4 Asbach Germany
207 F4 Asbestos Canada
197 E4 Asbestos Mountains S. Africa
221 F4 Asbury Park U.S.A.
184 F4 Ascea Italy
231 F7 Ascensión Bol.
191 C5 Ascension i. S. Atlantic Ocean
225 H4 Ascensión, Bahía de la b. Mex.
179 H5 Aschaffenburg Germany
179 F3 Ascheberg Germany
179 J3 Aschersleben Germany
184 E3 Ascoli Piceno Italy
171 K4 Åseda Sweden
170 L2 Åsele Sweden
185 K3 Asenovgrad Bulg.
140 D5 Aşgabat Turkm.
142 B5 Asharat Saudi Arabia
118 B4 Ashburton watercourse Australia
126 C5 Ashburton N.Z.
208 D1 Ashburton Bay Canada
120 F3 Ashburton Range hills Australia
141 F3 Ashchikol', Ozero salt l. Kazakh.
141 G4 Ashchysay Kazakh.
204 E4 Ashcroft Canada
138 E6 Ashdod Israel
217 E5 Ashdown U.S.A.
219 E5 Asheboro U.S.A.
219 D5 Asheville U.S.A.
125 I2 Ashford Australia
173 H6 Ashford U.K.
215 F4 Ash Fork U.S.A.
Ashgabat Turkm. see Aşgabat
158 H3 Ashibetsu Japan
159 F6 Ashikaga Japan
172 F2 Ashington U.K.
186 I3 Ashit r. Russia
159 C8 Ashizuri-misaki pt Japan
142 D4 Ashkezar Iran
217 D4 Ashland KS U.S.A.
220 B5 Ashland KY U.S.A.
221 I1 Ashland ME U.S.A.
212 F2 Ashland MT U.S.A.
221 H3 Ashland NH U.S.A.
220 B4 Ashland OH U.S.A.
213 B3 Ashland OR U.S.A.
221 E6 Ashland VA U.S.A.
208 B2 Ashland WI U.S.A.
125 H2 Ashley Australia
216 D2 Ashley U.S.A.
118 C3 Ashmore and Cartier Islands terr. Australia
120 C2 Ashmore Reef Australia
187 C4 Ashmyany Belarus
215 H5 Ash Peak U.S.A.
138 E6 Ashqelon Israel
139 I6 Ash Shabakah Iraq
139 H3 Ash Shaddādah Syria
139 J6 Ash Shanāfīyah Iraq
139 H7 Ash Shaqīq well Saudi Arabia
142 B5 Ash Sha'rā' Saudi Arabia
138 E6 Ash Sharāh reg. Jordan
Ash Shāriqah U.A.E. see Sharjah
139 I4 Ash Sharqāṭ Iraq
139 K6 Ash Shaṭrah Iraq
138 D7 Ash Shaṭṭ Egypt
138 E6 Ash Shawbak Jordan
137 F5 Ash Shaybānī well Saudi Arabia
146 C7 Ash Shiḥr Yemen
143 E5 Ash Shināş Oman
137 F6 Ash Shu'aybah Saudi Arabia
142 B4 Ash Shu'bah Saudi Arabia
142 B5 Ash Shumlūl Saudi Arabia
220 C4 Ashtabula U.S.A.
139 J1 Ashtarak Armenia
147 G2 Ashti Maharashtra India
148 D5 Ashti Maharashtra India
142 C3 Āshtīān Iran
196 D6 Ashton S. Africa
212 E2 Ashton U.S.A.
173 E4 Ashton-under-Lyne U.K.
203 L4 Ashuanipi Lake Canada
207 F4 Ashuapmushuan r. Canada
207 F4 Ashuapmushuan, Réserve Faunique nature res. Canada
219 C5 Ashville U.S.A.
139 F4 'Āṣī, Nahr al r. Asia
130 Asia
225 D3 Asientos Mex.
147 H2 Asifabad India
147 J2 Asika India
184 C4 Asinara, Golfo dell' b. Sardinia Italy
133 J4 Asino Russia
187 D4 Asipovichy Belarus
146 B5 'Asīr reg. Saudi Arabia
139 H2 Aşkale Turkey
140 D1 Askarovo Russia
171 J4 Asker Norway
171 K4 Askersund Sweden
171 J4 Askim Norway
139 I3 Askī Mawşil Iraq
150 B1 Askiz Russia
139 K2 Aşlāndūz Iran
194 D2 Asmara Eritrea
171 K4 Åsnen l. Sweden
148 C4 Asop India
139 L3 Aspar Iran
141 H4 Aspara Kazakh.
172 D3 Aspatria U.K.
213 F4 Aspen U.S.A.
179 H6 Asperg Germany
217 C5 Aspermont U.S.A.
126 B6 Aspiring, Mount N.Z.
205 H4 Asquith Canada
141 G4 Assa Kazakh.
139 F4 As Sa'an Syria
194 E2 Assab Eritrea
142 C5 As Sabsab well Saudi Arabia
138 C7 Aş Şaff Egypt
138 E6 Aş Şāfī Jordan
139 F3 As Safīrah Syria
Aş Şaḥrā' al Gharbīyah Egypt see Western Desert
Aş Şaḥrā' ash Sharqīyah des. Egypt see Eastern Desert
142 C5 As Saji well Saudi Arabia
140 D4 Assake-Audan, Vpadina depr. Uzbek.
142 B5 As Salamiyah Saudi Arabia
138 D6 Aş Şāliḥīyah Egypt
139 H4 Aş Şāliḥīyah Syria
136 B5 As Sallūm Egypt
139 J6 As Salmān Iraq
138 E5 As Salṭ Jordan
149 H4 Assam state India
139 J6 As Samāwah Iraq
139 F5 Aş Şanamayn Syria
193 E2 As Sarīr reg. Libya
221 F5 Assateague Island U.S.A.
221 F6 Assateague Island National Seashore nature res. U.S.A.
179 E1 Assen Neth.
178 B3 Assenede Belgium
178 D4 Assesse Belgium
149 F5 Assia Hills India
193 D1 As Sidrah Libya
205 H5 Assiniboia Canada
205 J5 Assiniboine r. Canada
204 F4 Assiniboine, Mount Canada
234 B3 Assis Brazil
184 E3 Assisi Italy
179 G4 Aßlar Germany
139 K7 Aş Şubayḥīyah Kuwait
142 B4 Aş Şufayrī well Saudi Arabia
139 G4 As Sukhnah Syria
139 J4 As Sulaymānīyah/Slêmânî Iraq
146 C5 As Sulayyil Saudi Arabia
142 C5 Aş Şulb reg. Saudi Arabia
142 B5 Aş Şummān plat. Saudi Arabia
146 B5 As Sūq Saudi Arabia
139 H4 Aş Şuwar Syria
139 F5 As Suwaydā' Syria
143 E6 As Suwayq Oman
139 J5 Aş Şuwayrah Iraq
As Suways Egypt see Suez
174 C2 Assynt, Loch l. U.K.
185 L7 Astakida i. Greece
135 F1 Astana Kazakh.
139 L3 Āstāneh-ye Ashrafīyeh Iran
137 H3 Astara Azer.
139 L2 Āstārā Azer.
184 C2 Asti Italy
214 A2 Asti U.S.A.
235 I1 Astica Arg.
143 F5 Astola Island Pak.
148 C2 Astor Pak.
148 C2 Astor r. Pak.
183 M1 Astorga Spain
212 B2 Astoria U.S.A.
171 K4 Åstorp Sweden
134 C2 Astrakhan' Russia
187 H6 Astrakhanskaya Oblast' admin. div. Russia
187 C4 Astravyets Belarus
127 K3 Astrid Ridge sea feature Southern Ocean
183 M1 Asturias aut. comm. Spain
185 L6 Astypalaia i. Greece
141 J2 Asubulak Kazakh.
232 E3 Asunción Para.
193 F2 Aswān Egypt
142 A5 Asyāḥ, Safrā' al esc. Saudi Arabia
193 F2 Asyūṭ Egypt
119 I4 Ata i. Tonga
233 K4 Atabapo r. Col./Venez.
141 G4 Atabay Kazakh.
Atabayeva, imeni Turkm. see Mäne
Atacama, Desierto de des. Chile see Atacama Desert
232 C2 Atacama, Salar de salt flat Chile
232 C2 Atacama Desert Chile
119 I2 Atafu atoll Tokelau
141 G4 Atakent Kazakh.

Bad Neuenahr-Ahrweiler

192 C4 Atakpamé Togo
185 J5 Atalanti Greece
224 I7 Atalaya Panama
230 D6 Atalaya Peru
141 F5 Atamyrat Turkm.
141 G1 Atansor, Ozero salt l. Kazakh.
192 A2 Atâr Mauritania
162 A1 Ataran r. Myanmar
215 H4 Atarque U.S.A.
214 B4 Atascadero U.S.A.
141 G2 Atasu Kazakh.
151 E7 Ataúro, Ilha de i. East Timor
185 L6 Atavyros mt. Greece
140 D4 Ataýap Turkm.
193 F3 Atbara Sudan
193 F3 Atbara r. Sudan
141 G2 Atbasar Kazakh.
141 H4 At-Bashy Kyrg.
217 F6 Atchafalaya Bay U.S.A.
217 E4 Atchison U.S.A.
224 C3 Atenguillo Mex.
184 E3 Aterno r. Italy
184 F3 Atessa Italy
178 B4 Ath Belgium
205 G4 Athabasca Canada
205 G3 Athabasca, Lake Canada
139 I6 'Athāmīn, Birkat al well Iraq
175 L4 Athboy Ireland
175 J4 Athenry Ireland
209 J3 Athens Canada
185 J6 Athens Greece
219 C5 Athens AL U.S.A.
219 D5 Athens GA U.S.A.
220 B5 Athens OH U.S.A.
219 C5 Athens TN U.S.A.
217 E5 Athens TX U.S.A.
173 F5 Atherstone U.K.
122 D3 Atherton Australia
178 A5 Athies France
Athina Greece see Athens
175 J4 Athleague Ireland
175 K4 Athlone Ireland
147 G2 Athni India
126 B6 Athol N.Z.
221 G3 Athol U.S.A.
174 E4 Atholl, Forest of reg. U.K.
185 K4 Athos mt. Greece
138 E7 Ath Thamad Egypt
175 L5 Athy Ireland
193 D3 Ati Chad
230 D7 Atico Peru
206 B4 Atikokan Canada
207 H3 Atikonak Lake Canada
161 I3 Atimonan Phil.
147 H4 Atirampattinam India
225 G5 Atitlán Guat.
225 G5 Átitlán, Volcán vol. Guat.
142 B5 'Atk, Wādī al watercourse Saudi Arabia
133 Q3 Atka Russia
187 H5 Atkarsk Russia
225 E4 Atlacomulco Mex.
219 C5 Atlanta GA U.S.A.
208 C5 Atlanta IL U.S.A.
209 E3 Atlanta MI U.S.A.
138 D2 Atlantı Turkey
216 E3 Atlantic U.S.A.
221 F5 Atlantic City U.S.A.
238 D9 Atlantic-Indian-Antarctic Basin sea feature S. Atlantic Ocean
238 D8 Atlantic-Indian Ridge sea feature Southern Ocean
239 Atlantic Ocean
196 C6 Atlantis S. Africa
Atlas Méditerranéen mts Alg. see Atlas Tellien
187 B1 Atlas Mountains Africa
192 C1 Atlas Saharien mts Alg.
180 D4 Atlas Tellien mts Alg.
204 C3 Atlin Canada
204 C3 Atlin Lake Canada
204 C3 Atlin Provincial Park Canada
138 E5 'Atlit Israel
225 E4 Atlixco Mex.
147 H3 Atmakur Andhra Pradesh India
147 H3 Atmakur Andhra Pradesh India
217 G6 Atmore U.S.A.
217 D5 Atoka U.S.A.
225 D3 Atotonilco el Alto Mex.
162 C1 Atouat mt. Laos
225 D4 Atoyac de Álvarez Mex.
149 G4 Atrai r. India
143 E2 Atrak, Rūd-e r. Iran alt. Atrek (Turkm.), alt. Etrek (Iran)
233 H3 Atrato r. Col.
142 D2 Atrek r. Turkm. alt. Atrak, Rūd-e (Iran), alt. Etrek (Iran)
221 F5 Atsion U.S.A.
156 G3 Atsonupuri, Vulkan vol. Russia
138 E6 Aṭ Ṭafīlah Jordan
146 B5 Aṭ Ṭā'if Saudi Arabia
219 C5 Attalla U.S.A.
181 H5 At Tamīmī Libya
162 C2 Attapu Laos
206 D3 Attawapiskat Canada
206 C3 Attawapiskat r. Canada
206 C3 Attawapiskat Lake Canada
139 G7 Aṭ Ṭawīl mts Saudi Arabia
142 A4 At Taysīyah plat. Saudi Arabia
179 F3 Attendorn Germany
176 F7 Attersee l. Austria
208 D5 Attica IN U.S.A.
220 B4 Attica OH U.S.A.
178 C5 Attigny France
221 H3 Attleboro U.S.A.
173 I5 Attleborough U.K.
139 F7 Aṭ Ṭubayq reg. Saudi Arabia
236 G2 Attu Island U.S.A.
142 B5 Aṭ Ṭulayḥī well Saudi Arabia
193 F2 Aṭ Ṭūr Egypt
147 H4 Attur India
235 I2 Atuel r. Arg.
235 I3 Atuel, Bañados del marsh Arg.
171 K4 Åtvidaberg Sweden
220 C4 Atwood Lake U.S.A.
169 P5 Atyashevo Russia
140 B3 Atyrau Kazakh.
140 B3 Atyrauskaya Oblast' admin. div. Kazakh.
179 I5 Aub Germany
183 G5 Aubagne France
178 D5 Aubange Belgium
161 I2 Aubarede Point Phil.
182 G4 Aubenas France
178 D5 Auboué France
215 F4 Aubrey Cliffs mts U.S.A.
202 F3 Aubry Lake Canada
124 C5 Auburn Australia
123 E5 Auburn r. Australia
209 G4 Auburn Canada
219 C5 Auburn AL U.S.A.
214 B2 Auburn CA U.S.A.
209 E5 Auburn IN U.S.A.
221 H2 Auburn ME U.S.A.
216 E3 Auburn NE U.S.A.
221 E3 Auburn NY U.S.A.
212 B2 Auburn WA U.S.A.
123 E5 Auburn Range hills Australia
182 F4 Aubusson France
235 I3 Auca Mahuida, Sierra de mt. Arg.
183 E5 Auch France
174 E4 Auchterarder U.K.
126 E2 Auckland N.Z.
119 G7 Auckland Islands N.Z.
221 H2 Audet Canada
173 I7 Audresselles France
178 A4 Audruicq France
179 K4 Aue Germany
179 K4 Auerbach Germany
179 J5 Auerbach in der Oberpfalz Germany
179 K4 Auersberg mt. Germany
141 J2 Auezov Kazakh.
123 D5 Augathella Australia
175 K3 Augher U.K.
175 L3 Aughnacloy U.K.
175 L5 Aughrim Ireland
196 D4 Augrabies S. Africa
196 D4 Augrabies Falls S. Africa
196 D4 Augrabies Falls National Park S. Africa
209 F3 Au Gres U.S.A.
176 E6 Augsburg Germany
121 A7 Augusta Australia
184 F6 Augusta Sicily Italy
219 D5 Augusta GA U.S.A.
217 D4 Augusta KS U.S.A.
221 I2 Augusta ME U.S.A.
208 B3 Augusta WI U.S.A.
177 K4 Augustów, Puszcza for. Poland
118 B4 Augustus, Mount Australia
121 C4 Auld, Lake salt flat Australia
141 F1 Auliyekol' Kazakh.
178 B4 Aulnoye-Aymeries France
173 I7 Ault France
Auminzatau, Gory h. Uzbek. see Ovminzatov tog'lari
195 B6 Auob watercourse Namibia
207 G2 Aupaluk Canada
162 C5 Aur i. Malaysia
171 M3 Aura Fin.
148 D4 Auraiya India
148 C6 Aurangabad India
179 F1 Aurich Germany
234 B2 Aurilândia Brazil
182 F4 Aurillac France
163 H3 Aurkuning Indon.
161 I5 Aurora Phil.
213 F4 Aurora CO U.S.A.
208 C5 Aurora IL U.S.A.
221 I2 Aurora ME U.S.A.
217 E4 Aurora MO U.S.A.
122 C2 Aurukun Australia
195 B6 Aus Namibia
209 F3 Au Sable U.S.A.
209 E3 Au Sable r. U.S.A.
221 G2 Ausable r. U.S.A.
221 G2 Au Sable Forks U.S.A.
208 D2 Au Sable Point MI U.S.A.
209 F3 Au Sable Point MI U.S.A.
175 F1 Auskerry i. U.K.
170 C2 Austari-Jökulsá r. Iceland
216 E3 Austin MN U.S.A.
215 D2 Austin NV U.S.A.
217 D6 Austin TX U.S.A.
121 B5 Austin, Lake salt flat Australia
123 B4 Austral Downs Australia
Australes, Îles is Fr. Polynesia see Tubuai Islands
118 C4 Australia country Oceania
239 P9 Australian-Antarctic Basin sea feature Southern Ocean
127 I7 Australian Antarctic Territory reg. Antarctica
125 H5 Australian Capital Territory admin. div. Australia
125 G9 Australian Convict Sites tourist site Australia
176 F7 Austria country Europe
170 K1 Austvågøy i. Norway
224 C4 Autlán Mex.
170 N2 Autti Fin.
182 G3 Autun France
182 F4 Auvergne reg. France
182 F3 Auxerre France
178 A4 Auxi-le-Château France
182 G3 Auxonne France
221 F3 Ava U.S.A.
139 L4 Āvaj Iran
182 F3 Avallon France
214 C5 Avalon U.S.A.
207 J4 Avalon Peninsula Canada
225 D2 Ávalos Mex.
142 B2 Avān Iran
138 E2 Avanos Turkey
234 C3 Avaré Brazil
139 K2 Āvārsīn Iran
215 D4 Avawatz Mountains U.S.A.
143 F3 Āvāz Iran
231 G4 Aveiro Brazil
183 L2 Aveiro Port.
183 L2 Aveiro, Ria de est. Port.
235 K2 Avellaneda Arg.
184 F4 Avellino Italy
214 B3 Avenal U.S.A.
125 F6 Avenel Australia
184 F4 Aversa Italy
178 B4 Avesnes-sur-Helpe France
171 L3 Avesta Sweden
182 F4 Aveyron r. France
184 E3 Avezzano Italy
174 E3 Aviemore U.K.
184 F4 Avigliano Italy
183 G5 Avignon France
183 N2 Ávila Spain
183 N1 Avilés Spain
178 A4 Avion France
147 I5 Avissawella Sri Lanka
186 H2 Avnyugskiy Russia
125 G8 Avoca Tas. Australia
125 E6 Avoca Vic. Australia
125 E6 Avoca r. Australia
175 L5 Avoca Ireland
216 E3 Avoca U.S.A.
184 F6 Avola Sicily Italy
173 E6 Avon r. England U.K.
173 E7 Avon r. England U.K.
173 F7 Avon r. England U.K.
208 B5 Avon U.S.A.
215 F5 Avondale U.S.A.
173 E6 Avonmouth U.K.
219 D7 Avon Park U.S.A.
182 D2 Avranches France
178 A5 Avre r. France
119 G2 Avuavu Solomon Is
159 D7 Awaji-shima i. Japan
126 E3 Awakino N.Z.
142 C5 'Awālī Bahrain
126 D1 Awanui N.Z.
126 B6 Awarua Point N.Z.
194 E3 Āwash Eth.
194 D3 Āwash r. Eth.
159 F5 Awa-shima i. Japan
194 D3 Āwash National Park Eth.
196 A2 Awasib Mountains Namibia
141 J4 Awat China
126 D4 Awatere r. N.Z.
193 D2 Awbārī Libya
193 D2 Awbārī, Idhān des. Libya
175 J5 Awbeg r. Ireland
139 K6 'Awdah, Hawr al imp. l. Iraq
194 E3 Aw Dheegle Somalia
174 C4 Awe, Loch l. U.K.
193 E4 Aweil South Sudan
192 C4 Awka Nigeria
161 J6 Awu vol. Indon.
125 F6 Axedale Australia
203 I2 Axel Heiberg Island Canada
192 B4 Axim Ghana
173 E7 Axminster U.K.
178 C5 Ay France
141 J3 Ay Kazakh.
159 D7 Ayabe Japan
180 C5 Ayachi, Jbel mt. Morocco
235 K3 Ayacucho Arg.
230 D6 Ayacucho Peru
141 J3 Ayagoz Kazakh.
141 I3 Ayagoz watercourse Kazakh.
Ayakkuduk Uzbek. see Oyoqquduq
150 A3 Ayakkum Hu salt l. China
183 M4 Ayamonte Spain
150 F1 Ayan Russia
187 E7 Ayancık Turkey
160 C4 Ayang N. Korea
133 R3 Ayanka Russia
233 I2 Ayapel Col.
138 D1 Ayaş Turkey
230 D6 Ayaviri Peru
141 G1 Aydabol Kazakh.
187 F5 Aydar r. Ukr.
141 F4 Aydarko'l ko'li l. Uzbek.
Aydarkul', Ozero l. Uzbek. see Aydarko'l ko'li
141 F3 Aydarly Kazakh.
138 A3 Aydın Turkey
138 A2 Aydın Dağları mts Turkey
140 C5 Aýdyň Turkm.
140 D2 Aydyrlinskiy Russia
162 □ Ayer Chawan, Pulau i. Sing.
162 □ Ayer Merbau, Pulau i. Sing.
Ayers Rock h. Australia see Uluṟu
141 J2 Aygyrzhal Kazakh.
140 E2 Ayke, Ozero l. Kazakh.
133 M3 Aykhal Russia
186 I2 Aykino Russia
141 J4 Aykol China
126 D5 Aylesbury N.Z.
173 G6 Aylesbury U.K.
221 E6 Aylett U.S.A.
183 O2 Ayllón Spain
209 G4 Aylmer Canada
205 H2 Aylmer Lake Canada
141 I3 Aynabulak Kazakh.
142 C4 'Ayn al 'Abd well Saudi Arabia
139 G3 'Ayn al 'Arab Syria
136 C6 'Ayn al Maqfī spring Egypt
136 B5 'Ayn az Zaytūn Egypt
136 B6 'Ayn Dāllah spring Egypt
141 G5 Aynī Tajik.
139 G3 'Ayn 'Īsá Syria
136 B5 'Ayn Tabaghbugh spring Egypt
136 B5 'Ayn Tumayrah spring Egypt
193 F4 Ayod South Sudan
133 R3 Ayon, Ostrov i. Russia
192 B3 'Ayoûn el 'Atroûs Mauritania
119 E3 Ayr Australia
174 D5 Ayr U.K.
174 D5 Ayr r. U.K.
138 D3 Ayrancı Turkey
172 C3 Ayre, Point of Isle of Man
141 G3 Ayshyrak Kazakh.
140 E3 Ayteke Bi Kazakh.
185 L3 Aytos Bulg.
163 D2 A Yun Pa Vietnam
162 B2 Ayutthaya Thai.
185 L5 Ayvacık Turkey
139 F2 Ayvalı Turkey
185 L5 Ayvalık Turkey
224 H5 Azacualpa Hond.
148 C2 Azad Kashmir admin. div. Pak.
149 E4 Azamgarh India
194 E3 Azania reg. Somalia
192 B3 Azaouâd reg. Mali
192 C3 Azaouagh, Vallée de watercourse Mali/Niger
141 G3 Azat, Gory h. Kazakh.
192 B3 Azawad reg. Mali
Azbine mts Niger see Aïr, Massif de l'
138 D1 Azdavay Turkey
139 K1 Azerbaijan country Asia
142 B2 Āzghān Iran
140 E3 Azhar Kazakh.
141 G2 Azhibeksor, Ozero salt l. Kazakh.
209 G2 Azilda Canada
221 H2 Aziscohos Lake U.S.A.
230 C4 Azogues Ecuador
132 F3 Azopol'ye Russia
166 A6 Azores terr. N. Atlantic Ocean
239 H3 Azores-Biscay Rise sea feature N. Atlantic Ocean
187 F6 Azov Russia
187 F6 Azov, Sea of Russia/Ukr.
139 F6 Azraq, Qaşr al Jordan
192 B1 Azrou Morocco
213 F4 Aztec U.S.A.
183 N3 Azuaga Spain
232 B3 Azúcar r. Chile
224 I7 Azuero, Península de pen. Panama
235 K3 Azul Arg.
225 G4 Azul r. Mex.
235 H4 Azul, Cerro mt. Arg.
230 C5 Azul, Cordillera mts Peru
234 A1 Azul, Serra hills Brazil
159 G6 Azuma-san vol. Japan
183 H5 Azur, Côte d' coastal area France
231 F8 Azurduy Bol.
142 C5 Az̧ Z̧a'āyin
184 B6 Azzaba Alg.
139 F5 Az Zabadānī Syria
139 I6 Az̧ Z̧afīrī reg. Iraq
Az̧ Z̧ahrān Saudi Arabia see Dhahran
193 F1 Az Zaqāzīq Egypt
139 F5 Az Zarqā' Jordan
193 D1 Az Zāwiyah Libya
139 J3 Az Zībār Iraq
142 B5 Az Zilfī Saudi Arabia
139 K6 Az Zubayr Iraq

B

163 D2 Ba, Sông r. Vietnam
120 C1 Baa Indon.
138 E5 Baabda Lebanon
137 E4 Ba'albek Lebanon
125 H3 Baan Baa Australia
194 E3 Baardheere Somalia
143 H3 Bābā, Kōh-e mts Afgh.
185 L5 Baba Burnu pt Turkey
139 L1 Babadağ mt. Azer.
185 M2 Babadag Romania
Babadaykhan Ahal Turkm. see Babadaýhan
140 D5 Babadurmaz Turkm.
187 C7 Babaeski Turkey
230 C4 Babahoyo Ecuador
147 H1 Babai India
149 E3 Babai r. Nepal
154 B1 Babai Gaxun China
139 K2 Bābājān Iran
161 J5 Babak Phil.
194 E2 Bāb al Mandab str. Africa/Asia
Babao China see Qilian
151 E7 Babar i. Indon.
141 H4 Babash-Ata, Khrebet mt. Kyrg.
195 D4 Babati Tanz.
186 E3 Babayevo Russia
187 H7 Babayurt Russia
208 B2 Babbitt U.S.A.
125 H7 Babel Island Australia
202 F4 Babine r. Canada
204 D4 Babine Lake Canada
151 F7 Babo Indon.
142 D2 Bābol Iran
140 C5 Bābolsar Iran
196 C6 Baboon Point S. Africa
215 G6 Baboquivari Peak U.S.A.
194 B3 Baboua C.A.R.
187 D4 Babruysk Belarus
156 D2 Babstovo Russia
148 B4 Babuhri India
148 C2 Babusar Pass Pak.
186 G3 Babushkina, imeni Russia
161 H4 Babuyan Phil.
161 I2 Babuyan i. Phil.
155 F7 Babuyan Channel Phil.
161 I2 Babuyan Islands Phil.
139 J5 Babylon tourist site Iraq
231 J4 Bacabal Brazil
138 C1 Bacakliyayla Tepesi mt. Turkey
225 G4 Bacalar Mex.
151 E7 Bacan i. Indon.
161 I2 Bacarra Phil.
177 M7 Bacău Romania
125 F6 Bacchus Marsh Australia
155 C6 Băc Giang Vietnam
156 D2 Bacha China
224 C1 Bachiniva Mex.
155 C6 Bach Long Vi, Đao i. Vietnam
141 I5 Bachu China
141 I5 Bachu Liuchang China
122 C3 Back r. Australia
205 I1 Back r. Canada
155 B6 Băc Kan Vietnam
185 H2 Bačka Palanka Serbia
204 D2 Backbone Ranges mts Canada
171 L3 Backe Sweden
124 B5 Backstairs Passage Australia
174 E4 Backwater Reservoir U.K.
162 C3 Bac Liêu Vietnam
155 C6 Băc Ninh Vietnam
161 I3 Baco, Mount Phil.
161 I4 Bacolod Phil.
Băc Quang Vietnam see Viêt Quang
207 F2 Bacqueville, Lac l. Canada
140 E5 Badabaýhan Ahal Turkm.
140 E5 Badabaýhan Ahal Turkm.
179 K6 Bad Abbach Germany
154 A1 Badain Jaran Shamo des. China
231 F4 Badajós, Lago l. Brazil
183 M3 Badajoz Spain
147 G3 Badami India
140 D2 Badamsha Kazakh.
139 H6 Badanah Saudi Arabia
149 H4 Badarpur India
209 F4 Bad Axe U.S.A.
179 G1 Bad Bederkesa Germany
179 K2 Bad Belzig Germany
179 F5 Bad Bergzabern Germany
179 G3 Bad Berleburg Germany
179 I1 Bad Bevensen Germany
179 J4 Bad Blankenburg Germany
179 G4 Bad Camberg Germany
207 H4 Baddeck Canada
143 G4 Baddo r. Pak.
179 H3 Bad Driburg Germany
179 K3 Bad Düben Germany
179 G5 Bad Dürkheim Germany
179 K3 Bad Dürrenberg Germany
Bademli Turkey see Aladağ
138 C3 Bademli Geçidi pass Turkey
179 F4 Bad Ems Germany
177 H6 Baden Austria
176 D7 Baden Switz.
176 D6 Baden-Baden Germany
174 D4 Badenoch reg. U.K.
179 G5 Baden-Württemberg land Germany
179 G2 Bad Essen Germany
179 H2 Bad Fallingbostel Germany
207 I4 Badger Canada
179 I3 Bad Grund (Harz) Germany
179 I3 Bad Harzburg Germany
179 H4 Bad Hersfeld Germany
176 F7 Bad Hofgastein Austria
179 G4 Bad Homburg vor der Höhe Germany
184 D2 Badia Polesine Italy
148 B4 Badin Pak.
224 C2 Badiraguato Mex.
176 F7 Bad Ischl Austria
Bādiyat ash Shām des. Asia see Syrian Desert
179 I4 Bad Kissingen Germany
179 J3 Bad Kösen Germany
179 K5 Bad Kötzting Germany
179 F5 Bad Kreuznach Germany
179 G4 Bad Laasphe Germany
216 C2 Badlands reg. U.S.A.
216 C3 Badlands National Park U.S.A.
179 I3 Bad Langensalza Germany
179 I3 Bad Lauterberg im Harz Germany
179 G3 Bad Lippspringe Germany
179 F4 Bad Marienberg (Westerwald) Germany
179 H5 Bad Mergentheim Germany
179 G4 Bad Nauheim Germany
179 F4 Bad Neuenahr-Ahrweiler Germany

Bad Neustadt an der Saale

179 I4 **Bad Neustadt an der Saale** Germany
179 I1 **Bad Oldesloe** Germany
155 D4 **Badong** China
162 C3 **Ba Đông** Vietnam
179 H3 **Bad Pyrmont** Germany
139 J5 **Badrah** Iraq
176 F7 **Bad Reichenhall** Germany
137 I4 **Bādrūd** Iran
179 I3 **Bad Sachsa** Germany
179 I2 **Bad Salzdetfurth** Germany
179 G2 **Bad Salzuflen** Germany
179 I4 **Bad Salzungen** Germany
179 G4 **Bad Schwalbach** Germany
176 E4 **Bad Schwartau** Germany
176 E4 **Bad Segeberg** Germany
179 F5 **Bad Sobernheim** Germany
179 I4 **Bad Staffelstein** Germany
119 E3 **Badu Island** Australia
147 I5 **Badulla** Sri Lanka
179 G4 **Bad Vilbel** Germany
179 J2 **Bad Wilsnack** Germany
179 I5 **Bad Windsheim** Germany
156 D2 **Badzhal** Russia
156 D2 **Badzhal'skiy Khrebet** *mts* Russia
179 G1 **Bad Zwischenahn** Germany
170 B1 **Bæir** Iceland
160 C5 **Baengnyeong-do** *i.* N. Korea
125 I4 **Baerami** Australia
179 E4 **Baesweiler** Germany
183 O4 **Baeza** Spain
193 D4 **Bafang** Cameroon
192 A3 **Bafatá** Guinea-Bissau
240 T2 **Baffin Basin** *sea feature* Arctic Ocean
203 L2 **Baffin Bay** *sea* Canada/Greenland
203 K2 **Baffin Island** Canada
193 D4 **Bafia** Cameroon
192 A3 **Bafing, Réserve du** *nature res.* Mali
192 A3 **Bafoulabé** Mali
193 D4 **Bafoussam** Cameroon
142 D4 **Bāfq** Iran
138 E1 **Bafra** Turkey
187 E7 **Bafra Burnu** *pt* Turkey
143 E4 **Bāft** Iran
194 C3 **Bafwasende** Dem. Rep. Congo
149 F4 **Bagaha** India
161 H5 **Bagahak, Gunung** *h. Sabah* Malaysia
147 G2 **Bagalkot** India
195 D4 **Bagamoyo** Tanz.
163 B2 **Bagan Datuk** Malaysia
195 C5 **Bagani** Namibia
162 B4 **Bagan Serai** Malaysia
162 B5 **Bagansiapiapi** Indon.
215 F4 **Bagdad** U.S.A.
153 J1 **Bagdarin** Russia
235 L1 **Bagé** Brazil
175 L5 **Bagenalstown** Ireland
149 G5 **Bagerhat** Bangl.
148 D3 **Bageshwar** India
213 F3 **Baggs** U.S.A.
173 C6 **Baggy Point** U.K.
148 C5 **Bagh** India
142 D4 **Bāgh, Chāh-e** *well* Iran
143 F2 **Baghbaghū** Iran
143 E4 **Bāghbāghū'īyeh** Iran
139 J5 **Baghdād** Iraq
142 C4 **Bāgh-e Malek** Iran
143 H2 **Baghlān** Afgh.
143 G3 **Baghrān** Afgh.
216 E2 **Bagley** U.S.A.
149 E3 **Baglung** Nepal
183 Q1 **Bagnères-de-Luchon** France
182 G4 **Bagnols-sur-Cèze** France
149 F4 **Bagnuiti** *r.* Nepal
154 C2 **Bag Nur** *l.* China
161 I4 **Bago** Phil.
177 J3 **Bagrationovsk** Russia
161 I2 **Baguio** *Benguet* Phil.
161 J5 **Baguio** *Davao del Sur* Phil.
148 D3 **Bahadurgarh** India
223 I3 **Bahamas, The** *country* Caribbean Sea
149 G4 **Baharampur** India
Bahariya Oasis Egypt *see* **Bahrīyah, Wāḥāt al**
140 D5 **Baharly** Turkm.
163 B2 **Bahau** Malaysia
148 C3 **Bahawalnagar** Pak.
148 B3 **Bahawalpur** Pak.
139 F3 **Bahçe** Turkey
155 C4 **Ba He** *r.* China
148 D3 **Baheri** India
195 D4 **Bahi** Tanz.
234 E1 **Bahia** *state* Brazil
224 H4 **Bahía, Islas de la** Hond.
235 J3 **Bahía Blanca** Arg.
224 B1 **Bahía Kino** Mex.
232 C7 **Bahía Laura** Arg.
232 E2 **Bahía Negra** Para.
224 A2 **Bahía Tortugas** Mex.
194 D2 **Bahir Dar** Eth.
147 E5 **Bahlā** Oman
142 C4 **Bahman Yārī** Iran
149 E4 **Bahraich** India
142 C5 **Bahrain** *country* Asia
142 C5 **Bahrain, Gulf of** Asia
139 L3 **Bahrāmābād** Iran
139 L3 **Bahrām Beyg** Iran
143 E4 **Bahrāmjerd** Iran
193 E2 **Bahrīyah, Wāḥāt al** *oasis* Egypt
230 E6 **Bahuaja-Sonene, Parque Nacional** *nat. park* Peru
143 F5 **Bāhū Kālāt** Iran
177 K7 **Baia Mare** Romania
150 E2 **Baicheng** *Jilin* China
141 J4 **Baicheng** *Xinjiang Uygur Zizhiqu* China
207 G4 **Baie-Comeau** Canada
Baie-du-Poste Canada *see* **Mistissini**
207 F4 **Baie-St-Paul** Canada
207 I4 **Baie Verte** Canada
154 E2 **Baigou He** *r.* China
149 E5 **Baihar** India
150 E2 **Baihe** *Jilin* China
154 D3 **Baihe** *Shaanxi* China
154 E1 **Bai He** *r.* China
150 C1 **Baikal, Lake** Russia
156 A1 **Baikalu Shan** *mt.* China
Baile an Bhuinneánaigh Ireland *see* **Ballybunion**
Baile an Chinnéidigh Ireland *see* **Newtown Mount Kennedy**
174 A3 **Baile Mhartainn** U.K.
175 J3 **Baile na Finne** Ireland
185 J2 **Băilești** Romania
185 J2 **Băileștilor, Câmpia** *plain* Romania
121 C6 **Bailey Range** *hills* Australia
175 L4 **Bailieborough** Ireland
154 D1 **Bailingmiao** China
178 A4 **Bailleul** France
205 H2 **Baillie** *r.* Canada
154 B3 **Bailong Jiang** *r.* China
150 C3 **Baima** *Qinghai* China
Baima *Xizang Zizhiqu* China *see* **Baxoi**
155 E4 **Baima Jian** *mt.* China
173 G4 **Bain** *r.* U.K.
219 C6 **Bainbridge** *GA* U.S.A.
221 F3 **Bainbridge** *NY* U.S.A.
Baingoin China *see* **Porong**
180 B3 **Baiona** Spain
156 B3 **Baiquan** China
139 F6 **Bā'ir** Jordan
139 F6 **Bā'ir, Wādī** *watercourse* Jordan
149 E2 **Bairab Co** *l.* China
149 F4 **Bairagnia** India
202 C3 **Baird Mountains** U.S.A.
117 G3 **Bairiki** Kiribati
154 F1 **Bairin Qiao** China
125 G6 **Bairnsdale** Australia
161 I4 **Bais** Phil.
155 C4 **Baise** China
155 C7 **Baisha** *Hainan* China
155 E5 **Baisha** *Jiangxi* China
155 C4 **Baisha** *Sichuan* China
160 D2 **Baishan** *Jilin* China
160 D3 **Baishan** *Jilin* China
154 B3 **Baishui Jiang** *r.* China
155 B7 **Bai Thường** Vietnam
157 C4 **Baitou Shan** *mt.* China/N. Korea
160 A2 **Baixingt** China
154 B2 **Baiyin** China
193 F3 **Baiyuda Desert** Sudan
185 H1 **Baja** Hungary
224 A2 **Baja California** *pen.* Mex.
176 C6 **Baja California** *state* Mex.
224 A2 **Baja California Sur** *state* Mex.
139 L3 **Bājalān** Iran
225 D2 **Bajan** Mex.
149 E3 **Bajang** Nepal
149 G5 **Baj Baj** India
143 E3 **Bajestān** Iran
142 E2 **Bājgīrān** Iran
233 H3 **Bajo Baudó** Col.
224 I6 **Bajo Boquete** Panama
235 J1 **Bajo Hondo** Arg.
141 I3 **Bakanas** Kazakh.
141 I3 **Bakanas** *watercourse* Kazakh.
141 G4 **Bakay-Ata** Kyrg.
192 A3 **Bakel** Senegal
215 D4 **Baker** *CA* U.S.A.
212 F2 **Baker** *MT* U.S.A.
215 E2 **Baker** *NV* U.S.A.
212 B1 **Baker, Mount** *vol.* U.S.A.
215 G4 **Baker Butte** *mt.* U.S.A.
212 C2 **Baker City** U.S.A.
119 I1 **Baker Island** *terr.* Pacific Ocean
204 C3 **Baker Island** U.S.A.
121 D5 **Baker Lake** *salt flat* Australia
205 J2 **Baker Lake** Canada
205 J2 **Baker Lake** *l.* Canada
206 E2 **Baker's Dozen Islands** Canada
214 C4 **Bakersfield** U.S.A.
162 C2 **Bâ Kêv** Cambodia
Bakhardok Turkm. *see* **Bokurdak**
143 F3 **Bākharz, Kūhhā-ye** *mts* Iran
148 B4 **Bakhasar** India
187 E6 **Bakhchysaray** Crimea
Bakherden Turkm. *see* **Baharly**
156 C2 **Bakhirevo** Russia
187 E5 **Bakhmach** Ukr.
Bakhma Dam Iraq *see* **Bēkma, Sadd**
142 D4 **Bakhtegan, Daryācheh-ye** *l.* Iran
Bakı Azer. *see* **Baku**
194 E3 **Baki** Somalia
138 B1 **Bakırköy** Turkey
194 D3 **Bako** Eth.
194 C3 **Bakouma** C.A.R.
195 B4 **Bakoumba** Gabon
187 G7 **Baksan** Russia
141 J3 **Bakty** Kazakh.
139 L1 **Baku** Azer.
194 C4 **Baku** Dem. Rep. Congo
138 D2 **Balâ** Turkey
173 D5 **Bala** U.K.
230 E6 **Bala, Cerros de** *mts* Bol.
161 H4 **Balabac** Phil.
161 H5 **Balabac** *i.* Phil.
163 I1 **Balabac Strait** Malaysia/Phil.
139 J4 **Balad** Iraq
142 C4 **Bālā Deh** Iran
142 C2 **Baladeh** *Māzandarān* Iran
142 C2 **Baladeh** *Māzandarān* Iran
156 D1 **Baladek** Russia
Balagar Gaole China *see* **Bayan Ul**
149 E5 **Balaghat** India
147 G2 **Balaghat Range** *hills* India
143 E4 **Bālā Ḥowz** Iran
139 K1 **Balakān** Azer.
186 G3 **Balakhna** Russia
124 C5 **Balaklava** Australia
187 E6 **Balaklava** Crimea
187 F5 **Balakliya** Ukr.
187 H4 **Balakovo** Russia
173 D5 **Bala Lake** U.K.
163 I1 **Balambangan** *i. Sabah* Malaysia
143 F3 **Bālā Murghāb** Afgh.
148 B4 **Balan** India
187 H5 **Balanda** *r.* Russia
138 B3 **Balan Dağı** *h.* Turkey
161 I3 **Balanga** Phil.
147 I1 **Balangir** India
147 I5 **Balangoda** Sri Lanka
140 B2 **Balashi** Russia
187 G5 **Balashov** Russia
148 C5 **Balasinor** India
177 H7 **Balaton, Lake** Hungary
177 H7 **Balatonboglár** Hungary
177 H7 **Balatonfüred** Hungary
231 G4 **Balbina, Represa de** *resr* Brazil
175 L4 **Balbriggan** Ireland
124 C3 **Balcanoona** Australia
235 K3 **Balcarce** Arg.
185 M3 **Balchik** Bulg.
143 G3 **Bal Chirāgh** Afgh.
126 B7 **Balclutha** N.Z.
217 F5 **Bald Knob** U.S.A.
215 E3 **Bald Mountain** U.S.A.
205 J3 **Baldock Lake** Canada
209 H3 **Baldwin** Canada
219 D6 **Baldwin** *FL* U.S.A.
209 E4 **Baldwin** *MI* U.S.A.
208 A3 **Baldwin** *WI* U.S.A.
221 E3 **Baldwinsville** U.S.A.
215 H5 **Baldy Peak** U.S.A.
Baleares, Islas *is* Spain *see* **Balearic Islands**
183 R3 **Balearic Islands** *is* Spain
163 H2 **Baleh** *r. Sarawak* Malaysia
234 E2 **Baleia, Ponta da** *pt* Brazil
207 F3 **Baleine, Grande Rivière de la** *r.* Canada
206 E2 **Baleine, Petite Rivière de la** *r.* Canada
207 G2 **Baleine, Rivière à la** *r.* Canada
194 D3 **Bale Mountains National Park** Eth.
161 I3 **Baler** Phil.
161 I3 **Baler Bay** Phil.
149 F5 **Baleshwar** India
171 I3 **Balestrand** Norway
184 C4 **Balestrieri, Punta** *mt. Sardinia* Italy
169 Q4 **Balezino** Russia
123 D4 **Balfes Creek** Australia
126 B6 **Balfour** N.Z.
121 C4 **Balfour Downs** Australia
121 D4 **Balgo** Australia
144 G3 **Balguntay** China
163 I4 **Bali** *i.* Indon.
193 D4 **Bali** Nigeria
163 I4 **Bali, Laut** *sea* Indon.
163 E2 **Balige** Indon.
147 I1 **Baligurha** India
154 F1 **Balihan** China
138 A2 **Balıkesir** Turkey
137 E4 **Balīkh** *r.* Syria/Turkey
163 I3 **Balikpapan** Indon.
147 I2 **Balimila Reservoir** India
119 E2 **Balimo** P.N.G.
176 D6 **Balingen** Germany
161 I2 **Balintang Channel** Phil.
174 E3 **Balintore** U.K.
Bali Sea Indon. *see* **Bali, Laut**
161 I5 **Baliungan** *i.* Phil.
141 G5 **Baljuvon** Tajik.
178 D2 **Balk** Neth.
140 C5 **Balkanabat** Turkm.
185 J3 **Balkan Mountains** Bulg./Serbia
141 H3 **Balkash** Kazakh.
141 G1 **Balkashino** Kazakh.
143 G2 **Balkh** *r.* Afgh.
141 H3 **Balkhash, Lake** Kazakh.
140 A3 **Balkuduk** Kazakh.
174 C4 **Ballachulish** U.K.
118 C5 **Balladonia** Australia
125 H3 **Balladoran** Australia
175 J4 **Ballaghaderreen** Ireland
125 F6 **Ballan** Australia
170 L1 **Ballangen** Norway
212 E2 **Ballantine** U.S.A.
174 D5 **Ballantrae** U.K.
125 E6 **Ballarat** Australia
118 C4 **Ballard, Lake** *salt flat* Australia
147 H3 **Ballari** India
148 D6 **Ballarpur** India
174 E3 **Ballater** U.K.
192 B3 **Ballé** Mali
232 B3 **Ballena, Punta** *pt* Chile
127 I6 **Balleny Islands** Antarctica
149 F4 **Ballia** India
125 J2 **Ballina** Australia
175 I3 **Ballina** Ireland
175 J3 **Ballinafad** Ireland
175 K4 **Ballinalack** Ireland
175 K3 **Ballinamore** Ireland
175 J4 **Ballinasloe** Ireland
175 J4 **Ballindine** Ireland
217 D6 **Ballinger** U.S.A.
174 E4 **Ballinluig** U.K.
175 I4 **Ballinrobe** Ireland
221 G3 **Ballston Spa** U.S.A.
175 L3 **Ballybay** Ireland
Ballybrack Ireland *see* **An Baile Breac**
175 I5 **Ballybunion** Ireland
175 L5 **Ballycanew** Ireland
175 I3 **Ballycastle** Ireland
175 L2 **Ballycastle** U.K.
175 M3 **Ballyclare** U.K.
175 H4 **Ballyconneely Bay** Ireland
175 K3 **Ballyconnell** Ireland
175 J4 **Ballygar** Ireland
175 K3 **Ballygawley** U.K.
175 K2 **Ballygorman** Ireland
175 J4 **Ballyhaunis** Ireland
175 I5 **Ballyheigue** Ireland
175 J5 **Ballyhoura Mountains** Ireland
175 K2 **Ballykelly** U.K.
175 K5 **Ballylynan** Ireland
175 K5 **Ballymacmague** Ireland
175 K4 **Ballymahon** Ireland
175 L3 **Ballymena** U.K.
175 L2 **Ballymoney** U.K.
175 J3 **Ballymote** Ireland
175 M3 **Ballynahinch** U.K.
175 J3 **Ballyshannon** Ireland
175 L5 **Ballyteige Bay** Ireland
175 I4 **Ballyvaughan** Ireland
175 L3 **Ballyward** U.K.
124 D6 **Balmoral** Australia
217 C6 **Balmorhea** U.S.A.
143 G4 **Balochistan** *prov.* Pak.
135 E4 **Balochistan** *reg.* Pak.
149 E5 **Balod** India
147 I1 **Baloda Bazar** India
125 H2 **Balonne** *r.* Australia
148 C4 **Balotra** India
141 I3 **Balpyk Bi** Kazakh.
149 E4 **Balrampur** India
125 E5 **Balranald** Australia
185 K2 **Balș** Romania
209 H2 **Balsam Creek** Canada
231 I5 **Balsas** Brazil
225 E4 **Balsas** Mex.
225 D4 **Balsas** *r.* Mex.
187 D6 **Balta** Ukr.
186 I3 **Baltasi** Russia
174 □ **Baltasound** U.K.
187 C6 **Bălți** Moldova
171 L5 **Baltic Sea** *g.* Europe
138 C6 **Balṭīm** Egypt
197 H1 **Baltimore** S. Africa
221 E5 **Baltimore** U.S.A.
175 L5 **Baltinglass** Ireland
148 C2 **Baltistan** *reg.* Pak.
177 I3 **Baltiysk** Russia
148 D2 **Baltoro Glacier** Pak.
143 E4 **Baluch Ab** *well* Iran
149 G4 **Balurghat** India
161 J5 **Balut** *i.* Phil.
179 F3 **Balve** Germany
171 N4 **Balvi** Latvia
185 L5 **Balya** Turkey
141 I4 **Balykchy** Kyrg.
140 B3 **Balykshi** Kazakh.
143 E4 **Bam** Iran
143 E2 **Bām** Iran
155 C5 **Bama** China
119 E3 **Bamaga** Australia
206 B3 **Bamaji Lake** Canada
192 B3 **Bamako** Mali
192 B3 **Bamba** Mali
161 I2 **Bambang** Phil.
194 C3 **Bambari** C.A.R.
162 A5 **Bambel** Indon.
179 I5 **Bamberg** Germany
219 D5 **Bamberg** U.S.A.
194 C3 **Bambili** Dem. Rep. Congo
197 G5 **Bamboesberg** *mts* S. Africa
121 C4 **Bamboo Creek** Australia
194 C3 **Bambouti** C.A.R.
234 D3 **Bambuí** Brazil
139 L6 **Bāmdezh** Iran
193 D4 **Bamenda** Cameroon
Bami Turkm. *see* **Bamy**
160 C2 **Bamiancheng** China
194 C3 **Bamingui-Bangoran, Parc National du** *nat. park* C.A.R.
143 F5 **Bamposht** *reg.* Iran
173 D7 **Bampton** U.K.
143 F5 **Bampūr** Iran
143 E5 **Bampūr** *watercourse* Iran
143 F3 **Bamrūd** Iran
140 D5 **Bamy** Turkm.
143 G3 **Bāmyān** Afgh.
120 F2 **Bamyili** Australia
119 G2 **Banaba** *i.* Kiribati
231 K5 **Banabuiu, Açude** *resr* Brazil
175 K4 **Banagher** Ireland
194 C3 **Banalia** Dem. Rep. Congo
197 J1 **Banamana, Lagoa** *l.* Moz.
192 B3 **Banamba** Mali
155 E4 **Banan** China
123 E5 **Banana** Australia
231 H6 **Bananal, Ilha do** *i.* Brazil
147 J2 **Banapur** India
148 D4 **Banas** *r.* India
138 B2 **Banaz** Turkey
162 B1 **Ban Ban** Laos
Banbar China *see* **Domartang**
175 L3 **Banbridge** U.K.
162 B2 **Ban Bua Yai** Thai.
173 F5 **Banbury** U.K.
161 H4 **Bancalan** *i.* Phil.
153 H7 **Ban Cang** Vietnam
124 D3 **Bancannia Lake** *salt flat* Australia
192 A2 **Banc d'Arguin, Parc National du** *nat. park* Mauritania
175 F3 **Banchory** U.K.
161 H5 **Bancoran** *i.* Phil.
209 I3 **Bancroft** Canada
194 C3 **Banda** Dem. Rep. Congo
149 E4 **Banda** India
151 E7 **Banda, Kepulauan** *is* Indon.
151 F7 **Banda, Laut** *sea* Indon.
163 E1 **Banda Aceh** Indon.
125 J3 **Banda Banda, Mount** Australia
148 B2 **Banda Daud Shah** Pak.
162 A5 **Bandahara, Gunung** *mt.* Indon.
159 F6 **Bandai-Asahi Kokuritsu-kōen** *nat. park* Japan
143 F4 **Bandān** Iran
143 F4 **Bandān Kūh** *mts* Iran
149 H5 **Bandarban** Bangl.
143 E5 **Bandar-e 'Abbās** Iran
142 C2 **Bandar-e Anzalī** Iran
142 C4 **Bandar-e Būshehr** Iran
142 D5 **Bandar-e Chārak** Iran
142 C5 **Bandar-e Dayyer** Iran
142 C4 **Bandar-e Deylam** Iran
142 C4 **Bandar-e Emām Khomeynī** Iran
142 C4 **Bandar-e Ganāveh** Iran
142 B2 **Bandar-e Ḥeydarābād** Iran
143 E5 **Bandar-e Jāsk** Iran
142 D5 **Bandar-e Kangān** Iran
142 D5 **Bandar-e Khamīr** Iran
142 D5 **Bandar-e Lengeh** Iran
142 C4 **Bandar-e Māhshahr** Iran
142 D5 **Bandar-e Moghūyeh** Iran
142 D5 **Bandar-e Moqām** Iran
142 C4 **Bandar-e Rīg** Iran
142 D2 **Bandar-e Torkaman** Iran
163 G4 **Bandar Lampung** Indon.
148 D3 **Bandarpunch** *mt.* India
163 H1 **Bandar Seri Begawan** Brunei
Banda Sea Indon. *see* **Banda, Laut**
Band-e Amir *r.* Afgh. *see* **Balkh**
Band-e Bābā *mts* Afgh. *see* **Band-e Bābā, Silsilah-ye Kōh-e**
143 F3 **Band-e Bābā, Silsilah-ye Kōh-e** *mts* Afgh.
143 F5 **Band-e Bamposht, Kūh-e** *mts* Iran
234 B1 **Bandeirante** Brazil
234 E3 **Bandeiras, Pico de** *mt.* Brazil
197 H1 **Bandelierkop** S. Africa
224 C3 **Banderas, Bahía de** *b.* Mex.
142 D3 **Band-e Sar Qom** Iran
Band-e Torkestān *mts* Afgh. *see* **Turkistān, Silsilah-ye Band-e**
148 C4 **Bandi** *r. Rajasthan* India
148 C4 **Bandi** *r. Rajasthan* India
149 E6 **Bandia** *r.* India
192 B3 **Bandiagara** Mali
193 F4 **Bandingilo National Park** South Sudan
143 E5 **Bandīnī** Iran
138 A1 **Bandırma** Turkey
175 J6 **Bandon** Ireland
175 J6 **Bandon** *r.* Ireland
162 A3 **Ban Don, Ao** *b.* Thai.
139 L2 **Bändovan Burnu** *pt* Azer.
139 L6 **Band Qīr** Iran
195 B4 **Bandundu** Dem. Rep. Congo
163 G4 **Bandung** Indon.
121 C5 **Bandya** Australia
142 B3 **Bāneh** Iran
223 I4 **Banes** Cuba
204 F4 **Banff** Canada
175 F3 **Banff** U.K.
204 F4 **Banff National Park** Canada
192 B3 **Banfora** Burkina Faso
195 C4 **Banga** Dem. Rep. Congo
161 J5 **Banga** Phil.
161 J5 **Bangai Point** Phil.
Bangalore India *see* **Bengaluru**
148 D4 **Banganga** *r.* India
149 G5 **Bangaon** India
161 I2 **Bangar** Phil.
194 C3 **Bangassou** C.A.R.
149 E2 **Bangdag Co** *salt l.* China
162 C1 **Bangfai, Xé** *r.* Laos
118 C2 **Banggai** Indon.
151 E7 **Banggai, Kepulauan** *is* Indon.
163 I1 **Banggi** *i. Sabah* Malaysia
162 C1 **Banghiang, Xé** *r.* Laos
163 G3 **Bangka** *i.* Indon.
163 H4 **Bangkalan** Indon.
162 A5 **Bangkaru** *i.* Indon.
163 B3 **Bangko** Indon.
162 B2 **Bangkok** Thai.
162 B2 **Bangkok, Bight of** *b.* Thai.
149 G5 **Bangladesh** *country* Asia

Bayan Har Shan

150 B3 **Bayan Har Shan** *mts* China
150 C2 **Bayanhongor** Mongolia
154 B2 **Bayan Hot** China
160 A1 **Bayan Huxu** China
142 B3 **Bayānlū** Iran
154 C1 **Bayannur** China
154 B1 **Bayan Nurun** China
154 C1 **Bayan Obo** China
Bayan-Ovoo *Govĭ-Altay* Mongolia *see* **Altay**
154 C1 **Bayan-Ovoo** *Ömnögovĭ* Mongolia
160 A1 **Bayan Qagan** China
154 D1 **Bayan Shutu** China
144 I2 **Bayantsagaan** Mongolia
150 D2 **Bayan Ul** China
150 D2 **Bayan-Uul** Mongolia
Bayasgalant Mongolia *see* **Mönhhaan**
142 D4 **Bayāẕ** Iran
142 D3 **Bayāẕīyeh** Iran
161 J4 **Baybay** Phil.
139 H1 **Bayburt** Turkey
209 F4 **Bay City** *MI* U.S.A.
217 D6 **Bay City** *TX* U.S.A.
132 H3 **Baydaratskaya Guba** Russia
194 E3 **Baydhabo** Somalia
179 K5 **Bayerischer Wald** *mts* Germany
179 I5 **Bayern** *land* Germany
141 J1 **Bayevo** Russia
208 B2 **Bayfield** U.S.A.
141 F3 **Baygekum** Kazakh.
140 E1 **Baygora** Kazakh.
185 L5 **Bayındır** Turkey
139 I4 **Bayjī** Iraq
Baykal, Ozero *l.* Russia *see* **Baikal, Lake**
156 C1 **Baykal-Amur Magistral** Russia
150 C1 **Baykal'skiy Khrebet** *mts* Russia
139 H2 **Baykan** Turkey
152 F1 **Bay-Khaak** Russia
141 F3 **Baykonur** Kazakh.
140 E3 **Baykonyr** Kazakh.
140 E3 **Baykozha** Kazakh.
141 H5 **Baykurt** China
140 D1 **Baymak** Russia
142 D6 **Baynūna'h** *reg.* U.A.E.
161 I2 **Bayombong** Phil.
Bayona Spain *see* **Baiona**
183 D5 **Bayonne** France
161 I4 **Bayo Point** Phil.
140 E5 **Baýramaly** Turkm.
185 L5 **Bayramiç** Turkey
179 J5 **Bayreuth** Germany
217 F6 **Bay St Louis** U.S.A.
140 C3 **Bayshonas** Kazakh.
221 G4 **Bay Shore** U.S.A.
173 E5 **Bayston Hill** U.K.
Baysun Uzbek. *see* **Boysun**
141 F5 **Baysuntau, Gory** *mts* Uzbek.
217 E6 **Baytown** U.S.A.
126 F3 **Bay View** N.Z.
181 G5 **Bayy al Kabīr, Wādī** *watercourse* Libya
141 G4 **Bayyrkum** Kazakh.
141 G4 **Bayzhansay** Kazakh.
183 O4 **Baza** Spain
141 H5 **Bāzā'ī Gunbad** Afgh.
141 J3 **Bazar** *watercourse* Kazakh.
143 H3 **Bāzārak** Afgh.
139 K1 **Bazardyuzyu, Gora** *mt.* Azer./Russia
139 L3 **Bāzār-e Jom'eh** Iran
143 G3 **Bāzār-e Mālistān** Afgh.
142 C2 **Bāzār-e Māsāl** Iran
139 J2 **Bāzargān** Iran
187 H4 **Bazarnyy Karabulak** Russia
140 B2 **Bazarsholan** Kazakh.
140 B2 **Bazartobe** Kazakh.
195 D6 **Bazaruto, Ilha do** *i.* Moz.
143 G5 **Bazdar** Pak.
155 C4 **Bazhong** China
154 E2 **Bazhou** China
143 F5 **Bazmān** Iran
143 F4 **Bazmān, Kūh-e** *mt.* Iran
142 C3 **Bāzoft, Āb-e** *r.* Iran
138 E4 **Bcharré** Lebanon
195 E5 **Bé, Nosy** *i.* Madag.
162 C3 **Be, Sông** *r.* Vietnam
216 C2 **Beach** U.S.A.
209 I3 **Beachburg** Canada
221 F5 **Beach Haven** U.S.A.
124 D6 **Beachport** Australia
221 F5 **Beachwood** U.S.A.
173 H7 **Beachy Head** U.K.
221 G4 **Beacon** U.S.A.
197 G6 **Beacon Bay** S. Africa
155 □ **Beacon Hill** *Hong Kong* China
173 G6 **Beaconsfield** U.K.
232 C8 **Beagle, Canal** *sea chan.* Arg.
120 C2 **Beagle Bank** *reef* Australia
120 C3 **Beagle Bay** Australia
118 C3 **Beagle Gulf** Australia
195 E5 **Bealanana** Madag.
175 I3 **Béal an Mhuirthead** Ireland
173 E7 **Beaminster** U.K.
213 E3 **Bear** *r.* U.S.A.
205 M2 **Bear Cove** *b.* Canada
206 C4 **Beardmore** Canada
Beardmore Reservoir Australia *see* **Kajarabie, Lake**
208 B5 **Beardstown** U.S.A.
206 D3 **Bear Island** Canada
204 D3 **Bear Lake** Canada
213 E3 **Bear Lake** *l.* U.S.A.
148 D4 **Bearma** *r.* India
212 E1 **Bear Paw Mountain** U.S.A.
206 B3 **Bearskin Lake** Canada
214 B2 **Bear Valley** U.S.A.
148 C3 **Beas** *r.* India
148 C3 **Beas Dam** India
223 J5 **Beata, Cabo** *c.* Dom. Rep.
223 J5 **Beata, Isla** *i.* Dom. Rep.
216 D3 **Beatrice** U.S.A.
122 B2 **Beatrice, Cape** Australia
204 E3 **Beatton** *r.* Canada
204 E3 **Beatton River** Canada
215 D3 **Beatty** U.S.A.
206 E4 **Beattyville** Canada
183 S1 **Beaucaire** France
232 E8 **Beauchene Island** Falkland Is
125 E6 **Beaufort** Australia
163 I1 **Beaufort** *Sabah* Malaysia
219 D5 **Beaufort** U.S.A.
202 D2 **Beaufort Sea** Canada/U.S.A.
197 E6 **Beaufort West** S. Africa
207 F4 **Beauharnois** Canada
173 D3 **Beauly** U.K.
174 D3 **Beauly Firth** *est.* U.K.
173 C4 **Beaumaris** U.K.
178 C4 **Beaumont** Belgium
126 B6 **Beaumont** N.Z.
217 F6 **Beaumont** *MS* U.S.A.
220 B5 **Beaumont** *OH* U.S.A.
217 E6 **Beaumont** *TX* U.S.A.
182 G3 **Beaune** France
182 D3 **Beaupréau** France
178 A4 **Beauquesne** France
178 C4 **Beauraing** Belgium
205 J4 **Beauséjour** Canada
182 F2 **Beauvais** France
205 H3 **Beauval** Canada
178 A4 **Beauval** France
203 H4 **Beaver** *r. Alta* Canada
206 C2 **Beaver** *r. Ont.* Canada
204 D2 **Beaver** *r. Y.T.* Canada
215 F2 **Beaver** U.S.A.
215 F2 **Beaver** *r.* U.S.A.
204 A2 **Beaver Creek** Canada
219 C4 **Beaver Dam** *KY* U.S.A.
208 C4 **Beaver Dam** *WI* U.S.A.
220 C4 **Beaver Falls** U.S.A.
212 D2 **Beaverhead Mountains** U.S.A.
205 I2 **Beaverhill Lake** Canada
209 E3 **Beaver Island** U.S.A.
217 E4 **Beaver Lake** *resr* U.S.A.
204 F3 **Beaverlodge** Canada
220 D4 **Beaver Run Reservoir** U.S.A.
148 C4 **Beawar** India
235 I2 **Beazley** Arg.
234 C3 **Bebedouro** Brazil
173 D4 **Bebington** U.K.
179 H4 **Bebra** Germany
207 F1 **Bécard, Lac** *l.* Canada
173 I5 **Beccles** U.K.
185 I2 **Bečej** Serbia
183 M1 **Becerreá** Spain
192 B1 **Béchar** Alg.
179 I5 **Bechhofen** Germany
220 C6 **Beckley** U.S.A.
179 G3 **Beckum** Germany
179 K4 **Bečov nad Teplou** Czech Rep.
172 F3 **Bedale** U.K.
179 E4 **Bedburg** Germany
221 I2 **Beddington** U.S.A.
194 D3 **Bedelē** Eth.
141 I4 **Bedel Pass** China/Kyrg.
221 G2 **Bedford** Canada
197 I4 **Bedford** S. Africa
173 G5 **Bedford** U.K.
219 C4 **Bedford** *IN* U.S.A.
221 H3 **Bedford** *MA* U.S.A.
220 D4 **Bedford** *PA* U.S.A.
220 D6 **Bedford** *VA* U.S.A.
122 D2 **Bedford, Cape** Australia
120 D3 **Bedford Downs** Australia
173 G5 **Bedford Level (North Level)** *lowland* U.K.
125 G4 **Bedgerebong** Australia
172 F2 **Bedlington** U.K.
162 □ **Bedok** Sing.
162 □ **Bedok Reservoir** Sing.
123 B5 **Bedourie** Australia
215 H2 **Bedrock** U.S.A.
179 E1 **Bedum** Neth.
173 F5 **Bedworth** U.K.
220 B5 **Beech Fork Lake** U.S.A.
208 C2 **Beechwood** U.S.A.
125 G6 **Beechworth** Australia
125 I5 **Beecroft Peninsula** Australia
179 K2 **Beelitz** Germany
125 J1 **Beenleigh** Australia
175 H5 **Beenoskee** *h.* Ireland
178 B3 **Beernem** Belgium
138 E6 **Beersheba** Israel
197 E6 **Beervlei Dam** S. Africa
125 J1 **Beerwah** Australia
120 F3 **Beetaloo** Australia
179 K2 **Beetzsee** *l.* Germany
217 D6 **Beeville** U.S.A.
194 C3 **Befale** Dem. Rep. Congo
195 E5 **Befandriana Avaratra** Madag.
125 H6 **Bega** Australia
148 B3 **Begari** *r.* Pak.
183 R2 **Begur, Cap de** *c.* Spain
149 F4 **Begusarai** India
143 E3 **Behābād** *Khorāsān-e Jonūbī* Iran
142 D4 **Behābād** *Yazd* Iran
231 H3 **Béhague, Pointe** Fr. Guiana
142 C4 **Behbahān** Iran
204 F2 **Behchokǫ̀** Canada
204 C3 **Behm Canal** *sea chan.* U.S.A.
142 D4 **Behrūsī** Iran
142 D2 **Behshahr** Iran
150 E2 **Bei'an** China
155 C4 **Beibei** China
155 F6 **Beigang** Taiwan
155 C6 **Beihai** China
155 D6 **Bei Jiang** *r.* China
154 E2 **Beijing** China
154 E1 **Beijing** *mun.* China
179 E2 **Beilen** Neth.
155 C7 **Beili** China
155 D6 **Beiliu** China
179 J5 **Beilngries** Germany
Beining China *see* **Beizhen**
174 C5 **Beinn an Oir** *h.* U.K.
174 D3 **Beinn Dearg** *mt.* U.K.
155 C5 **Beipan Jiang** *r.* China
160 A3 **Beipiao** China
195 D5 **Beira** Moz.
154 E3 **Beiru He** *r.* China
138 E5 **Beirut** Lebanon
144 I3 **Bei Shan** *mts* China
154 D2 **Beitai Ding** *mt.* China
195 C6 **Beitbridge** Zimbabwe
174 D5 **Beith** U.K.
177 K7 **Beiuș** Romania
160 A3 **Beizhen** China
183 M3 **Beja** Port.
192 C1 **Béja** Tunisia
192 C1 **Bejaïa** Alg.
183 N2 **Béjar** Spain
148 B3 **Beji** *r.* Pak.
140 E3 **Bekbauly** Kazakh.
140 C3 **Bekbike** Kazakh.
Bekdash Turkm. *see* **Garabogaz**
177 J7 **Békés** Hungary
177 J7 **Békéscsaba** Hungary
195 E6 **Bekily** Madag.
137 G3 **Bēkma, Sadd** *dam* Iraq
192 B4 **Bekwai** Ghana
149 E4 **Bela** India
143 G5 **Bela** Pak.
148 B3 **Belab** *r.* Pak.
197 H2 **Bela-Bela** S. Africa
193 D4 **Bélabo** Cameroon
185 I2 **Bela Crkva** Serbia
141 J2 **Bel'agash** Kazakh.
147 G3 **Belagavi** India
221 E5 **Bel Air** U.S.A.
183 N3 **Belalcázar** Spain
179 K5 **Bělá nad Radbuzou** Czech Rep.
Belaraboon Australia *see* **Paddington**
177 M4 **Belarus** *country* Europe
234 A3 **Bela Vista** Brazil
195 D6 **Bela Vista** Moz.
162 A5 **Belawan** Indon.
133 S3 **Belaya** *r.* Russia
187 G6 **Belaya Glina** Russia
187 G5 **Belaya Kalitva** Russia
186 I3 **Belaya Kholunitsa** Russia
177 I5 **Bełchatów** Poland
220 B6 **Belcher** U.S.A.
203 J4 **Belcher Islands** Canada
139 F2 **Belcik** Turkey
175 K3 **Belcoo** U.K.
209 I1 **Belcourt** Canada
214 B1 **Belden** U.S.A.
194 E3 **Beledweyne** Somalia
140 C5 **Belek** Turkm.
231 I4 **Belém** Brazil
232 C3 **Belén** Arg.
139 F3 **Belen** Turkey
213 F5 **Belen** U.S.A.
119 G3 **Belep, Îles** *is* New Caledonia
140 D3 **Beleuli** *tourist site* Uzbek.
187 F4 **Belev** Russia
126 D5 **Belfast** N.Z.
175 M3 **Belfast** U.K.
221 I2 **Belfast** U.S.A.
175 M3 **Belfast Lough** *inlet* U.K.
216 C2 **Belfield** U.S.A.
172 F2 **Belford** U.K.
182 H3 **Belfort** France
Belgaum India *see* **Belagavi**
179 L3 **Belgern** Germany
178 C4 **Belgium** *country* Europe
187 F5 **Belgorod** Russia
187 F5 **Belgorodskaya Oblast'** *admin. div.* Russia
185 I2 **Belgrade** Serbia
212 E2 **Belgrade** U.S.A.
127 J3 **Belgrano II** *research stn* Antarctica
184 E6 **Belice** *r. Sicily* Italy
187 G4 **Belinskiy** Russia
163 G3 **Belinyu** Indon.
163 G3 **Belitung** *i.* Indon.
225 G4 **Belize** Belize
225 G4 **Belize** *country* Central America
158 E2 **Belkina, Mys** *pt* Russia
133 O2 **Bel'kovskiy, Ostrov** *i.* Russia
125 I1 **Bell** Australia
125 H4 **Bell** *r.* Australia
204 D4 **Bella Bella** Canada
182 E3 **Bellac** France
204 D4 **Bella Coola** Canada
217 E6 **Bellaire** U.S.A.
Bellary India *see* **Ballari**
125 H2 **Bellata** Australia
235 L1 **Bella Unión** Uruguay
125 J3 **Bellbrook** Australia
123 E4 **Bell Cay** *reef* Australia
220 B4 **Bellefontaine** U.S.A.
221 E4 **Bellefonte** U.S.A.
216 C2 **Belle Fourche** U.S.A.
216 C2 **Belle Fourche** *r.* U.S.A.
182 G3 **Bellegarde-sur-Valserine** France
219 D7 **Belle Glade** U.S.A.
182 C3 **Belle-Île** *i.* France
207 J3 **Belle Isle** *i.* Canada
207 I3 **Belle Isle, Strait of** Canada
215 G4 **Bellemont** U.S.A.
208 A5 **Belle Plaine** U.S.A.
209 H2 **Belleterre** Canada
209 I3 **Belleville** Canada
217 D4 **Belleville** U.S.A.
213 D3 **Bellevue** *ID* U.S.A.
220 B4 **Bellevue** *OH* U.S.A.
212 B2 **Bellevue** *WA* U.S.A.
125 J3 **Bellingen** Australia
172 E2 **Bellingham** U.K.
212 B1 **Bellingham** U.S.A.
127 L2 **Bellingshausen** *research stn* Antarctica
127 I3 **Bellingshausen Sea** Antarctica
176 D7 **Bellinzona** Switz.
233 I3 **Bello** Col.
221 G3 **Bellows Falls** U.S.A.
148 B3 **Bellpat** Pak.
175 F4 **Bell Rock** *i.* U.K.
221 F5 **Belltown** U.S.A.
184 E1 **Belluno** Italy
235 J2 **Bell Ville** Arg.
196 C6 **Bellville** S. Africa
179 G2 **Belm** Germany
197 F4 **Belmont** S. Africa
174 □ **Belmont** U.K.
220 D3 **Belmont** U.S.A.
234 E1 **Belmonte** Brazil
225 G4 **Belmopan** Belize
125 J2 **Belmore, Mount** *h.* Australia
Belmullet Ireland *see* **Béal an Mhuirthead**
178 B4 **Belœil** Belgium
221 G2 **Belœil** Canada
150 E1 **Belogorsk** Russia
195 E6 **Beloha** Madag.
234 D2 **Belo Horizonte** Brazil
217 D4 **Beloit** *KS* U.S.A.
208 C4 **Beloit** *WI* U.S.A.
141 K2 **Belokurikha** Russia
186 E1 **Belomorsk** Russia
149 G5 **Belonia** India
187 F6 **Belorechensk** Russia
139 F3 **Belören** *Adıyaman* Turkey
136 D3 **Belören** *Konya* Turkey
140 D1 **Beloretsk** Russia
Belorussia *country* Europe *see* **Belarus**
195 E5 **Belo Tsiribihina** Madag.
141 J2 **Belousovka** Kazakh.
186 F1 **Beloye (abandoned)** Russia
186 F2 **Beloye, Ozero** *l.* Russia
Beloye More *sea* Russia *see* **White Sea**
186 F2 **Belozersk** Russia
220 C5 **Belpre** U.S.A.
212 E2 **Belt** U.S.A.
124 C3 **Beltana** Australia
124 B2 **Belt Bay** *salt flat* Australia
215 D3 **Belted Range** *mts* U.S.A.
217 D6 **Belton** U.S.A.
144 G2 **Belukha, Gora** *mt.* Kazakh./Russia
147 G3 **Belur** India
161 H5 **Beluran** *Sabah* Malaysia
169 P2 **Belush'ye** Russia
208 C4 **Belvidere** U.S.A.
123 D4 **Belyando** *r.* Australia
140 D2 **Belyayevka** Russia
186 H3 **Belyshevo** Russia
187 E4 **Belyy** Russia
132 I2 **Belyy, Ostrov** *i.* Russia
208 C6 **Bement** U.S.A.
216 E2 **Bemidji** U.S.A.
195 C4 **Bena Dibele** Dem. Rep. Congo
174 D2 **Ben Alder** *mt.* U.K.
125 F6 **Benalla** Australia
184 D6 **Ben Arous** Tunisia
183 N1 **Benavente** Spain
174 E3 **Ben Avon** *mt.* U.K.
175 I4 **Benbaun** *h.* Ireland
174 A3 **Benbecula** *i.* U.K.
175 J3 **Benbulben** *h.* Ireland
175 L3 **Benburb** U.K.
174 C4 **Ben Cruachan** *mt.* U.K.
212 B2 **Bend** U.S.A.
197 G5 **Bendearg** *mt.* S. Africa
125 I3 **Bendemeer** Australia
187 D6 **Bender** Moldova
194 E3 **Bender-Bayla** Somalia
125 F6 **Bendigo** Australia
125 H6 **Bendoc** Australia
195 D5 **Bene** Moz.
207 I3 **Benedict, Mount** *h.* Canada
221 I2 **Benedicta** U.S.A.
195 E6 **Benenitra** Madag.
176 G6 **Benešov** Czech Rep.
179 E6 **Bénestroff** France
184 F4 **Benevento** Italy
135 G5 **Bengal, Bay of** *sea* Asia
147 H3 **Bengaluru** India
194 C3 **Bengamisa** Dem. Rep. Congo
154 E3 **Bengbu** China
193 E1 **Benghazi** Libya
154 F3 **Beng He** *r.* China
162 B5 **Bengkalis** Indon.
163 B3 **Bengkulu** Indon.
171 K4 **Bengtsfors** Sweden
195 B5 **Benguela** Angola
174 B4 **Ben Hiant** *h.* U.K.
174 D2 **Ben Hope** *h.* U.K.
230 E6 **Beni** *r.* Bol.
194 C3 **Beni** Dem. Rep. Congo
192 B1 **Beni Abbès** Alg.
183 P3 **Benidorm** Spain
192 B1 **Beni Mellal** Morocco
192 C4 **Benin** *country* Africa
192 C4 **Benin, Bight of** *g.* Africa
192 C4 **Benin City** Nigeria
192 B1 **Beni Saf** Alg.
235 K3 **Benito Juárez** Arg.
161 I2 **Benito Soliven** Phil.
230 E4 **Benjamin Constant** Brazil
222 B2 **Benjamín Hill** Mex.
118 D2 **Benjina** Indon.
216 C3 **Benkelman** U.S.A.
174 D2 **Ben Klibreck** *h.* U.K.
174 D4 **Ben Lawers** *mt.* U.K.
125 I3 **Ben Lomond** *mt.* Australia
174 D4 **Ben Lomond** *h.* U.K.
125 G8 **Ben Lomond National Park** Australia
174 D2 **Ben Loyal** *h.* U.K.
174 D4 **Ben Lui** *mt.* U.K.
174 E3 **Ben Macdui** *mt.* U.K.
122 B3 **Benmara** Australia
174 B4 **Ben More** *h.* U.K.
174 D4 **Ben More** *mt.* U.K.
126 C6 **Benmore, Lake** N.Z.
174 D2 **Ben More Assynt** *h.* U.K.
171 M3 **Bennäs** Fin.
133 P2 **Bennetta, Ostrov** *i.* Russia
174 C4 **Ben Nevis** *mt.* U.K.
221 G3 **Bennington** U.S.A.
197 H3 **Benoni** S. Africa
193 D4 **Bénoué, Parc National de la** *nat. park* Cameroon
179 G5 **Bensheim** Germany
215 G6 **Benson** *AZ* U.S.A.
216 E2 **Benson** *MN* U.S.A.
143 E5 **Bent** Iran
163 D2 **Benta Seberang** Malaysia
220 D6 **Bent Creek** U.S.A.
151 E7 **Benteng** Indon.
118 D3 **Bentinck Island** Australia
162 A3 **Bentinck Island** Myanmar
193 E4 **Bentiu** South Sudan
173 F4 **Bentley** U.K.
221 J2 **Benton** Canada
217 E5 **Benton** *AR* U.S.A.
214 C3 **Benton** *CA* U.S.A.
219 B4 **Benton** *IL* U.S.A.
208 D4 **Benton Harbor** U.S.A.
162 C3 **Bên Tre** Vietnam
162 B5 **Bentung** Malaysia
193 D4 **Benue** *r.* Nigeria
174 D4 **Ben Vorlich** *h.* U.K.
175 I3 **Benwee Head** Ireland
174 D3 **Ben Wyvis** *mt.* U.K.
160 B3 **Benxi** *Liaoning* China
160 C3 **Benxi** *Liaoning* China
161 J5 **Beo** Indon.
Beograd Serbia *see* **Belgrade**
149 E5 **Beohari** India
192 B4 **Béoumi** Côte d'Ivoire
159 B8 **Beppu** Japan
119 H3 **Beqa** *i.* Fiji
148 C4 **Berach** *r.* India
185 H3 **Berane** Montenegro
207 G2 **Bérard, Lac** *l.* Canada
148 D5 **Berasia** India
162 A5 **Berastagi** Indon.
185 H4 **Berat** Albania
163 I3 **Beratus, Gunung** *mt.* Indon.
151 F7 **Berau, Teluk** *b.* Indon.
193 F3 **Berber** Sudan
194 E2 **Berbera** Somalia
194 B3 **Berbérati** C.A.R.
182 E1 **Berck** France
139 J1 **Berd** Armenia
133 N3 **Berdigestyakh** Russia
150 A1 **Berdsk** Russia
187 F6 **Berdyans'k** Ukr.
187 D5 **Berdychiv** Ukr.
220 A6 **Berea** U.S.A.
156 B1 **Beregovoy** Russia
187 B5 **Berehove** Ukr.
119 E2 **Bereina** P.N.G.
140 C5 **Bereket** Turkm.
141 K2 **Berel'** Kazakh.
205 J4 **Berens** *r.* Canada
205 J4 **Berens River** Canada
216 D3 **Beresford** U.S.A.
187 C5 **Berezhany** Ukr.
187 D6 **Berezivka** Ukr.
187 C5 **Berezne** Ukr.
186 G2 **Bereznik** Russia
156 B2 **Berezovka** *Amurskaya Oblast'* Russia
140 D1 **Berezovka** *Orenburgskaya Oblast'* Russia
132 H3 **Berezovo** Russia
156 D2 **Berezovyy** Russia
179 J3 **Berga** Germany
183 Q1 **Berga** Spain
185 L5 **Bergama** Turkey
184 C2 **Bergamo** Italy
171 L3 **Bergby** Sweden
179 H2 **Bergen** Germany
171 I3 **Bergen** Norway
176 F3 **Bergen auf Rügen** Germany
178 C3 **Bergen op Zoom** Neth.
182 E4 **Bergerac** France
178 C6 **Bergères-lès-Vertus** France
179 E4 **Bergheim** Germany
179 F4 **Bergisches Land** *reg.* Germany
179 F4 **Bergisch Gladbach** Germany
196 B1 **Bergland** Namibia
208 C2 **Bergland** U.S.A.
171 L3 **Bergsjö** Sweden
170 M2 **Bergsviken** Sweden
179 I5 **Bergtheim** Germany
178 A4 **Bergues** France
Bergum Neth. *see* **Burgum**

Bishrī, Jabal

197 H4 Bergville S. Africa
163 B3 Berhala, Selat sea chan. Indon.
133 R4 Beringa, Ostrov i. Russia
178 D3 Beringen Belgium
133 S3 Beringovskiy Russia
133 S4 Bering Sea Pacific Ocean
202 B3 Bering Strait Russia/U.S.A.
171 J3 Berkåk Norway
179 E2 Berkel r. Neth.
214 A3 Berkeley U.S.A.
220 D5 Berkeley Springs U.S.A.
178 D2 Berkhout Neth.
127 J3 Berkner Sub-glacial Island Antarctica
185 J3 Berkovitsa Bulg.
173 F6 Berkshire Downs hills U.K.
178 C3 Berlare Belgium
170 O1 Berlevåg Norway
179 L2 Berlin Germany
221 F5 Berlin MD U.S.A.
221 H2 Berlin NH U.S.A.
220 D5 Berlin PA U.S.A.
208 C4 Berlin WI U.S.A.
203 J2 Berlinguet Inlet Canada
220 C4 Berlin Lake U.S.A.
125 I6 Bermagui Australia
235 J4 Bermeja, Punta pt Arg.
225 D2 Bermejíllo Mex.
235 I1 Bermejo r. Arg.
232 D2 Bermejo r. Arg./Bol.
231 F8 Bermejo Bol.
223 M2 Bermuda terr. Atlantic Ocean
239 E4 Bermuda Rise sea feature N. Atlantic Ocean
176 C7 Bern Switz.
213 F5 Bernalillo U.S.A.
127 L2 Bernardo O'Higgins research stn Antarctica
232 A7 Bernardo O'Higgins, Parque Nacional nat. park Chile
235 J3 Bernasconi Arg.
179 J3 Bernburg (Saale) Germany
179 G1 Berne Germany
209 E5 Berne U.S.A.
176 C7 Berner Alpen mts Switz.
174 A3 Berneray i. Scotland U.K.
174 A4 Berneray i. Scotland U.K.
203 J2 Bernier Bay Canada
118 B4 Bernier Island Australia
176 E7 Bernina Pass Switz.
179 F5 Bernkastel-Kues Germany
195 E6 Beroroha Madag.
176 G6 Beroun Czech Rep.
176 F5 Berounka r. Czech Rep.
124 D5 Berri Australia
180 D5 Berriane Alg.
123 E8 Berridale Australia
174 E2 Berriedale U.K.
125 F5 Berrigan Australia
125 I5 Berrima Australia
183 R4 Berrouaghia Alg.
125 I5 Berry Australia
182 E3 Berry reg. France
214 A2 Berryessa, Lake U.S.A.
217 E7 Berry Islands Bahamas
196 B3 Berseba Namibia
179 F2 Bersenbrück Germany
187 D5 Bershad' Ukr.
140 E1 Bersuat Russia
163 B1 Bertam Malaysia
231 J5 Bertolínia Brazil
193 D4 Bertoua Cameroon
175 I4 Bertraghboy Bay Ireland
119 H2 Beru atoll Kiribati
Beruni Uzbek. see Beruniy
140 E4 Beruniy Uzbek.
231 F4 Beruri Brazil
125 F7 Berwick Australia
221 E4 Berwick U.S.A.
172 E2 Berwick-upon-Tweed U.K.
204 F3 Berwyn Canada
173 D5 Berwyn hills U.K.
187 E6 Beryslav Ukr.
195 E5 Besalampy Madag.
182 H3 Besançon France
140 C3 Besbay Kazakh.
141 G4 Beshariq Uzbek.
Besharyk Uzbek. see Beshariq
Beshir Turkm. see Beşir
141 F5 Beshkent Uzbek.
142 D4 Beshneh Iran
120 D1 Besikama Indon.
141 F5 Beşir Turkm.
139 H3 Beşiri Turkey
187 H7 Beslan Russia
205 H3 Besnard Lake Canada
139 F3 Besni Turkey
141 H2 Besoba Kazakh.
175 L3 Bessbrook U.K.
219 C5 Bessemer AL U.S.A.
208 B2 Bessemer MI U.S.A.
140 C3 Besshoky, Gora h. Kazakh.
140 C2 Bestamak Aktyubinskaya Oblast' Kazakh.
141 I2 Bestamak Vostochnyy Kazakhstan Kazakh.
141 H1 Bestobe Kazakh.
149 H5 Betalongchhip mt. India
195 E6 Betanty Madag.
183 L1 Betanzos Spain
193 D4 Bétaré Oya Cameroon
197 H3 Bethal S. Africa
196 B3 Bethanie Namibia
216 E3 Bethany MO U.S.A.
217 D5 Bethany OK U.S.A.
202 B3 Bethel AK U.S.A.
221 H2 Bethel ME U.S.A.
208 A6 Bethel MO U.S.A.
220 A5 Bethel OH U.S.A.
220 D4 Bethel Park U.S.A.
173 C4 Bethesda U.K.
221 E5 Bethesda MD U.S.A.
220 C4 Bethesda OH U.S.A.
197 F5 Bethesdaweg S. Africa
197 H4 Bethlehem S. Africa
221 F4 Bethlehem U.S.A.
138 E6 Bethlehem West Bank
197 F5 Bethulie S. Africa
178 A4 Béthune France
233 J2 Betijoque Venez.
195 E6 Betioky Madag.
162 B4 Betong Thai.
123 C5 Betoota (abandoned) Australia
141 G3 Betpak-Dala Kazakh.
141 G3 Betpakdala plain Kazakh.
195 E6 Betroka Madag.
138 E5 Bet She'an Israel
207 G4 Betsiamites Canada
207 G4 Betsiamites r. Canada
195 E5 Betsiboka r. Madag.
208 D3 Betsie, Point U.S.A.
158 I3 Betsukai Japan
209 E2 Betsy Lake U.S.A.
208 B5 Bettendorf U.S.A.
149 F4 Bettiah India
174 D2 Bettyhill U.K.
175 L4 Bettystown Ireland
148 D5 Betul India
163 H2 Betung Kerihun, Taman Nasional nat. park Indon./Malaysia
178 D3 Betuwe reg. Neth.
148 D4 Betwa r. India
173 D4 Betws-y-coed U.K.
179 F4 Betzdorf Germany
125 E5 Beulah Australia
208 D3 Beulah U.S.A.
173 H6 Beult r. U.K.
173 G4 Beverley U.K.
202 C4 Beverley, Lake U.S.A.
221 H3 Beverly MA U.S.A.
220 C5 Beverly OH U.S.A.
214 C4 Beverly Hills U.S.A.
205 I2 Beverly Lake Canada
179 G1 Beverstedt Germany
179 H3 Beverungen Germany
178 C2 Beverwijk Neth.
179 F5 Bexbach Germany
173 H7 Bexhill U.K.
142 D2 Beyārjomand Iran
138 C3 Bey Dağları mts Turkey
138 B1 Beykoz Turkey
192 B4 Beyla Guinea
139 K2 Beyläqan Azer.
140 C3 Beyneu Kazakh.
138 C1 Beypazarı Turkey
139 F2 Beypınarı Turkey
147 G4 Beypore India
Beyrouth Lebanon see Beirut
138 C3 Beyşehir Turkey
138 C3 Beyşehir Gölü l. Turkey
187 F6 Beysug r. Russia
156 B1 Beytonovo Russia
139 I3 Beytüşşebap Turkey
143 E3 Bezameh Iran
186 I3 Bezbozhnik Russia
186 D3 Bezhanitsy Russia
186 F3 Bezhetsk Russia
183 F5 Béziers France
148 B3 Bhabhar India
149 E4 Bhabua India
148 B5 Bhadar r. India
Bhadgaon Nepal see Bhaktapur
149 E4 Bhadohi India
148 C3 Bhadra India
147 I2 Bhadrachalam India
149 F5 Bhadrak India
147 G3 Bhadra Reservoir India
147 G3 Bhadravati India
148 A3 Bhag Pak.
148 D2 Bhaga r. India
149 F4 Bhagalpur India
149 G5 Bhagirathi r. India
148 D5 Bhainsdehi India
149 G4 Bhairab Bazar Bangl.
149 E4 Bhairawa Nepal
149 F4 Bhaktapur Nepal
147 H2 Bhalki India
151 B4 Bhamo Myanmar
147 I2 Bhamragarh India
148 C2 Bhandal India
148 D4 Bhander India
149 F6 Bhanjanagar India
148 C4 Bhanpura India
148 D5 Bhanrer Range hills India
127 K5 Bharati research stn India
148 D4 Bharatpur India
149 H4 Bhareli r. India
143 F5 Bhari r. Pak.
148 C5 Bharuch India
147 I1 Bhatapara India
147 G3 Bhatkal India
149 G5 Bhatpara India
147 H4 Bhavani India
147 H4 Bhavani r. India
148 C5 Bhavnagar India
148 C3 Bhawana Pak.
147 I2 Bhawanipatna India
197 I3 Bhekuzulu S. Africa
149 E3 Bheri r. Nepal
149 E5 Bhilai India
148 C4 Bhilwara India
147 H2 Bhima r. India
147 I2 Bhimavaram India
148 D4 Bhind India
148 C4 Bhindar India
149 E4 Bhinga India
148 C4 Bhinmal India
197 G6 Bhisho S. Africa
148 D3 Bhiwani India
149 F4 Bhojpur Nepal
147 H2 Bhongir India
197 H5 Bhongweni S. Africa
148 D5 Bhopal India
147 I2 Bhopalpatnam India
147 G2 Bhor India
149 F5 Bhuban India
149 F5 Bhubaneshwar India
148 B5 Bhuj India
148 C5 Bhusawal India
149 G4 Bhutan country Asia
148 D4 Bhuttewala India
143 E5 Bīābān mts Iran
148 C2 Biafo Glacier Pak.
151 F7 Biak Indon.
151 F7 Biak i. Indon.
177 K4 Biała Podlaska Poland
176 G4 Białogard Poland
177 K4 Białystok Poland
192 B4 Biankouma Côte d'Ivoire
160 B1 Bianzhao China
148 D5 Biaora India
183 D5 Biarritz France
142 B5 Bi'ār Tabrāk well Saudi Arabia
176 D7 Biasca Switz.
158 G3 Bibai Japan
195 B5 Bibala Angola
125 H6 Bibbenluke Australia
184 D3 Bibbiena Italy
176 D6 Biberach an der Riß Germany
149 G4 Bibiyana r. Bangl.
179 G5 Biblis Germany
138 C2 Biçer Turkey
173 F6 Bicester U.K.
125 H8 Bicheno Australia
156 D3 Bichevaya Russia
156 E1 Bichi r. Russia
187 G7 Bich'vinta Georgia
118 D3 Bickerton Island Australia
173 D7 Bickleigh U.K.
215 G2 Bicknell U.S.A.
195 B5 Bicuari, Parque Nacional do nat. park Angola
147 G2 Bid India
192 C4 Bida Nigeria
161 H5 Bidadari, Tanjung pt Sabah Malaysia
142 D4 Bīdākhavīd Iran
147 H2 Bidar India
143 E6 Bidbid Oman
221 H3 Biddeford U.S.A.
178 D2 Biddinghuizen Neth.
174 C4 Bidean nam Bian mt. U.K.
173 C6 Bideford U.K.
Bideford Bay U.K. see Barnstaple Bay
156 C3 Bidzhan Russia
177 K4 Biebrza r. Poland
179 G4 Biedenkopf Germany
177 H5 Bielawa Poland
176 C7 Biel/Bienne Switz.
179 G2 Bielefeld Germany
184 C2 Biella Italy
177 I6 Bielsko-Biała Poland
177 K4 Bielsk Podlaski Poland
179 I1 Bienenbüttel Germany
162 C3 Biên Hoa Vietnam
207 F2 Bienville, Lac l. Canada
123 D5 Bierbank Australia
197 F3 Biesiesvlei S. Africa
179 H6 Bietigheim-Bissingen Germany
178 D5 Bièvre Belgium
195 B4 Bifoun Gabon
207 I3 Big r. Canada
214 A2 Big r. U.S.A.
187 C7 Biga Turkey
138 B2 Bigadiç Turkey
185 L5 Biga Yarımadası pen. Turkey
208 D2 Big Bay U.S.A.
208 D3 Big Bay de Noc U.S.A.
215 D4 Big Bear Lake U.S.A.
212 E2 Big Belt Mountains U.S.A.
197 I3 Big Bend Swaziland
217 C6 Big Bend National Park U.S.A.
217 F5 Big Black r. U.S.A.
173 D7 Bigbury-on-Sea U.K.
219 D7 Big Cypress National Preserve U.S.A.
208 C3 Big Eau Pleine Reservoir U.S.A.
144 I2 Biger Nuur salt l. Mongolia
205 K5 Big Falls U.S.A.
205 H4 Biggar Canada
174 E5 Biggar U.K.
120 D2 Bigge Island Australia
123 F5 Biggenden Australia
204 B3 Bigger, Mount Canada
173 G5 Biggleswade U.K.
212 D2 Big Hole r. U.S.A.
212 F2 Bighorn r. U.S.A.
212 E2 Bighorn Canyon National Recreation Area park U.S.A.
212 F2 Bighorn Mountains U.S.A.
203 K3 Big Island Nunavut Canada
204 F2 Big Island N.W.T. Canada
221 J2 Big Lake U.S.A.
192 A3 Bignona Senegal
220 D6 Big Otter r. U.S.A.
214 C3 Big Pine U.S.A.
209 E4 Big Rapids U.S.A.
208 C3 Big Rib r. U.S.A.
205 H4 Big River Canada
208 D3 Big Sable Point U.S.A.
204 C2 Big Salmon r. Canada
205 J3 Big Sand Lake Canada
215 F4 Big Sandy watercourse U.S.A.
216 D2 Big Sioux r. U.S.A.
215 D2 Big Smokey Valley U.S.A.
217 C5 Big Spring U.S.A.
216 C3 Big Springs U.S.A.
220 B6 Big Stone Gap U.S.A.
214 B3 Big Sur U.S.A.
212 E2 Big Timber U.S.A.
206 C3 Big Trout Lake Canada
206 C3 Big Trout Lake l. Canada
215 G3 Big Water U.S.A.
209 H3 Bigwin Canada
184 F2 Bihać Bos. & Herz.
149 F4 Bihar state India
149 F4 Bihar Sharif India
177 K7 Bihor, Vârful mt. Romania
158 I3 Bihoro Japan
140 C3 Biikzhal Kazakh.
192 A3 Bijagós, Arquipélago dos is Guinea-Bissau
148 C4 Bijainagar India
147 I2 Bijapur Chhattisgarh India
Bijapur Karnataka India see Vijayapura
142 B3 Bījār Iran
185 H2 Bijeljina Bos. & Herz.
185 H3 Bijelo Polje Montenegro
155 B5 Bijie China
149 G4 Bijni India
148 D3 Bijnor India
148 B3 Bijnot Pak.
142 C5 Bijrān, Khashm h. Saudi Arabia
148 C3 Bikaner India
150 F2 Bikin Russia
158 D1 Bikin r. Russia
117 F2 Bikini atoll Marshall Is
195 B4 Bikoro Dem. Rep. Congo
154 B3 Bikou China
148 C4 Bilara India
147 I1 Bilaspur India
139 L2 Biläsuvar Azer.
187 D5 Bila Tserkva Ukr.
162 A2 Bilauktaung Range mts Myanmar/Thai.
183 O1 Bilbao Spain
138 C6 Bilbays Egypt
185 H3 Bileća Bos. & Herz.
138 B1 Bilecik Turkey
177 K5 Biłgoraj Poland
195 D4 Bilharamulo Tanz.
187 D6 Bilhorod-Dnistrovs'kyy Ukr.
194 C3 Bili Dem. Rep. Congo
133 R3 Bilibino Russia
161 J4 Biliran i. Phil.
160 B4 Biliu He r. China
213 F3 Bill U.S.A.
121 A5 Billabalong Australia
173 H6 Billericay U.K.
120 D3 Billiluna Australia
172 F3 Billingham U.K.
212 E2 Billings U.S.A.
173 E7 Bill of Portland hd U.K.
215 F4 Bill Williams r. U.S.A.
215 F4 Bill Williams Mountain U.S.A.
193 D3 Bilma Niger
193 D3 Bilma, Grand Erg de des. Niger
119 F4 Biloela Australia
187 E6 Bilohirs'k Crimea
177 M5 Bilohir"ya Ukr.
147 H3 Biloli India
187 F5 Bilolutsʼk Ukr.
187 E5 Bilopillya Ukr.
187 F5 Bilovods'k Ukr.
219 B6 Biloxi U.S.A.
118 D4 Bilpa Morea Claypan salt flat Australia
174 E5 Bilston U.K.
193 E3 Biltine Chad
162 A1 Bilugyun Island Myanmar
224 I5 Bilwascarma Nicaragua
187 I4 Bilyarsk Russia
187 D6 Bilyayivka Ukr.
178 D4 Bilzen Belgium
125 H5 Bimberi, Mount Australia
194 B3 Bimbo C.A.R.
219 E7 Bimini Islands Bahamas
148 D4 Bina-Etawa India
151 E7 Binaija, Gunung mt. Indon.
139 F2 Binboğa Daği mt. Turkey
125 G1 Bindebango Australia
149 E4 Bindki India
125 H1 Bindle Australia
195 B4 Bindu Dem. Rep. Congo
195 D5 Bindura Zimbabwe
183 Q2 Binéfar Spain
125 I2 Bingara N.S.W. Australia
125 F2 Bingara Qld Australia
122 B2 Bing Bong Australia
154 B2 Bingcaowan China
179 F5 Bingen am Rhein Germany
192 B4 Bingerville Côte d'Ivoire
221 I2 Bingham U.S.A.
221 F3 Binghamton U.S.A.
139 H2 Bingöl Turkey
139 H2 Bingol Dağı mt. Turkey
155 C6 Binh Gia Vietnam
Binh Sơn Vietnam see Châu Ô
149 H4 Bini India
147 I1 Binika India
162 A5 Binjai Indon.
142 D5 Bin Mürkhan well U.A.E.
125 H3 Binnaway Australia
162 C5 Bintan i. Indon.
161 I3 Bintuan Phil.
163 B3 Bintuhan Indon.
163 H2 Bintulu Sarawak Malaysia
156 B3 Binxian Heilongjiang China
154 C3 Binxian Shaanxi China
125 G5 Binya Australia
155 C6 Binyang China
154 F2 Binzhou China
235 H3 Biobío admin. reg. Chile
235 H3 Biobío r. Chile
184 F3 Biograd na Moru Croatia
192 C4 Bioko i. Equat. Guinea
185 G3 Biokovo mts Croatia
156 D2 Bira Russia
193 D2 Birāk Libya
156 C2 Birakan Russia
136 B5 Bi'r al Khamsah well Egypt
139 H5 Bi'r al Mulūsi Iraq
136 B5 Bi'r al Qaṭrānī well Egypt
Bi'r an Nuşf well Egypt see Bi'r an Nuşş
136 B5 Bi'r an Nuşş well Egypt
194 C2 Birao C.A.R.
136 B5 Bi'r ar Rābiyah well Egypt
138 D6 Bi'r ar Rummānah Egypt
140 E4 Birata Turkm.
149 F4 Biratnagar Nepal
136 B5 Bi'r Baylī well Egypt
139 G3 Bi'r Buṭaymān Syria
205 G3 Birch r. Canada
205 H4 Birch Hills Canada
125 E5 Birchip Australia
204 F4 Birch Island Canada
205 K4 Birch Lake Canada
205 G3 Birch Mountains Canada
205 I4 Birch River Canada
Birdaard Neth. see Burdaard
Bîr Dignâsh well Egypt see Bi'r Diqnāsh
136 B5 Bi'r Diqnāsh well Egypt
127 J1 Bird Island S. Georgia
215 G2 Birdseye U.S.A.
118 D4 Birdsville Australia
139 F3 Birecik Turkey
Bîr el Iṣṭabl well Egypt see Bi'r Iṣṭabl
Bîr el Khamsa well Egypt see Bi'r al Khamsah
Bîr el Nuşş well Egypt see Bi'r an Nuşş
Bîr el Qaṭrâni well Egypt see Bi'r al Qaṭrānī
Bîr el Râbia well Egypt see Bi'r ar Rābiyah
193 E3 Bir en Natrûn well Sudan
163 E1 Bireun Indon.
137 E5 Bi'r Fajr well Saudi Arabia
136 B5 Bi'r Fu'ād well Egypt
143 F5 Bīrg, Kūh-e mts Iran
142 B6 Bi'r Ghawdah well Saudi Arabia
Bi'r Ibn Hirmās Saudi Arabia see Al Bi'r
234 B3 Birigui Brazil
136 B5 Bi'r Iṣṭabl well Egypt
143 E3 Bīrjand Iran
136 B5 Bi'r Jubnī well Libya
139 J6 Birkát Hamad well Iraq
179 F5 Birkenfeld Germany
173 D4 Birkenhead U.K.
184 F7 Birkirkara Malta
139 J3 Bīrmē Iraq
121 E5 Birksgate Range hills Australia
192 B2 Bir Lahlou W. Sahara
141 H3 Birlik Zhambylskaya Oblast' Kazakh.
141 H4 Birlik Zhambylskaya Oblast' Kazakh.
173 F5 Birmingham U.K.
219 C5 Birmingham U.S.A.
192 A2 Bîr Mogreïn Mauritania
138 B6 Bi'r Nāḥid oasis Egypt
192 C3 Birnin-Kebbi Nigeria
192 C3 Birnin Konni Niger
150 F2 Birobidzhan Russia
136 B5 Bi'r Qaşīr as Sirr well Egypt
175 K4 Birr Ireland
125 G2 Birrie r. Australia
120 E3 Birrindudu Australia
139 I5 Bi'r Sābil Iraq
174 E1 Birsay U.K.
140 D2 Birshogyr Kazakh.
173 F5 Birstall U.K.
179 H4 Birstein Germany
138 E7 Bi'r Ṭābah Egypt
122 C2 Birthday Mountain h. Australia
205 I4 Birtle Canada
149 H3 Biru China
147 G3 Birur India
171 N4 Biržai Lith.
145 E6 Bisalpur India
215 H6 Bisbee U.S.A.
182 B4 Biscay, Bay of sea France/Spain
239 I3 Biscay Abyssal Plain sea feature N. Atlantic Ocean
219 D7 Biscayne National Park U.S.A.
176 F7 Bischofshofen Austria
127 I2 Biscoe Islands Antarctica
209 F2 Biscotasi Lake Canada
209 F2 Biscotasing Canada
155 C4 Bishan China
139 L5 Bīsheh Iran
141 H4 Bishkek Kyrg.
149 F5 Bishnupur India
214 C3 Bishop U.S.A.
172 F3 Bishop Auckland U.K.
173 H6 Bishop's Stortford U.K.
139 G4 Bishrī, Jabal hills Syria

Bishui

150 E1 **Bishui** China
192 C1 **Biskra** Alg.
161 J4 **Bislig** Phil.
216 C2 **Bismarck** U.S.A.
119 E2 **Bismarck Archipelago** *is* P.N.G.
119 E2 **Bismarck Range** *mts* P.N.G.
119 E2 **Bismarck Sea** P.N.G.
179 J2 **Bismark (Altmark)** Germany
139 H3 **Bismil** Turkey
171 J3 **Bismo** Norway
139 K4 **Bīsotūn** Iran
171 L3 **Bispgården** Sweden
179 I1 **Bispingen** Germany
183 Q4 **Bissa, Djebel** *mt.* Alg.
Bissagos Islands *is* Guinea-Bissau *see* **Bijagós, Arquipélago dos**
147 I2 **Bissamcuttak** India
192 A3 **Bissau** Guinea-Bissau
193 D4 **Bissaula** Nigeria
205 J4 **Bissett** Canada
204 F3 **Bistcho Lake** Canada
177 L7 **Bistrița** Romania
177 M7 **Bistrița** *r.* Romania
179 E5 **Bitburg** Germany
179 F5 **Bitche** France
140 B2 **Bitik** Kazakh.
193 D3 **Bitkine** Chad
139 I2 **Bitlis** Turkey
185 I4 **Bitola** Macedonia
185 G4 **Bitonto** Italy
142 B6 **Bitrān, Jabal** *h.* Saudi Arabia
145 D9 **Bitra Par** *reef* India
215 H2 **Bitter Creek** *r.* U.S.A.
179 K3 **Bitterfeld** Germany
196 C5 **Bitterfontein** S. Africa
138 D6 **Bitter Lakes** Egypt
212 D2 **Bitterroot Range** *mts* U.S.A.
179 J2 **Bittkau** Germany
187 G5 **Bityug** *r.* Russia
193 D3 **Biu** Nigeria
159 D7 **Biwa-ko** *l.* Japan
141 K1 **Biya** *r.* Russia
154 D3 **Biyang** China
194 E2 **Bīye K'obē Polīs T'abīya** Eth.
141 K1 **Biysk** Russia
197 H5 **Bizana** S. Africa
192 C1 **Bizerte** Tunisia
170 A2 **Bjargtangar** *hd* Iceland
171 L3 **Bjästa** Sweden
185 G2 **Bjelovar** Croatia
170 L1 **Bjerkvik** Norway
171 J4 **Bjerringbro** Denmark
171 L3 **Björklinge** Sweden
171 J3 **Bjorli** Norway
171 L3 **Björna** Sweden
132 C2 **Bjørnøya** *i.* Svalbard
171 L3 **Bjurholm** Sweden
192 B3 **Bla** Mali
174 B3 **Bla Bheinn** *h.* U.K.
217 F5 **Black** *r. AR* U.S.A.
215 H5 **Black** *r. AZ* U.S.A.
209 F4 **Black** *r. MI* U.S.A.
208 B3 **Black** *r. WI* U.S.A.
155 B6 **Black** *r.* Vietnam
119 E4 **Blackall** Australia
208 C1 **Black Bay** Canada
206 B3 **Blackbear** *r.* Canada
173 F6 **Black Bourton** U.K.
122 C3 **Blackbull** Australia
173 E4 **Blackburn** U.K.
125 J1 **Blackbutt** Australia
214 A2 **Black Butte** *mt.* U.S.A.
214 A2 **Black Butte Lake** U.S.A.
215 E4 **Black Canyon** *gorge* U.S.A.
215 F4 **Black Canyon City** U.S.A.
123 E4 **Blackdown Tableland National Park** Australia
216 E2 **Blackduck** U.S.A.
205 G4 **Blackfalds** Canada
213 D3 **Blackfoot** U.S.A.
212 D2 **Black Foot** *r.* U.S.A.
176 D6 **Black Forest** *mts* Germany
216 C2 **Black Hills** U.S.A.
174 D3 **Black Isle** *pen.* U.K.
205 H3 **Black Lake** Canada
205 H3 **Black Lake** *l.* Canada
209 E3 **Black Lake** *l.* U.S.A.
215 G3 **Black Mesa** *ridge* U.S.A.
173 D6 **Black Mountain** *hills* U.K.
215 D4 **Black Mountain** U.S.A.
173 D6 **Black Mountains** U.K.
215 E4 **Black Mountains** U.S.A.
196 C1 **Black Nossob** *watercourse* Namibia
155 □ **Black Point** *Hong Kong* China
173 D4 **Blackpool** U.K.
213 C3 **Black Rock Desert** U.S.A.
220 C6 **Blacksburg** U.S.A.
187 E7 **Black Sea** Asia/Europe
175 H3 **Blacksod Bay** Ireland
175 L5 **Blackstairs Mountain** *h.* Ireland
175 L5 **Blackstairs Mountains** Ireland
221 E6 **Blackstone** U.S.A.
125 I3 **Black Sugarloaf** *mt.* Australia
207 I3 **Black Tickle** Canada
192 B4 **Black Volta** *r.* Africa
123 E4 **Blackwater** Australia
175 L5 **Blackwater** Ireland
175 L4 **Blackwater** *r. Cavan/Meath* Ireland
175 K5 **Blackwater** *r.* Ireland
175 L3 **Blackwater** *r.* Ireland/U.K.
173 H6 **Blackwater** *r.* U.K.
221 E6 **Blackwater** *r.* U.S.A.
204 E2 **Blackwater Lake** Canada
174 D4 **Blackwater Reservoir** U.K.
217 D4 **Blackwell** U.S.A.
118 B5 **Blackwood** *r.* Australia
123 D4 **Blackwood National Park** Australia
123 C4 **Bladensburg National Park** Australia
173 D6 **Blaenavon** U.K.
187 G6 **Blagodarnyy** Russia
185 J3 **Blagoevgrad** Bulg.
141 I1 **Blagoveshchenka** Russia
150 E1 **Blagoveshchensk** Russia
221 E4 **Blain** U.S.A.
212 B1 **Blaine** U.S.A.
205 H4 **Blaine Lake** Canada
216 D3 **Blair** *NE* U.S.A.
208 B3 **Blair** *WI* U.S.A.
123 D4 **Blair Athol** Australia
174 E4 **Blair Atholl** U.K.
174 E4 **Blairgowrie** U.K.
219 C6 **Blakely** U.S.A.
173 I5 **Blakeney** U.K.
208 C1 **Blake Point** U.S.A.
163 H4 **Blambangan, Semenanjung** *pen.* Indon.
182 H4 **Blanc, Mont** *mt.* France/Italy
235 K3 **Blanca, Bahía** *b.* Arg.
235 I3 **Blanca de la Totora, Sierra** *hills* Arg.
213 F4 **Blanca Peak** U.S.A.
124 C2 **Blanche, Lake** *salt flat S.A.* Australia
121 C4 **Blanche, Lake** *salt flat W.A.* Australia
220 B5 **Blanchester** U.S.A.
124 C5 **Blanchetown** Australia
235 I1 **Blanco** *r.* Arg.
231 F6 **Blanco** *r.* Bol.
224 H6 **Blanco, Cabo** *c.* Costa Rica
213 A3 **Blanco, Cape** U.S.A.
207 I3 **Blanc-Sablon** Canada
125 G4 **Bland** *r.* Australia
170 B2 **Blanda** *r.* Iceland
173 E7 **Blandford Forum** U.K.
215 H3 **Blanding** U.S.A.
183 R2 **Blanes** Spain
209 E2 **Blaney Park** U.S.A.
162 □ **Blangah, Telok** Sing.
162 A5 **Blangkejeren** Indon.
178 B3 **Blankenberge** Belgium
179 E4 **Blankenheim** Germany
233 K2 **Blanquilla, Isla** *i.* Venez.
177 H6 **Blansko** Czech Rep.
195 D5 **Blantyre** Malawi
175 J6 **Blarney** Ireland
179 H5 **Blaufelden** Germany
170 L2 **Blåviksjön** Sweden
125 H4 **Blayney** Australia
120 E2 **Blaze, Point** Australia
179 I1 **Bleckede** Germany
126 D4 **Blenheim** N.Z.
173 F6 **Blenheim Palace** *tourist site* U.K.
179 E3 **Blerick** Neth.
175 L4 **Blessington Lakes** Ireland
173 G5 **Bletchley** U.K.
192 C1 **Blida** Alg.
179 F5 **Blies** *r.* Germany
119 H3 **Bligh Water** *b.* Fiji
209 F2 **Blind River** Canada
124 B3 **Blinman** Australia
213 D3 **Bliss** U.S.A.
209 F5 **Blissfield** U.S.A.
221 H4 **Block Island** U.S.A.
221 H4 **Block Island Sound** *sea chan.* U.S.A.
197 G4 **Bloemfontein** S. Africa
197 F3 **Bloemhof** S. Africa
197 F3 **Bloemhof Dam** S. Africa
179 H3 **Blomberg** Germany
170 B2 **Blönduós** Iceland
121 E5 **Bloods Range** *mts* Australia
221 E5 **Bloodsworth Island** U.S.A.
205 J4 **Bloodvein** *r.* Canada
175 J2 **Bloody Foreland** *pt* Ireland
209 I4 **Bloomfield** Canada
208 A5 **Bloomfield** *IA* U.S.A.
219 C4 **Bloomfield** *IN* U.S.A.
213 E4 **Bloomfield** *NM* U.S.A.
208 C5 **Bloomington** *IL* U.S.A.
219 C4 **Bloomington** *IN* U.S.A.
216 E2 **Bloomington** *MN* U.S.A.
221 E4 **Bloomsburg** U.S.A.
221 E4 **Blossburg** U.S.A.
203 P3 **Blosseville Kyst** *coastal area* Greenland
197 H1 **Blouberg** S. Africa
173 F5 **Bloxham** U.K.
215 H5 **Blue** *watercourse* U.S.A.
215 G1 **Bluebell** U.S.A.
215 G2 **Blue Bell Knoll** *mt.* U.S.A.
216 E3 **Blue Earth** U.S.A.
220 C6 **Bluefield** U.S.A.
224 I5 **Bluefields** Nicaragua
221 I2 **Blue Hill** U.S.A.
209 H5 **Blue Knob** *h.* U.S.A.
215 H1 **Blue Mountain** U.S.A.
221 F3 **Blue Mountain Lake** U.S.A.
197 G4 **Blue Mountain Pass** Lesotho
125 I4 **Blue Mountains** Australia
212 C2 **Blue Mountains** U.S.A.
125 I4 **Blue Mountains National Park** Australia
193 F3 **Blue Nile** *r.* Sudan *alt.* **Ābay Wenz (Ethiopia),** *alt.* **Azraq, Bahr el (Sudan)**
202 G3 **Bluenose Lake** Canada
219 C5 **Blue Ridge** U.S.A.
220 D6 **Blue Ridge** *mts* U.S.A.
204 F4 **Blue River** Canada
215 D2 **Blue Springs** U.S.A.
175 J3 **Blue Stack** *h.* Ireland
175 J3 **Blue Stack Mountains** Ireland
220 C6 **Bluestone Lake** U.S.A.
126 B7 **Bluff** N.Z.
215 H3 **Bluff** U.S.A.
155 □ **Bluff Island** *Hong Kong* China
121 B7 **Bluff Knoll** *mt.* Australia
209 E5 **Bluffton** *IN* U.S.A.
220 B4 **Bluffton** *OH* U.S.A.
233 G3 **Blumenau** Brazil
216 C2 **Blunt** U.S.A.
213 B3 **Bly** U.S.A.
124 C4 **Blyth** Australia
172 F2 **Blyth** *England* U.K.
173 H5 **Blyth** *England* U.K.
215 E5 **Blythe** U.S.A.
217 F5 **Blytheville** U.S.A.
171 J4 **Bø** Norway
192 A4 **Bo** Sierra Leone
161 I3 **Boac** Phil.
224 H5 **Boaco** Nicaragua
231 J5 **Boa Esperança, Açude** *resr* Brazil
154 D3 **Bo'ai** *Henan* China
155 C6 **Bo'ai** *Yunnan* China
194 B3 **Boali** C.A.R.
197 J3 **Boane** Moz.
220 C4 **Boardman** U.S.A.
197 F1 **Boatlaname** Botswana
125 G1 **Boatman** Australia
231 K5 **Boa Viagem** Brazil
233 L4 **Boa Vista** Brazil
192 □ **Boa Vista** *i.* Cape Verde
125 G4 **Bobadah** Australia
155 D6 **Bobai** China
195 E5 **Bobaomby, Tanjona** *c.* Madag.
147 I2 **Bobbili** India
192 B3 **Bobo-Dioulasso** Burkina Faso
195 C6 **Bobonong** Botswana
141 G4 **Boboyob, Gora** *mt.* Uzbek.
187 G5 **Bobrov** Russia
187 D5 **Bobrovytsya** Ukr.
187 E5 **Bobrynets'** Ukr.
195 E6 **Boby** *mt.* Madag.
233 K2 **Boca del Pao** Venez.
223 L7 **Boca de Macareo** Venez.
230 E5 **Boca do Acre** Brazil
231 H4 **Boca do Jari** Brazil
233 L2 **Boca Grande** *r. mouth* Venez.
234 D2 **Bocaiúva** Brazil
194 B3 **Bocaranga** C.A.R.
219 D7 **Boca Raton** U.S.A.
224 I6 **Bocas del Toro** Panama
177 J6 **Bochnia** Poland
179 E3 **Bocholt** Germany
179 F3 **Bochum** Germany
Bochum S. Africa *see* **Senwabarwana**
179 I2 **Bockenem** Germany
233 J2 **Boconó** Venez.
233 J2 **Boconó** *r.* Venez.
224 C2 **Bocoyna** Mex.
194 B3 **Boda** C.A.R.
125 I6 **Bodalla** Australia
121 B6 **Bodallin** Australia
150 D1 **Bodaybo** Russia
217 E5 **Bodcau Reservoir** U.S.A.
175 G3 **Boddam** U.K.
179 J3 **Bode** *r.* Germany
214 A2 **Bodega Head** U.S.A.
193 D3 **Bodélé** *reg.* Chad
170 M2 **Boden** Sweden
173 E5 **Bodenham** U.K.
Bodensee *l.* Germany/Switz. *see* **Constance, Lake**
179 I2 **Bodenteich** Germany
179 H3 **Bodenwerder** Germany
147 H2 **Bodhan** India
149 F4 **Bodh Gaya** India
147 H4 **Bodinayakkanur** India
173 C7 **Bodmin** U.K.
173 C7 **Bodmin Moor** *moorland* U.K.
170 K2 **Bodø** Norway
185 L6 **Bodrum** Turkey
178 C3 **Boechout** Belgium
195 C4 **Boende** Dem. Rep. Congo
192 A3 **Boffa** Guinea
Bogalay Myanmar *see* **Bogale**
145 I8 **Bogale** Myanmar
217 F6 **Bogalusa** U.S.A.
125 G3 **Bogan** *r.* Australia
192 B3 **Bogandé** Burkina Faso
125 G4 **Bogan Gate** Australia
186 I3 **Bogatyye Saby** Russia
138 E2 **Boğazlıyan** Turkey
149 F3 **Bogcang Zangbo** *r.* China
144 J3 **Bogd** Mongolia
140 C1 **Bogdanovka** Russia
150 A2 **Bogda Shan** *mts* China
140 E3 **Bogen** Kazakh.
141 H1 **Bogenbay** Kazakh.
125 I2 **Boggabilla** Australia
125 I3 **Boggabri** Australia
175 I5 **Boggeragh Mountains** Ireland
183 R5 **Boghar** Alg.
173 G7 **Bognor Regis** U.K.
161 J4 **Bogo** Phil.
141 G1 **Bogodukhovka** Kazakh.
175 K4 **Bog of Allen** *reg.* Ireland
187 F4 **Bogolyubovo** Russia
125 G6 **Bogong, Mount** Australia
158 D2 **Bogopol'** Russia
163 G4 **Bogor** Indon.
186 G3 **Bogorodsk** Russia
156 F1 **Bogorodskoye** *Khabarovskiy Kray* Russia
186 I3 **Bogorodskoye** *Kirovskaya Oblast'* Russia
233 I3 **Bogotá** Col.
150 A1 **Bogotol** Russia
149 G4 **Bogra** Bangl.
149 H3 **Bogu** India
133 L4 **Boguchanskoye Vodokhranilishche** *resr* Russia
133 K4 **Boguchany** Russia
187 G5 **Boguchar** Russia
192 A3 **Bogué** Mauritania
154 F2 **Bo Hai** *g.* China
160 A4 **Bohai Haixia** *sea chan.* China
182 F2 **Bohain-en-Vermandois** France
154 E2 **Bohai Wan** *b.* China
179 K3 **Böhlen** Germany
197 H4 **Bohlokong** S. Africa
179 K5 **Böhmer Wald** *mts* Germany
179 G2 **Bohmte** Germany
187 E5 **Bohodukhiv** Ukr.
161 J4 **Bohol** *i.* Phil.
161 J4 **Bohol Sea** Phil.
161 I4 **Bohol Strait** Phil.
Böhöt Mongolia *see* **Öndörshil**
135 G2 **Bohu** China
187 D5 **Bohuslav** Ukr.
235 D4 **Boi, Ponta do** *pt* Brazil
221 F4 **Boiceville** U.S.A.
197 E4 **Boichoko** S. Africa
197 G3 **Boikhutso** S. Africa
120 C3 **Boileau, Cape** Australia
231 G4 **Boim** Brazil
149 H5 **Boinu** *r.* Myanmar
234 E1 **Boipeba, Ilha** *i.* Brazil
234 C2 **Bois** *r.* Brazil
202 F3 **Bois, Lac des** *l.* Canada
209 E3 **Bois Blanc Island** U.S.A.
213 C3 **Boise** U.S.A.
217 C4 **Boise City** U.S.A.
205 I5 **Boissevain** Canada
197 F3 **Boitumelong** S. Africa
179 I1 **Boizenburg/Elbe** Germany
161 I2 **Bojeador, Cape** Phil.
143 E2 **Bojnūrd** Iran
149 H4 **Bokajan** India
140 E4 **Bo'kantov tog'lari** *hills* Uzbek.
149 F5 **Bokaro** India
195 B4 **Bokatola** Dem. Rep. Congo
192 A3 **Boké** Guinea
141 J2 **Boke** Kazakh.
195 C4 **Bokele** Dem. Rep. Congo
125 G2 **Bokhara** *r.* Australia
171 I4 **Boknafjorden** *sea chan.* Norway
141 I4 **Bökönbaev** Kyrg.
193 D3 **Bokoro** Chad
187 G5 **Bokovskaya** Russia
186 E3 **Boksitogorsk** Russia
196 D3 **Bokspits** Botswana
156 E2 **Boktor** Russia
140 D5 **Bokurdak** Turkm.
195 C4 **Bolaiti** Dem. Rep. Congo
192 A3 **Bolama** Guinea-Bissau
148 A3 **Bolan** *r.* Pak.
Bolangir India *see* **Balangir**
148 A3 **Bolan Pass** Pak.
182 E2 **Bolbec** France
142 C4 **Boldājī** Iran
179 L1 **Boldekow** Germany
140 D4 **Boldumsaz** Turkm.
141 J3 **Bole** China
192 B4 **Bole** Ghana
195 B4 **Boleko** Dem. Rep. Congo
156 D2 **Bolen** Russia
192 B3 **Bolgatanga** Ghana
187 D6 **Bolhrad** Ukr.
158 B2 **Boli** China
195 B4 **Bolia** Dem. Rep. Congo
170 M2 **Boliden** Sweden
161 H2 **Bolinao** Phil.
185 K2 **Bolintin-Vale** Romania
233 H3 **Bolívar** Col.
230 C5 **Bolívar** Peru
217 E4 **Bolivar** *MO* U.S.A.
219 B5 **Bolivar** *TN* U.S.A.
233 J2 **Bolívar, Pico** *mt.* Venez.
230 E7 **Bolivia** *country* S. America
138 E3 **Bolkar Dağları** *mts* Turkey
187 F4 **Bolkhov** Russia
209 F1 **Bolkow** Canada
182 G4 **Bollène** France
171 L3 **Bollnäs** Sweden
125 G2 **Bollon** Australia
171 L3 **Bollstabruk** Sweden
171 K4 **Bolmen** *l.* Sweden
187 H7 **Bolnisi** Georgia
195 B4 **Bolobo** Dem. Rep. Congo
161 I5 **Bolod Islands** Phil.
184 D2 **Bologna** Italy
177 O2 **Bologovo** Russia
186 E3 **Bologoye** Russia
197 F4 **Bolokanang** S. Africa
194 B3 **Bolomba** Dem. Rep. Congo
156 E2 **Bolon'** Russia
225 G3 **Bolonchén de Rejón** Mex.
161 I5 **Bolong** Phil.
133 J4 **Bolotnoye** Russia
149 F5 **Bolpur** India
184 D3 **Bolsena, Lago di** *l.* Italy
177 J3 **Bol'shakovo** Russia
140 B1 **Bol'shaya Chernigovka** Russia
141 F1 **Bol'shaya Churakovka** Kazakh.
140 B1 **Bol'shaya Glushitsa** Russia
170 P2 **Bol'shaya Imandra, Ozero** *l.* Russia
140 B1 **Bol'shaya Kinel'** *r.* Russia
187 G6 **Bol'shaya Martynovka** Russia
141 I2 **Bol'shaya Vladimirovka** Kazakh.
141 H1 **Bol'shegrivskoye** Russia
133 L2 **Bol'shevik, Ostrov** *i.* Russia
169 Q2 **Bol'shezemel'skaya Tundra** *lowland* Russia
140 D3 **Bol'shiye Barsuki, Peski** *des.* Kazakh.
186 H2 **Bol'shiye Chirki** Russia
140 B3 **Bol'shiye Peshnyye, Ostrova** *is* Kazakh.
140 D2 **Bol'shoy Ik** *r.* Russia
140 B2 **Bol'shoy Irgiz** *r.* Russia
158 C3 **Bol'shoy Kamen'** Russia
Bol'shoy Kavkaz *mts* Asia/Europe *see* **Caucasus**
187 I5 **Bol'shoy Uzen'** *r.* Russia
178 D1 **Bolsward** Neth.
173 E4 **Bolton** U.K.
220 B6 **Bolton** U.S.A.
138 C1 **Bolu** Turkey
170 B1 **Bolungarvík** Iceland
155 E6 **Boluo** China
138 C2 **Bolvadin** Turkey
184 D1 **Bolzano** Italy
195 B4 **Boma** Dem. Rep. Congo
125 I5 **Bomaderry** Australia
125 H6 **Bombala** Australia
Bombay India *see* **Mumbai**
151 F7 **Bomberai, Semenanjung** *pen.* Indon.
230 E5 **Bom Comércio** Brazil
234 D2 **Bom Despacho** Brazil
149 H4 **Bomdila** India
149 H3 **Bomi** China
234 D1 **Bom Jesus da Lapa** Brazil
234 E3 **Bom Jesus do Itabapoana** Brazil
171 I4 **Bømlo** *i.* Norway
193 D1 **Bon, Cap** *c.* Tunisia
142 B2 **Bonāb** *Āzarbāyjān-e Sharqī* Iran
139 L3 **Bonāb** *Zanjān* Iran
221 E6 **Bon Air** U.S.A.
223 K6 **Bonaire** *i.* Caribbean Sea
224 H5 **Bonanza** Nicaragua
118 C3 **Bonaparte Archipelago** *is* Australia
174 D3 **Bonar Bridge** U.K.
207 J4 **Bonavista** Canada
207 J4 **Bonavista Bay** Canada
124 A3 **Bon Bon** Australia
175 F5 **Bonchester Bridge** U.K.
194 C3 **Bondo** Dem. Rep. Congo
161 I3 **Bondoc Peninsula** Phil.
192 B4 **Bondoukou** Côte d'Ivoire
151 E7 **Bone, Teluk** *b.* Indon.
208 A3 **Bone Lake** U.S.A.
179 F3 **Bönen** Germany
151 E7 **Bonerate, Kepulauan** *is* Indon.
174 E4 **Bo'ness** U.K.
234 D2 **Bonfinópolis de Minas** Brazil
194 D3 **Bonga** Eth.
161 I3 **Bongabong** Phil.
149 G4 **Bongaigaon** India
194 C3 **Bongandanga** Dem. Rep. Congo
196 H3 **Bongani** S. Africa
161 H5 **Bongao** Phil.
149 G3 **Bong Co** *l.* China
161 J5 **Bongo** *i.* Phil.
194 C3 **Bongo, Massif des** *mts* C.A.R.
195 E5 **Bongolava** *mts* Madag.
193 D3 **Bongor** Chad
192 B4 **Bongouanou** Côte d'Ivoire
163 D2 **Bông Sơn** Vietnam
178 C3 **Bonheiden** Belgium
184 C4 **Bonifacio** *Corsica* France
184 C4 **Bonifacio, Strait of** France/Italy
151 G4 **Bonin Islands** Japan
234 A3 **Bonito** Brazil
179 F4 **Bonn** Germany
170 K2 **Bonnåsjøen** Norway
212 C1 **Bonners Ferry** U.S.A.
182 H3 **Bonneville** France
124 D6 **Bonney, Lake** Australia
118 B5 **Bonnie Rock** Australia
174 E5 **Bonnyrigg** U.K.
205 G4 **Bonnyville** Canada
161 H4 **Bonobono** Phil.
184 C4 **Bonorva** *Sardinia* Italy
125 I2 **Bonshaw** Australia
196 D7 **Bontebok National Park** S. Africa
192 A4 **Bonthe** Sierra Leone
161 I2 **Bontoc** Phil.
163 I4 **Bontosunggu** Indon.
197 F6 **Bontrug** S. Africa
197 G1 **Bonwapitse** Botswana
215 H2 **Book Cliffs** *ridge* U.S.A.
125 E4 **Boolaboolka Lake** *imp. l.* Australia
124 C4 **Booleroo Centre** Australia
175 K5 **Booley Hills** Ireland
125 F4 **Booligal** Australia
125 H2 **Boomi** Australia
125 J1 **Boonah** Australia
216 E3 **Boone** *IA* U.S.A.

177 H6 **Brno** Czech Rep.
219 D5 **Broad** *r.* U.S.A.
221 F3 **Broadalbin** U.S.A.
121 C6 **Broad Arrow (abandoned)** Australia
206 E3 **Broadback** *r.* Canada
125 F6 **Broadford** Australia
175 J5 **Broadford** Ireland
174 C3 **Broadford** U.K.
174 E5 **Broad Law** *h.* U.K.
122 A3 **Broadmere** Australia
123 E4 **Broad Sound** *sea chan.* Australia
173 I6 **Broadstairs** U.K.
212 F2 **Broadus** U.S.A.
205 I4 **Broadview** Canada
125 J2 **Broadwater** Australia
216 C3 **Broadwater** U.S.A.
126 D1 **Broadwood** N.Z.
171 M4 **Brocēni** Latvia
205 I3 **Brochet** Canada
205 I3 **Brochet, Lac** *l.* Canada
179 I3 **Brocken** *mt.* Germany
202 G2 **Brock Island** Canada
121 B4 **Brockman, Mount** Australia
221 E3 **Brockport** U.S.A.
221 H3 **Brockton** U.S.A.
209 J3 **Brockville** Canada
209 F4 **Brockway** *MI* U.S.A.
220 D4 **Brockway** *PA* U.S.A.
203 J2 **Brodeur Peninsula** Canada
208 C4 **Brodhead** U.S.A.
174 C5 **Brodick** U.K.
177 I4 **Brodnica** Poland
187 C5 **Brody** Ukr.
148 C1 **Brōghīl, Kōtal-e** Afgh.
217 E4 **Broken Arrow** U.S.A.
125 I4 **Broken Bay** Australia
216 D3 **Broken Bow** *NE* U.S.A.
217 E5 **Broken Bow** *OK* U.S.A.
124 D3 **Broken Hill** Australia
238 K7 **Broken Plateau** *sea feature* Indian Ocean
179 I2 **Brome** Germany
173 G6 **Bromley** U.K.
173 E5 **Bromsgrove** U.K.
171 J4 **Brønderslev** Denmark
197 H2 **Bronkhorstspruit** S. Africa
170 K2 **Brønnøysund** Norway
209 E5 **Bronson** U.S.A.
173 I5 **Brooke** U.K.
161 H4 **Brooke's Point** Phil.
208 C4 **Brookfield** U.S.A.
217 F6 **Brookhaven** U.S.A.
213 A3 **Brookings** *OR* U.S.A.
216 D2 **Brookings** *SD* U.S.A.
221 H3 **Brookline** U.S.A.
208 A5 **Brooklyn** *IA* U.S.A.
208 B5 **Brooklyn** *IL* U.S.A.
216 E2 **Brooklyn Center** U.S.A.
220 D6 **Brookneal** U.S.A.
205 G4 **Brooks** Canada
214 A2 **Brooks** *CA* U.S.A.
221 I2 **Brooks** *ME* U.S.A.
127 J3 **Brooks, Cape** Antarctica
202 D3 **Brooks Range** *mts* U.S.A.
219 D6 **Brooksville** U.S.A.
121 B7 **Brookton** Australia
220 D4 **Brookville** U.S.A.
174 C3 **Broom, Loch** *inlet* U.K.
118 C3 **Broome** Australia
174 E2 **Brora** U.K.
171 K5 **Brösarp** Sweden
175 K4 **Brosna** *r.* Ireland
213 B3 **Brothers** U.S.A.
155 □ **Brothers, The** *is* Hong Kong China
172 E3 **Brough** U.K.
174 E1 **Brough Head** U.K.
175 L3 **Broughshane** U.K.
124 C4 **Broughton** *r.* Australia
Broughton Island Canada *see* **Qikiqtarjuaq**
125 J4 **Broughton Islands** Australia
177 O5 **Brovary** Ukr.
123 E5 **Brovinia** Australia
171 J4 **Brovst** Denmark
124 C4 **Brown, Mount** *h.* Australia
121 D5 **Browne Range** *hills* Australia
217 C5 **Brownfield** U.S.A.
212 D1 **Browning** U.S.A.
208 D6 **Brownsburg** U.S.A.
221 F5 **Browns Mills** U.S.A.
219 B5 **Brownsville** *TN* U.S.A.
217 D7 **Brownsville** *TX* U.S.A.
221 I2 **Brownville** U.S.A.
221 I2 **Brownville Junction** U.S.A.
217 D6 **Brownwood** U.S.A.
120 C2 **Browse Island** Australia
177 N4 **Brozha** Belarus
182 F1 **Bruay-la-Buissière** France
208 C2 **Bruce Crossing** U.S.A.
206 D4 **Bruce Peninsula** Canada
209 G3 **Bruce Peninsula National Park** Canada
121 B6 **Bruce Rock** Australia
179 G5 **Bruchsal** Germany
179 K2 **Brück** Germany
176 G7 **Bruck an der Mur** Austria
173 E6 **Brue** *r.* U.K.
Bruges Belgium *see* **Brugge**
178 B3 **Brugge** Belgium
179 G5 **Brühl** *Baden-Württemberg* Germany
179 E4 **Brühl** *Nordrhein-Westfalen* Germany
149 I3 **Bruini** India
215 G2 **Bruin Point** *mt.* U.S.A.
196 C2 **Brukkaros** Namibia
208 B2 **Brule** U.S.A.
207 H3 **Brûlé, Lac** *l.* Canada
178 C5 **Brûly** Belgium
234 E1 **Brumado** Brazil
171 J3 **Brumunddal** Norway
175 L4 **Brú Na Bóinne** *tourist site* Ireland
179 J2 **Brunau** Germany
213 D3 **Bruneau** U.S.A.
213 D3 **Bruneau** *r.* U.S.A.
163 H2 **Brunei** *country* Asia
122 A3 **Brunette Downs** Australia
171 K3 **Brunflo** Sweden
184 D1 **Brunico** Italy
126 C5 **Brunner, Lake** N.Z.
205 H4 **Bruno** Canada
176 D4 **Brunsbüttel** Germany
219 D6 **Brunswick** *GA* U.S.A.
221 I3 **Brunswick** *ME* U.S.A.
220 C4 **Brunswick** *OH* U.S.A.
232 B8 **Brunswick, Península de** *pen.* Chile
120 D2 **Brunswick Bay** Australia
125 J2 **Brunswick Heads** Australia
177 H6 **Bruntál** Czech Rep.
127 J3 **Brunt Ice Shelf** Antarctica
197 I4 **Bruntville** S. Africa
125 G9 **Bruny Island** Australia
213 G3 **Brush** U.S.A.
Brussel Belgium *see* **Brussels**
178 C4 **Brussels** Belgium
209 G4 **Brussels** Canada
208 D3 **Brussels** U.S.A.
177 N5 **Brusyliv** Ukr.
125 G6 **Bruthen** Australia
Bruxelles Belgium *see* **Brussels**
220 A4 **Bryan** *OH* U.S.A.
217 D6 **Bryan** *TX* U.S.A.
124 C4 **Bryan, Mount** *h.* Australia
187 E4 **Bryansk** *Bryanskaya Oblast'* Russia
187 H6 **Bryansk** *Respublika Dagestan* Russia
187 E4 **Bryanskaya Oblast'** *admin. div.* Russia
215 F3 **Bryce Canyon National Park** U.S.A.
215 H5 **Bryce Mountain** U.S.A.
171 I4 **Bryne** Norway
187 F6 **Bryukhovetskaya** Russia
177 H5 **Brzeg** Poland
194 E3 **Bu'aale** Somalia
119 F2 **Buala** Solomon Is
160 D6 **Buan** S. Korea
192 A3 **Buba** Guinea-Bissau
139 L7 **Būbiyān, Jazīrat** Kuwait
161 I5 **Bubuan** *i.* Phil.
138 C1 **Bucak** Turkey
233 I3 **Bucaramanga** Col.
161 J4 **Bucas Grande** *i.* Phil.
120 C3 **Buccaneer Archipelago** *is* Australia
125 H6 **Buchan** Australia
192 A4 **Buchanan** Liberia
208 D5 **Buchanan** *MI* U.S.A.
220 D6 **Buchanan** *VA* U.S.A.
123 D4 **Buchanan, Lake** *salt flat* Australia
217 D6 **Buchanan, Lake** U.S.A.
203 K2 **Buchan Gulf** Canada
207 I4 **Buchans** Canada
185 L2 **Bucharest** Romania
179 I1 **Büchen** Germany
179 H5 **Buchen (Odenwald)** Germany
160 D5 **Bucheon** S. Korea
179 K1 **Buchholz** Germany
179 H1 **Buchholz in der Nordheide** Germany
214 B4 **Buchon, Point** U.S.A.
177 L7 **Bucin, Pasul** *pass* Romania
125 F3 **Buckambool Mountain** *h.* Australia
179 H2 **Bückeburg** Germany
179 H2 **Bücken** Germany
215 F5 **Buckeye** U.S.A.
220 B5 **Buckeye Lake** U.S.A.
220 C5 **Buckhannon** U.S.A.
220 C5 **Buckhannon** *r.* U.S.A.
174 E4 **Buckhaven** U.K.
209 H3 **Buckhorn** Canada
215 H5 **Buckhorn** U.S.A.
209 H3 **Buckhorn Lake** Canada
220 B6 **Buckhorn Lake** U.S.A.
175 F3 **Buckie** U.K.
209 J3 **Buckingham** Canada
173 G5 **Buckingham** U.K.
220 D6 **Buckingham** U.S.A.
118 D3 **Buckingham Bay** Australia
119 E4 **Buckland Tableland** *reg.* Australia
124 B4 **Buckleboo** Australia
127 I6 **Buckle Island** Antarctica
123 B4 **Buckley** *watercourse* Australia
215 F4 **Buckskin Mountains** U.S.A.
214 B2 **Bucks Mountain** U.S.A.
221 I2 **Bucksport** U.S.A.
179 K2 **Bückwitz** Germany
București Romania *see* **Bucharest**
220 B4 **Bucyrus** U.S.A.
177 O4 **Buda-Kashalyova** Belarus
145 I7 **Budalin** Myanmar
177 I7 **Budapest** Hungary
148 D3 **Budaun** India
125 F3 **Budda** Australia
175 F4 **Buddon Ness** *pt* U.K.
184 C4 **Buddusò** *Sardinia* Italy
173 C7 **Bude** U.K.
217 F6 **Bude** U.S.A.
187 H6 **Budennovsk** Russia
125 J1 **Buderim** Australia
179 H4 **Büdingen** Germany
148 D5 **Budni** India
186 E3 **Budogoshch'** Russia
149 H2 **Budongquan** China
184 C4 **Budoni** *Sardinia* Italy
142 C6 **Budū, Ḥadabat al** *plain* Saudi Arabia
142 C6 **Budū', Sabkhat al** *salt pan* Saudi Arabia
192 C4 **Buea** Cameroon
214 B4 **Buellton** U.S.A.
235 J2 **Buena Esperanza** Arg.
233 H4 **Buenaventura** Col.
222 C3 **Buenaventura** Mex.
233 H4 **Buenaventura, Bahía de** *b.* Col.
213 F4 **Buena Vista** *CO* U.S.A.
220 D6 **Buena Vista** *VA* U.S.A.
183 O2 **Buendía, Embalse de** *resr* Spain
235 H4 **Bueno** *r.* Chile
235 K3 **Buenos Aires** Arg.
235 K3 **Buenos Aires** *prov.* Arg.
232 B7 **Buenos Aires, Lago** *l.* Arg./Chile
232 C7 **Buen Pasto** Arg.
224 C2 **Búfalo** Mex.
205 G3 **Buffalo** *r.* Canada
220 D3 **Buffalo** *NY* U.S.A.
217 D4 **Buffalo** *OK* U.S.A.
216 C2 **Buffalo** *SD* U.S.A.
217 D6 **Buffalo** *TX* U.S.A.
212 F2 **Buffalo** *WY* U.S.A.
208 B3 **Buffalo** *r.* U.S.A.
125 G6 **Buffalo, Mount** *h.* Australia
208 B3 **Buffalo City** U.S.A.
204 F3 **Buffalo Head Hills** Canada
204 F2 **Buffalo Lake** Canada
205 H3 **Buffalo Narrows** Canada
196 B4 **Buffels** *watercourse* S. Africa
197 G1 **Buffels Drift** S. Africa
219 D5 **Buford** U.S.A.
185 K2 **Buftea** Romania
177 J4 **Bug** *r.* Poland
233 H4 **Buga** Col.
233 H3 **Bugalagrande** Col.
125 H3 **Bugaldie** Australia
Bugdayli Turkm. *see* **Bugdaýly**
140 C5 **Bugdaýly** Turkm.
163 H4 **Bugel, Tanjung** *pt* Indon.
178 C3 **Buggenhout** Belgium
185 G2 **Bugojno** Bos. & Herz.
169 P2 **Bugrino** Russia
161 H4 **Bugsuk** *i.* Phil.
153 L2 **Bugt** China
161 I2 **Buguey** Phil.
140 C1 **Buguruslan** Russia
195 D5 **Buhera** Zimbabwe
161 I3 **Buhi** Phil.
213 D3 **Buhl** *ID* U.S.A.
208 A2 **Buhl** *MN* U.S.A.
139 I3 **Bühtan** *r.* Turkey
177 M7 **Buhuşi** Romania
173 D5 **Builth Wells** U.K.
176 E7 **Buin, Piz** *mt.* Austria/Switz.
192 B4 **Bui National Park** Ghana
187 I4 **Buinsk** Russia
139 K4 **Bu'in Soflā** Iran
195 B6 **Buitepos** Namibia
185 I3 **Bujanovac** Serbia
195 C4 **Bujumbura** Burundi
150 D1 **Bukachacha** Russia
149 G1 **Bukadaban Feng** *mt.* China
119 F2 **Buka Island** P.N.G.
142 B2 **Būkān** Iran
142 D4 **Būkand** Iran
141 J1 **Bukanskoye** Russia
Bukantau, Gory *h.* Uzbek. *see* **Bo'kantov tog'lari**
195 C4 **Bukavu** Dem. Rep. Congo
Bukhara Uzbek. *see* **Buxoro**
161 J6 **Bukide** *i.* Indon.
163 H3 **Bukit Baka-Bukit Raya, Taman Nasional** *nat. park* Indon.
163 B4 **Bukit Barisan Selatan, Taman Nasional** Indon.
162 B5 **Bukit Fraser** Malaysia
163 B3 **Bukittinggi** Indon.
195 D4 **Bukoba** Tanz.
141 K2 **Buktyrma, Vodokhranilishche** *resr* Kazakh.
162 □ **Bukum, Pulau** *i.* Sing.
151 F7 **Bula** Indon.
187 I4 **Bula** *r.* Russia
176 D7 **Bülach** Switz.
125 J4 **Bulahdelah** Australia
161 I3 **Bulalacao** Phil.
161 I3 **Bulan** Phil.
139 G1 **Bulancak** Turkey
139 I2 **Bulanık** Turkey
156 F2 **Bulava** Russia
195 C6 **Bulawayo** Zimbabwe
141 G1 **Bulayevo** Kazakh.
139 F3 **Bulbul** Syria
138 B2 **Buldan** Turkey
148 D5 **Buldana** India
197 I2 **Bulembu** Swaziland
150 C2 **Bulgan** *Bulgan* Mongolia
144 H2 **Bulgan** *Hovd* Mongolia
154 B1 **Bulgan** *Ömnögovĭ* Mongolia
185 K3 **Bulgaria** *country* Europe
125 E1 **Bullawarra, Lake** *salt flat* Australia
124 D3 **Bullea, Lake** *salt flat* Australia
126 D4 **Buller** *r.* N.Z.
125 G6 **Buller, Mount** Australia
122 C3 **Bulleringa National Park** Australia
121 B6 **Bullfinch** Australia
215 E4 **Bullhead City** U.S.A.
215 D4 **Bullion Mountains** U.S.A.
120 E2 **Bullo** *r.* Australia
125 E2 **Bulloo** *watercourse* Australia
125 E2 **Bulloo Downs** Australia
125 E2 **Bulloo Lake** *salt flat* Australia
196 B2 **Büllsport** Namibia
120 F2 **Bulman** Australia
120 F2 **Bulman Gorge** Australia
162 □ **Buloh, Pulau** *i.* Sing.
125 E6 **Buloke, Lake** *dry lake* Australia
197 G4 **Bultfontein** S. Africa
161 J5 **Buluan** Phil.
187 H5 **Bulukhta, Ozero** *l.* Russia
118 C2 **Bulukumba** Indon.
133 N2 **Bulun** Russia
195 B4 **Bulungu** *Bandundu* Dem. Rep. Congo
195 C4 **Bulungu** *Kasaï-Occidental* Dem. Rep. Congo
141 F5 **Bulung'ur** Uzbek.
Bulungur Uzbek. *see* **Bulung'ur**
161 J3 **Bulusan** Phil.
194 C3 **Bumba** Dem. Rep. Congo
154 B1 **Bumbat** China
215 F4 **Bumble Bee (abandoned)** U.S.A.
161 H5 **Bum-Bum** *i. Sabah* Malaysia
195 B4 **Buna** Dem. Rep. Congo
194 D3 **Buna** Kenya
195 D4 **Bunazi** Tanz.
Bunbeg Ireland *see* **An Bun Beag**
118 B5 **Bunbury** Australia
175 L5 **Bunclody** Ireland
175 K2 **Buncrana** Ireland
195 D4 **Bunda** Tanz.
119 F4 **Bundaberg** Australia
125 G2 **Bundaleer** Australia
125 I3 **Bundarra** Australia
148 C4 **Bundi** India
125 J2 **Bundjalung National Park** Australia
175 J3 **Bundoran** Ireland
149 F5 **Bundu** India
173 I5 **Bungay** U.K.
125 H5 **Bungendore** Australia
Bungle Bungle National Park Australia *see* **Purnululu National Park**
159 C8 **Bungo-suidō** *sea chan.* Japan
194 D3 **Bunia** Dem. Rep. Congo
195 C4 **Bunianga** Dem. Rep. Congo
121 C6 **Buningonia** *well* Australia
125 E6 **Buninyong** Australia
193 D3 **Buni-Yadi** Nigeria
148 C2 **Bunji** Pak.
123 F4 **Bunker Group** *atolls* Australia
215 E3 **Bunkerville** U.S.A.
217 E6 **Bunkie** U.S.A.
219 D6 **Bunnell** U.S.A.
138 E2 **Bünyan** Turkey
161 H6 **Bunyu** *i.* Indon.
162 C2 **Buôn Đôn** Vietnam
163 D2 **Buôn Hô** Vietnam
163 D2 **Buôn Ma Thuôt** Vietnam
Buôn Mê Thuôt Vietnam *see* **Buôn Ma Thuôt**
133 O2 **Buor-Khaya, Guba** *b.* Russia
136 B5 **Buqbuq** Egypt
195 D4 **Bura** Kenya
Burang China *see* **Jirang**
234 E2 **Buranhaém** *r.* Brazil
140 C2 **Burannoye** Russia
Burao Somalia *see* **Burco**
161 J4 **Burauen** Phil.
146 B4 **Buraydah** Saudi Arabia
179 G4 **Burbach** Germany
214 C4 **Burbank** U.S.A.
125 G4 **Burcher** Australia
194 E3 **Burco** Somalia
178 D3 **Burdaard** Neth.
141 F5 **Burdalyk** Turkm.
138 C3 **Burdur** Turkey
194 D2 **Burē** Eth.
173 I5 **Bure** *r.* U.K.
170 M2 **Bureå** Sweden
150 F1 **Bureinskiy Khrebet** *mts* Russia
156 D2 **Bureinskiy Zapovednik** *nature res.* Russia
Bürenhayrhan Mongolia *see* **Bulgan**
148 C3 **Burewala** Pak.
156 C2 **Bureya** *r.* Russia
Bûr Fu'ad Egypt *see* **Port Fuad**
179 J2 **Burg** Germany
185 L3 **Burgas** Bulg.
219 E5 **Burgaw** U.S.A.
179 I5 **Burgbernheim** Germany
179 I2 **Burgdorf** Germany
207 I4 **Burgeo** Canada
197 G5 **Burgersdorp** S. Africa
197 I2 **Burgersfort** S. Africa
121 C6 **Burges, Mount** *h.* Australia
173 G7 **Burgess Hill** U.K.
179 H4 **Burghaun** Germany
176 F6 **Burghausen** Germany
174 E3 **Burghead** U.K.
178 B3 **Burgh-Haamstede** Neth.
184 F6 **Burgio, Serra di** *h. Sicily* Italy
179 K5 **Burglengenfeld** Germany
183 O1 **Burgos** Spain
179 K4 **Burgstädt** Germany
171 L4 **Burgsvik** Sweden
179 E1 **Burgum** Neth.
182 G3 **Burgundy** *reg.* France
150 B3 **Burhan Budai Shan** *mts* China
185 L5 **Burhaniye** Turkey
148 D5 **Burhanpur** India
149 E5 **Burhar-Dhanpuri** India
149 H4 **Burhi Dihing** *r.* India
149 F4 **Burhi Gandak** *r.* India
161 I3 **Burias** *i.* Phil.
140 D2 **Buribay** Russia
224 I6 **Burica, Punta** *pt* Costa Rica
149 E4 **Buri Gandak** *r.* Nepal
140 E1 **Burili** Kazakh.
207 I4 **Burin Peninsula** Canada
162 B2 **Buriram** Thai.
231 J5 **Buriti Bravo** Brazil
234 C1 **Buritis** Brazil
143 G4 **Burj Aziz Khan** Pak.
118 D3 **Burketown** Australia
192 B3 **Burkina Faso** *country* Africa
141 I2 **Burkitty** Kazakh.
209 H3 **Burk's Falls** Canada
141 I1 **Burla** Russia
141 I1 **Burla** *r.* Russia
213 D3 **Burley** U.S.A.
209 H4 **Burlington** Canada
217 C4 **Burlington** *CO* U.S.A.
208 B5 **Burlington** *IA* U.S.A.
208 D5 **Burlington** *IN* U.S.A.
221 I2 **Burlington** *ME* U.S.A.
221 G2 **Burlington** *VT* U.S.A.
208 C4 **Burlington** *WI* U.S.A.
140 D1 **Burly** Russia
Burma *country* Asia *see* **Myanmar**
217 D6 **Burnet** U.S.A.
213 B3 **Burney** U.S.A.
221 I2 **Burnham** U.S.A.
125 F8 **Burnie** Australia
172 G3 **Burniston** U.K.
173 E4 **Burnley** U.K.
213 C3 **Burns** U.S.A.
205 H1 **Burnside** *r.* Canada
121 C5 **Burnside, Lake** *salt flat* Australia
202 F4 **Burns Lake** Canada
220 C5 **Burnsville Lake** U.S.A.
174 E4 **Burntisland** U.K.
205 J3 **Burntwood** *r.* Canada
205 I3 **Burntwood Lake** Canada
125 E5 **Buronga** Australia
140 E4 **Burovoy** Uzbek.
133 J5 **Burqin** China
139 G5 **Burqu'** Jordan
124 C4 **Burra** Australia
174 □ **Burra** *i.* U.K.
174 □ **Burravoe** U.K.
175 F2 **Burray** *i.* U.K.
185 I4 **Burrel** Albania
125 H4 **Burrendong, Lake** Australia
125 H3 **Burren Junction** Australia
125 I5 **Burrewarra Point** Australia
Burriana Spain *see* **Borriana**
125 H5 **Burrinjuck** Australia
125 H5 **Burrinjuck Reservoir** Australia
225 D1 **Burro, Serranías del** *mts* Mex.
220 B5 **Burr Oak Reservoir** U.S.A.
174 D6 **Burrow Head** U.K.
120 E2 **Burrundie** Australia
215 G2 **Burrville** U.S.A.
138 B1 **Bursa** Turkey
193 F2 **Būr Safājah** Egypt
Būr Sa'īd Egypt *see* **Port Said**
179 G5 **Bürstadt** Germany
Būr Sudan Sudan *see* **Port Sudan**
124 D4 **Burta** Australia
209 E3 **Burt Lake** U.S.A.
209 F4 **Burton** U.S.A.
206 E3 **Burton, Lac** *l.* Canada
Burtonport Ireland *see* **Ailt an Chorráin**
173 F5 **Burton upon Trent** U.K.
170 M2 **Burträsk** Sweden
221 J1 **Burtts Corner** Canada
125 E4 **Burtundy** Australia
121 F4 **Burt Well** Australia
151 E7 **Buru** *i.* Indon.
138 C6 **Burullus, Lake** *lag.* Egypt
Burultokay China *see* **Fuhai**
195 D4 **Burundi** *country* Africa
195 C4 **Bururi** Burundi
204 B2 **Burwash Landing** Canada
175 F2 **Burwick** U.K.
141 H3 **Burylbaytal** Kazakh.
187 E5 **Buryn'** Ukr.
140 B3 **Burynshyk** Kazakh.
173 H5 **Bury St Edmunds** U.K.
148 C2 **Burzil Pass** Pak.
184 E6 **Busambra, Rocca** *mt. Sicily* Italy
160 E6 **Busan** S. Korea
195 C4 **Busanga** Dem. Rep. Congo
175 L2 **Bush** *r.* U.K.
149 E2 **Bushêngcaka** China
195 D4 **Bushenyi** Uganda
175 L2 **Bushmills** U.K.
208 B5 **Bushnell** U.S.A.
162 □ **Busing, Pulau** *i.* Sing.

Cann River

194 C3 **Businga** Dem. Rep. Congo
139 F5 **Buşrá ash Shām** Syria
156 B2 **Busse** Russia
118 B5 **Busselton** Australia
178 D2 **Bussum** Neth.
225 D2 **Bustamante** Mex.
224 C1 **Bustillos, Lago** Mex.
184 C2 **Busto Arsizio** Italy
161 H3 **Busuanga** *i.* Phil.
194 C3 **Buta** Dem. Rep. Congo
235 I3 **Buta Ranquil** Arg.
195 C4 **Butare** Rwanda
236 G6 **Butaritari** *atoll* Kiribati
124 B4 **Bute** Australia
174 C5 **Bute** *i.* U.K.
174 C5 **Bute, Sound of** *sea chan.* U.K.
204 D4 **Butedale (abandoned)** Canada
204 D4 **Bute Inlet** Canada
197 H4 **Butha-Buthe** Lesotho
Butha Qi China *see* **Zalantun**
179 G1 **Butjadingen** *reg.* Germany
209 E5 **Butler** *IN* U.S.A.
220 D4 **Butler** *PA* U.S.A.
175 K3 **Butlers Bridge** Ireland
151 E7 **Buton** *i.* Indon.
179 K1 **Bütow** Germany
212 D2 **Butte** U.S.A.
179 J3 **Buttelstedt** Germany
214 B1 **Butte Meadows** U.S.A.
163 B1 **Butterworth** Malaysia
Butterworth S. Africa *see* **Gcuwa**
175 J5 **Buttevant** Ireland
204 D5 **Buttle Lake** Canada
174 B2 **Butt of Lewis** *hd* U.K.
203 I4 **Button Bay** Canada
214 C4 **Buttonwillow** U.S.A.
161 J4 **Butuan** Phil.
155 B5 **Butuo** China
187 G5 **Buturlinovka** Russia
149 E4 **Butwal** Nepal
179 G4 **Butzbach** Germany
194 E3 **Buulobarde** Somalia
195 E4 **Buur Gaabo** Somalia
194 E3 **Buurhabaka** Somalia
144 I2 **Buutsagaan** Mongolia
149 F4 **Buxar** India
141 F5 **Buxoro** Uzbek.
179 H1 **Buxtehude** Germany
173 F4 **Buxton** U.K.
186 G3 **Buy** Russia
Buyant Mongolia *see* **Buutsagaan**
208 A1 **Buyck** U.S.A.
187 H7 **Buynaksk** Russia
143 G2 **Buynī Qarah** Afgh.
150 D2 **Buyr Nuur** *l.* Mongolia
138 A3 **Büyükmenderes** *r.* Turkey
160 B3 **Buyun Shan** *mt.* China
178 C5 **Buzancy** France
185 L2 **Buzău** Romania
195 D5 **Búzi** Moz.
140 C1 **Buzuluk** Russia
187 G5 **Buzuluk** *r.* Russia
141 F2 **Buzylyk** Kazakh.
221 H4 **Buzzards Bay** U.S.A.
185 K3 **Byala** Bulg.
185 J3 **Byala Slatina** Bulg.
177 N4 **Byalynichy** Belarus
203 H2 **Byam Martin Island** Canada
187 D4 **Byarezina** *r.* Belarus
187 C4 **Byaroza** Belarus
138 E4 **Byblos** *tourist site* Lebanon
177 I4 **Bydgoszcz** Poland
187 D4 **Byerazino** Belarus
213 F4 **Byers** U.S.A.
177 N3 **Byeshankovichy** Belarus
171 I4 **Bygland** Norway
187 D4 **Bykhaw** Belarus
171 I4 **Bykle** Norway
169 P6 **Bykovo** Russia
141 H2 **Bylkyldak** Kazakh.
203 K2 **Bylot Island** Canada
209 G3 **Byng Inlet** Canada
171 I3 **Byrkjelo** Norway
125 G3 **Byrock** Australia
208 C4 **Byron** *IL* U.S.A.
221 H2 **Byron** *ME* U.S.A.
125 J2 **Byron, Cape** Australia
125 J2 **Byron Bay** Australia
133 L2 **Byrranga, Gory** *mts* Russia
170 M2 **Byske** Sweden
156 C1 **Byssa** Russia
156 C1 **Byssa** *r.* Russia
141 K1 **Bystryy Istok** Russia
133 O3 **Bytantay** *r.* Russia
177 I5 **Bytom** Poland
177 H3 **Bytów** Poland

C

232 E3 **Caacupé** Para.
235 A4 **Caaguazú** Para.
235 A4 **Caaguazú, Cordillera de** *hills* Para.
234 A3 **Caarapó** Brazil
235 A4 **Caazapá** Para.
230 C6 **Caballas** Peru
230 D4 **Caballococha** Peru
225 D1 **Caballos Mesteños, Llano de los** *plain* Mex.
161 I3 **Cabanatuan** Phil.
207 G4 **Cabano** Canada
194 E2 **Cabdul Qaadir** Somalia
234 A1 **Cabeceira Rio Manso** Brazil
231 L5 **Cabedelo** Brazil
183 N3 **Cabeza del Buey** Spain
231 F7 **Cabezas** Bol.
235 K3 **Cabildo** Arg.
233 J2 **Cabimas** Venez.
195 B4 **Cabinda** Angola
195 B4 **Cabinda** *prov.* Angola
212 C1 **Cabinet Mountains** U.S.A.
233 I3 **Cable Way** *pass* Col.
234 D3 **Cabo Frio** Brazil
234 E3 **Cabo Frio, Ilha do** *i.* Brazil
206 E4 **Cabonga, Réservoir** *resr* Canada
217 E4 **Cabool** U.S.A.
125 J1 **Caboolture** Australia
231 H3 **Cabo Orange, Parque Nacional de** *nat. park* Brazil
230 C4 **Cabo Pantoja** Peru
195 D5 **Cabora Bassa, Lake** *resr* Moz.
222 B2 **Caborca** Mex.
224 B3 **Cabo San Lucas** Mex.
209 G3 **Cabot Head** Canada
207 I4 **Cabot Strait** Canada
Cabo Verde *country* Africa *see* **Cape Verde**
234 D2 **Cabral, Serra do** *mts* Brazil
139 K2 **Cäbrayıl** Azer.
183 R3 **Cabrera, Illa de** *i.* Spain
183 M1 **Cabrera, Sierra de la** *mts* Spain
183 P3 **Cabriel** *r.* Spain
233 K3 **Cabruta** Venez.
161 I2 **Cabugao** Phil.
232 F3 **Caçador** Brazil
225 E4 **Cacahuatepec** Mex.
185 I3 **Čačak** Serbia
235 M1 **Caçapava do Sul** Brazil
220 D5 **Cacapon** *r.* U.S.A.
233 I3 **Cácares** Col.
184 C4 **Caccia, Capo** *c. Sardinia* Italy
143 F2 **Çäçe** Turkm.
231 G7 **Cáceres** Brazil
183 M3 **Cáceres** Spain
213 D3 **Cache Peak** U.S.A.
192 A3 **Cacheu** Guinea-Bissau
232 C3 **Cachi** *r.* Arg.
232 C2 **Cachi, Nevados de** *mts* Arg.
231 H5 **Cachimbo, Serra do** *hills* Brazil
233 I3 **Cáchira** Col.
234 E1 **Cachoeira** Brazil
234 B2 **Cachoeira Alta** Brazil
235 M1 **Cachoeira do Sul** Brazil
234 E3 **Cachoeiro de Itapemirim** Brazil
192 A3 **Cacine** Guinea-Bissau
231 H3 **Caciporé, Cabo** *c.* Brazil
195 B5 **Cacolo** Angola
195 B4 **Caconda** Angola
215 D3 **Cactus Range** *mts* U.S.A.
234 B2 **Caçu** Brazil
234 D1 **Caculé** Brazil
177 I6 **Čadca** Slovakia
179 H1 **Cadenberge** Germany
225 D2 **Cadereyta** Mex.
124 A2 **Cadibarrawirracanna, Lake** *salt flat* Australia
161 I3 **Cadig Mountains** Phil.
209 H1 **Cadillac** *Que.* Canada
205 H5 **Cadillac** *Sask.* Canada
209 E3 **Cadillac** U.S.A.
161 I4 **Cadiz** Phil.
183 M4 **Cádiz** Spain
183 M4 **Cádiz, Golfo de** *g.* Spain
215 E4 **Cadiz Lake** U.S.A.
182 D2 **Caen** France
173 C4 **Caernarfon** U.K.
173 C4 **Caernarfon Bay** U.K.
173 D6 **Caerphilly** U.K.
220 B5 **Caesar Creek Lake** U.S.A.
138 E5 **Caesarea** *tourist site* Israel
234 D1 **Caetité** Brazil
232 C3 **Cafayate** Arg.
161 I4 **Cagayan** *i.* Phil.
161 I2 **Cagayan** *r.* Phil.
161 J4 **Cagayan de Oro** Phil.
161 H5 **Cagayan de Tawi-Tawi** *i.* Phil.
161 I4 **Cagayan Islands** Phil.
184 E3 **Cagli** Italy
184 C5 **Cagliari** *Sardinia* Italy
184 C5 **Cagliari, Golfo di** *b. Sardinia* Italy
233 I4 **Caguán** *r.* Col.
140 C4 **Çagyl** Turkm.
140 D4 **Çagyllyşor Çöketligi** *depr.* Turkm.
219 C5 **Cahaba** *r.* U.S.A.
175 I6 **Caha Mountains** Ireland
175 H6 **Cahermore** Ireland
175 K5 **Cahir** Ireland
175 H6 **Cahirsiveen** Ireland
Cahora Bassa, Lago de *resr* Moz. *see* **Cabora Bassa, Lake**
175 L5 **Cahore Point** Ireland
182 E4 **Cahors** France
230 C5 **Cahuapanas** Peru
230 D4 **Cahuinarí, Parque Nacional** *nat. park* Col.
187 D6 **Cahul** Moldova
195 D5 **Caia** Moz.
231 G6 **Caiabis, Serra dos** *hills* Brazil
195 C5 **Caianda** Angola
234 B2 **Caiapó** *r.* Brazil
234 B2 **Caiapó, Serra do** *mts* Brazil
234 B2 **Caiapônia** Brazil
223 I4 **Caibarién** Cuba
155 C6 **Cai Bâu, Đao** *i.* Vietnam
162 C3 **Cai Be** Vietnam
233 K3 **Caicara** Venez.
223 J4 **Caicos Islands** Turks and Caicos Is
155 E4 **Caidian** China
121 D7 **Caiguna** Australia
224 C3 **Caimanero, Laguna del** *lag.* Mex.
235 H1 **Caimanes** Chile
161 H3 **Caiman Point** Phil.
183 P2 **Caimodorro** *mt.* Spain
162 C3 **Cai Nước** Vietnam
174 E3 **Cairn Gorm** *mt.* U.K.
174 E3 **Cairngorm Mountains** U.K.
174 D4 **Cairngorms National Park** U.K.
174 C6 **Cairnryan** U.K.
122 D3 **Cairns** Australia
174 E3 **Cairn Toul** *mt.* U.K.
193 F1 **Cairo** Egypt
219 C6 **Cairo** U.S.A.
184 C2 **Cairo Montenotte** Italy
195 B5 **Caiundo** Angola
125 F2 **Caiwarro (abandoned)** Australia
230 C5 **Cajamarca** Peru
161 I3 **Cajidiocan** Phil.
185 G1 **Čakovec** Croatia
138 B2 **Çal** Turkey
197 G5 **Cala** S. Africa
192 C4 **Calabar** Nigeria
209 I3 **Calabogie** Canada
233 K2 **Calabozo** Venez.
185 J3 **Calafat** Romania
161 I3 **Calagua Islands** Phil.
183 P1 **Calahorra** Spain
195 B5 **Calai** Angola
182 E1 **Calais** France
221 J2 **Calais** U.S.A.
Calais, Pas de *str.* France/U.K. *see* **Dover, Strait of**
225 G4 **Calakmul** *tourist site* Mex.
231 F5 **Calama** Brazil
232 C2 **Calama** Chile
233 I2 **Calamar** *Bolívar* Col.
233 I4 **Calamar** *Guaviare* Col.
161 H4 **Calamian Group** *is* Phil.
183 P2 **Calamocha** Spain
195 B4 **Calandula** Angola
161 I3 **Calapan** Phil.
185 L2 **Călărași** Romania
183 P2 **Calatayud** Spain
161 I3 **Calauag** Phil.
161 H3 **Calauit** *i.* Phil.
161 I3 **Calavite, Cape** Phil.
161 I2 **Calayan** *i.* Phil.
161 J3 **Calbayog** Phil.
179 J3 **Calbe (Saale)** Germany
161 J4 **Calbiga** Phil.
235 H4 **Calbuco** Chile
231 K5 **Calcanhar, Ponta do** *pt* Brazil
217 E6 **Calcasieu Lake** U.S.A.
231 H3 **Calçoene** Brazil
Calcutta India *see* **Kolkata**
183 L3 **Caldas da Rainha** Port.
234 C2 **Caldas Novas** Brazil
179 H3 **Calden** Germany
232 B3 **Caldera** Chile
123 D5 **Caldervale** Australia
139 I2 **Çaldıran** Turkey
213 C3 **Caldwell** U.S.A.
220 D3 **Caledon** Canada
197 G5 **Caledon** *r.* Lesotho/S. Africa
196 C7 **Caledon** S. Africa
122 B2 **Caledon Bay** Australia
209 H4 **Caledonia** Canada
208 B4 **Caledonia** U.S.A.
232 C7 **Caleta Olivia** Arg.
215 E5 **Calexico** U.S.A.
172 C3 **Calf of Man** *i.* U.K.
205 G4 **Calgary** Canada
219 C5 **Calhoun** U.S.A.
233 H4 **Cali** Col.
161 J4 **Calicoan** *i.* Phil.
Calicut India *see* **Kozhikode**
214 C4 **Caliente** *CA* U.S.A.
215 E3 **Caliente** *NV* U.S.A.
214 B3 **California** *state* U.S.A.
California, Golfo de *g.* Mex. *see* **California, Gulf of**
224 B2 **California, Gulf of** Mex.
214 B3 **California Aqueduct** *canal* U.S.A.
214 C4 **California Hot Springs** U.S.A.
139 L2 **Cälilabad** Azer.
213 D5 **Calipatria** U.S.A.
214 A2 **Calistoga** U.S.A.
196 D6 **Calitzdorp** S. Africa
225 G3 **Calkiní** Mex.
124 D2 **Callabonna, Lake** *salt flat* Australia
215 D2 **Callaghan, Mount** U.S.A.
219 D6 **Callahan** U.S.A.
175 K5 **Callan** Ireland
209 H2 **Callander** Canada
174 D4 **Callander** U.K.
230 C6 **Callao** Peru
215 F2 **Callao** U.S.A.
225 E3 **Calles** Mex.
221 F4 **Callicoon** U.S.A.
173 C7 **Callington** U.K.
123 E5 **Calliope** Australia
209 G2 **Callum** Canada
205 G4 **Calmar** Canada
208 B4 **Calmar** U.S.A.
215 E4 **Cal-Nev-Ari** U.S.A.
219 D7 **Caloosahatchee** *r.* U.S.A.
225 G3 **Calotmul** Mex.
125 J1 **Caloundra** Australia
214 B2 **Calpine** U.S.A.
225 E4 **Calpulálpan** Mex.
184 F6 **Caltanissetta** *Sicily* Italy
208 C2 **Calumet** U.S.A.
195 B5 **Calunga** Angola
195 B5 **Caluquembe** Angola
161 I4 **Calusa** *i.* Phil.
194 F2 **Caluula** Somalia
215 G5 **Calva** U.S.A.
122 F1 **Calvados Chain** *is* P.N.G.
122 B3 **Calvert Hills** Australia
204 D4 **Calvert Island** Canada
184 C3 **Calvi** *Corsica* France
183 R3 **Calvià** Spain
225 D3 **Calvillo** Mex.
196 C5 **Calvinia** S. Africa
184 F4 **Calvo, Monte** *mt.* Italy
173 H5 **Cam** *r.* U.K.
234 E1 **Camaçari** Brazil
214 B2 **Camache Reservoir** U.S.A.
225 D2 **Camacho** Mex.
195 B5 **Camacuio** Angola
195 B5 **Camacupa** Angola
233 K2 **Camaguán** Venez.
223 I4 **Camagüey** Cuba
223 I4 **Camagüey, Archipiélago de** *is* Cuba
Çamalan Turkey *see* **Gülek**
230 D7 **Camaná** Peru
195 C5 **Camanongue** Angola
234 B2 **Camapuã** Brazil
235 M1 **Camaquã** Brazil
235 M1 **Camaquã** *r.* Brazil
138 E3 **Çamardı** Turkey
225 E2 **Camargo** Mex.
232 C6 **Camarones** Arg.
232 C6 **Camarones, Bahía** *b.* Arg.
212 B2 **Camas** U.S.A.
162 C3 **Ca Mau** Vietnam
162 C3 **Ca Mau, Mui** *c.* Vietnam
173 G6 **Camberley** U.K.
162 C2 **Cambodia** *country* Asia
173 B7 **Camborne** U.K.
182 F1 **Cambrai** France
214 B4 **Cambria** U.S.A.
173 D5 **Cambrian Mountains** U.K.
209 G4 **Cambridge** Canada
126 E2 **Cambridge** N.Z.
173 H5 **Cambridge** U.K.
208 B5 **Cambridge** *IL* U.S.A.
221 H3 **Cambridge** *MA* U.S.A.
221 E5 **Cambridge** *MD* U.S.A.
216 E2 **Cambridge** *MN* U.S.A.
221 G3 **Cambridge** *NY* U.S.A.
220 C4 **Cambridge** *OH* U.S.A.
207 G2 **Cambrien, Lac** *l.* Canada
196 F6 **Camdeboo National Park** S. Africa
125 I5 **Camden** Australia
219 C5 **Camden** *AL* U.S.A.
217 E5 **Camden** *AR* U.S.A.
221 I2 **Camden** *ME* U.S.A.
221 F5 **Camden** *NJ* U.S.A.
221 F3 **Camden** *NY* U.S.A.
219 D5 **Camden** *SC* U.S.A.
232 B8 **Camden, Isla** *i.* Chile
195 C5 **Cameia, Parque Nacional da** *nat. park* Angola
215 G4 **Cameron** *AZ* U.S.A.
217 E6 **Cameron** *LA* U.S.A.
217 E4 **Cameron** *MO* U.S.A.
217 D6 **Cameron** *TX* U.S.A.
208 B3 **Cameron** *WI* U.S.A.
204 F3 **Cameron Hills** Canada
214 B2 **Cameron Park** U.S.A.
193 D4 **Cameroon** *country* Africa
193 D4 **Cameroon Highlands** *slope* Cameroon/Nigeria
192 C4 **Cameroun, Mont** *vol.* Cameroon
231 I4 **Cametá** Brazil
161 I2 **Camiguin** *i.* Phil.
161 J4 **Camiguin** *i.* Phil.
161 I3 **Camiling** Phil.
219 C6 **Camilla** U.S.A.
231 F8 **Camiri** Bol.
231 J4 **Camocim** Brazil
118 D3 **Camooweal** Australia
123 B4 **Camooweal Caves National Park** Australia
145 H10 **Camorta** *i.* India
161 J4 **Camotes Sea** *g.* Phil.
235 K2 **Campana** Arg.
233 I4 **Campana, Cerro** *h.* Col.
232 A7 **Campana, Isla** *i.* Chile
235 H2 **Campanario** *mt.* Arg./Chile
204 D4 **Campania Island** Canada
197 E4 **Campbell** S. Africa
126 E4 **Campbell, Cape** N.Z.
121 E4 **Campbell, Mount** *h.* Australia
117 F7 **Campbell Island** N.Z.
236 G9 **Campbell Plateau** *sea feature* S. Pacific Ocean
120 D2 **Campbell Range** *hills* Australia
204 D4 **Campbell River** Canada
209 I3 **Campbell's Bay** Canada
219 C4 **Campbellsville** U.S.A.
207 G4 **Campbellton** Canada
125 G8 **Campbell Town** Australia
174 C5 **Campbeltown** U.K.
225 G4 **Campeche** Mex.
225 G4 **Campeche** *state* Mex.
225 F4 **Campeche, Bahía de** *g.* Mex.
125 E7 **Camperdown** Australia
185 K2 **Câmpina** Romania
231 K5 **Campina Grande** Brazil
234 C3 **Campinas** Brazil
234 C2 **Campina Verde** Brazil
192 C4 **Campo** Cameroon
233 I4 **Campoalegre** Col.
184 F4 **Campobasso** Italy
234 D3 **Campo Belo** Brazil
231 H6 **Campo de Diauarum** Brazil
234 C2 **Campo Florido** Brazil
232 D3 **Campo Gallo** Arg.
234 A3 **Campo Grande** Brazil
231 J4 **Campo Maior** Brazil
183 M3 **Campo Maior** Port.
233 J2 **Campo Mara** Venez.
235 B4 **Campo Mourão** Brazil
234 C2 **Campos Altos** Brazil
234 D3 **Campos do Jordão** Brazil
234 E3 **Campos dos Goytacazes** Brazil
174 D4 **Campsie Fells** *hills* U.K.
220 B6 **Campton** *KY* U.S.A.
221 H3 **Campton** *NH* U.S.A.
185 K2 **Câmpulung** Romania
177 L7 **Câmpulung Moldovenesc** Romania
215 G4 **Camp Verde** U.S.A.
Cam Ranh Vietnam *see* **Ba Ngoi**
205 G4 **Camrose** Canada
173 B6 **Camrose** U.K.
205 G2 **Camsell Lake** Canada
205 H3 **Camsell Portage** Canada
187 C7 **Çan** Turkey
163 D3 **Ca Na, Mui** *hd* Vietnam
221 G3 **Canaan** U.S.A.
202 G3 **Canada** *country* N. America
240 O1 **Canada Basin** *sea feature* Arctic Ocean
235 K2 **Cañada de Gómez** Arg.
221 H2 **Canada Falls Lake** U.S.A.
217 C5 **Canadian** *r.* U.S.A.
111 **Canadian Shield** N. America
233 L3 **Canaima, Parque Nacional** *nat. park* Venez.
221 F3 **Canajoharie** U.S.A.
187 C7 **Çanakkale** Turkey
Çanakkale Boğazı *str.* Turkey *see* **Dardanelles**
235 I2 **Canalejas** Arg.
221 E3 **Canandaigua** U.S.A.
221 E3 **Canandaigua Lake** U.S.A.
222 B2 **Cananea** Mex.
235 C4 **Cananéia** Brazil
233 J4 **Canapiare, Cerro** *h.* Col.
230 C4 **Cañar** Ecuador
Canarias, Islas *terr.* N. Atlantic Ocean *see* **Canary Islands**
192 A2 **Canary Islands** *terr.* N. Atlantic Ocean
221 F3 **Canastota** U.S.A.
234 C2 **Canastra, Serra da** *mts* Brazil
224 C2 **Canatlán** Mex.
219 D6 **Canaveral, Cape** U.S.A.
183 O2 **Cañaveras** Spain
234 E1 **Canavieiras** Brazil
125 G3 **Canbelego** Australia
125 H5 **Canberra** Australia
213 B3 **Canby** *CA* U.S.A.
216 D2 **Canby** *MN* U.S.A.
225 H3 **Cancún** Mex.
225 G4 **Candelaria** *Campeche* Mex.
213 F6 **Candelaria** *Chihuahua* Mex.
225 E5 **Candelaria Loxicha** Mex.
183 N2 **Candeleda** Spain
125 H6 **Candelo** Australia
231 I4 **Cândido Mendes** Brazil
138 D1 **Çandır** Turkey
205 H4 **Candle Lake** Canada
205 H4 **Candle Lake** *l.* Canada
229 G7 **Candlemas Island** S. Sandwich Is
221 G4 **Candlewood, Lake** U.S.A.
216 D1 **Cando** U.S.A.
161 I2 **Candon** Phil.
121 A4 **Cane** *r.* Australia
235 H1 **Canela Baja** Chile
235 L2 **Canelones** Uruguay
235 H3 **Cañete** Chile
183 P2 **Cañete** Spain
230 D6 **Cangallo** Peru
195 B5 **Cangamba** Angola
183 M1 **Cangas del Narcea** Spain
197 E6 **Cango Caves** S. Africa
231 K5 **Canguaretama** Brazil
235 M1 **Canguçu** Brazil
235 M1 **Canguçu, Serra do** *hills* Brazil
155 D6 **Cangwu** China
154 E2 **Cangzhou** China
207 G3 **Caniapiscau** Canada
207 G2 **Caniapiscau** *r.* Canada
207 G3 **Caniapiscau, Lac** Canada
203 K4 **Caniapiscau, Réservoir de** *l.* Canada
184 E6 **Canicattì** *Sicily* Italy
204 E4 **Canim Lake** Canada
204 E4 **Canim Lake** *l.* Canada
231 K4 **Canindé** Brazil
231 J5 **Canindé** *r.* Brazil
174 C2 **Canisp** *h.* U.K.
221 E3 **Canisteo** U.S.A.
221 E3 **Canisteo** *r.* U.S.A.
225 D3 **Cañitas de Felipe Pescador** Mex.
138 D1 **Çankırı** Turkey
161 I4 **Canlaon** Phil.
204 F4 **Canmore** Canada
121 A6 **Canna** Australia
174 B3 **Canna** *i.* U.K.
Cannanore India *see* **Kannur**
147 G4 **Cannanore Islands** India
183 H5 **Cannes** France
173 E5 **Cannock** U.K.
125 H6 **Cann River** Australia

Chazy

192 B4 Cavally r. Côte d'Ivoire
175 K4 Cavan Ireland
136 C3 Çavdır Turkey
217 F4 Cave City U.S.A.
234 E1 Caveira r. Brazil
125 E6 Cavendish Australia
235 B4 Cavernoso, Serra do mts Brazil
220 B5 Cave Run Lake U.S.A.
161 I4 Cavili reef Phil.
161 I3 Cavite Phil.
174 E3 Cawdor U.K.
124 D4 Cawndilla Lake imp. l. Australia
173 I5 Cawston U.K.
231 J4 Caxias Brazil
232 F3 Caxias do Sul Brazil
195 B4 Caxito Angola
138 C2 Çay Turkey
219 D5 Cayce U.S.A.
138 D1 Çaycuma Turkey
139 H1 Çayeli Turkey
231 H3 Cayenne Fr. Guiana
138 E3 Çayhan Turkey
138 C1 Çayırhan Turkey
223 I5 Cayman Brac i. Cayman Is
223 H5 Cayman Islands terr. Caribbean Sea
239 D4 Cayman Trench sea feature Caribbean Sea
194 E3 Caynaba Somalia
209 H4 Cayuga Canada
221 E3 Cayuga Lake U.S.A.
221 F3 Cazenovia U.S.A.
195 C5 Cazombo Angola
239 G6 Ceara Abyssal Plain sea feature S. Atlantic Ocean
224 I7 Cébaco, Isla de i. Panama
224 C2 Ceballos Mex.
235 L2 Cebollatí r. Uruguay
161 I4 Cebu Phil.
161 I4 Cebu i. Phil.
208 C3 Cecil U.S.A.
125 I1 Cecil Plains Australia
121 C5 Cecil Rhodes, Mount h. Australia
184 D3 Cecina Italy
208 A4 Cedar r. MI U.S.A.
216 C2 Cedar r. ND U.S.A.
208 D4 Cedarburg U.S.A.
215 F3 Cedar City U.S.A.
217 D5 Cedar Creek Reservoir U.S.A.
208 A4 Cedar Falls U.S.A.
208 D4 Cedar Grove WI U.S.A.
220 C5 Cedar Grove WV U.S.A.
221 F6 Cedar Island U.S.A.
205 I4 Cedar Lake Canada
208 D5 Cedar Lake U.S.A.
220 B4 Cedar Point U.S.A.
208 B5 Cedar Rapids U.S.A.
215 G3 Cedar Ridge U.S.A.
221 F5 Cedar Run U.S.A.
209 F4 Cedar Springs Canada
209 E4 Cedar Springs U.S.A.
219 C5 Cedartown U.S.A.
197 H5 Cedarville S. Africa
209 E3 Cedarville U.S.A.
224 A1 Cedros, Isla i. Mex.
118 D5 Ceduna Australia
194 E3 Ceeldheere Somalia
194 E2 Ceerigaabo Somalia
184 F5 Cefalù Sicily Italy
177 I7 Cegléd Hungary
155 B5 Ceheng China
138 E1 Çekerek Turkey
224 G5 Celaque, Parque Nacional nat. park Hond.
225 D3 Celaya Mex.
175 L4 Celbridge Ireland
163 I3 Celebes i. Indon.
151 E6 Celebes Sea Indon./Phil.
220 A4 Celina U.S.A.
184 F1 Celje Slovenia
179 I2 Celle Germany
239 I2 Celtic Shelf sea feature N. Atlantic Ocean
138 E1 Cemilbey Turkey
139 G2 Çemişgezek Turkey
151 F7 Cenderawasih, Teluk b. Indon.
197 H6 Centane S. Africa
215 F5 Centennial Wash watercourse U.S.A.
217 E6 Center U.S.A.
221 G4 Centereach U.S.A.
219 C5 Center Point U.S.A.
220 B5 Centerville U.S.A.
197 G1 Central admin. dist. Botswana
233 H4 Central, Cordillera mts Col.
224 I6 Central, Cordillera mts Panama
230 C5 Central, Cordillera mts Peru
161 I2 Central, Cordillera mts Phil.
193 D4 Central African Republic country Africa
143 G4 Central Brahui Range mts Pak.
208 B4 Central City IA U.S.A.
216 D3 Central City NE U.S.A.
219 B4 Centralia IL U.S.A.
212 B2 Centralia WA U.S.A.
194 D2 Central Island National Park Kenya
208 A2 Central Lakes U.S.A.
143 G5 Central Makran Range mts Pak.
121 F4 Central Mount Stuart h. Australia
236 G5 Central Pacific Basin sea feature Pacific Ocean
213 B3 Central Point U.S.A.
119 E2 Central Range mts P.N.G.
132 E4 Central Russian Upland hills Russia
133 L3 Central Siberian Plateau Russia
219 C5 Centreville U.S.A.
155 D6 Cenxi China
185 K6 Ceos i. Greece
185 I5 Cephalonia i. Greece
Ceram Sea Indon. see Seram, Laut
233 K3 Cerbatana, Sierra de la mt. Venez.
215 E4 Cerbat Mountains U.S.A.
205 G4 Cereal Canada
232 D3 Ceres Arg.
196 C6 Ceres S. Africa
233 I2 Cereté Col.
183 O2 Cerezo de Abajo Spain
184 F4 Cerignola Italy
138 D2 Çerikli Turkey
138 D1 Çerkeş Turkey
139 G3 Çermelik Deresi r. Syria
139 G2 Çermik Turkey
185 M2 Cernavodă Romania
225 E2 Cerralvo Mex.
224 B2 Cerralvo, Isla i. Mex.
185 H4 Cërrik Albania
225 D3 Cerritos Mex.
235 C4 Cerro Azul Brazil
225 E3 Cerro Azul Mex.
230 C6 Cerro de Pasco Peru
224 I7 Cerro Hoya, Parque Nacional nat. park Panama
233 K3 Cerro Jáua, Meseta del plat. Venez.
233 J2 Cerrón, Cerro mt. Venez.
224 C2 Cerro Prieto Mex.
235 I3 Cerros Colorados, Embalse resr Arg.
230 B4 Cerros de Amotape, Parque Nacional nat. park Peru
184 F4 Cervati, Monte mt. Italy
184 C3 Cervione Corsica France
183 M1 Cervo Spain
233 I2 Cesar r. Col.
184 E2 Cesena Italy
171 N4 Cēsis Latvia
176 G6 České Budějovice Czech Rep.
176 G6 Český Krumlov Czech Rep.
179 K5 Český les mts Czech Rep./Germany
185 L5 Çeşme Turkey
125 I4 Cessnock Australia
185 H3 Cetinje Montenegro
184 F5 Cetraro Italy
183 N5 Ceuta Spain
119 H4 Ceva-i-Ra reef Fiji
182 F4 Cévennes mts France
138 E3 Ceyhan Turkey
138 E3 Ceyhan r. Turkey
139 H3 Ceylanpınar Turkey
Chaacha Turkm. see Çäçe
178 A5 Chaalis, Abbaye de tourist site France
143 F5 Chābahār Iran
149 F3 Chabyêr Caka salt l. China
235 K2 Chacabuco Arg.
235 H4 Chacao Chile
235 I3 Chachahuén, Sierra mts Arg.
230 C5 Chachapoyas Peru
187 D4 Chachersk Belarus
162 B2 Chachoengsao Thai.
148 B4 Chachro Pak.
213 F4 Chaco Culture National Historical Park nat. park U.S.A.
204 C4 Chacon, Cape U.S.A.
193 D3 Chad country Africa
193 D3 Chad, Lake Africa
153 H2 Chadaasan Mongolia
135 H1 Chadan Russia
197 G1 Chadibe Botswana
Chadileo r. Arg. see Salado
216 C3 Chadron U.S.A.
162 A1 Chae Hom Thai.
141 H4 Chaek Kyrg.
160 C4 Chaeryŏng N. Korea
233 I4 Chafurray Col.
143 G4 Chagai Pak.
143 F4 Chagai Hills Afgh./Pak.
141 F3 Chagan Kazakh.
149 F2 Chagdo Kangri mt. China
143 G3 Chaghcharān Afgh.
141 G1 Chaglinka r. Kazakh.
182 G3 Chagny France
169 N4 Chagoda Russia
131 C7 Chagos Archipelago is British Indian Ocean Terr.
238 I5 Chagos-Laccadive Ridge sea feature Indian Ocean
238 I5 Chagos Trench sea feature Indian Ocean
156 C1 Chagoyan Russia
187 I4 Chagra r. Russia
224 J6 Chagres, Parque Nacional nat. park Panama
233 K2 Chaguaramas Venez.
Chagyl Turkm. see Çagyl
140 C4 Chagyllshor, Vpadina depr. Turkm.
149 G3 Cha'gyüngoinba China
143 H2 Chāh Āb Afgh.
142 D4 Chāhak Iran
143 E3 Chāh Ākhvor Iran
143 F4 Chahār Burjak Afgh.
143 H3 Chahār Dar Afgh.
142 C4 Chahār Rūstā'ī Iran
143 E3 Chahār Takāb Iran
139 K3 Chahār Ţāq Iran
142 D3 Chāh Badam Iran
143 E3 Chāh-e Khoshāb Iran
142 D3 Chāh-e Nūklok Iran
142 D4 Chāh-e Rāh Iran
142 D3 Chāh-e Shūr Iran
137 I5 Chāh Kūh Iran
143 E5 Chāh Lak Iran
143 F4 Chah Sandan Pak.
149 F5 Chaibasa India
207 G3 Chaigneau, Lac l. Canada
160 C2 Chai He r. China
162 B2 Chainat Thai.
162 B2 Chai Si r. Thai.
155 □ Chai Wan Hong Kong China
162 A3 Chaiya Thai.
162 B2 Chaiyaphum Thai.
235 L1 Chajarí Arg.
148 B3 Chakar r. Pak.
149 H5 Chakaria Bangl.
143 F4 Chakhānsūr Afgh.
149 E4 Chakia India
143 G5 Chakku Pak.
137 F2 Chakvi Georgia
230 D7 Chala Peru
224 G5 Chalatenango El Salvador
144 H4 Chalengkou China
207 G4 Chaleur Bay inlet Canada
155 D5 Chaling China
148 C5 Chalisgaon India
136 B3 Chalki i. Greece
185 J5 Chalkida Greece
126 A7 Chalky Inlet N.Z.
182 D3 Challans France
230 E7 Challapata Bol.
236 E5 Challenger Deep sea feature N. Pacific Ocean
212 D2 Challis U.S.A.
182 G2 Châlons-en-Champagne France
182 G3 Chalon-sur-Saône France
160 C2 Chaluhe China
142 C2 Chālūs Iran
179 K5 Cham Germany
163 D2 Cham, Cu Lao i. Vietnam
213 F4 Chama U.S.A.
233 J2 Chama r. Venez.
195 D5 Chama Zambia
163 B1 Chamah, Gunung mt. Malaysia
235 J2 Chamaico Arg.
196 A3 Chamais Bay Namibia
143 G4 Chaman Pak.
147 H4 Chamarajanagar India
152 C5 Chamba India
148 D4 Chambal r. India
207 G3 Chambeaux, Lac l. Canada
120 D3 Chamberlain r. Australia
205 H4 Chamberlain Canada
216 D3 Chamberlain U.S.A.
221 I1 Chamberlain Lake U.S.A.
215 H4 Chambers U.S.A.
221 E5 Chambersburg U.S.A.
182 G4 Chambéry France
195 D5 Chambeshi Zambia
184 C7 Chambi, Jebel mt. Tunisia
Chamdo China see Qamdo
182 G4 Chamechaude mt. France
142 C3 Cham-e Ḩannā Iran
142 C3 Chameshk Iran
235 I1 Chamical Arg.
149 F4 Chamlang mt. Nepal
162 B3 Châmnar Cambodia
Chamoli India see Gopeshwar
182 H4 Chamonix-Mont-Blanc France
147 I1 Champa India
204 B2 Champagne Canada
182 G2 Champagne France
197 H4 Champagne Castle mt. S. Africa
182 G3 Champagnole France
120 D2 Champagny Islands Australia
208 C5 Champaign U.S.A.
235 J1 Champaqui, Cerro mt. Arg.
162 C2 Champasak Laos
149 H5 Champhai India
208 D2 Champion U.S.A.
221 G2 Champlain U.S.A.
221 G2 Champlain, Lake Canada/U.S.A.
225 G4 Champotón Mex.
187 H4 Chamzinka Russia
162 B4 Chana Thai.
232 B3 Chañaral Chile
233 L3 Chanaro, Cerro mt. Venez.
235 H2 Chanco Chile
202 D3 Chandalar r. U.S.A.
147 I1 Chandarpur India
148 D3 Chandausi India
217 F6 Chandeleur Islands U.S.A.
149 E5 Chandia India
148 D3 Chandigarh India
215 G5 Chandler U.S.A.
209 I3 Chandos Lake Canada
149 G5 Chandpur Bangl.
148 D3 Chandpur India
149 H5 Chandraghona Bangl.
148 D6 Chandrapur India
148 D5 Chandur India
162 B2 Chang, Ko i. Thai.
195 D6 Changane r. Moz.
195 D5 Changara Moz.
160 E3 Changbai China
160 D3 Changbai Shan mts China/N. Korea
155 C7 Changcheng China
160 C2 Changchun China
160 C1 Changchunling China
154 F2 Changdao China
155 D4 Changde China
160 D4 Ch'angdo N. Korea
154 E3 Changfeng China
163 D1 Changhua Jiang r. China
162 □ Changi Sing.
144 G3 Changji China
155 C7 Changjiang China
155 E4 Chang Jiang r. China alt. Jinsha Jiang, alt. Tongtian He, alt. Zhi Qu, conv. Yangtze, long Yangtze Kiang
155 F4 Changjiang Kou China
160 D3 Changjin N. Korea
160 D3 Changjin-gang r. N. Korea
160 D3 Changjin-ho resr N. Korea
155 F5 Changle China
154 F2 Changli China
160 B1 Changling China
144 I4 Changma China
149 F3 Changna China
155 D5 Changning China
160 C4 Changnyŏn N. Korea
154 E1 Changping China
160 C4 Changsan-got pt N. Korea
155 D4 Changsha China
155 F4 Changshan China
160 B4 Changshan Qundao is China
155 C4 Changshou Chongqing China
155 D4 Changshou Hunan China
Changshoujie China see Changshou
155 F4 Changshu China
155 C5 Changshun China
155 E5 Changtai China
155 E5 Changting Fujian China
160 E1 Changting Heilongjiang China
160 C2 Changtu China
224 I6 Changuinola Panama
160 E6 Changwon S. Korea
154 C3 Changwu China
160 A4 Changxing Dao i. China
155 D4 Changyang China
154 F2 Changyi China
160 C4 Changyŏn N. Korea
154 E3 Changyuan China
154 D2 Changzhi China
155 F4 Changzhou China
185 K7 Chania Greece
154 B3 Chankou China
147 H3 Channapatna India
182 C2 Channel Islands English Chan.
214 C5 Channel Islands U.S.A.
214 B5 Channel Islands National Park U.S.A.
207 I4 Channel-Port-aux-Basques Canada
173 I6 Channel Tunnel France/U.K.
208 C2 Channing U.S.A.
183 M1 Chantada Spain
162 B2 Chanthaburi Thai.
182 F2 Chantilly France
217 E4 Chanute U.S.A.
132 I4 Chany, Ozero salt l. Russia
154 E2 Chaobai Xinhe r. China
155 E4 Chaohu China
155 E4 Chao Hu l. China
162 B2 Chao Phraya r. Thai.
149 H2 Chaowula Shan mt. China
155 E6 Chaoyang Guangdong China
Chaoyang Heilongjiang China see Jiayin
154 F1 Chaoyang Liaoning China
156 B2 Chaoyang Nei Mongol Zizhiqu China
155 E6 Chaozhou China
234 E1 Chapada Diamantina, Parque Nacional nat. park Brazil
234 A1 Chapada dos Guimarães Brazil
234 C1 Chapada dos Veadeiros, Parque Nacional da nat. park Brazil
225 D3 Chapala Mex.
225 D3 Chapala, Laguna de l. Mex.
143 G3 Chāpārī, Kōtal-e Afgh.
233 I4 Chaparral Col.
140 B2 Chapayevo Kazakh.
187 I4 Chapayevsk Russia
232 F3 Chapecó Brazil
232 F3 Chapecó r. Brazil
173 F4 Chapel-en-le-Frith U.K.
219 E5 Chapel Hill U.S.A.
178 C4 Chapelle-lez-Herlaimont Belgium
173 F4 Chapeltown U.K.
209 F2 Chapleau Canada
187 F4 Chaplygin Russia
187 E6 Chaplynka Ukr.
220 B6 Chapmanville U.S.A.
125 G8 Chappell Islands Australia
149 F4 Chapra India
230 E7 Chaqui Bol.
148 D2 Char India
225 D3 Charcas Mex.
149 H3 Char Chu r. China
127 I3 Charcot Island Antarctica
205 E2 Chard Canada
173 E7 Chard U.K.
139 K5 Chardāvol Iran
220 C4 Chardon U.S.A.
180 D5 Charef Alg.
180 C5 Charef, Oued watercourse Morocco
182 E3 Charente r. France
142 D4 Charg Iran
143 H3 Chārīkār Afgh.
216 E3 Chariton r. U.S.A.
209 F3 Charity Island U.S.A.
142 C4 Charkas Iran
132 G3 Charkayuvom Russia
148 D4 Charkhari India
178 C4 Charleroi Belgium
211 K4 Charles, Cape U.S.A.
208 A4 Charles City U.S.A.
120 E2 Charles Point Australia
126 C4 Charleston N.Z.
219 B4 Charleston IL U.S.A.
221 I2 Charleston ME U.S.A.
217 F4 Charleston MO U.S.A.
219 E5 Charleston SC U.S.A.
220 C5 Charleston WV U.S.A.
215 E3 Charleston Peak U.S.A.
175 J4 Charlestown Ireland
221 G3 Charlestown NH U.S.A.
221 H4 Charlestown RI U.S.A.
221 E5 Charles Town U.S.A.
119 E4 Charleville Australia
175 J5 Charleville Ireland
182 G2 Charleville-Mézières France
209 E3 Charlevoix U.S.A.
127 J5 Charlie, Dome ice feature Antarctica
204 E3 Charlie Lake Canada
209 E4 Charlotte MI U.S.A.
219 D5 Charlotte NC U.S.A.
219 D7 Charlotte Harbor b. U.S.A.
220 D5 Charlottesville U.S.A.
207 H4 Charlottetown Canada
233 L2 Charlotteville Trin. and Tob.
125 E6 Charlton Australia
206 E3 Charlton Island Canada
186 F2 Charozero Russia
148 B2 Charsadda Pak.
Charshangngy Turkm. see Köýtendag
119 E4 Charters Towers Australia
182 E2 Chartres France
Charvakskoye Vodokhranilishche resr Kazakh./Uzbek. see Chorvoq suv ombori
141 J1 Charysh r. Russia
141 J2 Charyshskoye Russia
235 K2 Chascomús Arg.
204 F4 Chase Canada
140 E5 Chashkent Turkm.
143 E3 Chashmeh Nūrī Iran
142 D3 Chashmeh-ye Palasi Iran
187 D4 Chashniki Belarus
126 B7 Chaslands Mistake c. N.Z.
160 D3 Chasŏng N. Korea
142 D3 Chastab, Kūh-e mts Iran
182 D3 Châteaubriant France
182 E3 Château-du-Loir France
182 E2 Châteaudun France
221 F2 Chateaugay U.S.A.
221 G2 Châteauguay Canada
182 B2 Châteaulin France
182 F3 Châteauneuf-sur-Loire France
182 E3 Châteauroux France
179 E6 Château-Salins France
182 F2 Château-Thierry France
178 C4 Châtelet Belgium
182 E3 Châtellerault France
208 A4 Chatfield U.S.A.
209 F4 Chatham Canada
173 H6 Chatham U.K.
221 H4 Chatham MA U.S.A.
221 G3 Chatham NY U.S.A.
220 D6 Chatham VA U.S.A.
119 I6 Chatham Islands N.Z.
237 H8 Chatham Rise sea feature S. Pacific Ocean
204 C4 Chatham Sound sea chan. Canada
204 C3 Chatham Strait U.S.A.
141 G4 Chatkal r. Kyrg.
141 G4 Chatkal Range mts Kyrg.
149 F4 Chatra India
209 G3 Chatsworth Canada
208 C5 Chatsworth U.S.A.
219 C5 Chattanooga U.S.A.
173 H5 Chatteris U.K.
162 B2 Chatturat Thai.
141 H4 Chatyr-Köl l. Kyrg.
141 I4 Chatyr-Tash Kyrg.
162 C3 Châu Đôc Vietnam
148 B4 Chauhtan India
149 H5 Chauk Myanmar
149 E4 Chauka r. India
148 D3 Chaukhamba mts India
182 G2 Chaumont France
162 A2 Chaungwabyin Myanmar
133 R3 Chaunskaya Guba b. Russia
182 F2 Chauny France
163 D2 Châu Ô Vietnam
149 F4 Chauparan India
220 D3 Chautauqua, Lake U.S.A.
141 H4 Chauvay Kyrg.
147 I4 Chavakachcheri Sri Lanka
142 B3 Chavār Iran
231 I4 Chaves Brazil
183 M2 Chaves Port.
206 E2 Chavigny, Lac l. Canada
187 D4 Chavusy Belarus
148 A3 Chawal r. Pak.
155 B6 Chay, Sông r. Vietnam
156 E1 Chayatyn, Khrebet ridge Russia
235 J2 Chazón Arg.
221 G2 Chazy U.S.A.

Cheadle

173 F5 **Cheadle** U.K.
220 D5 **Cheat** *r.* U.S.A.
176 F5 **Cheb** Czech Rep.
184 D7 **Chebba** Tunisia
169 P4 **Cheboksarskoye Vodokhranilishche** *resr* Russia
186 H3 **Cheboksary** Russia
209 E3 **Cheboygan** U.S.A.
187 H7 **Chechen', Ostrov** *i.* Russia
Chechenia *aut. rep.* Russia *see* **Chechenskaya Respublika**
187 H7 **Chechenskaya Respublika** *aut. rep.* Russia
Chechnia *aut. rep.* Russia *see* **Chechenskaya Respublika**
217 E5 **Checotah** U.S.A.
160 A5 **Chedao** China
173 E6 **Cheddar** U.K.
205 G3 **Cheecham** Canada
192 B1 **Chefchaouene** Morocco
202 B3 **Chefornak** U.S.A.
197 J1 **Chefu** Moz.
156 D2 **Chegdomyn** Russia
192 B2 **Chegga** Mauritania
195 D5 **Chegutu** Zimbabwe
212 B2 **Chehalis** U.S.A.
139 K5 **Cheharīz** *tourist site* Iraq
143 E4 **Chehel Pāyeh** Iran
Cheju S. Korea *see* **Jeju**
150 E3 **Cheju do** S. Korea
Cheju-do *i.* S. Korea *see* **Jeju-do**
187 F4 **Chekhov** *Moskovskaya Oblast'* Russia
156 F3 **Chekhov** *Sakhalinskaya Oblast'* Russia
156 D2 **Chekunda** Russia
212 B2 **Chelan, Lake** U.S.A.
Cheleken Turkm. *see* **Hazar**
235 I3 **Chelforó** Arg.
140 B2 **Chelkar** Kazakh.
177 K5 **Chełm** Poland
173 H6 **Chelmer** *r.* U.K.
177 I4 **Chełmno** Poland
173 H6 **Chelmsford** U.K.
221 H3 **Chelmsford** U.S.A.
173 E6 **Cheltenham** U.K.
183 P3 **Chelva** Spain
132 H4 **Chelyabinsk** Russia
195 D5 **Chemba** Moz.
148 D2 **Chêm Co** *l.* China
179 K4 **Chemnitz** Germany
221 E3 **Chemung** *r.* U.S.A.
143 H4 **Chenab** *r.* India/Pak.
192 B2 **Chenachane** Alg.
221 F3 **Chenango** *r.* U.S.A.
212 C2 **Cheney** U.S.A.
217 D4 **Cheney Reservoir** U.S.A.
147 I3 **Chengalpattu** India
154 E2 **Cheng'an** China
155 D5 **Chengbu** China
154 E1 **Chengde** China
155 B4 **Chengdu** China
154 C3 **Chenggu** China
155 B5 **Chengguan** China
155 E6 **Chenghai** China
155 B5 **Chengjiang Fossil Site** *tourist site* China
155 C4 **Chengkou** China
151 D5 **Chengmai** China
160 B5 **Chengshan** China
153 I5 **Chengxian** China
160 B4 **Chengzitan** China
154 F3 **Cheniu Shan** *i.* China
147 I3 **Chennai** India
208 C5 **Chenoa** U.S.A.
156 B2 **Chenqing** China
Chenqingqiao China *see* **Chenqing**
155 D5 **Chenxi** China
155 D5 **Chenzhou** China
160 D5 **Cheonan** S. Korea
160 E6 **Cheongdo** S. Korea
160 D5 **Cheongju** S. Korea
Cheo Reo Vietnam *see* **A Yun Pa**
160 D4 **Cheorwon** S. Korea
230 C5 **Chepén** Peru
235 I1 **Chepes** Arg.
173 E6 **Chepstow** U.K.
186 I3 **Cheptsa** *r.* Russia
139 K5 **Cheqād Kabūd** Iran
208 B2 **Chequamegon Bay** U.S.A.
182 F3 **Cher** *r.* France
225 D4 **Cherán** Mex.
219 E5 **Cheraw** U.S.A.
182 D2 **Cherbourg-Octeville** France
183 R4 **Cherchell** Alg.
187 I4 **Cherdakly** Russia
150 C1 **Cheremkhovo** Russia
141 J1 **Cheremnoye** Russia
158 D2 **Cheremshany** Russia
186 F3 **Cherepovets** Russia
186 H2 **Cherevkovo** Russia
180 C5 **Chergui, Chott ech** *imp. l.* Alg.
184 B7 **Chéria** Alg.
187 E5 **Cherkasy** Ukr.
187 G6 **Cherkessk** Russia
147 I2 **Cherla** India
141 H1 **Cherlak** Russia
141 H1 **Cherlakskoye** Russia
195 C5 **Chermenze** Angola
186 I3 **Chernaya Kholunitsa** Russia
158 C2 **Chernigovka** Russia
187 D5 **Chernihiv** Ukr.
187 F6 **Cherninivka** Ukr.
187 C5 **Chernivtsi** Ukr.
150 B1 **Chernogorsk** Russia
141 I1 **Chernoretsk** Kazakh.
186 H3 **Chernovskoye** Russia
187 D5 **Chernyakhiv** Ukr.
177 J3 **Chernyakhovsk** Russia
187 F5 **Chernyanka** Russia
156 B1 **Chernyayevo** Russia
153 K1 **Chernyshevsk** Russia
133 M3 **Chernyshevskiy** Russia
187 H6 **Chernyye Zemli** *reg.* Russia
Chernyy Irtysh *r.* China/Kazakh. *see* **Ertix He**
140 C2 **Chernyy Otrog** Russia
187 H5 **Chernyy Yar** Russia
216 E3 **Cherokee** *IA* U.S.A.
217 D4 **Cherokee** *OK* U.S.A.
217 E4 **Cherokees, Lake o' the** U.S.A.
219 E7 **Cherokee Sound** Bahamas
235 H3 **Cherquenco** Chile
149 G4 **Cherrapunji** India
215 E2 **Cherry Creek** U.S.A.
215 E1 **Cherry Creek Mountains** U.S.A.
221 J2 **Cherryfield** U.S.A.
119 G3 **Cherry Island** Solomon Is
209 I4 **Cherry Valley** Canada
221 F3 **Cherry Valley** U.S.A.
Cherskiy Range *mts* Russia *see* **Cherskogo, Khrebet**
133 P3 **Cherskogo, Khrebet** *mts Respublika Sakha (Yakutiya)* Russia
153 J1 **Cherskogo, Khrebet** *mts Zabaykal'skiy Kray* Russia
187 G5 **Chertkovo** Russia
186 I2 **Cherva** Russia
185 K3 **Cherven Bryag** Bulg.
187 C5 **Chervonohrad** Ukr.
187 E5 **Chervonozavods'ke** Ukr.
187 D4 **Chervyen'** Belarus
173 F6 **Cherwell** *r.* U.K.
187 D4 **Cherykaw** Belarus
209 E4 **Chesaning** U.S.A.
221 E6 **Chesapeake** U.S.A.
221 E5 **Chesapeake Bay** U.S.A.
173 G6 **Chesham** U.K.
221 G3 **Cheshire** U.S.A.
173 E4 **Cheshire Plain** U.K.
140 E5 **Cheshme Vtoroy** Turkm.
132 F3 **Cheshskaya Guba** *b.* Russia
141 H5 **Cheshtebe** Tajik.
173 G6 **Cheshunt** U.K.
140 E1 **Chesma** Russia
Chesnokovka Russia *see* **Novoaltaysk**
173 E4 **Chester** U.K.
214 B1 **Chester** *CA* U.S.A.
219 B4 **Chester** *IL* U.S.A.
212 E1 **Chester** *MT* U.S.A.
221 F5 **Chester** *PA* U.S.A.
219 D5 **Chester** *SC* U.S.A.
221 E5 **Chester** *r.* U.S.A.
173 F4 **Chesterfield** U.K.
119 F3 **Chesterfield, Îles** *is* New Caledonia
205 K2 **Chesterfield Inlet** Canada
205 K2 **Chesterfield Inlet** *inlet* Canada
172 F3 **Chester-le-Street** U.K.
221 E5 **Chestertown** *MD* U.S.A.
221 G3 **Chestertown** *NY* U.S.A.
221 F2 **Chesterville** Canada
220 D4 **Chestnut Ridge** U.S.A.
221 I1 **Chesuncook** U.S.A.
221 I1 **Chesuncook Lake** U.S.A.
184 B6 **Chetaïbi** Alg.
207 H4 **Chéticamp** Canada
147 G4 **Chetlat** *i.* India
225 G4 **Chetumal** Mex.
204 E3 **Chetwynd** Canada
155 □ **Cheung Chau** *Hong Kong* China
155 □ **Cheung Chau** *i. Hong Kong* China
126 D5 **Cheviot** N.Z.
172 E2 **Cheviot Hills** U.K.
123 C5 **Cheviot Range** *hills* Australia
212 C1 **Chewelah** U.S.A.
217 D5 **Cheyenne** *OK* U.S.A.
213 F3 **Cheyenne** *WY* U.S.A.
216 C3 **Cheyenne** *r.* U.S.A.
217 C4 **Cheyenne Wells** U.S.A.
121 B7 **Cheyne Bay** Australia
204 E4 **Chezacut** Canada
148 C4 **Chhapar** India
148 D4 **Chhatarpur** India
148 B3 **Chhatr** Pak.
149 E5 **Chhattisgarh** *state* India
148 D5 **Chhindwara** India
148 C5 **Chhota Udepur** India
148 C4 **Chhoti Sadri** India
162 C3 **Chhuk** Cambodia
149 G4 **Chhukha** Bhutan
162 C2 **Chi, Lam** *r.* Thai.
Chiai Taiwan *see* **Jiayi**
195 E4 **Chiamboni** Kenya
162 A1 **Chiang Dao** Thai.
162 B1 **Chiang Kham** Thai.
162 B1 **Chiang Khan** Thai.
162 A1 **Chiang Mai** Thai.
162 A1 **Chiang Rai** Thai.
225 F4 **Chiapas** *state* Mex.
184 C2 **Chiari** Italy
225 E4 **Chiautla** Mex.
Chiayi Taiwan *see* **Jiayi**
159 G7 **Chiba** Japan
155 D4 **Chibi** China
195 B5 **Chibia** Angola
195 D6 **Chiboma** Moz.
207 F4 **Chibougamau** Canada
207 F4 **Chibougamau, Lac** *l.* Canada
197 J2 **Chibuto** Moz.
149 G2 **Chibuzhang Co** *l.* China
Chibuzhang Hu *l.* China *see* **Chibuzhang Co**
208 D5 **Chicago** U.S.A.
208 D5 **Chicago Heights** U.S.A.
208 C5 **Chicago Ship Canal** U.S.A.
233 I3 **Chicamocha** *r.* Col.
233 L3 **Chicanán** *r.* Venez.
204 B3 **Chichagof** U.S.A.
204 B3 **Chichagof Island** U.S.A.
156 A1 **Chichatka** Russia
154 E1 **Chicheng** China
225 G3 **Chichén Itzá** *tourist site* Mex.
173 G7 **Chichester** U.K.
118 B4 **Chichester Range** *mts* Australia
159 F7 **Chichibu** Japan
159 F7 **Chichibu-Tama Kokuritsu-kōen** *nat. park* Japan
221 E6 **Chickahominy** *r.* U.S.A.
219 C5 **Chickamauga Lake** U.S.A.
217 D5 **Chickasha** U.S.A.
183 M4 **Chiclana de la Frontera** Spain
230 C5 **Chiclayo** Peru
232 C6 **Chico** *r. Chubut* Arg.
235 H4 **Chico** *r. Chubut* Arg.
232 C7 **Chico** *r. Santa Cruz* Arg.
214 B2 **Chico** U.S.A.
197 K2 **Chicomo** Moz.
225 F5 **Chicomucelo** Mex.
221 G3 **Chicopee** U.S.A.
161 I2 **Chico Sapocoy, Mount** Phil.
207 F4 **Chicoutimi** Canada
197 I1 **Chicualacuala** Moz.
147 H4 **Chidambaram** India
197 K2 **Chidenguele** Moz.
207 H1 **Chidley, Cape** Canada
197 K2 **Chiducuane** Moz.
219 D6 **Chiefland** U.S.A.
176 F7 **Chiemsee** *l.* Germany
178 D5 **Chiers** *r.* France
184 F3 **Chieti** Italy
225 E4 **Chietla** Mex.
154 F1 **Chifeng** China
234 E2 **Chifre, Serra do** *mts* Brazil
207 G4 **Chignecto Bay** Canada
233 H3 **Chigorodó** Col.
195 D6 **Chigubo** Moz.
149 G3 **Chigu Co** *l.* China
143 G3 **Chihil Abdālān, Kōh-e** *mts* Afgh.
224 C1 **Chihuahua** Mex.
224 C1 **Chihuahua** *state* Mex.
213 F6 **Chihuahua, Desierto de** *des.* Mex./U.S.A.
155 D6 **Chikan** China
186 D3 **Chikhachevo** Russia
148 D5 **Chikhli** India
147 H3 **Chikkaballapur** India
147 G3 **Chikkamagaluru** India
159 F6 **Chikuma-gawa** *r.* Japan
204 E4 **Chilanko Forks** Canada
225 E4 **Chilapa** Mex.
135 F3 **Chilas** Pak.
147 H5 **Chilaw** Sri Lanka
214 B2 **Chilcoot** U.S.A.
204 E4 **Chilcotin** *r.* Canada
123 F5 **Childers** Australia
217 C5 **Childress** U.S.A.
232 B5 **Chile** *country* S. America
237 N8 **Chile Basin** *sea feature* S. Pacific Ocean
232 C3 **Chilecito** Arg.
237 N8 **Chile Rise** *sea feature* S. Pacific Ocean
187 H6 **Chilgir** Russia
149 F6 **Chilika Lake** India
195 C5 **Chililabombwe** Zambia
204 E4 **Chilko** *r.* Canada
204 E4 **Chilko Lake** Canada
235 H3 **Chillán** Chile
235 H3 **Chillán, Nevado** *mts* Chile
235 K3 **Chillar** Arg.
208 C5 **Chillicothe** *IL* U.S.A.
217 E4 **Chillicothe** *MO* U.S.A.
220 B5 **Chillicothe** *OH* U.S.A.
148 C1 **Chillinji** Pak.
204 E5 **Chilliwack** Canada
Chil'mamedkum, Peski *des.* Turkm. *see* **Çilmämmetgum**
232 B6 **Chiloé, Isla de** *i.* Chile
213 B3 **Chiloquin** U.S.A.
225 E4 **Chilpancingo** Mex.
125 G6 **Chiltern** Australia
173 G6 **Chiltern Hills** U.K.
208 C3 **Chilton** U.S.A.
Chilung Taiwan *see* **Jilong**
189 H6 **Chilwa, Lake** *l.* Malawi
195 D4 **Chimala** Tanz.
224 J6 **Chimán** Panama
178 C4 **Chimay** Belgium
178 C4 **Chimay, Bois de** *for.* Belgium
235 I1 **Chimbas** Arg.
Chimbay Uzbek. *see* **Chimboy**
230 C4 **Chimborazo** *mt.* Ecuador
230 C5 **Chimbote** Peru
140 D4 **Chimboy** Uzbek.
233 I2 **Chimichagua** Col.
195 D5 **Chimoio** Moz.
144 C4 **Chimtargha, Qullai** *mt.* Tajik.
Chimtorga, Gora *mt.* Tajik. *see* **Chimtargha, Qullai**
150 B3 **China** *country* Asia
225 E2 **China** Mex.
233 I3 **Chinácota** Col.
155 D5 **China Danxia** *tourist site* China
225 G4 **Chinajá** Guat.
215 D4 **China Lake** *CA* U.S.A.
221 I2 **China Lake** *ME* U.S.A.
224 H5 **Chinandega** Nicaragua
214 C5 **China Point** U.S.A.
Chinaz Uzbek. *see* **Chinoz**
230 C6 **Chincha Alta** Peru
204 F3 **Chinchaga** *r.* Canada
123 E5 **Chinchilla** Australia
223 G5 **Chinchorro, Banco** *sea feature* Mex.
221 F6 **Chincoteague Bay** U.S.A.
195 D5 **Chinde** Moz.
150 B3 **Chindu** China
149 H5 **Chindwin** *r.* Myanmar
148 C2 **Chineni** India
233 I3 **Chingaza, Parque Nacional** *nat. park* Col.
160 C4 **Chinghwa** N. Korea
195 C5 **Chingola** Zambia
195 B5 **Chinguar** Angola
195 D5 **Chinhoyi** Zimbabwe
148 C3 **Chiniot** Pak.
224 B2 **Chinipas** Mex.
162 C2 **Chinit, Stœng** *r.* Cambodia
160 E6 **Chinju** S. Korea
194 C3 **Chinko** *r.* C.A.R.
215 H3 **Chinle** U.S.A.
215 H3 **Chinle Valley** U.S.A.
215 H3 **Chinle Wash** *watercourse* U.S.A.
Chinmen Tao *i.* Taiwan *see* **Jinmen Dao**
147 H2 **Chinnur** India
159 F7 **Chino** Japan
182 E3 **Chinon** France
237 H3 **Chinook Trough** *sea feature* N. Pacific Ocean
215 F4 **Chino Valley** U.S.A.
141 G4 **Chinoz** Uzbek.
195 D5 **Chinsali** Zambia
147 H3 **Chintamani** India
184 E2 **Chioggia** Italy
185 L5 **Chios** Greece
185 K5 **Chios** *i.* Greece
195 D5 **Chipata** Zambia
235 I4 **Chipchihua, Sierra de** *mts* Arg.
195 B5 **Chipindo** Angola
195 D6 **Chipinge** Zimbabwe
147 G2 **Chiplun** India
173 E6 **Chippenham** U.K.
208 B3 **Chippewa** *r.* U.S.A.
208 B3 **Chippewa Falls** U.S.A.
173 F6 **Chipping Norton** U.K.
173 E6 **Chipping Sodbury** U.K.
221 J2 **Chiputneticook Lakes** U.S.A.
Chiquibul, Parque Nacional *nat. park* Belize *see* **Chiquibul National Park**
225 G4 **Chiquibul National Park** Belize
225 G5 **Chiquimula** Guat.
233 I3 **Chiquinquirá** Col.
187 G5 **Chir** *r.* Russia
147 I3 **Chirada** India
147 G4 **Chirakkal** India
147 I3 **Chirala** India
143 G3 **Chīras** Afgh.
148 C3 **Chirawa** India
Chirchik Uzbek. *see* **Chirchiq**
141 G4 **Chirchiq** Uzbek.
195 D6 **Chiredzi** Zimbabwe
215 H5 **Chiricahua National Monument** *nat. park* U.S.A.
215 H6 **Chiricahua Peak** U.S.A.
233 I2 **Chiriguaná** Col.
202 C4 **Chirikof Island** U.S.A.
224 I6 **Chiriquí, Golfo de** *b.* Panama
224 I6 **Chiriquí, Laguna de** *b.* Panama
173 D5 **Chirk** U.K.
175 F5 **Chirnside** U.K.
185 K3 **Chirpan** Bulg.
224 I6 **Chirripó** *mt.* Costa Rica
195 C5 **Chirundu** Zambia
206 E3 **Chisasibi** Canada
225 G5 **Chisec** Guat.
208 A2 **Chisholm** U.S.A.
143 F3 **Chisht-e Sharīf** Afgh.
148 C3 **Chishtian** Pak.
155 B4 **Chishui** China
187 D6 **Chişinău** Moldova
177 J7 **Chişineu-Criş** Romania
187 I4 **Chistopol'** Russia
150 D1 **Chita** Russia
195 B5 **Chitado** Angola
195 D5 **Chitambo** Zambia
195 C4 **Chitato** Angola
205 H4 **Chitek Lake** Canada
195 B5 **Chitembo** Angola
195 D4 **Chitipa** Malawi
195 C5 **Chitokoloki** Zambia
158 G3 **Chitose** Japan
147 H3 **Chitradurga** India
148 B2 **Chitral** Pak.
148 B2 **Chitral** *r.* Pak.
224 I7 **Chitré** Panama
149 G5 **Chittagong** Bangl.
149 F5 **Chittaranjan** India
148 C4 **Chittaurgarh** India
147 H3 **Chittoor** India
147 H4 **Chittur** India
195 D5 **Chitungulu** Zambia
195 D5 **Chitungwiza** Zimbabwe
195 C5 **Chiume** Angola
224 A2 **Chívato, Punta** *pt* Mex.
195 D5 **Chivhu** Zimbabwe
235 K2 **Chivilcoy** Arg.
155 D6 **Chixixu** China
139 J4 **Chiyā Surkh** Iraq
155 E4 **Chizhou** China
159 D7 **Chizu** Japan
141 H1 **Chkalovo** Kazakh.
186 G3 **Chkalovsk** Russia
158 C2 **Chkalovskoye** Russia
192 C1 **Chlef** Alg.
183 Q4 **Chlef, Oued** *r.* Alg.
156 F1 **Chlya, Ozero** *l.* Russia
162 □ **Choa Chu Kang** Sing.
162 □ **Choa Chu Kang** *h.* Sing.
162 C2 **Chŏâm Khsant** Cambodia
235 H1 **Choapa** *r.* Chile
195 C5 **Chobe National Park** Botswana
215 E5 **Chocolate Mountains** U.S.A.
233 I3 **Chocontá** Col.
160 C4 **Cho-do** *i.* N. Korea
160 D6 **Cho-do** *i.* S. Korea
179 K4 **Chodov** Czech Rep.
235 J3 **Choele Choel** Arg.
156 D1 **Chogar** *r.* Russia
148 C2 **Chogo Lungma Glacier** Pak.
187 H6 **Chograyskoye Vodokhranilishche** *resr* Russia
205 I4 **Choiceland** Canada
119 F2 **Choiseul** *i.* Solomon Is
232 E8 **Choiseul Sound** *sea chan.* Falkland Is
224 B2 **Choix** Mex.
177 H4 **Chojnice** Poland
159 G5 **Chōkai-san** *vol.* Japan
217 D6 **Choke Canyon Lake** U.S.A.
194 D2 **Ch'ok'ē Mountains** Eth.
194 D2 **Ch'ok'ē Terara** *mt.* Eth.
149 F3 **Choksum** China
133 P2 **Chokurdakh** Russia
195 D6 **Chókwè** Moz.
182 D3 **Cholet** France
235 H4 **Cholila** Arg.
141 H4 **Cholpon** Kyrg.
141 I4 **Cholpon-Ata** Kyrg.
224 H5 **Choluteca** Hond.
195 C5 **Choma** Zambia
149 G4 **Chomo Lhari** *mt.* Bhutan
162 A1 **Chom Thong** Thai.
176 F5 **Chomutov** Czech Rep.
133 L3 **Chona** *r.* Russia
162 B2 **Chon Buri** Thai.
160 D3 **Ch'ŏnch'ŏn** N. Korea
230 B4 **Chone** Ecuador
160 C4 **Ch'ŏngch'ŏn-gang** *r.* N. Korea
160 E3 **Ch'ŏngjin** N. Korea
160 C4 **Chŏngju** N. Korea
Ch'ŏngju S. Korea *see* **Cheongju**
162 B2 **Chŏng Kal** Cambodia
153 L5 **Chongming Dao** *i.* China
160 D4 **Chŏngp'yŏng** N. Korea
155 C4 **Chongqing** China
155 C4 **Chongqing** *mun.* China
155 E5 **Chongren** China
197 J2 **Chonguene** Moz.
195 C5 **Chongwe** Zambia
155 D4 **Chongyang** China
155 F5 **Chongyang Xi** *r.* China
155 E5 **Chongyi** China
155 C6 **Chongzuo** China
Chŏnju S. Korea *see* **Jeonju**
Chonogol Mongolia *see* **Erdenetsagaan**
232 B7 **Chonos, Archipiélago de los** *is* Chile
149 F3 **Cho Oyu** *mt.* China
235 B4 **Chopim** *r.* Brazil
235 B4 **Chopinzinho** Brazil
221 F5 **Choptank** *r.* U.S.A.
148 B4 **Chor** Pak.
185 K7 **Chora Sfakion** Greece
173 E4 **Chorley** U.K.
187 D5 **Chornobyl'** Ukr.
187 E6 **Chornomors'ke** Crimea
187 C5 **Chortkiv** Ukr.
141 G4 **Chorvoq suv ombori** *resr* Kazakh./Uzbek.
160 C3 **Ch'osan** N. Korea
159 G7 **Chōshi** Japan
235 H4 **Chos Malal** Arg.
176 G4 **Choszczno** Poland
230 C5 **Chota** Peru
212 D2 **Choteau** U.S.A.
148 B3 **Choti** Pak.
192 A2 **Choûm** Mauritania
214 B3 **Chowchilla** U.S.A.
204 F4 **Chown, Mount** Canada
141 K2 **Choya** Russia
150 D2 **Choybalsan** Mongolia
150 C2 **Choyr** Mongolia
177 H6 **Chřiby** *hills* Czech Rep.
208 D6 **Chrisman** U.S.A.
197 I3 **Chrissiesmeer** S. Africa
126 D5 **Christchurch** N.Z.
173 F7 **Christchurch** U.K.
203 L2 **Christian, Cape** Canada
197 F3 **Christiana** S. Africa
209 G3 **Christian Island** Canada
220 C6 **Christiansburg** U.S.A.
Christianshåb Greenland *see* **Qasigiannguit**
204 C3 **Christian Sound** *sea chan.* U.S.A.
205 G3 **Christina** *r.* Canada
151 C8 **Christmas Island** *terr.* Indian Ocean

Colorado

235 J3 **Colorado** *r.* Arg.
215 E5 **Colorado** *r.* Mex./U.S.A.
217 D6 **Colorado** *r.* U.S.A.
213 F4 **Colorado** *state* U.S.A.
235 J3 **Colorado, Delta del Río** Arg.
215 F3 **Colorado City** *AZ* U.S.A.
217 C5 **Colorado City** *TX* U.S.A.
215 D5 **Colorado Desert** U.S.A.
215 H2 **Colorado National Monument** *nat. park* U.S.A.
215 G3 **Colorado Plateau** U.S.A.
215 E4 **Colorado River Aqueduct** *canal* U.S.A.
213 F4 **Colorado Springs** U.S.A.
225 D3 **Colotlán** Mex.
179 L1 **Cölpin** Germany
173 G5 **Colsterworth** U.K.
173 I5 **Coltishall** U.K.
215 D4 **Colton** *CA* U.S.A.
221 F2 **Colton** *NY* U.S.A.
215 G2 **Colton (abandoned)** U.S.A.
221 E5 **Columbia** *MD* U.S.A.
217 E4 **Columbia** *MO* U.S.A.
217 F6 **Columbia** *MS* U.S.A.
221 E4 **Columbia** *PA* U.S.A.
219 D5 **Columbia** *SC* U.S.A.
219 C5 **Columbia** *TN* U.S.A.
212 B2 **Columbia** *r.* U.S.A.
203 K1 **Columbia, Cape** Canada
221 E5 **Columbia, District of** *admin. dist.* U.S.A.
204 F4 **Columbia, Mount** Canada
209 E5 **Columbia City** U.S.A.
221 J2 **Columbia Falls** *ME* U.S.A.
212 D1 **Columbia Falls** *MT* U.S.A.
204 F4 **Columbia Mountains** Canada
212 C2 **Columbia Plateau** U.S.A.
196 B6 **Columbine, Cape** S. Africa
219 C5 **Columbus** *GA* U.S.A.
219 C4 **Columbus** *IN* U.S.A.
217 F5 **Columbus** *MS* U.S.A.
212 E2 **Columbus** *MT* U.S.A.
216 D3 **Columbus** *NE* U.S.A.
213 F6 **Columbus** *NM* U.S.A.
220 B5 **Columbus** *OH* U.S.A.
217 D6 **Columbus** *TX* U.S.A.
208 C4 **Columbus** *WI* U.S.A.
208 B5 **Columbus Junction** U.S.A.
219 F7 **Columbus Point** Bahamas
215 D2 **Columbus Salt Marsh** U.S.A.
214 A2 **Colusa** U.S.A.
126 E2 **Colville** N.Z.
212 C1 **Colville** U.S.A.
202 C3 **Colville** *r.* U.S.A.
126 E2 **Colville Channel** N.Z.
202 F3 **Colville Lake** Canada
173 D4 **Colwyn Bay** U.K.
184 E2 **Comacchio** Italy
184 E2 **Comacchio, Valli di** *lag.* Italy
149 G3 **Comai** China
235 H4 **Comallo** *r.* Arg.
217 D6 **Comanche** U.S.A.
127 L2 **Comandante Ferraz** *research stn* Antarctica
235 I2 **Comandante Salas** Arg.
177 M7 **Comănești** Romania
224 H5 **Comayagua** Hond.
235 H1 **Combarbalá** Chile
175 M3 **Comber** U.K.
209 I3 **Combermere** Canada
149 H6 **Combermere Bay** Myanmar
178 A4 **Combles** France
197 J1 **Combomune** Moz.
125 J3 **Comboyne** Australia
206 E3 **Comencho, Lac** *l.* Canada
175 K5 **Comeragh Mountains** Ireland
217 D6 **Comfort** U.S.A.
149 G5 **Comilla** Bangl.
178 A4 **Comines** Belgium
184 C4 **Comino, Capo** *c. Sardinia* Italy
225 F4 **Comitán de Domínguez** Mex.
221 G4 **Commack** U.S.A.
209 H3 **Commanda** Canada
203 J3 **Committee Bay** Canada
127 I6 **Commonwealth Bay** Antarctica
184 C2 **Como** Italy
184 C2 **Como, Lake** Italy
149 G3 **Como Chamling** *l.* China
232 C7 **Comodoro Rivadavia** Arg.
192 B4 **Comoé, Parc National de la** *nat. park* Côte d'Ivoire
147 H4 **Comorin, Cape** India
195 E5 **Comoros** *country* Africa
182 F2 **Compiègne** France
224 C3 **Compostela** Mex.
161 J5 **Compostela** Phil.
235 C4 **Comprida, Ilha** *i.* Brazil
208 C5 **Compton** U.S.A.
187 D6 **Comrat** Moldova
174 E4 **Comrie** U.K.
217 C6 **Comstock** U.S.A.
162 C1 **Con, Sông** *r.* Vietnam
149 H4 **Cona** China
192 A4 **Conakry** Guinea
235 I4 **Cona Niyeo** Arg.
125 G8 **Conara** Australia
234 C2 **Conceição** *r.* Brazil
234 E2 **Conceição da Barra** Brazil
231 I5 **Conceição do Araguaia** Brazil
232 C3 **Concepción** Arg.
231 F7 **Concepción** Bol.
235 H3 **Concepción** Chile
Concepción Panama *see* **La Concepción**
232 E2 **Concepción** Para.
235 K2 **Concepción del Uruguay** Arg.
214 B4 **Conception, Point** U.S.A.
207 J4 **Conception Bay South** Canada
219 F7 **Conception Island** Bahamas
234 C3 **Conchas** Brazil
213 F5 **Conchas Lake** U.S.A.
215 H4 **Concho** U.S.A.
224 C2 **Conchos** *r. Chihuahua* Mex.
225 E2 **Conchos** *r. Nuevo León/Tamaulipas* Mex.
214 A3 **Concord** *CA* U.S.A.
219 D5 **Concord** *NC* U.S.A.
221 H3 **Concord** *NH* U.S.A.
127 J6 **Concordia** *research stn* Antarctica
235 L1 **Concordia** Arg.
196 B4 **Concordia** S. Africa
217 D4 **Concordia** U.S.A.
141 H5 **Concord Peak** Afgh.
125 I1 **Condamine** Australia
162 C3 **Côn Đao** Vietnam
224 H5 **Condega** Nicaragua
234 E1 **Condeúba** Brazil
125 G4 **Condobolin** Australia
183 E5 **Condom** France
212 B2 **Condon** U.S.A.
178 D4 **Condroz** *reg.* Belgium
219 C6 **Conecuh** *r.* U.S.A.
184 E2 **Conegliano** Italy
225 D2 **Conejos** Mex.
220 D4 **Conemaugh** *r.* U.S.A.
209 G4 **Conestogo Lake** Canada
221 E3 **Conesus Lake** U.S.A.
Coney Island Sing. *see* **Serangoon, Pulau**
221 G4 **Coney Island** U.S.A.
119 F3 **Conflict Group** *is* P.N.G.
182 E3 **Confolens** France
215 F2 **Confusion Range** *mts* U.S.A.
149 F3 **Congdü** China
155 D6 **Conghua** China
155 C5 **Congjiang** China
173 E4 **Congleton** U.K.
195 B4 **Congo** *country* Africa
194 B3 **Congo** *r.* Africa
195 C4 **Congo, Democratic Republic of the** *country* Africa
111 **Congo Basin** *basin* Africa
239 J6 **Congo Cone** *sea feature* S. Atlantic Ocean
234 D3 **Congonhas** Brazil
215 F4 **Congress** U.S.A.
235 H3 **Conguillo, Parque Nacional** *nat. park* Chile
173 G4 **Coningsby** U.K.
206 D4 **Coniston** Canada
172 D3 **Coniston** U.K.
122 D3 **Conjuboy** Australia
205 G3 **Conklin** Canada
235 J2 **Conlara** Arg.
235 J2 **Conlara** *r.* Arg.
175 I3 **Conn, Lough** *l.* Ireland
220 C4 **Conneaut** U.S.A.
218 F3 **Connecticut** *r.* U.S.A.
221 G4 **Connecticut** *state* U.S.A.
220 D4 **Connellsville** U.S.A.
175 I4 **Connemara** *reg.* Ireland
221 I1 **Conners** Canada
219 C4 **Connersville** U.S.A.
123 E4 **Connors Range** *hills* Australia
125 F4 **Conoble** Australia
Co Nôi Vietnam *see* **Yên Châu**
221 E5 **Conowingo** U.S.A.
212 E1 **Conrad** U.S.A.
239 L9 **Conrad Rise** *sea feature* Southern Ocean
217 E6 **Conroe** U.S.A.
234 D3 **Conselheiro Lafaiete** Brazil
234 E2 **Conselheiro Pena** Brazil
172 F3 **Consett** U.K.
162 C3 **Côn Sơn, Đao** *i.* Vietnam
205 G4 **Consort** Canada
176 D7 **Constance, Lake** Germany/Switz.
231 F5 **Constância dos Baetas** Brazil
185 M2 **Constanța** Romania
183 N4 **Constantina** Spain
192 C1 **Constantine** Alg.
209 E5 **Constantine** U.S.A.
215 E6 **Constitución de 1857, Parque Nacional** *nat. park* Mex.
213 D3 **Contact** U.S.A.
230 C5 **Contamana** Peru
234 E1 **Contas** *r.* Brazil
215 G6 **Continental** U.S.A.
221 H3 **Contoocook** *r.* U.S.A.
205 G1 **Contwoyto Lake** Canada
217 E5 **Conway** *AR* U.S.A.
221 H3 **Conway** *NH* U.S.A.
219 E5 **Conway** *SC* U.S.A.
123 E4 **Conway, Cape** Australia
124 A2 **Conway, Lake** *salt flat* Australia
123 E4 **Conway National Park** Australia
173 D4 **Conwy** U.K.
173 D4 **Conwy** *r.* U.K.
118 D4 **Coober Pedy** Australia
121 E6 **Cook** Australia
208 A2 **Cook** U.S.A.
204 D4 **Cook, Cape** Canada
119 G3 **Cook, Grand Récif de** *reef* New Caledonia
Cook, Mount *mt.* N.Z. *see* **Aoraki/Mount Cook**
219 C4 **Cookeville** U.S.A.
197 F6 **Cookhouse** S. Africa
202 C3 **Cook Inlet** *sea chan.* U.S.A.
117 I5 **Cook Islands** Pacific Ocean
221 F3 **Cooksburg** U.S.A.
207 I3 **Cook's Harbour** Canada
122 D2 **Cooks Passage** Australia
175 L3 **Cookstown** U.K.
126 E4 **Cook Strait** N.Z.
119 E3 **Cooktown** Australia
125 G3 **Coolabah** Australia
125 H3 **Coolah** Australia
125 G5 **Coolamon** Australia
125 J2 **Coolangatta** Australia
118 C5 **Coolgardie** Australia
120 E2 **Coolibah** Australia
215 G5 **Coolidge** U.S.A.
215 G5 **Coolidge Dam** U.S.A.
123 F5 **Coolum Beach** Australia
125 H6 **Cooma** Australia
175 H6 **Coomacarrea** *h.* Ireland
124 D4 **Coombah** Australia
175 I6 **Coomnadiha** *h.* Ireland
123 E6 **Coonabarabran** Australia
124 C5 **Coonalpyn** Australia
125 H3 **Coonamble** Australia
124 D6 **Coonawarra** Australia
124 A3 **Coondambo** Australia
125 F1 **Coongoola** Australia
124 C2 **Cooper Creek** *watercourse* Australia
125 J3 **Coopernook** Australia
221 I2 **Coopers Mills** U.S.A.
219 E7 **Cooper's Town** Bahamas
216 D2 **Cooperstown** *ND* U.S.A.
221 F3 **Cooperstown** *NY* U.S.A.
121 F6 **Coorabie** Australia
121 B6 **Coorow** Australia
213 A3 **Coos Bay** U.S.A.
125 H5 **Cootamundra** Australia
175 K3 **Cootehill** Ireland
235 H3 **Copahue, Volcán** *vol.* Chile
225 F4 **Copainalá** Mex.
225 E4 **Copala** Mex.
225 E4 **Copalillo** Mex.
225 G5 **Copán** *tourist site* Hond.
213 G5 **Cope** U.S.A.
171 K5 **Copenhagen** Denmark
125 I2 **Copeton Reservoir** Australia
162 C1 **Cô Pi, Phou** *mt.* Laos/Vietnam
232 B3 **Copiapó** Chile
232 B3 **Copiapo** *r.* Chile
124 C3 **Copley** Australia
184 D2 **Copparo** Italy
209 G2 **Copper Cliff** Canada
208 D2 **Copper Harbor** U.S.A.
Coppermine Canada *see* **Kugluktuk**
202 G3 **Coppermine** *r.* Canada
209 E2 **Coppermine Point** Canada
197 E4 **Copperton** S. Africa
149 F3 **Coqên** China
235 H1 **Coquimbo** Chile
235 H1 **Coquimbo** *admin. reg.* Chile
185 K3 **Corabia** Romania
234 D2 **Coração de Jesus** Brazil
230 D7 **Coracora** Peru
125 J2 **Coraki** Australia
118 B4 **Coral Bay** Australia
219 D7 **Coral Gables** U.S.A.
203 J3 **Coral Harbour** Canada
119 F3 **Coral Sea** Coral Sea Is Terr.
236 F6 **Coral Sea Basin** S. Pacific Ocean
119 F3 **Coral Sea Islands Territory** *terr.* Pacific Ocean
208 B5 **Coralville Reservoir** U.S.A.
125 E7 **Corangamite, Lake** Australia
231 G3 **Corantijn** *r.* Suriname
139 L1 **Corat** Azer.
178 B5 **Corbeny** France
235 K2 **Corbett** Arg.
205 K2 **Corbett Inlet** Canada
178 A5 **Corbie** France
220 A6 **Corbin** U.S.A.
173 G5 **Corby** U.K.
214 C3 **Corcoran** U.S.A.
232 B6 **Corcovado, Golfo de** *sea chan.* Chile
224 I6 **Corcovado, Parque Nacional** *nat. park* Costa Rica
219 D6 **Cordele** U.S.A.
233 I4 **Cordillera de los Picachos, Parque Nacional** *nat. park* Col.
161 I4 **Cordilleras Range** *mts* Phil.
123 C5 **Cordillo Downs** Australia
235 J1 **Córdoba** *Córdoba* Arg.
235 I4 **Córdoba** *Río Negro* Arg.
235 J2 **Córdoba** *prov.* Arg.
225 D2 **Córdoba** *Durango* Mex.
225 E4 **Córdoba** *Veracruz* Mex.
183 N4 **Córdoba** Spain
235 J2 **Córdoba, Sierras de** *mts* Arg.
202 D3 **Cordova** U.S.A.
204 C4 **Cordova Bay** U.S.A.
221 J2 **Corea** U.S.A.
185 H5 **Corfu** *i.* Greece
183 M3 **Coria** Spain
125 I4 **Coricudgy** *mt.* Australia
185 G5 **Corigliano Calabro** Italy
122 E3 **Coringa Islands** Australia
125 F8 **Corinna** Australia
221 I2 **Corinna** U.S.A.
205 I4 **Corinne** Canada
185 J6 **Corinth** Greece
217 F5 **Corinth** *MS* U.S.A.
221 G3 **Corinth** *NY* U.S.A.
185 J5 **Corinth, Gulf of** *sea chan.* Greece
234 D2 **Corinto** Brazil
231 G7 **Corixa Grande** *r.* Bol./Brazil
234 A2 **Corixinha** *r.* Brazil
175 J6 **Cork** Ireland
184 E6 **Corleone** *Sicily* Italy
138 A1 **Çorlu** Turkey
205 I4 **Cormorant** Canada
197 H3 **Cornelia** S. Africa
234 B3 **Cornélio Procópio** Brazil
208 B3 **Cornell** U.S.A.
207 I4 **Corner Brook** Canada
125 G7 **Corner Inlet** *b.* Australia
239 F3 **Corner Seamounts** *sea feature* N. Atlantic Ocean
178 C5 **Cornillet, Mont** *h.* France
214 A2 **Corning** *CA* U.S.A.
221 E3 **Corning** *NY* U.S.A.
123 D4 **Cornish** *watercourse* Australia
Corn Islands Nicaragua *see* **Maíz, Islas del**
184 E3 **Corno Grande** *mt.* Italy
207 F4 **Cornwall** Canada
203 I2 **Cornwallis Island** Canada
124 B5 **Corny Point** Australia
233 J2 **Coro** Venez.
231 J4 **Coroatá** Brazil
230 E7 **Corocoro** Bol.
175 I5 **Corofin** Ireland
230 E7 **Coroico** Bol.
234 C2 **Coromandel** Brazil
135 G5 **Coromandel Coast** India
126 E2 **Coromandel Peninsula** N.Z.
126 E2 **Coromandel Range** *hills* N.Z.
161 I3 **Coron** Phil.
124 D3 **Corona** Australia
215 D5 **Corona** U.S.A.
215 D5 **Coronado** U.S.A.
224 I6 **Coronado, Bahía de** *b.* Costa Rica
235 H4 **Coronados, Golfo de los** *b.* Chile
205 G4 **Coronation** Canada
202 G3 **Coronation Gulf** Canada
127 J2 **Coronation Island** S. Atlantic Ocean
204 C3 **Coronation Island** U.S.A.
161 I4 **Coron Bay** Phil.
235 K1 **Coronda** Arg.
235 K2 **Coronel Brandsen** Arg.
235 K3 **Coronel Dorrego** Arg.
232 E3 **Coronel Oviedo** Para.
234 A1 **Coronel Ponce** Brazil
235 K3 **Coronel Pringles** Arg.
234 A3 **Coronel Sapucaia** Brazil
235 K3 **Coronel Suárez** Arg.
235 L3 **Coronel Vidal** Arg.
230 D7 **Coropuna, Nudo** *mt.* Peru
185 I4 **Çorovodë** Albania
125 G5 **Corowa** Australia
225 G4 **Corozal** Belize
217 D7 **Corpus Christi** U.S.A.
217 D6 **Corpus Christi, Lake** U.S.A.
230 E7 **Corque** Bol.
183 N3 **Corral de Cantos** *mt.* Spain
235 I1 **Corral de Isaac** Arg.
121 A5 **Corrandibby Range** *hills* Australia
231 I6 **Corrente** Brazil
234 D1 **Corrente** *r. Bahia* Brazil
234 C1 **Corrente** *r. Goiás* Brazil
234 B2 **Corrente** *r. Minas Gerais* Brazil
234 A2 **Correntes** Brazil
234 A2 **Correntes** *r.* Brazil
234 D1 **Correntina** Brazil
175 I4 **Corrib, Lough** *l.* Ireland
232 E3 **Corrientes** Arg.
232 E3 **Corrientes** *r.* Arg.
235 L3 **Corrientes, Cabo** *c.* Arg.
233 H3 **Corrientes, Cabo** *c.* Col.
224 C3 **Corrientes, Cabo** Mex.
217 E6 **Corrigan** U.S.A.
121 B7 **Corrigin** Australia
173 D5 **Corris** U.K.
220 D4 **Corry** U.S.A.
125 G6 **Corryong** Australia
Corse *i.* France *see* **Corsica**
184 C3 **Corse, Cap** *c. Corsica* France
173 E6 **Corsham** U.K.
183 I5 **Corsica** *i.* France
217 D5 **Corsicana** U.S.A.
184 C3 **Corte** *Corsica* France
183 M4 **Cortegana** Spain
215 H3 **Cortez** U.S.A.
215 D1 **Cortez Mountains** U.S.A.
184 E1 **Cortina d'Ampezzo** Italy
221 E3 **Cortland** U.S.A.
173 I5 **Corton** U.K.
184 D3 **Cortona** Italy
183 L3 **Coruche** Port.
139 H1 **Çoruh** *r.* Turkey
138 E1 **Çorum** Turkey
231 G7 **Corumbá** Brazil
234 C2 **Corumbá** *r.* Brazil
234 C2 **Corumbaíba** Brazil
233 L3 **Corumo** *r.* Venez.
212 B2 **Corvallis** U.S.A.
173 D5 **Corwen** U.K.
224 C2 **Cosalá** Mex.
185 G5 **Cosenza** Italy
220 C4 **Coshocton** U.S.A.
182 F3 **Cosne-Cours-sur-Loire** France
235 J1 **Cosquín** Arg.
183 P3 **Costa Blanca** *coastal area* Spain
183 R2 **Costa Brava** *coastal area* France/Spain
183 M4 **Costa de la Luz** *coastal area* Spain
183 N4 **Costa del Sol** *coastal area* Spain
224 H6 **Costa Rica** *country* Central America
224 C2 **Costa Rica** Mex.
185 K2 **Costești** Romania
221 I2 **Costigan** U.S.A.
179 K3 **Coswig (Anhalt)** Germany
161 J5 **Cotabato** Phil.
233 H4 **Cotacachi, Cerro** *mt.* Ecuador
230 E8 **Cotagaita** Bol.
234 E2 **Cotaxé** *r.* Brazil
204 C3 **Cote, Mount** U.S.A.
192 B4 **Côte d'Ivoire** *country* Africa
173 D5 **Cothi** *r.* U.K.
183 Q1 **Cotiella** *mt.* Spain
233 L3 **Cotingo** *r.* Brazil
192 C4 **Cotonou** Benin
230 C4 **Cotopaxi, Volcán** *vol.* Ecuador
173 E6 **Cotswold Hills** U.K.
213 B3 **Cottage Grove** U.S.A.
176 G5 **Cottbus** Germany
147 H3 **Cotteliar** *r.* India
173 H5 **Cottenham** U.K.
215 H5 **Cotton City** U.S.A.
215 F4 **Cottonwood** U.S.A.
215 G4 **Cottonwood Wash** *watercourse* U.S.A.
217 D6 **Cotulla** U.S.A.
220 D4 **Coudersport** U.S.A.
124 B6 **Couedic, Cape du** Australia
127 I5 **Coulman Island** Antarctica
182 F2 **Coulommiers** France
209 I2 **Coulonge** *r.* Canada
214 B3 **Coulterville** U.S.A.
212 C2 **Council** U.S.A.
216 E3 **Council Bluffs** U.S.A.
125 F7 **Councillor Island** Australia
205 G2 **Courageous Lake** Canada
171 M5 **Courland Lagoon** *b.* Lith./Russia
204 E5 **Courtenay** Canada
175 J6 **Courtmacsherry** Ireland
175 L5 **Courtown** Ireland
217 E5 **Coushatta** U.S.A.
182 D2 **Coutances** France
206 E2 **Couture, Lac** *l.* Canada
178 C4 **Couvin** Belgium
215 F2 **Cove Fort** U.S.A.
209 G3 **Cove Island** Canada
221 E5 **Cove Mountains** U.S.A.
173 F5 **Coventry** U.K.
221 E5 **Cove Point** U.S.A.
183 M2 **Covilhã** Port.
219 D5 **Covington** *GA* U.S.A.
208 D5 **Covington** *IN* U.S.A.
220 A5 **Covington** *KY* U.S.A.
219 B5 **Covington** *TN* U.S.A.
220 D6 **Covington** *VA* U.S.A.
209 F2 **Cow** *r.* Canada
125 G4 **Cowal, Lake** *dry lake* Australia
118 C5 **Cowan, Lake** *salt flat* Australia
221 G2 **Cowansville** Canada
121 B6 **Cowcowing Lakes** *salt flat* Australia
174 E4 **Cowdenbeath** U.K.
124 B4 **Cowell** Australia
125 F7 **Cowes** Australia
173 F7 **Cowes** U.K.
172 E3 **Cow Green Reservoir** U.K.
220 D5 **Cowpasture** *r.* U.S.A.
125 H4 **Cowra** Australia
122 A2 **Cox** *r.* Australia
234 D1 **Coxá** *r.* Brazil
235 L1 **Coxilha de Santana** *hills* Brazil/Uruguay
234 A2 **Coxim** Brazil
234 A2 **Coxim** *r.* Brazil
221 G3 **Coxsackie** U.S.A.
149 H5 **Cox's Bazar** Bangl.
224 B2 **Coyote, Punta** *pt* Mex.
215 D4 **Coyote Lake** U.S.A.
215 E5 **Coyote Peak** *h.* U.S.A.
214 C3 **Coyote Peak** U.S.A.
224 C3 **Coyotitán** Mex.
225 D4 **Coyuca de Benítez** Mex.
149 F2 **Cozhê** *Xizang Zizhiqu* China
149 F3 **Cozhê** *Xizang Zizhiqu* China
185 K2 **Cozia, Vârful** *mt.* Romania
225 H3 **Cozumel** Mex.
225 H3 **Cozumel, Isla de** *i.* Mex.
125 H4 **Craboon** Australia
123 E5 **Cracow** Australia
125 G8 **Cradle Mountain** Australia
125 G8 **Cradle Mountain Lake St Clair National Park** Australia
124 C3 **Cradock** Australia
197 F6 **Cradock** S. Africa
174 C3 **Craig** U.K.
204 C3 **Craig** *AL* U.S.A.
213 F3 **Craig** *CO* U.S.A.
175 L3 **Craigavon** U.K.
125 F6 **Craigieburn** Australia
220 D5 **Craigsville** U.S.A.
175 F4 **Crail** U.K.
179 I5 **Crailsheim** Germany
185 J2 **Craiova** Romania
172 F2 **Cramlington** U.K.

Daman

221 F2 **Cranberry Lake** U.S.A.
221 F2 **Cranberry Lake** *l.* U.S.A.
125 F7 **Cranbourne** Australia
204 F5 **Cranbrook** Canada
208 C3 **Crandon** U.S.A.
213 C3 **Crane** *OR* U.S.A.
217 C6 **Crane** *TX* U.S.A.
208 A1 **Crane Lake** U.S.A.
221 H4 **Cranston** U.S.A.
127 I5 **Crary Ice Rise** Antarctica
127 I4 **Crary Mountains** Antarctica
213 B3 **Crater Lake** U.S.A.
213 B3 **Crater Lake National Park** U.S.A.
213 D3 **Craters of the Moon National Monument** *nat. park* U.S.A.
231 J5 **Crateús** Brazil
231 K5 **Crato** Brazil
233 J3 **Cravo Norte** Col.
233 J3 **Cravo Sur** *r.* Col.
216 C3 **Crawford** U.S.A.
208 D5 **Crawfordsville** U.S.A.
219 C6 **Crawfordville** U.S.A.
173 G6 **Crawley** U.K.
212 E2 **Crazy Mountains** U.S.A.
174 D4 **Creag Meagaidh** *mt.* U.K.
205 H4 **Crean Lake** Canada
173 E5 **Credenhill** U.K.
173 D7 **Crediton** U.K.
205 H3 **Cree** *r.* Canada
224 C2 **Creel** Mex.
205 H3 **Cree Lake** Canada
205 I4 **Creighton** Canada
178 A5 **Creil** France
178 D2 **Creil** Neth.
179 I2 **Cremlingen** Germany
184 D2 **Cremona** Italy
178 C5 **Crépy-en-Valois** France
184 F2 **Cres** *i.* Croatia
213 A3 **Crescent City** U.S.A.
155 □ **Crescent Island** *Hong Kong* China
215 H2 **Crescent Junction** U.S.A.
214 B1 **Crescent Mills** U.S.A.
215 E4 **Crescent Peak** U.S.A.
208 A4 **Cresco** U.S.A.
235 K2 **Crespo** Arg.
125 E7 **Cressy** Australia
204 F5 **Creston** Canada
216 E3 **Creston** *IA* U.S.A.
213 F3 **Creston** *WY* U.S.A.
219 C6 **Crestview** U.S.A.
221 F5 **Crestwood Village** U.S.A.
125 E6 **Creswick** Australia
185 K7 **Crete** *i.* Greece
183 R1 **Creus, Cap de** *c.* Spain
182 E3 **Creuse** *r.* France
179 J5 **Creußen** Germany
179 E5 **Creutzwald** France
179 I3 **Creuzburg** Germany
173 E4 **Crewe** U.K.
220 D6 **Crewe** U.S.A.
173 E7 **Crewkerne** U.K.
174 D4 **Crianlarich** U.K.
173 C5 **Criccieth** U.K.
233 G3 **Criciúma** Brazil
174 E4 **Crieff** U.K.
Crifell *h.* U.K. *see* **Criffel**
174 E6 **Criffel** *h.* U.K.
184 F2 **Crikvenica** Croatia
187 E6 **Crimea** *disp. terr.* Europe
165 E6 **Crimea** *pen.* Europe
179 K4 **Crimmitschau** Germany
175 G3 **Crimond** U.K.
221 F6 **Crisfield** U.S.A.
234 C2 **Cristalina** Brazil
233 I2 **Cristóbal Colón, Pico** *mt.* Col.
234 C1 **Crixás** Brazil
234 C1 **Crixás Açu** *r.* Brazil
234 B1 **Crixás Mirim** *r.* Brazil
Crna Gora *aut. rep.* Europe *see* **Montenegro**
184 F2 **Črnomelj** Slovenia
175 I4 **Croagh Patrick** *h.* Ireland
125 H6 **Croajingolong National Park** Australia
184 F2 **Croatia** *country* Europe
163 I2 **Crocker, Banjaran** *mts* Malaysia
217 E6 **Crockett** U.S.A.
221 F3 **Croghan** U.S.A.
178 A4 **Croisilles** France
118 D3 **Croker Island** Australia
174 D3 **Cromarty** U.K.
174 D3 **Cromarty Firth** *est.* U.K.
174 E3 **Cromdale, Hills of** U.K.
173 I5 **Cromer** U.K.
126 B6 **Cromwell** N.Z.
172 F3 **Crook** U.K.
220 D4 **Crooked Creek Reservoir** U.S.A.
223 J4 **Crooked Island** Bahamas
155 □ **Crooked Island** *Hong Kong* China
223 J4 **Crooked Island Passage** Bahamas
208 B1 **Crooked Lake** Canada/U.S.A.
216 D2 **Crookston** U.S.A.
125 H5 **Crookwell** Australia
175 J5 **Croom** Ireland
125 I2 **Croppa Creek** Australia
173 D4 **Crosby** U.K.
205 I5 **Crosby** U.S.A.
205 K3 **Cross Bay** Canada
219 D6 **Cross City** U.S.A.
221 J1 **Cross Creek** Canada
217 E5 **Crossett** U.S.A.
172 E3 **Cross Fell** *h.* U.K.
175 M3 **Crossgar** U.K.
175 J6 **Crosshaven** Ireland
173 C5 **Cross Inn** U.K.
205 J4 **Cross Lake** Canada
205 J4 **Cross Lake** *l.* Canada
221 E3 **Cross Lake** *l.* U.S.A.
126 D5 **Crossley, Mount** N.Z.
175 L3 **Crossmaglen** U.K.
215 E4 **Crossman Peak** U.S.A.
204 B3 **Cross Sound** *sea chan.* U.S.A.
209 E3 **Cross Village** U.S.A.
219 C5 **Crossville** U.S.A.
209 F4 **Croswell** U.S.A.
185 G5 **Crotone** Italy
173 H6 **Crouch** *r.* U.K.
125 G3 **Crowal** *watercourse* Australia
173 H6 **Crowborough** U.K.
125 F4 **Crowl** *watercourse* Australia
173 G5 **Crowland** U.K.
217 E6 **Crowley** U.S.A.
214 C3 **Crowley, Lake** U.S.A.
208 D5 **Crown Point** *IN* U.S.A.
221 G3 **Crown Point** *NY* U.S.A.
125 J1 **Crows Nest** Australia
205 G5 **Crowsnest Pass** Canada
122 C3 **Croydon** Australia
173 G6 **Croydon** U.K.
238 H6 **Crozet, Îles** *is* Indian Ocean
239 N8 **Crozet Basin** *sea feature* Indian Ocean
238 G7 **Crozet Plateau** *sea feature* Indian Ocean
202 G2 **Crozier Channel** Canada
182 B2 **Crozon** France
233 I4 **Cruces, Paso de las** *mt.* Col.
175 G3 **Cruden Bay** U.K.
225 E2 **Cruillas** Mex.
175 L3 **Crumlin** U.K.
175 J5 **Crusheen** Ireland
223 I5 **Cruz, Cabo** *c.* Cuba
232 F3 **Cruz Alta** Brazil
235 J1 **Cruz del Eje** Arg.
234 D3 **Cruzeiro** Brazil
230 D5 **Cruzeiro do Sul** Brazil
215 H5 **Cruzville** U.S.A.
204 E3 **Crysdale, Mount** Canada
124 C4 **Crystal Brook** Australia
217 D6 **Crystal City** U.S.A.
208 C2 **Crystal Falls** U.S.A.
208 C4 **Crystal Lake** U.S.A.
177 J7 **Csongrád** Hungary
139 J5 **Ctesiphon** *tourist site* Iraq
233 K2 **Cúa** Venez.
162 C3 **Cửa Lớn, Sông** *r.* Vietnam
195 C5 **Cuando** *r.* Angola/Zambia
195 B5 **Cuangar** Angola
195 B4 **Cuango** *r.* Angola/Dem. Rep. Congo
195 B4 **Cuanza** *r.* Angola
233 K3 **Cuao** *r.* Venez.
235 L1 **Cuaró** *r.* Uruguay
235 J2 **Cuarto** *r.* Arg.
225 D2 **Cuatro Ciénegas** Mex.
224 C1 **Cuauhtémoc** Mex.
225 E4 **Cuautla** Mex.
223 I4 **Cuba** *country* Caribbean Sea
208 B5 **Cuba** *IL* U.S.A.
213 F4 **Cuba** *NM* U.S.A.
215 F6 **Cubabi, Cerro** *mt.* Mex.
195 B5 **Cubal** Angola
195 B5 **Cubango** *r.* Angola/Namibia
233 I3 **Cubará** Col.
205 I4 **Cub Hills** Canada
138 D1 **Çubuk** Turkey
235 L1 **Cuchilla Grande** *hills* Uruguay
235 L1 **Cuchilla Grande Inferior** *hills* Uruguay
235 J3 **Cuchillo-Có** Arg.
233 K3 **Cuchivero** *r.* Venez.
221 E6 **Cuckoo** U.S.A.
233 K4 **Cucuí** Brazil
233 I3 **Cúcuta** Col.
147 H4 **Cuddalore** India
Cuddapah India *see* **Kadapa**
205 H4 **Cudworth** Canada
121 B5 **Cue** Australia
183 N2 **Cuéllar** Spain
195 B5 **Cuemba** Angola
230 C4 **Cuenca** Ecuador
183 O2 **Cuenca** Spain
183 O2 **Cuenca, Serranía de** *mts* Spain
225 E4 **Cuernavaca** Mex.
217 D6 **Cuero** U.S.A.
214 B4 **Cuesta Pass** U.S.A.
225 E3 **Cuetzalán** Mex.
233 J2 **Cueva de la Quebrada del Toro, Parque Nacional** *nat. park* Venez.
185 J2 **Cugir** Romania
231 G5 **Cuiabá** *Amazonas* Brazil
234 A1 **Cuiabá** *Mato Grosso* Brazil
234 A2 **Cuiabá** *r.* Brazil
234 A1 **Cuiabá de Larga** Brazil
225 E4 **Cuicatlan** Mex.
178 D3 **Cuijk** Neth.
225 G5 **Cuilapa** Guat.
175 K3 **Cuilcagh** *h.* Ireland/U.K.
174 B3 **Cuillin Hills** U.K.
174 B3 **Cuillin Sound** *sea chan.* U.K.
195 B4 **Cuilo** Angola
156 C3 **Cuiluan** China
234 E2 **Cuité** *r.* Brazil
195 B5 **Cuito** *r.* Angola
195 B5 **Cuito Cuanavale** Angola
225 D4 **Cuitzeo, Laguna de** *l.* Mex.
163 B2 **Cukai** Malaysia
139 I3 **Çukurca** Turkey
212 F1 **Culbertson** *MT* U.S.A.
216 C3 **Culbertson** *NE* U.S.A.
125 G5 **Culcairn** Australia
183 M2 **Culebra, Sierra de la** *mts* Spain
139 J2 **Culfa** Azer.
125 G2 **Culgoa** *r.* Australia
224 C2 **Culiacán** Mex.
161 H4 **Culion** Phil.
161 H4 **Culion** *i.* Phil.
175 F3 **Cullen** U.K.
122 C1 **Cullen Point** Australia
183 P3 **Cullera** Spain
174 □ **Cullivoe** U.K.
219 C5 **Cullman** U.S.A.
139 H2 **Çullu** Turkey
175 L3 **Cullybackey** U.K.
174 C2 **Cul Mòr** *h.* U.K.
220 D5 **Culpeper** U.S.A.
143 D5 **Cultural Sites of Al Ain** *tourist site* U.A.E.
231 H6 **Culuene** *r.* Brazil
121 D7 **Culver, Point** Australia
126 D5 **Culverden** N.Z.
174 D5 **Culzean Bay** U.K.
233 K2 **Cumaná** Venez.
233 I4 **Cumare, Cerro** *h.* Col.
233 H4 **Cumbal, Nevado de** *vol.* Col.
220 D5 **Cumberland** *MD* U.S.A.
208 A3 **Cumberland** *WI* U.S.A.
219 C4 **Cumberland** *r.* U.S.A.
205 I4 **Cumberland House** Canada
205 I4 **Cumberland Lake** Canada
220 B6 **Cumberland Mountains** U.S.A.
203 L3 **Cumberland Peninsula** Canada
219 C4 **Cumberland Plateau** U.S.A.
208 C4 **Cumberland Point** U.S.A.
203 L3 **Cumberland Sound** *sea chan.* Canada
174 E5 **Cumbernauld** U.K.
225 D2 **Cumbres de Monterey, Parque Nacional** *nat. park* Mex.
179 J1 **Cumlosen** Germany
214 A2 **Cummings** U.S.A.
124 A5 **Cummins** Australia
120 D3 **Cummins Range** *hills* Australia
125 H4 **Cumnock** Australia
174 D5 **Cumnock** U.K.
138 D3 **Çumra** Turkey
224 B1 **Cumuripa** Mex.
121 B6 **Cunderdin** Australia
225 F4 **Cunduacán** Mex.
225 G5 **Cunén** Guat.
195 B5 **Cunene** *r.* Angola/Namibia *alt.* **Kunene**
184 B2 **Cuneo** Italy
124 A4 **Cungena** Australia
163 D2 **Cung Sơn** Vietnam
139 G2 **Çüngüş** Turkey
125 F2 **Cunnamulla** Australia
174 □ **Cunningsburgh** U.K.
233 K4 **Cunucunuma** *r.* Venez.
184 B2 **Cuorgnè** Italy
174 E4 **Cupar** U.K.
233 H3 **Cupica** Col.
233 H3 **Cupica, Golfo de** *b.* Col.
224 B2 **Cupula, Pico** *mt.* Mex.
231 K5 **Curaçá** Brazil
223 K6 **Curaçao** *terr.* Caribbean Sea
235 H3 **Curacautín** Chile
235 J3 **Curacó** *r.* Arg.
235 H3 **Curanilahue** Chile
230 D4 **Curaray** *r.* Ecuador
235 H2 **Curaumilla, Punta** *pt* Chile
124 B3 **Curdlawidny Lagoon** *salt flat* Australia
213 F4 **Curecanti National Recreation Area** *park* U.S.A.
235 H2 **Curicó** Chile
233 K5 **Curicuriari, Serra** *h.* Brazil
233 K5 **Curieuriari** *r.* Brazil
235 C4 **Curitiba** Brazil
124 C3 **Curnamona** Australia
125 I3 **Currabubula** Australia
231 K5 **Currais Novos** Brazil
192 □ **Curral Velho** Cape Verde
209 F3 **Curran** U.S.A.
175 H6 **Currane, Lough** *l.* Ireland
215 E2 **Currant** U.S.A.
125 F3 **Curranyalpa** Australia
123 C5 **Currawilla** Australia
123 D6 **Currawinya National Park** Australia
219 E7 **Current** Bahamas
125 E7 **Currie** Australia
215 E1 **Currie** U.S.A.
125 I5 **Currockbilly, Mount** Australia
123 F5 **Curtis Channel** Australia
125 G7 **Curtis Group** *is* Australia
119 F4 **Curtis Island** Australia
231 H5 **Curuá** *r.* Brazil
231 I4 **Curuçá** Brazil
163 B3 **Curup** Indon.
233 K4 **Curupira, Serra** *mts* Brazil/Venez.
231 J4 **Cururupu** Brazil
233 L3 **Curutú, Cerro** *mt.* Venez.
234 D2 **Curvelo** Brazil
230 D6 **Cusco** Peru
175 L2 **Cushendall** U.K.
175 L2 **Cushendun** U.K.
217 D4 **Cushing** U.S.A.
233 J3 **Cusiana** *r.* Col.
224 C1 **Cusihuiráchic** Mex.
219 C5 **Cusseta** U.S.A.
208 A1 **Cusson** U.S.A.
206 E1 **Cusson, Pointe** Canada
212 F2 **Custer** *MT* U.S.A.
216 C3 **Custer** *SD* U.S.A.
233 H4 **Cutanga, Pico de** *mt.* Col.
212 D1 **Cut Bank** U.S.A.
219 C6 **Cuthbert** U.S.A.
205 H4 **Cut Knife** Canada
221 J2 **Cutler** U.S.A.
219 D7 **Cutler Ridge** U.S.A.
235 I3 **Cutral-Có** Arg.
149 F5 **Cuttack** India
215 G5 **Cutter** U.S.A.
179 G1 **Cuxhaven** Germany
220 C4 **Cuyahoga Falls** U.S.A.
220 C4 **Cuyahoga Valley National Park** U.S.A.
214 C4 **Cuyama** *r.* U.S.A.
161 I3 **Cuyapo** Phil.
161 I4 **Cuyo** Phil.
161 I4 **Cuyo** *i.* Phil.
161 I4 **Cuyo East Passage** Phil.
161 I4 **Cuyo Islands** Phil.
161 I4 **Cuyo West Passage** Phil.
233 L3 **Cuyuni** *r.* Guyana
Cuzco Peru *see* **Cusco**
173 D6 **Cwmbrân** U.K.
195 C4 **Cyangugu** Rwanda
185 K6 **Cyclades** *is* Greece
125 G9 **Cygnet** Australia
220 A5 **Cynthiana** U.S.A.
205 G5 **Cypress Hills** Canada
138 D4 **Cyprus** *country* Asia
205 G4 **Czar** Canada
176 G6 **Czech Republic** *country* Europe
177 H4 **Czersk** Poland
177 I5 **Częstochowa** Poland

D

Đa, Sông *r.* Vietnam *see* **Black**
160 C1 **Da'an** China
233 J2 **Dabajuro** Venez.
192 B4 **Dabakala** Côte d'Ivoire
154 F1 **Daban** China
154 A2 **Daban Shan** *mts* China
154 C3 **Daba Shan** *mts* China
233 H3 **Dabeiba** Col.
179 J1 **Dabel** Germany
148 C5 **Dabhoi** India
147 G2 **Dabhol** India
155 E4 **Dabie Shan** *mts* China
148 D4 **Daboh** India
192 A3 **Dabola** Guinea
192 B4 **Daboya** Ghana
154 C2 **Dabqig** China
148 D4 **Dabra** India
177 I5 **Dąbrowa Górnicza** Poland
160 B1 **Dabs Nur** *l.* China
155 E5 **Dabu** China
Dacca Bangl. *see* **Dhaka**
176 E6 **Dachau** Germany
154 A2 **Dachechang** China
Dachengzi China *see* **Harqin**
147 H2 **Dachepalle** India
Đắc Lắc, Cao Nguyên *plat.* Vietnam *see* **Đắk Lắk, Cao Nguyên**
209 I3 **Dacre** Canada
194 E3 **Dadaab** Kenya
138 D1 **Daday** Turkey
219 D6 **Dade City** U.S.A.
148 C5 **Dadra** India
148 C5 **Dadra and Nagar Haveli** *union terr.* India
148 A4 **Dadu** Pak.
155 B4 **Dadu He** *r.* China
160 C5 **Daecheong-do** *i.* N. Korea
160 E6 **Daegu** S. Korea
160 C6 **Daeheuksan-gundo** *is* S. Korea
160 D5 **Daejeon** S. Korea
160 D7 **Daejeong** S. Korea
161 I3 **Daet** Phil.
155 B5 **Dafang** China
154 F3 **Dafeng** China
149 H4 **Dafla Hills** India
192 A3 **Dagana** Senegal
187 H7 **Dagestan, Respublika** *aut. rep.* Russia
Dağlıq Qarabağ *disp. terr* Azer. *see* **Nagorno-Karabakh**
155 B5 **Daguan** China
154 F2 **Dagu He** *r.* China
155 □ **D'Aguilar Peak** *h.* *Hong Kong* China
156 C3 **Daguokui Shan** *h.* China
161 I2 **Dagupan** Phil.
149 H1 **Dagur** China
149 G3 **Dagzê** China
149 F3 **Dagzê Co** *salt l.* China
148 C6 **Dahanu** India
158 C1 **Dahe** China
156 C3 **Daheiding Shan** *mt.* China
154 D1 **Dahei He** *r.* China
160 C2 **Dahei Shan** *mts* China
150 D2 **Da Hinggan Ling** *mts* China
194 E2 **Dahlak Archipelago** *is* Eritrea
194 E2 **Dahlak Marine National Park** Eritrea
179 E4 **Dahlem** Germany
179 I1 **Dahlenburg** Germany
184 C7 **Dahmani** Tunisia
179 F5 **Dahn** Germany
148 C5 **Dahod** India
148 D2 **Dahongliutan** China
179 I2 **Dähre** Germany
139 I3 **Dahūk/Dihok** Iraq
160 C3 **Dahuofang Shuiku** *resr* China
160 B3 **Dahushan** China
154 D1 **Dai Hai** *l.* China
163 B3 **Daik** Indon.
163 D2 **Đại Lanh, Mui** *pt* Vietnam
174 D5 **Dailly** U.K.
159 C6 **Daimanji-san** *h.* Japan
183 O3 **Daimiel** Spain
175 H5 **Daingean Uí Chúis** Ireland
122 D3 **Daintree National Park** Australia
235 K3 **Daireaux** Arg.
208 A2 **Dairyland** U.S.A.
159 C7 **Dai-sen** *vol.* Japan
158 H3 **Daisetsu-zan Kokuritsu-kōen** *nat. park* Japan
155 G4 **Daishan** China
155 F5 **Daiyun Shan** *mts* China
118 D4 **Dajarra** Australia
155 A4 **Dajin Chuan** *r.* China
154 B2 **Dajing** China
149 H1 **Da Juh** China
192 A3 **Dakar** Senegal
149 G3 **Dakelangsi** China
193 E2 **Dākhilah, Wāḥāt ad** *oasis* Egypt
149 G5 **Dakhin Shahbazpur Island** Bangl.
192 A2 **Dakhla** W. Sahara
Dakhla Oasis Egypt *see* **Dākhilah, Wāḥāt ad**
Dak Kon Vietnam *see* **Plei Kần**
163 D2 **Đắk Lắk, Cao Nguyên** *plat.* Vietnam
145 H10 **Dakoank** India
187 D4 **Dakol'ka** *r.* Belarus
216 D3 **Dakota City** U.S.A.
185 H2 **Đakovo** Croatia
156 B1 **Daktuy** Russia
195 C5 **Dala** Angola
192 A3 **Dalaba** Guinea
154 A1 **Dalain Hob** China
154 E1 **Dalai Nur** *l.* China
139 K4 **Dālā Khānī, Kūh-e** *mt.* Iraq
142 C4 **Dalaki, Rūd-e** *r.* Iran
169 J3 **Dalälven** *r.* Sweden
154 D1 **Dalamamiao** China
138 B3 **Dalaman** Turkey
138 B3 **Dalaman** *r.* Turkey
150 C2 **Dalandzadgad** Mongolia
161 I4 **Dalanganem Islands** Phil.
163 D3 **Đa Lat** Vietnam
Dalay Mongolia *see* **Bayandalay**
143 G4 **Dalbandin** Pak.
174 E6 **Dalbeattie** U.K.
123 D4 **Dalbeg** Australia
125 I1 **Dalby** Australia
172 C3 **Dalby** U.K.
171 I3 **Dale** *Hordaland* Norway
171 I3 **Dale** *Sogn og Fjordane* Norway
221 E5 **Dale City** U.S.A.
217 G4 **Dale Hollow Lake** U.S.A.
179 E2 **Dalen** Neth.
149 H6 **Dalet** Myanmar
149 H5 **Daletme** Myanmar
171 K3 **Dalfors** Sweden
143 E5 **Dalgān** Iran
125 H6 **Dalgety** Australia
121 A5 **Dalgety** *r.* Australia
217 C4 **Dalhart** U.S.A.
207 G4 **Dalhousie** Canada
154 D3 **Dali** *Shaanxi* China
151 C4 **Dali** *Yunnan* China
160 A4 **Dalian** China
155 B4 **Daliang Shan** *mts* China
160 B2 **Dalin** China
154 F1 **Daling He** *r.* China
160 D3 **Dalizi** China
174 E5 **Dalkeith** U.K.
149 F4 **Dalkola** India
221 F4 **Dallas** *PA* U.S.A.
217 D5 **Dallas** *TX* U.S.A.
208 B5 **Dallas City** U.S.A.
204 C4 **Dall Island** U.S.A.
142 D5 **Dalmā** *i.* U.A.E.
235 J2 **Dalmacio Vélez Sarsfield** Arg.
185 G3 **Dalmatia** *reg.* Croatia
149 E4 **Dalmau** India
174 D5 **Dalmellington** U.K.
158 D2 **Dal'negorsk** Russia
158 C2 **Dal'nerechensk** Russia
192 B4 **Daloa** Côte d'Ivoire
155 C5 **Dalou Shan** *mts* China
142 B5 **Dalqān** *well* Saudi Arabia
174 D5 **Dalry** U.K.
174 D5 **Dalrymple** U.K.
119 E4 **Dalrymple, Lake** Australia
119 E4 **Dalrymple, Mount** Australia
209 E1 **Dalton** Canada
197 I4 **Dalton** S. Africa
219 C5 **Dalton** *GA* U.S.A.
221 G3 **Dalton** *MA* U.S.A.
149 F4 **Daltonganj** India
172 D3 **Dalton-in-Furness** U.K.
209 E1 **Dalton Mills** Canada
175 J5 **Dalua** *r.* Ireland
161 I2 **Dalupiri** *i.* Phil.
161 J3 **Dalupiri** *i.* Phil.
170 C2 **Dalvík** Iceland
118 D3 **Daly** *r.* Australia
214 A3 **Daly City** U.S.A.
120 E2 **Daly River** Australia
118 D3 **Daly Waters** Australia
148 C5 **Daman** India

Eldorado

232 F3 **Eldorado** Arg.
224 C2 **El Dorado** Mex.
217 E5 **El Dorado** *AR* U.S.A.
217 D4 **El Dorado** *KS* U.S.A.
217 C6 **Eldorado** U.S.A.
233 L3 **El Dorado** Venez.
194 D3 **Eldoret** Kenya
212 E2 **Electric Peak** U.S.A.
192 B2 **El Eglab** *plat.* Alg.
183 O4 **El Ejido** Spain
Elemi Triangle *terr.* Africa *see* **Ilemi Triangle**
230 D4 **El Encanto** Col.
179 I3 **Elend** Germany
147 G2 **Elephanta Caves** *tourist site* India
213 F5 **Elephant Butte Reservoir** U.S.A.
127 I2 **Elephant Island** Antarctica
149 H5 **Elephant Point** Bangl.
139 I2 **Eleşkirt** Turkey
225 G5 **El Estor** Guat.
192 C1 **El Eulma** Alg.
219 E7 **Eleuthera** *i.* Bahamas
184 C6 **El Fahs** Tunisia
193 E3 **El Fasher** Sudan
179 H4 **Elfershausen** Germany
224 B2 **El Fuerte** Mex.
193 E3 **El Fula** Sudan
El Gara Egypt *see* **Qārah**
193 E3 **El Geneina** Sudan
193 F3 **El Geteina** Sudan
El Ghardaqa Egypt *see* **Hurghada**
174 E3 **Elgin** U.K.
208 C4 **Elgin** *IL* U.S.A.
216 C2 **Elgin** *ND* U.S.A.
215 E3 **Elgin** *NV* U.S.A.
215 G2 **Elgin (abandoned)** U.S.A.
133 P3 **El'ginskiy** Russia
225 D3 **El Gogorrón, Parque Nacional** *nat. park* Mex.
192 C1 **El Goléa** Alg.
193 F4 **Elgon, Mount** Uganda
184 B6 **El Hadjar** Alg.
El Ḥarra Egypt *see* **Al Ḥarrah**
El Ḥeiz Egypt *see* **Al Ḥayz**
192 A2 **El Hierro** *i.* Canary Is
225 E3 **El Higo** Mex.
192 C2 **El Homr** Alg.
185 L3 **Elhovo** Bulg.
175 F4 **Elie** U.K.
126 C5 **Elie de Beaumont, Mount** *mt.* N.Z.
202 B3 **Elim** U.S.A.
207 H2 **Eliot, Mount** Canada
187 H6 **Elista** Russia
208 B4 **Elizabeth** *IL* U.S.A.
221 F4 **Elizabeth** *NJ* U.S.A.
220 C5 **Elizabeth** *WV* U.S.A.
120 D3 **Elizabeth, Mount** *h.* Australia
219 E4 **Elizabeth City** U.S.A.
221 H4 **Elizabeth Islands** U.S.A.
219 D4 **Elizabethton** U.S.A.
219 C4 **Elizabethtown** *KY* U.S.A.
219 E5 **Elizabethtown** *NC* U.S.A.
221 G2 **Elizabethtown** *NY* U.S.A.
221 E4 **Elizabethtown** *PA* U.S.A.
183 P1 **Elizondo** Spain
192 B1 **El Jadida** Morocco
224 C2 **El Jaralito** Mex.
184 D7 **El Jem** Tunisia
224 H5 **El Jícaral** Nicaragua
205 G4 **Elk** *r.* Canada
177 K4 **Ełk** Poland
214 A2 **Elk** U.S.A.
220 C5 **Elk** *r.* U.S.A.
184 C6 **El Kala** Alg.
193 F3 **El Kamlin** Sudan
217 D5 **Elk City** U.S.A.
214 A2 **Elk Creek** U.S.A.
123 A4 **Elkedra** Australia
123 B4 **Elkedra** *watercourse* Australia
214 B2 **Elk Grove** U.S.A.
209 E5 **Elkhart** U.S.A.
192 B2 **El Khnâchîch** *esc.* Mali
208 C4 **Elkhorn** U.S.A.
216 D3 **Elkhorn** *r.* U.S.A.
220 D5 **Elkins** U.S.A.
205 G4 **Elk Island National Park** Canada
209 G2 **Elk Lake** Canada
209 E3 **Elk Lake** *l.* U.S.A.
221 E4 **Elkland** U.S.A.
204 F5 **Elko** Canada
213 D3 **Elko** U.S.A.
205 G4 **Elk Point** Canada
216 E2 **Elk River** U.S.A.
221 F5 **Elkton** *MD* U.S.A.
220 D5 **Elkton** *VA* U.S.A.
205 L2 **Ell Bay** Canada
203 H2 **Ellef Ringnes Island** Canada
215 G2 **Ellen, Mount** U.S.A.
148 C3 **Ellenabad** India
216 D2 **Ellendale** U.S.A.
212 B2 **Ellensburg** U.S.A.
221 F4 **Ellenville** U.S.A.
125 H6 **Ellery, Mount** Australia
126 D5 **Ellesmere, Lake** N.Z.
203 J2 **Ellesmere Island** Canada
173 E4 **Ellesmere Port** U.K.
203 H3 **Ellice** *r.* Canada
220 D3 **Ellicottville** U.S.A.
225 E3 **El Limón** Mex.
179 I5 **Ellingen** Germany
197 G5 **Elliot** S. Africa
122 D3 **Elliot, Mount** Australia
197 H5 **Elliotdale** S. Africa
209 F2 **Elliot Lake** Canada
120 F3 **Elliott** Australia
212 D2 **Ellis** U.S.A.
Ellisras S. Africa *see* **Lephalale**
124 A4 **Elliston** Australia
175 F3 **Ellon** U.K.
148 C5 **Ellora Caves** *tourist site* India
221 I2 **Ellsworth** *ME* U.S.A.
208 A3 **Ellsworth** *WI* U.S.A.
127 I3 **Ellsworth Land** *reg.* Antarctica
127 I3 **Ellsworth Mountains** Antarctica
179 I6 **Ellwangen (Jagst)** Germany
138 B3 **Elmalı** Turkey
215 D6 **El Maneadero** Mex.
233 L3 **El Manteco** Venez.
El Maṭarîya Egypt *see* **Al Maṭarīyah**
192 C1 **El Meghaïer** Alg.
233 L3 **El Miamo** Venez.
180 E4 **El Milia** Alg.
138 E4 **El Mîna** Lebanon
209 E3 **Elmira** *MI* U.S.A.
221 E3 **Elmira** *NY* U.S.A.
215 F5 **El Mirage** U.S.A.
183 O4 **El Moral** Spain
125 F6 **Elmore** Australia
235 J2 **El Morro** *mt.* Arg.
192 B2 **El Mreyyé** *reg.* Mauritania
179 H1 **Elmshorn** Germany
193 E3 **El Muglad** Sudan
209 G3 **Elmwood** Canada
208 C5 **Elmwood** *IL* U.S.A.
208 A3 **Elmwood** *WI* U.S.A.
171 I3 **Elnesvågen** Norway
233 I3 **El Nevado, Cerro** *mt.* Col.
161 H4 **El Nido** Phil.
193 F3 **El Obeid** Sudan
225 D2 **El Oro** Mex.
233 J3 **Elorza** Venez.
192 C1 **El Oued** Alg.
215 G5 **Eloy** U.S.A.
224 C2 **El Palmito** Mex.
233 L2 **El Pao** *Bolívar* Venez.
233 J2 **El Pao** *Cojedes* Venez.
208 C5 **El Paso** *IL* U.S.A.
213 F6 **El Paso** *TX* U.S.A.
174 C2 **Elphin** U.K.
214 C3 **El Portal** U.S.A.
224 J6 **El Porvenir** Panama
183 R2 **El Prat de Llobregat** Spain
El Progreso Guat. *see* **Guastatoya**
225 H5 **El Progreso** Hond.
224 B2 **El Puerto, Cerro** *mt.* Mex.
183 M4 **El Puerto de Santa María** Spain
El Quds Israel/West Bank *see* **Jerusalem**
El Qûsîya Egypt *see* **Al Qūṣīyah**
224 J6 **El Real de Santa María** Panama
217 D5 **El Reno** U.S.A.
225 D3 **El Retorno** Mex.
208 B4 **Elroy** U.S.A.
214 D3 **El Rucio** Mex.
204 B2 **Elsa** Canada
225 D2 **El Salado** Mex.
224 C3 **El Salto** Mex.
225 G5 **El Salvador** *country* Central America
225 D2 **El Salvador** Mex.
161 J4 **El Salvador** Phil.
233 J3 **El Samán de Apure** Venez.
209 F1 **Elsas** Canada
224 C1 **El Sauz** Mex.
179 G2 **Else** *r.* Germany
El Sellûm Egypt *see* **As Sallūm**
120 F2 **Elsey** Australia
120 F2 **El Sharana** Australia
233 K2 **El Sombrero** Venez.
235 I2 **El Sosneado** Arg.
225 E3 **El Tajín** *tourist site* Mex.
233 I3 **El Tama, Parque Nacional** *nat. park* Venez.
184 C6 **El Tarf** Alg.
183 M1 **El Teleno** *mt.* Spain
225 E4 **El Tepozteco, Parque Nacional** *nat. park* Mex.
233 K2 **El Tigre** Venez.
225 G4 **El Tigre, Parque Nacional** *nat. park* Guat.
179 I5 **Eltmann** Germany
233 J2 **El Tocuyo** Venez.
187 H5 **El'ton** Russia
187 H5 **El'ton, Ozero** *l.* Russia
212 C2 **Eltopia** U.S.A.
233 L2 **El Toro** Venez.
235 K2 **El Trébol** Arg.
224 B3 **El Triunfo** Mex.
233 J3 **El Tuparro, Parque Nacional** *nat. park* Col.
232 B8 **El Turbio** Arg.
147 I2 **Eluru** India
171 N4 **Elva** Estonia
233 H3 **El Valle** Col.
174 E5 **Elvanfoot** U.K.
183 M3 **Elvas** Port.
171 J3 **Elverum** Norway
233 I3 **El Viejo** *mt.* Col.
233 J2 **El Vigía** Venez.
230 D5 **Elvira** Brazil
194 E3 **El Wak** Kenya
El Wâṭya *well* Egypt *see* **Al Wāṭiyah**
209 E5 **Elwood** U.S.A.
179 I3 **Elxleben** Germany
173 H5 **Ely** U.K.
215 E2 **Ely** U.S.A.
220 B4 **Elyria** U.S.A.
179 G4 **Elz** Germany
179 H2 **Elze** Germany
119 G3 **Émaé** *i.* Vanuatu
196 C3 **eMakhazeni** S. Africa
197 I2 **eMakhazeni** S. Africa
197 H2 **eMalahleni** S. Africa
Emām Ṣaḥēb Afgh. *see* **Imām Ṣāḥib**
139 K5 **Emāmzādeh Naṣrod Dīn** Iran
171 L4 **Emån** *r.* Sweden
197 I5 **eManzimtoti** S. Africa
234 B2 **Emas, Parque Nacional das** *nat. park* Brazil
141 J3 **Emazar** Kazakh.
140 D2 **Emba** Kazakh.
197 H3 **Embalenhle** S. Africa
205 G3 **Embarras Portage** Canada
234 C2 **Emborcação, Represa de** *resr* Brazil
221 F2 **Embrun** Canada
195 D4 **Embu** Kenya
179 F1 **Emden** Germany
155 B4 **Emeishan** China
155 B4 **Emei Shan** *mt.* China
119 E4 **Emerald** *Qld* Australia
125 F6 **Emerald** *Vic.* Australia
207 G3 **Emeril** Canada
205 J5 **Emerson** Canada
138 B2 **Emet** Turkey
197 I2 **eMgwenya** S. Africa
197 I2 **Emgwenya** S. Africa
215 E3 **Emigrant Valley** U.S.A.
193 D3 **Emi Koussi** *mt.* Chad
224 C2 **Emiliano Martínez** Mex.
225 G4 **Emiliano Zapata** Mex.
141 J3 **Emin** China
185 L3 **Emine, Nos** *pt* Bulg.
141 J3 **Emin He** *r.* China
185 L3 **Eminska Planina** *hills* Bulg.
138 C2 **Emirdağ** Turkey
138 C2 **Emir Dağı** *mt.* Turkey
125 G8 **Emita** Australia
197 I2 **eMjindini** S. Africa
197 I3 **eMkhondo** S. Africa
171 K4 **Emmaboda** Sweden
171 M4 **Emmaste** Estonia
125 I2 **Emmaville** Australia
178 D2 **Emmeloord** Neth.
179 F4 **Emmelshausen** Germany
179 E2 **Emmen** Neth.
176 D7 **Emmen** Switz.
179 E3 **Emmerich am Rhein** Germany
123 D5 **Emmet** Australia
147 H3 **Emmiganuru** India
197 I3 **eMondlo** S. Africa
217 C6 **Emory Peak** U.S.A.
224 B2 **Empalme** Mex.
197 I4 **Empangeni** S. Africa
232 E3 **Empedrado** Arg.
236 G2 **Emperor Seamount Chain** *sea feature* N. Pacific Ocean
236 G2 **Emperor Trough** *sea feature* N. Pacific Ocean
184 D3 **Empoli** Italy
217 D4 **Emporia** *KS* U.S.A.
221 E6 **Emporia** *VA* U.S.A.
220 D4 **Emporium** U.S.A.
205 G4 **Empress** Canada
179 F2 **Ems** *r.* Germany
209 H3 **Emsdale** Canada
179 F2 **Emsdetten** Germany
179 F1 **Ems-Jade-Kanal** *canal* Germany
179 F2 **Emsland** *reg.* Germany
197 H3 **eMzinoni** S. Africa
171 K3 **Enafors** Sweden
151 F7 **Enarotali** Indon.
159 E7 **Ena-san** *mt.* Japan
235 M1 **Encantadas, Serra das** *hills* Brazil
224 A2 **Encantado, Cerro** *mt.* Mex.
161 I3 **Encanto, Cape** Phil.
225 D3 **Encarnación** Mex.
232 E3 **Encarnación** Para.
217 D6 **Encinal** U.S.A.
215 D5 **Encinitas** U.S.A.
213 F5 **Encino** U.S.A.
124 C5 **Encounter Bay** Australia
234 E1 **Encruzilhada** Brazil
235 M1 **Encruzilhada do Sul** Brazil
204 D4 **Endako** Canada
151 E7 **Ende** Indon.
119 E3 **Endeavour Strait** Australia
Endeh Indon. *see* **Ende**
239 L9 **Enderby Abyssal Plain** *sea feature* Southern Ocean
127 L4 **Enderby Land** *reg.* Antarctica
221 E3 **Endicott** U.S.A.
204 C3 **Endicott Arm** *est.* U.S.A.
202 C3 **Endicott Mountains** U.S.A.
140 D2 **Energetik** Russia
235 K3 **Energía** Arg.
187 E6 **Enerhodar** Ukr.
236 G5 **Enewetak** *atoll* Marshall Is
136 B2 **Enez** Turkey
184 D6 **Enfidaville** Tunisia
221 G3 **Enfield** U.S.A.
209 E2 **Engadine** U.S.A.
171 J3 **Engan** Norway
161 I2 **Engaño, Cape** Phil.
158 H2 **Engaru** Japan
219 F5 **Engelhard** U.S.A.
187 H5 **Engel's** Russia
178 C1 **Engelschmangat** *sea chan.* Neth.
124 A2 **Engenina** *watercourse* Australia
163 B4 **Enggano** *i.* Indon.
178 C4 **Enghien** Belgium
173 E5 **England** *admin. div.* U.K.
207 I3 **Englee** Canada
209 H2 **Englehart** Canada
211 H1 **English** *r.* Canada
173 D7 **English Channel** France/U.K.
187 G7 **Enguri** *r.* Georgia
197 I4 **Enhlalakahle** S. Africa
217 D4 **Enid** U.S.A.
158 G3 **Eniwa** Japan
178 D2 **Enkhuizen** Neth.
171 L4 **Enköping** Sweden
184 F6 **Enna** *Sicily* Italy
205 I2 **Ennadai Lake** Canada
193 E3 **En Nahud** Sudan
193 E3 **Ennedi, Massif** *mts* Chad
175 K4 **Ennell, Lough** *l.* Ireland
125 F2 **Enngonia** Australia
216 C2 **Enning** U.S.A.
175 J5 **Ennis** Ireland
212 E2 **Ennis** *MT* U.S.A.
217 D5 **Ennis** *TX* U.S.A.
175 L5 **Enniscorthy** Ireland
175 K3 **Enniskillen** U.K.
175 I5 **Ennistymon** Ireland
176 G7 **Enns** *r.* Austria
171 O3 **Eno** Fin.
215 F3 **Enoch** U.S.A.
170 M1 **Enontekiö** Fin.
155 D6 **Enping** China
161 I2 **Enrile** Phil.
178 D2 **Ens** Neth.
125 G6 **Ensay** Australia
179 E2 **Enschede** Neth.
179 G3 **Ense** Germany
235 K3 **Ensenada** Arg.
222 A2 **Ensenada** Mex.
155 C4 **Enshi** China
204 F2 **Enterprise** *N.W.T.* Canada
209 I3 **Enterprise** *Ont.* Canada
219 C6 **Enterprise** *AL* U.S.A.
212 C2 **Enterprise** *OR* U.S.A.
215 F3 **Enterprise** *UT* U.S.A.
204 F4 **Entrance** Canada
235 K2 **Entre Ríos** *prov.* Arg.
231 F8 **Entre Ríos** Bol.
183 L3 **Entroncamento** Port.
192 C4 **Enugu** Nigeria
133 U3 **Enurmino** Russia
230 D5 **Envira** Brazil
230 D5 **Envira** *r.* Brazil
126 C5 **Enys, Mount** N.Z.
178 D2 **Epe** Neth.
178 B5 **Épernay** France
185 L6 **Ephesus** *tourist site* Turkey
215 G2 **Ephraim** U.S.A.
221 E4 **Ephrata** *PA* U.S.A.
212 C2 **Ephrata** *WA* U.S.A.
119 G3 **Épi** *i.* Vanuatu
182 H2 **Épinal** France
138 D4 **Episkopi** Cyprus
184 E4 **Epomeo, Monte** *vol.* Italy
173 H6 **Epping** U.K.
123 D4 **Epping Forest National Park** Australia
179 G4 **Eppstein** Germany
173 D5 **Eppynt, Mynydd** *hills* U.K.
173 G6 **Epsom** U.K.
235 J3 **Epu-pel** Arg.
142 D4 **Eqlīd** Iran
192 C4 **Equatorial Guinea** *country* Africa
233 L3 **Equeipa** Venez.
161 H4 **Eran Bay** Phil.
139 F1 **Erbaa** Turkey
179 K5 **Erbendorf** Germany
179 F5 **Erbeskopf** *h.* Germany
139 J4 **Erbet** Iraq
139 I2 **Erçek** Turkey
139 I2 **Erciş** Turkey
138 E2 **Erciyes Dağı** *mt.* Turkey
177 I7 **Érd** Hungary
149 H2 **Erdaogou Bingzhan** China
160 D2 **Erdao Jiang** *r.* China
138 A1 **Erdek** Turkey
138 E3 **Erdemli** Turkey
153 H2 **Erdenedalay** Mongolia
153 H2 **Erdenet** Mongolia
153 K2 **Erdenetsagaan** Mongolia
Erdenetsogt Mongolia *see* **Bayan-Ovoo**
193 E3 **Erdi** *reg.* Chad
187 H6 **Erdniyevskiy** Russia
235 B4 **Eré, Campos** *hills* Brazil
233 K3 **Erebato** *r.* Venez.
127 I5 **Erebus, Mount** *vol.* Antarctica
139 J6 **Erech** *tourist site* Iraq
232 F3 **Erechim** Brazil
150 D2 **Ereentsav** Mongolia
138 E3 **Ereğli** *Konya* Turkey
138 C1 **Ereğli** *Zonguldak* Turkey
184 F6 **Erei, Monti** *mts Sicily* Italy
154 D1 **Erenhot** China
143 E3 **Eresk** Iran
183 N2 **Eresma** *r.* Spain
185 J5 **Eretria** Greece
179 J4 **Erfurt** Germany
139 G2 **Ergani** Turkey
192 B2 **'Erg Chech** *des.* Alg./Mali
Ergel Mongolia *see* **Hatanbulag**
185 L4 **Ergene** *r.* Turkey
171 N4 **Ērgļi** Latvia
158 A1 **Ergu** China
153 L1 **Ergun** China
Ergun Youqi China *see* **Ergun**
160 C3 **Erhulai** China
174 D2 **Eriboll, Loch** *inlet* U.K.
174 D4 **Ericht, Loch** *l.* U.K.
208 B5 **Erie** *IL* U.S.A.
217 E4 **Erie** *KS* U.S.A.
220 C3 **Erie** *PA* U.S.A.
209 G4 **Erie, Lake** Canada/U.S.A.
158 H3 **Erimo** Japan
158 H4 **Erimo-misaki** *c.* Japan
174 A3 **Eriskay** *i.* U.K.
194 D2 **Eritrea** *country* Africa
141 H5 **Erkech-Tam** Kyrg.
138 E2 **Erkilet** Turkey
179 J5 **Erlangen** Germany
118 D4 **Erldunda** Australia
121 C5 **Erlistoun** *watercourse* Australia
160 E2 **Erlong Shan** *mt.* China
160 C2 **Erlongshan Shuiku** *resr* China
178 D2 **Ermelo** Neth.
197 H3 **Ermelo** S. Africa
138 D3 **Ermenek** Turkey
185 K6 **Ermoupoli** Greece
147 H4 **Ernakulam** India
121 C5 **Ernest Giles Range** *hills* Australia
147 H4 **Erode** India
123 C5 **Eromanga** Australia
196 A1 **Erongo** *admin. reg.* Namibia
178 D3 **Erp** Neth.
121 A5 **Errabiddy Hills** Australia
192 B1 **Er Rachidia** Morocco
193 F3 **Er Rahad** Sudan
195 D5 **Errego** Moz.
184 D7 **Er Remla** Tunisia
175 J2 **Errigal** *h.* Ireland
175 H3 **Erris Head** Ireland
221 H2 **Errol** U.S.A.
119 G3 **Erromango** *i.* Vanuatu
185 I4 **Ersekë** Albania
216 D2 **Erskine** U.S.A.
171 M3 **Ersmark** Sweden
144 H2 **Ertai** China
187 G5 **Ertil'** Russia
144 G2 **Ertix He** *r.* China/Kazakh.
124 C3 **Erudina** Australia
139 I3 **Eruh** Turkey
220 D5 **Erwin** U.S.A.
179 G3 **Erwitte** Germany
179 J2 **Erxleben** *Sachsen-Anhalt* Germany
179 J2 **Erxleben** *Sachsen-Anhalt* Germany
152 G6 **Eryuan** China
179 K4 **Erzgebirge** *mts* Czech Rep./Germany
156 B2 **Erzhan** China
139 F3 **Erzin** Turkey
139 G2 **Erzincan** Turkey
139 H2 **Erzurum** Turkey
158 G4 **Esan-misaki** *pt* Japan
158 G4 **Esashi** *Hokkaidō* Japan
158 H2 **Esashi** *Hokkaidō* Japan
171 J5 **Esbjerg** Denmark
215 G3 **Escalante** U.S.A.
215 G3 **Escalante** *r.* U.S.A.
215 F3 **Escalante Desert** U.S.A.
224 C3 **Escalón** Mex.
208 D3 **Escanaba** U.S.A.
225 G4 **Escárcega** Mex.
161 I2 **Escarpada Point** Phil.
183 P2 **Escatrón** Spain
178 B4 **Escaut** *r.* Belgium
178 D3 **Esch** Neth.
179 E2 **Esche** Germany
179 I2 **Eschede** Germany
178 D5 **Esch-sur-Alzette** Lux.
179 I3 **Eschwege** Germany
179 E4 **Eschweiler** Germany
215 D5 **Escondido** U.S.A.
224 C3 **Escuinapa** Mex.
225 G5 **Escuintla** Guat.
225 F5 **Escuintla** Mex.
138 B3 **Eşen** Turkey
140 C5 **Esenguly** Turkm.
179 F1 **Esens** Germany
142 C3 **Eşfahān** Iran
142 D4 **Esfandārān** Iran
143 E2 **Esfarayen, Reshteh-ye** *mts* Iran
142 C4 **Esfarjān** Iran
142 D5 **Eshkanān** Iran
197 I4 **Eshowe** S. Africa
143 E3 **'Eshqābād** Iran
142 C3 **Eshtehārd** Iran
195 C6 **Esigodini** Zimbabwe
197 J4 **eSikhaleni** S. Africa
Esikhawini S. Africa *see* **eSikhaleni**
125 J1 **Esk** Australia
125 G8 **Esk** *r.* Australia
172 D2 **Esk** *r.* U.K.
174 E5 **Eskdalemuir** U.K.
207 G3 **Esker** Canada
170 D2 **Eskifjörður** Iceland
138 B2 **Eski Gediz** Turkey
171 L4 **Eskilstuna** Sweden
202 E3 **Eskimo Lakes** Canada
141 H4 **Eski-Nookat** Kyrg.
138 D1 **Eskipazar** Turkey
138 C2 **Eskişehir** Turkey
183 N1 **Esla** *r.* Spain
139 L4 **Eslāmābād** Iran
142 B3 **Eslāmābād-e Gharb** Iran
138 B3 **Esler Dağı** *mt.* Turkey
179 G3 **Eslohe (Sauerland)** Germany
171 K5 **Eslöv** Sweden
138 B2 **Eşme** Turkey
230 C3 **Esmeraldas** Ecuador
209 E1 **Esnagi Lake** Canada
178 B4 **Esnes** France
143 F5 **Espakeh** Iran
182 F4 **Espalion** France

Fériana

209 G2 **Espanola** Canada
213 F4 **Espanola** U.S.A.
230 □ **Española, Isla** *i. Galapagos Is* Ecuador
214 A2 **Esparto** U.S.A.
179 G2 **Espelkamp** Germany
118 C5 **Esperance** Australia
121 C7 **Esperance Bay** Australia
127 L2 **Esperanza** *research stn* Antarctica
235 K1 **Esperanza** Arg.
224 B2 **Esperanza** Mex.
161 J4 **Esperanza** Phil.
224 H5 **Esperanza, Sierra de la** *mts* Hond.
183 L3 **Espichel, Cabo** *c.* Port.
183 N1 **Espigüete** *mt.* Spain
225 D2 **Espinazo** Mex.
234 D2 **Espinhaço, Serra do** *mts* Brazil
234 D1 **Espinosa** Brazil
234 E2 **Espírito Santo** *state* Brazil
161 I2 **Espiritu** Phil.
119 G3 **Espiritu Santo** *i.* Vanuatu
225 H4 **Espíritu Santo, Bahía del** *b.* Mex.
224 B2 **Espíritu Santo, Isla** *i.* Mex.
171 N3 **Espoo** Fin.
183 P4 **Espuña** *mt.* Spain
232 B6 **Esquel** Arg.
204 E5 **Esquimalt** Canada
161 J5 **Essang** Indon.
192 B1 **Essaouira** Morocco
178 C3 **Essen** Belgium
179 F3 **Essen** Germany
179 F2 **Essen (Oldenburg)** Germany
231 G3 **Essequibo** *r.* Guyana
209 F4 **Essex** Canada
215 E4 **Essex** U.S.A.
221 G2 **Essex Junction** U.S.A.
209 F4 **Essexville** U.S.A.
192 A2 **Es-Smara** W. Sahara
133 Q4 **Esso** Russia
207 H4 **Est, Île de l'** *i.* Canada
221 I1 **Est, Lac de l'** *l.* Canada
232 D8 **Estados, Isla de los** *i.* Arg.
149 E4 **Eştahbān** Iran
209 G2 **Estaire** Canada
231 K6 **Estância** Brazil
183 Q1 **Estats, Pic d'** *mt.* France/Spain
197 H4 **Estcourt** S. Africa
179 H1 **Este** *r.* Germany
224 H5 **Estelí** Nicaragua
183 O1 **Estella** Spain
183 N4 **Estepa** Spain
183 N4 **Estepona** Spain
205 I4 **Esterhazy** Canada
214 B4 **Estero Bay** U.S.A.
232 D2 **Esteros** Para.
205 I5 **Estevan** Canada
216 E3 **Estherville** U.S.A.
219 D5 **Estill** U.S.A.
171 N4 **Estonia** *country* Europe
178 A5 **Estrées-St-Denis** France
183 M2 **Estrela, Serra da** *mts* Port.
183 O3 **Estrella** *mt.* Spain
215 F5 **Estrella, Sierra** *mts* U.S.A.
183 M3 **Estremoz** Port.
231 I5 **Estrondo, Serra** *hills* Brazil
139 L4 **Estūh** Iran
124 C2 **Etadunna** Australia
148 D4 **Etah** India
178 D5 **Étain** France
182 F2 **Étampes** France
182 E1 **Étaples** France
148 D4 **Etawah** India
197 I3 **Ethandakukhanya** S. Africa
121 C4 **Ethel Creek** Australia
197 E4 **E'Thembini** S. Africa
194 D3 **Ethiopia** *country* Africa
111 **Ethiopian Highlands** *mts* Africa
138 D2 **Etimesgut** Turkey
174 C4 **Etive, Loch** *inlet* U.K.
184 F6 **Etna, Mount** *vol. Sicily* Italy
171 I4 **Etne** Norway
204 C3 **Etolin Island** U.S.A.
195 B5 **Etosha National Park** Namibia
195 B5 **Etosha Pan** *salt pan* Namibia
Etrek *r.* Iran/Turkm. *see* **Atrek**
140 C5 **Etrek** Turkm.
185 K3 **Etropole** Bulg.
147 H4 **Ettaiyapuram** India
179 E5 **Ettelbruck** Lux.
178 C3 **Etten-Leur** Neth.
179 G6 **Ettlingen** Germany
174 E5 **Ettrick Forest** *reg.* U.K.
Etxarri Spain *see* **Etxarri-Aranatz**
183 O1 **Etxarri-Aranatz** Spain
224 C3 **Etzatlán** Mex.
125 G4 **Euabalong** Australia
118 C5 **Eucla** Australia
220 C4 **Euclid** U.S.A.
231 K6 **Euclides da Cunha** Brazil
125 H6 **Eucumbene, Lake** Australia
124 C5 **Eudunda** Australia
219 C6 **Eufaula** U.S.A.
217 E5 **Eufaula Lake** *resr* U.S.A.
212 B2 **Eugene** U.S.A.
213 D7 **Eugenia, Punta** *pt* Mex.
125 H4 **Eugowra** Australia
125 F2 **Eulo** Australia
125 H3 **Eumungerie** Australia
123 E4 **Eungella** Australia
123 E4 **Eungella National Park** Australia
217 E6 **Eunice** U.S.A.
179 E4 **Eupen** Belgium
139 J6 **Euphrates** *r.* Asia *alt.* **Al Furāt (Iraq/Syria),** *alt.* **Fırat (Turkey)**
171 M3 **Eura** Fin.
182 E2 **Eure** *r.* France
213 A3 **Eureka** *CA* U.S.A.
212 D1 **Eureka** *MT* U.S.A.
215 E2 **Eureka** *NV* U.S.A.
170 C3 **Eyjafjallajökull** *ice cap* Iceland
124 D3 **Eurinilla** *watercourse* Australia
124 D3 **Euriowie** Australia
125 F6 **Euroa** Australia
123 E5 **Eurombah** Australia
123 E5 **Eurombah Creek** *r.* Australia
195 E6 **Europa, Île** *i.* Indian Ocean
183 N4 **Europa Point** Gibraltar
166 **Europe**
179 E4 **Euskirchen** Germany
125 E5 **Euston** Australia
219 C5 **Eutaw** U.S.A.
204 D4 **Eutsuk Lake** Canada
179 K3 **Eutzsch** Germany
120 F3 **Eva Downs** Australia
197 H3 **Evander** S. Africa
206 E3 **Evans, Lac** *l.* Canada
213 F4 **Evans, Mount** U.S.A.
204 F4 **Evansburg** Canada
125 J2 **Evans Head** Australia
123 F6 **Evans Head** *hd* Australia
203 J3 **Evans Strait** Canada
208 D4 **Evanston** *IL* U.S.A.
213 E3 **Evanston** *WY* U.S.A.
209 F3 **Evansville** Canada
219 C4 **Evansville** *IN* U.S.A.
208 C4 **Evansville** *WI* U.S.A.
213 F3 **Evansville** *WY* U.S.A.
209 E4 **Evart** U.S.A.
197 G3 **Evaton** S. Africa
142 D5 **Evaz** Iran
208 A2 **Eveleth** U.S.A.
133 Q3 **Evensk** Russia
124 A3 **Everard, Lake** *salt flat* Australia
121 F4 **Everard, Mount** Australia
118 D4 **Everard Range** *hills* Australia
178 D3 **Everdingen** Neth.
149 F4 **Everest, Mount** China
221 J1 **Everett** Canada
212 B1 **Everett** U.S.A.
178 B3 **Evergem** Belgium
219 D7 **Everglades** *swamp* U.S.A.
219 D7 **Everglades National Park** U.S.A.
217 G6 **Evergreen** U.S.A.
123 C4 **Evesham** Australia
173 F5 **Evesham** U.K.
173 F5 **Evesham, Vale of** *val.* U.K.
171 M3 **Evijärvi** Fin.
193 D4 **Evinayong** Equat. Guinea
171 I4 **Evje** Norway
183 M3 **Évora** Port.
150 F1 **Evoron, Ozero** *l.* Russia
139 J2 **Evowghlī** Iran
182 E2 **Évreux** France
185 J6 **Evrotas** *r.* Greece
138 D4 **Evrychou** Cyprus
185 K5 **Evvoia** *i.* Greece
214 □[1] **'Ewa Beach** U.S.A.
122 D3 **Ewan** Australia
194 D3 **Ewaso Ngiro** *r.* Kenya
174 C3 **Ewe, Loch** *b.* U.K.
195 B4 **Ewo** Congo
230 E6 **Exaltación** Bol.
197 G4 **Excelsior** S. Africa
214 C2 **Excelsior Mountain** U.S.A.
214 C2 **Excelsior Mountains** U.S.A.
217 E4 **Excelsior Springs** U.S.A.
173 D6 **Exe** *r.* U.K.
127 I4 **Executive Committee Range** *mts* Antarctica
125 I5 **Exeter** Australia
209 G4 **Exeter** Canada
173 D7 **Exeter** U.K.
214 C3 **Exeter** *CA* U.S.A.
221 H3 **Exeter** *NH* U.S.A.
179 E2 **Exloo** Neth.
173 D7 **Exminster** U.K.
173 D6 **Exmoor** *hills* U.K.
173 D6 **Exmoor National Park** U.K.
221 F6 **Exmore** U.S.A.
121 A4 **Exmouth** Australia
173 D7 **Exmouth** U.K.
125 H3 **Exmouth, Mount** Australia
118 B4 **Exmouth Gulf** Australia
238 L6 **Exmouth Plateau** *sea feature* Indian Ocean
123 E5 **Expedition National Park** Australia
123 E5 **Expedition Range** *mts* Australia
183 N3 **Extremadura** *aut. comm.* Spain
219 E7 **Exuma Sound** *sea chan.* Bahamas
195 D4 **Eyasi, Lake** *salt l.* Tanz.
173 I5 **Eye** U.K.
175 F5 **Eyemouth** U.K.
174 B2 **Eye Peninsula** U.K.
170 C1 **Eyjafjörður** *inlet* Iceland
194 E3 **Eyl** Somalia
173 F6 **Eynsham** U.K.
123 B5 **Eyre Creek** *watercourse* Australia
126 B6 **Eyre Mountains** N.Z.
124 A4 **Eyre Peninsula** Australia
179 H2 **Eystrup** Germany
168 E3 **Eysturoy** *i.* Faroe Is
170 □ **Eysturoy** *i.* Faroe Is
197 I4 **Ezakheni** S. Africa
197 H3 **Ezenzeleni** S. Africa
235 I3 **Ezequiel Ramos Mexía, Embalse** *resr* Arg.
155 E4 **Ezhou** China
186 I2 **Ezhva** Russia
185 L5 **Ezine** Turkey
139 F1 **Ezinepazar** Turkey

F

171 J5 **Faaborg** Denmark
145 D10 **Faadhippolhu** *atoll* Maldives
217 B6 **Fabens** U.S.A.
162 □ **Faber, Mount** *h.* Sing.
204 F2 **Faber Lake** Canada
Fåborg Denmark *see* **Faaborg**
184 E3 **Fabriano** Italy
233 I3 **Facatativá** Col.
178 B4 **Faches-Thumesnil** France
193 D3 **Fachi** Niger
221 F4 **Factoryville** U.S.A.
232 B7 **Facundo** Arg.
193 E3 **Fada** Chad
192 C3 **Fada-N'Gourma** Burkina Faso
139 H4 **Fadghāmī** Syria
184 D2 **Faenza** Italy
Faeroes *terr.* Atlantic Ocean *see* **Faroe Islands**
151 F7 **Fafanlap** Indon.
194 E3 **Fafen Shet'** *watercourse* Eth.
185 K2 **Făgăraş** Romania
117 H3 **Fagatogo** American Samoa
171 J3 **Fagernes** Norway
171 K4 **Fagersta** Sweden
232 C8 **Fagnano, Lago** *l.* Arg./Chile
178 C4 **Fagne** *reg.* Belgium
192 B3 **Faguibine, Lac** *l.* Mali
170 C3 **Fagurhólsmýri** Iceland
193 F4 **Fagwir** South Sudan
142 C4 **Fahlīān, Rūdkhāneh-ye** *watercourse* Iran
143 E4 **Fahraj** Iran
138 D6 **Fā'id** Egypt
202 D3 **Fairbanks** U.S.A.
220 B5 **Fairborn** U.S.A.
216 D3 **Fairbury** U.S.A.
221 E5 **Fairfax** U.S.A.
214 A2 **Fairfield** *CA* U.S.A.
208 B5 **Fairfield** *IA* U.S.A.
219 C4 **Fairfield** *OH* U.S.A.
217 D6 **Fairfield** *TX* U.S.A.
221 G3 **Fair Haven** U.S.A.
175 L2 **Fair Head** U.K.
161 H4 **Fairie Queen Shoal** *sea feature* Phil.
175 G1 **Fair Isle** *i.* U.K.
126 C7 **Fairlie** N.Z.
216 E3 **Fairmont** *MN* U.S.A.
220 C5 **Fairmont** *WV* U.S.A.
213 F4 **Fairplay** U.S.A.
208 D3 **Fairport** U.S.A.
220 C4 **Fairport Harbor** U.S.A.
122 D2 **Fairview** Australia
204 F3 **Fairview** Canada
209 E3 **Fairview** *MI* U.S.A.
217 D4 **Fairview** *OK* U.S.A.
215 G2 **Fairview** *UT* U.S.A.
155 □ **Fairview Park** *Hong Kong* China
204 B3 **Fairweather, Cape** U.S.A.
204 B3 **Fairweather, Mount** Canada/U.S.A.
151 G6 **Fais** *i.* Micronesia
148 C3 **Faisalabad** Pak.
178 C5 **Faissault** France
216 C2 **Faith** U.S.A.
143 H2 **Faiẕābād** Afgh.
149 E4 **Faizabad** India
119 I2 **Fakaofo** *atoll* Tokelau
117 I5 **Fakarava** *atoll* Fr. Polynesia
173 H5 **Fakenham** U.K.
171 K3 **Fåker** Sweden
151 F7 **Fakfak** Indon.
142 D4 **Fakhrābād** Iran
160 B2 **Faku** China
173 C7 **Fal** *r.* U.K.
192 A4 **Falaba** Sierra Leone
182 D2 **Falaise** France
149 G4 **Falakata** India
149 H5 **Falam** Myanmar
142 C3 **Falāvarjān** Iran
217 D7 **Falcon Lake** Mex./U.S.A.
217 D7 **Falfurrias** U.S.A.
204 F3 **Falher** Canada
171 K4 **Falkenberg** Sweden
179 L3 **Falkenberg/Elster** Germany
179 K1 **Falkenhagen** Germany
179 K3 **Falkenhain** Germany
179 L2 **Falkensee** Germany
179 K5 **Falkenstein** Germany
174 E5 **Falkirk** U.K.
174 E4 **Falkland** U.K.
239 F9 **Falkland Escarpment** *sea feature* S. Atlantic Ocean
232 E8 **Falkland Islands** *terr.* Atlantic Ocean
239 F9 **Falkland Plateau** *sea feature* S. Atlantic Ocean
232 D8 **Falkland Sound** *sea chan.* Falkland Is
171 K4 **Falköping** Sweden
215 D5 **Fallbrook** U.S.A.
214 C2 **Fallon** U.S.A.
221 H4 **Fall River** U.S.A.
213 F3 **Fall River Pass** U.S.A.
216 E3 **Falls City** U.S.A.
173 B7 **Falmouth** U.K.
220 A5 **Falmouth** *KY* U.S.A.
221 H3 **Falmouth** *ME* U.S.A.
209 E3 **Falmouth** *MI* U.S.A.
196 C7 **False Bay** S. Africa
224 B3 **Falso, Cabo** *c.* Mex.
171 J5 **Falster** *i.* Denmark
177 M7 **Fălticeni** Romania
171 K3 **Falun** Sweden
138 D4 **Famagusta** Cyprus
179 E5 **Fameck** France
142 C3 **Fāmenīn** Iran
178 D4 **Famenne** *val.* Belgium
121 C5 **Fame Range** *hills* Australia
205 J4 **Family Lake** Canada
121 D4 **Family Well** Australia
155 F4 **Fanchang** China
175 L4 **Fane** *r.* Ireland
162 A1 **Fang** Thai.
154 D3 **Fangcheng** China
155 C4 **Fangdou Shan** *mts* China
155 F6 **Fangliao** Taiwan
154 E2 **Fangshan** *Beijing* China
154 D2 **Fangshan** *Shanxi* China
155 F6 **Fangshan** Taiwan
154 D3 **Fangxian** China
158 A2 **Fangzheng** China
155 □ **Fanling** *Hong Kong* China
174 C3 **Fannich, Loch** *l.* U.K.
143 E5 **Fannūj** Iran
184 E3 **Fano** Italy
155 F5 **Fanshan** China
154 D2 **Fanshi** China
Fan Si Pan *mt.* Vietnam *see* **Phăng Xi Păng**
194 C3 **Faradje** Dem. Rep. Congo
195 E6 **Farafangana** Madag.
193 E2 **Farāfirah, Wāḥāt al** *oasis* Egypt
Farafra Oasis Egypt *see* **Farāfirah, Wāḥāt al**
143 F3 **Farāh** Afgh.
143 F4 **Farāh Rōd** *watercourse* Afgh.
233 H4 **Farallones de Cali, Parque Nacional** *nat. park* Col.
192 A3 **Faranah** Guinea
143 F2 **Farap** Turkm.
146 B6 **Farasān, Jazā'ir** *is* Saudi Arabia
151 G6 **Faraulep** *atoll* Micronesia
173 F7 **Fareham** U.K.
203 N4 **Farewell, Cape** Greenland
126 D4 **Farewell, Cape** N.Z.
126 D4 **Farewell Spit** N.Z.
171 K4 **Färgelanda** Sweden
216 D2 **Fargo** U.S.A.
141 G4 **Farg'ona** Uzbek.
216 E2 **Faribault** U.S.A.
207 F2 **Faribault, Lac** *l.* Canada
148 D3 **Faridabad** India
148 C3 **Faridkot** India
149 G5 **Faridpur** Bangl.
192 A3 **Farim** Guinea-Bissau
143 E3 **Farīmān** Iran
171 L4 **Färjestaden** Sweden
141 G5 **Farkhor** Tajik.
139 L4 **Farmahīn** Iran
208 C5 **Farmer City** U.S.A.
206 D2 **Farmer Island** Canada
204 E3 **Farmington** Canada
208 B5 **Farmington** *IA* U.S.A.
208 B5 **Farmington** *IL* U.S.A.
221 H2 **Farmington** *ME* U.S.A.
221 H3 **Farmington** *NH* U.S.A.
215 H3 **Farmington** *NM* U.S.A.
213 E3 **Farmington** *UT* U.S.A.
204 D4 **Far Mountain** Canada
220 D6 **Farmville** U.S.A.
173 G6 **Farnborough** U.K.
172 F2 **Farne Islands** U.K.
173 G6 **Farnham** U.K.
121 D5 **Farnham, Lake** *salt flat* Australia
204 F4 **Farnham, Mount** Canada
231 G4 **Faro** Brazil
204 C2 **Faro** Canada
183 M4 **Faro** Port.
171 L4 **Fårö** *i.* Sweden
170 □[2] **Faroe Islands** *terr.* N. Atlantic Ocean
171 L4 **Fårösund** Sweden
191 I5 **Farquhar, Atoll de** *is* Seychelles
Farquhar Islands Seychelles *see* **Farquhar, Atoll de**
121 C5 **Farquharson Tableland** *hills* Australia
142 D4 **Farrāshband** Iran
220 C4 **Farrell** U.S.A.
209 J3 **Farrellton** Canada
143 E3 **Farrokhī** Iran
142 D3 **Farsakh** Iran
185 J5 **Farsala** Greece
213 E3 **Farson** U.S.A.
171 I4 **Farsund** Norway
140 D5 **Fārūj** Iran
Farvel, Kap *c.* Greenland *see* **Farewell, Cape**
217 C5 **Farwell** U.S.A.
143 E5 **Fāryāb** Iran
142 D4 **Fasā** Iran
185 G4 **Fasano** Italy
179 I2 **Faßberg** Germany
221 E4 **Fassett** U.S.A.
187 D5 **Fastiv** Ukr.
148 D4 **Fatehgarh** India
148 C4 **Fatehpur** *Rajasthan* India
149 E4 **Fatehpur** *Uttar Pradesh* India
148 D4 **Fatehpur Sikri** India
142 D4 **Fatḥābād** Iran
209 G3 **Fathom Five National Marine Park** Canada
192 A3 **Fatick** Senegal
182 H2 **Faulquemont** France
197 F4 **Fauresmith** S. Africa
170 K2 **Fauske** Norway
215 F1 **Faust** U.S.A.
184 E6 **Favignana, Isola** *i. Sicily* Italy
205 G4 **Fawcett** Canada
173 F7 **Fawley** U.K.
196 F6 **Fawley Court** S. Africa
206 C3 **Fawn** *r.* Canada
170 B2 **Faxaflói** *b.* Iceland
171 L3 **Faxälven** *r.* Sweden
193 D3 **Faya** Chad
208 D3 **Fayette (abandoned)** U.S.A.
217 E4 **Fayetteville** *AR* U.S.A.
219 E5 **Fayetteville** *NC* U.S.A.
219 C5 **Fayetteville** *TN* U.S.A.
139 L7 **Faylakah** *i.* Kuwait
192 C4 **Fazao Malfakassa, Parc National de** *nat. park* Togo
148 C3 **Fazilka** India
142 C5 **Fazrān, Jabal** *h.* Saudi Arabia
192 A2 **Fdérik** Mauritania
175 I5 **Feale** *r.* Ireland
219 E5 **Fear, Cape** U.S.A.
214 B2 **Feather, North Fork** *r.* U.S.A.
214 B2 **Feather Falls** U.S.A.
126 E4 **Featherston** N.Z.
125 G6 **Feathertop, Mount** Australia
182 E2 **Fécamp** France
235 L1 **Federación** Arg.
232 E4 **Federal** Arg.
140 E1 **Fedorovka** *Kostanayskaya Oblast'* Kazakh.
141 I1 **Fedorovka** *Pavlodarskaya Oblast'* Kazakh.
140 B2 **Fedorovka** *Zapadnyy Kazakhstan* Kazakh.
140 C1 **Fedorovka** Russia
176 E3 **Fehmarn** *i.* Germany
179 K2 **Fehrbellin** Germany
234 E3 **Feia, Lagoa** *lag.* Brazil
155 E4 **Feidong** China
154 F3 **Feihuanghe Kou** *r. mouth* China
230 D5 **Feijó** Brazil
126 E4 **Feilding** N.Z.
231 K6 **Feira de Santana** Brazil
155 E4 **Feixi** China
138 E3 **Feke** Turkey
183 R3 **Felanitx** Spain
208 D3 **Felch** U.S.A.
179 L1 **Feldberg** Germany
176 D7 **Feldberg** *mt.* Germany
176 D7 **Feldkirch** Austria
176 G7 **Feldkirchen in Kärnten** Austria
235 K1 **Feliciano** *r.* Arg.
225 G4 **Felipe C. Puerto** Mex.
234 D2 **Felixlândia** Brazil
173 I6 **Felixstowe** U.K.
184 D1 **Feltre** Italy
171 J3 **Femunden** *l.* Norway
171 K3 **Femundsmarka Nasjonalpark** *nat. park* Norway
184 D3 **Fenaio, Punta del** *pt* Italy
215 H4 **Fence Lake** U.S.A.
209 H3 **Fenelon Falls** Canada
185 K4 **Fengari** *mt.* Greece
155 E4 **Fengcheng** *Jiangxi* China
160 C3 **Fengcheng** *Liaoning* China
155 C4 **Fengdu** China
155 C5 **Fenggang** China
160 D1 **Fengguang** China
155 F4 **Fenghua** China
155 C5 **Fenghuang** China
155 C4 **Fengjie** China
155 D6 **Fengkai** China
155 F6 **Fenglin** Taiwan
160 D2 **Fengman** China
154 F2 **Fengnan** China
154 E1 **Fengning** China
154 E3 **Fengqiu** China
155 C5 **Fengshan** China
155 E6 **Fengshun** China
154 E3 **Fengtai** China
153 I5 **Fengxian** China
Fengxiang China *see* **Luobei**
155 E4 **Fengxin** China
154 E3 **Fengyang** China
154 D1 **Fengzhen** China
154 D2 **Fen He** *r.* China
149 G5 **Feni** Bangl.
119 F2 **Feni Islands** P.N.G.
183 F5 **Fenille, Col de la** *pass* France
208 B4 **Fennimore** U.S.A.
195 E5 **Fenoarivo Atsinanana** Madag.
209 F4 **Fenton** U.S.A.
154 D2 **Fenxi** China
154 D2 **Fenyang** China
155 E5 **Fenyi** China
187 E6 **Feodosiya** Crimea
184 B6 **Fer, Cap de** *c.* Alg.
Férai Greece *see* **Feres**
143 E3 **Ferdows** Iran
136 B2 **Feres** Greece
Fergana Uzbek. *see* **Farg'ona**
141 H4 **Fergana Too Tizmegi** *mts* Kyrg.
209 G4 **Fergus** Canada
216 D2 **Fergus Falls** U.S.A.
119 F2 **Fergusson Island** P.N.G.
184 C7 **Fériana** Tunisia

G

Granville

123 E4 **Glenden** Australia
212 F2 **Glendive** U.S.A.
205 G4 **Glendon** Canada
213 F3 **Glendo Reservoir** U.S.A.
124 D6 **Glenelg** *r.* Australia
175 F4 **Glen Esk** *val.* U.K.
174 A5 **Glengad Head** Ireland
174 C3 **Glen Garry** *val. Scotland* U.K.
174 D4 **Glen Garry** *val. Scotland* U.K.
175 K3 **Glengavlen** Ireland
123 B5 **Glengyle** Australia
125 I2 **Glen Innes** Australia
174 D6 **Glenluce** U.K.
174 D4 **Glen Lyon** *val.* U.K.
174 D3 **Glen More** *val.* U.K.
125 H1 **Glenmorgan** Australia
174 D3 **Glen Moriston** *val.* U.K.
215 G6 **Glenn, Mount** U.S.A.
202 D3 **Glennallen** U.S.A.
174 C4 **Glen Nevis** *val.* U.K.
209 F3 **Glennie** U.S.A.
221 E6 **Glenns** U.S.A.
204 C3 **Glenora** Canada
122 C3 **Glenore** Australia
123 B4 **Glenormiston** Australia
221 F2 **Glen Robertson** Canada
174 E4 **Glenrothes** U.K.
221 G3 **Glens Falls** U.S.A.
174 E4 **Glen Shee** *val.* U.K.
174 C3 **Glen Shiel** *val.* U.K.
175 J3 **Glenties** Ireland
175 K2 **Glenveagh National Park** Ireland
220 C5 **Glenville** U.S.A.
217 E5 **Glenwood** *AR* U.S.A.
215 H5 **Glenwood** *NM* U.S.A.
213 F4 **Glenwood Springs** U.S.A.
208 B2 **Glidden** U.S.A.
179 I1 **Glinde** Germany
177 I5 **Gliwice** Poland
215 G5 **Globe** U.S.A.
177 H5 **Głogów** Poland
170 K2 **Glomfjord** Norway
171 J4 **Glomma** *r.* Norway
195 E5 **Glorieuses, Îles** *is* Indian Ocean
125 I3 **Gloucester** Australia
173 E6 **Gloucester** U.K.
221 H3 **Gloucester** *MA* U.S.A.
221 E6 **Gloucester** *VA* U.S.A.
221 F3 **Gloversville** U.S.A.
179 K2 **Glöwen** Germany
158 D1 **Glubinnoye** Russia
152 G1 **Glubokiy** *Krasnoyarskiy Kray* Russia
187 G6 **Glubokiy** *Rostovskaya Oblast'* Russia
141 J2 **Glubokoye** Kazakh.
179 H1 **Glückstadt** Germany
170 □ **Gluggarnir** *h.* Faroe Is
173 F4 **Glusburn** U.K.
187 H5 **Gmelinka** Russia
176 G6 **Gmünd** Austria
176 F7 **Gmunden** Austria
171 L3 **Gnarp** Sweden
179 H1 **Gnarrenburg** Germany
177 H4 **Gniezno** Poland
121 B7 **Gnowangerup** Australia
121 B6 **Gnows Nest Range** *hills* Australia
147 G3 **Goa** India
147 G3 **Goa** *state* India
196 B3 **Goageb** Namibia
125 I6 **Goalen Head** Australia
149 G4 **Goalpara** India
175 C4 **Goat Fell** *h.* U.K.
194 E3 **Goba** Eth.
195 B6 **Gobabis** Namibia
196 C3 **Gobas** Namibia
235 K1 **Gobernador Crespo** Arg.
235 I3 **Gobernador Duval** Arg.
232 B7 **Gobernador Gregores** Arg.
150 C2 **Gobi Desert** Mongolia
159 D8 **Gobō** Japan
179 E3 **Goch** Germany
160 D6 **Gochang** S. Korea
195 B6 **Gochas** Namibia
173 G6 **Godalming** U.K.
147 I2 **Godavari** *r.* India
147 I2 **Godavari, Mouths of the** India
207 G4 **Godbout** Canada
214 C3 **Goddard, Mount** U.S.A.
194 E3 **Godere** Eth.
209 G4 **Goderich** Canada
148 C5 **Godhra** India
235 I2 **Godoy Cruz** Arg.
205 K3 **Gods** *r.* Canada
205 K4 **Gods Lake** Canada
205 L2 **God's Mercy, Bay of** Canada
Godthåb Greenland *see* **Nuuk**
Godwin-Austen, Mount China/Pak. *see* **K2**
178 B3 **Goedereede** Neth.
206 E4 **Goéland, Lac au** *l.* Canada
207 H2 **Goélands, Lac aux** *l.* Canada
178 B3 **Goes** Neth.
209 E2 **Goetzville** U.S.A.
215 E4 **Goffs** U.S.A.
209 G2 **Gogama** Canada
208 C2 **Gogebic, Lake** U.S.A.
208 C2 **Gogebic Range** *hills* U.S.A.
148 D4 **Gohad** India
160 D6 **Goheung** S. Korea
231 L5 **Goiana** Brazil
234 C2 **Goiandira** Brazil
234 C2 **Goiânia** Brazil
234 B1 **Goiás** Brazil
234 B2 **Goiás** *state* Brazil
145 D10 **Goidhoo** Maldives
235 B4 **Goioerê** Brazil
148 C3 **Gojra** Pak.
147 G2 **Gokak** India
187 C7 **Gökçeada** *i.* Turkey
187 B2 **Gökçedağ** Turkey
149 G3 **Gokhar La** *pass* China
138 E1 **Gökirmak** *r.* Turkey
140 D4 **Goklenkuy, Solonchak** *salt l.* Turkm.
136 B3 **Gökova Körfezi** *b.* Turkey
143 F5 **Gokprosh Hills** Pak.
139 F2 **Göksun** Turkey
138 E3 **Göksu Nehri** *r.* Turkey
195 C5 **Gokwe** Zimbabwe
171 J3 **Gol** Norway
149 E3 **Gola** India
149 H4 **Golaghat** India
143 E4 **Golbāf** Iran
139 F3 **Gölbaşı** Turkey
138 B1 **Gölcük** Turkey
177 K3 **Gołdap** Poland
179 K1 **Goldberg** Germany
125 J2 **Gold Coast** Australia
192 B4 **Gold Coast** *coastal area* Ghana
204 F4 **Golden** Canada
126 D4 **Golden Bay** N.Z.
179 I3 **Goldene Aue** *reg.* Germany
214 A3 **Golden Gate National Recreation Area** *park* U.S.A.
204 D5 **Golden Hinde** *mt.* Canada
179 G2 **Goldenstedt** Germany
175 J5 **Golden Vale** *lowland* Ireland
215 D3 **Goldfield** U.S.A.
215 D3 **Gold Point (abandoned)** U.S.A.
219 E5 **Goldsboro** U.S.A.
121 B4 **Goldsworthy (abandoned)** Australia
217 D6 **Goldthwaite** U.S.A.
139 I1 **Göle** Turkey
214 C4 **Goleta** U.S.A.
153 I1 **Golets-Davydov, Gora** *mt.* Russia
224 I6 **Golfito** Costa Rica
217 D6 **Goliad** U.S.A.
160 A1 **Golin Baixing** China
139 F1 **Gölköy** Turkey
179 K2 **Golm** Germany
139 J3 **Golmānkhāneh** Iran
150 B3 **Golmud** China
149 H1 **Golmud He** *r.* China
161 I3 **Golo** *i.* Phil.
158 I3 **Golovnino** Russia
142 C3 **Golpāyegān** Iran
138 C1 **Gölpazarı** Turkey
174 E3 **Golspie** U.K.
141 H1 **Golubovka** Kazakh.
143 F3 **Gol Vardeh** Iran
185 K4 **Golyama Syutkya** *mt.* Bulg.
185 K4 **Golyam Persenk** *mt.* Bulg.
Golyshi Russia *see* **Vetluzhskiy**
179 K2 **Golzow** Germany
149 G3 **Gomang Co** *salt l.* China
149 E4 **Gomati** *r.* India
162 □ **Gombak, Bukit** *h.* Sing.
193 D3 **Gombe** Nigeria
195 D4 **Gombe** *r.* Tanz.
193 D3 **Gombi** Nigeria
225 D2 **Gómez Palacio** Mex.
142 D2 **Gomīsh Tappeh** Iran
179 J2 **Gommern** Germany
149 F2 **Gomo Co** *salt l.* China
143 E2 **Gonābād** *Khorāsān-e Razavī* Iran
143 E3 **Gonābād** *Khorāsān-e Razavī* Iran
223 J5 **Gonaïves** Haiti
197 I1 **Gonarezhou National Park** Zimbabwe
223 J5 **Gonâve, Île de la** *i.* Haiti
142 D2 **Gonbad-e Kāvūs** Iran
149 E4 **Gonda** India
148 B5 **Gondal** India
194 D2 **Gonder** Eth.
149 E5 **Gondiya** India
138 A1 **Gönen** Turkey
155 D4 **Gong'an** China
Gongbalou China *see* **Gamba**
155 D5 **Gongcheng** China
155 A4 **Gongga Shan** *mt.* China
154 A2 **Gonghe** China
154 E1 **Gonghui** China
160 D5 **Gongju** S. Korea
141 J4 **Gongliu** China
234 E1 **Gongogi** *r.* Brazil
193 D3 **Gongola** *r.* Nigeria
125 G3 **Gongolgon** Australia
155 B4 **Gongquan** China
155 B5 **Gongwang Shan** *mts* China
Gongxian China *see* **Gongquan**
154 D3 **Gongyi** China
160 C2 **Gongzhuling** China
197 H6 **Gonubie** S. Africa
225 E3 **Gonzáles** Mex.
214 B3 **Gonzales** *CA* U.S.A.
217 D6 **Gonzales** *TX* U.S.A.
235 J2 **González Moreno** Arg.
156 B1 **Gonzha** Russia
221 E6 **Goochland** U.S.A.
127 J6 **Goodenough, Cape** Antarctica
119 F2 **Goodenough Island** P.N.G.
209 H3 **Gooderham** Canada
196 C7 **Good Hope, Cape of** S. Africa
213 D3 **Gooding** U.S.A.
217 C4 **Goodland** U.S.A.
125 G2 **Goodooga** Australia
173 G4 **Goole** U.K.
125 F5 **Goolgowi** Australia
125 H4 **Goolma** Australia
125 H4 **Gooloogong** Australia
124 C5 **Goolwa** Australia
121 B6 **Goomalling** Australia
125 F2 **Goombalie** Australia
125 I2 **Goondiwindi** Australia
121 C6 **Goongarrie, Lake** *salt flat* Australia
121 C6 **Goongarrie National Park** Australia
123 D4 **Goonyella** Australia
121 B6 **Goorly, Lake** *salt flat* Australia
207 H3 **Goose** *r.* Canada
213 B3 **Goose Lake** U.S.A.
147 H3 **Gooty** India
152 C5 **Gopeshwar** India
176 D6 **Göppingen** Germany
149 F4 **Gorakhpur** India
185 H3 **Goražde** Bos. & Herz.
186 G3 **Gorchukha** Russia
224 I5 **Gorda, Punta** *pt* Nicaragua
219 E7 **Gorda Cay** *i.* Bahamas
138 B2 **Gördes** Turkey
177 O4 **Gordeyevka** Russia
125 F9 **Gordon** *r.* Australia
175 F5 **Gordon** U.K.
125 G9 **Gordon, Lake** Australia
120 E3 **Gordon Downs** Australia
205 G2 **Gordon Lake** Canada
220 D5 **Gordon Lake** U.S.A.
220 D5 **Gordonsville** U.S.A.
193 D4 **Goré** Chad
194 D3 **Gorē** Eth.
126 B7 **Gore** N.Z.
209 F3 **Gore Bay** Canada
174 E5 **Gorebridge** U.K.
138 E2 **Göreme Milli Parkı** *nat. park* Turkey
175 L5 **Gorey** Ireland
143 E4 **Gorg** Iran
142 D2 **Gorgān** Iran
137 I3 **Gorgān, Khalīj-e** Iran
121 B4 **Gorge Range** *hills* Australia
233 H4 **Gorgona, Isla** *i.* Col.
221 H2 **Gorham** U.S.A.
187 H7 **Gori** Georgia
178 C3 **Gorinchem** Neth.
139 K2 **Goris** Armenia
184 E2 **Gorizia** Italy
Gor'kiy Russia *see* **Nizhniy Novgorod**
186 G3 **Gor'kovskoye Vodokhranilishche** *resr* Russia
141 J1 **Gor'koye, Ozero** *salt l.* Russia
177 J6 **Gorlice** Poland
176 G5 **Görlitz** Germany
148 D4 **Gormi** India
185 K3 **Gorna Oryahovitsa** Bulg.
185 I2 **Gornji Milanovac** Serbia
185 G3 **Gornji Vakuf** Bos. & Herz.
141 K2 **Gorno-Altaysk** Russia
158 G1 **Gornozavodsk** Russia
141 J2 **Gornyak** Russia
158 C2 **Gornyy** *Primorskiy Kray* Russia
187 I5 **Gornyy** *Saratovskaya Oblast'* Russia
187 H5 **Gornyy Balykley** Russia
158 C2 **Gornyye Klyuchi** Russia
186 G3 **Gorodets** Russia
187 H5 **Gorodishche** Russia
Gorodok Russia *see* **Zakamensk**
187 G6 **Gorodovikovsk** Russia
119 E2 **Goroka** P.N.G.
124 D6 **Goroke** Australia
186 G3 **Gorokhovets** Russia
192 B3 **Gorom Gorom** Burkina Faso
195 D5 **Gorongosa** Moz.
195 D5 **Gorongosa, Parque Nacional da** *nat. park* Moz.
151 E6 **Gorontalo** Indon.
187 F5 **Gorshechnoye** Russia
175 J4 **Gort** Ireland
Gortahork Ireland *see* **Gort an Choirce**
175 J2 **Gort an Choirce** Ireland
143 E4 **Gorūh** Iran
234 D1 **Gorutuba** *r.* Brazil
187 F6 **Goryachiy Klyuch** Russia
160 E6 **Goryeong** S. Korea
179 K2 **Görzke** Germany
176 G4 **Gorzów Wielkopolski** Poland
125 I4 **Gosford** Australia
172 F2 **Gosforth** U.K.
209 E5 **Goshen** *IN* U.S.A.
221 F4 **Goshen** *NY* U.S.A.
158 G4 **Goshogawara** Japan
179 I3 **Goslar** Germany
140 C4 **Goşoba** Turkm.
184 F2 **Gospić** Croatia
173 F7 **Gosport** U.K.
185 I4 **Gostivar** Macedonia
Göteborg Sweden *see* **Gothenburg**
171 K4 **Götene** Sweden
179 I4 **Gotha** Germany
171 J4 **Gothenburg** Sweden
216 C3 **Gothenburg** U.S.A.
171 L4 **Gotland** *i.* Sweden
159 A8 **Gotō** Japan
157 C6 **Gotō-rettō** *is* Japan
185 J4 **Gotse Delchev** Bulg.
171 L4 **Gotska Sandön** *i.* Sweden
159 C7 **Götsu** Japan
179 H3 **Göttingen** Germany
204 E4 **Gott Peak** Canada
140 C5 **Goturdepe** Turkm.
160 A3 **Goubangzi** China
178 C2 **Gouda** Neth.
192 A3 **Goudiri** Senegal
193 D3 **Goudoumaria** Niger
209 E1 **Goudreau** Canada
239 I8 **Gough Island** S. Atlantic Ocean
207 F4 **Gouin, Réservoir** *resr* Canada
209 E2 **Goulais River** Canada
125 H5 **Goulburn** Australia
125 I4 **Goulburn** *r. N.S.W.* Australia
125 F6 **Goulburn** *r. Vic.* Australia
118 D3 **Goulburn Islands** Australia
209 E2 **Gould City** U.S.A.
192 B3 **Goundam** Mali
183 Q4 **Gouraya** Alg.
193 D3 **Gouré** Niger
196 D7 **Gourits** *r.* S. Africa
192 B3 **Gourma-Rharous** Mali
182 E2 **Gournay-en-Bray** France
125 H6 **Gourock Range** *mts* Australia
178 A5 **Goussainville** France
221 F2 **Gouverneur** U.S.A.
205 H5 **Govenlock** Canada
234 E2 **Governador Valadares** Brazil
161 J5 **Governor Generoso** Phil.
219 E7 **Governor's Harbour** Bahamas
150 B2 **Govĭ Altayn Nuruu** *mts* Mongolia
149 E4 **Govind Ballash Pant Sagar** *resr* India
148 D3 **Govind Sagar** *resr* India
Govurdak Turkm. *see* **Magdanly**
220 D3 **Gowanda** U.S.A.
123 D5 **Gowan Range** *hills* Australia
142 D4 **Gowd-e Aḥmar** Iran
173 C6 **Gower** *pen.* U.K.
209 G2 **Gowganda** Canada
175 K4 **Gowna, Lough** *l.* Ireland
232 E3 **Goya** Arg.
139 K1 **Göyçay** Azer.
121 F5 **Goyder** *watercourse* Australia
137 G2 **Göygöl** Azer.
140 C4 **Goýmatdag** *hills* Turkm.
139 H2 **Göynük** *Bingöl* Turkey
181 J3 **Göynük** *Bolu* Turkey
159 G5 **Goyō-zan** *mt.* Japan
139 L2 **Göytäpä** Azer.
Gożareh Afgh. *see* **Guzarah**
139 G2 **Gözene** Turkey
141 F4 **G'ozg'on** Uzbek.
149 E2 **Gozha Co** *salt l.* China
184 F6 **Gozo** *i.* Malta
197 F6 **Graaff-Reinet** S. Africa
196 C6 **Graafwater** S. Africa
179 I4 **Grabfeld** *plain* Germany
192 B4 **Grabo** Côte d'Ivoire
196 C7 **Grabouw** S. Africa
179 J1 **Grabow** Germany
184 F2 **Gračac** Croatia
209 I2 **Gracefield** Canada
140 C1 **Grachevka** Russia
141 I2 **Grachi (abandoned)** Kazakh.
224 G5 **Gracias** Hond.
179 K3 **Gräfenhainichen** Germany
179 J5 **Grafenwöhr** Germany
125 J2 **Grafton** Australia
216 D1 **Grafton** *ND* U.S.A.
208 D4 **Grafton** *WI* U.S.A.
220 C5 **Grafton** *WV* U.S.A.
122 D3 **Grafton, Cape** Australia
215 E2 **Grafton, Mount** U.S.A.
122 D3 **Grafton Passage** Australia
217 D5 **Graham** U.S.A.
215 H5 **Graham, Mount** U.S.A.
Graham Bell Island Russia *see* **Greem-Bell, Ostrov**
204 C4 **Graham Island** *B.C.* Canada
203 I2 **Graham Island** *Nunavut* Canada
221 I2 **Graham Lake** U.S.A.
197 G6 **Grahamstown** S. Africa
175 L5 **Graigue** Ireland
192 A4 **Grain Coast** Liberia
231 I5 **Grajaú** Brazil
174 B1 **Gralisgeir** *i.* U.K.
185 I4 **Grammos** *mt.* Greece
174 D4 **Grampian Mountains** U.K.
125 E6 **Grampians National Park** Australia
196 C5 **Granaatboskolk** S. Africa
233 I4 **Granada** Col.
224 H6 **Granada** Nicaragua
183 O4 **Granada** Spain
217 C4 **Granada** U.S.A.
175 K4 **Granard** Ireland
207 F4 **Granby** Canada
192 A2 **Gran Canaria** *i.* Canary Is
232 D3 **Gran Chaco** *reg.* Arg./Para.
208 D4 **Grand** U.S.A.
216 E3 **Grand** *r.* U.S.A.
219 E7 **Grand Bahama** *i.* Bahamas
207 I4 **Grand Bank** Canada
239 F3 **Grand Banks of Newfoundland** *sea feature* N. Atlantic Ocean
192 B4 **Grand-Bassam** Côte d'Ivoire
207 G4 **Grand Bay-Westfield** Canada
209 G4 **Grand Bend** Canada
Grand Canal China *see* **Da Yunhe**
175 K4 **Grand Canal** Ireland
215 F3 **Grand Canyon** U.S.A.
215 F3 **Grand Canyon** *gorge* U.S.A.
215 F3 **Grand Canyon National Park** U.S.A.
215 F3 **Grand Canyon-Parashant National Monument** *tourist site* U.S.A.
223 H5 **Grand Cayman** *i.* Cayman Is
205 G4 **Grand Centre** Canada
212 C2 **Grand Coulee** U.S.A.
235 I3 **Grande** *r.* Arg.
231 F7 **Grande** *r.* Bol.
231 I6 **Grande** *r. Bahia* Brazil
234 B2 **Grande** *r. São Paulo* Brazil
235 L3 **Grande, Arroyo** *r.* Arg.
232 C8 **Grande, Bahía** *b.* Arg.
234 D3 **Grande, Ilha** *i.* Brazil
233 L4 **Grande, Serra** *mt.* Brazil
204 F4 **Grande Cache** Canada
182 H4 **Grande Casse, Pointe de la** *mt.* France
Grande Comore *i.* Comoros *see* **Ngazidja**
204 F3 **Grande Prairie** Canada
192 B1 **Grand Erg Occidental** *des.* Alg.
192 C2 **Grand Erg Oriental** *des.* Alg.
207 H4 **Grande-Rivière** Canada
212 C2 **Grande Ronde** *r.* U.S.A.
232 C4 **Grandes, Salinas** *salt flat* Arg.
207 G4 **Grande-Vallée** Canada
207 G4 **Grand Falls** Canada
207 I4 **Grand Falls-Windsor** Canada
204 F5 **Grand Forks** Canada
216 D2 **Grand Forks** U.S.A.
221 F3 **Grand Gorge** U.S.A.
221 J2 **Grand Harbour** Canada
208 D4 **Grand Haven** U.S.A.
204 F2 **Grandin, Lac** *l.* Canada
152 G1 **Grandioznyy, Pik** *mt.* Russia
216 D3 **Grand Island** U.S.A.
208 D2 **Grand Island** *i.* U.S.A.
217 F6 **Grand Isle** *LA* U.S.A.
221 I1 **Grand Isle** *ME* U.S.A.
215 H2 **Grand Junction** U.S.A.
192 B4 **Grand-Lahou** Côte d'Ivoire
207 G4 **Grand Lake** Canada
207 H3 **Grand Lake** *Nfld and Lab.* Canada
207 I4 **Grand Lake** *Nfld and Lab.* Canada
217 E6 **Grand Lake** *LA* U.S.A.
209 F3 **Grand Lake** *MI* U.S.A.
221 I1 **Grand Lake Matagamon** U.S.A.
220 A4 **Grand Lake St Marys** U.S.A.
221 I1 **Grand Lake Seboeis** U.S.A.
221 J2 **Grand Lake Stream** U.S.A.
209 E4 **Grand Ledge** U.S.A.
207 G5 **Grand Manan Island** Canada
209 E2 **Grand Marais** *MI* U.S.A.
208 B2 **Grand Marais** *MN* U.S.A.
207 F4 **Grand-Mère** Canada
183 L3 **Grândola** Port.
119 G3 **Grand Passage** New Caledonia
208 C2 **Grand Portage** U.S.A.
207 H4 **Grand Pré, Landscape of** *tourist site* Canada
205 J4 **Grand Rapids** Canada
209 E4 **Grand Rapids** *MI* U.S.A.
216 E2 **Grand Rapids** *MN* U.S.A.
215 G3 **Grand Staircase-Escalante National Monument** *nat. park* U.S.A.
213 E3 **Grand Teton** *mt.* U.S.A.
213 E3 **Grand Teton National Park** U.S.A.
209 E3 **Grand Traverse Bay** U.S.A.
223 J4 **Grand Turk** Turks and Caicos Is
212 C2 **Grandview** U.S.A.
215 F3 **Grand Wash** *watercourse* U.S.A.
215 E4 **Grand Wash Cliffs** *mts* U.S.A.
235 H2 **Graneros** Chile
175 K6 **Grange** Ireland
213 E3 **Granger** U.S.A.
171 K3 **Grängesberg** Sweden
212 C2 **Grangeville** U.S.A.
204 D3 **Granisle** Canada
216 E2 **Granite Falls** U.S.A.
207 I4 **Granite Lake** Canada
215 E4 **Granite Mountains** U.S.A.
212 E2 **Granite Peak** *MT* U.S.A.
215 F1 **Granite Peak** *UT* U.S.A.
141 H4 **Granitogorsk** Kazakh.
184 E6 **Granitola, Capo** *c. Sicily* Italy
232 C6 **Gran Laguna Salada** *l.* Arg.
171 K4 **Gränna** Sweden
184 B2 **Gran Paradiso** *mt.* Italy
176 E7 **Gran Pilastro** *mt.* Austria/Italy
179 K3 **Granschütz** Germany
179 L1 **Gransee** Germany
214 C2 **Grant, Mount** *NV* U.S.A.
215 D2 **Grant, Mount** *NV* U.S.A.
173 G5 **Grantham** U.K.
127 H4 **Grant Island** Antarctica
174 E3 **Grantown-on-Spey** U.K.
215 E2 **Grant Range** *mts* U.S.A.
213 F5 **Grants** U.S.A.
213 B3 **Grants Pass** U.S.A.
182 D2 **Granville** France
208 C5 **Granville** *IL* U.S.A.

155 D5 **Hengyang** *Hunan* China
187 E6 **Heniches'k** Ukr.
126 C6 **Henley** N.Z.
173 G6 **Henley-on-Thames** U.K.
221 F5 **Henlopen, Cape** U.S.A.
179 F4 **Hennef (Sieg)** Germany
197 G3 **Hennenman** S. Africa
179 L2 **Hennigsdorf** Germany
221 H3 **Henniker** U.S.A.
217 D5 **Henrietta** U.S.A.
206 D2 **Henrietta Maria, Cape** Canada
215 G3 **Henrieville** U.S.A.
208 C5 **Henry** U.S.A.
127 J3 **Henry Ice Rise** Antarctica
203 L3 **Henry Kater, Cape** Canada
215 G2 **Henry Mountains** U.S.A.
209 G4 **Hensall** Canada
179 H1 **Henstedt-Ulzburg** Germany
153 I2 **Henteyn Nuruu** *mts* Mongolia
195 B6 **Hentiesbaai** Namibia
125 G5 **Henty** Australia
Henzada Myanmar *see* **Hinthada**
205 H4 **Hepburn** Canada
155 E5 **Heping** China
155 C6 **Hepu** China
154 D2 **Hequ** China
122 E3 **Herald Cays** *atolls* Australia
143 F3 **Herāt** Afgh.
183 F5 **Hérault** *r.* France
205 H4 **Herbert** Canada
123 B4 **Herbert Downs** Australia
122 D3 **Herbert River Falls National Park** Australia
121 D5 **Herbert Wash** *salt flat* Australia
179 G4 **Herborn** Germany
179 H4 **Herbstein** Germany
127 J4 **Hercules Dome** *ice feature* Antarctica
179 F3 **Herdecke** Germany
179 F4 **Herdorf** Germany
217 H6 **Heredia** Costa Rica
173 E5 **Hereford** U.K.
217 C5 **Hereford** U.S.A.
117 J6 **Hereheretue** *atoll* Fr. Polynesia
178 C4 **Herent** Belgium
179 G2 **Herford** Germany
179 I4 **Heringen (Werra)** Germany
217 D4 **Herington** U.S.A.
142 B2 **Herīs** Iran
176 D7 **Herisau** Switz.
221 F3 **Herkimer** U.S.A.
Herlen Gol *r.* China/Mongolia *see* **Herlen He**
153 K2 **Herlen He** *r.* China/Mongolia
179 I3 **Herleshausen** Germany
225 D2 **Hermanas** Mex.
174 □ **Herma Ness** *hd* U.K.
179 I2 **Hermannsburg** Germany
196 C7 **Hermanus** S. Africa
137 E4 **Hermel** Lebanon
197 H5 **Hermes, Cape** S. Africa
125 G3 **Hermidale** Australia
212 C2 **Hermiston** U.S.A.
232 C9 **Hermite, Islas** Chile
119 E2 **Hermit Islands** P.N.G.
138 E5 **Hermon, Mount** Lebanon/Syria
Hermopolis Magna Egypt *see* **Al Ashmūnayn**
224 B1 **Hermosillo** Mex.
232 F3 **Hernandarias** Para.
179 F3 **Herne** Germany
173 I6 **Herne Bay** U.K.
171 J4 **Herning** Denmark
208 D1 **Heron Bay** Canada
225 D3 **Herradura** Mex.
183 N3 **Herrera del Duque** Spain
208 C5 **Herrick** Australia
179 I5 **Herrieden** Germany
221 E4 **Hershey** U.S.A.
173 G6 **Hertford** U.K.
197 F4 **Hertzogville** S. Africa
235 M2 **Herval** Brazil
178 D4 **Herve** Belgium
119 F4 **Hervey Bay** Australia
237 I7 **Hervey Islands** Cook Is
179 H2 **Herzberg** Germany
179 L3 **Herzberg (Elster)** Germany
179 F2 **Herzlake** Germany
179 I5 **Herzogenaurach** Germany
179 K1 **Herzsprung** Germany
139 L3 **Ḥeṣār** Iran
139 L4 **Ḥeṣār-e Valī-ye 'Asr** Iran
178 C4 **Hesbaye** *reg.* Belgium
179 F1 **Hesel** Germany
155 C6 **Heshan** China
154 C3 **Heshui** China
154 D2 **Heshun** China
215 D4 **Hesperia** U.S.A.
204 C2 **Hess** *r.* Canada
179 I5 **Heßdorf** Germany
179 I5 **Hesselberg** *h.* Germany
179 H4 **Hessen** *land* Germany
179 H3 **Hessisch Lichtenau** Germany
155 B6 **Het** *r.* Laos
214 B3 **Hetch Hetchy Aqueduct** *canal* U.S.A.
178 D3 **Heteren** Neth.
178 D2 **Het Loo, Paleis** *tourist site* Neth.
216 C2 **Hettinger** U.S.A.
172 E3 **Hetton** U.K.
179 J3 **Hettstedt** Germany
172 E3 **Hexham** U.K.
155 F4 **Hexian** China
154 B2 **Hexipu** China
196 C6 **Hex River Pass** S. Africa
155 D3 **Heyang** China
143 E4 **Ḥeydarābād** *Kermān* Iran
143 F4 **Ḥeydarābād** *Khorāsān-e Jonūbī* Iran
172 E3 **Heysham** U.K.
155 E6 **Heyuan** China
124 D7 **Heywood** Australia
173 E4 **Heywood** U.K.
208 C5 **Heyworth** U.S.A.
154 E3 **Heze** China
155 B5 **Hezhang** China
154 B3 **Hezheng** China
155 D5 **Hezhou** China
154 B3 **Hezuo** China
219 D7 **Hialeah** U.S.A.
217 E4 **Hiawatha** U.S.A.
208 A2 **Hibbing** U.S.A.
125 F9 **Hibbs, Point** Australia
120 C2 **Hibernia Reef** Australia
219 D5 **Hickory** U.S.A.
127 G2 **Hicks Bay** N.Z.
225 G4 **Hicks Cayes** *is* Belize
205 J2 **Hicks Lake** Canada
220 A4 **Hicksville** U.S.A.
217 D5 **Hico** U.S.A.
158 H3 **Hidaka** Japan
158 H3 **Hidaka-sanmyaku** *mts* Japan
225 E2 **Hidalgo** Mex.
225 E3 **Hidalgo** *state* Mex.
224 C2 **Hidalgo del Parral** Mex.
234 C2 **Hidrolândia** Brazil
159 C7 **Higashihiroshima** Japan
159 G5 **Higashine** Japan
159 D7 **Higashi-Ōsaka** Japan
159 A8 **Higashi-suidō** *sea chan.* Japan
221 F3 **Higgins Bay** U.S.A.
209 E3 **Higgins Lake** U.S.A.
213 B3 **High Desert** U.S.A.
208 C3 **High Falls Reservoir** U.S.A.
209 E3 **High Island** U.S.A.
155 □ **High Island Reservoir** *Hong Kong* China
208 D4 **Highland Park** U.S.A.
214 C2 **Highland Peak** *CA* U.S.A.
215 E3 **Highland Peak** *NV* U.S.A.
204 F3 **High Level** Canada
149 F5 **High Level Canal** India
219 E5 **High Point** U.S.A.
204 F3 **High Prairie** Canada
205 G4 **High River** Canada
219 E7 **High Rock** Bahamas
205 I3 **Highrock Lake** Canada
125 F9 **High Rocky Point** Australia
172 E3 **High Seat** *h.* U.K.
High Tatras *mts* Poland/Slovakia *see* **Tatry**
221 F4 **Hightstown** U.S.A.
173 G6 **High Wycombe** U.K.
224 B2 **Higuera de Zaragoza** Mex.
233 K2 **Higuerote** Venez.
171 M4 **Hiiumaa** *i.* Estonia
146 A4 **Hijaz** *reg.* Saudi Arabia
136 B5 **Ḥikmah, Ra's al** *pt* Egypt
215 E3 **Hiko** U.S.A.
159 E7 **Hikone** Japan
127 G2 **Hikurangi** *mt.* N.Z.
181 H5 **Hilāl, Ra's al** *pt* Libya
215 F3 **Hildale** U.S.A.
179 H2 **Hildburghausen** Germany
179 I4 **Hilders** Germany
179 H2 **Hildesheim** Germany
149 G4 **Hili** Bangl.
139 J5 **Hillah** Iraq
217 D4 **Hill City** U.S.A.
215 H2 **Hill Creek** *r.* U.S.A.
178 C2 **Hillegom** Neth.
171 K5 **Hillerød** Denmark
122 D3 **Hillgrove** Australia
216 D2 **Hillsboro** *ND* U.S.A.
221 H3 **Hillsboro** *NH* U.S.A.
220 B5 **Hillsboro** *OH* U.S.A.
217 D5 **Hillsboro** *TX* U.S.A.
208 B4 **Hillsboro** *WI* U.S.A.
220 C5 **Hillsboro** *WV* U.S.A.
209 E5 **Hillsdale** *MI* U.S.A.
221 G3 **Hillsdale** *NY* U.S.A.
221 E4 **Hillsgrove** U.S.A.
121 B4 **Hillside** Australia
175 F4 **Hillside** U.K.
215 F4 **Hillside** U.S.A.
125 F4 **Hillston** Australia
220 C6 **Hillsville** U.S.A.
125 I5 **Hill Top** Australia
214 □2 **Hilo** U.S.A.
123 B4 **Hilton** Australia
197 I4 **Hilton** S. Africa
221 E3 **Hilton** U.S.A.
209 F2 **Hilton Beach** Canada
219 D5 **Hilton Head Island** U.S.A.
139 G3 **Hilvan** Turkey
178 D2 **Hilversum** Neth.
148 D3 **Himachal Pradesh** *state* India
148 D2 **Himalaya** *mts* Asia
149 F3 **Himalchul** *mt.* Nepal
170 M2 **Himanka** Fin.
185 H4 **Himarë** Albania
148 C5 **Himatnagar** India
159 D7 **Himeji** Japan
159 G5 **Himekami-dake** *mt.* Japan
197 H4 **Himeville** S. Africa
159 E6 **Himi** Japan
Ḥimṣ Syria *see* **Homs**
161 J4 **Hinatuan** Phil.
177 N7 **Hîncești** Moldova
119 E3 **Hinchinbrook Island** Australia
173 F5 **Hinckley** U.K.
208 A2 **Hinckley** *MN* U.S.A.
215 F2 **Hinckley** *UT* U.S.A.
221 F3 **Hinckley Reservoir** U.S.A.
148 D4 **Hindaun** India
172 G3 **Hinderwell** U.K.
173 E4 **Hindley** U.K.
220 B6 **Hindman** U.S.A.
124 D6 **Hindmarsh, Lake** *dry lake* Australia
147 J1 **Hindola** India
143 G3 **Hindu Kush** *mts* Afgh./Pak.
147 H3 **Hindupur** India
204 F3 **Hines Creek** Canada
219 D6 **Hinesville** U.S.A.
148 D5 **Hinganghat** India
143 G5 **Hinglaj** Pak.
143 G5 **Hingol** *r.* Pak.
148 D6 **Hingoli** India
139 H2 **Hınıs** Turkey
215 D4 **Hinkley** U.S.A.
170 K1 **Hinnøya** *i.* Norway
161 I4 **Hinoba-an** Phil.
183 N3 **Hinojosa del Duque** Spain
159 C7 **Hino-misaki** *pt* Japan
221 G3 **Hinsdale** U.S.A.
179 F1 **Hinte** Germany
151 B5 **Hinthada** Myanmar
204 F4 **Hinton** Canada
220 C6 **Hinton** U.S.A.
Hiort *i.* U.K. *see* **St Kilda**
178 C2 **Hippolytushoef** Neth.
139 J2 **Hirabit Dağ** *mt.* Turkey
159 A8 **Hirado** Japan
159 A8 **Hirado-shima** *i.* Japan
159 G5 **Hiraizumi** *tourist site* Japan
147 I1 **Hirakud Reservoir** India
158 H3 **Hiroo** Japan
158 G4 **Hirosaki** Japan
159 C7 **Hiroshima** Japan
179 J5 **Hirschaid** Germany
179 J4 **Hirschberg** Germany
176 E7 **Hirschberg** *mt.* Germany
182 G2 **Hirson** France
171 J4 **Hirtshals** Denmark
148 C3 **Hisar** India
143 G3 **Ḥiṣār, Kōh-e** *mts* Afgh.
138 D1 **Hisarönü** Turkey
139 J6 **Ḥisb, Sha'īb** *watercourse* Iraq
141 G5 **Hisor** Tajik.
223 J4 **Hispaniola** *i.* Caribbean Sea
149 F4 **Hisua** India
139 I5 **Hīt** Iraq
159 G6 **Hitachi** Japan
157 F5 **Hitachinaka** Japan
159 G6 **Hitachiōta** Japan
159 B8 **Hitoyoshi** Japan
171 J3 **Hitra** *i.* Norway
179 J1 **Hitzacker (Elbe)** Germany
159 C7 **Hiuchi-nada** *b.* Japan
117 J5 **Hiva Oa** *i.* Fr. Polynesia
204 E4 **Hixon** Canada
123 F4 **Hixson Cay** *reef* Australia
139 I2 **Hizan** Turkey
171 K4 **Hjälmaren** *l.* Sweden
205 H2 **Hjalmar Lake** Canada
171 J3 **Hjerkinn** Norway
171 K4 **Hjo** Sweden
171 J4 **Hjørring** Denmark
152 G6 **Hkakabo Razi** *mt.* China/Myanmar
197 I4 **Hlabisa** S. Africa
197 I3 **Hlatikulu** Swaziland
187 E5 **Hlobyne** Ukr.
197 G4 **Hlohlowane** S. Africa
197 H4 **Hlotse** Lesotho
197 J4 **Hluhluwe** S. Africa
187 E5 **Hlukhiv** Ukr.
177 N4 **Hlusha** Belarus
187 C4 **Hlybokaye** Belarus
192 C4 **Ho** Ghana
155 B6 **Hoa Binh** *Hoa Binh* Vietnam
162 C1 **Hoa Binh** *Nghệ An* Vietnam
195 B6 **Hoachanas** Namibia
Hoan Lao Vietnam *see* **Bô Trach**
125 G9 **Hobart** Australia
217 D5 **Hobart** U.S.A.
217 C5 **Hobbs** U.S.A.
219 D7 **Hobe Sound** U.S.A.
154 D1 **Hobor** China
171 J4 **Hobro** Denmark
194 E3 **Hobyo** Somalia
179 H5 **Höchberg** Germany
179 I3 **Hochharz, Nationalpark** *nat. park* Germany
162 C3 **Ho Chi Minh City** Vietnam
176 G7 **Hochschwab** *mt.* Austria
179 G5 **Hockenheim** Germany
220 B5 **Hocking** *r.* U.S.A.
225 G3 **Hoctún** Mex.
148 D4 **Hodal** India
173 E4 **Hodder** *r.* U.K.
173 G6 **Hoddesdon** U.K.
146 B7 **Hodeidah** Yemen
221 J1 **Hodgdon** U.S.A.
120 F2 **Hodgson Downs** Australia
177 J7 **Hódmezővásárhely** Hungary
183 S5 **Hodna, Chott el** *salt l.* Alg.
160 D4 **Hodo-dan** *pt* N. Korea
Hoek van Holland Neth. *see* **Hook of Holland**
178 D4 **Hoensbroek** Neth.
160 E2 **Hoeryŏng** N. Korea
160 D4 **Hoeyang** N. Korea
179 J4 **Hof** Germany
179 I4 **Hofheim in Unterfranken** Germany
197 F5 **Hofmeyr** S. Africa
170 D2 **Höfn** Iceland
171 L3 **Hofors** Sweden
170 C2 **Hofsjökull** *ice cap* Iceland
159 B7 **Hōfu** Japan
171 K4 **Höganäs** Sweden
125 G7 **Hogan Group** *is* Australia
Hoggar *plat.* Alg. *see* **Ahaggar**
221 F6 **Hog Island** U.S.A.
171 L4 **Högsby** Sweden
171 I3 **Høgste Breakulen** *mt.* Norway
179 H5 **Hohenloher Ebene** *plain* Germany
179 K3 **Hohenmölsen** Germany
179 K2 **Hohennauen** Germany
179 J4 **Hohenwartetalsperre** *resr* Germany
179 H4 **Hohe Rhön** *mts* Germany
176 F7 **Hohe Tauern** *mts* Austria
179 E4 **Hohe Venn** *moorland* Belgium
154 D1 **Hohhot** China
144 H2 **Höhmorīt** Mongolia
149 H2 **Hoh Sai Hu** *l.* China
149 G2 **Hoh Xil Hu** *salt l.* China
149 G2 **Hoh Xil Shan** *mts* China
163 D2 **Hôi An** Vietnam
194 D3 **Hoima** Uganda
149 H4 **Hojai** India
141 F5 **Hojambaz** Turkm.
159 C8 **Hōjo** Japan
126 D1 **Hokianga Harbour** N.Z.
126 C5 **Hokitika** N.Z.
158 H3 **Hokkaidō** *i.* Japan
171 J4 **Hokksund** Norway
Hoktemberyan Armenia *see* **Armavir**
171 J3 **Hol** Norway
147 H3 **Holalkere** India
171 J5 **Holbæk** Denmark
173 H5 **Holbeach** U.K.
215 G4 **Holbrook** U.S.A.
208 B3 **Holcombe Flowage** *resr* U.S.A.
205 G4 **Holden** Canada
215 F2 **Holden** U.S.A.
217 D5 **Holdenville** U.S.A.
216 D3 **Holdrege** U.S.A.
147 H3 **Hole Narsipur** India
223 I4 **Holguín** Cuba
160 B1 **Holin He** *r.* China
171 K3 **Höljes** Sweden
Holland *country* Europe *see* **Netherlands**
208 D4 **Holland** U.S.A.
220 D4 **Hollidaysburg** U.S.A.
204 C3 **Hollis** *AL* U.S.A.
217 D5 **Hollis** *OK* U.S.A.
214 B3 **Hollister** U.S.A.
209 F4 **Holly** U.S.A.
217 F5 **Holly Springs** U.S.A.
214 C4 **Hollywood** *CA* U.S.A.
219 D7 **Hollywood** *FL* U.S.A.
170 K2 **Holm** Norway
Holman Canada *see* **Ulukhaktok**
122 D3 **Holmes Reef** Australia
171 J4 **Holmestrand** Norway
171 M3 **Holmön** *i.* Sweden
171 M3 **Holmsund** Sweden
196 B3 **Holoog** Namibia
120 D2 **Holothuria Banks** *reef* Australia
122 C2 **Holroyd** *r.* Australia
171 J4 **Holstebro** Denmark
219 D4 **Holston** *r.* U.S.A.
220 C6 **Holston Lake** U.S.A.
173 C7 **Holsworthy** U.K.
173 I5 **Holt** U.K.
209 E4 **Holt** U.S.A.
217 E4 **Holton** U.S.A.
178 D1 **Holwerd** Neth.
175 K5 **Holycross** Ireland
173 C4 **Holyhead** U.K.
173 C4 **Holyhead Bay** U.K.
172 F2 **Holy Island** *England* U.K.
173 C4 **Holy Island** *Wales* U.K.
221 G3 **Holyoke** U.S.A.
173 D4 **Holywell** U.K.
179 K3 **Holzhausen** Germany
176 E7 **Holzkirchen** Germany
179 H3 **Holzminden** Germany
179 H3 **Homberg (Efze)** Germany
192 B3 **Hombori** Mali
179 F5 **Homburg** Germany
203 L3 **Home Bay** Canada
178 D5 **Homécourt** France
217 E5 **Homer** U.S.A.
219 D6 **Homerville** U.S.A.
123 D4 **Homestead** Australia
219 D7 **Homestead** U.S.A.
219 C5 **Homewood** U.S.A.
147 H2 **Homnabad** India
139 F4 **Homs** Syria
187 D4 **Homyel'** Belarus
147 G3 **Honavar** India
233 I3 **Honda** Col.
161 H3 **Honda Bay** Phil.
215 H4 **Hon Dah** U.S.A.
196 B5 **Hondeklipbaai** S. Africa
154 C1 **Hondlon Ju** China
225 G4 **Hondo** *r.* Belize/Mex.
217 D6 **Hondo** U.S.A.
179 E1 **Hondsrug** *reg.* Neth.
224 H5 **Honduras** *country* Central America
224 H4 **Honduras, Gulf of** Belize/Hond.
171 J3 **Hønefoss** Norway
221 F4 **Honesdale** U.S.A.
214 B1 **Honey Lake** *salt l.* U.S.A.
221 E3 **Honeyoye Lake** U.S.A.
182 E2 **Honfleur** France
Hông, Sông *r.* Vietnam *see* **Red**
155 E4 **Hong'an** China
160 D5 **Hongcheon** S. Korea
Hông Gai Vietnam *see* **Ha Long**
155 E6 **Honghai Wan** *b.* China
155 B6 **Honghe** China
154 E3 **Hong He** *r.* China
155 B6 **Honghe Hani Rice Terraces** *tourist site* China
155 D4 **Honghu** China
155 C5 **Hongjiang** *Hunan* China
155 C5 **Hongjiang** *Hunan* China
155 E6 **Hong Kong** China
155 □ **Hong Kong** *aut. reg.* China
155 □ **Hong Kong Island** *Hong Kong* China
154 C2 **Hongliu He** *r.* China
Hongliuwan China *see* **Aksay**
144 I3 **Hongliuyuan** *Gansu* China
154 B2 **Hongliuyuan** *Gansu* China
162 C3 **Hông Ngư** Vietnam
Hongqizhen China *see* **Wuzhishan**
155 D4 **Hongshan** China
154 B2 **Hongshansi** China
160 D2 **Hongshilazi** China
155 D6 **Hongshui He** *r.* China
154 D2 **Hongtong** China
207 G4 **Honguedo, Détroit d'** *sea chan.* Canada
160 D3 **Hongwŏn** N. Korea
160 B1 **Hongxing** China
154 B3 **Hongyuan** China
154 F3 **Hongze** China
154 F3 **Hongze Hu** *l.* China
119 F2 **Honiara** Solomon Is
173 D7 **Honiton** U.K.
171 M3 **Honkajoki** Fin.
147 G3 **Honnali** India
170 N1 **Honningsvåg** Norway
214 □2 **Honoka'a** U.S.A.
214 □1 **Honolulu** U.S.A.
159 D6 **Honshū** *i.* Japan
212 B2 **Hood, Mount** *vol.* U.S.A.
118 B5 **Hood Point** Australia
179 E2 **Hoogeveen** Neth.
179 E1 **Hoogezand-Sappemeer** Neth.
217 C4 **Hooker** U.S.A.
175 L5 **Hook Head** Ireland
178 C3 **Hook of Holland** Neth.
122 E3 **Hook Reef** Australia
204 B3 **Hoonah** U.S.A.
202 B3 **Hooper Bay** U.S.A.
221 E5 **Hooper Island** U.S.A.
208 D5 **Hoopeston** U.S.A.
197 F3 **Hoopstad** S. Africa
171 K5 **Höör** Sweden
178 D2 **Hoorn** Neth.
119 I3 **Hoorn, Îles de** *is* Wallis and Futuna Is
221 G3 **Hoosick** U.S.A.
215 E3 **Hoover Dam** U.S.A.
220 B4 **Hoover Memorial Reservoir** U.S.A.
139 H1 **Hopa** Turkey
221 F4 **Hop Bottom** U.S.A.
204 E5 **Hope** Canada
126 D5 **Hope** *r.* N.Z.
217 E5 **Hope** *AR* U.S.A.
215 F5 **Hope** *AZ* U.S.A.
124 C2 **Hope, Lake** *salt flat S.A.* Australia
121 C7 **Hope, Lake** *salt flat W.A.* Australia
202 B3 **Hope, Point** U.S.A.
207 I2 **Hopedale** Canada
196 C6 **Hopefield** S. Africa
225 G4 **Hopelchén** Mex.
207 H3 **Hope Mountains** Canada
132 D2 **Hopen** *i.* Svalbard
126 D4 **Hope Saddle** *pass* N.Z.
207 G2 **Hopes Advance, Baie** *b.* Canada
125 E5 **Hopetoun** Australia
197 F4 **Hopetown** S. Africa
221 E6 **Hopewell** U.S.A.
206 E2 **Hopewell Islands** Canada
123 C8 **Hopkins** *r.* Australia
118 C4 **Hopkins, Lake** *salt flat* Australia
219 C4 **Hopkinsville** U.S.A.
214 A2 **Hopland** U.S.A.
212 B2 **Hoquiam** U.S.A.
154 A3 **Hor** China
139 K2 **Horadiz** Azer.
139 I1 **Horasan** Turkey
171 K5 **Hörby** Sweden
224 C1 **Horcasitas** Mex.
Horgo Mongolia *see* **Tariat**
141 J3 **Horgos Kou'an** China
154 B1 **Hörhiyn Nuruu** *mts* Mongolia
208 C4 **Horicon** U.S.A.
154 D1 **Horinger** China
237 H7 **Horizon Deep** *sea feature* S. Pacific Ocean
187 D4 **Horki** Belarus
127 I4 **Horlick Mountains** Antarctica
187 F5 **Horlivka** Ukr.
143 F4 **Hormak** Iran
143 E5 **Hormoz, Jazīreh-ye** *i.* Iran
143 E5 **Hormuz, Strait of** Iran/Oman
176 G6 **Horn** Austria

Isparta

138 C6 Idkū Egypt
139 F4 Idlib Syria
171 K3 Idre Sweden
179 G4 Idstein Germany
Idutywa S. Africa see Dutywa
171 N4 Iecava Latvia
234 B3 Iepê Brazil
178 A4 Ieper Belgium
185 K7 Ierapetra Greece
170 N1 Iešjávri l. Norway
195 D4 Ifakara Tanz.
195 E6 Ifanadiana Madag.
122 C3 Iffley Australia
170 N1 Ifjord Norway
192 C3 Ifôghas, Adrar des hills Mali
163 H2 Igan Sarawak Malaysia
234 C3 Igarapava Brazil
234 D3 Igarapé Brazil
133 J3 Igarka Russia
148 C6 Igatpuri India
137 G3 Igdir Iran
139 J2 Iğdır Turkey
171 L3 Iggesund Sweden
184 C5 Iglesias Sardinia Italy
203 J3 Igloolik Canada
206 B4 Ignace Canada
171 N5 Ignalina Lith.
187 C7 İğneada Turkey
185 M4 İğneada Burnu pt Turkey
173 P3 Igorevskaya Russia
185 I5 Igoumenitsa Greece
132 H3 Igrim Russia
235 B4 Iguaçu r. Brazil
235 A4 Iguaçu, Parque Nacional do nat. park Brazil
232 F3 Iguaçu Falls Arg./Brazil
234 E1 Iguaí Brazil
233 I4 Iguaje, Mesa de hills Col.
225 E4 Iguala Mex.
183 Q2 Igualada Spain
235 C4 Iguape Brazil
234 A3 Iguatemi Brazil
234 A3 Iguatemi r. Brazil
231 K5 Iguatu Brazil
235 B4 Iguazú, Parque Nacional del nat. park Arg.
195 A4 Iguéla Gabon
192 B2 Iguidi, Erg des. Alg./Mauritania
195 D4 Igunga Tanz.
195 E5 Iharaña Madag.
Ihbulag Mongolia see Hanbogd
195 E6 Ihosy Madag.
160 B2 Ih Tal China
185 J3 Ihtiman Bulg.
153 L1 Ih Tol Gol China
159 F6 Iide-san mt. Japan
170 N1 Iijärvi Fin.
170 N2 Iijoki r. Fin.
171 N3 Iisalmi Fin.
159 B8 Iizuka Japan
139 J1 Ijevan Armenia
178 C2 IJmuiden Neth.
178 D2 IJssel r. Neth.
178 D2 IJsselmeer l. Neth.
171 M3 Ikaalinen Fin.
197 G2 Ikageleng S. Africa
197 G3 Ikageng S. Africa
185 L6 Ikaria i. Greece
171 J4 Ikast Denmark
158 H3 Ikeda Japan
195 C4 Ikela Dem. Rep. Congo
197 F4 Ikhutseng S. Africa
158 H6 Iki-Burul Russia
159 A8 Iki-shima i. Japan
192 C4 Ikom Nigeria
195 E6 Ikongo Madag.
187 H6 Ikryanoye Russia
160 D6 Iksan S. Korea
195 D4 Ikungu Tanz.
161 I2 Ilagan Phil.
194 D3 Ilaisamis Kenya
142 B3 Īlām Iran
149 F4 Ilam Nepal
Ilan Taiwan see Yilan
192 C4 Ilaro Nigeria
177 I4 Iława Poland
205 H3 Île-à-la-Crosse Canada
205 H3 Île-à-la-Crosse, Lac l. Canada
195 C4 Ilebo Dem. Rep. Congo
140 C2 Ilek Kazakh.
140 C2 Ilek r. Russia
193 F4 Ilemi Triangle terr. Africa
194 D3 Ileret Kenya
186 G2 Ileza Russia
173 H6 Ilford U.K.
123 D4 Ilfracombe Australia
173 C6 Ilfracombe U.K.
138 D1 Ilgaz Turkey
138 D1 Ilgaz Dağları mts Turkey
138 C2 Ilgın Turkey
233 K5 Ilha Grande Brazil
234 B3 Ilha Grande resr Brazil
197 J2 Ilhas da Inhaca e dos Portugueses nature res. S. Africa
234 B3 Ilha Solteíra, Represa resr Brazil
183 L2 Ílhavo Port.
234 E1 Ilhéus Brazil
141 J4 Ili r. China
141 I3 Ili r. Kazakh.
202 C4 Iliamna Lake U.S.A.
139 G2 İliç Turkey
161 J4 Iligan Phil.
161 J4 Iligan Bay Phil.
140 D2 Il'inka Kazakh.
156 F3 Il'inskiy Russia
186 H2 Il'insko-Podomskoye Russia
221 F3 Ilion U.S.A.
147 H3 Ilkal India
173 F5 Ilkeston U.K.
173 F4 Ilkley U.K.
161 I5 Illana Bay Phil.
235 H1 Illapel Chile
235 H1 Illapel r. Chile
176 E7 Iller r. Germany
187 D6 Illichivs'k Ukr.
230 E7 Illimani, Nevado de mt. Bol.
208 C5 Illinois r. U.S.A.
208 C5 Illinois state U.S.A.
208 B5 Illinois and Mississippi Canal U.S.A.
187 D5 Illintsi Ukr.
192 C2 Illizi Alg.
123 A5 Illogwa watercourse Australia
179 J4 Ilm r. Germany
171 M3 Ilmajoki Fin.
186 D3 Il'men', Ozero l. Russia
179 I4 Ilmenau Germany
179 I1 Ilmenau r. Germany
173 E7 Ilminster U.K.
230 D7 Ilo Peru
161 H4 Iloc i. Phil.
161 I4 Iloilo Phil.
171 O3 Ilomantsi Fin.
192 C4 Ilorin Nigeria
187 F6 Ilovays'k Ukr.
187 G5 Ilovlya Russia
187 H5 Ilovlya r. Russia
179 I2 Ilsede Germany
125 J2 Iluka Australia
203 M3 Ilulissat Greenland
159 C7 Imabari Japan
Imaichi Japan see Nikkō
139 J6 Imām al Ḥamzah Iraq
139 J5 Imām Ḥamīd Iraq
136 D3 İmamoğlu Turkey
138 E3 İmamoğlu admin. dist. Turkey
143 H2 Imām Ṣāḥib Afgh.
158 D2 Iman r. Russia
159 A8 Imari Japan
233 L3 Imataca, Serranía de mts Venez.
171 O3 Imatra Fin.
159 E7 Imazu Japan
233 G3 Imbituba Brazil
235 B4 Imbituva Brazil
194 E3 Īmī Eth.
139 L2 İmişli Azer.
160 D6 Imja-do i. S. Korea
160 D4 Imjin-gang r. N. Korea
184 D2 Imola Italy
197 H4 Impendle S. Africa
231 I5 Imperatriz Brazil
184 C3 Imperia Italy
216 C3 Imperial U.S.A.
215 D5 Imperial Beach U.S.A.
215 E5 Imperial Valley plain U.S.A.
120 B3 Imperieuse Reef Australia
194 B3 Impfondo Congo
149 H4 Imphal India
185 K4 İmroz Turkey
160 D5 Imsil S. Korea
139 F5 Imtān Syria
161 H4 Imuruan Bay Phil.
156 D2 In r. Russia
159 F7 Ina Japan
230 E6 Inambari r. Peru
192 C2 In Aménas Alg.
197 I4 Inanda S. Africa
126 C4 Inangahua Junction N.Z.
151 F7 Inanwatan Indon.
170 N1 Inari Fin.
170 N1 Inarijärvi l. Fin.
170 N1 Inarijoki r. Fin./Norway
183 R3 Inca Spain
187 C7 İnce Burnu pt Turkey
187 E7 İnce Burun pt Turkey
138 D3 İncekum Burnu pt Turkey
138 E2 İncesu Turkey
175 L5 Inch Ireland
174 C2 Inchard, Loch b. U.K.
Inchcape Rock i. U.K. see Bell Rock
160 D5 Incheon S. Korea
174 E4 Inchkeith i. U.K.
197 J2 Incomati r. Moz.
174 B5 Indaal, Loch b. U.K.
234 D2 Indaiá r. Brazil
234 B2 Indaiá Grande r. Brazil
171 L3 Indalsälven r. Sweden
171 I3 Indalstø Norway
224 C2 Indé Mex.
214 C3 Independence CA U.S.A.
208 B4 Independence IA U.S.A.
217 E4 Independence KS U.S.A.
208 A2 Independence MN U.S.A.
217 E4 Independence MO U.S.A.
220 C6 Independence VA U.S.A.
208 B3 Independence WI U.S.A.
213 C3 Independence Mountains U.S.A.
156 A3 Inder China
140 B2 Inder, Ozero salt l. Kazakh.
140 B2 Inderbor Kazakh.
147 H2 Indi India
135 F4 India country Asia
208 D2 Indian r. U.S.A.
220 D4 Indiana U.S.A.
208 D5 Indiana state U.S.A.
208 D5 Indiana Dunes National Lakeshore nature res. U.S.A.
Indian-Antarctic Basin sea feature Southern Ocean see Australian-Antarctic Basin
238 L8 Indian-Antarctic Ridge sea feature Southern Ocean
208 D6 Indianapolis U.S.A.
Indian Desert India/Pak. see Thar Desert
207 I3 Indian Harbour Canada
221 F3 Indian Lake U.S.A.
208 D3 Indian Lake l. MI U.S.A.
220 B4 Indian Lake l. OH U.S.A.
220 D4 Indian Lake l. PA U.S.A.
238 Indian Ocean
216 E3 Indianola IA U.S.A.
217 F5 Indianola MS U.S.A.
215 F2 Indian Peak U.S.A.
209 E3 Indian River U.S.A.
215 E3 Indian Springs U.S.A.
215 G4 Indian Wells U.S.A.
169 P2 Indiga Russia
133 P2 Indigirka r. Russia
185 I2 Inđija Serbia
204 F2 Indin Lake Canada
215 D5 Indio U.S.A.
119 G3 Indispensable Reefs Solomon Is
129 C5 Indo-China reg. Asia
151 D7 Indonesia country Asia
148 C5 Indore India
163 G4 Indramayu, Tanjung pt Indon.
163 B3 Indrapura Indon.
147 I2 Indravati r. India
182 E3 Indre r. France
121 F5 Indulkana Australia
149 E2 Indus r. China
conv. Indus
148 B4 Indus r. China/Pak.
alt. Shiquan He (China)
148 A5 Indus, Mouths of the Pak.
238 I3 Indus Cone sea feature Indian Ocean
197 G5 Indwe S. Africa
187 E7 İnebolu Turkey
138 B1 İnegöl Turkey
220 B6 Inez U.S.A.
196 D7 Infanta, Cape S. Africa
225 D4 Infiernillo, Presa resr Mex.
162 B1 Ing, Nam Mae r. Thai.
208 D3 Ingalls U.S.A.
214 B2 Ingalls, Mount U.S.A.
205 I2 Ingalls Lake Canada
178 B4 Ingelmunster Belgium
235 I4 Ingeniero Jacobacci Arg.
209 G4 Ingersoll Canada
122 D3 Ingham Australia
141 F5 Ingichka Uzbek.
172 E3 Ingleborough h. U.K.
203 K2 Inglefield Land reg. Greenland
172 E3 Ingleton U.K.
125 I2 Inglewood Qld Australia
125 E6 Inglewood Vic. Australia
173 H4 Ingoldmells U.K.
176 E6 Ingolstadt Germany
121 F6 Ingomar Australia
207 H4 Ingonish Canada
149 G4 Ingraj Bazar India
204 F2 Ingray Lake Canada
Ingushetia aut. rep. Russia see Respublika Ingushetiya
197 J3 Ingwavuma S. Africa
197 J2 Inhaca Moz.
197 J3 Inhaca, Península pen. Moz.
195 D6 Inhambane Moz.
197 J1 Inhambane prov. Moz.
195 D5 Inhaminga Moz.
234 A3 Inhanduízinho r. Brazil
234 D1 Inhaúmas Brazil
233 K4 Inírida Col.
233 J4 Inírida r. Col.
175 H4 Inishark i. Ireland
175 H4 Inishbofin i. Ireland
175 H3 Inishkea North i. Ireland
175 H3 Inishkea South i. Ireland
175 I4 Inishmaan i. Ireland
175 I4 Inishmore i. Ireland
175 J3 Inishmurray i. Ireland
175 K2 Inishowen pen. Ireland
175 L2 Inishowen Head Ireland
175 K2 Inishtrahull i. Ireland
175 K2 Inishtrahull Sound sea chan. Ireland
175 H4 Inishturk i. Ireland
123 E5 Injune Australia
122 C3 Inkerman Australia
171 N3 Inkeroinen Fin.
140 E5 Inkylap Turkm.
126 D5 Inland Kaikoura Range mts N.Z.
Inland Sea Japan see Seto-naikai
181 F2 Inn r. Europe
203 L2 Innaanganeq c. Greenland
124 D1 Innamincka Australia
123 C5 Innamincka Regional Reserve nature res. Australia
170 K2 Inndyr Norway
Inner Mongolia aut. reg. China see Zizhiqu
174 C3 Inner Sound sea chan. U.K.
123 B7 Innes National Park Australia
119 E3 Innisfail Australia
156 C2 Innokent'yevka Russia
176 E7 Innsbruck Austria
175 K4 Inny r. Ireland
195 B4 Inongo Dem. Rep. Congo
136 C3 İnönü Turkey
177 I4 Inowrocław Poland
192 C2 In Salah Alg.
187 H4 Insar Russia
175 F3 Insch U.K.
122 B3 Inscription, Cape Australia
132 H3 Inta Russia
235 J2 Intendente Alvear Arg.
176 C7 Interlaken Switz.
216 E1 International Falls U.S.A.
145 H9 Interview Island India
159 G7 Inubō-zaki pt Japan
206 E2 Inukjuak Canada
202 E3 Inuvik Canada
174 C4 Inveraray U.K.
175 F4 Inverbervie U.K.
126 B7 Invercargill N.Z.
125 I2 Inverell Australia
174 D3 Invergordon U.K.
174 E4 Inverkeithing U.K.
122 C3 Inverleigh Australia
207 H4 Inverness Canada
174 D3 Inverness U.K.
219 D6 Inverness U.S.A.
175 F3 Inverurie U.K.
121 F7 Investigator Group is Australia
238 K5 Investigator Ridge sea feature Indian Ocean
124 B5 Investigator Strait Australia
135 G1 Inya Russia
213 C5 Inyokern U.S.A.
214 C3 Inyo Mountains U.S.A.
195 D4 Inyonga Tanz.
187 H4 Inza Russia
140 D1 Inzer Russia
187 G4 Inzhavino Russia
185 I5 Ioannina Greece
159 B9 Iō-jima i. Japan
217 E4 Iola U.S.A.
141 K2 Iolgo, Khrebet mts Russia
174 B4 Iona i. U.K.
212 C1 Ione U.S.A.
209 E4 Ionia U.S.A.
185 H5 Ionian Islands Greece
185 G6 Ionian Sea Greece/Italy
Ionoi Nisoi is Greece see Ionian Islands
150 G1 Iony, Ostrov i. Russia
139 K1 Iori r. Georgia
185 K6 Ios i. Greece
151 G4 Iō-tō i. Japan
170 O2 Iovskoye Vodokhranilishche l. Russia
208 B5 Iowa r. U.S.A.
208 A4 Iowa state U.S.A.
208 B5 Iowa City U.S.A.
216 E3 Iowa Falls U.S.A.
234 C2 Ipameri Brazil
230 D5 Iparía Peru
234 D2 Ipatinga Brazil
187 G6 Ipatovo Russia
197 F3 Ipelegeng S. Africa
233 H4 Ipiales Col.
234 E1 Ipiaú Brazil
235 B4 Ipiranga Brazil
163 B2 Ipoh Malaysia
231 K5 Ipojuca r. Brazil
234 B2 Iporá Brazil
194 C3 Ippy C.A.R.
185 L4 İpsala Turkey
125 J1 Ipswich Australia
173 I5 Ipswich U.K.
203 L3 Iqaluit Canada
232 B2 Iquique Chile
230 D4 Iquitos Peru
161 H4 Iraan Phil.
143 F5 Īrafshān reg. Iran
159 E7 Irago-misaki pt Japan
185 K6 Irakleia i. Greece
Irakleio Greece see Iraklion
185 K7 Iraklion Greece
234 E1 Iramaia Brazil
142 D3 Iran country Asia
163 H2 Iran, Pegunungan mts Indon.
143 F5 Īrānshahr Iran
225 D3 Irapuato Mex.
139 I5 Iraq country Asia
221 G2 Irasville U.S.A.
235 B4 Irati Brazil
138 E5 Irbid Jordan
132 H4 Irbit Russia
231 J6 Irecê Brazil
175 K4 Ireland country Europe
195 C4 Irema Dem. Rep. Congo
151 F7 Irian Jaya Indon.
139 K2 Īrī Dāgh mt. Iran
161 I3 Iriga Phil.
192 B3 Irîgui reg. Mali/Mauritania
195 D4 Iringa Tanz.
147 H4 Irinjalakuda India
231 H4 Iriri r. Brazil
173 B4 Irish Sea Ireland
231 I4 Irituia Brazil
142 C5 'Irj well Saudi Arabia
150 C1 Irkutsk Russia
138 D2 Irmak Turkey
239 G2 Irminger Basin sea feature N. Atlantic Ocean
124 B4 Iron Baron Australia
209 F2 Iron Bridge Canada
221 E3 Irondequoit U.S.A.
124 B4 Iron Knob Australia
208 C3 Iron Mountain U.S.A.
215 F3 Iron Mountain mt. U.S.A.
122 C2 Iron Range National Park Australia
208 C2 Iron River U.S.A.
217 F4 Ironton MO U.S.A.
220 B5 Ironton OH U.S.A.
208 B2 Ironwood U.S.A.
221 F2 Iroquois Canada
208 D5 Iroquois r. U.S.A.
161 J3 Irosin Phil.
159 F7 Irō-zaki pt Japan
187 D5 Irpin' Ukr.
149 H5 Irrawaddy r. China/Myanmar
151 B5 Irrawaddy, Mouths of the Myanmar
148 C1 Irshad Pass Afgh./Pak.
186 I2 Irta Russia
172 E3 Irthing r. U.K.
132 H3 Irtysh r. Kazakh./Russia
194 C3 Irumu Dem. Rep. Congo
183 P1 Irun Spain
174 D5 Irvine U.K.
215 D5 Irvine CA U.S.A.
220 B6 Irvine KY U.S.A.
217 D5 Irving U.S.A.
121 A6 Irwin r. Australia
123 E4 Isaac r. Australia
161 I5 Isabela Phil.
230 □ Isabela, Isla i. Galapagos Is Ecuador
224 H5 Isabelia, Cordillera mts Nicaragua
208 B2 Isabella U.S.A.
214 C4 Isabella Lake U.S.A.
208 D2 Isabelle, Point U.S.A.
170 B1 Ísafjarðardjúp est. Iceland
170 B1 Ísafjörður Iceland
159 B8 Isahaya Japan
148 B2 Isa Khel Pak.
186 G1 Isakogorka Russia
195 E6 Isalo, Massif de l' mts Madag.
195 E6 Isalo, Parc National de l' nat. park Madag.
233 J4 Isana r. Col.
174 □ Isbister U.K.
184 E4 Ischia, Isola d' i. Italy
235 I1 Ischigualasto, Parque Provincial nature res. Arg.
233 H4 Iscuande r. Col.
159 E7 Ise Japan
194 C3 Isengi Dem. Rep. Congo
182 H4 Isère r. France
179 F3 Iserlohn Germany
179 H2 Isernhagen Germany
184 F4 Isernia Italy
159 F6 Isesaki Japan
159 E7 Ise-shima Kokuritsu-kōen nat. park Japan
159 E7 Ise-wan b. Japan
192 C4 Iseyin Nigeria
Isfahan Iran see Eşfahān
141 G5 Isfana Kyrg.
141 G4 Isfara Tajik.
139 J5 Isḩāq Iraq
187 I4 Isheyevka Russia
153 L7 Ishigaki Japan
158 G3 Ishikari-gawa r. Japan
158 G3 Ishikari-wan b. Japan
141 F2 Ishimskoye Kazakh.
159 G5 Ishinomaki Japan
159 G5 Ishinomaki-wan b. Japan
159 G6 Ishioka Japan
159 C8 Ishizuchi-san mt. Japan
148 C1 Ishkuman Pak.
208 D2 Ishpeming U.S.A.
141 G5 Ishqoshim Kazakh.
141 F5 Ishtixon Uzbek.
Ishtykhan Uzbek. see Ishtixon
149 G4 Ishurdi Bangl.
230 E7 Isiboro Sécure, Parque Nacional nat. park Bol.
138 B2 Işıklı Turkey
138 B2 Işıklı Barajı resr Turkey
132 I4 Isil'kul' Russia
197 J3 iSimangaliso Wetland Park nature res. S. Africa
197 I4 Isipingo S. Africa
194 C3 Isiro Dem. Rep. Congo
123 D5 Isisford Australia
143 G2 Iskabad Canal (disused) Afgh.
141 G4 Iskandar Uzbek.
185 K3 Iskar r. Bulg.
139 F3 İskenderun Turkey
181 K4 İskenderun Körfezi b. Turkey
138 E1 İskilip Turkey
150 A1 Iskitim Russia
204 C3 Iskut Canada
204 C3 Iskut r. Canada
123 E5 Isla Gorge National Park Australia
139 F3 İslahiye Turkey
148 C2 Islamabad Pak.
148 C3 Islam Barrage Pak.
148 B4 Islamgarh Pak.
148 B4 Islamkot Pak.
219 D7 Islamorada U.S.A.
143 F3 Islam Qal'ah Afgh.
161 H4 Island Bay Phil.
221 I1 Island Falls U.S.A.
124 B3 Island Lagoon salt flat Australia
205 K4 Island Lake l. Canada
208 A2 Island Lake l. U.S.A.
214 A1 Island Mountain U.S.A.
212 E2 Island Park U.S.A.
221 H2 Island Pond U.S.A.
126 E1 Islands, Bay of N.Z.
174 B5 Islay i. U.K.
172 C3 Isle of Man terr. Irish Sea
221 E6 Isle of Wight U.S.A.
208 C2 Isle Royale National Park U.S.A.
139 L1 İsmayıllı Azer.
141 G5 Ismoili Somoní, Qullai mt. Tajik.
171 M3 Isojoki Fin.
195 D5 Isoka Zambia
170 N2 Isokylä Fin.
185 G5 Isola di Capo Rizzuto Italy
138 C3 Isparta Turkey

Kaduy

231 J5 **Jerumenha** Brazil
138 E6 **Jerusalem** Israel/West Bank
125 I5 **Jervis Bay** Australia
125 I5 **Jervis Bay** *b.* Australia
125 I5 **Jervis Bay Territory** *admin. div.* Australia
184 F1 **Jesenice** Slovenia
184 E3 **Jesi** Italy
179 K3 **Jessen (Elster)** Germany
171 J3 **Jessheim** Norway
149 G5 **Jessore** Bangl.
179 H1 **Jesteburg** Germany
219 D6 **Jesup** U.S.A.
225 F4 **Jesús Carranza** Mex.
235 J1 **Jesús María** Arg.
148 B5 **Jetalsar** India
217 D4 **Jetmore** U.S.A.
148 B5 **Jetpur** India
179 F1 **Jever** Germany
Jewish Autonomous Oblast *admin. div.* Russia *see* **Yevreyskaya Avtonomnaya Oblast'**
185 H3 **Jezercë, Maja** *mt.* Albania
149 F4 **Jha Jha** India
148 C4 **Jhajju** India
148 A3 **Jhal** Pak.
149 G5 **Jhalakati** Bangl.
143 G5 **Jhal Jhao** Pak.
148 C3 **Jhang** Pak.
148 D4 **Jhansi** India
149 F5 **Jharia** India
149 F4 **Jharkhand** *state* India
147 J1 **Jharsuguda** India
148 B3 **Jhatpat** Pak.
148 C2 **Jhelum** Pak.
148 C2 **Jhelum** *r.* Pak.
149 G5 **Jhenaidah** Bangl.
149 H4 **Jhingtubum** *mt.* India
148 B4 **Jhudo** Pak.
149 F4 **Jhumritilaiya** India
148 C3 **Jhunjhunun** India
154 C3 **Jiachuan** China
155 F4 **Jiading** China
155 D5 **Jiahe** China
155 B4 **Jiajiang** China
154 B3 **Jialing Jiang** *r.* China
158 B1 **Jiamusi** China
155 E5 **Ji'an** *Jiangxi* China
155 E5 **Ji'an** *Jiangxi* China
160 D3 **Ji'an** *Jilin* China
154 F1 **Jianchang** China
155 F4 **Jiande** China
155 B4 **Jiang'an** China
155 A6 **Jiangcheng** China
155 B5 **Jiangchuan** China
Jiange China *see* **Pu'an**
155 C4 **Jiangjin** China
144 G3 **Jiangjunmiao** China
155 C5 **Jiangkou** China
155 E5 **Jiangle** China
155 D6 **Jiangmen** China
155 F4 **Jiangshan** China
154 F3 **Jiangsu** *prov.* China
155 E5 **Jiangxi** *prov.* China
155 E4 **Jiangxia** China
154 D3 **Jiangxian** China
154 F3 **Jiangyan** China
155 F4 **Jiangyin** China
155 D5 **Jiangyong** China
155 B4 **Jiangyou** China
154 F3 **Jianhu** China
155 D6 **Jian Jiang** *r.* China
155 A5 **Jiankang** China
155 D4 **Jianli** China
155 E5 **Jianning** China
155 F5 **Jian'ou** China
154 F1 **Jianping** *Liaoning* China
154 F1 **Jianping** *Liaoning* China
154 E2 **Jianqiao** China
155 C4 **Jianshi** China
155 B6 **Jianshui** China
155 F5 **Jianyang** *Fujian* China
155 B4 **Jianyang** *Sichuan* China
154 D2 **Jiaocheng** China
160 D2 **Jiaohe** China
Jiaojiang China *see* **Taizhou**
160 A2 **Jiaolai He** *r. Nei Mongol Zizhiqu* China
154 F2 **Jiaolai He** *r. Shandong* China
155 E5 **Jiaoling** China
154 F3 **Jiaonan** China
154 F2 **Jiaozhou** China
154 F2 **Jiaozhou Wan** *b.* China
154 D3 **Jiaozuo** China
160 D2 **Jiapigou** China
141 I5 **Jiashi** China
154 D2 **Jiaxian** China
155 F4 **Jiaxing** China
155 F6 **Jiayi** Taiwan
156 C2 **Jiayin** China
155 D4 **Jiayu** China
150 B3 **Jiayuguan** China
155 E6 **Jiazi** China
224 I7 **Jicarón, Isla** *i.* Panama
Jiddah Saudi Arabia *see* **Jeddah**
138 D6 **Jiddī, Jabal al** *h.* Egypt
160 D6 **Jido** S. Korea
161 F1 **Jidong** China
154 B2 **Jieheba** China
170 L1 **Jiehkkevárri** *mt.* Norway
155 E6 **Jieshi** China
155 E6 **Jieshi Wan** *b.* China
154 E3 **Jieshou** China
Ješjávri *l.* Norway *see* **Iešjávri**
155 E6 **Jiexi** China
154 D2 **Jiexiu** China
155 E6 **Jieyang** China
171 N5 **Jieznas** Lith.
140 E4 **Jigerbent** Turkm.
154 A3 **Jigzhi** China
176 G6 **Jihlava** Czech Rep.
143 F3 **Jījah** Afgh.
180 E4 **Jijel** Alg.
194 E3 **Jijiga** Eth.
155 A4 **Jijü** China
193 E2 **Jilf al Kabīr, Haḍabat al** *plat.* Egypt
143 H3 **Jilgah** *r.* Afgh.
194 E3 **Jilib** Somalia
160 D2 **Jilin** China
160 C2 **Jilin** *prov.* China
154 A2 **Jiling** China
160 C2 **Jilin Hada Ling** *mts* China
155 F5 **Jilong** Taiwan
194 D3 **Jīma** Eth.
224 C2 **Jiménez** *Chihuahua* Mex.
225 D1 **Jiménez** *Coahuila* Mex.
225 E2 **Jiménez** *Tamaulipas* Mex.
154 F2 **Jimo** China
144 G3 **Jimsar** China
221 F4 **Jim Thorpe** U.S.A.
154 E2 **Jinan** China
Jinbi China *see* **Dayao**
154 B2 **Jinchang** China
154 D3 **Jincheng** *Shanxi* China
155 C4 **Jincheng** *Sichuan* China
155 B4 **Jinchuan** China
148 D3 **Jind** India
125 H6 **Jindabyne** Australia
125 G5 **Jindera** Australia
160 D6 **Jindo** S. Korea
160 D6 **Jin-do** *i.* S. Korea
176 G6 **Jindřichův Hradec** Czech Rep.
155 E4 **Jing'an** China
154 E2 **Jingbian** China
154 C3 **Jingchuan** China
155 F4 **Jingde** China
155 E4 **Jingdezhen** China
155 E4 **Jinggongqiao** China
154 E2 **Jinghai** China
160 B5 **Jinghai Wan** *b.* China
141 J3 **Jinghe** China
154 C3 **Jing He** *r.* China
151 C4 **Jinghong** China
154 F3 **Jingjiang** China
154 D2 **Jingle** China
154 D4 **Jingmen** China
154 B3 **Jingning** China
154 E1 **Jingpeng** China
160 E2 **Jingpo** China
160 E2 **Jingpo Hu** *l.* China
154 B2 **Jingtai** China
Jingtieshan China *see* **Sanchakou**
155 C6 **Jingxi** China
155 F4 **Jingxian** China
160 D2 **Jingyu** China
154 B2 **Jingyuan** China
155 D4 **Jingzhou** *Hubei* China
155 D4 **Jingzhou** *Hubei* China
155 C5 **Jingzhou** *Hunan* China
160 E6 **Jinhae** S. Korea
154 F3 **Jinhu** China
155 F4 **Jinhua** China
Jining *Nei Mongol Zizhiqu* China *see* **Ulan Qab**
154 E3 **Jining** *Shandong* China
194 D3 **Jinja** Uganda
155 F5 **Jinjiang** China
155 E4 **Jin Jiang** *r.* China
194 D3 **Jinka** Eth.
160 A3 **Jinlingsi** China
155 F5 **Jinmen** Taiwan
155 F5 **Jinmen Dao** *i.* Taiwan
155 C7 **Jinmu Jiao** *pt* China
224 H5 **Jinotega** Nicaragua
224 H6 **Jinotepe** Nicaragua
155 C5 **Jinping** *Guizhou* China
155 B6 **Jinping** *Yunnan* China
155 A5 **Jinping Shan** *mts* China
155 C5 **Jinsha** China
155 B4 **Jinsha Jiang** *r.* China *alt.* **Chang Jiang**, *alt.* **Tongtian He**, *alt.* **Zhi Qu**, *conv.* **Yangtze**, *long* **Yangtze Kiang**
154 F1 **Jinshan** *Nei Mongol Zizhiqu* China
Jinshan *Shanghai* China *see* **Zhujing**
155 D4 **Jinshi** China
155 B4 **Jintang** China
161 I4 **Jintotolo** *i.* Phil.
161 I4 **Jintotolo Channel** Phil.
148 D6 **Jintur** India
155 E5 **Jinxi** China
155 E4 **Jinxian** China
154 E3 **Jinxiang** *Shandong* China
155 F5 **Jinxiang** *Zhejiang* China
155 B5 **Jinyang** China
155 F4 **Jinyun** China
155 E4 **Jinzhai** China
154 D2 **Jinzhong** China
160 A3 **Jinzhou** *Liaoning* China
160 A4 **Jinzhou** *Liaoning* China
160 A4 **Jinzhou Wan** *b.* China
231 F6 **Ji-Paraná** Brazil
231 F5 **Ji-Paraná** *r.* Brazil
230 B4 **Jipijapa** Ecuador
149 H2 **Ji Qu** *r.* China
149 E3 **Jirang** China
141 G5 **Jirghatol** Tajik.
157 B6 **Jiri-san** *mt.* S. Korea
143 E4 **Jīroft** Iran
142 C6 **Jirwān** Saudi Arabia
142 C6 **Jirwan** *well* Saudi Arabia
155 C4 **Jishou** China
139 F4 **Jisr ash Shughūr** Syria
162 B4 **Jitra** Malaysia
154 C2 **Jiudengkou** China
155 B4 **Jiuding Shan** *mt.* China
154 C3 **Jiufoping** China
155 E4 **Jiujiang** *Jiangxi* China
155 E4 **Jiujiang** *Jiangxi* China
Jiulian China *see* **Mojiang**
155 E4 **Jiuling Shan** *mts* China
155 A4 **Jiulong** China
160 A2 **Jiumiao** China
144 I4 **Jiuquan** China
160 C1 **Jiutai** China
155 C5 **Jiuxu** China
154 B3 **Jiuzhaigou** China
143 F5 **Jiwani** Pak.
156 A2 **Jiwen** China
154 E3 **Jixi** *Anhui* China
161 F1 **Jixi** *Heilongjiang* China
158 B1 **Jixian** China
154 D3 **Jiyuan** China
154 E2 **Jizhou** China
159 C7 **Jizō-zaki** *pt* Japan
141 F4 **Jizzax** Uzbek.
235 M2 **João Maria, Albardão do** *coastal area* Brazil
231 L5 **João Pessoa** Brazil
234 C2 **João Pinheiro** Brazil
214 C2 **Job Peak** U.S.A.
160 D5 **Jochiwon** S. Korea
179 K4 **Jocketa** Germany
147 J1 **Joda** India
148 C4 **Jodhpur** India
171 O3 **Joensuu** Fin.
159 F6 **Jōetsu** Japan
195 D6 **Jofane** Moz.
204 F4 **Joffre, Mount** Canada
171 N4 **Jõgeva** Estonia
207 H4 **Joggins** Canada
197 G3 **Johannesburg** S. Africa
215 D4 **Johannesburg** U.S.A.
149 E5 **Johilla** *r.* India
212 C2 **John Day** U.S.A.
212 B2 **John Day** *r.* U.S.A.
204 F3 **John D'Or Prairie** Canada
221 G4 **John F. Kennedy** *airport* U.S.A.
220 D6 **John H. Kerr Reservoir** U.S.A.
174 E2 **John o' Groats** U.K.
219 D4 **Johnson City** U.S.A.
204 C2 **Johnson's Crossing** Canada
219 D5 **Johnston** U.S.A.
121 C7 **Johnston, Lake** *salt flat* Australia
117 H2 **Johnston Atoll** *terr.* N. Pacific Ocean
174 D5 **Johnstone** U.K.
121 B6 **Johnston Range** *hills* Australia
175 K5 **Johnstown** Ireland
221 F3 **Johnstown** *NY* U.S.A.
220 D4 **Johnstown** *PA* U.S.A.
209 F3 **Johnswood** U.S.A.
162 □ **Johor, Selat** *str.* Malaysia/Sing.
163 B2 **Johor Bahru** Malaysia
171 N4 **Jõhvi** Estonia
233 G3 **Joinville** Brazil
182 G2 **Joinville** France
127 I2 **Joinville Island** Antarctica
170 L2 **Jokkmokk** Sweden
170 D2 **Jökulsá á Dál** *r.* Iceland
170 C1 **Jökulsá á Fjöllum** *r.* Iceland
170 D2 **Jökulsá í Fljótsdal** *r.* Iceland
142 B2 **Jolfā** Iran
208 C5 **Joliet** U.S.A.
207 F4 **Joliette** Canada
161 I5 **Jolo** Phil.
161 I5 **Jolo** *i.* Phil.
161 I3 **Jomalig** *i.* Phil.
163 H4 **Jombang** Indon.
152 G5 **Jomda** China
225 G4 **Jonathan Point** Belize
171 N5 **Jonava** Lith.
154 B3 **Jonê** China
217 F5 **Jonesboro** *AR* U.S.A.
221 J2 **Jonesboro** *ME* U.S.A.
221 J2 **Jonesport** U.S.A.
203 J2 **Jones Sound** *sea chan.* Canada
220 B6 **Jonesville** U.S.A.
140 E4 **Jongeldi** Uzbek.
193 F4 **Jonglei Canal** South Sudan
147 I1 **Jonk** *r.* India
171 K4 **Jönköping** Sweden
207 F4 **Jonquière** Canada
225 F4 **Jonuta** Mex.
217 E4 **Joplin** U.S.A.
221 E5 **Joppatowne** U.S.A.
148 D4 **Jora** India
139 F6 **Jordan** *country* Asia
138 E6 **Jordan** *r.* Asia
212 F2 **Jordan** U.S.A.
213 E3 **Jordan** *r.* U.S.A.
213 C3 **Jordan Valley** U.S.A.
235 B4 **Jordão** *r.* Brazil
171 K3 **Jordet** Norway
149 H4 **Jorhat** India
141 I5 **Jor Hu** *l.* China
179 F1 **Jork** Germany
170 M2 **Jörn** Sweden
171 N3 **Joroinen** Fin.
171 I4 **Jørpeland** Norway
192 C4 **Jos** Nigeria
161 J5 **Jose Abad Santos** Phil.
225 E4 **José Cardel** Mex.
232 B6 **José de San Martín** Arg.
234 A2 **Joselândia** Brazil
235 L2 **José Pedro Varela** Uruguay
207 G3 **Joseph, Lac** *l.* Canada
118 C3 **Joseph Bonaparte Gulf** Australia
215 G4 **Joseph City** U.S.A.
159 F6 **Jōshinetsu-kōgen Kokuritsu-kōen** *nat. park* Japan
215 E5 **Joshua Tree National Park** U.S.A.
192 C4 **Jos Plateau** Nigeria
171 I3 **Jostedalsbreen Nasjonalpark** *nat. park* Norway
171 J3 **Jotunheimen Nasjonalpark** *nat. park* Norway
197 E6 **Joubertina** S. Africa
197 G3 **Jouberton** S. Africa
171 N4 **Jõuga** Estonia
136 D4 **Joûnié** Lebanon
178 D2 **Joure** Neth.
171 N3 **Joutsa** Fin.
171 O3 **Joutseno** Fin.
179 E5 **Jouy-aux-Arches** France
149 H4 **Jowai** India
143 G3 **Jowand** Afgh.
175 I4 **Joyce Country** *reg.* Ireland
225 D2 **Juan Aldama** Mex.
212 A1 **Juan de Fuca Strait** U.S.A.
195 E5 **Juan de Nova** *i.* Indian Ocean
228 E5 **Juan Fernández, Archipiélago** *is* S. Pacific Ocean
171 O3 **Juankoski** Fin.
224 H6 **Juan Santamaria** *airport* Costa Rica
225 D2 **Juárez** Mex.
231 J5 **Juazeiro** Brazil
231 K5 **Juazeiro do Norte** Brazil
193 F4 **Juba** South Sudan
Jubaland *reg.* Somalia *see* **Azania**
194 E3 **Jubba** *r.* Somalia
137 F5 **Jubbah** Saudi Arabia
121 D6 **Jubilee Lake** *salt flat* Australia
215 D4 **Jubilee Pass** U.S.A.
225 E4 **Juchatengo** Mex.
225 D3 **Juchipila** Mex.
225 F4 **Juchitán** Mex.
224 C3 **Juchitlán** Mex.
234 E2 **Jucuruçu** *r.* Brazil
171 I4 **Judaberg** Norway
139 H6 **Judaidat al Hamir** Iraq
139 G4 **Judaydat Khābūr** Syria
139 H6 **Judayyidat 'Ar'ar** *well* Iraq
176 G7 **Judenburg** Austria
171 J5 **Juelsminde** Denmark
154 C2 **Juh** China
154 F1 **Juhua Dao** *i.* China
224 H5 **Juigalpa** Nicaragua
179 F1 **Juist** *i.* Germany
234 D3 **Juiz de Fora** Brazil
230 E8 **Julaca** Bol.
216 C3 **Julesburg** U.S.A.
230 D7 **Juliaca** Peru
123 C4 **Julia Creek** Australia
178 C2 **Julianadorp** Neth.
231 G3 **Juliana Top** *mt.* Suriname
179 E4 **Jülich** Germany
184 E1 **Julijske Alpe** *mts* Slovenia
123 B4 **Julius, Lake** Australia
141 F5 **Juma** Uzbek.
230 C5 **Jumbilla** Peru
183 P3 **Jumilla** Spain
149 E3 **Jumla** Nepal
Jumna *r.* India *see* **Yamuna**
148 B5 **Junagadh** India
147 I2 **Junagarh** India
154 F3 **Junan** China
235 H1 **Juncal** *mt.* Chile
235 J4 **Juncal, Laguna** *l.* Arg.
217 D6 **Junction** *TX* U.S.A.
213 D4 **Junction** *UT* U.S.A.
217 D4 **Junction City** U.S.A.
234 C3 **Jundiaí** Brazil
204 C3 **Juneau** U.S.A.
125 G5 **Junee** Australia
Jungar Qi China *see* **Shagedu**
176 D7 **Jungfrau** *mt.* Switz.
135 G2 **Junggar Pendi** *basin* China
148 A4 **Jungshahi** Pak.
221 E4 **Juniata** *r.* U.S.A.
235 K2 **Junín** Arg.
235 H3 **Junín de los Andes** Arg.
221 J1 **Juniper** Canada
214 B3 **Junipero Serro Peak** U.S.A.
155 B4 **Junlian** China
147 G2 **Junnar** India
171 L3 **Junsele** Sweden
213 C3 **Juntura** U.S.A.
171 N4 **Juodup** Lith.
235 C4 **Juquiá** Brazil
193 E4 **Jur** *r.* South Sudan
182 H3 **Jura** *mts* France/Switz.
174 C4 **Jura** *i.* U.K.
142 B5 **Jur'ā, Nafūd al** *des.* Saudi Arabia
174 C5 **Jura, Sound of** *sea chan.* U.K.
234 E1 **Jurací** Brazil
233 H3 **Juradó** Col.
171 M5 **Jurbarkas** Lith.
138 E6 **Jurf ad Darāwīsh** Jordan
179 K1 **Jürgenstorf** Germany
160 A1 **Jurh** *Nei Mongol Zizhiqu* China
160 A1 **Jurh** *Nei Mongol Zizhiqu* China
149 G2 **Jurhen Ul** *mts* China
171 M4 **Jūrmala** Latvia
170 N2 **Jurmu** Fin.
155 F4 **Jurong** China
162 □ **Jurong** Sing.
162 □ **Jurong, Selat** *str.* Sing.
230 E4 **Juruá** *r.* Brazil
231 G6 **Juruena** *r.* Brazil
171 M3 **Jurva** Fin.
143 E2 **Jūshqān** Iran
235 J2 **Justo Daract** Arg.
230 E4 **Jutaí** *r.* Brazil
179 L3 **Jüterbog** Germany
234 A3 **Juti** Brazil
225 G5 **Jutiapa** Guat.
224 H5 **Juticalpa** Hond.
170 L2 **Jutis** Sweden
168 H4 **Jutland** *pen.* Denmark
171 O3 **Juuka** Fin.
171 N3 **Juva** Fin.
223 H4 **Juventud, Isla de la** *i.* Cuba
154 F3 **Juxian** China
154 A1 **Juyan** China
154 E3 **Juye** China
142 D4 **Jūyom** Iran
195 C6 **Jwaneng** Botswana
Jylland *pen.* Denmark *see* **Jutland**
141 I4 **Jyrgalang** Kyrg.
171 N3 **Jyväskylä** Fin.

K

148 D2 **K2** *mt.* China/Pak.
231 F7 **Kaa-Iya del Gran Chaco, Parque Nacional** *nat. park* Bol.
214 □[1] **Ka'ala** *mt.* U.S.A.
171 M3 **Kaarina** Fin.
179 J1 **Kaarßen** Germany
179 E3 **Kaarst** Germany
171 O3 **Kaavi** Fin.
Kaba China *see* **Habahe**
118 C2 **Kabaena** *i.* Indon.
Kabakly Turkm. *see* **Gabakly**
192 A4 **Kabala** Sierra Leone
195 C4 **Kabale** Uganda
195 C4 **Kabalo** Dem. Rep. Congo
195 C4 **Kabambare** Dem. Rep. Congo
141 F1 **Kaban'** Kazakh.
141 J3 **Kabanbay** *Almatinskaya Oblast'* Kazakh.
141 J3 **Kabanbay** *Almatinskaya Oblast'* Kazakh.
141 F1 **Kabanbay** *Severnyy Kazakhstan* Kazakh.
141 G2 **Kabanbay Batyr** Kazakh.
195 C5 **Kabangu** Dem. Rep. Congo
162 A5 **Kabanjahe** Indon.
140 B1 **Kabanovka** Russia
187 G7 **Kabardino-Balkarskaya Respublika** *aut. rep.* Russia
195 C4 **Kabare** Dem. Rep. Congo
170 M2 **Kåbdalis** Sweden
209 E1 **Kabenung Lake** Canada
206 D4 **Kabinakagami Lake** Canada
195 C4 **Kabinda** Dem. Rep. Congo
142 B3 **Kabīrkūh** *mts* Iran
148 B3 **Kabirwala** Pak.
194 B3 **Kabo** C.A.R.
Kābol *r.* Afgh. *see* **Kābul**
195 C5 **Kabompo** Zambia
195 C4 **Kabongo** Dem. Rep. Congo
192 B3 **Kaboré Tambi, Parc National de** *nat. park* Burkina Faso
142 C3 **Kabūdar Āhang** Iran
161 I2 **Kabugao** Phil.
143 H3 **Kābul** Afgh.
143 H3 **Kābul** *r.* Afgh.
120 B1 **Kabunduk** Indon.
161 J5 **Kabuntalan** Phil.
161 J6 **Kaburuang** *i.* Indon.
195 C5 **Kabwe** Zambia
140 E2 **Kabyrga** *r.* Kazakh.
143 F4 **Kachā Kūh** *mts* Iran/Pak.
187 H5 **Kachalinskaya** Russia
148 B5 **Kachchh, Gulf of** India
148 B5 **Kachchh, Little Rann of** *marsh* India
148 B4 **Kachchh, Rann of** *marsh* India
137 G2 **K'ach'reti** Georgia
150 C1 **Kachug** Russia
139 H1 **Kaçkar Dağı** *mt.* Turkey
147 H4 **Kadaiyanallur** India
148 A3 **Kadanai** *r.* Afgh./Pak.
162 A2 **Kadan Kyun** *i.* Myanmar
147 H3 **Kadapa** India
117 H3 **Kadavu** *i.* Fiji
119 H3 **Kadavu** *i.* Fiji
119 H3 **Kadavu Passage** Fiji
192 B4 **Kade** Ghana
148 C5 **Kadi** India
138 B1 **Kadıköy** Turkey
124 B4 **Kadina** Australia
138 D2 **Kadınhanı** Turkey
192 B3 **Kadiolo** Mali
147 H3 **Kadiri** India
139 F3 **Kadirli** Turkey
147 G4 **Kadmat** *atoll* India
160 C4 **Ka-do** *i.* N. Korea
216 C3 **Kadoka** U.S.A.
195 C5 **Kadoma** Zimbabwe
193 E3 **Kadugli** Sudan
192 C3 **Kaduna** Nigeria
192 C3 **Kaduna** *state* Nigeria
149 I3 **Kadusam** *mt.* China
186 F3 **Kaduy** Russia

Kaziranga National Park

187 C4 **Kapyl'** Belarus
141 I5 **Kaqung** China
192 C4 **Kara** Togo
139 H2 **Kara** *r.* Turkey
185 L5 **Kara Ada** *i.* Turkey
138 D2 **Karaali** Turkey
141 I2 **Karaauyl** Kazakh.
141 H4 **Kara-Balta** Kyrg.
140 E1 **Karabalyk** Kazakh.
141 H2 **Karabas** Kazakh.
140 C2 **Karabau** Kazakh.
140 C4 **Karabaur, Uval** *hills* Uzbek.
Karabil', Vozvyshennost' *hills* Turkm. *see* **Garabil Belentligi**
Kara-Bogaz-Gol, Zaliv *b.* Turkm. *see* **Garabogazköl Aýlagy**
Karabogazkel' Turkm. *see* **Garabogazköl**
138 D1 **Karabük** Turkey
141 I3 **Karabulak** *Almatinskaya Oblast'* Kazakh.
141 K3 **Karabulak** *Vostochnyy Kazakhstan* Kazakh.
141 H2 **Karabulakskaya (abandoned)** Kazakh.
136 B3 **Karaburun** Turkey
140 E2 **Karabutak** Kazakh.
138 B1 **Karacabey** Turkey
139 G3 **Karacadağ** Turkey
138 D3 **Karacadağ** *mts* Turkey
138 B1 **Karacaköy** Turkey
139 G3 **Karacalı Dağ** *mt.* Turkey
138 B3 **Karacasu** Turkey
138 C3 **Karaca Yarımadası** *pen.* Turkey
187 G7 **Karachayevo-Cherkesskaya Respublika** *aut. rep.* Russia
187 G7 **Karachayevsk** Russia
187 E4 **Karachev** Russia
143 G5 **Karachi** Pak.
139 I2 **Karaçoban** Turkey
147 G2 **Karad** India
138 D3 **Kara Dağ** *mt.* Turkey
139 I3 **Kara Dağ** *mt.* Turkey
141 H4 **Kara-Daryya** *r.* Kyrg.
141 G2 **Karagandinskaya Oblast'** *admin. div.* Kazakh.
141 H2 **Karagandy** Kazakh.
141 H2 **Karagayly** Kazakh.
133 R4 **Karaginskiy Zaliv** *b.* Russia
140 B4 **Karagiye, Vpadina** *depr.* Kazakh.
138 B2 **Karahallı** Turkey
138 E2 **Karahasanlı** Turkey
147 H4 **Karaikal** India
147 H4 **Karaikkudi** India
138 E3 **Karaisalı** Turkey
147 H4 **Karaitivu** *i.* Sri Lanka
142 C3 **Karaj** Iran
142 C3 **Karaj** *r.* Iran
Karakalpakiya Uzbek. *see* **Qoraqalpog'iston**
125 E6 **Kara Kara National Park** Australia
Karakatinskaya, Vpadina *depr.* Uzbek. *see* **Qoraqata botig'i**
149 E1 **Karakax He** *r.* China
139 G3 **Karakeçi** Turkey
138 D2 **Karakeçili** Turkey
151 E6 **Karakelong** *i.* Indon.
141 I3 **Karaketken** Kazakh.
139 H2 **Karakoçan** Turkey
140 C2 **Karakol'** Kazakh.
141 H4 **Kara-Köl** Kyrg.
141 I4 **Karakol** *Ysyk-Köl* Kyrg.
141 I4 **Karakol** *Ysyk-Köl* Kyrg.
148 D2 **Karakoram Pass** China/India
135 F3 **Karakoram Range** *mts* Asia
194 D2 **Kara K'orē** Eth.
Karakorum Range *mts* Asia *see* **Karakoram Range**
141 G3 **Karakoyyn, Ozero** *salt l.* Kazakh.
141 J2 **Karakozha** Kazakh.
Karakul' Uzbek. *see* **Qorako'l**
140 E1 **Karakul'skoye** Russia
141 I3 **Karakum** Kazakh.
Karakum, Peski *des.* Kazakh. *see* **Karakum Desert**
140 C3 **Karakum Desert** Kazakh.
143 F2 **Karakum Desert** Turkm.
Karakumskiy Kanal *canal* Turkm. *see* **Garagum Kanaly**
Kara Kumy *des.* Turkm. *see* **Garagum**
Karakumy, Peski *des.* Turkm. *see* **Karakum Desert**
139 I1 **Karakurt** Turkey
171 M4 **Karala** Estonia
121 B5 **Karalundi** Australia
138 D3 **Karaman** Turkey
138 B3 **Karamanlı** Turkey
135 G2 **Karamay** China
148 C1 **Karambar Pass** Afgh./Pak.
126 D4 **Karamea** N.Z.
126 C4 **Karamea Bight** *b.* N.Z.
141 F2 **Karamendy** Kazakh.
Karamet-Niyaz Turkm. *see* **Garamätnyýaz**
149 F1 **Karamiran** China
149 F1 **Karamiran Shankou** *pass* China
138 B1 **Karamürsel** Turkey
186 D3 **Karamyshevo** Russia
142 C5 **Karān** *i.* Saudi Arabia
148 D5 **Karanja** India
147 H2 **Karanja** *r.* India
149 F5 **Karanjia** India
148 C3 **Karanpura** India
141 I1 **Karaoba** Kazakh.
141 H3 **Karaoy (abandoned)** *Almatinskaya Oblast'* Kazakh.
141 H3 **Karaoy (abandoned)** *Almatinskaya Oblast'* Kazakh.
141 F3 **Karaozek** Kazakh.
138 D3 **Karapınar** Turkey
141 I4 **Karaqi** China
196 B3 **!Karas** *admin. reg.* Namibia
196 B3 **Karas** *watercourse* Namibia
152 D4 **Karasay** China
141 I4 **Kara-Say** Kyrg.
195 B6 **Karasburg** Namibia
132 I2 **Kara Sea** Russia
141 H2 **Karashoky** Kazakh.
Kárášjohka Norway *see* **Karasjok**
170 N1 **Karasjok** Norway
141 H2 **Karasor** Kazakh.
141 H1 **Karasor, Ozero** *salt l.* Kazakh.
141 H2 **Karasor, Ozero** *salt l.* Kazakh.
141 H3 **Karasu** *Karagandinskaya Oblast'* Kazakh.
141 F1 **Karasu** *Kostanayskaya Oblast'* Kazakh.
141 H1 **Karasu** *r.* Kazakh.
138 C1 **Karasu** Turkey
139 I2 **Karasu** *r.* Turkey
141 I1 **Karasuk** Russia
141 H4 **Kara-Suu** Kyrg.
141 K3 **Karatal** Kazakh.
138 E3 **Karataş** Turkey
138 E3 **Karataş Burun** *pt* Turkey
141 G4 **Karatau** Kazakh.
141 F3 **Karatau, Khrebet** *mts* Kazakh.
149 E2 **Karatax Shan** *mts* China
151 B4 **Karathuri** Myanmar
140 C2 **Karatobe** Kazakh.
140 D3 **Karatobe, Mys** *pt* Kazakh.
140 D2 **Karatogay** Kazakh.
141 I3 **Karatol** *r.* Kazakh.
140 E1 **Karatomarskoye Vodokhranilishche** *resr* Kazakh.
140 C3 **Karaton** Kazakh.
149 G4 **Karatoya** *r.* Bangl.
159 A8 **Karatsu** Japan
161 J5 **Karatung** *i.* Indon.
141 F2 **Kara-Turgay** *r.* Kazakh.
Karaulbazar Uzbek. *see* **Qorovulbozor**
148 D4 **Karauli** India
139 I1 **Karaurgan** Turkey
140 C2 **Karauylkel'dy** Kazakh.
163 G4 **Karawang** Indon.
141 K3 **Kara Yertis** *r.* Kazakh.
141 J4 **Karayulgun** China
141 G2 **Karazhal** Kazakh.
140 B3 **Karazhambas** Kazakh.
Karazhar Uzbek. *see* **Qorajar**
141 H3 **Karazhingil (abandoned)** Kazakh.
139 J5 **Karbalā'** Iraq
179 G4 **Karben** Germany
142 C3 **Karbūsh, Kūh-e** *mt.* Iran
177 J7 **Karcag** Hungary
179 F4 **Karden** Germany
185 I5 **Karditsa** Greece
171 M4 **Kärdla** Estonia
185 K4 **Kardzhali** Bulg.
197 G4 **Karee** S. Africa
196 D5 **Kareeberge** *mts* S. Africa
193 F3 **Kareima** Sudan
187 G7 **Kareli** Georgia
148 D5 **Kareli** India
186 E2 **Kareliya, Respublika** *aut. rep.* Russia
169 M2 **Karel'skiy Bereg** *coastal area* Russia
150 D1 **Karenga** *r.* Russia
148 D4 **Karera** India
170 M1 **Karesuando** Sweden
143 F5 **Kārevāndar** Iran
143 F3 **Kārēz** Afgh.
143 F3 **Kārēz Ilyās** Afgh.
187 H7 **Kargalinskaya** Russia
140 D2 **Kargaly** *Aktyubinskaya Oblast'* Kazakh.
141 H2 **Kargaly** *Karagandinskaya Oblast'* Kazakh.
141 J2 **Kargaly** *Vostochnyy Kazakhstan* Kazakh.
139 H2 **Kargapazarı Dağları** *mts* Turkey
138 E1 **Kargı** Turkey
148 D2 **Kargil** India
186 F2 **Kargopol'** Russia
143 E5 **Kargūshkī** Iran
195 C5 **Kariba** Zimbabwe
195 C5 **Kariba, Lake** *resr* Zambia/Zimbabwe
158 F3 **Kariba-yama** *vol.* Japan
197 E6 **Kariega** *r.* S. Africa
170 N1 **Karigasniemi** Fin.
121 B4 **Karijini National Park** Australia
171 M3 **Karijoki** Fin.
157 F4 **Karikachi-tōge** *pass* Japan
126 D1 **Karikari, Cape** N.Z.
142 D3 **Karīmābād** Iran
163 G3 **Karimata, Pulau-pulau** *is* Indon.
163 G3 **Karimata, Selat** *str.* Indon.
152 F7 **Karimganj** India
147 H2 **Karimnagar** India
163 H4 **Karimunjawa, Pulau-pulau** *is* Indon.
194 E2 **Karin** Somalia
147 G2 **Karjat** India
149 F5 **Karkai** *r.* India
147 G3 **Karkal** India
161 J5 **Karkaralong, Kepulauan** *is* Indon.
141 H2 **Karkaraly** Kazakh.
119 E2 **Karkar Island** P.N.G.
142 C4 **Karkheh, Rūdkhāneh-ye** *r.* Iran
187 E6 **Karkinits'ka Zatoka** *g.* Crimea
171 N3 **Kärkölä** Fin.
171 N4 **Karksi-Nuia** Estonia
Kar Lake *l.* India *see* **Tsokar Chumo**
171 L3 **Karlholmsbruk** Sweden
144 H3 **Karlik Shan** *mt.* China
139 H2 **Karlıova** Turkey
187 E5 **Karlivka** Ukr.
Karl-Marx-Stadt Germany *see* **Chemnitz**
184 F2 **Karlovac** Croatia
185 K3 **Karlovo** Bulg.
176 F5 **Karlovy Vary** Czech Rep.
179 G5 **Karlsbad** Germany
171 K4 **Karlsborg** Sweden
171 K4 **Karlshamn** Sweden
171 K4 **Karlskoga** Sweden
171 K4 **Karlskrona** Sweden
179 G5 **Karlsruhe** Germany
171 K4 **Karlstad** Sweden
216 D1 **Karlstad** U.S.A.
179 H5 **Karlstadt** Germany
187 D4 **Karma** Belarus
147 G2 **Karmala** India
Karmanovka Kazakh. *see* **Kyrkopa**
171 I4 **Karmøy** *i.* Norway
148 D3 **Karnal** India
149 E3 **Karnali** *r.* Nepal
149 H5 **Karnaphuli Reservoir** Bangl.
147 G3 **Karnataka** *state* India
185 L3 **Karnobat** Bulg.
143 G5 **Karodi** Pak.
195 C5 **Karoi** Zimbabwe
149 G3 **Karo La** *pass* China
149 H4 **Karong** India
195 D4 **Karonga** Malawi
121 C6 **Karonie** Australia
141 I4 **Karool-Döbö** Kyrg.
197 E6 **Karoo National Park** S. Africa
124 C5 **Karoonda** Australia
148 B3 **Karor** Pak.
194 D2 **Karora** Eritrea
120 B1 **Karossa, Tanjung** *pt* Indon.
179 K1 **Karow** Germany
185 L7 **Karpathos** *i.* Greece
185 L6 **Karpathou, Steno** *sea chan.* Greece
185 I5 **Karpenisi** Greece
186 H1 **Karpogory** Russia
118 B4 **Karratha** Australia
142 C4 **Karrī** Iran
139 I1 **Kars** Turkey
171 N3 **Kärsämäki** Fin.
171 N4 **Kārsava** Latvia
Karshi Turkm. *see* **Garşy**
Karshi Uzbek. *see* **Qarshi**
149 G4 **Karsiyang** India
132 G3 **Karskiye Vorota, Proliv** *str.* Russia
Karskoye More *sea* Russia *see* **Kara Sea**
179 J1 **Karstädt** Germany
171 N3 **Karstula** Fin.
138 B1 **Kartal** Turkey
140 E1 **Kartaly** Russia
171 N3 **Karttula** Fin.
143 F3 **Karukh** Afgh.
122 C3 **Karumba** Australia
142 C4 **Kārūn, Kūh-e** *h.* Iran
142 C4 **Kārūn, Rūd-e** *r.* Iran
120 B1 **Karuni** Indon.
147 H4 **Karur** India
171 M3 **Karvia** Fin.
171 M3 **Karvianjoki** *r.* Fin.
147 G3 **Karwar** India
185 K4 **Karyes** Greece
150 D1 **Karymskoye** Russia
140 C4 **Karynzharyk, Peski** *des.* Kazakh.
185 K5 **Karystos** Greece
138 B3 **Kaş** Turkey
206 C3 **Kasabonika** Canada
206 C3 **Kasabonika Lake** Canada
143 F3 **Kāsah Murgh** *mts* Afgh.
195 B4 **Kasaï** *r.* Dem. Rep. Congo
195 C5 **Kasaji** Dem. Rep. Congo
195 D5 **Kasama** Zambia
Kasan Uzbek. *see* **Koson**
195 C5 **Kasane** Botswana
195 B4 **Kasangulu** Dem. Rep. Congo
Kasansay Uzbek. *see* **Kosonsoy**
147 G3 **Kasaragod** India
156 C2 **Kasatkino** Russia
205 I2 **Kasba Lake** Canada
192 B1 **Kasba Tadla** Morocco
139 K4 **Kāseh Garān** Iran
195 C5 **Kasempa** Zambia
195 C5 **Kasenga** Dem. Rep. Congo
195 C4 **Kasese** Dem. Rep. Congo
194 D3 **Kasese** Uganda
148 D4 **Kasganj** India
142 C3 **Kāshān** Iran
206 D3 **Kashechewan** Canada
Kashgar China *see* **Kashi**
141 I5 **Kashi** China
159 D7 **Kashihara** Japan
159 B8 **Kashima** Japan
159 G6 **Kashima-nada** *b.* Japan
186 F3 **Kashin** Russia
148 D3 **Kashipur** India
159 F6 **Kashiwazaki** Japan
139 K5 **Kashkan** *r.* Iran
141 H3 **Kashkanteniz** Kazakh.
142 D4 **Kashkū'īyeh** Iran
143 E3 **Kāshmar** Iran
148 D2 **Kashmir** *reg.* Asia
148 C2 **Kashmir, Vale of** *reg.* India
148 B3 **Kashmore** Pak.
143 H3 **Kashmund Ghar** *reg.* Afgh.
141 I1 **Kashyr** Kazakh.
195 C4 **Kashyukulu** Dem. Rep. Congo
187 G4 **Kasimov** Russia
219 B4 **Kaskaskia** *r.* U.S.A.
205 K3 **Kaskattama** *r.* Canada
141 I4 **Kaskelen** Kazakh.
171 M3 **Kaskinen** Fin.
195 C4 **Kasongo** Dem. Rep. Congo
195 B4 **Kasongo-Lunda** Dem. Rep. Congo
185 L7 **Kasos** *i.* Greece
185 L7 **Kasou, Steno** *sea chan.* Greece
187 H7 **K'asp'i** Georgia
187 H7 **Kaspiysk** Russia
177 O3 **Kasplya** Russia
193 F3 **Kassala** Sudan
136 A3 **Kassandras, Akrotirio** *pt* Greece
185 J4 **Kassandras, Chersonisos** *pen.* Greece
185 J4 **Kassandras, Kolpos** *b.* Greece
179 H3 **Kassel** Germany
192 C1 **Kasserine** Tunisia
208 A3 **Kasson** U.S.A.
138 D1 **Kastamonu** Turkey
179 F4 **Kastellaun** Germany
185 J7 **Kastellia** Greece
Kastéllion Greece *see* **Kissamos**
178 C3 **Kasterlee** Belgium
185 I4 **Kastoria** Greece
181 K1 **Kastornoye** Russia
187 E4 **Kastsyukovichy** Belarus
159 E7 **Kasugai** Japan
195 D4 **Kasulu** Tanz.
159 G6 **Kasumiga-ura** *l.* Japan
187 I7 **Kasumkent** Russia
195 D5 **Kasungu** Malawi
148 C3 **Kasur** Pak.
221 I2 **Katahdin, Mount** U.S.A.
143 G3 **Katah Sang Srah** Afgh.
148 D2 **Kataklik** India
195 C4 **Katako-Kombe** Dem. Rep. Congo
148 D5 **Katangi** India
118 B5 **Katanning** Australia
145 H10 **Katchall** *i.* India
195 C4 **Katea** Dem. Rep. Congo
185 J4 **Katerini** Greece
204 C3 **Kate's Needle** *mt.* Canada/U.S.A.
195 D5 **Katete** Zambia
147 I1 **Katghora** India
151 B4 **Katha** Myanmar
Katherîna, Gebel *mt.* Egypt *see* **Kātrīnā, Jabal**
120 F2 **Katherine** Australia
118 D3 **Katherine** *r.* Australia
Katherine Gorge National Park Australia *see* **Nitmiluk National Park**
148 B5 **Kathiawar** *pen.* India
147 I4 **Kathiraveli** Sri Lanka
120 E2 **Kathleen Falls** Australia
149 F4 **Kathmandu** Nepal
197 E3 **Kathu** S. Africa
148 C2 **Kathua** India
192 B3 **Kati** Mali
149 F4 **Katihar** India
126 E2 **Katikati** N.Z.
197 G6 **Katikati** S. Africa
195 C5 **Katima Mulilo** Namibia
192 B4 **Katiola** Côte d'Ivoire
124 B2 **Kati Thanda-Lake Eyre (North)** *salt flat* Australia
124 B2 **Kati Thanda-Lake Eyre (South)** *salt flat* Australia
124 B2 **Kati Thanda-Lake Eyre National Park** Australia
196 D4 **Katkop Hills** S. Africa
197 H3 **Katlehong** S. Africa
149 E5 **Katni** India
185 I5 **Kato Achaïa** Greece
148 D5 **Katol** India
162 □ **Katong** Sing.
141 K2 **Katonkaragay** Kazakh.
125 I4 **Katoomba** Australia
177 I5 **Katowice** Poland
149 G5 **Katoya** India
136 D5 **Kātrīnā, Jabal** *mt.* Egypt
174 D4 **Katrine, Loch** *l.* U.K.
171 L4 **Katrineholm** Sweden
192 C3 **Katsina** Nigeria
192 C4 **Katsina-Ala** Nigeria
159 G7 **Katsuura** Japan
159 E6 **Katsuyama** Japan
207 G2 **Kattaktoc, Cap** *c.* Canada
Kattakurgan Uzbek. *see* **Kattaqo'rg'on**
121 D4 **Kattamudda Well** Australia
141 F5 **Kattaqo'rg'on** Uzbek.
171 J4 **Kattegat** *str.* Denmark/Sweden
141 K1 **Katun'** *r.* Russia
148 B3 **Katuri** Pak.
178 C2 **Katwijk aan Zee** Neth.
179 H5 **Katzenbuckel** *h.* Germany
214 □2 **Kaua'i** *i.* U.S.A.
214 □2 **Kaua'i Channel** U.S.A.
179 F4 **Kaub** Germany
179 H3 **Kaufungen** Germany
171 M3 **Kauhajoki** Fin.
171 M3 **Kauhava** Fin.
170 N2 **Kaukonen** Fin.
214 □2 **Ka'ula** *i.* U.S.A.
214 □2 **Kaulakahi Channel** U.S.A.
207 H2 **Kaumajet Mountains** Canada
214 □2 **Kaunakakai** U.S.A.
171 M5 **Kaunas** Lith.
171 N4 **Kaunata** Latvia
140 C4 **Kaundy, Vpadina** *depr.* Kazakh.
192 C3 **Kaura-Namoda** Nigeria
155 □ **Kau Sai Chau** *i. Hong Kong* China
171 M3 **Kaustinen** Fin.
170 M1 **Kautokeino** Norway
162 A3 **Kau-ye Kyun** *i.* Myanmar
185 J4 **Kavadarci** Macedonia
139 F1 **Kavak** Turkey
185 K4 **Kavala** Greece
158 D2 **Kavalerovo** Russia
147 I3 **Kavali** India
195 C5 **Kavango Zambezi Transfrontier Conservation Area** *nat. park* Africa
142 D4 **Kavār** Iran
145 D9 **Kavaratti** India
147 G4 **Kavaratti** *atoll* India
185 M3 **Kavarna** Bulg.
147 H4 **Kaveri** *r.* India
143 E3 **Kavīr, Chāh-e** *well* Iran
142 D3 **Kavīr, Dasht-e** *des.* Iran
159 F7 **Kawagoe** Japan
159 F7 **Kawaguchi** Japan
214 □2 **Kawaihae** U.S.A.
126 E1 **Kawakawa** N.Z.
195 C4 **Kawambwa** Zambia
208 H3 **Kawartha Highlands Signature Site** *res.* Canada
206 E5 **Kawartha Lakes** Canada
159 F7 **Kawasaki** Japan
126 E2 **Kawau Island** N.Z.
207 G2 **Kawawachikamach** Canada
126 F3 **Kawerau** N.Z.
126 E3 **Kawhia** N.Z.
126 E3 **Kawhia Harbour** N.Z.
215 D3 **Kawich Range** *mts* U.S.A.
162 A1 **Kawkareik** Myanmar
162 A1 **Kawludo** Myanmar
142 E6 **Kawr, Jabal** *mt.* Oman
162 A3 **Kawthaung** Myanmar
141 I5 **Kaxgar He** *r.* China
141 J4 **Kax He** *r.* China
148 D1 **Kaxtexi** China
192 B3 **Kaya** Burkina Faso
139 F2 **Kayadibi** Turkey
163 I2 **Kayan** *r.* Indon.
147 H4 **Kayankulam** India
163 I2 **Kayan Mentarang, Taman Nasional** *nat. park* Indon.
195 C4 **Kayanza** Burundi
213 F3 **Kaycee** U.S.A.
140 C3 **Kaydak, Sor** *dry lake* Kazakh.
195 C4 **Kayembe-Mukulu** Dem. Rep. Congo
215 G3 **Kayenta** U.S.A.
192 A3 **Kayes** Mali
141 F2 **Kayga** Kazakh.
192 A4 **Kayima** Sierra Leone
144 C4 **Kaylahgay (abandoned)** Afgh.
141 H1 **Kaymanachikha** Kazakh.
136 C3 **Kaymaz** Turkey
141 I2 **Kaynar** *Vostochnyy Kazakhstan* Kazakh.
141 H4 **Kaynar** *Zhambylskaya Oblast'* Kazakh.
139 F2 **Kaynar** Turkey
139 F3 **Kaypak** Turkey
187 H5 **Kaysatskoye** Russia
138 E2 **Kayseri** Turkey
147 H4 **Kayts Island** Sri Lanka
163 B3 **Kayuagung** Indon.
133 J3 **Kayyerkan** Russia
140 B2 **Kayyndy** Kazakh.
141 H4 **Kayyngdy** Kyrg.
133 O2 **Kazach'ye** Russia
Kazakhdar'ya Uzbek. *see* **Qozoqdaryo**
140 C4 **Kazakhskiy Zaliv** *b.* Kazakh.
140 D3 **Kazakhstan** *country* Asia
Kazakh Steppe *plain* Kazakh. *see* **Saryarka**
140 E3 **Kazaly** Kazakh.
205 J2 **Kazan** *r.* Canada
187 I4 **Kazan'** Russia
138 D3 **Kazancı** Turkey
187 I4 **Kazanka** *r.* Russia
185 K3 **Kazanlak** Bulg.
Kazan-rettō *is* Japan *see* **Volcano Islands**
187 G5 **Kazanskaya** Russia
141 H4 **Kazarman** Kyrg.
140 D2 **Kazatskiy** Kazakh.
187 H7 **Kazbek** *mt.* Georgia/Russia
185 L5 **Kaz Dağı** *mts* Turkey
142 C4 **Kāzerūn** Iran
143 F5 **Kazhmak** *r.* Pak.
186 I2 **Kazhym** Russia
177 J6 **Kazincbarcika** Hungary
149 H4 **Kaziranga National Park** India

K'azreti

187 H7 K'azreti Georgia
140 B2 Kaztalovka Kazakh.
158 G4 Kazuno Japan
141 G4 Kazygurt Kazakh.
132 H3 Kazym-Mys Russia
175 L3 Keady U.K.
214 □2 Kealakekua Bay U.S.A.
215 G4 Keams Canyon U.S.A.
216 D3 Kearney U.S.A.
215 G5 Kearny U.S.A.
139 G2 Keban Turkey
139 G2 Keban Barajı *resr* Turkey
192 A3 Kébémèr Senegal
180 E5 Kebili Tunisia
139 F4 Kebīr, Nahr al *r.* Lebanon/Syria
193 E3 Kebkabiya Sudan
170 L2 Kebnekaise *mt.* Sweden
174 B2 Kebock Head U.K.
194 E3 K'ebrī Dehar Eth.
163 G4 Kebumen Indon.
204 D3 Kechika *r.* Canada
138 C3 Keçiborlu Turkey
177 I7 Kecskemét Hungary
139 H1 Keda Georgia
171 M5 Kdainiai Lith.
148 D3 Kedar Kantha *mt.* India
148 D3 Kedarnath Peak India
207 G4 Kedgwick Canada
163 H4 Kediri Indon.
156 B3 Kedong China
192 A3 Kédougou Senegal
204 D2 Keele *r.* Canada
204 C2 Keele Peak Canada
213 C4 Keeler U.S.A.
Keeling Islands *terr.* Indian Ocean *see* Cocos (Keeling) Islands
Keelung Taiwan *see* Jilong
175 F4 Keen, Mount *h.* U.K.
161 H5 Keenapusan *i.* Phil.
221 G3 Keene U.S.A.
125 I3 Keepit, Lake *resr* Australia
120 E2 Keep River National Park Australia
178 C3 Keerbergen Belgium
122 C2 Keer-weer, Cape Australia
195 B6 Keetmanshoop Namibia
205 K6 Keewatin Canada
205 K5 Keewatin U.S.A.
Kefallonia *i.* Greece *see* Cephalonia
151 E7 Kefamenanu Indon.
170 B2 Keflavík Iceland
147 I5 Kegalla Sri Lanka
141 I4 Kegen Kazakh.
140 D4 Kegeyli Uzbek.
207 G2 Keglo, Baie de *b.* Canada
187 H6 Kegul'ta Russia
171 N4 Kehra Estonia
173 F4 Keighley U.K.
171 N4 Keila Estonia
196 D4 Keimoes S. Africa
171 N3 Keitele Fin.
171 N3 Keitele *l.* Fin.
124 D6 Keith Australia
175 F3 Keith U.K.
204 E1 Keith Arm *b.* Canada
207 G5 Kejimkujik National Park Canada
214 □2 Kekaha U.S.A.
177 J7 Kékes *mt.* Hungary
148 C4 Kekri India
135 F6 Kelaa *i.* Maldives
154 D2 Kelan China
Kelang Malaysia *see* Klang
162 B4 Kelantan *r.* Malaysia
179 E4 Kelberg Germany
141 J3 Kel'demurat Kazakh.
141 G4 Keles Uzbek.
179 J6 Kelheim Germany
184 D6 Kelibia Tunisia
141 F5 Kelif Turkm.
Kelifskiy Uzboy *marsh* Turkm. *see* Kelif Uzboýy
140 E5 Kelif Uzboýy *marsh* Turkm.
179 G4 Kelkheim (Taunus) Germany
139 G1 Kelkit Turkey
139 F1 Kelkit *r.* Turkey
204 E2 Keller Lake Canada
141 G1 Kellerovka Kazakh.
220 B4 Kelleys Island U.S.A.
212 C2 Kellogg U.S.A.
170 O2 Kelloselkä Fin.
175 L4 Kells Ireland
121 C5 Kelly Range *hills* Australia
171 M5 Kelm Lith.
179 E4 Kelmis Belgium
193 D4 Kélo Chad
204 F5 Kelowna Canada
214 A2 Kelseyville U.S.A.
175 F5 Kelso U.K.
212 B2 Kelso U.S.A.
215 E4 Kelso (abandoned) U.S.A.
163 B2 Keluang Malaysia
205 I4 Kelvington Canada
186 E1 Kem' Russia
186 E1 Kem' *r.* Russia
139 G2 Kemah Turkey
139 G2 Kemaliye Turkey
185 L5 Kemalpaşa Turkey
204 D4 Kemano (abandoned) Canada
138 C3 Kemer *Antalya* Turkey
138 B3 Kemer *Muğla* Turkey
138 B3 Kemer Barajı *resr* Turkey
150 A1 Kemerovo Russia
170 N2 Kemi Fin.
170 N2 Kemijärvi Fin.
170 N2 Kemijärvi *l.* Fin.
170 O2 Kemijoki *r.* Fin.
141 H4 Kemin Kyrg.
213 E3 Kemmerer U.S.A.
179 J5 Kemnath Germany
175 F3 Kemnay U.K.
217 D5 Kemp, Lake U.S.A.
170 N2 Kempele Fin.
178 C3 Kempen *reg.* Belgium
179 E3 Kempen Germany
127 K5 Kemp Land *pen.* Antarctica
127 J3 Kemp Peninsula Antarctica
219 E7 Kemp's Bay Bahamas
125 J3 Kempsey Australia
207 F4 Kempt, Lac *l.* Canada
176 E7 Kempten (Allgäu) Germany
125 G9 Kempton Australia
197 H3 Kempton Park S. Africa
209 J3 Kemptville Canada
163 H4 Kemujan *i.* Indon.
149 E4 Ken *r.* India
202 C3 Kenai U.S.A.
202 C4 Kenai Mountains U.S.A.
Kenâyis, Râs el *pt* Egypt *see* Ḥikmah, Ra's al
172 E3 Kendal U.K.
125 J3 Kendall Australia
205 L2 Kendall, Cape Canada
209 E5 Kendallville U.S.A.
163 G4 Kendang, Gunung *vol.* Indon.
151 E7 Kendari Indon.
163 H3 Kendawangan Indon.
193 D3 Kendégué Chad
140 C4 Kendirli-Kiyasan, Plato *plat.* Kazakh.
149 F5 Kendrapara India
212 C2 Kendrick U.S.A.
215 G4 Kendrick Peak U.S.A.
141 H4 Kendyktas *mts* Kazakh.
140 C4 Kendyrlisor, Solonchak *salt l.* Kazakh.
125 H3 Kenebri Australia
217 D6 Kenedy U.S.A.
192 A4 Kenema Sierra Leone
Keneurgench Turkm. *see* Köneürgenç
195 B4 Kenge Dem. Rep. Congo
140 D4 Keng-Peli Uzbek.
151 B4 Kengtung Myanmar
196 D4 Kenhardt S. Africa
192 A3 Kéniéba Mali
192 B1 Kenitra Morocco
154 F2 Kenli China
175 I6 Kenmare Ireland
216 C1 Kenmare U.S.A.
175 H6 Kenmare River *inlet* Ireland
179 E5 Kenn Germany
213 G5 Kenna U.S.A.
221 I2 Kennebec *r.* U.S.A.
221 H3 Kennebunk U.S.A.
221 H3 Kennebunkport U.S.A.
121 A5 Kennedy Range National Park Australia
217 F6 Kenner U.S.A.
173 F6 Kennet *r.* U.K.
121 B4 Kenneth Range *hills* Australia
217 F4 Kennett U.S.A.
212 C2 Kennewick U.S.A.
209 G1 Kenogami Lake Canada
209 G1 Kenogamissi Lake Canada
204 B2 Keno Hill Canada
205 K5 Kenora Canada
208 D4 Kenosha U.S.A.
186 F2 Kenozero, Ozero *l.* Russia
172 E3 Kent *r.* U.K.
221 G4 Kent *CT* U.S.A.
217 B6 Kent *TX* U.S.A.
212 B2 Kent *WA* U.S.A.
141 G4 Kentau Kazakh.
125 G7 Kent Group *is* Australia
208 D5 Kentland U.S.A.
220 B4 Kenton U.S.A.
211 J4 Kentucky *r.* U.S.A.
220 A6 Kentucky *state* U.S.A.
219 B4 Kentucky Lake U.S.A.
207 H4 Kentville Canada
217 F6 Kentwood *LA* U.S.A.
209 E4 Kentwood *MI* U.S.A.
194 D3 Kenya *country* Africa
194 D3 Kenya, Mount Kenya
208 A3 Kenyon U.S.A.
141 G2 Kenzharyk Kazakh.
214 □2 Kēōkea U.S.A.
208 B5 Keokuk U.S.A.
148 D4 Keoladeo National Park India
Keo Neua Pass *pass* Laos/Vietnam *see* Keo Nưa, Đeo
162 C1 Keo Nưa, Đeo *pass* Laos/Vietnam
208 B5 Keosauqua U.S.A.
119 F4 Keppel Bay Australia
162 □ Keppel Harbour *sea chan.* Sing.
138 B2 Kepsut Turkey
143 E4 Kerāh Iran
147 G4 Kerala *state* India
192 C4 Kéran, Parc National de la *nat. park* Togo
125 E5 Kerang Australia
171 N3 Kerava Fin.
183 Q4 Kerba Alg.
141 G4 Kerben Kyrg.
156 E1 Kerbi *r.* Russia
187 F6 Kerch Crimea
119 E2 Kerema P.N.G.
204 F5 Keremeos Canada
187 E7 Kerempe Burun *pt* Turkey
194 D2 Keren Eritrea
142 B3 Kerend-e Gharb Iran
Kerepakupai Merú Venez. *see* Angel Falls
141 G2 Kerey *watercourse* Kazakh.
141 G2 Kerey, Ozero *salt l.* Kazakh.
140 D5 Kergeli Turkm.
238 I8 Kerguelen, Îles *is* Indian Ocean
238 I8 Kerguelen Plateau *sea feature* Indian Ocean
195 D4 Kericho Kenya
126 D1 Kerikeri N.Z.
171 O3 Kerimäki Fin.
143 E3 Kerīmonj Iran
163 B3 Kerinci, Gunung *vol.* Indon.
163 B3 Kerinci Seblat, Taman Nasional Indon.
141 J5 Keriya He *watercourse* China
149 E2 Keriya Shankou *pass* China
179 E3 Kerken Germany
181 F5 Kerkennah, Îles *is* Tunisia
Kerki Turkm. *see* Atamyrat
Kerkichi Turkm. *see* Kerkiçi
141 F5 Kerkiçi Turkm.
185 J4 Kerkini, Limni *l.* Greece
185 H5 Kerkyra Greece
Kerkyra *i.* Greece *see* Corfu
193 F3 Kerma Sudan
117 H5 Kermadec Islands S. Pacific Ocean
237 H8 Kermadec Trench *sea feature* S. Pacific Ocean
143 E4 Kermān Iran
214 B3 Kerman U.S.A.
143 E4 Kermān, Bīābān-e *des.* Iran
Kermān Desert Iran *see* Kermān, Bīābān-e
142 B3 Kermānshāh *Kermānshāh* Iran
142 D4 Kermānshāh *Yazd* Iran
217 C6 Kermit U.S.A.
213 C5 Kern *r.* U.S.A.
214 C4 Kern, South Fork *r.* U.S.A.
207 G2 Kernertut, Cap *c.* Canada
214 C4 Kernville U.S.A.
186 J2 Keros Russia
185 K6 Keross *i.* Greece
192 B4 Kérouané Guinea
179 E4 Kerpen Germany
127 I5 Kerr, Cape Antarctica
205 H4 Kerrobert Canada
217 D6 Kerrville U.S.A.
175 I5 Kerry Head Ireland
162 B4 Kerteh Malaysia
171 J5 Kerteminde Denmark
Kerulen *r.* China/Mongolia *see* Herlen He
Keryneia Cyprus *see* Kyrenia
186 H3 Kerzhenets *r.* Russia
206 D3 Kesagami Lake Canada
171 O3 Kesälahti Fin.
187 C7 Keşan Turkey
139 G1 Keşap Turkey
159 G5 Kesennuma Japan
156 B2 Keshan China
148 B5 Keshod India
139 L5 Keshvar Iran
138 D2 Keskin Turkey
186 E2 Keskozero Russia
179 E3 Kessel Neth.
197 H4 Kestell S. Africa
170 O2 Kesten'ga Russia
170 N2 Kestilä Fin.
209 H3 Keswick Canada
172 D3 Keswick U.K.
177 H7 Keszthely Hungary
133 J4 Ket' *r.* Russia
192 C4 Keta Ghana
162 □ Ketam, Pulau *i.* Sing.
163 H3 Ketapang Indon.
204 C3 Ketchikan U.S.A.
178 D2 Ketelmeer *l.* Neth.
143 G5 Keti Bandar Pak.
141 J4 Ketmen', Khrebet *mts* China/Kazakh.
173 G5 Kettering U.K.
220 A5 Kettering U.S.A.
204 F5 Kettle *r.* Canada
208 A2 Kettle *r.* U.S.A.
221 E4 Kettle Creek *r.* U.S.A.
214 C3 Kettleman City U.S.A.
212 C1 Kettle River Range *mts* U.S.A.
221 E3 Keuka Lake U.S.A.
171 N3 Keuruu Fin.
208 D3 Kewaunee U.S.A.
208 C2 Keweenaw Bay U.S.A.
208 C2 Keweenaw Peninsula U.S.A.
208 D2 Keweenaw Point U.S.A.
233 L3 Keweigek Guyana
175 J5 Key, Lough *l.* Ireland
207 F3 Keyano Canada
209 G3 Key Harbour Canada
141 J4 Keyi China
156 A2 Keyihe China
219 D7 Key Largo U.S.A.
173 E6 Keynsham U.K.
220 D5 Keyser U.S.A.
220 D5 Keysers Ridge U.S.A.
215 G6 Keystone Peak U.S.A.
220 D6 Keysville U.S.A.
139 L4 Keytū Iran
169 N2 Keyvy, Vozvyshennost' *hills* Russia
219 D7 Key West *FL* U.S.A.
208 B4 Key West *IA* U.S.A.
221 H3 Kezar Falls U.S.A.
195 C6 Kezi Zimbabwe
177 J6 Kežmarok Slovakia
196 D2 Kgalagadi *admin. dist.* Botswana
196 D2 Kgalagadi Transfrontier Park Botswana/S. Africa
197 G2 Kgatleng *admin. dist.* Botswana
196 D1 Kgomofatshe Pan *salt pan* Botswana
197 F2 Kgoro Pan *salt pan* Botswana
197 G3 Kgotsong S. Africa
169 Q2 Khabarikha Russia
150 F2 Khabarovsk Russia
156 D2 Khabarovskiy Kray *admin. div.* Russia
Khabarovsk Kray *admin. div.* Russia *see* Khabarovskiy Kray
141 I1 Khabary Russia
139 H4 Khābūr, Nahr al *r.* Syria
139 I7 Khadd, Wādī al *watercourse* Saudi Arabia
143 G3 Khadīr Afgh.
142 B6 Khafs Daghrah Saudi Arabia
149 E4 Khaga India
149 G5 Khagrachari Bangl.
148 C3 Khairgarh Pak.
148 B4 Khairpur Pak.
148 D4 Khajuraho India
195 C6 Khakhea Botswana
143 G4 Khākrēz Afgh.
143 G4 Khākrēz *reg.* Afgh.
Khalach Turkm. *see* Halaç
142 C3 Khalajestan *reg.* Iran
148 D2 Khalatse India
139 L3 Khāleh Sarāy Iran
148 A3 Khalifat *mt.* Pak.
147 E6 Khalīj Maṣīrah *b.* Oman
143 E3 Khalīlābād Iran
Khalkabad Uzbek. *see* Xalqobod
142 C2 Khalkhāl Iran
Khálki *i.* Greece *see* Chalki
147 J2 Khallikot India
187 D4 Khalopyenichy Belarus
150 C1 Khamar-Daban, Khrebet *mts* Russia
148 C5 Khambhat India
148 B5 Khambhat, Gulf of India
148 D5 Khamgaon India
162 C1 Khamkeut Laos
142 B5 Khamma *well* Saudi Arabia
147 I2 Khammam India
133 M3 Khamra Russia
142 C3 Khamseh *reg.* Iran
Khamza Uzbek. *see* Hamza
162 B1 Khan, Nâm *r.* Laos
143 H2 Khānābād Afgh.
Khanabad Uzbek. *see* Xonobod
139 I5 Khān al Baghdādī Iraq
139 J5 Khān al Maḥāwīl Iraq
139 J5 Khān al Mashāhidah Iraq
139 J5 Khān al Muṣallá Iraq
147 G3 Khanapur India
142 B2 Khānaqāh Iran
139 J4 Khānaqīn Iraq
139 J6 Khān ar Raḥbah Iraq
139 J2 Khanasur Pass Iran/Turkey
139 F6 Khān az Zabīb *tourist site* Jordan
148 C2 Khanbari Pass Pak.
125 H6 Khancoban Australia
148 B2 Khand Pass Afgh./Pak.
141 H5 Khandūd Afgh.
148 D5 Khandwa India
133 O3 Khandyga Russia
148 B3 Khanewal Pak.
148 D4 Khaniadhana India
142 D4 Khānī Yek Iran
139 J5 Khān Jadwal Iraq
158 C2 Khanka, Lake China/Russia
148 C2 Khanki Weir Pak.
148 D3 Khanna India
140 A2 Khan Ordasy Kazakh.
148 B3 Khanpur *Balochistan* Pak.
148 B3 Khanpur *Punjab* Pak.
139 F4 Khān Shaykhūn Syria
141 H3 Khantau Kazakh.
133 K3 Khantayskoye, Ozero *l.* Russia
141 J4 Khan-Tengri, Pik *mt.* Kyrg.
132 H3 Khanty-Mansiysk Russia
138 E6 Khān Yūnus Gaza
162 A3 Khao Chum Thong Thai.
148 D5 Khapa India
144 E4 Khaplu Pak.
187 H6 Kharabali Russia
149 F5 Kharagpur India
143 E2 Kharakī Iran
142 D4 Kharāmeh Iran
143 E5 Khārān *r.* Iran
143 G4 Kharan Pak.
142 D3 Kharānaq Iran
142 D3 Kharānaq, Kūh-e *mt.* Iran
148 B2 Kharbin Pass Afgh.
148 C6 Khardi India
148 D2 Khardung La *pass* India
139 K6 Kharfiyah Iraq
156 D1 Kharga *r.* Russia
142 C4 Kharg Islands Iran
148 C5 Khargone India
148 C4 Khari *r. Rajasthan* India
148 C4 Khari *r. Rajasthan* India
148 C2 Kharian Pak.
147 I1 Khariar India
193 F2 Khārijah, Wāḥāt al *oasis* Egypt
187 F5 Kharkiv Ukr.
169 N2 Kharlovka Russia
186 G3 Kharovsk Russia
142 C3 Khar Rūd *r.* Iran
147 I1 Kharsia India
193 F3 Khartoum Sudan
Khasardag, Gora *mt.* Turkm. *see* Hasardag
187 H7 Khasavyurt Russia
143 F4 Khāsh Iran
143 F4 Khāsh, Dasht-e Afgh.
143 F4 Khāsh Rōd Afgh.
143 F4 Khāsh Rōd *r.* Afgh.
187 G7 Khashuri Georgia
149 G4 Khasi Hills India
133 L2 Khatanga Russia
133 L2 Khatangskiy Zaliv *b.* Russia
Khatmia Pass Egypt *see* Khutmīyah, Mamarr al
133 S3 Khatyrka Russia
Khavast Uzbek. *see* Xovos
148 B5 Khavda India
143 H3 Khāwāk, Kōtal-e Afgh.
143 E5 Khawr Fakkan U.A.E.
162 A2 Khawsa Myanmar
197 F5 Khayamnandi S. Africa
149 H4 Khayang *mt.* India
141 G5 Khaydarken Kyrg.
196 C7 Khayelitsha S. Africa
Khazarasp Uzbek. *see* Hazorasp
139 I3 Khāzir, Nahr al *r.* Iraq
Khê Bo Vietnam *see* Hoa Binh
147 G2 Khed India
148 C4 Khedbrahma India
149 E3 Khela India
183 R4 Khemis Miliana Alg.
162 C1 Khemmarat Thai.
192 C1 Khenchela Alg.
192 B1 Khenifra Morocco
142 C4 Khersan *r.* Iran
187 E6 Kherson Ukr.
142 C4 Khesht Iran
133 K2 Kheta *r.* Russia
142 D4 Kheyrābād Iran
142 D2 Khezerābād Iran
143 E3 Khezrī Dasht-e Bayāẕ Iran
148 D4 Khilchipur India
153 J1 Khilok Russia
153 I1 Khilok *r.* Russia
156 C2 Khinganskiy Zapovednik *nature res.* Russia
148 B4 Khipro Pak.
139 F4 Khirbat Isrīyah Syria
143 G3 Khisrow Afgh.
148 D2 Khitai Dawan China
Khiva Uzbek. *see* Xiva
142 B2 Khīyāv Iran
171 O3 Khiytola Russia
162 B2 Khlong, Mae *r.* Thai.
187 C5 Khmel'nyts'kyy Ukr.
187 C5 Khmil'nyk Ukr.
162 C3 Khoai, Hon *i.* Vietnam
137 F2 Khobi Georgia
142 B2 Khodā Āfarīn Iran
Khodzhambaz Turkm. *see* Hojambaz
Khodzheyli Uzbek. *see* Xo'jayli
196 D2 Khokhowe Pan *salt pan* Botswana
148 B4 Khokhropar Pak.
Kholm Afgh. *see* Khulm
169 M4 Kholm Russia
186 G1 Kholmogory Russia
150 G2 Kholmsk Russia
177 P3 Kholm-Zhirkovskiy Russia
139 L3 Khomām Iran
196 B1 Khomas *admin. reg.* Namibia
196 A1 Khomas Highland *hills* Namibia
142 C3 Khomeyn Iran
142 C3 Khomeynīshahr Iran
139 L4 Khondāb Iran
187 G7 Khoni Georgia
142 D5 Khonj Iran
162 B1 Khon Kaen Thai.
133 P3 Khonuu Russia
187 G5 Khoper *r.* Russia
150 F2 Khor Russia
150 F2 Khor *r.* Russia
143 H5 Khora Pak.
142 D3 Khorāsān, Chāh-e *well* Iran
149 F5 Khordha India
150 C1 Khorinsk Russia
195 B6 Khorixas Namibia
158 C2 Khorol Russia
187 E5 Khorol Ukr.
139 K2 Khoroslū Dāgh *hills* Iran
142 C3 Khorramābād Iran
139 L3 Khorramdarreh Iran
142 C4 Khorramshahr Iran
141 G5 Khorugh Tajik.
187 H6 Khosheutovo Russia
143 E4 Khoshkrūd Iran
139 J4 Khosravī *Kermānshāh* Iran
142 C4 Khosravī *Khūzestān* Iran
142 C4 Khosrowābād Iran
143 H3 Khōst Afgh.
142 D4 Khowrjān Iran
133 Q3 Khrebet Kolymskiy *mts* Russia
149 H5 Khreum Myanmar
149 G4 Khri *r.* India
186 H2 Khristoforovo Russia
133 P2 Khroma *r.* Russia
140 D2 Khromtau Kazakh.
158 D2 Khrustal'nyy Russia
177 N6 Khrystynivka Ukr.
143 G5 Khudo Range Pak.
197 F1 Khudumelapye Botswana
142 B5 Khuff Saudi Arabia
143 F5 Khūh Lab, Ra's *pt* Iran
196 D3 Khuis Botswana
141 G4 Khŭjand Tajik.
162 C2 Khu Khan Thai.
144 C4 Khulm Afgh.

Knud Rasmussen Land

143 G3 **Khulm, Daryā-ye** *r.* Afgh.
149 G5 **Khulna** Bangl.
139 I1 **Khulo** Georgia
197 G3 **Khuma** S. Africa
148 C2 **Khunjerab Pass** China/Pak.
149 F5 **Khunti** India
162 A1 **Khun Yuam** Thai.
142 D3 **Khūr** *Eşfahān* Iran
143 E3 **Khūr** *Khorāsān-e Razavī* Iran
148 D4 **Khurai** India
142 D5 **Khūran** *sea chan.* Iran
Khurda India *see* **Khordha**
148 D3 **Khurja** India
143 F3 **Khurmāliq** Afgh.
156 E2 **Khurmuli** Russia
139 I6 **Khurr, Wādī al** *watercourse* Saudi Arabia
143 E3 **Khūsf** Iran
148 C2 **Khushab** Pak.
139 L3 **Khūshāvar** Iran
143 F3 **Khuspās** Afgh.
187 B5 **Khust** Ukr.
138 D6 **Khutmīyah, Mamarr al** *pass* Egypt
197 G3 **Khutsong** S. Africa
156 E2 **Khutu** *r.* Russia
143 G5 **Khuzdar** Pak.
143 F3 **Khvāf** Iran
137 G3 **Khvājeh** Iran
187 I4 **Khvalynsk** Russia
142 C3 **Khvānsār** Iran
142 C4 **Khvormūj** Iran
140 B1 **Khvorostyanka** Russia
139 K3 **Khvosh Maqām** Iran
142 B2 **Khvoy** Iran
186 E3 **Khvoynaya** Russia
162 A2 **Khwae Noi** *r.* Thai.
143 F4 **Khwājah 'Alī Suflá** Afgh.
143 G2 **Khwājah Dū Kōh** *h.* Afgh.
143 H2 **Khwājah Muḥammad, Kōh-e** *mts* Afgh.
148 C2 **Khyber Pakhtunkhwa** *prov.* Pak.
148 B2 **Khyber Pass** Afgh./Pak.
125 I5 **Kiama** Australia
161 J5 **Kiamba** Phil.
195 D4 **Kiambi** Dem. Rep. Congo
217 E5 **Kiamichi** *r.* U.S.A.
170 O2 **Kiantajärvi** *l.* Fin.
142 D2 **Kīāsar** Iran
203 L2 **Kiatassuaq** *i.* Greenland
161 J5 **Kibawe** Phil.
195 D4 **Kibaya** Tanz.
195 D4 **Kibiti** Tanz.
195 C4 **Kibombo** Dem. Rep. Congo
195 D4 **Kibondo** Tanz.
185 I4 **Kičevo** Macedonia
186 H3 **Kichmengskiy Gorodok** Russia
140 C5 **Kiçi Balkan Daglary** *h.* Turkm.
192 C3 **Kidal** Mali
173 E5 **Kidderminster** U.K.
194 D3 **Kidepo Valley National Park** Uganda
192 A3 **Kidira** Senegal
148 D2 **Kidmang** India
126 F3 **Kidnappers, Cape** N.Z.
173 E4 **Kidsgrove** U.K.
176 E3 **Kiel** Germany
208 C4 **Kiel** U.S.A.
176 D3 **Kiel Canal** Germany
177 J5 **Kielce** Poland
172 E2 **Kielder Water** *resr* U.K.
176 E3 **Kieler Bucht** *b.* Germany
195 C5 **Kienge** Dem. Rep. Congo
179 F3 **Kierspe** Germany
187 D5 **Kiev** Ukr.
192 A3 **Kiffa** Mauritania
185 J5 **Kifisia** Greece
139 J4 **Kifrī** Iraq
195 D4 **Kigali** Rwanda
139 H2 **Kiğı** Turkey
207 H2 **Kiglapait Mountains** Canada
195 C4 **Kigoma** Tanz.
170 M2 **Kihlanki** Fin.
171 M3 **Kihniö** Fin.
141 H3 **Kiik** Kazakh.
170 N2 **Kiiminki** Fin.
159 D8 **Kii-sanchi** *mts* Japan
159 D8 **Kii-suidō** *sea chan.* Japan
185 I2 **Kikinda** Serbia
143 F5 **Kikki** Pak.
186 H3 **Kiknur** Russia
158 G4 **Kikonai** Japan
195 C4 **Kikondja** Dem. Rep. Congo
119 E2 **Kikori** P.N.G.
119 E2 **Kikori** *r.* P.N.G.
195 B4 **Kikwit** Dem. Rep. Congo
171 L3 **Kilafors** Sweden
147 H4 **Kilakkarai** India
148 D2 **Kilar** India
214 □2 **Kīlauea** U.S.A.
214 □2 **Kīlauea Volcano** U.S.A.
174 C5 **Kilbrannan Sound** *sea chan.* U.K.
160 E3 **Kilchu** N. Korea
175 L4 **Kilcoole** Ireland
175 K4 **Kilcormac** Ireland
125 J1 **Kilcoy** Australia
175 L4 **Kildare** Ireland
170 P1 **Kil'dinstroy** Russia
195 B4 **Kilembe** Dem. Rep. Congo
174 C5 **Kilfinan** U.K.
217 E5 **Kilgore** U.S.A.
172 E2 **Kilham** U.K.
162 B2 **Kiliěk** Cambodia
195 D4 **Kilifi** Kenya
195 D4 **Kilimanjaro** *vol.* Tanz.
195 D4 **Kilimanjaro National Park** Tanz.
119 F2 **Kilinailau Islands** P.N.G.
195 D4 **Kilindoni** Tanz.
171 N4 **Kilingi-Nõmme** Estonia
139 F3 **Kilis** Turkey
187 D6 **Kiliya** Ukr.
175 I5 **Kilkee** Ireland
175 M3 **Kilkeel** U.K.
175 K5 **Kilkenny** Ireland
173 C7 **Kilkhampton** U.K.
185 J4 **Kilkis** Greece
175 I3 **Killala** Ireland
175 I3 **Killala Bay** Ireland
175 J5 **Killaloe** Ireland
209 I3 **Killaloe Station** Canada
205 G4 **Killam** Canada
120 E3 **Killarney** *N.T.* Australia
125 J2 **Killarney** *Qld* Australia
209 G3 **Killarney** Canada
175 I5 **Killarney** Ireland
175 I6 **Killarney National Park** Ireland
209 G2 **Killarney Provincial Park** Canada
175 I4 **Killary Harbour** *b.* Ireland
217 D6 **Killeen** U.S.A.
175 K5 **Killenaule** Ireland
175 J4 **Killimor** Ireland
174 D4 **Killin** U.K.
175 M3 **Killinchy** U.K.
175 L5 **Killinick** Ireland
207 H1 **Killiniq (abandoned)** Canada
207 H1 **Killiniq Island** Canada
175 I5 **Killorglin** Ireland
175 L5 **Killurin** Ireland
175 J3 **Killybegs** Ireland
175 K2 **Kilmacrenan** Ireland
175 I4 **Kilmaine** Ireland
175 J5 **Kilmallock** Ireland
174 B3 **Kilmaluag** U.K.
174 D5 **Kilmarnock** U.K.
174 C4 **Kilmelford** U.K.
186 I3 **Kil'mez'** Russia
186 I3 **Kil'mez'** *r.* Russia
175 J5 **Kilmona** Ireland
125 F6 **Kilmore** Australia
175 L5 **Kilmore Quay** Ireland
195 D4 **Kilosa** Tanz.
170 M1 **Kilpisjärvi** Fin.
170 P1 **Kilp"yavr** Russia
175 I3 **Kilrea** U.K.
175 I5 **Kilrush** Ireland
174 D5 **Kilsyth** U.K.
147 G4 **Kiltan** *atoll* India
175 J4 **Kiltullagh** Ireland
195 C4 **Kilwa** Dem. Rep. Congo
195 D4 **Kilwa Masoko** Tanz.
174 D5 **Kilwinning** U.K.
141 F2 **Kima** Kazakh.
195 D4 **Kimambi** Tanz.
124 B4 **Kimba** Australia
195 B4 **Kimba** Congo
216 C3 **Kimball** U.S.A.
119 F2 **Kimbe** P.N.G.
204 F5 **Kimberley** Canada
197 F4 **Kimberley** S. Africa
118 C3 **Kimberley Plateau** Australia
121 B5 **Kimberley Range** *hills* Australia
126 E4 **Kimbolton** N.Z.
160 E3 **Kimch'aek** N. Korea
Kimhae S. Korea *see* **Gimhae**
171 M3 **Kimito** Fin.
160 D3 **Kimjŏngsuk** N. Korea
203 L3 **Kimmirut** Canada
185 K6 **Kimolos** *i.* Greece
187 F4 **Kimovsk** Russia
195 B4 **Kimpese** Dem. Rep. Congo
186 F3 **Kimry** Russia
195 B4 **Kimvula** Dem. Rep. Congo
163 I1 **Kinabalu, Gunung** *mt. Sabah* Malaysia
161 H5 **Kinabatangan** *r. Sabah* Malaysia
185 L6 **Kinaros** *i.* Greece
204 F4 **Kinbasket Lake** Canada
174 E2 **Kinbrace** U.K.
209 G3 **Kincardine** Canada
174 E4 **Kincardine** U.K.
125 E4 **Kinchega National Park** Australia
Kincolith Canada *see* **Gingolx**
195 C4 **Kinda** Dem. Rep. Congo
149 H5 **Kindat** Myanmar
217 E6 **Kinder** U.S.A.
173 F4 **Kinder Scout** *h.* U.K.
205 H4 **Kindersley** Canada
192 A3 **Kindia** Guinea
195 C4 **Kindu** Dem. Rep. Congo
140 B1 **Kinel'** Russia
186 G3 **Kineshma** Russia
146 A5 **King Abdullah Economic City** Saudi Arabia
Kingaok Canada *see* **Bathurst Inlet (abandoned)**
119 F4 **Kingaroy** Australia
214 B3 **King City** U.S.A.
127 J1 **King Edward Point** *research stn* Antarctica
221 E3 **King Ferry** U.S.A.
221 H2 **Kingfield** U.S.A.
217 D5 **Kingfisher** U.S.A.
127 I2 **King George Island** Antarctica
206 E2 **King George Islands** Canada
121 C4 **King Hill** Australia
186 D3 **Kingisepp** Russia
125 F8 **King Island** Australia
204 D4 **King Island** Canada
209 H1 **King Kirkland** Canada
125 F6 **Kinglake National Park** Australia
120 D3 **King Leopold Range National Park** Australia
118 C3 **King Leopold Ranges** *hills* Australia
215 E4 **Kingman** *AZ* U.S.A.
217 D4 **Kingman** *KS* U.S.A.
221 I2 **Kingman** *ME* U.S.A.
117 I3 **Kingman Reef** *terr.* N. Pacific Ocean
204 D3 **King Mountain** Canada
124 A3 **Kingoonya** Australia
175 K5 **Kings** *r.* Ireland
214 C3 **Kings** *r.* U.S.A.
173 D7 **Kingsbridge** U.K.
214 C3 **Kingsburg** U.S.A.
221 I2 **Kingsbury** U.S.A.
214 C3 **Kings Canyon National Park** U.S.A.
125 J2 **Kingscliff** Australia
124 B5 **Kingscote** Australia
175 L4 **Kingscourt** Ireland
127 L2 **King Sejong** *research stn* Antarctica
208 C3 **Kingsford** U.S.A.
219 D6 **Kingsland** *GA* U.S.A.
209 E5 **Kingsland** *IN* U.S.A.
173 H5 **King's Lynn** U.K.
119 H2 **Kingsmill Group** *is* Kiribati
173 H6 **Kingsnorth** U.K.
118 C3 **King Sound** *b.* Australia
213 E3 **Kings Peak** U.S.A.
220 B6 **Kingsport** U.S.A.
209 I3 **Kingston** Canada
223 I5 **Kingston** Jamaica
126 B6 **Kingston** N.Z.
208 B6 **Kingston** *IL* U.S.A.
221 F4 **Kingston** *NY* U.S.A.
125 G9 **Kingston**
215 E4 **Kingston Peak** U.S.A.
124 C6 **Kingston South East** Australia
173 G4 **Kingston upon Hull** U.K.
223 L6 **Kingstown** St Vincent
217 D7 **Kingsville** U.S.A.
173 E6 **Kingswood** U.K.
173 D5 **Kington** U.K.
174 D3 **Kingussie** U.K.
203 I3 **King William Island** Canada
197 G6 **King William's Town** S. Africa
217 E6 **Kingwood** *TX* U.S.A.
220 D5 **Kingwood** *WV* U.S.A.
205 I4 **Kinistino** Canada
159 G5 **Kinka-san** *i.* Japan
126 B6 **Kinloch** N.Z.
174 E3 **Kinloss** U.K.
209 H3 **Kinmount** Canada
171 K4 **Kinna** Sweden
175 K4 **Kinnegad** Ireland
Kinneret, Yam *l.* Israel *see* **Galilee, Sea of**
147 I4 **Kinniyai** Sri Lanka
171 N3 **Kinnula** Fin.
205 I3 **Kinoosao** Canada
159 F5 **Kinpoku-san** *mt.* Japan
174 E4 **Kinross** U.K.
175 J6 **Kinsale** Ireland
195 B4 **Kinshasa** Dem. Rep. Congo
217 D4 **Kinsley** U.S.A.
219 E5 **Kinston** U.S.A.
171 M5 **Kintai** Lith.
192 B4 **Kintampo** Ghana
175 F3 **Kintore** U.K.
174 C5 **Kintyre** *pen.* U.K.
204 F3 **Kinuso** Canada
193 F4 **Kinyeti** *mt.* South Sudan
140 D2 **Kinzhaly** Kazakh.
179 H4 **Kinzig** *r.* Germany
209 H2 **Kiosk** Canada
206 E4 **Kipawa, Lac** *l.* Canada
221 F6 **Kiptopeke** U.S.A.
195 C5 **Kipushi** Dem. Rep. Congo
119 G3 **Kirakira** Solomon Is
147 I2 **Kirandul** India
187 D4 **Kirawsk** Belarus
179 G2 **Kirchdorf** Germany
179 G5 **Kirchheimbolanden** Germany
175 M3 **Kircubbin** U.K.
151 C1 **Kirenga** *r.* Russia
150 C1 **Kirensk** Russia
141 H4 **Kirghiz Range** *mts* Asia
117 H4 **Kiribati** *country* Pacific Ocean
139 H1 **Kırık** Turkey
139 F3 **Kırıkhan** Turkey
138 D2 **Kırıkkale** Turkey
186 F3 **Kirillov** Russia
156 F3 **Kirillovo (abandoned)** Russia
Kirinyaga *mt.* Kenya *see* **Kenya, Mount**
186 E3 **Kirishi** Russia
159 B9 **Kirishima-yama** *vol.* Japan
117 I4 **Kiritimati** *atoll* Kiribati
138 A2 **Kırkağaç** Turkey
142 B2 **Kirk Bulāg Dāgi** *mt.* Iran
173 E4 **Kirkby** U.K.
173 F4 **Kirkby in Ashfield** U.K.
172 E3 **Kirkby Lonsdale** U.K.
172 E3 **Kirkby Stephen** U.K.
174 E4 **Kirkcaldy** U.K.
174 C6 **Kirkcolm** U.K.
174 D6 **Kirkcudbright** U.K.
171 K3 **Kirkenær** Norway
170 O1 **Kirkenes** Norway
209 H3 **Kirkfield** Canada
174 D5 **Kirkintilloch** U.K.
171 N3 **Kirkkonummi** Fin.
215 F4 **Kirkland** U.S.A.
215 F4 **Kirkland Junction** U.S.A.
209 G1 **Kirkland Lake** Canada
187 C7 **Kırklareli** Turkey
172 C3 **Kirk Michael** U.K.
172 E3 **Kirkoswald** U.K.
127 J5 **Kirkpatrick, Mount** Antarctica
216 E3 **Kirksville** U.S.A.
139 J4 **Kirkūk** Iraq
175 F2 **Kirkwall** U.K.
197 F6 **Kirkwood** S. Africa
214 B2 **Kirkwood** *CA* U.S.A.
217 F4 **Kirkwood** *MO* U.S.A.
138 C1 **Kırmır** *r.* Turkey
179 F5 **Kirn** Germany
187 E4 **Kirov** *Kaluzhskaya Oblast'* Russia
186 I3 **Kirov** *Kirovskaya Oblast'* Russia
Kirovabad Azer. *see* **Gäncä**
140 C2 **Kirovo** Kazakh.
186 I3 **Kirovo-Chepetsk** Russia
187 E5 **Kirovohrad** Ukr.
186 D3 **Kirovsk** *Leningradskaya Oblast'* Russia
170 P2 **Kirovsk** *Murmanskaya Oblast'* Russia
186 I3 **Kirovskaya Oblast'** *admin. div.* Russia
156 B1 **Kirovskiy** *Amurskaya Oblast'* Russia
158 C2 **Kirovskiy** *Primorskiy Kray* Russia
140 D5 **Kirpili** Turkm.
174 E4 **Kirriemuir** U.K.
186 J3 **Kirs** Russia
187 G4 **Kirsanov** Russia
138 E2 **Kırşehir** Turkey
143 G5 **Kirthar Range** *mts* Pak.
179 H4 **Kirtorf** Germany
170 M2 **Kiruna** Sweden
195 C4 **Kirundu** Dem. Rep. Congo
187 H4 **Kirya** Russia
159 F6 **Kiryū** Japan
171 K4 **Kisa** Sweden
194 C3 **Kisangani** Dem. Rep. Congo
195 B4 **Kisantu** Dem. Rep. Congo
163 E2 **Kisaran** Indon.
156 E2 **Kiselevka** Russia
150 A1 **Kiselevsk** Russia
142 D5 **Kīsh, Jazīreh-ye** *i.* Iran
149 F4 **Kishanganj** India
148 B4 **Kishangarh** *Rajasthan* India
148 C4 **Kishangarh** *Rajasthan* India
148 C2 **Kishen Ganga** *r.* India/Pak.
192 C4 **Kishi** Nigeria
141 G3 **Kishi Kamkaly** Kazakh.
159 B9 **Kishika-zaki** *pt* Japan
143 H2 **Kishim** Afgh.
143 G2 **Kishindih-ye Bālā** Afgh.
Kishinev Moldova *see* **Chişinău**
159 D7 **Kishiwada** Japan
141 H1 **Kishkenekol'** Kazakh.
149 G4 **Kishoreganj** Bangl.
Kishorganj Bangl. *see* **Kishoreganj**
148 C2 **Kishtwar** India
Kisi Nigeria *see* **Kishi**
195 D4 **Kisii** Kenya
205 J4 **Kiskittogisu Lake** Canada
177 I7 **Kiskunfélegyháza** Hungary
177 I7 **Kiskunhalas** Hungary
187 G7 **Kislovodsk** Russia
195 E4 **Kismaayo** Somalia
159 E7 **Kiso-sanmyaku** *mts* Japan
181 H4 **Kissamos** Greece
192 A4 **Kissidougou** Guinea
219 D6 **Kissimmee** U.S.A.
219 D7 **Kissimmee, Lake** U.S.A.
195 D4 **Kisumu** Kenya
192 B3 **Kita** Mali
Kitab Uzbek. *see* **Kitob**
153 N6 **Kita-Daitō-jima** *i.* Japan
159 G6 **Kitaibaraki** Japan
159 G5 **Kitakami** Japan
159 G5 **Kitakami-gawa** *r.* Japan
159 F6 **Kitakata** Japan
159 B8 **Kita-Kyūshū** Japan
194 D3 **Kitale** Kenya
133 P5 **Kitami** Japan
213 G4 **Kit Carson** U.S.A.
209 G4 **Kitchener** Canada
171 O3 **Kitee** Fin.
194 D3 **Kitgum** Uganda
204 D4 **Kitimat** Canada
170 N2 **Kitinen** *r.* Fin.
141 F5 **Kitob** Uzbek.
195 B4 **Kitona** Dem. Rep. Congo
159 B8 **Kitsuki** Japan
124 C2 **Kittakittaooloo, Lake** *salt flat* Australia
220 D4 **Kittanning** U.S.A.
221 F4 **Kittatinny Mountains** U.S.A.
221 H3 **Kittery** U.S.A.
170 N2 **Kittilä** Fin.
219 F4 **Kitty Hawk** U.S.A.
195 D4 **Kitunda** Tanz.
204 D3 **Kitwanga** Canada
195 C5 **Kitwe** Zambia
176 F7 **Kitzbüheler Alpen** *mts* Austria
179 I5 **Kitzingen** Germany
179 K3 **Kitzscher** Germany
171 N3 **Kiuruvesi** Fin.
171 N3 **Kivijärvi** Fin.
171 N4 **Kiviõli** Estonia
195 C4 **Kivu, Lac** Dem. Rep. Congo/Rwanda
141 G2 **Kiyakty, Ozero** *salt l.* Kazakh.
141 G2 **Kiyevka** Kazakh.
158 C3 **Kiyevka** Russia
185 M4 **Kıyıköy** Turkey
132 G4 **Kizel** Russia
186 H2 **Kizema** Russia
141 J4 **Kizil** China
138 B3 **Kızılca Dağ** *mt.* Turkey
138 D1 **Kızılcahamam** Turkey
139 G2 **Kızıl Dağı** *mt.* Turkey
138 D1 **Kızılırmak** Turkey
138 D2 **Kızılırmak** *r.* Turkey
138 C3 **Kızılkaya** Turkey
138 D3 **Kızılören** Turkey
140 D1 **Kizil'skoye** Russia
139 H3 **Kızıltepe** Turkey
187 H7 **Kizilyurt** Russia
187 H7 **Kizlyar** Russia
137 G1 **Kizlyarskiy Zaliv** *b.* Russia
Kizylayak Turkm. *see* **Gyzylaýak**
170 N1 **Kjøllefjord** Norway
170 L1 **Kjøpsvik** Norway
176 G5 **Kladno** Czech Rep.
176 G7 **Klagenfurt am Wörthersee** Austria
215 H4 **Klagetoh** U.S.A.
171 M5 **Klaipda** Lith.
170 □ **Klaksvík** Faroe Is
213 B3 **Klamath** *r.* U.S.A.
213 B3 **Klamath Falls** U.S.A.
213 B3 **Klamath Mountains** U.S.A.
163 B2 **Klang** Malaysia
171 K4 **Klarälven** *r.* Sweden
176 F6 **Klatovy** Czech Rep.
196 C5 **Klawer** S. Africa
204 C3 **Klawock** U.S.A.
179 E2 **Klazienaveen** Neth.
204 E4 **Kleena Kleene** Canada
196 D4 **Kleinbegin** S. Africa
196 C3 **Klein Karas** Namibia
197 F6 **Kleinpoort** S. Africa
196 D6 **Klein Roggeveldberge** *mts* S. Africa
196 B4 **Kleinsee** S. Africa
196 D6 **Klein Swartberg** *mt.* S. Africa
204 D4 **Klemtu** Canada
197 G3 **Klerksdorp** S. Africa
187 E4 **Kletnya** Russia
187 G5 **Kletskaya** Russia
179 E3 **Kleve** Germany
187 D4 **Klimavichy** Belarus
187 E4 **Klimovo** Russia
187 F4 **Klimovsk** Russia
186 F3 **Klin** Russia
204 D4 **Klinaklini** *r.* Canada
179 H5 **Klingenberg am Main** Germany
179 K4 **Klingenthal** Germany
179 K1 **Klink** Germany
176 F5 **Klínovec** *mt.* Czech Rep.
171 L4 **Klintehamn** Sweden
187 I5 **Klintsovka** Russia
187 E4 **Klintsy** Russia
196 C5 **Kliprand** S. Africa
185 G2 **Ključ** Bos. & Herz.
177 H5 **Kłodzko** Poland
204 C3 **Klondike Gold Rush National Historical Park** *nat. park* U.S.A.
179 E2 **Kloosterhaar** Neth.
177 H6 **Klosterneuburg** Austria
207 F1 **Klotz, Lac** *l.* Canada
179 J2 **Klötze (Altmark)** Germany
204 A2 **Kluane Game Sanctuary** *nature res.* Canada
204 B2 **Kluane Lake** Canada
204 B2 **Kluane National Park** Canada
177 I5 **Kluczbork** Poland
137 F2 **Klukhorskiy, Pereval** Georgia/Russia
187 C4 **Klyetsk** Belarus
133 R4 **Klyuchevskaya Sopka, Vulkan** *vol.* Russia
141 I1 **Klyuchi** *Altayskiy Kray* Russia
156 B2 **Klyuchi** *Amurskaya Oblast'* Russia
171 K3 **Knåda** Sweden
172 F3 **Knaresborough** U.K.
205 K3 **Knee Lake** Canada
179 I5 **Knetzgau** Germany
208 B1 **Knife Lake** Canada/U.S.A.
204 D4 **Knight Inlet** Canada
173 D5 **Knighton** U.K.
185 G2 **Knin** Croatia
176 G7 **Knittelfeld** Austria
185 J3 **Knjaževac** Serbia
120 E2 **Knob Peak** *h.* Australia
175 J4 **Knock** Ireland
175 I5 **Knockacummer** *h.* Ireland
175 J3 **Knockalongy** *h.* Ireland
175 I5 **Knockalough** Ireland
175 I6 **Knockboy** *h.* Ireland
175 F3 **Knock Hill** U.K.
175 L2 **Knocklayd** *h.* U.K.
178 B3 **Knokke-Heist** Belgium
179 L1 **Knorrendorf** Germany
185 K7 **Knossos** *tourist site* Greece
173 F5 **Knowle** U.K.
127 I3 **Knowles, Cape** Antarctica
221 I1 **Knowles Corner** U.S.A.
221 G2 **Knowlton** Canada
208 D5 **Knox** U.S.A.
204 C4 **Knox, Cape** Canada
214 A2 **Knoxville** *CA* U.S.A.
208 B5 **Knoxville** *IL* U.S.A.
219 D4 **Knoxville** *TN* U.S.A.
174 C3 **Knoydart** *mts* U.K.
203 M1 **Knud Rasmussen Land** *reg.* Greenland

Knysna

197 E7 **Knysna** S. Africa
156 E3 **Ko, Gora** *mt.* Russia
Kobanê Syria *see* **'Ayn al 'Arab**
159 B9 **Kobayashi** Japan
170 O1 **Kobbfoss** Norway
140 C2 **Kobda** Kazakh.
159 D7 **Kōbe** Japan
København Denmark *see* **Copenhagen**
192 B3 **Kobenni** Mauritania
179 F4 **Koblenz** Germany
156 D1 **Koboldo** Russia
186 I3 **Kobra** Russia
151 F7 **Kobroör** *i.* Indon.
187 C4 **Kobryn** Belarus
187 G7 **Kobuleti** Georgia
Kocaeli Turkey *see* **İzmit**
185 J4 **Kočani** Macedonia
138 B1 **Kocasu** *r.* Turkey
184 F2 **Kočevje** Slovenia
149 G4 **Koch Bihar** India
179 H5 **Kocher** *r.* Germany
169 Q4 **Kochevo** Russia
147 H4 **Kochi** India
159 C8 **Kōchi** Japan
141 H4 **Kochkor** Kyrg.
187 H4 **Kochkurovo** Russia
187 H6 **Kochubey** Russia
187 G6 **Kochubeyevskoye** Russia
147 H4 **Kodaikanal** India
147 J2 **Kodala** India
202 C4 **Kodiak** U.S.A.
202 C4 **Kodiak Island** U.S.A.
197 G1 **Kodibeleng** Botswana
186 F2 **Kodino** Russia
193 F4 **Kodok** South Sudan
187 G7 **K'odori** *r.* Georgia
187 D5 **Kodyma** Ukr.
185 K4 **Kodzhaele** *mt.* Bulg./Greece
196 D6 **Koedoesberg** *mts* S. Africa
196 D4 **Koegrabie** S. Africa
196 C5 **Koekenaap** S. Africa
149 E4 **Koel** *r.* India
178 D3 **Koersel** Belgium
195 B6 **Koës** Namibia
215 F5 **Kofa Mountains** U.S.A.
197 F4 **Koffiefontein** S. Africa
192 B4 **Koforidua** Ghana
159 F7 **Kōfu** Japan
206 E2 **Kogaluc** *r.* Canada
206 E2 **Kogaluc, Baie de** *b.* Canada
207 H2 **Kogaluk** *r.* Canada
141 I3 **Kogaly** Kazakh.
125 I1 **Kogan** Australia
171 K5 **Køge** Denmark
141 F5 **Kogon** Uzbek.
147 G5 **Kohan** Pak.
148 B2 **Kohat** Pak.
171 N4 **Kohila** Estonia
149 H4 **Kohima** India
148 B3 **Kohlu** Pak.
171 N4 **Kohtla-Järve** Estonia
126 E2 **Kohukohunui** *h.* N.Z.
204 A2 **Koidern** Canada
192 A4 **Koidu-Sefadu** Sierra Leone
147 H3 **Koilkuntla** India
160 D3 **Koin** N. Korea
158 F4 **Ko-jima** *i.* Japan
159 F8 **Ko-jima** *i.* Japan
121 B7 **Kojonup** Australia
162 A1 **Kok, Nam Mae** *r.* Thai.
221 I2 **Kokadjo** U.S.A.
141 F2 **Kokalaat** Kazakh.
Kokand Uzbek. *see* **Qo'qon**
171 M4 **Kökar** Fin.
140 E3 **Kokaral (abandoned)** Kazakh.
141 H4 **Kök-Art** Kyrg.
141 H4 **Kök-Aygyr** Kyrg.
143 H2 **Kökchah, Daryā-ye** *r.* Afgh.
171 M3 **Kokemäenjoki** *r.* Fin.
196 C4 **Kokerboom** Namibia
177 N3 **Kokhanava** Belarus
186 G3 **Kokhma** Russia
141 H4 **Kök-Janggak** Kyrg.
147 I4 **Kokkilai** Sri Lanka
171 M3 **Kokkola** Fin.
119 E2 **Kokoda** P.N.G.
214 □1 **Koko Head** U.S.A.
208 D5 **Kokomo** U.S.A.
197 E2 **Kokong** Botswana
197 G3 **Kokosi** S. Africa
141 J2 **Kokpekty** Kazakh.
160 D4 **Koksan** N. Korea
141 G4 **Koksaray** Kazakh.
186 H3 **Koksharka** Russia
141 G1 **Kokshetau** Kazakh.
207 G2 **Koksoak** *r.* Canada
197 H5 **Kokstad** S. Africa
141 I3 **Koksu** *Almatinskaya Oblast'* Kazakh.
141 G4 **Koksu** *Yuzhnyy Kazakhstan* Kazakh.
141 I3 **Koktal** Kazakh.
141 H2 **Koktas** Kazakh.
141 I3 **Kokterek** *Almatinskaya Oblast'* Kazakh.
140 B2 **Kokterek** *Zapadnyy Kazakhstan* Kazakh.
141 I2 **Koktobe** Kazakh.
140 D2 **Koktubek** Kazakh.
141 J3 **Koktuma** Kazakh.
141 I5 **Kokyar** China
141 J2 **Kokzhayyk** Kazakh.
170 P1 **Kola** Russia
143 G5 **Kolachi** *r.* Pak.
148 C2 **Kolahoi** *mt.* India
151 E7 **Kolaka** Indon.
162 A4 **Ko Lanta** Thai.
132 E3 **Kola Peninsula** Russia
149 E6 **Kolar** *Chhattisgarh* India
147 H3 **Kolar** *Karnataka* India
148 D4 **Kolaras** India
147 H3 **Kolar Gold Fields** India
170 M2 **Kolari** Fin.
148 C4 **Kolayat** India
186 F3 **Kol'chugino** Russia
192 A3 **Kolda** Senegal
171 J5 **Kolding** Denmark
195 C4 **Kole** *Kasaï-Oriental* Dem. Rep. Congo
194 C3 **Kole** *Orientale* Dem. Rep. Congo
183 R4 **Koléa** Alg.
170 M2 **Koler** Sweden
132 F3 **Kolguyev, Ostrov** *i.* Russia
149 F5 **Kolhan** *reg.* India
147 G2 **Kolhapur** India
171 M4 **Kõljala** Estonia
171 M4 **Kolkasrags** *pt* Latvia
149 G5 **Kolkata** India
141 G5 **Kolkhozobod** Tajik.
147 H4 **Kollam** India
147 H3 **Kollegal** India
147 I2 **Kolleru Lake** India
147 H4 **Kollidam** *r.* India
179 E1 **Kollum** Neth.
Köln Germany *see* **Cologne**
176 G3 **Kołobrzeg** Poland
186 H3 **Kologriv** Russia
192 B3 **Kolokani** Mali
119 F2 **Kolombangara** *i.* Solomon Is
187 F4 **Kolomna** Russia
187 C5 **Kolomyya** Ukr.
192 B3 **Kolondiéba** Mali
118 C2 **Kolonedale** Indon.
Kolonkwane Botswana *see* **Kolonkwaneng**
196 D3 **Kolonkwaneng** Botswana
140 B2 **Kolovertnoye** Kazakh.
133 J4 **Kolpashevo** Russia
187 F4 **Kolpny** Russia
140 E4 **Koʻlquduq** Uzbek.
Kol'skiy Poluostrov *pen.* Russia *see* **Kola Peninsula**
140 B1 **Koltubanovskiy** Russia
146 B7 **Koluli** Eritrea
141 G2 **Koluton** Kazakh.
147 G2 **Kolvan** India
170 J2 **Kolvereid** Norway
170 N1 **Kolvik** Norway
143 G5 **Kolwa** *reg.* Pak.
195 C5 **Kolwezi** Dem. Rep. Congo
133 Q3 **Kolyma** *r.* Russia
133 Q3 **Kolymskaya Nizmennost'** *lowland* Russia
187 H4 **Kolyshley** Russia
185 J3 **Kom** *mt.* Bulg.
158 G3 **Komaga-take** *vol.* Japan
196 B3 **Komaggas** S. Africa
196 B4 **Komaggas Mountains** S. Africa
157 E6 **Komaki** Japan
156 E2 **Komandnaya, Gora** *mt.* Russia
133 R4 **Komandorskiye Ostrova** *is* Russia
177 I7 **Komárno** Slovakia
197 I2 **Komatipoort** S. Africa
159 E6 **Komatsu** Japan
159 D7 **Komatsushima** Japan
195 C4 **Kombe** Dem. Rep. Congo
192 B3 **Kombissiri** Burkina Faso
163 B3 **Komering** *r.* Indon.
197 G6 **Komga** S. Africa
186 I2 **Komi, Respublika** *aut. rep.* Russia
187 D6 **Kominternivs'ke** Ukr.
185 G3 **Komiža** Croatia
185 H1 **Komló** Hungary
195 B4 **Komono** Congo
159 F6 **Komoro** Japan
185 K4 **Komotini** Greece
196 D6 **Komsberg** *mts* S. Africa
140 C3 **Komsomol** Kazakh.
140 E5 **Komsomol** Turkm.
133 K1 **Komsomolets, Ostrov** *i.* Russia
140 C3 **Komsomolets, Zaliv** *b.* Kazakh.
186 G3 **Komsomol'sk** Russia
Komsomol'sk Turkm. *see* **Komsomol**
187 E5 **Komsomol's'k** Ukr.
187 H6 **Komsomol'skiy** *Respublika Kalmykiya-Khalm'g-Tangch* Russia
187 H4 **Komsomol'skiy** *Respublika Mordoviya* Russia
150 F1 **Komsomol'sk-na-Amure** Russia
Komsomol'sk-na-Ustyurte Uzbek. *see* **Kubla Ustyurt**
140 E2 **Komsomol'skoye** Kazakh.
139 I1 **Kömürlü** Turkey
215 F6 **Kom Vo** U.S.A.
186 F3 **Konakovo** Russia
149 F6 **Konarka** India
149 F5 **Konar Reservoir** India
143 F3 **Konār Tapah** Afgh.
148 D4 **Konch** India
147 I2 **Kondagaon** India
209 I2 **Kondiaronk, Lac** *l.* Canada
121 B7 **Kondinin** Australia
195 D4 **Kondoa** Tanz.
186 E2 **Kondopoga** Russia
187 E4 **Kondrovo** Russia
Kondūz Afgh. *see* **Kunduz**
Kondūz *r.* Afgh. *see* **Kunduz, Daryā-ye**
140 D4 **Köneürgenç** Turkm.
162 B3 **Kŏng, Kaôh** *i.* Cambodia
162 C2 **Kŏng, Tônlé** *r.* Cambodia
162 C2 **Kong, Xé** *r.* Laos
203 O3 **Kong Christian IX Land** *reg.* Greenland
203 N3 **Kong Frederik VI Kyst** *coastal area* Greenland
132 D2 **Kong Karls Land** *is* Svalbard
163 I2 **Kongkemul** *mt.* Indon.
195 C4 **Kongolo** Dem. Rep. Congo
203 P2 **Kong Oscars Fjord** *inlet* Greenland
192 B3 **Kongoussi** Burkina Faso
171 J4 **Kongsberg** Norway
171 K3 **Kongsvinger** Norway
141 H5 **Kongur Shan** *mt.* China
195 D4 **Kongwa** Tanz.
203 P2 **Kong Wilhelm Land** *reg.* Greenland
141 G4 **Konibodom** Tajik.
179 J4 **Königsee** Germany
179 F4 **Königswinter** Germany
177 I4 **Konin** Poland
150 F1 **Konin** *r.* Russia
185 G3 **Konjic** Bos. & Herz.
196 B3 **Konkiep** *watercourse* Namibia
192 B3 **Konna** Mali
179 J3 **Könnern** Germany
171 N3 **Konnevesi** Fin.
186 G2 **Konosha** Russia
159 F6 **Kōnosu** Japan
187 E5 **Konotop** Ukr.
163 D2 **Kon Plông** Vietnam
144 G3 **Konqi He** *r.* China
194 D3 **Konso** Eth.
156 B2 **Konstantinovka** Russia
179 K5 **Konstantinovy Lázně** Czech Rep.
176 D7 **Konstanz** Germany
192 C3 **Kontagora** Nigeria
171 O3 **Kontiolahti** Fin.
170 N2 **Konttila** Fin.
162 C2 **Kon Tum** Vietnam
163 D2 **Kon Tum, Cao Nguyên** *plat.* Vietnam
Kontum, Plateau du Vietnam *see* **Kon Tum, Cao Nguyên**
138 D3 **Konya** Turkey
141 H3 **Konyrat** *Karagandinskaya Oblast'* Kazakh.
141 H3 **Konyrat** *Karagandinskaya Oblast'* Kazakh.
141 I3 **Konyrolen** Kazakh.
140 C2 **Konystanu** Kazakh.
179 E5 **Konz** Germany
121 C6 **Kookynie** Australia
214 □1 **Koʻolau Range** *mts* U.S.A.
121 B6 **Koolyanobbing** Australia
125 F5 **Koondrook** Australia
220 D5 **Koon Lake** U.S.A.
125 H5 **Koorawatha** Australia
121 A4 **Koordarrie** Australia
212 C2 **Kooskia** U.S.A.
204 F5 **Kootenay** *r.* Canada
204 F5 **Kootenay Lake** Canada
204 F4 **Kootenay National Park** Canada
196 D5 **Kootjieskolk** S. Africa
141 I3 **Kopa** Kazakh.
187 H6 **Kopanovka** Russia
148 C6 **Kopargaon** India
170 C1 **Kópasker** Iceland
141 I3 **Kopbirlik** Kazakh.
184 E2 **Koper** Slovenia
140 D5 **Kopet Dag** *mts* Iran/Turkm.
149 G4 **Kopili** *r.* India
171 L4 **Köping** Sweden
171 L3 **Köpmanholmen** Sweden
197 F2 **Kopong** Botswana
147 H3 **Koppal** India
171 J3 **Koppang** Norway
171 K4 **Kopparberg** Sweden
156 F2 **Koppi** *r.* Russia
197 G3 **Koppies** S. Africa
196 D3 **Koppieskraal Pan** *salt pan* S. Africa
185 G1 **Koprivnica** Croatia
138 C3 **Köprü** *r.* Turkey
181 J4 **Köprülü Kanyon Milli Parkı** *nat. park* Turkey
142 D4 **Kor, Rūd-e** *watercourse* Iran
187 G4 **Korablino** Russia
143 G5 **Korak** Pak.
206 E1 **Korak, Baie** *b.* Canada
152 E4 **Koramlik** China
147 H2 **Korangal** India
143 G5 **Korangi** Pak.
147 I2 **Koraput** India
147 I1 **Korba** India
184 D6 **Korba** Tunisia
179 G3 **Korbach** Germany
162 B4 **Korbu, Gunung** *mt.* Malaysia
185 I4 **Korçë** Albania
141 J1 **Korchino** Russia
185 G3 **Korčula** Croatia
185 G3 **Korčula** *i.* Croatia
185 G3 **Korčulanski Kanal** *sea chan.* Croatia
141 H4 **Korday** Kazakh.
142 D2 **Kord Kūy** Iran
143 F5 **Kords** *reg.* Iran
157 B5 **Korea, North** *country* Asia
157 B5 **Korea, South** *country* Asia
160 B4 **Korea Bay** *g.* China/N. Korea
159 A7 **Korea Strait** Japan/S. Korea
147 G2 **Koregaon** India
187 F6 **Korenovsk** Russia
187 C5 **Korets'** Ukr.
138 B1 **Körfez** Turkey
127 J3 **Korff Ice Rise** Antarctica
156 D2 **Korfovskiy** Russia
141 G2 **Korgalzhyn** Kazakh.
141 F2 **Korgasyn** Kazakh.
170 K2 **Korgen** Norway
192 B4 **Korhogo** Côte d'Ivoire
148 B5 **Kori Creek** *inlet* India
177 H7 **Kris-hegy** *h.* Hungary
143 E3 **Korīt** Iran
185 I3 **Koritnik** *mt.* Albania
159 G6 **Kōriyama** Japan
138 C3 **Korkuteli** Turkey
144 G3 **Korla** China
138 D4 **Kormakitis, Cape** Cyprus
177 H7 **Körmend** Hungary
141 H2 **Korneyevka** *Karagandinskaya Oblast'* Kazakh.
141 G1 **Korneyevka** *Severnyy Kazakhstan* Kazakh.
141 J1 **Kornilovo** Russia
192 B4 **Koro** Côte d'Ivoire
119 H3 **Koro** *i.* Fiji
192 B3 **Koro** Mali
187 F5 **Korocha** Russia
138 D1 **Köroğlu Dağları** *mts* Turkey
138 D1 **Köroğlu Tepesi** *mt.* Turkey
195 D4 **Korogwe** Tanz.
125 E7 **Koroit** Australia
185 J4 **Koroneia, Limni** *l.* Greece
125 E6 **Korong Vale** Australia
119 H3 **Koro Sea** Fiji
187 D5 **Korosten'** Ukr.
187 D5 **Korostyshiv** Ukr.
193 D3 **Koro Toro** Chad
171 N3 **Korpilahti** Fin.
171 M3 **Korpo** Fin.
140 C3 **Korsak** Kazakh.
150 G2 **Korsakov** Russia
186 I3 **Korshik** Russia
171 M3 **Korsnäs** Fin.
171 J5 **Korsør** Denmark
187 D5 **Korsun'-Shevchenkivs'kyy** Ukr.
177 J3 **Korsze** Poland
171 M3 **Kortesjärvi** Fin.
186 I2 **Kortkeros** Russia
178 B4 **Kortrijk** Belgium
186 G3 **Kortsovo** Russia
125 F7 **Korumburra** Australia
193 D4 **Korup, Parc National de** *nat. park* Cameroon
170 N2 **Korvala** Fin.
148 D4 **Korwai** India
150 H1 **Koryakskaya Sopka, Vulkan** *vol.* Russia
133 R3 **Koryakskoye Nagor'ye** *mts* Russia
186 H2 **Koryazhma** Russia
187 E5 **Koryukivka** Ukr.
140 C2 **Korzhyn** Kazakh.
185 L6 **Kos** *i.* Greece
169 Q4 **Kosa** Russia
140 E2 **Kosagal** Kazakh.
141 H1 **Kosagash** Kazakh.
160 D4 **Kosan** N. Korea
141 F2 **Kosay** Kazakh.
177 H4 **Kościan** Poland
217 F5 **Kosciusko** U.S.A.
204 C3 **Kosciusko Island** U.S.A.
125 H6 **Kosciuszko, Mount** Australia
125 H6 **Kosciuszko National Park** Australia
139 G1 **Köse** Turkey
139 F1 **Köse Dağı** *mt.* Turkey
147 H2 **Kosgi** India
135 G2 **Kosh-Agach** Russia
140 B2 **Koshankol'** Kazakh.
141 H4 **Kosh-Döbö** Kyrg.
159 A9 **Koshikijima-rettō** *is* Japan
140 B2 **Koshim** Kazakh.
140 B2 **Koshim** *r.* Kazakh.
143 F3 **Koshkak** Iran
141 J3 **Koshkarkol', Ozero** *l.* Kazakh.
208 C4 **Koshkonong, Lake** U.S.A.
Koshkupyr Uzbek. *see* **Qoʻshkoʻpir**
Koshoba Turkm. *see* **Goşoba**
Koshrabad Uzbek. *see* **Qoʻshrabot**
159 F7 **Kōshū** Japan
148 D4 **Kosi** India
148 D3 **Kosi** *r.* India
197 J3 **Kosi Bay** S. Africa
177 J6 **Košice** Slovakia
147 H3 **Kosigi** India
140 D2 **Kosistek** Kazakh.
141 F2 **Kosköl'** Kazakh.
141 I3 **Koskudyk** Kazakh.
170 M2 **Koskullskulle** Sweden
186 I2 **Koslan** Russia
141 F5 **Koson** Uzbek.
160 E3 **Kosŏng** *Hamgyŏng-namdo* N. Korea
160 E4 **Kosŏng** *Kangwŏn-do* N. Korea
141 G4 **Kosonsoy** Uzbek.
Kosova *country* Europe *see* **Kosovo**
185 I3 **Kosovo** *country* Europe
117 F2 **Kosrae** *atoll* Micronesia
179 J5 **Kösseine** *h.* Germany
140 C3 **Kosshagyl** Kazakh.
192 B4 **Kossou, Lac de** *l.* Côte d'Ivoire
140 E1 **Kostanay** Kazakh.
140 E1 **Kostanayskaya Oblast'** *admin. div.* Kazakh.
185 J3 **Kostenets** Bulg.
197 G2 **Koster** S. Africa
193 F3 **Kosti** Sudan
185 J3 **Kostinbrod** Bulg.
133 J3 **Kostino** Russia
186 D1 **Kostomuksha** Russia
187 C5 **Kostopil'** Ukr.
186 G3 **Kostroma** Russia
186 G3 **Kostroma** *r.* Russia
186 G3 **Kostromskaya Oblast'** *admin. div.* Russia
176 G4 **Kostrzyn nad Odrą** Poland
187 F5 **Kostyantynivka** Ukr.
169 R3 **Kos'yu** Russia
177 H3 **Koszalin** Poland
177 H7 **Kszeg** Hungary
147 I1 **Kota** *Chhattisgarh* India
148 C4 **Kota** *Rajasthan* India
163 B4 **Kotaagung** Indon.
148 C4 **Kota Barrage** India
163 H3 **Kotabaru** *Kalimantan Barat* Indon.
163 I3 **Kotabaru** *Kalimantan Selatan* Indon.
163 B1 **Kota Bharu** Malaysia
163 B3 **Kotabumi** Indon.
148 C4 **Kota Dam** India
163 I1 **Kota Kinabalu** *Sabah* Malaysia
141 I3 **Kotanemel', Gora** *mt.* Kazakh.
147 I2 **Kotaparh** India
162 B5 **Kotapinang** Indon.
148 C4 **Kotari** *r.* India
163 B2 **Kota Tinggi** Malaysia
186 I3 **Kotel'nich** Russia
187 G6 **Kotel'nikovo** Russia
133 O2 **Kotel'nyy, Ostrov** *i.* Russia
148 D3 **Kotgarh** India
179 J3 **Köthen (Anhalt)** Germany
149 E4 **Kothi** India
156 D3 **Kotikovo** Russia
171 N3 **Kotka** Fin.
148 C3 **Kot Kapura** India
169 Q2 **Kotkino** Russia
186 H2 **Kotlas** Russia
148 C2 **Kotli** Pak.
202 B3 **Kotlik** U.S.A.
170 C3 **Kötlutangi** *pt* Iceland
171 O4 **Kotly** Russia
185 G2 **Kotor Varoš** Bos. & Herz.
192 B4 **Kotouba** Côte d'Ivoire
187 H5 **Kotovo** Russia
187 G4 **Kotovsk** Russia
187 D6 **Kotovs'k** Ukr.
148 C4 **Kotra** India
149 E6 **Kotri** *r.* India
148 B4 **Kotri** Pak.
148 A5 **Kot Sarae** Pak.
147 I2 **Kottagudem** India
147 H4 **Kottarakara** India
147 H4 **Kottayam** India
147 H3 **Kotturu** India
Koturdepe Turkm. *see* **Goturdepe**
133 L2 **Kotuy** *r.* Russia
140 D2 **Kotyrtas** Kazakh.
202 B3 **Kotzebue** U.S.A.
202 B3 **Kotzebue Sound** *sea chan.* U.S.A.
192 A3 **Koubia** Guinea
192 B3 **Koudougou** Burkina Faso
197 E6 **Koueveldberge** *mts* S. Africa
193 D3 **Koufey** Niger
185 L7 **Koufonisi** *i.* Greece
197 E6 **Kougaberge** *mts* S. Africa
138 D4 **Kouklia** Cyprus
195 B4 **Koulamoutou** Gabon
192 B3 **Koulikoro** Mali
119 G4 **Koumac** New Caledonia
193 D4 **Koumra** Chad
192 A3 **Koundâra** Guinea
192 B3 **Koupéla** Burkina Faso
231 H2 **Kourou** Fr. Guiana
192 B3 **Kouroussa** Guinea
193 D3 **Kousséri** Cameroon
192 B3 **Koutiala** Mali
171 N3 **Kouvola** Fin.
170 O2 **Kovdor** Russia
187 C5 **Kovel'** Ukr.
186 G3 **Kovernino** Russia
147 H4 **Kovilpatti** India
186 G3 **Kovrov** Russia
187 G4 **Kovylkino** Russia
186 F2 **Kovzhskoye, Ozero** *l.* Russia
122 C2 **Kowanyama** Australia
126 C5 **Kowhitirangi** N.Z.
155 □ **Kowloon Peak** *h. Hong Kong* China
155 □ **Kowloon Peninsula** *Hong Kong* China
160 D4 **Kowŏn** N. Korea
141 I5 **Koxrap** China
141 I5 **Koxtag** China
159 B7 **Kōyama-misaki** *pt* Japan
141 F1 **Koybagar, Ozero** *l.* Kazakh.
138 B3 **Köyceğiz** Turkey
186 I2 **Koygorodok** Russia
Koymatdag, Gory *hills* Turkm. *see* **Goýmatdag**
147 G2 **Koyna Reservoir** India
186 H1 **Koynas** Russia
144 C4 **Köýtendag** Turkm.
202 C3 **Koyukuk** *r.* U.S.A.
139 F1 **Koyulhisar** Turkey
186 F3 **Koza** Russia
Kozağacı Turkey *see* **Günyüzü**
159 A7 **Kō-zaki** *pt* Japan
138 E3 **Kozan** Turkey
185 I4 **Kozani** Greece

185 G2 **Kozara** *mts* Bos. & Herz.
187 D5 **Kozelets'** Ukr.
187 E4 **Kozel'sk** Russia
147 G4 **Kozhikode** India
138 C1 **Kozlu** Turkey
186 H3 **Koz'modem'yansk** Russia
141 G4 **Kozmoldak** Kazakh.
185 J4 **Kožuf** *mts* Greece/Macedonia
159 F7 **Kōzu-shima** *i.* Japan
187 D5 **Kozyatyn** Ukr.
162 A3 **Kra, Isthmus of** Thai.
162 A3 **Krabi** Thai.
162 A3 **Kra Buri** Thai.
162 C2 **Krâchéh** Cambodia
170 L2 **Kraddsele** Sweden
171 J4 **Kragerø** Norway
178 D2 **Kraggenburg** Neth.
185 I2 **Kragujevac** Serbia
179 G5 **Kraichgau** *reg.* Germany
163 G4 **Krakatau** *i.* Indon.
162 C2 **Krâkôr** Cambodia
177 I5 **Kraków** Poland
179 K1 **Krakower See** *l.* Germany
162 B2 **Krâlănh** Cambodia
233 J1 **Kralendijk** Neth. Antilles
187 F5 **Kramators'k** Ukr.
171 L3 **Kramfors** Sweden
178 C3 **Krammer** *est.* Neth.
185 J6 **Kranidi** Greece
184 F1 **Kranj** Slovenia
162 □ **Kranji Reservoir** Sing.
197 I4 **Kranskop** S. Africa
186 H2 **Krasavino** Russia
132 G2 **Krasino** Russia
158 B3 **Kraskino** Russia
171 N5 **Krāslava** Latvia
179 K4 **Kraslice** Czech Rep.
177 O4 **Krasnapollye** Belarus
187 D4 **Krasnaya Gora** Russia
141 H2 **Krasnaya Polyana** Kazakh.
187 H5 **Krasnoarmeysk** Russia
187 F5 **Krasnoarmiys'k** Ukr.
186 H2 **Krasnoborsk** Russia
187 F6 **Krasnodar** Russia
187 F6 **Krasnodarskiy Kray** *admin. div.* Russia
187 F6 **Krasnodarskoye Vodokhranilishche** *resr* Russia
187 F5 **Krasnodon** Ukr.
186 D3 **Krasnogorodsk** Russia
156 F2 **Krasnogorsk** Russia
187 G6 **Krasnogvardeyskoye** Russia
187 E5 **Krasnohrad** Ukr.
187 E6 **Krasnohvardiys'ke** Crimea
140 C2 **Krasnokholm** Russia
177 Q2 **Krasnomayskiy** Russia
187 E6 **Krasnoperekops'k** Crimea
156 F2 **Krasnopol'ye** Russia
158 D2 **Krasnorechenskiy** Russia
171 O3 **Krasnosel'skoye** Russia
187 G4 **Krasnoslobodsk** Russia
140 D1 **Krasnousol'skiy** Russia
140 C5 **Krasnovodsk, Mys** *pt* Turkm.
Krasnovodskiy Zaliv *b.* Turkm. *see* **Türkmenbaşy Aýlagy**
140 C4 **Krasnovodskoye Plato** *plat.* Turkm.
156 C2 **Krasnoyarovo** Russia
150 B1 **Krasnoyarsk** Russia
177 O3 **Krasnyy** Russia
153 I1 **Krasnyy Chikoy** Russia
186 H3 **Krasnyye Baki** Russia
187 H6 **Krasnyye Barrikady** Russia
186 F3 **Krasnyy Kholm** Russia
187 H5 **Krasnyy Kut** Russia
186 D3 **Krasnyy Luch** Russia
187 F5 **Krasnyy Lyman** Ukr.
141 I3 **Krasnyy Oktyabr'** Kazakh.
141 G1 **Krasnyy Yar** Kazakh.
187 I6 **Krasnyy Yar** *Astrakhanskaya Oblast'* Russia
140 B1 **Krasnyy Yar** *Samarskaya Oblast'* Russia
187 H5 **Krasnyy Yar** *Volgogradskaya Oblast'* Russia
187 C5 **Krasyliv** Ukr.
187 H7 **Kraynovka** Russia
179 E3 **Krefeld** Germany
187 E5 **Kremenchuk** Ukr.
187 E5 **Kremenchuts'ke Vodoskhovyshche** *resr* Ukr.
187 G5 **Kremenskaya** Russia
176 G6 **Křemešník** *h.* Czech Rep.
213 F3 **Kremmling** U.S.A.
176 G6 **Krems an der Donau** Austria
133 T3 **Kresta, Zaliv** *g.* Russia
186 E3 **Kresttsy** Russia
171 M5 **Kretinga** Lith.
179 E4 **Kreuzau** Germany
179 F4 **Kreuztal** Germany
177 M3 **Kreva** Belarus
192 C4 **Kribi** Cameroon
Kriel S. Africa *see* **Ga-Nala**
185 I5 **Krikellos** Greece
158 H2 **Kril'on, Mys** *c.* Russia
135 F5 **Krishna** *r.* India
135 G5 **Krishna, Mouths of the** India
147 H3 **Krishnagiri** India
149 G5 **Krishnanagar** India
147 H3 **Krishnaraja Sagara** *l.* India
171 I4 **Kristiansand** Norway
171 K4 **Kristianstad** Sweden
171 I3 **Kristiansund** Norway
Kristiinankaupunki Fin. *see* **Kristinestad**
171 K4 **Kristinehamn** Sweden
171 M3 **Kristinestad** Fin.
Kriti *i.* Greece *see* **Crete**
185 K6 **Kritiko Pelagos** *sea* Greece
Krivoy Rog Ukr. *see* **Kryvyy Rih**
185 G1 **Križevci** Croatia
184 F2 **Krk** *i.* Croatia
171 K3 **Krokom** Sweden
171 J3 **Krokstadøra** Norway
170 K2 **Krokstranda** Norway
187 E5 **Krolevets'** Ukr.
179 J4 **Kronach** Germany
171 M3 **Kronoby** Fin.
203 O3 **Kronprins Frederik Bjerge** *nunataks* Greenland
162 A2 **Kronwa** Myanmar
197 G3 **Kroonstad** S. Africa
187 G6 **Kropotkin** Russia
179 K3 **Kropstädt** Germany
177 J6 **Krosno** Poland
177 H5 **Krotoszyn** Poland
197 I2 **Kruger National Park** S. Africa
156 D2 **Kruglikovo** Russia
177 N3 **Kruhlaye** Belarus
163 B4 **Krui** Indon.
197 F7 **Kruisfontein** S. Africa
185 H4 **Krujë** Albania
185 K4 **Krumovgrad** Bulg.
Krung Thep Thai. *see* **Bangkok**
177 N3 **Krupki** Belarus
185 I3 **Kruševac** Serbia
179 K4 **Krušné hory** *mts* Czech Rep.
204 B3 **Kruzof Island** U.S.A.
187 D4 **Krychaw** Belarus
239 H4 **Krylov Seamount** *sea feature* N. Atlantic Ocean
Krym' *pen.* Europe *see* **Crimea**
187 F6 **Krymsk** Russia
Kryms'kyy Pivostriv *pen.* Europe *see* **Crimea**
141 H3 **Krypsalo (abandoned)** Kazakh.
187 E6 **Kryvyy Rih** Ukr.
192 B2 **Ksabi** Alg.
192 C1 **Ksar el Boukhari** Alg.
192 B1 **Ksar el Kebir** Morocco
169 R3 **Ksenofontova** Russia
187 F5 **Kshenskiy** Russia
184 D7 **Ksour Essaf** Tunisia
186 H3 **Kstovo** Russia
142 B5 **Kū', Jabal al** *h.* Saudi Arabia
162 A4 **Kuah** Malaysia
162 B4 **Kuala Kangsar** Malaysia
162 B4 **Kuala Kerai** Malaysia
162 B5 **Kuala Kubu Baharu** Malaysia
163 B2 **Kuala Lipis** Malaysia
163 B2 **Kuala Lumpur** Malaysia
162 B4 **Kuala Nerang** Malaysia
162 B5 **Kuala Pilah** Malaysia
162 B5 **Kuala Rompin** Malaysia
163 H3 **Kualasampit** Indon.
162 A4 **Kualasimpang** Indon.
163 B1 **Kuala Terengganu** Malaysia
161 H5 **Kuamut** *Sabah* Malaysia
160 C3 **Kuandian** China
163 B2 **Kuantan** Malaysia
187 G6 **Kuban'** *r.* Russia
139 G4 **Kubār** Syria
139 I5 **Kubaysah** Iraq
186 F3 **Kubenskoye, Ozero** *l.* Russia
140 D4 **Kubla Ustyurt** Uzbek.
187 H4 **Kubnya** *r.* Russia
185 L3 **Kubrat** Bulg.
148 C4 **Kuchaman** India
148 C4 **Kuchera** India
163 H2 **Kuching** *Sarawak* Malaysia
159 A10 **Kuchino-shima** *i.* Japan
143 G4 **Küchnay Darwēshān** Afgh.
141 I1 **Kuchukskoye, Ozero** *salt l.* Russia
185 H4 **Kuçovë** Albania
147 G3 **Kudal** India
163 I1 **Kudat** *Sabah* Malaysia
147 H3 **Kudligi** India
147 G3 **Kudremukh** *mt.* India
163 H4 **Kudus** Indon.
176 F7 **Kufstein** Austria
203 J3 **Kugaaruk** Canada
186 H3 **Kugesi** Russia
202 G3 **Kugluktuk** Canada
202 E3 **Kugmallit Bay** Canada
143 E5 **Kūh, Ra's-al-** *pt* Iran
142 D3 **Kūh, Sīāh** *mts* Iran
143 F5 **Kūhak** Iran
149 E3 **Kuhanbokano** *mt.* China
143 E4 **Kūhbanān** Iran
179 K1 **Kuhbier** Germany
142 B3 **Kūhdasht** Iran
139 L3 **Kūhīn** Iran
170 O2 **Kuhmo** Fin.
171 N3 **Kuhmoinen** Fin.
142 D3 **Kūhpāyeh** Iran
179 K3 **Kühren** Germany
143 F3 **Kuhsān** Afgh.
162 A2 **Kui Buri** Thai.
196 B2 **Kuis** Namibia
196 A1 **Kuiseb Pass** Namibia
195 B5 **Kuito** Angola
204 C3 **Kuiu Island** U.S.A.
170 N2 **Kuivaniemi** Fin.
149 F5 **Kujang** India
160 C4 **Kujang** N. Korea
158 G4 **Kuji** Japan
159 B8 **Kujū-san** *vol.* Japan
156 D2 **Kukan** Russia
209 F1 **Kukatush** Canada
118 E2 **Kuk Early Agricultural Site** *tourist site* P.N.G.
185 I3 **Kukës** Albania
186 I3 **Kukmor** Russia
162 B5 **Kukup** Malaysia
140 D5 **Kükürtli** Turkm.
142 D5 **Kūl** *r.* Iran
138 B2 **Kula** Turkey
149 G3 **Kula Kangri** *mt.* Bhutan
140 B3 **Kulaly, Ostrov** *i.* Kazakh.
141 H4 **Kulan** Kazakh.
141 H4 **Kulanak** Kyrg.
143 F5 **Kulanch** *reg.* Pak.
140 D3 **Kulandy** Kazakh.
140 D3 **Kulandy, Poluostrov** *pen.* Kazakh.
141 G2 **Kulanotpes** *watercourse* Kazakh.
141 I4 **Kulansarak** China
143 G4 **Kulao** *r.* Pak.
133 O2 **Kular** Russia
161 I5 **Kulassein** *i.* Phil.
149 H4 **Kulaura** Bangl.
171 M4 **Kuldīga** Latvia
156 C2 **Kul'dur** Russia
Kul'dzhuktau, Gory *h.* Uzbek. *see* **Quljuqtov tog'lari**
196 D1 **Kule** Botswana
187 G4 **Kulebaki** Russia
162 C3 **Kulên** Cambodia
140 E1 **Kulevchi** Russia
121 F5 **Kulgera** Australia
186 H2 **Kulikovo** Russia
162 B4 **Kulim** Malaysia
121 B7 **Kulin** Australia
121 B6 **Kulja** Australia
Kulkuduk Uzbek. *see* **Ko'lquduq**
125 F3 **Kulkyne** *watercourse* Australia
148 D3 **Kullu** India
179 J4 **Kulmbach** Germany
141 G5 **Kŭlob** Tajik.
139 H2 **Kulp** Turkey
148 D4 **Kulpahar** India
221 F4 **Kulpsville** U.S.A.
140 C3 **Kul'sary** Kazakh.
179 H5 **Külsheim** Germany
138 D2 **Kulu** Turkey
138 C3 **Kulübe Tepe** *mt.* Turkey
141 I1 **Kulunda** Russia
141 J1 **Kulunda** *r.* Russia
141 H1 **Kulundinskaya Ravnina** *plain* Kazakh./Russia
141 I1 **Kulundinskoye, Ozero** *salt l.* Russia
142 D4 **Kūlvand** Iran
125 E5 **Kulwin** Australia
141 H1 **Kulykol'** Kazakh.
187 H6 **Kuma** *r.* Russia
159 F6 **Kumagaya** Japan
163 H3 **Kumai, Teluk** *b.* Indon.
158 F3 **Kumaishi** Japan
140 E2 **Kumak** Russia
140 D2 **Kumak** *r.* Russia
159 B8 **Kumamoto** Japan
159 E8 **Kumano** Japan
185 I3 **Kumanovo** Macedonia
156 B2 **Kumara** Russia
192 B4 **Kumasi** Ghana
192 C4 **Kumba** Cameroon
147 H4 **Kumbakonam** India
138 C2 **Kümbet** Turkey
197 E1 **Kumchuru** Botswana
142 D3 **Kumel** *well* Iran
169 P4 **Kumeny** Russia
140 C1 **Kumertau** Russia
160 E4 **Kŭmgang-san** *mt.* N. Korea
171 K4 **Kumla** Sweden
179 L2 **Kummersdorf-Alexanderdorf** Germany
193 D3 **Kumo** Nigeria
141 F3 **Kumola** *watercourse* Kazakh.
152 G6 **Kumon Range** *mts* Myanmar
162 B1 **Kumphawapi** Thai.
196 C4 **Kums** Namibia
147 G3 **Kumta** India
187 H7 **Kumukh** Russia
143 H3 **Kunaṛ Sīnd** *r.* Afgh.
150 G2 **Kunashir, Ostrov** *i.* Russia
149 E2 **Kunchuk Tso** *salt l.* China
171 N4 **Kunda** Estonia
149 E4 **Kunda** India
147 G3 **Kundapura** India
148 B2 **Kundar** *r.* Afgh./Pak.
143 H2 **Kunduz** Afgh.
143 H2 **Kunduz, Daryā-ye** *r.* Afgh.
143 H3 **Kunduz, Daryā-ye** *r.* Afgh.
141 H2 **Kundykol'** Kazakh.
195 B5 **Kunene** *r.* Angola/Namibia *alt.* **Cunene**
Künes China *see* **Xinyuan**
141 J4 **Künes Chang** China
141 J4 **Künes He** *r.* China
171 J4 **Kungälv** Sweden
141 I4 **Kungei Alatau** *mts* Kazakh./Kyrg.
204 C4 **Kunghit Island** Canada
Kungrad Uzbek. *see* **Qo'ng'irot**
140 E4 **Kungradkol'** Uzbek.
171 K4 **Kungsbacka** Sweden
171 J4 **Kungshamn** Sweden
194 B3 **Kungu** Dem. Rep. Congo
148 D6 **Kuni** *r.* India
159 B8 **Kunimi-dake** *mt.* Japan
149 F5 **Kunjabar** India
149 G4 **Kunlui** *r.* India/Nepal
135 F3 **Kunlun Shan** *mts* China
149 H2 **Kunlun Shankou** *pass* China
155 B5 **Kunming** China
148 D4 **Kuno** *r.* India
155 F4 **Kunshan** China
118 C3 **Kununurra** Australia
148 D4 **Kunwari** *r.* India
186 D3 **Kun'ya** Russia
179 H5 **Künzelsau** Germany
179 J3 **Künzels-Berg** *h.* Germany
155 F4 **Kuocang Shan** *mts* China
171 N3 **Kuohijärvi** *l.* Fin.
170 O2 **Kuoloyarvi** Russia
171 N3 **Kuopio** Fin.
171 M3 **Kuortane** Fin.
184 2 **Kupa** *r.* Croatia/Slovenia
151 E8 **Kupang** Indon.
171 N5 **Kupiškis** Lith.
204 C3 **Kupreanof Island** U.S.A.
187 F5 **Kup"yans'k** Ukr.
141 J4 **Kuqa** China
139 L2 **Kür** *r.* Azer.
156 D2 **Kur** *r.* Russia
139 J1 **Kura** *r.* Azer./Georgia
137 G2 **Kura** *r.* Georgia
187 G7 **Kura** *r.* Russia
141 H4 **Kuragaty** Kazakh.
187 H7 **Kurakh** Russia
140 D2 **Kurashasayskiy** Kazakh.
159 C7 **Kurashiki** Japan
149 E5 **Kurasia** India
159 C7 **Kurayoshi** Japan
138 B1 **Kurban Dağı** *mt.* Turkey
187 E5 **Kurchatov** Russia
143 G3 **Kürd, Kōh-e** *mt.* Afgh.
139 K1 **Kürdämir** Azer.
141 H4 **Kurday (abandoned)** Kazakh.
139 L2 **Kür Dili** *pt* Azer.
142 A2 **Kurdistan** *reg.* Asia
147 G2 **Kurduvadi** India
159 C7 **Kure** Japan
138 D1 **Küre** Turkey
117 G1 **Kure Atoll** U.S.A.
171 M4 **Kuressaare** Estonia
132 H4 **Kurgan** Russia
187 G6 **Kurganinsk** Russia
143 H2 **Kūrī** Afgh.
148 B4 **Kuri** India
Kuria Muria Islands Oman *see* **Ḥalāniyāt, Juzur al**
149 G4 **Kuri Chhu** *r.* Bhutan
123 C4 **Kuridala (abandoned)** Australia
171 M3 **Kurikka** Fin.
159 G5 **Kurikoma-yama** *vol.* Japan
236 E2 **Kuril Basin** *sea feature* Sea of Okhotsk
150 G2 **Kuril Islands** Russia
140 B2 **Kurilovka** Russia
150 G2 **Kuril'sk** Russia
Kuril'skiye Ostrova *is* Russia *see* **Kuril Islands**
236 E3 **Kuril Trench** *sea feature* N. Pacific Ocean
140 B1 **Kurmanayevka** Russia
193 F3 **Kurmuk** Sudan
147 H3 **Kurnool** India
138 E6 **Kurnub** *tourist site* Israel
159 E6 **Kurobe** Japan
158 G4 **Kuroishi** Japan
159 A9 **Kuro-shima** *i.* Japan
126 C6 **Kurow** N.Z.
148 B2 **Kurram** *r.* Afgh./Pak.
125 I4 **Kurri Kurri** Australia
137 F1 **Kursavka** Russia
141 J2 **Kurshim** Kazakh.
187 F5 **Kursk** Russia
187 H6 **Kurskaya** Russia
187 F5 **Kurskaya Oblast'** *admin. div.* Russia
138 D1 **Kurşunlu** Turkey
139 H3 **Kurtalan** Turkey
141 I3 **Kurtty** *r.* Kazakh.
136 D2 **Kurucaşile** Turkey
139 G2 **Kuruçay** Turkey
148 D3 **Kurukshetra** India
150 A2 **Kuruk Tag** *mts* China
197 E3 **Kuruman** S. Africa
196 D3 **Kuruman** *watercourse* S. Africa
159 B8 **Kurume** Japan
150 D1 **Kurumkan** Russia
147 I5 **Kurunegala** Sri Lanka
193 F2 **Kurush, Jebel** *hills* Sudan
141 J2 **Kur'ya** *Altayskiy Kray* Russia
169 R3 **Kur'ya** *Respublika Komi* Russia
140 B4 **Kuryk** Kazakh.
185 L6 **Kuşadası** Turkey
185 L6 **Kuşadası, Gulf of** *b.* Turkey
204 B2 **Kusawa Lake** Canada
179 F5 **Kusel** Germany
138 A1 **Kuş Gölü** *l.* Turkey
187 F6 **Kushchëvskaya** Russia
159 D8 **Kushimoto** Japan
158 I3 **Kushiro** Japan
158 I3 **Kushiro-Shitsugen Kokuritsu-kōen** *nat. park* Japan
139 L5 **Kūshkak** Iran
143 F3 **Kushk-e Kuhnah** Afgh.
147 H3 **Kushtagi** India
149 G5 **Kushtia** Bangl.
154 C2 **Kushui He** *r.* China
202 C3 **Kuskokwim** *r.* U.S.A.
202 B4 **Kuskokwim Bay** U.S.A.
202 C3 **Kuskokwim Mountains** U.S.A.
141 F1 **Kusmuryn** Kazakh.
160 C4 **Kusŏng** N. Korea
158 I3 **Kussharo-ko** *l.* Japan
179 F1 **Küstenkanal** *canal* Germany
162 B3 **Kut, Ko** *i.* Thai.
139 L6 **Kūt 'Abdollāh** Iran
162 A5 **Kutacane** Indon.
138 B2 **Kütahya** Turkey
187 G7 **Kutaisi** Georgia
187 H6 **Kutan** Russia
158 G3 **Kutchan** Japan
139 L5 **Kūt-e Gapu** *tourist site* Iran
185 G2 **Kutina** Croatia
185 G2 **Kutjevo** Croatia
177 I4 **Kutno** Poland
142 C4 **Kūt Seyyed Na'īm** Iran
195 B4 **Kutu** Dem. Rep. Congo
149 G5 **Kutubdia Island** Bangl.
202 G2 **Kuujjua** *r.* Canada
207 G2 **Kuujjuaq** Canada
206 E2 **Kuujjuarapik** Canada
Kuuli-Mayak Turkm. *see* **Guwlumaýak**
170 O2 **Kuusamo** Fin.
171 N3 **Kuusankoski** Fin.
140 D2 **Kuvandyk** Russia
195 B5 **Kuvango** Angola
186 E3 **Kuvshinovo** Russia
139 K7 **Kuwait** *country* Asia
139 K7 **Kuwait** Kuwait
139 K7 **Kuwait Jun** *b.* Kuwait
159 E7 **Kuwana** Japan
186 G1 **Kuya** Russia
139 J3 **Kūyah/Koye** Iraq
132 I4 **Kuybyshev** *Novosibirskaya Oblast'* Russia
Kuybyshev *Samarskaya Oblast'* Russia *see* **Samara**
187 I4 **Kuybyshevskoye Vodokhranilishche** *resr* Russia
154 D2 **Kuye He** *r.* China
141 H3 **Kuygan** Kazakh.
135 G2 **Kuytun** China
153 H1 **Kuytun** Russia
141 J3 **Kuytun He** *r.* China
185 M6 **Kuyucak** Turkey
141 F2 **Kuyukkol', Ozero** *salt l.* Kazakh.
141 K2 **Kuyus** Russia
140 D3 **Kuyushe** Kazakh.
171 O3 **Kuznechnoye** Russia
187 H4 **Kuznetsk** Russia
158 F1 **Kuznetsovo** Russia
187 C5 **Kuznetsovs'k** Ukr.
170 M1 **Kvænangen** *sea chan.* Norway
170 L1 **Kvaløya** *i.* Norway
170 M1 **Kvalsund** Norway
140 D1 **Kvarkeno** Russia
184 F2 **Kvarnerić** *sea chan.* Croatia
202 C4 **Kvichak Bay** U.S.A.
204 D3 **Kwadacha Wilderness Provincial Park** Canada
197 I4 **KwaDukuza** S. Africa
155 □ **Kwai Tau Leng** *h. Hong Kong* China
236 G6 **Kwajalein** *atoll* Marshall Is
193 E4 **Kwajok** South Sudan
162 A5 **Kwala** Indon.
197 I4 **KwaMashu** S. Africa
197 H2 **KwaMhlanga** S. Africa
Kwangju S. Korea *see* **Gwangju**
195 B4 **Kwango** *r.* Dem. Rep. Congo
195 D4 **Kwangwazi** Tanz.
160 E3 **Kwanmo-bong** *mt.* N. Korea
197 F6 **KwaNobuhle** S. Africa
197 F6 **KwaNojoli** S. Africa
197 G6 **Kwanonqubela** S. Africa
197 F5 **KwaNonzame** S. Africa
197 G6 **Kwatinidubu** S. Africa
197 H3 **KwaZamokuhle** S. Africa
197 F6 **KwaZamukucinga** S. Africa
197 F5 **Kwazamuxolo** S. Africa
197 H3 **KwaZanele** S. Africa
197 I4 **KwaZulu-Natal** *prov.* S. Africa
195 C5 **Kwekwe** Zimbabwe
197 F1 **Kweneng** *admin. dist.* Botswana
195 B4 **Kwenge** *r.* Dem. Rep. Congo
197 G5 **Kwezi-Naledi** S. Africa
177 I4 **Kwidzyn** Poland
202 B4 **Kwigillingok** U.S.A.
119 E2 **Kwikila** P.N.G.
195 B4 **Kwilu** *r.* Angola/Dem. Rep. Congo
151 F7 **Kwoka** *mt.* Indon.
155 □ **Kwun Tong** *Hong Kong* China
193 D4 **Kyabé** Chad
123 C5 **Kyabra** Australia
125 F6 **Kyabram** Australia
162 A1 **Kya-in Seikkyi** Myanmar
150 C1 **Kyakhta** Russia
125 E5 **Kyalite** Australia
123 A7 **Kyancutta** Australia
186 F1 **Kyanda** Russia
162 A1 **Kyaukhnyat** Myanmar
149 H6 **Kyaukpyu** Myanmar
149 H5 **Kyauktaw** Myanmar
171 M5 **Kybartai** Lith.
124 D6 **Kybybolite** Australia
155 C6 **Ky Cung, Sông** *r.* Vietnam
145 H8 **Kyeintali** Myanmar
148 D2 **Kyelang** India
154 A2 **Kyikug** China
Kyiv Ukr. *see* **Kiev**
187 D5 **Kyivs'ke Vodoskhovyshche** *resr* Ukr.
Kyklades *is* Greece *see* **Cyclades**
205 H4 **Kyle** Canada
174 C3 **Kyle of Lochalsh** U.K.
179 E5 **Kyll** *r.* Germany

Lubango

213 F4 Littleton CO U.S.A.
221 H2 Littleton NH U.S.A.
220 C5 Littleton WV U.S.A.
209 E3 Little Traverse Bay U.S.A.
195 D5 Litunde Moz.
204 B3 Lituya Bay U.S.A.
154 C3 Liuba China
155 C5 Liuchong He r. China
160 B5 Liugong Dao i. China
154 F1 Liugu He r. China
160 C2 Liuhe China
160 B2 Liu He r. China
155 D4 Liujiachang China
155 C5 Liujiang China
154 B3 Liujiaxia Shuiku resr China
156 B3 Liukesong China
154 C3 Liupan Shan mts China
155 B5 Liupanshui China
155 F6 Liuqiu Yu i. Taiwan
155 D4 Liuyang China
156 B2 Liuzhan China
156 B5 Liuzhi China
155 C5 Liuzhou China
185 J5 Livadeia Greece
158 C3 Livadiya Russia
171 N4 Līvāni Latvia
214 B2 Live Oak CA U.S.A.
219 D6 Live Oak FL U.S.A.
118 C3 Liveringa Australia
214 B3 Livermore U.S.A.
217 B6 Livermore, Mount U.S.A.
221 H2 Livermore Falls U.S.A.
125 I4 Liverpool Australia
207 H5 Liverpool Canada
173 E4 Liverpool U.K.
203 K2 Liverpool, Cape Canada
202 E3 Liverpool Bay Canada
173 D4 Liverpool Bay U.K.
125 I3 Liverpool Plains Australia
125 I3 Liverpool Range mts Australia
224 G5 Livingston Guat.
174 E5 Livingston U.K.
214 B3 Livingston CA U.S.A.
212 E2 Livingston MT U.S.A.
219 C4 Livingston TN U.S.A.
219 E6 Livingston TX U.S.A.
217 E6 Livingston, Lake U.S.A.
195 C5 Livingstone Zambia
127 I2 Livingston Island Antarctica
185 G3 Livno Bos. & Herz.
187 F4 Livny Russia
170 N2 Livojoki r. Fin.
209 F4 Livonia U.S.A.
184 D3 Livorno Italy
234 E1 Livramento de Nossa Senhora Brazil
143 E5 Liwā Oman
195 D4 Liwale Tanz.
154 B3 Lixian Gansu China
155 D4 Lixian Hunan China
155 B4 Lixian Sichuan China
154 E3 Lixin China
155 F4 Liyang China
173 B8 Lizard U.K.
173 B8 Lizard Point U.K.
178 B5 Lizy-sur-Ourcq France
184 F1 Ljubljana Slovenia
171 L4 Ljugarn Sweden
171 L3 Ljungan r. Sweden
171 L3 Ljungaverk Sweden
171 K4 Ljungby Sweden
171 L3 Ljusdal Sweden
171 L3 Ljusnan r. Sweden
171 L3 Ljusne Sweden
232 B5 Llaima, Volcán vol. Chile
173 C5 Llanbadarn Fawr U.K.
173 D5 Llanbister U.K.
235 I2 Llancanelo, Salina salt flat Arg.
173 D6 Llandeilo U.K.
173 C6 Llandissilio U.K.
173 D6 Llandovery U.K.
173 D5 Llandrindod Wells U.K.
173 D4 Llandudno U.K.
173 C5 Llandysul U.K.
173 C5 Llanegwad U.K.
173 C6 Llanelli U.K.
173 D5 Llanfair Caereinion U.K.
173 C4 Llangefni U.K.
173 D5 Llangollen U.K.
173 D5 Llangurig U.K.
173 C4 Llanllyfni U.K.
173 C4 Llannerch-y-medd U.K.
173 C5 Llannor U.K.
217 D6 Llano U.S.A.
217 D6 Llano r. U.S.A.
217 C5 Llano Estacado plain U.S.A.
233 J3 Llanos plain Col./Venez.
235 H4 Llanquihue, Lago l. Chile
173 C5 Llanrhystud U.K.
173 D6 Llantrisant U.K.
173 D5 Llanuwchllyn U.K.
173 D5 Llanwnog U.K.
173 D4 Llay U.K.
183 Q2 Lleida Spain
183 M3 Llerena Spain
183 P3 Llíria Spain
Llodio Spain see Laudio
202 F4 Lloyd George, Mount Canada
205 H3 Lloyd Lake Canada
205 G4 Lloydminster Canada
183 R3 Llucmajor Spain
232 C2 Llullaillaco, Volcán vol. Chile
155 B6 Lô, Sông r. China/Vietnam
232 C2 Loa r. Chile
215 G2 Loa U.S.A.
195 B4 Loango Congo
186 I3 Loban' r. Russia
183 N4 Lobatejo mt. Spain
195 C6 Lobatse Botswana
179 J3 Löbejün Germany
193 D4 Lobéké, Parc National de nat. park Cameroon
179 K3 Löbenberg h. Germany
235 K3 Loberia Arg.
195 B5 Lobito Angola
235 K2 Lobos Arg.
224 B2 Lobos, Isla i. Mex.
179 K2 Loburg Germany
174 D4 Lochaber reg. U.K.
174 C4 Lochaline U.K.
209 E1 Lochalsh Canada
174 A3 Lochboisdale U.K.
174 C3 Lochcarron U.K.
172 C1 Lochearnhead U.K.
179 E2 Lochem Neth.
123 C5 Lochern National Park Australia
182 E3 Loches France
174 E4 Lochgelly U.K.
174 C4 Lochgilphead U.K.
174 C2 Lochinver U.K.
174 E3 Loch Lomond and the Trossachs National Park U.K.
174 A3 Lochmaddy U.K.
174 E4 Lochnagar mt. U.K.
221 E5 Loch Raven Reservoir U.S.A.
174 D4 Lochy, Loch l. U.K.
124 A4 Lock Australia
174 E5 Lockerbie U.K.
125 G5 Lockhart Australia
217 D6 Lockhart U.S.A.
221 E4 Lock Haven U.S.A.
220 D3 Lockport U.S.A.
162 C3 Lôc Ninh Vietnam
220 B5 Locust Grove U.S.A.
138 E6 Lod Israel
125 E5 Loddon r. Australia
183 F5 Lodève France
186 E2 Lodeynoye Pole Russia
212 F2 Lodge Grass U.S.A.
148 B3 Lodhran Pak.
184 C2 Lodi Italy
214 B2 Lodi CA U.S.A.
220 B4 Lodi OH U.S.A.
170 K1 Lødingen Norway
195 C4 Lodja Dem. Rep. Congo
194 D3 Lodwar Kenya
177 I5 Łódź Poland
162 B1 Loei Thai.
196 C5 Loeriesfontein S. Africa
170 K1 Lofoten is Norway
187 G5 Log Russia
125 J1 Logan r. Australia
213 G5 Logan NM U.S.A.
220 B5 Logan OH U.S.A.
213 E3 Logan UT U.S.A.
220 C6 Logan WV U.S.A.
204 A2 Logan, Mount Canada
123 D4 Logan Creek r. Australia
204 D2 Logan Mountains Canada
208 D5 Logansport U.S.A.
184 F2 Logatec Slovenia
183 O1 Logroño Spain
197 E4 Lohatlha S. Africa
179 H3 Lohfelden Germany
170 N2 Lohiniva Fin.
149 H4 Lohit r. India
171 M3 Lohjanjärvi l. Fin.
179 G2 Löhne Germany
179 G2 Lohne (Oldenburg) Germany
170 M2 Lohtaja Fin.
162 A1 Loikaw Myanmar
152 G7 Loi-lem Myanmar
171 M3 Loimaa Fin.
182 E3 Loire r. France
230 C4 Loja Ecuador
183 N4 Loja Spain
163 I1 Lokan r. Sabah Malaysia
170 N2 Lokan tekojärvi resr Fin.
143 H3 Lōkār Afgh.
178 C3 Lokeren Belgium
196 D2 Lokgwabe Botswana
194 D3 Lokichar Kenya
194 D3 Lokichokio Kenya
171 J4 Løkken Denmark
171 J3 Løkken Norway
177 O2 Loknya Russia
192 C4 Lokoja Nigeria
192 C4 Lokossa Benin
187 E4 Lokot' Russia
171 N4 Loksa Estonia
203 L3 Loks Land i. Canada
149 H4 Loktak Lake India
192 B4 Lola Guinea
214 B2 Lola, Mount U.S.A.
195 D4 Loliondo Tanz.
171 J5 Lolland i. Denmark
212 D2 Lolo U.S.A.
197 E3 Lolwane S. Africa
185 J3 Lom Bulg.
171 J3 Lom Norway
195 C4 Lomami r. Dem. Rep. Congo
235 J3 Loma Negra, Planicie de la plain Arg.
143 G3 Lomar Pass Afgh.
235 K2 Lomas de Zamora Arg.
118 C2 Lomblen i. Indon.
163 I4 Lombok i. Indon.
163 I4 Lombok, Selat sea chan. Indon.
192 C4 Lomé Togo
195 C4 Lomela Dem. Rep. Congo
195 C4 Lomela r. Dem. Rep. Congo
178 A4 Lomme France
178 D3 Lommel Belgium
174 D4 Lomond, Loch l. U.K.
141 F1 Lomonosovka Kazakh.
240 M1 Lomonosov Ridge sea feature Arctic Ocean
186 G1 Lomovoye Russia
151 D7 Lompobattang, Gunung mt. Indon.
214 B4 Lompoc U.S.A.
162 B1 Lom Sak Thai.
177 K4 Łomża Poland
163 D2 Lơn, Hon i. Vietnam
148 D6 Lonar India
235 H3 Loncoche Chile
235 H3 Loncopué Arg.
156 D2 Londoko Russia
209 G4 London Canada
173 G6 London U.K.
220 A6 London KY U.S.A.
220 B5 London OH U.S.A.
175 K3 Londonderry U.K.
221 G3 Londonderry U.S.A.
118 C3 Londonderry, Cape Australia
232 B9 Londonderry, Isla i. Chile
234 B3 Londrina Brazil
214 C3 Lone Pine U.S.A.
162 A1 Long Thai.
174 D4 Long, Loch inlet U.K.
133 S2 Longa, Proliv sea chan. Russia
155 C6 Long'an China
173 E6 Long Ashton U.K.
235 H3 Longaví, Nevado de mt. Chile
219 E5 Long Bay U.S.A.
126 C6 Longbeach N.Z.
214 C5 Long Beach CA U.S.A.
221 G4 Long Beach NY U.S.A.
221 F4 Long Branch U.S.A.
208 A6 Long Branch Lake U.S.A.
155 B4 Longchang China
155 E5 Longchuan China
173 F5 Long Eaton U.K.
160 D1 Longfengshan Shuiku resr China
175 K4 Longford Ireland
155 E5 Longhai China
155 □ Long Harbour Hong Kong China
172 F2 Longhoughton U.K.
163 I3 Longiram Indon.
223 I4 Long Island Bahamas
206 E3 Long Island Canada
119 E2 Long Island P.N.G.
221 G4 Long Island U.S.A.
221 G4 Long Island Sound sea chan. U.S.A.
156 A3 Longjiang China
155 C5 Long Jiang r. China
149 H3 Longju China
154 F2 Longkou China
154 F2 Longkou Gang b. China
206 C4 Longlac Canada
206 C4 Long Lake l. Canada
221 F3 Long Lake U.S.A.
221 I1 Long Lake l. ME U.S.A.
209 E3 Long Lake l. MI U.S.A.
209 F3 Long Lake l. MI U.S.A.
216 C2 Long Lake l. ND U.S.A.
221 F2 Long Lake l. NY U.S.A.
155 C5 Longli China
155 B5 Longlin China
173 H5 Long Melford U.K.
155 E6 Longmen Guangdong China
156 B2 Longmen Heilongjiang China
154 B3 Longmen Shan mts China
213 F3 Longmont U.S.A.
154 B3 Longnan Gansu China
155 E5 Longnan Jiangxi China
209 G4 Long Point Canada
126 B7 Long Point N.Z.
209 G4 Long Point Bay Canada
172 E3 Long Preston U.K.
155 F4 Longquan China
155 F4 Longquan Xi r. China
207 I4 Long Range Mountains Nfld and Lab. Canada
207 I4 Long Range Mountains Nfld and Lab. Canada
119 E4 Longreach Australia
154 B3 Longriba China
155 C4 Longshan China
Longshanlu China see Shizhong
155 D5 Longsheng China
155 D5 Longshi China
213 F3 Longs Peak U.S.A.
173 I5 Long Stratton U.K.
155 D4 Longtian China
172 E2 Longtown U.K.
207 F4 Longueuil Canada
178 D5 Longuyon France
214 A2 Longvale U.S.A.
215 F3 Long Valley Junction U.S.A.
217 E5 Longview TX U.S.A.
212 B2 Longview WA U.S.A.
158 C2 Longwangmiao Russia
154 B3 Longxi China
154 C3 Longxian China
155 E5 Longxi Shan mt. China
162 C3 Long Xuyên Vietnam
155 E5 Longyan China
154 E2 Longyao China
166 D1 Longyearbyen Svalbard
156 B2 Longzhen China
155 C6 Longzhou China
179 F2 Löningen Germany
171 K4 Lönsboda Sweden
125 E6 Lonsdale, Lake Australia
182 G3 Lons-le-Saunier France
234 B3 Lontra r. Brazil
161 I3 Looc Phil.
209 E4 Looking Glass r. U.S.A.
221 F4 Lookout U.S.A.
206 D2 Lookout, Cape Canada
219 E5 Lookout, Cape U.S.A.
125 J1 Lookout, Point Australia
209 F3 Lookout, Point U.S.A.
214 C3 Lookout Mountain U.S.A.
121 B7 Lookout Point Australia
208 C1 Loon Canada
204 F3 Loon r. Canada
121 D6 Loongana Australia
205 H4 Loon Lake Canada
221 I1 Loon Lake l. U.S.A.
175 I5 Loop Head Ireland
149 E1 Lop China
150 G1 Lopatina, Gora mt. Russia
187 H4 Lopatino Russia
162 B2 Lop Buri Thai.
195 B4 Lopé, Parc National de la nat. park Gabon
161 I3 Lopez Phil.
221 E4 Lopez U.S.A.
150 B2 Lop Nur salt flat China
194 C3 Lopori r. Dem. Rep. Congo
170 M1 Lopphavet b. Norway
186 I2 Loptyuga Russia
124 A2 Lora watercourse Australia
233 I2 Lora r. Venez.
143 G4 Lora, Hāmūn-i- dry lake Pak.
183 N4 Lora del Río Spain
220 B4 Lorain U.S.A.
148 B3 Loralai Pak.
148 B3 Loralai r. Pak.
220 A4 Loramie, Lake U.S.A.
183 P4 Lorca Spain
179 F4 Lorch Germany
161 H4 Lord Auckland Shoal sea feature Phil.
142 C4 Lordegān Iran
119 F5 Lord Howe Island Pacific Ocean
236 F7 Lord Howe Rise sea feature S. Pacific Ocean
215 H5 Lordsburg U.S.A.
179 F4 Loreley tourist site Germany
234 D3 Lorena Brazil
151 F7 Lorentz r. Indon.
225 E3 Lorenzo del Real Mex.
231 F7 Loreto Bol.
231 I5 Loreto Brazil
224 B2 Loreto Mex.
161 J4 Loreto Phil.
233 I2 Lorica Col.
182 C3 Lorient France
205 K1 Lorillard r. Canada
174 C4 Lorn, Firth of est. U.K.
123 D5 Lorne Qld Australia
125 E7 Lorne Vic. Australia
122 B3 Lorne watercourse Australia
149 H3 Loro r. China
192 B3 Loropéni Burkina Faso
122 B3 Lorraine Australia
182 G2 Lorraine reg. France
179 G5 Lorsch Germany
179 F2 Lorup Germany
148 C4 Losal India
213 F5 Los Alamos U.S.A.
235 H2 Los Andes Chile
235 H3 Los Ángeles Chile
214 C5 Los Angeles U.S.A.
214 C4 Los Angeles Aqueduct canal U.S.A.
214 B3 Los Banos U.S.A.
232 D2 Los Blancos Arg.
215 D5 Los Coronados, Islas Mex.
214 B3 Los Gatos U.S.A.
224 C1 Los Gigantes, Llanos de plain Mex.
232 B8 Los Glaciares, Parque Nacional nat. park Arg.
179 E5 Losheim am See Germany
184 F2 Lošinj i. Croatia
233 H3 Los Katios, Parque Nacional nat. park Col.
197 H2 Loskop Dam S. Africa
235 H4 Los Lagos admin. reg. Chile
213 F5 Los Lunas U.S.A.
225 E3 Los Mármoles, Parque Nacional nat. park Mex.
235 I4 Los Menucos Arg.
224 B2 Los Mochis Mex.
214 A1 Los Molinos U.S.A.
194 B3 Losombo Dem. Rep. Congo
225 D4 Los Reyes Mex.
233 K2 Los Roques, Islas Venez.
179 E2 Losser Neth.
174 E3 Lossie r. U.K.
174 E3 Lossiemouth U.K.
179 K4 Lößnitz Germany
233 J2 Los Taques Venez.
233 K2 Los Teques Venez.
233 L2 Los Testigos is Venez.
214 C4 Lost Hills U.S.A.
212 D2 Lost Trail Pass U.S.A.
173 C7 Lostwithiel U.K.
232 C2 Los Vientos Chile
235 H1 Los Vilos Chile
180 D3 Lot r. France
235 H3 Lota Chile
140 D5 Loṭfābād Iran
197 I3 Lothair S. Africa
194 D3 Lotikipi Plain Kenya
195 C4 Loto Dem. Rep. Congo
186 E3 Lotoshino Russia
197 G1 Lotsane r. Botswana
170 O1 Lotta r. Fin./Russia
179 F2 Lotte Germany
151 C4 Louangnamtha Laos
Louang Namtha Laos see Louangnamtha
151 C5 Louangphabang Laos
Louangphabang Laos see Louangphabang
Loubomo Congo see Dolisie
182 C2 Loudéac France
155 D5 Loudi China
195 B4 Loudima Congo
220 B4 Loudonville U.S.A.
192 A3 Louga Senegal
173 F5 Loughborough U.K.
173 C6 Loughor r. U.K.
175 J4 Loughrea Ireland
173 H6 Loughton U.K.
220 B5 Louisa KY U.S.A.
221 E5 Louisa VA U.S.A.
175 I4 Louisburgh Ireland
204 C4 Louise Island Canada
119 F3 Louisiade Archipelago is P.N.G.
217 E6 Louisiana state U.S.A.
Louis Trichardt S. Africa see Makhado
219 D5 Louisville GA U.S.A.
219 C4 Louisville KY U.S.A.
217 F5 Louisville MS U.S.A.
237 H8 Louisville Ridge sea feature S. Pacific Ocean
206 E3 Louis-XIV, Pointe Canada
132 E3 Loukhi Russia
183 L4 Loulé Port.
205 K4 Lount Lake Canada
176 F5 Louny Czech Rep.
216 D3 Loup r. U.S.A.
207 F2 Loups Marins, Lacs des lakes Canada
207 I4 Lourdes Canada
183 D5 Lourdes France
183 L2 Lousã Port.
160 E1 Loushan China
125 F3 Louth Australia
173 G4 Louth U.K.
185 J5 Loutra Aidipsou Greece
Louvain Belgium see Leuven
196 B1 Louwater-Suid Namibia
197 I3 Louwsburg S. Africa
170 M2 Lövånger Sweden
186 D3 Lovat' r. Russia
185 K3 Lovech Bulg.
213 F3 Loveland U.S.A.
212 E2 Lovell U.S.A.
214 C1 Lovelock U.S.A.
178 B3 Lovendegem Belgium
171 N3 Loviisa Fin.
220 D6 Lovingston U.S.A.
208 C6 Lovington IL U.S.A.
217 C5 Lovington NM U.S.A.
169 M2 Lovozero Russia
209 J3 Low Canada
205 L2 Low, Cape Canada
206 E3 Low, Lac l. Canada
195 C4 Lowa Dem. Rep. Congo
148 B2 Lowarai Pass Pak.
221 H3 Lowell MA U.S.A.
209 E4 Lowell MI U.S.A.
221 G2 Lowell VT U.S.A.
204 F5 Lower Arrow Lake Canada
Lower California pen. Mex. see Baja California
124 D7 Lower Glenelg National Park Australia
215 F4 Lower Granite Gorge U.S.A.
126 E4 Lower Hutt N.Z.
214 A2 Lower Lake U.S.A.
175 K3 Lower Lough Erne l. U.K.
162 □ Lower Peirce Reservoir Sing.
204 D3 Lower Post Canada
207 H5 Lower Sackville Canada
173 I5 Lowestoft U.K.
177 I4 Łowicz Poland
125 F9 Low Rocky Point Australia
174 E5 Lowther Hills U.K.
221 F3 Lowville U.S.A.
179 G1 Loxstedt Germany
124 D5 Loxton Australia
197 E5 Loxton S. Africa
143 H3 Lōyah Ḍakah Afgh.
221 E4 Loyalsock Creek r. U.S.A.
214 B2 Loyalton U.S.A.
119 G4 Loyauté, Îs is New Caledonia
187 D5 Loyew Belarus
185 H2 Loznica Serbia
187 F5 Lozova Ukr.
141 I1 Lozovoye Kazakh.
195 C5 Lucano Angola
155 E4 Lu'an China
154 D3 Luanchuan China
195 B4 Luanda Angola
155 B7 Luang, Huai r. Thai.
162 A3 Luang, Khao mt. Thai.
162 B4 Luang, Thale lag. Thai.
195 D5 Luangwa r. Zambia
149 H2 Luanhaizi China
154 F1 Luan He r. China
154 F2 Luannan China
154 E1 Luanping China
195 C5 Luanshya Zambia
154 F2 Luanxian China
195 C4 Luanza Dem. Rep. Congo
163 H2 Luar, Danau l. Indon.
183 M1 Luarca Spain
195 C5 Luau Angola
225 G4 Lubaantum tourist site Belize
177 K5 Lubaczów Poland
171 N4 Lubānas ezers l. Latvia
161 I3 Lubang Phil.
161 I3 Lubang i. Phil.
161 H3 Lubang Islands Phil.
195 B5 Lubango Angola

Lubao

195 C4 **Lubao** Dem. Rep. Congo
177 K5 **Lubartów** Poland
179 G2 **Lübbecke** Germany
196 C4 **Lubbeskolk** *salt pan* S. Africa
217 C5 **Lubbock** U.S.A.
179 J2 **Lübbow** Germany
179 I1 **Lübeck** Germany
160 A1 **Lubei** China
177 K5 **Lubelska, Wyżyna** *hills* Poland
140 C2 **Lubenka** Kazakh.
195 C4 **Lubero** Dem. Rep. Congo
177 H5 **Lubin** Poland
177 K5 **Lublin** Poland
187 E5 **Lubny** Ukr.
163 H2 **Lubok Antu** *Sarawak* Malaysia
179 J1 **Lübstorf** Germany
179 J1 **Lübtheen** Germany
161 I2 **Lubuagan** Phil.
195 C4 **Lubudi** Dem. Rep. Congo
163 B3 **Lubuklinggau** Indon.
162 A5 **Lubukpakam** Indon.
162 B2 **Lubuksikaping** Indon.
195 C5 **Lubumbashi** Dem. Rep. Congo
195 C5 **Lubungu** Zambia
195 C4 **Lubutu** Dem. Rep. Congo
179 K1 **Lübz** Germany
195 B4 **Lucala** Angola
175 L4 **Lucan** Ireland
204 A2 **Lucania, Mount** Canada
195 C4 **Lucapa** Angola
219 E7 **Lucaya** Bahamas
184 D3 **Lucca** Italy
174 D6 **Luce Bay** U.K.
234 B3 **Lucélia** Brazil
161 I3 **Lucena** Phil.
183 N4 **Lucena** Spain
177 I6 **Lučenec** Slovakia
184 F4 **Lucera** Italy
176 D7 **Lucerne** Switz.
158 D1 **Luchegorsk** Russia
155 D6 **Luchuan** China
155 B6 **Lüchun** China
124 D6 **Lucindale** Australia
195 B5 **Lucira** Angola
Luckeesarai India *see* **Lakhisarai**
179 L2 **Luckenwalde** Germany
197 F4 **Luckhoff** S. Africa
209 G4 **Lucknow** Canada
149 E4 **Lucknow** India
195 C5 **Lucusse** Angola
123 B4 **Lucy Creek** Australia
186 F1 **Luda** Russia
155 F6 **Lü Dao** *i.* Taiwan
179 F3 **Lüdenscheid** Germany
195 B6 **Lüderitz** Namibia
179 I1 **Lüdersdorf** Germany
148 C3 **Ludhiana** India
155 B5 **Ludian** China
208 D4 **Ludington** U.S.A.
173 E5 **Ludlow** U.K.
215 D4 **Ludlow** *CA* U.S.A.
221 I1 **Ludlow** *ME* U.S.A.
221 G3 **Ludlow** *VT* U.S.A.
185 L3 **Ludogorie** *reg.* Bulg.
171 K3 **Ludvika** Sweden
179 H6 **Ludwigsburg** Germany
179 L2 **Ludwigsfelde** Germany
179 G5 **Ludwigshafen am Rhein** Germany
179 J1 **Ludwigslust** Germany
171 N4 **Ludza** Latvia
195 C4 **Luebo** Dem. Rep. Congo
195 B5 **Luena** Angola
233 L3 **Luepa** Venez.
154 C3 **Lüeyang** China
155 E6 **Lufeng** China
217 E6 **Lufkin** U.S.A.
186 D3 **Luga** Russia
186 D3 **Luga** *r.* Russia
184 C1 **Lugano** Switz.
179 K4 **Lugau/Erzgebirge** Germany
179 H3 **Lügde** Germany
195 D5 **Lugenda** *r.* Moz.
173 D5 **Lugg** *r.* U.K.
175 L5 **Lugnaquilla** *h.* Ireland
184 D2 **Lugo** Italy
183 M1 **Lugo** Spain
185 I2 **Lugoj** Romania
141 H4 **Lugovoy** Kazakh.
161 I5 **Lugus** *i.* Phil.
187 F5 **Luhans'k** Ukr.
154 F3 **Luhe** China
179 I1 **Luhe** *r.* Germany
195 D4 **Luhombero** Tanz.
153 H5 **Luhuo** China
187 D5 **Luhyny** Ukr.
195 C5 **Luiana** Angola
195 C4 **Luilaka** *r.* Dem. Rep. Congo
174 C4 **Luing** *i.* U.K.
184 C2 **Luino** Italy
170 N2 **Luiro** *r.* Fin.
225 D3 **Luis Moya** Mex.
195 C4 **Luiza** Dem. Rep. Congo
235 K2 **Luján** *r.* Arg.
235 I2 **Luján de Cuyo** Arg.
155 E4 **Lujiang** China
156 D1 **Lukachek** Russia
185 H2 **Lukavac** Bos. & Herz.
195 C4 **Lukenie** *r.* Dem. Rep. Congo
215 F6 **Lukeville** U.S.A.
186 G3 **Lukh** *r.* Russia
187 F4 **Lukhovitsy** Russia
185 K3 **Lukovit** Bulg.
177 K5 **Łuków** Poland
187 H4 **Lukoyanov** Russia
195 C5 **Lukulu** Zambia
195 D4 **Lukumburu** Tanz.
170 M2 **Luleå** Sweden
170 M2 **Luleälven** *r.* Sweden
138 A1 **Lüleburgaz** Turkey
154 D2 **Lüliang** China
155 B5 **Luliang** China
154 D2 **Lüliang Shan** *mts* China
217 D6 **Luling** U.S.A.
154 F2 **Lulong** China
149 F3 **Lumachomo** China
163 H4 **Lumajang** Indon.
149 E2 **Lumajangdong Co** *salt l.* China
139 K5 **Lūmār** Iran
195 C5 **Lumbala Kaquengue** Angola
195 C5 **Lumbala N'guimbo** Angola
219 E5 **Lumberton** U.S.A.
183 M2 **Lumbrales** Spain
149 H4 **Lumding** India
170 N2 **Lumijoki** Fin.
162 C2 **Lumphăt** Cambodia
126 B6 **Lumsden** N.Z.
163 G3 **Lumut, Tanjung** *pt* Indon.
161 I2 **Luna** Phil.
215 H5 **Luna** U.S.A.
175 F4 **Lunan Bay** U.K.
205 K2 **Lunan Lake** Canada
209 F5 **Luna Pier** U.S.A.
148 C5 **Lunavada** India
148 B4 **Lund** Pak.
171 K5 **Lund** Sweden
215 F2 **Lund** U.S.A.
205 J4 **Lundar** Canada
195 D5 **Lundazi** Zambia
173 C6 **Lundy** *i.* U.K.
Lundy Island U.K. *see* **Lundy**
172 E3 **Lune** *r.* U.K.
179 I1 **Lüneburg** Germany
179 I1 **Lüneburger Heide** *reg.* Germany
179 F3 **Lünen** Germany
182 H2 **Lunéville** France
195 C5 **Lunga** *r.* Zambia
149 E2 **Lungdo** China
149 E3 **Lunggar** China
192 A4 **Lungi** Sierra Leone
155 □ **Lung Kwu Chau** *i.* Hong Kong China
149 H5 **Lunglei** India
195 C5 **Lungwebungu** *r.* Zambia
148 C4 **Luni** India
148 C4 **Luni** *r.* India
148 B3 **Luni** *r.* Pak.
214 C2 **Luning** U.S.A.
187 H4 **Lunino** Russia
187 C4 **Luninyets** Belarus
148 C1 **Lunkho** *mt.* Afgh./Pak.
179 F2 **Lünne** Germany
192 A4 **Lunsar** Sierra Leone
197 H2 **Lunsklip** S. Africa
135 G2 **Luntai** China
156 C3 **Luobei** China
144 G4 **Luobuzhuang** China
155 C5 **Luocheng** China
154 C3 **Luochuan** China
155 C5 **Luodian** China
155 D6 **Luoding** China
155 D6 **Luodou Sha** *i.* China
154 E3 **Luohe** China
154 D3 **Luo He** *r. Henan* China
154 C3 **Luo He** *r. Shaanxi* China
154 D3 **Luoning** China
155 B5 **Luoping** China
154 E3 **Luoshan** China
155 E4 **Luotian** China
Luoto Fin. *see* **Larsmo**
154 D3 **Luoyang** China
155 F5 **Luoyuan** China
161 F2 **Luozigou** China
195 C5 **Lupane** Zimbabwe
Lupanshui China *see* **Liupanshui**
163 H2 **Lupar** *r. Sarawak* Malaysia
185 J2 **Lupeni** Romania
195 D5 **Lupilichi** Moz.
161 J5 **Lupon** Phil.
215 H4 **Lupton** U.S.A.
154 B3 **Luqu** China
154 E2 **Luquan** *Hebei* China
155 B5 **Luquan** *Yunnan* China
139 J3 **Lūrā Shīrīn** Iran
195 B4 **Luremo** Angola
174 C2 **Lurgainn, Loch** *l.* U.K.
175 L3 **Lurgan** U.K.
195 E5 **Lúrio** Moz.
195 D5 **Lurio** *r.* Moz.
195 C5 **Lusaka** Zambia
195 C4 **Lusambo** Dem. Rep. Congo
119 F2 **Lusancay Islands and Reefs** P.N.G.
204 F4 **Luscar** Canada
205 H4 **Luseland** Canada
120 D3 **Lush, Mount** *h.* Australia
154 D3 **Lushi** China
185 H4 **Lushnjë** Albania
160 D2 **Lushuihe** China
160 A4 **Lüshunkou** China
197 H5 **Lusikisiki** S. Africa
213 F3 **Lusk** U.S.A.
123 D5 **Lussvale** Australia
Lūt, Dasht-e *des.* Iran *see* **Lūt, Kavīr-e**
143 E4 **Lūt, Kavīr-e** *des.* Iran
209 G4 **Luther Lake** Canada
173 G6 **Luton** U.K.
163 H2 **Lutong** *Sarawak* Malaysia
205 G2 **Łutselk'e** Canada
187 C5 **Luts'k** Ukr.
178 D2 **Luttelgeest** Neth.
179 E2 **Luttenberg** Neth.
179 H5 **Lützelbach** Germany
127 L4 **Lützow-Holm Bay** Antarctica
196 D4 **Lutzputs** S. Africa
196 C5 **Lutzville** S. Africa
161 I5 **Luuk** Phil.
171 N3 **Luumäki** Fin.
194 E3 **Luuq** Somalia
216 D3 **Luverne** U.S.A.
195 C4 **Luvua** *r.* Dem. Rep. Congo
197 I1 **Luvuvhu** *r.* S. Africa
194 D3 **Luwero** Uganda
151 E7 **Luwuk** Indon.
179 E5 **Luxembourg** *country* Europe
179 E5 **Luxembourg** Lux.
182 H3 **Luxeuil-les-Bains** France
Luxi *Hunan* China *see* **Wuxi**
Luxi *Yunnan* China *see* **Mangshi**
155 B5 **Luxi** *Yunnan* China
197 F5 **Luxolweni** S. Africa
193 F2 **Luxor** Egypt
154 E3 **Luyi** China
178 D3 **Luyksgestel** Neth.
186 H2 **Luza** Russia
186 I2 **Luza** *r.* Russia
Luzern Switz. *see* **Lucerne**
155 C5 **Luzhai** China
155 B4 **Luzhou** China
186 D3 **Luzhskaya** Russia
234 C2 **Luziânia** Brazil
231 J4 **Luzilândia** Brazil
161 I3 **Luzon** *i.* Phil.
161 I1 **Luzon Strait** Phil.
182 F3 **Luzy** France
187 C5 **L'viv** Ukr.
Lvov Ukr. *see* **L'viv**
143 G4 **Lwarah Rōd** *r.* Afgh.
186 D3 **Lyady** Russia
187 C4 **Lyakhavichy** Belarus
205 G5 **Lyall, Mount** Canada
Lyangar Uzbek. *see* **Langar**
170 L2 **Lycksele** Sweden
173 H7 **Lydd** U.K.
127 J3 **Lyddan Ice Rise** Antarctica
Lydenburg S. Africa *see* **Mashishing**
173 E6 **Lydney** U.K.
187 D5 **Lyel'chytsy** Belarus
214 C3 **Lyell, Mount** U.S.A.
121 E4 **Lyell Brown, Mount** *h.* Australia
204 C4 **Lyell Island** Canada
187 D4 **Lyepyel'** Belarus
221 E4 **Lykens** U.S.A.
213 E3 **Lyman** U.S.A.
173 E7 **Lyme Bay** U.K.
173 E7 **Lyme Regis** U.K.
173 F7 **Lymington** U.K.
220 D6 **Lynchburg** U.S.A.
221 H2 **Lynchville** U.S.A.
125 H4 **Lyndhurst** *N.S.W.* Australia
122 D3 **Lyndhurst** *Qld* Australia
124 C3 **Lyndhurst** *S.A.* Australia
121 A4 **Lyndon** Australia
121 A4 **Lyndon** *r.* Australia
221 G2 **Lyndonville** U.S.A.
174 E2 **Lyness** U.K.
171 I4 **Lyngdal** Norway
221 H3 **Lynn** U.S.A.
204 B3 **Lynn Canal** *sea chan.* U.S.A.
215 F2 **Lynndyl** U.S.A.
205 I3 **Lynn Lake** Canada
173 D6 **Lynton** U.K.
205 H2 **Lynx Lake** Canada
182 G4 **Lyon** France
221 G2 **Lyon Mountain** U.S.A.
121 F6 **Lyons** Australia
219 D5 **Lyons** *GA* U.S.A.
221 E3 **Lyons** *NY* U.S.A.
221 F3 **Lyons Falls** U.S.A.
187 D4 **Lyozna** Belarus
119 F2 **Lyra Reef** P.N.G.
171 J4 **Lysekil** Sweden
186 H3 **Lyskovo** Russia
163 D2 **Ly Sơn, Đao** *i.* Vietnam
132 G4 **Lys'va** Russia
187 F5 **Lysychans'k** Ukr.
169 O5 **Lysyye Gory** Russia
173 D4 **Lytham St Anne's** U.K.
204 E4 **Lytton** Canada
187 D4 **Lyuban'** Belarus
169 N4 **Lyubertsy** Russia
187 C5 **Lyubeshiv** Ukr.
187 E4 **Lyudinovo** Russia
186 H3 **Lyunda** *r.* Russia

M

155 B6 **Ma, Sông** *r.* Laos/Vietnam
147 G5 **Maalhosmadulu Uthuruburi** *atoll* Maldives
195 C5 **Maamba** Zambia
138 E6 **Ma'ān** Jordan
171 N3 **Maaninka** Fin.
170 O2 **Maaninkavaara** Fin.
155 F4 **Ma'anshan** China
171 N4 **Maardu** Estonia
139 F4 **Ma'arrat an Nu'mān** Syria
178 D2 **Maarssen** Neth.
179 E3 **Maas** *r.* Neth. *alt.* **Meuse (Belgium/France)**
178 D3 **Maaseik** Belgium
161 J4 **Maasin** Phil.
178 D4 **Maasmechelen** Belgium
178 D3 **Maas-Schwalm-Nette, Naturpark** *nat. park* Neth.
197 H1 **Maasstroom** S. Africa
178 D4 **Maastricht** Neth.
125 G9 **Maatsuyker Group** *is* Australia
136 C6 **Maaza Plateau** Egypt
161 I3 **Mabalacat** Phil.
195 D6 **Mabalane** Moz.
231 G2 **Mabaruma** Guyana
121 F6 **Mabel Creek** Australia
120 D3 **Mabel Downs** Australia
209 I3 **Maberly** Canada
155 B4 **Mabian** China
173 H4 **Mablethorpe** U.K.
197 H2 **Mabopane** S. Africa
195 D6 **Mabote** Moz.
197 E2 **Mabuasehube Game Reserve** *nature res.* Botswana
161 I1 **Mabudis** *i.* Phil.
197 F2 **Mabule** Botswana
197 E2 **Mabutsane** Botswana
232 B7 **Macá, Monte** *mt.* Chile
235 J3 **Macachín** Arg.
121 B5 **Macadam Plains** Australia
234 E3 **Macaé** Brazil
161 J4 **Macajalar Bay** Phil.
125 G6 **Macalister** *r.* Australia
195 D5 **Macaloge** Moz.
203 H3 **MacAlpine Lake** Canada
197 J1 **Macandze** Moz.
155 D6 **Macao** China
231 H3 **Macapá** Brazil
230 C4 **Macará** Ecuador
234 E1 **Macarani** Brazil
233 I4 **Macarena, Cordillera** *mts* Col.
233 L2 **Macareo, Caño** *r.* Venez.
197 J2 **Macarretane** Moz.
125 E7 **Macarthur** Australia
230 C4 **Macas** Ecuador
Macassar Strait Indon. *see* **Selat Makassar**
231 K5 **Macau** Brazil
231 H6 **Macaúba** Brazil
234 D1 **Macaúbas** Brazil
233 I4 **Macaya** *r.* Col.
233 I4 **Macayarí** Col.
173 E4 **Macclesfield** U.K.
118 C4 **Macdonald, Lake** *salt flat* Australia
120 D2 **Macdonald Range** *hills* Australia
118 D4 **Macdonnell Ranges** *mts* Australia
206 B3 **MacDowell Lake** Canada
175 F3 **Macduff** U.K.
183 M2 **Macedo de Cavaleiros** Port.
125 F6 **Macedon** *mt.* Australia
185 I4 **Macedonia** *country* Europe
185 J4 **Macedonia** *reg.* Greece/Macedonia
231 K5 **Maceió** Brazil
192 B4 **Macenta** Guinea
184 E3 **Macerata** Italy
124 B4 **Macfarlane, Lake** *salt flat* Australia
175 I6 **Macgillycuddy's Reeks** *mts* Ireland
148 A3 **Mach** Pak.
230 C4 **Machachi** Ecuador
234 D3 **Machado** Brazil
195 D6 **Machaila** Moz.
194 D4 **Machakos** Kenya
230 C4 **Machala** Ecuador
150 B3 **Machali** China
195 D6 **Machanga** Moz.
123 B5 **Machattie, Lake** *salt flat* Australia
197 J2 **Machatuine** Moz.
178 C5 **Machault** France
155 E4 **Macheng** China
147 H2 **Macherla** India
147 I2 **Machhakund Reservoir** India
221 J2 **Machias** *ME* U.S.A.
220 D3 **Machias** *NY* U.S.A.
221 I1 **Machias** *r.* U.S.A.
147 I2 **Machilipatnam** India
233 I2 **Machiques** Venez.
174 C5 **Machrihanish** U.K.
230 D6 **Machu Picchu** *tourist site* Peru
173 D5 **Machynlleth** U.K.
197 J2 **Macia** Moz.
185 M2 **Măcin** Romania
192 B3 **Macina** Mali
125 I2 **Macintyre** *r.* Australia
125 I2 **Macintyre Brook** *r.* Australia
215 H2 **Mack** U.S.A.
139 G1 **Maçka** Turkey
119 E4 **Mackay** Australia
212 D2 **Mackay** U.S.A.
118 C4 **Mackay, Lake** *salt flat* Australia
205 G2 **MacKay Lake** Canada
123 E4 **Mackenzie** *r.* Australia
204 E3 **Mackenzie** *B.C.* Canada
208 C1 **Mackenzie** *Ont.* Canada
202 E3 **Mackenzie** *r.* Canada
127 L5 **Mackenzie Bay** Antarctica
202 E3 **Mackenzie Bay** Canada
204 F2 **Mackenzie Bison Sanctuary** *nature res.* Canada
202 G2 **Mackenzie King Island** Canada
204 C2 **Mackenzie Mountains** Canada
Mackillop, Lake *salt flat* Australia *see* **Yamma Yamma, Lake**
209 E3 **Mackinac, Straits of** *lake channel* U.S.A.
209 E3 **Mackinac Island** U.S.A.
208 C5 **Mackinaw** *r.* U.S.A.
209 E3 **Mackinaw City** U.S.A.
121 D5 **Mackintosh Range** *hills* Australia
205 H4 **Macklin** Canada
125 J3 **Macksville** Australia
125 J2 **Maclean** Australia
197 H5 **Maclear** S. Africa
125 J3 **Macleay** *r.* Australia
118 B4 **MacLeod, Lake** *dry lake* Australia
204 C2 **Macmillan** *r.* Canada
208 B5 **Macomb** U.S.A.
184 C4 **Macomer** *Sardinia* Italy
182 G3 **Mâcon** France
219 D5 **Macon** *GA* U.S.A.
217 E4 **Macon** *MO* U.S.A.
195 C5 **Macondo** Angola
125 G3 **Macquarie** *r. N.S.W.* Australia
125 G8 **Macquarie** *r. Tas.* Australia
125 I4 **Macquarie, Lake** *b.* Australia
125 F9 **Macquarie Harbour** Australia
135 F7 **Macquarie Island** S. Pacific Ocean
125 G3 **Macquarie Marshes** Australia
125 H4 **Macquarie Mountain** Australia
236 F9 **Macquarie Ridge** *sea feature* S. Pacific Ocean
162 □ **MacRitchie Reservoir** Sing.
127 L5 **Mac. Robertson Land** *reg.* Antarctica
175 J6 **Macroom** Ireland
233 J1 **Macuira, Parque Nacional** *nat. park* Col.
233 I4 **Macuje** Col.
123 A5 **Macumba** Australia
118 D4 **Macumba** *watercourse* Australia
230 D6 **Macusani** Peru
225 F4 **Macuspana** Mex.
224 B2 **Macuzari, Presa** *resr* Mex.
221 I2 **Macwahoc** U.S.A.
138 E6 **Mādabā** Jordan
197 I3 **Madadeni** S. Africa
193 D3 **Madagali** Nigeria
195 E6 **Madagascar** *country* Africa
238 H6 **Madagascar** *i.* Africa
238 H6 **Madagascar Basin** *sea feature* Indian Ocean
238 G7 **Madagascar Ridge** *sea feature* Indian Ocean
146 A4 **Madā'in Şāliḩ** Saudi Arabia
147 H3 **Madakasira** India
193 D2 **Madama** Niger
185 K4 **Madan** Bulg.
147 H3 **Madanapalle** India
119 E2 **Madang** P.N.G.
192 C3 **Madaoua** Niger
149 G5 **Madaripur** Bangl.
209 I3 **Madawaska** Canada
209 I3 **Madawaska** *r.* Canada
221 I1 **Madawaska** U.S.A.
192 A1 **Madeira** *terr.* Atlantic Ocean
231 F5 **Madeira** *r.* Brazil
239 H3 **Madeira, Arquipélago da** *is* Port.
207 H4 **Madeleine, Îles de la** *is* Canada
208 B2 **Madeline Island** U.S.A.
139 G2 **Maden** Turkey
141 I3 **Madeniyet** Kazakh.
222 C3 **Madera** Mex.
214 B3 **Madera** U.S.A.
149 F4 **Madhepura** India
147 I2 **Madhira** India
149 F4 **Madhubani** India
148 D5 **Madhya Pradesh** *state* India
197 F3 **Madibogo** S. Africa
230 E6 **Madidi** *r.* Bol.
124 B2 **Madigan Gulf** *salt flat* Australia
147 G3 **Madikeri** India
197 G2 **Madikwe Game Reserve** *nature res.* S. Africa
142 C5 **Madīnat ash Shamāl**
195 B4 **Madingou** Congo
195 E5 **Madirovalo** Madag.
219 C4 **Madison** *IN* U.S.A.
221 I2 **Madison** *ME* U.S.A.
216 D2 **Madison** *MN* U.S.A.
216 D3 **Madison** *NE* U.S.A.
216 D2 **Madison** *SD* U.S.A.
208 C4 **Madison** *WI* U.S.A.
220 C5 **Madison** *WV* U.S.A.
210 D2 **Madison** *r.* U.S.A.
219 C4 **Madisonville** *KY* U.S.A.
217 E6 **Madisonville** *TX* U.S.A.
163 H4 **Madiun** Indon.
121 C5 **Madley, Mount** *h.* Australia
209 I3 **Madoc** Canada
194 D3 **Mado Gashi** Kenya
171 N4 **Madona** Latvia
148 B4 **Madpura** India
185 L5 **Madra Dağı** *mts* Turkey
Madras India *see* **Chennai**
212 B2 **Madras** U.S.A.
225 E2 **Madre, Laguna** *lag.* Mex.
217 D7 **Madre, Laguna** *lag.* U.S.A.
161 I2 **Madre, Sierra** *mt.* Phil.
225 F4 **Madre de Chiapas, Sierra** *mts* Mex.
230 D6 **Madre de Dios** *r.* Peru
232 A8 **Madre de Dios, Isla** *i.* Chile
225 D4 **Madre del Sur, Sierra** *mts* Mex.
224 B1 **Madre Occidental, Sierra** *mts* Mex.
225 D2 **Madre Oriental, Sierra** *mts* Mex.
161 J4 **Madrid** Phil.
183 O2 **Madrid** Spain

Mangalagiri

161 I4 **Madridejos** Phil.
183 O3 **Madridejos** Spain
147 I2 **Madugula** India
163 H4 **Madura** *i.* Indon.
163 H4 **Madura, Selat** *sea chan.* Indon.
147 H4 **Madurai** India
149 E4 **Madwas** India
148 C2 **Madyan** Pak.
187 H7 **Madzhalis** Russia
159 F6 **Maebashi** Japan
162 A1 **Mae Hong Son** Thai.
162 A1 **Mae Sai** Thai.
162 A1 **Mae Sariang** Thai.
162 A1 **Mae Sot** Thai.
223 I5 **Maestra, Sierra** *mts* Cuba
195 E5 **Maevatanana** Madag.
119 G3 **Maéwo** *i.* Vanuatu
205 I4 **Mafeking** Canada
197 G4 **Mafeteng** Lesotho
125 G6 **Maffra** Australia
195 D4 **Mafia Island** Tanz.
Mafikeng S. Africa *see* **Mahikeng**
195 D4 **Mafinga** Tanz.
235 C4 **Mafra** Brazil
197 I5 **Magabeni** S. Africa
133 Q4 **Magadan** Russia
195 D4 **Magadi** Kenya
221 J2 **Magaguadavic Lake** Canada
197 J1 **Magaiza** Moz.
161 I3 **Magallanes** Phil.
233 I2 **Magangué** Col.
138 D3 **Mağara** Turkey
137 H2 **Magaramkent** Russia
187 H7 **Magas** Russia
161 I2 **Magat** *r.* Phil.
156 B1 **Magdagachi** Russia
235 L2 **Magdalena** Arg.
231 F6 **Magdalena** Bol.
233 I3 **Magdalena** *r.* Col.
222 B2 **Magdalena** Mex.
213 E6 **Magdalena** *r.* Mex.
213 F5 **Magdalena** U.S.A.
224 A2 **Magdalena, Bahía** *b.* Mex.
232 B6 **Magdalena, Isla** *i.* Chile
224 A2 **Magdalena, Isla** *i.* Mex.
161 H5 **Magdaline, Gunung** *mt. Sabah* Malaysia
141 F5 **Magdanly** Turkm.
179 J2 **Magdeburg** Germany
122 E3 **Magdelaine Cays** *atoll* Australia
175 M3 **Magee, Island** *pen.* U.K.
236 E4 **Magellan Seamounts** *sea feature* N. Pacific Ocean
121 B7 **Magenta, Lake** *salt flat* Australia
170 N1 **Magerøya** *i.* Norway
159 B9 **Mage-shima** *i.* Japan
184 C2 **Maggiorasca, Monte** *mt.* Italy
184 C2 **Maggiore, Lake** Italy
Maghâgha Egypt *see* **Maghāghah**
136 C5 **Maghāghah** Egypt
192 A3 **Maghama** Mauritania
175 L3 **Maghera** U.K.
175 L3 **Magherafelt** U.K.
173 E4 **Maghull** U.K.
213 D3 **Magna** U.S.A.
184 F6 **Magna Grande** *mt. Sicily* Italy
127 L5 **Magnet Bay** Antarctica
119 E3 **Magnetic Island** Australia
122 D3 **Magnetic Passage** Australia
170 P1 **Magnetity** Russia
140 D1 **Magnitogorsk** Russia
217 E5 **Magnolia** U.S.A.
156 F1 **Mago** Russia
207 F4 **Magog** Canada
225 E3 **Magozal** Mex.
207 H3 **Magpie** Canada
209 E1 **Magpie** *r.* Canada
207 H3 **Magpie, Lac** *l.* Canada
205 G5 **Magrath** Canada
215 D3 **Magruder Mountain** U.S.A.
192 A3 **Magta' Laḥjar** Mauritania
140 D5 **Magtymguly** Turkm.
195 D4 **Magu** Tanz.
156 E1 **Magu, Khrebet** *mts* Russia
155 B6 **Maguan** China
231 I4 **Maguarinho, Cabo** *c.* Brazil
197 J2 **Magude** Moz.
221 J2 **Magundy** Canada
205 J2 **Maguse Lake** Canada
149 H5 **Magwe** Myanmar
149 H5 **Magyichaung** Myanmar
142 B2 **Mahābād** Iran
147 G2 **Mahabaleshwar** India
149 F4 **Mahabharat Range** *mts* Nepal
195 E6 **Mahabo** Madag.
147 G2 **Mahad** India
148 D5 **Mahadeo Hills** India
194 D3 **Mahagi** Dem. Rep. Congo
195 E5 **Mahajamba** *r.* Madag.
148 C3 **Mahajan** India
195 E5 **Mahajanga** Madag.
163 H2 **Mahakam** *r.* Indon.
195 C6 **Mahalapye** Botswana
195 E5 **Mahalevona** Madag.
142 C3 **Maḩallāt** Iran
148 D3 **Maham** India
143 E4 **Māhān** Iran
147 J1 **Mahanadi** *r.* India
195 E5 **Mahanoro** Madag.
148 C5 **Maharashtra** *state* India
147 I1 **Mahasamund** India
162 B1 **Maha Sarakham** Thai.
195 E6 **Mahatalaky** Madag.
195 E5 **Mahavanona** Madag.
195 E5 **Mahavavy** *r.* Madag.
147 I5 **Mahaweli Ganga** *r.* Sri Lanka
162 C1 **Mahaxai** Laos
147 I2 **Mahbubabad** India
147 H2 **Mahbubnagar** India
142 D5 **Maḩḑah** Oman
231 G2 **Mahdia** Guyana
184 D7 **Mahdia** Tunisia
137 E3 **Mahdūm** Syria
191 I5 **Mahé** *i.* Seychelles
147 J2 **Mahendragiri** *mt.* India
148 C5 **Mahesana** India
148 C5 **Maheshwar** India
148 C5 **Mahi** *r.* India
143 E4 **Māhī** *watercourse* Iran
126 F3 **Mahia Peninsula** N.Z.
197 F2 **Mahikeng** S. Africa
187 D4 **Mahilyow** Belarus
143 F5 **Māhīrūd** Iran
147 I5 **Mahiyangana** Sri Lanka
197 I4 **Mahlabatini** S. Africa
179 J2 **Mahlsdorf** Germany
Maḩmūd-e 'Erāqī Afgh. *see* **Maḩmūd-e Rāqī**
143 H3 **Maḩmūd-e Rāqī** Afgh.
139 L4 **Māhnīān** Iran
216 D2 **Mahnomen** U.S.A.
148 D4 **Mahoba** India
Mahón Spain *see* **Maó**
220 D4 **Mahoning Creek Lake** U.S.A.
149 H5 **Mahudaung** *mts* Myanmar
148 B5 **Mahuva** India
185 L4 **Mahya Dağı** *mt.* Turkey
142 C3 **Mahyār** Iran
149 H4 **Maibong** India
233 I2 **Maicao** Col.
206 E4 **Maicasagi, Lac** *l.* Canada
155 C6 **Maichen** China
143 H3 **Maīdān Shahr** Afgh.
173 G6 **Maidenhead** U.K.
205 H4 **Maidstone** Canada
173 H6 **Maidstone** U.K.
193 D3 **Maiduguri** Nigeria
233 K3 **Maigualida, Sierra** *mts* Venez.
175 J5 **Maigue** *r.* Ireland
149 E4 **Maihar** India
154 C3 **Maiji Shan** *mt.* China
149 E5 **Maikala Range** *hills* India
195 C4 **Maiko, Parc National de la** *nat. park* Dem. Rep. Congo
149 E3 **Mailani** India
143 G3 **Maīmanah** Afgh.
179 H5 **Main** *r.* Germany
175 L3 **Main** *r.* U.K.
207 I3 **Main Brook** Canada
209 F3 **Main Channel** *lake channel* Canada
195 B4 **Mai-Ndombe, Lac** *l.* Dem. Rep. Congo
179 J5 **Main-Donau-Kanal** *canal* Germany
Maindong China *see* **Coqên**
209 I4 **Main Duck Island** Canada
221 I2 **Maine** *state* U.S.A.
193 D3 **Maïné-Soroa** Niger
162 A2 **Maingy Island** Myanmar
179 H5 **Mainhardt** Germany
161 J4 **Mainit** Phil.
161 J4 **Mainit, Lake** Phil.
174 E1 **Mainland** *i. Scotland* U.K.
174 □ **Mainland** *i. Scotland* U.K.
179 J4 **Mainleus** Germany
120 F2 **Mainoru** Australia
149 E5 **Mainpat** *reg.* India
148 D4 **Mainpuri** India
125 J1 **Main Range National Park** Australia
195 E5 **Maintirano** Madag.
179 G4 **Mainz** Germany
192 □ **Maio** *i.* Cape Verde
235 I2 **Maipó, Volcán** *vol.* Chile
235 L3 **Maipú** *Buenos Aires* Arg.
235 I2 **Maipú** *Mendoza* Arg.
233 K2 **Maiquetía** Venez.
149 G5 **Maiskhal Island** Bangl.
195 C6 **Maitengwe** Botswana
125 I4 **Maitland** *N.S.W.* Australia
124 B5 **Maitland** *S.A.* Australia
121 B4 **Maitland** *r.* Australia
127 K3 **Maitri** *research stn* Antarctica
120 E3 **Maiyu, Mount** *h.* Australia
224 I5 **Maíz, Islas del** Nicaragua
149 G3 **Maizhokunggar** China
159 D7 **Maizuru** Japan
147 H2 **Majalgaon** India
233 L4 **Majari** *r.* Brazil
138 E5 **Majdel Aanjar** *tourist site* Lebanon
163 I3 **Majene** Indon.
142 C6 **Majḩūd** *well* Saudi Arabia
194 D3 **Majī** Eth.
154 E2 **Majia He** *r.* China
155 D6 **Majiang** China
156 B2 **Majiazi** China
143 F3 **Majnābād** Iran
183 R3 **Major, Puig** *mt.* Spain
183 R3 **Majorca** *i.* Spain
149 H4 **Majuli Island** India
197 G4 **Majwemasweu** S. Africa
195 B4 **Makabana** Congo
214 □[1] **Mākaha** U.S.A.
151 D7 **Makale** Indon.
149 F4 **Makalu** *mt.* China
195 C4 **Makamba** Burundi
141 J3 **Makanshy** Kazakh.
214 □[1] **Makapu'u Head** U.S.A.
156 F2 **Makarov** Russia
240 M1 **Makarov Basin** *sea feature* Arctic Ocean
185 G3 **Makarska** Croatia
186 I2 **Makar-Yb** Russia
169 O4 **Makar'yev** Russia
163 I4 **Makassar** Indon.
140 C3 **Makat** Kazakh.
197 J3 **Makatini Flats** *lowland* S. Africa
192 A4 **Makeni** Sierra Leone
195 C6 **Makgadikgadi** *depr.* Botswana
187 H7 **Makhachkala** Russia
197 H1 **Makhado** S. Africa
140 B3 **Makhambet** Kazakh.
139 I4 **Makhmūr/Mexmûr** Iraq
141 G1 **Makhorovka** Kazakh.
195 D4 **Makindu** Kenya
141 G1 **Makinsk** Kazakh.
119 G3 **Makira** *i.* Solomon Is
187 F5 **Makiyivka** Ukr.
Makkah Saudi Arabia *see* **Mecca**
207 I2 **Makkovik** Canada
207 I2 **Makkovik, Cape** Canada
178 D1 **Makkum** Neth.
185 I1 **Makó** Hungary
194 B3 **Makokou** Gabon
195 D4 **Makongolosi** Tanz.
197 E2 **Makopong** Botswana
195 B4 **Makotipoko** Congo
143 F5 **Makran** *reg.* Iran/Pak.
148 C4 **Makrana** India
143 F5 **Makran Coast Range** *mts* Pak.
147 I2 **Makri** India
185 K6 **Makronisos** *i.* Greece
186 E3 **Maksatikha** Russia
158 E1 **Maksimovka** Russia
143 F4 **Maksotag** Iran
142 B2 **Mākū** Iran
149 H4 **Makum** India
195 D4 **Makumbako** Tanz.
195 D5 **Makunguwiro** Tanz.
159 B9 **Makurazaki** Japan
192 C4 **Makurdi** Nigeria
142 D4 **Makūyeh** Iran
197 F3 **Makwassie** S. Africa
170 L2 **Malå** Sweden
224 I7 **Mala, Punta** *pt* Panama
161 J5 **Malabang** Phil.
147 G3 **Malabar Coast** India
192 C4 **Malabo** Equat. Guinea
161 H4 **Malabuñgan** Phil.
163 E2 **Malacca, Strait of** Indon./Malaysia
213 D3 **Malad City** U.S.A.
187 C4 **Maladzyechna** Belarus
183 N4 **Málaga** Spain
221 F5 **Malaga** *NJ* U.S.A.
213 F5 **Malaga** *NM* U.S.A.
175 J3 **Málainn Mhóir** Ireland
119 G2 **Malaita** *i.* Solomon Is
193 F4 **Malakal** South Sudan
119 G3 **Malakula** *i.* Vanuatu
148 C2 **Malakwal** Pak.
151 E7 **Malamala** Indon.
143 G5 **Malan, Ras** *pt* Pak.
163 H4 **Malang** Indon.
195 B4 **Malanje** Angola
235 I1 **Malanzán, Sierra de** *mts* Arg.
147 H4 **Malappuram** India
171 L4 **Mälaren** *l.* Sweden
235 I2 **Malargüe** Arg.
209 H1 **Malartic** Canada
209 H1 **Malartic, Lac** *l.* Canada
204 A3 **Malaspina Glacier** U.S.A.
139 G2 **Malatya** Turkey
148 C3 **Malaut** India
139 K5 **Malāvī** Iran
161 H5 **Malawali** *i. Sabah* Malaysia
195 D5 **Malawi** *country* Africa
Malawi, Lake Africa *see* **Nyasa, Lake**
186 E3 **Malaya Vishera** Russia
161 J4 **Malaybalay** Phil.
142 C3 **Malāyer** Iran
131 F6 **Malay Peninsula** Asia
122 E3 **Malay Reef** Australia
141 I3 **Malaysary** Kazakh.
163 G2 **Malaysia** *country* Asia
163 B2 **Malaysia, Peninsular** Malaysia
139 I2 **Malazgirt** Turkey
123 C4 **Malbon** Australia
177 I3 **Malbork** Poland
179 E5 **Malborn** Germany
179 K1 **Malchin** Germany
179 K1 **Malchiner See** *l.* Germany
121 C6 **Malcolm (abandoned)** Australia
121 C7 **Malcolm, Point** Australia
149 G4 **Maldah** India
178 B3 **Maldegem** Belgium
217 F4 **Malden** U.S.A.
117 I4 **Malden Island** Kiribati
130 C6 **Maldives** *country* Indian Ocean
173 H6 **Maldon** U.K.
235 L2 **Maldonado** Uruguay
130 C6 **Male** Maldives
185 J6 **Maleas, Akrotirio** *pt* Greece
135 F6 **Male Atholhu** Maldives
197 F4 **Malebogo** S. Africa
147 H2 **Malegaon** *Maharashtra* India
148 C5 **Malegaon** *Maharashtra* India
137 I4 **Malek, Chāh-e** *well* Iran
139 K5 **Malek 'Alī** Iran
139 K3 **Malekān** Iran
177 H6 **Malé Karpaty** *hills* Slovakia
142 C4 **Māl-e Khalīfeh** Iran
195 B4 **Malele** Dem. Rep. Congo
195 D5 **Malema** Moz.
148 C3 **Maler Kotla** India
187 H7 **Malgobek** Russia
170 L2 **Malgomaj** *l.* Sweden
142 B5 **Malham** Saudi Arabia
213 C3 **Malheur Lake** U.S.A.
192 B3 **Mali** *country* Africa
195 C4 **Mali** Dem. Rep. Congo
192 A3 **Mali** Guinea
154 C3 **Malian He** *r.* China
144 I3 **Malianjing** China
148 C4 **Malihabad** India
143 F4 **Malik Naro** *mt.* Pak.
162 A2 **Mali Kyun** *i.* Myanmar
151 E7 **Malili** Indon.
163 G4 **Malimping** Indon.
195 E4 **Malindi** Kenya
175 K2 **Malin Head** Ireland
Malin More Ireland *see* **Málainn Mhóir**
141 G2 **Malinovka** Kazakh.
158 D2 **Malinovka** *r.* Russia
141 I2 **Malinovoye Ozero** Russia
155 B6 **Malipo** China
184 F2 **Mali Raginac** *mt.* Croatia
161 J5 **Malita** Phil.
162 A3 **Maliwun** Myanmar
148 B5 **Maliya** India
137 G2 **Malka** *r.* Russia
147 I2 **Malkangiri** India
148 D5 **Malkapur** India
187 C7 **Malkara** Turkey
177 M4 **Mal'kavichy** Belarus
185 L4 **Malko Tarnovo** Bulg.
125 H6 **Mallacoota** Australia
125 H6 **Mallacoota Inlet** *b.* Australia
174 C4 **Mallaig** U.K.
124 C5 **Mallala** Australia
136 C6 **Mallawī** Egypt
125 E5 **Mallee Cliffs National Park** Australia
205 J2 **Mallery Lake** Canada
Mallorca *i.* Spain *see* **Majorca**
175 J5 **Mallow** Ireland
121 D4 **Mallowa Well** Australia
173 D5 **Mallwyd** U.K.
170 J2 **Malm** Norway
170 M2 **Malmberget** Sweden
179 E4 **Malmedy** Belgium
196 C6 **Malmesbury** S. Africa
173 E6 **Malmesbury** U.K.
171 K5 **Malmö** Sweden
186 I3 **Malmyzh** Russia
119 G3 **Malo** *i.* Vanuatu
117 G2 **Maloelap** *i.* Marshall Is
161 I3 **Malolos** Phil.
221 F2 **Malone** U.S.A.
155 B5 **Malong** China
195 C5 **Malonga** Dem. Rep. Congo
186 F2 **Maloshuyka** Russia
171 I3 **Måløy** Norway
187 F4 **Maloyaroslavets** Russia
169 P2 **Malozemel'skaya Tundra** *lowland* Russia
230 B3 **Malpelo, Isla de** *i.* Col.
147 G3 **Malprabha** *r.* India
184 F7 **Malta** *country* Europe
171 N4 **Malta** Latvia
212 F1 **Malta** U.S.A.
184 F6 **Malta Channel** Italy/Malta
195 B6 **Maltahöhe** Namibia
173 F4 **Maltby** U.K.
173 H4 **Maltby le Marsh** U.K.
172 G3 **Malton** U.K.
Maluku *is* Indon. *see* **Moluccas**
151 E7 **Maluku, Laut** *sea* Indon.
171 K3 **Malung** Sweden
197 H4 **Maluti Mountains** Lesotho
119 G2 **Malu'u** Solomon Is
147 G2 **Malvan** India
217 E5 **Malvern** U.S.A.
187 D5 **Malyn** Ukr.
133 R3 **Malyy Anyuy** *r.* Russia
Malyy Balkhan, Khrebet *h.* Turkm. *see* **Kiçi Balkan Daglary**
187 H6 **Malyye Derbety** Russia
140 B1 **Malyy Irgiz** *r.* Russia
Malyy Kavkaz *mts* Asia *see* **Lesser Caucasus**
133 P2 **Malyy Lyakhovskiy, Ostrov** *i.* Russia
169 Q4 **Mamadysh** Russia
197 H3 **Mamafubedu** S. Africa
147 I3 **Mamallapuram** India
161 H5 **Mambahenauhan** *i.* Phil.
161 J4 **Mambajao** Phil.
194 C3 **Mambasa** Dem. Rep. Congo
194 B3 **Mambéré** *r.* C.A.R.
161 I3 **Mamburao** Phil.
197 H2 **Mamelodi** S. Africa
192 C4 **Mamfe** Cameroon
141 F1 **Mamlyutka** Kazakh.
215 G5 **Mammoth** U.S.A.
219 C4 **Mammoth Cave National Park** U.S.A.
214 C3 **Mammoth Lakes** U.S.A.
230 E6 **Mamoré** *r.* Bol./Brazil
192 A3 **Mamou** Guinea
195 E5 **Mampikony** Madag.
192 B4 **Mampong** Ghana
235 H3 **Mamuil Malal, Paso** *pass* Arg./Chile
163 I3 **Mamuju** Indon.
196 D1 **Mamuno** Botswana
140 D2 **Mamyt** Kazakh.
192 B4 **Man** Côte d'Ivoire
172 C3 **Man, Isle of** *terr.* Irish Sea
233 I3 **Manacacias** *r.* Col.
231 F4 **Manacapuru** Brazil
183 R3 **Manacor** Spain
151 E6 **Manado** Indon.
224 H5 **Managua** Nicaragua
224 H5 **Managua, Lago de** *l.* Nicaragua
195 E6 **Manakara** Madag.
126 D5 **Manakau** *mt.* N.Z.
142 C5 **Manama** Bahrain
119 E2 **Manam Island** P.N.G.
233 L2 **Manamo, Caño** *r.* Venez.
214 □[1] **Mānana** *i.* U.S.A.
195 E6 **Mananara** *r.* Madag.
195 E5 **Mananara Avaratra** Madag.
195 E5 **Mananara Nord, Parc National de** *nat. park* Madag.
125 E5 **Manangatang** Australia
122 B3 **Manangoora** Australia
195 E6 **Mananjary** Madag.
147 H4 **Mananthavady** India
148 D3 **Mana Pass** India
233 K2 **Manapire** *r.* Venez.
126 A6 **Manapouri, Lake** N.Z.
195 E5 **Manarantsandry** Madag.
149 G4 **Manas** *r.* Bhutan
144 G2 **Manas He** *r.* China
150 A2 **Manas Hu** *l.* China
149 F3 **Manaslu** *mt.* Nepal
149 G4 **Manas National Park** *nature res.* Bhutan
221 E5 **Manassas** U.S.A.
151 E7 **Manatuto** East Timor
152 F8 **Man-aung Kyun** Myanmar
231 F4 **Manaus** Brazil
138 C3 **Manavgat** Turkey
126 E4 **Manawatu** *r.* N.Z.
161 J5 **Manay** Phil.
139 F3 **Manbij** Syria
173 H4 **Manby** U.K.
209 E3 **Mancelona** U.S.A.
173 E4 **Manchester** U.K.
214 A2 **Manchester** *CA* U.S.A.
221 G4 **Manchester** *CT* U.S.A.
208 B4 **Manchester** *IA* U.S.A.
220 B6 **Manchester** *KY* U.S.A.
209 E4 **Manchester** *MI* U.S.A.
221 H3 **Manchester** *NH* U.S.A.
220 B5 **Manchester** *OH* U.S.A.
219 C5 **Manchester** *TN* U.S.A.
221 G3 **Manchester** *VT* U.S.A.
148 A4 **Manchhar Lake** Pak.
Manchurian Plain *plain* China *see* **Dongbei Pingyuan**
139 F2 **Mancılık** Turkey
215 H3 **Mancos** U.S.A.
215 H3 **Mancos** *r.* U.S.A.
143 F5 **Mand** Pak.
142 D4 **Mand, Rūd-e** *r.* Iran
193 D4 **Manda, Parc National de** *nat. park* Chad
195 E6 **Mandabe** Madag.
163 B2 **Mandah** Indon.
162 □ **Mandai** Sing.
148 C4 **Mandal** India
171 I4 **Mandal** Norway
151 G7 **Mandala, Puncak** *mt.* Indon.
151 B4 **Mandalay** Myanmar
150 C2 **Mandalgovĭ** Mongolia
139 J5 **Mandalī** Iraq
153 H3 **Mandal-Ovoo** Mongolia
154 D1 **Mandalt** China
216 C2 **Mandan** U.S.A.
161 I3 **Mandaon** Phil.
193 D3 **Mandara Mountains** Cameroon/Nigeria
184 C5 **Mandas** *Sardinia* Italy
194 E3 **Mandera** Kenya
215 F2 **Manderfield** U.S.A.
179 E4 **Manderscheid** Germany
223 I5 **Mandeville** Jamaica
126 B6 **Mandeville** N.Z.
148 B4 **Mandha** India
145 E5 **Mandi** India
192 B3 **Mandiana** Guinea
162 B4 **Mandi Angin, Gunung** *mt.* Malaysia
195 D5 **Mandié** Moz.
195 D5 **Mandimba** Moz.
197 I4 **Mandini** S. Africa
149 F5 **Mandira Dam** India
149 E5 **Mandla** India
195 E5 **Mandritsara** Madag.
148 C4 **Mandsaur** India
161 H6 **Mandul** *i.* Indon.
118 B5 **Mandurah** Australia
185 G4 **Manduria** Italy
148 B5 **Mandvi** *Gujarat* India
148 C5 **Mandvi** *Gujarat* India
147 H3 **Mandya** India
140 E5 **Māne** Turkm.
147 H2 **Maner** *r.* India
184 D2 **Manerbio** Italy
139 K5 **Manesht Kūh** *mt.* Iran
177 L5 **Manevychi** Ukr.
184 F4 **Manfredonia** Italy
185 G4 **Manfredonia, Golfo di** *g.* Italy
234 D1 **Manga** Brazil
192 B3 **Manga** Burkina Faso
195 B4 **Mangai** Dem. Rep. Congo
117 I5 **Mangaia** *i.* Cook Is
126 E3 **Mangakino** N.Z.
147 I2 **Mangalagiri** India

Mehamn

142 D4 **Marvast** Iran
182 F4 **Marvejols** France
215 G2 **Marvine, Mount** U.S.A.
205 G4 **Marwayne** Canada
120 E2 **Mary** *r.* Australia
143 F2 **Mary** Turkm.
119 F4 **Maryborough** *Qld* Australia
125 E6 **Maryborough** *Vic.* Australia
196 H3 **Marydale** S. Africa
187 I4 **Mar'yevka** Russia
205 H2 **Mary Frances Lake** Canada
221 E5 **Maryland** *state* U.S.A.
172 D3 **Maryport** U.K.
207 I3 **Mary's Harbour** Canada
207 J4 **Marystown** Canada
215 F2 **Marysvale** U.S.A.
207 G4 **Marysville** Canada
214 B2 **Marysville** *CA* U.S.A.
217 D4 **Marysville** *KS* U.S.A.
220 B4 **Marysville** *OH* U.S.A.
121 F5 **Maryvale** *N.T.* Australia
122 D3 **Maryvale** *Qld* Australia
216 E3 **Maryville** *MO* U.S.A.
219 C5 **Maryville** *TN* U.S.A.
179 K2 **Marzahna** Germany
224 H6 **Masachapa** Nicaragua
138 E6 **Masada** *tourist site* Israel
142 D4 **Masāhūn, Kūh-e** *mt.* Iran
195 D4 **Masaka** Uganda
197 G5 **Masakhane** S. Africa
139 L2 **Masallı** Azer.
118 C2 **Masamba** Indon.
160 E6 **Masan** S. Korea
221 I1 **Masardis** U.S.A.
195 D5 **Masasi** Tanz.
231 F7 **Masavi** Bol.
224 H6 **Masaya** Nicaragua
161 I3 **Masbate** Phil.
161 I4 **Masbate** *i.* Phil.
192 C1 **Mascara** Alg.
238 H6 **Mascarene Basin** *sea feature* Indian Ocean
238 H6 **Mascarene Plain** *sea feature* Indian Ocean
238 H5 **Mascarene Ridge** *sea feature* Indian Ocean
221 G2 **Mascouche** Canada
197 G4 **Maseru** Lesotho
197 H4 **Mashai** Lesotho
155 C6 **Mashan** China
148 D2 **Masherbrum** *mt.* Pak.
143 E2 **Mashhad** Iran
148 C4 **Mashi** *r.* India
139 K2 **Mashīrān** Iran
197 I2 **Mashishing** S. Africa
143 F4 **Mashkel, Hamun-i-** *salt flat* Pak.
143 F5 **Mashkel, Rudi-i** *r.* Pak.
143 F4 **Mashki Chah** Pak.
143 F5 **Māshkīd, Rūdkhāneh-ye** *r.* Iran
170 M1 **Masi** Norway
224 B2 **Masiáca** Mex.
197 G5 **Masibambane** S. Africa
197 G4 **Masilo** S. Africa
194 D3 **Masindi** Uganda
161 H3 **Masinloc** Phil.
197 E5 **Masinyusane** S. Africa
147 E5 **Maşīrah, Jazīrat** *i.* Oman
139 J1 **Masis** Armenia
142 C4 **Masjed Soleymān** Iran
175 I4 **Mask, Lough** *l.* Ireland
139 G3 **Maskanah** Syria
143 E5 **Maskūtān** Iran
143 G4 **Maslti** Pak.
195 E5 **Masoala, Parc National** Madag.
195 F5 **Masoala, Tanjona** *c.* Madag.
209 E4 **Mason** *MI* U.S.A.
214 C2 **Mason** *NV* U.S.A.
217 D6 **Mason** *TX* U.S.A.
121 B5 **Mason, Lake** *salt flat* Australia
126 A7 **Mason Bay** N.Z.
216 E3 **Mason City** *IA* U.S.A.
208 C5 **Mason City** *IL* U.S.A.
220 D5 **Masontown** U.S.A.
Masqaţ Oman *see* **Muscat**
184 D2 **Massa** Italy
221 G3 **Massachusetts** *state* U.S.A.
221 H3 **Massachusetts Bay** U.S.A.
215 H1 **Massadona** U.S.A.
185 G4 **Massafra** Italy
193 D3 **Massakory** Chad
184 D3 **Massa Marittima** Italy
195 D6 **Massangena** Moz.
195 B4 **Massango** Angola
194 D2 **Massawa** Eritrea
221 G2 **Massawippi, Lac** *l.* Canada
221 F2 **Massena** U.S.A.
193 D3 **Massenya** Chad
204 C4 **Masset** Canada
209 F2 **Massey** Canada
182 F4 **Massif Central** *mts* France
220 C4 **Massillon** U.S.A.
195 D6 **Massinga** Moz.
195 D6 **Massingir** Moz.
197 J1 **Massingir, Barragem de** *resr* Moz.
197 J2 **Massintonto** *r.* Moz./S. Africa
209 J3 **Masson-Angers** Canada
139 L1 **Maştağa** Azer.
141 G5 **Mastchoh** Tajik.
141 G2 **Masteksay** Kazakh.
126 E4 **Masterton** N.Z.
219 E7 **Mastic Point** Bahamas
148 C1 **Mastuj** Pak.
143 G4 **Mastung** Pak.
187 C4 **Masty** Belarus
159 B7 **Masuda** Japan
139 L3 **Māsūleh** Iran
195 D6 **Masvingo** Zimbabwe
139 F4 **Maşyāf** Syria
209 G2 **Matachewan** Canada
224 C1 **Matachic** Mex.
233 K4 **Matacuni** *r.* Venez.
150 D2 **Matad** Mongolia
195 B4 **Matadi** Dem. Rep. Congo
224 H5 **Matagalpa** Nicaragua
206 E4 **Matagami** Canada
206 E4 **Matagami, Lac** *l.* Canada
217 D6 **Matagorda Island** U.S.A.
154 C2 **Mataigou** China
162 C5 **Matak** *i.* Indon.
141 H2 **Matak** Kazakh.
126 F2 **Matakana Island** N.Z.
195 B5 **Matala** Angola
147 I5 **Matale** Sri Lanka
192 A3 **Matam** Senegal
225 D2 **Matamoros** *Coahuila* Mex.
225 E2 **Matamoros** *Tamaulipas* Mex.
161 I5 **Matanal Point** Phil.
195 D4 **Matandu** *r.* Tanz.
207 G4 **Matane** Canada
148 B2 **Matanni** Pak.
223 H4 **Matanzas** Cuba
207 G4 **Matapédia** *r.* Canada
235 H2 **Mataquito** *r.* Chile
147 I5 **Matara** Sri Lanka
163 I4 **Mataram** Indon.
230 D7 **Matarani** Peru
118 D3 **Mataranka** Australia
183 R2 **Mataró** Spain
197 H5 **Matatiele** S. Africa
126 B7 **Mataura** N.Z.
126 B7 **Mataura** *r.* N.Z.
119 J3 **Matā'utu** Wallis and Futuna Is
233 J3 **Mataveni** *r.* Col.
126 F3 **Matawai** N.Z.
144 E2 **Matay** Kazakh.
231 F6 **Mategua** Bol.
225 D3 **Matehuala** Mex.
195 D5 **Matemanga** Tanz.
185 G4 **Matera** Italy
184 C6 **Mateur** Tunisia
206 D4 **Matheson** Canada
217 D6 **Mathis** U.S.A.
125 F5 **Mathoura** Australia
148 D4 **Mathura** India
161 J5 **Mati** Phil.
149 G4 **Matiali** India
155 D5 **Matian** China
Matianxu China *see* **Matian**
148 B4 **Matiari** Pak.
225 F4 **Matías Romero** Mex.
207 G3 **Matimekosh** Canada
209 F2 **Matinenda Lake** Canada
221 I3 **Matinicus Island** U.S.A.
149 G5 **Matla** *r.* India
197 G2 **Matlabas** S. Africa
197 G2 **Matlabas** *r.* S. Africa
148 B4 **Matli** Pak.
173 F4 **Matlock** U.K.
233 K3 **Mato** *r.* Venez.
233 K3 **Mato, Cerro** *mt.* Venez.
234 A1 **Mato Grosso** *state* Brazil
234 A3 **Mato Grosso do Sul** *state* Brazil
197 J2 **Matola** Moz.
183 L2 **Matosinhos** Port.
147 E5 **Maţraḩ** Oman
196 C6 **Matroosberg** *mt.* S. Africa
197 F4 **Matsue** Japan
158 G4 **Matsumae** Japan
159 E6 **Matsumoto** Japan
159 D7 **Matsusaka** Japan
159 C8 **Matsuyama** Japan
206 D4 **Mattagami** *r.* Canada
209 H2 **Mattawa** Canada
221 I2 **Mattawamkeag** U.S.A.
176 C7 **Matterhorn** *mt.* Italy/Switz.
213 D3 **Matterhorn** *mt.* U.S.A.
117 G2 **Matthew Island** S. Pacific Ocean
233 L3 **Matthews Ridge** Guyana
223 J4 **Matthew Town** Bahamas
142 D6 **Maţţī, Sabkhat** *salt pan* Saudi Arabia
219 B4 **Mattoon** U.S.A.
147 I5 **Matugama** Sri Lanka
119 H3 **Matuku** *i.* Fiji
233 L2 **Maturín** Venez.
161 J5 **Matutuang** *i.* Indon.
197 G4 **Matwabeng** S. Africa
149 E4 **Mau** India
149 E4 **Mau Aimma** India
178 B4 **Maubeuge** France
145 I8 **Maubin** Myanmar
183 E5 **Maubourguet** France
174 D5 **Mauchline** U.K.
239 J10 **Maud Seamount** *sea feature* S. Atlantic Ocean
231 G4 **Maués** Brazil
149 E4 **Mauganj** India
214 $\square^2$ **Maui** *i.* U.S.A.
117 I5 **Mauke** *atoll* Cook Is
179 G6 **Maulbronn** Germany
235 H2 **Maule** *admin. reg.* Chile
235 H2 **Maule** *r.* Chile
235 H4 **Maullín** Chile
175 I3 **Maumakeogh** *h.* Ireland
220 B4 **Maumee** U.S.A.
220 B4 **Maumee** *r.* U.S.A.
209 F5 **Maumee Bay** U.S.A.
175 I4 **Maumtrasna** *h.* Ireland
175 I4 **Maumturk Mountains** Ireland
195 C5 **Maun** Botswana
214 $\square^2$ **Mauna Kea** *vol.* U.S.A.
214 $\square^2$ **Mauna Loa** *vol.* U.S.A.
214 $\square^1$ **Maunalua Bay** U.S.A.
149 E4 **Maunath Bhanjan** India
197 G1 **Maunatlala** Botswana
126 E2 **Maungaturoto** N.Z.
149 H5 **Maungdaw** Myanmar
162 A2 **Maungmagan Islands** Myanmar
202 F3 **Maunoir, Lac** *l.* Canada
124 B5 **Maupertuis Bay** Australia
118 D4 **Maurice, Lake** *salt flat* Australia
178 D3 **Maurik** Neth.
192 A3 **Mauritania** *country* Africa
191 I6 **Mauritius** *country* Indian Ocean
208 B4 **Mauston** U.S.A.
233 K4 **Mavaca** *r.* Venez.
195 C5 **Mavinga** Angola
197 G5 **Mavuya** S. Africa
148 D3 **Mawana** India
195 B4 **Mawanga** Dem. Rep. Congo
155 D4 **Ma Wang Dui** *tourist site* China
162 A3 **Mawdaung Pass** Myanmar/Thai.
127 G3 **Mawhai Point** N.Z.
152 G7 **Mawkmai** Myanmar
162 A1 **Mawlamyaing** Myanmar
127 L5 **Mawson** *research stn* Antarctica
127 K5 **Mawson Escarpment** Antarctica
127 I6 **Mawson Peninsula** Antarctica
162 A3 **Maw Taung** *mt.* Myanmar
216 C2 **Max** U.S.A.
225 G3 **Maxcanú** Mex.
184 C5 **Maxia, Punta** *mt. Sardinia* Italy
208 D5 **Maxinkuckee, Lake** U.S.A.
171 M3 **Maxmo** Fin.
209 F2 **Maxton** U.S.A.
141 J5 **Maxüt** China
214 A2 **Maxwell** U.S.A.
175 F4 **May, Isle of** *i.* U.K.
163 G3 **Maya** *i.* Indon.
150 F1 **Maya** *r.* Russia
223 J4 **Mayaguana** *i.* Bahamas
223 K5 **Mayagüez** Puerto Rico
192 C3 **Mayahi** Niger
156 E2 **Mayak** Russia
143 H2 **Mayakovskiy, Qullai** *mt.* Tajik.
141 G4 **Mayakum** Kazakh.
195 B4 **Mayama** Congo
142 D2 **Mayāmey** Iran
225 G4 **Maya Mountains** Belize
155 C5 **Mayang** China
154 B3 **Mayanhe** China
159 F5 **Maya-san** *mt.* Japan
174 D5 **Maybole** U.K.
139 J4 **Maydān Sarāy** Iraq
Maydān Shahr Afgh. *see* **Maīdān Shahr**
125 G9 **Maydena** Australia
179 F4 **Mayen** Germany
182 D2 **Mayenne** France
182 D2 **Mayenne** *r.* France
215 F4 **Mayer** U.S.A.
204 F4 **Mayerthorpe** Canada
126 C5 **Mayfield** N.Z.
219 B4 **Mayfield** U.S.A.
213 F5 **Mayhill** U.S.A.
160 E1 **Mayi He** *r.* China
141 I3 **Maykamys** Kazakh.
141 H2 **Maykayyn** Kazakh.
141 G5 **Maykhura** Tajik.
187 G6 **Maykop** Russia
141 H4 **Mayluu-Suu** Kyrg.
140 E3 **Maylybas** Kazakh.
141 K1 **Mayma** Russia
141 G4 **Maymak** Kazakh.
Maymyo Myanmar *see* **Pyin-U-Lwin**
150 B1 **Mayna** *Respublika Khakasiya* Russia
169 P5 **Mayna** *Ul'yanovskaya Oblast'* Russia
147 G2 **Mayni** India
209 I3 **Maynooth** Canada
204 B2 **Mayo** Canada
161 J5 **Mayo Bay** Phil.
195 B4 **Mayoko** Congo
204 B2 **Mayo Lake** Canada
161 I3 **Mayon** *vol.* Phil.
235 J3 **Mayor Buratovich** Arg.
126 F2 **Mayor Island** N.Z.
232 D1 **Mayor Pablo Lagerenza** Para.
195 E5 **Mayotte** *terr.* Africa
161 I2 **Mayraira Point** Phil.
150 E1 **Mayskiy** *Amurskaya Oblast'* Russia
137 G2 **Mayskiy** *Kabardino-Balkarskaya Respublika* Russia
220 B5 **Maysville** U.S.A.
195 B4 **Mayumba** Gabon
149 E3 **Mayum La** *pass* China
147 H4 **Mayuram** India
209 F4 **Mayville** *MI* U.S.A.
216 D2 **Mayville** *ND* U.S.A.
220 D3 **Mayville** *NY* U.S.A.
208 C4 **Mayville** *WI* U.S.A.
216 C3 **Maywood** U.S.A.
235 J3 **Maza** Arg.
186 F3 **Maza** Russia
195 C5 **Mazabuka** Zambia
231 H4 **Mazagão** Brazil
183 F5 **Mazamet** France
148 D1 **Mazar** China
143 G3 **Mazār, Kōh-e** *mt.* Afgh.
184 E6 **Mazara del Vallo** *Sicily* Italy
143 G2 **Mazār-e Sharīf** Afgh.
233 L3 **Mazaruni** *r.* Guyana
224 B1 **Mazatán** Mex.
225 G5 **Mazatenango** Guat.
224 C3 **Mazatlán** Mex.
215 G4 **Mazatzal Peak** U.S.A.
142 C3 **Mazdaj** Iran
143 F2 **Mazdāvand** Iran
171 M4 **Mažeikiai** Lith.
139 G2 **Mazgirt** Turkey
142 A5 **Maẕhūr, 'Irq al** *des.* Saudi Arabia
171 M4 **Mazirbe** Latvia
195 D4 **Mazomora** Tanz.
144 I3 **Mazongshan** China
177 J4 **Mazowiecka, Nizina** *lowland* Poland
139 L3 **Mazr'eh** Iran
139 L5 **Māzū** Iran
155 F5 **Mazu Dao** *i.* Taiwan
195 C6 **Mazunga** Zimbabwe
187 D4 **Mazyr** Belarus
197 I3 **Mbabane** Swaziland
192 B4 **Mbahiakro** Côte d'Ivoire
194 B3 **Mbaïki** C.A.R.
217 D4 **Mbala** Zambia
194 D3 **Mbale** Uganda
193 D4 **Mbalmayo** Cameroon
195 B4 **Mbandaka** Dem. Rep. Congo
192 C4 **Mbanga** Cameroon
195 B4 **M'banza Congo** Angola
195 D4 **Mbarara** Uganda
194 C3 **Mbari** *r.* C.A.R.
197 J3 **Mbaswana** S. Africa
193 D4 **Mbengwi** Cameroon
195 D4 **Mbeya** Tanz.
197 H6 **Mbhashe** *r.* S. Africa
195 D5 **Mbinga** Tanz.
195 D6 **Mbizi** Zimbabwe
197 I2 **Mbombela** S. Africa
194 B3 **Mbomo** Congo
193 D4 **Mbouda** Cameroon
192 A3 **Mbour** Senegal
192 A3 **Mbout** Mauritania
195 D4 **Mbozi** Tanz.
195 C4 **Mbuji-Mayi** Dem. Rep. Congo
195 D4 **Mbulu** Tanz.
195 D4 **Mbuyuni** Tanz.
221 J2 **McAdam** Canada
217 E5 **McAlester** U.S.A.
221 E4 **McAlevys Fort** U.S.A.
125 H5 **McAlister** *mt.* Australia
217 D7 **McAllen** U.S.A.
122 B2 **McArthur** *r.* Australia
220 B5 **McArthur** U.S.A.
209 I3 **McArthur Mills** Canada
204 E4 **McBride** Canada
212 C2 **McCall** U.S.A.
217 C6 **McCamey** U.S.A.
213 D3 **McCammon** U.S.A.
204 C4 **McCauley Island** Canada
203 H2 **McClintock Channel** Canada
120 D3 **McClintock Range** *hills* Australia
214 B3 **McClure, Lake** U.S.A.
202 F2 **McClure Strait** Canada
217 F6 **McComb** U.S.A.
216 C3 **McConaughy, Lake** U.S.A.
220 C5 **McConnelsville** U.S.A.
216 C3 **McCook** U.S.A.
205 J4 **McCreary** Canada
215 E4 **McCullough Range** *mts* U.S.A.
204 D3 **McDame (abandoned)** Canada
213 C3 **McDermitt** U.S.A.
238 I8 **McDonald Islands** Indian Ocean
212 D2 **McDonald Peak** U.S.A.
124 C2 **McDonnell Creek** *watercourse* Australia
196 B4 **McDougall's Bay** S. Africa
215 G5 **McDowell Peak** U.S.A.
214 C4 **McFarland** U.S.A.
205 H3 **McFarlane** *r.* Canada
215 E2 **McGill** U.S.A.
202 C3 **McGrath** U.S.A.
204 E4 **McGregor** *r.* Canada
196 C6 **McGregor** S. Africa
208 A2 **McGregor** U.S.A.
209 G2 **McGregor Bay** Canada
123 C5 **McGregor Range** *hills* Australia
212 D2 **McGuire, Mount** U.S.A.
195 D4 **Mchinga** Tanz.
122 C2 **McIlwraith Range** *hills* Australia
221 G2 **McIndoe Falls** U.S.A.
216 C2 **McIntosh** U.S.A.
121 C4 **McKay Range** *hills* Australia
119 I2 **McKean** *i.* Kiribati
220 A6 **McKee** U.S.A.
220 D4 **McKeesport** U.S.A.
221 F3 **McKeever** U.S.A.
219 B4 **McKenzie** U.S.A.
123 C4 **McKinlay** *r.* Australia
202 C3 **McKinley, Mount** U.S.A.
217 D5 **McKinney** U.S.A.
214 C4 **McKittrick** U.S.A.
216 C2 **McLaughlin** U.S.A.
204 F3 **McLennan** Canada
204 F4 **McLeod** *r.* Canada
204 E3 **McLeod Lake** Canada
213 B3 **McLoughlin, Mount** U.S.A.
209 E2 **McMillan** U.S.A.
212 B2 **McMinnville** *OR* U.S.A.
219 C5 **McMinnville** *TN* U.S.A.
127 I5 **McMurdo** *research stn* Antarctica
215 H4 **McNary** U.S.A.
204 F4 **McNaughton Lake** Canada
215 H6 **McNeal** U.S.A.
217 D4 **McPherson** U.S.A.
125 J2 **McPherson Range** *mts* Australia
204 B2 **McQuesten** *r.* Canada
219 D5 **McRae** U.S.A.
204 E1 **McVicar Arm** *b.* Canada
197 G6 **Mdantsane** S. Africa
184 B6 **M'Daourouch** Alg.
163 D2 **M'Đrăk** Vietnam
162 C1 **Mê, Hon** *i.* Vietnam
215 E3 **Mead, Lake** *resr* U.S.A.
217 C4 **Meade** U.S.A.
121 A5 **Meadow** Australia
205 H4 **Meadow Lake** Canada
205 H4 **Meadow Lake Provincial Park** Canada
215 E3 **Meadow Valley Wash** *r.* U.S.A.
220 C4 **Meadville** U.S.A.
209 G3 **Meaford** Canada
158 I3 **Meaken-dake** *vol.* Japan
174 A2 **Mealasta Island** U.K.
183 L2 **Mealhada** Port.
174 D4 **Meall a' Bhuiridh** *mt.* U.K.
207 I3 **Mealy Mountains** Canada
125 H1 **Meandarra** Australia
204 F3 **Meander River** Canada
161 J5 **Meares** *i.* Indon.
182 F2 **Meaux** France
195 B4 **Mebridege** *r.* Angola
146 A5 **Mecca** Saudi Arabia
221 H2 **Mechanic Falls** U.S.A.
220 B4 **Mechanicsburg** U.S.A.
208 B5 **Mechanicsville** U.S.A.
178 C3 **Mechelen** Belgium
178 D4 **Mechelen** Neth.
192 B1 **Mecheria** Alg.
179 E4 **Mechernich** Germany
138 E1 **Mecitözü** Turkey
179 F4 **Meckenheim** Germany
176 E3 **Mecklenburger Bucht** *b.* Germany
179 J1 **Mecklenburgische Seenplatte** *reg.* Germany
179 K1 **Mecklenburg-Vorpommern** *land* Germany
195 D5 **Mecula** Moz.
120 C3 **Meda** *r.* Australia
183 M2 **Meda** Port.
147 H2 **Medak** India
163 E2 **Medan** Indon.
235 J3 **Médanos** Arg.
232 C7 **Medanosa, Punta** *pt* Arg.
147 I4 **Medawachchiya** Sri Lanka
147 H2 **Medchal** India
221 J2 **Meddybemps Lake** U.S.A.
183 R4 **Médéa** Alg.
179 G3 **Medebach** Germany
233 I3 **Medellín** Col.
173 F4 **Meden** *r.* U.K.
193 D1 **Medenine** Tunisia
192 A3 **Mederdra** Mauritania
213 B3 **Medford** *OR* U.S.A.
208 B3 **Medford** *WI* U.S.A.
221 F5 **Medford Farms** U.S.A.
185 M2 **Medgidia** Romania
208 B5 **Media** U.S.A.
235 I2 **Media Luna** Arg.
177 L7 **Mediaş** Romania
212 C2 **Medical Lake** U.S.A.
213 F3 **Medicine Bow** U.S.A.
213 F3 **Medicine Bow Mountains** U.S.A.
213 F3 **Medicine Bow Peak** U.S.A.
205 G4 **Medicine Hat** Canada
217 D4 **Medicine Lodge** U.S.A.
234 E2 **Medina** Brazil
146 A5 **Medina** Saudi Arabia
220 D3 **Medina** *NY* U.S.A.
220 C4 **Medina** *OH* U.S.A.
183 O2 **Medinaceli** Spain
183 N2 **Medina del Campo** Spain
183 N2 **Medina de Rioseco** Spain
149 F5 **Medinipur** India
166 F5 **Mediterranean Sea** Africa/Europe
184 B6 **Medjerda, Monts de la** *mts* Alg.
140 D2 **Mednogorsk** Russia
182 D4 **Médoc** *reg.* France
152 G6 **Mêdog** China
186 H3 **Medvedevo** Russia
187 H5 **Medveditsa** *r.* Russia
184 F2 **Medvednica** *mts* Croatia
133 R2 **Medvezh'i, Ostrova** *is* Russia
150 F2 **Medvezh'ya, Gora** *mt.* Russia
186 E2 **Medvezh'yegorsk** Russia
173 H6 **Medway** *r.* U.K.
118 B4 **Meekatharra** Australia
215 H1 **Meeker** U.S.A.
214 B2 **Meeks Bay** U.S.A.
207 I4 **Meelpaeg Reservoir** Canada
179 K4 **Meerane** Germany
179 E3 **Meerlo** Neth.
148 D3 **Meerut** India
212 E2 **Meeteetse** U.S.A.
194 D3 **Mēga** Eth.
163 B3 **Mega** *i.* Indon.
149 G4 **Meghalaya** *state* India
149 F5 **Meghasani** *mt.* India
149 G5 **Meghna** *r.* Bangl.
139 K2 **Meghri** Armenia
138 B3 **Megisti** *i.* Greece
170 N1 **Mehamn** Norway

Monga

206 B4 **Mille Lacs, Lac des** *l.* Canada
124 A2 **Miller** *watercourse* Australia
216 D2 **Miller** U.S.A.
208 B3 **Miller Dam Flowage** *resr* U.S.A.
209 G3 **Miller Lake** Canada
187 G5 **Millerovo** Russia
215 G6 **Miller Peak** U.S.A.
220 C4 **Millersburg** *OH* U.S.A.
221 E4 **Millersburg** *PA* U.S.A.
124 B3 **Millers Creek** Australia
221 E6 **Millers Tavern** U.S.A.
214 C3 **Millerton Lake** U.S.A.
174 C5 **Milleur Point** U.K.
124 D6 **Millicent** Australia
209 F4 **Millington** *MI* U.S.A.
219 B5 **Millington** *TN* U.S.A.
221 I2 **Millinocket** U.S.A.
127 K6 **Mill Island** Antarctica
125 I1 **Millmerran** Australia
172 D3 **Millom** U.K.
174 D5 **Millport** U.K.
221 F5 **Millsboro** U.S.A.
204 F2 **Mills Lake** Canada
220 C5 **Millstone** U.S.A.
121 B4 **Millstream-Chichester National Park** Australia
207 G4 **Milltown** Canada
122 C3 **Millungera** Australia
221 J1 **Millville** Canada
221 F5 **Millville** U.S.A.
121 B5 **Milly Milly** Australia
221 I2 **Milo** U.S.A.
158 D3 **Milogradovo** Russia
185 K6 **Milos** *i.* Greece
187 F4 **Miloslavskoye** Russia
124 D2 **Milparinka** Australia
221 E4 **Milroy** U.S.A.
209 H4 **Milton** Canada
126 B7 **Milton** N.Z.
219 C6 **Milton** *FL* U.S.A.
208 A5 **Milton** *IA* U.S.A.
221 E4 **Milton** *PA* U.S.A.
221 G2 **Milton** *VT* U.S.A.
220 C4 **Milton, Lake** U.S.A.
214 C2 **Milton-Freewater** U.S.A.
173 G5 **Milton Keynes** U.K.
175 I5 **Miltown Malbay** Ireland
155 D4 **Miluo** China
208 D4 **Milwaukee** U.S.A.
239 E4 **Milwaukee Deep** *sea feature* Caribbean Sea
141 H2 **Milybulak** Kazakh.
187 G5 **Milyutinskaya** Russia
121 F5 **Mimili** Australia
182 D4 **Mimizan** France
195 B4 **Mimongo** Gabon
182 D2 **Mina** Mex.
214 C2 **Mina** U.S.A.
143 E5 **Mīnāb** Iran
151 E6 **Minahasa, Semenanjung** *pen.* Indon.
142 D5 **Mīnā' Jabal 'Alī** U.A.E.
205 K4 **Minaki** Canada
159 B8 **Minamata** Japan
120 F2 **Minamia** Australia
159 E7 **Minami-arupusu Kokuritsu-kōen** *nat. park* Japan
153 N6 **Minami-Daitō-jima** *i.* Japan
159 G5 **Minamisanriku** Japan
159 B9 **Minami-Satsuma** Japan
163 B2 **Minas** Indon.
235 L2 **Minas** Uruguay
225 G5 **Minas, Sierra de las** *mts* Guat.
139 L7 **Mīnā' Sa'ūd** Kuwait
207 H4 **Minas Basin** *b.* Canada
235 L1 **Minas de Corrales** Uruguay
234 D2 **Minas Gerais** *state* Brazil
234 D2 **Minas Novas** Brazil
225 F4 **Minatitlán** Mex.
149 H5 **Minbu** Myanmar
149 H5 **Minbya** Myanmar
232 B6 **Minchinmávida** *vol.* Chile
184 D2 **Mincio** *r.* Italy
139 K2 **Mincivan** Azer.
161 J5 **Mindanao** *i.* Phil.
124 D5 **Mindarie** Australia
192 □ **Mindelo** Cape Verde
209 H3 **Minden** Canada
179 G2 **Minden** Germany
217 E5 **Minden** *LA* U.S.A.
214 C2 **Minden** *NV* U.S.A.
149 H6 **Mindon** Myanmar
125 E4 **Mindona Lake** *imp. l.* Australia
161 I3 **Mindoro** *i.* Phil.
161 H3 **Mindoro Strait** Phil.
195 B4 **Mindouli** Congo
140 D1 **Mindyak** Russia
175 K6 **Mine Head** Ireland
173 D6 **Minehead** U.K.
234 B2 **Mineiros** Brazil
217 E5 **Mineola** U.S.A.
214 B1 **Mineral** U.S.A.
214 C3 **Mineral King** U.S.A.
187 G6 **Mineral'nyye Vody** Russia
208 B4 **Mineral Point** U.S.A.
217 D5 **Mineral Wells** U.S.A.
215 F2 **Minersville** U.S.A.
185 G4 **Minervino Murge** Italy
149 E1 **Minfeng** China
195 C5 **Minga** Dem. Rep. Congo
139 K1 **Mingäçevir** Azer.
139 K1 **Mingäçevir Su Anbarı** *resr* Azer.
207 H3 **Mingan** Canada
154 E1 **Ming'antu** China
124 D4 **Mingary** Australia
Mingbulak Uzbek. *see* **Mingbuloq**
140 E4 **Mingbuloq** Uzbek.
121 A6 **Mingenew** Australia
154 E3 **Minggang** China
154 F3 **Mingguang** China
152 G7 **Mingin Range** *mts* Myanmar
141 H4 **Ming-Kush** Kyrg.
183 P3 **Minglanilla** Spain
195 D5 **Mingoyo** Tanz.
155 B4 **Mingshan** China
144 I3 **Mingshui** *Gansu* China
150 E2 **Mingshui** *Heilongjiang* China
174 A4 **Mingulay** *i.* U.K.
155 E5 **Mingxi** China
154 B2 **Minhe** China
145 I8 **Minhla** Myanmar
155 F5 **Minhou** China
147 G4 **Minicoy** *atoll* India
121 C6 **Minigwal, Lake** *salt flat* Australia
118 B4 **Minilya** Australia
121 A4 **Minilya** *r.* Australia
207 H3 **Minipi Lake** Canada
205 I4 **Minitonas** Canada
155 F5 **Min Jiang** *r. Fujian* China
155 B4 **Min Jiang** *r. Sichuan* China
194 B3 **Minkébé, Parc National de** *nat. park* Gabon
154 A2 **Minle** China
192 C4 **Minna** Nigeria
171 K3 **Minne** Sweden
216 E2 **Minneapolis** U.S.A.
205 J4 **Minnedosa** Canada
211 G2 **Minnesota** *r.* U.S.A.
208 A2 **Minnesota** *state* U.S.A.
124 A4 **Minnipa** Australia
206 B4 **Minnitaki Lake** Canada
183 L2 **Miño** *r.* Port./Spain
208 C3 **Minocqua** U.S.A.
208 B2 **Minong** U.S.A.
208 C5 **Minonk** U.S.A.
183 S2 **Minorca** *i.* Spain
216 C1 **Minot** U.S.A.
154 B2 **Minqin** China
155 F5 **Minqing** China
154 B3 **Min Shan** *mts* China
149 H4 **Minsin** Myanmar
187 C4 **Minsk** Belarus
177 J4 **Mińsk Mazowiecki** Poland
173 E5 **Minsterley** U.K.
148 C1 **Mintaka Pass** China/Pak.
154 A3 **Mintang** China
207 G4 **Minto** Canada
207 F2 **Minto, Lac** *l.* Canada
202 G2 **Minto Inlet** Canada
213 F4 **Minturn** U.S.A.
138 C6 **Minūf** Egypt
150 B1 **Minusinsk** Russia
149 I3 **Minutang** India
154 B3 **Minxian** China
125 E6 **Minyip** Australia
209 E3 **Mio** U.S.A.
206 E4 **Miquelon** Canada
207 I4 **Miquelon** *i.* N. America
233 H4 **Mira** *r.* Col.
143 F4 **Mīrābād** Afgh.
221 F2 **Mirabel** Canada
234 D2 **Mirabela** Brazil
231 I5 **Miracema do Tocantins** Brazil
231 I5 **Mirador, Parque Nacional de** *nat. park* Brazil
225 G4 **Mirador-Dos Lagunos-Río Azul, Parque Nacional** *nat. park* Guat.
233 I4 **Miraflores** Col.
139 H5 **Mīrah, Wādī al** *watercourse* Iraq/Saudi Arabia
234 D2 **Miralta** Brazil
235 L3 **Miramar** Arg.
225 G4 **Miramar, Lago** *l.* Mex.
183 G5 **Miramas** France
207 G4 **Miramichi** Canada
185 K7 **Mirampellou, Kolpos** *b.* Greece
234 A3 **Miranda** Brazil
234 A3 **Miranda** *r.* Brazil
214 A1 **Miranda** U.S.A.
121 C5 **Miranda, Lake** *salt flat* Australia
183 O1 **Miranda de Ebro** Spain
183 M2 **Mirandela** Port.
184 D2 **Mirandola** Italy
234 B3 **Mirandópolis** Brazil
139 J4 **Mirane** Iraq
148 B2 **Miran Shah** Pak.
146 D6 **Mirbāṭ** Oman
183 E5 **Mirepoix** France
163 H2 **Miri** *Sarawak* Malaysia
143 F4 **Miri** *mt.* Pak.
147 H2 **Mirialguda** India
235 M2 **Mirim, Lagoa** *l.* Brazil
143 F4 **Mīrjāveh** Iran
127 K6 **Mirny** *research stn* Antarctica
186 G2 **Mirnyy** *Arkhangel'skaya Oblast'* Russia
133 M3 **Mirnyy** *Respublika Sakha (Yakutiya)* Russia
205 I3 **Mirond Lake** Canada
179 K1 **Mirow** Germany
148 C2 **Mirpur** Pak.
148 B4 **Mirpur Batoro** Pak.
148 B4 **Mirpur Khas** Pak.
148 A4 **Mirpur Sakro** Pak.
205 G4 **Mirror** Canada
155 □ **Mirs Bay** *Hong Kong* China
160 E6 **Miryang** S. Korea
142 D3 **Mirzā, Chāh-e** *well* Iran
149 E4 **Mirzapur** India
159 C8 **Misaki** Japan
141 J5 **Misalay** China
158 G4 **Misawa** Japan
207 H4 **Miscou Island** Canada
148 C1 **Misgar** Pak.
145 H10 **Misha** India
158 B2 **Mishan** China
208 D5 **Mishawaka** U.S.A.
209 E1 **Mishibishu Lake** Canada
159 B7 **Mi-shima** *i.* Japan
149 H3 **Mishmi Hills** India
119 F3 **Misima Island** P.N.G.
224 I5 **Miskitos, Cayos** *is* Nicaragua
177 J6 **Miskolc** Hungary
151 F7 **Misoöl** *i.* Indon.
208 B2 **Misquah Hills** U.S.A.
193 D1 **Miṣrātah** Libya
149 E4 **Misrikh** India
209 E1 **Missanabie** Canada
206 D3 **Missinaibi** *r.* Canada
209 F1 **Missinaibi Lake** Canada
205 I3 **Missinipe** Canada
204 E5 **Mission** Canada
216 C3 **Mission** *SD* U.S.A.
225 E2 **Mission** *TX* U.S.A.
122 D3 **Mission Beach** Australia
206 D3 **Missisa Lake** Canada
209 F2 **Mississagi** *r.* Canada
209 H4 **Mississauga** Canada
209 E5 **Mississinewa Lake** U.S.A.
209 I3 **Mississippi** *r.* Canada
217 F6 **Mississippi** *r.* U.S.A.
217 F5 **Mississippi** *state* U.S.A.
217 F6 **Mississippi Delta** U.S.A.
212 D2 **Missoula** U.S.A.
216 C2 **Missouri** *r.* U.S.A.
208 A6 **Missouri** *state* U.S.A.
216 E3 **Missouri Valley** U.S.A.
203 K4 **Mistassibi** *r.* Canada
207 F4 **Mistassini** *r.* Canada
207 F3 **Mistassini, Lac** *l.* Canada
207 H2 **Mistastin Lake** Canada
177 H6 **Mistelbach** Austria
207 H2 **Mistinibi, Lac** *l.* Canada
207 F3 **Mistissini** Canada
204 C3 **Misty Fiords National Monument Wilderness** *nat. park* U.S.A.
224 C3 **Mita, Punta de** *pt* Mex.
119 E4 **Mitchell** Australia
125 J2 **Mitchell** *r. N.S.W.* Australia
119 E3 **Mitchell** *r. Qld* Australia
125 G6 **Mitchell** *r. Vic.* Australia
209 G4 **Mitchell** Canada
216 D3 **Mitchell** U.S.A.
122 D3 **Mitchell, Lake** Australia
209 E3 **Mitchell, Lake** U.S.A.
219 D5 **Mitchell, Mount** U.S.A.
122 C2 **Mitchell and Alice Rivers National Park** Australia
120 E1 **Mitchell Point** Australia
175 J5 **Mitchelstown** Ireland
138 C6 **Mīt Ghamr** Egypt
148 B3 **Mithankot** Pak.
148 B3 **Mithi** Pak.
148 B4 **Mithrani Canal** *canal* Pak.
185 L5 **Mithymna** Greece
204 C3 **Mitkof Island** U.S.A.
159 G6 **Mito** Japan
195 D4 **Mitole** Tanz.
126 E4 **Mitre** *mt.* N.Z.
119 H3 **Mitre Island** Solomon Is
185 I3 **Mitrovicë** Kosovo
125 I5 **Mittagong** Australia
125 G6 **Mitta Mitta** Australia
179 G2 **Mittellandkanal** *canal* Germany
179 K5 **Mitterteich** Germany
179 K4 **Mittweida** Germany
233 J4 **Mitú** Col.
233 J4 **Mituas** Col.
195 C5 **Mitumba, Chaîne des** *mts* Dem. Rep. Congo
195 C4 **Mitumba, Monts** *mts* Dem. Rep. Congo
194 B3 **Mitzic** Gabon
159 F7 **Miura** Japan
139 G4 **Miyāh, Wādī al** *watercourse* Syria
159 F7 **Miyake-jima** *i.* Japan
159 G5 **Miyako** Japan
159 B9 **Miyakonojō** Japan
155 B4 **Miyaluo** China
140 C2 **Miyaly** Kazakh.
148 B5 **Miyani** India
159 B9 **Miyanoura-dake** *mt.* Japan
159 B9 **Miyazaki** Japan
159 D7 **Miyazu** Japan
155 B5 **Miyi** China
159 C7 **Miyoshi** Japan
154 E1 **Miyun** China
154 E1 **Miyun Shuiku** *resr* China
143 G3 **Mīzān 'Alāqahdārī** Afgh.
194 D3 **Mīzan Teferī** Eth.
193 D1 **Mizdah** Libya
175 I6 **Mizen Head** Ireland
187 B5 **Mizhhir"ya** Ukr.
154 D2 **Mizhi** China
149 H5 **Mizoram** *state* India
171 K4 **Mjölby** Sweden
195 D4 **Mkata** Tanz.
195 D4 **Mkomazi** Tanz.
195 C5 **Mkushi** Zambia
176 G5 **Mladá Boleslav** Czech Rep.
185 I2 **Mladenovac** Serbia
177 J4 **Mława** Poland
185 G3 **Mljet** *i.* Croatia
197 G5 **Mlungisi** S. Africa
162 C2 **Mlu Prey** Cambodia
177 L5 **Mlyniv** Ukr.
197 F2 **Mmabatho** S. Africa
197 G1 **Mmamabula** Botswana
197 F2 **Mmathethe** Botswana
171 I3 **Mo** Norway
215 H2 **Moab** U.S.A.
119 E3 **Moa Island** Australia
119 H3 **Moala** *i.* Fiji
142 D3 **Mo'allā** Iran
197 J2 **Moamba** Moz.
124 D2 **Moanba, Lake** *salt flat* Australia
215 E3 **Moapa** U.S.A.
175 K4 **Moate** Ireland
195 C4 **Moba** Dem. Rep. Congo
159 G7 **Mobara** Japan
142 C3 **Mobārakeh** *Eşfahān* Iran
142 D4 **Mobārakeh** *Yazd* Iran
194 C3 **Mobayi-Mbongo** Dem. Rep. Congo
217 E4 **Moberly** U.S.A.
219 B6 **Mobile** *AL* U.S.A.
215 F5 **Mobile** *AZ* U.S.A.
219 B6 **Mobile Bay** U.S.A.
216 C2 **Mobridge** U.S.A.
231 I4 **Mocajuba** Brazil
195 E5 **Moçambique** Moz.
233 K2 **Mocapra** *r.* Venez.
155 B6 **Môc Châu** Vietnam
146 B7 **Mocha** Yemen
233 K2 **Mochirma, Parque Nacional** *nat. park* Venez.
195 C6 **Mochudi** Botswana
195 E5 **Mocimboa da Praia** Moz.
179 J2 **Möckern** Germany
179 H5 **Möckmühl** Germany
170 M2 **Mockträsk** Sweden
233 H4 **Mocoa** Col.
234 C3 **Mococa** Brazil
224 C2 **Mocorito** Mex.
225 D3 **Moctezuma** Mex.
195 D5 **Mocuba** Moz.
182 H4 **Modane** France
148 C5 **Modasa** India
197 F4 **Modder** *r.* S. Africa
184 D2 **Modena** Italy
215 F3 **Modena** U.S.A.
214 B3 **Modesto** U.S.A.
197 H2 **Modimolle** S. Africa
197 I1 **Modjadjiskloof** S. Africa
Modot Mongolia *see* **Tsenhermandal**
125 G7 **Moe** Australia
173 D5 **Moel Sych** *h.* U.K.
171 J3 **Moelv** Norway
170 L1 **Moen** Norway
215 G3 **Moenkopi** U.S.A.
126 C6 **Moeraki Point** N.Z.
179 E3 **Moers** Germany
174 E5 **Moffat** U.K.
148 C3 **Moga** India
194 E3 **Mogadishu** Somalia
220 C4 **Mogadore Reservoir** U.S.A.
197 H1 **Mogalakwena** *r.* S. Africa
197 H2 **Moganyaka** S. Africa
152 G6 **Mogaung** Myanmar
156 D2 **Mogdy** Russia
179 K2 **Mögelin** Germany
234 C3 **Mogi das Cruzes** Brazil
234 C3 **Mogi Mirim** Brazil
141 F5 **Mogiyon** Tajik.
150 D1 **Mogocha** Russia
184 C6 **Mogod** *mts* Tunisia
197 F2 **Mogoditshane** Botswana
151 B4 **Mogok** Myanmar
215 H5 **Mogollon Mountains** U.S.A.
215 G4 **Mogollon Plateau** U.S.A.
197 H1 **Mogwadi** S. Africa
197 H1 **Mogwadi** *r.* S. Africa
197 G2 **Mogwase** S. Africa
153 J1 **Mogzon** Russia
185 H2 **Mohács** Hungary
126 F3 **Mohaka** *r.* N.Z.
197 G5 **Mohale's Hoek** Lesotho
205 I5 **Mohall** U.S.A.
143 E3 **Moḥammad** Iran
143 E4 **Moḥammadābād** Iran
183 Q5 **Mohammadia** Alg.
149 E3 **Mohan** *r.* India/Nepal
215 E4 **Mohave, Lake** U.S.A.
215 F5 **Mohawk** U.S.A.
221 F3 **Mohawk** *r.* U.S.A.
215 F5 **Mohawk Mountains** U.S.A.
Mohéli *i.* Comoros *see* **Mwali**
143 H5 **Mohenjo Daro** *tourist site* Pak.
175 K4 **Mohill** Ireland
179 G3 **Möhne** *r.* Germany
215 F4 **Mohon Peak** U.S.A.
195 D4 **Mohoro** Tanz.
187 C5 **Mohyliv-Podil's'kyy** Ukr.
171 I4 **Moi** Norway
197 G1 **Moijabana** Botswana
152 D5 **Moincêr** China
197 J2 **Moine** Moz.
177 M7 **Moinești** Romania
221 F2 **Moira** U.S.A.
170 K2 **Mo i Rana** Norway
149 H4 **Moirang** India
171 N4 **Mõisaküla** Estonia
235 K1 **Moisés Ville** Arg.
207 G3 **Moisie** Canada
207 G3 **Moisie** *r.* Canada
182 E4 **Moissac** France
214 C4 **Mojave** U.S.A.
215 D4 **Mojave** *r.* U.S.A.
215 D4 **Mojave Desert** U.S.A.
159 B8 **Moji** Japan
153 H7 **Mojiang** China
234 C3 **Moji-Guaçu** *r.* Brazil
197 F4 **Mokala National Park** S. Africa
149 F4 **Mokama** India
214 □[1] **Mōkapu Peninsula** U.S.A.
126 E3 **Mokau** N.Z.
126 E3 **Mokau** *r.* N.Z.
214 B2 **Mokelumne** *r.* U.S.A.
142 D4 **Mokh, Gowd-e** *l.* Iran
197 H4 **Mokhoabong Pass** Lesotho
197 H4 **Mokhotlong** Lesotho
184 D7 **Moknine** Tunisia
126 E1 **Mokohinau Islands** N.Z.
193 D3 **Mokolo** Cameroon
197 G2 **Mokolo** *r.* S. Africa
197 H2 **Mokopane** S. Africa
160 D6 **Mokpo** S. Korea
187 G4 **Moksha** *r.* Russia
187 H4 **Mokshan** Russia
214 □[1] **Moku 'Āuia** *i.* U.S.A.
214 □[1] **Moku Lua** *is* U.S.A.
141 I3 **Molaly** Kazakh.
225 E3 **Molango** Mex.
183 P3 **Molatón** *mt.* Spain
Moldavia *country* Europe *see* **Moldova**
171 I3 **Molde** Norway
170 K2 **Moldjord** Norway
187 D6 **Moldova** *country* Europe
185 K2 **Moldoveanu, Vârful** *mt.* Romania
173 D7 **Mole** *r.* U.K.
192 B4 **Mole National Park** Ghana
195 C6 **Molepolole** Botswana
171 N5 **Moltai** Lith.
185 G4 **Molfetta** Italy
183 P2 **Molina de Aragón** Spain
208 B5 **Moline** U.S.A.
171 K4 **Molkom** Sweden
139 L4 **Mollā Bodāgh** Iran
137 I3 **Mollagara** Turkm.
Mollakara Turkm. *see* **Mollagara**
149 H4 **Mol Len** *mt.* India
179 L1 **Möllenbeck** Germany
230 D7 **Mollendo** Peru
179 I1 **Mölln** Germany
171 K4 **Mölnlycke** Sweden
186 F3 **Molochnoye** Russia
170 P1 **Molochnyy** Russia
141 G1 **Molodogvardeyskoye** Kazakh.
186 E3 **Molodoy Tud** Russia
214 □[2] **Moloka'i** *i.* U.S.A.
186 I3 **Moloma** *r.* Russia
125 H4 **Molong** Australia
197 F2 **Molopo** *watercourse* Botswana/S. Africa
193 D4 **Moloundou** Cameroon
205 J4 **Molson Lake** Canada
151 E7 **Moluccas** *is* Indon.
Molucca Sea Indon. *see* **Maluku, Laut**
Molukken *is* Indon. *see* **Moluccas**
195 D5 **Moma** Moz.
133 P3 **Moma** *r.* Russia
125 E3 **Momba** Australia
195 D4 **Mombasa** Kenya
149 H4 **Mombi New** India
234 B2 **Mombuca, Serra da** *hills* Brazil
187 C7 **Momchilgrad** Bulg.
208 D5 **Momence** U.S.A.
233 I2 **Mompós** Col.
171 K5 **Møn** *i.* Denmark
215 G2 **Mona** U.S.A.
223 K5 **Mona, Isla** *i.* Puerto Rico
174 A3 **Monach, Sound of** *sea chan.* U.K.
174 A3 **Monach Islands** U.K.
183 H5 **Monaco** *country* Europe
239 H4 **Monaco Basin** *sea feature* N. Atlantic Ocean
174 D3 **Monadhliath Mountains** U.K.
175 L3 **Monaghan** Ireland
217 C6 **Monahans** U.S.A.
223 K5 **Mona Passage** Dom. Rep./Puerto Rico
195 E5 **Monapo** Moz.
174 C3 **Monar, Loch** *l.* U.K.
204 D4 **Monarch Mountain** Canada
213 F4 **Monarch Pass** U.S.A.
204 F4 **Monashee Mountains** Canada
184 D7 **Monastir** Tunisia
177 O3 **Monastyrshchina** Russia
187 D5 **Monastyryshche** Ukr.
158 H2 **Monbetsu** *Hokkaidō* Japan
Monbetsu *Hokkaidō* Japan *see* **Hidaka**
184 B2 **Moncalieri** Italy
183 P2 **Moncayo** *mt.* Spain
170 P2 **Monchegorsk** Russia
179 E3 **Mönchengladbach** Germany
183 L4 **Monchique** Port.
219 E5 **Moncks Corner** U.S.A.
225 D2 **Monclova** Mex.
207 H4 **Moncton** Canada
183 M2 **Mondego** *r.* Port.
184 B2 **Mondovì** Italy
208 B3 **Mondovi** U.S.A.
184 E4 **Mondragone** Italy
153 H1 **Mondy** Russia
185 J6 **Monemvasia** Greece
158 G1 **Moneron, Ostrov** *i.* Russia
220 D4 **Monessen** U.S.A.
209 J1 **Monet** Canada
175 K5 **Moneygall** Ireland
175 L3 **Moneymore** U.K.
184 E2 **Monfalcone** Italy
183 M1 **Monforte de Lemos** Spain
194 C3 **Monga** Dem. Rep. Congo

Mystic Island

173 B7 **Mount's Bay** U.K.
173 F5 **Mountsorrel** U.K.
208 B6 **Mount Sterling** *IL* U.S.A.
220 B5 **Mount Sterling** *KY* U.S.A.
220 D5 **Mount Storm** U.S.A.
123 A4 **Mount Swan** Australia
221 E4 **Mount Union** U.S.A.
121 B5 **Mount Vernon** Australia
219 B6 **Mount Vernon** *AL* U.S.A.
208 B5 **Mount Vernon** *IA* U.S.A.
219 B4 **Mount Vernon** *IL* U.S.A.
220 A6 **Mount Vernon** *KY* U.S.A.
220 B4 **Mount Vernon** *OH* U.S.A.
212 B1 **Mount Vernon** *WA* U.S.A.
124 A4 **Mount Wedge** Australia
125 H8 **Mount William National Park** Australia
121 F5 **Mount Willoughby** Australia
119 E4 **Moura** Australia
231 F4 **Moura** Brazil
193 E3 **Mourdi, Dépression du** *depr.* Chad
175 K3 **Mourne** *r.* U.K.
175 L3 **Mourne Mountains** U.K.
178 B4 **Mouscron** Belgium
193 D3 **Moussoro** Chad
151 E6 **Moutong** Indon.
178 A5 **Mouy** France
192 C2 **Mouydir, Monts du** *plat.* Alg.
178 D5 **Mouzon** France
142 C4 **Moveyleh** Iran
125 I1 **Mowbullan, Mount** Australia
219 E7 **Moxey Town** Bahamas
175 J4 **Moy** *r.* Ireland
194 D3 **Moyale** Eth.
192 A4 **Moyamba** Sierra Leone
147 H4 **Moyar** *r.* India
192 B1 **Moyen Atlas** *mts* Morocco
197 G5 **Moyeni** Lesotho
175 L4 **Moyer** *h.* Ireland
152 G1 **Moynalyk** Russia
140 D4 **Mo'ynoq** Uzbek.
141 I5 **Moyu** China
141 H3 **Moyynkum** Kazakh.
141 F3 **Moyynkum, Peski** *des. Karagandinskaya Oblast'* Kazakh.
141 G3 **Moyynkum, Peski** *des. Yuzhnyy Kazakhstan/Zhambylskaya Oblast'* Kazakh.
141 H3 **Moyynty** Kazakh.
195 D6 **Mozambique** *country* Africa
195 E5 **Mozambique Channel** Africa
238 G6 **Mozambique Ridge** *sea feature* Indian Ocean
187 H7 **Mozdok** Russia
187 F4 **Mozhaysk** Russia
149 H5 **Mozo** Myanmar
195 C4 **Mpala** Dem. Rep. Congo
195 D4 **Mpanda** Tanz.
195 D5 **Mpika** Zambia
197 I4 **Mpolweni** S. Africa
195 D4 **Mporokoso** Zambia
197 H2 **Mpumalanga** *prov.* S. Africa
197 H5 **Mqanduli** S. Africa
149 H5 **Mrauk-U** Myanmar
185 G2 **Mrkonjić-Grad** Bos. & Herz.
193 D1 **M'Saken** Tunisia
186 D3 **Mshinskaya** Russia
183 S5 **M'Sila** Alg.
186 E3 **Msta** *r.* Russia
187 D4 **Mstsislaw** Belarus
197 H5 **Mthatha** S. Africa
187 F4 **Mtsensk** Russia
197 J4 **Mtubatuba** S. Africa
197 I4 **Mtunzini** S. Africa
195 E5 **Mtwara** Tanz.
160 D6 **Muan** S. Korea
195 B4 **Muanda** Dem. Rep. Congo
163 B2 **Muang Hiam** Laos
162 B1 **Muang Hôngsa** Laos
Muang Khammouan Laos *see* **Thakhèk**
162 C2 **Muang Không** Laos
162 C2 **Muang Khôngxédôn** Laos
155 B6 **Muang Khoua** Laos
162 A3 **Muang Kirirath** *r.* Thai.
162 C1 **Muang Mok** Laos
155 B6 **Muang Ngoy** Laos
162 C1 **Muang Nong** Laos
155 A6 **Muang Ou Nua** Laos
Muang Pakxan Laos *see* **Pakxan**
162 C1 **Muang Phalan** Laos
162 B1 **Muang Phiang** Laos
162 C1 **Muang Phin** Laos
153 H7 **Muang Sing** Laos
162 B1 **Muang Souy** Laos
155 B6 **Muang Va** Laos
162 B1 **Muang Vangviang** Laos
Muang Xaignabouri Laos *see* **Xaignabouli**
Muang Xay Laos *see* **Oudômxai**
155 B6 **Muang Xon** Laos
163 B2 **Muar** Malaysia
162 B5 **Muar** *r.* Malaysia
163 B3 **Muarabungo** Indon.
163 B3 **Muaradua** Indon.
163 E3 **Muarasiberut** Indon.
163 E2 **Muarasipongi** Indon.
163 B3 **Muaratembesi** Indon.
149 E4 **Mubarakpur** India
Mubarek Uzbek. *see* **Muborak**
139 H7 **Mubarraz** *well* Saudi Arabia
194 D3 **Mubende** Uganda
193 D3 **Mubi** Nigeria
141 F5 **Muborak** Uzbek.
233 L4 **Mucajaí** *r.* Brazil
233 L4 **Mucajaí, Serra do** *mts* Brazil
121 C4 **Muccan** Australia
179 F4 **Much** Germany
195 D5 **Muchinga Escarpment** Zambia
155 B4 **Muchuan** China
174 B4 **Muck** *i.* U.K.
174 □ **Muckle Roe** *i.* U.K.
233 J3 **Muco** *r.* Col.
195 C5 **Muconda** Angola
233 L4 **Mucucuaú** *r.* Brazil
138 E2 **Mucur** Turkey
234 E2 **Mucuri** Brazil
234 E2 **Mucuri** *r.* Brazil
195 C5 **Mucussueje** Angola
143 E3 **Mūd** Iran
162 B4 **Muda** *r.* Malaysia
147 G3 **Mudabidri** India
160 E1 **Mudanjiang** China
160 E1 **Mudan Jiang** *r.* China
157 B4 **Mudan Ling** *mts* China
138 B1 **Mudanya** Turkey
139 K7 **Mudayrah** Kuwait
220 C5 **Muddlety** U.S.A.
170 L2 **Muddus nationalpark** *nat. park* Sweden
215 G2 **Muddy Creek** *r.* U.S.A.
215 E3 **Muddy Peak** U.S.A.
179 F4 **Mudersbach** Germany
125 H4 **Mudgee** Australia
147 G2 **Mudhol** India
148 C3 **Mudki** India
215 D3 **Mud Lake** U.S.A.
162 A1 **Mudon** Myanmar
138 C1 **Mudurnu** Turkey
186 F2 **Mud'yuga** Russia
195 D5 **Mueda** Moz.
120 D3 **Mueller Range** *hills* Australia
225 F4 **Muerto, Mar** *lag.* Mex.
186 H1 **Muftyuga** Russia
195 C5 **Mufulira** Zambia
195 C5 **Mufumbwe** Zambia
155 E4 **Mufu Shan** *mts* China
139 L2 **Muğan Düzü** *lowland* Azer.
155 C5 **Mugarripug** China
149 E4 **Mughal Sarai** India
142 D3 **Mūghār** Iran
139 F7 **Mughayrā'** Saudi Arabia
141 G5 **Mughsu** *r.* Tajik.
138 B3 **Muğla** Turkey
140 D3 **Mugodzhary, Gory** *mts* Kazakh.
149 H2 **Mug Qu** *r.* China
149 E3 **Mugu Karnali** *r.* Nepal
149 H2 **Mugxung** China
193 F2 **Muḩammad, Ra's** *pt* Egypt
148 B4 **Muhammad Ashraf** Pak.
193 F2 **Muhammad Qol** Sudan
142 B5 **Muḩayriqah** Saudi Arabia
179 K3 **Mühlanger** Germany
179 L3 **Mühlberg/Elbe** Germany
179 I3 **Mühlhausen/Thüringen** Germany
170 N2 **Muhos** Fin.
195 C4 **Muhulu** Dem. Rep. Congo
Muine Bheag Ireland *see* **Bagenalstown**
174 D5 **Muirkirk** U.K.
174 B2 **Muirneag** *h.* U.K.
174 D3 **Muir of Ord** U.K.
214 A3 **Muir Woods National Monument** *nat. park* U.S.A.
195 D5 **Muite** Moz.
142 D3 **Mūjān, Chāh-e** *well* Iran
225 H3 **Mujeres, Isla** *i.* Mex.
160 D6 **Muju** S. Korea
187 B5 **Mukacheve** Ukr.
163 H2 **Mukah** *Sarawak* Malaysia
146 C7 **Mukalla** Yemen
149 F3 **Mükangsar** China
162 C1 **Mukdahan** Thai.
156 E2 **Mukhen** Russia
156 B1 **Mukhino** Russia
118 B5 **Mukinbudin** Australia
163 B3 **Mukomuko** Indon.
141 F5 **Mukry** Turkm.
148 C3 **Muktsar** India
205 J4 **Mukutawa** *r.* Canada
208 C4 **Mukwonago** U.S.A.
140 C3 **Mukyr** *Atyrauskaya Oblast'* Kazakh.
141 J2 **Mukyr** *Vostochnyy Kazakhstan* Kazakh.
148 D5 **Mul** India
147 G2 **Mula** *r.* India
148 A3 **Mula** *r.* Pak.
147 G3 **Mulainagir** *mt.* India
158 A2 **Mulan** China
161 I3 **Mulanay** Phil.
195 D5 **Mulanje, Mount** Malawi
142 B5 **Mulayḩ** Saudi Arabia
217 E5 **Mulberry** U.S.A.
235 H3 **Mulchén** Chile
179 K3 **Mulde** *r.* Germany
195 D4 **Muleba** Tanz.
215 H5 **Mule Creek** *NM* U.S.A.
213 F3 **Mule Creek** *WY* U.S.A.
224 A2 **Mulegé** Mex.
217 C5 **Muleshoe** U.S.A.
121 E5 **Mulga Park** Australia
121 F6 **Mulgathing** Australia
183 O4 **Mulhacén** *mt.* Spain
179 E3 **Mülheim an der Ruhr** Germany
182 H3 **Mulhouse** France
155 A5 **Muli** China
Muli Russia *see* **Vysokogorniy**
161 F1 **Muling** *Heilongjiang* China
161 F1 **Muling** *Heilongjiang* China
160 G1 **Muling He** *r.* China
174 C4 **Mull** *i.* U.K.
174 B4 **Mull, Sound of** *sea chan.* U.K.
139 L3 **Mulla Ali** Iran
175 I6 **Mullaghanattin** *h.* Ireland
175 I5 **Mullaghareirk Mountains** Ireland
147 I4 **Mullaittivu** Sri Lanka
125 H3 **Mullaley** Australia
125 G3 **Mullengudgery** Australia
121 F4 **Muller** *watercourse* Australia
163 H2 **Muller, Pegunungan** *mts* Indon.
209 E3 **Mullett Lake** U.S.A.
118 B4 **Mullewa** Australia
175 F1 **Mull Head** U.K.
221 F5 **Mullica** *r.* U.S.A.
175 K4 **Mullingar** Ireland
125 H4 **Mullion Creek** Australia
174 D6 **Mull of Galloway** *c.* U.K.
174 C5 **Mull of Kintyre** *hd* U.K.
174 B5 **Mull of Oa** *hd* U.K.
195 C5 **Mulobezi** Zambia
147 G2 **Mulshi Lake** India
148 D5 **Multai** India
148 B3 **Multan** Pak.
171 N3 **Multia** Fin.
178 A6 **Multien** *reg.* France
143 F5 **Mūmān** Iran
147 G2 **Mumbai** India
125 H4 **Mumbil** Australia
195 C5 **Mumbwa** Zambia
Mŭ'minobod Tajik. *see* **Leningrad**
187 H6 **Mumra** Russia
162 C2 **Mun, Mae Nam** *r.* Thai.
118 C2 **Muna** *i.* Indon.
225 G3 **Muna** Mex.
133 M3 **Muna** *r.* Russia
170 B1 **Munaðarnes** Iceland
140 C3 **Munayly** Kazakh.
140 C4 **Munayshy** Kazakh.
179 J4 **Münchberg** Germany
München Germany *see* **Munich**
179 G4 **Münchhausen** Germany
233 H4 **Munchique, Cerro** *mt.* Col.
204 D3 **Muncho Lake** Canada
204 D3 **Muncho Lake Provincial Park** Canada
160 D4 **Munch'ŏn** N. Korea
209 E5 **Muncie** U.S.A.
123 B5 **Muncoonie West, Lake** *salt flat* Australia
221 E4 **Muncy** U.S.A.
147 H5 **Mundel Lake** Sri Lanka
173 I5 **Mundesley** U.K.
173 H5 **Mundford** U.K.
121 C4 **Mundiwindi (abandoned)** Australia
118 C5 **Mundrabilla** Australia
123 E5 **Mundubbera** Australia
148 C4 **Mundwa** India
147 I2 **Muneru** *r.* India
123 D5 **Mungallala** Australia
125 G2 **Mungallala Creek** *r.* Australia
122 D3 **Mungana** Australia
148 D4 **Mungaoli** India
160 D5 **Mungap-do** *i.* S. Korea
194 C3 **Mungbere** Dem. Rep. Congo
147 I1 **Mungeli** India
149 F4 **Munger** India
124 C2 **Mungeranie** Australia
163 D5 **Mungguresak, Tanjung** *pt* Indon.
125 H2 **Mungindi** Australia
125 E4 **Mungo National Park** Australia
160 D5 **Mun'gyeong** S. Korea
176 E6 **Munich** Germany
231 J4 **Munim** *r.* Brazil
208 D2 **Munising** U.S.A.
234 E3 **Muniz Freire** Brazil
170 O1 **Munkebakken** Norway
171 J4 **Munkedal** Sweden
171 K4 **Munkfors** Sweden
153 H1 **Munku-Sardyk, Gora** *mt.* Mongolia/Russia
179 I4 **Münnerstadt** Germany
197 H1 **Munnik** S. Africa
125 H8 **Munro, Mount** Australia
160 D5 **Munsan** S. Korea
176 C7 **Münsingen** Switz.
179 G5 **Münster** *Hessen* Germany
179 I2 **Munster** Germany
179 F3 **Münster** *Nordrhein-Westfalen* Germany
179 F3 **Münsterland** *reg.* Germany
121 B6 **Muntadgin** Australia
170 O2 **Muojärvi** *l.* Fin.
155 B6 **Mường Nhe** Vietnam
170 M2 **Muonio** Fin.
170 M2 **Muonioälven** *r.* Fin./Sweden
160 A5 **Muping** China
Muqdisho Somalia *see* **Mogadishu**
143 G3 **Muqêr** Afgh.
139 L1 **Müqtädır** Azer.
139 I2 **Muradiye** Turkey
162 □ **Murai Reservoir** Sing.
159 F5 **Murakami** Japan
232 B7 **Murallón, Cerro** *mt.* Chile
195 C4 **Muramvya** Burundi
186 I3 **Murashi** Russia
139 H2 **Murat** *r.* Turkey
138 B2 **Murat Dağı** *mts* Turkey
138 A1 **Muratlı** Turkey
159 G5 **Murayama** Japan
136 B5 **Muraysah, Ra's al** *pt* Libya
142 C3 **Mürcheh Khvort** Iran
125 F6 **Murchison** Australia
118 B4 **Murchison** *watercourse* Australia
121 B5 **Murchison, Mount** *h.* Australia
194 D3 **Murchison Falls National Park** Uganda
183 P4 **Murcia** Spain
183 P4 **Murcia** *aut. comm.* Spain
216 C3 **Murdo** U.S.A.
207 G4 **Murdochville** Canada
195 D5 **Murehwa** Zimbabwe
177 L7 **Mureşul** *r.* Romania
183 E5 **Muret** France
219 E4 **Murfreesboro** *NC* U.S.A.
219 C5 **Murfreesboro** *TN* U.S.A.
140 E5 **Murgap** Turkm.
143 F2 **Murgap** *r.* Turkm.
143 H3 **Murgh, Kōtal-e** Afgh.
148 B3 **Murgha Kibzai** Pak.
141 H5 **Murghob** Tajik.
141 H5 **Murghob** *r.* Tajik.
123 E5 **Murgon** Australia
121 B5 **Murgoo** Australia
154 A2 **Muri** China
149 F5 **Muri** India
143 E2 **Mūrī** Iran
234 D3 **Muriaé** Brazil
143 F3 **Mūrichāq** Afgh.
195 C4 **Muriege** Angola
179 K1 **Müritz** *l.* Germany
179 L1 **Müritz, Nationalpark** *nat. park* Germany
179 K1 **Müritz Seenpark** *nature res.* Germany
170 P1 **Murmansk** Russia
170 O1 **Murmanskaya Oblast'** *admin. div.* Russia
169 M2 **Murmanskiy Bereg** *coastal area* Russia
184 C4 **Muro, Capo di** *c. Corsica* France
187 G4 **Murom** Russia
158 G3 **Muroran** Japan
183 L1 **Muros** Spain
159 D8 **Muroto** Japan
159 D8 **Muroto-zaki** *pt* Japan
213 C3 **Murphy** *ID* U.S.A.
219 D5 **Murphy** *NC* U.S.A.
214 B2 **Murphys** U.S.A.
125 I5 **Murramarang National Park** Australia
125 G2 **Murra Murra** Australia
124 D5 **Murray** *r. S.A.* Australia
121 A7 **Murray** *r. W.A.* Australia
204 E3 **Murray** *r.* Canada
219 B4 **Murray** *KY* U.S.A.
213 E3 **Murray** *UT* U.S.A.
119 E2 **Murray, Lake** P.N.G.
219 D5 **Murray, Lake** U.S.A.
124 C5 **Murray Bridge** Australia
121 F4 **Murray Downs** Australia
121 E5 **Murray Range** *hills* Australia
197 E5 **Murraysburg** S. Africa
123 C7 **Murray Sunset National Park** Australia
124 D5 **Murrayville** Australia
179 H6 **Murrhardt** Germany
125 H5 **Murringo** Australia
175 I4 **Murrisk** *reg.* Ireland
175 I4 **Murroogh** Ireland
125 H5 **Murrumbateman** Australia
125 F5 **Murrumbidgee** *r.* Australia
195 D5 **Murrupula** Moz.
125 I3 **Murrurundi** Australia
185 G1 **Murska Sobota** Slovenia
124 D2 **Murteree, Lake** *salt flat* Australia
125 E6 **Murtoa** Australia
147 G2 **Murud** India
160 A2 **Muruin Sum Shuiku** *resr* China
121 B4 **Murujuga National Park** Australia
147 I4 **Murunkan** Sri Lanka
126 F3 **Murupara** N.Z.
117 J6 **Mururoa** *atoll* Fr. Polynesia
Murwara India *see* **Katni**
125 J2 **Murwillumbah** Australia
140 E5 **Murzechirla** Turkm.
193 D2 **Murzūq** Libya
193 D2 **Murzuq, Idhān** *des.* Libya
176 G7 **Mürzzuschlag** Austria
139 H2 **Muş** Turkey
148 B3 **Musakhel** Pak.
185 J3 **Musala** *mt.* Bulg.
163 E2 **Musala** *i.* Indon.
160 E2 **Musan** N. Korea
143 E5 **Musandam Peninsula** Oman
143 G3 **Mūsá Qal'ah** Afgh.
Musa Qala Rūd *r.* Afgh. *see* **Dê Mūsá Qal'ah Rōd**
147 E5 **Muscat** Oman
208 B5 **Muscatine** U.S.A.
208 B4 **Muscoda** U.S.A.
221 I3 **Muscongus Bay** U.S.A.
122 C2 **Musgrave** Australia
118 D4 **Musgrave Ranges** *mts* Australia
175 J5 **Musheramore** *h.* Ireland
195 B4 **Mushie** Dem. Rep. Congo
147 H2 **Musi** *r.* India
163 B3 **Musi** *r.* Indon.
215 F4 **Music Mountain** U.S.A.
197 I1 **Musina** S. Africa
215 G2 **Musinia Peak** U.S.A.
204 E2 **Muskeg** *r.* Canada
221 H4 **Muskeget Channel** U.S.A.
208 D4 **Muskegon** U.S.A.
208 D4 **Muskegon** *r.* U.S.A.
220 C5 **Muskingum** *r.* U.S.A.
217 E5 **Muskogee** U.S.A.
209 H3 **Muskoka** Canada
209 H3 **Muskoka, Lake** Canada
204 E3 **Muskwa** *r.* Canada
139 F3 **Muslimīyah** Syria
193 F3 **Musmar** Sudan
195 D4 **Musoma** Tanz.
119 E2 **Mussau Island** P.N.G.
174 E5 **Musselburgh** U.K.
179 F2 **Musselkanaal** Neth.
212 E2 **Musselshell** *r.* U.S.A.
138 B1 **Mustafakemalpaşa** Turkey
140 C2 **Mustayevo** Russia
171 M4 **Mustjala** Estonia
160 E3 **Musu-dan** *pt* N. Korea
125 I4 **Muswellbrook** Australia
193 E2 **Mūţ** Egypt
138 D3 **Mut** Turkey
234 E1 **Mutá, Ponta do** *pt* Brazil
195 D5 **Mutare** Zimbabwe
151 E7 **Mutis, Gunung** *mt.* Indon.
124 D4 **Mutooroo** Australia
195 D5 **Mutorashanga** Zimbabwe
158 G4 **Mutsu** Japan
158 G4 **Mutsu-wan** *b.* Japan
123 D4 **Muttaburra** Australia
126 B7 **Muttonbird Islands** N.Z.
175 I5 **Mutton Island** Ireland
195 D5 **Mutuali** Moz.
234 C1 **Mutunópolis** Brazil
147 I4 **Mutur** Sri Lanka
170 N1 **Mutusjärvi** *r.* Fin.
170 N2 **Muurola** Fin.
154 C2 **Mu Us Shadi** *des.* China
195 B4 **Muxaluando** Angola
186 E2 **Muyezerskiy** Russia
195 D4 **Muyinga** Burundi
Muynak Uzbek. *see* **Mo'ynoq**
155 D4 **Muyu** China
195 C4 **Muyumba** Dem. Rep. Congo
148 C2 **Muzaffarabad** Pak.
148 B3 **Muzaffargarh** Pak.
148 D3 **Muzaffarnagar** India
149 F4 **Muzaffarpur** India
197 J1 **Muzamane** Moz.
141 J4 **Muzat He** *r.* China
143 F5 **Mūzin** Iran
204 C4 **Muzon, Cape** U.S.A.
225 D2 **Múzquiz** Mex.
149 E2 **Muz Shan** *mt.* China
Muztag *mt.* China *see* **Muz Tag**
149 F1 **Muz Tag** *mt.* China
141 H5 **Muztagata** *mt.* China
193 E4 **Mvolo** South Sudan
195 D4 **Mvomero** Tanz.
195 D5 **Mvuma** Zimbabwe
195 E5 **Mwali** *i.* Comoros
195 C4 **Mwanza** Dem. Rep. Congo
195 D4 **Mwanza** Tanz.
195 C4 **Mwaro** Burundi
175 I4 **Mweelrea** *h.* Ireland
195 C4 **Mweka** Dem. Rep. Congo
195 C5 **Mwenda** Zambia
195 C4 **Mwene-Ditu** Dem. Rep. Congo
195 D6 **Mwenezi** Zimbabwe
195 C4 **Mweru, Lake** Dem. Rep. Congo/Zambia
195 C4 **Mwimba** Dem. Rep. Congo
195 C5 **Mwinilunga** Zambia
187 C4 **Myadzyel** Belarus
149 H5 **Myaing** Myanmar
148 B4 **Myajlar** India
125 J4 **Myall Lake** Australia
150 B2 **Myanmar** *country* Asia
174 E2 **Mybster** U.K.
185 J6 **Mycenae** *tourist site* Greece
149 H5 **Myebon** Myanmar
162 A2 **Myeik** Myanmar
162 A3 **Myeik Kyunzu** *is* Myanmar
151 B4 **Myingyan** Myanmar
162 A2 **Myinmoletkat** *mt.* Myanmar
151 B4 **Myitkyina** Myanmar
145 I7 **Myitson** Myanmar
162 A2 **Myitta** Myanmar
145 I7 **Myittha** Myanmar
149 H5 **Myittha** *r.* Myanmar
187 E6 **Mykolayiv** Ukr.
185 K6 **Mykonos** Greece
185 K6 **Mykonos** *i.* Greece
132 G3 **Myla** Russia
149 G4 **Mymensingh** Bangl.
171 M3 **Mynämäki** Fin.
141 H3 **Mynaral** Kazakh.
Myohaung Myanmar *see* **Mrauk-U**
159 F6 **Myōkō** Japan
160 E3 **Myŏnggan** N. Korea
187 C4 **Myory** Belarus
170 C3 **Mýrdalsjökull** *ice cap* Iceland
170 K1 **Myre** Norway
170 M2 **Myrheden** Sweden
187 E5 **Myrhorod** Ukr.
187 D5 **Myronivka** Ukr.
219 E5 **Myrtle Beach** U.S.A.
125 G6 **Myrtleford** Australia
213 A3 **Myrtle Point** U.S.A.
185 J6 **Myrtoo Pelagos** *sea* Greece
141 G4 **Myrzakent** Kazakh.
Mys Lazareva Russia *see* **Lazarev**
176 G4 **Myślibórz** Poland
Mysore India *see* **Mysuru**
133 T3 **Mys Shmidta** Russia
221 F5 **Mystic Island** U.S.A.

Mysuru

147 H3 **Mysuru** India
162 C3 **My Tho** Vietnam
185 L5 **Mytilini** Greece
136 B3 **Mytilini Strait** Greece/Turkey
187 F4 **Mytishchi** Russia
170 C2 **Mývatn-Laxá** *nature res.* Iceland
197 G5 **Mzamomhle** S. Africa
179 K5 **Mže** *r.* Czech Rep.
195 D5 **Mzimba** Malawi
195 D5 **Mzuzu** Malawi

N

155 B6 **Na, Nam** *r.* China/Vietnam
179 J5 **Naab** *r.* Germany
214 □2 **Nā'ālehu** U.S.A.
171 M3 **Naantali** Fin.
175 L4 **Naas** Ireland
204 D2 **Nááts'ihch'oh National Park Reserve** *nat. park* Canada
152 G7 **Naba** Myanmar
196 B4 **Nababeep** S. Africa
147 I2 **Nabarangapur** India
159 E7 **Nabari** Japan
161 I4 **Nabas** Phil.
138 E5 **Nabatîyé et Tahta** Lebanon
Nabatiyet et Tahta Lebanon *see* **Nabatîyé et Tahta**
121 C5 **Nabberu, Lake** *salt flat* Australia
179 K5 **Nabburg** Germany
195 D4 **Naberera** Tanz.
132 G4 **Naberezhnyye Chelny** Russia
193 D1 **Nabeul** Tunisia
148 D3 **Nabha** India
125 J4 **Nabiac** Australia
156 F2 **Nabil'skiy Zaliv** *lag.* Russia
151 F7 **Nabire** Indon.
138 E5 **Nāblus** West Bank
136 D5 **Nabq Protected Area** *nature res.* Egypt
162 A2 **Nabule** Myanmar
195 E5 **Nacala** Moz.
224 H5 **Nacaome** Hond.
212 B2 **Naches** U.S.A.
148 B4 **Nachna** India
145 H9 **Nachuge** India
214 B4 **Nacimiento Reservoir** U.S.A.
217 E6 **Nacogdoches** U.S.A.
222 C2 **Nacozari de García** Mex.
156 D2 **Nadezhdinskoye** Russia
148 C5 **Nadiad** India
142 D4 **Nadīk** Iran
192 B1 **Nador** Morocco
142 D3 **Nadūshan** Iran
187 C5 **Nadvirna** Ukr.
132 E3 **Nadvoitsy** Russia
132 I3 **Nadym** Russia
171 J5 **Næstved** Denmark
185 I5 **Nafpaktos** Greece
185 J6 **Nafplio** Greece
139 J5 **Nafṭ, Āb** *r.* Iraq
137 G2 **Naftalan** Azer.
142 C4 **Naft-e Safīd** Iran
139 J5 **Nafṭ Khāneh** Iraq
142 B3 **Naft Shahr** Iran
181 F5 **Nafūsah, Jabal** *hills* Libya
142 A5 **Nafy** Saudi Arabia
149 G2 **Nag, Co** *l.* China
161 I3 **Naga** Phil.
206 D4 **Nagagami** *r.* Canada
159 C8 **Nagahama** Japan
149 H4 **Naga Hills** India
159 G5 **Nagai** Japan
149 H4 **Nagaland** *state* India
125 F6 **Nagambie** Australia
159 F6 **Nagano** Japan
159 F6 **Nagaoka** Japan
149 H4 **Nagaon** India
147 H4 **Nagapattinam** India
148 D2 **Nagar** India
147 H2 **Nagarjuna Sagar Reservoir** India
148 B4 **Nagar Parkar** Pak.
149 G3 **Nagarzê** China
159 A8 **Nagasaki** Japan
159 B7 **Nagato** Japan
148 C4 **Nagaur** India
147 I2 **Nagavali** *r.* India
148 C5 **Nagda** India
147 H4 **Nagercoil** India
143 G5 **Nagha Kalat** Pak.
148 D3 **Nagina** India
149 E3 **Nagma** Nepal
139 K2 **Nagorno-Karabakh** *disp. terr* Azer.
186 I3 **Nagorsk** Russia
159 E7 **Nagoya** Japan
148 D5 **Nagpur** India
149 H3 **Nagqu** China
161 J3 **Nagumbuaya Point** Phil.
132 F1 **Nagurskoye** Russia
185 G1 **Nagyatád** Hungary
177 H7 **Nagykanizsa** Hungary
151 E4 **Naha** Japan
148 D3 **Nahan** India
143 F5 **Nahang** *r.* Iran/Pak.
204 E2 **Nahanni Butte** Canada
Nahanni National Park Canada *see* **Nahanni National Park Reserve**
204 D2 **Nahanni National Park Reserve** Canada
138 E5 **Nahariyya** Israel
142 C3 **Nahāvand** Iran
179 F5 **Nahe** *r.* Germany
143 H2 **Nahrīn** Afgh.
143 H3 **Nahrīn** *reg.* Afgh.
235 H3 **Nahuelbuta, Parque Nacional** *nat. park* Chile
235 H4 **Nahuel Huapí, Lago** *l.* Arg.
235 H4 **Nahuel Huapí, Parque Nacional** *nat. park* Arg.
219 D6 **Nahunta** U.S.A.
224 C2 **Naica** Mex.
149 H2 **Naij Tal** China
120 C1 **Naikliu** Indon.
207 H2 **Nain** Canada
142 D3 **Nā'īn** Iran
148 D3 **Nainital** India
149 E5 **Nainpur** India
174 E3 **Nairn** U.K.
209 G2 **Nairn Centre** Canada
195 D4 **Nairobi** Kenya
195 D4 **Naivasha** Kenya
160 D2 **Naizishan** China
140 B5 **Na'jān** Saudi Arabia
146 B4 **Najd** *reg.* Saudi Arabia
183 O1 **Nájera** Spain
156 A2 **Naji** China
148 D3 **Najibabad** India
161 F2 **Najin** N. Korea
Najitun China *see* **Naji**
146 B6 **Najrān** Saudi Arabia
159 A8 **Nakadōri-shima** *i.* Japan
162 C1 **Na Kae** Thai.
159 B8 **Nakama** Japan
Nakamura Japan *see* **Shimanto**
133 L3 **Nakanno** Russia
159 F6 **Nakano** Japan
159 C6 **Nakano-shima** *i.* Japan
143 H3 **Naka Pass** Afgh.
159 B8 **Nakatsu** Japan
159 E7 **Nakatsugawa** Japan
160 E6 **Nakdong-gang** *r.* S. Korea
194 D2 **Nakfa** Eritrea
193 F1 **Nakhl** Egypt
150 F2 **Nakhodka** Russia
162 B2 **Nakhon Nayok** Thai.
162 B2 **Nakhon Pathom** Thai.
162 C1 **Nakhon Phanom** Thai.
162 B2 **Nakhon Ratchasima** Thai.
162 B2 **Nakhon Sawan** Thai.
162 A3 **Nakhon Si Thammarat** Thai.
148 B5 **Nakhtarana** India
204 C3 **Nakina** B.C. Canada
206 C3 **Nakina** Ont. Canada
202 C4 **Naknek** U.S.A.
194 D4 **Nakonde** Zambia
171 J5 **Nakskov** Denmark
195 D4 **Nakuru** Kenya
204 F4 **Nakusp** Canada
143 G5 **Nal** Pak.
143 G5 **Nal** *r.* Pak.
197 J2 **Nalázi** Moz.
149 G4 **Nalbari** India
187 G7 **Nal'chik** Russia
147 H2 **Naldurg** India
147 H2 **Nalgonda** India
147 H3 **Nallamala Hills** India
138 C1 **Nallıhan** Turkey
141 G1 **Nalobino** Kazakh.
193 D1 **Nālūt** Libya
197 J2 **Namaacha** Moz.
197 H3 **Namahadi** S. Africa
142 C3 **Namak, Daryācheh-ye** *salt flat* Iran
143 E3 **Namak, Kavīr-e** *salt flat* Iran
143 E4 **Namakzar-e Shadad** *salt flat* Iran
195 D4 **Namanga** Kenya
141 G4 **Namangan** Uzbek.
195 D5 **Namapa** Moz.
196 B4 **Namaqualand** *reg.* S. Africa
139 J3 **Namashīr** Iran
119 F2 **Namatanai** P.N.G.
125 J1 **Nambour** Australia
125 J3 **Nambucca Heads** Australia
121 A6 **Nambung National Park** Australia
162 C3 **Năm Căn** Vietnam
Namch'ŏn N. Korea *see* **P'yŏngsan**
150 B3 **Nam Co** *salt l.* China
170 K2 **Namdalen** *val.* Norway
170 J2 **Namdalseid** Norway
155 C6 **Nam Định** Vietnam
208 B3 **Namekagon** *r.* U.S.A.
160 D4 **Nam-gang** *r.* N. Korea
160 E6 **Namhae-do** *i.* S. Korea
196 B3 **Namib Desert** Namibia
195 B5 **Namibe** Angola
195 B6 **Namibia** *country* Africa
239 J8 **Namibia Abyssal Plain** *sea feature* N. Atlantic Ocean
159 G6 **Namie (abandoned)** Japan
137 H3 **Namīn** Iran
149 H3 **Namjagbarwa Feng** *mt.* China
151 E7 **Namlea** Indon.
162 A1 **Nammekon** Myanmar
125 H3 **Namoi** *r.* Australia
204 F3 **Nampa** Canada
149 E3 **Nampa** *mt.* Nepal
213 C3 **Nampa** U.S.A.
192 B3 **Nampala** Mali
162 B1 **Nam Pat** Thai.
162 B1 **Nam Phong** Thai.
160 C4 **Namp'o** N. Korea
195 D5 **Nampula** Moz.
135 H4 **Namrup** India
149 H4 **Namsai** India
149 E3 **Namsê La** *pass* Nepal
170 J2 **Namsen** *r.* Norway
149 G3 **Namsi La** *pass* Bhutan
170 J2 **Namsos** Norway
162 C1 **Nam Theun 2** *resr* Laos
133 N3 **Namtsy** Russia
151 B4 **Namtu** Myanmar
178 C4 **Namur** Belgium
195 C5 **Namwala** Zambia
160 D6 **Namwon** S. Korea
152 G6 **Namya Ra** Myanmar
162 B1 **Nan** Thai.
162 B2 **Nan, Mae Nam** *r.* Thai.
194 B3 **Nana Bakassa** C.A.R.
204 E5 **Nanaimo** Canada
214 □1 **Nānākuli** U.S.A.
160 E3 **Nanam** N. Korea
155 F5 **Nan'an** China
196 B2 **Nananib Plateau** Namibia
159 E6 **Nanao** Japan
155 E6 **Nan'ao Dao** *i.* China
159 E6 **Nanatsu-shima** *i.* Japan
155 C4 **Nanbu** China
158 A1 **Nancha** China
155 E4 **Nanchang** *Jiangxi* China
155 E4 **Nanchang** *Jiangxi* China
155 E5 **Nancheng** China
155 C4 **Nanchong** China
155 C4 **Nanchuan** China
145 H10 **Nancowry** *i.* India
182 H2 **Nancy** France
149 E3 **Nanda Devi** *mt.* India
149 E3 **Nanda Kot** *mt.* India
155 C5 **Nandan** China
147 H2 **Nanded** India
125 I3 **Nandewar Range** *mts* Australia
148 C5 **Nandgaon** India
155 D6 **Nandu Jiang** *r.* China
148 C5 **Nandurbar** India
147 H3 **Nandyal** India
155 D6 **Nanfeng** *Guangdong* China
155 E5 **Nanfeng** *Jiangxi* China
149 H3 **Nang** China
193 D4 **Nanga Eboko** Cameroon
163 H3 **Nangahpinoh** Indon.
160 E2 **Nangang Ling** *mts* China/N. Korea
148 C2 **Nanga Parbat** *mt.* Pak.
163 H3 **Nangatayap** Indon.
162 A3 **Nangin** Myanmar
160 D3 **Nangnim** N. Korea
160 D3 **Nangnim-sanmaek** *mts* N. Korea
154 E2 **Nangong** China
152 G5 **Nangqên** China
195 D4 **Nangulangwa** Tanz.
154 A2 **Nanhua** China
155 F4 **Nanhui** China
147 H3 **Nanjangud** India
154 C3 **Nanjiang** China
155 E5 **Nanjing** *Fujian* China
154 F3 **Nanjing** *Jiangsu* China
155 E5 **Nankang** China
Nanking China *see* **Nanjing**
159 C8 **Nankoku** Japan
195 B5 **Nankova** Angola
154 E2 **Nanle** China
155 F4 **Nanling** China
155 D5 **Nan Ling** *mts* China
155 C6 **Nanliu Jiang** *r.* China
121 B5 **Nannine (abandoned)** Australia
155 C6 **Nanning** China
121 A7 **Nannup** Australia
162 B1 **Na Noi** Thai.
203 N3 **Nanortalik** Greenland
155 C5 **Nanpan Jiang** *r.* China
160 A3 **Nanpiao** China
155 F5 **Nanping** China
155 F5 **Nanri Dao** *i.* China
Nansei-shotō *is* Japan *see* **Ryukyu Islands**
240 B1 **Nansen Basin** *sea feature* Arctic Ocean
203 I1 **Nansen Sound** *sea chan.* Canada
182 D3 **Nantes** France
178 A5 **Nanteuil-le-Haudouin** France
147 I4 **Nanthi Kadal Lagoon** *lag.* Sri Lanka
209 G4 **Nanticoke** Canada
221 F5 **Nanticoke** *r.* U.S.A.
205 G4 **Nanton** Canada
155 F4 **Nantong** China
155 F6 **Nantou** Taiwan
221 H4 **Nantucket** U.S.A.
221 H4 **Nantucket Island** U.S.A.
221 H4 **Nantucket Sound** *g.* U.S.A.
173 E4 **Nantwich** U.K.
119 H2 **Nanumanga** *i.* Tuvalu
119 H2 **Nanumea** *atoll* Tuvalu
234 E2 **Nanuque** Brazil
161 J5 **Nanusa, Kepulauan** *is* Indon.
155 B4 **Nanxi** China
155 D4 **Nanxian** China
155 E5 **Nanxiong** China
154 D3 **Nanyang** China
160 C3 **Nanzamu** China
155 D4 **Nanzhang** China
154 D3 **Nanzhao** China
183 Q3 **Nao, Cabo de la** *c.* Spain
207 F3 **Naococane, Lac** *l.* Canada
149 G4 **Naogaon** Bangl.
158 C1 **Naoli He** *r.* China
143 F3 **Nāomīd, Dasht-e** *des.* Afgh./Iran
148 C2 **Naoshera** India
155 D6 **Naozhou Dao** *i.* China
214 A2 **Napa** U.S.A.
221 J1 **Napadogan** Canada
205 G1 **Napaktulik Lake** Canada
209 I3 **Napanee** Canada
148 C4 **Napasar** India
203 M3 **Napasoq** Greenland
208 C5 **Naperville** U.S.A.
126 F3 **Napier** N.Z.
120 D3 **Napier Range** *hills* Australia
221 G2 **Napierville** Canada
184 F4 **Naples** Italy
219 D7 **Naples** *FL* U.S.A.
221 H3 **Naples** *ME* U.S.A.
155 B6 **Napo** China
230 D4 **Napo** *r.* Ecuador/Peru
220 A4 **Napoleon** U.S.A.
Napoli Italy *see* **Naples**
235 J3 **Naposta** Arg.
235 J3 **Naposta** *r.* Arg.
209 E5 **Nappanee** U.S.A.
139 J3 **Naqadeh** Iran
139 L4 **Naqqash** Iran
159 D7 **Nara** Japan
192 B3 **Nara** Mali
177 M3 **Narach** Belarus
124 D6 **Naracoorte** Australia
125 G4 **Naradhan** Australia
148 C4 **Naraina** India
224 B2 **Naranjo** Mex.
225 E3 **Naranjos** Mex.
147 J2 **Narasannapeta** India
147 I2 **Narasapatnam, Point** India
147 I2 **Narasapur** India
147 I2 **Narasaraopet** India
149 F5 **Narasinghapur** India
162 B4 **Narathiwat** Thai.
147 G2 **Narayangaon** India
149 E6 **Narayanpur** India
173 C6 **Narberth** U.K.
183 F5 **Narbonne** France
183 M1 **Narcea** *r.* Spain
142 D2 **Nardīn** Iran
184 H4 **Nardò** Italy
235 K1 **Naré** Arg.
148 B3 **Narechi** *r.* Pak.
121 B7 **Narembeen** Australia
239 E4 **Nares Abyssal Plain** *sea feature* S. Atlantic Ocean
239 E4 **Nares Deep** *sea feature* N. Atlantic Ocean
203 L1 **Nares Strait** Canada/Greenland
121 D6 **Naretha** Australia
177 J4 **Narew** *r.* Poland
160 D2 **Narhong** China
148 A3 **Nari** *r.* Pak.
195 B6 **Narib** Namibia
196 B5 **Nariep** S. Africa
187 H6 **Narimanov** Russia
139 G3 **Narince** Turkey
149 H1 **Narin Gol** *watercourse* China
159 G7 **Narita** Japan
224 B2 **Narizon, Punta** *pt* Mex.
148 C5 **Narmada** *r.* India
139 H1 **Narman** Turkey
148 D3 **Narnaul** India
184 E3 **Narni** Italy
169 S3 **Narodnaya, Gora** *mt.* Russia
177 N5 **Narodychi** Ukr.
187 F4 **Naro-Fominsk** Russia
125 I6 **Narooma** Australia
187 G4 **Narovchat** Russia
187 D5 **Narowlya** Belarus
171 M3 **Närpes** Fin.
125 H3 **Narrabri** Australia
221 H4 **Narragansett Bay** U.S.A.
125 G2 **Narran** *r.* Australia
125 G5 **Narrandera** Australia
125 G2 **Narran Lake** Australia
121 B7 **Narrogin** Australia
125 H4 **Narromine** Australia
205 I4 **Narrow Hills Provincial Park** Canada
220 C6 **Narrows** U.S.A.
221 F4 **Narrowsburg** U.S.A.
148 D5 **Narsimhapur** India
149 G5 **Narsingdi** Bangl.
148 D5 **Narsinghgarh** India
Narsinghpur India *see* **Narsimhapur**
147 I2 **Narsipatnam** India
154 E1 **Nart** China
137 F2 **Nartkala** Russia
159 D7 **Naruto** Japan
171 O4 **Narva** Estonia
171 N4 **Narva Bay** Estonia/Russia
161 I2 **Narvacan** Phil.
171 O4 **Narva Reservoir** Estonia/Russia
170 L1 **Narvik** Norway
Narvskoye Vodokhranilishche *resr* Estonia/Russia *see* **Narva Reservoir**
148 D3 **Narwana** India
148 D4 **Narwar** India
132 G3 **Nar'yan-Mar** Russia
141 H4 **Naryn** Kyrg.
141 H4 **Naryn** *r.* Kyrg.
141 K2 **Naryn, Khrebet** *mts* Kazakh.
141 J4 **Narynkol** Kazakh.
171 L3 **Nåsåker** Sweden
Na Scealagae Skelligs *is* Ireland *see* **The Skelligs**
215 H3 **Naschitti** U.S.A.
126 C6 **Naseby** N.Z.
148 C5 **Nashik** India
208 A4 **Nashua** *IA* U.S.A.
221 H3 **Nashua** *NH* U.S.A.
219 C4 **Nashville** U.S.A.
139 F5 **Naşīb** Syria
171 M3 **Näsijärvi** *l.* Fin.
193 F4 **Nasir** South Sudan
193 F2 **Nāşir, Buḩayrat** *resr* Egypt
148 B3 **Nasirabad** Pak.
195 C5 **Nasondoye** Dem. Rep. Congo
138 C6 **Naşr** Egypt
143 E3 **Naşrābād** Iran
Nasratabad *Sīstān va Balūchestān* Iran *see* **Mehrestān**
139 K5 **Naşrīān** Iran
204 D3 **Nass** *r.* Canada
122 C2 **Nassau** *r.* Australia
219 E7 **Nassau** Bahamas
237 H6 **Nassau** *i.* Cook Is
171 K4 **Nässjö** Sweden
203 M3 **Nassuttooq** *inlet* Greenland
206 E2 **Nastapoca** *r.* Canada
206 E2 **Nastapoka Islands** Canada
159 F6 **Nasu-dake** *vol.* Japan
161 I3 **Nasugbu** Phil.
159 G6 **Nasushiobara** Japan
177 O2 **Nasva** Russia
195 C6 **Nata** Botswana
195 D4 **Nata** Tanz.
233 I4 **Natagaima** Col.
231 K5 **Natal** Brazil
Natal *prov.* S. Africa *see* **KwaZulu-Natal**
238 G7 **Natal Basin** *sea feature* Indian Ocean
142 C3 **Naţanz** Iran
207 H3 **Natashquan** Canada
207 H3 **Natashquan** *r.* Canada
217 F6 **Natchez** U.S.A.
217 E6 **Natchitoches** U.S.A.
176 G4 **Natecka, Puszcza** *for.* Poland
125 F6 **Nathalia** Australia
162 B4 **Na Thawi** Thai.
148 C4 **Nathdwara** India
183 R2 **Nati, Punta** *pt* Spain
124 D6 **Natimuk** Australia
215 D5 **National City** U.S.A.
192 C3 **Natitingou** Benin
231 I6 **Natividade** Brazil
224 B1 **Nátora** Mex.
159 G5 **Natori** Japan
195 D4 **Natron, Lake** *salt l.* Tanz.
162 A1 **Nattaung** *mt.* Myanmar
207 H2 **Natuashish** Canada
163 G2 **Natuna, Kepulauan** *is* Indon.
163 G2 **Natuna Besar** *i.* Indon.
221 F2 **Natural Bridge** U.S.A.
215 G3 **Natural Bridges National Monument** *nat. park* U.S.A.
121 A7 **Naturaliste, Cape** Australia
238 L7 **Naturaliste Plateau** *sea feature* Indian Ocean
215 H2 **Naturita** U.S.A.
209 E2 **Naubinway** U.S.A.
195 B6 **Nauchas** Namibia
179 K2 **Nauen** Germany
221 G4 **Naugatuck** U.S.A.
161 I3 **Naujan** Phil.
161 I3 **Naujan, Lake** Phil.
171 M4 **Naujoji Akmen** Lith.
148 C4 **Naukh** India
148 B4 **Naukot** Pak.
179 H3 **Naumburg (Hessen)** Germany
179 J3 **Naumburg (Saale)** Germany
162 A1 **Naungpale** Myanmar
138 E6 **Na'ūr** Jordan
143 G4 **Nauroz Kalat** Pak.
137 G2 **Naurskaya** Russia
119 G2 **Nauru** *country* Pacific Ocean
148 B4 **Naushara** Pak.
171 I3 **Naustdal** Norway
230 D4 **Nauta** Peru
196 C3 **Naute Dam** Namibia
225 E3 **Nautla** Mex.
149 G5 **Navadwip** India
187 C4 **Navahrudak** Belarus
215 H4 **Navajo** U.S.A.
213 F4 **Navajo Lake** U.S.A.
215 G3 **Navajo Mountain** U.S.A.
161 J4 **Naval** Phil.
183 N3 **Navalmoral de la Mata** Spain
183 N3 **Navalvillar de Pela** Spain
175 L4 **Navan** Ireland
187 D4 **Navapolatsk** Belarus
133 S3 **Navarin, Mys** *c.* Russia
232 C9 **Navarino, Isla** *i.* Chile
183 P1 **Navarra** *aut. comm.* Spain
125 E6 **Navarre** Australia
214 A2 **Navarro** U.S.A.
187 G4 **Navashino** Russia
217 D6 **Navasota** U.S.A.
174 D2 **Naver, Loch** *l.* U.K.
171 K3 **Näverede** Sweden
235 H2 **Navidad** Chile
147 G2 **Navi Mumbai** India
187 E4 **Navlya** Russia
185 M2 **Năvodari** Romania
Navoi Uzbek. *see* **Navoiy**
141 F4 **Navoiy** Uzbek.
224 B2 **Navojoa** Mex.
186 G3 **Navoloki** Russia
148 C5 **Navsari** India
148 C4 **Nawa** India
139 F5 **Nawá** Syria
149 G4 **Nawabganj** Bangl.
148 B4 **Nawabshah** Pak.
149 F4 **Nawada** India
143 G3 **Nāwah** Afgh.
148 C4 **Nawalgarh** India
152 G7 **Nawngleng** Myanmar

Niellé

Ohrid

174 □ Noss, Isle of i. U.K.
234 A1 Nossa Senhora do Livramento Brazil
171 K4 Nossebro Sweden
196 C2 Nossob watercourse Africa alt. Nosop
195 E6 Nosy Varika Madag.
215 F2 Notch Peak U.S.A.
177 H4 Noteć r. Poland
184 F6 Noto, Golfo di g. Sicily Italy
171 J4 Notodden Norway
159 E6 Noto-hantō pen. Japan
207 G4 Notre-Dame, Monts mts Canada
207 J4 Notre Dame Bay Canada
209 J3 Notre-Dame-de-la-Salette Canada
221 H2 Notre-Dame-des-Bois Canada
209 J2 Notre-Dame-du-Laus Canada
209 H2 Notre-Dame-du-Nord Canada
209 G3 Nottawasaga Bay Canada
206 E3 Nottaway r. Canada
173 F5 Nottingham U.K.
215 E6 Nottoway r. U.S.A.
179 F3 Nottuln Germany
205 H5 Notukeu Creek r. Canada
194 B3 Nouabalé-Ndoki, Parc National de nat. park Congo
192 A2 Nouâdhibou Mauritania
192 A3 Nouakchott Mauritania
192 A3 Nouâmghâr Mauritania
162 C2 Nouei Vietnam
119 G4 Nouméa New Caledonia
192 B3 Nouna Burkina Faso
197 F5 Noupoort S. Africa
170 O2 Nousu Fin.
119 G4 Nouvelle-Calédonie i. S. Pacific Ocean
141 G4 Nov Tajik.
234 C1 Nova América Brazil
234 B3 Nova Esperança Brazil
234 D3 Nova Friburgo Brazil
185 G2 Nova Gradiška Croatia
234 C3 Nova Granada Brazil
234 D3 Nova Iguaçu Brazil
187 E6 Nova Kakhovka Ukr.
234 D2 Nova Lima Brazil
187 D4 Novalukoml' Belarus
187 D6 Nova Odesa Ukr.
234 C2 Nova Ponte Brazil
234 C2 Nova Ponte, Represa resr Brazil
184 C2 Novara Italy
234 C1 Nova Roma Brazil
207 H5 Nova Scotia prov. Canada
214 A2 Novato U.S.A.
234 E2 Nova Venécia Brazil
234 B1 Nova Xavantina Brazil
169 M3 Novaya Ladoga Russia
137 E2 Novaya Matsesta Russia
133 Q2 Novaya Sibir', Ostrov i. Russia
132 G2 Novaya Zemlya is Russia
185 L3 Nova Zagora Bulg.
183 P3 Novelda Spain
177 I7 Nové Zámky Slovakia
186 E3 Novgorodskaya Oblast' admin. div. Russia
187 E5 Novhorod-Sivers'kyy Ukr.
141 J1 Novichikha Russia
185 J3 Novi Iskar Bulg.
158 H1 Novikovo Russia
184 C2 Novi Ligure Italy
185 I3 Novi Pazar Bulg.
185 I3 Novi Pazar Serbia
185 H2 Novi Sad Serbia
187 G6 Novoaleksandrovsk Russia
152 D1 Novoaltaysk Russia
187 G5 Novoanninskiy Russia
231 F5 Novo Aripuanã Brazil
187 F6 Novoazovs'k Ukr.
141 G5 Novobod Tajik.
186 I3 Novocheboksarsk Russia
187 G6 Novocherkassk Russia
141 H2 Novodolinka Kazakh.
186 G1 Novodvinsk Russia
156 B2 Novogeorgiyevka Russia
232 F3 Novo Hamburgo Brazil
234 C3 Novo Horizonte Brazil
176 G6 Novohradské hory mts Czech Rep.
187 C5 Novohrad-Volyns'kyy Ukr.
141 F1 Novoishimskiy Kazakh.
140 D1 Novokaolinovyy Russia
156 C2 Novokiyevskiy Uval Russia
187 G6 Novokubansk Russia
140 B1 Novokuybyshevsk Russia
150 A1 Novokuznetsk Russia
127 K3 Novolazarevskaya research stn Antarctica
141 H2 Novomarkovka Kazakh.
184 F2 Novo mesto Slovenia
187 F4 Novomichurinsk Russia
187 F6 Novomikhaylovskiy Russia
187 F4 Novomoskovsk Russia
187 E5 Novomoskovs'k Ukr.
187 D5 Novomyrhorod Ukr.
187 G5 Novonikolayevskiy Russia
141 G1 Novonikolskoye Kazakh.
187 E6 Novooleksiyivka Ukr.
140 D2 Novoorsk Russia
141 F1 Novopokrovka Kostanayskaya Oblast' Kazakh.
141 F1 Novopokrovka Severnyy Kazakhstan Kazakh.
141 J2 Novopokrovka Vostochnyy Kazakhstan Kazakh.
158 D2 Novopokrovka Russia
187 G6 Novopokrovskaya Russia
187 I5 Novorepnoye Russia
156 C1 Novorossiyka Russia
187 F6 Novorossiysk Russia
133 L2 Novorybnaya Russia
177 N2 Novorzhev Russia
187 E6 Novoselivs'ke Crimea
Novoselskoye Russia see Achkhoy-Martan
177 N1 Novosel'ye Russia
140 C1 Novosergiyevka Russia
187 F6 Novoshakhtinsk Russia
158 C2 Novoshakhtinskiy Russia
133 J4 Novosibirsk Russia
Novosibirskiye Ostrova is Russia see New Siberia Islands
186 D3 Novosokol'niki Russia
187 H4 Novospasskoye Russia
140 D2 Novotroitsk Russia
187 E6 Novotroyits'ke Ukr.
187 D5 Novoukrayinka Ukr.
140 D2 Novoural'sk Russia
156 E2 Novoussuri (abandoned) Russia
187 I5 Novouzensk Russia
141 H1 Novovarshavka Russia
187 C5 Novovolyns'k Ukr.
187 F5 Novovoronezh Russia
156 B1 Novovoskresenovka Russia
141 J2 Novoyegor'yevskoye Russia
187 D4 Novozybkov Russia
177 H6 Nový Jičín Czech Rep.
Novyy Afon Georgia see Akhali Atoni
187 F5 Novyy Oskol Russia
132 I3 Novyy Port Russia
186 I3 Novyy Tor''yal Russia
132 I3 Novyy Urengoy Russia
150 F1 Novyy Urgal Russia
142 D4 Now Iran
217 E4 Nowata U.S.A.
142 C3 Nowbarān Iran
142 D3 Now Deh Iran
139 L3 Nowdī Iran
148 D4 Nowgong India
205 I2 Nowleye Lake Canada
176 G4 Nowogard Poland
125 I5 Nowra Australia
142 C2 Nowshahr Ardabīl Iran
142 C2 Nowshahr Māzandarān Iran
148 C2 Nowshera Pak.
177 J6 Nowy Sącz Poland
177 J6 Nowy Targ Poland
143 G3 Now Zād Afgh.
221 E4 Noxen U.S.A.
162 C1 Noy, Xé r. Laos
162 C1 Noy, Xé r. Laos
132 I3 Noyabr'sk Russia
204 C3 Noyes Island U.S.A.
182 F2 Noyon France
152 C2 Noyon Mongolia
197 F5 Nozizwe S. Africa
197 I4 Nqutu S. Africa
195 D5 Nsanje Malawi
197 H5 Ntabankulu S. Africa
195 B4 Ntandembele Dem. Rep. Congo
197 G3 Ntha S. Africa
185 K5 Ntoro, Kavo pt Greece
195 D4 Ntungamo Uganda
193 F3 Nuba Mountains Sudan
139 J1 Nubarashen Armenia
193 F2 Nubian Desert Sudan
235 H3 Ñuble r. Chile
Nüden Mongolia see Ulaanbadrah
217 D6 Nueces r. U.S.A.
205 J2 Nueltin Lake Canada
224 G5 Nueva Arcadia Hond.
224 H5 Nueva Armenia Hond.
233 J2 Nueva Florida Venez.
235 L2 Nueva Helvecia Uruguay
235 H3 Nueva Imperial Chile
233 H4 Nueva Loja Ecuador
232 B6 Nueva Lubecka Arg.
225 G5 Nueva Ocotepeque Hond.
225 D2 Nueva Rosita Mex.
Nueva San Salvador El Salvador see Santa Tecla
223 I4 Nuevitas Cuba
235 J4 Nuevo, Golfo g. Arg.
222 C2 Nuevo Casas Grandes Mex.
224 C2 Nuevo Ideal Mex.
225 E2 Nuevo Laredo Mex.
225 E2 Nuevo León state Mex.
194 E3 Nugaal watercourse Somalia
194 E3 Nugaaleed, Dooxo val. Somalia
126 B7 Nugget Point N.Z.
119 F2 Nuguria Islands P.N.G.
126 F3 Nuhaka N.Z.
119 H2 Nui atoll Tuvalu
Nu Jiang r. China see Salween
124 A4 Nukey Bluff h. Australia
142 D3 Nūklok, Chāh-e well Iran
119 I4 Nuku'alofa Tonga
119 H2 Nukufetau atoll Tuvalu
117 J5 Nuku Hiva i. Fr. Polynesia
119 H2 Nukulaelae atoll Tuvalu
119 F2 Nukumanu Islands P.N.G.
Nukunono i. Pacific Ocean see Nukunonu
119 I2 Nukunonu atoll Pacific Ocean
140 D4 Nukus Uzbek.
118 C4 Nullagine Australia
121 E6 Nullarbor Australia
121 E6 Nullarbor National Park Australia
118 C5 Nullarbor Plain Australia
121 E6 Nullarbor Regional Reserve park Australia
154 F1 Nulu'erhu Shan mts China
125 F2 Numalla, Lake salt flat Australia
193 D4 Numan Nigeria
159 F6 Numata Japan
159 F7 Numazu Japan
122 A2 Numbulwar Australia
171 J3 Numedal val. Norway
151 F7 Numfoor i. Indon.
156 B3 Numin He r. China
125 F6 Numurkah Australia
207 H2 Nunaksaluk Island Canada
203 N3 Nunakuluut i. Greenland
Nunap Isua c. Greenland see Farewell, Cape
206 E2 Nunavik reg. Canada
203 H3 Nunavut admin. div. Canada
221 E3 Nunda U.S.A.
125 I3 Nundle Australia
173 F5 Nuneaton U.K.
153 K2 Nungnain Sum China
202 B4 Nunivak Island U.S.A.
148 D2 Nunkun mt. India
133 T3 Nunligran Russia
183 M2 Nuñomoral Spain
178 D2 Nunspeet Neth.
184 C4 Nuoro Sardinia Italy
119 G3 Nupani i. Solomon Is
146 B4 Nuqrah Saudi Arabia
233 H3 Nuquí Col.
149 E1 Nur China
142 C2 Nūr Iran
141 H2 Nura Kazakh.
141 G2 Nura r. Kazakh.
142 C4 Nūrābād Iran
Nurata Uzbek. see Nurota
Nuratau, Khrebet mts Uzbek. see Nurota tizmasi
136 D3 Nur Dağları mts Turkey
179 J5 Nuremberg Germany
143 H3 Nūrestān reg. Afgh.
139 I2 Nurettin Turkey
224 B1 Nuri Mex.
124 C5 Nuriootpa Australia
187 I4 Nurlaty Russia
171 O3 Nurmes Fin.
171 M3 Nurmo Fin.
Nürnberg Germany see Nuremberg
141 F4 Nurota Uzbek.
141 F4 Nurota tizmasi mts Uzbek.
125 G3 Nurri, Mount h. Australia
142 D2 Nūr Rūd r. Iran
149 H1 Nur Turu China
139 H3 Nusaybin Turkey
139 F4 Nuşayrīyah, Jabal an mts Syria
142 C3 Nūshābād Iran
152 G6 Nu Shan mts China
143 G4 Nushki Pak.
207 H2 Nutak Canada
215 H5 Nutrioso U.S.A.
148 B3 Nuttal Pak.
120 F2 Nutwood Downs Australia
240 U2 Nuuk Greenland
170 N2 Nuupas Fin.
203 M2 Nuussuaq Greenland
203 M2 Nuussuaq pen. Greenland
147 I5 Nuwara Eliya Sri Lanka
136 D5 Nuwaybi' al Muzayyinah Egypt
Nuweiba el Muzeina Egypt see Nuwaybi' al Muzayyinah
196 C5 Nuwerus S. Africa
196 D6 Nuweveldberge mts S. Africa
121 B7 Nuyts, Point Australia
121 F7 Nuyts Archipelago is Australia
139 J4 Nuzi tourist site Iraq
197 I1 Nwanedi Nature Reserve S. Africa
132 H3 Nyagan' Russia
125 E5 Nyah West Australia
149 G3 Nyainqêntanglha Feng mt. China
149 G3 Nyainqêntanglha Shan mts China
149 H2 Nyainrong China
171 L3 Nyåker Sweden
193 E3 Nyala Sudan
Nyalam China see Congdü
195 C5 Nyamandhlovu Zimbabwe
186 G2 Nyandoma Russia
186 F2 Nyandomskaya Vozvyshennost' hills Russia
195 B4 Nyanga r. Gabon
195 D5 Nyanga Zimbabwe
149 G3 Nyang Qu r. Xizang Zizhiqu China
149 H3 Nyang Qu r. Xizang Zizhiqu China
148 D3 Nyar r. India
195 D5 Nyasa, Lake Africa
187 C4 Nyasvizh Belarus
171 J5 Nyborg Denmark
170 O1 Nyborg Norway
171 K4 Nybro Sweden
203 M1 Nyeboe Land reg. Greenland
149 G3 Nyêmo China
195 D4 Nyeri Kenya
151 B4 Nyinghci China
177 J7 Nyíregyháza Hungary
171 M3 Nykarleby Fin.
171 J5 Nykøbing Falster Denmark
171 J5 Nykøbing Sjælland Denmark
171 L4 Nyköping Sweden
171 L3 Nyland Sweden
Nylstroom S. Africa see Modimolle
125 G4 Nymagee Australia
125 J2 Nymboida Australia
125 J2 Nymboida r. Australia
171 L4 Nynäshamn Sweden
125 G3 Nyngan Australia
177 K4 Nyoman r. Belarus/Lith.
176 C7 Nyon Switz.
149 F3 Nyonni Ri mt. China
182 G4 Nyons France
132 G3 Nyrob Russia
177 H5 Nysa Poland
156 F2 Nysh Russia
186 I2 Nyuchpas Russia
159 F5 Nyūdō-zaki pt Japan
195 C4 Nyunzu Dem. Rep. Congo
133 M3 Nyurba Russia
186 I2 Nyuvchim Russia
156 F1 Nyyskiy Zaliv lag. Russia
187 E6 Nyzhn'ohirs'kyy Crimea
195 D4 Nzega Tanz.
192 B4 Nzérékoré Guinea
195 B4 N'zeto Angola
197 I1 Nzhelele Dam S. Africa

O

216 C2 Oahe, Lake U.S.A.
Oahu i. U.S.A. see O'ahu
214 □1 O'ahu i. U.S.A.
124 D4 Oakbank Australia
215 F2 Oak City U.S.A.
217 E6 Oakdale U.S.A.
216 D2 Oakes U.S.A.
125 I1 Oakey Australia
173 G5 Oakham U.K.
212 B1 Oak Harbor U.S.A.
220 C6 Oak Hill U.S.A.
214 C3 Oakhurst U.S.A.
208 B2 Oak Island U.S.A.
214 A3 Oakland CA U.S.A.
220 D5 Oakland MD U.S.A.
216 D3 Oakland NE U.S.A.
213 B3 Oakland OR U.S.A.
125 G5 Oaklands Australia
208 D5 Oak Lawn U.S.A.
217 C4 Oakley U.S.A.
118 C4 Oakover r. Australia
213 B3 Oakridge U.S.A.
219 C4 Oak Ridge U.S.A.
124 D4 Oakvale Australia
209 H4 Oakville Canada
126 C6 Oamaru N.Z.
126 D5 Oaro N.Z.
161 I3 Oas Phil.
213 D3 Oasis U.S.A.
127 I6 Oates Land reg. Antarctica
125 G9 Oatlands Australia
215 E4 Oatman U.S.A.
225 E4 Oaxaca Mex.
225 E4 Oaxaca state Mex.
132 H3 Ob' r. Russia
141 J2 Oba r. Kazakh.
193 D4 Obala Cameroon
159 D7 Obama Japan
174 C4 Oban U.K.
159 G5 Obanazawa Japan
183 M1 O Barco Spain
207 F4 Obatogamau, Lac Canada
204 F4 Obed Canada
143 F3 Ōbêh Afgh.
126 B6 Obelisk mt. N.Z.
179 H4 Oberaula Germany
179 I3 Oberdorla Germany
179 E3 Oberhausen Germany
217 C4 Oberlin KS U.S.A.
220 B4 Oberlin OH U.S.A.
179 F5 Obermoschel Germany
125 H4 Oberon Australia
179 K5 Oberpfälzer Wald mts Germany
179 H4 Obersinn Germany
179 H4 Oberthulba Germany
179 G4 Obertshausen Germany
179 H3 Oberwälder Land reg. Germany
151 E7 Obi i. Indon.
231 G4 Óbidos Brazil
141 G5 Obigarm Tajik.
158 H3 Obihiro Japan
187 H6 Obil'noye Russia
233 J2 Obispos Venez.
150 F2 Obluch'ye Russia
187 F4 Obninsk Russia
194 C3 Obo C.A.R.
154 A2 Obo China
194 E2 Obock Djibouti
160 E3 Ŏbŏk N. Korea
195 C4 Obokote Dem. Rep. Congo
144 H4 Obo Liang China
187 F5 Oboyan' Russia
186 G2 Obozerskiy Russia
149 E4 Obra India
149 E4 Obra Dam India
224 B1 Obregón, Presa resr Mex.
185 I2 Obrenovac Serbia
138 D2 Obruk Turkey
121 F6 Observatory Hill Australia
140 B2 Obshchiy Syrt hills Russia
132 I2 Obskaya Guba sea chan. Russia
192 B4 Obuasi Ghana
187 D5 Obukhiv Ukr.
186 I2 Ob''yachevo Russia
219 D6 Ocala U.S.A.
233 K4 Ocamo r. Venez.
225 D2 Ocampo Mex.
233 I2 Ocaña Col.
183 O3 Ocaña Spain
230 E7 Occidental, Cordillera mts Chile
233 H4 Occidental, Cordillera mts Col.
230 C6 Occidental, Cordillera mts Peru
204 B3 Ocean Cape U.S.A.
221 F5 Ocean City MD U.S.A.
221 F5 Ocean City NJ U.S.A.
204 D4 Ocean Falls Canada
215 D5 Oceanside U.S.A.
217 F6 Ocean Springs U.S.A.
187 D6 Ochakiv Ukr.
187 G7 Ochamchire Georgia
157 G4 Ochiishi-misaki pt Japan
174 E4 Ochil Hills U.K.
148 C1 Ochili Pass Afgh.
179 I5 Ochsenfurt Germany
179 F2 Ochtrup Germany
171 L3 Ockelbo Sweden
177 L7 Ocolaşul Mare, Vârful mt. Romania
211 J5 Oconee r. U.S.A.
208 C4 Oconomowoc U.S.A.
208 D3 Oconto U.S.A.
225 F4 Ocosingo Mex.
224 H5 Ocotal Nicaragua
215 D5 Ocotillo Wells U.S.A.
225 D3 Ocotlán Mex.
120 D1 Ocussi enclave East Timor
192 B4 Oda Ghana
159 C7 Ōda Japan
170 C2 Ódáðahraun lava field Iceland
160 E3 Ŏdaejin N. Korea
158 G4 Ōdate Japan
159 F7 Odawara Japan
171 I3 Odda Norway
205 J3 Odei r. Canada
208 C5 Odell U.S.A.
183 L4 Odemira Port.
138 A2 Ödemiş Turkey
197 G3 Odendaalsrus S. Africa
171 J5 Odense Denmark
179 G5 Odenwald reg. Germany
179 I3 Oder r. Germany alt. Odra (Poland)
176 G3 Oderbucht b. Germany
Odesa Ukr. see Odessa
171 K4 Ödeshög Sweden
187 D6 Odessa Ukr.
217 C6 Odessa U.S.A.
141 H1 Odesskoye Russia
183 M4 Odiel r. Spain
192 B4 Odienné Côte d'Ivoire
187 F4 Odintsovo Russia
147 J1 Odisha state India
162 C3 Ŏdŏngk Cambodia
176 G4 Odra r. Poland alt. Oder (Germany)
231 J5 Oeiras Brazil
216 C3 Oelrichs U.S.A.
179 K4 Oelsnitz/Vogtland Germany
208 B4 Oelwein U.S.A.
178 D1 Oenkerk Neth.
120 F2 Oenpelli Australia
139 H1 Of Turkey
185 G4 Ofanto r. Italy
179 G4 Offenbach am Main Germany
179 F6 Offenburg Germany
185 L6 Ofidoussa i. Greece
159 G5 Ōfunato Japan
159 F5 Oga Japan
194 E3 Ogadēn reg. Eth.
159 F5 Oga-hantō pen. Japan
159 E7 Ōgaki Japan
216 C3 Ogallala U.S.A.
Ogasawara-shotō is Japan see Bonin Islands
209 H2 Ogascanane, Lac l. Canada
Ogbomosho Nigeria see Ogbomoso
192 C4 Ogbomoso Nigeria
216 E3 Ogden IA U.S.A.
213 E3 Ogden UT U.S.A.
204 C3 Ogden, Mount Canada
221 F2 Ogdensburg U.S.A.
202 E3 Ogilvie r. Canada
202 E3 Ogilvie Mountains Canada
140 C5 Oglanly Turkm.
219 C5 Oglethorpe, Mount U.S.A.
184 D1 Oglio r. Italy
156 E1 Oglongi Russia
123 E4 Ogmore Australia
156 D1 Ogodzha Russia
192 C4 Ogoja Nigeria
206 C3 Ogoki r. Canada
206 C3 Ogoki Reservoir Canada
156 C1 Ogoron Russia
185 J3 Ogosta r. Bulg.
171 N4 Ogre Latvia
Ogurchinskiy, Ostrov i. Turkm. see Ogurjaly Adasy
140 C5 Ogurjaly Adasy i. Turkm.
139 K1 Oğuz Azer.
126 A6 Ohai N.Z.
126 E3 Ohakune N.Z.
158 G4 Ōhata Japan
126 B6 Ohau, Lake N.Z.
235 H2 O'Higgins admin. reg. Chile
232 B7 O'Higgins, Lago l. Chile
219 C4 Ohio r. U.S.A.
220 B4 Ohio state U.S.A.
179 G4 Ohm r. Germany
179 I4 Ohrdruf Germany
179 K4 Ohře r. Czech Rep.
179 J2 Ohre r. Germany
185 I4 Ohrid Macedonia

Palmdale

171 J3 Os Norway
224 I6 Osa, Península de Costa Rica
208 A4 Osage U.S.A.
217 E4 Osage r. U.S.A.
159 D7 Ōsaka Japan
141 H2 Osakarovka Kazakh.
159 G5 Ōsaki Japan
185 K3 Osam r. Bulg.
171 K4 Osby Sweden
217 F5 Osceola AR U.S.A.
216 E3 Osceola IA U.S.A.
179 L3 Oschatz Germany
179 J2 Oschersleben (Bode) Germany
184 C4 Oschiri Sardinia Italy
209 F3 Oscoda U.S.A.
187 F4 Osetr r. Russia
159 A8 Ōse-zaki pt Japan
209 J3 Osgoode Canada
141 H4 Osh Kyrg.
195 B5 Oshakati Namibia
158 G3 Oshamanbe Japan
209 H4 Oshawa Canada
159 G5 Oshika-hantō pen. Japan
158 F4 Ō-shima i. Japan
159 F7 Ō-shima i. Japan
216 C3 Oshkosh NE U.S.A.
208 C3 Oshkosh WI U.S.A.
142 B2 Oshnavīyeh Iran
139 L5 Oshtorān Kūh mt. Iran
139 L5 Oshtorīnān Iran
159 G5 Ōshū Japan
195 B4 Oshwe Dem. Rep. Congo
185 H2 Osijek Croatia
184 E3 Osimo Italy
148 C4 Osiyan India
197 I3 oSizweni S. Africa
185 G2 Osječenica mts Bos. & Herz.
171 K3 Ösjön l. Sweden
216 E3 Oskaloosa U.S.A.
171 L4 Oskarshamn Sweden
209 J1 Oskélanéo Canada
187 F5 Oskol r. Russia
171 J4 Oslo Norway
161 I4 Oslob Phil.
171 J4 Oslofjorden sea chan. Norway
147 H2 Osmanabad India
138 E1 Osmancık Turkey
138 B1 Osmaneli Turkey
139 F3 Osmaniye Turkey
171 O4 Os'mino Russia
179 G2 Osnabrück Germany
192 C4 Osogbo Nigeria
185 J3 Osogovska Planina mts Bulg./Macedonia
235 H4 Osorno Chile
183 N1 Osorno Spain
235 H4 Osorno, Volcán vol. Chile
204 F5 Osoyoos Canada
171 I3 Osøyro Norway
119 E3 Osprey Reef Coral Sea Is Terr.
178 D3 Oss Neth.
125 G8 Ossa, Mount Australia
209 F3 Ossineke U.S.A.
221 H3 Ossipee Lake U.S.A.
179 J3 Oßmannstedt Germany
207 H3 Ossokmanuan Lake Canada
178 D5 Ossuaire, Cimetière d' tourist site France
186 E3 Ostashkov Russia
179 F2 Ostbevern Germany
179 H1 Oste r. Germany
178 A3 Ostend Belgium
177 O5 Oster Ukr.
179 J2 Osterburg (Altmark) Germany
171 K4 Österbymo Sweden
171 K3 Österdalälven l. Sweden
171 J3 Østerdalen val. Norway
179 J3 Osterfeld Germany
179 G1 Osterholz-Scharmbeck Germany
179 I3 Osterode am Harz Germany
171 K3 Östersund Sweden
179 I3 Osterwieck Germany
179 F1 Ostfriesland reg. Germany
171 L3 Östhammar Sweden
177 I6 Ostrava Czech Rep.
177 I4 Ostróda Poland
187 F5 Ostrogozhsk Russia
179 K4 Ostrov Czech Rep.
186 D3 Ostrov Russia
177 J5 Ostrowiec Świętokrzyski Poland
177 J4 Ostrów Mazowiecka Poland
177 H5 Ostrów Wielkopolski Poland
159 B9 Ōsumi-kaikyō sea chan. Japan
159 B9 Ōsumi-shotō is Japan
183 N4 Osuna Spain
221 F2 Oswegatchie U.S.A.
208 C5 Oswego IL U.S.A.
221 E3 Oswego NY U.S.A.
221 E3 Oswego r. U.S.A.
173 D5 Oswestry U.K.
159 F6 Ōta Japan
126 C6 Otago Peninsula N.Z.
126 E4 Otaki N.Z.
170 N2 Otanmäki Fin.
141 H4 Otar Kazakh.
233 I4 Otare, Cerro h. Col.
158 G3 Otaru Japan
126 B7 Otatara N.Z.
230 C3 Otavalo Ecuador
195 B5 Otavi Namibia
159 G6 Ōtawara Japan
141 I4 Otegen Batyr Kazakh.
126 C6 Otematata N.Z.
171 N4 Otepää Estonia
140 C3 Otes Kazakh.
144 I2 Otgon Tenger Uul mt. Mongolia
212 C2 Othello U.S.A.
197 I4 oThongathi S. Africa
224 C2 Otinapa Mex.
126 C5 Otira N.Z.
221 E3 Otisco Lake U.S.A.
207 F3 Otish, Monts hills Canada
195 B6 Otjiwarongo Namibia
173 F4 Otley U.K.
158 H2 Otoineppu Japan
126 E3 Otorohanga N.Z.
206 C3 Otoskwin r. Canada
140 B1 Otradnyy Russia
185 H4 Otranto Italy
185 H4 Otranto, Strait of Albania/Italy
209 E4 Otsego U.S.A.
209 E3 Otsego Lake MI U.S.A.
221 F3 Otsego Lake NY U.S.A.
221 F3 Otselic U.S.A.
159 D7 Ōtsu Japan
171 J3 Otta Norway
209 J3 Ottawa Canada
209 H2 Ottawa r. Canada
208 C5 Ottawa IL U.S.A.
217 E4 Ottawa KS U.S.A.
220 A4 Ottawa OH U.S.A.
206 D2 Ottawa Islands Canada
172 E2 Otterburn U.K.
215 G2 Otter Creek Reservoir U.S.A.
208 D1 Otter Island Canada
206 D3 Otter Rapids Canada
179 H1 Ottersberg Germany
173 C7 Ottery r. U.K.
178 C4 Ottignies Belgium
203 J1 Otto Fiord inlet Canada
141 H4 Ottuk Kyrg.
208 A5 Ottumwa U.S.A.
179 F5 Ottweiler Germany
192 C4 Otukpo Nigeria
232 D3 Otumpa Arg.
230 C5 Otuzco Peru
125 E7 Otway, Cape Australia
155 B6 Ou, Nâm r. Laos
217 E5 Ouachita r. U.S.A.
217 E5 Ouachita, Lake U.S.A.
217 E5 Ouachita Mountains U.S.A.
192 A2 Ouadâne Mauritania
194 C3 Ouadda C.A.R.
193 E3 Ouaddaï reg. Chad
192 B3 Ouagadougou Burkina Faso
192 B3 Ouahigouya Burkina Faso
192 B3 Oualâta Mauritania
194 C3 Ouanda Djallé C.A.R.
192 B2 Ouarâne reg. Mauritania
192 C1 Ouargla Alg.
192 B1 Ouarzazate Morocco
197 F6 Oubergpas pass S. Africa
178 B4 Oudenaarde Belgium
179 F1 Oude Pekela Neth.
155 B6 Oudômxai Laos
197 E6 Oudtshoorn S. Africa
178 C3 Oud-Turnhout Belgium
183 P5 Oued Tlélat Alg.
192 B1 Oued Zem Morocco
184 B6 Oued Zénati Alg.
182 B2 Ouessant, Île d' i. France
194 B3 Ouesso Congo
180 B5 Ouezzane Morocco
192 C4 Ouidah Benin
224 B2 Ouiriego Mex.
192 B1 Oujda Morocco
170 N2 Oulainen Fin.
180 E5 Ouled Djellal Alg.
183 Q4 Ouled Farès Alg.
180 D5 Ouled Naïl, Monts des mts Alg.
170 N2 Oulu Fin.
170 N2 Oulujärvi l. Fin.
170 N2 Oulujoki r. Fin.
170 N2 Oulunsalo Fin.
182 H4 Oulx Italy
193 E3 Oum-Chalouba Chad
192 B4 Oumé Côte d'Ivoire
193 D3 Oum-Hadjer Chad
170 N2 Ounasjoki r. Fin.
173 G5 Oundle U.K.
193 E3 Ounianga Kébir Chad
178 D4 Oupeye Belgium
179 E5 Our r. Lux.
176 C6 Our, Vallée de l' Germany/Lux.
185 L5 Oura, Akrotirio pt Greece
213 F4 Ouray CO U.S.A.
215 H1 Ouray UT U.S.A.
183 M1 Ourense Spain
231 J5 Ouricuri Brazil
234 C3 Ourinhos Brazil
234 C1 Ouro r. Brazil
234 D3 Ouro Preto Brazil
178 D4 Ourthe r. Belgium
173 G4 Ouse r. England U.K.
173 H7 Ouse r. England U.K.
195 B5 Outapi Namibia
207 G3 Outardes, Rivière aux r. Canada
197 E6 Outeniekpas pass S. Africa
174 A2 Outer Hebrides is U.K.
208 B2 Outer Island U.S.A.
214 C5 Outer Santa Barbara Channel U.S.A.
195 B6 Outjo Namibia
203 H4 Outlook Canada
171 O3 Outokumpu Fin.
174 □ Out Skerries is U.K.
119 G4 Ouvéa atoll New Caledonia
155 D5 Ouyanghai Shuiku resr China
125 E5 Ouyen Australia
173 G5 Ouzel r. U.K.
184 C4 Ovace, Punta d' mt. Corsica France
139 G2 Ovacık Turkey
184 C2 Ovada Italy
119 H3 Ovalau i. Fiji
235 H1 Ovalle Chile
183 L2 Ovar Port.
235 J2 Oveja mt. Arg.
125 G6 Ovens r. Australia
179 F4 Overath Germany
170 M2 Överkalix Sweden
121 A5 Overlander Roadhouse Australia
215 E3 Overton U.S.A.
170 M2 Övertorneå Sweden
171 L4 Överum Sweden
178 C3 Overveen Neth.
209 E4 Ovid U.S.A.
183 N1 Oviedo Spain
140 E4 Ovminzatov tog'lari hills Uzbek.
Ovoot Mongolia see Dariganga
170 N1 Øvre Anárjohka Nasjonalpark nat. park Norway
170 L1 Øvre Dividal Nasjonalpark nat. park Norway
171 J3 Øvre Rendal Norway
187 D5 Ovruch Ukr.
156 B1 Ovsyanka Russia
126 B7 Owaka N.Z.
195 B4 Owando Congo
159 E7 Owase Japan
216 E2 Owatonna U.S.A.
221 E3 Owego U.S.A.
175 I3 Owenmore r. Ireland
126 D4 Owen River N.Z.
214 C3 Owens r. U.S.A.
219 C4 Owensboro U.S.A.
215 D3 Owens Lake U.S.A.
209 G3 Owen Sound Canada
209 G3 Owen Sound inlet Canada
119 E2 Owen Stanley Range mts P.N.G.
192 C4 Owerri Nigeria
204 D4 Owikeno Lake Canada
220 B5 Owingsville U.S.A.
221 I2 Owls Head U.S.A.
192 C4 Owo Nigeria
209 E4 Owosso U.S.A.
139 K4 Owrāmān, Kūh-e mts Iran/Iraq
213 C3 Owyhee U.S.A.
213 C3 Owyhee r. U.S.A.
213 C3 Owyhee Mountains U.S.A.
230 C6 Oxapampa Peru
170 C1 Öxarfjörður b. Iceland
205 I5 Oxbow Canada
221 I1 Oxbow U.S.A.
171 L4 Oxelösund Sweden
126 D5 Oxford N.Z.
173 F6 Oxford U.K.
209 F4 Oxford MI U.S.A.
217 F5 Oxford MS U.S.A.
221 F3 Oxford NY U.S.A.
221 F5 Oxford PA U.S.A.
125 F5 Oxley Australia
125 I3 Oxleys Peak Australia
123 F6 Oxley Wild Rivers National Park Australia
175 J3 Ox Mountains Ireland
214 C4 Oxnard U.S.A.
209 H3 Oxtongue Lake Canada
170 K2 Øya Norway
159 F6 Oyama Japan
231 H3 Oyapock r. Brazil/Fr. Guiana
194 B3 Oyem Gabon
Oygon Mongolia see Tüdevtey
174 D3 Oykel r. U.K.
182 G3 Oyonnax France
141 F4 Oyoqog'itma botig'i depr. Uzbek.
141 F4 Oyoqquduq Uzbek.
141 J3 Oyshilik Kazakh.
149 H5 Oyster Island Myanmar
141 H4 Oy-Tal Kyrg.
179 H1 Oyten Germany
149 F1 Oyyaylak China
141 G4 Oyyk Kazakh.
140 C2 Oyyl Kazakh.
140 C2 Oyyl r. Kazakh.
139 I2 Özalp Turkey
161 I4 Ozamis Phil.
219 C6 Ozark AL U.S.A.
209 E2 Ozark MI U.S.A.
217 E4 Ozark Plateau U.S.A.
217 E4 Ozarks, Lake of the U.S.A.
143 E3 Ozbakūh Iran
150 H1 Ozernovskiy Russia
140 E1 Ozernoye Kazakh.
140 B2 Ozernoye Russia
140 E2 Ozernyy Orenburgskaya Oblast' Russia
187 E4 Ozernyy Smolenskaya Oblast' Russia
156 F1 Ozerpakh Russia
177 K3 Ozersk Russia
156 F3 Ozerskiy Russia
187 F4 Ozery Russia
156 C2 Ozeryane Russia
141 H4 Özgön Kyrg.
184 C4 Ozieri Sardinia Italy
140 B2 Ozinki Russia
Oznachennoye Russia see Sayanogorsk
217 C6 Ozona U.S.A.
159 B7 Ozuki Japan
187 G7 Ozurgeti Georgia

P

203 N3 Paamiut Greenland
Pa-an Myanmar see Hpa-an
196 C6 Paarl S. Africa
196 D4 Paballelo S. Africa
160 E3 P'abal-li N. Korea
174 A3 Pabbay i. Scotland U.K.
174 A4 Pabbay i. Scotland U.K.
177 I5 Pabianice Poland
149 G4 Pabna Bangl.
171 N5 Pabradė Lith.
143 G5 Pab Range mts Pak.
231 F6 Pacaás Novos, Parque Nacional nat. park Brazil
230 C5 Pacasmayo Peru
213 E6 Pacheco Chihuahua Mex.
225 D2 Pacheco Zacatecas Mex.
186 H2 Pachikha Russia
184 F6 Pachino Sicily Italy
147 H1 Pachmarhi India
148 D5 Pachor India
225 E3 Pachuca Mex.
237 I9 Pacific-Antarctic Ridge sea feature Pacific Ocean
236 Pacific Ocean
161 J4 Pacijan i. Phil.
163 H4 Pacitan Indon.
123 C6 Packsaddle Australia
231 H4 Pacoval Brazil
234 D2 Pacuí r. Brazil
177 H5 Paczków Poland
161 J5 Padada Phil.
233 K4 Padamo r. Venez.
163 B3 Padang Indon.
162 B5 Padang Endau Malaysia
163 B3 Padangpanjang Indon.
163 E2 Padangsidimpuan Indon.
163 G3 Padangtikar i. Indon.
186 E2 Padany Russia
139 L5 Padatha, Kūh-e mt. Iran
233 K4 Padauiri r. Brazil
231 F8 Padcaya Bol.
125 F4 Paddington Australia
204 F3 Paddle Prairie Canada
220 C5 Paden City U.S.A.
179 G3 Paderborn Germany
185 J2 Padeşu, Vârful mt. Romania
231 F7 Padilla Bol.
170 L2 Padjelanta nationalpark nat. park Sweden
149 G5 Padma r. Bangl. alt. Ganga, conv. Ganges
Padova Italy see Padua
217 D7 Padre Island U.S.A.
184 C3 Padro, Monte mt. Corsica France
173 C7 Padstow U.K.
177 M3 Padsvillye Belarus
124 D6 Padthaway Australia
147 I2 Padua India
184 D2 Padua Italy
219 B4 Paducah KY U.S.A.
217 C5 Paducah TX U.S.A.
148 D2 Padum India
160 E3 Paegam N. Korea
Paektu-san mt. China/N. Korea see Baitou Shan
126 E2 Paeroa N.Z.
161 I3 Paete Phil.
Pafos Cyprus see Paphos
197 I1 Pafuri Moz.
184 F2 Pag Croatia
184 F2 Pag i. Croatia
161 I5 Pagadian Phil.
163 B3 Pagai Selatan i. Indon.
163 B3 Pagai Utara i. Indon.
151 G5 Pagan i. N. Mariana Is
163 I3 Pagatan Indon.
215 G3 Page U.S.A.
171 M5 Pagėgiai Lith.
232 □ Paget, Mount Atlantic Ocean
122 F3 Paget Cay reef Australia
213 F4 Pagosa Springs U.S.A.
149 G4 Pagri China
206 C3 Pagwa River Canada
214 □2 Pāhala U.S.A.
163 B2 Pahang r. Malaysia
149 G4 Paharpur tourist site Bangl.
148 B2 Paharpur Pak.
126 A7 Pahia Point N.Z.
214 □2 Pāhoa U.S.A.
219 D7 Pahokee U.S.A.
215 E3 Pahranagat Range mts U.S.A.
148 D4 Pahuj r. India
215 D3 Pahute Mesa plat. U.S.A.
162 A1 Pai Thai.
171 N4 Paide Estonia
173 D7 Paignton U.K.
171 N3 Päijänne l. Fin.
149 F3 Paikü Co l. China
162 B2 Pailĭn Cambodia
235 H4 Paillaco Chile
214 □2 Pailolo Channel U.S.A.
171 M3 Paimio Fin.
235 H2 Paine Chile
220 C4 Painesville U.S.A.
215 G3 Painted Desert U.S.A.
215 F5 Painted Rock Reservoir U.S.A.
124 C3 Painter, Mount h. Australia
205 J3 Paint Lake Provincial Recreation Park Canada
220 B6 Paintsville U.S.A.
209 G3 Paisley Canada
174 D5 Paisley U.K.
230 B5 Paita Peru
161 H5 Paitan, Teluk b. Sabah Malaysia
155 D4 Paizhouwan China
170 M2 Pajala Sweden
231 K5 Pajeú r. Brazil
162 B4 Paka Malaysia
233 L4 Pakaraima Mountains Brazil
231 F2 Pakaraima Mountains Guyana
160 C4 Pakch'ŏn N. Korea
209 G3 Pakesley (abandoned) Canada
133 R3 Pakhachi Russia
140 D2 Pakhar' Kazakh.
Pakhtaabad Uzbek. see Paxtaobod
143 G4 Pakistan country Asia
152 G7 Pakokku Myanmar
126 D1 Pakotai N.Z.
148 C3 Pakpattan Pak.
162 B3 Pak Phanang Thai.
162 B4 Pak Phayun Thai.
171 M5 Pakruojis Lith.
177 I7 Paks Hungary
162 B2 Pak Thong Chai Thai.
143 H3 Paktīkā prov. Afgh.
162 B1 Pakxan Laos
162 C2 Pakxé Laos
193 D4 Pala Chad
162 A2 Pala Myanmar
163 G4 Palabuhanratu Indon.
163 G4 Palabuhanratu, Teluk b. Indon.
185 G3 Palagruža i. Croatia
185 J7 Palaiochora Greece
182 F2 Palaiseau France
147 H4 Palakkad India
Palakkat India see Palakkad
147 J1 Pala Laharha India
197 E1 Palamakoloi Botswana
183 R2 Palamós Spain
148 C4 Palana India
133 Q4 Palana Russia
161 I2 Palanan Phil.
161 I2 Palanan Point Phil.
142 B3 Palangān Iran
143 F4 Palangān, Kūh-e mts Iran
163 H3 Palangkaraya Indon.
147 H4 Palani India
148 C4 Palanpur India
143 G5 Palantak Pak.
161 J3 Palapag Phil.
195 C6 Palapye Botswana
147 H3 Palar r. India
149 G4 Palasbari India
133 Q3 Palatka Russia
151 F6 Palau country Pacific Ocean
161 I2 Palaui i. Phil.
161 H3 Palauig Phil.
236 D5 Palau Islands Palau
162 A2 Palauk Myanmar
236 D5 Palau Trench sea feature N. Pacific Ocean
162 A2 Palaw Myanmar
161 H4 Palawan i. Phil.
236 C5 Palawan Trough sea feature N. Pacific Ocean
161 I3 Palayan Phil.
171 N4 Paldiski Estonia
149 H5 Pale Myanmar
163 B3 Palembang Indon.
232 B6 Palena Chile
183 N1 Palencia Spain
225 G4 Palenque Mex.
184 E5 Palermo Sicily Italy
217 E6 Palestine U.S.A.
149 H5 Paletwa Myanmar
Palghat India see Palakkad
121 A4 Palgrave, Mount h. Australia
148 C4 Pali India
117 F2 Palikir Micronesia
161 J5 Palimbang Phil.
192 C4 Palimé Togo
184 F4 Palinuro, Capo c. Italy
215 H2 Palisade U.S.A.
178 D5 Paliseul Belgium
148 B5 Palitana India
171 M4 Palivere Estonia
147 H4 Palk Bay Sri Lanka
186 D3 Palkino Russia
147 I2 Palkohda India
147 H3 Palkonda Range mts India
147 H4 Palk Strait India/Sri Lanka
125 I2 Pallamallawa Australia
175 J5 Pallas Green New Ireland
187 H5 Pallasovka Russia
170 M1 Pallas-Yllästunturin kansallispuisto nat. park Fin.
147 I3 Pallavaram India
147 H2 Palleru r. India
126 E4 Palliser, Cape N.Z.
126 E4 Palliser Bay N.Z.
148 C3 Pallu India
183 N4 Palma del Río Spain
183 R3 Palma de Mallorca Spain
233 I2 Palmar r. Venez.
233 J3 Palmarito Venez.
231 I6 Palmas Brazil
192 B4 Palmas, Cape Liberia
234 D1 Palmas de Monte Alto Brazil
219 D7 Palm Bay U.S.A.
219 D7 Palm Beach U.S.A.
214 C4 Palmdale U.S.A.

Palmeira

Pielavesi

214 □[1] Pearl City U.S.A.
214 □[1] Pearl Harbor inlet U.S.A.
217 D6 Pearsall U.S.A.
219 D6 Pearson U.S.A.
203 H2 Peary Channel Canada
206 C2 Peawanuck Canada
195 D5 Pebane Moz.
Peć Kosovo see Pejë
234 D2 Peçanha Brazil
170 O1 Pechenga Russia
132 G3 Pechora Russia
240 D2 Pechora r. Russia
186 C3 Pechory Russia
209 F4 Peck U.S.A.
204 E3 Peck, Mount Canada
162 C2 Pe Cô, Krông r. Vietnam
217 C6 Pecos U.S.A.
217 C6 Pecos r. U.S.A.
185 H1 Pécs Hungary
224 I7 Pedasí Panama
125 G9 Pedder, Lake Australia
197 G6 Peddie S. Africa
224 C1 Pedernales Mex.
Pêdo La pass China see Pindu Pass
234 E1 Pedra Azul Brazil
233 J3 Pedraza la Vieja Venez.
233 J2 Pedregal Venez.
234 C3 Pedregulho Brazil
231 J4 Pedreiras Brazil
225 D2 Pedriceña Mex.
147 I4 Pedro, Point Sri Lanka
231 I5 Pedro Afonso Brazil
233 J4 Pedro Chico Col.
232 C2 Pedro de Valdivia Chile
234 A2 Pedro Gomes Brazil
224 J6 Pedro González, Isla i. Panama
231 J4 Pedro II Brazil
233 K4 Pedro II, Ilha reg. Brazil
232 E2 Pedro Juan Caballero Para.
235 M1 Pedro Osório Brazil
Pedro Segundo Brazil see Pedro II
174 E5 Peebles U.K.
219 E5 Pee Dee r. U.S.A.
221 G4 Peekskill U.S.A.
125 I3 Peel r. Australia
202 E3 Peel r. Canada
172 C3 Peel U.K.
178 D3 Peer Belgium
123 B5 Peera Peera Poolanna Lake salt flat Australia
204 F4 Peers Canada
125 E3 Peery Lake salt l. Australia
126 D5 Pegasus Bay N.Z.
179 I5 Pegnitz Germany
179 J5 Pegnitz r. Germany
151 B5 Pegu Myanmar
152 G8 Pegu Yoma mts Myanmar
186 I2 Pegysh Russia
235 K2 Pehuajó Arg.
179 I2 Peine Germany
171 N4 Peipus, Lake Estonia/Russia
Pei Shan mts China see Bei Shan
179 J3 Peißen Germany
154 E3 Peitun China
231 I6 Peixe Brazil
234 B1 Peixe r. Goiás Brazil
234 B3 Peixe r. São Paulo Brazil
154 E3 Peixian China
234 A2 Peixo de Couro r. Brazil
185 I3 Pejë Kosovo
197 G4 Peka Lesotho
163 G4 Pekalongan Indon.
162 B5 Pekan Malaysia
163 B2 Pekanbaru Indon.
208 C5 Pekin U.S.A.
Pelabuhan Kelang Malaysia see Pelabuhan Klang
162 B5 Pelabuhan Klang Malaysia
209 F5 Pelee Island Canada
209 F5 Pelee Point Canada
151 E7 Peleng i. Indon.
186 I2 Peles Russia
208 A1 Pelican Lake MN U.S.A.
208 C3 Pelican Lake WI U.S.A.
205 I3 Pelican Narrows Canada
170 N2 Pelkosenniemi Fin.
196 C4 Pella S. Africa
205 H1 Pellatt Lake Canada
119 E2 Pelleluhu Islands P.N.G.
208 C4 Pell Lake U.S.A.
170 M2 Pello Fin.
204 B2 Pelly r. Canada
Pelly Bay Canada see Kugaaruk
204 B2 Pelly Crossing Canada
205 I1 Pelly Lake Canada
204 C2 Pelly Mountains Canada
235 M1 Pelotas Brazil
232 F3 Pelotas, Rio das r. Brazil
138 D6 Pelusium tourist site Egypt
221 I2 Pemadumcook Lake U.S.A.
163 G4 Pemalang Indon.
163 G2 Pemangkat Indon.
163 E2 Pematangsiantar Indon.
195 E5 Pemba Moz.
195 C5 Pemba Zambia
195 D4 Pemba Island Tanz.
204 F4 Pembina r. Canada
216 D1 Pembina U.S.A.
209 I3 Pembroke Canada
173 C6 Pembroke U.K.
221 J2 Pembroke U.S.A.
173 B5 Pembrokeshire Coast National Park U.K.
147 G2 Pen India
149 H5 Pen r. Myanmar
183 O2 Peñalara mt. Spain
183 E3 Peñamiller Mex.
225 E3 Peña Nevada, Cerro mt. Mex.
234 B3 Penápolis Brazil
183 N2 Peñaranda de Bracamonte Spain
125 E5 Penarie Australia
183 P2 Peñarroya mt. Spain
183 N3 Peñarroya-Pueblonuevo Spain
173 D6 Penarth U.K.
183 N1 Peñas, Cabo de c. Spain
232 A7 Penas, Golfo de g. Chile
233 L2 Peñas, Punta pt Venez.
224 H6 Peñas Blancas Nicaragua
148 D5 Pench r. India
127 K6 Penck, Cape Antarctica
235 I2 Pencoso, Alto de hills Arg.
192 C3 Pendjari, Parc National de la nat. park Benin
173 E4 Pendle Hill U.K.
212 C2 Pendleton U.S.A.
204 D4 Pendleton Bay Canada
212 C1 Pend Oreille r. U.S.A.
212 C2 Pend Oreille Lake U.S.A.
147 I1 Pendra India
209 H3 Penetanguishene Canada
154 C3 Peng'an China
148 D6 Penganga r. India
155 □ Peng Chau i. Hong Kong China
195 C4 Penge Dem. Rep. Congo
197 I2 Penge S. Africa
155 F6 Penghu Dao i. Taiwan
155 F6 Penghu Qundao is Taiwan
155 G5 Pengjia Yu i. Taiwan
162 □ Peng Kang h. Sing.
154 F2 Penglai China
154 B3 Pengshan China
155 C4 Pengshui China
155 B4 Pengxi China
155 E4 Pengze China
197 G5 Penhoek Pass S. Africa
183 L3 Peniche Port.
174 E5 Penicuik U.K.
179 K4 Penig Germany
186 E2 Peninga Russia
184 E3 Penne Italy
147 H3 Penner r. India
124 B5 Penneshaw Australia
172 E3 Pennines hills U.K.
197 I5 Pennington S. Africa
221 F5 Pennsville U.S.A.
220 D4 Pennsylvania state U.S.A.
221 E3 Penn Yan U.S.A.
203 L3 Penny Icecap Canada
221 I2 Penobscot r. U.S.A.
221 I2 Penobscot Bay U.S.A.
124 D6 Penola Australia
224 C2 Peñón Blanco Mex.
118 D5 Penong Australia
224 I6 Penonomé Panama
117 I4 Penrhyn atoll Cook Is
237 I6 Penrhyn Basin sea feature Pacific Ocean
172 E3 Penrith U.K.
219 C6 Pensacola U.S.A.
127 J4 Pensacola Mountains Antarctica
139 L2 Pensär Azer.
125 E6 Penshurst Australia
148 D2 Pensi La pass India
119 G3 Pentecost Island Vanuatu
204 F5 Penticton Canada
173 B7 Pentire Point U.K.
123 D4 Pentland Australia
174 E2 Pentland Firth sea chan. U.K.
174 E5 Pentland Hills U.K.
208 D4 Pentwater U.S.A.
147 H3 Penukonda India
173 D5 Penygadair h. U.K.
172 E3 Pen-y-Ghent h. U.K.
205 H2 Penylan Lake Canada
187 H4 Penza Russia
173 B7 Penzance U.K.
187 H4 Penzenskaya Oblast' admin. div. Russia
133 R3 Penzhinskaya Guba b. Russia
215 F5 Peoria AZ U.S.A.
208 C5 Peoria IL U.S.A.
122 C2 Pera Head Australia
162 B4 Perai Malaysia
162 A4 Perak i. Malaysia
162 B4 Perak r. Malaysia
183 P2 Perales del Alfambra Spain
147 H4 Perambalur India
207 H4 Percé Canada
121 D4 Percival Lakes salt flat Australia
221 H2 Percy U.S.A.
119 F4 Percy Isles Australia
209 I3 Percy Reach l. Canada
183 Q1 Perdido, Monte mt. Spain
132 H3 Peregrebnoye Russia
233 I3 Pereira Col.
234 B3 Pereira Barreto Brazil
186 D3 Perekhoda r. Russia
187 G5 Perelazovskiy Russia
140 B2 Perelyub Russia
208 D4 Pere Marquette r. U.S.A.
140 B2 Peremetnoye Kazakh.
177 L6 Peremyshlyany Ukr.
121 B6 Perenjori Australia
186 F3 Pereslavl'-Zalesskiy Russia
140 C2 Perevolotskiy Russia
187 H4 Perevoz Russia
156 D3 Pereyaslavka Russia
187 D5 Pereyaslav-Khmel'nyts'kyy Ukr.
235 K2 Pergamino Arg.
162 B4 Perhentian Besar, Pulau i. Malaysia
171 N3 Perho Fin.
Péribonca, Lac l. Canada see Péribonka, Lac
207 F3 Péribonka, Lac l. Canada
232 C2 Perico Arg.
224 C2 Pericos Mex.
182 E4 Périgueux France
233 I2 Perijá, Parque Nacional nat. park Venez.
233 I2 Perijá, Sierra de mts Venez.
232 B7 Perito Moreno Arg.
208 D3 Perkins U.S.A.
224 I5 Perlas, Laguna de lag. Nicaragua
224 I5 Perlas, Punta de pt Nicaragua
179 J1 Perleberg Germany
132 G4 Perm' Russia
186 H3 Permas Russia
239 H6 Pernambuco Plain sea feature S. Atlantic Ocean
124 B3 Pernatty Lagoon salt flat Australia
185 J3 Pernik Bulg.
120 E2 Peron Islands Australia
182 F2 Péronne France
225 E4 Perote Mex.
182 F5 Perpignan France
173 B7 Perranporth U.K.
215 D5 Perris U.S.A.
182 C2 Perros-Guirec France
219 D6 Perry FL U.S.A.
219 D5 Perry GA U.S.A.
216 E3 Perry IA U.S.A.
217 D4 Perry OK U.S.A.
220 B4 Perrysburg U.S.A.
217 C4 Perryton U.S.A.
217 F4 Perryville U.S.A.
Persepolis tourist site Iran see Takht-e Jamshīd
173 E5 Pershore U.K.
Persian Gulf Asia see The Gulf
139 G2 Pertek Turkey
118 B5 Perth Australia
209 I3 Perth Canada
174 E4 Perth U.K.
221 F4 Perth Amboy U.S.A.
221 J1 Perth-Andover Canada
238 L6 Perth Basin sea feature Indian Ocean
186 F1 Pertominsk Russia
183 G5 Pertuis France
171 N3 Pertunmaa Fin.
184 C4 Pertusato, Capo c. Corsica France
230 C5 Peru country S. America
208 C5 Peru U.S.A.
237 M7 Peru Basin sea feature S. Pacific Ocean
237 N6 Peru-Chile Trench sea feature S. Pacific Ocean
184 E3 Perugia Italy
235 C4 Peruíbe Brazil
178 B4 Péruwelz Belgium
187 G4 Pervomaysk Russia
187 D5 Pervomays'k Ukr.
186 J2 Pervomayskaya Russia
187 E6 Pervomays'ke Crimea
141 J2 Pervomayskiy Kazakh.
140 C2 Pervomayskiy Orenburgskaya Oblast' Russia
187 G4 Pervomayskiy Tambovskaya Oblast' Russia
187 F5 Pervomays'kyy Ukr.
133 R3 Pervorechenskiy (abandoned) Russia
156 F1 Pervyy Brat, Gora h. Russia
184 E3 Pesaro Italy
214 A3 Pescadero U.S.A.
215 H4 Pescado U.S.A.
Pescadores is Taiwan see Penghu Qundao
184 F3 Pescara Italy
184 F3 Pescara r. Italy
187 G6 Peschanokopskoye Russia
140 B4 Peschanyy, Mys pt Kazakh.
162 □ Pesek, Pulau i. Sing.
148 B2 Peshawar Pak.
185 I4 Peshkopi Albania
185 K3 Peshtera Bulg.
208 D3 Peshtigo U.S.A.
208 C3 Peshtigo r. U.S.A.
141 F1 Peski Kazakh.
140 E5 Peski Turkm.
184 F1 Pesnica Slovenia
182 D4 Pessac France
179 K2 Pessin Germany
186 E3 Pestovo Russia
187 G4 Pet r. Russia
225 D4 Petacalco, Bahía de b. Mex.
138 E5 Petah Tiqwa Israel
171 N3 Petäjävesi Fin.
185 K5 Petalioi i. Greece
214 A2 Petaluma U.S.A.
178 D5 Pétange Lux.
163 I3 Petangis Indon.
233 K2 Petare Venez.
225 D4 Petatlán Mex.
195 D5 Petauke Zambia
209 I3 Petawawa Canada
225 G4 Petén Itzá, Lago l. Guat.
208 C3 Petenwell Lake U.S.A.
124 C4 Peterborough S.A. Australia
125 E7 Peterborough Vic. Australia
209 H3 Peterborough Canada
173 G5 Peterborough U.K.
175 F3 Peterculter U.K.
175 G3 Peterhead U.K.
127 I3 Peter I Island Antarctica
205 K2 Peter Lake Canada
172 F3 Peterlee U.K.
118 C4 Petermann Ranges mts Australia
235 H2 Peteroa, Volcán vol. Chile
205 H3 Peter Pond Lake Canada
207 F2 Peters, Lac l. Canada
179 H4 Petersberg Germany
204 C3 Petersburg AK U.S.A.
208 C6 Petersburg IL U.S.A.
221 E6 Petersburg VA U.S.A.
220 D5 Petersburg WV U.S.A.
173 G6 Petersfield U.K.
179 G2 Petershagen Germany
185 G5 Petilia Policastro Italy
221 J2 Petit Manan Point U.S.A.
207 H3 Petit Mécatina r. Nfld and Lab./Que. Canada
204 E3 Petitot r. Canada
225 E4 Petlalcingo Mex.
225 G3 Peto Mex.
209 E3 Petoskey U.S.A.
138 E6 Petra tourist site Jordan
150 F2 Petra Velikogo, Zaliv b. Russia
209 I4 Petre, Point Canada
185 J4 Petrich Bulg.
215 H4 Petrified Forest National Park U.S.A.
185 G2 Petrinja Croatia
152 E2 Petroglyphic Complexes of the Mongolian Altai tourist site Mongolia
185 J3 Petrohanski Prohod pass Bulg.
209 F4 Petrolia Canada
231 J5 Petrolina Brazil
141 J3 Petropavlovka Kazakh.
187 G5 Petropavlovka Russia
150 H1 Petropavlovsk-Kamchatskiy Russia
141 G1 Petropavlovskoye Kazakh.
185 J2 Petroșani Romania
141 G1 Petrovka Kazakh.
140 B1 Petrovka Russia
187 H4 Petrovsk Russia
150 C1 Petrovsk-Zabaykal'skiy Russia
187 H5 Petrov Val Russia
186 E2 Petrozavodsk Russia
197 F4 Petrusburg S. Africa
197 H3 Petrus Steyn S. Africa
197 F5 Petrusville S. Africa
178 C2 Petten Neth.
175 K3 Pettigo U.K.
132 H4 Petukhovo Russia
162 A4 Peureula Indon.
133 S3 Pevek Russia
169 O2 Peza r. Russia
177 H6 Pezinok Slovakia
179 F5 Pfälzer Wald hills Germany
179 G6 Pforzheim Germany
176 D7 Pfullendorf Germany
179 G5 Pfungstadt Germany
197 H2 Phagameng S. Africa
148 C3 Phagwara India
197 G4 Phahameng S. Africa
197 I1 Phalaborwa S. Africa
148 C4 Phalodi India
148 B4 Phalsund India
147 G2 Phaltan India
162 A1 Phan Thai.
162 B2 Phanat Nikhom Thai.
162 B3 Phangan, Ko i. Thai.
162 A3 Phangnga Thai.
155 B6 Phăng Xi Păng mt. Vietnam
162 C2 Phanom Dong Rak, Thiu Khao mts Cambodia/Thai.
Phan Rang Vietnam see Phan Rang-Thap Cham
163 D3 Phan Rang-Thap Cham Vietnam
163 D3 Phan Ri Cửa Vietnam
163 D3 Phan Thiêt Vietnam
Phapon Myanmar see Pyapon
217 D7 Pharr U.S.A.
155 C6 Phat Diêm Vietnam
162 B4 Phatthalung Thai.
149 H5 Phawngpui mt. India
162 A1 Phayao Thai.
149 H4 Phek India
205 I3 Phelps Lake Canada
162 B1 Phen Thai.
219 C5 Phenix City U.S.A.
162 A2 Phet Buri Thai.
162 B1 Phetchabun Thai.
162 C2 Phiafai Laos
162 B1 Phichai Thai.
162 B1 Phichit Thai.
217 F5 Philadelphia MS U.S.A.
221 F2 Philadelphia NY U.S.A.
221 F5 Philadelphia PA U.S.A.
216 C2 Philip U.S.A.
178 C4 Philippeville Belgium
220 C5 Philippi U.S.A.
123 B5 Philippi, Lake salt flat Australia
178 B3 Philippine Neth.
236 D4 Philippine Basin sea feature N. Pacific Ocean
161 Philippines country Asia
161 J2 Philippine Sea Phil.
236 D4 Philippine Trench sea feature N. Pacific Ocean
197 F5 Philippolis S. Africa
179 G5 Philippsburg Germany
220 D4 Philipsburg U.S.A.
178 C3 Philipsdam barrage Neth.
202 D3 Philip Smith Mountains U.S.A.
197 F5 Philipstown S. Africa
125 F7 Phillip Island Australia
221 H2 Phillips ME U.S.A.
208 B3 Phillips WI U.S.A.
217 D4 Phillipsburg KS U.S.A.
221 F4 Phillipsburg NJ U.S.A.
203 I1 Phillips Inlet Canada
120 D3 Phillips Range hills Australia
220 D4 Phillipston U.S.A.
221 G3 Philmont U.S.A.
205 G3 Philomena Canada
220 C6 Philpott Reservoir U.S.A.
162 B2 Phimae tourist site Thai.
162 C2 Phimun Mangsahan Thai.
197 G3 Phiritona S. Africa
162 B1 Phitsanulok Thai.
162 C3 Phnom Penh Cambodia
Phnum Pénh Cambodia see Phnom Penh
162 B4 Pho, Laem pt Thai.
215 F5 Phoenix U.S.A.
119 I2 Phoenix Islands Pacific Ocean
119 I2 Phoenix Islands Protected Area res. Kiribati
197 G3 Phomolong S. Africa
162 B2 Phon Thai.
151 C4 Phôngsali Laos
155 B6 Phong Thô Vietnam
162 B1 Phon Phisai Thai.
162 B1 Phônsavan Laos
162 B1 Phônsavan mt. Laos
162 B1 Phon Thong Thai.
125 E7 Phoques Bay Australia
123 C4 Phosphate Hill Australia
162 B1 Phrae Thai.
162 A1 Phrao Thai.
162 B2 Phra Phutthabat Thai.
162 A3 Phra Thong, Ko i. Thai.
162 C1 Phu Bai Vietnam
155 B6 Phuc Yên Vietnam
Phu Hôi Vietnam see Van Gia
162 A4 Phuket Thai.
162 A4 Phuket, Ko i. Thai.
148 C4 Phulera India
149 G5 Phultala Bangl.
155 B6 Phu Ly Vietnam
163 D2 Phu My Vietnam
162 C3 Phước Hai Vietnam
162 C3 Phước Long Vietnam
Phu Quôc Vietnam see Dương Đông
162 B3 Phu Quôc, Đao i. Vietnam
163 D3 Phu Quy, Đao i. Vietnam
197 H4 Phuthaditjhaba S. Africa
155 B6 Phu Tho Vietnam
162 B1 Phu Wiang Thai.
152 G8 Phyu Myanmar
231 I5 Piaca Brazil
184 C2 Piacenza Italy
125 H3 Pian r. Australia
154 D2 Pianguan China
184 D3 Pianosa, Isola i. Italy
177 M7 Piatra Neamț Romania
231 J5 Piauí r. Brazil
184 E1 Piave r. Italy
193 F4 Pibor r. South Sudan
193 F4 Pibor Post South Sudan
208 D1 Pic r. Canada
215 F4 Pica U.S.A.
215 G5 Picacho U.S.A.
215 E5 Picacho (abandoned) U.S.A.
182 F2 Picardy reg. France
219 B6 Picayune U.S.A.
224 C1 Picháchic Mex.
232 D2 Pichanal Arg.
235 I2 Pichi Ciego Arg.
235 H2 Pichilemu Chile
224 B2 Pichilingue Mex.
235 J3 Pichi Mahuida Arg.
148 D4 Pichor India
225 F4 Pichucalco Mex.
208 D1 Pic Island Canada
172 G3 Pickering U.K.
172 G3 Pickering, Vale of val. U.K.
209 E2 Pickford U.S.A.
206 B3 Pickle Lake Canada
166 A6 Pico, Ponta do i. Azores
224 H5 Pico Bonito, Parque Nacional nat. park Hond.
233 K4 Pico da Neblina, Parque Nacional do nat. park Brazil
225 E4 Pico de Orizaba, Parque Nacional nat. park Mex.
231 J5 Picos Brazil
232 C7 Pico Truncado Arg.
208 D1 Pic River Canada
125 I5 Picton Australia
209 I4 Picton Canada
125 G9 Picton, Mount Australia
207 H4 Pictou Canada
208 D2 Pictured Rocks National Lakeshore nature res. U.S.A.
235 I3 Picún Leufú r. Arg.
143 F5 Pidarak Pak.
147 I5 Pidurutalagala mt. Sri Lanka
233 I3 Piedecuesta Col.
235 I1 Pie de Palo, Sierra mts Arg.
219 C5 Piedmont U.S.A.
220 C4 Piedmont Lake U.S.A.
235 L2 Piedras, Punta pt Arg.
230 D6 Piedras, Río de las r. Peru
225 D1 Piedras Negras Coahuila Mex.
225 E4 Piedras Negras Veracruz Mex.
208 C1 Pie Island Canada
171 N3 Pieksämäki Fin.
171 N3 Pielavesi Fin.

Pielinen

Princeton

221 F4 Princeton NJ U.S.A.
208 C4 Princeton WI U.S.A.
220 C6 Princeton WV U.S.A.
221 J2 Prince William Canada
202 D3 Prince William Sound b. U.S.A.
192 C4 Príncipe i. São Tomé and Príncipe
212 B2 Prineville U.S.A.
132 C2 Prins Karls Forland i. Svalbard
224 I5 Prinzapolka Nicaragua
186 D2 Priozersk Russia
177 L5 Pripet r. Belarus/Ukr. alt. Pryp"yat' (Ukraine), alt. Prypyats' (Belarus)
181 H1 Pripet Marshes Belarus/Ukr.
170 O1 Prirechnyy Russia
185 I3 Prishtinë Kosovo
Priština Kosovo see Prishtinë
179 J1 Pritzier Germany
179 K1 Pritzwalk Germany
182 G4 Privas France
184 F2 Privlaka Croatia
186 G3 Privolzhsk Russia
187 H4 Privolzhskaya Vozvyshennost' hills Russia
140 B1 Privolzh'ye Russia
187 G6 Priyutnoye Russia
185 I3 Prizren Kosovo
163 H4 Probolinggo Indon.
179 J4 Probstzella Germany
173 C7 Probus U.K.
208 A2 Proctor MN U.S.A.
221 G3 Proctor VT U.S.A.
231 G3 Professor van Blommestein Meer resr Suriname
Progreso Hond. see El Progreso
225 D2 Progreso Coahuila Mex.
225 E3 Progreso Hidalgo Mex.
225 G3 Progreso Yucatán Mex.
127 K5 Progress research stn Antarctica
156 C2 Progress Russia
187 H7 Prokhladnyy Russia
133 J4 Prokop'yevsk Russia
185 I3 Prokuplje Serbia
186 D3 Proletariy Russia
187 G6 Proletarsk Russia
187 G6 Proletarskoye Vodokhranilishche l. Russia
234 A2 Promissão Brazil
202 F4 Prophet r. Canada
204 E3 Prophet River Canada
208 C5 Prophetstown U.S.A.
119 E4 Proserpine Australia
221 F3 Prospect U.S.A.
161 J4 Prosperidad Phil.
196 D7 Protem S. Africa
208 A4 Protivin U.S.A.
185 L3 Provadia Bulg.
183 H5 Provence reg. France
221 H4 Providence U.S.A.
126 A7 Providence, Cape N.Z.
209 F3 Providence Bay Canada
224 I5 Providencia, Isla de i. Col.
202 A3 Provideniya Russia
221 H3 Provincetown U.S.A.
215 G1 Provo U.S.A.
205 G4 Provost Canada
235 B4 Prudentópolis Brazil
202 D2 Prudhoe Bay U.S.A.
179 E4 Prüm Germany
179 E4 Prüm r. Germany
184 C3 Prunelli-di-Fiumorbo Corsica France
177 J4 Pruszków Poland
187 D6 Prut r. Moldova/Romania
127 L5 Prydz Bay Antarctica
187 E5 Pryluky Ukr.
187 F6 Prymors'k Ukr.
211 G4 Pryor U.S.A.
177 L5 Pryp"yat r. Ukr. alt. Prypyats' (Belarus), conv. Pripet
177 O5 Pryp"yat' (abandoned) Ukr.
177 M4 Prypyats' r. Belarus alt. Pryp"yat' (Ukraine), conv. Pripet
177 K6 Przemyśl Poland
Przheval'sk Kyrg. see Karakol
185 K5 Psara i. Greece
187 G6 Psebay Russia
187 F6 Pshish r. Russia
186 D3 Pskov Russia
171 N4 Pskov, Lake Estonia/Russia
186 D3 Pskovskaya Oblast' admin. div. Russia
185 I4 Ptolemaïda Greece
184 F1 Ptuj Slovenia
162 B1 Pua Thai.
235 J3 Puán Arg.
155 B5 Pu'an Guizhou China
155 B4 Pu'an Sichuan China
155 C6 Pubei China
230 D5 Pucallpa Peru
155 F5 Pucheng Fujian China
154 C3 Pucheng Shaanxi China
186 G3 Puchezh Russia
161 I4 Pucio Point Phil.
177 I3 Puck Poland
208 C4 Puckaway Lake U.S.A.
235 H3 Pucón Chile
143 F4 Pūdah Tal, Shēlah-ye watercourse Afgh.
142 D3 Pūdanū Iran
170 N2 Pudasjärvi Fin.
197 F3 Pudimoe S. Africa
155 F4 Pudong China
186 F2 Pudozh Russia
173 F4 Pudsey U.K.
Puducheri India see Puducherry
147 H4 Puducherry India
147 B4 Puducherry union terr. India
147 H4 Pudukkottai India
225 E4 Puebla Mex.
225 E4 Puebla state Mex.
183 M1 Puebla de Sanabria Spain
213 F4 Pueblo U.S.A.
233 J2 Pueblo Nuevo Venez.
225 F4 Pueblo Viejo tourist site Mex.
235 J3 Puelches Arg.
235 I3 Puelén Arg.
235 H2 Puente Alto Chile
225 E4 Puente de Ixtla Mex.
183 N4 Puente Genil Spain
233 J2 Puente Torres Venez.
232 B7 Puerto Aisén Chile
231 F6 Puerto Alegre Bol.
225 E5 Puerto Ángel Mex.
225 F5 Puerto Arista Mex.
224 I6 Puerto Armuelles Panama
233 H4 Puerto Asís Col.
233 K3 Puerto Ayacucho Venez.
230 □ Puerto Baquerizo Moreno Galapagos Is Ecuador
224 G5 Puerto Barrios Guat.
233 I3 Puerto Berrío Col.
233 J2 Puerto Cabello Venez.
224 I5 Puerto Cabezas Nicaragua
224 I5 Puerto Cabo Gracias a Dios Nicaragua
233 K3 Puerto Carreño Col.
232 E2 Puerto Casado Para.
232 B6 Puerto Cisnes Chile
232 C8 Puerto Coig (abandoned) Arg.
233 I4 Puerto Concordia Col.
225 H5 Puerto Cortés Hond.
224 B2 Puerto Cortés Mex.
233 J2 Puerto Cumarebo Venez.
225 H3 Puerto de Morelos Mex.
232 C7 Puerto Deseado Arg.
225 E5 Puerto Escondido Mex.
233 J1 Puerto Estrella Col.
231 F6 Puerto Frey Bol.
232 E2 Puerto Guarani Para.
230 E6 Puerto Heath Bol.
231 G7 Puerto Isabel Bol.
224 H6 Puerto Jesús Costa Rica
225 H3 Puerto Juáres Mex.
233 K2 Puerto La Cruz Venez.
230 D4 Puerto Leguízamo Col.
225 I5 Puerto Lempira Hond.
224 I6 Puerto Limón Costa Rica
183 N3 Puertollano Spain
235 J4 Puerto Lobos Arg.
233 I3 Puerto López Col.
225 F5 Puerto Madero Mex.
235 J4 Puerto Madryn Arg.
230 E6 Puerto Maldonado Peru
230 B4 Puerto Máncora Peru
233 K3 Puerto Miranda Venez.
235 H4 Puerto Montt Chile
224 H5 Puerto Morazán Nicaragua
232 B8 Puerto Natales Chile
233 J3 Puerto Nuevo Col.
224 J6 Puerto Obaldia Panama
233 L2 Puerto Ordaz Venez.
233 K3 Puerto Páez Venez.
222 B2 Puerto Peñasco Mex.
232 E2 Puerto Pinasco Para.
235 J4 Puerto Pirámides Arg.
223 J5 Puerto Plata Dom. Rep.
230 D5 Puerto Portillo Peru
161 H4 Puerto Princesa Phil.
233 H2 Puerto Rey Col.
223 K5 Puerto Rico terr. Caribbean Sea
239 E4 Puerto Rico Trench sea feature Caribbean Sea
233 J3 Puerto Rondón Col.
224 H5 Puerto Sandino Nicaragua
225 G5 Puerto San José Guat.
232 C7 Puerto San Julián Arg.
232 C8 Puerto Santa Cruz Arg.
232 E2 Puerto Sastre Para.
233 H4 Puerto Tejada Col.
224 C3 Puerto Vallarta Mex.
235 H4 Puerto Varas Chile
187 I4 Pugachev Russia
148 C3 Pugal India
155 B5 Puge China
142 D5 Pūhāl-e Khamīr, Kūh-e mts Iran
154 C3 Pu He r. China
183 R1 Puigmal mt. France/Spain
155 □ Pui O Wan b. Hong Kong China
155 F4 Pujiang China
160 D3 Pujŏn-ho resr N. Korea
160 E3 Pujonryong-sanmaek mts N. Korea
126 C6 Pukaki, Lake N.Z.
237 H6 Pukapuka atoll Cook Is
209 E1 Pukaskwa r. Canada
209 E1 Pukaskwa National Park Canada
205 I3 Pukatawagan Canada
160 C3 Pukchin N. Korea
160 E3 Pukch'ŏng N. Korea
126 E2 Pukekohe N.Z.
126 D5 Puketeraki Range mts N.Z.
126 F4 Puketoi Range hills N.Z.
126 C6 Pukeuri Junction N.Z.
177 O3 Pukhnovo Russia
186 G2 Puksoozero Russia
160 D3 Puksubaek-san mt. N. Korea
184 E2 Pula Croatia
180 E4 Pula Sardinia Italy
230 E8 Pulacayo Bol.
160 A4 Pulandian China
160 A4 Pulandian Wan b. China
161 J5 Pulangi r. Phil.
221 E3 Pulaski NY U.S.A.
219 C5 Pulaski TN U.S.A.
220 C6 Pulaski VA U.S.A.
208 C3 Pulaski WI U.S.A.
177 J5 Puławy Poland
143 H3 Pul-e 'Alam Afgh.
143 H3 Pul-e Khumrī Afgh.
141 G4 Pülgön Kyrg.
179 E3 Pulheim Germany
147 I3 Pulicat Lake inlet India
147 H3 Pulivendla India
147 H4 Puliyangudi India
170 N2 Pulkkila Fin.
212 C2 Pullman U.S.A.
170 P1 Pulozero Russia
224 B2 Púlpito, Punta pt Mex.
149 E1 Pulu China
139 G2 Pülümür Turkey
161 J5 Pulutan Indon.
149 G3 Puma Yumco l. China
230 B4 Puná, Isla i. Ecuador
149 G4 Punakha Bhutan
148 C2 Punch India
204 E4 Punchaw Canada
149 G3 Püncogling China
197 I1 Punda Maria S. Africa
148 D3 Pundri India
147 G2 Pune India
162 □ Punggol Sing.
160 E3 P'ungsan N. Korea
195 D5 Púnguè r. Moz.
195 C4 Punia Dem. Rep. Congo
235 H1 Punitaqui Chile
148 C3 Punjab state India
148 B3 Punjab prov. Pak.
148 D2 Punmah Glacier Pak.
149 F4 Punpun r. India
223 K5 Punta, Cerro de mt. Puerto Rico
235 J3 Punta Alta Arg.
232 B8 Punta Arenas Chile
235 L2 Punta del Este Uruguay
235 J4 Punta Delgada Arg.
224 G4 Punta Gorda Belize
224 I6 Punta Gorda Nicaragua
219 D7 Punta Gorda U.S.A.
235 J4 Punta Norte Arg.
224 H6 Puntarenas Costa Rica
194 E3 Puntland reg. Somalia
233 J2 Punto Fijo Venez.
220 D4 Punxsutawney U.S.A.
170 N2 Puokio Fin.
170 N2 Puolanka Fin.
143 E5 Pūr Iran
132 I3 Pur r. Russia
233 H4 Puracé, Parque Nacional nat. park Col.
233 H4 Puracé, Volcán de vol. Col.
217 D5 Purcell U.S.A.
204 F4 Purcell Mountains Canada
235 H3 Purén Chile
213 G4 Purgatoire r. U.S.A.
149 F6 Puri India
178 C2 Purmerend Neth.
147 H2 Purna India
148 D5 Purna r. Maharashtra India
148 D6 Purna r. Maharashtra India
149 G4 Purnabhaba r. India
149 F4 Purnia India
120 E3 Purnululu National Park Australia
235 H4 Purranque Chile
225 D3 Puruandíro Mex.
149 F5 Puruliya India
231 F4 Purus r. Brazil
171 O3 Puruvesi l. Fin.
163 G4 Purwakarta Indon.
163 H4 Purwodadi Indon.
163 G4 Purwokerto Indon.
160 E2 Puryŏng N. Korea
148 D6 Pus r. India
148 D6 Pusad India
Pusan S. Korea see Busan
221 I2 Pushaw Lake U.S.A.
148 C4 Pushkar India
186 D3 Pushkin Russia
187 H5 Pushkino Russia
156 F3 Pushkinskaya, Gora mt. Russia
186 D3 Pushkinskiye Gory Russia
186 H2 Pushma Russia
Pusht-i-Rud reg. Afgh. see Zamīndāwar
177 N2 Pustoshka Russia
120 D1 Putain Indon.
151 B4 Putao Myanmar
155 F5 Putian China
163 H3 Puting, Tanjung pt Indon.
141 K2 Putintsevo Kazakh.
225 E4 Putla Mex.
143 G4 Putla Khan Afgh.
179 L1 Putlitz Germany
185 L2 Putna r. Romania
221 H4 Putnam U.S.A.
221 G3 Putney U.S.A.
133 K3 Putorana, Plato plat. Russia
135 I6 Putrajaya Indon.
149 H3 Putrang La pass China
196 D4 Putsonderwater S. Africa
147 H4 Puttalam Sri Lanka
147 H4 Puttalam Lagoon Sri Lanka
179 E5 Puttelange-aux-Lacs France
178 D2 Putten Neth.
178 C3 Puttershoek Neth.
176 E3 Puttgarden Germany
230 D4 Putumayo r. Col.
139 G2 Pütürge Turkey
163 H2 Putusibau Indon.
187 G4 Putyatino Russia
187 E5 Putyvl' Ukr.
171 O3 Puumala Fin.
214 □2 Pu'uwai U.S.A.
206 E1 Puvirnituq Canada
212 B2 Puyallup U.S.A.
154 E3 Puyang China
180 D2 Puy de Sancy mt. France
235 H4 Puyehue Chile
235 H4 Puyehue, Parque Nacional nat. park Chile
183 F5 Puylaurens France
126 A7 Puysegur Point N.Z.
195 C4 Pweto Dem. Rep. Congo
173 C5 Pwllheli U.K.
186 E2 Pyal'ma Russia
187 H4 P'yana r. Russia
170 O2 Pyaozero, Ozero l. Russia
170 O2 Pyaozerskiy Russia
145 I8 Pyapon Myanmar
133 J2 Pyasina r. Russia
187 G6 Pyatigorsk Russia
140 B2 Pyatimarskoye Kazakh.
187 E5 P"yatykhatky Ukr.
151 B5 Pyè Myanmar
126 B7 Pye, Mount h. N.Z.
160 E5 Pyeongchang S. Korea
160 E5 Pyeonghae S. Korea
160 D5 Pyeongtaek S. Korea
187 D4 Pyetrykaw Belarus
170 N2 Pyhäjoki Fin.
170 N2 Pyhäjoki r. Fin.
170 N2 Pyhäntä Fin.
171 N3 Pyhäsalmi Fin.
171 O3 Pyhäselkä l. Fin.
149 H5 Pyingaing Myanmar
152 G8 Pyinmana Myanmar
151 B4 Pyin-U-Lwin Myanmar
173 D6 Pyle U.K.
133 J3 Pyl'karamo Russia
185 I6 Pylos Greece
220 C4 Pymatuning Reservoir U.S.A.
160 C5 Pyŏksŏng N. Korea
160 C3 Pyŏktong N. Korea
160 D4 P'yŏnggang N. Korea
160 D4 P'yŏngsan N. Korea
160 C4 P'yŏngsong N. Korea
160 C4 P'yŏngyang N. Korea
125 F6 Pyramid Hill Australia
214 C1 Pyramid Lake U.S.A.
209 E3 Pyramid Point U.S.A.
214 C3 Pyramid Range mts U.S.A.
138 C7 Pyramids of Giza tourist site Egypt
183 F5 Pyrenees mts France/Spain
185 I6 Pyrgos Greece
187 E5 Pyryatyn Ukr.
176 G4 Pyrzyce Poland
186 H3 Pyshchug Russia
177 M2 Pytalovo Russia
185 J5 Pyxaria mt. Greece

Q

139 F4 Qaa Lebanon
Qaanaaq Greenland see Thule
142 D6 Qābil Oman
139 I6 Qabr Bandar tourist site Iraq
197 H5 Qacha's Nek Lesotho
139 J4 Qadir Kerem Iraq
139 I4 Qādisīyah, Sadd dam Iraq
142 D2 Qā'emshahr Iran
143 E3 Qā'en Iran
153 K2 Qagan China
154 C2 Qagan Nur Nei Mongol Zizhiqu China
154 E1 Qagan Nur Nei Mongol Zizhiqu China
154 E1 Qagan Nur l. China
154 E1 Qagan Nur resr China
160 C1 Qagan Nur salt l. China
154 D1 Qagan Obo Mongolia
154 D1 Qagan Teg China
141 J3 Qagan Tungge China
154 E1 Qagan Us China
149 H3 Qagbasêrag China
149 E2 Qagcaka China
150 B3 Qaidam Pendi basin China
143 G3 Qaişār Afgh.
Qaisar, Koh-i- mt. Afgh. see Qeyşār, Kūh-e
143 F3 Qal'ah-ye Fārsī Afgh.
143 F3 Qal'ah-ye Now Afgh.
143 G4 Qal'ah-ye Rashīd Afgh.
143 G3 Qal'ah-ye Sang-e Takht Afgh.
143 F3 Qal'ah-ye Walī Afgh.
141 G5 Qalaikhumb Tajik.
143 G3 Qalāt Afgh.
142 D4 Qalāt Iran
137 E6 Qal'at al Mu'aẓẓam Saudi Arabia
Qal'at Dizah Iraq see Qeładize
139 K6 Qal'at Şāliḥ Iraq
139 K6 Qal'at Sukkar Iraq
142 B2 Qal'eh Dāgh mt. Iran
139 L5 Qal'eh-ye Now Iraq
139 J7 Qalīb Bāqūr well Iraq
138 C6 Qalyūb Egypt
205 J2 Qamanirjuaq Lake Canada
141 F5 Qamashi Uzbek.
197 G5 Qamata S. Africa
139 K4 Qāmchīān Iran
152 G5 Qamdo China
148 B3 Qamruddin Karez Pak.
142 C3 Qamşar Iran
142 B2 Qandarānbāshī, Kūh-e mt. Iran
140 D4 Qanliko'l Uzbek.
141 J4 Qapqal China
139 L2 Qaraçala Azer.
139 I4 Qarachōq, Jabal mts Iraq
139 J4 Qara Dāgh mt. Iraq
Qara Ertis r. China/Kazakh. see Ertix He
136 B5 Qārah Egypt
139 H7 Qārah Saudi Arabia
142 A5 Qa'rah, Jabal al h. Saudi Arabia
139 K3 Qarah Āghāj Iran
143 H3 Qarah Bāgh Afgh.
139 K3 Qaranqu r. Iran
194 E3 Qardho Somalia
139 K2 Qareh Dāgh mts Iran
139 K3 Qareh Dāsh, Kūh-e mt. Iran
142 B2 Qareh Sū r. Iran
139 K3 Qareh Urgān, Kūh-e mt. Iran
149 H1 Qarhan China
136 D5 Qarn al Kabsh, Jabal mt. Egypt
Qarn el Kabsh, Gebel mt. Egypt see Qarn al Kabsh, Jabal
141 H5 Qarokŭl l. Tajik.
144 G4 Qarqan He r. China
141 J4 Qarqi China
143 G3 Qarqīn Afgh.
141 F5 Qarshi Uzbek.
138 C7 Qārūn, Birkat salt l. Egypt
139 J6 Qaryat al Gharab Iraq
142 B5 Qaryat al Ulyā Saudi Arabia
143 E3 Qasamī Iran
142 C4 Qash Qā'ī reg. Iran
203 M3 Qasigiannguit Greenland
154 D1 Qasq China
139 I5 Qaşr al Khubbāz Iraq
139 L7 Qaşr aş Şabīyah Kuwait
143 F5 Qaşr-e Qand Iran
142 B3 Qaşr-e Shīrīn Iran
203 N3 Qassimiut Greenland
142 C5 Qatar country Asia
138 C7 Qaṭrānī, Jabal esc. Egypt
142 D4 Qaṭrūyeh Iran
Qaṭṭâra, Râs esc. Egypt see Qaṭṭārah, Ra's
193 E2 Qattara Depression Egypt
136 B5 Qaṭṭārah, Ra's esc. Egypt
139 F4 Qaṭṭīnah, Buḥayrat resr Syria
Qausuittuq Canada see Resolute
139 K1 Qax Azer.
141 J4 Qaxi China
149 H3 Qayü China
139 I4 Qayyārah Iraq
139 K2 Qazangöldağ mt. Azer.
139 J1 Qazax Azer.
148 B4 Qazi Ahmad Pak.
142 C2 Qazvīn Iran
154 A1 Qeh China
139 J3 Qeładize Iraq
203 M3 Qeqertarsuaq i. Greenland
203 M3 Qeqertarsuatsiaat Greenland
203 M3 Qeqertarsuup Tunua b. Greenland
139 K4 Qeshlāq Iran
142 B3 Qeshlāq, Rūdkhāneh-ye r. Iran
143 E5 Qeshm Iran
142 C2 Qeydār Iran
142 D4 Qeyşar, Chāh-e well Iran
143 G3 Qeyşār, Kūh-e mt. Afgh.
142 C2 Qezel Owzan, Rūdkhāneh-ye r. Iran
138 E6 Qeẓi'ot Israel
154 F2 Qian'an Hebei China
160 C1 Qian'an Jilin China
155 F4 Qiandao Hu resr China
141 J4 Qianfodong China
160 C1 Qian Gorlos China
154 C3 Qian He r. China
155 C4 Qianjiang Chongqing China
155 D4 Qianjiang Hubei China
156 D3 Qianjin Heilongjiang China
160 E1 Qianjin Jilin China
160 B1 Qianqihao China
160 B3 Qian Shan mts China
154 E2 Qianshangjie China
239 R4 Qiansuo China
155 C5 Qianxi China
154 C3 Qianxian China
154 C3 Qianyang China
154 D2 Qiaocun China
155 B5 Qiaojia China
144 I3 Qiaowan China
139 J2 Qīās Iran
142 B5 Qibā' Saudi Arabia
197 G4 Qibing S. Africa
155 D5 Qidong Hunan China
155 F4 Qidong Jiangsu China
149 H2 Qidukou China
135 G3 Qiemo China
154 E2 Qihe China
155 C4 Qijiang China
133 K5 Qijiaojing China
203 L3 Qikiqtarjuaq Canada
143 G4 Qila Abdullah Pak.
143 F5 Qila Ladgasht Pak.
154 E1 Qilaotu Shan mts China
143 F4 Qila Safed Pak.
148 B3 Qila Saifullah Pak.
144 J4 Qilian China

Raquette Lake

150 B3 **Qilian Shan** *mts* China
203 O3 **Qillak** *i.* Greenland
149 G1 **Qiman Tag** *mts* China
155 E4 **Qimen** China
203 L2 **Qimusseriarsuaq** *b.* Greenland
193 F2 **Qinā** Egypt
154 B3 **Qin'an** China
156 B3 **Qing'an** China
154 C2 **Qingcheng** China
160 B3 **Qingchengzi** China
154 F2 **Qingdao** China
156 B3 **Qinggang** China
Qinggil China *see* **Qinghe**
154 A2 **Qinghai** *prov.* China
154 A2 **Qinghai Hu** *salt l.* China
150 B3 **Qinghai Nanshan** *mts* China
158 A1 **Qinghe** *Heilongjiang* China
144 H2 **Qinghe** *Xinjiang Uygur Zizhiqu* China
160 C2 **Qing He** *r.* China
160 C3 **Qinghecheng** China
154 D2 **Qingjian** China
155 D4 **Qing Jiang** *r.* China
155 E5 **Qingliu** China
155 B5 **Qinglong** *Guizhou* China
154 F1 **Qinglong** *Hebei* China
154 F2 **Qinglong He** *r.* China
155 C6 **Qingping** China
155 F4 **Qingpu** China
Qingshan China *see* **Wudalianchi**
154 C3 **Qingshui** China
154 D2 **Qingshuihe** *Nei Mongol Zizhiqu* China
152 G5 **Qingshuihe** *Qinghai* China
141 J3 **Qingshuihe** *Xinjiang Uygur Zizhiqu* China
155 F4 **Qingtian** China
154 C2 **Qingtongxia** China
154 E2 **Qingxian** China
154 D2 **Qingxu** China
155 E4 **Qingyang** *Anhui* China
154 C3 **Qingyang** *Gansu* China
155 D6 **Qingyuan** *Guangdong* China
160 C2 **Qingyuan** *Liaoning* China
155 F5 **Qingyuan** *Zhejiang* China
Qingzang Gaoyuan *plat.* China *see* **Tibet, Plateau of**
155 C5 **Qingzhen** China
155 D4 **Qingzhou** *Hubei* China
154 F2 **Qingzhou** *Shandong* China
154 D3 **Qin He** *r.* China
154 F2 **Qinhuangdao** China
154 C3 **Qin Ling** *mts* China
154 D2 **Qinxian** China
154 D3 **Qinyang** China
154 D2 **Qinyuan** China
155 C6 **Qinzhou** China
155 C6 **Qinzhou Wan** *b.* China
155 D7 **Qionghai** China
155 B4 **Qionglai** China
155 B4 **Qionglai Shan** *mts* China
155 D7 **Qiongshan** China
Qiongzhou Haixia *str.* China *see* **Hainan Strait**
153 L1 **Qiqian** China
150 E2 **Qiqihar** China
142 D4 **Qīr** *Fārs* Iran
139 L5 **Qīr** *Lorestān* Iran
149 E1 **Qira** China
138 E6 **Qiryat Gat** Israel
139 F6 **Qitab ash Shāmah** *vol. crater* Saudi Arabia
158 B2 **Qitaihe** China
155 B5 **Qiubei** China
154 F2 **Qixia** China
154 E3 **Qixian** *Henan* China
154 D2 **Qixian** *Shanxi* China
158 C1 **Qixing He** *r.* China
155 D5 **Qiyang** China
154 C2 **Qiying** China
155 D7 **Qizhou Liedao** *i.* China
139 L2 **Qızılağac Körfäzi** *b.* Azer.
141 H5 **Qizilrabot** Tajik.
142 D3 **Qobād, Chāh-e** *well* Iran
139 L1 **Qobustan** Azer.
139 L1 **Qobustan Qoruğu** *nature res.* Azer.
Qogir Feng *mt.* China/Pak. *see* **K2**
142 B2 **Qojūr** Iran
142 C3 **Qom** Iran
Qomolangma Feng *mt.* China *see* **Everest, Mount**
Qomsheh Iran *see* **Shahreẓā**
142 C3 **Qonāq, Kūh-e** *h.* Iran
139 L1 **Qonaqkänd** Azer.
149 G3 **Qonggyai** China
140 D4 **Qo'ng'irot** Uzbek.
Qongj China *see* **Chuanjing**
149 E2 **Qong Muztag** *mt.* China
141 G4 **Qo'qon** Uzbek.
140 D4 **Qorajar** Uzbek.
140 E5 **Qorako'l** *Buxoro* Uzbek.
140 E5 **Qorako'l** *Buxoro* Uzbek.
140 D3 **Qoraqalpog'iston** Uzbek.
141 F4 **Qoraqata botig'i** *depr.* Uzbek.
139 F4 **Qornet es Saouda** *mt.* Lebanon
141 F5 **Qorovulbozor** Uzbek.
142 B3 **Qorveh** Iran
140 E4 **Qo'shko'pir** Uzbek.
141 F4 **Qo'shrabot** Uzbek.
143 E5 **Qoṭbābād** Iran
139 J2 **Qoṭūr** Iran
140 D4 **Qozoqdaryo** Uzbek.
221 G3 **Quabbin Reservoir** U.S.A.
215 D4 **Quail Mountains** U.S.A.
121 B7 **Quairading** Australia
179 F2 **Quakenbrück** Germany
221 F4 **Quakertown** U.S.A.
125 E5 **Quambatook** Australia
125 G3 **Quambone** Australia
123 C4 **Quamby** Australia
217 D5 **Quanah** U.S.A.
154 D3 **Quanbao Shan** *mt.* China
163 D2 **Quang Ngai** Vietnam
162 C1 **Quang Tri** Vietnam
155 C6 **Quang Yên** Vietnam
155 B6 **Quan Hoa** Vietnam
155 E5 **Quannan** China
155 F5 **Quanzhou** *Fujian* China
155 D5 **Quanzhou** *Guangxi Zhuangzu Zizhiqu* China
205 I4 **Qu'Appelle** Canada
205 I4 **Qu'Appelle** *r.* Canada
235 L1 **Quaraí** Brazil
235 L1 **Quaraí** *r.* Brazil
155 □ **Quarry Bay** *Hong Kong* China
184 C5 **Quartu Sant'Elena** *Sardinia* Italy
215 D3 **Quartzite Mountain** U.S.A.
215 E5 **Quartzsite** U.S.A.
204 D4 **Quatsino Sound** *inlet* Canada
140 A4 **Quba** Azer.
143 E2 **Qūchān** Iran
125 H5 **Queanbeyan** Australia
207 F4 **Québec** Canada
203 K4 **Québec** *prov.* Canada
234 C2 **Quebra Anzol** *r.* Brazil
235 H4 **Quedal, Cabo** *c.* Chile
179 J3 **Quedlinburg** Germany
204 E4 **Queen Bess, Mount** Canada
204 C4 **Queen Charlotte** Canada
Queen Charlotte Islands Canada *see* **Haida Gwaii**
204 D4 **Queen Charlotte Sound** *sea chan.* Canada
204 D4 **Queen Charlotte Strait** Canada
203 H1 **Queen Elizabeth Islands** Canada
194 D3 **Queen Elizabeth National Park** Uganda
127 K6 **Queen Mary Land** *reg.* Antarctica
203 H3 **Queen Maud Gulf** Canada
127 K3 **Queen Maud Land** *reg.* Antarctica
127 J4 **Queen Maud Mountains** Antarctica
119 E4 **Queensland** *state* Australia
125 F9 **Queenstown** Australia
126 B6 **Queenstown** N.Z.
197 G5 **Queenstown** S. Africa
162 □ **Queenstown** Sing.
221 E5 **Queenstown** U.S.A.
212 A2 **Queets** U.S.A.
235 L2 **Queguay Grande** *r.* Uruguay
235 J3 **Quehué** Arg.
231 H4 **Queimada, Ilha** *i.* Brazil
195 D5 **Quelimane** Moz.
232 B6 **Quellón** Chile
Quelpart Island *i.* S. Korea *see* **Jeju-do**
215 H4 **Quemado** U.S.A.
235 H4 **Quemchi** Chile
235 J3 **Quemú-Quemú** Arg.
235 K3 **Quequén Grande** *r.* Arg.
234 B3 **Querência do Norte** Brazil
225 D3 **Querétaro** Mex.
225 E3 **Querétaro** *state* Mex.
179 J3 **Querfurt** Germany
154 E3 **Queshan** China
204 E4 **Quesnel** Canada
204 E4 **Quesnel** *r.* Canada
204 E4 **Quesnel Lake** Canada
208 B1 **Quetico Provincial Park** Canada
148 A3 **Quetta** Pak.
225 G5 **Quetzaltenango** Guat.
235 H3 **Queuco** Chile
235 H3 **Queule** Chile
Quezaltenango Guat. *see* **Quetzaltenango**
161 H4 **Quezon** Phil.
161 I3 **Quezon City** Phil.
154 E3 **Qufu** China
195 B5 **Quibala** Angola
195 B4 **Quibaxe** Angola
233 H3 **Quibdó** Col.
182 C3 **Quiberon** France
195 B4 **Quiçama, Parque Nacional do** *nat. park* Angola
215 F5 **Quijotoa** U.S.A.
235 J1 **Quilino** Arg.
183 F5 **Quillan** France
205 I4 **Quill Lakes** Canada
235 H2 **Quillota** Chile
235 K2 **Quilmes** Arg.
Quilon India *see* **Kollam**
119 E4 **Quilpie** Australia
235 H2 **Quilpué** Chile
195 B4 **Quimbele** Angola
232 D3 **Quimilí** Arg.
182 B3 **Quimper** France
182 C3 **Quimperlé** France
230 D6 **Quince Mil** Peru
214 B2 **Quincy** *CA* U.S.A.
219 C6 **Quincy** *FL* U.S.A.
208 B6 **Quincy** *IL* U.S.A.
221 H3 **Quincy** *MA* U.S.A.
235 J2 **Quines** Arg.
Qui Nhơn Vietnam *see* **Quy Nhơn**
215 E3 **Quinn Canyon Range** *mts* U.S.A.
183 O3 **Quintanar de la Orden** Spain
225 G4 **Quintana Roo** *state* Mex.
235 H2 **Quintero** Chile
235 J2 **Quinto** *r.* Arg.
183 P2 **Quinto** Spain
195 E5 **Quionga** Moz.
195 B5 **Quipungo** Angola
225 G5 **Quiriguá** *tourist site* Guat.
235 H3 **Quirihue** Chile
195 B5 **Quirima** Angola
195 E5 **Quirimbas, Parque Nacional das** *nat. park* Moz.
125 I3 **Quirindi** Australia
235 K2 **Quiroga** Arg.
195 B5 **Quitapa** Angola
234 B2 **Quitéria** *r.* Brazil
219 D6 **Quitman** *GA* U.S.A.
219 B5 **Quitman** *MS* U.S.A.
230 C4 **Quito** Ecuador
213 D6 **Quitovac** Mex.
215 F4 **Quivero** U.S.A.
231 K4 **Quixadá** Brazil
155 D5 **Qujiang** China
155 C4 **Qu Jiang** *r.* China
155 D6 **Qujie** China
155 B5 **Qujing** China
139 K7 **Qulbān Layyah** *well* Iraq
140 E4 **Quljuqtov tog'lari** *hills* Uzbek.
149 H2 **Qumar He** *r.* China
149 H2 **Qumarheyan** China
149 H2 **Qumarrabdün** China
197 H5 **Qumbu** S. Africa
149 H3 **Qumdo** China
197 G6 **Qumrha** S. Africa
142 B5 **Qunayfidhah, Nafūd** *des.* Saudi Arabia
142 B6 **Qunayy** *well* Saudi Arabia
205 K2 **Quoich** *r.* Canada
174 C3 **Quoich, Loch** *l.* U.K.
175 M3 **Quoile** *r.* U.K.
196 C7 **Quoin Point** S. Africa
197 F1 **Quoxo** *r.* Botswana
143 E6 **Qurayat** Oman
141 G5 **Qŭrghonteppa** Tajik.
139 J2 **Qūrū Gol** *pass* Iran
140 A4 **Qusar** Azer.
155 B4 **Qushan** China
142 B2 **Qūshchī** Iran
139 K2 **Qūsheh Dāgh** *mts* Iran
142 C3 **Quṭīābād** Iran
154 B2 **Quwu Shan** *mts* China
155 C4 **Quxian** China
149 G3 **Qūxü** China
162 C1 **Quy Châu** Vietnam
Quynh Lưu Vietnam *see* **Câu Giat**
155 B6 **Quynh Nhai** Vietnam
163 D2 **Quy Nhơn** Vietnam
209 I3 **Quyon** Canada
154 E2 **Quzhou** *Hebei* China
155 F4 **Quzhou** *Zhejiang* China
187 H7 **Q'vareli** Georgia

R

177 H7 **Raab** *r.* Austria
170 N2 **Raahe** Fin.
171 O3 **Rääkkylä** Fin.
179 E2 **Raalte** Neth.
170 N2 **Raanujärvi** Fin.
163 H4 **Raas** *i.* Indon.
174 B3 **Raasay** *i.* U.K.
174 B3 **Raasay, Sound of** *sea chan.* U.K.
163 I4 **Raba** Indon.
149 E2 **Rabang** China
141 G4 **Rabat** Kazakh.
184 F7 **Rabat** Malta
192 B1 **Rabat** Morocco
119 F2 **Rabaul** P.N.G.
204 D3 **Rabbit** *r.* Canada
121 E4 **Rabbit Flat** Australia
146 A5 **Rābigh** Saudi Arabia
149 G5 **Rabnabad Islands** Bangl.
143 E4 **Rābor** Iran
Rabyānah, Ramlat *des.* Libya *see* **Rebiana Sand Sea**
220 B5 **Raccoon Creek** *r.* U.S.A.
207 J4 **Race, Cape** Canada
221 H3 **Race Point** U.S.A.
138 E5 **Rachaïya** Lebanon
217 D7 **Rachal** U.S.A.
215 E3 **Rachel** U.S.A.
162 C3 **Rach Gia** Vietnam
162 C3 **Rach Gia, Vinh** *b.* Vietnam
177 I5 **Racibórz** Poland
208 D4 **Racine** U.S.A.
209 F1 **Racine Lake** Canada
209 E2 **Raco** U.S.A.
177 L7 **Rădăuți** Romania
219 C4 **Radcliff** U.S.A.
156 C2 **Radde** Russia
220 C6 **Radford** U.S.A.
148 B5 **Radhanpur** India
140 A1 **Radishchevo** Russia
206 E3 **Radisson** Canada
204 F4 **Radium Hot Springs** Canada
185 K3 **Radnevo** Bulg.
177 J5 **Radom** Poland
185 J3 **Radomir** Bulg.
193 E4 **Radom National Park** Sudan
177 I5 **Radomsko** Poland
187 D5 **Radomyshl'** Ukr.
185 J4 **Radoviš** Macedonia
173 E6 **Radstock** U.K.
121 F7 **Radstock, Cape** Australia
187 C4 **Radun'** Belarus
171 M5 **Radviliškis** Lith.
177 L5 **Radyvyliv** Ukr.
149 E4 **Rae Bareli** India
Rae-Edzo Canada *see* **Behchokò**
Rae Lakes Canada *see* **Gamètì**
121 C6 **Raeside, Lake** *salt flat* Australia
126 E3 **Raetihi** N.Z.
137 E5 **Rāf** *h.* Saudi Arabia
235 K1 **Rafaela** Arg.
138 E6 **Rafaḥ** Gaza
194 C3 **Rafaï** C.A.R.
146 B4 **Rafḥā'** Saudi Arabia
143 E4 **Rafsanjān** Iran
161 J5 **Ragang, Mount** *vol.* Phil.
161 I3 **Ragay Gulf** Phil.
179 K1 **Rägelin** Germany
121 C7 **Ragged, Mount** *h.* Australia
221 I3 **Ragged Island** U.S.A.
142 B4 **Raghwah** Saudi Arabia
179 K2 **Ragösen** Germany
179 K3 **Raguhn** Germany
184 F6 **Ragusa** *Sicily* Italy
154 A3 **Ra'gya** China
118 C2 **Raha** Indon.
187 D4 **Rahachow** Belarus
179 G2 **Rahden** Germany
147 G2 **Rahimatpur** India
148 B3 **Rahimyar Khan** Pak.
142 C3 **Rāhjerd** Iran
143 E4 **Raḥmān, Chāh-e** *well* Iran
185 I3 **Rahovec** Kosovo
235 H3 **Rahue** *mt.* Chile
147 G2 **Rahuri** India
162 C3 **Rai, Hon** *i.* Vietnam
237 I7 **Raiatea** *i.* Fr. Polynesia
147 H2 **Raichur** India
149 G4 **Raiganj** India
147 I1 **Raigarh** India
120 C1 **Raijua** *i.* Indon.
215 E2 **Railroad Valley** U.S.A.
207 G3 **Raimbault, Lac** *l.* Canada
125 E5 **Rainbow** Australia
215 G3 **Rainbow Bridge National Monument** *nat. park* U.S.A.
204 F3 **Rainbow Lake** Canada
122 D1 **Raine Island** Australia
220 C6 **Rainelle** U.S.A.
148 B3 **Raini** *r.* Pak.
212 B2 **Rainier, Mount** *vol.* U.S.A.
206 B4 **Rainy** *r.* U.S.A.
203 I5 **Rainy Lake** Canada
205 K5 **Rainy River** Canada
147 I1 **Raipur** *Chhattisgarh* India
148 C4 **Raipur** *Rajasthan* India
171 M3 **Raisio** Fin.
178 B4 **Raismes** France
148 D5 **Raitalai** India
237 J7 **Raivavae** *i.* Fr. Polynesia
147 I2 **Rajahmundry** India
170 O1 **Raja-Jooseppi** Fin.
147 H3 **Rajampet** India
163 H2 **Rajang** *r. Sarawak* Malaysia
147 H4 **Rajapalayam** India
147 G2 **Rajapur** India
148 C4 **Rajasthan** *state* India
148 C3 **Rajasthan Canal** India
149 F4 **Rajauli** India
Rajauri India *see* **Rajouri**
149 G5 **Rajbari** Bangl.
148 C3 **Rajgarh** *Rajasthan* India
148 D4 **Rajgarh** *Rajasthan* India
139 F6 **Rājil, Wādī** *watercourse* Jordan
147 I1 **Rajim** India
148 B5 **Rajkot** India
149 F4 **Rajmahal** India
149 F4 **Rajmahal Hills** India
149 E5 **Rajnandgaon** India
145 D5 **Rajouri** India
148 D3 **Rajpura** India
149 G4 **Rajshahi** Bangl.
147 H2 **Rajura** India
149 F3 **Raka** China
117 I4 **Rakahanga** *atoll* Pacific Ocean
126 C5 **Rakaia** *r.* N.Z.
148 C1 **Rakaposhi** *mt.* Pak.
187 C5 **Rakhiv** Ukr.
148 B3 **Rakhni** Pak.
148 B3 **Rakhni** *r.* Pak.
143 G5 **Rakhshan** *r.* Pak.
187 E5 **Rakitnoye** *Belgorodskaya Oblast'* Russia
158 D2 **Rakitnoye** *Primorskiy Kray* Russia
171 N4 **Rakke** Estonia
171 J4 **Rakkestad** Norway
140 C3 **Rakusha** Kazakh.
140 B4 **Rakushechnyy, Mys** *pt* Kazakh.
171 N4 **Rakvere** Estonia
219 E5 **Raleigh** U.S.A.
117 G2 **Ralik Chain** *is* Marshall Is
208 D2 **Ralph** U.S.A.
204 E2 **Ram** *r.* Canada
207 H2 **Ramah** Canada
215 H4 **Ramah** U.S.A.
234 D1 **Ramalho, Serra do** *hills* Brazil
138 E6 **Rāmallāh** West Bank
147 H3 **Ramanagaram** India
147 H4 **Ramanathapuram** India
236 E3 **Ramapo Deep** *sea feature* N. Pacific Ocean
147 G3 **Ramas, Cape** India
197 F2 **Ramatlabama** S. Africa
119 E2 **Rambutyo Island** P.N.G.
193 F4 **Ramciel** South Sudan
147 G3 **Ramdurg** India
173 C7 **Rame Head** U.K.
195 E5 **Ramena** Madag.
186 F3 **Rameshki** Russia
147 H4 **Rameswaram** India
148 D4 **Ramganga** *r.* India
149 G5 **Ramgarh** Bangl.
149 F5 **Ramgarh** *Jharkhand* India
148 B4 **Ramgarh** *Rajasthan* India
142 C4 **Rāmhormoz** Iran
122 A2 **Ramingining** Australia
138 E6 **Ramla** Israel
138 E7 **Ramm, Jabal** *mts* Jordan
148 D3 **Ramnagar** India
185 L2 **Râmnicu Sărat** Romania
185 K2 **Râmnicu Vâlcea** Romania
215 D5 **Ramona** U.S.A.
209 G1 **Ramore** Canada
195 C6 **Ramotswa** Botswana
148 D3 **Rampur** India
148 C4 **Rampura** India
149 F4 **Rampur Hat** India
149 H6 **Ramree Island** Myanmar
142 C2 **Rāmsar** Iran
171 L3 **Ramsele** Sweden
209 F2 **Ramsey** Canada
172 C3 **Ramsey** Isle of Man
173 G5 **Ramsey** U.K.
173 B6 **Ramsey Island** U.K.
209 F2 **Ramsey Lake** Canada
173 I6 **Ramsgate** U.K.
142 C4 **Rāmshīr** Iran
148 D5 **Ramtek** India
171 N5 **Ramygala** Lith.
233 J4 **Rana, Cerro** *h.* Col.
149 G5 **Ranaghat** India
148 C5 **Ranapur** India
163 I1 **Ranau** *Sabah* Malaysia
235 H2 **Rancagua** Chile
149 F5 **Ranchi** India
235 H4 **Ranco, Lago** *l.* Chile
125 G5 **Rand** Australia
175 L3 **Randalstown** U.K.
184 F6 **Randazzo** *Sicily* Italy
171 J4 **Randers** Denmark
221 H3 **Randolph** *MA* U.S.A.
221 G3 **Randolph** *VT* U.S.A.
171 K3 **Randsjö** Sweden
170 M2 **Råneå** Sweden
126 C6 **Ranfurly** N.Z.
162 B4 **Rangae** Thai.
149 H5 **Rangamati** Bangl.
126 D1 **Rangaunu Bay** N.Z.
221 H2 **Rangeley** U.S.A.
221 H2 **Rangeley Lake** U.S.A.
215 H1 **Rangely** U.S.A.
209 F2 **Ranger Lake** Canada
126 D5 **Rangiora** N.Z.
126 F2 **Rangipoua** *mt.* N.Z.
117 I5 **Rangiroa** *atoll* Fr. Polynesia
126 F3 **Rangitaiki** *r.* N.Z.
126 C5 **Rangitata** *r.* N.Z.
126 E4 **Rangitikei** *r.* N.Z.
141 H5 **Rangkŭl** Tajik.
151 B5 **Rangoon** Myanmar
149 G4 **Rangpur** Bangl.
147 G3 **Ranibennur** India
149 F5 **Raniganj** India
147 I1 **Ranijula Peak** India
148 B4 **Ranipur** Pak.
139 J3 **Rānīyah/Ranye** Iraq
217 C6 **Rankin** U.S.A.
205 K2 **Rankin Inlet** Canada
205 K2 **Rankin Inlet** *inlet* Canada
125 G4 **Rankins Springs** Australia
171 N4 **Ranna** Estonia
123 E5 **Rannes** Australia
140 C2 **Ranneye** Russia
174 D4 **Rannoch, Loch** U.K.
174 D4 **Rannoch Moor** *moorland* U.K.
162 A3 **Ranong** Thai.
162 B4 **Ranot** Thai.
187 G4 **Ranova** *r.* Russia
139 L5 **Rānsa** Iran
171 K3 **Ransby** Sweden
151 F7 **Ransiki** Indon.
171 O3 **Rantasalmi** Fin.
163 E2 **Rantauprapat** Indon.
208 C5 **Rantoul** U.S.A.
177 Q2 **Rantsevo** Russia
170 N2 **Rantsila** Fin.
170 N2 **Ranua** Fin.
158 C1 **Raohe** China
155 E6 **Raoping** China
180 C6 **Raoui, Erg er** *des.* Alg.
119 J4 **Raoul Island** N.Z.
117 I6 **Rapa** *i.* Fr. Polynesia
184 C2 **Rapallo** Italy
Rapa Nui *i.* S. Pacific Ocean *see* **Easter Island**
148 B5 **Rapar** India
143 E5 **Rapch** *watercourse* Iran
235 H2 **Rapel** *r.* Chile
203 L3 **Raper, Cape** Canada
175 K3 **Raphoe** Ireland
221 E5 **Rapidan** *r.* U.S.A.
124 C5 **Rapid Bay** Australia
216 C2 **Rapid City** U.S.A.
209 H2 **Rapide-Deux** Canada
209 H2 **Rapide-Sept** Canada
208 D3 **Rapid River** U.S.A.
171 N4 **Rapla** Estonia
221 E5 **Rappahannock** *r.* U.S.A.
149 E4 **Rapti** *r.* India
148 B5 **Rapur** India
161 J3 **Rapurapu** *i.* Phil.
221 F2 **Raquette** *r.* U.S.A.
221 F3 **Raquette Lake** U.S.A.

Rucheng

235 J1 **Río Primero** Arg.
213 F5 **Rio Rancho** U.S.A.
215 G6 **Rio Rico** U.S.A.
235 J1 **Río Segundo** Arg.
233 H3 **Riosucio** Col.
235 J2 **Río Tercero** Arg.
230 C4 **Río Tigre** Ecuador
161 H4 **Rio Tuba** Phil.
234 B2 **Rio Verde** Brazil
225 G4 **Río Verde** *Quintana Roo* Mex.
225 E3 **Río Verde** *San Luis Potosí* Mex.
234 A2 **Rio Verde de Mato Grosso** Brazil
214 B2 **Rio Vista** U.S.A.
234 A2 **Riozinho** *r.* Brazil
177 O5 **Ripky** Ukr.
172 F3 **Ripley** *England* U.K.
173 F4 **Ripley** *England* U.K.
220 B5 **Ripley** *OH* U.S.A.
219 B5 **Ripley** *TN* U.S.A.
220 C5 **Ripley** *WV* U.S.A.
183 R1 **Ripoll** Spain
172 F3 **Ripon** U.K.
214 B3 **Ripon** *CA* U.S.A.
208 C4 **Ripon** *WI* U.S.A.
173 D6 **Risca** U.K.
158 G2 **Rishiri-tō** *i.* Japan
138 E6 **Rishon LeZiyyon** Israel
143 F5 **Rīsh Pīsh Bālā** Iran
171 J4 **Risør** Norway
171 J3 **Rissa** Norway
171 N3 **Ristiina** Fin.
170 O2 **Ristijärvi** Fin.
170 O1 **Ristikent** Russia
197 F4 **Ritchie** S. Africa
145 H9 **Ritchie's Archipelago** *is* India
127 K3 **Ritscher Upland** *mts* Antarctica
170 L2 **Ritsem** Sweden
214 C3 **Ritter, Mount** U.S.A.
179 G1 **Ritterhude** Germany
183 O2 **Rituerto** *r.* Spain
212 C2 **Ritzville** U.S.A.
235 J2 **Rivadavia** *Buenos Aires* Arg.
235 I2 **Rivadavia** *Mendoza* Arg.
232 D2 **Rivadavia** *Salta* Arg.
235 H1 **Rivadavia** Chile
184 D2 **Riva del Garda** Italy
224 C1 **Riva Palacio** Mex.
224 H6 **Rivas** Nicaragua
143 E3 **Rīvash** Iran
235 J3 **Rivera** Arg.
235 L1 **Rivera** Uruguay
192 B4 **River Cess** Liberia
221 G4 **Riverhead** U.S.A.
121 C6 **Riverina** Australia
125 F5 **Riverina** *reg.* Australia
196 D7 **Riversdale** S. Africa
197 H5 **Riverside** S. Africa
215 D5 **Riverside** U.S.A.
122 B3 **Riversleigh** Australia
124 C5 **Riverton** Australia
205 J4 **Riverton** Canada
126 B7 **Riverton** N.Z.
214 B2 **Riverton** *CA* U.S.A.
213 E3 **Riverton** *WY* U.S.A.
207 H4 **Riverview** Canada
183 F5 **Rivesaltes** France
219 D7 **Riviera Beach** U.S.A.
221 I1 **Rivière-Bleue** Canada
207 G4 **Rivière-du-Loup** Canada
187 C5 **Rivne** Ukr.
126 D4 **Riwaka** N.Z.
146 C5 **Riyadh** Saudi Arabia
142 D3 **Riza** *well* Iran
139 H1 **Rize** Turkey
Rizhao China *see* **Donggang**
138 E4 **Rizokarpason** Cyprus
143 E4 **Rīzū'īyeh** Iran
171 J4 **Rjukan** Norway
171 I4 **Rjuvbrokkene** *mt.* Norway
192 A3 **Rkîz** Mauritania
171 J3 **Roa** Norway
173 G5 **Roade** U.K.
170 J2 **Roan** Norway
215 H2 **Roan Cliffs** *ridge* U.S.A.
182 G3 **Roanne** France
219 C5 **Roanoke** *AL* U.S.A.
208 C5 **Roanoke** *IL* U.S.A.
220 D6 **Roanoke** *VA* U.S.A.
219 E4 **Roanoke** *r.* U.S.A.
219 E4 **Roanoke Rapids** U.S.A.
215 H2 **Roan Plateau** U.S.A.
175 I6 **Roaringwater Bay** Ireland
224 H5 **Roatán** Hond.
171 M3 **Röbäck** Sweden
143 E4 **Robāţ** Iran
143 E3 **Robāţ-e Kamānī** Iran
143 E3 **Robāţ-e Khān** Iran
125 F8 **Robbins Island** Australia
124 C6 **Robe** Australia
121 A4 **Robe** *r.* Australia
175 I4 **Robe** *r.* Ireland
124 D3 **Robe, Mount** *h.* Australia
179 K1 **Röbel/Müritz** Germany
206 E3 **Robert-Bourassa, Réservoir** *resr* Canada
217 C6 **Robert Lee** U.S.A.
213 D3 **Roberts** U.S.A.
125 J2 **Roberts, Mount** Australia
215 D2 **Roberts Creek Mountain** U.S.A.
170 M2 **Robertsfors** Sweden
149 E4 **Robertsganj** India
217 E5 **Robert S. Kerr Reservoir** U.S.A.
196 C6 **Robertson** S. Africa
121 C4 **Robertson Range** *hills* Australia
192 A4 **Robertsport** Liberia
124 C4 **Robertstown** Australia
207 F4 **Roberval** Canada
203 L1 **Robeson Channel** Canada/Greenland
172 G3 **Robin Hood's Bay** U.K.
155 □ **Robin's Nest** *h.* Hong Kong China
219 C4 **Robinson** U.S.A.
118 B4 **Robinson Ranges** *hills* Australia
122 B3 **Robinson River** Australia
125 E5 **Robinvale** Australia
215 G5 **Robles Junction** U.S.A.
215 G5 **Robles Pass** U.S.A.
205 I4 **Roblin** Canada
204 F4 **Robson, Mount** Canada
217 D7 **Robstown** U.S.A.
225 F4 **Roca Partida, Punta** *pt* Mex.
235 L2 **Rocha** Uruguay
173 E4 **Rochdale** U.K.
234 A2 **Rochedo** Brazil
178 D4 **Rochefort** Belgium
182 D4 **Rochefort** France
207 F2 **Rochefort, Lac** *l.* Canada
186 G2 **Rochegda** Russia
208 C5 **Rochelle** U.S.A.
125 F6 **Rochester** Australia
173 H6 **Rochester** U.K.
208 D5 **Rochester** *IN* U.S.A.
208 A3 **Rochester** *MN* U.S.A.
221 H3 **Rochester** *NH* U.S.A.
221 E3 **Rochester** *NY* U.S.A.
173 H6 **Rochford** U.K.
179 K3 **Rochlitz** Germany
182 C2 **Roc'h Trévezel** *h.* France
204 D2 **Rock** *r.* Canada
166 C4 **Rockall** *i.* N. Atlantic Ocean
239 H2 **Rockall Bank** *sea feature* N. Atlantic Ocean
127 I4 **Rockefeller Plateau** Antarctica
208 C4 **Rockford** U.S.A.
205 H5 **Rockglen** Canada
119 F4 **Rockhampton** Australia
208 C1 **Rock Harbor** U.S.A.
219 D5 **Rock Hill** U.S.A.
118 B5 **Rockingham** Australia
219 E5 **Rockingham** U.S.A.
122 D3 **Rockingham Bay** Australia
221 G2 **Rock Island** Canada
208 B5 **Rock Island** U.S.A.
216 D1 **Rock Lake** U.S.A.
221 F2 **Rockland** Canada
221 H3 **Rockland** *MA* U.S.A.
221 I2 **Rockland** *ME* U.S.A.
208 C2 **Rockland** *MI* U.S.A.
125 E6 **Rocklands Reservoir** Australia
215 H3 **Rock Point** U.S.A.
221 H3 **Rockport** U.S.A.
216 D3 **Rock Rapids** U.S.A.
212 F2 **Rock Springs** *MT* U.S.A.
213 E3 **Rock Springs** *WY* U.S.A.
217 C6 **Rocksprings** U.S.A.
220 D3 **Rockton** Canada
208 D6 **Rockville** *IN* U.S.A.
220 E5 **Rockville** *MD* U.S.A.
221 I2 **Rockwood** U.S.A.
213 G4 **Rocky Ford** U.S.A.
220 B5 **Rocky Fork Lake** U.S.A.
209 F2 **Rocky Island Lake** Canada
219 E5 **Rocky Mount** *NC* U.S.A.
220 D6 **Rocky Mount** *VA* U.S.A.
205 G4 **Rocky Mountain House** Canada
213 F3 **Rocky Mountain National Park** U.S.A.
210 D2 **Rocky Mountains** Canada/U.S.A.
204 F4 **Rocky Mountains Forest Reserve** *nature res.* Canada
178 B5 **Rocourt-St-Martin** France
178 C5 **Rocroi** France
171 J3 **Rødberg** Norway
171 J5 **Rødbyhavn** Denmark
207 I3 **Roddickton** Canada
174 B3 **Rodel** U.K.
179 E1 **Roden** Neth.
179 J4 **Rödental** Germany
235 I1 **Rodeo** Arg.
224 C2 **Rodeo** Mex.
215 H6 **Rodeo** U.S.A.
182 F4 **Rodez** France
179 K5 **Roding** Germany
141 J1 **Rodino** Russia
143 G5 **Rodkhan** Pak.
186 G3 **Rodniki** Russia
140 D2 **Rodnikovka** Kazakh.
Rodos Greece *see* **Rhodes**
Rodos *i.* Greece *see* **Rhodes**
238 I6 **Rodrigues Island** Mauritius
118 B4 **Roebourne** Australia
118 C3 **Roebuck Bay** Australia
197 H2 **Roedtan** S. Africa
121 D6 **Roe Plains** Australia
178 D3 **Roermond** Neth.
178 B4 **Roeselare** Belgium
203 J3 **Roes Welcome Sound** *sea chan.* Canada
179 J2 **Rogätz** Germany
217 E4 **Rogers** U.S.A.
209 F3 **Rogers City** U.S.A.
215 D4 **Rogers Lake** U.S.A.
213 D3 **Rogerson** U.S.A.
220 B6 **Rogersville** U.S.A.
206 E3 **Roggan** *r.* Canada
237 N8 **Roggeveen Basin** *sea feature* S. Pacific Ocean
196 D6 **Roggeveld** *plat.* S. Africa
196 D6 **Roggeveldberge** *esc.* S. Africa
170 K2 **Rognan** Norway
213 A3 **Rogue** *r.* U.S.A.
214 A2 **Rohnert Park** U.S.A.
176 F6 **Rohrbach in Oberösterreich** Austria
179 F5 **Rohrbach-lès-Bitche** France
148 B4 **Rohri Sangar** Pak.
148 D3 **Rohtak** India
162 B1 **Roi Et** Thai.
117 J5 **Roi-Georges, Îles du** *is* Fr. Polynesia
178 B5 **Roisel** France
171 M4 **Roja** Latvia
235 K2 **Rojas** Arg.
148 B3 **Rojhan** Pak.
225 E3 **Rojo, Cabo** Mex.
163 B2 **Rokan** *r.* Indon.
122 C2 **Rokeby** Australia
122 C2 **Rokeby National Park** Australia
171 N5 **Rokiškis** Lith.
170 M2 **Roknäs** Sweden
187 C5 **Rokytne** Ukr.
234 B3 **Rolândia** Brazil
217 F4 **Rolla** U.S.A.
171 J3 **Rollag** Norway
123 E5 **Rolleston** Australia
126 D5 **Rolleston** N.Z.
209 H2 **Rollet** Canada
219 F7 **Rolleville** Bahamas
209 I2 **Rolphton** Canada
119 E4 **Roma** Australia
Roma Italy *see* **Rome**
197 G4 **Roma** Lesotho
171 L4 **Roma** Sweden
219 E5 **Romain, Cape** U.S.A.
207 H3 **Romaine** *r.* Canada
177 M7 **Roman** Romania
181 H3 **Română, Câmpia** *plain* Romania
239 H6 **Romanche Gap** *sea feature* S. Atlantic Ocean
151 E7 **Romang, Pulau** *i.* Indon.
185 K1 **Romania** *country* Europe
136 D1 **Roman-Kosh** *mt.* Crimea
150 D1 **Romanovka** *Respublika Buryatiya* Russia
187 G5 **Romanovka** *Saratovskaya Oblast'* Russia
141 J1 **Romanovo** Russia
182 G4 **Romans-sur-Isère** France
202 B3 **Romanzof, Cape** U.S.A.
182 H2 **Rombas** France
161 I3 **Romblon** Phil.
161 I3 **Romblon** *i.* Phil.
Rombo, Ilhéus do *i.* Cape Verde *see* **Secos, Ilhéus**
184 E4 **Rome** Italy
219 C5 **Rome** *GA* U.S.A.
221 I2 **Rome** *ME* U.S.A.
221 F3 **Rome** *NY* U.S.A.
209 F4 **Romeo** U.S.A.
173 H6 **Romford** U.K.
182 F2 **Romilly-sur-Seine** France
Romitan Uzbek. *see* **Romiton**
141 F5 **Romiton** Uzbek.
220 D5 **Romney** U.S.A.
173 H6 **Romney Marsh** *reg.* U.K.
187 E5 **Romny** Ukr.
171 J5 **Rømø** *i.* Denmark
182 E3 **Romorantin-Lanthenay** France
162 B5 **Rompin** *r.* Malaysia
173 F7 **Romsey** U.K.
147 G3 **Ron** India
162 C1 **Ron** Vietnam
174 C1 **Rona** *i. Scotland* U.K.
174 C3 **Rona** *i. Scotland* U.K.
174 □ **Ronas Hill** U.K.
231 H6 **Roncador, Serra do** *hills* Brazil
119 F2 **Roncador Reef** Solomon Is
183 N4 **Ronda** Spain
171 J3 **Rondane Nasjonalpark** *nat. park* Norway
233 L4 **Rondon, Pico** *h.* Brazil
234 A2 **Rondonópolis** Brazil
135 F3 **Rondu** Pak.
155 C5 **Rong'an** China
155 B4 **Rongchang** China
160 B5 **Rongcheng** China
160 B5 **Rongcheng Wan** *b.* China
149 G3 **Rong Chu** *r.* China
236 G6 **Rongelap** *atoll* Marshall Is
155 C5 **Rongjiang** China
155 C6 **Rong Jiang** *r.* China
149 H5 **Rongklang Range** *mts* Myanmar
126 E4 **Rongotea** N.Z.
155 C5 **Rongshui** China
155 D6 **Rongxian** *Guangxi Zhuangzu Zizhiqu* China
155 B4 **Rongxian** *Sichuan* China
171 K5 **Rønne** Denmark
171 K4 **Ronneby** Sweden
127 I3 **Ronne Entrance** *str.* Antarctica
127 I3 **Ronne Ice Shelf** Antarctica
179 H2 **Ronnenberg** Germany
178 B4 **Ronse** Belgium
197 G3 **Roodepoort** S. Africa
179 E1 **Roodeschool** Neth.
Roordahuizum Neth. *see* **Reduzum**
148 D3 **Roorkee** India
178 C3 **Roosendaal** Neth.
215 G5 **Roosevelt** *AZ* U.S.A.
215 G1 **Roosevelt** *UT* U.S.A.
204 D3 **Roosevelt, Mount** Canada
127 I5 **Roosevelt Sub-glacial Island** Antarctica
204 E2 **Root** *r.* Canada
208 B4 **Root** *r.* U.S.A.
186 J2 **Ropcha** Russia
122 A2 **Roper** *r.* Australia
120 F2 **Roper Bar** Australia
182 D4 **Roquefort** France
233 L4 **Roraima** *state* Brazil
231 F2 **Roraima, Mount** Guyana
171 J3 **Røros** Norway
170 J2 **Rørvik** Norway
177 O6 **Ros'** *r.* Ukr.
230 □ **Rosa, Cabo** *c. Galapagos Is* Ecuador
219 D2 **Rosa, Lake** Bahamas
224 B2 **Rosa, Punta** *pt* Mex.
214 C4 **Rosamond** U.S.A.
214 C4 **Rosamond Lake** U.S.A.
235 K2 **Rosario** Arg.
222 A2 **Rosario** *Baja California* Mex.
225 D2 **Rosario** *Coahuila* Mex.
224 C3 **Rosario** *Sinaloa* Mex.
224 B2 **Rosario** *Sonora* Mex.
161 I3 **Rosario** *Batangas* Phil.
161 I2 **Rosario** *La Union* Phil.
233 I2 **Rosario** Venez.
235 K2 **Rosario del Tala** Arg.
235 L1 **Rosário do Sul** Brazil
234 A1 **Rosário Oeste** Brazil
224 A1 **Rosarito** *Baja California* Mex.
224 B2 **Rosarito** *Baja California Sur* Mex.
184 F5 **Rosarno** Italy
221 F4 **Roscoe** U.S.A.
182 C2 **Roscoff** France
175 J4 **Roscommon** Ireland
209 E3 **Roscommon** U.S.A.
175 K5 **Roscrea** Ireland
122 A2 **Rose** *r.* Australia
214 C2 **Rose, Mount** U.S.A.
223 L5 **Roseau** Dominica
205 J5 **Roseau** U.S.A.
123 B5 **Roseberth** Australia
125 F8 **Rosebery** Australia
207 I4 **Rose Blanche** Canada
213 B3 **Roseburg** U.S.A.
209 E3 **Rose City** U.S.A.
172 G3 **Rosedale Abbey** U.K.
193 F3 **Roseires Reservoir** Sudan
117 H4 **Rose Island** *atoll* American Samoa
217 E6 **Rosenberg** U.S.A.
171 I4 **Rosendal** Norway
197 G4 **Rosendal** S. Africa
176 F7 **Rosenheim** Germany
204 C4 **Rose Point** Canada
184 F3 **Roseto degli Abruzzi** Italy
205 H4 **Rosetown** Canada
205 I4 **Rose Valley** Canada
214 B2 **Roseville** *CA* U.S.A.
208 B5 **Roseville** *IL* U.S.A.
125 J1 **Rosewood** Australia
186 D2 **Roshchino** *Leningradskaya Oblast'* Russia
158 D2 **Roshchino** *Primorskiy Kray* Russia
196 B3 **Rosh Pinah** Namibia
143 E3 **Roshtkhvār** Iran
141 G5 **Roshtqal'a** Tajik.
183 J5 **Rosignano Marittimo** Italy
185 K2 **Roşiori de Vede** Romania
171 K5 **Roskilde** Denmark
187 E4 **Roslavl'** Russia
170 P1 **Roslyakovo** Russia
169 O4 **Roslyatino** Russia
125 G9 **Ross** Australia
204 C2 **Ross** *r.* Canada
126 C5 **Ross** N.Z.
126 E4 **Ross, Mount** *h.* N.Z.
185 G5 **Rossano** Italy
175 J3 **Rossan Point** Ireland
217 F5 **Ross Barnett Reservoir** U.S.A.
207 G3 **Ross Bay Junction** Canada
175 I6 **Rosscarbery** Ireland
127 H5 **Ross Dependency** *reg.* Antarctica
119 F3 **Rossel Island** P.N.G.
127 I5 **Ross Ice Shelf** Antarctica
207 H5 **Rossignol, Lake** Canada
127 I5 **Ross Island** Antarctica
175 L5 **Rosslare** Ireland
173 A5 **Rosslare Harbour** Ireland
179 K3 **Roßlau** Germany
209 I3 **Rossmore** Canada
192 A3 **Rosso** Mauritania
184 C3 **Rosso, Capo** *c. Corsica* France
173 E6 **Ross-on-Wye** U.K.
187 F5 **Rossosh'** Russia
208 D1 **Rossport** Canada
204 C2 **Ross River** Canada
127 I5 **Ross Sea** Antarctica
179 I5 **Roßtal** Germany
170 K2 **Røssvatnet** *l.* Norway
208 D5 **Rossville** U.S.A.
179 L3 **Roßwein** Germany
204 D3 **Rosswood** Canada
142 D5 **Rostāq** Iran
205 H4 **Rosthern** Canada
139 J3 **Rostī** Iraq
176 F3 **Rostock** Germany
186 F3 **Rostov** Russia
187 F6 **Rostov-na-Donu** Russia
187 G6 **Rostovskaya Oblast'** *admin. div.* Russia
170 M2 **Rosvik** Sweden
219 C5 **Roswell** *GA* U.S.A.
213 F5 **Roswell** *NM* U.S.A.
151 G5 **Rota** *i.* N. Mariana Is
179 I5 **Rot am See** Germany
151 E8 **Rote** *i.* Indon.
179 H1 **Rotenburg (Wümme)** Germany
179 J4 **Roter Main** *r.* Germany
179 J5 **Roth** Germany
179 G4 **Rothaargebirge** *hills* Germany
172 F2 **Rothbury** U.K.
172 F2 **Rothbury Forest** U.K.
179 I5 **Rothenburg ob der Tauber** Germany
173 G7 **Rother** *r.* U.K.
127 L2 **Rothera** *research stn* Antarctica
126 D5 **Rotherham** N.Z.
173 F4 **Rotherham** U.K.
174 E3 **Rothes** U.K.
174 C5 **Rothesay** U.K.
208 C3 **Rothschild** U.S.A.
173 G5 **Rothwell** U.K.
120 C1 **Roti** Indon.
125 F4 **Roto** Australia
126 C5 **Rotomanu** N.Z.
184 C3 **Rotondo, Monte** *mt. Corsica* France
126 D4 **Rotoroa, Lake** N.Z.
126 F3 **Rotorua** N.Z.
126 F3 **Rotorua, Lake** N.Z.
176 F6 **Rott** *r.* Germany
179 J5 **Röttenbach** Germany
179 I5 **Rottendorf** Germany
176 G7 **Rottenmann** Austria
178 C3 **Rotterdam** Neth.
179 I3 **Rottleberode** Germany
121 A7 **Rottnest Island** Australia
179 E1 **Rottumeroog** *i.* Neth.
179 E1 **Rottumerplaat** *i.* Neth.
176 D6 **Rottweil** Germany
119 H3 **Rotuma** *i.* Fiji
171 K3 **Rötviken** Sweden
179 K5 **Rötz** Germany
182 F1 **Roubaix** France
182 E2 **Rouen** France
126 B6 **Rough Ridge** N.Z.
Roulers Belgium *see* **Roeselare**
207 F3 **Roundeyed Lake** Canada
172 F3 **Round Hill** U.K.
125 J3 **Round Mountain** *mt.* Australia
215 D2 **Round Mountain** U.S.A.
215 H3 **Round Rock** U.S.A.
212 E2 **Roundup** U.S.A.
174 E1 **Rousay** *i.* U.K.
221 G2 **Rouses Point** U.S.A.
183 F5 **Roussillon** *reg.* France
197 G5 **Rouxville** S. Africa
209 H1 **Rouyn-Noranda** Canada
170 N2 **Rovaniemi** Fin.
187 F5 **Roven'ki** Russia
184 D2 **Rovereto** Italy
162 C2 **Rôviĕng** Cambodia
184 D2 **Rovigo** Italy
184 E2 **Rovinj** Croatia
187 H5 **Rovnoye** Russia
125 H2 **Rowena** Australia
120 B3 **Rowley Shoals** *sea feature* Australia
161 I4 **Roxas** *Capiz* Phil.
161 I2 **Roxas** *Isabela* Phil.
161 I3 **Roxas** *Oriental Mindoro* Phil.
161 H4 **Roxas** *Palawan* Phil.
219 E4 **Roxboro** U.S.A.
126 B6 **Roxburgh** N.Z.
124 B3 **Roxby Downs** Australia
213 F4 **Roy** U.S.A.
175 L4 **Royal Canal** Ireland
149 F4 **Royal Chitwan National Park** Nepal
208 C1 **Royale, Isle** *i.* U.S.A.
173 F5 **Royal Leamington Spa** U.K.
197 H4 **Royal Natal National Park** S. Africa
209 F4 **Royal Oak** U.S.A.
160 D5 **Royal Tombs of the Joseon Dynasty** *tourist site* South Korea
173 H6 **Royal Tunbridge Wells** U.K.
173 F6 **Royal Wootton Bassett** U.K.
182 D4 **Royan** France
178 A5 **Roye** France
121 B4 **Roy Hill** Australia
173 G5 **Royston** U.K.
143 F3 **Rōzanak** Afgh.
187 D6 **Rozdil'na** Ukr.
187 E6 **Rozdol'ne** Crimea
187 F6 **Rozivka** Ukr.
142 C3 **Rozveh** Iran
187 G4 **Rtishchevo** Russia
173 D5 **Ruabon** U.K.
195 B5 **Ruacana** Namibia
195 D4 **Ruaha National Park** Tanz.
126 F3 **Ruahine Range** *mts* N.Z.
126 E3 **Ruapehu, Mount** *vol.* N.Z.
126 B7 **Ruapuke Island** N.Z.
127 G2 **Ruatoria** N.Z.
187 D4 **Ruba** Belarus
146 C6 **Rub' al Khālī** *des.* Saudi Arabia
143 F4 **Rubāţ Māndêh** *r.* Afgh.
158 H3 **Rubeshibe** Japan
214 B2 **Rubicon** *r.* U.S.A.
187 F5 **Rubizhne** Ukr.
141 J2 **Rubtsovsk** Russia
202 C3 **Ruby** U.S.A.
215 E1 **Ruby Lake** U.S.A.
215 E1 **Ruby Mountains** U.S.A.
155 D5 **Rucheng** China

329

Seattle

234 C3 **São Bernardo do Campo** Brazil
232 E3 **São Borja** Brazil
234 C3 **São Carlos** Brazil
234 C1 **São Domingos** Brazil
234 B2 **São Domingos** *r.* Brazil
231 H6 **São Félix do Araguaia** Brazil
231 H5 **São Félix do Xingu** Brazil
234 E3 **São Fidélis** Brazil
192 □ **São Filipe** Cape Verde
234 D1 **São Francisco** Brazil
231 K5 **São Francisco** *r.* Brazil
233 G3 **São Francisco do Sul** Brazil
235 L1 **São Gabriel** Brazil
233 K5 **São Gabriel da Cachoeira** Brazil
234 D3 **São Gonçalo** Brazil
234 D2 **São Gotardo** Brazil
234 E3 **São João da Barra** Brazil
234 C3 **São João da Boa Vista** Brazil
234 C1 **São João d'Aliança** Brazil
183 L2 **São João da Madeira** Port.
234 D1 **São João do Paraíso** Brazil
234 D3 **São João Nepomuceno** Brazil
234 C3 **São Joaquim da Barra** Brazil
166 A6 **São Jorge** *i.* Azores
233 K5 **São José** Brazil
234 E3 **São José do Calçado** Brazil
235 M2 **São José do Norte** Brazil
234 C3 **São José do Rio Preto** Brazil
234 D3 **São José dos Campos** Brazil
235 C4 **São José dos Pinhais** Brazil
234 D3 **São Lourenço** Brazil
234 A2 **São Lourenço** *r.* Brazil
234 A2 **São Lourenço, Pantanal de** *marsh* Brazil
235 M1 **São Lourenço do Sul** Brazil
231 J4 **São Luís** Brazil
234 C3 **São Manuel** Brazil
234 C2 **São Marcos** *r.* Brazil
231 J4 **São Marcos, Baía de** *b.* Brazil
234 E2 **São Mateus** Brazil
234 E2 **São Mateus** *r.* Brazil
166 A6 **São Miguel** *i.* Azores
234 C2 **São Miguel** *r.* Brazil
182 G3 **Saône** *r.* France
192 □ **São Nicolau** *i.* Cape Verde
234 C3 **São Paulo** Brazil
234 C3 **São Paulo** *state* Brazil
239 H5 **São Pedro e São Paulo** *is* N. Atlantic Ocean
231 J5 **São Raimundo Nonato** Brazil
234 D2 **São Romão** Brazil
231 K5 **São Roque, Cabo de** *c.* Brazil
234 D3 **São Sebastião** Brazil
234 D3 **São Sebastião, Ilha do** *i.* Brazil
234 C3 **São Sebastião do Paraíso** Brazil
235 M1 **São Sepé** Brazil
234 B2 **São Simão** Brazil
234 B2 **São Simão, Barragem de** *resr* Brazil
151 E6 **Sao-Siu** Indon.
São Tiago *i.* Cape Verde *see* **Santiago**
192 C4 **São Tomé** *i.* São Tomé and Príncipe
234 E3 **São Tomé, Cabo de** *c.* Brazil
192 C4 **São Tomé and Príncipe** *country* Africa
180 C6 **Saoura, Oued** *watercourse* Alg.
234 C3 **São Vicente** Brazil
192 □ **São Vicente** *i.* Cape Verde
183 L4 **São Vicente, Cabo de** *c.* Port.
138 C1 **Sapanca** Turkey
140 D4 **Saparmyrat Türkmenbaşy** Turkm.
118 C2 **Saparua** Indon.
138 C2 **Şaphane Dağı** *mt.* Turkey
224 J7 **Sapo, Serranía del** *mts* Panama
192 B4 **Sapo National Park** Liberia
158 G3 **Sapporo** Japan
184 F4 **Sapri** Italy
163 H4 **Sapudi** *i.* Indon.
217 D4 **Sapulpa** U.S.A.
143 E3 **Sāqī** Iran
142 B2 **Saqqez** Iran
139 K3 **Sarā** Iran
142 B2 **Sarāb** Iran
162 B3 **Sara Buri** Thai.
143 F2 **Saragt** *Ahal* Turkm.
144 B4 **Saragt** *Ahal* Turkm.
230 C4 **Saraguro** Ecuador
185 H3 **Sarajevo** Bos. & Herz.
143 F2 **Sarakhs** Iran
140 D2 **Saraktash** Russia
140 C2 **Saralzhin** Kazakh.
149 H4 **Saramati** *mt.* India
141 H2 **Saran'** Kazakh.
163 H3 **Saran, Gunung** *mt.* Indon.
221 G2 **Saranac** *r.* U.S.A.
221 F2 **Saranac Lake** U.S.A.
185 I5 **Sarandë** Albania
235 L2 **Sarandí del Yí** Uruguay
235 L2 **Sarandí Grande** Uruguay
161 J5 **Sarangani** *i.* Phil.
161 J5 **Sarangani Bay** Phil.
161 J5 **Sarangani Islands** Phil.
161 J5 **Sarangani Strait** Phil.
187 H4 **Saransk** Russia
162 A1 **Saraphi** Thai.
132 G4 **Sarapul** Russia
233 J3 **Sarare** *r.* Venez.
219 D7 **Sarasota** U.S.A.
148 B5 **Saraswati** *r.* India
187 D6 **Sarata** Ukr.
213 F3 **Saratoga** U.S.A.
221 G3 **Saratoga Springs** U.S.A.
163 H2 **Saratok** *Sarawak* Malaysia
187 H5 **Saratov** Russia
187 H5 **Saratovskaya Oblast'** *admin. div.* Russia
187 I4 **Saratovskoye Vodokhranilishche** *resr* Russia
185 K5 **Saratsina, Akrotirio** *pt* Greece
143 F5 **Sarāvān** Iran
Saravan Laos *see* **Salavan**
162 A2 **Sarawa** *r.* Myanmar
163 H2 **Sarawak** *state* Malaysia
138 A1 **Saray** Turkey
138 B3 **Sarayköy** Turkey
138 D2 **Sarayönü** Turkey
141 F5 **Sarazm** *tourist site* Tajik.
141 G5 **Sarband** Tajik.
143 F5 **Sarbāz** Iran
143 F5 **Sarbāz** *r.* Iran
143 E3 **Sar Bīsheh** Iran
184 D2 **Sarca** *r.* Italy
139 L3 **Sarcham-e Soflá** Iran
149 E3 **Sarda** *r.* India/Nepal
149 E3 **Sarda** *r.* Nepal
148 C3 **Sardarshahr** India
142 B2 **Sardasht** Iran
Sardegna *i.* Italy *see* **Sardinia**
233 I2 **Sardinata** Col.
184 C4 **Sardinia** *i.* Italy
139 K3 **Sardrūd** Iran
142 C5 **Sareb, Rās as** *pt* U.A.E.
170 L2 **Sareks nationalpark** *nat. park* Sweden
170 L2 **Sarektjåkkå** *mt.* Sweden
142 B3 **Sar-e Pol-e Żahāb** Iran
143 G2 **Sar-e Pul** *Sar-e Pul* Afgh.
143 G2 **Sar-e Pul** *Sar-e Pul* Afgh.
141 H5 **Sarez, Kŭli** *l.* Tajik.
239 E4 **Sargasso Sea** Atlantic Ocean
148 C2 **Sargodha** Pak.
193 D4 **Sarh** Chad
142 D2 **Sārī** Iran
185 L7 **Saria** *i.* Greece
148 D2 **Sarigh Jilganang Kol** *salt l.* China
138 B2 **Sarıgöl** Turkey
139 I1 **Sarıkamış** Turkey
138 D3 **Sarıkavak** Turkey
148 D4 **Sarila** India
162 □ **Sarimbun Reservoir** Sing.
119 E4 **Sarina** Australia
138 E2 **Sarıoğlan** *Kayseri* Turkey
Sarıoğlan *Konya* Turkey *see* **Belören**
Sar-i-Pul Afgh. *see* **Sar-e Pul**
139 I2 **Sarısu** Turkey
160 C4 **Sariwŏn** N. Korea
138 C2 **Sarıyar Barajı** *resr* Turkey
138 B1 **Sarıyer** Turkey
139 F2 **Sarız** Turkey
149 E4 **Sarju** *r.* India
141 I3 **Sarkand** Kazakh.
148 B4 **Sarkari Tala** India
138 C2 **Şarkikaraağaç** Turkey
139 F2 **Şarkışla** Turkey
187 C7 **Şarköy** Turkey
143 G4 **Sarlath Range** *mts* Afgh./Pak.
182 E4 **Sarlat-la-Canéda** France
140 C5 **Şarlawuk** Turkm.
151 F7 **Sarmi** Indon.
171 K3 **Särna** Sweden
139 K5 **Sarneh** Iran
184 C1 **Sarnen** Switz.
209 F4 **Sarnia** Canada
187 C5 **Sarny** Ukr.
143 H3 **Sarōbī** Afgh.
163 B3 **Sarolangun** Indon.
158 H2 **Saroma-ko** *l.* Japan
185 J6 **Saronikos Kolpos** *g.* Greece
187 C7 **Saros Körfezi** *b.* Turkey
148 C4 **Sarotra** India
187 G4 **Sarov** Russia
187 H5 **Sarpa, Ozero** *l.* Russia
187 H6 **Sarpa, Ozero** *l.* Russia
171 J4 **Sarpsborg** Norway
182 H2 **Sarrebourg** France
179 F5 **Sarreguemines** France
183 M1 **Sarria** Spain
183 P2 **Sarrión** Spain
178 C6 **Sarry** France
184 C4 **Sartène** *Corsica* France
142 C3 **Sarud, Rūdkhāneh-ye** *r.* Iran
143 G5 **Saruna** Pak.
139 L4 **Sārūq** Iran
139 J2 **Şärur** Azer.
139 K4 **Sarvābād** Iran
177 H7 **Sárvár** Hungary
137 I4 **Sarv-e Bālā** Iran
142 D4 **Sarvestān** Iran
141 G4 **Saryagash** Kazakh.
141 G2 **Saryarka** *plain* Kazakh.
142 D4 **Sar Yazd** Iran
140 E3 **Sarybasat** Kazakh.
141 H4 **Sary-Bulak** Kyrg.
141 I4 **Sary-Jaz** *r.* Kyrg.
140 C3 **Sarykamys** *Atyrauskaya Oblast'* Kazakh.
141 F2 **Sarykamys** *Karagandinskaya Oblast'* Kazakh.
140 D4 **Sarykamyshskoye Ozero** *salt l.* Turkm./Uzbek.
141 G4 **Sarykemer** Kazakh.
141 H2 **Sarykiyak** Kazakh.
141 F1 **Sarykol'** Kazakh.
141 H5 **Sarykol Range** *mts* China/Tajik.
141 H3 **Sarykomey** Kazakh.
141 I3 **Saryozek** Kazakh.
140 B2 **Saryozen** *r.* Kazakh./Russia
141 H3 **Saryshagan** Kazakh.
141 F3 **Sarysu** *watercourse* Kazakh.
140 B3 **Sarytash** Kazakh.
141 H5 **Sary-Tash** Kyrg.
Sary Yazikskoye Vodokhranilishche *resr* Turkm. *see* **Saryýazy Suw Howdany**
143 F2 **Saryýazy Suw Howdany** *resr* Turkm.
141 H3 **Saryyesik-Atyrau, Peski** *des.* Kazakh.
141 I4 **Saryzhaz** Kazakh.
140 B4 **Sarzha** Kazakh.
215 G4 **Sasabe** U.S.A.
120 B1 **Sasar, Tanjung** *pt* Indon.
149 F4 **Sasaram** India
159 A8 **Sasebo** Japan
205 H4 **Saskatchewan** *prov.* Canada
205 I4 **Saskatchewan** *r.* Canada
205 H4 **Saskatoon** Canada
133 M2 **Saskylakh** Russia
224 H5 **Saslaya** *mt.* Nicaragua
224 H5 **Saslaya, Parque Nacional** *nat. park* Nicaragua
197 G3 **Sasolburg** S. Africa
187 G4 **Sasovo** Russia
221 F5 **Sassafras** U.S.A.
192 B4 **Sassandra** Côte d'Ivoire
184 C4 **Sassari** *Sardinia* Italy
179 G3 **Sassenberg** Germany
176 F3 **Sassnitz** Germany
141 J3 **Sasykkol', Ozero** *l.* Kazakh.
187 H6 **Sasykoli** Russia
192 A3 **Satadougou** Mali
159 B9 **Sata-misaki** *c.* Japan
148 C5 **Satana** India
147 G2 **Satara** India
197 I2 **Satara** S. Africa
Sätbaev Kazakh. *see* **Satpayev**
187 G4 **Satinka** Russia
149 G5 **Satkhira** Bangl.
148 C3 **Satluj** *r.* Pak.
147 H2 **Satmala Range** *hills* India
149 E4 **Satna** India
141 F2 **Satpayev** *Karagandinskaya Oblast'* Kazakh.
144 C2 **Satpayev** *Karagandinskaya Oblast'* Kazakh.
148 C5 **Satpura Range** *mts* India
159 B9 **Satsuma-hantō** *pen.* Japan
159 B9 **Satsuma-Sendai** Japan
162 B2 **Sattahip** Thai.
179 I5 **Satteldorf** Germany
148 D2 **Satti** India
177 K7 **Satu Mare** Romania
162 B4 **Satun** Thai.
235 K1 **Sauce** Arg.
225 D2 **Sauceda** Mex.
215 F5 **Sauceda Mountains** U.S.A.
224 C1 **Saucillo** Mex.
171 I4 **Sauda** Norway
141 G4 **Saudakent** Kazakh.
170 C2 **Sauðárkrókur** Iceland
146 B4 **Saudi Arabia** *country* Asia
179 F3 **Sauerland** *reg.* Germany
208 D4 **Saugatuck** U.S.A.
221 G3 **Saugerties** U.S.A.
216 E2 **Sauk Center** U.S.A.
208 C4 **Sauk City** U.S.A.
182 G3 **Saulieu** France
209 E2 **Sault Sainte Marie** Canada
209 E2 **Sault Sainte Marie** U.S.A.
141 G1 **Saumalkol'** Kazakh.
123 F4 **Saumarez Reef** Australia
151 F7 **Saumlakki** Indon.
182 D3 **Saumur** France
120 E2 **Saunders, Mount** *h.* Australia
229 G7 **Saunders Island** S. Sandwich Is
149 F4 **Saura** *r.* India
140 B3 **Saura** Kazakh.
195 C4 **Saurimo** Angola
148 D5 **Sausar** India
185 I2 **Sava** *r.* Europe
125 F8 **Savage River** Australia
119 I3 **Savai'i** *i.* Samoa
187 G5 **Savala** *r.* Russia
192 C4 **Savalou** Benin
219 D6 **Savannah** *GA* U.S.A.
219 B5 **Savannah** *TN* U.S.A.
219 D5 **Savannah** *r.* U.S.A.
219 E7 **Savannah Sound** Bahamas
162 C1 **Savannakhét** Laos
223 I5 **Savanna-la-Mar** Jamaica
206 B3 **Savant Lake** Canada
147 G3 **Savanur** India
171 M3 **Sävar** Sweden
185 L5 **Savaştepe** Turkey
192 C4 **Savè** Benin
195 D6 **Save** *r.* Moz.
142 C3 **Sāveh** Iran
171 O3 **Saviaho** Fin.
132 F3 **Savinskiy** Russia
184 C2 **Savona** Italy
171 O3 **Savonlinna** Fin.
171 O3 **Savonranta** Fin.
182 H4 **Savoy** *reg.* France
139 I1 **Şavşat** Turkey
171 K4 **Sävsjö** Sweden
120 C1 **Savu** *i.* Indon.
170 O2 **Savukoski** Fin.
139 H3 **Savur** Turkey
Savu Sea Indon. *see* **Sawu, Laut**
148 D4 **Sawai Madhopur** India
162 A1 **Sawankhalok** Thai.
213 F4 **Sawatch Range** *mts* U.S.A.
174 A4 **Sawel Mountain** *h.* U.K.
162 A3 **Sawi, Ao** *b.* Thai.
125 J3 **Sawtell** Australia
208 B2 **Sawtooth Mountains** U.S.A.
120 C1 **Sawu** Indon.
Sawu *i.* Indon. *see* **Savu**
151 E7 **Sawu, Laut** *sea* Indon.
173 G4 **Saxilby** U.K.
173 I5 **Saxmundham** U.K.
170 K2 **Saxnäs** Sweden
141 I3 **Sayak** Kazakh.
152 F1 **Sayanogorsk** Russia
150 B1 **Sayano-Shushenskoye Vodokhranilishche** *resr* Russia
153 H1 **Sayansk** Russia
140 E5 **Saýat** Turkm.
Sayat Turkm. *see* **Saýat**
225 G4 **Sayaxché** Guat.
142 D4 **Sāyen** Iran
153 H2 **Sayhan-Ovoo** Mongolia
146 D6 **Sayḩūt** Yemen
140 A2 **Saykyn** Kazakh.
Sāylac Somalia *see* **Saylac**
194 E2 **Saylac** Somalia
150 D2 **Saynshand** Mongolia
Sayn-Ust Mongolia *see* **Höhmorīt**
141 J3 **Sayram Hu** *salt l.* China
217 D5 **Sayre** *OK* U.S.A.
221 E4 **Sayre** *PA* U.S.A.
225 D4 **Sayula** *Jalisco* Mex.
225 F4 **Sayula** *Veracruz* Mex.
204 D4 **Sayward** Canada
140 B3 **Sazdy** Kazakh.
148 C2 **Sazin** Pak.
186 E3 **Sazonovo** Russia
192 B2 **Sbaa** Alg.
192 C1 **Sbeitla** Tunisia
121 C7 **Scaddan** Australia
172 D3 **Scafell Pike** *h.* U.K.
174 B4 **Scalasaig** U.K.
184 F5 **Scalea** Italy
174 □ **Scalloway** U.K.
175 J5 **Scalp** *h.* Ireland
174 B3 **Scalpay** *i. Scotland* U.K.
174 C3 **Scalpay** *i. Scotland* U.K.
125 H8 **Scamander** Australia
174 E2 **Scapa Flow** *inlet* U.K.
174 C4 **Scarba** *i.* U.K.
209 H4 **Scarborough** Canada
233 L2 **Scarborough** Trin. and Tob.
172 G3 **Scarborough** U.K.
161 H3 **Scarborough Reef** *sea feature* Phil.
174 A2 **Scarp** *i.* U.K.
179 I1 **Schaale** *r.* Germany
179 I1 **Schaalsee** *l.* Germany
178 C4 **Schaerbeek** Belgium
176 D7 **Schaffhausen** Switz.
179 J3 **Schafstädt** Germany
178 C2 **Schagen** Neth.
178 C2 **Schagerbrug** Neth.
196 B3 **Schakalskuppe** Namibia
143 F4 **Schao** *watercourse* Afgh./Iran
176 F6 **Schärding** Austria
178 B3 **Scharendijke** Neth.
179 H1 **Scheeßel** Germany
207 G3 **Schefferville** Canada
Schelde *r.* Belgium *see* **Scheldt**
178 C3 **Scheldt** *r.* Belgium
215 E2 **Schell Creek Range** *mts* U.S.A.
179 I2 **Schellerten** Germany
221 G3 **Schenectady** U.S.A.
179 H1 **Schenefeld** Germany
178 C2 **Schermerhorn** Neth.
174 D4 **Schiehallion** *mt.* U.K.
179 K6 **Schierling** Germany
179 E1 **Schiermonnikoog** Neth.
179 E1 **Schiermonnikoog** *i.* Neth.
179 E1 **Schiermonnikoog, Nationaal Park** *nat. park* Neth.
179 G1 **Schiffdorf** Germany
179 J1 **Schilde** *r.* Germany
178 D4 **Schinnen** Neth.
184 D2 **Schio** Italy
179 K3 **Schkeuditz** Germany
179 E4 **Schleiden** Germany
179 J4 **Schleiz** Germany
176 D3 **Schleswig** Germany
179 H1 **Schleswig-Holstein** *land* Germany
179 I4 **Schleusingen** Germany
179 H4 **Schlitz** Germany
179 G3 **Schloß Holte-Stukenbrock** Germany
179 H4 **Schlüchtern** Germany
179 I5 **Schlüsselfeld** Germany
179 I4 **Schmalkalden** Germany
179 G3 **Schmallenberg** Germany
Schmidt Peninsula Russia *see* **Shmidta, Poluostrov**
179 K4 **Schneeberg** Germany
179 J3 **Schneidlingen** Germany
179 H1 **Schneverdingen** Germany
221 G3 **Schodack Center** U.S.A.
208 C3 **Schofield** U.S.A.
214 □[1] **Schofield Barracks** *military base* U.S.A.
178 D2 **Schokland** *tourist site* Neth.
179 K1 **Schönebeck** Germany
179 J2 **Schönebeck (Elbe)** Germany
179 I2 **Schöningen** Germany
179 H5 **Schöntal** Germany
221 I2 **Schoodic Lake** U.S.A.
209 E4 **Schoolcraft** U.S.A.
178 C3 **Schoonhoven** Neth.
179 I5 **Schopfloch** Germany
179 I2 **Schöppenstedt** Germany
179 F1 **Schortens** Germany
125 H9 **Schouten Island** Australia
119 E2 **Schouten Islands** P.N.G.
208 D1 **Schreiber** Canada
221 G3 **Schroon Lake** U.S.A.
215 F5 **Schuchuli** U.S.A.
175 I6 **Schull** Ireland
205 J2 **Schultz Lake** Canada
214 C2 **Schurz** U.S.A.
179 F2 **Schüttorf** Germany
221 G3 **Schuylerville** U.S.A.
179 J5 **Schwabach** Germany
176 D6 **Schwäbische Alb** *mts* Germany
179 H5 **Schwäbisch Hall** Germany
176 E6 **Schwabmünchen** Germany
179 G2 **Schwaförden** Germany
179 H4 **Schwalmstadt-Ziegenhain** Germany
179 K5 **Schwandorf** Germany
163 H3 **Schwaner, Pegunungan** *mts* Indon.
179 G1 **Schwanewede** Germany
179 H2 **Schwarmstedt** Germany
179 L3 **Schwarze Elster** *r.* Germany
179 I1 **Schwarzenbek** Germany
179 K4 **Schwarzenberg/Erzgebirge** Germany
179 E4 **Schwarzer Mann** *h.* Germany
196 B2 **Schwarzrand** *mts* Namibia
Schwarzwald *mts* Germany *see* **Black Forest**
176 E7 **Schwaz** Austria
179 I5 **Schwebheim** Germany
176 G4 **Schwedt/Oder** Germany
179 G5 **Schwegenheim** Germany
179 E5 **Schweich** Germany
179 I4 **Schweinfurt** Germany
179 L3 **Schweinitz** Germany
179 K1 **Schweinrich** Germany
197 F3 **Schweizer-Reneke** S. Africa
179 F3 **Schwelm** Germany
176 D6 **Schwenningen** Germany
179 J1 **Schwerin** Germany
179 J1 **Schweriner See** *l.* Germany
179 G5 **Schwetzingen** Germany
176 D7 **Schwyz** Switz.
184 E6 **Sciacca** *Sicily* Italy
184 F6 **Scicli** *Sicily* Italy
173 A8 **Scilly, Isles of** U.K.
220 B5 **Scioto** *r.* U.S.A.
215 F2 **Scipio** U.S.A.
212 F1 **Scobey** U.S.A.
173 I5 **Scole** U.K.
125 I4 **Scone** Australia
174 E4 **Scone** U.K.
221 I1 **Scopan Lake** U.S.A.
203 P2 **Scoresby Land** *reg.* Greenland
121 D7 **Scorpion Bight** *b.* Australia
239 F9 **Scotia Ridge** *sea feature* S. Atlantic Ocean
239 G9 **Scotia Sea** S. Atlantic Ocean
209 G4 **Scotland** Canada
174 D4 **Scotland** *admin. div.* U.K.
120 E2 **Scott, Cape** Australia
204 D4 **Scott, Cape** Canada
127 I5 **Scott Base** *research stn* Antarctica
197 I5 **Scottburgh** S. Africa
217 C4 **Scott City** U.S.A.
127 I5 **Scott Coast** Antarctica
220 D4 **Scottdale** U.S.A.
203 K2 **Scott Inlet** Canada
127 H6 **Scott Island** Antarctica
205 H3 **Scott Lake** Canada
127 L4 **Scott Mountains** Antarctica
120 C2 **Scott Reef** Australia
216 C3 **Scottsbluff** U.S.A.
219 C5 **Scottsboro** U.S.A.
219 C4 **Scottsburg** U.S.A.
125 G8 **Scottsdale** Australia
213 E5 **Scottsdale** U.S.A.
214 A3 **Scotts Valley** U.S.A.
208 D4 **Scottville** U.S.A.
215 D3 **Scottys Junction** U.S.A.
174 C2 **Scourie** U.K.
174 □ **Scousburgh** U.K.
174 E2 **Scrabster** U.K.
221 F4 **Scranton** U.S.A.
174 B4 **Scridain, Loch** *inlet* U.K.
173 G4 **Scunthorpe** U.K.
121 B6 **Seabrook, Lake** *salt flat* Australia
173 H7 **Seaford** U.K.
221 F5 **Seaford** U.S.A.
209 G4 **Seaforth** Canada
161 H4 **Seahorse Shoal** *sea feature* Phil.
205 J3 **Seal** *r.* Canada
197 E7 **Seal, Cape** S. Africa
125 E5 **Sea Lake** Australia
221 I3 **Seal Island** U.S.A.
207 H3 **Seal Lake** Canada
197 F7 **Seal Point** S. Africa
215 E3 **Seaman Range** *mts* U.S.A.
172 G3 **Seamer** U.K.
215 E4 **Searchlight** U.S.A.
217 F5 **Searcy** U.S.A.
215 D4 **Searles Lake** U.S.A.
209 E4 **Sears** U.S.A.
221 I2 **Searsport** U.S.A.
214 B3 **Seaside** *CA* U.S.A.
212 B2 **Seaside** *OR* U.S.A.
174 E6 **Seaton** U.K.
212 B2 **Seattle** U.S.A.

Sibay

155 E4 Shangrao *Jiangxi* China
141 J3 Shangsanshilipu China
154 E3 Shangshui China
155 C6 Shangsi China
155 E4 Shangtang China
154 D1 Shangyi China
155 E5 Shangyou China
141 J4 Shangyou Shuiku *resr* China
155 F4 Shangyu China
160 D1 Shangzhi China
Shangzhou China *see* Shangluo
160 D1 Shanhe China
154 F3 Shanhou He *r.* China
175 I6 Shanlaragh Ireland
175 J5 Shannon *est.* Ireland
175 J4 Shannon *r.* Ireland
175 I5 Shannon, Mouth of the Ireland
121 B7 Shannon National Park Australia
200 G1 Shannon Ø Greenland
160 D2 Shansonggang China
149 G5 Shantipur India
155 E6 Shantou China
155 E6 Shanwei China
154 D2 Shanxi *prov.* China
154 E3 Shanxian China
154 C3 Shanyang China
154 D2 Shanyin China
155 D5 Shaodong China
155 D5 Shaoguan China
155 E5 Shaowu China
155 F4 Shaoxing China
155 D5 Shaoyang *Hunan* China
155 D5 Shaoyang *Hunan* China
172 E3 Shap U.K.
155 D6 Shapa China
175 F1 Shapinsay *i.* U.K.
144 G1 Shapshal'skiy Khrebet *mts* Russia
146 C4 Shaqrā' Saudi Arabia
139 K6 Shaqrah, Qaşr *tourist site* Iraq
141 J2 Shar Kazakh.
139 I6 Sharaf *well* Iraq
148 B3 Sharan Jogizai Pak.
141 I1 Sharbakty Kazakh.
Sharbulag Mongolia *see* Dzavhan
141 J1 Sharchino Russia
141 F4 Shardara Kazakh.
141 F4 Shardara, Step' *plain* Kazakh.
141 G4 Shardarinskoye Vodokhranilishche *resr* Kazakh./Uzbek.
Sharga Mongolia *see* Tsagaan-Uul
Shargun' Uzbek. *see* Sharg'un
141 F5 Sharg'un Uzbek.
187 D5 Sharhorod Ukr.
Sharhulsan Mongolia *see* Mandal-Ovoo
139 J4 Shārī, Buḩayrat *imp. l.* Iraq
158 I3 Shari-dake *vol.* Japan
147 E4 Sharjah U.A.E.
177 M3 Sharkawshchyna Belarus
118 B4 Shark Bay Australia
122 D2 Shark Reef Australia
Sharlouk Turkm. *see* Şarlawuk
140 C1 Sharlyk Russia
136 D6 Sharm ash Shaykh Egypt
Sharm el Sheikh Egypt *see* Sharm ash Shaykh
221 G4 Sharon *CT* U.S.A.
220 C4 Sharon *PA* U.S.A.
155 □ Sharp Peak *Hong Kong* China
138 E5 Sharqī, Jabal ash *mts* Lebanon/Syria
140 D4 Sharqiy Ustyurt Chink *esc.* Uzbek.
186 H3 Shar'ya Russia
141 I4 Sharyn Kazakh.
141 I4 Sharyn *r.* Kazakh.
195 C6 Shashe *r.* Botswana/Zimbabwe
194 D3 Shashemenē Eth.
141 H3 Shashubay Kazakh.
213 B3 Shasta, Mount *vol.* U.S.A.
213 B3 Shasta Lake U.S.A.
155 □ Sha Tin *Hong Kong* China
187 H4 Shatki Russia
169 O5 Shatsk Russia
236 F3 Shatsky Rise *sea feature* Pacific Ocean
142 C4 Shaţţ, Ra's osh *pt* Iran
139 L7 Shatt al Arab *r.* Iran/Iraq
139 J6 Shaţţ al Hillah *r.* Iraq
187 F4 Shatura Russia
141 G4 Shauil'dir Kazakh.
205 H5 Shaunavon Canada
220 D5 Shavers Fork *r.* U.S.A.
121 B4 Shaw *r.* Australia
221 F4 Shawangunk Mountains U.S.A.
208 C3 Shawano U.S.A.
208 C3 Shawano Lake U.S.A.
207 F4 Shawinigan Canada
139 F4 Shawmarīyah, Jabal ash *mts* Syria
217 D5 Shawnee U.S.A.
155 F5 Sha Xi *r.* China
155 E5 Shaxian China
141 G4 Shayan Kazakh.
155 D4 Shayang China
118 C4 Shay Gap (abandoned) Australia
143 H3 Shaykarī, Darah-ye *r.* Afgh.
139 K5 Shaykh Jūwī Iraq
139 K5 Shaykh Sa'd Iraq
187 F4 Shchekino Russia
169 Q2 Shchel'yayur Russia
187 F5 Shchigry Russia
187 D5 Shchors Ukr.
141 G1 Shchuchinsk Kazakh.
187 C4 Shchuchyn Belarus
141 K2 Shebalino Russia
187 F5 Shebekino Russia
194 E3 Shebelē Wenz, Wabē *r.* Eth./Somalia
194 E3 Shebelē Wenz, Wabē *r.* Somalia
208 D4 Sheboygan U.S.A.
193 D4 Shebshi Mountains Nigeria
156 F3 Shebunino Russia
207 H4 Shediac Canada
204 D3 Shedin Peak Canada
137 F1 Shedok Russia
175 K4 Sheelin, Lough *l.* Ireland
175 K2 Sheep Haven *b.* Ireland
197 I3 Sheepmoor S. Africa
215 E3 Sheep Peak U.S.A.
173 H6 Sheerness U.K.
207 H5 Sheet Harbour Canada
125 G8 Sheffield Australia
126 D5 Sheffield N.Z.
173 F4 Sheffield U.K.
219 C5 Sheffield *AL* U.S.A.
208 C5 Sheffield *IL* U.S.A.
220 D4 Sheffield *PA* U.S.A.
217 C6 Sheffield *TX* U.S.A.
209 G3 Sheguiandah Canada
139 J3 Shehedan Iraq
155 B4 Shehong China
Sheikh, Jebel esh *mt.* Lebanon/Syria *see* Hermon, Mount
148 C3 Sheikhupura Pak.
155 □ Shek Kwu Chau *i.* *Hong Kong* China
155 □ Shek Pik Reservoir *Hong Kong* China
186 F3 Sheksna Russia
155 □ Shek Uk Shan *mt.* *Hong Kong* China
133 S2 Shelagskiy, Mys *pt* Russia
143 F4 Shēlah, Rōd-e *watercourse* Afgh./Iran
208 A6 Shelbina U.S.A.
207 G5 Shelburne *N.S.* Canada
209 G3 Shelburne *Ont.* Canada
122 C1 Shelburne Bay Australia
221 G3 Shelburne Falls U.S.A.
208 D4 Shelby *MI* U.S.A.
212 E1 Shelby *MT* U.S.A.
219 D5 Shelby *NC* U.S.A.
220 B4 Shelby *OH* U.S.A.
219 C4 Shelbyville *IN* U.S.A.
208 A6 Shelbyville *MO* U.S.A.
219 C5 Shelbyville *TN* U.S.A.
215 H5 Sheldon *AZ* U.S.A.
208 D5 Sheldon *IL* U.S.A.
214 C2 Sheldon Springs U.S.A.
207 H3 Sheldrake Canada
133 Q3 Shelikhova, Zaliv *g.* Russia
202 C4 Shelikof Strait U.S.A.
205 H4 Shellbrook Canada
213 D3 Shelley U.S.A.
125 I5 Shellharbour Australia
214 A1 Shell Mountain U.S.A.
204 F4 Shelter Bay Canada
214 A1 Shelter Cove U.S.A.
155 □ Shelter Island *Hong Kong* China
221 G4 Shelter Island U.S.A.
126 B7 Shelter Point N.Z.
141 J2 Shemonaikha Kazakh.
216 E3 Shenandoah *IA* U.S.A.
221 E4 Shenandoah *PA* U.S.A.
220 D5 Shenandoah *VA* U.S.A.
220 D5 Shenandoah *r.* U.S.A.
220 D5 Shenandoah Mountains U.S.A.
220 D5 Shenandoah National Park U.S.A.
220 C4 Shenango River Lake U.S.A.
155 E6 Shen'ao China
140 E2 Shenbertal Kazakh.
192 C4 Shendam Nigeria
158 C1 Shending Shan *h.* China
140 E3 Shengel'dy Kazakh.
156 B3 Shengping China
155 G4 Shengsi China
155 F4 Shengzhou China
186 G2 Shenkursk Russia
154 D2 Shenmu China
155 D4 Shennong Ding *mt.* China
155 D4 Shennongjia China
154 E3 Shenqiu China
158 A1 Shenshu China
121 C6 Shenton, Mount *h.* Australia
160 B3 Shenwo Shuiku *resr* China
160 B3 Shenyang China
155 E6 Shenzhen China
155 □ Shenzhen He *r.* *Hong Kong* China
Shenzhen Wan *b.* *Hong Kong* China *see* Deep Bay
Sheoigheach, Dúiche *reg.* Ireland *see* Joyce Country
187 C5 Shepetivka Ukr.
119 G3 Shepherd Islands Vanuatu
125 F6 Shepparton Australia
173 H6 Sheppey, Isle of *i.* U.K.
Sherabad Uzbek. *see* Sherobod
173 E7 Sherborne U.K.
207 H4 Sherbrooke *N.S.* Canada
207 F4 Sherbrooke *Que.* Canada
221 F3 Sherburne U.S.A.
175 L4 Shercock Ireland
143 H3 Sher Dahan Pass Afgh.
193 F3 Shereiq Sudan
148 C4 Shergarh India
217 E5 Sheridan *AR* U.S.A.
212 F2 Sheridan *WY* U.S.A.
124 A4 Sheringa Australia
173 I5 Sheringham U.K.
217 D5 Sherman U.S.A.
221 I2 Sherman Mills U.S.A.
215 E1 Sherman Mountain U.S.A.
141 F5 Sherobod Uzbek.
149 G4 Sherpur Bangl.
205 I3 Sherridon Canada
178 D3 's-Hertogenbosch Neth.
173 F4 Sherwood Forest *reg.* U.K.
204 C3 Sheslay Canada
132 A3 Shetland Islands U.K.
140 C3 Shetpe Kazakh.
155 □ Sheung Shui *Hong Kong* China
155 □ Sheung Sze Mun *sea chan.* *Hong Kong* China
147 H4 Shevaroy Hills India
140 E3 Shevchenko, Zaliv *l.* Kazakh.
156 D1 Shevli *r.* Russia
143 H2 Shēwah, Kōl-e *l.* Afgh.
155 F4 Shexian China
154 F3 Sheyang China
216 D2 Sheyenne U.S.A.
216 D2 Sheyenne *r.* U.S.A.
142 D4 Sheyţūr Iran
140 B2 Shezhin II Kazakh.
174 B3 Shiant Islands U.K.
150 H2 Shiashkotan, Ostrov *i.* Russia
209 E4 Shiawassee *r.* U.S.A.
146 C6 Shibām Yemen
143 H3 Shibar, Kōtal-e Afgh.
159 F6 Shibata Japan
156 B1 Shibazhan China
158 H2 Shibetsu *Hokkaidō* Japan
158 I3 Shibetsu *Hokkaidō* Japan
138 C6 Shibīn al Kawm Egypt
143 G2 Shibirghān Afgh.
Shibotsu-jima *i.* Russia *see* Zelenyy, Ostrov
159 F6 Shibukawa Japan
155 E5 Shicheng China
160 B4 Shicheng Dao *i.* China
221 E4 Shickshinny U.S.A.
139 G6 Shidād al Mismā' *h.* Saudi Arabia
160 B5 Shidao China
160 B5 Shidao Wan *b.* China
141 H2 Shiderty *r.* Kazakh.
174 C4 Shiel, Loch *l.* U.K.
122 B2 Shield, Cape Australia
136 D5 Shifa, Jabal ash *mts* Saudi Arabia
155 B4 Shifang China
187 I4 Shigony Russia
154 D1 Shiguai China
135 G2 Shihezi China
154 E2 Shijiazhuang China
143 F4 Shikar *r.* Pak.
147 G3 Shikarpur India
148 B4 Shikarpur Pak.
159 C8 Shikoku *i.* Japan
159 C8 Shikoku-sanchi *mts* Japan
157 G4 Shikotan, Ostrov *i.* Russia
Shikotan-tō *i.* Russia *see* Shikotan, Ostrov
158 G3 Shikotsu-Tōya Kokuritsu-kōen *nat. park* Japan
140 D2 Shil'da Russia
172 F3 Shildon U.K.
186 H1 Shilega Russia
149 G4 Shiliguri India
141 I4 Shilik Kazakh.
155 D4 Shilipu China
148 D2 Shilla *mt.* India
175 L5 Shillelagh Ireland
209 G1 Shillington Canada
149 G4 Shillong India
149 G4 Shillong Peak *mt.* India
140 B2 Shil'naya Balka Kazakh.
221 F5 Shiloh U.S.A.
154 D2 Shilou China
187 G4 Shilovo Russia
159 B8 Shimabara Japan
159 F7 Shimada Japan
150 E1 Shimanovsk Russia
159 C8 Shimanto Japan
155 D4 Shimen China
155 B4 Shimian China
159 F7 Shimizu Japan
148 D3 Shimla India
159 F7 Shimoda Japan
Shimoga India *see* Shivamogga
157 F4 Shimokita-hantō *pen.* Japan
195 D4 Shimoni Kenya
159 B8 Shimonoseki Japan
148 C1 Shimshal Pak.
186 D3 Shimsk Russia
174 D2 Shin, Loch *l.* U.K.
143 F3 Shīndand Afgh.
148 B3 Shinghar Pak.
148 C1 Shinghshal Pass Pak.
208 D2 Shingleton U.S.A.
159 E8 Shingū Japan
197 I1 Shingwedzi S. Africa
197 I1 Shingwedzi *r.* S. Africa
173 E4 Shining Tor *h.* U.K.
209 G2 Shining Tree Canada
159 G5 Shinjō Japan
143 G4 Shīnkaī Afgh.
159 E6 Shinminato Japan
221 I1 Shin Pond U.S.A.
195 D4 Shinyanga Tanz.
159 G5 Shiogama Japan
159 D8 Shiono-misaki *c.* Japan
159 G6 Shioya-zaki *pt* Japan
155 E4 Shipai China
219 E7 Ship Chan Cay *i.* Bahamas
155 B6 Shiping China
148 D3 Shipki La China/India
173 F4 Shipley U.K.
207 H4 Shippagan Canada
221 E4 Shippensburg U.S.A.
215 H3 Shiprock U.S.A.
215 H3 Shiprock Peak U.S.A.
155 F4 Shipu China
141 J1 Shipunovo Russia
155 C5 Shiqian China
154 C3 Shiquan China
Shiquanhe China *see* Ali
154 C3 Shiquan Shuiku *resr* China
139 L2 Shīrābād Iran
158 G4 Shirakami-sanchi *tourist site* Japan
159 G6 Shirakawa Japan
159 E6 Shirakawa-go and Gokayama *tourist site* Japan
150 F3 Shirane-san *mt.* Japan
159 F6 Shirane-san *vol.* Japan
127 L4 Shirase Glacier Antarctica
142 D4 Shīrāz Iran
138 C6 Shirbīn Egypt
158 I2 Shiretoko-misaki *c.* Japan
140 E3 Shirikrabat *tourist site* Kazakh.
141 G4 Shirin Uzbek.
143 G4 Shirinab *r.* Pak.
158 G4 Shiriya-zaki *c.* Japan
140 D3 Shirkala *reg.* Kazakh.
221 G4 Shirley U.S.A.
221 I2 Shirley Mills U.S.A.
159 E7 Shirotori Japan
148 C5 Shirpur India
144 I3 Shirten Holoy Gobi *des.* China
143 E2 Shīrvān Iran
156 B2 Shisanzhan China
155 D4 Shishou China
155 E4 Shitai China
155 F4 Shitang China
139 I5 Shithāthah Iraq
148 B4 Shiv India
147 G3 Shivamogga India
150 C2 Shiveegovĭ Mongolia
133 R4 Shiveluch, Vulkan *vol.* Russia
219 C4 Shively U.S.A.
148 D4 Shivpuri India
215 F3 Shivwits Plateau U.S.A.
155 C6 Shiwan Dashan *mts* China
160 B3 Shiwen China
155 E5 Shixing China
154 D3 Shiyan China
141 F3 Shiyeli Kazakh.
154 E3 Shizhong China
155 C4 Shizhu China
155 B5 Shizong China
154 C2 Shizuishan China
159 F7 Shizuoka Japan
146 B1 Shkhara *mt.* Georgia/Russia
187 D4 Shklow Belarus
185 H3 Shkodër Albania
133 J1 Shmidta, Ostrov *i.* Russia
156 F1 Shmidta, Poluostrov *pen.* Russia
159 C7 Shōbara Japan
141 G5 Shoh Tajik.
158 G3 Shokanbetsu-dake *mt.* Japan
141 H4 Shokpar Kazakh.
141 G4 Sholakkorgan Kazakh.
141 F2 Sholaksay Kazakh.
140 D3 Shomishkol' Kazakh.
186 I2 Shomvukovo Russia
174 C4 Shona, Eilean *i.* U.K.
239 J9 Shona Ridge *sea feature* S. Atlantic Ocean
141 I4 Shonzhy Kazakh.
140 D3 Shoptykol' *Aktyubinskaya Oblast'* Kazakh.
141 H2 Shoptykol' *Pavlodarskaya Oblast'* Kazakh.
148 D2 Shor India
143 G4 Shōrābak *reg.* Afgh.
147 H4 Shoranur India
143 G5 Shorap Pak.
141 F5 Sho'rchi Uzbek.
139 J3 Shor Gol Iran
148 C3 Shorkot Pak.
140 C4 Shorkozakhly, Solonchak *salt flat* Turkm.
141 G4 Shornak Kazakh.
141 G2 Shortandy Kazakh.
158 G2 Shosanbetsu Japan
215 D4 Shoshone *CA* U.S.A.
213 D3 Shoshone *ID* U.S.A.
212 E2 Shoshone *r.* U.S.A.
212 E2 Shoshone Lake U.S.A.
213 C4 Shoshone Mountains U.S.A.
197 G1 Shoshong Botswana
213 E3 Shoshoni U.S.A.
187 E5 Shostka Ukr.
142 D3 Shotoran, Chashmeh-ye *well* Iran
143 G3 Shotor Khūn Afgh.
154 F2 Shouguang China
155 F5 Shouning China
154 E3 Shouxian China
154 D2 Shouyang China
154 C3 Shouyang Shan *mt.* China
215 G4 Show Low U.S.A.
187 D5 Shpola Ukr.
217 E5 Shreveport U.S.A.
173 E5 Shrewsbury U.K.
147 G2 Shrigonda India
149 G5 Shrirampur India
141 H4 Shu Kazakh.
132 H5 Shu *r.* Kazakh.
139 K6 Shu'aiba Iraq
155 A5 Shuangbai China
160 D1 Shuangcheng China
155 C4 Shuanghe China
156 C2 Shuanghedagang China
160 B2 Shuangliao China
155 D5 Shuangpai China
Shuangshipu China *see* Fengxian
160 A3 Shuangtaizihe Kou *r. mouth* China
160 C2 Shuangyang China
158 B1 Shuangyashan China
140 D2 Shubarkudyk Kazakh.
140 D2 Shubarshi Kazakh.
139 C6 Shubrā al Khaymah Egypt
155 E4 Shucheng China
141 H5 Shufu China
154 F3 Shu He *r.* China
155 F5 Shuiji China
155 D5 Shuikou China
141 H3 Shu-Ile, Gory *mts* Kazakh.
154 A2 Shuiquanzi China
148 B3 Shujaabad Pak.
160 D1 Shulan China
141 I5 Shule China
154 D1 Shulinzhao China
140 D4 Shumanay Uzbek.
158 H2 Shumarinai-ko *l.* Japan
195 C5 Shumba Zimbabwe
185 L3 Shumen Bulg.
187 H4 Shumerlya Russia
177 N3 Shumilina Belarus
215 G4 Shumway U.S.A.
187 E4 Shumyachi Russia
141 H3 Shunak, Gora *mt.* Kazakh.
159 B7 Shūnan Japan
155 E5 Shunchang China
160 B3 Shuncheng China
155 D6 Shunde China
202 C3 Shungnak U.S.A.
154 E1 Shunyi China
155 C6 Shuolong China
154 D2 Shuozhou China
146 C7 Shuqrah Yemen
142 D4 Shūr *r.* Iran
142 D4 Shūr *r.* Iran
143 F3 Shūr *r.* Iran
142 D4 Shūr *watercourse* Iran
142 D5 Shūr *watercourse* Iran
143 E3 Shur *watercourse* Iran
142 D3 Shūr, Chāh-e *well* Iran
143 E4 Shūr, Rūd-e *watercourse* Iran
142 C3 Shūr Āb Iran
142 D3 Shūrāb *Yazd* Iran
143 E3 Shūrāb *Yazd* Iran
143 E4 Shūr Āb *watercourse* Iran
Shurchi Uzbek. *see* Sho'rchi
142 D3 Shūreghestān Iran
143 E4 Shūr Gaz Iran
142 D4 Shūrjestān Iran
141 G4 Shūrob Tajik.
195 D5 Shurugwi Zimbabwe
139 J6 Shuruppak *tourist site* Iraq
143 F4 Shūsf Iran
142 C3 Shūsh Iran
142 C3 Shūshtar Iran
204 F4 Shuswap Lake Canada
139 G4 Shuwayḩān Syria
139 F6 Shuwaysh, Tall ash *h.* Jordan
186 G3 Shuya Russia
154 F3 Shuyang China
169 O4 Shuyskoye Russia
137 F6 Shuẓāẓ, Jabal *mt.* Saudi Arabia
162 A1 Shwegun Myanmar
141 G3 Shyganak *Zhambylskaya Oblast'* Kazakh.
141 H3 Shyganak *Zhambylskaya Oblast'* Kazakh.
141 H3 Shygys Konyrat Kazakh.
141 G4 Shymkent Kazakh.
140 C2 Shyngyrlau Kazakh.
140 C2 Shyngyrlau *r.* Kazakh.
141 I2 Shyngystau, Khrebet *mts* Kazakh.
141 J3 Shynkozha Kazakh.
148 D2 Shyok India
148 D2 Shyok *r.* India
187 F5 Shypuvate Ukr.
187 E6 Shyroke Ukr.
151 F7 Sia Indon.
148 D2 Siachen Glacier India
143 F5 Siahan Range *mts* Pak.
139 J2 Sīah Cheshmeh Iran
142 D3 Sīāh Kūh, Kavīr-e *salt flat* Iran
148 C2 Sialkot Pak.
156 B1 Sian Russia
225 H4 Sian Ka'an, Reserva de la Biósfera *nature res.* Mex.
162 C5 Siantan *i.* Indon.
233 K4 Siapa *r.* Venez.
143 F4 Sīāreh Iran
161 J4 Siargao *i.* Phil.
161 I5 Siasi Phil.
161 I5 Siasi *i.* Phil.
149 H5 Siatlai Myanmar
161 I4 Siaton Phil.
171 M5 Šiauliai Lith.
143 F5 Sīb Iran
142 C3 Sībak Iran
197 I1 Sibasa S. Africa
161 I4 Sibay *i.* Phil.
140 D1 Sibay Russia

South Nesting Bay

174 □ **South Nesting Bay** U.K.
239 G10 **South Orkney Islands** S. Atlantic Ocean
137 G2 **South Ossetia** *disp. terr* Georgia
119 H5 **South Pacific Ocean**
221 H2 **South Paris** U.S.A.
213 G3 **South Platte** *r.* U.S.A.
127 J4 **South Pole** Antarctica
209 G1 **South Porcupine** Canada
125 J1 **Southport** Australia
173 D4 **Southport** U.K.
221 H3 **South Portland** U.S.A.
209 H3 **South River** Canada
175 F2 **South Ronaldsay** *i.* U.K.
221 G3 **South Royalton** U.S.A.
197 I5 **South Sand Bluff** *pt* S. Africa
239 H9 **South Sandwich Islands** S. Atlantic Ocean
239 H9 **South Sandwich Trench** *sea feature* S. Atlantic Ocean
205 H4 **South Saskatchewan** *r.* Canada
205 J3 **South Seal** *r.* Canada
127 I2 **South Shetland Islands** Antarctica
239 E10 **South Shetland Trough** *sea feature* S. Atlantic Ocean
172 F2 **South Shields** U.K.
208 A5 **South Skunk** *r.* U.S.A.
236 F6 **South Solomon Trench** *sea feature* Pacific Ocean
193 E4 **South Sudan** *country* Africa
126 E3 **South Taranaki Bight** *b.* N.Z.
238 N8 **South Tasman Rise** *sea feature* Southern Ocean
215 G2 **South Tent** *mt.* U.S.A.
149 E4 **South Tons** *r.* India
206 E3 **South Twin Island** Canada
172 E3 **South Tyne** *r.* U.K.
174 A3 **South Uist** *i.* U.K.
122 B3 **South Wellesley Islands** Australia
125 G9 **South West Cape** Australia
126 A7 **South West Cape** N.Z.
122 E1 **South West Entrance** *sea chan.* P.N.G.
238 G7 **Southwest Indian Ridge** *sea feature* Indian Ocean
207 G4 **Southwest Miramichi** *r.* Canada
125 G9 **South West National Park** Australia
237 I8 **Southwest Pacific Basin** *sea feature* S. Pacific Ocean
South-West Peru Ridge *sea feature* S. Pacific Ocean *see* **Nazca Ridge**
125 J3 **South West Rocks** Australia
209 E5 **South Whitley** U.S.A.
221 H3 **South Windham** U.S.A.
173 I5 **Southwold** U.K.
197 H1 **Soutpansberg** *mts* S. Africa
185 G5 **Soverato** Italy
187 B4 **Sovetsk** *Kaliningradskaya Oblast'* Russia
186 I3 **Sovetsk** *Kirovskaya Oblast'* Russia
150 G2 **Sovetskaya Gavan'** Russia
132 H3 **Sovetskiy** *Khanty-Mansiyskiy Avtonomnyy Okrug-Yugra* Russia
186 D2 **Sovetskiy** *Leningradskaya Oblast'* Russia
186 I3 **Sovetskiy** *Respublika Mariy El* Russia
197 G3 **Soweto** S. Africa
139 L3 **Şowma'eh Sarā** Iran
141 G5 **So'x** Tajik.
225 F4 **Soyaló** Mex.
158 G2 **Sōya-misaki** *c.* Japan
160 D4 **Soyang-ho** *l.* S. Korea
141 G3 **Sozak** Kazakh.
177 O4 **Sozh** *r.* Belarus
185 L3 **Sozopol** Bulg.
178 D4 **Spa** Belgium
183 N2 **Spain** *country* Europe
173 G5 **Spalding** U.K.
173 D6 **Span Head** *h.* U.K.
209 F2 **Spanish** Canada
209 G2 **Spanish** *r.* Canada
215 G1 **Spanish Fork** U.S.A.
223 I5 **Spanish Town** Jamaica
214 C2 **Sparks** U.S.A.
Sparta Greece *see* **Sparti**
220 C6 **Sparta** U.S.A.
219 D5 **Spartanburg** U.S.A.
185 J6 **Sparti** Greece
185 G6 **Spartivento, Capo** *c.* Italy
205 G5 **Sparwood** Canada
187 E4 **Spas-Demensk** Russia
169 O4 **Spas-Klepiki** Russia
186 E2 **Spasskaya Guba** Russia
150 F2 **Spassk-Dal'niy** Russia
185 J7 **Spatha, Akrotirio** *pt* Greece
204 D3 **Spatsizi Plateau Wilderness Provincial Park** Canada
216 C2 **Spearfish** U.S.A.
217 C4 **Spearman** U.S.A.
221 F3 **Speculator** U.S.A.
216 E3 **Spencer** *IA* U.S.A.
212 D2 **Spencer** *ID* U.S.A.
220 C5 **Spencer** *WV* U.S.A.
124 B5 **Spencer, Cape** Australia
204 B3 **Spencer, Cape** U.S.A.
124 B5 **Spencer Gulf** *est.* Australia
120 E2 **Spencer Range** *hills* Australia
204 E4 **Spences Bridge** Canada
172 F3 **Spennymoor** U.K.
195 B6 **Sperrgebiet National Park** Namibia
175 K3 **Sperrin Mountains** U.K.
220 D5 **Sperryville** U.S.A.
179 H5 **Spessart** *reg.* Germany
185 J6 **Spetses** *i.* Greece
174 E3 **Spey** *r.* U.K.
179 G5 **Speyer** Germany
143 G4 **Spezand** Pak.
179 F1 **Spiekeroog** *i.* Germany
176 C7 **Spiez** Switz.
179 E1 **Spijk** Neth.
178 C3 **Spijkenisse** Neth.
184 E1 **Spilimbergo** Italy
173 H4 **Spilsby** U.K.
143 G4 **Spīn Böldak** Afgh.
148 B3 **Spintangi** Pak.
204 F3 **Spirit River** Canada
208 C3 **Spirit River Flowage** *resr* U.S.A.
205 H4 **Spiritwood** Canada
143 G3 **Spirsang Pass** Afgh.
177 J6 **Spišská Nová Ves** Slovakia
139 J1 **Spitak** Armenia
148 D3 **Spiti** *r.* India
132 C2 **Spitsbergen** *i.* Svalbard
176 F7 **Spittal an der Drau** Austria
185 G3 **Split** Croatia
205 J3 **Split Lake** Canada
205 J3 **Split Lake** *l.* Canada
212 C2 **Spokane** U.S.A.
184 E3 **Spoleto** Italy
162 C2 **Spóng** Cambodia
208 B3 **Spooner** U.S.A.
179 J1 **Spornitz** Germany
212 F2 **Spotted Horse** U.S.A.
209 F2 **Spragge** Canada
204 E4 **Spranger, Mount** Canada
151 D6 **Spratly Islands** S. China Sea
212 C2 **Spray** U.S.A.
176 G5 **Spree** *r.* Germany
178 D4 **Sprimont** Belgium
209 F3 **Spring Bay** Canada
196 B4 **Springbok** S. Africa
207 I4 **Springdale** Canada
217 E4 **Springdale** U.S.A.
179 H2 **Springe** Germany
213 F4 **Springer** U.S.A.
215 H4 **Springerville** U.S.A.
217 C4 **Springfield** *CO* U.S.A.
208 C6 **Springfield** *IL* U.S.A.
221 G3 **Springfield** *MA* U.S.A.
221 I2 **Springfield** *ME* U.S.A.
216 E2 **Springfield** *MN* U.S.A.
217 E4 **Springfield** *MO* U.S.A.
220 B5 **Springfield** *OH* U.S.A.
217 C4 **Springfield** *OR* U.S.A.
221 G3 **Springfield** *VT* U.S.A.
220 D5 **Springfield** *WV* U.S.A.
208 C6 **Springfield, Lake** U.S.A.
197 F5 **Springfontein** S. Africa
208 B4 **Spring Green** U.S.A.
208 B4 **Spring Grove** U.S.A.
207 H4 **Springhill** Canada
219 D6 **Spring Hill** U.S.A.
208 D4 **Spring Lake** U.S.A.
215 E3 **Spring Mountains** U.S.A.
126 D5 **Springs Junction** N.Z.
123 E5 **Springsure** Australia
208 A4 **Spring Valley** U.S.A.
220 D3 **Springville** *NY* U.S.A.
215 G1 **Springville** *UT* U.S.A.
173 I5 **Sprowston** U.K.
205 G4 **Spruce Grove** Canada
220 D5 **Spruce Knob-Seneca Rocks National Recreation Area** *park* U.S.A.
213 D3 **Spruce Mountain** U.S.A.
173 H4 **Spurn Head** U.K.
204 E5 **Spuzzum** Canada
204 E5 **Squamish** Canada
221 H3 **Squam Lake** U.S.A.
221 I1 **Square Lake** U.S.A.
185 G5 **Squillace, Golfo di** *g.* Italy
121 D5 **Squires, Mount** *h.* Australia
Srbija *country* Europe *see* **Serbia**
162 B3 **Srê Âmběl** Cambodia
185 H2 **Srebrenica** Bos. & Herz.
185 L3 **Sredets** Bulg.
133 Q4 **Sredinnyy Khrebet** *mts* Russia
185 J3 **Sredna Gora** *mts* Bulg.
133 Q3 **Srednekolymsk** Russia
Sredne-Russkaya Vozvyshennost' *hills* Russia *see* **Central Russian Upland**
Sredne-Sibirskoye Ploskogor'ye *plat.* Russia *see* **Central Siberian Plateau**
170 O2 **Sredneye Kuyto, Ozero** *l.* Russia
162 C2 **Srêpôk, Tônlé** *r.* Cambodia
150 D1 **Sretensk** Russia
163 H2 **Sri Aman** *Sarawak* Malaysia
147 I3 **Sriharikota Island** India
147 H5 **Sri Jayewardenepura Kotte** Sri Lanka
147 J2 **Srikakulam** India
147 H3 **Sri Kalahasti** India
148 D3 **Srikanta** *mt.* India
147 I5 **Sri Lanka** *country* Asia
148 C2 **Srinagar** *Jammu and Kashmir* India
148 D3 **Srinagar** *Uttarakhand* India
Sri Pada *mt.* Sri Lanka *see* **Adam's Peak**
147 H4 **Srirangam** India
162 B1 **Sri Thep** *tourist site* Thai.
147 H4 **Srivaikuntam** India
147 G2 **Srivardhan** India
147 H4 **Srivilliputtur** India
141 K1 **Srostki** Russia
147 I2 **Srungavarapukota** India
122 C3 **Staaten** *r.* Australia
122 C3 **Staaten River National Park** Australia
179 H1 **Stade** Germany
178 B4 **Staden** Belgium
179 E2 **Stadskanaal** Neth.
179 H4 **Stadtallendorf** Germany
179 H2 **Stadthagen** Germany
179 J4 **Stadtilm** Germany
179 E3 **Stadtlohn** Germany
179 H3 **Stadtoldendorf** Germany
179 J4 **Stadtroda** Germany
174 B4 **Staffa** *i.* U.K.
179 J4 **Staffelberg** *h.* Germany
173 E5 **Stafford** U.K.
220 E5 **Stafford** U.S.A.
171 N4 **Staicele** Latvia
173 G6 **Staines-upon-Thames** U.K.
187 F5 **Stakhanov** Ukr.
173 E7 **Stalbridge** U.K.
173 I5 **Stalham** U.K.
Stalingrad Russia *see* **Volgograd**
177 K5 **Stalowa Wola** Poland
185 K3 **Stamboliyski** Bulg.
123 C4 **Stamford** Australia
173 G5 **Stamford** U.K.
221 G4 **Stamford** *CT* U.S.A.
221 F3 **Stamford** *NY* U.S.A.
195 B6 **Stampriet** Namibia
170 K1 **Stamsund** Norway
216 E3 **Stanberry** U.S.A.
178 C3 **Standdaarbuiten** Neth.
197 H3 **Standerton** S. Africa
209 F4 **Standish** U.S.A.
219 C4 **Stanford** U.S.A.
Stanger S. Africa *see* **KwaDukuza**
219 E7 **Staniard Creek** Bahamas
179 L5 **Staňkov** Czech Rep.
125 F8 **Stanley** Australia
221 J1 **Stanley** Canada
155 □ **Stanley** *Hong Kong* China
232 E8 **Stanley** Falkland Is
172 F3 **Stanley** U.K.
212 D2 **Stanley** *ID* U.S.A.
216 C1 **Stanley** *ND* U.S.A.
208 B3 **Stanley** *WI* U.S.A.
121 E4 **Stanley, Mount** *h. N.T.* Australia
125 F8 **Stanley, Mount** *h. Tas.* Australia
147 H4 **Stanley Reservoir** India
172 F2 **Stannington** U.K.
150 D1 **Stanovoye Nagor'ye** *mts* Russia
150 E1 **Stanovoy Khrebet** *mts* Russia
121 E4 **Stansmore Range** *hills* Australia
125 I2 **Stanthorpe** Australia
173 H5 **Stanton** U.K.
220 B6 **Stanton** *KY* U.S.A.
209 E4 **Stanton** *MI* U.S.A.
216 C3 **Stapleton** U.S.A.
177 J5 **Starachowice** Poland
Stara Planina *mts* Bulg./Serbia *see* **Balkan Mountains**
187 H4 **Staraya Kulatka** Russia
187 H5 **Staraya Poltavka** Russia
186 D3 **Staraya Russa** Russia
177 O2 **Staraya Toropa** Russia
185 K3 **Stara Zagora** Bulg.
117 I4 **Starbuck Island** Kiribati
122 D2 **Starcke National Park** Australia
176 G4 **Stargard Szczeciński** Poland
186 E3 **Staritsa** Russia
219 D6 **Starke** U.S.A.
217 F5 **Starkville** U.S.A.
176 E7 **Starnberger See** *l.* Germany
141 J2 **Staroaleyskoye** Russia
187 F5 **Starobil's'k** Ukr.
177 P4 **Starodub** Russia
177 I4 **Starogard Gdański** Poland
187 C5 **Starokostyantyniv** Ukr.
187 F6 **Starominskaya** Russia
187 F6 **Staroshcherbinovskaya** Russia
140 D1 **Starosubkhangulovo** Russia
214 C1 **Star Peak** U.S.A.
173 D7 **Start Point** U.K.
177 N4 **Staryya Darohi** Belarus
140 D2 **Staryy Karabutak** Kazakh.
133 L2 **Staryy Kayak** Russia
187 F5 **Staryy Oskol** Russia
179 J3 **Staßfurt** Germany
221 E4 **State College** U.S.A.
219 D5 **Statesboro** U.S.A.
219 D5 **Statesville** U.S.A.
240 W1 **Station Nord** Greenland
179 L3 **Stauchitz** Germany
179 G4 **Staufenberg** Germany
220 D5 **Staunton** U.S.A.
171 I4 **Stavanger** Norway
173 F4 **Staveley** U.K.
179 K1 **Stavenhagen** Germany
187 G6 **Stavropol'** Russia
141 F1 **Stavropolka** Kazakh.
187 G6 **Stavropol'skaya Vozvyshennost'** *hills* Russia
187 G6 **Stavropol'skiy Kray** *admin. div.* Russia
125 E6 **Stawell** Australia
197 H4 **Steadville** S. Africa
214 C2 **Steamboat** U.S.A.
213 F3 **Steamboat Springs** U.S.A.
221 E4 **Steelton** U.S.A.
179 E2 **Steenderen** Neth.
197 I2 **Steenkampsberge** *mts* S. Africa
204 F3 **Steen River** Canada
213 C3 **Steens Mountain** U.S.A.
Steenstrup Gletscher *glacier* Greenland *see* **Sermersuaq**
178 A4 **Steenvoorde** France
179 E2 **Steenwijk** Neth.
203 H2 **Stefansson Island** Canada
179 I5 **Steigerwald** *mts* Germany
179 J5 **Stein** Germany
179 J4 **Steinach** Germany
205 J5 **Steinbach** Canada
179 G2 **Steinfeld (Oldenburg)** Germany
179 F2 **Steinfurt** Germany
195 B6 **Steinhausen** Namibia
179 H3 **Steinheim** Germany
179 H2 **Steinhuder Meer** *l.* Germany
170 J2 **Steinkjer** Norway
196 B4 **Steinkopf** S. Africa
215 H5 **Steins (abandoned)** U.S.A.
170 J2 **Steinsdalen** Norway
197 F3 **Stella** S. Africa
219 F7 **Stella Maris** Bahamas
196 C6 **Stellenbosch** S. Africa
184 C3 **Stello, Monte** *mt. Corsica* France
178 D5 **Stenay** France
179 J2 **Stendal** Germany
155 □ **Stenhouse, Mount** *h. Hong Kong* China
174 E4 **Stenhousemuir** U.K.
171 J4 **Stenungsund** Sweden
Stepanakert Azer. *see* **Xankändi**
187 H7 **Step'anavan** Armenia
205 J5 **Stephen** U.S.A.
124 D4 **Stephens** *watercourse* Australia
126 D4 **Stephens, Cape** N.Z.
124 D3 **Stephens Creek** Australia
208 D3 **Stephenson** U.S.A.
204 C3 **Stephens Passage** U.S.A.
207 I4 **Stephenville** Canada
217 D5 **Stephenville** U.S.A.
141 G1 **Stepnogorsk** Kazakh.
141 H4 **Stepnoy** Kyrg.
140 E1 **Stepnoye** *Chelyabinskaya Oblast'* Russia
187 H5 **Stepnoye** *Saratovskaya Oblast'* Russia
141 G1 **Stepnyak** Kazakh.
197 H4 **Sterkfontein Dam** *resr* S. Africa
197 G5 **Sterkstroom** S. Africa
140 C1 **Sterlibashevo** Russia
196 D5 **Sterling** S. Africa
213 G3 **Sterling** *CO* U.S.A.
216 C2 **Sterling** *ND* U.S.A.
215 G2 **Sterling** *UT* U.S.A.
217 C6 **Sterling City** U.S.A.
209 F4 **Sterling Heights** U.S.A.
140 C1 **Sterlitamak** Russia
179 J1 **Sternberg** Germany
205 G4 **Stettler** Canada
208 D2 **Steuben** U.S.A.
220 C4 **Steubenville** U.S.A.
173 G6 **Stevenage** U.K.
205 J4 **Stevenson Lake** Canada
208 C3 **Stevens Point** U.S.A.
202 D3 **Stevens Village** U.S.A.
204 D3 **Stewart** Canada
204 B2 **Stewart** *r.* Canada
204 B2 **Stewart Crossing** Canada
126 A7 **Stewart Island** N.Z.
119 G2 **Stewart Islands** Solomon Is
203 J3 **Stewart Lake** Canada
174 D5 **Stewarton** U.K.
208 A4 **Stewartville** U.S.A.
197 F5 **Steynsburg** S. Africa
176 G6 **Steyr** Austria
197 F6 **Steytlerville** S. Africa
178 D1 **Stiens** Neth.
204 C3 **Stikine** *r.* Canada
204 C3 **Stikine Plateau** Canada
196 D7 **Stilbaai** S. Africa
208 A3 **Stillwater** *MN* U.S.A.
214 C2 **Stillwater** *NV* U.S.A.
217 D4 **Stillwater** *OK* U.S.A.
213 C4 **Stillwater Range** *mts* U.S.A.
173 G5 **Stilton** U.K.
185 J4 **Štip** Macedonia
121 F4 **Stirling** *N.T.* Australia
124 C5 **Stirling** *S.A.* Australia
174 E4 **Stirling** U.K.
214 B2 **Stirling City** U.S.A.
120 E3 **Stirling Creek** *r.* Australia
124 B4 **Stirling North** Australia
121 B7 **Stirling Range National Park** Australia
171 J3 **Stjørdalshalsen** Norway
177 H6 **Stockerau** Austria
179 J4 **Stockheim** Germany
171 L4 **Stockholm** Sweden
221 I1 **Stockholm** U.S.A.
173 E4 **Stockport** U.K.
239 G6 **Stocks Seamount** *sea feature* S. Atlantic Ocean
214 B3 **Stockton** *CA* U.S.A.
217 D4 **Stockton** *KS* U.S.A.
215 F1 **Stockton** *UT* U.S.A.
208 B2 **Stockton Island** U.S.A.
217 E4 **Stockton Lake** U.S.A.
172 F3 **Stockton-on-Tees** U.K.
221 I2 **Stockton Springs** U.S.A.
171 L3 **Stöde** Sweden
162 C2 **Stœng Trêng** Cambodia
174 C2 **Stoer, Point of** U.K.
173 E4 **Stoke-on-Trent** U.K.
172 F3 **Stokesley** U.K.
125 E8 **Stokes Point** Australia
120 E3 **Stokes Range** *hills* Australia
170 B3 **Stokkseyri** Iceland
170 K2 **Stokkvågen** Norway
170 K1 **Stokmarknes** Norway
185 G3 **Stolac** Bos. & Herz.
179 E4 **Stolberg (Rheinland)** Germany
141 K2 **Stolboukha (abandoned)** Kazakh.
187 C5 **Stolin** Belarus
179 K4 **Stollberg** Germany
179 H2 **Stolzenau** Germany
173 E5 **Stone** U.K.
209 I2 **Stonecliffe** Canada
221 F5 **Stone Harbor** U.S.A.
175 F4 **Stonehaven** U.K.
123 C5 **Stonehenge** Australia
173 F6 **Stonehenge** *tourist site* U.K.
204 E3 **Stone Mountain Provincial Park** Canada
215 H3 **Stoner** U.S.A.
221 F4 **Stone Ridge** U.S.A.
205 J4 **Stonewall** Canada
220 C5 **Stonewall Jackson Lake** U.S.A.
209 F4 **Stoney Point** Canada
221 I2 **Stonington** U.S.A.
214 A2 **Stonyford** U.S.A.
221 E3 **Stony Point** U.S.A.
205 H3 **Stony Rapids** Canada
170 L2 **Stora Lulevatten** *l.* Sweden
170 L2 **Stora Sjöfallets nationalpark** *nat. park* Sweden
170 L2 **Storavan** *l.* Sweden
Store Bælt *sea chan.* Denmark *see* **Great Belt**
171 J3 **Støren** Norway
170 K2 **Storforshei** Norway
170 K2 **Storjord** Norway
203 H2 **Storkerson Peninsula** Canada
125 G9 **Storm Bay** Australia
197 G5 **Stormberg** S. Africa
197 G5 **Stormberge** *mts* S. Africa
216 E3 **Storm Lake** U.S.A.
168 H3 **Stornosa** *mt.* Norway
174 B2 **Stornoway** U.K.
186 J2 **Storozhevsk** Russia
187 C5 **Storozhynets'** Ukr.
221 G4 **Storrs** U.S.A.
170 L2 **Storseleby** Sweden
171 K3 **Storsjön** *l.* Sweden
171 J3 **Storskrymten** *mt.* Norway
170 M1 **Storslett** Norway
178 D1 **Stortemelk** *sea chan.* Neth.
170 L2 **Storuman** Sweden
170 L2 **Storuman** *l.* Sweden
171 L3 **Storvik** Sweden
171 J4 **Storvorde** Denmark
171 L4 **Storvreta** Sweden
173 G5 **Stotfold** U.K.
208 C4 **Stoughton** U.S.A.
173 E7 **Stour** *r. England* U.K.
173 F5 **Stour** *r. England* U.K.
173 H6 **Stour** *r. England* U.K.
173 I6 **Stour** *r. England* U.K.
173 E5 **Stourbridge** U.K.
173 E5 **Stourport-on-Severn** U.K.
205 K4 **Stout Lake** Canada
187 C4 **Stowbtsy** Belarus
221 F4 **Stowe** U.S.A.
173 H5 **Stowmarket** U.K.
156 C1 **Stoyba** Russia
175 K3 **Strabane** U.K.
175 K4 **Stradbally** Ireland
173 I5 **Stradbroke** U.K.
184 C2 **Stradella** Italy
125 F9 **Strahan** Australia
215 G3 **Straight Cliffs** *ridge* U.S.A.
232 B8 **Strait of Magellan** Chile
176 F6 **Strakonice** Czech Rep.
176 F3 **Stralsund** Germany
196 C7 **Strand** S. Africa
171 I3 **Stranda** Norway
219 E7 **Strangers Cay** *i.* Bahamas
175 M3 **Strangford** U.K.
175 M3 **Strangford Lough** *inlet* U.K.
120 F2 **Strangways** *r.* Australia
174 C6 **Stranraer** U.K.
182 H2 **Strasbourg** France
220 D5 **Strasburg** U.S.A.
125 G6 **Stratford** Australia
209 G4 **Stratford** Canada
126 E3 **Stratford** N.Z.
217 C4 **Stratford** *TX* U.S.A.
208 B3 **Stratford** *WI* U.S.A.
173 F5 **Stratford-upon-Avon** U.K.
124 C5 **Strathalbyn** Australia
174 D5 **Strathaven** U.K.
175 G3 **Strathbeg, Loch of** *l.* U.K.
174 D3 **Strathcarron** *val.* U.K.
204 D5 **Strathcona Provincial Park** Canada
174 D3 **Strathconon** *val.* U.K.
174 D3 **Strath Dearn** *val.* U.K.
174 D2 **Strath Fleet** *val.* U.K.
205 G4 **Strathmore** Canada
204 E4 **Strathnaver** Canada
174 D2 **Strathnaver** *val.* U.K.
174 E2 **Strath of Kildonan** *val.* U.K.
209 G4 **Strathroy** Canada
174 E3 **Strathspey** *val.* U.K.
174 E3 **Strathy** U.K.
174 D2 **Strathy Point** U.K.
173 C7 **Stratton** U.K.
221 H2 **Stratton** U.S.A.

Teren'ga

126 D4 **Tapuae-o-Uenuku** *mt.* N.Z.
161 I5 **Tapul** Phil.
161 I5 **Tapul Group** *is* Phil.
233 K5 **Tapurucuara** Brazil
234 B1 **Taquaral, Serra do** *hills* Brazil
231 G7 **Taquarí** *r.* Brazil
234 A2 **Taquarí, Pantanal do** *marsh* Brazil
234 A2 **Taquari, Serra do** *hills* Brazil
234 C3 **Taquaritinga** Brazil
234 B3 **Taquaruçu** *r.* Brazil
175 K5 **Tar** *r.* Ireland
125 I1 **Tara** Australia
175 L4 **Tara, Hill of** Ireland
193 D4 **Taraba** *r.* Nigeria
230 E7 **Tarabuco** Bol.
Ţarābulus Libya *see* **Tripoli**
233 J4 **Taracua** Brazil
149 E4 **Tarahuwan** India
149 G4 **Tarai** *reg.* India
163 I2 **Tarakan** Indon.
161 H6 **Tarakan** *i.* Indon.
138 C1 **Taraklı** Turkey
125 H5 **Taralga** Australia
177 I3 **Taran, Mys** *pt* Russia
125 H4 **Tarana** Australia
148 D5 **Tarana** India
148 C3 **Taranagar** India
126 E3 **Taranaki, Mount** *vol.* N.Z.
183 O2 **Tarancón** Spain
174 A3 **Taransay** *i.* U.K.
185 G4 **Taranto** Italy
185 G4 **Taranto, Golfo di** *g.* Italy
230 C5 **Tarapoto** Peru
126 E4 **Tararua Range** *mts* N.Z.
177 O6 **Tarashcha** Ukr.
230 D5 **Tarauacá** Brazil
230 E5 **Tarauacá** *r.* Brazil
117 G3 **Tarawa** *atoll* Kiribati
126 F3 **Tarawera** N.Z.
126 F3 **Tarawera, Mount** *vol.* N.Z.
141 G4 **Taraz** Kazakh.
183 P2 **Tarazona** Spain
183 P3 **Tarazona de la Mancha** Spain
141 J3 **Tarbagatay** Kazakh.
141 J3 **Tarbagatay, Khrebet** *mts* Kazakh.
174 E3 **Tarbat Ness** *pt* U.K.
148 C2 **Tarbela Dam** Pak.
175 I5 **Tarbert** Ireland
174 B3 **Tarbert** *Scotland* U.K.
174 C5 **Tarbert** *Scotland* U.K.
183 E5 **Tarbes** France
219 E5 **Tarboro** U.S.A.
124 A3 **Tarcoola** Australia
125 G3 **Tarcoon** Australia
121 F5 **Tarcoonyinna** *watercourse* Australia
125 G5 **Tarcutta** Australia
150 F2 **Tardoki-Yangi, Gora** *mt.* Russia
125 J3 **Taree** Australia
125 E3 **Tarella** Australia
142 C6 **Ţarfā', Baţn aţ** *depr.* Saudi Arabia
Targan China *see* **Talin Hiag**
212 E2 **Targhee Pass** U.S.A.
185 L3 **Targovishte** Bulg.
185 K2 **Târgovişte** Romania
185 J2 **Târgu Jiu** Romania
177 L7 **Târgu Mureş** Romania
177 M7 **Târgu Neamţ** Romania
177 M7 **Târgu Secuiesc** Romania
142 B3 **Tarhān** Iran
193 D1 **Tarhūnah** Libya
154 C2 **Tarian Gol** China
144 I2 **Tariat** Mongolia
142 D5 **Tarif** U.A.E.
183 N4 **Tarifa** Spain
183 N4 **Tarifa, Punta de** *pt* Spain
231 F8 **Tarija** Bol.
151 F7 **Tariku** *r.* Indon.
146 C6 **Tarīm** Yemen
135 G3 **Tarim Basin** China
141 J4 **Tarim He** *r.* China
Tarim Pendi *basin* China *see* **Tarim Basin**
143 G3 **Tarīn Kōţ** Afgh.
151 F7 **Taritatu** *r.* Indon.
139 J4 **Tarjīl** Iraq
197 F6 **Tarka** *r.* S. Africa
197 G6 **Tarkastad** S. Africa
216 E3 **Tarkio** U.S.A.
132 I3 **Tarko-Sale** Russia
192 B4 **Tarkwa** Ghana
161 I3 **Tarlac** Phil.
150 B3 **Tarlag** China
179 H1 **Tarmstedt** Germany
182 F4 **Tarn** *r.* France
170 K2 **Tärnaby** Sweden
143 G3 **Tarnak Rōd** *r.* Afgh.
177 L7 **Târnăveni** Romania
177 J5 **Tarnobrzeg** Poland
186 G2 **Tarnogskiy Gorodok** Russia
177 J5 **Tarnów** Poland
149 E3 **Taro Co** *salt l.* China
142 D4 **Ţārom** Iran
123 E5 **Taroom** Australia
192 B1 **Taroudannt** Morocco
122 B3 **Tarpaulin Swamp** Australia
124 D6 **Tarpeena** Australia
219 E7 **Tarpum Bay** Bahamas
142 C3 **Ţarq** Iran
150 E2 **Tarqi** China
184 D3 **Tarquinia** Italy
122 A3 **Tarrabool Lake** *salt flat* Australia
192 □ **Tarrafal** Cape Verde
183 Q2 **Tarragona** Spain
170 L2 **Tårrajaur** Sweden
125 G9 **Tarraleah** Australia
124 G4 **Tarran Hills** Australia
122 B3 **Tarrant Point** Australia
126 B6 **Tarras** N.Z.
183 Q2 **Tàrrega** Spain
138 E3 **Tarsus** Turkey
140 C4 **Tarta** Turkm.
232 D2 **Tartagal** Arg.
139 K1 **Tärtär** Azer.
139 K1 **Tärtär** *r.* Azer.
183 D5 **Tartas** France
171 N4 **Tartu** Estonia
138 E4 **Ţarţūs** Syria
234 E2 **Tarumirim** Brazil
187 H6 **Tarumovka** Russia
162 A4 **Tarutao, Ko** *i.* Thai.
162 A5 **Tarutung** Indon.
184 E1 **Tarvisio** Italy
143 E4 **Ţarz** Iran
141 H3 **Tasaral** Kazakh.
141 F3 **Tasbuget** Kazakh.
206 E4 **Taschereau** Canada
147 G2 **Tasgaon** India
160 A3 **Tashan** China
Tashigang Bhutan *see* **Trashigang**
148 C1 **Tashikuzuke Shan** *mts* China
139 J1 **Tashir** Armenia
142 D4 **Tashk, Daryācheh-ye** *l.* Iran
Tashkepri Turkm. *see* **Daşköpri**
141 H4 **Tash-Kömür** Kyrg.
140 C2 **Tashla** Russia
152 E1 **Tashtagol** Russia
152 E1 **Tashtyp** Russia
207 F2 **Tasialujjuaq, Lac** *l.* Canada
207 F2 **Tasiat, Lac** *l.* Canada
203 O3 **Tasiilaq** Greenland
163 G4 **Tasikmalaya** Indon.
207 G2 **Tasiujaq** Canada
140 B2 **Taskala** Kazakh.
141 J3 **Taskesken** Kazakh.
138 E1 **Taşköprü** Turkey
139 I2 **Taşlıçay** Turkey
236 F8 **Tasman Abyssal Plain** *sea feature*
238 O7 **Tasman Basin** *sea feature* Tasman Sea
126 D4 **Tasman Bay** N.Z.
125 G9 **Tasman Head** Australia
125 F9 **Tasmania** *state* Australia
126 D4 **Tasman Mountains** N.Z.
125 H9 **Tasman Peninsula** Australia
119 F5 **Tasman Sea** Pacific Ocean
139 F1 **Taşova** Turkey
214 B3 **Tassajara Hot Springs** U.S.A.
141 G3 **Tasty** Kazakh.
141 F2 **Tasty-Taldy** Kazakh.
139 J2 **Tasūj** Iran
133 M3 **Tas-Yuryakh** Russia
177 I7 **Tatabánya** Hungary
151 E7 **Tatamailau, Foho** *mt.* East Timor
Tata Mailau, Gunung *mt.* East Timor *see* **Tatamailau, Foho**
181 F5 **Tataouine** Tunisia
187 D6 **Tatarbunary** Ukr.
133 I4 **Tatarsk** Russia
140 C2 **Tatarskaya Kargala** Russia
150 G1 **Tatarskiy Proliv** *str.* Russia
187 I4 **Tatarstan, Respublika** *aut. rep.* Russia
142 B2 **Tatavi** *r.* Iran
122 C3 **Tate** *r.* Australia
159 F7 **Tateyama** Japan
159 E6 **Tate-yama** *vol.* Japan
204 F2 **Tathlina Lake** Canada
146 B5 **Tathlīth, Wādī** *watercourse* Saudi Arabia
125 H6 **Tathra** Australia
205 J2 **Tatinnai Lake** Canada
187 H5 **Tatishchevo** Russia
212 A1 **Tatla Lake** Canada
204 D3 **Tatlatui Provincial Park** Canada
125 G6 **Tatong** Australia
Tatra Mountains Poland/Slovakia *see* **Tatry**
181 G2 **Tatry** *mts* Poland/Slovakia
204 B3 **Tatshenshini** *r.* Canada
187 G5 **Tatsinskaya** Russia
159 D7 **Tatsuno** Japan
141 H4 **Tatty** Kazakh.
204 E4 **Tatuk Mountain** Canada
217 C5 **Tatum** U.S.A.
125 F6 **Tatura** Australia
139 I2 **Tatvan** Turkey
171 I4 **Tau** Norway
231 J5 **Tauá** Brazil
231 I8 **Taubaté** Brazil
179 H5 **Tauber** *r.* Germany
179 H5 **Tauberbischofsheim** Germany
179 K3 **Taucha** Germany
179 H4 **Taufstein** *h.* Germany
141 H3 **Taukum, Peski** *des.* Kazakh.
197 F3 **Taung** S. Africa
151 B4 **Taunggyi** Myanmar
151 B5 **Taung-ngu** Myanmar
162 A2 **Taungnyo Range** *mts* Myanmar
152 F8 **Taungup** Myanmar
173 D6 **Taunton** U.K.
221 H4 **Taunton** U.S.A.
179 F4 **Taunus** *hills* Germany
126 F3 **Taupo** N.Z.
126 E3 **Taupo, Lake** N.Z.
171 M5 **Taurag** Lith.
126 F2 **Tauranga** N.Z.
185 G5 **Taurianova** Italy
126 D1 **Tauroa Point** N.Z.
138 D3 **Taurus Mountains** Turkey
140 B3 **Taushyk** Kazakh.
Tauu Islands P.N.G. *see* **Takuu Islands**
138 B3 **Tavas** Turkey
173 I5 **Taverham** U.K.
183 M4 **Tavira** Port.
173 C7 **Tavistock** U.K.
Tavoy Myanmar *see* **Dawei**
162 A2 **Tavoy Point** Myanmar
158 B3 **Tavrichanka** Russia
138 B2 **Tavşanlı** Turkey
173 C6 **Taw** *r.* U.K.
161 H5 **Tawai, Bukit** *mt. Sabah* Malaysia
141 J5 **Tawakkul** China
209 F3 **Tawas Bay** U.S.A.
209 F3 **Tawas City** U.S.A.
163 I2 **Tawau** *Sabah* Malaysia
173 D6 **Tawe** *r.* U.K.
148 C2 **Tawi** *r.* India
161 H5 **Tawi-Tawi** *i.* Phil.
225 E4 **Taxco** Mex.
140 D4 **Taxiatosh** Uzbek.
148 C2 **Taxila** *tourist site* Pak.
141 H5 **Taxkorgan** China
140 E4 **Taxtako'pir** Uzbek.
204 C2 **Tay** *r.* Canada
174 E4 **Tay** *r.* U.K.
174 E4 **Tay, Firth of** *est.* U.K.
121 C7 **Tay, Lake** *salt flat* Australia
174 D4 **Tay, Loch** *l.* U.K.
161 I3 **Tayabas Bay** Phil.
143 F3 **Taybād** Iran
170 P1 **Taybola** Russia
174 C5 **Tayinloan** U.K.
204 E3 **Taylor** Canada
215 G4 **Taylor** *AZ* U.S.A.
209 F4 **Taylor** *MI* U.S.A.
208 B6 **Taylor** *MO* U.S.A.
216 D3 **Taylor** *NE* U.S.A.
217 D6 **Taylor** *TX* U.S.A.
221 E5 **Taylors Island** U.S.A.
219 B4 **Taylorville** U.S.A.
146 A4 **Taymā'** Saudi Arabia
143 F3 **Taymanī** *reg.* Afgh.
133 K3 **Taymura** *r.* Russia
133 L2 **Taymyr, Ozero** *l.* Russia
Taymyr, Poluostrov *pen.* Russia *see* **Taymyr Peninsula**
133 K2 **Taymyr Peninsula** Russia
141 G1 **Tayncha** Kazakh.
162 C3 **Tây Ninh** Vietnam
224 C2 **Tayoltita** Mex.
140 B2 **Taypak** Kazakh.
140 C2 **Taysoygan, Peski** *des.* Kazakh.
161 H4 **Taytay** *Palawan* Phil.
161 I3 **Taytay** *Rizal* Phil.
161 H4 **Taytay Bay** Phil.
156 B2 **Tayuan** China
143 G3 **Taywarah** Afgh.
133 J2 **Taz** *r.* Russia
192 B1 **Taza** Morocco
139 J4 **Tāza Khurmātū** Iraq
139 K2 **Tāzeh Kand** Azer.
220 B6 **Tazewell** *TN* U.S.A.
220 C6 **Tazewell** *VA* U.S.A.
205 H2 **Tazin** *r.* Canada
205 H3 **Tazin Lake** Canada
193 E2 **Tāzirbū** Libya
183 S4 **Tazmalt** Alg.
132 I3 **Tazovskaya Guba** *sea chan.* Russia
187 H7 **Tbilisi** Georgia
187 G6 **Tbilisskaya** Russia
195 B4 **Tchibanga** Gabon
193 D2 **Tchigaï, Plateau du** Niger
193 D4 **Tcholliré** Cameroon
177 I3 **Tczew** Poland
224 C3 **Teacapán** Mex.
121 C5 **Teague, Lake** *salt flat* Australia
126 A6 **Te Anau** N.Z.
126 A6 **Te Anau, Lake** N.Z.
225 F4 **Teapa** Mex.
127 G2 **Te Araroa** N.Z.
126 E2 **Te Aroha** N.Z.
126 E3 **Te Awamutu** N.Z.
172 E3 **Tebay** U.K.
205 J2 **Tebesjuak Lake** Canada
192 C1 **Tébessa** Alg.
184 B7 **Tébessa, Monts de** *mts* Alg.
232 E3 **Tebicuary** *r.* Para.
163 B3 **Tebingtinggi** *Sumatera Selatan* Indon.
163 E2 **Tebingtinggi** *Sumatera Utara* Indon.
184 C6 **Tébourba** Tunisia
184 C6 **Téboursouk** Tunisia
187 H7 **T'ebulos Mta** Georgia/Russia
192 B4 **Techiman** Ghana
232 B6 **Tecka** Arg.
179 F2 **Tecklenburger Land** *reg.* Germany
225 E3 **Tecolutla** Mex.
225 D4 **Tecomán** Mex.
215 D4 **Tecopa** U.S.A.
224 B1 **Tecoripa** Mex.
225 D4 **Técpan** Mex.
177 M7 **Tecuci** Romania
209 F5 **Tecumseh** U.S.A.
Tedzhen Turkm. *see* **Tejen**
Tedzhen *r.* Turkm. *see* **Tejen**
143 F2 **Tedzhenstroy** Turkm.
215 H3 **Teec Nos Pos** U.S.A.
135 H1 **Teeli** Russia
172 F3 **Tees** *r.* U.K.
172 E3 **Teesdale** *val.* U.K.
230 E4 **Tefé** *r.* Brazil
138 B3 **Tefenni** Turkey
163 G4 **Tegal** Indon.
179 L2 **Tegel** *airport* Germany
Tegid, Llyn *l.* U.K. *see* **Bala Lake**
224 H5 **Tegucigalpa** Hond.
192 C3 **Teguidda-n-Tessoumt** Niger
214 C4 **Tehachapi** U.S.A.
213 C5 **Tehachapi Mountains** U.S.A.
214 C4 **Tehachapi Pass** U.S.A.
205 J2 **Tehek Lake** Canada
Teheran Iran *see* **Tehrān**
192 B4 **Téhini** Côte d'Ivoire
142 C3 **Tehrān** Iran
225 E4 **Tehuacán** Mex.
225 F5 **Tehuantepec, Gulf of** Mex.
225 F4 **Tehuantepec, Istmo de** *isth.* Mex.
237 M5 **Tehuantepec Ridge** *sea feature* N. Pacific Ocean
225 E4 **Tehuitzingo** Mex.
173 C5 **Teifi** *r.* U.K.
173 D7 **Teign** *r.* U.K.
173 D7 **Teignmouth** U.K.
Te Ika-a-Māui N.Z. *see* **North Island**
234 E2 **Teixeira de Freitas** Brazil
140 E5 **Tejen** Turkm.
143 F2 **Tejen** *r.* Turkm.
183 L3 **Tejo** *r.* Port. *alt.* **Tajo (Spain),** *conv.* **Tagus**
214 C4 **Tejon Pass** U.S.A.
225 D4 **Tejupan, Punta** *pt* Mex.
126 D1 **Te Kao** N.Z.
126 C5 **Tekapo, Lake** N.Z.
149 F4 **Tekari** India
225 G3 **Tekax** Mex.
141 H1 **Teke, Ozero** *salt l.* Kazakh.
140 E2 **Tekeli** *Aktyubinskaya Oblast'* Kazakh.
141 I3 **Tekeli** *Almatinskaya Oblast'* Kazakh.
141 J4 **Tekes** China
141 J4 **Tekes** Kazakh.
141 J3 **Tekes He** *r.* China
194 D2 **Tekezē Wenz** *r.* Eritrea/Eth.
149 E1 **Tekiliktag** *mt.* China
156 D2 **Tekin** Russia
138 A1 **Tekirdağ** Turkey
147 J2 **Tekkali** India
139 H2 **Tekman** Turkey
149 H5 **Teknaf** Bangl.
209 E4 **Tekonsha** U.S.A.
126 E3 **Te Kuiti** N.Z.
147 I2 **Tel** *r.* India
224 H5 **Tela** Hond.
147 H2 **Telangana** *state* India
187 H7 **Telavi** Georgia
138 E5 **Tel Aviv-Yafo** Israel
176 G6 **Telč** Czech Rep.
225 G3 **Telchac Puerto** Mex.
204 C3 **Telegraph Creek** Canada
235 B4 **Telêmaco Borba** Brazil
235 J3 **Telén** Arg.
163 I2 **Telen** *r.* Indon.
185 K2 **Teleorman** *r.* Romania
215 D3 **Telescope Peak** U.S.A.
231 G5 **Teles Pires** *r.* Brazil
173 E5 **Telford** U.K.
179 F3 **Telgte** Germany
138 E5 **Tel Hazor** *tourist site* Israel
224 H5 **Telica** Nicaragua
192 A3 **Télimélé** Guinea
204 D4 **Telkwa** Canada
Tell Atlas *mts* Alg. *see* **Atlas Tellien**
202 B3 **Teller** U.S.A.
178 D4 **Tellin** Belgium
139 K6 **Telloh** Iraq
156 D2 **Tel'mana, imeni** Russia
156 F2 **Tel'novskiy** Russia
225 E4 **Teloloapán** Mex.
169 R3 **Telpoziz, Gora** *mt.* Russia
235 I4 **Telsen** Arg.
171 M5 **Telšiai** Lith.
179 L2 **Teltow** Germany
Teluk Anson Malaysia *see* **Teluk Intan**
163 E2 **Telukdalam** Indon.
163 B2 **Teluk Intan** Malaysia
209 H2 **Temagami** Canada
209 G2 **Temagami Lake** Canada
163 H4 **Temanggung** Indon.
225 G3 **Temax** Mex.
197 H2 **Temba** S. Africa
133 K3 **Tembenchi** *r.* Russia
163 B3 **Tembilahan** Indon.
197 H3 **Tembisa** S. Africa
195 B4 **Tembo Aluma** Angola
173 E5 **Teme** *r.* U.K.
215 D5 **Temecula** U.S.A.
138 D2 **Temelli** Turkey
163 B2 **Temerluh** Malaysia
139 L5 **Temīleh** Iran
140 D2 **Temir** *Aktyubinskaya Oblast'* Kazakh.
141 G4 **Temir** *Yuzhnyy Kazakhstan* Kazakh.
141 G4 **Temirlan** Kazakh.
141 H2 **Temirtau** Kazakh.
209 H2 **Témiscaming** Canada
209 H2 **Témiscamingue, Lac** *l.* Canada
207 G4 **Témiscouata, Lac** *l.* Canada
125 F8 **Temma** Australia
170 N2 **Temmes** Fin.
187 G4 **Temnikov** Russia
125 G5 **Temora** Australia
224 C1 **Temósachic** Mex.
215 G5 **Tempe** U.S.A.
121 F5 **Tempe Downs** Australia
184 C4 **Tempio Pausania** *Sardinia* Italy
209 E3 **Temple** *MI* U.S.A.
217 D6 **Temple** *TX* U.S.A.
173 C5 **Temple Bar** U.K.
175 K5 **Templemore** Ireland
161 H4 **Templer Bank** *sea feature* Phil.
172 E3 **Temple Sowerby** U.K.
123 B4 **Templeton** *watercourse* Australia
179 L1 **Templin** Germany
225 E3 **Tempoal** Mex.
187 F6 **Temryuk** Russia
235 H3 **Temuco** Chile
126 C6 **Temuka** N.Z.
230 C4 **Tena** Ecuador
215 D1 **Tenabo, Mount** U.S.A.
147 I2 **Tenali** India
225 E4 **Tenancingo** Mex.
162 A2 **Tenasserim** Myanmar
162 A2 **Tenasserim** *r.* Myanmar
173 E5 **Tenbury Wells** U.K.
173 C6 **Tenby** U.K.
209 F2 **Tenby Bay** Canada
194 E2 **Tendaho** Eth.
182 H4 **Tende** France
135 H6 **Ten Degree Channel** India
159 G5 **Tendō** Japan
139 I2 **Tendürek Dağı** *mt.* Turkey
192 B3 **Ténenkou** Mali
193 D3 **Ténéré** *reg.* Niger
193 D3 **Ténéré, Erg du** *des.* Niger
193 D2 **Ténéré du Tafassâsset** *des.* Niger
192 A2 **Tenerife** *i.* Canary Is
183 Q4 **Ténès** Alg.
163 I4 **Tengah, Kepulauan** *is* Indon.
140 C4 **Tenge** Kazakh.
162 □ **Tengeh Reservoir** Sing.
154 B2 **Tengger Shamo** *des.* China
162 B4 **Tenggul** *i.* Malaysia
141 G2 **Tengiz, Ozero** *salt l.* Kazakh.
192 B3 **Tengréla** Côte d'Ivoire
155 D6 **Tengxian** China
154 E3 **Tengzhou** China
141 F1 **Teniz, Ozero** *l.* Kazakh.
195 C5 **Tenke** Dem. Rep. Congo
133 P2 **Tenkeli** Russia
192 B3 **Tenkodogo** Burkina Faso
121 C5 **Ten Mile Lake** *salt flat* Australia
118 D3 **Tennant Creek** Australia
219 C5 **Tennessee** *r.* U.S.A.
220 B6 **Tennessee** *state* U.S.A.
213 F4 **Tennessee Pass** U.S.A.
170 L1 **Tennevoll** Norway
235 H2 **Teno** *r.* Chile
170 O1 **Tenojoki** *r.* Fin./Norway
225 G4 **Tenosique** Mex.
212 F2 **Ten Sleep** U.S.A.
118 C2 **Tenteno** Indon.
173 H6 **Tenterden** U.K.
125 J2 **Tenterfield** Australia
219 D7 **Ten Thousand Islands** U.S.A.
183 M3 **Tentudia** *mt.* Spain
234 B3 **Teodoro Sampaio** Brazil
234 E2 **Teófilo Otoni** Brazil
225 F4 **Teopisca** Mex.
225 E4 **Teotihuacán** *tourist site* Mex.
213 E6 **Tepache** Mex.
126 D1 **Te Paki** N.Z.
225 D4 **Tepalcatepec** Mex.
225 D3 **Tepatitlán** Mex.
139 H3 **Tepe** Turkey
139 I3 **Tepe Gawra** *tourist site* Iraq
224 C2 **Tepehuanes** Mex.
225 E4 **Tepeji** Mex.
185 I4 **Tepelenë** Albania
225 E4 **Tepelmeme de Morelos** Mex.
179 K5 **Tepelská vrchovina** *hills* Czech Rep.
233 L4 **Tepequem, Serra** *mts* Brazil
224 C3 **Tepic** Mex.
126 C5 **Te Pirita** N.Z.
176 F5 **Teplice** Czech Rep.
186 J2 **Teplogorka** Russia
156 C2 **Teplozersk** Russia
187 F4 **Teploye** Russia
Teploye Ozero Russia *see* **Teplozersk**
126 F2 **Te Puke** N.Z.
139 J4 **Teq Teq** Iraq
225 F4 **Tequisistlán** Mex.
225 E3 **Tequisquiapán** Mex.
183 R1 **Ter** *r.* Spain
117 I3 **Teraina** *i.* Kiribati
148 D2 **Teram Kangri** *mt.* China
184 E3 **Teramo** Italy
125 E7 **Terang** Australia
179 F2 **Ter Apel** Neth.
187 F4 **Terbuny** Russia
139 H2 **Tercan** Turkey
166 A6 **Terceira** *i.* Azores
177 L6 **Terebovlya** Ukr.
187 H7 **Terek** Russia
187 H7 **Terek** *r.* Russia
141 G2 **Terekty** *Karagandinskaya Oblast'* Kazakh.
141 K2 **Terekty** *Vostochnyy Kazakhstan* Kazakh.
187 I4 **Teren'ga** Russia

Treinta y Tres

148 B1 **Tirich Mir** *mt.* Pak.
147 H2 **Tirna** *r.* India
147 G3 **Tirthahalli** India
149 F5 **Tirtol** India
147 H4 **Tiruchchendur** India
147 H4 **Tiruchchirappalli** India
147 H4 **Tiruchengodu** India
147 H4 **Tirunelveli** India
147 H3 **Tirupati** India
147 H3 **Tiruppattur** India
147 H4 **Tiruppur** India
147 H4 **Tirutturaippundi** India
147 H3 **Tiruvannamalai** India
121 D4 **Tiru Well** Australia
147 H4 **Tisaiyanvilai** India
205 I4 **Tisdale** Canada
147 I5 **Tissamaharama** Sri Lanka
183 Q5 **Tissemsilt** Alg.
149 G4 **Tista** *r.* India
127 J4 **Titan Dome** *ice feature* Antarctica
133 N2 **Tit-Ary** Russia
230 E7 **Titicaca, Lake** Bol./Peru
147 I1 **Titlagarh** India
121 F4 **Ti Tree** Australia
209 E4 **Tittabawassee** *r.* U.S.A.
185 K2 **Titu** Romania
219 D6 **Titusville** *FL* U.S.A.
220 D4 **Titusville** *PA* U.S.A.
209 G3 **Tiverton** Canada
173 D7 **Tiverton** U.K.
184 E4 **Tivoli** Italy
225 G3 **Tixkokob** Mex.
225 E4 **Tixtla** Mex.
225 D3 **Tizapán el Alto** Mex.
225 G3 **Tizimín** Mex.
183 S4 **Tizi Ouzou** Alg.
233 K2 **Tiznados** *r.* Venez.
141 I5 **Tiznap He** *r.* China
192 B2 **Tiznit** Morocco
225 D2 **Tizoc** Mex.
197 I2 **Tjaneni** Swaziland
170 L2 **Tjappsåive** Sweden
178 D2 **Tjeukemeer** *l.* Neth.
171 I4 **Tjorhom** Norway
225 E4 **Tlacolula** Mex.
225 F4 **Tlacotalpán** Mex.
225 D2 **Tlahualilo** Mex.
225 E4 **Tlalnepantla** Mex.
225 E4 **Tlapa** Mex.
225 D3 **Tlaquepaque** Mex.
225 E4 **Tlaxcala** Mex.
225 E4 **Tlaxcala** *state* Mex.
225 E4 **Tlaxiaco** Mex.
192 B1 **Tlemcen** Alg.
197 E4 **Tlhakalatlou** S. Africa
197 H4 **Tlholong** S. Africa
197 F2 **Tlokweng** Botswana
137 G2 **Tlyarata** Russia
162 C3 **Tnaôt, Prêk** *l.* Cambodia
204 D3 **Toad River** Canada
195 E5 **Toamasina** Madag.
162 □ **Toa Payoh** Sing.
235 J3 **Toay** Arg.
159 E7 **Toba** Japan
162 A5 **Toba, Danau** *l.* Indon.
148 A3 **Toba and Kakar Ranges** *mts* Pak.
231 F1 **Tobago** *i.* Trin. and Tob.
Tobar an Choire Ireland *see* **Tobercurry**
151 E6 **Tobelo** Indon.
175 J3 **Tobercurry** Ireland
123 B4 **Tobermorey** Australia
123 C5 **Tobermory** Australia
209 G3 **Tobermory** Canada
174 B4 **Tobermory** U.K.
161 I4 **Tobias Fornier** Phil.
121 D4 **Tobin, Lake** *salt flat* Australia
215 D1 **Tobin, Mount** U.S.A.
205 I4 **Tobin Lake** Canada
221 J1 **Tobique** *r.* Canada
159 F5 **Tobi-shima** *i.* Japan
163 G3 **Toboali** Indon.
169 Q2 **Tobseda** Russia
140 E1 **Tobyl** Kazakh.
132 H4 **Tobyl** *r.* Kazakh./Russia
231 I5 **Tocantinópolis** Brazil
231 I4 **Tocantins** *r.* Brazil
234 C1 **Tocantinzinha** *r.* Brazil
219 D5 **Toccoa** U.S.A.
148 B2 **Tochi** *r.* Pak.
171 J4 **Töcksfors** Sweden
232 B2 **Tocopilla** Chile
125 F5 **Tocumwal** Australia
233 J2 **Tocuyo** *r.* Venez.
123 A5 **Todd** *watercourse* Australia
184 E3 **Todi** Italy
176 D7 **Todi** *mt.* Switz.
141 J3 **Todog** China
159 H5 **Todoga-saki** *pt* Japan
158 G4 **Todohokke** Japan
230 E7 **Todos Santos** Bol.
224 B3 **Todos Santos** Mex.
215 D6 **Todos Santos, Bahía de** *b.* Mex.
205 G4 **Tofield** Canada
204 D5 **Tofino** Canada
174 □ **Toft** U.K.
208 B2 **Tofte** U.S.A.
119 I3 **Tofua** *i.* Tonga
151 E7 **Togian, Kepulauan** *is* Indon.
192 C4 **Togo** *country* Africa
208 A2 **Togo** U.S.A.
154 D1 **Togrog Ul** China
154 D1 **Togtoh** China
149 H2 **Togton He** *r.* China
140 E3 **Togyz** Kazakh.
215 H4 **Tohatchi** U.S.A.
171 N3 **Toholampi** Fin.
154 B1 **Tohom** China
149 G3 **Toiba** China
171 M3 **Toijala** Fin.
159 B9 **Toi-misaki** *pt* Japan
171 N3 **Toivakka** Fin.
215 D2 **Toiyabe Range** *mts* U.S.A.
141 G5 **Tojikobod** Tajik.
140 C1 **Tok** *r.* Russia
202 D3 **Tok** U.S.A.
159 F6 **Tōkamachi** Japan
126 B7 **Tokanui** N.Z.
193 F3 **Tokar** Sudan
151 E4 **Tokara-rettō** *is* Japan
139 F1 **Tokat** Turkey
160 D4 **Tŏkch'ŏn** N. Korea
119 I2 **Tokelau** *terr.* Pacific Ocean
187 E6 **Tokmak** Ukr.
141 H4 **Tokmok** Kyrg.
127 G3 **Tokomaru Bay** N.Z.
126 E3 **Tokoroa** N.Z.
197 H3 **Tokoza** S. Africa
133 J5 **Toksun** China
141 H4 **Toktogul** Kyrg.
141 H4 **Toktogul Suu Saktagychy** *resr* Kyrg.
141 J3 **Tokty** Kazakh.
156 D1 **Tokur** Russia
159 D7 **Tokushima** Japan
159 F7 **Tōkyō** Japan
159 F7 **Tōkyō-wan** *b.* Japan
127 G3 **Tolaga Bay** N.Z.
195 E6 **Tôlañaro** Madag.
140 C1 **Tolbazy** Russia
144 H2 **Tolbo** Mongolia
156 B1 **Tolbuzino** Russia
224 I6 **Tolé** Panama
225 E3 **Toleant** *tourist site* Mex.
141 H4 **Tole Bi** Kazakh.
235 B4 **Toledo** Brazil
183 N3 **Toledo** Spain
208 A5 **Toledo** *IA* U.S.A.
220 B4 **Toledo** *OH* U.S.A.
183 N3 **Toledo, Montes de** *mts* Spain
217 E6 **Toledo Bend Reservoir** U.S.A.
235 H3 **Tolhuaca, Parque Nacional** *nat. park* Chile
141 J3 **Toli** China
195 E6 **Toliara** Madag.
233 I3 **Tolima, Nevado del** *vol.* Col.
151 E6 **Tolitoli** Indon.
133 J3 **Tol'ka** Russia
179 L1 **Tollensesee** *l.* Germany
186 D3 **Tolmachevo** Russia
184 E1 **Tolmezzo** Italy
155 □ **Tolo Channel** *Hong Kong* China
155 □ **Tolo Harbour** *b. Hong Kong* China
183 O1 **Tolosa** Spain
209 F3 **Tolsmaville** Canada
174 B2 **Tolsta Head** U.K.
233 I2 **Tolú** Col.
225 E4 **Toluca** Mex.
To-lun China *see* **Duolun**
187 I4 **Tol'yatti** Russia
140 E2 **Tolybay** *Aktyubinskaya Oblast'* Kazakh.
140 E2 **Tolybay** *Aktyubinskaya Oblast'* Kazakh.
156 B2 **Tom'** *r.* Russia
208 C3 **Tomahawk** U.S.A.
158 G3 **Tomakomai** Japan
158 G2 **Tomamae** Japan
119 H3 **Tomanivi** *mt.* Fiji
233 L5 **Tomar** Brazil
183 L3 **Tomar** Port.
156 F3 **Tomari** Russia
138 E2 **Tomarza** Turkey
235 L1 **Tomás Gomensoro** Uruguay
177 K5 **Tomaszów Lubelski** Poland
177 J5 **Tomaszów Mazowiecki** Poland
174 E3 **Tomatin** U.K.
224 C4 **Tomatlán** Mex.
219 B6 **Tombigbee** *r.* U.S.A.
195 B4 **Tomboco** Angola
234 D3 **Tombos** Brazil
Tombouctou Mali *see* **Timbuktu**
215 G6 **Tombstone** U.S.A.
195 B5 **Tombua** Angola
197 H1 **Tom Burke** S. Africa
141 F4 **Tomdibuloq** Uzbek.
235 H3 **Tomé** Chile
197 K1 **Tome** Moz.
171 K5 **Tomelilla** Sweden
183 O3 **Tomelloso** Spain
141 F4 **Tomenaryk** Kazakh.
141 H2 **Tomengi Kayrakty** Kazakh.
209 H2 **Tomiko** Canada
125 H4 **Tomingley** Australia
151 E7 **Tomini, Teluk** *g.* Indon.
192 B3 **Tominian** Mali
174 E3 **Tomintoul** U.K.
185 G3 **Tomislavgrad** Bos. & Herz.
121 E5 **Tomkinson Ranges** *mts* Australia
170 K2 **Tømmerneset** Norway
133 N4 **Tommot** Russia
233 K4 **Tomo** Col.
233 J3 **Tomo** *r.* Col.
154 D1 **Tomortei** China
133 O3 **Tompo** Russia
118 B4 **Tom Price** Australia
150 A1 **Tomsk** Russia
171 K4 **Tomtabacken** *h.* Sweden
133 P3 **Tomtor** Russia
158 H3 **Tomuraushi-yama** *mt.* Japan
187 G6 **Tomuzlovka** *r.* Russia
225 F4 **Tonalá** Mex.
215 G3 **Tonalea** U.S.A.
230 E4 **Tonantins** Brazil
212 C1 **Tonasket** U.S.A.
142 D5 **Tonb-e Bozorg, Jazīreh-ye** *i.* Iran
173 H6 **Tonbridge** U.K.
151 E6 **Tondano** Indon.
171 J5 **Tønder** Denmark
145 E10 **Tondi** India
173 E6 **Tone** *r.* U.K.
142 C2 **Tonekābon** Iran
119 I4 **Tonga** *country* Pacific Ocean
125 F6 **Tongala** Australia
155 F5 **Tong'an** China
126 E3 **Tongariro National Park** N.Z.
119 I4 **Tongatapu Group** *is* Tonga
237 H7 **Tonga Trench** *sea feature* S. Pacific Ocean
154 D3 **Tongbai** China
154 D3 **Tongbai Shan** *mts* China
155 E4 **Tongcheng** *Anhui* China
155 D4 **Tongcheng** *Hubei* China
160 D4 **T'ongch'ŏn** N. Korea
154 C3 **Tongchuan** China
155 C5 **Tongdao** China
154 A3 **Tongde** China
178 D4 **Tongeren** Belgium
155 E4 **Tonggu** China
155 D7 **Tonggu Zui** *pt* China
155 B5 **Tonghai** China
158 A2 **Tonghe** China
160 C3 **Tonghua** *Jilin* China
160 C3 **Tonghua** *Jilin* China
156 D3 **Tongjiang** *Heilongjiang* China
155 C4 **Tongjiang** *Sichuan* China
156 B2 **Tongjiangkou** China
160 D4 **Tongjosŏn-man** *b.* N. Korea
155 C6 **Tongking, Gulf of** China/Vietnam
155 C4 **Tongliang** China
160 B2 **Tongliao** China
155 E4 **Tongling** China
155 F4 **Tonglu** China
155 B4 **Tongnan** China
125 E3 **Tongo** Australia
125 E3 **Tongo Lake** *salt flat* Australia
161 I5 **Tongquil** *i.* Phil.
155 C5 **Tongren** *Guizhou* China
154 A3 **Tongren** *Qinghai* China
155 E4 **Tongshan** *Hubei* China
Tongshan *Jiangsu* China *see* **Xuzhou**
Tongtian He *r.* China *see* **Yangtze**
174 D2 **Tongue** U.K.
212 F2 **Tongue** *r.* U.S.A.
219 E7 **Tongue of the Ocean** *sea chan.* Bahamas
154 B3 **Tongwei** China
154 B2 **Tongxin** China
155 E4 **Tongyang** China
160 E6 **Tongyeong** S. Korea
160 B1 **Tongyu** China
160 B3 **Tongyuanpu** China
154 E2 **Tongzhou** *Beijing* China
154 F3 **Tongzhou** *Jiangsu* China
155 C4 **Tongzi** China
208 C5 **Tonica** U.S.A.
224 B1 **Tónichi** Mex.
148 C4 **Tonk** India
155 B6 **Tonkin** *reg.* Vietnam
186 H3 **Tonkino** Russia
Tônlé Sab, Bœng *l.* Cambodia *see* **Tonle Sap**
162 B2 **Tonle Sap** *l.* Cambodia
159 G5 **Tōno** Japan
215 D2 **Tonopah** U.S.A.
233 L2 **Tonoro** *r.* Venez.
224 I7 **Tonosí** Panama
195 C6 **Tonota** Botswana
148 D3 **Tons** *r.* India
171 J4 **Tønsberg** Norway
171 I4 **Tonstad** Norway
215 G5 **Tonto National Monument** *nat. park* U.S.A.
149 H5 **Tonzang** Myanmar
125 H2 **Toobeah** Australia
213 D3 **Tooele** U.S.A.
125 J1 **Toogoolawah** Australia
125 E5 **Tooleybuc** Australia
124 A4 **Tooligie** Australia
125 H6 **Tooma** *r.* Australia
123 D5 **Toompine** Australia
125 G7 **Toora** Australia
125 H3 **Tooraweenah** Australia
197 F6 **Toorberg** *mt.* S. Africa
125 I1 **Toowoomba** Australia
215 G6 **Topawa** U.S.A.
214 C2 **Topaz** U.S.A.
141 J1 **Topchikha** Russia
217 E4 **Topeka** U.S.A.
224 C2 **Topia** Mex.
204 D4 **Topley Landing** Canada
179 K2 **Töplitz** Germany
235 H2 **Topocalma, Punta** *pt* Chile
215 E4 **Topock** U.S.A.
177 I6 **Topoľčany** Slovakia
140 B3 **Topoli** Kazakh.
224 B2 **Topolobampo** Mex.
185 L3 **Topolovgrad** Bulg.
170 P2 **Topozero, Ozero** *l.* Russia
212 B2 **Toppenish** U.S.A.
221 J2 **Topsfield** U.S.A.
215 F3 **Toquerville** U.S.A.
185 L5 **Torbalı** Turkey
143 E3 **Torbat-e Ḩeydarīyeh** Iran
143 F3 **Torbat-e Jām** Iran
121 B7 **Torbay Bay** Australia
187 G4 **Torbeyevo** Russia
209 E3 **Torch Lake** U.S.A.
183 N2 **Tordesillas** Spain
170 M2 **Töre** Sweden
183 R1 **Torelló** Spain
178 D2 **Torenberg** *h.* Neth.
179 K3 **Torgau** Germany
141 H2 **Torgay** *Akmolinskaya Oblast'* Kazakh.
140 E2 **Torgay** *Kostanayskaya Oblast'* Kazakh.
187 H5 **Torgun** *r.* Russia
178 B3 **Torhout** Belgium
194 D3 **Torī** Eth.
Torino Italy *see* **Turin**
159 G9 **Tori-shima** *i.* Japan
193 F4 **Torit** South Sudan
234 B2 **Torixoréu** Brazil
139 K3 **Torkamānchāy** Iran
186 G3 **Tor'kovskoye Vodokhranilishche** *resr* Russia
183 N2 **Tormes** *r.* Spain
170 M2 **Torneälven** *r.* Fin./Sweden
170 L1 **Torneträsk** Sweden
170 L1 **Torneträsk** *l.* Sweden
207 H2 **Torngat Mountains** Canada
207 H2 **Torngat Mountains National Park** Canada
170 N2 **Tornio** Fin.
235 J3 **Tornquist** Arg.
183 N2 **Toro** Spain
225 D2 **Toro, Pico del** *mt.* Mex.
156 D1 **Torom** Russia
150 F1 **Torom** *r.* Russia
125 I4 **Toronto** Australia
209 H4 **Toronto** Canada
215 D5 **Toro Peak** U.S.A.
186 D3 **Toropets** Russia
194 D3 **Tororo** Uganda
Toros Dağları *mts* Turkey *see* **Taurus Mountains**
175 F3 **Torphins** U.K.
173 D7 **Torquay** U.K.
214 C5 **Torrance** U.S.A.
183 L3 **Torrão** Port.
183 M2 **Torre** *mt.* Port.
183 Q2 **Torreblanca** Spain
183 N1 **Torrecerredo** *mt.* Spain
184 F4 **Torre del Greco** Italy
183 N1 **Torrelavega** Spain
183 N4 **Torremolinos** Spain
124 B3 **Torrens, Lake** *imp. l.* Australia
123 D4 **Torrens Creek** Australia
183 P3 **Torrent** Spain
225 D2 **Torreón** Mex.
224 B1 **Torres** Mex.
119 G3 **Torres Islands** Vanuatu
183 L3 **Torres Novas** Port.
119 E2 **Torres Strait** Australia
183 L3 **Torres Vedras** Port.
183 P4 **Torrevieja** Spain
215 G2 **Torrey** U.S.A.
173 C7 **Torridge** *r.* U.K.
174 C3 **Torridon, Loch** *b.* U.K.
183 N3 **Torrijos** Spain
125 I2 **Torrington** Australia
221 G4 **Torrington** *CT* U.S.A.
213 F3 **Torrington** *WY* U.S.A.
183 R1 **Torroella de Montgrí** Spain
171 K3 **Torsby** Sweden
170 □ **Tórshavn** Faroe Is
141 G4 **Tortkol'** Kazakh.
140 E4 **To'rtko'l** Uzbek.
141 H2 **Tortkuduk** Kazakh.
184 C5 **Tortolì** *Sardinia* Italy
184 C2 **Tortona** Italy
183 Q2 **Tortosa** Spain
224 I6 **Tortuguero, Parque Nacional** *nat. park* Costa Rica
139 H1 **Tortum** Turkey
141 I4 **Toru-Aygyr** Kyrg.
142 D3 **Ţorūd** Iran
139 G1 **Torul** Turkey
177 I4 **Toruń** Poland
175 J2 **Tory Island** Ireland
175 J2 **Tory Sound** *sea chan.* Ireland
186 E3 **Torzhok** Russia
159 C8 **Tosa** Japan
159 C8 **Tosashimizu** Japan
170 K2 **Tosbotn** Norway
197 E2 **Tosca** S. Africa
184 C3 **Toscano, Arcipelago** *is* Italy
158 G4 **Tōshima-yama** *mt.* Japan
141 G4 **Toshkent** Uzbek.
186 D3 **Tosno** Russia
232 D3 **Tostado** Arg.
179 H1 **Tostedt** Germany
159 B8 **Tosu** Japan
138 E1 **Tosya** Turkey
186 G3 **Tot'ma** Russia
225 E4 **Totolapan** Mex.
117 H3 **Totoya** *i.* Fiji
140 C1 **Totskoye** Russia
173 F7 **Totton** U.K.
159 D7 **Tottori** Japan
192 B4 **Touba** Côte d'Ivoire
192 A3 **Touba** Senegal
192 B1 **Toubkal, Jebel** *mt.* Morocco
154 B2 **Toudaohu** China
192 B3 **Tougan** Burkina Faso
192 C1 **Touggourt** Alg.
192 A3 **Tougué** Guinea
182 G2 **Toul** France
183 G5 **Toulon** France
183 E5 **Toulouse** France
192 B4 **Toumodi** Côte d'Ivoire
192 B2 **Tounassine, Hamada** *des.* Alg.
Toungoo Myanmar *see* **Taung-ngu**
155 D5 **Toupai** China
162 B1 **Tourakom** Laos
178 B4 **Tourcoing** France
178 B4 **Tournai** Belgium
182 G4 **Tournon-sur-Rhône** France
182 G3 **Tournus** France
231 K5 **Touros** Brazil
182 E3 **Tours** France
156 B3 **Toutai** China
196 D6 **Touwsrivier** S. Africa
179 K4 **Toužim** Czech Rep.
233 J2 **Tovar** Venez.
173 F5 **Tove** *r.* U.K.
139 J1 **Tovuz** Azer.
158 G4 **Towada** Japan
159 G5 **Towada-Hachimantai Kokuritsu-kōen** *nat. park* Japan
158 G4 **Towada-ko** *l.* Japan
126 E1 **Towai** N.Z.
221 E4 **Towanda** U.S.A.
215 H3 **Towaoc** U.S.A.
173 G5 **Towcester** U.K.
175 J6 **Tower** Ireland
208 A2 **Tower** U.S.A.
205 I5 **Towner** U.S.A.
215 D3 **Townes Pass** U.S.A.
212 E2 **Townsend** U.S.A.
125 H6 **Townsend, Mount** Australia
123 E4 **Townshend Island** Australia
119 E3 **Townsville** Australia
151 E7 **Towori, Teluk** *b.* Indon.
221 E5 **Towson** U.S.A.
141 I4 **Toxkan He** *r.* China
158 G3 **Tōya-ko** *l.* Japan
159 E6 **Toyama** Japan
159 E6 **Toyama-wan** *b.* Japan
159 E7 **Toyohashi** Japan
159 E7 **Toyokawa** Japan
159 D7 **Toyonaka** Japan
159 D7 **Toyooka** Japan
159 E7 **Toyota** Japan
141 G4 **To'ytepa** Uzbek.
192 C1 **Tozeur** Tunisia
187 G7 **T'q'ibuli** Georgia
187 G7 **T'q'varcheli** Georgia
179 F5 **Traben** Germany
Trâblous Lebanon *see* **Tripoli**
185 J4 **Trabotivište** Macedonia
139 G1 **Trabzon** Turkey
221 J2 **Tracy** Canada
214 B3 **Tracy** *CA* U.S.A.
216 E2 **Tracy** *MN* U.S.A.
208 A4 **Traer** U.S.A.
183 M4 **Trafalgar, Cabo** *c.* Spain
235 H3 **Traiguén** Chile
204 F5 **Trail** Canada
171 N5 **Trakai** Lith.
186 I2 **Trakt** Russia
175 I5 **Tralee** Ireland
175 I5 **Tralee Bay** Ireland
233 L3 **Tramán Tepuí** *mt.* Venez.
175 K5 **Tramore** Ireland
171 K4 **Tranås** Sweden
232 C3 **Trancas** Arg.
171 K4 **Tranemo** Sweden
175 F5 **Tranent** U.K.
162 A4 **Trang** Thai.
151 F7 **Trangan** *i.* Indon.
155 B6 **Trang An** *tourist site* Vietnam
125 G4 **Trangie** Australia
235 L1 **Tranqueras** Uruguay
127 I5 **Transantarctic Mountains** Antarctica
205 G4 **Trans Canada Highway** Canada
205 J5 **Transcona** Canada
177 N7 **Transnistria** *disp. terr* Moldova
185 J2 **Transylvanian Alps** *mts* Romania
184 E5 **Trapani** *Sicily* Italy
125 G7 **Traralgon** Australia
149 G4 **Trashigang** Bhutan
184 E3 **Trasimeno, Lago** *l.* Italy
183 O3 **Trasvase, Canal de** Spain
162 B2 **Trat** Thai.
148 B3 **Tratani** *r.* Pak.
176 F7 **Traunsee** *l.* Austria
176 F7 **Traunstein** Germany
125 E4 **Travellers Lake** *imp. l.* Australia
126 D5 **Travers, Mount** N.Z.
229 G7 **Traversay Islands** S. Sandwich Is
209 E3 **Traverse City** U.S.A.
162 C3 **Tra Vinh** Vietnam
217 D6 **Travis, Lake** U.S.A.
185 G2 **Travnik** Bos. & Herz.
184 F1 **Trbovlje** Slovenia
119 F2 **Treasury Islands** Solomon Is
179 L2 **Trebbin** Germany
176 G6 **Třebíč** Czech Rep.
185 H3 **Trebinje** Bos. & Herz.
177 J6 **Trebišov** Slovakia
184 F2 **Trebnje** Slovenia
179 G5 **Trebur** Germany
179 I3 **Treffurt** Germany
208 B3 **Trego** U.S.A.
122 E3 **Tregosse Islets and Reefs** Australia
174 D4 **Treig, Loch** *l.* U.K.
235 L2 **Treinta y Tres** Uruguay

Trelew

232 C6 **Trelew** Arg.
171 K5 **Trelleborg** Sweden
178 C4 **Trélon** France
173 C5 **Tremadog Bay** U.K.
207 F4 **Tremblant, Mont** *h.* Canada
184 F3 **Tremiti, Isole** Italy
213 D3 **Tremonton** U.S.A.
183 Q1 **Tremp** Spain
208 B3 **Trempealeau** *r.* U.S.A.
173 B7 **Trenance** U.K.
177 I6 **Trenčín** Slovakia
179 H3 **Trendelburg** Germany
235 J2 **Trenque Lauquén** Arg.
173 G4 **Trent** *r.* U.K.
184 D1 **Trento** Italy
209 I3 **Trenton** Canada
216 E3 **Trenton** *MO* U.S.A.
221 F4 **Trenton** *NJ* U.S.A.
173 D6 **Treorchy** U.K.
207 J4 **Trepassey** Canada
235 L2 **Tres Árboles** Uruguay
235 K3 **Tres Arroyos** Arg.
173 A8 **Tresco** *i.* U.K.
234 D3 **Três Corações** Brazil
233 I4 **Tres Esquinas** Col.
Tres Forcas, Cabo *c.* Morocco *see* **Trois Fourches, Cap des**
174 B4 **Treshnish Isles** U.K.
234 B3 **Três Irmãos, Represa** *resr* Brazil
234 B3 **Três Lagoas** Brazil
232 B7 **Tres Lagos** Arg.
235 J3 **Tres Lomas** Arg.
234 D2 **Três Marias, Represa** *resr* Brazil
235 H4 **Tres Picos** *mt.* Arg.
225 F5 **Tres Picos** Mex.
235 K3 **Tres Picos, Cerro** *mt.* Arg.
213 F4 **Tres Piedras** U.S.A.
234 D3 **Três Pontas** Brazil
232 C7 **Tres Puntas, Cabo** *c.* Arg.
234 D3 **Três Rios** Brazil
225 E4 **Tres Valles** Mex.
225 F4 **Tres Zapotes** *tourist site* Mex.
171 J3 **Tretten** Norway
179 I6 **Treuchtlingen** Germany
179 K2 **Treuenbrietzen** Germany
171 J4 **Treungen** Norway
184 C2 **Treviglio** Italy
184 E2 **Treviso** Italy
173 B7 **Trevose Head** U.K.
125 G9 **Triabunna** Australia
185 L6 **Tria Nisia** *i.* Greece
185 M6 **Trianta** Greece
148 B2 **Tribal Areas** *admin. div.* Pak.
185 H5 **Tricase** Italy
Trichur India *see* **Thrissur**
178 A5 **Tricot** France
125 F4 **Trida** Australia
179 E5 **Trier** Germany
184 E2 **Trieste** Italy
184 E1 **Triglav** *mt.* Slovenia
185 I5 **Trikala** Greece
138 D4 **Trikomon** Cyprus
151 F7 **Trikora, Puncak** *mt.* Indon.
175 L4 **Trim** Ireland
147 I4 **Trincomalee** Sri Lanka
234 C2 **Trindade** Brazil
239 H7 **Trindade, Ilha da** *i.* S. Atlantic Ocean
231 F6 **Trinidad** Bol.
233 J3 **Trinidad** Col.
223 I4 **Trinidad** Cuba
231 F1 **Trinidad** *i.* Trin. and Tob.
235 L2 **Trinidad** Uruguay
213 F4 **Trinidad** U.S.A.
223 L2 **Trinidad and Tobago** *country* Caribbean Sea
207 J4 **Trinity Bay** Canada
202 C4 **Trinity Islands** U.S.A.
214 C1 **Trinity Range** *mts* U.S.A.
219 C5 **Trion** U.S.A.
179 J1 **Tripkau** Germany
185 J6 **Tripoli** Greece
138 E4 **Tripoli** Lebanon
193 D1 **Tripoli** Libya
193 D1 **Tripolitania** *reg.* Libya
147 H4 **Tripunittura** India
149 G5 **Tripura** *state* India
239 I8 **Tristan da Cunha** *i.* S. Atlantic Ocean
148 D3 **Trisul** *mt.* India
149 F4 **Trisul Dam** Nepal
179 I1 **Trittau** Germany
179 E5 **Trittenheim** Germany
Trivandrum India *see* **Thiruvananthapuram**
184 F4 **Trivento** Italy
177 H6 **Trnava** Slovakia
119 F2 **Trobriand Islands** P.N.G.
170 K2 **Trofors** Norway
185 G3 **Trogir** Croatia
184 F4 **Troia** Italy
179 F4 **Troisdorf** Germany
180 C4 **Trois Fourches, Cap des** *c.* Morocco
178 D4 **Trois-Ponts** Belgium
207 F4 **Trois-Rivières** Canada
140 E1 **Troitsk** Russia
169 R3 **Troitsko-Pechorsk** Russia
141 K1 **Troitskoye** *Altayskiy Kray* Russia
156 E2 **Troitskoye** *Khabarovskiy Kray* Russia
140 C1 **Troitskoye** *Orenburgskaya Oblast'* Russia
140 D1 **Troitskoye** *Respublika Bashkortostan* Russia
187 H6 **Troitskoye** *Respublika Kalmykiya-Khalm'g-Tangch* Russia
127 K3 **Troll** *research stn* Antarctica
171 K4 **Trollhättan** Sweden
231 G3 **Trombetas** *r.* Brazil
191 I6 **Tromelin, Île** *i.* Indian Ocean
235 H3 **Tromen, Volcán** *vol.* Arg.
197 F5 **Trompsburg** S. Africa
170 L1 **Tromsø** Norway
215 D4 **Trona** U.S.A.
235 H4 **Tronador, Monte** *mt.* Arg.
171 J3 **Trondheim** Norway
171 J3 **Trondheimsfjorden** *sea chan.* Norway
149 G4 **Trongsa Chhu** *r.* Bhutan
138 D4 **Troödos** Cyprus
174 D5 **Troon** U.K.
234 D1 **Tropeiros, Serra dos** *hills* Brazil
215 F3 **Tropic** U.S.A.
122 G4 **Tropic of Capricorn**
175 L2 **Trostan** *h.* U.K.
175 F3 **Troup Head** U.K.
204 E2 **Trout** *r.* Canada
209 H3 **Trout Creek** Canada
215 F2 **Trout Creek** U.S.A.
205 G3 **Trout Lake** *Alta* Canada
204 E2 **Trout Lake** *N.W.T.* Canada
204 E2 **Trout Lake** *l. N.W.T.* Canada
205 K4 **Trout Lake** *l. Ont.* Canada
209 E2 **Trout Lake** U.S.A.
208 C2 **Trout Lake** *l.* U.S.A.
212 E2 **Trout Peak** U.S.A.
221 E4 **Trout Run** U.S.A.
173 E6 **Trowbridge** U.K.
125 F8 **Trowutta** Australia
185 L5 **Troy** *tourist site* Turkey
219 C6 **Troy** *AL* U.S.A.
212 D2 **Troy** *MT* U.S.A.
221 G3 **Troy** *NH* U.S.A.
221 G3 **Troy** *NY* U.S.A.
220 A4 **Troy** *OH* U.S.A.
221 E4 **Troy** *PA* U.S.A.
185 K3 **Troyan** Bulg.
182 G2 **Troyes** France
215 D4 **Troy Lake** U.S.A.
215 E2 **Troy Peak** U.S.A.
185 I3 **Trstenik** Serbia
187 E4 **Trubchevsk** Russia
183 M1 **Truchas** Spain
186 E3 **Trud** Russia
158 C3 **Trudovoye** Russia
224 H5 **Trujillo** Hond.
230 C5 **Trujillo** Peru
183 N3 **Trujillo** Spain
233 J2 **Trujillo** Venez.
179 F5 **Trulben** Germany
221 G4 **Trumbull** U.S.A.
215 F3 **Trumbull, Mount** U.S.A.
163 E2 **Trumon** Indon.
125 G4 **Trundle** Australia
162 C2 **Trưng Hiệp** Vietnam
155 C6 **Trưng Khanh** Vietnam
207 H4 **Truro** Canada
173 B7 **Truro** U.K.
175 J3 **Truskmore** *h.* Ireland
204 E3 **Trutch** Canada
213 F5 **Truth or Consequences** U.S.A.
176 G5 **Trutnov** Czech Rep.
Truva *tourist site* Turkey *see* **Troy**
185 K7 **Trypiti, Akrotirio** *pt* Greece
171 K3 **Trysil** Norway
176 G3 **Trzebiatów** Poland
150 A2 **Tsagaannuur** Mongolia
144 I2 **Tsagaan-Uul** Mongolia
187 H6 **Tsagan Aman** Russia
187 H6 **Tsagan Nur** Russia
187 G7 **Tsageri** Georgia
137 F2 **Ts'alenjikha** Georgia
139 J1 **Ts'alk'a** Georgia
195 E5 **Tsaratanana, Massif du** *mts* Madag.
185 L3 **Tsarevo** Bulg.
196 B2 **Tsaris Mountains** Namibia
187 H5 **Tsatsa** Russia
196 A3 **Tsaukaib** Namibia
195 D4 **Tsavo East National Park** Kenya
187 G6 **Tselina** Russia
153 I2 **Tsenhermandal** Mongolia
195 B6 **Tses** Namibia
144 H2 **Tsetseg** Mongolia
Tsetsegnuur Mongolia *see* **Tsetseg**
195 C6 **Tsetseng** Botswana
150 C2 **Tsetserleg** *Arhangay* Mongolia
144 I2 **Tsetserleg** *Hövsgöl* Mongolia
195 C6 **Tshabong** Botswana
195 C6 **Tshane** Botswana
195 B4 **Tshela** Dem. Rep. Congo
195 C4 **Tshibala** Dem. Rep. Congo
195 C4 **Tshikapa** Dem. Rep. Congo
195 C4 **Tshikapa** *r.* Dem. Rep. Congo
197 G3 **Tshing** S. Africa
197 I1 **Tshipise** S. Africa
195 C4 **Tshitanzu** Dem. Rep. Congo
195 C4 **Tshofa** Dem. Rep. Congo
197 I2 **Tshokwane** S. Africa
195 C4 **Tshuapa** *r.* Dem. Rep. Congo
Tshwane S. Africa *see* **Pretoria**
187 G6 **Tsimlyansk** Russia
187 G6 **Tsimlyanskoye Vodokhranilishche** *resr* Russia
156 E2 **Tsimmermanovka** Russia
197 E3 **Tsineng** S. Africa
Tsing Shan Wan *b.* China *see* **Castle Peak Bay**
Tsingtao China *see* **Qingdao**
155 □ **Tsing Yi** *i. Hong Kong* China
Tsining China *see* **Ulan Qab**
195 E6 **Tsiombe** Madag.
195 E5 **Tsiroanomandidy** Madag.
197 E6 **Tsitsikamma Forest and Coastal National Park** S. Africa
204 D4 **Tsitsutl Peak** Canada
187 H4 **Tsivil'sk** Russia
187 G7 **Tskhinvali** Georgia
187 G4 **Tsna** *r.* Russia
137 G2 **Ts'nori** Georgia
154 B1 **Tsogttsetsiy** Mongolia
148 D2 **Tsokar Chumo** *l.* India
197 H5 **Tsolo** S. Africa
197 G6 **Tsomo** S. Africa
187 G7 **Ts'q'alt'ubo** Georgia
159 E7 **Tsu** Japan
159 G6 **Tsuchiura** Japan
155 □ **Tsuen Wan** *Hong Kong* China
158 G4 **Tsugarū-kaikyō** *str.* Japan
195 B5 **Tsumeb** Namibia
195 B6 **Tsumis Park** Namibia
195 C5 **Tsumkwe** Namibia
149 G4 **Tsunthang** India
159 E7 **Tsuruga** Japan
159 D8 **Tsurugi-san** *mt.* Japan
Tsurukhaytuy Russia *see* **Priargunsk**
159 F5 **Tsuruoka** Japan
159 A7 **Tsushima** Japan
159 A7 **Tsushima** *is* Japan
159 D7 **Tsuyama** Japan
196 D1 **Tswaane** Botswana
197 F4 **Tswaraganang** S. Africa
197 F3 **Tswelelang** S. Africa
177 L4 **Tsyelyakhany** Belarus
170 P1 **Tsypnavolok** Russia
187 E6 **Tsyurupyns'k** Ukr.
151 F7 **Tual** Indon.
175 J4 **Tuam** Ireland
126 D4 **Tuamarina** N.Z.
Tuamotu, Archipel des *is* Fr. Polynesia *see* **Tuamotu Islands**
117 J5 **Tuamotu Islands** Fr. Polynesia
155 B6 **Tuân Giao** Vietnam
162 A5 **Tuangku** *i.* Indon.
187 F6 **Tuapse** Russia
162 □ **Tuas** Sing.
126 A7 **Tuatapere** N.Z.
174 B2 **Tuath, Loch a'** *b.* U.K.
215 G3 **Tuba City** U.S.A.
163 H4 **Tuban** Indon.
233 G3 **Tubarão** Brazil
161 H4 **Tubbataha Reefs** Phil.
Tubbercurry Ireland *see* **Tobercurry**
176 D6 **Tübingen** Germany
192 A4 **Tubmanburg** Liberia
161 I4 **Tubod** Phil.
193 E1 **Tubruq** Libya
237 J7 **Tubuai** *i.* Fr. Polynesia
117 I6 **Tubuai Islands** Fr. Polynesia
231 K6 **Tucano** Brazil
235 H3 **Tucapel, Punta** *pt* Chile
231 G7 **Tucavaca** Bol.
179 K1 **Tüchen** Germany
179 K2 **Tuchheim** Germany
204 D2 **Tuchitua** Canada
221 F5 **Tuckerton** U.S.A.
215 G5 **Tucson** U.S.A.
215 G5 **Tucson Mountains** U.S.A.
233 I2 **Tucuco** *r.* Venez.
213 G5 **Tucumcari** U.S.A.
233 L2 **Tucupita** Venez.
231 I4 **Tucuruí** Brazil
231 I4 **Tucuruí, Represa de** *resr* Brazil
139 L5 **Tū Dār** Iran
183 P1 **Tudela** Spain
144 I2 **Tüdevtey** Mongolia
183 M2 **Tuela** *r.* Port.
155 □ **Tuen Mun** *Hong Kong* China
149 H4 **Tuensang** India
142 C5 **Ţufayḩ** Saudi Arabia
237 J2 **Tufts Abyssal Plain** *sea feature* N. Pacific Ocean
161 J4 **Tugnug Point** Phil.
161 I2 **Tuguegarao** Phil.
133 O4 **Tugur** Russia
141 K3 **Tugyl** Kazakh.
154 F2 **Tuhai He** *r.* China
162 A5 **Tuhemberua** Indon.
183 L1 **Tui** Spain
224 J6 **Tuira** *r.* Panama
140 D1 **Tukan** Russia
151 E7 **Tukangbesi, Kepulauan** *is* Indon.
206 E2 **Tukarak Island** Canada
141 H5 **Tükhtamish** Tajik.
202 E3 **Tuktoyaktuk** Canada
171 M4 **Tukums** Latvia
156 B1 **Tukuringra, Khrebet** *mts* Russia
143 G3 **Tukzār** Afgh.
225 E3 **Tula** Mex.
187 F4 **Tula** Russia
149 H1 **Tulagt Ar Gol** *r.* China
225 E3 **Tulancingo** Mex.
214 C3 **Tulare** U.S.A.
214 C4 **Tulare Lake Bed** U.S.A.
213 F5 **Tularosa** U.S.A.
147 I2 **Tulasi** *mt.* India
196 C6 **Tulbagh** S. Africa
230 C3 **Tulcán** Ecuador
185 M2 **Tulcea** Romania
187 D5 **Tul'chyn** Ukr.
214 C3 **Tule** *r.* U.S.A.
142 D3 **Tuleh** Iran
149 G4 **Tule La** *pass* Bhutan
205 I2 **Tulemalu Lake** Canada
217 C5 **Tulia** U.S.A.
204 D2 **Tulita** Canada
138 E5 **Ţūlkarm** West Bank
175 J5 **Tulla** Ireland
125 F8 **Tullah** Australia
219 C5 **Tullahoma** U.S.A.
125 G4 **Tullamore** Australia
175 K4 **Tullamore** Ireland
182 E4 **Tulle** France
171 K3 **Tulleråsen** Sweden
125 G4 **Tullibigeal** Australia
217 E6 **Tullos** U.S.A.
175 L5 **Tullow** Ireland
119 E3 **Tully** Australia
122 D3 **Tully** *r.* Australia
175 K3 **Tully** U.K.
221 E3 **Tully** U.S.A.
186 D2 **Tulos** Russia
217 D4 **Tulsa** U.S.A.
187 F4 **Tul'skaya Oblast'** *admin. div.* Russia
233 H3 **Tuluá** Col.
202 B3 **Tuluksak** U.S.A.
225 H3 **Tulum** *tourist site* Mex.
235 I1 **Tulum, Valle de** *val.* Arg.
150 C1 **Tulun** Russia
163 H4 **Tulungagung** Indon.
149 H4 **Tulung La** *pass* China
161 H4 **Tuluran** *i.* Phil.
233 H4 **Tumaco** Col.
197 G3 **Tumahole** S. Africa
187 I6 **Tumak** Russia
147 H3 **Tumakuru** India
171 L4 **Tumba** Sweden
195 B4 **Tumba, Lac** *l.* Dem. Rep. Congo
163 H3 **Tumbangsamba** Indon.
230 B4 **Tumbes** Peru
204 E3 **Tumbler Ridge** Canada
124 B5 **Tumby Bay** Australia
154 B2 **Tumen** *Gansu* China
160 E2 **Tumen** *Jilin* China
160 E2 **Tumen** *r.* China/N. Korea
231 F2 **Tumereng** Guyana
161 H5 **Tumindao** *i.* Phil.
149 G3 **Tum La** *pass* China
174 E4 **Tummel, Loch** *l.* U.K.
150 G2 **Tumnin** *r.* Russia
143 F5 **Tump** Pak.
162 B4 **Tumpat** Malaysia
192 B3 **Tumu** Ghana
231 G3 **Tumucumaque, Parque Indígena do** *res.* Brazil
231 G3 **Tumucumaque, Serra** *hills* Brazil
125 H5 **Tumut** Australia
125 H5 **Tumut** *r.* Australia
141 J4 **Tumxuk** China
139 G2 **Tunceli** Turkey
155 D7 **Tunchang** China
125 J4 **Tuncurry** Australia
143 F3 **Tundī** *imp. l.* Afgh.
195 D5 **Tunduru** Tanz.
185 L3 **Tundzha** *r.* Bulg.
147 H3 **Tungabhadra** *r.* India
147 G3 **Tungabhadra Reservoir** India
149 H3 **Tunga La** China/India
161 I5 **Tungawan** Phil.
155 □ **Tung Chung Wan** *b. Hong Kong* China
170 C2 **Tungnaá** *r.* Iceland
156 F1 **Tungor** Russia
Tung Pok Liu Hoi Hap China *see* **East Lamma Channel**
204 D2 **Tungsten (abandoned)** Canada
186 E1 **Tunguda** Russia
155 □ **Tung Wan** *b. Hong Kong* China
147 I2 **Tuni** India
193 D1 **Tunis** Tunisia
184 D6 **Tunis, Golfe de** *g.* Tunisia
192 C1 **Tunisia** *country* Africa
233 I3 **Tunja** Col.
154 D2 **Tunliu** China
170 K2 **Tunnsjøen** *l.* Norway
173 I5 **Tunstall** U.K.
170 O2 **Tuntsa** Fin.
170 O2 **Tuntsayoki** *r.* Fin./Russia
207 G2 **Tunulic** *r.* Canada
207 H2 **Tunungayualok Island** Canada
235 I2 **Tunuyán** Arg.
235 I2 **Tunuyán** *r.* Arg.
154 E3 **Tuo He** *r.* China
154 F2 **Tuoji Dao** *i.* China
162 C3 **Tuŏl Khpós** Cambodia
214 B3 **Tuolumne** U.S.A.
210 B4 **Tuolumne** *r.* U.S.A.
214 C3 **Tuolumne Meadows** U.S.A.
155 B5 **Tuoniang Jiang** *r.* China
Tuotuo He *r.* China *see* **Togton He**
141 I4 **Tüp** Kyrg.
234 B3 **Tupã** Brazil
234 C2 **Tupaciguara** Brazil
139 K3 **Tūp Āghāj** Iran
232 F3 **Tupanciretã** Brazil
233 J3 **Tuparro** *r.* Col.
217 F5 **Tupelo** U.S.A.
153 K1 **Tupik** Russia
230 E8 **Tupiza** Bol.
140 B3 **Tupkaragan, Mys** *pt* Kazakh.
221 F2 **Tupper Lake** U.S.A.
221 F2 **Tupper Lake** *l.* U.S.A.
235 I2 **Tupungato** Arg.
235 I2 **Tupungato, Cerro** *mt.* Arg./Chile
139 J7 **Tuqayyid** *well* Iraq
160 A1 **Tuquan** China
233 H4 **Túquerres** Col.
149 G4 **Tura** India
133 L3 **Tura** Russia
146 B5 **Turabah** Saudi Arabia
233 K3 **Turagua, Serranía** *mt.* Venez.
126 E4 **Turakina** N.Z.
143 E3 **Turan** Iran
152 F1 **Turan** Russia
150 F1 **Turana, Khrebet** *mts* Russia
126 E3 **Turangi** N.Z.
143 E2 **Turan Lowland** Asia
141 G4 **Turar Ryskulov** Kazakh.
139 G6 **Ţurayf** Saudi Arabia
142 C5 **Ţurayf** *well* Saudi Arabia
171 N4 **Turba** Estonia
233 I2 **Turbaco** Col.
143 F5 **Turbat** Pak.
233 H2 **Turbo** Col.
177 K7 **Turda** Romania
142 C3 **Tūreh** Iran
Turfan China *see* **Turpan**
140 E3 **Turgay** *r.* Kazakh.
140 E2 **Turgayskaya Dolina** *val.* Kazakh.
140 E2 **Turgayskaya Stolovaya Strana** *reg.* Kazakh.
138 C2 **Turgut** Turkey
138 A2 **Turgutlu** Turkey
139 F1 **Turhal** Turkey
171 N4 **Türi** Estonia
183 P3 **Turia** *r.* Spain
233 K2 **Turiamo** Venez.
184 B2 **Turin** Italy
158 B2 **Turiy Rog** Russia
187 C5 **Turiys'k** Ukr.
194 D3 **Turkana, Lake** *salt l.* Eth./Kenya
185 L4 **Türkeli Adası** *i.* Turkey
141 G5 **Turkestan Range** *mts* Asia
138 E2 **Turkey** *country* Asia
208 B4 **Turkey** *r.* U.S.A.
187 G5 **Turki** Russia
Turkish Republic of Northern Cyprus *disp. terr* Asia *see* **Northern Cyprus**
141 G4 **Turkistan** Kazakh.
143 F3 **Turkistān, Silsilah-ye Band-e** *mts* Afgh.
140 E5 **Türkmenabat** Turkm.
Turkmenabat Turkm. *see* **Türkmenabat**
140 C5 **Türkmen Aýlagy** *b.* Turkm.
Turkmenbashi Turkm. *see* **Türkmenbaşy**
140 C4 **Türkmenbaşy** Turkm.
140 C5 **Türkmenbaşy Aýlagy** *b.* Turkm.
138 C2 **Türkmen Dağı** *mt.* Turkey
140 E5 **Türkmengala** Turkm.
Turkmengala Turkm. *see* **Türkmengala**
140 C5 **Turkmenistan** *country* Asia
Turkmenskiy Zaliv *b.* Turkm. *see* **Türkmen Aýlagy**
139 F3 **Türkoğlu** Turkey
223 J4 **Turks and Caicos Islands** *terr.* Caribbean Sea
223 J4 **Turks Islands** Turks and Caicos Is
171 M3 **Turku** Fin.
194 D3 **Turkwel** *watercourse* Kenya
214 B3 **Turlock** U.S.A.
214 B3 **Turlock Lake** U.S.A.
126 F4 **Turnagain, Cape** N.Z.
174 D5 **Turnberry** U.K.
215 G5 **Turnbull, Mount** U.S.A.
225 H4 **Turneffe Islands** *atoll* Belize
209 F3 **Turner** U.S.A.
178 C3 **Turnhout** Belgium
205 H3 **Turnor Lake** Canada
185 K3 **Turnu Măgurele** Romania
Turnu Severin Romania *see* **Drobeta-Turnu Severin**
125 H4 **Turon** *r.* Australia
186 G3 **Turovets** Russia
150 A2 **Turpan** China
150 A2 **Turpan Pendi** *depr.* China
223 I4 **Turquino, Pico** *mt.* Cuba
175 F3 **Turriff** U.K.
139 J5 **Tursāq** Iraq
Turtkul' Uzbek. *see* **To'rtko'l**
208 B2 **Turtle Flambeau Flowage** *resr* U.S.A.
205 H4 **Turtleford** Canada
208 A3 **Turtle Lake** U.S.A.
141 H4 **Turugart Pass** China/Kyrg.
234 B2 **Turvo** *r. São Paulo* Brazil
234 C3 **Turvo** *r. São Paulo* Brazil
140 D3 **Turysh** Kazakh.
215 F4 **Tusayan** U.S.A.
219 C5 **Tuscaloosa** U.S.A.
220 C4 **Tuscarawas** *r.* U.S.A.
221 E4 **Tuscarora Mountains** U.S.A.
208 C6 **Tuscola** *IL* U.S.A.
217 D5 **Tuscola** *TX* U.S.A.
219 C5 **Tuskegee** U.S.A.
220 D4 **Tussey Mountains** U.S.A.
139 I2 **Tutak** Turkey
186 F3 **Tutayev** Russia
147 H4 **Tuticorin** India

W

Williamsburg

219 C4 Waverly TN U.S.A.
221 E6 Waverly VA U.S.A.
178 C4 Wavre Belgium
209 E1 Wawa Canada
192 C4 Wawa Nigeria
209 E5 Wawasee, Lake U.S.A.
214 C3 Wawona U.S.A.
217 D5 Waxahachie U.S.A.
144 G4 Waxxari China
121 C5 Way, Lake salt flat Australia
219 D6 Waycross U.S.A.
220 B6 Wayland KY U.S.A.
208 B5 Wayland MO U.S.A.
216 D3 Wayne U.S.A.
219 D5 Waynesboro GA U.S.A.
217 F6 Waynesboro MS U.S.A.
221 E5 Waynesboro PA U.S.A.
220 D5 Waynesboro VA U.S.A.
220 C5 Waynesburg U.S.A.
217 E4 Waynesville U.S.A.
217 D4 Waynoka U.S.A.
193 D3 Waza, Parc National de nat. park Cameroon
148 C2 Wazirabad Pak.
192 C3 W du Niger, Parc National du nat. park Niger
163 E1 We, Pulau i. Indon.
206 B3 Weagamow Lake Canada
172 E3 Wear r. U.K.
119 E3 Weary Bay Australia
217 D5 Weatherford U.S.A.
213 B3 Weaverville U.S.A.
121 E4 Webb, Mount h. Australia
209 G2 Webbwood Canada
206 C3 Webequie Canada
204 D3 Weber, Mount Canada
238 M5 Weber Basin sea feature Indon.
221 H3 Webster MA U.S.A.
216 D2 Webster SD U.S.A.
208 A3 Webster WI U.S.A.
216 E3 Webster City U.S.A.
220 C5 Webster Springs U.S.A.
238 B9 Weddell Abyssal Plain sea feature Southern Ocean
232 D8 Weddell Island Falkland Is
127 J3 Weddell Sea Antarctica
125 E6 Wedderburn Australia
179 H1 Wedel Germany
213 B3 Weed U.S.A.
220 D4 Weedville U.S.A.
125 H2 Weemelah Australia
197 I4 Weenen S. Africa
179 F1 Weener Germany
178 D3 Weert Neth.
125 G4 Weethalle Australia
125 H3 Wee Waa Australia
179 E3 Wegberg Germany
177 J3 Węgorzewo Poland
154 E1 Weichang China
179 K4 Weida Germany
179 J5 Weidenberg Germany
179 K5 Weiden in der Oberpfalz Germany
154 F2 Weifang China
160 B5 Weihai China
154 B2 Wei He r. Henan China
154 D3 Wei He r. Shaanxi China
154 E3 Weihui China
160 D2 Weihu Ling mts China
179 G4 Weilburg Germany
125 G2 Weilmoringle Australia
179 J4 Weimar Germany
154 C3 Weinan China
179 G5 Weinheim Germany
155 B5 Weining China
179 H5 Weinsberg Germany
119 E3 Weipa Australia
125 H2 Weir r. Australia
205 K3 Weir River Canada
220 C4 Weirton U.S.A.
212 C2 Weiser U.S.A.
154 E3 Weishan China
154 E3 Weishan Hu l. China
154 E3 Weishi China
179 I5 Weißenburg in Bayern Germany
179 J3 Weißenfels Germany
219 C5 Weiss Lake U.S.A.
196 C2 Weissrand Mountains Namibia
179 G5 Weiterstadt Germany
155 B5 Weixin China
144 H3 Weiya China
153 B3 Weiyuan Gansu China
155 B4 Weiyuan Sichuan China
176 G7 Weiz Austria
155 C6 Weizhou Dao i. China
160 B3 Weizi China
177 I3 Wejherowo Poland
205 J4 Wekusko Canada
205 J4 Wekusko Lake Canada
205 G2 Wekweètì Canada
121 F5 Welbourn Hill Australia
220 C6 Welch U.S.A.
221 H2 Weld U.S.A.
194 D2 Weldiya Eth.
214 C4 Weldon U.S.A.
123 C5 Welford National Park Australia
197 G2 Welgevonden Game Reserve nature res. S. Africa
194 D3 Welk'īt'ē Eth.
197 G3 Welkom S. Africa
209 H4 Welland Canada
173 G5 Welland r. U.K.
209 H4 Welland Canal Canada
147 I5 Wellawaya Sri Lanka
209 G4 Wellesley Canada
118 D3 Wellesley Islands Australia
204 B2 Wellesley Lake Canada
221 H4 Wellfleet U.S.A.
178 D4 Wellin Belgium
173 G5 Wellingborough U.K.
125 H4 Wellington N.S.W. Australia
124 C5 Wellington S.A. Australia
126 E4 Wellington N.Z.
196 C6 Wellington S. Africa
173 D7 Wellington England U.K.
173 E5 Wellington England U.K.
213 F3 Wellington CO U.S.A.
217 D4 Wellington KS U.S.A.
214 C2 Wellington NV U.S.A.
220 B4 Wellington OH U.S.A.
217 C5 Wellington TX U.S.A.
215 G2 Wellington UT U.S.A.
232 A7 Wellington, Isla i. Chile
125 G7 Wellington, Lake Australia
120 F2 Wellington Range hills N.T. Australia
121 C5 Wellington Range hills W.A. Australia
208 B5 Wellman U.S.A.
204 E4 Wells Canada
173 E6 Wells U.K.
213 D3 Wells NV U.S.A.
221 F3 Wells NY U.S.A.
118 C4 Wells, Lake salt flat Australia
221 E4 Wellsboro U.S.A.
126 E2 Wellsford N.Z.
204 E4 Wells Gray Provincial Park Canada
173 H5 Wells-next-the-Sea U.K.
220 B5 Wellston U.S.A.
221 E3 Wellsville U.S.A.
215 E5 Wellton U.S.A.
176 G6 Wels Austria
221 J2 Welshpool Canada
173 D5 Welshpool U.K.
179 L3 Welsickendorf Germany
173 G6 Welwyn Garden City U.K.
179 H6 Welzheim Germany
173 E5 Wem U.K.
197 H4 Wembesi S. Africa
204 F3 Wembley Canada
206 E3 Wemindji Canada
219 E7 Wemyss Bight Bahamas
212 B2 Wenatchee U.S.A.
234 C3 Wenceslau Braz Brazil
155 D7 Wencheng Hainan China
155 F5 Wencheng Zhejiang China
192 B4 Wenchi Ghana
155 B4 Wenchuan China
179 J5 Wendelstein Germany
179 F4 Wenden Germany
215 F5 Wenden U.S.A.
160 B5 Wendeng China
194 D3 Wendo Eth.
213 D3 Wendover U.S.A.
209 F2 Wenebegon Lake Canada
155 C5 Weng'an China
155 A4 Wengda China
155 E5 Wengyuan China
154 F3 Wen He r. China
155 B4 Wenjiang Sichuan China
155 B4 Wenjiang Sichuan China
155 F5 Wenling China
122 C2 Wenlock r. Australia
208 C5 Wenona U.S.A.
141 J3 Wenquan China
155 B6 Wenshan China
141 J4 Wensu China
173 H5 Wensum r. U.K.
179 I1 Wentorf bei Hamburg Germany
124 D5 Wentworth Australia
221 H3 Wentworth U.S.A.
154 B3 Wenxian China
155 F5 Wenzhou China
179 K2 Wenzlow Germany
197 G4 Wepener S. Africa
179 J2 Werben (Elbe) Germany
197 E2 Werda Botswana
179 K4 Werdau Germany
179 K2 Werder (Havel) Germany
179 F3 Werdohl Germany
179 F3 Werl Germany
179 K5 Wernberg-Köblitz Germany
179 F3 Werne Germany
204 C2 Wernecke Mountains Canada
179 I3 Wernigerode Germany
179 H3 Werra r. Germany
124 D5 Werrimull Australia
125 I3 Werris Creek Australia
179 H5 Wertheim Germany
178 B4 Wervik Belgium
179 E3 Wesel Germany
179 E3 Wesel-Datteln-Kanal canal Germany
179 K1 Wesenberg Germany
179 I2 Wesendorf Germany
179 H2 Weser r. Germany
179 G1 Weser sea chan. Germany
179 G2 Wesergebirge hills Germany
217 C4 Weskan U.S.A.
209 I3 Weslemkoon Lake Canada
221 J2 Wesley U.S.A.
207 J4 Wesleyville Canada
118 D3 Wessel, Cape Australia
118 D3 Wessel Islands Australia
197 H3 Wesselton S. Africa
216 D2 Wessington Springs U.S.A.
121 F7 Westall, Point Australia
208 C4 West Allis U.S.A.
127 I4 West Antarctica reg. Antarctica
238 K6 West Australian Basin sea feature Indian Ocean
148 B5 West Banas r. India
138 E5 West Bank disp. terr Asia
207 I3 West Bay Canada
217 F6 West Bay b. U.S.A.
208 C4 West Bend U.S.A.
149 F5 West Bengal state India
209 E3 West Branch U.S.A.
173 F5 West Bromwich U.K.
221 H3 Westbrook U.S.A.
West Burra i. U.K. see Burra
125 G8 Westbury Australia
173 E6 Westbury U.K.
125 G5 Westby Australia
121 B7 West Cape Howe Australia
236 E5 West Caroline Basin sea feature N. Pacific Ocean
221 F5 West Chester U.S.A.
221 G2 West Danville U.S.A.
209 F3 West Duck Island Canada
219 E7 West End Bahamas
215 D4 Westend U.S.A.
219 E7 West End Point Bahamas
179 F4 Westerburg Germany
179 F1 Westerholt Germany
176 D3 Westerland Germany
178 C3 Westerlo Belgium
221 H4 Westerly U.S.A.
205 H1 Western r. Canada
118 C4 Western Australia state Australia
196 D6 Western Cape prov. S. Africa
193 E2 Western Desert Egypt
Western Dvina r. Europe see Zapadnaya Dvina
147 G2 Western Ghats mts India
125 F7 Western Port b. Australia
192 A2 Western Sahara disp. terr Africa
178 B3 Westerschelde est. Neth.
179 F1 Westerstede Germany
179 F4 Westerwald hills Germany
232 D8 West Falkland i. Falkland Is
216 D2 West Fargo U.S.A.
208 D5 Westfield IN U.S.A.
221 G3 Westfield MA U.S.A.
221 J1 Westfield ME U.S.A.
220 D3 Westfield NY U.S.A.
178 C1 West Frisian Islands Neth.
179 E1 Westgat sea chan. Neth.
123 D5 Westgate Australia
221 J2 West Grand Lake U.S.A.
179 I6 Westhausen Germany
175 F3 Westhill U.K.
216 C1 Westhope U.S.A.
127 L5 West Ice Shelf Antarctica
111 West Indies is Caribbean Sea
178 B3 Westkapelle Neth.
155 □ West Lamma Channel China
220 B5 West Lancaster U.S.A.
123 C4 Westland Australia
126 B5 Westland Tai Poutini National Park N.Z.
173 I5 Westleton U.K.
214 B3 Westley U.S.A.
220 B6 West Liberty KY U.S.A.
220 B4 West Liberty OH U.S.A.
174 E5 West Linton U.K.
174 B2 West Loch Roag b. U.K.
205 G4 Westlock Canada
209 G4 West Lorne Canada
121 F4 West MacDonnell National Park Australia
178 C3 Westmalle Belgium
236 E4 West Mariana Basin sea feature Pacific Ocean
217 F5 West Memphis U.S.A.
221 E5 Westminster MD U.S.A.
219 D5 Westminster SC U.S.A.
122 B3 Westmoreland Australia
220 C5 Weston U.S.A.
173 E6 Weston-super-Mare U.K.
221 F5 Westover U.S.A.
219 D7 West Palm Beach U.S.A.
217 F4 West Plains U.S.A.
124 A5 West Point pt S.A. Australia
125 F8 West Point pt Tas. Australia
217 F5 West Point MS U.S.A.
221 F4 West Point NY U.S.A.
209 I3 Westport Canada
175 I4 Westport Ireland
126 C4 Westport N.Z.
214 A2 Westport U.S.A.
205 I4 Westray Canada
174 E1 Westray i. U.K.
209 G2 Westree Canada
179 F5 Westrich reg. Germany
204 E4 West Road r. Canada
133 J3 West Siberian Plain Russia
125 G7 West Sister Island Australia
221 H2 West Stewartstown U.S.A.
178 D1 West-Terschelling Neth.
221 H4 West Tisbury U.S.A.
221 G2 West Topsham U.S.A.
221 G3 West Townshend U.S.A.
208 B4 West Union IA U.S.A.
220 B5 West Union OH U.S.A.
220 C5 West Union WV U.S.A.
208 D5 Westville U.S.A.
220 C5 West Virginia state U.S.A.
214 C2 West Walker r. U.S.A.
214 B1 Westwood U.S.A.
125 G4 West Wyalong Australia
212 E2 West Yellowstone U.S.A.
178 C2 Westzaan Neth.
151 E7 Wetar i. Indon.
205 G4 Wetaskiwin Canada
208 D2 Wetmore U.S.A.
179 G4 Wetter r. Germany
179 J3 Wettin Germany
179 G4 Wetzlar Germany
119 E2 Wewak P.N.G.
175 L5 Wexford Ireland
205 H4 Weyakwin Canada
208 C3 Weyauwega U.S.A.
173 G6 Weybridge U.K.
205 I5 Weyburn Canada
179 G2 Weyhe Germany
173 E7 Weymouth U.K.
221 H3 Weymouth U.S.A.
179 E2 Wezep Neth.
126 F2 Whakaari i. N.Z.
126 F2 Whakatane N.Z.
126 F3 Whakatane r. N.Z.
162 A3 Whale Bay Myanmar
204 B3 Whale Bay U.S.A.
219 E7 Whale Cay i. Bahamas
205 K2 Whale Cove Canada
174 □ Whalsay i. U.K.
126 E2 Whangamata N.Z.
126 E3 Whangamomona N.Z.
126 E3 Whanganui National Park N.Z.
126 E1 Whangarei N.Z.
206 E2 Whapmagoostui Canada
173 F4 Wharfe r. U.K.
209 F2 Wharncliffe Canada
205 I2 Wharton Lake Canada
208 A5 What Cheer U.S.A.
204 F2 Whatî Canada
213 F3 Wheatland U.S.A.
208 C5 Wheaton U.S.A.
213 F4 Wheeler Peak NM U.S.A.
215 E2 Wheeler Peak NV U.S.A.
220 C4 Wheeling U.S.A.
235 K2 Wheelwright Arg.
172 E3 Whernside h. U.K.
124 A5 Whidbey, Point Australia
121 E5 Whinham, Mount Australia
213 B3 Whiskeytown Shasta Trinity National Recreation Area park U.S.A.
174 E5 Whitburn U.K.
209 H4 Whitby Canada
172 G3 Whitby U.K.
173 E5 Whitchurch U.K.
204 A2 White r. Canada/U.S.A.
217 E4 White r. AR U.S.A.
213 E3 White r. CO U.S.A.
219 C4 White r. IN U.S.A.
208 D4 White r. MI U.S.A.
215 E2 White r. NV U.S.A.
216 C3 White r. SD U.S.A.
208 B2 White r. WI U.S.A.
215 G5 White watercourse U.S.A.
118 C4 White, Lake salt flat Australia
207 I3 White Bay Canada
216 C2 White Butte mt. U.S.A.
125 E3 White Cliffs Australia
209 E4 White Cloud U.S.A.
204 F4 Whitecourt Canada
208 A2 Whiteface Lake U.S.A.
221 H2 Whitefield U.S.A.
209 G2 Whitefish Canada
212 D1 Whitefish U.S.A.
208 D3 Whitefish r. U.S.A.
205 H2 Whitefish Lake Canada
209 E2 Whitefish Point U.S.A.
175 F1 Whitehall U.K.
221 G3 Whitehall NY U.S.A.
208 B3 Whitehall WI U.S.A.
172 D3 Whitehaven U.K.
175 M3 Whitehead U.K.
173 G6 Whitehill U.K.
204 B2 Whitehorse Canada
173 F6 White Horse, Vale of val. U.K.
215 E1 White Horse Pass U.S.A.
217 E6 White Lake LA U.S.A.
208 D4 White Lake MI U.S.A.
214 C3 White Mountain Peak U.S.A.
221 H2 White Mountains U.S.A.
123 D4 White Mountains National Park Australia
193 F3 White Nile r. Africa alt. Abiad, Bahr el, alt. Jabal, Bahr el
196 C1 White Nossob watercourse Namibia
215 E2 White Pine Range mts U.S.A.
221 G4 White Plains U.S.A.
206 C4 White River Canada
215 H5 Whiteriver U.S.A.
221 G3 White River Junction U.S.A.
215 E2 White River Valley U.S.A.
215 E2 White Rock Peak U.S.A.
213 F5 White Sands National Monument nat. park U.S.A.
220 B6 Whitesburg U.S.A.
132 E3 White Sea Russia
205 J4 Whiteshell Provincial Park Canada
212 E2 White Sulphur Springs MT U.S.A.
220 C6 White Sulphur Springs WV U.S.A.
219 E5 Whiteville U.S.A.
192 B4 White Volta r. Ghana
208 C4 Whitewater U.S.A.
215 H5 Whitewater Baldy mt. U.S.A.
206 C3 Whitewater Lake Canada
123 C4 Whitewood Australia
205 I4 Whitewood Canada
125 G6 Whitfield Australia
173 I6 Whitfield U.K.
174 D6 Whithorn U.K.
126 E2 Whitianga N.Z.
221 J2 Whiting U.S.A.
173 C6 Whitland U.K.
172 F2 Whitley Bay U.K.
219 D5 Whitmire U.S.A.
209 H3 Whitney Canada
214 C3 Whitney, Mount U.S.A.
221 J2 Whitneyville U.S.A.
173 I6 Whitstable U.K.
123 E4 Whitsunday Group is Australia
119 E4 Whitsunday Island Australia
123 E4 Whitsunday Island National Park Australia
125 F6 Whittlesea Australia
173 G5 Whittlesey U.K.
125 G5 Whitton Australia
205 H2 Wholdaia Lake Canada
215 F5 Why U.S.A.
124 B4 Whyalla Australia
162 B1 Wiang Sa Thai.
209 G3 Wiarton Canada
178 B3 Wichelen Belgium
217 D4 Wichita U.S.A.
217 D5 Wichita Falls U.S.A.
217 D5 Wichita Mountains U.S.A.
174 E2 Wick U.K.
215 F5 Wickenburg U.S.A.
173 H6 Wickford U.K.
120 E3 Wickham r. Australia
125 E7 Wickham, Cape Australia
120 E3 Wickham, Mount h. Australia
175 L5 Wicklow Ireland
175 M5 Wicklow Head Ireland
175 L5 Wicklow Mountains Ireland
175 L4 Wicklow Mountains National Park Ireland
125 G2 Widgeegoara watercourse Australia
121 C6 Widgiemooltha (abandoned) Australia
173 E4 Widnes U.K.
160 D6 Wi-do i. S. Korea
179 G2 Wiehengebirge hills Germany
179 F4 Wiehl Germany
177 I5 Wieluń Poland
Wien Austria see Vienna
177 H7 Wiener Neustadt Austria
179 E2 Wierden Neth.
179 I2 Wieren Germany
178 C2 Wieringermeer Polder Neth.
178 D2 Wieringerwerf Neth.
179 G4 Wiesbaden Germany
179 K5 Wiesenfelden Germany
179 I5 Wiesentheid Germany
179 G5 Wiesloch Germany
179 F1 Wiesmoor Germany
179 H2 Wietze Germany
179 H2 Wietzendorf Germany
177 I3 Wieżyca h. Poland
173 E4 Wigan U.K.
217 F6 Wiggins U.S.A.
173 F7 Wight, Isle of i. U.K.
205 H2 Wignes Lake Canada
173 F5 Wigston U.K.
172 D3 Wigton U.K.
174 D6 Wigtown U.K.
174 D6 Wigtown Bay U.K.
178 D3 Wijchen Neth.
179 E2 Wijhe Neth.
178 C3 Wijnegem Belgium
215 F4 Wikieup U.S.A.
209 G3 Wikwemikong Canada
122 B1 Wilberforce, Cape Australia
212 C2 Wilbur U.S.A.
125 E3 Wilcannia Australia
179 K2 Wildberg Germany
205 I4 Wildcat Hill Provincial Wilderness Park Canada
215 D2 Wildcat Peak U.S.A.
197 H5 Wild Coast S. Africa
179 G2 Wildeshausen Germany
208 C1 Wild Goose Canada
204 F4 Wildhay r. Canada
208 A2 Wild Rice Lake U.S.A.
176 E7 Wildspitze mt. Austria
219 D6 Wildwood FL U.S.A.
221 F5 Wildwood NJ U.S.A.
197 H3 Wilge r. Free State S. Africa
197 H2 Wilge r. Gauteng/Mpumalanga S. Africa
124 A3 Wilgena Australia
220 C4 Wilhelm, Lake U.S.A.
119 E2 Wilhelm, Mount P.N.G.
179 G1 Wilhelmshaven Germany
179 H3 Wilhelmshöhe, Bergpark tourist site Germany
221 F4 Wilkes-Barre U.S.A.
127 J6 Wilkes Land reg. Antarctica
205 H4 Wilkie Canada
127 I3 Wilkins Ice Shelf Antarctica
121 F6 Wilkinson Lakes salt flat Australia
204 D3 Will, Mount Canada
212 B2 Willamette r. U.S.A.
173 D7 Willand U.K.
125 F4 Willandra Billabong watercourse Australia
125 F4 Willandra National Park Australia
212 B1 Willapa Bay U.S.A.
220 B4 Willard U.S.A.
221 F5 Willards U.S.A.
215 H5 Willcox U.S.A.
179 H3 Willebadessen Germany
178 C3 Willebroek Belgium
223 K6 Willemstad Neth. Antilles
120 E2 Willeroo Australia
205 H3 William r. Canada
125 E6 William, Mount Australia
124 B2 William Creek Australia
215 F4 Williams AZ U.S.A.
214 A2 Williams CA U.S.A.
208 A5 Williamsburg IA U.S.A.

141 J1 Zav'yalovo Russia
154 A2 Zawa China
177 I5 Zawiercie Poland
143 H3 Zayd Ābād Afgh.
141 K3 Zaysan Kazakh.
141 J2 Zaysan, Lake Kazakh.
Zayü China see Zhigang
176 G6 Žd'ár nad Sázavou Czech Rep.
187 C5 Zdolbuniv Ukr.
171 J5 Zealand i. Denmark
197 H2 Zebediela S. Africa
178 B3 Zedelgem Belgium
178 B3 Zeebrugge Belgium
125 F8 Zeehan Australia
197 G2 Zeerust S. Africa
178 B3 Zeeuwsch-Vlaanderen reg. Neth.
138 E5 Zefat Israel
179 L2 Zehdenick Germany
118 D4 Zeil, Mount Australia
179 I4 Zeil am Main Germany
178 D2 Zeist Neth.
179 K3 Zeitz Germany
154 A3 Zêkog China
141 H1 Zelenaya Roshcha Kazakh.
170 P2 Zelenoborskiy Russia
187 I4 Zelenodol'sk Russia
171 O3 Zelenogorsk Russia
186 F3 Zelenograd Russia
187 B4 Zelenogradsk Russia
187 G6 Zelenokumsk Russia
186 H3 Zelentsovo Russia
157 G4 Zelennyy, Ostrov i. Russia
141 G2 Zelenyy Gay Kazakh.
176 F7 Zell am See Austria
179 H5 Zellingen Germany
178 B3 Zelzate Belgium
154 A3 Zêmdasam China
187 G4 Zemetchino Russia
194 C3 Zémio C.A.R.
183 Q5 Zemmora Alg.
225 E4 Zempoala, Pirámides de tourist site Mex.
225 F4 Zempoaltépetl, Nudo de mt. Mex.
155 D6 Zengcheng China
160 E2 Zengfeng Shan mt. China
214 A1 Zenia U.S.A.
185 G2 Zenica Bos. & Herz.
173 B7 Zennor U.K.
214 C2 Zephyr Cove U.S.A.
141 I5 Zepu China
143 F4 Zerah, Gowd-e depr. Afgh.
Zeravshan r. Uzbek. see Zarafshon
179 K3 Zerbst/Anhalt Germany
Zereh, Lake plain Afgh. see Zerah, Gowd-e
141 G1 Zerendy Kazakh.
179 E5 Zerf Germany
179 I1 Zernien Germany
179 K2 Zernitz Germany
187 G6 Zernograd Russia
187 G7 Zest'aponi Georgia
Zêtang China see Nêdong
179 F1 Zetel Germany
179 J4 Zeulenroda Germany
179 H1 Zeven Germany
179 E3 Zevenaar Neth.
150 E1 Zeya Russia
150 E1 Zeya r. Russia
142 D4 Zeydābād Iran
143 E2 Zeydar Iran
143 E4 Zeynalābād Iran
156 B1 Zeyskiy Zapovednik nature res. Russia
156 C2 Zeysko-Bureinskaya Vpadina depr. Russia
150 E1 Zeyskoye Vodokhranilishche resr Russia

183 M3 Zêzere r. Port.
177 I5 Zgierz Poland
187 C4 Zhabinka Belarus
Zhaggo China see Luhuo
141 F2 Zhaksy Kazakh.
141 G2 Zhaksy-Kon watercourse Kazakh.
140 E3 Zhaksykylysh Kazakh.
140 E3 Zhaksykylysh, Ozero salt l. Kazakh.
141 F3 Zhalagash Kazakh.
141 J2 Zhalgyztobe Kazakh.
140 B2 Zhalpaktal Kazakh.
141 G2 Zhaltyr Akmolinskaya Oblast' Kazakh.
141 I2 Zhaltyr Pavlodarskaya Oblast' Kazakh.
140 B3 Zhaltyr, Ozero l. Kazakh.
140 E2 Zhamanakkol', Ozero salt l. Kazakh.
140 C3 Zhamansor Kazakh.
141 G3 Zhambyl Kazakh.
141 G3 Zhambylskaya Oblast' admin. div. Kazakh.
141 J3 Zhameuka Kazakh.
141 G3 Zhanabas (abandoned) Kazakh.
140 B3 Zhanakala Kazakh.
140 B2 Zhanakazan Kazakh.
140 E3 Zhanakentkala tourist site Kazakh.
141 F4 Zhanakorgan Kazakh.
140 E3 Zhanakurylys Kazakh.
141 F3 Zhanala tourist site Kazakh.
141 H3 Zhanaortalyk Kazakh.
140 C4 Zhanaozen Kazakh.
141 I4 Zhanatalan Kazakh.
141 G4 Zhanatas Kazakh.
140 E3 Zhanay Kazakh.
140 B3 Zhanbay Kazakh.
156 B2 Zhanbei China
154 E1 Zhangbei China
160 E1 Zhangguangcai Ling mts China
160 B2 Zhanggutai China
154 E2 Zhang He r. China
155 F5 Zhanghua Taiwan
155 D4 Zhangjiajie China
154 E1 Zhangjiakou China
154 A3 Zhangla China
156 A1 Zhangling China
155 E5 Zhangping China
155 E5 Zhangpu China
160 B2 Zhangqiang China
155 E4 Zhangshu China
154 E2 Zhangwei Xinhe r. China
160 B2 Zhangwu China
154 B3 Zhangxian China
154 A2 Zhangye China
155 E5 Zhangzhou China
154 D2 Zhangzi China
160 B4 Zhangzi Dao i. China
Zhanhe China see Zhanbei
154 F2 Zhanhua China
140 A2 Zhanibek Kazakh.
155 D6 Zhanjiang China
141 I3 Zhansugirov Kazakh.
140 C3 Zhanterek Kazakh.
155 B5 Zhanyi China
155 E6 Zhao'an China
156 B3 Zhaodong China
155 B4 Zhaojue China
155 D5 Zhaoping China
155 D6 Zhaoqing China
141 J4 Zhaosu China
160 B2 Zhaosutai He r. China
155 B5 Zhaotong China
154 E2 Zhaoxian China
160 C1 Zhaoyuan China
156 B3 Zhaozhou China
155 D6 Zhapo China

141 J3 Zharbulak Kazakh.
149 F3 Zhari Namco salt l. China
140 D3 Zharkamys Kazakh.
141 J3 Zharkent Kazakh.
187 E4 Zharkovskiy Russia
140 C4 Zharma Mangystauskaya Oblast' Kazakh.
141 J2 Zharma Vostochnyy Kazakhstan Kazakh.
141 J3 Zharsuat (abandoned) Kazakh.
141 F3 Zharyk Kazakh.
187 D5 Zhashkiv Ukr.
154 C3 Zhashui China
Zhaslyk Uzbek. see Jaslïq
149 F2 Zhaxi Co salt l. China
148 D2 Zhaxigang China
141 G2 Zhayrem Kazakh.
154 E3 Zhecheng China
155 F4 Zhejiang prov. China
141 H2 Zhekezhal Kazakh.
132 H2 Zhelaniya, Mys c. Russia
141 H1 Zhelezinka Kazakh.
187 E4 Zheleznogorsk Russia
141 H3 Zheltorangy Kazakh.
140 C3 Zhem r. Kazakh.
154 C3 Zhen'an China
154 C3 Zhenba China
155 C4 Zheng'an China
154 E2 Zhengding China
155 F5 Zhenghe China
Zhenglan Qi China see Shangdu
154 E3 Zhengning China
Zhengxiangbai Qi China see Ming'antu
154 E3 Zhengyang China
154 D3 Zhengzhou China
155 F4 Zhenhai China
154 F3 Zhenjiang China
154 B3 Zhenjiangguan China
156 A3 Zhenlai China
155 B5 Zhenning China
154 D3 Zhenping China
155 B5 Zhenxiong China
154 C3 Zhenyuan Gansu China
155 C5 Zhenyuan Guizhou China
187 G5 Zherdevka Russia
155 F5 Zherong China
186 I2 Zheshart Russia
140 C4 Zhetybay Kazakh.
140 C2 Zhetykol', Ozero l. Russia
135 F2 Zhetysuskiy Alatau mts China/Kazakh.
155 D4 Zhexi Shuiku resr China
141 F2 Zhezdy Kazakh.
141 F3 Zhezkazgan Karagandinskaya Oblast' Kazakh.
141 F3 Zhezkazgan Karagandinskaya Oblast' Kazakh.
155 D4 Zhicheng China
154 C2 Zhidan China
149 H2 Zhidoi China
153 I1 Zhigalovo Russia
151 B4 Zhigang China
133 N3 Zhigansk Russia
149 G3 Zhigung China
155 D4 Zhijiang Hubei China
155 C5 Zhijiang Hunan China
155 B5 Zhijin China
Zhi Qu r. China see Yangtze
187 H5 Zhirnovsk Russia
Zhishan China see Lingling
140 E1 Zhitikara Kazakh.
187 H5 Zhitkur Russia
139 K4 Zhīvār Iran
187 D4 Zhlobin Belarus

187 D5 Zhmerynka Ukr.
148 B3 Zhob Pak.
148 B3 Zhob r. Pak.
133 Q2 Zhokhova, Ostrov i. Russia
141 J2 Zholnuskau Kazakh.
141 G2 Zholymbet Kazakh.
149 F3 Zhongba China
Zhongdian China see Xamgyi'nyilha
155 B4 Zhongjiang China
154 B2 Zhongning China
127 L5 Zhongshan research stn Antarctica
155 D6 Zhongshan Guangdong China
155 D5 Zhongshan Guangxi Zhuangzu Zizhiqu China
Zhongshan Guizhou China see Liupanshui
154 D3 Zhongtiao Shan mts China
154 B2 Zhongwei China
155 C4 Zhongxian China
155 E5 Zhongxin China
155 F6 Zhongyang Shanmo mts Taiwan
156 B2 Zhongyaozhan China
Zhongyicun China see Gucheng
154 D7 Zhongyuan China
141 F3 Zhosaly Kazakh.
154 E3 Zhoucheng China
155 C4 Zhou He r. China
154 B2 Zhoujiajing China
154 E3 Zhoukou China
155 F5 Zhouning China
155 G4 Zhoushan China
153 L5 Zhoushan Dao i. China
187 C5 Zhovti Vody Ukr.
160 B4 Zhuanghe China
154 B3 Zhuanglang China
154 D3 Zhuantobe Kazakh.
154 F3 Zhucheng China
160 C1 Zhuchengzi China
155 F5 Zhudong Taiwan
154 C3 Zhugqu China
155 D6 Zhuhai China
155 F4 Zhuji China
155 F4 Zhujing China
187 E4 Zhukovka Russia
154 E2 Zhulong He r. China
154 D3 Zhumadian China
140 B3 Zhumysker Kazakh.
155 C4 Zhuo He r. China
154 E1 Zhuolu China
154 E2 Zhuozhou China
154 D1 Zhuozi China
141 G2 Zhuravlevka Kazakh.
140 D2 Zhuryn Kazakh.
141 H3 Zhusandala, Step' plain Kazakh.
154 D3 Zhushan China
154 C3 Zhuxi China
155 D5 Zhuzhou Hunan China
155 D6 Zhuzhou Hunan China
187 C5 Zhydachiv Ukr.
140 C2 Zhympity Kazakh.
140 B3 Zhyngyldy Kazakh.
187 C4 Zhytkavichy Belarus
187 D5 Zhytomyr Ukr.
177 I6 Žiar nad Hronom Slovakia
139 I3 Zībār Iraq
154 F2 Zibo China
154 C2 Zichang China
176 G5 Zielona Góra Poland
179 H3 Zierenberg Germany
179 K2 Ziesar Germany
138 C6 Ziftá Egypt
139 L1 Zığ Azer.
149 H5 Zigaing Myanmar
149 G2 Zigê Tangco l. China

155 B4 Zigong China
192 A3 Ziguinchor Senegal
171 N4 Žiguri Latvia
154 F2 Zi He r. China
225 D4 Zihuatanejo Mex.
155 E6 Zijin China
179 E3 Zijpenberg h. Neth.
138 E5 Zikhron Ya'aqov Israel
140 D1 Zilair Russia
138 E5 Zile Turkey
177 I6 Žilina Slovakia
150 C1 Zima Russia
225 E4 Zimapán Mex.
225 E4 Zimatlán Mex.
195 C5 Zimba Zambia
195 C5 Zimbabwe country Africa
142 B3 Zīmkān, Rūdkhāneh-ye r. Iran
192 A4 Zimmi Sierra Leone
185 K3 Zimnicea Romania
169 N2 Zimniy Bereg coastal area Russia
187 G6 Zimovniki Russia
138 E4 Zimrīn Syria
143 F3 Zindah Jān Afgh.
192 C3 Zinder Niger
192 B3 Ziniaré Burkina Faso
215 G5 Zion National Park U.S.A.
206 B3 Zionz Lake Canada
233 I3 Zipaquirá Col.
149 F2 Ziqudukou China
179 I5 Zirndorf Germany
149 H4 Ziro India
155 E5 Zi Shui r. China
177 H6 Zistersdorf Austria
225 D4 Zitácuaro Mex.
176 G5 Zittau Germany
139 J3 Zīveh Iran
155 E5 Zixi China
154 E2 Ziya He r. China
154 B1 Zizhiqu aut. reg. China
155 B5 Zizhong China
185 K3 Zlatitsa Bulg.
156 D1 Zlatoustovsk Russia
177 H6 Zlín Czech Rep.
187 D4 Zlynka Russia
141 J2 Zmeinogorsk Russia
181 K1 Zmiyevka Russia
187 F5 Zmiyiv Ukr.
141 I1 Znamenka Altayskiy Kray Russia
187 E4 Znamenka Orlovskaya Oblast' Russia
140 D1 Znamenskiy Russia
187 E5 Znam"yanka Ukr.
177 H6 Znojmo Czech Rep.
176 D6 Zoar S. Africa
139 K4 Zobeyrī Iran
178 C2 Zoetermeer Neth.
Zoganiawar China see Huashixia
152 G6 Zogang China
139 J4 Zohāb Iran
154 B3 Zoigê China
140 D4 Zoir Uzbek.
178 D3 Zolder Belgium
187 E5 Zolochiv Kharkivs'ka Oblast' Ukr.
187 C5 Zolochiv L'vivs'ka Oblast' Ukr.
187 E5 Zolotonosha Ukr.

141 G1 Zolotorunnoye Kazakh.
187 F4 Zolotukhino Russia
195 D5 Zomba Malawi
141 G5 Zomin Uzbek.
138 C1 Zonguldak Turkey
149 G3 Zongxoi China
155 E4 Zongyang China
184 C4 Zonza Corsica France
179 K3 Zörbig Germany
192 B3 Zorgho Burkina Faso
141 H5 Zorkül l. Afgh./Tajik.
192 B4 Zorzor Liberia
178 B4 Zottegem Belgium
193 D2 Zouar Chad
154 E3 Zoucheng China
192 A2 Zouérat Mauritania
154 E2 Zouping China
180 C5 Zousfana, Oued watercourse Alg.
155 D4 Zoushi China
185 I2 Zrenjanin Serbia
179 L3 Zschopau Germany
179 K3 Zschornewitz Germany
233 K2 Zuata r. Venez.
142 A4 Zubālah, Birkat waterhole Saudi Arabia
235 J3 Zubillaga Arg.
187 G4 Zubova Polyana Russia
192 B4 Zuénoula Côte d'Ivoire
176 D7 Zug Switz.
187 G4 Zugdidi Georgia
176 D7 Zuger See l. Switz.
176 E7 Zugspitze mt. Austria/Germany
Zuider Zee l. Neth. see IJsselmeer
179 E1 Zuidhorn Neth.
178 C2 Zuid-Kennemerland, Nationaal Park nat. park Neth.
183 N3 Zújar r. Spain
233 I2 Zulia r. Col.
179 E2 Zülpich Germany
195 D5 Zumbo Moz.
208 A3 Zumbro r. U.S.A.
208 A3 Zumbrota U.S.A.
225 E4 Zumpango Mex.
192 C4 Zungeru Nigeria
154 F1 Zunhua China
215 H4 Zuni U.S.A.
215 H4 Zuni Mountains U.S.A.
155 C5 Zunyi Guizhou China
155 C5 Zunyi Guizhou China
155 C6 Zuo Jiang r. China/Vietnam
154 D2 Zuoquan China
154 D2 Zuoyun China
139 K5 Zurbāṭīyah Iraq
176 D7 Zürich Switz.
143 H3 Zurmat reg. Afgh.
179 E2 Zutphen Neth.
193 D1 Zuwārah Libya
186 I3 Zuyevka Russia
171 N4 Zvejniekciems Latvia
187 I4 Zvenigovo Russia
187 D5 Zvenyhorodka Ukr.
141 G1 Zverinogolovskoye Russia
195 D6 Zvishavane Zimbabwe
177 I6 Zvolen Slovakia
185 H2 Zvornik Bos. & Herz.
192 B4 Zwedru Liberia
179 E2 Zweeloo Neth.
179 F5 Zweibrücken Germany
179 L3 Zwethau Germany
176 G7 Zwettl Austria
179 K4 Zwickau Germany
179 K3 Zwochau Germany
179 E2 Zwolle Neth.
179 K4 Zwönitz Germany
133 Q3 Zyryanka Russia
141 K2 Zyryanovsk Kazakh.

ACKNOWLEDGEMENTS
ATLAS OF THE WORLD
Maps, design and origination by Collins Bartholomew, HarperCollins Publishers, Glasgow

Illustrations created by HarperCollins Publishers unless otherwise stated.

Cover: Vatnajökull Glacier, Iceland © Image Source/Alamy

Pages 2–15 SATELLITE IMAGES

2–13
Blue Marble: Next Generation. NASA's Earth Observatory
14–15
Landsat Image Mosaic of Antarctica (LIMA) Project and
Blue Marble: Next Generation. NASA's Earth Observatory

Pages 64–87 GEOGRAPHICAL INFORMATION

64–65
Babylonian World map: © British Museum, London, UK
Smith Geological map: © The Natural History Museum, London, UK
Ptolemaic World map: The British Library, London, UK
Carte de France: Reproduced by permission of the Trustees of the
National Library of Scotland, Edinburgh, UK
Sydney Harbour: Google – Data SIO, NOAA, U.S. Navy, NGA GEBCO
Venice: NASA Earth Observatory images by Jesse Allen and Robert
Simmon, using Landsat data from the U.S. Geological Survey.
Collaborative mapping: OpenStreetMap under Creative Commons
Attribution-Share Alike 2.0 license
Earthquakes data USGS. Map Mashp http://sunild.com/proto/
Earthquakes2/Earthquakes.html
66–67
MODIS/NASA
68–69
Earthquake data: United States Geological Survey (USGS) National
Earthquakes Information Center, Denver, USA
Japan: NASA Earth Observatory images created by Jesse Allen, using
data provided courtesy of NASA/GSFC/METI/ERSDAC/JAROS, and
U.S./Japan ASTER Science Team.
Barðarbunga: Marisa Estivill/Shutterstock
70–71
Arkansas: NASA Earth Observatory image by Jesse Allen and Robert
Simmon, using EO-1 ALI data provided courtesy of the NASA EO-1
team.
Cyclone Pam: NASA images courtesy Jeff Schmaltz, LANCE/EOSDIS
MODIS Rapid Response Team at NASA GSFC. NASA VIIRS image
by Jesse Allen, using data from the Suomi National Polar-orbiting
Partnership.
Köppen classification map: Kottek, M., J. Grieser, C. Beck, B. Rudolf,
and F. Rubel, 2006: World Map of the Köppen-Geiger climate
classification updated. Meteorol. Z., 15, 259–263.
http://koeppen-geiger.vu-wien.ac.at
72–73
Climate: Tracks of tropical storms from National Oceanic and
Atmospheric Administration (NOAA) National Hurricane Centre.
IPCC, 2013: Summary for Policymakers. In: Climate Change 2013:
The Physical Science Basis. Contribution of Working Group I to
the Fifth Assessment Report of the Intergovernmental Panel on
Climate Change [Stocker, T.F., D. Qin, G.-K. Plattner, M. Tignor, S.K.
Allen, J. Boschung, A. Nauels, Y. Xia, V. Bex and P.M. Midgley (eds.)].
Cambridge University Press, Cambridge, United Kingdom and New
York, NY, USA, in press.
Scripps Institution of Oceanography/NOAA Earth Systems Research
Laboratory
Pedersen Glacier, top: NSIDC/Louis H. Pedersen;
bottom: NSIDC/Bruce F. Molina
Male: Shahee Ilyas
74–75
Land Cover map data: © ESA 2010 and UCLouvain.
Arino, O., Ramos, J., Kalogirou, V., Defourny, P., Achard, F., 2010.
GlobCover 2009. ESA Living Planet Symposium 2010,
28th June – 2nd July, Bergen, Norway, SP-686, ESA,
www.esa.int/due/globcover
Living Planet Index: McRae L, Freeman R & Deinet S (2014) 'The
Living Planet Index' in: Living Planet Report 2014: species and
spaces, people and places [McLellan, R., Iyengar, L., Jeffries, B. and
N. Oerlemans (Eds)]. WWF, Gland, Switzerland.
Protected Area of the World: UNEP-WCMC and World Database on
Protected Areas for terrestrial ecoregions as identified by the World
Wide Fund for Nature (WWF). www.unep-wcmc.org/wdpa
Sea Around Us Project (L. Wood, 2007), University of British
Columbia Fisheries Centre, in collaboration with UNEP-WCMC and
WWF, for large marine ecosystems. www.mpaglobal.org
Hamoun Wetlands: USGS
Water data: 1962 Aquastat data © The Food and Agriculture
Organization of the United Nations.
http://www.fao.org/nr/water/aquastat/main/index.stm
2013: World Bank
http://data.worldbank.org/data-catalog/world-development-indicators
76–77
Population statistics: UN Department of Economic and Social Affairs
Population Division
Population map: 2005. Gridded Population of the World Version
3 (GPWv3). Palisades, NY: Socioeconomic Data and Applications
Center (SEDAC), Columbia University.
Available at: http://sedac.ciesin.columbia.edu/gpw http://www.ciesin.
columbia.edu
Shanghai: TonyV3112/Shutterstock.com

78–79
USGS EROS DATA CENTER
80–81
Edgar Cleijne/Robert Harding
82–83
Statistics from International Telecommunication Union (ITU), ICT
statistics http://www.itu.int/en/ITU-D/Statistics/Pages/stat/default.
aspx and Groupe Speciale Mobile Association (GSMA) Intelligence
https://gsmaintelligence.com/
84–85
Lake Eyre: MODIS/NASA
New Guinea: NASA/Goddard Space Flight Center/USGS
Borneo: NASA/Goddard Space Flight Center/USGS
Mt Everest: Blazej Lyjak/Shutterstock
Volga: MODIS/NASA
Caspian Sea: MODIS/NASA
Madagascar: MODIS/NASA
Kilimanjaro: enote/Shutterstock
86–87
Mississippi: ASTER/NASA
Greenland: MODIS/NASA
Mt McKinley: PhotosbyElliot/Shutterstock
Lake Titicaca: NASA
Cerro Aconcagua: Leonardo Azevedo/Shutterstock
Amazon: MODIS/NASA
Mount Sidley: NASA Earth Observatory/USGS

Pages 110–240 ATLAS OF THE WORLD

110–111
Great Barrier Reef: Provided by the SeaWiFS Project, NASA/Goddard
Space Flight Center, and OrbImage
Kamchatka Peninsula: NASA/MODIS
Desert Oasis: faberfoto/Shutterstock
Great Plains: Dirk Ercken/Shutterstock
112–113
SVLuma/Shutterstock
120-121
NASA/GSFC/MITI/ERSDAC/JAROS, and U.S./Japan ASTER Science
Team
124–125
Rodney Haywood
127
Sea ice extents data: National Snow and Ice Data Center (NSIDC),
University of Colorado, USA
132–133
top: Jaques Descloitres, MODIS Land Rapid Response Team, NASA/
GSFC
bottom: withGod/shutterstock
136–137
NASA/JSC Gateway to Astronaut Photography of Earth
138–139
Ryan Rodrick Beiler/Shutterstock.com
140–141
left: USGS, EROS Data Center, Sioux Falls, SD
right: MODIS/NASA
142–143
left: NASA/JSC Gateway to Astronaut Photography of Earth
right: NASA image created by Jesse Allen, using data from NASA/
GSFC/METI/ERSDAC/JAROS, and the U.S./Japan ASTER Science
Team.
144–145
Oatta/Shutterstock
150–151
NASA/JSC Gateway to Astronaut Photography of Earth
152–153
BartlomiejMagierowski/Shutterstock.com
154–155
USGS
156–157
NASA images by Jesse Allen and Robert Simmon, using ALI data
from the EO-1 team, and data from the NASA/GSFC/METI/ERSDAC/
JAROS, and U.S./Japan ASTER Science Team.
158–159
NASA/GSFC/METI/ERSDAC/JAROS, and U.S./Japan ASTER Science
Team
160–161
NASA/GSFC/MITI/ERSDAC/JAROS, and U.S./Japan ASTER Science
Team
162–163
top: Alexey Stiop/Shutterstock
bottom: NASA/GSFC/METI/ERSDAC/JAROS, and the U.S./Japan
ASTER Science Team.
168–169
S-F/Shutterstock
170–171
Marisa Estivill/Shutterstock
172–173
ASA/GSFC/METI/ERSDAC/JAROS, and U.S./Japan ASTER Science
Team

176–177
SRTM Team NASA/JPL/NIMA
178–179
NASA
180–181
MODIS/ NASA
186–187
MODIS/ NASA
192-193
Image courtesy of MODIS Rapid Response Project at NASA/GSFC
196–197
top: SRTM Team NASA/JPL/NIMA
bottom: MODIS/NASA
202–203
National Snow and Ice Data Center. Boulder, CO. USA
204–205
Gregor Turk
206–207
NASA/GSFC/METI/ERSDAC/JAROS, and U.S./Japan ASTER Science
Team
208–209
top: MODIS/NASA
bottom: Aqua–MODIS
212–213
kavram/Shutterstock
214–215
top: SRTM Team NASA/JPL/NIMA and Landsat 7 Science Team
NASA GSFC/USGS
bottom: Alisha Vargas CC by 2.0
216–217
USGS
220–221
Image courtesy Stu Snodgrass, NASA GSFC Scientific Visualization
Studio
222–223
NASA/GSFC/MITI/ERSDAC/JAROS, and the U.S./Japan ASTER
Science Team
224–225
top: National Archives/CORBIS
bottom: B. Franklin/Shutterstock.com
232–233
top: Jason Maehl/Shutterstock
bottom: Dmitry V. Petrenko/Shutterstock
234–235
gary yim/Shutterstock.com
240
National Oceanic and Atmospheric Administration (NOAA)
Sea ice extents data: National Snow and Ice Data Center (NSIDC),
University of Colorado, USA

Pages 242–256 IMAGES OF EARTH

242–243
NASA/JSC Gateway to Astronaut Photography of Earth.
244–245
NASA Earth Observatory images by Jesse Allen, using Landsat data
from the U.S. Geological Survey.
246–247
NASA Earth Observatory images by Robert Simmon, using Landsat 8
data from the USGS Earth Explorer.
248–249
NASA/JSC Gateway to Astronaut Photography of Earth.
250–251
NASA Earth Observatory image created by Jesse Allen and Robert
Simmon, using EO-1 ALI data provided courtesy of the NASA EO-1
team.
252–253
NASA Earth Observatory images by Jesse Allen and Norman Kuring,
using Landsat 8 data from the U.S. Geological Survey.
254–255
NASA Earth Observatory images by Jesse Allen and Robert Simmon,
using Landsat data from the U.S. Geological Survey.
256
NASA Landsat 8 – OLI

Creative Commons Licensing
    creativecommons.org/licenses/
ITU   www.itu.int
National Snow and Ice Data Center. Boulder, CO. USA
    nsidc.org
NASA   earthobservatory.nasa.gov
NASA   rapidfire.sci.gsfc.nasa.gov
NASA   asterweb.jpl.nasa.gov/index.asp
NOAA   www.noaa.gov
United Nations Environment Programme
    www.na.unep.net
United States Geological Survey
    www.usgs.gov

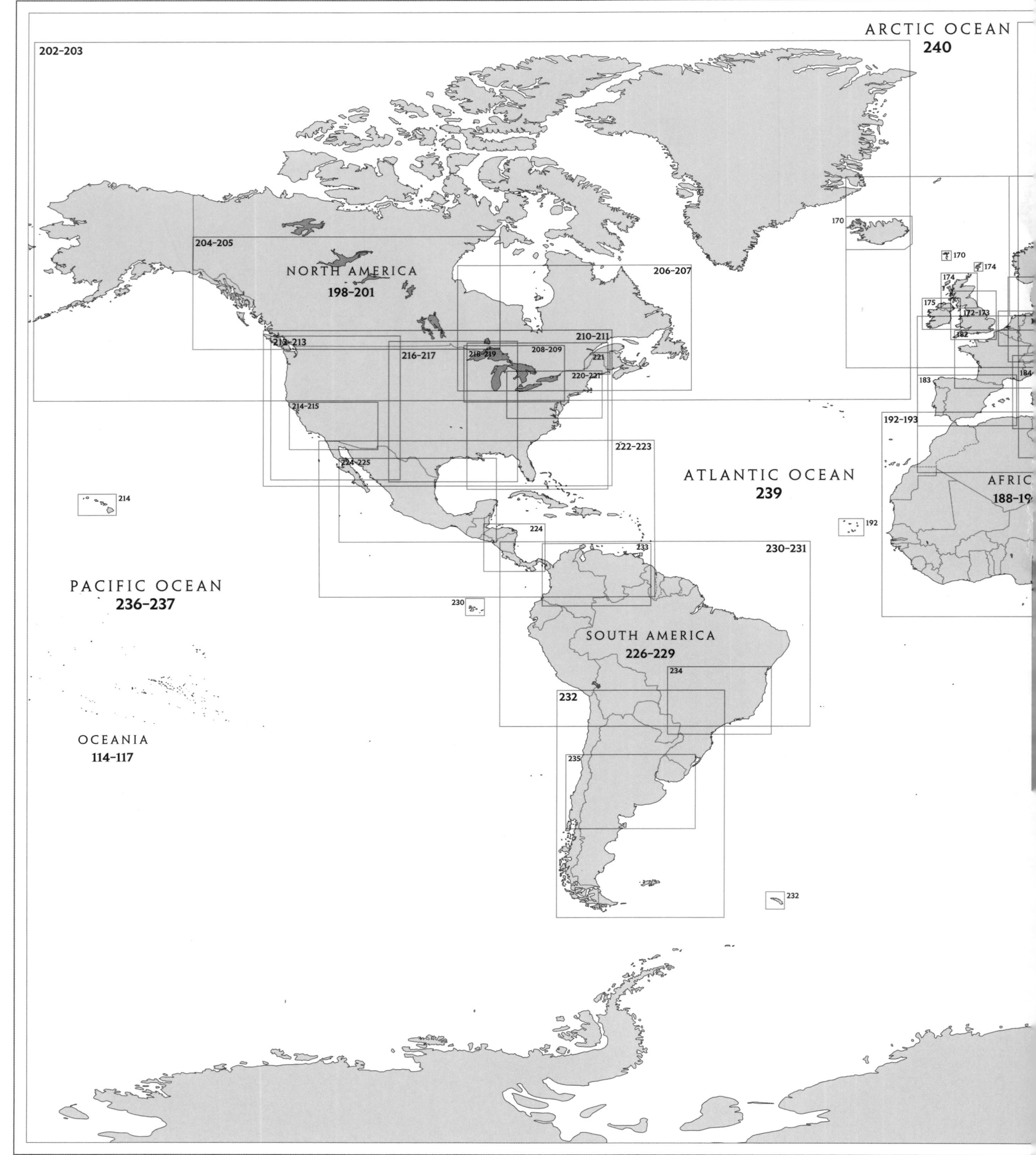

ARCTIC OCEAN
240

202-203

204-205

NORTH AMERICA
198-201

206-207

212-213

216-217

218-219

210-211

208-209

221

220-221

214-215

222-223

ATLANTIC OCEAN
239

224-225

214

192

224

233

230-231

PACIFIC OCEAN
236-237

230

SOUTH AMERICA
226-229

OCEANIA
114-117

234

232

235

232

170

170

174

174

175

172-173

182

183

184

192-193

AFRIC
188-19

232